Guide to Collective Biographies for Children and Young Adults

Sue Barancik

The Scarecrow Press, Inc.
Lanham, Maryland • Toronto • Oxford

SCARECROW PRESS, INC.

Published in the United States of America
by Scarecrow Press, Inc.
A wholly owned subsidiary of
The Rowman & Littlefield Publishing Group, Inc.
4501 Forbes Boulevard, Suite 200, Lanham, Maryland 20706
www.scarecrowpress.com

PO Box 317
Oxford
OX2 9RU, UK

British Library Cataloguing in Publication Information Available

Library of Congress Cataloging-in-Publication Data

Barancik, Sue, 1944–
  Guide to collective biographies for children and young adults / Sue Barancik.
    p. cm.
  Includes bibliographical references and index.
  ISBN 0-8108-5033-8 (pbk. : alk. paper)
  1. Biography—Juvenile literature—Bibliography. I. Title.

Z5301.B27 2005
[CT104]
016.92—dc22

                                                          2004019560

Contents

Preface   v

A Brief Guide to Using This Book   vii

Part I   Titles Indexed and Their Codes   1

Part II   The Biographees   27

Part III   List of Subject Headings   161

Part IV   Subject Guide to Biographees   169

About the Author   447

Preface

As a youth services librarian for the past twenty years, I have responded to hundreds of requests from children and teenagers seeking biographical information on notable people in all fields of endeavor. The students need information on African-American heroes during Black History Month, famous females to commemorate Women's History Month, Holocaust rescuers and survivors to supplement the Holocaust curriculum, and renowned scientists to support their science fair projects.

Although librarians select and purchase new individual biographies on a regular basis, the collection may be quickly snatched up by the first eager student, leaving others without a book to take home. Encyclopedias may not be an option as many teachers forbid the students to use them for their reports. Online sources, including biographical databases, may also not be allowed, and, if they are, it is not possible to find many of the more obscure personages. And, very often, the youngster has to have the work handed in the *next day*, not even allowing the librarian the time to attempt to gather information from other sources.

Collective biographies provide concise information focusing on the lives and accomplishments of a number of people, grouping the individuals together generally by occupation, racial or ethnic group, or some other distinguishing characteristic. Often these books, with their entries ranging from paragraphs to pages to lengthy chapters, are just what the student needs to fulfill the assignment's demands. Publishers for children and young adults have been ably publishing fine collective biographies, both as individual books, as well as series entries, to fulfill school assignments.

With this in mind, *Guide to Collective Biographies for Children and Young Adults* was created to organize and utilize the growing number of collective biographies in an efficient way, therefore easing the searches of librarians, media specialists, teachers, and students. Extensive efforts were made to locate as many titles as possible published between 1988-2002. Besides using my library system's collection, other books were procured through our Inter-Library Loan Department and through direct requests to publishers for the newest titles. Attempts were made to check and recheck facts, especially birth and death dates, for accuracy. I apologize for any factual errors since no matter how many print and online sources I contacted, I could not always locate or verify desired information.

Seven hundred twenty-one titles are included in this guide resulting in a combined total of 5,760 people. The book has two main sections. The biographees section lists each person alphabetically with data about the individual's birthdate, death, nationality, and identifying occupational or other field of activity. The entry concludes with the codes of the book(s) in which one can find the person.

The second section is the subject guide to biographees, and from abolitionists to zoologists, the searcher will find the same individuals indexed according to their distinguishing characteristics of career, nationality, or ethnic group. Students will find this particularly helpful when trying to cull lists of people working in a particular field, or from a certain immigrant group, to research.

I could not have accomplished this book without the efforts of many others. My colleagues at the Somerset County Library System in Bridgewater, New Jersey, have been wonderful. The Youth Services Department not only gave me the impetus to do this book, but their never-ceasing support and encouragement will never be forgotten. The patient women of the Inter-Library Loan Department enthusiastically searched the country for the titles I requested. I cannot neglect to mention the assistance of my more computer savvy colleagues who helped me time and again with my formatting concerns. Thank you all very much. And to my husband, Marty, my biggest and forever fan as well as the source of a wealth of information, a very special thank you from the bottom of my heart.

A Brief Guide to Using This Book

Titles Indexed and Their Codes

This section is an alphabetical listing of all 721 titles indexed in this book with full bibliographic information and the letter code used to indicate the title. Not all books are still in print for purchasing; however, many libraries already own copies of these titles and this will make those books more accessible.

The Biographees

In this major section of the guide, the reader will find each individual listed alphabetically with accompanying identifying information of birthdate, death date when relevant, nationality, and career or other significant information. Attempts were made to ascertain the place of birth and to determine if the person became a citizen of the United States. It was not always possible to locate this information. Athletes originating from different countries, such as baseball players from Latin American countries playing on teams in the United States, are listed under their country of origin. If no country is listed for an individual, it should be understood that the person is an American.

Sample entry of American:
Aaron, Henry "Hank." (1934-) Baseball player, Presidential Medal of
Freedom recipient. DEA; DEA2; ITA; KRAMS; SEHN; SULG7; USC2.

Sample entry of someone whose nationality is not American:
Austen, Jane. (1775-1817) English author. HER; KRULL6; NIN; SMIL.

Sample entry of someone who was born in one country but then emigrated to another country:
Albright, Madeleine. (1937-) Secretary of State, born Czechoslovakia. GUL;
HARN; JONV.

Subject Guide to Biographees

The biographees are listed under subject headings of occupation, nationality, or other distinguishing characteristic. Many individuals are listed under more than one subject. For the people in the examples above, the searcher would find Hank Aaron under *Baseball Players* and *Presidential Medal of Freedom Recipients.* Jane Austen will be found with *Authors, Fiction-English* as well under the heading *English.* Madeleine Albright's name is listed as a *Cabinet Member* as well as under *Immigrants-Czechoslovakia.* Birth and death dates are repeated in this section to enable the researcher to find people in appropriate eras. For certain subjects, such as Explorers,

Inventors, and Medical Researchers, more specific information is added to each person's entry delineating *what* they invented, *where* they explored, or *which* state they governed.

For the most part, proper names are used as the main entry with references from the pseudonym, stage name, pen name, or more popular name. You will see a reference from *Landers, Ann to Lederer, Pauline Esther, Calamity Jane to Cannary, Martha Jane, Black Bart to Boles, Charles.*

Part I

TITLES INDEXED
AND
THEIR CODES

Titles Indexed and Their Codes

AAS   Aaseng, Nathan. *American dinosaur hunters.* (Collective Biographies) Berkeley Heights, NJ: Enslow Publishers, 1996.

AAS2   ——. *America's third party presidential candidates.* (Profiles) Minneapolis: Oliver Press, 1995.

AAS3   ——. *Better mousetraps: Product improvements that led to success.* Minneapolis: Lerner, 1990.

AAS4   ——. *Black inventors.* (American Profiles) New York: Facts on File, 1997.

AAS5   ——. *Business builders in computers.* (Business Builders) Minneapolis: Oliver Press, 2000.

AAS6   ——. *Business builders in fast food.* (Business Builders) Minneapolis: Oliver Press, 2001.

AAS7   ——. *Business builders in oil.* (Business Builders) Minneapolis: Oliver Press, 2000.

AAS8   ——. *Business builders in real estate.* (Business Builders) Minneapolis: Oliver Press, 2002.

AAS9   ——. *Business builders in toys.* (Business Builders) Minneapolis: Oliver Press, 2002.

AAS10   ——. *Close calls: From the brink of ruin to financial success.* New York: Lerner, 1990.

AAS11   ——. *Constructions: Building the impossible.* (Innovators) Minneapolis: Oliver Press, 2000.

AAS12   ——. *From rags to riches: People who started businesses from scratch.* New York: Lerner, 1990.

AAS13   ——. *Genetics: Unlocking the secrets of life.* (Innovators) Mineapolis: Oliver Press, 1996.

AAS14   ——. *Great justices of the Supreme Court.* (Profiles) Minneapolis: Oliver Press, 1996.

AAS15   ——. *The inventors: Nobel prizes in Chemistry, Physics and Medicine.* New York: Lerner, 1988.

AAS16   ——. *Midstream changes: People who started over and made it work.* New York:. Lerner, 1990.

AAS17   ——. *Top ten basketball scoring small forwards.* (Sports Top 10) Berkeley Heights, NJ: Enslow Publishers, 1998.

AAS18   ——. *Treacherous traitors.* (Profiles) Minneapolis: Oliver Press, 1997.

AAS19   ——. *Twentieth-Century inventors.* (American Profiles) New York: Facts on File, 1991.

AAS20   ——. *Women Olympic champions.* (History Makers) San Diego: Lucent, 2001.

ADA   Adams, Simon. *The Presidents of the United States.* Princeton, NJ: Two-Can Publishing, 2001.

AFR   *African-American voices of triumph: Creative fire.* Alexandria, VA: Time-Life Books, 1994.

AFR2   African-American voices of triumph: Leadership. Alexandria, VA: Time-Life Books, 1993.

ALLP   Allen, Paula Gunn and Patricia Clark Smith. *As long as the rivers flow: The stories of nine Native Americans.* New York: Scholastic, 1996.

ALLZ   Allen, Zita. *Black women leaders of the civil rights movement.* (African American Experience) Danbury, CT: Franklin Watts, 1996.

ALTE   Alter, Judy. *Extraordinary explorers and adventurers.* (Extraordinary People) New York: Children's Press, 2001.

ALTE2   ———. Extraordinary women of the American west. (Extraordinary People) New York: Children's Press, 1999.

ALTML   Altman, Linda Jacobs. *Women inventors.* (American Profiles) New York: Facts on File, 1997.

ALTMS   Altman, Susan. *Extraordinary Black Americans from colonial to contemporary times.* (Extraordinary People) New York: Children's Press, 1989.

AMR   Amram, Fred M. B. *African American inventors I.* (African American Inventors) Mankato, MN: Capstone Press, 1996.

AND   Anderson, Margaret and Karen Stephenson. *Scientists of the ancient world.* (Collective Biographies) Berkeley Heights, NJ: Enslow Publishers, 1999.

ANT   Anthony, Carl. *America's most influential First Ladies.* (Profiles) Minneapolis: Oliver Press, 1992.

ARC   Archer, Jules. *Breaking barriers: The feminist revolution from Susan B. Anthony to Margaret Sanger to Betty Friedan.* (Epoch) New York: Viking Press, 1991.

ARC2   ———. They had a dream: The Civil Rights struggle from Frederick Douglass to Marcus Garvey to Martin Luther King and Malcolm X. (Epoch) New York: Viking Press, 1993.

ARM   Armstrong, Carole. *Lives and legends of the Saints.* New York: Simon & Schuster, 1995.

ARM2   ———. Women of the Bible: With paintings from the great art museums of the world. New York: Simon & Schuster, 1998.

ARO   Aronson, Virginia. *Literature.* (Female Firsts in their Fields) Philadelphia: Chelsea House, 1999.

AUT   Author talk: Conversations with Judy Blume. Leonard Marcus, Editor. New York: Simon & Schuster, 2000.

AVE   Avery, Susan and Linda Skinner. *Extraordinary American Indians.* (Extraordinary People) New York: Children's Press, 1992.

AXE   Axelrod, Toby. *Rescuers defying the Nazis: Non-Jewish teens who rescued Jews.* (Teen Witnesses to the Holocaust) New York: Rosen, 1999.

AXEC   Axelrod-Contrada, Joan. *Women who led nations.* (Profiles) Minneapolis: Oliver Press, 1999.

BAIL   Bailer, Darice. *Great women athletes.* (Step into Reading) New York: Random House, 2001.

BAIR   Baird, Anne. *The U.S. Space Camp book of astronauts* New York: William Morrow, 1996.

BAKR   Baker, Rosalie F. and Charles F. Baker III. *Ancient Egyptians: People of the pyramids.* (Oxford Profiles) New York: Oxford University Press, 2001.

BAKR2   ———. Ancient Greeks: Creating the classical tradition. (Oxford Profiles) New York: Oxford University Press, 1997.

BAKR3   ———. Ancient Romans: Expanding the classical tradition. (Oxford Profiles) New York: Oxford University Press, 1998.

BAKS   Baker, Susan. *Explorers of North America.* (Tales of Courage) Austin, TX: Raintree Steck Vaughn, 1989.

BARB   Barber, James and Amy Pastan. *Smithsonian Presidents and First Ladies.* New York: Dorling-Kindersley, 2002.

BART   Barter, James. *Artists of the Renaissance.* (History Makers) San Diego: Lucent Press, 1999.

BAU   Bausum, Ann. *Our country's Presidents.* Washington: National Geographic Society, 2002.

BECKM   Beckman, Wendy Hart. *Artists and writers of the Harlem Renaissance.* (Collective Biographies) Berkeley Heights, NJ: Enslow Publishers, 2002.

BECKN   Beckner, Chrisanne. *100 African-Americans who shaped history.* (100 Series) San Francisco: Bluewood Books,

1995.

BERL   Berliner, Don. *Aviation: Reaching for the sky.* (Innovators) Minneapolis: Oliver Press, 1997.

BERL2   ———. *Before the Wright brothers.* Minneapolis: Lerner, 1990.

BERS   Berson, Robin Kadison. *Young heroes in world history.* Greenwood Press, 1999.

BJA   Bjarkman, Peter C. *Slam dunk superstars.* Avenel, NJ: Crescent Books, 1994.

BJA2   ———. *Top ten baseball base stealers.* (Sports Top Ten) Berkeley Heights, NJ: Enslow Publishers, 1995.

BJA3   ———. *Top ten basketball slam dunkers.* (Sports Top Ten) Berkeley Heights, NJ: Enslow Publishers, 1995.

BLACA   Blackwood, Alan. *Twenty names in art.* (Twenty Names) New York: Marshall Cavendish, 1988.

BLACA2   ———. *Twenty names in classical music.* (Twenty Names) New York: Marshall Cavendish, 1988.

BLACG   Blackwood, Gary. *Gangsters.* (Bad Guys). New York: Marshall Cavendish, 2002.

BLACG2   ———. *Highwaymen.* (Bad Guys) New York: Marshall Cavendish, 2002.

BLACG3   ———. *Outlaws.* (Bad Guys) New York: Marshall Cavendish, 2002.

BLACG4   ———. *Pirates.* (Bad Guys) New York: Marshall Cavendish, 2002.

BLACG5   ———. *Swindlers.* (Bad Guys) New York: Marshall Cavendish, 2002.

BLASH   Blashfield, Jean. *Women at the front: Their changing roles in the Civil War.* Danbury, CT: Franklin Watts, 1997.

BLASH2   ———. *Women inventors I.* (Capstone Short Biographies) Mankato, MN: Capstone Press, 1996.

BLASH3   ———. *Women inventors II.* (Capstone Short Biographies) Mankato, MN: Capstone Press, 1996.

BLASH4   ———. *Women inventors III.* (Capstone Short Biographies) Mankato, MN: Capstone Press, 1996.

BLASH5   ———. *Women inventors IV.* (Capstone Short Biographies) Mankato, MN: Capstone Press, 1996.

BLASS   Blassingame, Wyatt. *Look-it-up book of Presidents.* New York: Random House, 1996.

BLU   Blue, Rose and Corrine J. Naden. *People of peace.* Brookfield, CT: Millbrook Press, 1994.

BOL   Bolden, Tanya. *And not afraid to dare: The stories of ten African-American women.* New York: Scholastic, 1998.

BOOK   *Book of firsts: Leaders of America.* Edited by Richard Rennert. (Profiles of Great Black Americans) Philadelphia: Chelsea House, 1994.

BOOK2   *Book of firsts: Sports heroes.* Edited by Richard Rennert. (Profiles of Great Black Americans) Philadelphia: Chelsea House, 1994.

BOR   Borklund, C. W. *Military leaders since World War II.* (American Profiles) New York: Facts on File, 1992.

BOY   *Boys who rocked the world: From King Tut to Tiger Woods.* Edited by Lar DeSouza. Hillsboro, OR: Beyond Words Publishing, 2001.

BRED   Bredeson, Carmen. *American writers of the twentieth century.* (Collective Biographies) Berkeley Heights, NJ: Enslow Publishers, 1996.

BRED2   ———. *Presidential Medal of Freedom winners.* (Collective Biographies) Berkeley Heights, NJ: Enslow Publishers, 1996.

BRED3   Bredeson, Carmen and Ralph Thibodeau. *Ten great American composers.* (Collective Biographies) Berkeley Heights, NJ: Enslow Publishers, 2002.

BREH   Brehm, Mike and Michael Russo. *Rising stars: The best young players in the NHL.* (Rising Stars) New York: Rosen/Sports Illustrated for Kids, 2002.

BREW   Brewster, Hugh and Laurie Coulter. *To be a princess: The fascinating life of real princesses.* New York: HarperCollins, 2001.

BRIGG   Briggs, Carole S. *At the controls: Women in aviation.* New York: Lerner, 1991.

BRIGG2   ———. *Women in space.* (A & E Biographies) New York: Lerner, 1999.

BRIGH   Brighton, Catherine. *The Brontes: Scenes from the childhood of Charlotte, Bramwell, Emily and Anne.* San Francisco:

Chronicle, 1994.

BRIL   Brill, Marlene Targ. *Extraordinary young people.* (Extraordinary People) New York: Children's Press, 1996.

BRIL2   ———. *Winning women in baseball and softball.* (Sport Success) Hauppauge, NY: Barron's Educational Services, 2000.

BRIL3   ———. *Winning women in basketball.* (Sport Success) Hauppauge, NY: Barron's Educational Services, 2000.

BRIL4   ———. *Winning women in ice hockey.* (Sport Success) Hauppauge, NY: Barron's Educational Services, 1999.

BRIL5   ———. *Winning women in soccer.* (Sport Success) Hauppauge, NY: Barron's Educational Services, 1999.

BRO   Brooks, Philip. *Extraordinary Jewish Americans.* (Extraordinary People) New York: Children's Press, 1998.

BRY   Bryant, Jill. *Amazing women athletes.* (Women's Hall of Fame) Toronto: Orca/Second Story, 2002.

BUCH   Buchanan, Doug. *Air and space.* (Female Firsts in their Fields) Philadelphia: Chelsea House, 1999.

BUCK   Buckley, James, Jr. *Rumbling running backs.* (Proficient Readers) New York: DK Publishing, 2001.

BUCK2   ———. *Strikeout kings.* (Proficient Readers) New York: DK Press, 2001.

BUCK3   ———. *Super Bowl heroes.* (Reading Alone) New York: DK Press, 2000.

BUCK4   ———. *Super shortstops: Jeter, Nomar and A-Red.* (Proficient Readers) New York: DK Press, 2001.

BUR   Burns, Kepra and Willliam Miles. *Black stars in orbit: NASA's African-American astronauts.* New York: Harcourt, Brace, 1995.

BUS   Bussing-Burks, Marie. *Influential economists.* (Profiles) Minneapolis: Oliver Press, 2002.

BYR   Byrnes, Patricia. *Environmental pioneers.* (Profiles) Minneapolis: Oliver Press, 1998.

CALA   Calabro, Marian. *Great courtroom lawyers: Fighting the cases that made history.* (American Profiles) New York: Facts on File, 1996.

CALV   Calvert, Patricia. *Great lives: The American frontier.* New York: Atheneum, 1997.

CAM   Camp, Carole Ann. *American astronomers: Searchers and wanderers.* (Collective Biographies) Berkeley Heights, NJ: Enslow Publishers, 1996.

CAM2   ———. *American women of science.* (Collective Biographies) Berkeley Heights, NJ: Enslow Publishers, 2001.

CARA   Caravantes, Peggy. *Petticoat spies: Six women spies of the Civil War.* Greensboro, NC: Morgan Reynolds, 2002.

CARR   Carruthers, Margaret W. and Susan Clinton. *Pioneers of ecology: Discovering earth's secrets.* (Lives in Science) Danbury, CT: Franklin Watts, 2001.

CEL   *Celebrating women in mathematics and science.* Reston, Va: National Council of Teachers of Mathematics, 1996.

CHA   Chang, Ina. *A separate battle: Women and the Civil War.* (Young Reader's History of the Civil War) New York: Dutton, 1991.

CHI   Chiu, Christina. *Lives of notable Asian-Americans: Literature and education.* (The Asian-American Experience) Philadelphia: Chelsea House, 1996.

CHRISP   Chrisp, Peter. *Dinosaur detectives.* (Proficient Readers) New York: Dorling Kindersley, 2001.

CHRIST   Christopher, Andre. *Top ten men's tennis players.* (Sports Top Ten) Berkeley Heights, NJ: Enslow Publishers, 1998.

CIV   *Civil rights leaders.* Edited by Richard Rennert. (Profiles of Great Black Americans) Philadelphia: Chelsea House, 1993.

CLA   Clarke, Brenda. *Caring for others.* (Tales of Courage) Austin, TX: Raintree Steck Vaughn, 1990.

CLA2   ———. *Fighting for their faith.* (Tales of Courage) Austin, TX: Raintree Steck Vaughn, 1990.

CLI   Clinton, Susan. *Reading between the bones: The pioneers of dinosaur palentology.* (Lives in Science) Danbury, CT: Franklin Watts, 1997.

COLE   Cole, Melanie, Barbara Marvis and Valerie Menard. *Famous people of Hispanic heritage, vol. 9.* (Contemporary American Success Stories) Bear, DE: Mitchell Lane Publishers, 1997.

COLL Collins, James. *The mountain men.* Danbury, CT: Franklin Watts, 1996.

COLM Colman, Penny. *Where the action was: Women war correspondents in World War II.* New York: Crown Publishers, 2002.

COOL *Cool women.* Edited by Pam Nelson. Los Angeles: Girl Press, 1998.

COOLI Coolidge, Olivia. *Lives of famous Romans.* North Haven, CT: Linnet Books, 1992.

COX Cox, Clinton. *African-American healers.* (Black Stars) New York: John Wiley & Sons, 2000.

COX2 ———. *African-American teachers.* (Black Stars) New York: John Wiley & Sons, 2000.

CRO Crompton, Samuel Willard. *100 Americans who shaped world history.* (100 Series) San Francisco: Bluewood Books, 1999.

CRO2 ———. *100 colonial leaders who shaped North America.* (100 Series) San Francisco: Bluewood Books, 1999.

CRO3 ———. *100 military heroes who shaped world history.* (100 Series) San Francisco: Bluewood Books, 1998.

CRO4 ———. *100 relationships that shaped world history.* (100 Series) San Francisco: Bluewood Books, 2000.

CRO5 ———. *100 religious leaders who shaped world history.* (100 Series) San Francisco: Bluewood Books, 2001.

CRO6 ———. *The Presidents of the United States.* New York: Smithmark Publishers, 1992.

CUM Cumming, Robert. *Great artists: The lives of fifty painters explored through their work.* New York:. Dorling-Kindersley, 1998.

CURR Currie, Stephen. *Polar explorers.* (History Makers) San Diego: Lucent, 2002.

CURR2 ———. *Women inventors.* (History Makers) San Diego: Lucent, 2001.

CURT Curtis, Robert H. *Great lives-medicine.* (Great Lives) New York: Charles Scribner's Sons, 1993.

CUS Cush, Cathie. *Artists who created great works.* (Twenty Events) Austin, TX: Raintree Steck Vaughn, 1995.

CUS2 ———. *Women who achieved great-ness.* (Twenty Events) Austin, TX: Raintree Steck Vaughn, 1995.

DAN Danenberg, Julie. *Women artists of the West: Five portraits of creativity and courage.* Fulcrum, 2002.

DAS Dash, Joan. *The triumph of discovery: Women scientists who won the Nobel prize.* Englewood Cliffs, NJ: Messner, 1991.

DAT Datnow, Claire. *American science fiction and fantasy writers.* Berkeley Heights, NJ: Enslow Publishers, 1999.

DAV Davis, Kenneth C. *Don't know much about the Kings and Queens of England.* New York: HarperCollins, 2002.

DAV2 ———. *Don't know much about the Presidents.* New York: HarperCollins, 2002.

DE De Angelis, Gina. *Science and medicine.* (Female Firsts in their Fields) Philadelphia: Chelsea House, 1999.

DEA Deane, Bill. *Top ten baseball hitters.* (Sports Top Ten) Berkeley Heights, NJ: Enslow Publishers, 1998.

DEA2 ———. *Top ten baseball home run hitters.* (Sports Top Ten) Berkeley Heights, NJ: Enslow Publishers, 1997.

DEA3 ———. *Top ten baseball shortstops.* (Sports Top Ten) Berkeley Heights, NJ: Enslow Publishers, 1999.

DEE Deegan, Paul. *Basketball legends.* (Legendary Sports Heroes) Bloomington, MN: Abdo and Daughters, 1990.

DEI Deitsch, Richard and Alan Schwartz. *Rising stars: The ten best young players in the NFL.* New York: Rosen/Sports Illustrated for Kids, 2002.

DEN Denenberg, Dennis and Lorraine Roscoe. *Fifty American heroes every kid should meet.* Brookfield, CT: Millbrook Press, 2001.

DEV Devaney, John. *Winners of the Heisman Trophy.* New York: Walker & Company, 1990.

DID Di Domenico, Kelly. *Super women in science.* (Women's Hall of Fame) Toronto: Second Story Press, 2002.

DIN Dineen, Jacqueline. *Twenty inventors.* (Twenty Names) New York: Marshall Cavendish, 1988.

DIT Ditchfield, Christin. *Top ten American women's Olympic Gold Medalists.* (Sports Top Ten) Berkeley Heights, NJ: Enslow

Publishers, 2000.

DOH   Doherty, Kieran. *Congressional Medal of Honor Recipients.* (Collective Biographies) Berkeley Heights, NJ: Enslow Publishers, 1998.

DOH2   ———. *Explorers, missionaries, and trappers: trailblazers of the west.* (Shaping America) Minneapolis: Oliver Press, 2000.

DOH3   ———. *Puritans, pilgrims, and merchants: Founders of the northeastern colonies.* (Shaping America) Minneapolis: Oliver Press, 1999.

DOH4   ———. *Ranchers, homesteaders and traders: Frontiersmen of the south central states.* (Shaping America) Minneapolis: Oliver Press, 2001.

DOH5   ———. *Soldiers, cavaliers and planters: Settlers of the southeastern colonies.* (Shaping America) Minneapolis: Oliver Press, 1999.

DON   Donkin, Andrew. *Crime busters.* (Proficient Readers). New York: DK Books, 2001.

DON2   ———. *Going for gold.* (Eyewitness Books) New York: DK Books, 1999.

DRI   Drimmer, Frederick. *Born different: The amazing stories of some very special people.* New York: Atheneum, 1988.

DUB   Dubovoy, Sina. *Civil rights leaders.* (American Profiles) New York: Facts on File, 1997.

DUD   Dudley, Karen. *Great African-Americans in government.* (Outstanding African-Americans) New York: Crabtree Publishing Company, 1997.

DUM   Dumbeck, Kristina. *Leaders of women's suffrage.* (History Makers) San Diego: Lucent, 2001.

DUN   Dungworth, Richard and Philippa Wingate. *The Usborne book of famous women.* Tulsa, OK: EDC Publishing, 1997.

EIG   *The eighteenth century: Artists, writers and composers.* Edited by Sarah Halliwell. (Who and When) Austin, TX: Raintree Steck Vaughn, 1998.

EME   Emert, Phyllis. *Top lawyers and their famous cases.* (Profiles) Minneapolis: Oliver Press, 1996.

FAB   Faber, Doris and Harold. *Great lives: American government.* (Great Lives) New York: Charles Scribner's Sons, 1988.

FAB2   ———. *Great lives: American literature.* (Great Lives) New York: Charles Scribner's Sons, 1995.

FAB3   ———. *Great lives: Nature and the environment.* (Great Lives) New York: Charles Scribner's Sons, 1991.

FAG   Fagan, Brian. *Archaeologists: Explorers of the human past.* (Oxford Profiles) New York: Oxford University Press, 2002.

FEM   *Female leaders.* Edited by Richard Rennert. (Profiles of Great Black Americans) Philadelphia: Chelsea House, 1994.

FEM2   *Female writers.* Edited by Richard Rennert. (Profiles of Great Black Americans) Philadelphia: Chelsea House, 1994.

FIR   Fireside, Bryna. *Is there a woman in the House . . . or Senate?* Morton Grove, Il: Albert Whitman and Company, 1994.

FIS   Fisher, Leonard Everett. *The gods and goddesses of Ancient Egypt.* New York: Holiday House, 1997.

FIS2   ———. *Gods and goddesses of the Ancient Maya.* New York: Holiday House, 1999.

FIS3   ———. *Gods and goddesses of the Ancient Norse.* New York: Holiday House, 2001.

FLE   Fleming, Constance. *Women of the lights.* Morton Grove, Il: Albert Whitman and Company, 1996.

FOR   Ford, Carin T. *Legends of American dance and choreography.* (Collective Biographies) Berkeley Heights, NJ: Enslow Publishers, 2000.

FOX   Fox, Karen. *The chain reaction: Pioneers of nuclear science.* (Lives in Science) Danbury, CT: Franklin Watts, 1998.

FRA   Fradin, Dennis Brindell. *Bound for the North Star: True stories of fugitive slaves.* New York: Clarion Books, 2000.

FRA2   ———. *The signers: The 56 stories behind the Declaration of Independence.* New York: Walker and Company, 2002.

FRA3   ———. *"We have conquered pain.". The discovery of anesthesia.* New York: Simon & Schuster/Margaret K. McElderry Books, 1996.

FREM   Fremon, David J. *The Holocaust heroes.* (The Holocaust Remembered) Berkeley Heights, NJ: Enslow Publishers,

1998.

FREN French, Laura. *Internet pioneers: The cyber elite.* (Collective Biographies) Berkeley Heights, NJ: Enslow Publishers, 2001.

FRID Fridell, Ron. *Solving crimes: Pioneers of forensic science.* (Lives in Science) Danbury, CT: Franklin Watts, 2000.

FRIT Fritz, Jean. *Around the world in a hundred years from Henry the Navigator to Magellan.* New York: G.P. Putnam's Sons, 1994.

FUR Furbee, Mary Rodd. *Outrageous women of colonial America.* New York: John Wiley and Sons, 2001.

FUR2 ———. *Outrageous women of the American frontier.* New York: John Wiley and Sons, 2002.

FUR3 ———. *Women of the American Revolution.* (History Makers) San Diego: Lucent Books, 1999.

GAI Gaines, Ann. *American photographers: Capturing the image.* (Collective Biographies) Berkeley Heights, NJ: Enslow Publishers, 2002.

GAI2 ———. *Entertainment and performing arts.* (Female Firsts in their Fields) Philadelphia: Chelsea House, 1999.

GAI3 ———. *Sports and athletics.* (Female Firsts in their Fields) Philadelphia: Chelsea House, 1999.

GAN Gan, Geraldine. *Lives of notable Asian-Americans: Arts, entertainment, sports.* (The Asian-American Experience) Philadelphia: Chelsea House, 1995.

GAR Garrison, Mary. *Slaves who dared: The stories of ten African-American heroes.* Shippensburg, PA: White Mane Kids, 2002.

GID Giddens, Sandra. *Escape: Teens who escaped the Holocaust to freedom.* (Teen Witnesses to the Holocaust) New York: Rosen Publishing Group, 1999.

GLA Glass, Andrew. *Bad guys: True stories of legendary gunslingers, sidewinders, four flushers, dry gulchers, bushwackers, freebooters, and downright bad guys and gals of the Wild West.* New York: Doubleday, 1998.

GLA2 ———. *Mountain men: True grit and tall tales.* New York: Random House Doubleday, 2001.

GLU Glubock, Shirley. *Great lives: Paint-ing.* (Great Lives) New York: Charles Scribner's Sons, 1994.

GOLDE Goldenstern, Joyce. *American women against violence.* (Collective Biographies) Berkeley Heights, NJ: Enslow Publishers, 1998.

GOLDM Goldman, Elizabeth. *Believers: Spiritual leaders of the world.* (Oxford Profiles) New York: Oxford University Press, 1995.

GOM Gombar, Christina. *Great women writers 1900-1950.* (American Profiles) New York: Facts on File, 1996.

GON Gonzales, Doreen. *AIDS: Ten stories of courage.* (Collective Biographies) Berkeley Heights, NJ: Enslow Publishers, 1996.

GOR Gormley, Beatrice. *First Ladies: Women who called the White House home.* New York: Scholastic Press, 1997.

GOU Gourse, Leslie. *Blowing on the changes: The art of the jazz horn players.* (Art of Jazz) Danbury, CT: Franklin Watts, 1997.

GOU2 ———. *Deep down in music: The art of the great jazz bassists.* (Art of Jazz) Danbury, CT: Franklin Watts, 1998.

GOU3 ———. *Fancy fretwork: The great jazz guitarists.* (Art of Jazz) Danbury, CT: Franklin Watts, 1995.

GOU4 ———. *Striders to beboppers and beyond: The art of jazz piano.* (Art of Jazz) Danbury, CT: Franklin Watts, 1997.

GOU5 ———. *Swingers and crooners: The art of jazz singing.* (Art of Jazz) Danbury, CT: Franklin Watts, 1997.

GOU6 ———. *Time keepers: The great jazz drummers.* (Art of Jazz) Danbury, CT: Franklin Watts, 1999.

GRAH Graham, Kevin. *Contemporary environmentalists.* (Global Profiles) New York: Facts on File, 1996.

GRAN Grant, Neil. *Heroes of World War II.* (Tales of Courage) Austin, TX: Raintree Steck Vaughn, 1990.

GREA *Great women in the struggle: An introduction for young readers.* Edited by Toymi Igus. (Book of Black Heroes) Orange, NJ: Just Us Books, 1991.

GREEC Green, Carl R. and William R. Sanford. *American tycoons.* (Collective Biographies) Berkeley Heights, NJ: Enslow Publishers, 1999.

GREEC2 ———. *Confederate Generals of the Civil War.* (Collective Biographies) Berkeley Heights, NJ: Enslow Publishers, 1998.

GREEC3 ———. *Union Generals of the Civil War.* (Collective Biographies) Berkeley Heights, NJ: Enslow Publishers, 1998.

GREENBJ Greenberg, Jan. *The American eye: Eleven artists of the 20th century.* New York: Delacorte Press, 1995.

GREENBL Greenberg, Lorna and Margot F. Horwitz. *Digging into the past: Pioneers of archaeology.* (Lives in Science) Danbury, CT: Franklin Watts, 2001.

GREENF Greenfeld, Howard. *After the Holocaust.* New York: Greenwillow Books, 2001.

GREER Green, Robert. *Dictators.* (History Makers) San Diego: Lucent Books, 2000.

GREES Green, Septima. *Top ten women gymnasts.* (Sports Top Ten) Berkeley Heights, NJ: Enslow Publishers, 1999.

GUL Gulotta, Charles. *Extraordinary women in politics.* (Extraordinary People) New York: Children's Press, 1998.

GUZ Guzzetti, Paula. *A family called Bronte.* (People in Focus) New York: Dillon Press, 1994.

HAC Hacker, Carlotta. *Explorers.* (Women in Profile) New York: Crabtree Publishing Company, 1998.

HAC2 ———. *Great African-Americans in history.* (Outstanding African-Americans) New York: Crabtree Publishing Company, 1997.

HAC3 ———. *Great African-Americans in jazz.* (Outstanding African-Americans) New York: Crabtree Publishing Company, 1997.

HAC4 ———. *Great African-Americans in the arts.* (Outstanding African-Americans) New York: Crabtree Publishing Company, 1997.

HAC5 ———. *Humanitarians.* (Women in Profile) New York: Crabtree Publishing Company, 1999.

HAC6 ———. *Nobel Prize winners.* (Women in Profile) New York: Crabtree Publishing Company, 1998.

HAC7 ———. *Rebels.* (Women in Profile) New York: Crabtree Publishing Company, 1999.

HAC8 ———. *Scientists.* (Women in Profile) New York: Crabtree Publishing Company, 1998.

HAM Hamilton, Virginia. *Many thousand gone: African-Americans from slavery to freedom.* New York: Alfred A. Knopf, 1993.

HAN Hansen, Joyce. *"Bury me not in a land of slaves." African-Americans in the time of reconstruction.* New York: Franklin Watts, 2000.

HAN2 ———. *Women of hope: African-Americans who made a difference.* New York: Scholastic Press, 1998.

HARD Hardy, P. Stephen. *Extraordinary people of the Harlem Renaissance.* (Extraordinary People) New York: Children's Press, 2000.

HARM Harmon, Rod. *American civil rights leaders.* (Collective Biographies) Berkeley Heights, NJ: Enslow Press, 2000.

HARR Harrington, Denis J. *Top ten women tennis players.* (Sports Top Ten) Berkeley Heights, NJ: Enslow Publishers, 1995.

HASK Haskins, James, *African American entrepreneurs.* (Black Stars) New York: John Wiley and Sons, 1998.

HASK2 ———. *African American military heroes.* (Black Stars) New York: John Wiley and Sons, 1998.

HASK3 ———. *Against all opposition: Black explorers in America.* New York: Walker and Company, 1992.

HASK4 ———. *Black stars of colonial times and the Revolutionary War.* (Black Stars) New York: John Wiley and Sons, 2002.

HASK5 ———. *Black stars of the Harlem Renaissance.* (Black Stars) John Wiley and Sons, 2002.

HASK6 ———. *Conjure times: Black magicians in America.* New York: Walker and Company, 2001.

HASK7 ———. *One more river to cross: The stories of twelve Black Americans.* New York: Scholastic Press, 1992.

HASK8 ———. *Outward dreams: Black inventors and their inventions.* New York: Walker and Company, 1991.

HAV Haven, Kendall and Donna Clark.

100 most popular scientists for young adults: Biographical sketches and professional paths. Englewood, CO: Libraries Unlimited, 1999.

HAY Hayden, Robert C. *Eleven African American doctors.* (Achievers: African Americans in Science and Technology) Frederick, MD: Twenty First Century Books, 1992.

HAY2 ———. *Nine African American inventors.* (Achievers: African Americans in Science and Technology) Frederick, MD: Twenty First Century Books, 1992.

HAY3 ———. *Seven African American scientists.* (Achievers: African Americans in Science and Technology) Frederick, MD: Twenty First Century Books, 1992.

HAZ Hazell, Rebecca. *Heroes: Great men through the ages.* New York: Abbeville Press, 1997.

HAZ2 ———. *Heroines: Great women through the ages.* New York: Abbeville Press, 1996.

HEA Head, Judith. *America's daughters: 400 years of American women.* Los Angeles: Perspective Publishing, 1999.

HEL Helmer, Diana Star. *Women suffragists.* (American Profiles) New York: Facts on File, 1998.

HENH Henderson, Harry. *Modern mathematicians.* (Global Profiles) New York: Facts on File, 1996.

HENH2 ———. *Pioneers of the Internet.* (History Makers) San Diego: Lucent Books, 2002.

HENS Henderson, Susan K. *African-American inventors II.* (Capstone Short Biographies) Mankato, MN: Capstone Press, 1998.

HENS2 ———. *African-American inventors III.* (Capstone Short Biographies) Mankato, MN: Capstone Press, 1998.

HER *Herstory: Women who changed the world.* Edited by Ruth Ashby and Deborah Gore Ohrn. New York: Viking Press, 1995.

HILA Hill, Anne E. *Broadcasting and journalism.* (Female Firsts in their Fields) Philadelphia: Chelsea House, 1999.

HILA2 ———. *Ten American movie directors: The men behind the camera.* (Collec-

tive Biographies) Berkeley Heights, NJ: Enslow Publishers, 2002.

HILC Hill, Christine M. *Ten Hispanic American authors.* (Collective Biographies) Berkeley Heights, NJ: Enslow Publishers, 2002.

HILC2 ———. *Ten terrific authors for teens.* (Collective Biographies) Berkeley Heights, NJ: Enslow Publishers, 2000.

HON *Honoring our ancestors: Stories and pictures by fourteen artists.* Edited by Harriet Rohmer. San Francisco: Children's Book Press, 1999.

HOOB Hoobler, Dorothy and Thomas. *Chinese portraits.* (Images Across the Ages) Austin, TX: Raintree Steck Vaughn, 1993.

HOOB2 ———. *French portraits.* (Images Across the Ages) Austin, TX: Raintree Steck Vaughn, 1994.

HOOB3 ———. *Italian portraits.* (Images Across the Ages) Austin, TX: Raintree Steck Vaughn, 1993.

HOOB4 ———. *Japanese portraits.* (Images Across the Ages) Austin, TX: Raintree Steck Vaughn, 1994.

HOOB5 ———. *Russian portraits.* (Images Across the Ages) Austin, TX: Raintree Steck Vaughn, 1994.

HOOB6 ———. *South American portraits.* (Images Across the Ages) Austin, TX: Raintree Steck Vaughn, 1994.

HOOS Hoose, Phillip. *We were there too!: Young people in US history.* New York: Farrar, Straus & Giroux, 2001.

HOR Horwitz, Margot. *A female focus: Great women photographers.* (Women then—Women now) Danbury, CT: Franklin Watts, 1996.

HUD Hudson, Wade. *Five brave explorers.* (Great Black Heroes/Hello Readers) New York: Scholastic Press, 1995.

HUD2 ———. *Five notable inventors.* (Great Black Heroes/Hello Readers) New York: Scholastic Press, 1995.

HUNT Hunt, Donald. *Top ten football legends.* (Sports Top Ten) Berkeley Heights, NJ: Enslow Publishers, 2001.

HUNTE Hunter, Shaun. *Great African Americans in the Olympics.* (Outstanding

African Americans) New York: Crabtree
Publishing Company, 1997.

HUNTE2 ———. *Leaders in medicine.*
(Women in Profile) New York: Crabtree
Publishing Company, 1999.

HUNTE3 ———. *Visual and performing
artists.* (Women in Profile) New York:
Crabtree Publishing Company, 1999.

HUNTE4 ———. *Writers.* (Women in Profile) New York: Crabtree Publishing Company, 1998.

IMP *Impressionism and post-
impressionism: artists, writers and composers.* Edited by Sarah Halliwell. (Who
and When) Austin, TX: Raintree Steck
Vaughn, 1998.

ISH Ishizuka, Kathy. *Asian American authors.* (Collective Biographies) Berkeley
Heights, NJ: Enslow Publishers, 2000.

ITA Italia, Bob. *Baseball legends.* (Legendary Sports Heroes) Bloomington, MN:
Abdo and Daughters, 1990.

ITA2 ———. *Boxing legends.* (Legendary
Sports Heroes) Bloomington, MN: Abdo
and Daughters, 1990.

ITA3 ———. *Courageous crime fighters.*
(Profiles) Minneapolis: Oliver Press, 1995.

ITA4 ———. *Golf legends.* (Legendary
Sports Heroes) Bloomington, MN: Abdo
and Daughters, 1990.

ITA5 ———. *Great auto makers and their
cars.* (Profiles) Minneapolis: Oliver Press,
1993.

JACK Jackel, Molly. *WNBA superstars.*
New York: Scholastic Press, 1998.

JACKD Jackson, Dave and Neta. *Hero
tales: A family treasury of true stories from
the lives of Christian Heroes, volume 1.*
Minneapolis: Bethany House, 1996.

JACKD2 ———. *Hero tales: A family
treasury of true stories from the lives of
Christian heroes, volume 2.* Minneapolis:
Bethany House, 1997.

JACKD3 ———. *Hero tales: A family
treasury of true stories from the lives of
Christian heroes, volume 3.* Minneapolis:
Bethany House, 1997.

JACKD4 ———. *Hero tales: A family
treasury of true stories from the lives of
Christian heroes, volume 4.* Minneapolis:

Bethany House, 2001.

JACKN Jackson, Nancy Jane. *Photographers: History and culture through the
camera.* (American Profiles) New York:
Facts on File, 1997.

JACT Jacobs, Timothy. *100 athletes who
shaped sports history.* (100 Series) San
Francisco: Bluewood Books, 1994.

JACW Jacobs, William Jay. *Great lives:
Human rights.* (Great Lives) New York:
Charles Scribner's Sons, 1990.

JACW2 ———. *Great lives: World
religions.* (Great Lives) New York:
Atheneum, 1996.

JACW3 ———. *They shaped the game.*
New York: Charles Scribner's Sons, 1994.

JAN Janulewicz, Mike and Richard Wid-
dows. *The big book of American heroes: A
young person's guide.* Philadelphia: Courage Books, 1998.

JAZ *Jazz stars.* Edited by Richard Rennert.
(Profile of Great Black Americans) Philadelphia: Chelsea House, 1994.

JEF Jeffrey, Laura. *American inventors of
the 20th century.* (Collective Biographies)
Berkeley Heights, NJ: Enslow Publishers,
1996.

JEF2 ———. *Great American business-
women.* (Collective Biographies) Berkeley
Heights, NJ: Enslow Publishers, 1996.

JEN Jennings, Jay. *Comebacks: Heroic
returns.* (Sports triumphs) Englewood
Cliffs, NJ: Silver Burdett Press, 1991.

JEN2 ———. *Long shots: They beat the
odds.* (Sports triumphs) Englewood Cliffs,
NJ: Silver Burdett Press, 1990.

JONH Jones, Hettie. *Big star falling mama:
Five women in Black music.* New York:
Viking Press, 1995.

JONL Jones, Lynda. *Five brilliant scientists.* (Great Black Heroes/Hello Readers)
New York: Scholastic Press, 2000.

JONR Jones, Rebecca C. *The President has
been shot!: True stories of the attacks on
ten US Presidents.* New York: Dutton,
1996.

JONS Jones, Stanley and L. Octavia Tripp.
African-American astronauts. (Capstone
Short Biographies) Mankato, MN: Cap-
stone Press, 1998.

JONS2 ———. *African American aviators.*

(Capstone Short Biographies) Mankato, MN: Capstone Press, 1998.

JONV   Jones, Veda Boyd. *Government and politics.* (Female Firsts in their Fields) Philadelphia: Chelsea House, 1999.

KAH   Kahn, Jetty. *Women in agricultural science careers.* (Capstone Short Biographies) Mankato, MN: Capstone Press, 2000.

KAH2   ———. *Women in chemistry careers.* (Capstone Short Biographies) Mankato, MN: Capstone Press, 2000.

KAH3   ———. *Women in computer science careers.* (Capstone Short Biographies) Mankato, MN: Capstone Press, 2000.

KAH4   ———. *Women in earth science careers.* (Capstone Short Biographies) Mankato, MN: Capstone Press, 1999.

KAH5   ———. *Women in engineering careers.* (Capstone Short Biographies) Mankato, MN: Capstone Press, 1999.

KAH6   ———. *Women in life science careers.* (Capstone Short Biographies) Mankato, MN: Capstone Press, 1999.

KAH7   ———. *Women in medical science careers.* (Capstone Short Biographies) Mankato, MN: Capstone Press, 2000.

KAH8   ———. *Women in physical science careers.* (Capstone Short Biographies) Mankato, MN: Capstone Press, 1999.

KAL   Kallen, Stuart A. *Great composers.* (History Makers) San Diego: Lucent Books, 2001.

KAL2   ———. *Great male comedians.* (History Makers) San Diego: Lucent Books, 2001.

KAL3   ———. *Native American Chiefs and Warriors.* (History Makers) Lucent Books, 1999.

KALLN   Kallner, Donna Jackson. *The bug scientists.* (Scientists in the field) Boston: Houghton Mifflin, 2002.

KAM   Kaminsky, Marty. *Uncommon champions: Fifteen athletes who battled back.* Honesdale, PA: Boyds Mill Press, 2000.

KAT   Katz, William Loren. *Black women of the Old West.* New York: Atheneum, 1995.

KAT2   ———. *Proudly red and black: stories of African and Native Americans.* New York: Atheneum, 1993.

KEEL   Keeley, Jennifer. *Women pop stars.* (History Makers) San Diego: Lucent Books, 2001.

KEEN   Keene, Ann. *Earthkeepers: Observers and protectors.* (Oxford Profiles) New York: Oxford University Press, 1994.

KEEN2   ———. *Peacemakers: Winners of the Nobel Peace Prize.* (Oxford Profiles) New York: Oxford University Press, 1997.

KELLA   Kellaher, Karen Burns. *Cult leaders.* (History Makers) San Diego: Lucent Books, 2000.

KELLY   Kelly, J. *Superstars of women's basketball.* (Female Sports Stars) Philadelphia: Chelsea House, 1997.

KEND   Kent, Deborah and Kathryn Quinlan. *Extraordinary people with disabilities.* (Extraordinary People) New York: Children's Press, 1996.

KENJ   Kent, Jacqueline. *Business builders in fashion.* (Business Builders) Minneapolis: Oliver Press, 2002.

KENJ2   ———. *Women of medicine.* (Profiles) Minneapolis: Oliver Press, 1998.

KET   Ketchum, Liza. *Into a new country: Eight remarkable women of the West.* Boston: Little, Brown, 2000.

KIR   Kirsh, Sharon and Florence Kirsh. *Fabulous female physicians.* (Women's Hall of Fame) Toronto: Orca/Second Story, 2001.

KLE   Kleinbaum, N. H. *The magnificent seven: The authorized story of American gold.* New York: Bantam Books, 1996.

KNA   Knapp, Ron. *American Generals of World War II.* (Collective Biographies) Berkeley Heights, NJ: Enslow Publishers, 1998.

KNA2   ———. *American legends of rock.* (Collective Biographies) Berkeley Heights, NJ: Enslow Publishers, 1996.

KNA3   ———. *Top ten American men sprinters.* (Sports Top Ten) Berkeley Heights, NJ: Enslow Publishers, 1999.

KNA4   ———. *Top ten America's men's Olympic Gold Medalists.* (Sports Top Ten) Berkeley Heights, NJ: Enslow Publishers, 2000.

KNA5   ———. *Top ten basketball centers.* (Sports Top Ten) Berkeley Heights, NJ: Enslow Publishers, 1994.

KNA6 ———. *Top ten basketball scorers.* (Sports Top Ten) Berkeley Heights, NJ: Enslow Publishers, 1994.

KNA7 ———. *Top ten heavyweight boxers.* (Sports Top Ten) Berkeley Heights, NJ: Enslow Publishers, 1997.

KNA8 ———. *Top ten hockey scorers.* (Sports Top Ten) Berkeley Heights, NJ: Enslow Publishers, 1994.

KNA9 ———. *Top ten NFL Super Bowl most valuable players.* (Sports Top Ten) Berkeley Heights, NJ: Enslow Publishers, 2000.

KNA10 ———. *Top ten professional basketball coaches.* (Sports Top Ten) Berkeley Heights, NJ: Enslow Publishers, 1998.

KNA11 ———. *Top ten stars of the NCAA's Men's Basketball Tournament.* (Sports Top Ten) Berkeley Heights, NJ: Enslow Publishers, 2001.

KNI Knight, Brenda. *Women who love books too much: Bibliophiles, bluestockings and prolific pens from the Algonquin Hotel to the Ya Ya Sisterhood.* Berkeley, CA: Conari Press, 2000.

KRAL Krall, Sarah. *100 folk heroes who shaped world history.* (100 Series) San Francisco: Bluewood Books, 1995.

KRAMB Kramer, Barbara. *The founders of famous food companies.* (Collective Biographies) Berkeley Heights, NJ: Enslow Publishers, 2002.

KRAMB2 ———. *Trailblazing American women.* (Collective Biographies) Berkeley Heights, NJ: Enslow Publishers, 2000.

KRAMS Kramer, S.A. *Baseball's greatest hitters.* (Step into Reading) New York: Random House, 1995.

KRAMS2 ———. *Hockey stars.* (All Aboard Reading) New York: Grosset & Dunlap, 1997.

KRAMS3 ———. *Hoop stars.* (All Aboard Reading) New York: Grosset & Dunlap, 1995.

KRAMS4 ———. *Ice stars.* (All Aboard Reading) New York: Grosset & Dunlap, 1997.

KRAMS5 ———. *Wonder women of sports.* (All Aboard Reading) New York: Grosset

& Dunlap, 1997.

KRE Krensky, Stephen. *Four against the odds: The struggle to save our environment.* (Scholastic Biography) New York: Scholastic Press, 1992.

KRO Krohn, Katherine. *Women of the Wild West.* (A & E Biography) Minneapolis: Lerner Publications, 2000.

KRULI Krulik Nancy. *Pop goes Latin!* New York: Grosset & Dunlap, 1999.

KRULL Krull, Kathleen. *Lives of extraordinary women: Rulers, rebels (and what the neighbors thought)* San Diego: Harcourt Brace, 2000.

KRULL2 ———. *Lives of the artists: Masterpieces, messes (and what the neighbors thought)* San Diego: Harcourt Brace 1995.

KRULL3 ———. *Lives of the athletes: Thrills, spills (and what the neighbors thought)* San Diego: Harcourt Brace 1997.

KRULL4 ———. *Lives of the musicians: Good times, bad times (and what the neighbors thought)* San Diego: Harcourt Brace, 1993.

KRULL5 ———. *Lives of the Presidents: Fame, shame (and what the neighbors thought)* San Diego: Harcourt Brace, 1998.

KRULL6 ———. *Lives of the writers: Comedies, tragedies (and what the neighbors thought)* San Diego: Harcourt Brace, 1994.

KRULL7 ———. *They saw the future: Oracles, psychics, scientists, great thinkers and pretty good guessers.* New York: Atheneum, 1999.

KRY Krystal, Barbara. *100 artists who shaped world history.* (100 Series) San Francisco: Bluewood Books, 1997.

KUH Kuhn, Betsy. *Top ten jockeys.* (Sports Top Ten) Berkeley Heights, NJ: Enslow Publishers, 1999.

KUS Kustanowitz, Esther. *The hidden children of the Holocaust: Teens who hid from the Nazis.* (Teen Witnessses to the Holocaust) New York: Rosen Publishing Group, 1999.

LAC Lace, William W. *Leaders and Generals of World War II.* (American War Library) San Diego: Lucent Books, 2000.

LAC2 ———. *Top ten football quarterbacks.*

(Sports Top Ten) Berkeley Heights, NJ: Enslow Publishers, 1994.

LAC3 ———. *Top ten football rushers.* (Sports Top Ten) Berkeley Heights, NJ: Enslow Publishers, 1994.

LAE Laezman, Rick. *100 Hispanic Americans who shaped American history.* (100 Series) San Francisco: Bluewood Books, 2002.

LAK Lake, A.I. *Women of the West.* (The Wild West in American History) Vero Beach, FL: Rourke, 1990.

LAND Landau, Elaine. *Holocaust memories: Speaking the truth.* (In Their Own Words) New York: Franklin Watts, 2001.

LAND2 ———. *Nazi war criminals.* New York: Franklin Watts, 1990.

LAND3 ———. *Slave narratives: The journey to freedom.* Danbury, CT: Franklin Watts, 2001.

LAND4 ———. *We survived the Holocaust.* New York: Franklin Watts, 1991.

LANG Langley, Andrew. *Twenty explorers.* (Twenty Names) New York: Marshall Cavendish, 1990.

LAS Lassieur, Allison. *Serial killers.* (History Makers) San Diego: Lucent Books, 2000.

LAY Layden, Joe. *Superstars of USA Women's Gymnastics.* (Women Athletes of the 2000 Olympics) New York: Simon & Schuster/Aladdin, 2000.

LAY2 ———. *Superstars of USA Women's Soccer.* (Women Athletes of the 2000 Olympics) New York: Simon & Schuster/Aladdin, 2000.

LEO Leon, Vicki. *Outrageous women of ancient times.* (Outrageous Women) New York: John Wiley and Sons, 1998.

LEO2 ———. *Outrageous women of the Middle Ages.* (Outrageous Women) New York: John Wiley and Sons, 1998.

LEO3 ———. *Outrageous women of the Renaissance.* (Outrageous Women) New York: John Wiley and Sons, 1999.

LES Lester, Julius. *The blues singers: Ten who rocked the world.* Jump at the Sun/Hyperion Books, 2001.

LEU Leuzzi, Linda. *Life connections: Pioneers in ecology* (Lives in Science). Danbury, CT: Franklin Watts, 2000.

LEVE LeVert, Suzanne. *The Doubleday Book of Famous Americans.* New York: Doubleday, 1989.

LEVI Levite, Christine. *Princesses.* New York: Franklin Watts, 1989.

LIL Lilley, Stephen R. *Fighters against American slavery.* (History Makers) San Diego: Lucent Books, 1999.

LINE Lindop, Edmund. *Presidents by accident.* New York: Franklin Watts, 1991.

LINL Lindop, Laurie. *Athletes.* (Dynamic Modern Women) New York: Henry Holt, 1996.

LINL2 ———. *Champions of equality.* (Dynamic Modern Women) New York, Henry Holt, 1997.

LINL3 ———. *Scientists and doctors.* (Dynamic Modern Women) New York: Henry Holt, 1997.

LIT Littlefield, Bill. *Champions: Stories of ten remarkable athletes.* Boston: Little, Brown, 1993.

LOM Lomask, Milton. *Great lives: Exploration.* (Great Lives) New York: Charles Scribner's Sons, 1988.

LOM2 ———. *Great lives: Invention and technology.* (Great Lives) New York: Charles Scribner's Sons, 1991.

LUC Lucas, Eileen. *Contemporary human rights activists.* (Global Profiles) New York: Facts on File, 1997.

LUC2 ———. *Naturalists, conservationists, and environmentalists.* (American Profiles) New York: Facts on File, 1994.

LUT Lutz, Norma Jean. *Business and industry.* (Female Firsts in their Fields) Philadelphia: Chelsea House, 1999.

LYM Lyman, Darryl. *Holocaust rescuers: Ten stories of courage.* (Collective Biographies) Berkeley Heights, NJ: Enslow Publishers, 1999.

LYO Lyons, Mary E. *Keeping secrets: The girlhood diaries of seven women writers.* New York: Henry Holt, 1995.

MAC Macht, Norman L. *Famous financeers and innovators.* (Exploring Business and Economics) Philadelphia: Chelsea House, 2002.

MAD Madison, Bob. *American horror writers.* (Collective Biographies) Berkeley Heights, NJ: Enslow Publishers, 2001.

MAL *Male writers.* Edited by Richard Rennert. (Profiles of Great Black Americans) Philadelphia: Chelsea House, 1994.

MAN Mandell, Sherri Lederman. *Writers of the Holocaust.* (Global Profiles) New York: Facts on File, 1999.

MARC Marcus, Leonard S. *A Caldecott celebration: Six artists and their paths to the Caldecott Medal.* New York: Walker & Company, 1998.

MARC2 ———. *Side by side: Five favorite picture book teams go to work.* New York: Walker & Company, 2001.

MARC3 ———. *Ways of telling: Conversations on the art of the picture book.* New York: Dutton, 2002.

MART Martini, Teri. *The secret is out: True spy stories.* Boston: Little, Brown, 1990.

MARV Marvis, Barbara. *Famous people of Hispanic heritage, volume 1.* (Contemporary American Success Stories) Bear, DE: Mitchell Lane, 1996.

MARV2 ———. *Famous people of Hispanic heritage, volume 2.* (Contemporary American Success Stories) Bear, DE: Mitchell Lane, 1996.

MARV3 ———. *Famous people of Hispanic heritage, volume 3.* (Contemporary American Success Stories) Bear, DE: Mitchell Lane, 1996.

MARV4 ———. *Famous people of Hispanic heritage, volume 4.* (Contemporary American Success Stories) Bear, DE: Mitchell Lane, 1996.

MARV5 ———. *Famous people of Hispanic heritage, volume 5.* (Contemporary American Success Stories) Bear, DE: Mitchell Lane, 1996.

MARV6 Marvis, Barbara and Theresa Scott Sevansen. *Famous people of Hispanic heritage, volume 6.* (Contemporary American Success Stories) Bear, DE: Mitchell Lane, 1997.

MARV7 Marvis, Barbara, Melanie Cole and Tony Centu. *Famous people of Hispanic heritage, volume 7.* (Contemporary American Success Stories) Bear, DE: Mitchell Lane, 1997.

MARV8 Marvis, Barbara. *Famous people of Hispanic heritage, volume 10.* (Contemporary American Success Stories) Bear, DE: Mitchell Lane, 1997.

MARX Marx, Trish. *Echoes of World War II.* Minneapolis: Lerner Books, 1994.

MARZ Marzollo, Jean. *My first book of biographies: Great men and women every child should know.* New York: Scholastic Press, 1994.

MAS Mass, Wendy. *Great authors of children's literature.* (History Makers) San Diego: Lucent Books, 2000.

MAYB Mayberry, Jodine. *Business leaders who built financial empires.* (20 Events) Austin, TX: Raintree Steck Vaughn, 1995.

MAYB2 ———. *Leaders who changed the 20th century.* (20 Events) Austin, TX: Raintree Steck Vaughn, 1994.

MAYE Mayer, Marianna. *The twelve apostles.* New York: Penguin Putnam, 2000.

MAYE2 ———. *Women warriors: Myths and legends of heroic women.* New York: William Morrow, 1999.

MCD McDonough, Yona Zeldis. *Sisters of strength: American women who made a difference.* New York: Henry Holt, 2000.

MCK McKissack, Patricia and Frederick. *African-American inventors.* (A Proud Heritage) Brookfield, CT: Millbrook Press, 1994.

MCK2 ———. *African-American scientists.* (A Proud Heritage) Brookfield, CT: Millbrook Press, 1994.

MCLE McLean, Jacqueline. *Women of adventure.* (Profiles) Minneapolis: Oliver Press, 2002.

MCLE2 ———. *Women with wings.* (Profiles) Minneapolis: Oliver Press, 2001.

MCLO McLoone, Margo. *Women explorers in Africa.* (Capstone Short Biographies) Mankato, MN: Capstone Press, 1997.

MCLO2 ———. *Women explorers in Asia.* (Capstone Short Biographies) Mankato, MN: Capstone Press, 1997.

MCLO3 ———. *Women explorers in North and South America.* (Capstone Short Biographies) Mankato, MN: Capstone Press, 1997.

MCLO4 ———. *Women explorers in polar regions.* (Capstone Short Biographies) Mankato, MN: Capstone Press, 1997.

MCLO5 ———. *Women explorers of the air.* (Capstone Short Biographies) Mankato, MN: Capstone Press, 2000.

MCLO6 ———. *Women explorers of the mountains.* (Capstone Short Biographies) Mankato, MN: Capstone Press, 2000.

MCLO7 ———. *Women explorers of the ocean.* (Capstone Short Biographies) Mankato, MN: Capstone Press, 2000.

MCLO8 ———. *Women explorers of the world.* (Capstone Short Biographies) Mankato, MN: Capstone Press, 2000.

MCLU McLuskey, Krista. *Entrepreneurs.* (Women in Profile) New York: Crabtree Publishing Company, 1999.

MED Medearis, Angela Shelf. *Come this far to freedom: A history of African Americans.* New York: Atheneum, 1993.

MEE Meehan, Elizabeth. *Twentieth century American writers.* (History Makers) San Diego: Lucent Books, 2000.

MEI Meisner, James, Jr. and Amy Ruth Meisner. *American Revolutionaries and founders of the nation.* (Collective Biographies) Berkeley Heights, NJ: Enslow Publishers, 1999.

MEL Meltzer, Milton. *Ten kings and the worlds they ruled.* New York: Orchard Books, 2002.

MEL2 ———. *Ten queens: Portraits of women in power.* New York: Dutton Books, 1998.

MEN Menard, Valerie and Melanie Cole. *Famous people of Hispanic heritage, volume 8.* (Contemporary American Success Stories) Bear, DE: Mitchell Lane, 1997.

MILE Miles, Ellen. *Superstars of women's tennis.* (Women Athletes of the New Millennium) New York: Simon & Schuster/Aladdin, 2000.

MILM Miller, Marla. *All-American Girls Soccer: The U.S. Women's National Soccer Team.* New York: Pocket Books, 1999.

MILR Miller, Robert H. *Reflections of a black cowboy.* (Mountain Men) Englewood Cliffs, NJ: Silver Burdett, 1992.

MILT Milton, Steve. *Figure skating champions.* Toronto: Firefly Books, 2002.

MOL Molzahn, Arlene Bourgeois. *Top ten American women sprinters.* (Sports Top Ten) Berkeley Heights, NJ: Enslow Publishers, 1998.

MON Monceaux, Morgan. *Jazz: My music, my people.* New York: Alfred A. Knopf, 1994.

MON2 ———. *My heroes, my people: African Americans and Native Americans in the West.* New York: Frances Foster Books/Farrar Straus, 1999.

MOO Moore, Reavis. *Native artists of North America.* Santa Fe: John Muir Publications, 1993.

MORE Morey, Janet Namura and Wendy Dunn. *Famous Asian Americans.* New York: Cobblehill Books, 1992.

MORE2 *Famous Hispanic Americans.* New York: Cobblehill Books, 1996.

MORI Morin, Isabel. *Women chosen for public office.* (Profiles) Minneapolis: Oliver Press, 1995.

MORI2 ———. *Women of the U.S. Congress.* (Profiles) Minneapolis: Oliver Press, 1994.

MORI3 ———. *Women who reformed politics.* (Profiles) Minneapolis: Oliver Press, 1994.

MORR Morris, Juddi. *At home with the Presidents.* New York: John Wiley and Sons, 1999.

MOU Mour, Stanley. *American jazz musicians.* (Collective Biographies) Berkeley Heights, NJ: Enslow Publishers, 1998.

MUL Mulcahy, Robert. *Diseases: Finding the cure.* (Innovators) Minneapolis: Oliver Press, 1996.

MUL2 ———. *Medical technology: Inventing the instruments.* (Innovators) Minneapolis: Oliver Press, 1997.

NAR Nardo, Don. *Leaders of Ancient Greece.* (History Makers) San Diego: Lucent Books, 1999.

NAR2 ———. *Rulers of Ancient Rome.* (History Makers) San Diego: Lucent Books, 1999.

NAR3 ———. *Scientists of Ancient Greece.* (History Makers) San Diego: Lucent Books, 1999.

NAR4 ———. *Women leaders of nations.* (History Makers) San Diego: Lucent Books, 1999.

NEL Nelson, Glenn, Dalton Ross and Andrea Whitaker. *Rising stars: The ten best young players in the NBA.* New York:

Rosen/Sports Illustrated for Kids, 2002.

NET   Netzley, Patricia D. *Presidential assassins.* (History Makers) San Diego: Lucent Books, 2000.

NIC   Nichols, Janet. *American music makers.* New York: Walker & Company, 1990.

NIC2 ———. *Women music makers: An introduction to women composers.* New York: Walker & Company, 1992.

NIE   Nieuwsma, Milton. *Kinderlager: An oral history of young Holocaust survivors.* New York: Holiday House, 1998.

NIN   *The nineteenth century: Artists, writers and composers.* Edited by Sarah Halliwell. (Who and When) Austin, TX: Raintree Steck Vaughn, 1998.

NOO   Noonan, Jon. *Nineteenth century inventors.* (American Profiles) New York: Facts on File, 1992.

NOR   Northup, Mary. *American computer pioneers.* (Collective Biographies) Berkeley Heights, NJ: Enslow Publishers, 1998.

OCO   O'Connor, Jim. *Comeback! Four true stories.* (Step into Reading) New York: Random House, 1992.

OFT   Oftinoski, Steven. *Great Black writers.* (American Profiles) New York: Facts on File, 1994.

OFT2 ———. *Nineteenth century writers.* (American Profiles) New York: Facts on File, 1991.

OLE   Oleksy, Walter. *Hispanic-American scientists.* (American Profiles) New York: Facts on File, 1998.

OLE2 ———. *Military leaders of World War II.* (American Profiles) New York: Facts on File, 1994.

ORE   O'Reilly, Wenda. *Van Gogh and friends.* Palo Alto, CA: Birdcage Books, 2002.

ORG   Orgill, Roxane. *Shout, sister, shout: Ten girl singers who shaped a century.* New York: Margaret K. McElderry Books, 2001.

PAL   Palacios, Argentina. *Standing tall: The stories of ten Hispanic-Americans.* New York: Scholastic Press, 1994.

PAP   Paperchontis, Kathy. *100 world leaders who shaped world history.* (100 Series) San Francisco: Bluewood Books, 2001.

PARJ   Parker, Janice. *Great African Americans in film.* (Outstanding African Americans) New York: Crabtree Publishing Company, 1997.

PARJ2 ———. *Political leaders.* (Women in Profile) New York: Crabtree Publishing Company, 1998.

PARN   Parker, Nancy Winslow. *Land Ho!: Fifty glorious years in the age of exploration.* New York: HarperCollins, 2001.

PASA   Pasachoff, Naomi. *Links in the chain: Shapers of the Jewish tradition.* (Oxford Profiles) New York: Oxford University Press, 1997.

PAST   Pastan, Amy. *First Ladies.* (Eyewitness Books) New York: Dorling Kindersley, 2001.

PAU   Paul, Alan and Jon Kramer. *Basketball all-stars: The NBA's best.* New York: Rosen/Sports Illustrated for Kids, 2002.

PER   Perkins, Christine M. *100 authors who shaped world history.* (100 Series) San Francisco: Bluewood Books, 1996.

PET   Pettit, Jayne. *A place to hide: True stories of Holocaust rescuers.* (Scholastic Biography) New York: Scholastic Press, 1993.

PIE   Pietrusza, David. *Top ten baseball managers.* (Sports Top Ten) Berkeley Heights, NJ: Enslow Publishers, 1999.

PIL   Pile, Robert B. *Top entrepreneurs and their businesses.* (Profiles) Minneapolis: Oliver Press, 1999.

PIL2 ———. *Women business leaders.* (Profiles) Minneapolis: Oliver Press, 1995.

PIN   Pinkney, Andrea Davis. *Let it shine: Stories of Black women freedom fighters.* San Diego: Harcourt Brace, 2000.

PIO   *Pioneers of discovery.* Edited by Richard Rennert. (Profiles of Great Black Americans) Philadelphia: Chelsea House, 1993.

PLO   Plowden, Martha Ward. *Famous firsts of Black women.* Gretna,LA: Pelican Press, 1993.

POD   Podell, Janet and Steven Anzovin. *Old world to new: The age of exploration and discovery.* (They Changed the World) New York: H.W. Wilson, 1993.

POLK   Polk, Milbry and Mary Tiegreen. *Women of discovery: A celebration of intrepid women who explored the world.* New York: Clarkson Potter, 2001.

POLKI   Polking, Kirk. *Oceanographers and*

explorers of the sea. (Collective Biographies) Berkeley Heights, NJ: Enslow Publishers, 1999.

PON Ponti, James. *WNBA: Stars of women's basketball.* New York: Pocket Books, 1999.

POT Potter, Joan and Constance Clayton. *African Americans who were first.* New York: Dutton/Cobblehill Books, 1997.

POY Poynter, Margaret. *Top Ten American women's figure skaters.* (Sports Top Ten) Berkeley Heights, NJ: Enslow Publishers, 1998.

PRE Prescott, Jerome. *100 explorers who shaped world history.* (100 Series) San Francisco: Bluewood Books, 1996.

PRI Price-Groff, Claire. *Extraordinary women journalists.* (Extraordinary People) New York: Children's Press, 1997.

PRI2 ———. *Great conquerors.* (History Makers) San Diego: Lucent Books, 2000.

PRI3 ———. *Twentieth century women political leaders.* (Global Profiles) New York: Facts on File, 1998.

QUI Quinn, Brother C. Edward. *The signers of the Declaration of Independence.* New York: Bronx County Historical Society, 1988.

RAG Ragaza, Angelo. *Lives of notable Asian Americans: Business, politics, science.* (The Asian American Experience) Philadelphia: Chelsea House, 1995.

RAPD Rappaport, Doreen. *Living dangerously: American women who risked their lives for adventure.* New York: HarperCollins, 1991.

RAPD2 ———. *We are the many: A picture book of American Indians.* New York: HarperCollins, 2002.

RAPK Rappoport, Ken. *Guts and glory: Making it in the NBA.* New York: Walker & Company, 1997.

RAPK2 ———. *Top ten basketball legends.* (Sports Top Ten) Berkeley Heights, NJ: Enslow Publishers, 1995.

RAS Rasmussen, R. Kent. *Modern African political leaders.* (Global Profiles) New York: Facts on File, 1998.

RED Rediger, Pat. *Great African Americans in business.* (Outstanding African Americans) New York: Crabtree Publishing Company, 1996.

RED2 ———. *Great African Americans in civil rights.* (Outstanding African Americans) New York: Crabtree Publishing Company, 1996.

RED3 ———. *Great African Americans in entertainment.* (Outstanding African Americans) New York: Crabtree Publishing Company, 1996.

RED4 ———. *Great African Americans in literature.* (Outstanding African Americans) New York: Crabtree Publishing Company, 1996.

RED5 ———. *Great African Americans in music.* (Outstanding African Americans) New York: Crabtree Publishing Company, 1996.

RED6 ———. *Great African Americans in sports.* (Outstanding African Americans) New York: Crabtree Publishing Company, 1996.

REE Reef, Catherine. *Black explorers.* (American Profiles) New York: Facts on File, 1996.

REE2 ———. *Black fighting men: A proud history.* (African American Soldiers) New York: 21st Century Books, 1994.

REG Reger, James P. *Civil War Generals of the Confederacy.* (History Makers) San Diego: Lucent Books, 1999.

REN *The Renaissance: Artists and writers.* Edited by Sarah Halliwell. (Who and When) Austin, TX: Raintree Steck Vaughn, 1998.

REY Reynolds, Moira Davison. *American women scientists: 23 inspiring biographies 1900-2000.* Jefferson, NC: McFarland and Company, 1999.

RIC Richie, Jason. *Secretaries of State: Making foreign policy.* (In the Cabinet) Minneapolis: Oliver Press, 2002.

RIC2 ———. *Secretaries of War, Navy and Defense: Ensuring national security.* (In the Cabinet) Minneapolis: Oliver Press, 2002.

RIC3 ———. *Space flight: Crossing the last frontier.* (Innovators) Minneapolis: Oliver Press, 2001.

RIC4 ———. *Spectacular space travelers.* (Profiles) Minneapolis: Oliver Press, 2001.

RIC5 ———. *Weapons: Designing the tools of war.* (Innovators) Minneapolis: Oliver Press, 2001.

RIL Riley, Gail Blasser. *Top ten Nascar Drivers.* (Sports Top Ten) Berkeley Heights, NJ: Enslow Publishers, 1995.

RIT Ritchie, Donald A. *American journalists: Getting the story.* (Oxford Profiles) New York: Oxford University Press, 1997.

ROBB Robb, Jacqueline. *Go Girl!: Young women superstars of pop music.* Greensboro, NC: Avisson Press, Inc., 2000.

ROBE Roberts, Russell. *American women of medicine.* (Collective Biographies) Berkeley Heights, NJ: Enslow Publishers, 2002.

ROBE2 ———. *Presidents and scandals.* (History Makers) San Diego: Lucent Books, 2001.

ROBE3 ———. *Rulers of Ancient Egypt.* (History Makers) San Diego: Lucent Books, 1999.

ROC Rochelle, Belinda. *Witnesses to freedom: Young people who fought for civil rights.* New York: Dutton Lodestar, 1993.

ROE Roehm, Michelle. *Girls who rocked the world 2: Heroines from Harriet Tubman to Mia Hamm.* Hillsboro, OR: Beyond Words Publishing, 2000.

ROL Rolka, Gail Meyer. *100 women who shaped world history.* (100 Series) San Francisco: Bluewood Books, 1994.

ROM *The Romantics: artists, writers, and composers.* Edited by Sarah Halliwell. (Who and When) Austin, TX: Raintree Steck Vaughn, 1998.

ROS Rosenbaum, Robert A. *Aviators.* (American Profiles) New York: Facts on File, 1992.

RUT Rutledge, Rachel. *The best of the best in basketball.* (Women of Sports) Brookfield, CT: Millbrook Press, 1998.

RUT2 ———. *The best of the best in figure skating.* (Women of Sports) Brookfield, CT: Millbrook Press, 1998.

RUT3 ———. *The best of the best in gymnastics.* (Women of Sports) Brookfield, CT: Millbrook Press, 1999.

RUT4 ———. The *best of the best in soccer.* (Women of Sports) Brookfield, CT: Millbrook Press, 1998.

RUT5 ———. *The best of the best in tennis.* (Women of Sports) Brookfield, CT: Millbrook Press, 1998.

RUT6 ———. The *best of the best in track and field.* (Women of Sports) Brookfield, CT: Millbrook Press, 1999.

RYL Rylant, Cynthia. *Margaret, Frank and Andy: Three writers' stories.* San Diego: Harcourt Brace, 1996.

SAB Sabbeth, Carol. *Monet and the Impressionists for kids.* Chicago: Chicago Review Press, 2002.

SAT Satter, James. *Journalists who made history.* (Profiles) Minneapolis: Oliver Press, 1998.

SAV Savage, Jeff. *Gunfighters of the Old West.* (Trailblazers of the Wild West) Berkeley Heights, NJ: Enslow Publishers, 1995.

SAV2 ———. *Pioneering women of the Wild West.* (Trailblazers of the Wild West) Berkeley Heights, NJ: Enslow Publishers, 1995.

SAV3 ———. *Scouts of the Wild West.* (Trailblazers of the Wild West) Berkeley Heights, NJ: Enslow Publishers, 1995.

SAV4 ———. *Top Ten African-American men's athletes.* (Sports Top Ten) Berkeley Heights, NJ: Enslow Publishers, 2001.

SAV5 ———. *Top ten basketball point guards.* (Sports Top Ten) Berkeley Heights, NJ: Enslow Publishers, 1997.

SAV6 ———. *Top ten basketball power forwards.* (Sports Top Ten) Berkeley Heights, NJ: Enslow Publishers, 1997.

SAV7 ———. *Top ten football sackers.* (Sports Top Ten) Berkeley Heights, NJ: Enslow Publishers, 1997.

SAV8 ———. *Top ten Heisman trophy winners.* (Sports Top Ten) Berkeley Heights, NJ: Enslow Publishers, 1999.

SAV9 ———. *Top ten in-line skaters.* (Sports Top Ten) Berkeley Heights, NJ: Enslow Publishers, 1999.

SAV10 ———. *Top ten physically challenged athletes.* (Sports Top Ten) Berkeley Heights, NJ: Enslow Publishers, 2000.

SAV11 ———. *Top ten professional football coaches.* (Sports Top Ten) Berkeley Heights, NJ: Enslow Publishers, 1998.

SAV12 ———. *Top ten sports bloopers and who made them.* (Sports Top Ten) Berkeley Heights, NJ: Enslow Publishers, 2000.

SAV13 ———. *Top ten women's basketball stars.* (Sports Top Ten) Berkeley Heights, NJ: Enslow Publishers, 2001.

SAV14 ———. *Top ten women's sports legends.* (Sports Top Ten) Berkeley Heights, NJ: Enslow Publishers, 2001.

SAW Sawyers, June. *Famous firsts of Scottish-Americans.* Gretna, LA: Pelican Publishers, 1997.

SAY Sayre, April Pulley. *Secrets of sound: Studying the calls and songs of whales, elephants, and birds.* (Scientists in the Field) Boston: Houghton Mifflin, 2002.

SCHEL Scheller, William. *Amazing archaeologists and their finds.* (Profiles) Minneapolis: Oliver Press, 1994.

SCHEL2 ———. *The world's greatest explorers.* (Profiles) Minneapolis: Oliver Press, 1992.

SCHER Scher, Jon. *Baseball's best sluggers.* New York: Rosen/Sports Illustrated for Kids, 2000.

SCHM Schmittroth, Linda and Mary Kay Rosteck. *American Revolution: Biographies, vol. 1.* Detroit: UXL, 2000.

SCHM2 ———. *American Revolution: Biographies: vol. 2.* Detroit: UXL, 2000.

SCHM3 ———. *People of the Holocaust, A-J.* Detroit: UXL, 1998.

SCHM4 ———. *People of the Holocaust, K-Z.* Detroit: UXL, 1998.

SCHR Schraff, Anne. *American heroes of exploration and flight.* (Collective Biographies) Berkeley Heights, NJ: Enslow Publishers, 1996.

SCHR2 ———. *Women of peace: Nobel Prize winners.* (Collective Biographies) Berkeley Heights, NJ: Enslow Publishers, 1994.

SCHWAB Schwabacher, Martin. *Superstars of women's tennis.* (Female Sports Stars) Philadelphia: Chelsea House, 1997.

SCHWAR Schwarz, Alan. *Baseball All-Stars.* New York: Rosen/Sports Illustrated for Kids, 1999.

SCHWAR2 ———. *Rising stars: The ten best young players in baseball.* New York: Sports Illustrated for Kids, 2000.

SEHN Sehnert, Chris. *Sluggers.* (Top Ten Champions) Bloomington, MN: Abdo and Daughters, 1997.

SEV *The seventeenth century: Artists, writers and composers.* Edited by Sarah Halliwell. (Who and When) Austin, TX: Raintree Steck Vaughn, 1998.

SHAP *Shapers of America.* Edited by Richard Rennert. (Profiles of Great African Americans) Philadelphia: Chelsea House, 1993.

SHAR Sharp, Anne Wallace. *Daring pirate women.* (A & E Biography) Minneapolis: Lerner Books, 2002.

SHAW Shaw, Maura D. *Ten amazing people and how they changed the world.* Woodstock, VT: Skylights Path Publishers, 2002.

SHEA Sheafer, Silvia. *Women in America's wars.* (Collective Biographies) Berkeley Heights, NJ: Enslow Publishers, 1996.

SHER Sherrow, Victoria. *Great Scientists.* (American Profiles) New York: Facts on File, 1992.

SHER2 ———. *Political leaders and peacemakers.* (American Indian Lives) New York: Facts on File, 1994.

SHIP Shipton, Allyn. *Jazzmakers: Vanguards of sound.* (Oxford Profiles) New York: Oxford University Press, 2002.

SHIR Shirey, Lynn M. *Latin American writers.* (Global Profiles) New York: Facts on File, 1997.

SILC Silcox-Jarrett, Diane. *Heroines of the American Revolution: America's founding mothers.* Chapel Hill, NC: Green Angel Press, 1998.

SILL Sills, Leslie. *In real life: Six women photographers.* New York: Holiday House, 2000.

SILL2 ———. *Inspirations: Stories about women artists.* Morton Grove, IL: Albert Whitman & Company, 1989.

SILL3 ———. *Visions: Stories about women artists.* Morton Grove, IL: Albert Whitman & Company, 1993.

SIN Sinnott, Susan. *Extraordinary Asian Pacific Americans.* (Extraordinary People) New York: Children's Press, 1993.

SIN2 ———. *Extraordinary Hispanic Americans.* (Extraordinary People) New York: Children's Press, 1991.

SIR Sirch, Willow Ann. *Eco-women: Protectors of the earth.* Golden, CO: Fulcrum Press, 1996.

SLO   Sloate, Susan. *Hotshots baseball: Greats of the game when they were kids.* New York: Rosen/Sports Illustrated for Kids, 1991.

SMIL   Smith, Lucinda Irwin. *Women who write: From the past and the present to the future.* Englewood Cliffs, NJ: Julian Messner, 1989.

SMIL2 ———. *Women who write: From the past and the present to the future, volume 2.* Englewood Cliffs, NJ: Julian Messner, 1994.

SMIP   Smith, Pohla. *Superstars of women's figure skating.* (Female Sports Stars) Philadelphia: Chelsea House, 1997.

SPA   Spangenberg, Ray and Diane K. Moser. *Disease fighters since 1950.* (Global Profiles) Facts on File, 1996.

SPI   Spiros, Dean. *Top ten hockey goalies.* (Sports Top Ten) Berkeley Heights, NJ: Enslow Publishers, 1998.

STA   Stanley, Phyllis. *American environmental heroes.* (Collective Biographies) Berkeley Heights, NJ: Enslow Publishers, 1996.

STEFF   Steffens, Bradley and Robyn M. Weaver. *Cartoonists.* (History Makers) San Diego: Lucent Books, 2000.

STEFO   Stefoff, Rebecca. *Scientific explorers: Travels in search of knowledge.* (Extraordinary Explorers) New York: Oxford University Press, 1992.

STEFO2 ———. *Women of the world: Women travelers and explorers.* (Extraordinary Explorers) New York: Oxford University Press, 1992.

STEFO3 ———. *Women pioneers.* (American Profiles) New York: Facts on File, 1995.

STEW   Stewart, Gail. *Great women comedians.* (History Makers) San Diego: Lucent Books, 2002.

STEWM   Stewart, Mark with Mike Kennedy. *Latino baseball's finest fielders.* Brookfield, CT: Millbrook Press, 2002.

STEWM ———. *Latino baseball's hottest hitters.* Brookfield, CT: Millbrook Press, 2002.

STG   St. George, Judith. *In the line of fire: Presidents lives at stake.* New York: Holiday House, 1999.

STI   Stille, Darlene. *Extraordinary women of medicine.* (Extraordinary People) New York: Children's Press, 1997.

STI2 ———. *Extraordinary women scientists.* (Extraordinary People) New York: Children's Press, 1995.

STJ   St. John, Jetty. *African-American scientists.* (Capstone Short Biographies) Mankato, MN: Capstone Press, 1996.

STJ2 ———. *Hispanic scientists.* (Capstone Short Biographies) Mankato, MN: Capstone Press, 1996.

STJ3 ———. *Native American scientists.* (Capstone Short Biographies) Mankato, MN: Capstone Press, 1996.

STRE   Streissguth, Thomas. *Charismatic cult leaders.* (Profiles) Minneapolis: Oliver Press, 1995.

STRE2 ———. *Communication: Sending the message.* (Innovators) Minneapolis: Oliver Press, 1997.

STRE3 ———. *Hatemongers and demagogues.* (Profiles) Minneapolis: Oliver Press, 1995.

STRE4 ———. *International terrorists.* (Profiles) Minneapolis: Oliver Press, 1993.

STRE5 ———. *Legendary labor leaders.* (Profiles) Minneapolis: Oliver Press, 1998.

STRE6 ———. *Utopian visionaries.* (Profiles) Minneapolis: Oliver Press, 1999.

STRI   Strickland, Michael. *African American poets.* (Collective Biographies) Berkeley Heights, NJ: Enslow Publishers, 1996.

STRU   Strudwick, Leslie. *Athletes.* (Women in Profile) New York: Crabtree Publishing Company, 1999.

STRU2 ———. *Musicians.* (Women in Profile) New York: Crabtree Publishing Company, 1998.

STU   Stux, Erica. *Eight who made a difference: Pioneer women in the arts.* Greensboro, NC: Avisson Press, 1999.

SULG   Sullivan, George. *Black artists in photography 1840-1940.* New York: Cobblehill/Dutton, 1996.

SULG2 ———. *Glovemen: 27 of baseball's greatest.* New York: Atheneum, 1996.

SULG3 ———. *Great lives: Sports.* (Great Lives) New York: Charles Scribner's Sons, 1988.

SULG4 ———. *In the line of fire: Eight women war spies.* New York: Scholastic Press, 1996.

SULG5 ———. *Pitchers: 27 of baseball's greatest.* New York: Atheneum, 1994.

SULG6 ———. *Portraits of war: Civil War photographers and their work.* Brookfield, CT: Twenty First Century Books, 1998.

SULG7 ———. *Quarterbacks.* New York: Atheneum, 1998.

SULG8 ———. *Sluggers.* New York: Atheneum, 1991.

SULG9 ———. *They shot the President: Ten true stories.* New York: Scholastic Press, 1993.

SULM Sullivan, Michael J. *Top ten baseball pitchers.* (Sports Top Ten) Berkeley Heights, NJ: Enslow Publishers, 1994.

SULO Sullivan, Otha Richard. *African American inventors.* (Black Stars) New York: John Wiley and Sons, 1998.

SULO2 ———. *African American women scientists and inventors.* (Black Stars) New York: John Wiley and Sons, 2002.

TAI Taitz, Emily and Sondra Henry. *Remarkable Jewish women: Rebels, rabbis and other women from biblical times to the present.* Philadelphia: Jewish Publication Society, 1996.

TALAD *Talking with adventurers.* Edited by Pat and Linda Cummings. Washington, D.C.: National Geographic Press, 1998.

TALAR *Talking with artists, volume 1.* Edited by Pat Cummings. New York: Bradbury Press, 1992.

TALAR2 *Talking with artists, volume 2.* Edited by Pat Cummings. New York: Simon & Schuster, 1995.

TALAR3 *Talking with artists, volume 3.* Edited by Pat Cummings. New York: Clarion Press, 1999.

TAT Tate, Eleanora E. *African American musicians.* (Black Stars) New York: John Wiley and Sons, 2000.

TAYK Taylor, Kimberly. *Black abolitionists and freedom fighters.* (Profiles) Minneapolis: Oliver Press, 1996.

TAYK2 ———. *Black civil rights champions.* (Profiles) Minneapolis: Oliver Press, 1995.

TAYS Taylor, Sherri Peel. *Influential First Ladies.* (History Makers) San Diego: Lucent Books, 2001.

TAYS2 ———. *Pioneers of the American West.* (History Makers) San Diego: Lucent Books, 2002.

TES Tessendorf, K. C. *Over the edge: Flying with the Arctic heroes.* New York: Atheneum, 1998.

THI Thimmesh, Catherine. *Girls think of everything: Stories of ingenious inventions.* Boston: Houghton Mifflin, 2000.

THI2 ———. *The sky's the limit: Stories of discovery by girls and women.* Boston: Houghton Mifflin, 2002.

THIR *33 things every girl should know about women's history: From suffragettes to skirt lengths to the ERA.* Edited by Tanya Bolden. New York: Crown Publishers, 2002.

THOM Thomas, Paul. *Campaigners.* (Rebels with a Cause) Austin, TX: Raintree Steck Vaughn, 1998.

THOM2 ———. *Outlaws.* (Rebels with a Cause) Austin, TX: Raintree Steck Vaughn, 1998.

THOM3 ———. *Revolutionaries.* (Rebels with a Cause) Austin, TX: Raintree Steck Vaughn, 1998.

THOM4 ———. *Undercover agents.* (Rebels with a Cause) Austin, TX: Raintree Steck Vaughn, 1998.

THOR Thornley, Stew. *Top ten football receivers.* (Sports Top Ten) Berkeley Heights, NJ: Enslow Publishers, 1995.

THRA Thrasher, Thomas. *Gunfighters of the American West.* (History Makers) San Diego: Lucent Books, 2000.

THRO Thro, Ellen. *Twentieth century women politicians.* (American Profiles) New York: Facts on File, 1998.

TIN Tiner, John Hudson. *100 scientists who shaped world history.* (100 Series) San Francisco: Bluewood Books, 2000.

TIT Tito, E. Tina. *Teens in the concentration camps and the soldiers who liberated them.* (Teen Witnesses to the Holocaust) New York: Rosen Publishing Group, 1999.

TOR Torres, John A. *Home-run hitters: Heroes of the four home-run games.* New York: Macmillan Books for Young Readers, 1995.

TOR2 ———. *Top ten baseball legends.* (Sports Top Ten) Berkeley Heights, NJ: Enslow Publishers, 2001.

TOR3 ———. *Top ten basketball three-point shooters.* (Sports Top Ten) Berkeley Heights, NJ: Enslow Publishers, 1999.

TOR4 ———. *Top ten NBA finals most valuable players.* (Sports Top Ten) Berkeley Heights, NJ: Enslow Publishers, 2000.

TRAC Tracey, Patrick Austin. *Military leaders of the Civil War.* (American Profiles) New York: Facts on File, 1993.

TRAC2 ———. *Political and reform leaders in Eastern Europe and the former Soviet Union.* (Global Profiles) New York: Facts on File, Inc., 1996.

TRAU Traub, Carol. *Philanthropists and their legacies* (Profiles) Minneapolis: Oliver Press, 1997.

TUR Turner, Glennette Tilley. *Follow in their footsteps.* New York: Cobblehill Books/Dutton, 1997.

TUR2 ———. *Take a walk in their shoes.* New York: Dutton, 1989.

TWEPO *The twentieth century: Post-1945: Artists, writers and composers.* Edited by Sarah Halliwell. (Who and When) Austin, TX: Raintree Steck Vaughn, 1998.

TWEPR *The twentieth century: Pre-1945: Artists, writers and composers.* Edited by Sarah Halliwell. (Who and When) Austin, TX: Raintree Steck Vaughn, 1998.

UNG Unger, Harlow G. *Teachers and educators.* (American Profiles) New York: Facts on File, 1994.

USC Uschan, Michael V. *America's founders.* (History Makers) San Diego: Lucent Books, 2000.

USC2 ———. *Home run kings.* (History Makers) San Diego: Lucent Books, 2000.

USC3 ———. *The Kennedys.* (History Makers) San Diego: Lucent Books, 2002.

USC4 ———. *Male Olympic champions.* (History Makers) San Diego: Lucent Books, 2000.

VAR Vare, Ethlie Ann and Greg Ptacek. *Women inventors and their discoveries.* (Profiles) Minneapolis: Oliver Press, 1993.

VEG Veglahn, Nancy. *Women scientists.* (American Profiles) New York: Facts on File, 1991.

VEN Ventura, Piero. *Great composers.* New York: G.P. Putnam's Sons, 1989.

VERD Verde, Tom. *Twentieth-Century writers 1950-1990.* (American Profiles) New York: Facts on File, 1996.

VERN Vernell, Marjorie. *Leaders of Black civil rights.* (History Makers) San Diego: Lucent Books, 2000.

WAK Wakin, Edward. *Contemporary political leaders of the Middle East.* (Global Profiles) New York: Facts on File, 1996.

WAKI Wakin, Eric. *Asian independence leaders.* (Global Profiles) New York: Facts on File, Inc, 1997.

WAL Walker, Paul Robert. *Great figures of the Wild West.* (American Profiles) New York: Facts on File, 1992.

WAT Waterlow, Julia. *The explorer through history.* London: Thomson Learning, 1994.

WE *We are witnesses: Five diaries of teenagers who died in the Holocaust.* Edited by Jacob Boas. New York: Henry Holt, 1995.

WE2 *We rode the wind: Recollections of Native American life.* Edited by Jane B. Katz. Minneapolis: Runestone Press/Lerner Publishing Group, 1995.

WEA Weatherly, Myra. *Women pirates: Eight stories of adventure.* Greensboro, NC: Morgan Reynolds, 1998.

WEI Weitzman, David. *Great lives: Human culture.* (Great Lives) New York: Charles Scribner's Sons, 1994.

WEI2 ———. *Great lives: Theatre.* (Great Lives) New York: Atheneum, 1996.

WEL Welden, Amelie. *Girls who rocked the world: Heroines from Sacagawea to Sheryl Swoopes.* Hillsboro, OR: Beyond Words Publishing, 1998.

WHI Whitelaw, Nancy. *They wrote their own headlines: American women journalists.* (World Writers) Greensboro, NC: Morgan Reynolds, 1994.

WILKB Wilkinson, Brenda. *African American women writers.* (Black Stars) New York: John Wiley and Sons, 2000.

WILKP Wilkinson, Philip and Michael Pollard. *Generals who changed the world.* (Turning Points in History) Philadelphia:

Chelsea House, 1994.

WILKP2   Wilkinson, Philip and Jacqueline Dineen. *People who changed the world.* (Turning Points in History) Philadelphia: Chelsea House, 1994.

WILKP3   Wilkinson, Philip and Michael Pollard. *Scientists who changed the world.* (Turning Points in History) Philadelphia: Chelsea House, 1994.

WILKP4   Wilkinson, Philip and Jacqueline Dineen. *Statesmen who changed the world.* (Turning Points in History) Philadelphia: Chelsea House, 1994.

WILLI   Williams, Brian. *Pioneers of flight.* (Tales of Courage) Austin, TX: Raintree Steck Vaughn, 1990.

WILLI2   ———. *Voyages of discovery.* (Tales of Courage) Austin, TX: Raintree Steck Vaughn, 1990.

WILLS   Wills, Susan and Steven. *Astronomy: Looking at the stars.* (Innovators) Minneapolis: Oliver Press, 2001.

WIN   Winter, Jonah. *Beisbol! Latino baseball pioneers and legends.* New York: Lee & Low, 2001.

WIN2   ———. *Fair ball! 14 great stars from baseball's Negro Leagues.* New York: Scholastic Press, 1999.

WOL   Wolf, Sylvia. *Focus: Five women photographers.* Morton Grove, IL: Albert Whitman and Company, 1994.

WOO   Woog, Adam. *Gangsters.* (History Makers) San Diego: Lucent Books, 2000.

WOO2   ———. *Magicians and illusionists.* (History Makers) San Diego: Lucent Books, 2000.

WOO3   ———. *Rock and roll legends.* (History Makers) San Diego: Lucent Books, 2001.

WYB   Wyborny, Sheila. *Astronauts.* (History Makers) San Diego: Lucent Books, 2001.

YAN   Yancey, Diane. *Civil War Generals of the Union.* (History Makers) San Diego: Lucent Books, 1999.

YEA   Yeatts, Tabitha. *Forensics: Solving the crime.* (Innovators) Minneapolis: Oliver Press, 2001.

YEN   Yenne, Bill. *100 men who shaped world history.* (100 Series) San Francisco: Bluewood Books, 1994.

YOUNG   Young, Jeff C. *Top ten basketball shot-blockers.* (Sports Top Ten) Berkeley Heights, NJ: Enslow Publishers, 2000.

YOUNG2   ———. *Top ten World Series MVP.* (Sports Top Ten) Berkeley Heights, NJ: Enslow Publishers, 2001.

YOUNT   Yount, Lisa. *Asian-American scientists.* (American Profiles) New York: Facts on File, 1998.

YOUNT2   ———. *Black scientists.* (American Profiles) New York: Facts on File, 1991.

YOUNT3   ———. *Contemporary women scientists.* (American Profiles) New York: Facts on File, 1994.

YOUNT4   ———. *Disease detectives.* (History Makers) San Diego: Lucent Books, 2001.

YOUNT5   ———. *Pirates.* (History Makers) San Diego: Lucent Books, 2002.

YOUNT6   ———. *Twentieth century women scientists.* (Global Profiles) New York: Facts on File, 1996.

YOUNT7   ———. *Women aviators.* (American Profiles) New York: Facts on File, 1995.

YUN   Yunghans, Penelope. *Prize winners: Ten writers for young people.* (World Writers) Greensboro, NC: Morgan Reynolds, 1995.

ZAU   Zaunders, Bo. *Crocodiles, camels and dugout canoes: Eight adventurous episodes.* New York: Dutton Publishing Company, 1998.

ZAU2   ———. *Feathers, flaps and flops: Fabulous early flyers.* New York: Dutton Publishing Company, 2001.

ZEI   Zeinert, Karen. *Those courageous women of the Civil War.* Brookfield, CT: Millbrook Press, 1998.

ZEI2   ———. *Those extraordinary women of World War I.* Brookfield, CT: Millbrook Press, 2001.

ZEI3   ———. *Those incredible women of World War II.* Brookfield, CT: Millbrook Press, 1994.

ZEI4   ———. *Those remarkable women of the American Revolution.* Brookfield, CT: Millbrook Press, 1996.

ZEI5   ———. *Women in politics: In the running.* Brookfield, CT: Twenty first Century Books, 2002.

Part II

THE BIOGRAPHEES

The Biographees

A

Aaron, Henry "Hank" (1934-) Baseball player. Presidential Medal of Freedom recipient. DEA; DEA2; ITA; KRAMS; SEHN; SULG8; USC2.

Abbott, Berenice. (1898-1991) Photographer. HOR.

Abbott, Jim. (1967-) Baseball player. JEN2; KEND; SAV10; SLO; SULG2.

Abbott, Maude Elizabeth Seymour. (1869-1940) Medical researcher, physician. STI.

Abbott, Robert Sengstacke. (1870-1940) Civil rights activist, newspaper editor. AFR; ALTMS; BECKN.

Abbott, Teddy. (1860-?) Cowboy. HOOS.

Abdul-Jabbar, Kareem. (1947-) Basketball player. DEE; JACT; KNA5; KNA11; SAV4; YOUNG.

Abdul-Rauf, Mahmoud. (Chris Jackson) (1969-) Basketball player. RAPK.

Abdur-Rahim, Ahareef. (1976-) Basketball player. NEL.

Abel, Rudolf Ivanovich. (1920-1971) Russian spy. MART.

Abelard, Pierre. (1097-1142) French orator. KRAL.

Abernathy, Ralph David. (1926-1990) Civil rights activist, spiritual leader. RED2.

Abigail. Biblical character. ARM2.

Abrabanel, Benvenida. (d. 1560) Italian political activist, scholar, born Spain. TAI.

Abraham. (c. 1800 B.C.) Biblical character. CRO5.

Abrahamson, James A. (1933-) Space Flight director, Vietnam War Air Force lieutenant general. BOR.

Abrams, Creighton W. (1914-1974) Vietnam War Army Chief of Staff, World War II general. BOR.

Abrams, George. (1939-) Seneca Indian anthropologist. AVE.

Abreu, Bobby. (1974-) Baseball player, born Venezuela. STEWM2.

Abu Bakr. (1050-1087) Islamic general. WILKP.

Abzug, Bella. (1920-1998) Congresswoman, peace activist. FIR; GUL.

Acheson, Dean. (1893-1971) Attorney, author, cabinet member. Presidential Medal of Freedom recipient, Pulitzer Prize winner. RIC.

Adams, Abigail. (1744-1818) American Revolutionary War patriot, First Lady, women's rights activist. BARB; CRO4; FUR; FUR3; GOR; HARN; PAST; SCHM; SILC; ZEI4.

Adams, Ansel. (1902-1984) Photographer. Presidential Medal of Freedom recipient. CUS; GAI.

Adams, Eugene W. (1920-) Medical researcher, pathologist, veterinarian. HAY.

Adams, Harriet Chalmers. (1875-1937) Adventurer, geographer, photographer. MCLE.

Adams, John. (1735-1826) American Revolutionary War patriot, attorney, Declaration of Independence signer, 2nd president of U.S. ADA; BARB; BAU; BLASS; CRO; CRO4; CRO6; DAV2; EME; FAB; FRA2;

KRULL5; MEI; MORR; QUI; SCHM; USC.

Adams, John Quincy. (1767-1848) Ambassador, cabinet member, congressman, 6th president of U.S., senator. ADA; BARB; BAU; BLASS; BRIL; CRO; CRO6; DAV2; FAB; HOOS; MORR; RIC.

Adams, Louisa Catherine Johnson. (1775-1852) First Lady. BARB; GOR; PAST.

Adams, Michael. (1963-) Basketball player. TOR3.

Adams, Samuel. (1722-1803) American Revolutionary War patriot, brewer, Declaration of Independence signer, governor, publisher. CRO2; FRA2; QUI; SCHM.

Adams, Scott. (1957-) Cartoonist. STEF.

Adams, William. (1564-1620) English explorer. POD.

Adcock, Joe. (1927-) Baseball player. TOR.

Addams, Jane. (1860-1935) Community activist, human rights activist, social worker. Nobel Peace Prize winner. BLU; CLA; DEN; DUN; HARN; HER; JACW; KEEN2; KRAMB2; MAYB2; ROL; SCHR2; THIR.

Ader, Clement. (1841-1926) French aviation pioneer, electrical engineer, inventor. BERL2.

Adler, Henny. (1925-) German Jewish Holocaust survivor. LAND4.

Adler, Sam. (unknown) German Jewish Holocaust survivor. LAND4.

Aebi, Tania. (1966-) Adventurer, sailor. MCLO7.

Aeschylus. (c. 525-456 B.C.) Greek playwright. BAKR2.

Aesop. (c. 600 B.C.) Greek storyteller. BAKR2; KRAL; PER.

Africanus, Leo. (Giovanni Leone) (1495-1553) Spanish explorer. POD.

Agassi, Andre. (1970-) Olympic tennis player. CHRIST.

Agassiz, Louis. (1807-1873) Educator, naturalist, born Switzerland. FAB3; KEEN; PRE; TIN.

Agnesi, Maria Gaetana. (1718-1799) Italian mathematician. CEL.

Agnodice. (c. 300 B.C.) Greek physician. HAZ2.

Agrippa. (Marcus Vippsanius Agrippa) (63-12 B.C.) Roman general. BAKR3.

Agrippina the Young. (Agrippina Minor) (15-59) Roman wife of Claudius, mother of Nero. BAKR3.

Aguilera, Christina. (1966-) Pop singer. KRULI.

Aguilar, Grace. (1816-1847) English author, scholar. TAI.

Aguinaldo, Emilio. (1869-1964) Filipino military leader, revolutionary. WAKI.

Agustin, Maria. (La Saragosa) (1786-1857) Spanish soldier. ROL.

Ah Puch. Mayan god of death. FIS2.

Ahad Ha'am. See Ginzberg, Asher.

Ahmose (fl. 1535 B.C.) Egyptian navy captain. BAKR.

Ahn, Chang-Ho. (1878-1938) Human rights activist, born Korea. SIN.

Ahn, Philip. (1911-1978) Actor. SIN.

Ahyokah. (1811-?) Cherokee Indian lexicographer, daughter of Sequoyah. HOOS.

Aiken, Howard. (1900-1973) Computer pioneer. AAS19.

Aikman, Troy. (1966-) Football player. SULG7.

Ailey, Alvin. (1931-1989) Dancer and choreographer. FOR; HAC4.

Ainge, Danny. (1959-) Basketball player. TOR3.

Aiyaruk, Princess. (c. 1280) Tartan wrestler. JACT.

Akeley, Delia. (1875-1970) Explorer. MCLO; POLK; RAPD.

Akeley, Mary Leonore Jobe. (1878-1966) Explorer. POLK.

Akers, Michelle. (1966-) Olympic soccer player. BRIL5; KAM; LAY2; MILM; RUT4.

Akhmatova, Anna. (1889-1966) Russian poet. HAZ2; KNI.

Akiba ben Joseph. (c. 50-135) Hebrew scholar, spiritual leader, founder of Rabbinic Judaism. PASA.

Akiyoshi, Toshiko. (1929-) Bandleader, composer, jazz musician, born China. SIN.

al-Ghazali. (1058-1111) Islamic Iranian spiritual leader. CRO5.

al-Kahina, Damia. (fl. 680) North African political activist. LEO2.

al-Sharki, Amatalrauf. (1958-) Yemenite

women's rights activist. WEL.

Alaminos, Antón de. (1482-1520) Spanish explorer, navigator. SIN2.

Alaric the Goth. (370-410) Romanian military warlord. CRO3.

Albéniz, Isaac. (1860-1909) Spanish composer, musician. VEN.

Albert, Prince. (1819-1861) English ruler, husband of Queen Victoria. CRO4.

Albright, Madeleine. (1937-) Cabinet member, born Czechoslovakia. GUL; HARN; JONV.

Albright, Tenley. (1935-) Olympic figure skater, physician. HASD; POY.

Alburquerque, Afonso de. (1453-1515) Portuguese explorer. POD.

Alcibiades.(450-405 B.C.) Greek general, traitor. BAKR2; CRO3; NAR.

Alcock, Sir John. (1892-1919) English aviation pioneer, World War I captain. WILLI.

Alcott, Louisa May. (1832-1888) Children's author. CHA; FAB2; HARN; HER; KRULL6; LYO; NIN; PER; ROL; THIR.

Alcuin of York. (732-804) English scholar. CRO4.

Alden, Howard. (1948-) Jazz musician. GOU3.

Alden, John. (1599-1687) Colonist, born England. KRAL.

Aldrin, Edwin, Jr. "Buzz" (1930-) Astronaut. Presidential Medal of Freedom winner. MARZ; PRE.

Aleu, Moises. (1966-) Baseball player, born Dominican Republic. STEWM2.

Alexander, Annie Montague. (1867-1950) Naturalist, palentologist. POLK.

Alexander, Grover Cleveland. (1887-1950) Baseball player. SAV10; SULG5; SULM

Alexander, Hattie Elizabeth. (1901-1968) Bacteriologist, medical researcher, physician. STI.

Alexander the Great. (356-323 B.C.) Greek military leader, ruler. ALTE; BAKR2; CRO3; CRO4; MEL; NAR; PRI2; WILKP; YEN.

Alexander, William. (1916-) Filmmaker. AFR.

Alexandra. (1872-1918) Russian czarina. CRO4.

Alexeyev, Vasily. (1942-) Russian olympic weight lifter. JACT; USC4.

Alexie, Sherman. (1966-) Spokane-Coeur D'Alene Indian author, poet, screenwriter. RAPD2.

Alfhild (Alvida) (c. 1000) Viking pirate. SHAR; WEA.

Alfonzo, Edgardo. (1974-) Baseball player, born Venezuela. STEWM.

Alfred the Great. (849-901) English navy founder. CRO3.

Alger, Horatio. (1832-1899) Children's author. KRAL.

Ali, Muhammad. (1942-) Olympic boxer. BECKN; ITA2; JACT; JAN; KNA7; LEVE; LIT; POT; RED6; SAV4; SULG3.

Aliengena, Tony. (1978-) Child pilot. BRIL.

Aliquipso. (unknown) Oneida Indian legendary heroine. MAYE2.

Allen, Christina M. (1970-) Ecologist. TALAD.

Allen, Debbie. (1956-) Actor, dancer, singer. HAC4.

Allen, Ethan. (1738-1789) American Revolutionary War military leader. SCHM.

Allen, Florence Ellinwood. (1884-1966) Attorney, U.S. Appeals Court jurist. MORI; ZEI5.

Allen, Geri. (1957-) Bandleader, jazz musician. SHIP.

Allen, Gracie. (1900-1964) Comedian. CRO4; STEWG.

Allen, Henry "Red" (1908-1967) Jazz musician. GOU.

Allen, Marcus. (1960-) Football player. Heisman Trophy winner. KNA9; SAV8.

Allen, Paul. (1953-) Computer pioneer, entrepreneur computers. CRO4.

Allen, Paula Gunn (1939-) Laguna Pueblo Sioux Indian author, poet. SMIL2.

Allen, Richard. (1760-1831) Abolitionist, spiritual leader. AFR2; ALTMS; BECKN; GOLDM; HASK4; SHAP; TAYK.

Allen, Thomas B. (1928-) Children's author, illustrator. TALAR2.

Allen, Woody. (1935-) Actor, filmmaker, screenwriter. BRO; HILA2; LEVE.

Allende, Isabel. (1942-) Chilean author. COLE; SHIR.

Allison, Bobby. (1937-) Race car driver. RIL.

Allison, Clay. (1840-1877) Outlaw. SAV.

Allston, Washington. (1779-1843) Painter. KRY.

Allyón, Lucas Vásquez de. (1475-1526)
Spanish entrepreneur sugar refining, explorer. SIN2.

Almonaster y Rojas, Andrés. (1725-1798)
Entrepreneur shipping industry, philanthropist. SIN2.

Almonaster y Rojas, Michaela. (1795-1874)
Baroness of Pontalba, philanthropist. SIN2.

Alomar, Roberto. (1968-) Baseball player,
born Puerto Rico. SCHWAR; STEWM.

Alonso, Alicia. (1921-) Cuban ballet dancer.
KEND; LAE.

Alou, Felipe. (1935-) Baseball coach, born
Dominican Republic. MORE2; PIE; WIN.

Alsop, Joseph. (1910-1989) Journalist. RIT.

Alvarez, Eduardo. (unknown) Argentine police inspector, forensic scientist. DON.

Alvarez, Everett, Jr. (1937-) Navy pilot, Vietnam War pilot. SIN2.

Alvarez, Julia (1950-) Author. HILC.

Alvarez, Luis Walter. (1911-1988) Physicist.
Nobel Prize winner. HAV; LAE; OLE;
SIN2; TIN.

Alvarez de Toledo, Fernando. (Duke of Alva)
(1507-1583) Spanish military leader.
CRO3.

Alving, Amy. (unknown) Aerospace engineer, educator. KAH5.

Alworth, Lance. (1940-) Football player.
THOR.

Amado, Jorge. (1912-2001) Brazilian author.
SHIR.

Amanar, Simona. (1979-) Romanian olympic
gymnast. RUT3.

Amanpour, Christiane. (1958-) English
broadcast journalist, Gulf War correspondent. PRI.

Amenemhet I (fl. 1991-1962 B.C.) Egyptian
king. BAKR.

Amenemhet III (fl. 1842-1797 B.C.) Egyptian
king. BAKR.

Amenhotep III (fl. 1886-1849 B.C.) Egyptian
king. BAKR.

Amenhotep IV (Akhantenen) (1370-1340
B.C.) Egyptian king, spiritual leader.
BAKR; CRO5; JACW2; ROBE3.

Ames, Aldrich. (1941-) Spy, traitor. AAS18.

Ames, Jessie Daniel. (1883-1972) Civil rights
activist, suffragist, women's rights activist.
ALTE2.

Amherst, Jeffrey. (1717-1797) English

American Revolutionary War military
leader. CRO2.

Ammons, Albert. (1907-1949) Bandleader,
jazz musician. SHIP.

Amos, Wally. (1936-) Entrepreneur cookies.
KRAMB.

Amundsen, Roald Engebreth Gravning.
(1872-1928) Arctic explorer. ALTE;
CURR; LANG; LOM; PRE; SCHEL2;
TES; WAT.

Anacreon. (c. 570-485 B.C.) Greek poet.
BAKR2.

Anaya, Rudolfo. (1937-) Author. HILC.

Andersen, Dorothy. (1901-1963) Medical
researcher, pathologist, physician.
HUNTE2; STI.

Andersen, Hans Christian. (1805-1875) Danish children's writer, storyteller. KRAL;
KRULL6.

Anderson, Elizabeth Garrett. (1836-1917)
English physician. CEL; STI.

Anderson, Garland. (1886-1939) Playwright.
POT.

Anderson, Ivie. (1904-1949) Jazz singer.
GOU5; MON.

Anderson, John. (1831-?) Fugitive slave.
FRA.

Anderson, John. (1922-) Presidential candidate. AAS2.

Anderson, Laurie. (1947-) Composer. NIC2.

Anderson, Marian. (1897-1993) Opera singer.
Presidential Medal of Freedom recipient.
ALTMS; BECKN; BRED2; CUS2; GREA;
HAC4; HARN; HASK7; HER; PLO; POT;
ROE; ROL; STU; TAT.

Anderson, Mary. (1866-1953) Inventor.
BLASH3.

Anderson, Mary. (1872-1964) Labor leader,
Director U.S. Women's Bureau, born Sweden. MORI; THI.

Anderson, Poul. (1926-2001) Author. DAT.

Anderson, Robert O. (1917-) Entrepreneur oil
refinery. AAS7.

Anderson, Walter. (1880-?) Entrepreneur restaurants. AAS6.

André, Captain John. (1750-1780) American
Revolutionary War spy. MART.

Andrée, August. (1854-1897) Swedish aviation pioneer, engineer, arctic explorer. TES;
ZAU.

Andreessen, Marc. (1971-) Internet pioneer.

HENH2; NOR.

Andretti, Mario. (1940-) Auto racer, born Italy. JACT.

Andrew. (1st century) Apostle, saint. ARM; MAYE.

Andrew, Brother. (1928-) Dutch missionary, Holocaust resistance worker. JACKD3.

Andrews, Julie. (1935-) Actor, singer, born England. HUNTE3.

Andrews, Roy Chapman. (1884-1960) Naturalist, paleontologist. AAS; FAB3; PRE.

Andrianov, Nikolai. (1952-) Russian olympic gymnast. JACT.

Andros, Edmund. (1637-1714) Colonial governor, born England. CRO2.

Angel, Carl. (1968-) Painter. HON.

Angell, Sir Norman. (1873-1967) English author, peace activist. Nobel Peace Prize winner. KEEN2.

Angelou, Maya. (1928-) Author, poet. BECKN; BRED; CUS2; DUN; FEM2; GREA; HAN2; HARN; HUNTE4; JAN; KNI; RED4; SMIL2; STRI; WILKB.

Anguissola, Sofonisba. (1532-1625) Italian painter. KRULL2; KRY.

Anielewicz, Mordecai. (1919-1943) Polish Jewish Holocaust resistance worker, victim. SCHM3.

Anissina, Mariana. (1975-) Russian olympic figure skater. MILT.

Anne. (1665-1714) English queen. DAV.

Annenberg, Walter. (1908-2002) Editor, media entrepreneur, philanthropist, publisher. Presidential Medal of Freedom recipient. MAYD.

Anning, Mary. (1799-1847) English paleontologist. CHRISP; DID; STI2; THI2; WEL.

Anno, Mitsumasa. (1926-) Japanese children's author, illustrator. MARC3.

Anokye, Okomfo. (17th century) West African priest. AFR2.

Anthony, Marc. (1968-) Pop singer. KRULI.

Anthony, Susan B. (1820-1906) Suffragist, women's rights activist. ARC; CRO; CRO4; DEN; DUM; GUL; HARN; HEA; HEL; HER; JACW; MARZ; MCD; ROL; ZEI5.

Antigonus I (c. 382-301 B.C.) Greek general. BAKR2.

Antokoletz, Maria Adele de. (unknown) Argentine human rights activist. LUC.

Antolin, Jeanette. (1981-) Olympic gymnast. LAY.

Antony, Marc. (Marcus Antonius) (83?-30 B.C.) Roman general, statesman. BAKR3; CRO4.

Anubis. Egyptian god of the dead. FIS.

Anza, Juan Bautista de. (1735-1788) Mexican explorer, settler California. LAE.

Aparicio, Luis. (1934-) Baseball player, born Venezuela. BJA2; DEA3; SULG2; WIN.

Apgar, Virginia. (1909-1974) Medical researcher, physician. HUNTE2; KENJ2; REY; STI.

Apollonia. Saint. ARM.

Apollonius, Rhodius. (c. 290-247 B.C.) Greek author, scholar. BAKR2.

Appelfeld, Aharon. (1932-) Ukrainian Jewish Holocaust survivor, author. MAN.

Appleseed, Johnny. See Chapman, Jonathan.

Appling, Luke. (1907-1991) Baseball player. DEA3.

Aquinas, Thomas. See Thomas Aquinas.

Aquino, Corazon. (1933-) Filipino political activist, president. AXEC; DUN; GUL; HER; PARJ2; PRI3; ROL.

Arad, Yael. (1967-) Israeli olympic judo athlete. SEG.

Arafat, Yasir. (1929-) Palestinian political leader, terrorist. Nobel Peace Prize winner. CRO4; KEEN2; STRE4; WAK.

Arbus, Diane. (1923-1971) Photographer. GAI; HER; HOR.

Arcaro, Eddie. (1916-1997) Jockey. KUH.

Arce, Elmer Figuero. (Chayanne) (1968-) Puerto Rican pop singer. KRULI.

Archibald, Nate "Tiny." (1948-) Basketball player. LIT; SAV5.

Archimedes. (287-212 B.C.) Greek inventor, mathematician. AND; BAKR2; DIN; NAR3; TIN; YEN.

Arcimboldo, Giuseppe. (1527-1593) Italian painter. KRY.

Arden, Elizabeth. (1878-1966) Entrepreneur cosmetics industry, born Canada. SAW.

Arias Sánchez, Oscar. (1941-) Costa Rican president. Nobel Peace Prize winner. BLU; KEEN2.

Aristophanes. (c. 455-388 B.C.) Greek playwright. BAKR2.

Aristotle. (384-322 B.C.) Greek biologist, philosopher, scholar. AND; BAKR2;

NAR3; TIN; YEN.

Arius (c. 256-336) Alexandrian spiritual leader, founder of Arianism. CRO5.

Arizin, Paul. (1928-) Basketball player. AAS17.

Arkwright, Sir Richard. (1732-1792) English inventor. DIN.

Armistead, James. (1760-1832) American Revolutionary War soldier, spy. ALTMS.

Armstrong, Edwin Howard. (1890-1954) Electrical engineer, inventor. STRE2.

Armstrong, Ellen. (1914-) Cartoonist, magician. HASK6.

Armstrong, John Hartford. (1886-1939) Magician. HASK6.

Armstrong, Louis. (1901-1971) Bandleader, composer, jazz musician. ALTMS; BECKN; GOU; GOU5; HAC3; HARD; HASK5; JAN; JAZ; LEVE; MON; SHIP; TAT; VEN.

Armstrong, Neil. (1930-) Astronaut. Presidential Medal of Freedom recipient. BAIR; BRED2; CRO; JAN; LEVE; MARZ; PRE; RIC4; SAW; SCHR; WAT; WYB.

Arnaz y de Acha, Desiderio Alberto, III. (Desi Arnaz) (1917-1986) Actor, bandleader, born Cuba. CRO4; LAE; MARV3; SIN2.

Arnett, Hannah. (unknown) American Revolutionary War patriot. SILC.

Arnold, Benedict. (1741-1801) American Revolutionary War patriot, traitor. AAS18; SCHM; THOM4.

Arnold, Eve. (1913-) Photographer. HOR.

Arnold, Henry H. (1886-1950) World War I pilot, World War II Air Force general. KNA.

Arnold, Peggy Shippen. (1760-1804) American Revolutionary War traitor, wife of Benedict Arnold. FUR.

Arnold, Roseanne. (Roseanne) (1952-) Comedian. STEWG.

Arnoldson, Klas. (1844-1916) Swedish journalist, peace activist. Nobel Peace Prize winner. KEEN2.

Arouet, François Marie. (Voltaire) (1694-1778) French author, philosopher, playwright. EIG; PER; YEN.

Arrington, Richard, Jr. (1934-) Mayor. AFR2.

Arthur. (6th century) English king, possibly legendary. KRAL.

Arthur, Chester A. (1829-1886) Attorney, 21st president of U.S., vice-president. ADA; BARB; BAU; BLASS; CRO6; DAV2; LINE; MORR.

Arthur, Elizabeth Ann. (1953-) Author. POLK.

Arthur, Ellen Lewis Herndon. (1837-1880) First Lady. BARB; GOR; PAST.

Aruego, Jose. (1932-) Children's author, illustrator, born Philippines. MORE; SIN.

Arviga, Rosita. (1941-) Botanist. POLK.

Ascarelli, Devorah. (16th century) Italian poet, scholar. TAI.

Ash, Mary Kay. (1915-2001) Entrepreneur cosmetics industry. AAS16; LUT; PIL2.

Ashburn, Richie. (1927-1997) Baseball player. SULG2.

Ashby, Irving. (1920-1987) Jazz musician. GOU3.

Ashe, Arthur. (1943-1993) Tennis player. Presidential Medal of Freedom recipient. BOOK2; CHRIST; GON; KRULL3; POT; RED6; SAV4.

Ashford, Evelyn. (1957-) Olympic track and field athlete. HUNTE; MOL.

Asimov, Isaac. (1920-1992) Author. DAT; HAV.

Askia the Great. (1444?-1538) African king. MED.

Asóka the Great. (292?-232 B.C.) Indian emperor, spiritual leader. GOLDM; WILKP4; YEN.

Aspasia. (c. 470-410 B.C.) Greek women's rights activist. CRO4; HER; ROL.

Assad, Hafiz-al. (1930-2000) Syrian president. WAK.

Asser, Tobias. (1838-1913) Dutch attorney, Institute of International Law cofounder. Nobel Peace Prize winner. KEEN2.

Astaire, Fred. (1899-1987) Actor, dancer. CRO4; FOR; LEVE.

Aster, John Jacob. (1763-1848) Entrepreneur real estate, born Germany. AAS8.

Atahualpa. (1502-1533) Inca emperor. MEL; POD.

Atatürk, Mustapha Kemal. (1881-1938) Turkish president. PAP.

Athena. Greek goddess. COOL.

Atkinson, Lucy. (1820-1863?) Explorer. MCLO2.

Atler, Vanessa. (1982-) Olympic gymnast.

LAY; RUT3.

Attila the Hun. (400-453) German conqueror, king. CRO3; MEL; PRI2.

Attucks, Crispus. (1732-1770) American Revolutionary War patriot, military hero. ALTMS; BECKN; CRO2; HASK4; HASK7; LEVE; REE2; SCHM.

Atwood, Margaret. (1939-) Canadian author, poet. KNI; SMIL2.

Aud the Deep Minded. (c. 900) Viking philosopher, scholar. COOL; LEO2; POLK.

Audubon, John James. (1785-1851) Ornithologist, painter, born Haiti. FAB3; KEEN; KRY; LEVE; LUC2.

Auerbach, Arnold Jacob "Red." (1917-) Basketball coach. BRO; KNA10.

Augusta, Alexander T. (1825-1890) Civil War physician. COX.

Augustine. (354-430) North African saint, spiritual leader. CRO5; GOLDM; JACW2; YEN.

Augustus. (Gaius Octavius) (31 B.C-14 A.D.) Roman emperor. BAKR3; COOLI, CRO4; NAR2; PRI2; YEN.

Aung San. (1915-1947) Burmese political leader. WAKI.

Austen, Jane. (1775-1817) English author. HER; KNI; KRULL6; NIN; SMIL.

Austin, Stephen Fuller. (1793-1836) Founder Texas, pioneer. DOH4; LEVE; TAYS2.

Avery, Byllye. (1937-) Women's rights activist. THIR.

Avery, Oswald. (1877-1955) Canadian bacteriologist. AAS13.

Avila, Bobby. (1924-) Baseball player, born Mexico. WIN.

Avvakum. (1620-1682) Russian spiritual leader. HOOB5.

Aylward, Gladys. (1902-1970) English missionary, World War I spy. CLA2; DUN; JACKD.

Axene, Harry. (1905-) Entrepreneur restaurants. AAS6.

Azzi, Jennifer. (1968-) Olympic basketball player. PON.

B

Ba'al Shem Tov (Israel Ben Eliezer) (1700-1760) Polish Jewish spiritual leader, founder Hasidism movement of Judaism. CRO5; PASA.

Babur, Zahir un-Din Muhammed. (Babur the Conqueror) (1483-1530) Indian Mughal military leader, emperor. CRO4; WILKP.

Babbage, Charles. (1791-1871) English computer pioneer, mathematician. HENH; LOM2; TIN.

Babbitt, Milton. (1916-) Composer, musician. NIC.

Babur, Zahir un-Din Muhammed. (Babur the Conqueror) (1483-1530) Indian Mughal military leader. CRO4; WILKP.

Baca, Judy. (1946-) Human rights activist. GOLDE; LAE.

Bach, Johann Sebastian. (1685-1750) German composer, musician. BLACA2; EIG; KAL; KRULL4; VEN; YEN.

Bache, Benjamin Franklin. (1769-1798) Editor newspaper. RIT.

Bacon, Nathaniel. (1647-1676) Colonist, born England. CRO2.

Bader, Sir Douglas. (1910-1982) English pilot, World War II hero. GRAN; KEND.

Baeck, Leo. (1873-1956) German Jewish author, Holocaust resistance worker, survivor. SCHM3.

Baekeland, Leo. (1863-1944) Chemist, inventor, born Belgium. AAS19.

Baez, Joan. (1941-) Political activist, folk singer. LAE; LUC; MARV3; ORG; SIN2.

Bagwell, Jeff. (1968-) Baseball player. SCHWAR.

Bahrami, Mansour. (1956-) Iranian tennis player. KAM.

Bahaullah. (1817-1892) Persian spiritual leader, founder Baha'i faith. CRO5; JACW2.

Bai, Lakshmi. (1830-1858) Indian military leader, ruler, disguised as man. COOL; DUN; HER; ROL.

Bailey, Anne Trotter. (1743-1825) American Revolutionary War patriot, colonist, Indian scout, disguised as man. FUR.

Bailey, F. Lee. (1933-) Attorney. CALA.

Bailey, Jerry. (1957-) Jockey. KUH.

Bailey, Liberty Hyde. (1858-1954) Botanist, educator. FAB3.

Bailey, Pearl. (1918-1990) Jazz singer. Presidential Medal of Freedom recipient. MON.

Baird, John Logie. (1888-1946) English inventor. DIN; WILKP3.

Baiul, Oksana (1977-) Ukrainian olympic figure skater. KRAMS4; RUT2.

Bajer, Fredrik. (1837-1922) Danish peace activist, political activist. Nobel Peace Prize winner. KEEN2.

Baker, Ella Josephine. (1903-1986) Civil rights activist. ALLZ; GREA; HAN2; HARM; TAYK2.

Baker, Florence von Sass. (1841-1916) English explorer, born Romania. LANG; MCLO; STEFO2.

Baker, George, Jr. "Father Divine." (1882-1965) Cult leader. KELLA; STRE.

Baker, James. (1930-) Attorney, cabinet member. Presidential Medal of Freedom recipient. RIC.

Baker, John Franklin "Home Run." (1886-1964) Baseball player. SULG8.

Baker, Josephine. (1906-1975) Jazz singer, World War II resistance worker. BECKM; COOL; MON.

Baker, Sir Samuel White. (1821-1893) English explorer. LANG.

Baker, Sara Josephine. (1873-1945) Physician, public health pioneer. ALTML; HUNTE2; REY; STI; VAR.

Baker, Vernon J. (1919-) World War II lieutenant. Medal of Honor recipient. HASK2.

Bakker, Robert. (1945-) Paleontologist. AAS; HAV.

Balanchine, George. (1904-1983) Choreographer, dancer, educator, born Russia. Presidential Medal of Freedom recipient. FOR; MARZ.

Balboa, Vasco Nunez de. (1475-1519) Spanish explorer. ALTE; FRIT; LOM; PARN; POD; PRE.

Balch, Emily Greene. (1867-1961) Civil rights activist, peace activist, women's rights activist. Nobel Peace Prize winner. KEEN2; SCHR2.

Balchen, Bernt. (1899-1973) World War II Army Air Force, born Norway. ROS.

Baldur. Norse god of peace and light. FIS3.

Baldwin, James. (1924-1987) Author, civil rights activist, playwright. AFR; ALTMS; BECKN; BRED; MAL; MEE; OFT; RED4; VERD.

Ball, James P. (1825-1904) Entrepreneur photo studios, photographer. SULG.

Ball, Lucille. (1911-1989) Comedian. Presidential Medal of Freedom recipient. COOL; CRO4; GAI2; HARN; STEWG.

Ballard, Louis. (1931-) Quapaw and Cherokee Indian composer. AVE.

Ballard, Robert. (1942-) Oceanographer. ALTE; HAV; POLKI; TALAD.

Bambera, Toni Cade. (1939-1995) Author. WILKB.

Bamberger, Niels. (1928-) Danish Holocaust survivor. AXE.

Ban Chao. (d. 102) Chinese historian, military leader. HOOB; LEO.

Ban Gu. (32-92) Chinese historian. HOOB.

Ban Piao. (unknown) Chinese historian, scholar. HOOB.

Ban Zhao. (45-116) Chinese historian. HOOB.

Bancroft, Ann. (1955-) Arctic explorer. MCLE.

Bandaranaike, Sirimavo. (1916-2000) Sri Lankan prime minister. GUL.

Banks, Ernie. (1931-) Baseball player. DEA3.

Banneker, Benjamin. (1731-1806) Abolitionist, astronomer, inventor, mathematician. AFR2; ALTMS; BECKN; COX2; HASK4; HASK8; HAY3; MCK2; PIO; POT; SULO.

Banning, James Herman. (1900-1933) Aviation pioneer, engineer. HART; JONS2.

Bannister, Roger. (1929-) English olympic runner, track and field athlete. JACT; SULG3.

Banting, Sir Frederick Grant. (1891-1941) Canadian medical researcher, physician. Nobel Prize winner. CURT; MUL.

Banuelos, Romana Acosta. (1925-) Banker, treasurer of U.S. LAE.

Baraka, Amiri. (1934-) Poet. AFR; STRI; WEI2.

Baranova, Elena. (1976-) Russian basketball player. JACK.

Barbarin, Louis. (1902-1997) Jazz musician. MON.

Barber, Samuel. (1910-1981) Composer. Pulitzer Prize winner. BRED3.

Barbie, Klaus. (1913-1991) German Nazi war criminal LAND2; SCHM3.

Barceló, Maria Gertrudes "Tules." (1800-1852) Pioneer, women's rights activist. ALTE2; FUR2; LAE; SIN2.

Bardeen, John. (1908-1991) Inventor, physicist. Nobel Prize winner, Presidential Medal of Freedom recipient. AAS15; HAV; TIN.

Barden, Don. (1943-) Media entrepreneur. AFR2.

Barents, Willem. (1550-1597) Dutch arctic explorer. POD; PRE.

Baret, Jeanne. (1740?-1803?) French naturalist, disguised as man. POLK.

Barker, Danny. (1908-1994) Jazz musician. GOU3; MON.

Barker, Penelope. (unknown) American Revolutionary War patriot. SILC.

Barkley, Charles. (1963-) Basketball player. BJA; BJA3; KRAMS3; PAU; SAV6.

Barkow, Bill. (unknown) Acoustic biologist. SAY.

Barnard, George N. (1819-1902) Civil War photographer. SULG6.

Barnard, Henry. (1811-1900) Educator, U.S. Commissioner of Education. UNG.

Barnardo, Thomas. (1845-1905) Irish missionary. CLA.

Barnes, Djuna. (1892-1982) Author, journalist, playwright. KNI.

Barnes, Sharon J. (1955-) Chemist. SULO2.

Barnett, Claude. (1890-1967) Publisher. RIT.

Barnhart, Cynthia. (unknown) Civil and transportation engineer, educator. KAH5.

Barnum, Phineas "P. T." (1810-1891) Showman. CRO; JAN; KRAL; LEVE; WEI2.

Barrault, Jean-Louis. (1910-1994) French actor, theatrical director, producer. WEI2.

Barré-Sinoussi, Françoise. (1947-) French chemist, medical researcher. SPA.

Barringer, Emily Dunning. (1876-1961) World War II physician. ZEI3.

Barrow, Claude. (1909-1934) Outlaw. BLACG; CRO4; KRAL; THOM2.

Barry, Catherine Moore. (unknown) American Revolutionary War patriot. SILC.

Barry, James. *see* Stuart, Miranda.

Barry, Rick. (1944-) Basketball player. AAS17; RAPK2; TOR4.

Barrymore, Ethel. (1879-1959) Actor. WEI2.

Barsosio, Sally. (1978-) Kenyan olympic track and field athlete. RUT6.

Barthé, Richmond. (1901-1989) Sculptor. HARD.

Bartholomew. Apostle, Saint. MAYE.

Bartlett, Josiah. (1729-1795) American Revolutionary War patriot, congressman, Declaration of Independence signer, physician. FRA2; QUI.

Bartok, Bela. (1861-1945) Hungarian composer. BLACA2.

Barton, Bruce. (1886-1967) Author, congressman, entrepreneur advertising. PIL.

Barton, Clara. (1821-1912) Civil War nurse, founder American Red Cross. BLASH; CHA; CLA; CRO; DE; DEN; HARN; HER; JACW; LEVE; MCD; ROBE; ROL; STI; THIR; ZEI.

Barton, Greg. (1959-) Olympic kayaker. KNA4.

Bartram, John. (1699-1777) Botanist. FAB3; KEEN.

Bartram, William. (1739-1822) Botanist. FAB3; KEEN.

Baryshnikov, Mikhail. (1948-) Ballet dancer, born Russia. FOR.

Basch, Civia Gelber. (1928-) Romanian Holocaust survivor. GREENF.

Bascom, Florence. (1862-1945) Educator, geologist. CAM2; REY; STI2.

Basho. (1644-1694) Japanese poet. HOOB4.

Basie, William "Count." (1904-1984) Bandleader, composer, jazz musician. Presidential Medal of Freedom recipient. AFR; GOU4; JAZ; MON; SHIP.

Baskin, Leonard. (1922-) Illustrator, printmaker, sculptor. KRY.

Bassett, Angela. (1959-) Actor. PARJ.

Bassi, Laura. (1711-1778) Italian physicist. ROE.

Bat Ha-Levi (12th century) Iraqi scholar. TAI.

Bateman, Ray, Jr. (1974-) Canadian teenage medical researcher. BRIL.

Bates, Abigail. (1799-?) Lighthouse keeper. HOOS.

Bates, Billy. (1848-1909) Civil War teenage soldier. HOOS.

Bates, Daisy. (1914-1999) Civil rights activist. GREA.

Bates, Rebecca. (1795-?) Lighthouse keeper. HOOS.

Bath, Patricia. (1942-) Medical researcher, physician. HENS2; SULO2.

Bathsheba. Biblical character. ARM2.

Battey, Cornelius M. (1873-1927) Photographer. SULG.

Bauduc, Ray. (1909-1988) Jazz musician. GOU6.

Bauer, Billy. (1915-) Jazz musician. GOU3.

Baugh, Sammy. (1914-) Football player. LAC2; SULG7.

Baum, L. Frank. (1856-1919) Children's author. PER; RYL.

Bayerzid I. (1354-1403) Turkish military leader. CRO3.

Baylor, Elgin. (1934-) Basketball player. AAS17.

Beach, Amy. (1867-1944) Composer. NIC2.

Beach Boys. Rock and Roll group. KNA2.

Beach, Sheryl Luzzadder. (unknown) Educator, geographer, geologist. KAH4.

Beadle, George. (1903-1989) Educator, geneticist. Nobel Prize winner. HAV.

Beals, Melba Pattilo. (1941-) Civil rights activist. ALLZ; BERS.

Bean, Alan. (1932-) Aeronautical engineer, astronaut, Navy pilot. PRE.

Bean, Leon Leonwood "L. L." (1872-1967) Entrepreneur retail establishments. PIL

Bean, Roy. (1825-1903) Jurist, Wild West lawman. KRAL; WAL.

Beard, Andrew Jackson. (1849-1941) Inventor, slave. SULO.

Bearden, Romare. (1912-1988) Painter. GREENBJ; HASK7.

Beatles. Musical group. VEN.

Beauharnais, Josephine. (1763-1814) French empress, wife of Napoleon Bonaparte. CRO4.

Beauvoir, Simone de. (1908-1986) French author, philosopher, women's rights activist. CRO4; DUN; HER; KNI.

Bechet, Sidney. (1897-1959) Bandleader, composer, educator, jazz musician. MON; SHIP.

Beckenbauer, Franz. (1946-) German soccer player. JACT.

Beckerman, Alyssa. (1981-) Olympic gymnast. LAY.

Beckmann, Max. (1884-1950) German painter, printmaker. KRY.

Beckwourth, James. (1798-1866) Fur trapper, pioneer, slave, soldier Seminole War. ALTE; ALTMS; COLL; GLA2; HASK3; HUD; MILR; MON2; PIO; REE.

Becoat, Bill. (1938-) Inventor. HENS.

Becquerel, Antoine Henri. (1852-1908) French physicist. Nobel Prize winner. TIN.

Bedard, Myriam. (1969-) Canadian olympic biathlon athlete. HASD.

Beebe, Charles William. (1877-1962) Naturalist, ornithologist. PRE.

Beech, Olive Ann. (1903-1993) Entrepreneur aircraft. JEF2.

Beecher, Catherine. (1800-1878) Author, educator, women's rights activist. HER; ROL; UNG.

Beecher, Lyman. (1775-1863) Puritan hate-monger, spiritual leader. STRE3.

Beernaert, Auguste. (1829-1912) Belgian attorney, peace activist, political activist. Nobel Peace Prize winner. KEEN2.

Beethoven, Ludwig von. (1770-1827) German composer. BLACA2; KAL; KEND; KRULL4; ROM; VEN; YEN.

Begay, Fred. (1932-) Navajo and Ute Indian physicist. STJ3.

Begin, Mary Jane. (1963-) Illustrator. TALAR2.

Begin, Menachem. (1913-1992) Israeli prime minister, born Poland. Nobel Peace Prize winner. KEEN2; MAYB2; PASA.

Behn, Aphra Johnson. (1640?-1689) English playwright, poet, spy.. KNI; POLK.

Beiderbecke, Leon "Bix." (1903-1931) Jazz musician. GOU; SHIP.

Belafonte, Harry. (1927-) Singer. BECKN.

Belaney, Archibald (Grey Owl) (1888-1938) Canadian fur trapper, naturalist, born England. KEEN.

Belfour, Ed. (1965-) Canadian hockey player. SPI.

Belisarius. (505-565) Byzantian military leader. CRO3.

Bell, Alexander Graham. (1847-1922) Inventor, born Scotland. DIN; LEVE; LOM2; NOO; SAW; STRE2; WILKP3; YEN.

Bell, Gertrude. (1868-1926) English adventurer, archaeologist, explorer. COOL; DUN; FAG; GREENBL; KRULL; MCLO8; POLK; ROL.

Bell, James Thomas "Cool Papa." (1903-1991) Baseball player. WIN2.

Belle, Albert. (1966-) Baseball player. SCHER.

Belline, Germaine. (unknown) Belgian Holocaust rescuer. PET.

Bellini, Giovanni. (1430-1516) Italian painter. CUM; KRY.

Bellini, Vincenzo. (1801-1835) Italian sacred music composer. VEN.

Bellow, Saul. (1915-) Author. Nobel Prize winner, Pulitzer Prize winner. TWEPO; VERD.

Bellows, George Wesley. (1882-1925) Painter. KRY.

Belo, Carlos Felipe Ximenes. (1948-) East Timorian peace activist, spiritual leader. Nobel Peace Prize winner. KEEN2.

Beltran, Carlos. (1977-) Baseball player, born Puerto Rico. SCHWAR.

Beltré, Adrián. (1979-) Baseball player, born Dominican Republic. STEWM.

Belzoni, Giovanni. (1778-1823) Italian archaeologist. FAG; GREENBL.

Bemis, Polly. (Lalu Nathay) (1853-1933) Pioneer, born China. SIN; STEFO3.

Ben-Gurion, David. (1886-1973) Israeli prime minister. PASA.

Ben-Yehuda, Eliezer. (1858-1922) Israeli linguist. PASA.

Benavidez, Roy. (1935-) Vietnam War Army military hero. Medal of Honor recipient. COLE.

Bench, Johnny. (1947-) Baseball player. SULG2; YOUNG2.

Bender, Charles Albert "Chief." (1884-1954) Chippewa Indian baseball player. SULG5.

Benedict of Nursia. (c. 480-550) Italian saint, spiritual leader. CRO5.

Benedict, Ruth. (1887-1948) Anthropologist. STI2; WEI.

Benenson, Peter. (1921-) Attorney, human rights activist, founder Amnesty International. LUC.

Benerito, Ruth. (1916-) Physical chemist, inventor. BLASH3.

Benham, Gertrude. (1867-1938) English mountaineer. MCLO6.

Benjamin, Judah Philip. (1811-1854) Attorney, confederate statesman. BRO.

Benjamin, Miriam E. (unknown) Inventor. SULO2.

Bennett, Floyd. (1890-1928) Arctic explorer, aviator, Navy pilot. TES.

Bennett, Hugh Hammond. (1881-1960) Agricultural chemist. FAB3.

Bennett, James Gordon. (1795-1872) Newspaper editor, publisher, born Scotland. RIT.

Bennett, Lerone, Jr. (1928-) Author, historian, journalist. BECKN.

Benny, Jack. (1894-1974) Comedian. BRO.

Benson, George. (1943-) Jazz musician. GOU3.

Benton, Thomas Hart. (1889-1975) Painter. GREENBJ.

Benz, Karl. (1844-1929) German automaker, engineer, inventor. ITA6; LOM2.

Berezhnaya, Elena. (1977-) Russian olympic figure skater. MILT.

Berg, Alan Alban. (1885-1935) Austrian composer. VEN.

Berg, Patty. (1918-) Golfer, World War II Marine Corps lieutenant. HASD; JACT.

Bering, Vitus Jonassen. (1681-1741) Danish explorer. ALTE; LANG; POD; PRE.

Berk, Allan. (1918-) Czech Jewish Holocaust survivor. LAND.

Berkeley, John. (1602-1678) Colonist. DOH3.

Berkeley, William. (1606-1677) Colonial governor. CRO2.

Berlin, Irving. (1888-1989) Composer, born Russia. Presidential Medal of Freedom recipient. BRO.

Berlioz, Hector. (1803-1869) French composer. BLACA2; ROM.

Bermúdez, Diego. (1480-?) Spanish page for Columbus. HOOS.

Bernadotte, Folke. (1895-1948) Swedish diplomat, Holocaust rescuer. SCHM3.

Bernard of Clairvaux. (1090-1153) French saint, spiritual leader. CRO5.

Berners-Lee, Tim. (1955-) English internet pioneer. HENH2.

Bernhardt, Sarah. (1844-1923) French actor. DUN; HER; KRAL; WEI2; WEL.

Bernini, Gian Lorenzo. (1598-1680) Italian sculptor. CUS; SEV.

Bernoulli, Daniel. (1700-1782) Swiss mathematician. TIN.

Bernstein, Carl. (1944-) Journalist. RIT; SAT.

Bernstein, Leonard. (1918-1990) Composer, conductor. BLACA2; BRED3; BRO; LEVE; TWEPO.

Bernstein, Peter. (1967-) Jazz musician. GOU3.

Berry, Carrie. (1854-?) Southern girl during Civil War. HOOS.

Berry, Chuck. (1926-) Composer, rock musician, singer. KNA2; RED5; TAT.

Berry, Raymond. (1933-) Football player. THOR.

Berry, Wendell. (1934-) Ecologist, poet. KEEN.

Bertillon, Alphonse. (1853-1914) French forensic scientist. FRID.

Bertoncini, Gene. (1937-) Jazz musician. GOU3.

Beruriah. (2nd century) Hebrew scholar. PASA; TAI.

Berzelius, Jöns Jakob. (1779-1848) Swedish chemist. TIN.

Besant, Annie. (1847-1933) English human rights activist, journalist, orator, reformer. ROL.

Best, Daniel. (1838-1923) Entrepreneur tractors. AAS3.

Bethune, Mary McLeod. (1875-1955) Civil rights activist, educator. AFR2; ALTMS; BECKN; BOL; COX2; DEN; GREA; HAC2; HARN; HER; PIN; PLO; POT; ROL; SHAP; THIR; TUR2.

Bethune, Thomas "Blind Tom" Greene. (1849-1908) Musician, slave. TAT.

Bettelheim, Bruno. (1903-1990) Holocaust survivor, psychotherapist, born Austria. SCHM3.

Beukels, Jan. (John of Leiden) (1509-1536) German cult leader, spiritual leader. STRE.

Beurton, Ruth Kuczynski. (1907-) World War II spy. COOL.

Bezos, Jeffrey. (1964-) Entrepreneur computers, Internet pioneer. FREN; HENH2.

Bhutto, Benazir. (1953-) Pakistani prime minister. AXE; GUL; NAR4; PARJ2; PRI3.

Biaggi, Cristina Shelley. (1937-) Archaeologist, historian. POLK.

Bibb, Henry. (unknown) Slave. GAR.

Bickerdyke, Mary Ann "Mother." (1817-1901) Civil War nurse. BLASH; CHA; ZEI.

Bienville, Jean Baptiste le Moyne. (1680-1767) French colonial governor. CRO2; DOH5.

Biggio, Craig. (1965-) Baseball player. SCHWAR.

Bihaly, Judith. (1934-) Hungarian Holocaust survivor. GREENF.

Billiris, Manuel. (1975-) Australian in-line skater. SAV9.

Billy the Kid. *See* McCarthy, Henry.

Bingham, George Caleb. (1811-1879) Painter. NIN.

Bingham, Hiram. (1878-1956) Archaeologist, senator, World War I Army pilot. GREENBL; SCHEL2.

Bird, Larry. (1956-) Basketball player. AAS17; DEE; KNA6; RAPK2; SULG3; TOR3; TOR4.

Biro, Ladislao. (1900-1944) Hungarian inventor. DIN.

Bishop, Isabella Lucy "Bird." (1831-1904) English adventurer. HAC; MCLO8; POLK; STEFO2.

Bismarck, Otto Eduard Leopold von. (1815-1898) German chancellor, statesman. WILKP4; YEN.

Bizet, Georges. (1838-1875) French opera composer. VEN.

Bjerknes, Jacob. (1897-1975) Meterologist, born Sweden. HAV.

Bjork. (singer) *See* Gudmundsdorttir, Bjork.

Black Bart. *See* Boles, Charles.

Black Elk. (1863-1950) Oglala Lakota Sioux Indian medicine man, showman. AVE; KRU7; SHAW; WE2.

Black Herman. *See* Rucker, Herman.

Black, Hugo. (1886-1971) Attorney, Supreme Court jurist. AAS14.

Black Kettle. (1807-1868) Cheyenne Indian chief, peace activist. SHER2.

Blackbeard. *See* Teach, Edward L.

Blackburn, Robert. (1920-2003) Educator, painter, printmaker. AFR.

Blackman, Cindy. (1959-) Composer, jazz musician. HAC3.

Blackwell, Antoinette Brown. (1825-1921) Spiritual leader, suffragist. HER; THIR.

Blackwell, Elizabeth. (1821-1910) Physician, born England. CEL; CURT; DE; DEN; HARN; HEA; HER; KENJ2; ROBE; ROL; STI; THIR.

Blackwell, Emily. (1826-1910) Physician, born England. STI; THIR.

Blackwell, Otis. (1931-2002) Songwriter. AFR.

Blades, Ruben. (1948-) Actor, composer, singer. LAE; SIN2.

Blair, Bonnie. (1964-) Olympic speed skater. DIT; HASD; JACT; LINL; STRU.

Blair, Tonia Rotkopf. (1925-) Polish Holocaust survivor. GREENF.

Blake, James Hubert "Eubie." (1883-1983) Composer, jazz musician. Presidential Medal of Freedom recipient. GOU4; HARD; HASK5; TAT.

Blake, William. (1757-1827) English engraver, painter, poet. KRY; PER.

Blakey, Art. (1919-1990) Bandleader, jazz musician. GOU6; SHIP.

Blakey, Michael L. (1953-) Anthropologist. TALAD.

Blanchard, Felix Anthony "Doc." (1924-) Football player. Heisman Trophy winner. DEV.

Blanchard, Jean-Pierre. (aka François Blanchard) (1754-1809) French aviation pioneer. WILLI.

Blanchfield, Florence Aby. (1882-1971) World War I Army nurse, World War II Superintendent Army Nurse Corps. SHEA; STI.

Blankers-Koen, Fanny. (1918-2004) Dutch olympic track and field athlete. AAS20.

Blanton, Jimmy. (1918-1942) Jazz musician. GOU2.

Blavatsky, Helena Petrovna. (1831-1891) Russian spiritual leader, founder of theosophical movement. CRO5.

Bleier, Robert Patrick "Rocky.". (1946-) Football player, Vietnam War army soldier. JEN.

Blériot, Louis. (1872-1936) French aviation pioneer. WILLI.

Bloch, Robert. (1917-1994) Author, screenwriter. MAD.

Blodgett, Katherine. (1898-1979) Chemist. ALTML.

Blom, Gertrude Elizabeth Loertscher Doby. (1901-1993) Swiss conservationist, photographer. POLK; SIR.

Bloomer, Amelia Jenks. (1818-1894) Editor, publisher, suffragist, women's rights activist. HARN; HEL; PRI.

Bloomfield, Michael. (unknown) Canadian environmentalist, organization founder. GRAH.

Bluford, Guion Steward. (1942-) Astronaut, Vietnam War pilot. AFR2; ALTMS; BAIR; BUR; HASK2; HASK3; JONS; PIO; POT; REE; SCHR.

Blume, Judy. (1938-) Children's and young adult author. ARO; AUT; BRO; HILC2; HUNTE4; MAS.

Blunt, Lady Anne. (1837-1917) English explorer. POLK.

Bly, Nellie. *See* Cochrane, Elizabeth.

Blyleven, Bert. (1951-) Baseball player, born Holland. SULG5.

Boaz, Franz. (1858-1942) German anthropologist, linguist. WEI.

Boccaccio, Giovanni. (1313-1375) Italian author. PER.

Boccherini, Luigi. (1741-1805) Italian composer. VEN.

Boccioni, Umberto. (1882-1916) Italian painter, sculptor. KRY.

Boehm, Helen. (1909-) Entrepreneur porcelain art. PIL2.

Bogues, Tyrone "Muggsy." (1965-) Basketball player. RAPK.

Boguinskaia, Svetlana. (1973-) Russian olympic gymnast. GREES.

Bohr, Niels. (1885-1962) Danish physicist. Nobel Prize winner. HAV; TIN.

Boissevain, Inez Milholland. (1886-1916) Suffragist, women's rights activist. THIR.

Boissonnault, Masako. (1944-) Entrepreneur interior design. PIL2.

Bojaxhiu, Agnes. (Mother Teresa) (1910-1997) Indian/Albanian human rights activist, missionary, born Yugoslavia. Nobel Peace Prize winner, Presidential Medal of Freedom recipient. CLA; CRO5; CUS2; DUN; GOLDM; HAC5; HER; JACW2; KEEN2; LUC; ROL; SCHR2; SHAW; WEL.

Bol, Manute. (1962-) Sudanese basketball player. YOUNG.

Bolden, Buddy. (1868-1931) Bandleader, jazz musician. AFR; GOU; MON.

Bolden, Charles. (1946-) Astronaut, Marine Corps pilot. AFR2; BUR; JONS.

Boles, Charles. (Black Bart) (1829-1917) Outlaw. BLACG3; GLA.

Boleyn, Anne. (1507-1536) English wife of Henry VIII. CRO4; KRAL.

Bolivar, Simón. (1783-1830) Venezuelan political leader, revolutionary. CRO3; CRO4; HOOB6; KRAL; THOM3;

WILKP4; YEN.

Bolling, Thomas Spottswood, Jr. (1939-1990) Civil rights activist. ROC.

Bolontiku. Mayan god of the lower world. FIS2.

Bolton-Holifield, Ruthie. (1967-) Basketball player. JACK.

Bombeck, Erma. (1927-1996) Journalist. PRI.

Bonafini, Hebe de. (unknown) Argentine human rights activist. LUC.

Bonaly, Surya. (1973-) French olympic figure skater. RUT2.

Bonaparte, Napoleon. (1768-1821) French military leader. CRO3; CRO4; PRI2; WILKP.

Bond, Julian. (1940-) Civil rights activist, organization head, state legislator, DUD; HARM.

Bonds, Barry. (1964-) Baseball player. SCHER; SCHWAR; SULG2.

Bonga, George. (1802-1880) Ojibwa Indian fur trader. MON2.

Bonheur, Rosa. (1822-1899) French painter. KRY.

Bonhoeffer, Dietrich. (1906-1945) German Holocaust resistance worker, victim, spiritual leader. CLA2; JACKD2; SCHM3.

Boniface. (672-754) German missionary, saint. CLA2; CRO5.

Bonner, Elena. (1923-) Russian political activist. HOOB5.

Bonnett, Neil. (1946-1994) Nascar auto racer. RIL.

Bonney, Anne. (1697-1721) Irish pirate, disguised as man. BLACG4; COOL; DUN; FUR; SHAR; WEA; YOUNT5.

Bonnin, Gertrude Simmons. (1876-1938) Yankton Dakota Indian author, Native American rights activist, social reformer. AVE.

Bontemps, Arnaud "Arna." (1902-1973) Author, educator, librarian, poet. BECKM; HARD.

Boole, George. (1815-1864) English mathematician. HENH.

Boone, Daniel. (1734-1820) Frontiersman, hunter, pioneer, soldier in French-Indian War. ALTE; BAKS; CALV; CRO; DOH4; JAN; KRAL; LEVE; POD; TAYS2.

Boone, Sarah. (unknown) Inventor. SULO2.

Booth, Catherine. (1829-1890) English cofounder Salvation Army, human rights activist. JACKD.

Booth, Eva. (1865-1950) Brought Salvation Army movement to U.S., human rights activist, born England. CLA.

Booth, John Wilkes. (1838-1865) Assassin of President Abraham Lincoln. JONR; NET; STG; SULG9.

Booth, William. (1829-1912) English human rights activist, spiritual leader, cofounder of Salvation Army movement. CLA; JACKD.

Booth, William. (1833-1893) Actor. WEI2.

Borden, Amanda. (1977-) Olympic gymnast. KLE.

Borden, Lizzie. (1860-1927) Murdered parents, legendary folk hero. DUN.

Borders, Ila. (1975-) Baseball player. BRIL3.

Bordin, Alexander Porfiervich. (1833-1889) Russian chemist, opera composer, physician. VEN.

Borg, Björn. (1956-) Swedish tennis player. CHRIST; CRO4.

Borges, Jorge Luis. (1899-1986) Argentine author, poet. HAZ; SHIR.

Borgia, Lucrezia. (1480-1519) Italian criminal, ruler, folk hero. DUN

Borglum, Gutzon. (1867-1941) Sculptor. KRY.

Bori, Lucrezia. (1887-1960) Opera singer, born Spain. LAE.

Borkowska, Anna. (c. 1900-) Polish Holocaust rescuer, spiritual leader. LYM.

Borlaug, Norman Ernest. (1914-) Agricultural scientist, chemist. Nobel Peace Prize winner, Presidential Medal of Freedom recipient. KEEN2.

Bormann, Martin. (1900-1945) German Nazi war criminal. SCHM3.

Born, Max. (1882-1970) English physicist, born Poland. Nobel Prize winner. HAV.

Boru, Brian. (941-1014) Irish military leader. CRO3.

Bosch, Hieronymous. (1450-1516) Dutch painter. BLACA; REN.

Bosley, Freeman R., Jr. (1954-) Mayor. AFR2.

Boswell, James. (1740-1795) Scottish author. CRO4.

Botticelli, Sandro. (1444-1510) Italian painter. CUM; KRY; REN.

Boudicca. (28-62) Celtic queen. DUN; HER;

MAYE2; MEL2; ROL.

Boudinot, Elias. (1800-1839) Cherokee Indian editor, newspaper. RIT.

Boudreau, Lou. (1917-2001) Baseball player, manager, sportscaster. DEA3.

Boulanger, Nadia. (1887-1979) French composer, conductor. KRULL4; STU.

Bourgeois, Léon. (1851-1925) French attorney, prime minister, statesman. Nobel Peace Prize winner. KEEN2.

Bourke-White, Margaret. (1906-1971) World War II photojournalist. COLM; COOL; CUS2; GAI; HARN; HER; HOR; JACKN; MCLO8; PRI; RIT; ROL; SHEA; STU; WHI; WOL; ZEI3.

Bourne, Shae-Lynn. (1976-) Canadian olympic figure skater. MILT.

Bourne, St. Clair. (unknown) Filmmaker. AFR.

Bowie, James. (1796-1836) Adventurer, crime fighter, frontiersman. CALV.

Bowles, Ann. (1956-) Acoustic biologist. TALAD.

Boxer, Barbara. (1940-) Congresswoman, women's rights activist. GUL.

Boyd, Belle. (1843-1900) Civil War spy. BLASH; CARA; CHA; HARN; SULG4; ZEI.

Boyd, Henry. (1802-1886) Inventor, slave. MCK.

Boyd, Liona. (1949-) Canadian musician. STRU2.

Boyd, Louise Arner. (1887-1972) Arctic explorer. JAN; MCLE; MCLO4; POLK; ROL; STEFO2.

Boyd, Richard Henry. (1843-1922) Banker, entrepreneur Black dolls, slave. HASK.

Boyle, Robert. (1627-1691) English chemist, inventor, physicist. TIN.

Boylston, Zabadiel. (1679-1766) Colonist, physician. CRO2.

Bradbury, Ray. (1920-) Author. DAT.

Bradford, William. (1590-1657) Colonial governor, born England. CRO2; DOH3; POD.

Bradley, Benjamin. (1830-?) Inventor. HASK8.

Bradley, Bill. (1943-) Olympic basketball player, presidential candidate, senator. KNA11.

Bradley, Milton. (1836-1911) Entrepreneur board games. AAS9; AAS16.

Bradley, Omar N. (1893-1981) World War II Army general. Presidential Medal of Freedom recipient. KNA; OLE2.

Bradley, Shawn. (1972-) Basketball player. YOUNG.

Bradley, Thomas. (1917-1998) Mayor. AFR2.

Bradshaw, Terry. (1948-) Football player. KNA9; LAC2; SULG7.

Bradstreet, Anne. (1612-1672) Colonist, poet. CRO2; KNI.

Bradstreet, Simon. (1603-1697) Colonist. CRO2.

Brady, James "Diamond Jim." (1856-1917) Financier. KRAL.

Brady, Matthew B. (1823-1896) Civil War photographer. GAI; JACKN; KRY; SULG6.

Bragg, Janet Harmon. (1907-1993) Aviator, nurse. HASK.

Bragi. Norse god of poetry. FIS3.

Brahe, Sophie. (1556-1643) Danish astronomer. LEO3.

Brahe, Tyche. (1546-1601) Danish astronomer. POD; WILLS.

Brahms. Johannes. (1833-1897) German composer. KRULL4; VEN.

Braille, Louis. (1809-1852) French inventor. BOY; BRIL; DIN; KEND.

Brand, Elton. (1979-) Basketball player. PAU.

Brandeis, Louis. (1856-1941) Attorney, chief justice Supreme Court. AAS14; BRO.

Brandt, Karl. (1904-1948) German Nazi war criminal, physician. SCHM3.

Brandt, Willy. (1913-1992) German journalist, statesman. Nobel Peace Prize winner. KEEN2.

Brandy (singer) See Norwood, Brandy.

Brant, Joseph. (1742-1807) American Revolutionary War loyalist, Mohawk Indian war chief. AVE; SCHM.

Brant, Mary "Molly." (Degonwadonti) (1736-1796) Mohawk Indian American Revolutionary War patriot. RAPD2; SCHM.

Branting, Karl. (1860-1925) Swedish astronomer, journalist, prime minister, statesman. Nobel Peace Prize winner. KEEN2.

Braque, Georges. (1882-1963) French painter. KRY.

Brattain, Walter Houser. (1902-1987) Inventor, physicist. Nobel Prize winner. AAS15.

Bratton, Martha. (unknown) American Revolutionary War patriot. SILC.

Braud, Wellman. (1891-1966) Jazz musician. GOU2.

Braun, E. Lucy. (1889-1971) Ecologist, geologist. LEU.

Braun, Eva. (1912-1945) German mistress of Adolf Hitler. SCHM3.

Bravo, Lola Alvarez. (1907-1993) Mexican photographer. SILL.

Braxton, Anthony. (1945-) Bandleader, composer, jazz musician. SHIP.

Braxton, Carter. (1736-1797) American Revolutionary War patriot, congressman, Declaration of Independence signer. FRA2; QUI.

Breasted, James Henry. (1865-1935) Egyptologist. WEI.

Brebeuf, Jean de, Father. (1593-1649) Colonist, missionary, spiritual leader. CLA2; CRO2.

Brecht, Bertolt. (1898-1956) German playwright, poet. WEI2.

Brecker, Michael. (1949-) Bandleader, jazz musician. SHIP.

Breckinridge, Mary Marvin. (1905-2002) World War II broadcast journalist, photographer. COLM.

Brendan the Navigator. (484-577) Irish explorer, saint. ALTE; PRE; WILLI2.

Brent, Margaret. (1601-1671) Colonist, women's rights activist. CRO2; FUR.

Brents, Frank. (1926-) Magician. HASK6.

Breuil, Henri. (1877-1961) French archaeologist. FAG.

Brewster, William. (1567-1643) Colonial pilgrim. CRO2.

Briand, Aristide. (1862-1932) French attorney, prime minister, statesman. Nobel Peace Prize winner. KEEN2.

Bridger, Jim. (1804-1881) Civil War soldier, frontiersman, fur trapper, Indian agent and scout, pioneer. ALTE; BAKS; CALV; COLL; GLA2; PRE; SAV3.

Bridges, Marilyn. (1948-) Photographer. POLK.

Brigman, Anne. (1869-1950) Photographer. HOR.

Brill, Yvonne. (1924-) Aerospace chemist, inventor, space scientist, born Canada. BLASH4.

Briones, Juana. (1802-1889) Human rights activist, pioneer, rancher. FUR2.

Brisco-Hooks, Valerie. (1960-) Olympic track and field athlete. MOL.

Britten, Benjamin. (1913-1976) English opera composer. VEN.

Brittin, Louis. (fl. 1926) Entrepreneur airlines. PIL.

Brizi, Luigi. (unknown) Italian Holocaust rescuer. PET.

Brock, Lou. (1939-) Baseball player. BJA2.

Brodeur, Martin. (1972-) Canadian hockey player. SPI.

Brodie, William. (1741-1798) Scottish city official, model for Dr. Jekyll. KRAL.

Brody, Jane. (1941-1987) Author, journalist, nutritionist. HAV.

Bromfield, Louis. (1896-1956) Author, ecologist, World War I hero. Pulitzer Prize winner. KEEN.

Bronte, Anne. (1820-1849) English author. BRIGH; DUN; GUZ; KNI; ROE; ROM.

Bronte, Branwell. (1817-1848) English painter. BRIGH; GUZ.

Bronte, Charlotte. (1816-1855) English author, poet. BRIGH; DUN; GUZ; HER; KNI; KRULL6; PER; ROE; ROL; ROM.

Bronte, Emily. (1818-1848) English author, poet. BRIGH; DUN; GUZ; HER; KNI; KRULL6; PER; ROE; ROL; ROM.

Brooks, Bruce. (1950-) Children's and young adult author. AUT.

Brooks, Gwendolyn. (1917-2000) Poet. Pulitzer Prize winner. BECKN; FEM2; GREA; PLO; POT; STRI; WILKB.

Broonzy, "Big" Bill. (1893-1959) Jazz musician, singer. GOU3.

Brosius, Scott. (1966-) Baseball player. YOUNG2.

Brower, David. (1912-2000) Environmental activist, mountaineer, Sierra Club president. BYR; GRAH; HAV; KEEN; LUC2; STA.

Brown, Arthur Whitten. (1886-1948) Aviation pioneer. WILLI.

Brown, Barnum. (1873-1963) Paleontologist. AAS.

Brown, Christy. (1932-1981) Author, poet. KEND.

Brown, Clara. (1803-1885) Pioneer, slave. KAT; MON2; SAV2; STEFO3.

Brown, Dorothy Lavinia. (1919-) Physician, state legislator. KENJ2.

Brown, George. (1818-1880) Canadian editor, publisher. SAT.

Brown, George S. (1918-1978) Korean War, Vietnam War Joint Chiefs of Staff, World War II Air Force general. BOR.

Brown, Helen Gurley. (1922-) Magazine editor. PRI.

Brown, Henry "Box." (1816-?) Magician, slave. HAM; HASK6.

Brown, Henry. (1857-1884) Law marshal, outlaw. SAV.

Brown, James. (1933-) Civil rights activist, jazz musician, singer. LES; TAT.

Brown, Jim. (1936-) Football player. BUCK; ITA4; JACT; LAC3; SAV4; SULG3.

Brown, John. (1800-1859) Abolitionist. AAS18; CRO; LIL; THOM.

Brown, John "Fed." (1810-1876) Author, slave. FRA.

Brown, Kevin. (1968-) Baseball player. SCHWAR.

Brown, Marcia. (1918-) Children's author, illustrator. MARC.

Brown, Margaret Tobin "Molly." (1867-1932) Titanic survivor, women's rights activist. KRO.

Brown, Margaret Wise. (1910-1952) Children's author. RYL.

Brown, Marie Van Brittan. (fl. 1969) Inventor. SULO2.

Brown, Mordecai Peter Centennial "Three Finger." (1876-1948) Baseball player. SAV10; SULG5.

Brown, Paul. (1908-1996) Football coach. SAV11.

Brown, Rachel. (1898-1980) Biochemist, medical researcher. ALTML; BLASH2.

Brown, Ray. (1926-2002) Jazz musician. GOU2.

Brown, Ronald. (1941-1996) Attorney, cabinet member. POT.

Brown, Sterling Allen. (1901-1989) Author, poet. HARD.

Brown, Steve. (1890-1965) Jazz musician. GOU2.

Brown, Tabitha. (1780-1858) Pioneer. STEFO3.

Brown, Tim. (1966-) Football player. Heisman Trophy winner. DEV; SAV8.

Brown, Wesley A. (1927-) Navy lieutenant commander. POT.

Brown, William Wells. (1814-1884) Abolitionist, author, playwright, slave. FRA.

Browne, Marjorie Lee. (1914-1979) Mathematician. SULO2.

Brownell, Kady. (1842-?) Civil war heroine. BLASH; CHA; ZEI.

Browning, Elizabeth Barrett. (1806-1861) English poet. CRO4.

Browning, Robert. (1812-1889) English poet. CRO4.

Bruce, Blanche K. (1841-1898) Political activist, senator. BOOK.

Bruce, Robert. (1274-1329) Scottish military leader. CRO3; KRAL.

Brueghel, Jan. (1568-1625) Flemish painter. CUM.

Brueghel, Pieter. (1525-1569) Flemish painter. KRULL2; REN.

Brule, Etienne. (1592-1632) French explorer. PRE.

Brundtland, Gro Harlem. (1939-) Norwegian environmental activist, physician, prime minister, World Health Organization head. AXEC; GRAH; GUL; PRI3.

Brunel, Marc. (1769-1849) French civil engineer. AAS11.

Brunelleschi. (1377-1466) Italian architect. BART.

Bruno, Giordano. (1548-1600) Italian scholar. POD.

Bryan, Ashley. (1923-) Children's author, illustrator. MARC3.

Bryan, William Jennings. (1860-1925) Cabinet member, congressman, human rights activist. CRO; CRO4; FAB; JACW.

Bryant, Kobe. (1978-) Basketball player. NEL; PAU.

Buade, Louis de. (Frontenac et Palluau, Comte) (1622-1698) French colonist, military leader. CRO2.

Buber, Martin. (1878-1965) Austrian philosopher, spiritual leader. CRO5; PASA.

Buchanan, James. (1791-1868) Cabinet member, congressman, 15th president of U.S. ADA; BARB; BAU; BLASS; CRO6; DAV2; MORR.

Buck, Pearl S. (1892-1973) Author. Nobel

Prize winner, Pulitzer Prize winner. ARO; FAB2; GOM; KNI; KRAMB2; PER; SMIL2.

Buck, Rufus. (d. 1896) Native American gang leader. MON2.

Buckner, Bill. (1949-) Baseball player. SAV12.

Buddha. *See* Gautama, Siddhartha.

Budge, Don. (1915-2000) Tennis player. CHRIST.

Buffalo Bill. *See* Cody, William.

Buffet, Warren. (1930-) Financier. MAC.

Buffon, Georges. (1707-1788) French author, naturalist. KEEN.

Bugbee, Emma. (1888-1981) Journalist. PRI.

Buick, David Dunbar. (1854-1929) Automaker, born Scotland. SAW.

Bujones, Fernando. (1955-) Ballet dancer. PAL.

Bukovsky, Vladimir. (1942-) Russian human rights activist. BERS.

Bulkeley, John. (1911-1996), Navy vice admiral, World War II hero. Medal of Honor recipient. DOH.

Bullett, Vicki. (unknown) Basketball player. JACK.

Bullock, Anna Mae. (Tina Turner) (1939-) Singer. KEEL.

Bulosan, Carlos (1911-1956) Author, born Philippines. ISH; SIN.

Bulwer-Lytton, Edward. (1803-1873) English author. PER

Bunche, Ralph Johnson. (1904-1971) Diplomat, statesman. Nobel Peace Prize winner, Presidential Medal of Freedom recipient. ALTMS; BECKN; BLU; BOOK; BRED2; DUD; HASK7; KEEN2; POT.

Bundy, Ted. (1946-1989) Serial killer. LAS.

Bunn, Teddy. (1909-1978) Jazz musician. GOU3.

Bunyan, John. (1628-1688) English author, spiritual leader. JACKD2; PER.

Burbank, Luther. (1849-1926) Horticulturalist. FAB3; HAV; TIN.

Burbridge, E. Margaret. (1919-) English astronomer. YOUNT6.

Burgess, Abbie. (1839-1892) Lighthouse keeper. FLE.

Burgin, Elizabeth. (unknown) American Revolutionary War heroine. SILC.

Burgoyne, John. (1723-1792) English military leader in American Revolutionary War, playwright. CRO3; SCHM.

Burke, Arleigh A. (1901-1996) Navy admiral, Korean War Chief of Naval Operations. Presidential Medal of Freedom recipient. BOR.

Burke, Chris. (1965-) Actor. KEND.

Burke, Edmund. (1729-1797) English author, orator, philosopher, statesman. SCHM.

Burke, Robert O'Hara. (1820-1861) Irish explorer. LANG; LOM; PRE.

Burke, Yvonne Braithwaite. (1932-) Attorney, congresswoman, human rights activist. DUD; GREA.

Burkitt, Denis Parsons. (1911-1993) Irish medical researcher, physician. SPA.

Burland, Rebecca. (1793-1872) Pioneer, born England. STEFO3.

Burnell, Jocelyn Bell. (1943-) Irish astronomer. HAC8; HAV; STI2.

Burnet, Sir Frank MacFarlane. (1899-1985) Australian medical researcher, physician. Nobel Prize winner. SPA.

Burnett, Charles. (1944-) Filmmaker. AFR.

Burnett, Frances Hodgson. (1849-1924) Children's author, born England. KRULL6.

Burns, Anthony. (1834-1862) Abolitionist, slave. HAM.

Burns, George. (1896-1996) Actor, comedian. CRO4.

Burns, Robert. (1759-1796) Scottish poet. PER.

Burns, Ursula. (1958-) Engineer. SULO2.

Burnside, Ambrose Everett. (1824-1881) Civil War general. GREEC3; YAN.

Burpee, W. Atlee. (1858-1915) Entrepreneur gardening seeds and supplies. AAS16.

Burr, Aaron. (1756-1836) Attorney, presidential candidate, senator, vice president of U.S. CRO4.

Burrell, Kenny. (1931-) Jazz musician. GOU3.

Burrell, Stanley Kirk. (Hammer) (1963-) Dancer, singer, songwriter. RED5.

Burroughs, Edgar Rice. (1875-1950) Author. PER.

Burroughs, John. (1837-1921) Author, environmentalist. FAB3; KEEN.

Burson, Nancy. (1948-) Photographer. HOR.

Burton, Richard. (1925-1984) Welsh actor. CRO4.

Burton, Sir Richard Francis. (1821-1890) English explorer, linguist, soldier, translator. ALTE; LOM; POD; PRE; ZAU.

Bush, Barbara Pierce. (1925-) First Lady. BARB; GOR; PAST; TAYS.

Bush, George Herbert Walker. (1924-) Entrepreneur oil, 41st president of U.S., vice president, World War II Navy pilot. ADA; BARB; BAU; BLASS; CRO6; DAV2; KRULL5; MORR.

Bush, George W. (1791-1867) Cattle trader, explorer, pioneer. HASK3.

Bush, George Walker. (1946-) Governor, 43rd president of U.S. ADA; BARB; BAU; DAV2.

Bush, Laura Welch. (1946-) First Lady, librarian. BARB; PAST.

Bushnell, David. (1742-1824) Inventor. RIC5.

Bushnell, Nolan. (1943-) Electrical engineer, entrepreneur computer games, inventor. HAV.

Butcher, Susan. (1956-) Sled dog racer. ALTE2; LIT.

Butkus, Dick. (1942-) Football player. HUNT; ITA4.

Butler, Benjamin Franklin. (1818-1893) Attorney, Civil War general, congressman, governor. YAN.

Butler, Beverly. (1932-) Children's author. KEND.

Butler, Nicholas Murray. (1862-1947) Educator, peace activist. Nobel Peace Prize winner. KEEN2.

Butler, Octavia. (1947-) Author. DAT; RED4; WILKB.

Button, Dick. (1929-) Olympic figure skater, sportscaster. KNA4.

Byars, Betsy. (1928-) Children's author. YUN.

Byrd, Charlie. (1925-1999) Jazz musician. GOU3.

Byrd, Richard Evelyn. (1888-1957) Arctic explorer, aviation pioneer, World War I and II Navy pilot. ALTE; LOM; SCHR; TES.

Byrd, William. (1674-1744) Colonist. CRO2.

Byrdsong, Ricky. (1957-1999) Basketball coach, human rights activist. JACKD4.

Byrdsong, Sherialyn. (1957-) Basketball coach, human rights activist. JACKD4.

Byrne, David. (1952-) Composer, singer, songwriter, born Scotland. SAW.

Byrne, Jane. (1934-) Mayor. GUL

Byron, Lord. See Gordon, George.

C

C Note. Pop music group. KRULI.

Cabeza de Vaca, Álvar Núñez. (1490-1557) Spanish explorer. ALTE; CRO2; PARN; SIN2.

Cabot, John. (1450-1499) English explorer, born Italy. ALTE; CRO2; FRIT; LOM; PARN; PRE; WILLI2.

Cabot, Sebastian. (1476-1557) Italian explorer. ALTE; PRE.

Cabral, Pedro Álvares. (1460-1526) Portuguese explorer. FRIT; POD; PRE.

Cabrillo, Juan Rodriguez. (1520?-1543) Portuguese explorer. PARN; PRE.

Cadoria, Sherian. (1940-) Army brigadier general, Vietnam War military police. HASK2.

Caesar, Julius. (100-44 B.C.) Roman dictator, ruler. BAKR3; COOLI; CRO3; CRO4; HOOB3; NAR2; WILKP4; YEN.

Caglistro, Alessandro di. (1743-1795) Italian magician. HOOB3.

Cahan, Abraham. (1860-1951) Author, editor newspaper, born Lithuania. RIT.

Cailliaud, Frederic. (1787-1869) French explorer. PRE.

Caillié, René. (1799-1838) French explorer. PRE.

Calamity Jane. See Cannary, Martha Jane.

Calder, Alexander. (1898-1966) Painter, sculptor. Presidential Medal of Freedom recipient. CUS; KRY; SAW.

Calhoun, John Caldwell. (1782-1850) Cabinet member, congressman, senator, vice president. CRO; FAB.

Callahan, John. (1951-) Cartoonist, disability rights activist. KEND.

Callas, Maria. (1923-1977) Greek opera singer. BRIL; COOL; DUN.

Callendar, George "Red." (1916-) Jazz musician. GOU2.

Calloway, Cab. (1907-1994) Bandleader, composer, singer. MON; SHIP.

Calvert, Cecil. (1606-1675) Colonist, settler

of Maryland. DOH5.

Calvert, Leonard. (1607-1647) Colonial governor, settler of Maryland. CRO2; DOH5.

Calvin, John. (1509-1564) French spiritual leader, Protestant theologian. CRO5; GOLDM; JACW2.

Cameron, Agnes Deans. (1863-1912) Arctic explorer. MCLO4.

Cameron, Evelyn. (1868-1928) Photographer. ALTE2; FUR2.

Cameron, Julia Margaret. (1815-1878) Photographer. KRY; WOL.

Camillus. (Marcus Furius Camillus) (450-365 B.C.) Roman general, statesman. BAKR3.

Cammermeyer, Margarethe. (1942-) Army colonel, Vietnam War nurse. LINL2.

Campanella, Roy. (1921-1993) Baseball player. KEND; SULG2.

Campbell, Bebe Moore. (1950-) Author. SMIL2.

Campbell, Ben Nighthorse. (1933-) Cheyenne Indian jewelry designer, Korean Conflict military, olympic judo athlete, senator. ALLP.

Campbell, Bonnie. (1948-) Attorney, government agency director, human rights activist, women's rights activist. GOLDE.

Campbell, Earl. (1955-) Football player. Heisman Trophy winner. DEV; LAC3.

Campbell, Fanny. (1755-?) Pirate. WEA.

Campbell, Kim. (1947-) Canadian prime minister. GUL.

Campbell, Naomi. (1970-) Fashion model. DUN.

Campbell, Tunis G. (1812-1891) State legislator. AFR2.

Canady, Alexa. (1950-) Physician. HAN2; SULO2.

Canaletto. (Giovanni Antonio Canale) (1697-1768) Italian painter. CUM; EIG; KRY.

Cannary, Martha Jane. (Calamity Jane) (1852-1903) Adventurer, Indian scout, pioneer. CALV; COOL; FUR2; GLA; HARN; JAN; KRAL; KRO; LAK; SAV2.

Cannon, Annie Jump. (1863-1941) Astronomer. CAM; HARN; REY; STI2; VEG.

Cannon, Walter Bradford. (1871-1945) Educator, physiologist. CURT.

Canseco, Jose. (1964-) Baseball player, born Cuba. SAV12; SCHWAR; SULG8.

Cantor, Georg. (1845-1918) German mathematician. HENH.

Canute II. (994-1035) Danish military leader. CRO3.

Capa, Robert. (1913-1954) Photojournalist, born Hungary. KRY.

Capone, Al. (1899-1947) Gangster. BLACG; DON.

Capra, Frank. (1897-1991) Filmmaker, born Italy. HILA2.

Capriati, Jennifer. (1976-) Olympic tennis player. DON.

Caravaggio. (Michelangelo Merisi) (1573-1610) Italian painter. CUM; KRY; SEV.

Carbajal, Michael. (1968-) Boxer. SIN2.

Cardin, Shoshana. (1926-) Organizational head. SEG.

Cardona, Manuel. (1934-) Physicist, born Spain. OLE.

Cardozo, Francis Louis. (1837-1903) Educator. COX2.

Cardus, David. (1922-) Physician, born Spain. OLE.

Careme, Antonin. (1784-1833) French chef. HOOB2.

Carey, Mariah. (1969-) Singer. MARV7; ROBB.

Carl, William. (unknown) Magician. HASK6.

Carle, Eric. (1929-) Children's author, illustrator. MARC3.

Carlson, Chester. (1906-1968) Inventor. AAS19.

Carlson, Evans. (1896-1947) World War I Army, World War II Marine commander, lieutenant colonel. OLE2.

Carlton, Steve. (1944-) Baseball player. SULG5.

Carmichael, Amy. (1867-1951) Irish missionary. JACKD.

Carnegie, Andrew. (1835-1919) Entrepreneur steel, philanthropist, born Scotland. BLU; CRO; GREEC; JACW; MAC; MAYB; SAW; TRAU.

Carney, William H. (1840-1908) Civil War Army hero. Medal of Honor recipient. DOH; HASK2; MED; POT.

Carnot, Lazare Nicolas Marguerite. (1753-1823) French military leader. CRO3.

Caro, Joseph Ben Ephraim. (1488-1575) Israeli legal scholar. PASA.

Caron, Nadine. (1970-) Canadian physician. KIR.

Carothers, Wallace. (1896-1937) Organic chemist, editor magazine, inventor. HAV.

Carpenter, Iris. (unknown) English journalist, World War II correspondent. COLM.

Carr, Emma Perry. (1880-1972) Physical chemist. STI2.

Carr, Henry. (1942-) Olympic sprinter, track and field athlete. KNA3.

Carr, Vicki. (1940-) Singer. LAE.

Carré, Lily. (1908-) French World War II double spy. SULG4.

Carrey, Jim. (1962-) Actor, comedian. KAL2.

Carrington, Leonora. (1917-) Painter. SILL3.

Carroll, Charles. (1737-1832) American Revolutionary War patriot, congressman, Declaration of Independence signer. FRA2; QUI.

Carroll, Diahann. (1935-) Actor. PLO.

Carroll, Lewis. See Dodgson, Charles.

Carruthers, George E. (1939-) Astrophysicist. AFR2; HENS; SULO.

Carson, Benjamin Solomon. (1951-) Human rights activist, physician. AFR2; COX; JACKD4; POT.

Carson, Christopher "Kit." (1809-1868) Civil War soldier, fur trapper, hunter, Indian agent and scout. ALTE; BAKS; CALV; COLL; GLA2; JAN; KRAL; LEVE; SAV3.

Carson, Rachel. (1907-1964) Author, environmental activist. Presidential Medal of Freedom recipient. BRIL; BYR; CAM2; CUS2; DE; DEN; DID; FAB3; HAC6; HARN; HAV; HEA; HER; KEEN; KNI; KRE; LEU; LEVE; LUC2; MARZ; REY; ROL; SAW; SIR; STA; STI2; VEG.

Carter, Benny. (1907-) Jazz musician. GOU.

Carter, Don. (1926-) Bowler. JACT.

Carter, Howard. (1873-1939) English archaeologist, egyptologist. FAG; GREENBL; SCHEL; WEI.

Carter, Iola O. (unknown) Inventor. SULO2.

Carter, James Earl "Jimmy." (1924-) Governor, 39th president of U.S., World War II Navy. Nobel Peace Prize winner, Presidential Medal of Freedom recipient. ADA; BARB; BAU; BLASS; BLU; CRO6; DAV2; DEN; KRULL5; LUC; MORR.

Carter, Pamela. (1950-) Attorney, state attorney general. POT.

Carter, Robert. (1663-1732) Colonist, settled Virginia. CRO2.

Carter, Ron. (1937-) Jazz musician. GOU2.

Carter, Rosalynn Smith. (1927-) First Lady. Presidential Medal of Freedom recipient. ANT; BARB; GOR; PAST.

Carter, Vince. (1977-) Basketball player. NEL; PAU.

Carteret, Sir George. (1610-1680) Colonist, settled New Jersey. DOH3.

Cartier, Jacques. (1491-1557) French explorer. ALTE; BAKS; CRO2; HOOB2; LOM; PARN; POD; PRE; WILLI2.

Cartland, Barbara. (1901-2000) English author. KNI.

Cartwright, Peter. (1785-1872) Abolitionist, spiritual leader. JACKD2.

Caruso, Enrico. (1873-1921) Italian opera singer. KRAL.

Carver, George Washington. (1864-1943) Agricultural scientist. AFR2; ALTMS; BECKN; BOY; DEN; FAB3; HAC2; HASK8; HAV; HAY3; JONL; LEVE; LOM2; MARZ; MCK2; PIO; STA; SULO; TIN; YOUNT2.

Cary, Mary Ann Shadd. (1822-1893) Abolitionist, attorney, educator, journalist. HEA; POT; TUR.

Casals, Pablo. (1876-1973) Composer, conductor, musician, born Spain. Presidential Medal of Freedom recipient. SIN2.

Casals, Rosemary. (1948-) Tennis player. LAE.

Casanova de Seingalt, Giovanni Giacomo (1725-1798) Italian adventurer. KRAL.

Case, Steve. (1958-) Entrepreneur computers, Internet pioneer. AAS4; FREN.

Casey, Al. (1915-) Jazz musician. GOU3.

Casey, Sean. (1974-) Baseball player. SCHWAR; SCHWAR2.

Cashier, Albert. See Hodgers, Jenny.

Cashman, Nellie. (1845-1925) Gold miner, explorer, pioneer. ALTE2; FUR2; MCLO3; SAV2.

Caslavska. Vera. (1942-) Czech olympic gymnast. GREES.

Cassatt, Mary. (1844-1926) Painter. DEN; GLU; HARN; HER; IMP; KRULL2; KRY; MCD; SAB; SILL3; STU.

Cassidy, Butch. See Parker, Robert Leroy.

Cassin, René. (1887-1976) French attorney,

human rights activist, legal scholar, UNESCO co-founder. Nobel Peace Prize winner. KEEN2.

Castaneda, Carlos. (1896-1958) Historian, born Mexico. LAE; SIN2.

Castellanos, Rosario. (1925-1974) Mexican author. SHIR.

Castillo, Luis. (1975-) Baseball player, born Dominican Republic. STEWG.

Castner, Mattie. (1848-1920) Pioneer hotel-keeper. ALTE2.

Castro, Fidel. (1926-) Cuban dictator. CRO4; GREER; MAYB2.

Catalanotto, Peter. (1959-) Children's author, illustrator. TALAR3.

Cather, Willa. (1873-1947) Author. Pulitzer Prize winner. ALTE2; BRED; FAB2; GOM.

Catherine of Alexandria. (4th century) Saint. ARM.

Catherine of Aragon. (1485-1536) English queen. ROL.

Catherine de Medici. (1519-1589) French queen. GUL; HER; ROL.

Catherine of Siena. (1353-1386) Human rights activist, mystic, poet, spiritual leader. KNI.

Catherine the Great. (1729-1796) Russian empress. CRO4; DUN; GUL; HER; HOOB5; KRULL; MEL2; NAR4; ROL.

Catlett, Elizabeth. (1915-) Painter, print-maker, sculptor. AFR.

Catlett, "Big" Sid. (1910-1951) Jazz musician. GOU6.

Catlin, George. (1796-1872) Attorney, painter. CALV.

Cato the Elder (Marcus Porcius Cato) (234-149 B.C.) Roman statesman. BAKR3.

Caton-Thompson, Gertrude. (1888-1985) English archaeologist. FAG.

Catt, Carrie Chapman. (1859-1947) Suffragist, women's rights activist. DUM; HEL; MORI3; ROL; ZEI2; ZEI5.

Catullus. (Gaius Valerius Catullus) (84-54 B.C.) Roman poet. BAKR3.

Caulkins, Tracy. (1963-) Olympic swimmer. HASD.

Cauthen, Steve. (1960-) Jockey. KUH.

Cavanagh, Kit. (Christian Walsh) (1667-1739) English soldier, disguised self as man. DUN.

Cavazos, Lauro F. (1927-) Anatomist, cabinet member, educator, physiologist. LAE.

Cavell, Edith. (1865-1915) English educator, World War I nurse and heroine. DUN.

Cavendish, Henry. (1731-1810) English chemist, physicist. TIN.

Cayce, Edgar. (1877-1945) Psychic. CRO4; KRULL7.

Cayley, George. (1773-1857) English aviation pioneer. BERL2.

Ceballos, Cedric. (1969-) Basketball player. BJA.

Cecil, Robert. (1864-1958) English attorney, peace activist, statesman. Nobel Peace Prize winner. KEEN2.

Cecilia. Saint. ARM.

Celleni, Benvenuto. (1500-1571) Italian goldsmith, jewelry designer, sculptor. KRY.

Cepeda, Perucho. (1906-1955) Baseball player, born Puerto Rico. WIN.

Cerf, Vinton. (1943-) Internet pioneer. HENH2.

Cernan, Eugene. (1934-) Astronaut, Navy aviator. PRE.

Cervantes, Miguel de. (1547-1616) Spanish author. KRULL6; PER; REN.

Cervenka, Valerie. (unknown) Forensic entomologist. KALLN.

Cézanne, Paul. (1839-1906) French painter. CUM; IMP; KRY; ORE; SAB.

Chac. Mayan god of rain. FIS2.

Chacon, Rafael. (1833-1925) Civil War soldier. SIN2.

Chagall, Marc. (1887-1985) French painter, born Russia. GLU; KRULL2; KRY; TWEPO.

Chagoya, Enrique. (1953-) Painter. HON.

Chain, Sir Ernst Boris. (1906-1979) English biochemist, medical researcher, born Germany. Nobel Prize Winner. CURT.

Chamberlain, J. Austen. (1863-1937) English political activist, statesman. Nobel Peace Prize winner. KEEN2.

Chamberlain, Neville. (1869-1940) English prime minister. PAP.

Chamberlain, Wilt. (1936-) Basketball player. CRO4; DEE; JACT; JAN; KNA5; KNA6; POT; SULG3.

Chamberlin, Judi. (1944-) Disability rights activist. KEND.

Chambers, Paul. (1935-1969) Jazz musician.

GOU2.

Chamorro, Violeta Barrios de. (1929-) Nicaraguan president. AXEC; CUS2; GUL; HER; PRI3.

Champlain, Samuel de. (1567-1635) French explorer. ALTE; BAKS; CRO2; POD; PRE; SCHEL2.

Champollion, Jean-François. (1790-1832) French egyptologist. POD; WEI.

Chandrasekhar, Subrahmanyan. (1910-1995) Astrophysicist, born Pakistan. Nobel Prize winner. RAG; YOUNT.

Chanel, Gabrielle "Coco." (1883-1971) French fashion designer and entrepreneur. DUN; HER; KENJ; MCLU; ROE.

Chang, Michael. (1972-) Tennis player. GAN; MORE; SIN.

Chang-Diaz, Franklin R. (1950-) Astronaut, physicist, born Venezuela. BAIR; PAL.

Chanute, Octave. (1832-1910) Aviation pioneer, civil engineer, born France. BERL2.

Chaplin, Charlie. (1889-1997) Comedian, showman. KAL2; YEN.

Chapman, Jonathan. (Johnny Appleseed) (1774-1845) Agricultural scientist, botanist, folk hero, frontiersman. CALV; KEEN; KRAL.

Chappelle, Georgette "Dickey" Meyer. (1918-1965) World War II photojournalist. COLM; PRI.

Charlemagne. (742-814) French conqueror, emperor. CRO3; CRO4; HOOB2; MEL; PRI2; YEN.

Charles. (1947-) English Prince of Wales. CRO4.

Charles I. (1600-1649) English king. DAV.

Charles II. (1630-1685) English king. DAV.

Charles V. (1500-1558) Holy Roman Emperor. PAP.

Charles XII. (1682-1718) Swedish king. CRO3.

Charles, Eugenia. (1919-) Dominica prime minister. GUL.

Charles, Ray. (1930-2004) Jazz musician, singer. AFR; LES; RED5; TAT.

Charleston, Oscar McKinley. (1896-1954) Baseball player. WIN2.

Charlot, Olivia. (1913-) Jazz singer. MON.

Chase, Hal. (1883-1947) Baseball player. SULG2.

Chase, Samuel. (1741-1811) American Revolutionary War patriot, congressman, Declaration of Independence signer. FRA2; QUI.

Chastain, Brandi. (1968-) Olympic soccer player. LAY2; MILM.

Chaucer, Geoffrey. (1343-1400) English diplomat, poet, scholar. REN.

Chávez, César. (1927-1993) Workers' rights activist. Presidential Medal of Freedom recipient. BRED2; DEN; JACW; LAE; LEVE; MARV2; MARZ; SIN2; STRE5.

Chávez, Denise. (1948) Playwright. SMIL2.

Chavez, Dennis. (1888-1962) Senator, state legislator. LAE; SIN2.

Chávez-Thompson, Linda. (1944-) Workers' rights activist. MARV8.

Chayanne. (singer) See Arce, Elmer Figuero.

Cheeks, Maurice. (1956-) Basketball player. SAV5.

Cheesman, Lucy Evelyn. (1881-1969) English entomologist. POLK.

Cheever, Susan. (1943-) Author. SMIL2.

Chekhov, Anton. (1860-1904) Russian author, playwright. NIN; WEI2.

Cheng Ho. See Zheng He.

Cheng I Sao. (Lady Ching) (1775-1844) Chinese pirate. SHAR; WEA.

Cheng, Nien. (1915-) Author, political activist, born China. SMIL2.

Chennault, Anna. (1925-) Journalist, political activist, born China. SIN.

Chennault, Claire Lee. (1890-1958) World War I fighter pilot, World War II Army Air Force major general. OLE2.

Chenzira, Ayoka. (1956-) Filmmaker. AFR.

Cher. See Sarkisan, Cherilyn.

Chern, Shiing-Shen. (1911-) Educator, mathematician, born China. HENH.

Cherry, Fred V. (1928-) Vietnam War soldier. REE2.

Chesnut, Mary Boykin. (1823-1886) Author, Civil War diarist. BLASH; ZEI.

Chesnutt, Charles. (1858-1932) Author. AFR; MAL; OFT.

Chess, Victoria. (1939-) Children's author, illustrator. TALAR.

Chiang Kai-Shek. (1887-1975) Chinese military leader. CRO3.

Chikatilo, Andrei. (1936-1994) Russian serial killer. LAS.

Childe, Vere Gordon. (1892-1957) Australian archaeologist. FAG.

Childress, Alice. (1920-1994) Actor, author, playwright. GREA; HAC4.

Chin, Ch'iu. (1879-1907) Chinese women's rights activist. DUN.

Chin, Karen. (1952-) Paleontologist, born Canada. HAV; KAH6.

Chin, Leann. (1933-) Entrepreneur restaurants. PIL2.

Chinn, May Edward. (1896-1980) Physician. KENJ2.

Chisholm, Mairí. (1896-?) Scottish suffragist, World War I nurse. BERS.

Chisholm, Sallie. (unknown) Biologist. KAH6.

Chisholm, Shirley. (1924-) Congresswoman, presidential candidate. BECKN; BOOK; DUD; FEM; FIR; GREA; GUL; HARN; HASK7; HER; MORI2; PIN: PLO; POT; ROL.

Chizick, Sarah. (1897-) Israeli settler. TAI.

Cho, Margaret. (1969-) Actor. GAN.

Choi, Sook Nyul. (1937-) Children's and young adult author, born Korea. ISH.

Chopin, Frederic. (1810-1849) Polish composer. CRO4; KRULL4; ROM; VEN.

Chopin, Kate. (1850-1904) Author, women's rights activist. KNI; LYO.

Chorn, Arn. (1967-) Cambodian political activist and prisoner. HOOS.

Chotek, Sophie. (1868-1914) Austrian political activist, wife of Archduke Ferdinand, World War I victim. ZEI2.

Chou En-Lai. (1898-1976) Chinese communist leader, political activist. CRO4.

Chouet, Bernard. (1945-) Geophysicist, volcanologist, born Switzerland. HAV.

Chouteau, Auguste. (1749-1829) Fur trader, pioneer. DOH4.

Chow, Amy. (1978-) Olympic gymnast. KLE; LAY.

Christian, Charlie. (1916-1942) Jazz musician. GOU3.

Christian, Sara. (1920-) Nascar auto racer. RIL.

Christiansen, Ole Kirk. (1891-1958) Danish entrepreneur toys. AAS9.

Christie, Agatha. (1891-1976) English author. KNI; PER; ROL; SMIL.

Christina. (1626-1689) Swedish queen. COOL; LEO3; MEL2.

Christopher. (3rd century) Saint. ARM.

Chrysler, Walter P. (1875-1940) Automaker. AAS10.

Chu, Paul Ching-Wu. (1941-) Physicist, born China. YOUNT.

Chuang Tzu. (369-286 B.C.) Chinese philosopher, spiritual leader, cofounder of Taoism. GOLDM.

Chuka. (c. 1890) Hopi Indian child sent to boarding school. HOOS.

Chung, Constance Vu-Hwa "Connie." (1946-) Broadcast journalist. MORE; RAG; SIN.

Chung, Myung-Whun. (1953-) Conductor, musician, born Korea. MORE; SIN.

Church, Benjamin. (1639-1718) Colonist and soldier. CRO2.

Church, Frederick E. (1826-1900) Painter. GLU.

Churchill, John. (1650-1722) English military leader. CRO3.

Churchill, Odette Brailly Sansom. (1912-1995) French World War II resistance fighter. GRAN; SCHM4; THOM4.

Churchill, Sir Winston Leonard Spencer. (1874-1965) English author, prime minister. Nobel Prize Winner. CRO4; MARZ; MAYB2; YEN.

Ciccione, Madonna Louise Veronica. (Madonna) (1958-) Pop singer. HUNTE3; KEEL; ORG.

Cicero. (Marcus Tollius Cicero) (106-43 B.C.) Roman attorney, orator, philosopher. BAKR3; COOLI; NAR2.

Cid Campeadore, El. (Rodrigo Diaz de Viver) (1043-1099) Spanish military leader. CRO3; KRAL.

Ciller, Tansu. (1946-) Turkish prime minister. GUL.

Cimabue. (1240?-1302) Italian painter. KRY.

Cimarosa, Domenico. (1749-1801) Italian opera composer. VEN.

Cinque, Joseph. (1817-1879) African patriot, slave insurrectionist. ALTMS.

Cisneros, Evelyn. (1958-) Ballet dancer. SIN2.

Cisneros, Henry. (1947-) Cabinet member, mayor. LAE; SIN2.

Cisneros, Sandra. (1954-) Author. HILC; LAE.

Claiborne, William. (1587-1677) Colonist. CRO2.

Clalin, Frances. (unknown) Civil War soldier,

disguised as man. CHA.

Clancy, Tom. (1947-) Author. PER.

Clapp, Cornelia. (1849-1934) Educator, zoologist. REY.

Clappe, Louise Amelia. (1819-1906) Gold mine camp owner, journalist, pioneer. STEFO3.

Clark, Christopher. (unknown) Acoustic biologist, educator. SAY.

Clark, Eugenie. (1922-) Ichthyologist, oceanographer. HAV; MCLO7; POLK; POLKI; RAPD; YOUNT3.

Clark, Grahame. (1907-1995) English archaeologist, author. FAG.

Clark, Kenneth B. (1914-) Civil rights activist, psychologist. BECKN.

Clark, Joan. (unknown) Inventor. SULO2.

Clark, John Desmond. (1916-2002) Archaeologist. FAG.

Clark, Marcellus R. (d. 1971) Magician. HASK6.

Clark, Peter Humphries. (1829-1925) Civil rights activist, educator. COX2.

Clark, Septima Poinsette. (1898-1987) Civil rights activist, educator. GREA; HAN2.

Clark, William. (1770-1838) Army, explorer, Indian official. ALTE; BAKS; CALV; CRO; CRO4; DEN; JAN; LANG; POD; PRE; SCHEL2; WAT; YEN.

Clarke, Kenny. (1914-1985) Jazz musician. GOU6.

Clarke, Kim. (1954-) Jazz musician. GOU2.

Claude, Albert. (1899-1983) English biologist, World War I British intelligence. Nobel Prize winner. HAV.

Claudel, Camille. (1864-1943) French sculptor. KRY.

Claudius. (Tiberius Claudius Nero Germanicus) (10 B.C.-13 A.D.) Roman emperor. BAKR3.

Clausewitz, Karl von. (1780-1831) Prussian (German) military leader. CRO3.

Clay, Henry. (1777-1852) Cabinet member, congressman, senator. CRO; FAB.

Cleary, Beverly. (1912-) Children's author. PER; YUN.

Clem, Johnny. (1852-1937) Civil War child soldier. HOOS.

Clémenceau, Georges. (1841-1929) French prime minister, World War I military leader. PAP.

Clemens, Roger. (1962-) Baseball player. BUCK2; SCHWAR; SULG5; SULM.

Clemens, Samuel. (Mark Twain) (1835-1910) Author, journalist. CRO; FAB2; KRAL; KRU6; LEVE; NIN; OFT2; PER; RIT; YEN.

Clemente, Roberto. (1934-1972) Baseball player, born Puerto Rico. DEN; KRULL3; LAE; LIT; PAL; SEHN; SIN2; SLO; SULG2; TOR2; WIN; YOUNG2.

Cleopatra VII. (69-30 B.C.) Egyptian ruler. COOL; CRO4; GUL; HER; KRAL; KRULL; LEO; MARZ; MEL2; NAR4; ROBE3; ROL; WEL.

Cleopatra Selene of Mauretania. (40 B.C.-6 A.D.) Daughter of Cleopatra. LEO.

Cleveland, Emeline Horton. (1829-1878) Physician. STI.

Cleveland, Frances Folsom. (1864-1947) First Lady. BARB; GOR; PAST.

Cleveland, Grover. (1837-1908) Governor, mayor, 22nd and 24th president of U.S. ADA; BARB; BAU; BLASS; CRO6; DAV2; MORR.

Clifford, Esther. (1921-) German Jewish Holocaust survivor. LAND4.

Clifton, Lucille. (1936-) Children's author. WILKB.

Clinton, Hillary Rodham. (1947-) Attorney, First Lady, senator. BARB; GOR; GUL; PAST; TAYS.

Clinton, William Jefferson "Bill." (1946) Attorney, governor, 42nd president of U.S. ADA; BARB; BAU; BLASS; CRO6; DAV2; KRULL5; MORR; ROBE2.

Clicquot-Ponsardin, Nicole-Barbe. (1777-1866) French winemaker. DUN.

Clotilda. (470-545) French saint, spiritual leader. CRO4.

Clovis. (466-511) French military and spiritual leader. CRO3; CRO4.

Clugney, Odode. (879-942) French composer, singer, spiritual leader. VEN.

Clymer, George. (1739-1813) American Revolutionary War patriot, congressman, Declaration of Independence signer. FRA2; QUI.

Coachman, Alice. (1923-) Olympic track and field athlete. GREA; HUNTE; POT.

Cobain, Kurt. (1967-1994) Rock musician. WOO3.

Cobb, Geraldyn. (1931-) Aviator, missionary. BRIGG; BRIGG2; YOUNT7.

Cobb, Jewel Plummer. (1924-) Cell biologist, educator, medical researcher. GREA; HAV; HUNTE2; STI2; SULO2; YOUNT3.

Cobb, Ty. (1886-1961) Baseball player. BJA2; DEA; JACW3; KRAMS; SLO; SULG3; TOR2.

Cobb, William Montague. (1904-1990) Anatomist, educator, historian, physician. HAY.

Cochise. (1812-1874) Apache chief. JAN; MON2.

Cochran, Jacqueline. (1910-1980) Aviator, World War II Air Force Female Service Pilots director. ALTE; BRIGG; HARN; MCLE2; MCLO5; OLE2; SCHR; YOUNT7; ZEI3.

Cochrane, Elizabeth. (Nellie Bly) (1865-1922) Adventurer, disability rights activist, human rights activist, journalist. BERS; COOL; HARN; JAN; KRAL; MCLO8; PRE; PRI; RIT; THIR; ZEI2.

Cody, William. (Buffalo Bill) (1846-1917) Civil War soldier, hunter, Indian guide, pioneer. CALV; CRO4; HOOS; KRAL; SAV3; WAL.

Cofer, Judith Ortiz. (1952-) Author, educator, poet. HILC.

Coffin, Katie. (unknown) Abolitionist. FRA.

Coffin, Levi. (1798-1877) Abolitionist. FRA.

Cohen, Ben. (1951-) Entrepreneur ice cream. BRO; KRAMB; MAYB.

Cohen, Rose. (1880-1925) Labor leader, workers' rights activist. HOOS.

Cohen, Sasha. (1984-) Olympic figure skater. MILT.

Cohen, Stanley. (1922-) Biochemist. Nobel Prize winner. HAV.

Cohn, Marianne. (1924-1944) German Holocaust resistance worker, victim. BERS.

Coimbre, Pancho. (1909-1989) Baseball player, born Puerto Rico. WIN.

Coker, Daniel. (1780-1846) Abolitionist, civil rights activist, educator. COX2; HASK4.

Colavito, Rocky. (1933-) Baseball player. TOR.

Cole, Joanne. (1944-) Children's author. MARC2.

Cole, Nat King Cole. (1916-1965) Jazz musician, singer. AFR; GOU5; MON; POT; RED5.

Cole, Natalie. (1950-) Singer. RED5.

Cole, Rebecca J. (1846-1922) Civil rights activist, human rights activist, physician. AFR2; GREA.

Cole, Thomas. (1801-1848) Painter, born England. NIN.

Cole, William "Cozy." (1909-1981) Jazz musician. GOU6.

Coleman, Bessie. (1893-1926) Aviator. ALTE2; BECKN; GREA; HAC2; HART; JONS2; MCLE2; MCLO5; POLK; POT; RAPD; TUR; YOUNT7; ZAU2.

Coleman, Derrick. (1967-) Basketball player. BJA; SAV6.

Coleman, Ornette. (1930-) Bandleader, composer, jazz musician. GOU; SHIP.

Coleman, William. (1870-1957) Entrepreneur camping supplies. AAS16.

Colfax, Harriet. (1824-1904) Lighthouse keeper. FLE.

Collazo, Oscar. (1914-1994) Puerto Rican assassin, attempted to kill President Harry Truman. JONR; STG; SULG9.

Collett-Vare, Glenna. (1903-1989) Golfer. JACT.

Collins, Cardiss. (1931-) Congresswoman. GREA.

Collins, Daniel A. (1916-) Dentist, medical researcher, physician. HAY.

Collins, Eddie. (1887-1951) Baseball player. BJA2.

Collins, Eileen M. (1956-) Air Force pilot, astronaut. ALTE; BRIGG2; BUCH; RIC4.

Collins, Kathleen. (1942-1988) Filmmaker. AFR.

Collins, Marva Delores. (1936-) Children's rights activist, educator. AFR2; COX2; GREA.

Collins, Michael. (1890-1922) Irish terrorist. STRE4; THOM3.

Colmenaaves, Margarita. (1957-) Environmental engineer. OLE.

Colon, Raul. (1952-) Puerto Rican illustrator. TALAR3.

Colonna, Vittoria. (1490-1547) Italian religious reformer. LEO3.

Colosimo, James "Big Jim." (1878-1920) Gangster, born Italy. BLACG.

Colt, Samuel (1814-1862) Inventor. RIC5.

Colter, John. (1775-1813) Explorer, fur trapper, hunter, pioneer. BAKS; COLL; GLA2.

Colton, Mary-Russell. (1889-1971) Painter, sculptor. DAN.

Coltrane, John. (1926-1967) Bandleader, jazz musician. AFR; GOU; JAZ; MOU; SHIP.

Columba. (521-597) Irish missionary, saint. CRO4.

Columbus, Christopher. (1451-1506) Italian explorer. ALTE; FRI; LANG; LOM; MARZ; PARN; POD; PRE; WILKP2; WILLI2; YEN.

Colvin, Claudette. (1940-) Civil rights activist. HOOS; ROC.

Comaneci, Nadia. (1961-) Romanian olympic gymnast. AAS20; GREES; HASD; JACT; LAY; STRU; SULG3; WEL.

Comer, James P. (1934-) Community activist, physician, psychiatrist. COX2.

Commoner, Barry. (1917-) Biologist, environmentalist. HAV; STA.

Comnena, Anna. (1083-1148) Byzantian historian, princess, religious reformer. LEO2.

Compton, Arthur Holly. (1892-1962) Nuclear physicist. Nobel Prize winner. SHER; TIN.

Comstock, Anna Botsford. (1854-1930) Entomologist, naturalist. KEEN.

Comstock, Will. (1842-1868) Indian scout, pioneer. SAV3.

Condon, Eddie. (1905-1973) Author, bandleader, journalist, jazz musician. GOU3.

Confucius. (551-479 B.C.) Chinese philosopher, spiritual leader, founder of Confucianism. CRO5; GOLDM; HOOB; JACW2; KRAL; WILKP2; YEN.

Conley, Helena. (1867-1958) Wyandotte Indian Native American rights activist. RAPD2.

Conley, Ida. (1862-1948) Wyandotte Indian Native American rights activist. RAPD2.

Conley, Lyda. (1869-1946) Wyandotte Indian attorney, Native American rights activist. RAPD2.

Conly, Elvira. (1845-?) Pioneer, slave. KAT.

Connelly, Joan Breton. (1954-) Archaeologist. POLK.

Conner, Bart. (1958-) Olympic gymnast. OCO.

Connolly, Maureen. (1934-1969) Tennis player. HARR; KRULL3.

Connor, Roger. (1857-1931) Baseball player. SULG8.

Connors, Jimmy. (1952-) Tennis player. CHRIST; JACT.

Conrad, Charles "Pete," Jr. (1930-1999) Astronaut. BAIR; PRE.

Conrad, Joseph. (1857-1924) English author. PER.

Conradt, Jody. (1941-) Basketball coach. HASD.

Constable, John. (1776-1837) English painter. CUM; ROM.

Constant, Paul D'Estournelles. (1852-1924) French diplomat, peace activist, statesman. Nobel Peace Prize winner. KEEN2.

Constantine. (c. 280-337) Roman emperor, military leader, spiritual leader. BAKR3; COOLI; CRO3; NAR2; WILKP4; YEN.

Conway, John H. (1937-) English mathematician. HENH.

Cook, George S. (1819-1902) Civil War photographer. SULG6.

Cook, James. (1728-1779) English explorer. ALTE; LANG; LOM; POD; PRE; SCHEL2; STEFO; WAT; WILKP2; WILLI2; YEN.

Cooley, Chloe. (unknown) Slave. HAM.

Coolidge, Calvin. (1872-1923) Attorney, governor, 30th president of U.S., vice-president. ADA; BARB; BAU; BLASS; CRO6; DAV2; LINE; MORR.

Coolidge, Grace Anna Goodhue. (1879-1957) First Lady. BARB; GOR; PAST.

Cooper, Anna Julia. (1858-1964) Educator. THIR.

Cooper, Chuck. (1926-1984) Basketball player. BOOK2.

Cooper, Cynthia. (1963-) Olympic basketball player. HASD; PON; RUT; SAV13.

Cooper, Dan B. "D. B." (unknown) Hijacker, folk hero. KRAL.

Cooper, Floyd. (1959-) Children's author, illustrator. TALAR2.

Cooper, Jackie. (1922-) Actor. HOOS.

Cooper, James Fenimore. (1789-1851) Author. FAB2; OFT2; PER.

Cope, Edward. (1840-1897) Paleontologist. AAS; CHRISP.

Copeland, John Anthony, Jr. (1836-1859) Abolitionist. ALTMS.

Copernicus, Nicolaus. (1473-1543) Polish astronomer. POP; TIN; WILLS; YEN.

Copland, Aaron. (1900-1990) Composer.

Presidential Medal of Freedom recipient, Pulitzer Prize winner. BRED3; TWEPR.

Copley, John Singleton. (1738-1815) Painter. EIG.

Copperfield, David. (1956-) Magician. WOO2.

Coppin, Fannie Jackson. (1836-1913) Educator, slave. GREA.

Coppola, Francis Ford. (1939-) Filmmaker. HILA2.

Coram, Thomas. (1668-1751) English children's rights activist, human rights activist. CLA.

Corbin, Margaret. (1751-1800) American Revolutionary War heroine. HARN; SCHM; SILC; ZEI4.

Cordero, Angel, Jr. (1942-) Jockey. KUH.

Cordova, Dorothy. (1932-) Archivist, community leader. SIN.

Cordova, France. (unknown) Physicist. KAH8.

Cordova, Fred. (1931-) Archivist, community leader. SIN.

Corea, Anthony "Chick." (1941-) Bandleader, composer, jazz musician. GOU4; SHIP.

Cori, Gerty Radnitz. (1896-1957) Biochemist, born Czechoslovakia. Nobel Prize winner. HAV; HUNTE2; REY; ROBE; STI; STI2; VEG.

Cornelius, Don. (1936-) Entrepreneur music business. RED.

Cornish, Samuel E. (1795-1858) Editor newspaper, journalist. BECKN.

Cornstalk. (1720-1777) Shawnee Indian warrior. CRO2.

Corona, Bert. (1918-2001) Labor leader, workers' rights activist. LAE.

Coronado, Francisco Vásquez de. (1510-1554) Spanish explorer. ALTE; CRO2; PARN; POD; PRE; SIN2.

Correggio. (Antonio Allegri) (1489-1534) Italian painter. KRY.

Corrigan, Douglas "Wrong Way." (1907-1995) Aviator. ZAU2.

Corrigan, Mairead. (1944-) Irish peace activist. Nobel Peace Prize winner. BLU; HAC6; HER; KEEN2; SCHR2.

Corso, Sandra. (unknown) Geophysicist, oceanographer. KAH4.

Cortazar, Julio. (1914-1984) Argentine author. SHIR.

Corte Real, Gaspar. (1455-1501) Portuguese explorer. WILLI2.

Corte Real, Miguel. (1450-1502) Portuguese explorer. WILLI2.

Cortes, Hernan. (1485-1547) Spanish explorer. ALTE; CRO3; CRO4; POD; WILKP4.

Cosby, Bill. (1937-) Actor, comedian. Presidential Medal of Freedom recipient. BECKN; DEN; KAL2; LEVE; RED3.

Coston, Martha. (1826-1886) Inventor. VAR.

Cotera, Martha P. (1938-) Mexican civil rights activist, educator, historian. LAE.

Coughlin, Father Charles Edward. (1891-1979) Broadcast journalist, hatemonger, radio personality, spiritual leader, born Canada. SCHM3; STRE3.

Courbet, Gustave. (1819-1877) French painter. CUM.

Court, Margaret Smith. (1942-) Australian tennis player. HARR; HASD; JACT.

Cousins, Margaret. (1905-1996) Editor, journalist. PRI.

Cousteau, Jacques-Yves. (1910-1997) French environmentalist, explorer, inventor, World War II resistance fighter. Presidential Medal of Freedom recipient. ALTE; FAB3; GRAH; HAV; LEO; PRE; THOM; TIN.

Cousy, Bob. (1928-) Basketball player. JACT; RAPK2; SAV5.

Covilla, Peroda. (1460-1526) Portuguese explorer. POD.

Cowan, Ruth. (1902-) Journalist, World War II correspondent. COLM.

Cowell, Henry. (1897-1965) Composer. NIC.

Cowen, Joshua Lionel. (1880-1965) Entrepreneur toy trains. AAS9.

Cowens, Dave. (1948-) Basketball player. KNA5.

Cowings, Patricia. (1948-) Physiologist, psychologist, space scientist. AFR2; SULO2.

Cox, Bobby. (1941-) Baseball manager. PIE.

Cox, Ida. (1889-1967) Singer. AFR.

Crabtree, Lotta. (1847-1924) Actor. KET.

Craft, Ellen. (1826-1897) Abolitionist, slave, disguised as man. BOL; FRA; GAR; GREA.

Craft, William. (1824-1900) Slave. FRA; GAR.

Craig, Daniel H. (1811-1895) Entrepreneur news service, journalist. RIT.

Craig, Lulu Sadler. (1868-1972?) Educator. KAT.

Crane, Stephen. (1871-1900) Author. OFT2.

Cranmer, Thomas. (1489-1556) English spiritual leader. CLA2; CRO5.

Crassus. (Marcus Licinius Crassus) (c. 115-53 B.C.) Roman financier, military leader, statesman. BAKR3.

Crawford, Jimmy. (1910-1980) Jazz musician. GOU6.

Crawford, Samuel Earl "Whoo Sam." (1880-1968) Baseball player. SULG8.

Cray, Seymour. (1925-1996) Computer pioneer, electrical engineer, World War II decoder. AAS5.

Crazy Horse. (1841-1877) Lakota Oglala Sioux Indian chief. AVE; BOY; CALV; CRO; KAL3.

Cremer, Sir William Randal. (1828-1908) English labor leader, organization co-founder, workers' rights activist. Nobel Peace Prize winner. KEEN2.

Crespi, Ann. (unknown) Chemist, medical researcher. KAH2.

Crespo, Elvis. (1970-) Puerto Rican pop singer. KRULI.

Crespo, George. (1962-) Painter. HON.

Cresson, Edith. (1934-) French prime minister. GUL.

Cressy-Marcks, Violet. (1890-1976) Explorer. MCLO3.

Crevecoeur, Hector St. John de. (1735-1813) American Revolutionary War author, soldier, born France. SCHM.

Crews, Jeanne Lee. (unknown) Aerospace engineer, space scientist. THI.

Crichton, Michael. (1942-) Author, physician, screenwriter. PER.

Crick, Francis H. C. (1916-2004) English molecular biologist. Nobel Prize winner. AAS13; CRO4; CURT; HAV.

Cristina. (1965-) Spanish princess. LEVI.

Crockett, Davy. (1786-1836) Congressman, folk hero, frontiersman, hunter. ALTE; CALV; CRO; JAN; KRAL.

Croly, Jane Cunningham. (Jennie June) (1829-1901) Journalist. PRI; THIR.

Cromwell, Oliver. (1599-1658) English general, puritan colonist, statesman. CRO3; DAV; DOH3; YEN.

Cronin, Joe. (1906-1984) Baseball player. DEA3.

Cronkite, Walter. (1916-) Broadcast journalist. Presidential Medal of Freedom recipient. LEVE; RIT.

Crosby, Bing. (1904-1977) Singer. CRO4; GOU5.

Crosby, Israel. (1919-1962) Jazz musician. GOU2.

Croslin, Michael. (1933-) Mechanical engineer, inventor, medical researcher, Korean War, Vietnam War Air Force, born Virgin Islands. SULO.

Crosthwait, David Nelson, Jr. (1898-1976) Electrical engineer, inventor. SULO.

Croteau, Julie. (1970-) Baseball player. BRIL2.

Crowe, Cameron. (1957-) Filmmaker, journalist. BOY.

Crowe, Frank. (1882-1946) Civil engineer. AAS11.

Crowfoot. (1821-1890) Blackfoot Indian chief, peace activist. SHER2.

Crown, Frank Fools. (1890-1989) Oglala Indian spiritual leader. AVE.

Cruise, Tom. (1962-) Actor. KEND.

Crumb, George. (1929-) Composer, musician. NIC.

Crumpler, Rebecca Lee. (1833-1895) Physician. AFR2; COX; POT.

Cruz, Celia. (1924-2003) Singer, born Cuba. LAE.

Cruz, Jose, Jr. (1974-) Baseball player, born Puerto Rico. STEWM2.

Cruz, Juana Inés de la. (1651-1695) Mexican poet, scholar, spiritual leader. HER; LEO3; WEL.

Cruz, Philip Vera. (1904-) Labor leader, born Philippines. SIN.

Cuffe, Paul. (1759-1817) Colonist, entrepreneur sailmaker, founder Sierra Leone, philanthropist. AFR2; ALTMS; BECKN; HASK; HASK4; KAT2.

Cugat, Xavier. (1900-1990) Bandleader, musician, born Spain. LAE.

Cukier, Sam. (1920-) Polish Jewish Holocaust survivor. GID.

Cullen, Countee. (1903-1946) Children's and adult author, educator, poet. BECKM; HARD; OFT.

Cummings, Nathan. (1896-1985) Entrepreneur food industry, born Canada. PIL.

Cummings, Pat. (1950-) Children's author, illustrator. TALAR.

Cunha, Tristao da. (1460-1540) Portuguese explorer. PRE

Cunningham, Imogen. (1883-1976) Photographer. HOR; KRY; SILL.

Curie, Marie Sklodowska. (1867-1934) French chemist, inventor, physicist, born Poland. Nobel Prize winner. CEL; COOL; CURT; DE; DIN; DUN; FOX; HAC6; HAV; HAZ; HER; MARZ; MUL2; ROL; STI2; TIN; WILKP3.

Curie, Pierre. (1859-1906) French inventor, physicist. Nobel Prize winner. MARZ.

Curtis, Austin Maurice. (1868-1939) Physician. COX.

Curtis, Edward S. (1868-1952) Photographer. JACKN.

Curtis, Jennie. (c. 1878) Child laborer. HOOS.

Curtiss, Glenn H. (1878-1930) Aviation pioneer, entrepreneur aircraft. BERL; ROS.

Cushman, Karen. (1941-) Children's and young adult author. AUT.

Cushman, Pauline. (Harriet Wood) (1833-1893) Civil War spy. CARA.

Custer, George Armstrong. (1839-1876) Civil War soldier, frontiersman. CALV; KRAL.

Custer, Libbie. (1842-1933) Author, pioneer, women's rights activist. FUR2.

Cuvier, Georges. (1769-1832) French anatomist, paleontologist. KEEN; TIN.

Cuza, Fernando. (unknown) Baseball agent. MARV5.

Cyril. (827-869) Greek missionary, saint, spiritual leader. CRO5.

Cyrus the Great. (600-530 B.C.) Iranian (Persian) military leader. CRO3; YEN.

Czerniakóv, Adam. (1880-1942) Polish Jewish Holocaust resistance, victim. SCHM3.

Czolgosz, Leon. (1873-1901) Assassin, killed President McKinley, born Poland. JONR; NET; STG; SULG9.

D

Da Fu. (712-?) Chinese poet. HOOB.

Da Gama, Gaspar. (1458-1526) Portuguese explorer, born Poland. POD.

Da Gama, Vasco. (1460-1524) Portuguese explorer. ALTE; FRI; LOM; POD; PRE; SCHEL2; WILLI2.

Da Silva, Fabriola. (1979-) Brazilian in-line skater. SAV9.

Dabney, Austin. (1799-1821) American Revolutionary War soldier, slave. HASK2; HASK4.

Dahia al-Kahina. (fl. 680) North African political activist, queen. LEO2.

Dahl, Roald. (1916-1990) English children's author. MAS; YUN.

Dahl-Wolfe, Louise. (1895-1989) Photographer. HOR.

Dahmer, Jeffrey. (1960-1994) Serial killer. LAS.

Daimler, Gottlieb. (1834-1900) German automaker, mechanical engineer, inventor. DIN.

Dalai Lama. *See* Gyatso, Sonam.

Dalai Lama. *See* Gyatso, Tenzin.

Dali, Salvador. (1904-1989) Spanish painter. BLACA; CUS; KRULL2; KRY; TWEPO.

Dallmeier, Francisco. (1953-) Wildlife biologist, born Venezuela. OLE.

Dalton, Bob. (1870-1892) Outlaw. SAV.

Dalton, Emmett. (1871-1937) Outlaw. SAV.

Dalton, Grattan. (1861-1892) Outlaw. SAV.

Dalton, John. (1766-1844) English chemist. TIN.

Daly, Chuck. (1930-) Basketball coach. KNA10.

Damien, Father. *See* de Veuster, Joseph.

Dampier, William. (1652-1715) English adventurer, explorer, pirate. WILLI2; YOUNT5.

Dandridge, Dorothy. (1923-1965) Actor, singer. AFR; MON; PARJ.

Dante Alighieri. (1265-1321) Italian poet. HOOB3; PER; REN.

Danton, Georges. (1759-1794) French revolutionary, military leader. THOM3.

Dantzscher, Jamie. (1982-) Olympic gymnast. LAY.

D'Arcy, William Knox. (1849-1917) English attorney, entrepreneur oil. AAS7.

Darden, Christine. (1942-) Aeronautical engineer, mathematician, space scientist. AFR2.

D'Aresso, Guido. (992-1050) Italian composer, spiritual leader. VEN.

Darius III. (380-330 B.C.) Greek ruler. CRO4.

Darling, Grace. (1815-1842) English lighthouse keeper's daughter who rescued people when very young. DUN.

Darling, Jay Norwood "Ding." (1876-1962) Cartoonist, conservationist. Pulitzer Prize winner. BYR.

Darragh, John. (unknown) American Revolutionary War spy. HOOS.

Darragh, Lydia. (1725-1789) American Revolutionary War spy. SULG4; ZEI4.

Darrow, Clarence. (1857-1938) Attorney, human rights activist. CALA; CRO4; EME; JACW; LEVE.

Darwin, Charles. (1809-1882) English naturalist. AAS13; FAB3; KEEN; STEFO; TIN; WILKP3.

Dash, Julie. (1952-) Filmmaker. AFR.

Dater, Judy. (1941-) Photographer. HOR.

Daumier, Honoré. (1808-1879) French caricaturist, painter, sculptor. KRY.

Dausset, Jean. (1916-) French immunologist, physician, physiologist. Nobel Prize winner. HAV.

Davenport, Lindsay. (1976-) Tennis player. MILE; RUT5.

David. (fl. 1010-970 B.C.) Hebrew king of Israel. MEL.

David, Jacques-Louis. (1784-1825) French painter. CUM; EIG; GLU.

David-Neel, Alexandra. (1868-1969) French adventurer, explorer. DUN; HER; MCLE; MCLO2; POLK; STEFO2.

Davies, Henry. (unknown) Spy. MART.

Davis, Angela. (1944-) Educator, political activist. GREA; THIR.

Davis, Benjamin O., Jr. (1912-2002) Air Force career officer retired as lieutenant general, Korean War commander, World War II Tuskegee airman. BOOK; CRO3; HASK2; JONS2.

Davis, Benjamin O., Sr. (1877-1970) Army career officer Spanish American War, World War I commander, World War II brigadier general. BOOK; HASK2; POT; REE2.

Davis, Ernie. (1939-1963) Football player. Heisman Trophy winner. SAV8.

Davis, Glenn. (1925-) Football player. Heisman Trophy winner. DEV.

Davis, Jefferson. (1808-1889) Cabinet member, Civil War president confederate states, congressman, senator. CRO; FAB.

Davis, John. (1921-1984) Olympic weightlifter. JACT.

Davis, John W. (1873-1955) Attorney, congressman, presidential candidate. CALA.

Davis, Lonnie. (1958-) Gulf War Army military hero. REE2.

Davis, Miles Dewey III. (1926-1991) Bandleader, composer, jazz musician. AFR; GOU; HAC3; MON; MOU; SHIP.

Davis, N. Jan. (1953-) Astronaut, mechanical engineer. BAIR.

Davis, Ossie. (1917-) Actor, civil rights activist. BECKN.

Davis, Richard. (1930-) Educator, jazz musician. GOU2.

Davis, Richard Harding. (1864-1916) Author, journalist. RIT.

Davis, Sammy, Jr. (1925-1990) Actor, showman, singer. BRIL.

Davis, Stuart. (1894-1964) Painter. GREENBJ; KRY.

Davis, Terrell. (1972-) Football player. BUCK; KNA9.

Davis, Tice. (unknown) Slave. HAM.

Davis, Varina Howell. (1826-1906) Civil War author, wife of Jefferson Davis. ZEI.

Davison, Anne. (1913-1992) Adventurer, aviator, sailor, born England. MCLO7.

Davy, Humphrey. (1778-1829) English chemist, inventor. TIN.

Dawes, Charles Gates. (1865-1951) Attorney, banker, diplomat, philanthropist, vicepresident. Nobel Peace Prize winner. KEEN2.

Dawes, Dominique. (1976-) Olympic gymnast. GREES; KLE; RUT3.

Dawkins, Darryl. (1957-) Basketball player. BJA3.

Dawson, Len. (1935-) Football player. SULG8.

Day, Dorothy. (1897-1980) Journalist, spiritual leader, women's rights activist. CRO5; JACW; JACW2; SHAW.

Day, Pat. (1953-) Jockey. KUH.

Dayan, Moshe. (1915-1981) Israeli foreign minister, military leader. CRO3

de Dios Unanue, Manuel. (1943-1992) Editor, publisher, born Cuba. RIT.

De Forest, Lee. (1873-1961) Inventor. STRE2.

De Gaulle, Charles. (1890-1970) French World War I lieutenant, World War II general. HOOB2; YEN.

De Generes, Ellen. (1958-) Actor, comedian. STEWG.

de Klerk, Fredrik Willem "F. W." (1936-) South African attorney, civil rights activist, president. Nobel Peace Prize winner. KEEN2.

de Kooning, Willem. (1904-1997) Painter, sculptor, born Holland. KRY.

de la Cruz, Jessie Lopez. (1919-) Workers' rights activist. HER.

de la Hoya, Oscar. (1973-) Boxer. COLE; LAE.

de la Renta, Oscar. (1932-) Fashion designer, born Dominican Republic. LAE.

De Mille, Agnes. (1905-1993) Choreographer. FOR.

De Mille, Cecil B. (1881-1959) Filmmaker. CRO.

De Moss, Edward "Bingo." (1889-1965) Baseball player. WIN2.

De Palma, Brian. (1940-) Filmmaker. HILA2.

De Passe, Suzanne. (1946-) Filmmaker. GREA.

De Priest, Oscar. (1871-1951) Congressman. AFR2.

De Smet, Pierre Jean. (1801-1873) Missionary, spiritual leader, born Belgium. DOH2.

de Soto, Hernando. (1496?-1542) Spanish explorer. ALTE; CRO2; PARN; PRE.

De Veuster, Joseph. (Father Damien) (1840-1889) Belgian human rights activist, missionary, spiritual leader. CLA.

De Vincenzo, Roberto. (1923-) Argentine golfer. SAV12.

Dean, James. (1931-1955) Actor, folk hero. KRAL.

Dean, Jay Hanna "Dizzy." (1911-1974) Baseball player. SLO; SULG5.

Dean, Paul "Daffy." (1914-1981) Baseball player. SLO.

Debo, Angie. (1890-1988) Historian. ALTE2.

Deborah. (c. 1150 B.C.) Biblical character, mother of Israel. ARM2; LEO; ROL; TAI.

Debs, Eugene. (1855-1926) Labor leader, presidential candidate. AAS2; LEVE; STRE5.

DeBusschere, Dave. (1940-2002) Basketball player, coach. SAV6

Debussy, Claude. (1862-1918) French composer. IMP; VEN.

Dede, Edmund. (1827-1903) Jazz musician. TAT.

Dee, Ruby. (1924-) Actor. BECKN; GREA; HAN2.

Deer, Ada. (1935-) Menominee Indian attorney, Assistant Secretary Indian Affairs, Native American rights activist, social worker. SHER2.

Deere, John. (1804-1886) Entrepreneur transportation, frontiersman, inventor. CALV.

Dees, Morris. (1936-) Attorney, civil rights activist. EME.

Defoe, Daniel. (1660-1731) English author, secret agent. EIG; PER; THOM4.

DeFrantz, Anita. (1952-) Olympic rower. HASD

Deganwidah. (c. 1400) Huron Indian chief, peace activist. SHER2.

Degas, Edgar. (1834-1917) French painter. CUM; GLU; IMP; KRY; SAB.

Degen, Bruce. (1945-) Illustrator. MARC2.

del Mundo, Fe. (1911-) Filipino human rights activist, physician. KIR.

Delacroix, Eugène. (1798-1863) French painter. CUM; CUS; ROM.

Delaney, Annie Elizabeth. (1891-1995) Author, educator. HAN2.

Delaney, Martin Robison. (1812-1885) Abolitionist, Civil War major, journalist, physician. AFR2; BECKN; COX; HAN; HASK2; RIT.

Delaney, Sarah Louise "Sadie." (1889-1998) Author, educator. HAN2.

Delano, Jane Arminda. (1862-1919) World War I superintendent Army Air Corps nurses. STI.

Deledda, Grazia. (1871-1936) Italian author. Nobel Prize winner. KNI.

Delgado, Carlos. (1972-) Baseball player, born Puerto Rico. STEWM2.

Delilah. Biblical character. ARM2.

Deloria, Ella Cara. (1889-1971) Yankton Dakota Indian anthropologist, linguist. AVE; STI2

Deloria, Philip Sam. (unknown) Yankton Dakota Indian attorney. AVE.

Deloria, Vine, Jr. (1939-) Yankton Dakota

Indian author, Native American rights activist. AVE.

Deloria, Vine, Sr. (1901-1990) Yankton Dakota Indian spiritual leader. AVE.

Demara, Fred. (1921-1982) Swindler. BLACG5.

DeMédici, Cosimo. (1389-1464) Italian financier. CRO4.

Demetrius. (336-283 B.C.) Greek military leader, ruler. BAKR2.

Demjanjuk, John "Ivan the Terrible." (1920-) Nazi war criminal, born Ukraine. SCHM3.

Democritus. (460-370 B.C.) Greek scientist. NAR3.

Demosthenes. (384-322 B.C.) Greek orator. BAKR2.

Dempsey, Jack. (1895-1983) Boxer. KNA7.

Dempsey, Sister Mary Joseph. (1856-1939) Nurse, spiritual leader. STI.

Dempsey, Tom. (1947-) Football player. SAV10.

Denetclaw, Wilfred F., Jr. (1959-) Navajo Indian geologist. STJ3.

Deneuve, Catherine. (1943-) French actor. HOOB2.

Derham, James. (1762-1804) Physician, slave. COX; HASK4; MCK2; POT.

Descartes, René. (1596-1650) French mathematician, philosopher. POD; TIN.

Desimini, Lisa. (1964-) Children's author, illustrator. TALAR3.

Desormeaux, Kent. (1970-) Jockey. KUH.

Despres, Josquin. (1440-1521) French composer, conductor. VEN.

D'Este, Beatrice. (1475-1497) Italian patron of the arts. HOOB3.

D'Este, Isabella. (1474-1539) Italian patron of the arts. HOOB3.

Devers, Gail. (1966-) Olympic track and field athlete. HASD; HUNTE; KAM; KRAMS5; MOL; RUT6.

Devi. (unknown) East Indian goddess, warrior queen, legendary. MAYE2.

Devi, Gayatri "Ayesha." (1919-) Indian political activist, ruler. BREW.

Devi, Phoolan. (1963-) Indian criminal, political activist. DUN.

Dewey, John. (1859-1952) Educator, philosopher. CRO; UNG.

Dewson, Molly. (1874-1962) Suffragist, women's rights activist. MORI3.

Dezhnev, Semyon. (1610-1672) Russian explorer, fur trapper, pioneer. POD.

di Lasso, Orlando. (1532-1594) Belgian composer, singer. VEN.

Diana. Greek goddess. COOL.

Diana. Princess of Wales. (1961-1997) English human rights activist, princess. CRO4; DUN; HAC5; LEVI.

Dias, Bartholomeu. (1450-1500) Portuguese explorer. FRI; POD; PRE; WILLI2.

Diaz, Henry. (1948-) Meteorologist. OLE.

Dick, Gladys Rowena. (1881-1963) Medical researcher, physician. STI.

Dickens, Charles. (1812-1870) English author. KRULL6; NIN; PER; YEN.

Dickerson, Eric. (1960-) Football player. LAC3.

Dickinson, Anna Elizabeth. (1842-1932) Abolitionist, orator, suffragist. WEL.

Dickinson, Emily. (1830-1886) Poet. FAB2; HARN; HER; KNI; KRULL6; LEVE; MCD; NIN; OFT2; PER; SMIL.

Dickinson, John. (1732-1808) American Revolutionary War soldier, attorney. SCHM.

Diderot, Denis. (1713-1784) French scholar. CRO4.

Didrikson, Mildred "Babe." *See* Zaharias, Mildred "Babe" Didrikson.

Dietrich, Amalie Nelle. (1821-1891) German botanist. POLK.

Dietrichson, Leif. (d.1928) Norwegian explorer, navy officer. TES.

Dihigo, Martin "El Maestro." (1905-1971) Baseball player, born Cuba. WIN; WIN2.

Dillard, Annie. (1945-) Author, poet. Pulitzer Prize winner. SMIL2.

Dillinger, John. (1903-1934) Gangster. BLACG.

Dillon, Diane. (1933-) Children's author, illustrator. TALAR.

Dillon, Leo. (1933-) Children's author, illustrator. TALAR.

Dimaggio, Joe. (1914-1999) Baseball player. Presidential Medal of Freedom recipient. BRED2; ITA; JACT; SEHN; SLO; SULG2; SULG8.

Dimas, Trent. (1970-) Olympic gymnast. MEN.

Dinkins, David. (1927-) Attorney, mayor. AFR2; DUD.

Diocletian. (Diocles) (245-313) Roman emperor. BAKR3; COOLI.

Dionysia. (unknown) Roman olympic track and field athlete. LEO.

Dior, Christian. (1905-1957) French fashion designer. KENJ.

Dirac, Paul Adrien Maurice. (1902-1984) English physicist. Nobel Prize winner. HAV.

Disney, Walt. (1901-1966) Entrepreneur real estate, filmmaker, showman. Presidential Medal of Freedom recipient. AAS8; CRO; DEN; KRAL; LEVE; MAC; MARZ; MAYB; PIL.

Disraeli, Benjamin. (1804-1881) English political activist, prime minister. CRO4; YEN.

Divine, Father. *See* Baker, George F. Jr.

Dix, Dorothea. (1802-1887) Civil War Army nurse superintendent, educator, human rights activist, social reformer. BLASH; CLA; CRO; HER; JACW; MOR; ROBE; ROL; STI; THIR; ZEI.

Dix, Dorothy. *See* Gilmer, Elizabeth Meriwether.

Dixie, Florence. (1857-1905) English adventurer, author, women's rights activist. MCLO8.

Dixon, Jeane. (1918-1997) Psychic. KRULL7.

Djoser. (fl. 2668-2649 B.C.) Egyptian king. BAKR.

Doby, Larry. (1923-2003) Baseball player. SLO.

Dockstader, Frederick L. (1919-1998) Oneida and Navajo Indian anthropologist, author, silversmith artist. AVE.

Dodds, Warren "Baby." (1898-1959) Jazz musician. GOU6.

Dodge, Horace. (1868-1920) Automaker. ITA6.

Dodge, John. (1864-1920) Automaker. ITA6.

Dodgson, Charles. (Lewis Carroll) (1832-1898) English children's author. NIN; PER.

Dodwell, Christina. (1951-) English adventurer, author, explorer. MCLO.

Dogen. (1200-1253) Japanese spiritual leader, founder of Soto Zen school of Buddhism. CRO5.

Dole, Robert. (1923-) Congressman, presidential candidate, senator, World War II lieutenant. Presidential Medal of Freedom recipient. KEND.

Dolphy, Eric. (1928-1964) Jazz musician. GOU.

Domitian. (Titus Flavius Domitianus) (51-96) Roman emperor. BAKR3.

Donatello. (Donato de Betto di Bardi) (1387-1466) Italian sculptor. BART; CRO4; KRY.

Donizetti, Gaetano. (1797-1848) Italian opera composer. VEN.

Donne, John. (1572-1631) English poet, spiritual leader. SEV.

Donovan, Anne. (1961-) Olympic basketball player. SAV12.

Doolittle, Hilda "H. D." (1886-1961) Author, poet, translator. KNI.

Doolittle, Jimmy. (1896-1993) Army Air Corps aviator, World War II military leader. Medal of Honor recipient, Presidential Medal of Freedom recipient. ZAU2.

Doors. Rock and roll group. KNA2.

Dorantz, Stephen. (Esteban, Estevanico) (1500-1539) Spanish colonist, explorer. ALTMS; CRO2; HASK3; HASK4; HUD; MILR; POD; REE.

Dorfman, Elsa. (1937-) Photographer. SILL.

Dorgon. (1612-1650) Chinese emperor, prince. WILKP4.

Dorman, Pamela Davis. (1952-) Gulf War Navy chaplain. SHEA.

Dornberger, Walter. (1895-1980) German inventor, World War I army. RIC5.

Dorothy. Saint. ARM.

Dorr, Rheta Childe. (1866-1948) Journalist, suffragist, World War I correspondent. PRI.

Dorsett, Tony. (1954-) Football player. Heisman Trophy winner. DEV; LAC3; SAV8.

Dorsey, James "Jimmy." (1904-1957) Bandleader, jazz musician. SHIP.

Dorsey, Thomas "Tommy." (1905-1956) Bandleader, jazz musician. SHIP.

Dorsey, Thomas Andrew. (1899-1993) Composer gospel music, musician. AFR; HASK5; POT; RED5; TAT.

Dostoevski, Fyodor. (1821-1881) Russian author. PER.

Doubilet, David. (1946-) Photographer. TALAD.

Douglas, Aaron. (1899-1979) Painter. BECKM; HARD.

Douglas, Helen Gahagan. (1900-1980) Actor,

congresswoman, singer. ALTE2; MORI2.

Douglas, Lizzie. (Memphis Minnie) (1897-1973) Jazz musician. COOL.

Douglas, Marjorie Stoneman. (1890-1998) Author, conservationist, World War I Navy. Presidential Medal of Freedom recipient. KEEN; LUC2; SIR.

Douglas, Stephen A. (1813-1861) Presidential candidate, senator. CRO.

Douglass, Earl. (1862-1931) Paleontologist. AAS.

Douglass, Frederick. (1817-1895) Abolitionist, journalist, orator, slave. ALTMS; ARC2; BECKN; CRO; CRO4; DEN; DUB; GAR; HAC2; HAM; HAN; HOOS; JACW; JAN; LEVE; LIL; MARZ; MED; RIT; SHAP; TAYK; THOM; TUR2.

Douglass, Sarah Mapps. (1806-1882) Educator. COX2.

Dove, Arthur. (1880-1946) Painter. GREENBJ.

Dove, Rita. (1952-) Poet. Pulitzer Prize winner. POT; SMIL2; STRI.

Dow, Charles Henry. (1851-1902) Financier, journalist. AAS12.

Dow, Herbert Henry. (1866-1930) Entrepreneur chemicals. AAS10.

Dowland, John. (1562-1626) English composer, musician. VEN.

Dowling, Arthur. (d. 1922) Magician. HASK6.

Downing, Julie. (1956-) Children's author, illustrator. TALAR2.

Doyle, Sir Arthur Conan. (1859-1930) Scottish author, physician. PER.

Draenger, Shimson. (1917-1943) Polish Jewish Holocaust resistance worker, victim. SCHM3.

Draenger, Tova. (1917-1943) Polish Jewish Holocaust resistance worker, victim. SCHM3.

Dragila, Stacy. (1971-) Olympic track and field athlete. RUT6.

Drake, Sir Francis. (1540-1596) English adventurer, explorer, navy admiral. ALTE; CRO3; DOH5; POD; PRE; WILKP; WILLI2.

Draper, Margaret Green. (1727-1804) American Revolutionary War loyalist, newspaper publisher. RIT.

Dravecky, Dave. (1956-) Baseball player. JEN.

Drayton, Daniel. (unknown) Slave insurrectionist. HAM.

Dreiser, Theodore. (1871-1945) Author. FAB2.

Dresselhaus, Mildred. (1930-) Physicist. LINL3; VEG.

Drew, Charles Richard. (1904-1950) Educator, medical researcher, physician. AFR2; ALTMS; BECKN; COX; CURT; HASK7; HAY; MCK2; PIO; POT; SULO; TUR2; YOUNT2.

Drexler, Clyde. (1962-) Basketball player. BJA; BJA3.

Driscoll, Jean. (1966-) Wheelchair athlete. KAM; KEND.

Drury, Chris. (1976-) Hockey player. BREH.

Dryden, Ken. (1947-) Canadian hockey player, SPI.

Drysdale, Don. (1936-) Baseball player. SULG5.

Du Bois, W. E. B. (1868-1963) Author, civil rights activist, editor, educator, founder of NAACP. AFR2; ALTMS; BECKN; COX; CRO; HAC2; HAN; HARD; HASK5; SHAP; TAYK2; UNG.

Du Chaillu, Paul. (1836-1903) Explorer, born France. LANG.

du Chatelet, Marquise Gabrielle-Emilie. (1706-1749) French mathematician, physicist. CEL; ROL.

Du Pont, Eleuthera Ireneee. (1771-1834) Entrepreneur chemicals, gunpowder, born France. AAS10.

Du Sable, Jean Baptiste Pointe. (1745-1818) Founder Chicago, frontiersman, fur trapper, born Haiti. ALTMS; HASK3; HASK4; HUD; MILR; POD; REE.

Du Temple, Felix. (1823-1890) French aviation pioneer, naval officer. BERL2.

Dubcek, Alexander. (1921-1992) Czech political activist. TRAC2.

Duchamp, Marcel. (1887-1968) French painter. KRULL2; KRY.

Ducommon, Élie. (1833-1906) Swiss journalist, peace activist. Nobel Peace Prize winner. KEEN2.

Dudley, Joseph. (1647-1720) Colonial governor. CRO2.

Duggar, Benjamin. (1872-1956) Botanist, medical researcher, physician. HAV.

Duke, Charles. (1935-) Aeronautical engineer, Air Force pilot, astronaut. PRE.

Duke, Mark. (1958-) Painter. HON.

Duke, Patty. (1946-) Actor. KEND.

Dukepoo, Frank C. (1943-) Hopi Indian educator. STJ3.

Dulcie of Worms. (12th century) German banker, scholar. TAI.

Dulles, John Foster. (1888-1959) Attorney, cabinet member, diplomat. RIC.

Dunant, Henri. (1828-1910) Swiss human rights activist, founder International Red Cross. Nobel Peace Prize winner. CLA; KEEN2; WILKP2.

Dunbar, Bonnie. (1949-) Astronaut, mechanical engineer. BRIGG2.

Dunbar, Paul Laurence. (1872-1906) Poet. AFR; BECKN; MAL; STRI.

Duncan, Tim. (1976-) Basketball player, born Virgin Islands. NEL; PAU.

Duncanson, Robert Scott. (1821-1872) Painter. AFR.

Dunham, Katherine. (1909-) Anthropologist, choreographer, dancer. BECKN; FOR; GREA; HARN.

Duniway, Abigail Scott. (1834-1915) Journalist, suffragist, women's rights activist. ALTE2; HARN; LAK.

Dunlop, John. (1840-1921) Scottish inventor. DIN.

Dunn, Oscar. (1820-1871) Civil War Army captain, state lieutenant governor. AFR2.

Dunn, Warrick. (1975-) Football player. DEI.

Dupin, Amandine Aurore Lucie. (George Sand) (1804-1876) French author, disguised as man. CRO4; DUN; HOOB2; PER.

Durant, Ida Kaufman "Ariel." (1898-1981) Author, historian, born Russia. Presidential Medal of Freedom recipient, Pulitzer Prize winner. CRO4.

Durant, Will. (1885-1981) Author, historian. Presidential Medal of Freedom recipient. Pulitzer Prize winner. CRO4.

Durazo, Maria Elena. (1954-) Labor leader, workers' rights activist, born Mexico. LAE.

Dürer, Albrecht. (1471-1528) German engraver, painter. BLACA; CUM; CUS; GLU; KRY; REN.

Durgan, Beverly. (unknown) Agricultural scientist. KAH.

Durham, Eddie. (1906-1987) Jazz musician. GOU3.

Durrell, Gerald. (1925-1995) English environmentalist, zoologist. KEEN.

Durocher, Leo. (1908-1991) Baseball manager. PIE.

Duse, Eleanora. (1859-1924) Italian actor. WEI2.

Duston, Hannah. (1657-1736) Colonist, Indian captive. CRO2.

Duvivier, George. (1920-1985) Jazz musician. GOU2.

Dvorak, Antonin. (1841-1904) Czech composer. BLACA2; VEN.

Dwight, Edward J., Jr. (1933-) Air Force pilot, astronaut, sculptor. BUR.

Dyer, Jane. (1945-) Illustrator. TALAR3.

Dyer, Mary. (1610-1660) Colonist. CRO2; DOH3.

Dylan, Bob. (1941-) Composer, singer. BOY; BRO; KNA2; LEVE.

E

Eagan, Eddie. (1898-1967) Olympic boxer, bobsledder. KNA4.

Earhart, Amelia. (1897-1937) Aviation pioneer, aviator. ALTE; BUCH; COOL; CUS2; DUN; HAC; HARN; HAZ2; HEA; HER; JAN; KRAL; LEVE; MARZ; MCD; MCLE2; MCLO5; POLK; PRE; ROL; ROS; SCHR; WILLI; YOUNT7.

Earle, Sylvia. (1935-) Marine biologist, oceanographer. HARN; MCLO7; POLK; POLKI; STA.

Earley, Charity Adams. (1918-2002) World War II WAAC lieutenant colonel. HASK2.

Earp, Wyatt. (1848-1929) Lawman, wild west. JAN; KRAL; WAL.

Eastman, Charles Alexander. (1858-1939) Santee Dakota Indian author, physician. AVE; BERS; WE2.

Eastman, Crystal. (1881-1928) Attorney, women's rights activist, workers' rights activist. THIR.

Eastman, George. (1854-1932) Entrepreneur cameras, inventor, philanthropist. AAS3; LOM2; TRAU.

Eastman, Monk. *See* Osterman, Edward.

Eastwood, Alice. (1859-1953) Canadian botanist. POLK; STI2.

Eaton, Mark. (1957-) Basketball player. YOUNG.

Echohawk, Brummett. (1922-) Pawnee Indian actor, author, painter, World War II military hero. AVE.

Echohawk, John. (1945-) Pawnee Indian attorney. AVE.

Echohawk, Larry. (1948-) Pawnee Indian attorney, state legislator. AVE.

Eckert, J. Presper. (1919-1995) Computer pioneer. NOR.

Eckford, Elizabeth. (1942-) Civil rights activist. ALLZ; HOOS; ROC.

Eckhart, Meister. (1280-1327) German mystic, spiritual leader. CRO5.

Eckstine, Billy. (1904-1993) Singer. AFR.

Eddy, Mary Baker. (1821-1910) Spiritual leader, founder Christian Science religion. CRO; CRO5; GOLDM; JACW2; KNI; LEVE; ROL.

Edelman, Marian Wright. (1939-) Attorney, children's rights activist, civil rights activist, human rights activist. Presidential Medal of Freedom recipient. BECKN; FEM; GOLDE; GREA; HAN2; HER; LINL2; RED2; ROL.

Ederle, Gertrude. (1905-2003) Olympic swimmer. DUN; HARN; HASD; KRULL3.

Edge, Rosalie. (1877-1962) Conservationist, suffragist. BYR.

Edinger, Tilly. (1897-1967) Paleontologist. STI2.

Edison, Thomas Alva. (1847-1931) Inventor. BOY; BRIL; CRO; CRO4; DEN; DIN; JAN; LOM2; MARZ; NOO; SAW; STRE3; TIN; YEN.

Edmonds, Sarah Emma. (1841-1898) Civil war soldier, disguised as man, nurse, spy. BLASH; CARA; CHA; HARN; SHEA; SULG4; ZEI.

Edmondson, Belle. (1840-1873) Civil War spy. CARA.

Edward I. (1239-1307) English king. CRO3; DAV.

Edward II. (1287-1327) English king. DAV.

Edward VIII. (1894-1972) English duke of Windsor. CRO4.

Edward the Black Prince. (1330-1376) English prince of Wales. CRO3.

Edwards, Chris. (1973-) Entrepreneur skating equipment, in-line skater. SAV9.

Edwards, Eileen Regina. (Shania Twain) (1965-) Canadian singer, songwriter. KEEL.

Edwards, Jonathan. (1703-1758) Colonist, educator, spiritual leader. CRO2; JACW2.

Edwards, Teresa. (1964-) Olympic basketball player. PON; RUT.

Egeria. (4th century) Spanish adventurer, author, pilgrim. POLK.

Egielski, Richard. (1952-) Children's author, illustrator. MARC2; TALAR.

Eglin, Ellen F. (1849-?) Inventor. SULO2.

Ehlert, Lois. (1934-) Children's author, illustrator. TALAR.

Ehrlich, Paul. (1854-1915) German bacteriologist, medical researcher. Nobel Prize winner. CURT; MUL.

Ehrlich, Paul. (1932-) Author, educator, entomologist, zoologist. HAV.

Eichmann, Adolf. (1906-1962) German Nazi war criminal LAND2; SCHM3.

Eielson, Carl Ben. (1897-1929) Aviator, World War I pilot. TES.

Eiffel, Alexandre Gustave. (1832-1923) French mechanical engineer. AAS11.

Eilberg, Amy. (1954-) Spiritual leader. TAI.

Einstein, Albert. (1879-1955) Physicist, born Germany. Nobel Prize winner. BOY; DEN; HAV; HAZ; MARZ; SHER; TIN; WILKP3; YEN.

Einthoven, Willem. (1860-1927) Dutch medical researcher, physician. Nobel Prize winner. AAS14; MUL.

Eiseley, Loren. (1907-1977) Anthropologist, author. HAV.

Eisen, Renata. (1929-) Yugoslavian Jewish Holocaust survivor. GID.

Eisenberg, Arlo. (1973-) Entrepreneur skating equipment, in-line skater. SAV9.

Eisenhower, Dwight David. (1890-1969) Army military leader, 34th president of U.S., World War II Allied military commander. ADA; BARB; BAU; BLASS; CRO; CRO4; CRO6; DAV2; FAB; JAN; KNA; KRULL5; LAC; MORR; OLE2; WILKP; YEN.

Eisenhower, Mamie Geneva Doud. (1896-1979) First Lady. BARB; GOR; PAST.

Eisenreich, Jim. (1959-) Baseball player. KAM.

Eisenstein, Judith Kaplan. (1909-1996) Educator, songwriter. TAI.

Eisenstein, Sergei. (1898-1948) Russian filmmaker. HOOB5.

Ek Chuah. Mayan god of war. FIS2.

El Cid. *See* Cid Campeador, El.

Elders, Jocelyn Jones. (1933-) Physician, surgeon general of U.S. COX.

Eldredge, Todd. (1971-) Olympic figure skater. MILT.

Eldridge, Roy. (1911-1989) Jazz musician. GOU.

Eleanor of Aquitaine. (1122-1204) French queen. COOL; CRO4; HAZ2; KRULL; LEO2; MEL2; ROL.

Elena. (1964-) Spanish princess. LEVI.

Elgar, Edward. (1857-1934) English composer. BLACA2.

El Greco. *See* Greco, El.

Elias, Patrick. (1976-) Czech hockey player. BREH.

Elijah ben Solomon. (1720-1797) Polish Jewish scholar, spiritual leader. CRO5.

Elion, Gertrude Belle. (1918-1999) Biochemist. Nobel Prize winner. HAV; JEF; REY; SPA; STI; STI2; YOUNT3.

Eliot, George. *See* Evans, Mary Ann.

Eliot, John. (1604-1690) English colonist, puritan missionary. CRO2.

Eliot, Thomas Stearns "T. S." (1888-1965) English playwright, poet. Nobel Prize winner, Presidential Medal of Freedom recipient. PER.

Elisabeth. Biblical character. ARM2.

Elizabeth I. (1533-1603) English queen. BREW; CRO4; DAV; HAZ2; HER; KRULL; LEO3; MARZ; MEL2; NAR4; ROL.

Elizabeth II. (1926-) English queen. BREW; DAV.

Elizabeth, Princess of Toro (Uganda) (1941-) African princess. LEVI.

Ella bat Moses. (17th century) German printer. TAI.

Ellery, William. (1727-1820) American Revolutionary War patriot, congressman, Declaration of Independence signer. FRA2; QUI.

Ellington, Edward Kennedy "Duke." (1899-1974) Bandleader, composer, jazz musician. Presidential Medal of Freedom recipient. AFR; ALTMS; BECKM; BECKN; BRED3; CRO; CRO4; GOU4; HAC3; HARD; HASK5; JAZ; MARZ; MON; MOU; SHIP; TAT; TWEPO; VEN.

Elliot, Jim. (1927-1956) Missionary. JACKD2.

Elliott, Bill. (1956-) Nascar auto racer. RIL.

Ellis, Dale. (1960-) Basketball player. TOR3.

Ellis, Herb. (1921-) Jazz musician. GOU3.

Ellison, Lawrence. (1944-) Entrepreneur computers, Internet pioneer. FREN.

Ellison, Ralph. (1919-1994) Author, educator. Presidential Medal of Freedom recipient. AFR; MAL; POT; RED4.

Ellsworth, Lincoln. (1880-1951) Explorer, financier. TES.

Elway, John. (1960-) Football player. BUCK3; KNA9; LAC2; SULG7.

Emeagwali, Philip. (1954-) Computer scientist, civil engineer, born Nigeria. HENS2.

Emerson, Ralph Waldo. (1803-1882) Author, philosopher. CRO; CRO4; FAB2; PER.

Endicott, John. (1589-1665) Colonial governor, puritan leader. CRO2.

Eng and Chang. (1811-1874) Showmen, Siamese twins. DRI.

Engels, Friedrich. (1820-1895) German political activist. CRO4; WILKP2.

English, Alex. (1954-) Basketball player. AAS17.

Enheduana of Sumer. (fl. 2300 B.C.) Sumerian poet, priestess. KNI; LEO.

Epaminondas. (410-323 B.C.) Greek military leader. NAR.

Epicurus. (341-270 B.C.) Greek philosopher. BAKR2.

Epstein, Sir Michael Anthony. (1921-) English medical researcher, physician. SPA.

Equiano, Olaudah. (1745-1799) African author, slave. BERS; HAM; HOOS; MED.

Erasmus, Desiderius. (1469-1536) Dutch philosopher, scholar, spiritual leader. JACW2; YEN.

Eratostheses. (276-194 B.C.) Greek astronomer, geographer. AND.

Erauso, Catalina de. (1585-1650) Spanish

outlaw, disguised as male. LEO3; POLK.

Erdrich, Louise. (1954-) Chippewa Indian author. ALLP; SMIL2; TWEPO.

Ericsson, John. (1803-1889) Civil War Navy, inventor, born Sweden. RIC5.

Ericsson, Leif. (970-1020) Viking explorer. ALTE; LOM; POD; PRE; WAT; WILLI2.

Ericsson-Jackson, Aprille Joy. (unknown) Aerospace engineer, space scientist. SULO2.

Erik the Red. *See* Thorvaldson, Erik.

Eriksdottir, Freydis. (971-1010) Viking explorer. POD; POLK

Ernst, Lisa Campbell. (1957-) Children's author, illustrator. TALAR.

Erving, Julius. (1950-) Basketball player. AAS17; BJA3; KNA6; RAPK2; SULG3.

Escalante, Jaime. (1930-) Educator, born Bolivia. LAE; MORE2; PAL.

Escobar, Marisol. (Marisol) (1930-) Sculptor, born Venezuela. LAE; SIN2.

Espinel, Luisa Ronstadt. (1892-1963) Actor, singer. SIN2.

Esposito, Phil. (1942-) Canadian hockey player. JACT; KNA8.

Esposito, Tony. (1944-) Canadian hockey player. SPI.

Esquiroz, Margarita. (1945-) Attorney, jurist. MARV2.

Esquivel, Adolfo Pérez. (1931-) Argentine human rights activist, sculptor. Nobel Peace Prize winner. KEEN2.

Esteban. *See* Dorantz, Stephen.

Estefan, Gloria. (1957-) Singer, born Cuba. LAE; MARV5; MORE2; PAL.

Estés, Clarissa Pinkol. (1943-) Author, psychologist, storyteller. LAE.

Estevanico. *See* Dorantz, Stephen.

Esther. (5th century B.C.) Biblical character, Persian queen. ARM2; MEL2; TAI.

Estrada, Alfredo. (unknown) Mechanical engineer, publisher magazine. MARV4.

Esu-Williams, Eka. (1956-) Nigerian community leader, AIDS activist, educator, immunologist, physician. HER.

Eubanks, Kevin. (1957-) Jazz musician. GOU3.

Euclid. (325-270 B.C.) Greek mathematician. TIN.

Euler, Leonard. (1707-1783) Swiss mathematician. TIN.

Euripides. (484-406 B.C.) Greek playwright. BAKR2.

Europe, James Reese. (1881-1939) Bandleader, composer, jazz musician, World War I military hero. HASK5.

Eustace. Saint. ARM.

Evans, Arthur. (1851-1941) English archaeologist. FAG; SCHEL; WEI.

Evans, Bill. (unknown) Acoustic biologist. SAY.

Evans, Dale. (1912-2001) Actor, cowgirl. ALTE2; DEN; KRAL.

Evans, Henry. (1760-1810) Spiritual leader. AFR2.

Evans, Janet. (1971-) Olympic swimmer. HASD.

Evans, John. (1823-1908) English archaeologist. FAG.

Evans, Mary Ann. (George Eliot) (1819-1880) English author, disguised as man. ROL; SMIL.

Evans, Matilda Arabella. (1872-1935) Human rights activist, physician. KIR.

Evans, William "Bill." (1929-1980) Jazz musician. GOU4; SHIP.

Eve. Biblical character. ARM2; TAI.

Everett, Dawn. (1979-) In-line skater. SAV9.

Everett, Milton Hutchin "M. H." (mid 1800's-early 1900's) Magician, showman. HASK6.

Evers, Medger. (1925-1963) Civil rights activist. ALTMS.

Evers-Williams, Myrlie. (1933-) Civil rights activist. LINL2; VERN.

Everson, Carrie. (1842-1914) Inventor. ALTML.

Evert, Chris. (1954-) Tennis player. HARR; HASD; JACT; SAV14; SCHWAB.

Every, Henry. (1653-?) English pirate. BLACG4.

Ewing, Maurice. (1906-1974) Geologist, oceanographer, physicist. POLKI.

Ewing, Patrick. (1962-) Basketball player. BJA; KNA5; YOUNG.

F

Faber, Sandra. (unknown) Astronomer. KAH8.

Fabius. (d. 203 B.C.) Roman ruler. NAR2.

Fabre, Jean Henri. (1823-1915) French entomologist. FAB3.

Faget, Maxim. (1921-2004) Aeronautical engineer, space scientist. RIC3.

Fair, Lorrie. (1978-) Olympic soccer player.
MILM.

Fairstein, Linda. (1947-) Attorney, author,
crimefighter. CALA; GOLDE.

Falla, Manuel de. (1876-1946) Spanish ballet
composer. VEN

Fang, Lizhi. (1936-) Chinese human rights
activist, astrophysicist. LUC.

Faraday, Michael. (1791-1867) English chemist, inventor. LOM2; TIN.

Farlow, Tal. (1921-1998) Jazz musician.
GOU3.

Farmer, Fannie Merritt. (1857-1915) Author,
chef. HER; VAR.

Farmer, James. (1920-1999) Civil rights activist. Presidential Medal of Freedom recipient. TAYK2.

Farnsworth, Philo Taylor. (1906-1971) Electrical engineer, inventor. HAV; JEF;
LOM2; STRE2.

Farragut, David Glasgow. (1801-1870) Civil
War Navy admiral. CRO3; LAE; PAL;
SIN2.

Farrakhan, Louis. (1933-) Civil rights activist,
hatemonger. STRE3.

Faulds, Henry. (fl. 1880) English forensic
scientist, physician. YEA.

Faulkner, William. (1897-1962) Author. No-
bel Prize winner, Pulitzer Prize winner.
BRED; FAB2; LEVE; MEE; PER;
TWEPR.

Fauset, Jessie Redmon. (1882-1961) Author.
HARD; WILKB.

Favre, Brett. (1969-) Football player. SULG7.

Fawcett, Joy. (1968-) Olympic soccer player.
LAY2; MILM; RUT4.

Fawkes, Guy. (1570-1606) English undercover agent, folk hero. KRAL; THOM4.

Feelings, Tom. (1933-2003) Children's author, illustrator. TALAR.

Fegen, Edward Fogarty. (1895-1940) English
World War II Navy commander. GRAN.

Feinstein, Dianne. (1933-) Mayor, senator.
BRO; GUL; THRO.

Feller, Bob. (1918-) Baseball player. SULG5.

Fenno, John. (1751-1798) Editor, publisher.
RIT.

Fenwick, Millicent. (1910-1992) Ambassador, congresswoman, state legislator. FIR.

Ferdinand. (1452-1516) Spanish king. CRO4.

Ferenz, Ludmilla "Lou." (1921-) World War
II Army nurse corps flight nurse. SHEA.

Fergus, Pamelia. (1824-1902) Pioneer.
STEFO3.

Ferguson, Angella D. (1925-) Medical researcher, physician. HAY; SULO2.

Ferguson, Catherine "Katy." (1779-1854)
Educator, slave. COX2; HASK4.

Ferguson, Miriam "Mo." (1875-1961) Governor. ALTE2.

Ferlette, Diane. (1945-) Storyteller. AFR.

Fermi, Enrico. (1901-1954) Inventor, physicist, born Italy. Nobel Prize winner. FOX;
HAV; LOM2; SHER; TIN.

Fernandez, Beatriz Christina "Gigi." (1967)
Puerto Rican tennis player. MORE2.

Fernandez, Giselle. (1961-) Broadcast journalist, journalist, born Mexico. MARV3.

Fernandez, Lisa. (1971-) Olympic softball
player. BRIL2.

Fernandez, Mary Joe. (1971-) Tennis player,
born Dominican Republic. MARV7.

Ferrari, Enzo. (1898-1988) Italian automaker.
ITA6.

Ferraro, Geraldine. (1935-) Attorney,
congresswoman. FIR; GUL; JONV; THRO.

Feynman, Richard Philips. (1918-1988)
Physicist. Nobel Prize winner. HAV; TIN.

Field, Kate. (1838-1896) Abolitionist, journalist. PRI; RIT.

Fielding, Henry. (1707-1754) English attorney, author, crimefighter, editor, jurist,
playwright. BLACG2.

Fieldler, Molly. (unknown) Chemist. KAH2.

Fields, Debbi. (1956-) Entrepreneur cookies.
JEF2; KRAMB.

Fields, Mary. (1832-1914) Pioneer businesswoman, slave disguised as man. ALTE2;
BOL; FUR2; KAT; MON2.

Filipovic, Zlata. (1980-) Yugoslavian author.
BRIL.

Fillmore, Millard. (1800-1874) Attorney,
congressman, 13th president of U.S., vice-
president. ADA; BARB; BAU; BLASS;
CRO6; DAV2; LINE; MORR.

Fillmore, Abigail Powers. (1798-1853) First
Lady. BARB; GOR; PAST.

Fine, Vivian. (1913-) Composer. NIC2.

Fingers, Rollie. (1946-) Baseball player. SULG5.

Fink, Ida. (1921-) Israeli children's and adult author, Holocaust survivor, playwright, born Poland. MAN.

Fink, Mike. (1770?-1823?) Frontiersman, fur trapper. GLA2; KRAL.

Finlay, Carlos Juan. (1833-1915) Cuban medical researcher, physician. LAE.

Finnbogadottir, Vigadis. (1930-) Icelandic president. GUL.

Fish, Albert. (1870-1936) Serial killer. LAS.

Fish, Emily. (1843-1931) Lighthouse keeper. FLE.

Fish, Juliet. (1859-1947) Lighthouse keeper. FLE.

Fisher, John King. (1854-1884) Lawman, outlaw. SAV.

Fitzgerald, Ella. (1918-1996) Jazz singer. Presidential Medal of Freedom recipient. GOU5; GREA; JAZ; MON; RED5; SHIP; TAT.

Fitzgerald, F. Scott. (1896-1940) Author. BRED; CRO4; FAB2; PER; TWEPR.

Fitzgerald, Zelda Sayre. (1900-1948) Wife of F. Scott. CRO4; KNI.

Fitzpatrick, Tom "Broken Hand." (1799-1854) Fur trader, Indian agent. COLL; SAV3.

Fix, Georgia Arbuckle. (1852-1918) Physician. ALTE2.

Flagg, Fannie. (1944-) Author, screenwriter. SMIL2.

Flaggs, Gail. (unknown) Geneticist, medical researcher. KAH7.

Flanner, Janet. (Genét) (1892-1978) Journalist. COOL.

Fleetwood, Christian A. (1840-1914) Civil War Army hero. Medal of Honor recipient. HASK2.

Fleischman, Solomon. (1928-) Hungarian Jewish Holocaust survivor. LAND4.

Fleming, Sir Alexander. (1881-1955) Scottish bacteriologist, medical researcher. Nobel Prize winner. CURT; MUL; TIN.

Fleming, Denise. (1950-) Children's author, illustrator. TALAR2.

Fleming, John Ambrose. (1849-1945) English physicist. TIN.

Fleming, Peggy. (1948-) Olympic figure skater. DIT; HASD; POY; SMIP; SULG3.

Fleming, Williamina Patron Stevens. (1857-1911) Astronomer, born Scotland. CAM; STI2.

Fletcher, Alice Cunningham. (1838-1923) Anthropologist, archaeologist. LAK; WEI.

Fletcher, Alphonse, Jr. "Buddy." (1966-) Entrepreneur stock brokerage, mathematician. HASK.

Flinker, Moshe. (1926-1944) Dutch author, Holocaust victim. WE.

Flipper, Henry O. (1856-1940) Slave, World War I lieutenant. HASK2; POT.

Florey, Lord Howard Walter. (1898-1968) Australian medical researcher, pathologist. Nobel Prize winner. CURT.

Floyd, William. (1734-1821) American Revolutionary War patriot, congressman, Declaration of Independence signer. FRA2; QUI.

Flutie, Doug. (1962-) Football player. Heisman Trophy winner. DEV; SAV8.

Flynn, Elizabeth Gurley. (1890-1964) Cofounder of American Civil Liberties Union, suffragist, workers' rights activist. THIR.

Foch, Ferdinand. (1851-1929) French World War I army general. CRO3.

Folger, James A. (1835-1889) Entrepreneur coffee and spices. AAS10.

Fong, Hiram. (1907-) Senator. SIN.

Fontana, Lavinia. (1552-1614) Italian painter. KRY.

Foote, Mary Hallock. (1847-1938) Author. ALTE2.

Ford, Edward Charles "Whitey." (1928-) Baseball player. SULG5.

Ford, Eileen. (1922-) Entrepreneur modeling agency. JEF2.

Ford, Elizabeth Bloomer "Betty." (1918-) First Lady. ANT; BARB; GOR; PAST; TAYS.

Ford, Gerald R. (1913-) Attorney, congressman, 38th president of U.S., vice-president, World War II Navy. Presidential Medal of Freedom recipient. ADA; BARB; BAU; BLASS; CRO6; DAV2; JONR; KRULL5; LINE; MORR; STG.

Ford, Henry. (1863-1947) Automaker. CRO; CRO4; GREEC; ITA6; LEVE; MAC; WILKP3; YEN.

Ford, John. (1895-1973) Filmmaker. Presidential Medal of Freedom recipient. LEVE.

Ford, Justina Laurena. (1871-1952) Physician. AFR2; COX.

Foreman, George. (1949-) Olympic boxer. HUNTE; KNA7.

Fornés, Maria Irene. (1930-) Playwright, born Cuba. LAE.

Forrest, Nathan Bedford. (1821-1877) Civil War Army general. REG.

Forrestal, James. (1892-1949) Banker, cabinet member. RIC2.

Forsythe, Ruby Middleton. (1905-1992) Educator. AFR2.

Fort, Cornelia. (1919-1943) World War II Air Force pilot. ZEI3.

Forten, Charlotte. *See* Grimke, Charlotte Forten.

Forten, James. (1766-1842) Abolitionist, entrepreneur sailmaker. AFR2; ALTMS; BECKN; HASK; HASK4; HASK8; HOOS; MCK; SCHM.

Fortune, T. Thomas. (1856-1928) Civil rights activist, journalist, state legislator. BECKN.

Fosse, Bob. (1927-1987) Choreographer, dancer. FOR.

Fossey, Dian. (1932-1985) Primatologist. CEL; HAC8; HARN; HAV; POLK; STI2.

Foster, Abby Kelley. (1811-1887) Abolitionist. MORI3.

Foster, Andrew "Rube." (1879-1930) Baseball player, manager. PIE; WIN2.

Foster, George Murphy "Pops." (1892-1969) Jazz musician. GOU2.

Foster, Jodie. (1962-) Actor. GAI2.

Foster, Sarah Jane. (1839-1868) Civil rights activist, educator. LYO.

Foster, Stephen. (1826-1864) Composer. KRULL4.

Foster, William Hendrick "Willie." (1904-1978) Baseball player. WIN2.

Foucault, Jean Bernard Léon. (1819-1868) French physicist. TIN.

Foudy, Julie. (1971-) Olympic soccer player. LAY2; MILM; RUT4.

Fountaine, Margaret. (1862-1940) English author, environmentalist, lepidopterist. POLK.

Fowler, Lydia Folger. (1822-1879) Physician. STI.

Fowler-Billings, Katharine Stevens. (1902-1997) Conservationist, geologist. POLK.

Fox, George. (1624-1691) English spiritual leader, founder Quaker religion. CRO5;

JACW2.

Foxx, Jimmie. (1907-1967) Baseball player. DEA2; SULG8.

Foyt, A. J. (1935-) Auto racer. JACT.

Fragonard, Jean-Honoré. (1732-1806) French painter. CUM; EIG.

Francesca, Piero Della. (c. 1415-1492) Italian mathematician, painter. CUM; REN.

Francis of Assissi. (1181-1226) Italian saint, spiritual leader, founder Franciscan order. ARM; CRO5; GOLDM; HOOB3.

Francis, Steve. (1977-) Basketball player. PAU.

Franco, Francisco. (1892-1975) Spanish political leader, dictator. GREER.

Frank, Anne. (1929-1945) Dutch author, Holocaust victim, born Germany. BRIL; DUN; FREM; GRAN; KNI; KUS; MAN; ROL; SCHM3; SMIL; WE; WEL.

Frank, Hans. (1900-1946) German attorney, Nazi political activist. SCHM3.

Frank, Henry. (unknown) German Jewish Holocaust survivor. LAND4.

Frank, Irene. (1927-) German Jewish Holocaust survivor. LAND4.

Frank, Mary. (1933-) Painter. SILL3.

Frankl, Viktor E. (1905-1997) Austrian Jewish Holocaust survivor, physician, psychotherapist. SCHM3.

Franklin, Aretha. (1942-) Jazz singer. AFR; GREA; JONH; KNA2; LES; POT; RED5; TAT.

Franklin, Benjamin. (1706-1790) American Revolutionary War patriot, author, congressman, Declaration of Independence signer, diplomat, political activist, printer. CRO; DEN; FAB; FRA2; HAZ; JACW; JAN; MARZ; QUI; RIT; SCHM; TIN; USC; YEN.

Franklin, Chester A. (1880-1955) Publisher newspaper. AFR.

Franklin, Deborah Read. (1707-1774) American Revolutionary War patriot, entrepreneur. SCHM.

Franklin, Sir John. (1786-1847) English explorer. ALTE; CURR; PRE.

Franklin, John Hope. (1915-) Historian. Presidential Medal of Freedom recipient. AFR2.

Franklin, Rosalind Elsie. (1920-1958) English molecular biologist, x-ray crystallographer. DID; DIN; DUN; HAV; STI2; TIN; YOUNT6.

Fraser, Dawn. (1937-) Australian olympic swimmer. AAS20; DUN.

Fraser-Reid, Bertram O. (1934-) Organic chemist. YOUNT2.

Fratianne, Linda. (1960-) Olympic figure skater. POY.

Frazier, E. Franklin. (1894-1962) Educator, sociologist. BECKN.

Frazier, Joe. (1944-) Boxer. KNA7.

Frederick I. (Barbarossa.) (1123-1190) German ruler Holy Roman Empire. PAP.

Frederick II, the Great. (1712-1786) Prussian king. CRO3; CRO4; YEN.

Freedman, Russell. (1929-) Children's author. AUT.

Freeman, Cathy. (1973-) Australian olympic track and field athlete. BRY; RUT6.

Freeman, Elizabeth "Mumbet." (1742-1829) Abolitionist, nurse, slave. ALTMS; BECKN; FUR; HAM; SCHM.

Freeman, Louis. (1952-) Pilot. POT.

Freeman, Morgan. (1937-) Actor. PARJ.

Fremont, Jessie Benton. (1824-1902) Author, pioneer. ALTE2.

Fremont, John Charles. (1813-1890) Civil War Army general, explorer. ALTE; BAKS; CRO; PRE; TAYS2.

Freneau, Philip. (1752-1832) American Revolutionary War patriot, editor, poet. RIT.

Freud, Anna. (1895-1982) English physician, psychoanalyst, born Austria. HUNTE2; ROL; STI.

Freud, Sigmund. (1856-1939) Austrian physician, psychoanalyst. CRO4; CURT; TIN; WILKP2; YEN.

Frey. Norse god of rain and sunshine. FIS3.

Freya. Norse goddess of love and beauty. FIS3.

Fried, Alfred. (1864-1921) Austrian journalist, peace activist, publisher. Nobel Peace Prize winner. KEEN2.

Friedan, Betty Goldstein. (1921-) Women's rights activist. ARC; BRO; CRO; HARN; HEA; HER; KNI; ROL; TAI.

Friedman, Milton. (1912-) Economist. Nobel Prize winner, Presidential Medal of Freedom recipient. BUS.

Friedman, Tova Grossman. (1938-) Holocaust survivor, social worker, born Poland. NIE.

Friedrich, Caspar David. (1774-1840) German painter. CUM; ROM.

Frietchie, Barbara Hauer. (1766-1862) Civil War heroine, perhaps legendary. KRAL.

Friezen, Jeff. (1976-) Canadian hockey player. BREH.

Frigga. Norse goddess of marriage. FIS3.

Frith, Mary "Moll Cutpurse." (1590-1659) English criminal. BLACG2; DUN; LEO3.

Frobisher, Martin. (1535-1594) English explorer. POD; PRE; WILLI2.

Frome, Lynette "Squeaky." (1948-) Assassin (attempted) of President Gerald Ford. JONR; NET; STG; SULG9.

Frommet of Arwyller. (15th century) German scribe. TAI.

Frontenac et Palluau, Comte de. *See* Buade, Louis de.

Frost, Robert. (1874-1963) Poet. Pulitzer Prize winner. FAB2; PER; TWEPR.

Fry, Elizabeth. (1780-1845) English human rights activist, reformer. CLA; DUN; JACKD2; ROL; THOM.

Fry, Varian. (1907-1967) Holocaust rescuer. LYM; SCHM3.

Fryman, Travis. (1969-) Baseball player. SCHWAR.

Fuentes, Carlos. (1928-) Mexican author. SHIR.

Fuertes, Louis Agassiz. (1874-1927) Naturalist, painter. SIN2.

Fuhr, Grant. (1962-) Canadian hockey player. SPI.

Fuller, Alfred. (1885-1973) Entrepreneur brushes, born Canada. MAYB.

Fuller, Meta Vaux Warrick. (1877-1968) Sculptor. HARD.

Fuller, R. Buckminster. (1895-1983) Architect, inventor. Presidential Medal of Freedom winner. LEVE.

Fuller, Solomon Carter. (1872-1953) Medical researcher, pathologist, physician, born Liberia. HAY.

Fulton, Robert. (1765-1815) Civil engineer, inventor. CRO; LOM2; NOO.

Furcal, Rafael. (1980-) Baseball player, born Dominican Republic. STEWM.

Futrell, Mary Hatwood. (1940-) Educator. GREA.

G

Gabe, Frances. (1915-) Inventor. BLASH5.

Gable, Clark. (1901-1960) Actor. LEVE.

Gable, Dan. (1948-) Olympic wrestler. JACT.

Gabo, Naum. (1890-1977) Russian painter, sculptor. KRY.

Gabor, Dennis. (1900-1979) Hungarian electrical engineer, inventor, physicist. Nobel Prize winner. HAV.

Gabrieli, Andrea. (1510-1586) Italian composer, educator, musician. VEN.

Gacy, John Wayne. (1942-1994) Serial killer. LAS.

Gaes, Jason. (1978-) Author, cancer patient. BRIL.

Gagarin, Yuri. (1934-1968) Russian aviator, cosmonaut. PRE; RIC4; WYB.

Gage, Thomas. (1721-1787) American Revolutionary War military leader, governor. SCHM.

Gaines, Ernest. (1933-) Author. RED4.

Gainsborough, Thomas. (1727-1788) English painter. GLU; KRY.

Galahad, Sir. (6th century) English knight of round table, legendary. KRAL.

Galarraga, Andrés. (1962-) Baseball player, born Venezuela. MARV7; STEWM.

Galbraith, John Kenneth. (1908-) Author, diplomat, economist, born Canada. Presidential Medal of Honor winner. LEVE.

Galdikas, Birute. (1946-) Canadian primatologist, born Germany. DID; LINL3; YOUNT6.

Galen. (130-200) Greek physician. AND; CURT; NAR3; TIN.

Galilei, Galileo. (1564-1642) Italian astronomer, mathematician, physicist. BOY; HOOB3; LOM2; POD; TIN; WILKP3; WILLS; YEN.

Gallatin, Albert. (1761-1849) Ambassador, cabinet member, congressman, born Switzerland. FAB.

Galloway, Abraham. (1837-1870) Slave, state legislator. AFR2.

Gallego, Luis Miguel. (Luis Miguel) (1970-) Puerto Rican pop singer. KRULI.

Galluppi, Baldassarre. (1706-1785) Italian opera composer. VEN.

Gálvez, Bernardo de. (1746-1782) American Revolutionary War patriot, colonial governor, born Spain. CRO2; LAE; SCHM; SIN2.

Gamble, James. (1803-1891) Entrepreneur soaps. AAS12.

Gandhi, Indira. (1917-1984) Indian prime minister. AXEC; CUS2; DUN; GUL; HER; KRULL; PARJ2; PRI3; ROL; WEL.

Gandhi, Mohandas. (1869-1948) Indian ruler, peace activist, spiritual leader. BLU; CRO5; GOLDM; HAZ; JACW2; MARZ; MAYB2; SHAW; THOM; WAKI; WILKP4; YEN.

Gannett, Deborah Sampson. *See* Sampson, Deborah.

Gantt, Harvey B. (1943-) Architect, civil rights activist, mayor. ROC.

Garbarek, Jan. (1947-) Norwegian bandleader, jazz musician. SHIP.

Garbo, Greta. (1905-1990) Actor, born Sweden. HER; KRAL.

Garcia. (fl. 1813) Native American slave, soldier. ALTMS.

Garcia, Andy. (1957-) Actor, born Cuba. MORE2.

Garcia, Dawn. (unknown) Journalist. SMIL.

Garcia, Emma. (1972-) Community organizer. BRIL.

Garcia, Hector Perez. (1914-1996) Civil rights activist, physician, World War II Army military hero, born Mexico. Presidential Medal of Honor recipient. BRED2; LAE; SIN2.

Garciaparra, Nomar. (1973-) Baseball player. BUCK4; SCHWAR; SCHWAR2; STEWM.

Garden, Mary. (1874-1967) Opera singer, born Scotland. SAW.

Gardiner, Lion. (1599-1663) Colonist, born England. CRO2.

Gardner, Alexander. (1821-1882) Civil War photographer, born Scotland. SULG6.

Garduño, Flor. (1957-) Mexican photographer. WOL.

Garfield, James A. (1831-1881) Civil War union general, congressman, 20th president of U.S. ADA; BARB; BAU; BLASS; CRO6; DAV2; JONR; MORR; STG.

Garfield, Lucretia Rudolph. (1832-1918) First Lady. BARB; GOR; PAST.

Garibaldi, Giuseppe. (1807-1882) Italian military leader. CRO3; YEN.

Garland, Judy. (1922-1969) Singer. ORG.

Garner, Margaret. (1833-?) Fugitive slave. HAM.

Garnet, Henry Highland. (1815-1882) Abolitionist, orator, spiritual leader. BECKN; TAYK.

Garnett, Kevin. (1976-) Basketball player. NEL; PAU.

Garrick, David. (1717-1779) English actor, playwright. WEI2.

Garrison, William Lloyd. (1805-1879) Abolitionist, publisher. JACW; LIL.

Garrison-Jackson, Zina. (1963-) Tennis player. HARR; KAM; RED6.

Garrod, Dorothy. (1892-1968) English archaeologist. FAG.

Garvey, Amy-Jacques. (1896-1973) Civil rights activist. GREA.

Garvey, Marcus. (1887-1940) Civil rights activist, orator, born Jamaica. ALTMS; ARC2; BECKN; HARD; HASK5; SHAP; THOM.

Garzarelli, Elaine. (1952-) Financial analyst. JEF2.

Gaston, Arthur George. (1892-1996) Entrepreneur multi-businesses, World War I Army. AFR2; HASK; RED; TUR.

Gates, Bill. (1955-) Computer pioneer, entrepreneur computers, Internet pioneer. AAS5; BOY; CRO; CRO4; FREN; GREEC; HAV; HOOS; MAC; NOR; YEN.

Gatty, Harold Charles. (1903-1957) Australian aviation pioneer. WILLI.

Gauguin, Paul. (1848-1903) French painter. CUM; GLU; IMP; KRY; ORE; SAB.

Gauss, Carl Friedrich. (1777-1855) German mathematician. BRIL; TIN.

Gautama, Siddhartha. (Buddha) (560-480 B.C.) Indian philosopher, spiritual leader, founder Buddhism. CRO5; GOLDM; JACW2; WILKP2; YEN.

Gay-Lussac, Joseph Louis. (1778-1850) French chemist. TIN.

Geb. Egyptian god of the earth. FIS.

Gehrig, Lou. (1903-1941) Baseball player. CRO4; SLO; SULG8; TOR.

Geiger, Abraham. (1810-1874) German Jewish spiritual leader. PASA.

Geiger, Emily. (1760-1813) American Revolutionary War heroine, patriot. SILC.

Geiger, Hans. (1882-1945) German inventor, physicist. HAV.

Gein, Ed. (1906-1984) Serial killer. LAS.

Geisel, Theodor Seuss. (Dr. Seuss) (1904-1991) Children's author, illustrator. Pulitzer Prize winner. MAS.

Gela bat Moses. (18th century) German printer. TAI.

Gellhorn, Martha. (1908-1998) Journalist, World War II correspondent. COLM.

Genét. *See* Flanner, Janet.

Genghis Khan. (1165-1227) Mongol conqueror, general, political leader. BRIL; CRO3; PRI2; WILKP; YEN.

Gengo, Kate. (1964-) In-line skater. SAV9.

Gentileschi, Artemisia. (1593-1652) Italian painter. CUM; DUN; HER; KRY; NIN.

Geoffrin, Thérèse Roget. (1699-1777) French patron of arts. HOOB2.

George. Saint. ARM.

George III. (1738-1820) English king during American Revolutionary War. DAV; SCHM.

George V. (1865-1936) English king. DAV.

George VI. (1895-1952) English king. DAV.

George, Eddie. (1973-) Football player. Heisman Trophy winner. DEI; SAV8.

George, Eliza Davis. (1879-1979) Missionary. JACKD4.

George, Emma. (1974-) Australian olympic track and field athlete. RUT6.

Gerima, Haile. (1946-) Filmmaker, born Ethiopia. AFR.

Germain, Sophie. (1776-1831) French mathematician. CEL; ROL.

Geronimo. (1829-1909) Apache chief, military leader. ALLP; AVE; CRO3; JAN; KAL3; KRAL; MON2; THOM3; WAL.

Gerry, Elbridge. (1744-1814) American Revolutionary War patriot, colonial governor, congressman, Declaration of Independence signer, vice-president of U.S. FRA2; QUI.

Gershwin, George. (1898-1937) Composer, songwriter. BLACA2; BRED3; BRO; CRO4; KAL; KRULL4; LEVE; NIC; TWEPR; VEN.

Gershwin, Ira. (1896-1983) Composer, songwriter. CRO4; KAL.

Gertz, Alison. (1966-1992) AIDS activist. GON.

Getty, J(ean). Paul. (1892-1976) Entrepreneur oil. AAS7.

Getz, Stan. (1927-1991) Bandleader, jazz musician. SHIP.

Geyer, Georgie Anne. (1933-) Journalist. PRI; RIT.

Ghermezian brothers (Bahman 1946, Eskander 1940, Nader 1941, Raphael 1944) Canadian entrepreneurs real estate. AAS8.

Giaconda, Lisa. (1479-1509) Italian art model. KRAL.

Giancana, Salvatore "Sam." (1908-1975) Gangster, born Italy. WOO.

Gianninni, A. P. (1870-1949) Banker, financier. MAYB.

Giap, Vo Nguygen. (1911-) North Vietnamese military leader. CRO3.

Gibbs, Joe. (1940-) Football coach. SAV11.

Gibbs, Lois Marie. (1951-) Environmental activist. KRE.

Gibbs, Mifflin. (1823-1915) Abolitionist, attorney, educator, jurist. AFR2.

Gibran, Kahlil. (1883-1931) Lebanese author, mystic. CRO5.

Gibson, Althea. (1927-2003) Tennis player. BOOK2; COOL; GAI3; GREA; HARR; HASD; KRAMB2; PLO; RED6.

Gibson, Bob. (1939-) Baseball player. SULG5; SULM; YOUNG2.

Gibson, James F. (unknown) Civil War photographer, born Scotland. SULG6.

Gibson, Josh. (1911-1947) Baseball player. SULG8; WIN2.

Gies, Miep. (1909-) Dutch Holocaust rescuer, born Austria. FREM; PET; SCHM3.

Gilbert, G. K. (1843-1918) Geologist. CARR.

Gilbert, Sir Humphrey. (1539-1583) English explorer. PRE.

Gilbert, Sir William. (1836-1911) English comic opera composer. CRO4; KRULL4.

Gilgamesh. (c. 2700 B.C.) Babylonian adventurer, explorer, ruler. ALTE.

Gillars, Mildred "Axis Sally." (1900-1988) World War II traitor. AAS18; SCHM3.

Gillepsie, John Birks "Dizzy." (1917-1993) Bandleader, composer, jazz musician. AFR, GOU; HAC3; JAZ; MON; MOU; SHIP.

Gillette, King C. (1855-1932) Entrepreneur razors, inventor. AAS3.

Gillom, Jennifer. (1964-) Olympic basketball player. PON.

Gilman, Charlotte Perkins. (1860-1935) Author, women's rights activist. HER; KNI; LYO.

Gilmer, Elizabeth Meriwether. (Dorothy Dix) (1861-1951) Journalist. PRI.

Gilpin, Charles. (1878-1930) Actor. HARD.

Gilpin, Laura. (1891-1979) Photographer. ALTE2; DAN; HOR.

Gimbel, Adam. (1817-1896) Entrepreneur retail stores, born Germany. BRO.

Gimbutas, Marija Birute Alseikaite. (1921-1994) Archaeologist, born Lithuania. POLK.

Gini, Mari. (unknown) Computer scientist, educator, physicist, born Italy. KAH3.

Ginsberg, Allen. (1926-1997) Poet. CRO4.

Ginsburg, Charles. (1920-1992) Inventor. JEF.

Ginsburg, Ruth Bader. (1933-) Attorney, Supreme Court justice. BRO; MORI; TAI; THIR.

Ginzberg, Asher. (Ahad Ha'am) (1856-1922) Russian spiritual leader, founder Spiritual Judaism. PASA.

Giorgione. (Giorgio Barbarelli) (1447-1510) Italian painter. CUM.

Giotto di Bondone. (1276-1337) Italian painter. BART; REN.

Giovanni, Nikki. (1943-) Children's author, poet. FEM2; RED4; SMIL; STRI; WILKB.

Girard, Jami. (unknown) Mining engineer. KAH4.

Girrard, Henri. (1825-1882) French aviation pioneer, inventor. BERL.

Girty, Simon. (1741-1818) American Revolutionary War traitor, frontiersman, Indian scout, translator. SCHM.

Gist, Christopher. (1706-1759) Colonist, explorer. CRO2.

Gittis, Kelley Anne. (unknown) Paleontologist. KAH4.

Gladney, Edna Kahly. (1886-1961) Human rights activist, reformer. ALTE2.

Gladstone, William. (1809-1898) English prime minister. CRO4; YEN.

Glaser, Elizabeth. (1947-1994) AIDS activist, children's rights activist. GON; LINL2.

Glass, Hugh. (1780-1833?) Frontiersman, fur trapper. GLA2.

Glass, Philip. (1937-) Composer. BRED3; NIC.

Glavine, Tom. (1966-) Baseball player. SCHWAR; YOUNG2.

Glenn, John. (1921-) Astronaut, engineer. ALTE; BAIR; DEN; JAN; WYB.

Gloria von Thurn und Taxis. (1960-) German princess. LEVI.

Glover, Savion. (1974-) Actor, dancer. BRIL.

Gluck, Christoph Willibald. (1714-1787) German opera composer. VEN.

Gluckel of Hameln. (1646-1724) German author. TAI.

Gobat, Albert. (1843-1914) Swiss attorney, International Peace Bureau director, peace activist. Nobel Peace Prize winner. KEEN2.

Gobright, Lawrence A. (1816-1879) Journalist. RIT

Goddard, Calvin Hooker. (1891-1955) Forensic scientist, historian, World War II colonel. YEA.

Goddard, Mary Katherine. (1738-1816) American Revolutionary War patriot, printer, publisher. SCHM.

Goddard, Robert. (1882-1945) Inventor, physicist, space scientist. AAS19; HAV; LOM2; RIC3; SHER.

Godiva, Lady. (1010-1067) English reformer, ruler, folk heroine. KRAL.

Godkin, Edwin L. (1831-1902) Journalist, born Ireland. RIT.

Goebbels, Joseph. (1897-1945) German Nazi war criminal. SCHM3.

Goebel, Timothy. (1980-) Olympic figure skater. MILT.

Goeppert-Mayer, Maria. (1906-1972) Physicist, born Germany. Nobel Prize winner. CAM; DAS; DID; FOX; HAV; REY; STI2; TIN; YOUNT3.

Goethals, George W. (1858-1928) Army career, engineer. AAS11.

Goforth, Jonathan. (1859-1936) Canadian missionary. JACKD3.

Goforth, Rosalind Smith. (1864-1942) Canadian missionary. JACKD3.

Goizueta, Roberto C. (1931-1997) Entrepreneur cola, born Cuba. LAE; MORE2.

Goldberg, Whoopi. (1950-) Actor, comedian. AFR; RED3; STEWG.

Golden, Diana. (1963-2001) Olympic skier. KAM; LIT.

Goldman, Emma. (1869-1940) Human rights activist, political activist, women's rights activist, born Lithuania. HER; JACW; TAI; THIR; THOM3.

Goldsby, Crawford. (1876-1896) Cherokee Indian criminal. MON2.

Goldwyn, Samuel. (1882-1974) Filmmaker, born Poland. Presidential Medal of Freedom recipient. LEVE.

Gomez, Eddie. (1944-) Jazz musician. GOU2.

Gomez, Scott. (1979-) Hockey player. BREH.

Gompers, Samuel. (1850-1924) Labor leader, workers' rights activist, born England. BRO; CRO; JACW; STRE5.

Gonzáles, Henry Barbosa. (1916-2000) Congressman. LAE; SIN2.

Gonzáles, Jovita Mireles. (1904-1983) Historian, storyteller. SIN2.

Gonzales, Richard "Pancho." (1928-1995) Tennis player. CHRIST; LAE; SIN2.

Gonzales, Rodolfo "Corkey."(1928-) Boxer, civil rights activist, poet. LAE.

Gonzalez, Juan. (1969-) Baseball player, born Puerto Rico. SCHWAR; STEWM2.

Gonzalez, Luis. (1967-) Baseball player. STEWM2.

Gonzalez, Maya Christina. (1964-) Painter. HON.

Gonzalez, Melissa Eve. (1980-) Actor. MARV.

Gonzalez, Ruben. (1951-) Racquetball player. KAM.

Good, Mary. (1931-) Chemist. REY.

Goodall, Jane. (1934-) English primatologist. CEL; COOL; CUS2; HAV; KEEN; POLK; SIR; STI2; TALAD; THI2; WEI.

Goode, Mal. (1908-1995) Radio, TV broadcast journalist. POT.

Goode, Sara E. (1850-?) Inventor, slave. SULO2.

Goode, W. Wilson. (1938-) Army captain, mayor. DUD.

Goodman, Benjamin David "Benny." (1909-1986) Composer, jazz musician. BRO; MOU; SHIP; VEN.

Goodman, Ellen. (1941-) Journalist. HILA.

Goodman, Robert O. (1956-) Naval commander, born Puerto Rico. HASK2.

Goodnight, Molly. (1839-1926) Rancher. ALTE2.

Goodrich, Annie W. (1866-1954) Educator, nurse. STI.

Goodridge, Glenalvin. (1829-1866) Entrepreneur photo studios, photographer. SULG.

Goodridge, Wallace. (1841-1922) Entrepreneur photo studios, photographer. AFR; SULG.

Goodridge, William. (1846-1891) Entrepreneur photo studios, photographer. AFR; SULG.

Goodwin, Jan. (1944-) English journalist. SMIL.

Goodyear, Charles. (1800-1860) Inventor. NOO.

Gorbachev, Mikhail. (1931-) Russian political activist. Nobel Peace Prize winner. CRO4; KEEN2; MAYB2; TRAC2; WILKP4; YEN.

Gordimer, Nadine. (1923-) South African author, playwright. Nobel Prize winner. HAC6; KNI.

Gordon, George. (Lord Byron) (1788-1824) English poet. ROM.

Gordy, Berry, Jr. (1929-) Entrepreneur music business. AFR2; HASK; LEVE; RED.

Göring, Hermann. (1893-1946) German air force general, Nazi war criminal. SCHM3.

Gotti, John. (1940-2002) Gangster. WOO.

Gottschalk, Louis Moreau. (1829-1869) Composer. NIC.

Gould, Gordon. (1920-) Inventor, physicist. AAS19; HAV; JEF.

Gould, Stephen Jay. (1941-) Paleontologist. HAV.

Gounod, Charles. (1818-1893) French sacred music and opera composer. VEN.

Gourdine, Meredith. (1929-1998) Electrical engineer, inventor, olympic track and field athlete. AFR2; HENS; SULO.

Govea, Jessica. (c. 1950) Workers' rights activist. HOOS.

Goya, Francisco de. (1746-1828) Spanish painter. CUM; CUS; KRY; ROM.

Goyens, William. (1794-1856) Army military leader Texas Revolution. HASK2.

Gracchus, Gaius. (153-121 B.C.) Roman statesman. BAKR3.

Gracchus, Tiberius. (167-133 B.C.) Roman statesman. BAKR3.

Graf, Steffi. (1969-) German tennis player. HARR; HASD; RUT5; SCHWAB.

Grafton, Sue. (1940-) Author. SMIL2.

Graham, Bette Nesmith. (1924-1980) Inventor. ALTML; BLASH3; THI; VAR.

Graham, Billy. (1918-) Author, spiritual leader. Presidential Medal of Freedom recipient. CRO5.

Graham, Calvin. (1929-1992) World War II teen serving in Navy. HOOS.

Graham, Katharine. (1917-2001) Author, publisher. Presidential Medal of Freedom recipient, Pulitzer Prize winner. CUS2; HARN; JEF2; LUT; PRI.

Graham, Martha. (1894-1991) Choreographer, dancer. COOL; DEN; FOR; HER; LEVE; ROL.

Graham, Otto. (1921-2003) Football player, coach. LAC2; SULG7.

Gramm, Wendy Lee. (1945-) Economist. MORE; SIN.

Granato, Cammi. (1971-) Olympic hockey player, sportscaster. BRIL4.

Granados, Enrique. (1867-1916) Spanish composer. VEN.

Grandin, Temple. (1974-) Inventor. CURR2; KEND.

Grandmaison y Bruno Godin, Isabel. (1729-1792) Peruvian adventurer. POLK.

Grange, Red. (1903-1991) Football player. HUNT; ITA4; JACT; KRULL3; SULG3.

Grant, Bud. (1927-) Football coach. SAV11.

Grant, Horace Junior. (1965-) Basketball player. BJA.

Grant, Jehu. (1752?-?)) American Revolutionary War military, slave. SCHM.

Grant, Julia Dent. (1826-1902) First Lady. BARB; GOR; PAST.

Grant, Ulysses S. (1822-1885) Civil War general, 18th president of U.S. ADA; BARB; BAU; CRO; CRO3; CRO4; CRO6; DAV2; GREEC3; JAN; KRULL5; MORR; ROBE2; SAW; TRAC; YAN.

Granville, Evelyn Boyd. (1924-) Educator, government employee, mathematician. CEL; SULO2.

Grasso, Ella. (1919-1981) Governor, state legislator. Presidential Medal of Freedom recipient. GUL.

Gratz, Rebecca. (1781-1869) Educator, philanthropist. PASA; TAI.

Gravely, Samuel L., Jr. (1922-) Naval admiral, World War II military. HASK2.

Graves, Earl G. (1935-) Publisher magazines. HASK.

Gray, Asa. (1810-1888) Botanist, educator.

KEEN.

Gray, Martha. (unknown) Medical engineer, educator, medical researcher. KAH5.

Gray, Mary. (1938-) Mathematician. CEL.

Gray, Pete. (1915-2002) Baseball player. SAV10.

Gray, William H. "Bill." (1941-) Congressman, educator. BECKN.

Greatbatch, Wilson. (1919-) Biomedical engineer, medical researcher. AAS19.

Greaves, William. (1926-) Actor, filmmaker. AFR.

Grebel, Conrad. (1498-1526) Swiss spiritual leader. CRO5.

Greco, El. *See* Theotokópoulous, Doménikos.

Greeley, Horace. (1811-1872) Author, editor newspaper, journalist. RIT; SAT.

Green, Dannellia Gladden. (1966-) Engineer. SULO2.

Green, Freddie. (1911-1987) Jazz musician. GOU3.

Green, Grant. (1931-1978) Jazz musician. GOU3.

Green, Hetty. (1834-1916) Financier. MAC.

Green, Lear. (c. 1830-1850) Fugitive slave. FRA.

Green, Shawn. (1972-) Baseball player. SCHWAR; SCHWAR2.

Greenberg, Hank. (1911-1986) Baseball player. SULG8.

Greene, Bette. (1920-1997) Aviator, missionary. JACKD3.

Greene, Catherine Littlefield. (1755-1814) Inventor. BLASH4; ROL.

Greene, Charles Edward "Mean Joe." (1946-) Football player. SAV7.

Greene, Nathanael. (1742-1786) American Revolutionary War military commander. CRO3.

Greenfield, Elizabeth Taylor. (1809-1876) Singer. TAT.

Greenfield, Eloise. (1929-) Children's author, poet. STRI.

Greenfield, Jerry. (1951-) Entrepreneur ice cream. BRO; KRAMB; MAYB.

Greenhow, Rose O'Neal. (1817-1864) Civil War spy. BLASH; CARA; CHA; SULG4; ZEI.

Greenspan, Alan. (1926-) Economist. BUS.

Greer, Pedro Jose, Jr. (1956-) Human rights activist, physician. MARV6.

Greer, William Alexander "Sunny." (1895?-1982) Jazz musician. GOU6.

Gregory I. (Pope Gregory the Great) (540-604) Italian composer, saint, spiritual leader. VEN.

Gregory VII. (1015-1085) Italian pope. CRO4.

Gregory, Dick. (1932-) Civil rights activist, comedian, presidential candidate. RED3.

Gregory, Frederick. (1941-) Air Force colonel, astronaut, aviator. AFR2; BUR; JONS.

Gresham, Thomas. (1518-1579) English financier. BUS.

Gretzky, Wayne. (1961-) Canadian hockey player. BRIL; JACT; KNA8; KRAMS2; SULG3.

Grieg, Edvard. (1843-1907) Norwegian composer, conductor, musician. VEN.

Griffey, Ken, Jr. (1969-) Baseball player. SCHER; SCHWAR; TOR2.

Griffin, Archie. (1954) Football player, Heisman Trophy winner. DEV; SAV8.

Griffin, Bessie Blount. (1913-) Inventor, physical therapist. SULO2.

Griffin, Susan. (1943-) Author, poet. SMIL2.

Griffith, Darrell. (1958-) Basketball player. BJA3.

Griffith, Linda. (unknown) Chemical engineer, medical researcher. KAH2.

Grimes, Lloyd " Tiny." (1916-1989) Jazz musician. GOU3.

Grimke, Angelina. (1805-1879) Abolitionist, human rights activist. CHA; HER; JACW; KNI; THIR.

Grimke, Charlotte Forten. (1837-1914) Abolitionist, author, educator. AFR2; ALTMS; BOL; CHA; COX2; GREA; HAN; LYO.

Grimke, Sarah Moore. (1792-1873) Abolitionist, human rights activist. HARN; HER; JACW; KNI; THIR.

Grimm, Jacob. (1785-1863) German folklorist, storyteller. KRAL; PER.

Grimm, Wilhelm. (1786-1859) German folklorist, storyteller. KRAL; PER.

Grimmesey, Tevry. (1931-) World War II Japanese-American girl. HOOS.

Grinnell, George Bird. (1849-1938) Author, naturalist. CALV; KEEN.

Grissom, Virgil I. "Gus." (1926-1967) Astronaut, aviator, Korean War Air Force combat pilot. BAIR.

Groening, Matt. (1954-) Cartoonist. BOY; STEFF.

Gronniosaw, Ukawsaw. (1725-1786) African prince, slave. HAM.

Groseilliers, Médard Chouat des. (1618?-1695?) French explorer. BAKS.

Grossman, Mendel. (1917-1945) Polish Jewish Holocaust victim, photographer. SCHM3.

Grotefend, Georg Friedrich. (1775-1853) German scholar, translator. WEI.

Grove, Andrew. (1936-) Entrepreneur computers, Internet pioneer. FREN.

Grove, Robert Moses "Lefty." (1900-1975) Baseball player. SULG5.

Gruenewald, Matthias. (1475-1528) German painter. KRY.

Grynszpan, Herschel. (1921-1942) German Jewish Holocaust resistance worker, victim. SCHM3.

Guastavino, Rafael. (1842-1908) Architect, born Spain. LAE.

Guderian, Heinz. (1888-1954) World War II German military hero CRO3.

Gudmundsdottir, Bjork. (Bjork) (1966-) Icelandic pop singer. ROBB

Guerra, Jackie. (1967-) Actor, comedian, human rights activist, workers' rights activist. COLE.

Guerrero, Vladimir. (1976-) Baseball player, born Dominican Republic. SCHWAR; SCHWAR2; STEWM2.

Guevara, Che. (1928-1967) Argentine revolutionary. CRO4.

Guffey, James M. (1839-1930) Entrepreneur oil. AAS7.

Guggenheim, Meyer. (1828-1905) Entrepreneur copper, born Switzerland. BRO.

Guinevere. (6th century) English princess, married to King Arthur, legendary. KRAL.

Guiscard, Robert. (1015-1085) French military leader. CRO3.

Guisewite, Cathy. (1950-) Cartoonist. STEFF.

Guiteau, Charles Julius. (1841-1882) Assassin, killed President James Garfield. JONR; NET; STG; SULG9.

Guiteras, Juan. (1852-1925) Medical researcher, physician, born Cuba. LAE; SIN2.

Guiterrez, Jose Angel. (1944-) Civil rights activist for Mexican-Americans. LAE.

Gustavus Adolphus II. (1594-1632) Swedish military leader, ruler. CRO3.

Gutenberg, Johann. (1399-1468) German inventor, printer. DIN; LOM2; STRE2; WILKP3; YEN.

Guthrie, Janet. (1938-) Auto racer. GAI3; SAW.

Guthrie, Woody. (1912-1967) Folksinger, songwriter. KRULL4; SAW.

Gutman, Sarel. (17th century) Czech merchant. TAI.

Guy, Fred. (1897-1971) Jazz musician. GOU3.

Guzman, Cristian. (1978-) Baseball player, born Dominican Republic. STEWM2.

Gwaltney, John Langston. (1928-1998) Anthropologist. KEND.

Gwendolen. (fl. 1075-1060 B.C.) English warrior queen. MAYE2.

Gwinnett, Button. (1735-1777) American Revolutionary War patriot, colonial governor, congressman, Declaration of Independence signer, born England. FRA2; QUI.

Gwynn, Tony. (1960-) Baseball player. DEA; SCHWAR.

Gyatso, Sonam. (Dalai Lama) (1543-1588) Tibetan spiritual leader. CRO5.

Gyatso, Tenzin. (Dalai Lama) (1935-) Tibetan spiritual leader. Nobel Peace Prize winner. BOY; CRO5; GOLDM; KEEN2.

Gygax, Gary. (1938-) Author, entrepreneur games. AAS9.

H

Haden, Charlie. (1937-) Jazz musician. GOU2.

Hadjidaki-Marder, Elpida. (1948-) Greek marine archaeologist. POLK.

Hadley, Leila Eliott Burton. (1925-) Adventurer, author. POLK.

Hadrian. (Publius Aelius Handrianus) (76-138) Roman general and emperor. BAKR3; COOLI.

Hagar. Biblical character. ARM2.

Hagedorn, Jessica. (1949-) Author, born Philippines. CHI.

Hahn, Emily. (1905-1997) Adventurer, author, women's rights activist. POLK.

Halas, George. (1895-1983) Football coach. SAV11.

Hale, Clara. (1905-1992) Children's rights activist, human rights activist. BOL; GREA.

Hale, George Ellery. (1868-1938) Astronomer. CAM; HAV.

Hale, Nathan. (1755-1776) American Revolutionary War patriot, spy. BERS; SCHM.

Hale, Sarah Josepha Buell. (1788-1879) Children's author, editor magazine, women's rights activist. HARN; PRI.

Halevi, Judah. (1075-1141) Spanish physician, poet, scholar, spiritual leader. PASA.

Haley, Alex. (1921-1992) Author, journalist, World War II Coast Guard. Pulitzer Prize winner. BECKN; MAL; OFT; RED4; TUR.

Haley, Charles. (1964-) Football player. SAV7.

Hall, Al. (1915-) Jazz musician. GOU2.

Hall, George Cleveland. (1864-1930) Physician. COX.

Hall, Glenn. (1931-) Canadian hockey player. SPI.

Hall, Jim. (1930-) Jazz musician. GOU3.

Hall, Joyce C. (1891-1982) Entrepreneur greeting cards. AAS10.

Hall, Lyman. (1724-1790) American Revolutionary War patriot, congressman, Declaration of Independence signer, physician. FRA2; QUI.

Hall, Radclyffe. (1886-1943) English author, poet, dressed as man. KNI.

Halloren, Mary. (1907-) Army career officer. THIR.

Halleck, Henry Wager. (1815-1872) Civil War general. GREEC3.

Halley, Edmund. (1656-1742) English astronomer. TIN.

Hals, Frans. (1581-1666) Dutch painter. SEV.

Halsey, William F. "Bull." (1882-1959) World War II Navy commander. CRO3; OLE2.

Hamanaka, Sheila. (1949-) Children's author, illustrator. TALAR2.

Hamer, Fannie Lou. (1917-1977) Civil rights activist. ALLZ; ALTMS; BECKN; DUB; GREA; HAC2; HAN2; HARM; HASK7; MORI3; PIN; VERN.

Hamer, Victoria. (unknown) Veterinarian. KAH.

Hamill, Dorothy. (1956-) Olympic figure skater. POY; SMIP.

Hamilton, Alexander. (1753-1804) American Revolutionary War patriot, cabinet member, political activist. CRO; CRO4; FAB; LEVE; MEI; SAW; SCHM; USC.

Hamilton, Alice. (1869-1970) Children's rights activist, educator, human rights activist, pathologist, physician, public health activist. HAV; HUNTE2; REY; ROL; STI; VEG; YOUNT4.

Hamilton, Andrew. (1676-1741) Attorney, colonist. EME.

Hamilton, Marilyn. (1947-) Disability rights activist, inventor. PIL2.

Hamilton, Richard. (1978-) Basketball player. KNA11.

Hamilton, Virginia. (1936-2002) Children's and young adult author. HILC2; YUN.

Hamm, Mia. (1972-) Olympic soccer player. BAIL; HASD; LAY2; MILM; ROE; RUT4; SAV14.

Hammarskjöld, Dag. (1905-1961) Swedish diplomat, peace activist. Nobel Peace Prize winner. BLU; KEEN2.

Hammer. See Burrell, Stanley Kirk.

Hammerstein, Oscar, II. (1895-1960) Playwright, songwriter. Pulitzer Prize winner. CRO4; WEI2.

Hammett, Dashiell. (1894-1961) Author, screenwriter. PER.

Hammonds, Julia T. (unknown) Inventor. SULO2.

Hammons, David. (1943-) Mixed-media artist. AFR.

Hammurabi. (fl. 1792-1750 B.C.) Babylonian king. MEL; YEN.

Hanagid, Samuel. (993-1056) Spanish military leader, scholar. PASA.

Hanasi, Judah. (135-217) Hebrew scholar, spiritual leader. PASA.

Hanauer, Chip. (1954-) Power boat racer. JACT.

Hancock, Herbie. (1940-) Bandleader, jazz musician. GOU4; SHIP.

Hancock, John. (1737-1793) American Revolutionary War patriot, businessman, political leader. CRO; SCHM.

Hancock, Joy Bright. (1898-1986) Naval career, WAVES director, World War I, World War II. ZEI2.

Hancock, Winfield Scott. (1824-1886) Civil
War general. GREEC3.

Handali, Esther Kiera. (16th century) Turkish
human rights activist. TAI.

Handel, George Frideric. (1685-1759) English
composer. BLACA2; EIG; VEN.

Handler, Ruth. (1916-2002) Entrepreneur
dolls, inventor. AAS9; ALTML; BLASH2;
JEF2; VAR.

Handsome Lake. (1735-1818) Iroquois Indian
spiritual leader. GOLDM.

Handy, William Christopher. (1873-1958)
Composer, musician. ALTMS; BECKN;
HARD; HASK5; MON; POT; TAT.

Hanh, Thich Nhat. (1926-) Vietnamese author, Buddhist spiritual leader, Vietnam
War peace activist. SHAW.

Hani Motoko. (1873-1957) Japanese journalist. HOOB4.

Hannah. Biblical character. TAI.

Hannah, Marc. (1956-) Computer pioneer.
NOR.

Hannibal. (247-183 B.C.) Carthaginian general. CRO3.

Hanno. (c. 450 B.C.) Carthaginian explorer
and Navy. WAT.

Hannum, Alex. (1923-2002) Basketball
coach. KNA10.

Hansberry, Lorraine. (1930-1965) Playwright.
AFR; ALTMS; BECKN; FEM2; GREA;
KNI; OFT; POT; SMIL; WEI2; WILKB.

Hansberry, William Leo. (1894-1965) Anthropologist, educator. COX2.

Hanson, Harriet. (1825-1911) Civil rights
activist, suffragist, workers' rights activist.
HOOS.

Hardaga, Mustafa. (unknown) Muslim Holocaust rescuer. LAE.

Hardaway, Anfernee. (1972-) Basketball
player. SAV5.

Hardaway, Tim. (1966-) Basketball player.
SAV5.

Hardee, William Joseph. (1815-1873) Civil
War general. GREEC2.

Hardin, John Wesley. (1853-1895) Outlaw.
BLACG3; THRA.

Harding, Florence Kling De Wolfe. (1860-
1924) First Lady. BARB; GOR; PAST.

Harding, Tonya. (1970-) Olympic figure
skater. SAV12.

Harding, Warren G. (1865-1923) 29th president of U.S., senator. ADA; BARB; BAU;
BLASS; CRO6; DAV2; MORR; ROBE2.

Hardy, Oliver. (1892-1957) Comedian.
CRO4.

Hardy, Thomas. (1840-1928) English author,
poet. NIN; PER.

Hardy-Garcia, Dianne. (1965-) Gay rights
activist, human rights activist, social
worker. GOLDE.

Hare, Joseph Thompson. (1780-1818) Outlaw. BLACG2.

Haring, Keith. (1958-1990) AIDS activist,
cartoonist, painter. GON.

Harkhuf. (c. 2275 B.C.) Egyptian adventurer,
explorer. BAKR.

Harlan, John. (1833-1911) Attorney, Supreme
Court justice. AAS14.

Harmsworth, Alfred. (1865-1922) English
publisher. SAT.

Harper, Frances E. W. (1825-1911) Abolitionist, author, poet, suffragist, women's
rights activist. AFR; GREA; THIR;
WILKB.

Harper, John. (1872-1912) Scottish orator,
spiritual leader. JACKD4.

Harris, Bernard. (1956-) Astronaut, physician.
AFR2; JONS.

Harris, Betty Wright. (1940-) Chemist.
SULO2.

Harris, Eliza. (uknown) Fugitive slave. FRA.

Harris, Franco. (1950-) Football player.
LAC3.

Harris, LaDonna. (1931-) Comanche Indian
Native American rights activist. AVE.

Harris, Patricia Roberts. (1924-1985) Attorney, cabinet member, diplomat. DUD;
MORI; PLO.

Harris, Wesley. (1941-) Aerospace engineer,
civil rights activist, educator, space scientist. HAV.

Harrison, Anna Tuthill Symmes. (1775-1864)
First Lady. BARB; GOR; PAST.

Harrison, Benjamin. (1833-1901) Attorney,
Civil War military leader, 23rd president of
U.S., senator. ADA; BARB; BAU;
BLASS; CRO6; DAV2; MORR.

Harrison, Caroline Scott. (1832-1892) First
Lady. BARB; GOR; PAST.

Harrison, Marguerite Baker. (1879-1967)
Adventurer, spy. MCLE; STEFO2.

Harrison, William Henry. (1773-1862) Congressman, governor, military leader War of 1812, 9th president of U.S. ADA; BARB; BAU; BLASS; CRO6; DAV2; MORR.

Hart, John. (1711-1779) American Revolutionary War patriot, congressman, Declaration of Independence signer. FRA2; QUI.

Hart, Nancy. (1744-1841) American Revolutionary War patriot, spy. SCHM; SILC.

Hart, Pearl. (1871-1925) Canadian outlaw. BLACG3; SAV2.

Harte, Bret. (1836-1902) Author, diplomat, poet. PER.

Harvard, Beverly. (1950-) Police chief. POT.

Harvard, Claude. (1911-1999) Inventor. SULO.

Harvey, Fred. (1835-1901) Entrepreneur restaurants, born England. AAS6.

Harvey, William. (1578-1657) English anatomist. CURT; POD; TIN.

Haskells, Ella Knowles. (1860-1911) Attorney. ALTE2.

Hasselaar, Kenau. (1526-1588) Dutch political activist. LEO3.

Hastie, William H. (1904-1976) Attorney, jurist. BOOK.

Hata, Prateep Ungsongtham. (1952-) Thai educator, human rights activist. BERS.

Hathhor. Egyptian goddess of love. FIS.

Hatshepsut. (1500-1460 B.C.) Egyptian pharoah. DUN; HER; LEO; ROBE3; ROE; ROL.

Hauptman, Judith. (unknown) Educator. TAI.

Havel, Vaclav. (1936-) Czech playwright, political activist, president. TRAC2.

Havlicek, John. (1940-) Basketball player. AAS17.

Hawes, Harriet Ann Boyd. (1871-1945) Archaeologist. FAG; STI2.

Hawk, Tony. (1968-) Skateboarder. BOY.

Hawkes, Kevin. (1959-) Children's author, illustrator. TALAR3.

Hawking, Stephen. (1942-) English astrophysicist. HAV; KEND; TIN; YEN.

Hawkins, Coleman. (1904-1969) Jazz musician. GOU; SHIP.

Hawkins, Connie. (1942-) Basketball player. BJA3.

Hawthorne, Nathaniel. (1804-1864) Author. CRO4; FAB2; OFT2; PER.

Hay, John. (1838-1905) Author, cabinet member, diplomat. RIC.

Hayakawa, Samuel Ichiye. (1906-1992) Educator, scholar, senator, born Canada. SIN.

Hayakawa, Sessue. (Kintaro) (1890-1973) Actor, born Japan. SIN.

Hayden, Ferdinand Vandeveer. (1829-1887) Geologist. PRE.

Hayden, Lewis. (1815-1889) Abolitionist, state legislator. ALTMS.

Hayden, Palmer C. (1890-1973) Painter. HARD.

Hayden, Sophia. (1868-1953) Architect, born Chile. HER.

Haydn, Franz Joseph. (1732-1809) Austrian composer. EIG; VEN.

Hayenwatha. (c. 1400) Mohawk Indian chief, peace activist. SHER2.

Hayes, Bob. (1942-2002) Football player, olympic sprinter, track and field athlete. KNA3.

Hayes, Elvin. (1945-) Basketball player. SAV6.

Hayes, Ira. (1922-1955) Pim Indian World War II Marine hero. AVE.

Hayes, Isaac. (1943-) Jazz musician, singer. AFR.

Hayes, Lucy Ware Webb. (1831-1889) First Lady. BARB; GOR; PAST.

Hayes, Randy. (unknown) Environmentalist. GRAH.

Hayes, Rutherford B. (1822-1893) Attorney, Civil War soldier, congressman, governor, 19th president of U.S. ADA; BARB; BAU; BLASS; CRO6; DAV2; MORR.

Haymes, Dick. (1917-1980) Singer. GOU5.

Haynes, Lemuel. (1753-1833) American Revolutionary War military, spiritual leader. AFR2; HASK2; HASK4.

Haynes, Ray. (1925-) Jazz musician. GOU6.

Hayward, John T. (1908-1999) World War II Navy admiral. BOR.

Haywood, William D. "Big Bill." (1869-1928) Labor leader. STRE5.

Hazen, Elizabeth. (1885-1975) Bacteriologist, medical researcher. ALTML; BLASH2.

Healy, Bernadine. (1944-) National Institute of Health Director, physician. STI.

Healy, Michael A. (1839-1904) Captain U.S. Revenue Cutter service. HASK2.

Healy, Patrick Francis. (1834-1910) Educator, spiritual leader. COX2.

Heard, J.C. (1917-1988) Jazz musician. GOU6.

Hearst, William Randolph. (1863-1951) Philanthropist, publisher newspapers. CRO; CRO4; MAYB; RIT; SAT.

Heath, Percy. (1923-) Jazz musician. GOU2.

Hecox, Laura. (1854-1919) Lighthouse keeper. FLE.

Hedea. (?) Roman olympic track and field athlete. LEO.

Hedin, Sven. (1865-1952) Swedish explorer, geographer. LANG.

Heiden, Eric. (1958-) Olympic speed skater. USC4.

Heifetz, Jascha. (1901-1987) Musician, born Russia. BRO.

Height, Dorothy Irene. (1912-) Civil rights activist, National Council of Negro Women director, social worker. Presidential Medal of Freedom recipient. GREA; PIN; RED2; TUR.

Heimdall. Norse god "The watchman." FIS3.

Heinlein, Robert. (1907-1988) Author. DAT.

Heinrichs, April. (1964-) Olympic soccer player, coach. BRIL5.

Heinz, Henry John. (1844-1919) Entrepreneur canned foods and sauces. AAS10.

Heisenberg, Werner. (1901-1976) German physicist. Nobel Prize winner. HAV; TIN.

Heiss, Carol. (1940-) Olympic figure skater. POY.

Hejduk, Milan. (1976-) Czech olympic hockey player. BREH.

Hela. Norse goddess of death. FIS3.

Helen of Troy. (1200-1150 B.C.) Greek heroine, perhaps legendary. KRAL.

Helena. (250-330) Roman saint, spiritual leader. CRO5; ROL.

Héloise. (1098-1164) French spiritual leader. KRAL.

Hemingway, Ernest Miller. (1899-1961) Author. Nobel Prize winner, Pulitzer Prize winner. BRED; FAB2; KRAL; LEVE; MEE; PER; TWEPR.

Henderson, Arthur. (1863-1935) Scottish labor leader. Nobel Peace Prize winner. KEEN2.

Henderson, Fletcher. (1897-1952) Bandleader, jazz musician, singer. HARD; HASK5; SHIP.

Henderson, Rickey. (1958-) Baseball player. BJA2.

Hendrickson, Sue. (1950-) Adventurer, paleontologist. POLK; THI2.

Hendrix, Jimi. (1942-1970) Rock musician. KNA2; WOO.

Henie, Sonia. (1912-1969) Norwegian olympic figure skater. AAS20; HASD; JACT; KRULL3; ROE; SMIP; STRU.

Henkes, Kevin. (1960-) Children's author, illustrator. TALAR2.

Henley, Beth. (1952-) Playwright. SMIL.

Henri, Robert. (1865-1929) Painter. KRY.

Henry II. (1133-1189) English king. CRO4; DAV.

Henry III. (1207-1272) English king. DAV.

Henry IV. (1050-1106) German emperor. CRO4.

Henry V. (1387-1422) English king. DAV.

Henry VI. (1421-1471) English king. DAV.

Henry VII. (1457-1509) English king. DAV.

Henry VIII. (1491-1547) English king. CRO4; DAV; YEN.

Henry. Prince of Portugal. (Henry the Navigator) (1394-1460) Portuguese explorer, prince. FRIT; LOM; POD; PRE; WILLI2.

Henry, Caryl. (1955-) Painter. HON.

Henry, Sir Edward. (1859-1931) English forensic scientist. FRID.

Henry, John. (1840-1871) Railroad worker, folk hero. KRAL.

Henry, Joseph. (1797-1878) Inventor, physicist. TIN.

Henry, O. See Porter, William Sydney.

Henry, Patrick. (1736-1799) American Revolutionary War patriot, colonial governor, orator, political activist. CRO; SAW; SCHM.

Henry, Warren. (1909-2001) Physical chemist. HAV.

Hensel, Fanny Mendelssohn. (1805-1847) German composer. NIC2.

Henson, Jim. (1937-1990) Television personality. BRIL.

Henson, Josiah. (1789-1883) Abolitionist, fugitive slave, spiritual leader. GAR; HAM.

Henson, Matthew. (1866-1955) Arctic explorer. ALTE; ALTMS; BECKN; CRO4; CURR; DEN; HAC2; HASK3; HASK7; HAV; HAY3; HUD; PIO; POT; REE;

SCHEL2; SCHR.

Henson, William. (1812-1888) Aviation pioneer, engineer, born England. BERL2.

Hepburn, Katherine. (1907-2003) Actor. GAI2; LEVE.

Hepworth, Barbara. (1903-1975) English sculptor. DUN.

Herbert, Frank. (1920-1986) Author. DAT.

Herbert, George. (1866-1923) English archaeologist, egyptologist. GREENBL; WEI.

Hercules. Greek adventurer. ALTE.

Hermod. Norse god of courage. FIS3.

Hernandez, Keith. (1953-) Baseball player. SULG2.

Hernandez, Maria Latigo. (1893-1986) Author, civil rights activist, political activist, television personality, born Mexico. LAE.

Herodias. (1st century C.E.) Israeli queen. ARM2.

Herodotus. (c. 484-420 B.C.) Greek historian. BAKR2; PRE; YEN.

Herrera, Caroline. (1939-) Fashion designer, born Venezuela. LAE; MORE2.

Herring, Augustus. (1867-1926) Aviation pioneer. BERL2.

Herschel, Caroline. (1750-1848) English astronomer, born Germany. CEL; DUN; POD; ROL.

Herschel, Sir John. (1792-1871) English astronomer. POD.

Herschel, William. (1738-1822) English astronomer. POD; TIN; WILLS.

Hershey, Milton. (1857-1945) Entrepreneur chocolate. AAS12; DEN; KRAMB.

Hershiser, Orel. (1958-) Baseball player. YOUNG2.

Herzl, Theodor. (1860-1904) Austrian author, journalist, born Hungary. PASA.

Heschel, Abraham Joshua. (1907-1972) Author, civil rights activist, educator, political activist, born Poland. PASA.

Hess, Harry. (1906-1969) Geologist, minerologist, World War II Navy commander. CARR; HAV.

Hess, Rudolf. (1894-1987) German aviator, Nazi war criminal. SCHM3.

Hesse, Eva. (1936-1970) Painter, sculptor, born Germany. GREENBJ.

Hesse, Herman. (1877-1962) Swiss author, born Germany. Nobel Prize winner. PER.

Heuman, Judy. (1947-) Government employee. KEND.

Hewes, Joseph. (1730-1779) American Revolutionary War patriot, congressman, Declaration of Independence signer. FRA2; QUI.

Hewlett, Bill. (1913-2001) Computer pioneer, entrepreneur computers. AAS12.

Heydrich, Reinhard. (1904-1942) German Nazi war criminal. SCHM3.

Heyerdahl, Thor. (1914-2002) Norwegian adventurer, biologist. ALTE; LANG; WILLI2.

Heyman, Eva. (1931-1944) Hungarian author, Holocaust victim. WE.

Heyward, Thomas, Jr. (1746-1809) American Revolutionary War patriot, attorney, congressman, Declaration of Independence signer, jurist. FRA2; QUI.

Hiawatha. (fl. 1440) Iroquois chief, spiritual leader, legendary. CRO5; KRAL.

Hickok, James Butler "Wild Bill." (1837-1876) Civil War union scout, crimefighter, outlaw. GLA; JAN; KRAL; SAV; SAV3; THRA.

Hickson, Catherine. (1955-) Canadian geologist, volcanologist. DID.

Hidalgo, Richard. (1975-) Baseball player, born Venezuela. STEWM2.

Hiera. Amazon warrior queen. MAYE2.

Higgins, Marguerite. (1920-1966) Photojournalist Korean War, Vietnam War, World War II. Pulitzer Prize winner. COLM; PRI; RIT; SHEA; WHI; ZEI3.

Higgins, Patillo. (1863-1955) Entrepreneur oil. AAS7.

Hijuelos, Oscar. (1948-) Author. Pulitzer Prize winner. HILC; LAE; SIN2.

Hilda of Whitby. (614-680) English educator, saint, spiritual leader. KNI.

Hildegarde von Bingen. (1098-1179) German spiritual leader, visionary. CRO5; GOLDM; KNI; KRULL7; LEO2.

Hill, Ambrose Powell. (1825-1865) Civil War general. GREEC2.

Hill, Grant. (1972-) Basketball player. AAS17.

Hill, James J. (1838-1916) Entrepreneur railroads, born Canada. CALV.

Hill, Lauryn. (1975-) Singer, songwriter. KEEL; ROE.

Hill, Lynn. (1961-) Rock climber. ROE.

Hill, Mozell Clarence. (1911-1969) Civil rights activist, educator. COX2.

Hillary, Sir Edmund. (1919-) New Zealander adventurer, author, mountaineer. ALTE; CRO4; KRULL3; PRE.

Hillel. (60-10 B.C.E.) Hebrew scholar, spiritual leader. CRO5; PASA.

Hillerich, Bud. (1866-1946) Entrepreneur baseball bats. PIL.

Hilton, Conrad. (1887-1979) Entrepreneur hotels, state legislator. AAS16.

Himes, Chester. (1909-1984) Author, criminal. MAL.

Himmler, Heinrich. (1900-1945) German Nazi war criminal. SCHM3.

Hinckley, John Warnock, Jr. (1966-) Assassin, attempted to kill President Ronald Reagan. JONR; NET; STG; SULG9.

Hindenburg, Paul von. (1847-1934) German president, World War I military leader. CRO3.

Hine, Lewis W. (1874-1940) Photographer, workers' rights activist. GAI; JACKN.

Hines, Earl "Fatha." (1903-1983) Bandleader, jazz musician. GOU4; SHIP.

Hines, Jim. (1946-) Olympic track and field athlete. HUNTE; KNA3.

Hingis, Martina. (1980-) Swiss tennis player, born Czechoslovakia. HASD; MILE; RUT5; WEL.

Hinton, Milt. (1910-2000) Jazz musician. GOU2.

Hinton, Susan E. "S. E." (1949-) Young adult author. BRIL; WEL.

Hinton, William Augustus. (1883-1959) Educator, medical researcher, physician. COX; HAY.

Hipparchia of Athens. (c. 330 B.C.) Greek philosopher. LEO.

Hippocrates. (460?-370? B.C.) Greek physician. AND; BAKR2; CURT; TIN; YEN.

Hirohito. (1901-1989) Japanese emperor. PAP.

Hirsch, Elroy "Crazy Legs." (1923-2004) Football player. THOR.

Hirsch, Samson Raphael. (1808-1888) German author, educator. PASA.

Hirschfeld, Magnus. (1868-1935) Polish gay rights activist, human rights activist, physician. SCHM3.

Hiss, Alger. (1904-1996) Attorney, government official, spy, traitor. AAS18.

Hitchcock, Alfred. (1899-1980) Filmmaker, born England. HILA2.

Hitchcock, Edward. (1793-1864) Geologist, spiritual leader. AAS.

Hitler, Adolf. (1889-1945) German dictator, World War II Nazi war criminal. CRO4; GREER; MAYB2; SCHM3; YEN.

Ho Chi Minh. (1890-1969) Vietnamese dictator, political activist, revolutionary. MAYB2; WAKI.

Ho, David. (1952-) AIDS researcher, medical researcher, physician, born Taiwan. RAG; YOUNT.

Hoagland, Jesse. (1939-) Inventor. HENS.

Hoban, Tana. (unknown) Children's author, illustrator. MARC3.

Hobby, Oveta Culp. (1905-1995) Cabinet member, publisher, World War II Army commander WAACS. ALTE2; ZEI3.

Hoben, Patricia. (unknown) Agricultural scientist, biologist, medical researcher. KAH7.

Hockenberry, John. (1956-) Author, broadcast journalist, journalist. KEND.

Hodgers, Jenny. (Albert Cashier) (1844-1915) Civil War soldier, disguised as man, born Ireland. ZEI.

Hodges, Gil. (1924-1972) Baseball player, World War II marine. TOR.

Hodgins, Jessica. (unknown) Computer scientist. KAH3.

Hodgkin, Dorothy Crowfoot. (1910-1994) English physical chemist, x-ray crystallographer. Nobel Prize winner. STI2; TIN.

Hodgson, Tasha. (1972-) New Zealander in-line skater. SAV9.

Hoei-shin. (5th century) Chinese explorer, spiritual leader. ALTE; LOM.

Hoff, Ted. (1937-) Computer scientist, electrical engineer, inventor. HAV.

Hoffa, James R. (1913-1975) Labor leader. STRE5.

Hoffman, Trevor. (1967-) Baseball player. SCHWAR.

Hofstadter, Robert. (1915-1990) Physicist. Nobel Prize winner. HAV.

Hogan, Ben. (1912-1997) Golfer. JACT; SAV10.

Hogarth, William. (1697-1764) English painter. BLACA; CUM; EIG; KRY.

Hogg, Helen Battles Sawyer. (1905-1993)

Canadian astronomer. STI2.

Hokusai, Katsushika. (1760-1849) Japanese painter, printmaker. BLACA; HOOB4; KRULL2; MARZ.

Holdsclaw, Chamique. (1977-) Basketball player. SAV13.

Holiday, Billie. (1915-1959) Jazz singer. AFR; BECKN; GOU5; HAC3; JAZ; JONH; LES; MON; SHIP.

Holland, Dave. (1946-) English jazz musician. GOU2.

Holland, Elizabeth. (unknown) Biogeochemist. KAH.

Hollerith, Herman. (1860-1929) Computer pioneer. NOO; NOR.

Holley, Major. (1924-1991) Jazz musician, singer. GOU2.

Holliday, John "Doc." (1852-1887) Dentist, outlaw. GLA.

Holly, Buddy. (1936-1959) Rock singer. KNA2.

Holmes, Arthur. (1890-1965) English geologist. HAV.

Holmes, Herman Mudget "H. H." (1866-1896) Physician, serial killer. LAS.

Holmes, Larry. (1949-) Boxer. KNA7.

Holmes, Oliver Wendell. (1841-1935) Attorney, Supreme Court justice. AAS14; CRO; FAB; LEVE.

Holt, Benjamin. (1849-1920) Entrepreneur tractors. AAS3.

Holzman, William "Red." (1920-1998) Basketball coach. KNA10.

Hom, Nancy. (1949-) Painter. HON.

Homer. (c. 750 B.C.) Greek poet. BAKR2; KRAL; PER; YEN.

Homer, Winslow. (1836-1910) Painter. GLU.

Honda, Soichiero. (1906-1991) Japanese automaker. ITA6.

Hood, John Bell. (1821-1879) Civil War general. GREEC2.

Hood, Robin. (1290-1346) English outlaw, political activist, folk hero. KRAL; THOM2.

Hooke, Robert. (1635-1703) English inventor. TIN.

Hooker, Joseph. (1814-1878) Civil War general. GREEC3.

Hooker, Thomas. (1586-1647) Puritan preacher, founder of Connecticut. CRO2; DOH3.

Hooper, William. (1742-1790) American Revolutionary War patriot, attorney, congressman, Declaration of Independence signer. FRA2; QUI.

Hoover, Herbert. (1874-1964) Cabinet member, engineer, 31st president of U.S. ADA; BARB; BAU; BLASS; CRO6; DAV2; MORR.

Hoover, J. Edgar. (1895-1972) Crimefighter, FBI director. CRO; KRAL.

Hoover, Lou Henry. (1874-1944) First Lady. BARB; GOR; PAST.

Hope, John. (1868-1936) Civil rights activist, educator. BECKN; COX2.

Hope, Leslie Townes " Bob." (1903-2003) Actor, comedian, human rights activist, born England. Presidential Medal of Freedom recipient. CRO4.

Hopkins, Harry L. (1890-1946) Government employee, social work administrator. CRO.

Hopkins, Lee Bennett. (1938-) Children's author, poet. AUT.

Hopkins, Stephen. (1707-1785) American Revolutionary patriot, congressman, Declaration of Independence signer, publisher newspaper. FRA2; QUI.

Hopkinson, Francis. (1737-1791) American Revolutionary War patriot, composer, congressman, Declaration of Independence signer. FRA2; QUI.

Hopper, Edward. (1882-1967) Painter. CUM; GREENBJ; KRY; TWEPO.

Hopper, Grace. (1906-1972) Computer pioneer. CAM; CEL; CURR2; HARN; NOR; REY; THI; TIN; VAR; YOUNT3.

Horace. (Quintus Horatius Flaccus) (65-8 B.C.) Roman poet. BAKR3.

Horemheb. (fl. 1321-1293 B.C.) Egyptian king. BAKR.

Horn, Tom. (1806-1903) Cowboy, frontiersman, Indian scout, French-Indian War soldier. THRA.

Hornaday, William Temple. (1854-1937) Wildlife conservationist. KEEN.

Horne, Lena. (1917-) Jazz singer. AFR; GREA; MON.

Horner, Bob. (1957-) Baseball player. TOR.

Horner, Jack. (1946-) Paleontologist. AAS; CHRISP.

Horney, Karen Danielsen. (1885-1952) Psychiatrist, born Germany. REY; ROL; STI.

Hornsby, Rogers. (1896-1963) Baseball player. DEA; JACT; SULG8.

Hornung, Paul. (1935-) Football player. Heisman Trophy winner. DEV.

Horowitz, Sarah Rebecca Rachel Leah. (18th century) Polish scholar. TAI.

Horse, John. (1812-1852) Black Seminole Indian military leader. KAT2; MON2.

Hortensia. (1st century B.C.) Roman orator, women's rights activist. DUN; LEO.

Horus. Egyptian god of life. FIS.

Hose, Louise. (1952-) Geologist. POLK.

Hosier, Harry "Black Harry." (1750-1806) Spiritual leader. AFR2.

Hosmer, Harriet. (1830-1908) Inventor, sculptor. BLASH4.

Höss, Rudolf. (1900-1947) German Nazi war criminal. SCHM3.

Hostetter, Margaret. (unknown) Medical researcher, physician. KAH7.

Houbolt, John. (fl. 1960s) Aeronautical engineer, mathematician, space scientist. RIC3.

Houdini, Harry. (1874-1926) Magician. BRO; KRAL; LEVE; WOO.

Hounsfield, Sir Godfrey N. (1919-) English biomedical engineer, inventor. Nobel Prize winner. AAS15.

Houston, Charles H. (1895-1950) Attorney, civil rights activist, educator. BECKN; HARM.

Houston, Sam. (1793-1863) Congressman, governor, president republic Texas, senator. CALV; CRO; DOH4; FAB.

Houston, Whitney. (1963-) Actor, singer. RED5.

Howard, Edward Lee. (1951-2002) Spy, traitor. AAS18.

Howard, John. (1726-1790) English reformer. CLA.

Howard, Mildred. (1945-) Mixed-media artist. AFR.

Howe, Gordie. (1928-) Hockey player, born Canada. JACT; KNA8; SULG3.

Howe, James. (1946-) Children's author. AUT.

Howe, James Wong. (1899-1976) Filmmaker, born China. SIN.

Howe, Oscar. (1915-1983) Yankton Dakota Indian painter. AVE.

Howe, William. (1729-1814) American Revolutionary War military leader, loyalist. SCHM.

Hsüan-tsang. (c. 602-664) Chinese spiritual leader. CRO5.

Hua Mu-Lan. (c. 400) Chinese warrior, disguised as man.

Hubbard, L. Ron. (1911-1986) Author, cult leader, spiritual leader. CRO5; KELLA; STRE.

Hubbard, Mina Benson. (1870-1956) Canadian explorer. POLK.

Hubbell, Carl. (1903-1988) Baseball player. SULG5.

Hubble, Edwin. (1889-1953) Astronomer. CAM; HAV; TIN.

Hübener, Helmut. (1925-1942) German anti-Nazi youth World War II, Holocaust victim. BERS.

Huddleston, Ned. (AKA Isum Dart, Tan Mex, Quick-Shot, Old Black Fox) (1849-1900) Outlaw, slave. MON2.

Hudson, Henry. (1565-1631) English explorer. ALTE; BAKS; LANG; POD; PRE; WILLI2.

Huerta, Dolores. (1930-) Labor leader. DEN; HAC5; HEA; LAE; LINL2; THIR.

Hughes, Charles Evan. (1862-1948) Attorney, cabinet member, governor, Supreme Court justice. AAS14; RIC.

Hughes, Howard. (1905-1976) Aviator, entrepreneur aircraft, filmmaker. KRAL.

Hughes, James Mercer Langston. (1902-1967) Poet. AFR; ALTMS; BECKM; BECKN; DEN; FAB2; HARD; HASK5; KRULL6; MAL; OFT; STRI; TWEPO.

Hughes, Lewis. (1832-?) Author, slave. LAND3.

Hughes, Sarah. (1985-) Olympic figure skater. MILT.

Hugo, Victor. (1802-1885) French author, playwright, poet. PER; ROM.

Hull, Bobby. (1939-) Canadian hockey player. KNA8.

Hull, Brett. (1964-) Canadian hockey player. KNA8.

Hull, Cordell. (1871-1955) Attorney, cabinet member, congressman, senator. Nobel Peace Prize winner. KEEN2.

Hull, Peggy. (1890-1967) World War I correspondent. ZEI2.

Humboldt, Alexander von. (1769-1859) German botanist, geographer. FAB3; KEEN; LANG; LEU; POD; STEFO; TIN.

Hume, Hamilton. (1797-1873) Australian explorer. ALTE.

Hunt, Fern. (unknown) Computer scientist, mathematician. KAH3.

Hunter, Alberta. (1895-1984) Singer. AFR.

Hunter, Clarence. (1920-1993) Magician. HASK6.

Hunter, Clementine. (1886-1988) Painter. AFR; HAC4.

Hunter, Jim "Catfish." (1946-) Baseball player. OCO.

Hunter-Gault, Charlayne. (1942-) Broadcast journalist, civil rights activist. ALLZ; PRI; SMIL2; WHI.

Huntingdon, Samuel. (1731-1796) American Revolutionary patriot, attorney, congressman, Declaration of Independence signer. FRA2; QUI.

Hurd, Henriette Wyeth. (1907-1997) Painter. ALTE2.

Hurley, Bobby. (1971-) Basketball player. RAPK.

Hurston, Zora Neale. (1901-1960) Anthropologist, author. AFR; BECKM; BECKN; COOL; FEM2; GOM; GREA; HARD; HASK5; HER; KNI; KRULL6; MED; OFT; POLK; RED4; SMIL2; TWEPR; WEI; WILKB.

Hurwitz, Johanna. (1937-) Children's author. AUT.

Hus, Jan. (1369-1415) Czech scholar, spiritual leader. CRO5.

Hussein, Ibn Talal. (1935-1999) Jordanian king. WAK.

Hussein, Saddam. (1937-) Iraqi dictator, president. GREER; WAK.

Hutchinson, Anne Marbury (1591-1643) Human rights activist, spiritual leader, women's rights activist, born England. CRO2; CRO5; FUR; GOLDM; JACW; JACW2; POD.

Hutchinson, Thomas. (1711-1780) Colonial governor, congressman, political activist. CRO2.

Hutson, Don. (1913-1997) Football player. HUNT; THOR.

Hutson, Jean Blackwell. (1914-1998) Librarian. GREA.

Hutton, James. (1726-1797) Scottish geologist, physician. CARR.

Hutton, May Arkwright. (1860-1915) Pioneer, suffragist. ALTE2.

Huxley, Aldous. (1894-1963) English author. PER.

Huygens, Christiaan. (1629-1695) Dutch astronomer. TIN.

Hwang, David Henry. (1957-) Playwright. CHI; SIN.

Hyams, Rachel. (1937-) Holocaust survivor. NIE.

Hyde, Ida Henrietta. (1857-1945) Physiologist. STI2.

Hyman, Flo. (1954-1986) Olympic volleyball player. KRULL3.

Hyman, Libbie. (1888-1969) Zoologist. REY.

Hypathia. (355-415) Egyptian astronomer, mathematician, philosopher. AND; CEL; DID; HER; ROL.

I

Iacocca, Lee. (1924-) Entrepreneur automobiles. LEVE.

Iaia of Cyzicus. (fl. 90 B.C.) Turkish painter. LEO.

Ibarurri, Dolores. (1895-1989) Spanish political activist, revolutionary. HAC7.

Iberville, Pierre le Moyne de. (1661-1706) Canadian colonist, founder of Louisiana, naval captain, soldier, born France. CRO2; DOH5.

Ibn al-Walid, Khalid. (d. 642) Arab general. CRO3.

Ibn Battuta, Muhammad. (1304-1369) Muslim Berber adventurer, explorer, born Morocco. LANG; POD; SCHEL2; WAT.

Ibn-e-Sina, Hakim. (980-1037) Islamic physician. TIN.

Ibn Ziyad, Tariq. (d. 700) Berber general. CRO3.

Ibsen, Henrik. (1828-1906) Norwegian playwright, poet. NIN; WEI2.

Ichikawa Fusae. (1893-1981) Japanese political activist, suffragist, women's rights activist. HER.

Idunn. Norse goddess of youth. FIS3.

Iglesias, Enrique. (1975-) Pop singer, born Spain. KRULI.

Ignatius of Loyola. (1491-1556) Spanish military leader, saint, spiritual leader. CRO5; GOLDM.

Ima Shalom. (50-?) Hebrew woman in Talmud. TAI.

Imhotep. (3000-2950 B.C.) Egyptian architect. AAS11.

Ingles, Mary Draper. (1731-1815) Colonist, Indian captive. FUR.

Inglis, Elsie. (1864-1917) Scottish physician, women's rights activist, World War I surgeon. STI.

Ingram, Billy. (1880-?) Entrepreneur restaurants. AAS6.

Ingres, Jean-Auguste. (1780-1867) French painter. CUM.

Innocent III, Pope. (Lothario de Segni) (1160-1216) Italian pope. PAP.

Inouye, Daniel. (1924-) Attorney, senator, World War II Army captain. BERS; KEND; MORE; RAG; SIN.

Ireland, Patricia. (1945-) Attorney, human rights activist, National Organization for Women president, women's rights activist. LINL2.

Ireland, William Henry. (1777-1835) English swindler. BLACG5.

Irvine, Andrew. (1896-1924) English explorer, mountaineer. ALTE.

Irving, Henry. (1838-1905) English actor. WEI2.

Irving, John. (1942-) Author. PER.

Irving, Washington. (1783-1859) Author. FAB2; OFT2; SAW.

Irwin, James. (1930-1991) Aerospace engineer, Air Force test pilot, astronaut. PRE.

Isaacs, Susan. (1943-) Author. SMIL2.

Isabella I. (1451-1504) Spanish queen. COOL; CRO4; DUN; GUL; HER; KRULL; LEO3; MEL2; NAR4; ROL.

Ishi. (1862-1916) Yani Indian. AVE.

Isis. (c. 3000 B.C.) Egyptian goddess. COOL.

Itzámna. Mayan god of all. FIS2.

Ivan IV. (Ivan the Terrible) (1530-1584) Russian czar. WILKP4.

Iverson, Allen. (1975-) Basketball player. NEL; PAU.

Ives, Charles. (1874-1954) Composer. Pulitzer Prize winner. BRED3; KRULL4; NIC; TWEPR.

Ivins, Marsha. (1951-) Aerospace engineer, astronaut, space scientist. BRIGG2.

Ixchal. Mayan goddess of childbirth. FIS2.

Ix Tab. Mayan goddess of suicide. FIS2.

J

Jackson, Andrew. (1767-1863) Congressman, 7th president of U.S., senator. ADA; BARB; BAU; BLASS; CRO; CRO6; DAV2; FAB; JONR; KRULL5; MORR; STG.

Jackson, "Blind Lemon." (1897-1930) Jazz musician. GOU3.

Jackson, Bo. (1962-) Baseball player, football player. Heisman Trophy winner. DEV; SLO; SULG8.

Jackson, Charles T. (1805-1880) Chemist, medical researcher. FRA3.

Jackson, Chris. See Abdul-Rauf, Mahmad.

Jackson, Janet. (1966-) Actor, dancer, singer. RED5.

Jackson, Janis. (unknown) Biologist, medical researcher, physician. KAH7.

Jackson, Jesse. (1941-) Civil rights activist, political activist, presidential candidate, spiritual leader. Presidential Medal of Freedom recipient. ALTMS; BECKN; CIV; HARM; VERN.

Jackson, Jim. (1970-) Basketball player. BJA.

Jackson, Mahalia. (1911-1972) Jazz singer. GREA; JONH; LES; TAT.

Jackson, May Howard. (1877-1931) Sculptor. HARD.

Jackson, Michael. (1958-) Showman, singer. TAT.

Jackson, Phil. (1945-) Basketball coach. KNA10.

Jackson, Rachel Donelson Robards. (1767-1828) First Lady. BARB; GOR; PAST.

Jackson, Reggie. (1946-) Baseball player. SEHN; SULG8; YOUNG2.

Jackson, Robert H. (1892-1954) Attorney, Nuremberg trial judge, Supreme Court justice. CALA; EME.

Jackson, Shirley. (1919-1965) Author. MAD.

Jackson, Shirley Ann. (1946-) Educator, Nuclear Regulatory Commission head, physicist. AFR2; CAM; HAV; HAY3; JONL; KAH8; SULO; SULO2.

Jackson, Thomas "Stonewall." (1824-1863)

Civil War general. CRO3; GREEC2; REG; TRAC.

Jacob, Mary Phelps. (Caresse Crosby) (1892-1970) Inventor. DIN.

Jacobi, Mary Putnam. (1842-1906) Educator, physician, born England. STI.

Jacobs, Harriet. (1813-1897) Abolitionist, author, slave. GAR; WILKB.

Jael of Israel. (120-100 B.C.E.) Hebrew political activist. LEO.

Jahan, Shah. (1592-1666) Indian ruler. CRO4.

James I. (1566-1625) English king. DAV.

James the Elder. Apostle, saint. MAYE.

James the Younger. Apostle, saint. MAYE.

James, Alice. (1848-1892) Author. KNI.

James, Daniel "Chappie," Jr. (1920-1978) Air Force general, Korean War, Vietnam War, World War II. ALTMS; BECKN; HASK2; JONS2; TUR2.

James, Edgerrin. (1978-) Football player. BUCK; DEI.

James, Frank. (1843-1915) Outlaw. SAV.

James, Henry. (1843-1916) Author. FAB2.

James, Jesse. (1847-1882) Outlaw. GLA; KRAL; SAV; THOM2; WAL.

James, Naomi. (1949-) New Zealander adventurer, sailor. DUN; MCLO7.

James, Ryan. (1975-) AIDS activist. BRIL.

James-Rodman, Charmayne. (1970-) Rodeo rider. ALTE2.

Jamison, Judith. (1944-) Choreographer, dancer. GREA.

Janensch, Werner. (1878-1969) German paleontologist. CHRISP.

Janowitz,Tama. (1957-) Author. SMIL.

Jans, Megan C. (1952-) Gulf War Army lieutenant colonel, helicopter pilot. SHEA.

Jarrett, Keith. (1945-) Jazz musician. GOU4.

Jason. Greek adventurer. ALTE.

Jasper, John. (1812-1901) Slave, spiritual leader. AFR2.

Jathro, Karl. (1873-1933) German aviation pioneer. BERL2.

Jay, Allen. (1831-1910) Abolitionist, civil rights activist, spiritual leader. HOOS.

Jay, John. (1745-1829) American Revolutionary War patriot, attorney, diplomat, governor. MEI; SCHM.

Jean-Murat, Carolle. (1950-) Haitian educator, human rights activist, physician, public health worker. KIR.

Jefferson, Arthur Stanley. (Stan Laurel) (1890-1965) Comedian, born England. CRO4.

Jefferson, Martha Waylee Skelton. (1748-1782) First Lady. BARB; GOR; PAST.

Jefferson, Thomas. (1743-1826) American Revolutionary patriot, architect, cabinet member, congressman, Declaration of Independence signer, inventor, 3rd president of U.S. ADA; BARB; BAU; BLASS; CRO; CRO6; DAV2; DEN; FAB; FRA2; KRULL5; LEVE; MARZ; MEI; MORR; QUI; SCHM; USC; YEN.

Jeffreys, Sir Alec. (1950-) English forensic scientist, geneticist. FRID; YEA.

Jemison, Mae C. (1956-) Astronaut, educator, physician. AFR2; ALTE; BOL; BRIGG2; BUCH; COX2; DID; GREA; HAN2; HUD; HUNTE2; JONS; LINL3; MCK2; MED; POT; REE; ROBE; SULO2; WYB.

Jemison, Mary. (1742-1833) American Revolutionary War patriot, Indian captive. ZEI4.

Jenner, Edward. (1749-1823) English medical researcher, physician. CURT; MUL; TIN.

Jennings, Thomas L. (1791-1859) Entrepreneur tailoring/dry cleaning. HASK.

Jeremiah. (650-585 B.C.E.) Hebrew scholar, spiritual leader. JACW2.

Jernigan, Tamara. (1955-) Astronomer, physicist. BRIGG2.

Jerome. (342-420) Saint. ARM.

Jesus Christ. Founder of Christianity. CRO5; GOLDM; JACW2; WILKP2; YEN.

Jeter, Derek. (1974-) Baseball player. BUCK4; SCHWAR; SCHWAR2.

Jex-Blake, Sophia. (1840-1912) English educator, physician. ROL; STI.

Jhirad, Jerusha. (1891-1948) Indian physician. KIR.

Jie, Ling. (1982-) Chinese olympic gymnast. RUT3.

Jimenez y Muro, Dolores. (1848-1925) Mexican revolutionary. COOL.

Jinnah, Mohammad Ali. (1876-1948) Indian governor general of Pakistan. WAKI.

Joan of Arc. (1412-1431) French military leader, saint. ARM; BRIL; CLA; COOL; CRO3; CRO5; DUN; GOLDM; HAZ2; HER; HOOB2; KRAL; KRULL; LEO3; ROL; WEL.

Jobs, Steve. (1955-) Entrepreneur computers,

Internet pioneer. AAS5; AAS12; CRO; FREN; MAYB; NOR; YEN.

Joel, Lawrence. (1928-1984) Vietnam War soldier, Medal of Honor recipient. REE2.

JoeSam. (1939-) Painter, sculptor. HON.

Johanan ben Zakkai. (15-70) Hebrew spiritual leader. PASA.

John. (1167-1216) English king. WILKP4.

John III Sobieski. (1624-1696) Polish military commander, king. WILKP.

John XXIII. (Angelo Roncalli) (1881-1963) Italian author, pope. Presidential Medal of Freedom recipient. CRO5; GOLDM.

John of Leiden. *See* Beukels, Jan.

John Paul II. (Karol Wojtyla) (1920-) Polish pope. CRO5.

John Stands in Timber. (1884-1967) Cheyenne Indian historian. WE2.

John the Baptist. Saint. ARM.

John the Evangelist. Apostle, saint. MAYE.

Johnetta. (1927-1983) Jazz singer. MON.

Johnny Rotten. *See* Lydon, John Joseph.

Johns, Barbara. (1935-1991) Civil rights activist. ROC.

Johnson, Amy. (1903-1941) English aviator, World War II pilot. DUN; WILLI.

Johnson, Andrew. (1808-1875) 17th president of U.S., vice-president. ADA; BARB; BAU; BLASS; CRO6; DAV2; KRULL5; LINE; MORR.

Johnson, Anthony. (c. 1678) Civil rights activist, slave. HASK4.

Johnson, Bill. (c. 1870) Jazz musician. GOU2.

Johnson, Claudia "Lady Bird" Alta. (1912-) First Lady. Presidential Medal of Freedom recipient. ALTE2; ANT; BARB; GOR; PAST.

Johnson, Earvin "Magic" (1959-) Basketball player. DEE; GON; JACT; KNA11; RAPK2; RED6; SAV5; TOR4.

Johnson, Eliza McCardle. (1810-1876) First Lady. BARB; GOR; PAST.

Johnson, Francis "Hall." (1883?-1970) Composer, conductor. HASK5; TAT.

Johnson, George. (1948-) Basketball player. YOUNG.

Johnson, Halle Tanner Dillon. (1864-1901) Physician. AFR2.

Johnson, Hazel W. (1927-) Army nurse corps chief, brigadier general, educator. HASK2.

Johnson, Henry. (1897-1929) World War I military hero. ALTMS; HASK2; REE2.

Johnson, Jack. (1878-1946) Boxer. BECKN; BOOK2; KNA7.

Johnson, James P. (1891-1976) Composer, jazz musician. HARD.

Johnson, James Weldon. (1871-1938) Attorney, author, civil rights activist, diplomat, educator, journalist, songwriter. AFR; BECKM; BECKN; CIV; HARD; OFT.

Johnson, Jimmy. (1943-) Football coach. SAV11.

Johnson, John H. (1918-) Publisher magazines. Presidential Medal of Freedom recipient. AFR2; BECKN; GREEC; HASK; PIL; RED.

Johnson, Katherine (1918-) Aerospace engineer, space scientist. AFR2.

Johnson, Keyshawn. (1972-) Football player. DEI.

Johnson, Kory. (1979-) Environmental activist. HOOS.

Johnson, Larry. (1969-) Basketball player. BJA; SAV6.

Johnson, Lonnie. (1889-1970) Jazz musician. GOU3.

Johnson, Lonnie. (1949-) Inventor. AMR; JEF.

Johnson, Lyndon Baines. (1908-1973) Congressman, 36th president of U.S., senator, vice-president, World War II Navy. Presidential Medal of Freedom recipient. ADA; BARB; BAU; BLASS; CRO; CRO6; DAV2; KRULL5; LINE; MORR.

Johnson, Michael. (1967-) Olympic track and field athlete. HUNTE; KNA3.

Johnson, Mordecai. (1890-1976) Educator, spiritual leader. BECKN; COX2.

Johnson, Noble. (1881-1978) Actor, entrepreneur film studio, filmmaker. AFR.

Johnson, Osa Leighty. (1894-1953) Explorer, filmmaker. POLK.

Johnson, Rafer. (1935-) Olympic track and field athlete. HUNTE.

Johnson, Randy. (1963-) Baseball player. BUCK2; SCHWAR.

Johnson, Robert. (1911-1938) Jazz singer. GOU3; LES.

Johnson, Samuel. (1709-1784) English journalist, lexicographer. CRO4.

Johnson, Sargent Claude. (1887-1967) Sculptor. HARD.

Johnson, Walter. (1887-1946) Baseball player. SULG3; SULG5; SULM.

Johnson, William. (1714-1774) English colonist, superintendent of Indian Affairs. CRO2.

Johnson, William Henry. (1901-1970) Painter. HAC4; HARD; KRULL2.

Johnson, William Julius "Judy." (1900-1989) Baseball player. WIN2.

Johnston, Frances Benjamin. (1864-1952) Photographer. HOR.

Johnston, Harriet Lane. *See* Lane, Harriet.

Johnston, Joe. (1807-1891) Civil War general. GREEC2.

Joliet, Louis. (1645-1700) Canadian adventurer, explorer. ALTE; CRO2; PRE.

Joliot-Curie, Irène. (1897-1956) French chemist, physicist. Nobel Prize winner. STI2; TIN; WEL.

Jolson, Al. (1886-1950) Showman, singer. BRO.

Jones, Albert Jose. (unknown) Marine biologist, explorer, Korean War soldier. REE.

Jones, Amanda Theodosia. (1835-1914) Inventor. ALTML; BLASH3.

Jones, Andruw. (1977-) Baseball player. SCHWAR; SCHWAR2; STEWM.

Jones, Bobby. (1902-1971) Golfer. ITA5; JACT.

Jones, Casey. (1863-1900) Railroad man, folk hero. KRAL.

Jones, Charles Martin "Chuck." (1912-2002) Cartoonist. STEFF.

Jones, Charles Wesley. (1900-1986) Missionary, broadcast journalist. JACKD3.

Jones, Chipper. (1972-) Baseball player. SCHWAR.

Jones, David "Deacon." (1938-) Football player. SAV7.

Jones, Edward. (1856-?) Entrepreneur financier. AAS12.

Jones, Elvin. (1927-) Jazz musician. GOU6.

Jones, Frederick McKinley. (1892-1961) Inventor. AAS4; ALTMS; AMR; BECKN; HAY2; MCK; SULO.

Jones, Jim. (1931-1978) Cult leader. KELLA; STRE.

Jones, John Paul. (1747-1792) American Revolutionary War military, Navy leader, born Scotland. JAN; SAW.

Jones, Jonathan "Papa Jo." (1911-1985) Jazz musician. GOU6.

Jones, Marion. (1975-) Basketball player, olympic track and field athlete. BAIL; HASD; RUT6; SAV14.

Jones, Mary "Mother." (1830-1930) Labor leader, workers' rights activist, born Ireland. COOL; HARN; HER; JAN; ROL; STRE5; THIR.

Jones, Quincy. (1933-) Entrepreneur music companies, jazz musician. HASK.

Jones, Robert. (1951-) Food science chemist. STJ.

Jones, Sam. (1924-1981) Jazz musician. GOU2.

Jong, Erica. (1942-) Author, poet. PER.

Joplin, Janis. (1943-1970) Rock musician, singer. WOO3.

Joplin, Scott. (1868-1917) Composer, musician. Pulitzer Prize winner. AFR; ALTMS; BECKN; BRED3; KRULL4; NIN; SHIP; TAT.

Joques, Isaac. (1607-1646) French colonist in Canada. CRO2.

Jordan, Barbara. (1936-1996) Attorney, civil rights activist, congresswoman. Presidential Medal of Freedom recipient. ALTE2; CUS2; FEM; FIR; GREA; GUL; HARN; HER; JONV; MORI2; PLO; PRI3.

Jordan, George. (1847-1904) Indian Wars soldier. ALTMS

Jordan, Irving King. (1943-) Educator. KEND.

Jordan, Lynda. (unknown) Chemist, medical researcher. KAH2.

Jordan, Michael. (1963-) Basketball player. BJA; BJA3; DEE; JACT; JAN; RAPK2; RED6; SAV4; TOR4.

Jordan, Vernon E., Jr. (1935-) Attorney, civil rights activist, National Urban League organizer. RED2.

Joseph. Saint. ARM.

Joseph. (1840-1904) Nez Percé chief, Native American rights activist. AVE; CRO3; JACW; MON2.

Joubert, Beverly. (1957-) Wildlife photographer. TALAD.

Joubert, Dereck. (1956-) Wildlife photographer. TALAD.

Jouhaux, Léon. (1879-1954) French labor leader, International Labor Organization cofounder, political activist. Nobel Peace Prize winner. KEEN2.

Joule, James Prescott. (1818-1889) English physicist. TIN.

Joyce, James. (1882-1941) Irish author, playwright. PER.

Joyce, William. (1957-) Children's author, illustrator. TALAR2.

Joyner, Florence Griffith. (1959-1998) Olympic track and field athlete. DIT; GREA; HASD; HUNTE; JACT; LINL; MOL.

Joyner-Kersee, Jackie. (1962-) Olympic track and field athlete. AAS20; BOL; DEN; DIT; HASD; HEA; JACT; KEND; RED6; SAV10.

Joyner, Marjorie Stewart. (1896-1994) Entrepreneur cosmetics. AMR; SULO2.

Juarez, Benito. (1806-1872) Mexican president. PAP.

Judas. Apostle. MAYE.

Jude Thaddeus. Apostle, saint. MAYE.

Judith. Biblical character. ARM2; TAI.

Judith of Ethiopia. (10th century) Warrior queen. TAI.

Judson, Adoniram. (1788-1850) Missionary. JACKD.

Judson, Ann Hassletine. (unknown) Missionary. JACKD.

Julia, Raul. (1940-1994) Actor, born Puerto Rico. MARV7.

Julian, Hubert Fauntelroy. (1897-?) Aviation pioneer, born Trinidad. HART.

Julian of Norwich. (1342-1416) English mystic, spiritual leader. CRO5; KNI.

Julian, Percy Lavon. (1899-1975) Chemist, medical researcher. AAS4; AFR2; ALTMS; BECKN; COX; HASK8; HAY3; JONL; MCK2; SULO; YOUNT2.

Julius II. (1443-1513) Italian pope. CRO4.

Jung, Carl. (1875-1961) Swiss psychiatrist. CRO4.

Just, Ernest Everett. (1883-1941) Biologist, educator. AFR2; HAY3; JONL; MCK2; PIO; POLKI; SULO; YOUNT2.

Justice, David. (1966-) Baseball player. SEHN.

Justinian I, the Great. (482-565) Turkish emperor. CRO4.

Juvenal. (Decimus Junius Juvenalis) (55?-127) Roman author. BAKR3.

K

Kaat, Jim. (1938-) Baseball player. SULG2.

Kabir. (1440-1518) Indian Muslim philosopher, poet. CRO5.

Kahanamoku, Duke. (1890-1968) Hawaiian surfer, Olympic swimmer. KRULL3.

Kahlo, Frida. (1907-1954) Mexican painter. CRO4; HAZ2; HER; HUNTE3; KEND; KRULL2; KRY; SILL2; TWEPR; WEL.

Kalman, Maira. (1949-) Children's author, illustrator. TALAR2.

Ka'lulani. (1875-1899) Hawaiian princess. BREW.

Kaminska, Ida. (1899-1980) Actor, born Russia. SEG.

Kandel, Lenore. (1932-) Poet. KNI.

Kandinsky, Wassily. (1866-1944) Russian painter. CUM; KRY; TWEPR.

Kang, Younghill. (1903-1973) Author, educator, born Korea. SIN.

Kaplan, Mordecai Menahem. (1881-1983) Educator, spiritual leader, founded Reconstructionist movement in Judaism, born Lithuania. PASA.

Kapuscinski, Anne. (unknown) Agricultural scientist, educator, born France. KAH.

Karan, Donna. (1948-) Fashion designer. KENJ.

Karas, G. Brian. (1957-) Children's author, illustrator. TALAR3.

Kariya, Paul. (1974-) Canadian hockey player. BREH.

Karpis, Alvin. (1908-1979) Canadian gangster. BLACG.

Kasebier, Gertrude. (1852-1934) Photographer. HOR.

Kassebaum, Nancy Landon. (1932-) Senator. FIR; GUL; MORI2; THRO.

Kato, Sawao. (1946-) Japanese olympic gymnast. JACT.

Katz, Ralph. (1932-) German Jewish Holocaust survivor. LAND4.

Katznelson, Yitzhak. (1886-1944) Polish Jewish author, Holocaust victim, poet. MAN; PASA.

Kauffmann, Angelica. (1741-1807) Italian artist. EIG.

Kean, Edmund. (1787-1833) English actor. WEI2.

Kearse, Jevon. (1976-) Football player. DEI.

Keaton, Buster. (1895-1966) Comedian. LEVE.

Keats, John. (1795-1821) English poet. ROM.

Keckley, Elizabeth. (1818-1907) Abolitionist, entrepreneur dressmaking, slave. HASK.

Kefauver, Estes. (1903-1963) Crime fighter, senator. ITA3.

Keillor, Garrison. (1942-) Author, radio personality, storyteller. PER.

Kekulé, Friedrich August. (1829-1896) German chemist. TIN.

Kellar, Harry. (1849-1922) Magician. WOO2.

Keller, Helen. (1880-1968) Author, disability rights activist. Presidential Medal of Freedom recipient. BRIL; CRO4; CUS2; DEN; DUN; HAC5; HARN; HER; KEND; LEVE; MARZ; MCD; ROL; WEL.

Kelley, Florence. (1859-1932) Attorney, human rights activist, social worker. THIR.

Kellogg, Frank Billings. (1856-1937) Ambassador, attorney, cabinet member, senator. Nobel Peace Prize winner. KEEN2.

Kellogg, Steven. (1941-) Children's author, illustrator. TALAR.

Kellogg, Will Keith. (1860-1951) Entrepreneur cereals, philanthropist. KRAMB; MAYB; TRAU.

Kelly, Emmett. (1898-1979) Clown. KRAL.

Kelly, Grace. (1929-1982) Actor, wife of Prince Rainier. CRO4; KRAL.

Kelly, Jim. (1960-) Football player. SULG8.

Kelly, Ned. (1855-1880) Australian outlaw. THOM2.

Kelly, Patrick. (1954-1990) Fashion designer. AFR; RED.

Kelly, Paul. See Vaccarelli, Paulo Antonio.

Kelly, Sharon Pratt. (1944-) Attorney, mayor. AFR2; DUD.

Kelly, Wynton. (1931-1971) Jazz musician, born Jamaica. GOU4.

Kemp, Shawn. (1969-) Basketball player. BJA; BJA3.

Kempe, Margery. (1373-1440) English author. KNI.

Kendall, Jason. (1974-) Baseball player. SCHWAR; SCHWAR2.

Kennedy, Cortez. (1968-) Football player. SAV7.

Kennedy, Edward Moore "Ted." (1932-) Senator. USC3.

Kennedy, Florence. (1916-2000) Attorney, women's rights activist. THIR.

Kennedy, Jacqueline Lee Bouvier. See Onassis, Jacqueline Lee Bouvier Kennedy.

Kennedy, John Fitzgerald. (1917-1963) 35th president of U.S., senator, World War II Navy commander. Presidential Medal of Freedom recipient. ADA; BARB; BAU; BLASS; CRO; CRO4; CRO6; DAV2; JAN; JONR; KRULL5; MORR; STG; USC3; YEN.

Kennedy, John Fitzgerald, Jr. (1960-1998) Attorney, publisher magazine. USC3.

Kennedy, Joseph Patrick. (1888-1969) Diplomat, financier. CRO4; USC3.

Kennedy, Robert Francis. (1925-1968) Attorney, presidential candidate, senator. USC3.

Kennedy, Rose Fitzgerald. (1890-1995) Matriarch Kennedy family. CRO4.

Kenner, Beatrice. (1912-) Inventor. BLASH5; JEF; SULO2.

Kenny, Elizabeth. (1880-1952) Australian medical researcher, World War I nurse. HUNTE2; ROL; STI.

Kenyatta, Jomo. (1894-1978) African political leader, Kenyan president, prime minister. MAYB2.

Kenyatta, Julius K. (1922-) Tanzanian prime minister. RAS.

Kenyon, Kathleen. (1906-1978) English archaeologist. FAG; GREENBL; SCHEL.

Kepler, Johannes. (1571-1630) German astronomer. POD; TIN; WILLS.

Kerouac, Jack. (1922-1969) Author. CRO4; VERD.

Kerr, Barbara. (unknown) Author, educator, inventor. SIR.

Kerrigan, Nancy. (1969-) Olympic figure skater. KRAMS4; POY; RUT2.

Kessel, Barney. (1923-) Jazz musician. GOU3.

Keynes, John Maynard. (1883-1946) English economist. BUS.

Khadijah. (Khadika bint Khuwaylid) (555-620) Arab prophet Muhammad's wife. LEO2.

Khan, Genghis. See Genghis Khan.

Khan, Kublai. See Kublai Khan.

Khan, Noor Inayat. (1914-1944) Indian Holocaust resistance worker, victim. GRAN; SCHM4.

Khan, Yasmin Aga. (1949-) Princess, born
    Switzerland. LEVI.
Khayyam, Omar. (1048-1131) Persian as-
    tronomer, mathematician, poet. PER.
Khomeini, Ayatollah Ruholla. (1900-1989)
    Iranian Muslim political activist, spiritual
    leader. CRO5; JACW2; MAYB2.
Khorana, Har Gobind. (1922-) Chemist, ge-
    neticist, born India. Nobel Prize winner.
    AAS13; TIN. YOUNT.
Khorkina, Svetlana. (1979-) Russian olympic
    gymnast. RUT3.
Khreiss, Betty Jane. (unknown) Forensic sci-
    entist. KAH7.
Khrushchev, Nikita. (1894-1971) Russian
    president. PAP.
Khufu. (fl. 2589-2566 B.C.) Egyptian king.
    BAKR.
Khwarizmi, Abu Jafar Muhammad Ibn Musa-
    al (780-850) Arab astronomer, mathemati-
    cian. AND.
Kidd, Jason. (1973-) Basketball player. NEL;
    PAU; SAV5.
Kidd, William "Captain." (1645-1701) Scot-
    tish pirate. KRAL; YOUNT5.
Kidder, Alfred Vincent. (1885-1963) Archae-
    ologist. FAG.
Kieler, Jorgen. (1920-) Danish Holocaust
    rescuer. LYM.
Kilby, Jack St. Clair. (1923-) Computer scien-
    tist, electrical engineer. Nobel Prize winner.
    HAV; JEF; LOM2; NOR.
Kilgallen, Dorothy M. (1913-1965) Journal-
    ist, television personality. PRI.
Killebrew, Harmon. (1936-) Baseball player.
    DEA2; SULG8.
Killigrew, Lady Elizabeth. (1530-1570)
    English pirate. SHAR.
Killy, Jean-Claude. (1943-) French olympic
    skier. SULG3; USC4.
Kim, Willyce. (1946-) Author, poet. CHI.
Kiner, Ralph. (1922-) Baseball player, sports-
    caster. SULG8.
King, B. B. (1925-) Jazz musician, singer.
    LES; TAT.
King, Billie Jean. (1943-) Tennis player.
    HARN; HARR; HASD; HER; JAN; LIT;
    SCHWAB; SULG3.
King, Charles Edward. (1879-1950) Band-
    leader, composer, publisher, born Hawaii.
    SIN.

King, Coretta Scott. (1927?-) Author, civil
    rights activist, singer. CRO4; FEM; GREA;
    MED; RED2.
King, Dick. (1845-?) Civil War soldier as
    teenager. HOOS.
King, Larry. (1933-) Television personality.
    BRO.
King, Martin Luther, Jr. (1929-1968) Civil
    rights activist, orator. Nobel Peace Prize
    winner. ALTMS; ARC2; BECKN; CIV;
    CRO; CRO4; CRO5; DEN; DUB;
    GOLDM; HARM; HAZ; JACW; JACW2;
    JAN; KEEN2; LEVE; MARZ; MAYB;
    MED; RED2; SHAW; TAYK2; THOM;
    TUR2; VERN; WILKP2; YEN.
King, Mary-Claire. (1946-) Geneticist.
    LINL3; YOUNT4.
King, Reatha Clark. (1938-) Chemist, Na-
    tional Bureau of Standards governmental
    agency employee. SULO2.
King, Stephen. (1947-) Author. BOY; MAD;
    PER.
Kingman, Dong. (1911-2000) Painter. SIN.
Kingsley, Mary. (1862-1900) English adven-
    turer, author, explorer. DUN; HAC; LANG;
    LOM; MCLE; MCLO; POLK; ROL;
    STEFO2; WAT; ZAU.
Kingston, Maxine Hong. (1940-) Author,
    educator. CHI; ISH; MORE; SIN; SMIL.
Kinich Ahau. Mayan god of the Sun. FIS2.
Kino, Eusebio. (1645-1711) Austrian ex-
    plorer, missionary, spiritual leader. DOH2.
Kintpuash (Captain Jack). (1837-1873) Mo-
    dac Indian chief. MON2.
Kipling, Rudyard. (1865-1936) English au-
    thor, born India. Nobel Prize winner. PER.
Kirby, John. (1908-1952) Jazz musician.
    GOU2.
Kirkpatrick, Helen. (1909-1997) Journalist,
    World War II correspondent. COLM.
Kirkpatrick, Jeane. (1926-) Ambassador.
    Presidential Medal of Freedom recipient.
    GUL
Kisor, Henry. (1940-) Journalist. KEND.
Kissinger, Henry. (1923-) Cabinet member,
    born Germany. Nobel Peace Prize winner.
    BRO; KEEN2; RIC.
Kivengere, Festo. (1919-1988) Ugandan hu-
    man rights activist, spiritual leader.
    JACKD2
Klarsfeld, Beate. (1939-) German Nazi

hunter. SCHM4.

Klarsfeld, Serge. (1935-) Hungarian Nazi hunter, scholar. SCHM4.

Klee, Paul. (1879-1940) Swiss painter. CUM; KRY; TWEPR.

Klein, Chuck. (1904-1958) Baseball player. TOR.

Klein, Norma. (1938-1989) Young adult author. SMIL.

Klimt, Gustav. (1862-1918) Austrian painter. CUM.

Knight, Margaret. (1838-1914) Inventor. BLASH2; CURR2; ROE; THI.

Knight, Nancy Lopez. *See* Lopez, Nancy.

Knight, Phil. (1938-) Entrepreneur athletic shoes. MAYB.

Knopfler, Clara. (unknown) Transylvanian Holocaust survivor. LAND4.

Koch, Ilse. (1906-1967) German Nazi war criminal. SCHM4.

Koch, Karl. (1897-1945) German Nazi war criminal. SCHM4.

Koch, Robert. (1843-1910) German bacteriologist. Nobel Prize winner. CURT.

Kohane, Akiva. (1929-) Polish Jewish Holocaust survivor. GREENF.

Kohut, Rebekah Bettelheim. (1864-1951) Human rights activist. TAI.

Koken. (718-770) Japanese empress, Buddhist nun. LEO2.

Kolbe, Fritz. (1903-1961) German World War II spy. MART.

Kollontai, Alexandra. (1872-1952) Russian ambassador, human rights activist, political activist, revolutionary, women's rights activist. DUN; GUL; HER.

Kollwitz, Kaethe. (1867-1945) German painter, sculptor. BLACA; KRULL2.

Kolzig, Olaf. (1970-) Olympic hockey player, born Germany. BREH.

Komyo. (701-760) Japanese empress, Buddhist nun. LEO2.

Koningsburg, Elaine "E. L." (1930-) Children's author. AUT.

Koontz, Dean. (1945-) Author. MAD.

Koontz, Elizabeth Duncan. (1919-1989) Civil rights activist, educator, National Education Association president. PLO.

Korbut, Olga. (1955-) Russian Olympic gymnast. GREES; HASD; JEN.

Korczak, Janusz. (1878-1942) Polish children's author, Holocaust rescuer and victim, human rights activist, physician. SCHM4; SHAW.

Koresh, David. (1959-1993) Cult leader. KELLA; STRE.

Korolev, Sergei. (1906-1966) Russian engineer, space scientist. RIC3.

Kosciuszko, Thaddeus. (1746-1817) Polish American Revolutionary War military leader. SCHM2.

Kosinski, Jerzy. (1933-1991) Author, Holocaust survivor, born Poland. MAN.

Kosmodemianskaya, Zoya. (1925-1943) Polish Holocaust resistance worker, victim. GRAN.

Kouchner, Bernard. (1939-) French human rights activist, founder Doctors Without Walls, physician. SPA.

Koufax, Sandy. (1935-) Baseball player. BRO; JACT; SLO; SULG5; SULM; YOUNG2.

Kournikova, Anna. (1981-) Russian tennis player. MILE; RUT5.

Kovalevskaia, Sofia. (1850-1891) Russian mathematician. HENH.

Kovner, Abba. (1918-1987) Russian Jewish Holocaust resistance worker, survivor, poet. MAN.

Kovner, Vitka Kempner. (1920-) Polish Jewish Holocaust resistance worker. TAI.

Kowalyk, Jonka. (unknown) Ukrainian Holocaust rescuer. PET.

Kraatz, Victor. (1971-) Canadian olympic figure skater. MILT.

Krecek, Joseph. (unknown) Environmentalist. GRAH.

Kroc, Ray. (1902-1984) Entrepreneur restaurants. AAS6; CRO; KRAMB; MAC; MAYB.

Kroeber, Alfred. (1875-1960) Anthropologist. WEI.

Krone, Julie. (1963-) Jockey. BRY; KUH; LINL; LIT; SAV14.

Kruger, Paul. (1825-1904) South African general, statesman. WILKP.

Krupa, Gene. (1900-1973) Jazz musician. GOU6.

Krupp, Alfred. (1907-1967) German entrepreneur arms manufacturing, Nazi war criminal. SCHM4.

Kublai Khan. (1215-1294) Chinese Mongol

emperor. CRO3; CRO4; MEL; WAT.

Kübler-Ross, Elisabeth. (1926-2004) Author, psychiatrist, born Switzerland. HUNTE2; STI.

Kuehn, Ruth. (unknown) German World War II spy. SULG4.

Kuhn, Maggie. (1905-1995) Human rights activist, reformer. LINL2.

Kukai. (774-835) Japanese spiritual leader, founder of Shingon sect of Buddhism. CRO5.

Kukulcán. Mayan god of the wind. FIS2.

Kundla, John. (1916-) Basketball coach. KNA10.

Kunin, Madeleine. (1933-) Governor, born Switzerland. GUL.

Kuntzler, William. (1919-1999) Attorney, civil rights activist. CALA.

Kuramato, June. (1948-) Jazz musician, born Japan. MORE; SIN.

Kuskin, Karla. (1933-) Children's author, illustrator. MARC3.

Kuznetsova, Irina Mihailovna. (1961-) Russian arctic explorer. POLK.

Kuznetsova, Valentina Mihailovna. (1937-) Russian arctic explorer. POLK.

Kwan, Michelle. (1980-) Olympic figure skater. KRAMS4; MILT; POY; RUT2.

Kwolek, Stephanie. (1923-) Chemist, inventor. BLASH5; CAM; JEF; THI; VAR.

Kyoko, Ina. (1972-) Olympic figure skater, born Japan. MILT.

L

La Faro, Scott. (1940-1969) Jazz musician. GOU2.

La Flesche, Francis. (1857-1932) Ponca and Omaha Indian anthropologist, author. AVE.

La Follette, Robert. (1855-1925) Congressman, governor, presidential candidate, senator. AAS2; FAB.

La Fontaine, Henri. (1854-1943) Belgian attorney, educator, politicial activist. Nobel Peace Prize winner. KEEN2.

La Salle, René Robert Cavalier. (1643-1687) French explorer. ALTE; BAKS; CRO2; DOH4; DOH5; LOM; POD; PRE.

La Tour, Charles Turquis de Sainte-Étienne de. (1593-1666) French colonist, military

leader. CRO2.

Labosky, Bonnie. (unknown) Computer scientist, mathematician. KAH3.

Laclède Liguest, Pierre de. (1729-1778) French explorer. DOH4.

Laettner, Christian. (1969-) Olympic basketball player. KNA11.

Lafayette, Marie Joseph Paul Yves Roch Gilbert du Motier, Marquis de. (1757-1834) French American Revolutionary War military leader. CRO4; SCHM2.

Lafitte, Jean. (1781-1826) Pirate. BLACG4; KRAL.

Lafleur, Guy. (1951-) Canadian hockey player. KNA8.

Lai Cho San. (1922-1939) Chinese pirate. SHAR.

Laitman, Helen Kornitzer. (unknown) Czech Holocaust survivor. LAND4.

Lajoie, Nap. (1874-1959) Baseball player. SULG2.

Lamarck, Jean Baptiste. (1744-1829) French author, botanist, environmentalist. KEEN.

Lamas, Carlos Saavedra. (1878-1959) Argentine attorney, educator, peace activist, statesman. Nobel Peace Prize winner. KEEN2.

Lamb, William Frederick. (1883-1952) Architect. AAS11.

Lambeau, Earl Louis "Curly." (1898-1965) Football coach. SAV11.

Lamborghi, Feruccio. (1916-1993) Italian automaker. ITA6.

Lancelot, Sir. (6th century) English knight, warrior, folk hero. KRAL.

Land, Edwin. (1909-1991) Inventor, physicist. Presidential Medal of Freedom recipient. BRO; HAV.

Landers, Ann. See Lederer, Esther Pauline.

Landry, Tom. (1924-2000) Football coach. SAV11.

Landsteiner, Karl. (1868-1943) Forensic scientist, pathologist, physician, physiologist, born Austria. Nobel Prize winner. FRID.

Lane, Harriet. (1830-1903) First Lady (niece of James Buchanan). BARB; GOR; PAST.

Lanennec, René T.H. (1781-1826) French medical researcher, physician. CURT; MUL2.

Laney, Lucy Craft. (1854-1933) Educator, slave. GREA.

Lang, Eddie. (1902-1933) Jazz musician. GOU3.

Lang, Naomi. (1978-) Karuk Indian olympic figure skater. MILT.

Lange, Christian. (1869-1938) Norwegian author, educator, peace activist. Nobel Peace Prize winner. KEEN2.

Lange, Dorothea. (1895-1965) Photographer. DAN; GAI; HOR; JACKN; KEND; LEVE; SILL.

Langley, Samuel Pierpont. (1834-1906) Astronomer, aviation pioneer, physicist. BERL; BERL2; WILLI.

Langston, Dicey. (1766-1837) American Revolutionary War patriot, spy. HOOS.

Lanier, Bob. (1948-) Basketball player. KNA5.

Lansing, Sherry. (1944-) Filmmaker. LUT.

Lansky, Meyer. (1902-1983) Gangster, born Russia. WOO.

Lao-Tzu. (604-531 B.C.) Chinese philosopher, spiritual leader, founder Taoism. CRO5; GOLDM; YEN.

Lappe, Frances Moore. (1944-) Nutritionist. STA.

Larguent, Steve. (1954-) Football player. ITA4; THOR.

Larkin, Barry. (1964-) Baseball player. DEA3; SCHWAR.

Laroche, Raymonde de. (1886-1919) French aviation pioneer.WILLI.

Lars, Byron. (1965-) Fashion designer. AFR2.

Larsen, Don. (1929-) Baseball player. YOUNG2.

Larsen, Nella. (1891-1964) Author. COOL; HARD.

Las Casas, Bartolomé de. (1474-1566) Spanish soldier, spiritual leader. CRO5; POD.

Lasorda, Tommy. (1927-) Baseball manager. PIE.

Latham, Hubert. (1883-1912) French aviation pioneer. WILLI.

Lathrop, Julia. (1858-1932) Children's rights activist, U.S. Children's Bureau Director, social reformer, social worker. MORI.

Latifah, Queen. See Owens, Dana Elaine.

Latimer, Lewis Howard. (1848-1928) Inventor. AAS4; ALTMS; BECKN; HASK8; HAY2; MCK; PIO; SULO.

Lattimore, Deborah Nourse. (1949-) Children's author, illustrator. TALAR2.

Latynina, Larissa. (1934-) Russian olympic gymnast. GREES; HASD; JACT.

Laumann, Silken. (1965-) Canadian olympic rower. HASD.

Laurel, Stan. See Jefferson, Arthur Stanley.

Laver, Rod. (1938-) Australian tennis player. CHRIST; JACT.

Laveran, Charles Louis Alphonse. (1845-1932) French bacteriologist, medical researcher. Nobel Prize winner. CURT.

Lavoisier, Antoine Laurent. (1743-1794) French chemist. TIN.

Lavoisier, Marie. (1758-1836) French chemist. ROL.

Lawless, Theodore K. (1892-1971) Philanthropist, physician. MCK2.

Lawrence, D. H. (1885-1930) English author. CRO4; PER; TWEPR.

Lawrence, Ernest Orlando. (1901-1958) Inventor, physicist. Nobel Prize winner. FOX; HAV; LOM2.

Lawrence, Jacob. (1917-2000) Painter. AFR; MED.

Lawrence, Richard. (1800-1861) Assassin, tried to kill President Andrew Jackson. JONR; STG; SULG9.

Lawrence, Thomas Edward. (Lawrence of Arabia) (1888-1935) English archaeologist, World War I intelligence officer. KRAL; MART.

Lawson, Louisa. (1848-1920) Poet, suffragist. HER.

Layard, Austen Henry. (1817-1894) English adventurer, archaeologist. FAG; SCHEL; WEI.

Layne, Bobby. (1926-1986) Football player. SULG7.

Lazarus, Emma. (1849-1887) Poet. BRO; ROL; TAI; WEL.

Lazebnik, Faye. (unknown) Polish Jewish Holocaust resistance worker. FREM.

Le-Duc-Tho. (1911-1990) Vietnamese political leader, Vietnam War peace activist Nobel Peace Prize winner. KEEN2.

Le Guin, Ursula K. (1929-) Young adult author. DAT.

Le Sueur, Meridel. (1900-1996) Children's author, novelist, journalist, revolutionary. KNI.

Leach, Molly. (1960-) Illustrator. MARC2.

Lead, Jane. (1624-1704) English mystic. KNI.

Leah. Biblical character. ARM2; TAI.

Leakey, Louis S. B. (1903-1972) English anthropologist, archaeologist, paleontologist. FAG; HAV; WEI.

Leakey, Mary. (1913-1996) English anthropologist, archaeologist. CRO4; FAG; HAC8; HER; LINL3; POLK; STI2; THI2; WEI; WEL.

Leakey, Richard. (1944-) Kenyan archaeologist, paleontologist. CRO4; WEI.

Lear, Norman. (1922-) Filmmaker. LEVE.

Lear, William. (1902-1978) Aeronautical engineer, entrepreneur aircraft. JEF.

Leavitt, Henrietta Swan. (1868-1921) Astronomer. STI2; TIN.

Lecavalier, Vincent. (1980-) Canadian hockey player. BREH.

Ledbetter, Huddy "Leadbelly." (1885-1949) Jazz musician, singer, songwriter. GOU3; MON.

Lederer, Esther Pauline "Eppie." (Ann Landers) (1918-2002) Journalist. PRI; WHI.

Lee, Ann. (1736-1784) Spiritual leader, founder of Shaker community, born England. CRO5; GOLDM; HARN; KELLA; STRE6; ZEI4.

Lee, Bruce. (1940-1973) Actor, martial arts athlete. BOY; KRULL3; SIN.

Lee, Carlos. (1976-) Panamanian baseball player. STEWM2.

Lee, Francis Lightfoot. (1734-1797) American Revolutionary War patriot, congressman, Declaration of Independence signer. FRA2; QUI.

Lee, Jarena. (1783-1850) Spiritual leader. AFR2.

Lee, K. W. (1928-) Journalist, born Korea. SIN.

Lee, Li-Young. (1957-) Poet, born Indonesia. CHI.

Lee, Marie G. (1964-) Young adult author. CHI; ISH.

Lee, Mark C. (1952-) Air Force lieutenant, astronaut, mechanical engineer. BAIR.

Lee, Richard Henry. (1732-1794) American Revolutionary War patriot, congressman, Declaration of Independence signer, senator. FRA2; MEI; QUI.

Lee, Robert E. (1807-1870) Civil War general. CRO3; CRO4; DEN; GREEC2; JAN;

LEVE; REG; TRAC; WILKP.

Lee, Sammy. (1920-) Olympic diver, physician. GAN; SIN.

Lee, Shelton Jackson "Spike." (1957-) Filmmaker, screenwriter. HASK; HILA2; RED3.

Lee, Tsung Dao. (1926-) Physicist, born China. Nobel Prize winner. SIN; TIN; YOUNT.

Leeuwenhoek, Anton van. (1632-1728) Dutch biologist, medical researcher, physician. CURT; MUL2; POD; TIN.

Leibovitz, Annie. (1949-) Photographer. HOR; PRI.

Leibowitz, Nehama. (1905-1997) Israeli broadcast journalist, scholar. SEG; TAI.

Leidy, Joseph. (1823-1891) Paleontologist, physician. AAS.

Leigh, Samuel. (1785-1852) English missionary. JACKD4.

Leisdorff, William A. (1810-1848) Diplomat, entrepreneur steamboats. HASK.

Leisler, Jacob. (1640-1691) Colonist, born Germany. CRO2.

Leitch, Peter. (1944-) Canadian jazz musician. GOU3.

Leitner, Isabella Katz. (1924-) Author, Holocaust survivor, born Hungary. SCHM4.

LeMay, Curtis E. (1906-1990) Air Force pilot, aviator, World War II general. KNA; OLE2.

Lemieux, Mario. (1965-) Canadian hockey player. KNA8; KRAMS2.

Lemlich, Clara. *See* Shavelson, Clara Lemlich.

LeMond, Greg. (1961-) Bicyclist. JACT; JEN; KAM; OCO.

L'Enfant, Pierre Charles. (1754-1825) American Revolutionary War Army officer, architect, engineer, born France. SCHM2.

L'Engle, Madeline. (1918-) Children's and young adult author. DAT; YUN.

Lenin, Nikolai (Vladimir Ilich) (1870-1924) Russian political leader. CRO4; MAYB2; WILKP4; YEN.

Lennon, John. (1940-1980) English rock musician, singer. CRO4; VEN; WOO3.

Leo III, the Isaurian. (680-741) Syrian military leader. CRO3.

Leo X. (1475-1521) Italian pope. CRO4.

Leonard, Andy. (1968-) Power weightlifter,

born Vietnam. SIN.

Leonard, Charles "Sugar Ray." (1956-) Olympic boxer. BRIL; HUNTE.

Leonard, Walter Fenner "Buck." (1907-1997) Baseball player. WIN2.

Leonardo da Vinci. (1452-1519) Italian architect, engineer, painter, sculptor. BART; BLACA; CUM; CUS; GLU; HAZ; HOOB3; KRULL2; KRULL7; KRY; LOM2; MARZ; REN; YEN.

Leonidas I. (575-490 B.C.) Greek military leader, ruler. BAKR2.

Leonov, Alexei. (1934-) Russian cosmonaut. RIC4.

Leonowens, Anna. (1834-1915) Welsh author, educator. CRO4.

Leopold II. (1835-1909) Belgian king. WILKP2.

Leopold, Aldo. (1886-1948) Author, conservationist. BYR; FAB3; KEEN; LEU; LUC2; STA.

Lerner, Bianca. (1929-) Polish Jewish Holocaust survivor. LAND.

Leroux, Antoine. (1635-1708) Fur trapper, Indian scout, born France. SAV3.

Leslie, Lisa. (1972-) Olympic basketball player. BRIL3; JACK; PON; RUT; SAV13.

Leslie, Miriam "Frank" Florence Folline. (1836-1914) Editor magazine. PRI.

L'Esperance, Elsie Strong. (1878-1959) Pathologist, physician. STI.

Lester, Julius. (1939-) Children's and adult author. HILC2; MARC2.

Levertov, Denise. (1923-1997) Poet, born England. SMIL.

Levi, Primo. (1919-1987) Italian author, chemist, Holocaust survivor. MAN.

Levi-Montalcini, Rita. (1909-) Cell biologist, born Italy. Nobel Prize winner. DAS; LINL3; REY; SPA; STI; STI2; YOUNT6.

Levitt, William. (1907-1994) Entrepreneur real estate. AAS8; CRO.

Levy, Hans. (1928-) German Jewish Holocaust survivor. MARX.

Levy, Uriah P. (1797-1862) Naval officer, War of 1812. BRO.

Lew Chew. (1866-?) Gold miner, born China. HOOS.

Lewin, Betsy. (1937-) Children's author, illustrator. TALAR3.

Lewin, Ted. (1935-) Children's author, illus-trator. TALAR3.

Lewis, Carl. (1961-) Olympic track and field athlete. JACT; KNA3; RED6.

Lewis, Clive Staples "C. S." (1898-1963) Irish children's author. CRO5; MAS.

Lewis, Francis. (1713-1802) American Revolutionary War patriot, congressman, Declaration of Independence signer, entrepreneur clothing merchant. FRA2; QUI.

Lewis, Ida. (1842-1911) Lighthouse keeper. BRIL; DUN; FLE.

Lewis, John L. (1880-1969) Labor leader. Presidential Medal of Freedom recipient. CRO; STRE5.

Lewis, Loida Nicolas. (1942-) Attorney, author, entrepreneur foods conglomerate, born Philippines. RAG.

Lewis, Mary Edmonia. (1845-1890) Sculptor. AFR; GREA; HARD; KAT2; PLO; POT; TUR.

Lewis, Meriwether. (1774-1809) Explorer. ALTE; BAKS; CALV; CRO; CRO4; DEN; JAN; LANG; LOM2; POD; PRE; SCHEL2; WAT; YEN.

Lewis, Reginald. (1942-1993) Attorney, entrepreneur foods conglomerate. AFR2; HASK.

Lewis, Sinclair. (1885-1951) Author. Nobel Prize winner, Pulitzer Prize winner. FAB2; PER.

Leyster, Judith. (1609-1660) Dutch painter. HER.

Li Bo (or Li Po) (701-762) Chinese poet. HOOB; PER.

Li Ch'ing-Chao. (1084-1151) Chinese poet. LEO2.

Libby, Willard. (1908-1980) Chemist, inventor. Nobel Prize winner. AAS15.

Liddell, Eric. (1902-1945) Scottish missionary, olympic runner. JACKD2.

Lieberman-Cline, Nancy. (1958-) Olympic basketball player, coach. BRIL3; HASD; KELLY; SAV13.

Liebmann, Hanne Eve Hirsch. (1924-) German Jewish Holocaust survivor. KUS.

Lifshitz, Aliza. (1951-) Mexican AIDS activist, author, editor magazine, educator, physician. LAE.

Lilienthal, Otto. (1848-1896) German aeronautical engineer, aviation pioneer. BERL; BERL2; WILLI.

Liliuokalani, Lydia. (1838-1917) Hawaiian
composer, musician, queen. GUL; HER;
SIN.

Lilly, Bob. (1939-) Football player. SAV7.

Lilly, Kristine. (1971-) Olympic soccer
player. BRIL5; LAY2; MILM; RUT4.

Limbourg, Herman. (fl. 1400) Dutch painter.
CUM

Limbourg, Jean. (fl. 1400) Dutch painter.
CUM.

Limbourg, Paul. (fl. 1400) Dutch painter.
CUM.

Limón, José Arcadia. (1908-1972) Choreographer, dancer, born Mexico. LAE; SIN2.

Lin, Maya Ying. (1960-) Architect, sculptor.
GAN; HARN; HEA; ROE; SIN.

Lin Xezu. (1785-1850) Chinese anti-drug
educator, reformer. HOOB.

Lincoln, Abbey. (1930-) Actor, composer,
jazz singer. HAC3.

Lincoln, Abraham. (1809-1865) Attorney,
congressman, 16th president of U.S., state
legislator. ADA; BARB; BAU; BLASS;
CRO; CRO4; CRO6; DAV2; DEN; EME;
FAB; JONR; KRULL5; MARZ; MORR;
STG; YEN.

Lincoln, Mary Todd. (1818-1882) First Lady.
ANT; BARB; GOR; PAST; ZEI.

Lincoln, Trebitsch. (1872-1943) Hungarian
spy. MART.

Lind, James. (1716-1794) Scottish medical
researcher, physician. MUL.

Lindbergh, Anne Morrow. (1906-2001) Author, aviator. MCLE2; YOUNT7.

Lindbergh, Charles A. Jr. (1902-1974) Avia-
tor. Pulitzer Prize winner. ALTE; CRO;
JAN; KRAL; LEVE; PRE; ROS; SCHR;
WILLI.

Lindgren, Astrid. (1902-2002) Swedish children's author. HUNTE4.

Lindros, Eric. (1973-) Canadian hockey
player. KRAMS2.

Lindsay, John. (1894-1950) Jazz musician.
GOU2.

Ling, Chai. (1966-) Chinese political activist.
BERS.

Linnaeus, Carl. (1707-1778) Swedish botanist. FAB3; KEEN; POD; TIN.

Lion, Jules. (1810-1866) Photographer.
SULG.

Lipinski, Tara. (1982-) Olympic figure skater.

POY; RUT2.

Lippmann, Walter. (1889-1974) Author, journalist, World War I Army captain military
intelligence. Presidential Medal of Freedom
recipient, Pulitzer Prize winner. RIT.

Lisa, Manuel. (1772-1820) Explorer, fur
trader. COLL; LAE; SIN2.

Lisboa, Antonio Francisco. (1738-1814) Brazilian architect, sculptor. HOOB6.

Lister, Joseph. (1827-1912) English medical
researcher, physician. CURT; TIN;
WILKP3.

Liszt, Franz. (1811-1886) Hungarian composer. BLACA2; GREA; ROM.

Little, Frank. (1879-1917) Cherokee Indian
labor leader, Native American rights activist, workers' rights activist. AVE.

Little, Jean. (1932-) Canadian children's author. HUNTE4; YUN.

Little, Larry. (1945-) Football player. HUNT.

Little Raven. (d. 1889) Arapaho chief, peace
activist. MON2.

Little Richard. *See* Penniman, Richard
Wayne.

Litvak, Lily. (1921-1943) Russian World War
II fighter pilot. COOL.

Liu, Hung. (1948-) Painter, born China.
HON.

Liu Pang. (256-195 B.C.) Chinese emperor.
PAP.

Livia. (Livia Drusilla) (58 B.C.-19 A.D.)
Roman wife of Augustus, mother of Tiberius. BAKR3; CRO4.

Livingston, Philip. (1716-1778) American
Revolutionary War patriot, congressman,
Declaration of Independence signer, entre-
preneur merchant, philanthropist. FRA2;
QUI.

Livingstone, David. (1813-1873) Scottish
anthropologist, astronomer, botanist, chemist, explorer, geographer, missionary.
ALTE; JACKD; KRAL; LOM; POD; PRE.

Livy. (Titus Livius) (59 or 64 BC-17 AD)
Roman historian. BAKR3.

Llewellyn, J. Bruce. (1927-) Entrepreneur soft
drink bottler. AFR2.

Llosa, Mario Vargas. (1936-) Peruvian author. SHIR.

Lloyd, John Henry "Pop." (1884-1965) Baseball player. WIN2.

Lloyd George, David. (1863-1945) English

prime minister, World War I military leader. PAP.

Lobo, Rebecca. (1973-) Olympic basketball player. BAIL; BRIL3; JACK; KELLY; KRAMS5; MARV8; PON; RUT; SAV13.

Locard, Edmond. (1877-1966) French forensic scientist. FRID.

Locke, Alain Leroy. (1886-1954) Composer, educator. BECKM; HARD.

Locklear, Ormer. (1891-1929) Stunt pilot, World War I Army Air Service pilot. ALTE.

Lockwood, Belva Ann. (1830-1917) Attorney, Native American rights activist, presidential candidate, women's rights activist. CALA; EME; HARN; HEA; THIR.

Locusta of Gaul. (fl. 50 A.D.) Roman poisoner. LEO.

Loeb, Ilse. (unknown) Austrian Jewish Holocaust survivor. LAND4.

Lofton, Kenny. (1967-) Baseball player. BJA2.

Logan, Arthur C. (1909-1973) Physician. HAY.

Logan, James. (1674-1751) Colonist, born Ireland. CRO2.

Loguen, Jermain Wesley. (1813-1872) Abolitionist. ALTMS.

Loki. Norse god of mischief. FIS3.

L'Olonnois, François. (1630-1671) French pirate. BLACG4.

Lombardi, Vincent. (1913-1970) Football coach. SAV11.

London, Jack. (1876-1916) Adventurer, author. FAB2; KRULL6; NIN; PER.

Lone Dog. (Shunka-Ishnala) (1780-1871) Yankton Dakota Indian historian. RAPD2.

Long, Crawford. (1815-1878) Medical researcher, physician. FRA3.

Longabaugh, Harry "Sundance Kid." (1863-1909) Outlaw. SAV.

Longfellow, Henry Wadsworth. (1807-1882) Poet. FAB.

Longshore, Hannah E. Myers. (1810-1901) Educator, physician. STI.

Longstreet, James. (1821-1904) Civil War general. GREEC2; REG; TRAC.

López, Javy. (1970-) Baseball player, born Puerto Rico. STEWM.

Lopez, Jennifer. (1970-) Actor, pop singer. KRULI.

Lopez, Josefina. (1969-) Playwright, born Mexico. MARV4.

Lopez, Lourdes. (1958-) Ballet dancer, born Cuba. MORE2.

Lopez, Nancy. (1957-) Golfer. HASD; LAE; LINL; MARV6.

Lord, Audre. (1934-1992) Human rights activist, poet. KEND; WILKB.

Lord, Bette Bao. (1938-) Children's and adult author, born China. ISH; SIN.

Lorenz, Edward. (1917-) Meterologist. HAV.

Lorrain, Claude. (1605-1682) French painter. SEV.

Louganis, Greg. (1960-) Olympic diver. JACT; KNA4; SIN.

Louis II de Bourbon. (1621-1686) French army commander. CRO3.

Louis XIV. (1638-1715) French king. MEL.

Louis XVI. (1754-1792) French king. CRO4; SCHM2; WILKP4.

Louis, Joe. (1914-1981) Boxer. ALTMS; ITA2; JACT; KNA7; SAV4.

Love, Nancy Harkness. (1914-1976) World War II pilot. ZEI3.

Love, Nat. (1854-1921) Cowboy. ALTMS; BECKN; GAR; MED; MON2.

Love, Susan. (1948-) Medical researcher, physician. LINL3.

Lovecraft, H. P. (1890-1937) Author. MAD.

Lovejoy, Elijah P. (1802-1837) Abolitionist, editor. RIT; SAT.

Lovejoy, Esther Pohl. (1869-1967) Physician, reformer, women's rights activist, World War I Red Cross doctor. STI.

Lovelace, Lady Ada Byron. (1815-1852) English computer pioneer, mathematician. CEL; DUN; HENH; ROL; TIN.

Low, Juliette Gordon "Daisy." (1860-1927) Girl Scouts of America founder. HARN; KEND; SAW.

Lowe, Ann. (1899-?) Fashion designer. AFR2.

Lowe, Mundell. (1922-) Jazz musician. GOU3.

Lowell, Amy. (1874-1925) Poet. Pulitzer Prize winner. KNI.

Lowell, Percival. (1855-1916) Astronomer. CAM.

Lowie, Robert Harry. (1883-1957) Anthropologist, born Austria. WEI.

Lowry, Judith. (1948-) Pit River Indian

painter. HON.

Lowry, Lois. (1937-) Children's and young adult author. AUT; HILC2.

Lozano, Ignacio E. (1886-1953) Mexican editor newspaper. LAE.

Lozen. (1840-1890) Apache Indian woman warrior. COOL.

Lu, Chen. (1976-) Chinese olympic figure skater. BRY; RUT2.

Lubetkin, Zivia. (1914-1978) Polish Jewish Holocaust resistance leader, survivor. SEG; TAI.

Lucas, Adetokonbo. (1931-) Nigerian medical researcher, physician, founder World Health Organization. SPA.

Lucas, Anthony Francis. (1855-1921) Engineer, entrepreneur oil, geologist, born Austria. AAS7.

Lucas, George. (1944-) Filmmaker. HILA2.

Lucas, John. (1953-) Basketball player, coach. KAM.

Lucas, Tad. (1902-1990) Rodeo rider. ALTE2.

Luce, Clare Boothe. (1903-1987) Ambassador, congresswoman, playwright. Presidential Medal of Freedom recipient. LEVE.

Luce, Henry R. (1898-1967) Editor, publisher. RIT.

Luciano, Salvatore "Lucky." (1897-1962) Gangster, born Italy. WOO.

Lucid, Shannon W. (1943-) Astronaut. ALTE; BRIGG2; BUCH; HAV.

Luckman, Sid. (1916-1990) Football player. SULG7.

Lucy. Saint. ARM.

Ludewig, Marion. (1914-) Bowler. JACT.

Ludington, Sybil. (1761-1839) American Revolutionary War patriot. BERS; BRIL; HARN; HOOS; SILC; ZEI4.

Luke. Saint. ARM.

Lundy, Benjamin. (1789-1839) Abolitionist, journalist. LIL.

Luque, Dolf. (1890-1957) Baseball player, born Cuba. WIN.

Luria, Isaac. (1534-1572) Israeli educator, mystic, scholar. CRO5; GOLDM; PASA.

Lustig, Arnost. (1926-) Czech Jewish Holocaust survivor, author, screenwriter. MAN.

Luther, Martin. (1483-1546) German spiritual leader, Protestantism. CRO4; CRO5; GOLDM; JACKD; JACW2; WILKP2;

YEN.

Luther Standing Bear. (1868-1937) Oglala Lakota Sioux Indian chief. WE2.

Luthuli, Albert. (1898-1967) South African educator, political activist. Nobel Peace Prize winner. KEEN2.

Luwum, Janani. (1922-1977) Ugandan archbishop, political activist. CLA2.

Luxemburg, Rosa. (1870-1919) German political activist, revolutionary, workers' rights activist, born Poland. DUN; ROL; TAI.

Lycurgus. (7th century B.C.) Greek statesman. BAKR2.

Lydon, John Joseph. (Johnny Rotten) (1956-) Rock musician. WOO3.

Lyell, Sir Charles. (1797-1875) English attorney, geologist. CARR; KEEN.

Lynch, John R. (1847-1939) Congressman, slave. HAN.

Lynch, Thomas, Jr. (1749-1779) American Revolutionary War patriot, attorney, congressman, Declaration of Independence signer. FRA2; QUI.

Lyon, Mary. (1797-1849) Educator. UNG.

Lyons, Sir William. (1901-1985) English automaker. ITA6.

M

Ma, Yo-Yo. (1955-) Musician, born France. DEN; GAN; MARZ; SIN.

Ma Yuan. (1165-1225) Chinese painter. HOOB.

Maass, Clara. (1875-1901) Medical researcher, nurse. ROBE.

Maathai, Wangari. (1940-) Kenyan environmentalist, political activist. HAC5; SIR.

MacArthur, Catherine. (1906-1981) Philanthropist. TRAU.

MacArthur, Douglas. (1880-1964) World War I Army officer, World War II Army commander general. CRO3; CRO4; KNA; LAC; OLE2; YEN.

MacArthur, John D. (1897-1978) Financier, philanthropist. TRAU.

MacBride, Seán. (1904-1988) Irish attorney, International Peace Bureau President, peace activist. Nobel Peace Prize winner. KEEN2.

MacDonald, Flora. (1722-1790) Scottish

American Revolutionary War musician. SCHM2.

MacDowell, Edward. (1861-1908) Composer, musician. NIC.

MacDowell Marian. (1857-1956) Patron of arts. SAW.

Machel, Gracia Simbine. (1945-) Mozambican children's rights activist. HAC5.

Machiavelli, Niccolo. (1469-1527) Italian historian, political activist. KRAL.

Mack, Connie. (1862-1956) Baseball manager. PIE.

MacKaye, Benton. (1879-1975) Conservationist, forester. KEEN.

MacKenzie, Sir Alexander. (1764-1820) Scottish explorer, fur trader. ALTE; LOM2; SCHEL2.

Mackey, Raleigh "Biz." (1897-1965) Baseball player. WIN2.

MacLeish, Archibald. (1892-1982) Author, poet. Presidential Medal of Freedom recipient, Pulitzer Prize winner. SAW.

Maclure, William. (1763-1840) Geologist, cofounder Harmonist utopian society, born Scotland. SAW.

Macmillan, Shannon. (1974-) Soccer player. MILM; RUT4.

Maddux, Greg. (1966-) Baseball player. SCHWAR.

Madhubuti, Haki R. (1942-) Poet. STRI.

Madison, Dolley Payne Todd. (1768-1849) First Lady. ANT; BARB; GOR; HARN; PAST.

Madison, James. (1751-1836) Cabinet member, 4th president of U.S. ADA; BARB; BAU; BLASS; CRO; CRO6; DAV2; FAB; KRULL5; MEI; MORR; SCHM2.

Madonna. (singer) *See* Ciccione, Madonna Louise Veronica.

Magellan, Ferdinand. (1480-1521) Portuguese explorer. ALTE; FRI; LANG; LOM; PARN; POD; PRE; WILKP2; WILLI2; YEN.

Magoffin, Susan Shelby. (1827-1855) Pioneer. KET.

Magritte, René. (1896-1967) Belgian painter. KRY.

Mahan, Larry. (1943-) Rodeo cowboy. JACT.

Mahavira, Vardhamana. (599-527 B.C.) Indian spiritual leader, founder of Jainism. CRO5; GOLDM; JACW2.

Mahaut, Countess of Artois. (1275-1329) French noblewoman. LEO2.

Mahler, Gustav. (1860-1911) Austrian composer, conductor. ROM; VEN.

Mahoney, Mary Eliza. (1845-1926) Civil rights activist, nurse, women's rights activist. COX; GREA; STI.

Mahowald, Misha. (1963-) Biologist, computer scientist. KAH3.

Mailer, Norman. (1923-) Author, playwright. Pulitzer Prize winner. PER.

Maimonides. (Moses ben Maimon) (1135-1204) Spanish Hebrew philosopher, spiritual leader. CRO5; GOLDM; PASA.

Maisonneuve, Paul. (1612-1676) French founder of Montreal. CRO2.

Majerle, Dan. (1968-) Basketball player. TOR3.

Makarova, Natalia. (1940-) Ballet dancer, born Russia. HUNTE3.

Makeba, Miriam. (1932-) South African political activist, singer. GREA.

Makeda. (960-930 B.C.) Ethiopian queen. AFR2.

Makhubu, Lydia Phindile. (1937-) Swasiland chemist, educator. YOUNT6.

Malcolm X. (1925-1965) Civil rights activist. ALTMS; ARC2; BECKN; CIV; CRO; CRO4; GOLDM; HARM; HASK7; RED2; SHAW; TAYK2; TUR; VERN.

Malinche, La. (Malintzin) (1500-1527) Mexican princess, slave, translator. CRO4; HER; LEO3; POD; POLK.

Mallon, Mary "Typhoid Mary." (1870-1938) Irish cook, maid, legendary spreader of typhoid disease. KRAL.

Mallory, George. (1886-1924) English explorer, mountainer. ALTE.

Mallowan, Max. (1904-1978) English archaeologist. WEI.

Malo, Davida. (1795-1853) Hawaiian translator. SIN.

Malone, Annie Turnbo. (1869-1957) Inventor. SULO2.

Malone, Karl. (1963-) Basketball player. BJA; PAU; SAV6.

Malone, Russell. (1963-) Jazz musician. GOU3.

Maloney, Kris. (1981-) Olympic gymnast. LAY; RUT3.

Malthaus, Thomas Robert. (1766-1834)

English economist. BUS.

Man Ray. *See* Radnitsky, Emmanuel.

Manalapit, Pablo. (1891-1969) Labor leader, born Philippines. SIN.

Mandel, Basia. (1925-) Polish Jewish Holocaust survivor. LAND.

Mandela, Nelson. (1918-) South African attorney, human rights activist, political activist. Nobel Peace Prize winner, Presidential Medal of Freedom recipient. BOY; CRO4; KEEN2; MAYB2; THOM; TUR.

Mandela, Winnie Madikizela. (1934-) South African political activist. CRO4; DUN; GREA; PRI3.

Mandelbrot, Benoit. (1924-) Polish mathematician. HENH.

Manet, Édouard. (1832-1883) French painter. CUM; IMP.

Mangeshkar, Lata. (1929-2001) Indian singer. DUN.

Mangin, Anna M. (unknown) Inventor. SULO2.

Mani. (216-277) Persian spiritual leader, founder of Manichaeism. CRO5; GOLDM.

Manik. Mayan god of human sacrifice. FIS2.

Manjiro. (1827-1898) Japanese fisherman. HOOS.

Mankiller, Wilma. (1945-) Cherokee Indian chief. Presidential Medal of Freedom recipient. ALLP; ALTE2; AVE; CUS2; GUL; HER; KAL3; KEND; KRULL; LINL2; PRI3; RAPD2; SHER2; THIR.

Manley, Mary. (1663-1724) English author, journalist, women's rights activist. KNI.

Mann, Horace. (1796-1859) Abolitionist, congressman, educator, state legislator, women's rights activist. UNG.

Mann, Shelley. (1939-) Olympic swimmer. DON2.

Manning, Peyton. (1976-) Football player. DEI.

Mansa Musa I. (1312-1337) King of Mali. HAZ.

Mansfield, Katherine. (1888-1923) English author, born New Zealand.

Mansi, Paula dei. (13th century) Italian scribe, scholar. TAI.

Mansur, Abu Jafar ibn Muhammad al- (714-775) Islamic military leader. PAP.

Mantell, Gideon. (1790-1852) English geologist, physician. CHRISP.

Mantilla, Ray. (1934-) Jazz musician. GOU6.

Mantle, Mickey. (1931-1995) Baseball player. DEA2; SEHN; SLO; SULG8; TOR2.

Mantz, Matt. (1981-) In-line skater. SAV7.

Mao Tse-Tung. (1893-1976) Chinese dictator, political activist, revolutionary. CRO3; CRO4; GREER; MAYB2; THOM3; WAKI; WILKP4; YEN.

Maradona, Diego. (1960-) Argentine soccer player. JACT.

Maravich, Pete. (1947-1988) Basketball player. KRULL3.

Marbury, Stephon. (1977-) Basketball player. NEL; PAU.

Marcello, Benedetto. (1686-1739) Italian opera composer. VEN.

Marchbanks, Vance. (1905-1988) Air Force colonel, medical researcher, physician, space scientist, World War II Tuskegee airman. AFR2; BUR.

Marchetti, Gino. (1927-) Football player. SAV7.

Marciano, Rocky (Rocco Francis Marchegiano) (1923-1969) Boxer. ITA2; JACT; KNA8.

Marconi, Guglielmo. (1874-1937) Italian inventor, physicist. Nobel Prize winner. AAS15; DIN; LOM2; STRE2; YEN.

Marcos de Niza, Fray. (1495-1558) Spanish missionary. SIN2.

Marcos, Ferdinand. (1917-1989) Filipino dictator, political activist. PAP.

Marcovaldi, Maria "Neca." (1948-) Brazilian conservationist. GRAH.

Marcus Aurelius. (Marcus Annius Verus) (121-180) Roman emperor. BAKR3; COOLI.

Margaret. (1930-2002) English princess. BREW.

Margaret I. (1353-1412) Scandinavian queen. ROL.

Maria, "Madame." (unknown) French Holocaust rescuer. PET.

Maria Theresa. (1717-1780) Austrian archduchess, empress. MEL2.

Marichal, Juan. (1937-) Baseball player, born Dominican Republic. WIN.

Marie Antoinette. (1755-1793) French princess, queen. BREW; CRO4; KRAL; KRULL.

Marie-Benoit, Father. (unknown) French Holocaust rescuer, spiritual leader. FREM.

Mariette, Auguste. (1821-1881) French archaeologist. FAG.

Marin, Richard Anthony "Cheech." (1946-) Actor, comedian, filmmaker. MARV5.

Marino, Dan. (1961-) Football player. LAC2; SULG7.

Marion, Marty. (1917-) Baseball player. SULG2.

Maris, Roger. (1934-1985) Baseball player. DEA2.

Marius. (Gaius Marius) (157-86 B.C.) Roman emperor. BAKR3; NAR2.

Mark, Mary Ellen. (1940-) Photographer. HOR.

Markham, Beryl. (1902-1986) English author, aviation pioneer, pilot. MCLE2; MCLO5; POLK; WILLI; ZAU2.

Markiewiecz, Constance. (1867-1927) Irish political activist. DUN.

Marlin, Sterling. (1957-) Nascar auto racer. RIL.

Marlowe, Christopher. (1564-1593) English playwright. PER.

Marquard, Richard William "Rube." (1889-1980) Baseball player. SULG5.

Marquette, Jacques. (1637-1675) French explorer, missionary, spiritual leader. ALTE; CRO2; PRE; SCHEL2.

Marquez, Gabriel Garcia. (1928-) Colombian author. Nobel Prize winner. SHIR; TWEPO.

Marriott, John Willard. (1900-1985) Entrepreneur hotels and restaurants, philanthropist. Presidential Medal of Freedom recipient. AAS12.

Marsalis, Wynton. (1961-) Bandleader, composer, educator, jazz musician. Pulitzer Prize winner. HAC3; MOU; SHIP.

Marsden, Kate. (1859-1931) Arctic explorer. MCLO4.

Marsh, George Perkins. (1801-1882) Ambassador, attorney, author, conservationist, state legislator. KEEN; LUC2.

Marsh, James. (fl. 1832) Scottish chemist, forensic scientist. YEA.

Marsh, Othniel Charles. (1831-1899) Paleontologist. AAS; CHRISP.

Marshall, Andrew Cox. (1775-1856) Spiritual leader. AFR2.

Marshall, George Catlett. (1880-1959) Army Chief of Staff, cabinet member, World War I military leader, World War II general. Nobel Peace Prize winner. CRO; DEN; FAB; KEEN2; KNA.

Marshall, James. (1942-1992) Children's author, illustrator. MARC3.

Marshall, Jim. (1937-) Football player. SAV12.

Marshall, John. (1755-1835) Attorney, cabinet member, Supreme Court chief justice. AAS14; CRO; FAB.

Marshall, Paule. (1929-) Author. WILKB.

Marshall, Thurgood. (1908-1993) Attorney, civil rights activist, Supreme Court justice. Presidential Medal of Freedom recipient. ALTMS; BECKN; BOOK; CALA; CIV; DUB; FAB; HARM; MED; POT; RED2; TAYK2; TUR; VERN.

Martel, Charles. (689-741) French military leader. CRO3.

Martha. Biblical character. ARM2.

Martha Louise. (1971-) Norwegian princess. LEVI.

Martí, José. (1853-1895) Cuban revolutionary. BERS.

Martial. (Marcus Valerius Martialis) (40-103) Roman poet. BAKR3.

Martin. (de Porres). (1579-1639) Peruvian saint. CRO5.

Martin. (of Tours). (316-397) French saint. ARM.

Martin, Ann M. (1955-) Children's and young adult author. AUT.

Martin, Billy. (1928-1989) Baseball player, manager. PIE.

Martin, Casey. (1972-) Golfer. SAV10.

Martin, Grace. (unknown) American Revolutionary War patriot, heroine. SILC.

Martin, Joseph Plumb. (1762-1852) American Revolutionary War child soldier, author. HOOS.

Martin, Louise. (1911-) Photographer. HOR.

Martin, Rachel. (unknown) American Revolutionary War patriot, heroine. SILC.

Martin, Ricky. (1971-) Puerto Rican pop singer. KRULI.

Martinez, Father Antonio José, (1793-1867) Mexican educator, human rights activist, spiritual leader. LAE; SIN2.

Martinez, Edgar. (1963-) Baseball player,

born Puerto Rico. STEWM2.

Martinez, José P. (1920-1943) World War II military hero. LAE.

Martinez, Julian. (1897-1943) San Idlefonso Pueblo potter. RAPD2.

Martinez, Maria Montoya. (1887-1980) San Idlefonso Pueblo potter. ALTE2; AVE; DAN; HEA; RAPD2.

Martinez, Pedro. (1971-) Baseball player, born Dominican Republic. BUCK2; SCHWAR.

Martinez, Tino. (1967-) Baseball player. STEWM2.

Martinez, Vilma. (1943-) Attorney, civil rights activist. LAE; LINL2; PAL.

Martinez-Canas, Maria. (1960-) Puerto Rican photographer, born Cuba. HOR.

Martino, Pat. (1944-) Jazz musician. GOU3.

Marx, Groucho. (1890-1977) Comedian. BRO; KAL2.

Marx, Karl Heinrich. (1818-1883) German economist, philosopher. BUS; CRO4; WILKP2.

Mary. Biblical character. ARM2.

Mary I. (Mary Tudor) (1516-1558) English princess, queen. BREW; DAV; DUN.

Mary II. (1662-1694) English queen. DAV.

Mary Magdalen. Saint. ARM; ARM2; GOLDM.

Mary Prophetetissa of Alexandra. (1st century A.D.) Egyptian chemist, inventor. LEO.

Mary, Queen of Scots. (1547-1587) Scottish queen. CRO4; GUL; HER.

Mary Tudor. *See* Mary I.

Mary, Virgin. (22 B.C.-1st century A.D.) Biblical character. ARM2; CRO5; GOLDM; ROL.

Masih, Igbal. (1982-1995) Pakistani slave, workers' rights activist.

Maskelyne, Jasper. (1902-1973) English magician, World War II hero. WOO2.

Mason, Andrée-Paule. (1923-1991) French World War II resistance fighter. MARX.

Mason, Biddy. (1818-1891) Civil rights activist, entrepreneur, pioneer, slave. FUR2; GREA; KAT; KET; MON2; PIN.

Mason, George. (1725-1792) American Revolutionary War patriot. MEI; SCHM2.

Massaccio, Tommaso. (1401-1428) Italian painter. CUM; REN.

Massasoit. (1600-1661) Wampanoag Indian chief, colonist. CRO2.

Massey, Walter. (1938-) Physicist. STJ.

Masters, Sybilla. (d. 1720) Inventor. BLASH5.

Masters, William. (1915-2001) Author, medical researcher, physician. CRO4.

Masterson, Martha Gay. (1837-1916) Pioneer. STEFO3.

Masterson, William Barclay "Bat." (1853-1921) Law marshal. SAV.

Mata Hari. *See* Zelle, Margareta Gertrude.

Mathai-Davis, Prema. (1950-) Human rights activist, women's rights activist, YWCA director, born India. GOLDE.

Mather, Cotton. (1663-1728) Author, colonist, puritan, spiritual leader. CRO2; GOLDM.

Mather, Increase. (1639-1723) Colonist, educator, puritan, spiritual leader. CRO2.

Mathewson, Christopher "Christy." (1880-1925) Baseball player. SULG5; SULM.

Mathias, Bob. (1930-) Olympic decathlon athlete. SULG3.

Mathis, Johnny. (1935-) Singer. AFR.

Mathison, Melissa. (1949-) Screenwriter. SMIL2.

Matilda of England. (1102-1167) English empress of Holy Roman Empire. LEO2.

Matisse, Henri. (1869-1954) French painter, sculptor. CUM; CUS; KRULL2; KRY; TWEPR.

Matlin, Marlee. (1965-) Actor. GAI2; KEND.

Matsui, Robert. (1941-) Congressman. RAG.

Matsunaga, Masayuki "Spark." (1916-1990) Attorney, senator, World War II Army captain. SIN.

Matthew. Apostle. MAYE.

Matthews, Eddie. (1913-2001) Baseball player. SULG8.

Matthias. Apostle, saint. MAYE.

Mattingly, Don. (1961-) Baseball player. SULG2.

Matzeliger, Jan Ernst. (1852-1889) Inventor. AAS4; AFR2; ALTMS; HASK8; HAY2; HUD2; MCK; SULO2.

Mauchaut, Guillaumede. (1300-1377) French composer. VEN.

Mauchly, John W. (1907-1980) Computer pioneer. NOR.

Maugham, W. Somerset. (1874-1965) English author, playwright. PER.

Maurice of Nassau. (Prince of Orange) (1567-1625) Dutch military leader, ruler. CRO3.

Maury, Antonia C. (1866-1952) Astronomer. STI2.

Maury, Matthew Fontaine. (1806-1873) Oceanographer. TIN.

Maxim, Sir Hiram Stevens. (1840-1916) English aviation pioneer, inventor. BERL2; RIC5.

Maximinus, Gaius Valerius. (186-238) Roman olympic runner, wrestler. JACT.

Maxwell, James Clerk. (1831-1879) Scottish physicist. TIN.

Maxwell, Nicole Hughes. (1905-1998) Ethnobiologist. POLK.

Mayer, Louis B. (1885-1957) Filmmaker. GREEC.

Maynard, Don. (1937-) Football player. THOR.

Mays, Benjamin E. (1895-1984) Educator, spiritual leader. BECKN.

Mays, Willie. (1931-) Baseball player. ITA; RED6; SEHN; SLO; SULG2; SULG3; SULG8; TOR; TOR2.

Mazeroski, Bill. (1936-) Baseball player. SULG2.

Mazuchelli, Nina. (1832-1914) English explorer, mountaineer. MCLO6.

Mbandi, Jinga. *See* Nzinga, Anna.

McAliskey, Bernadette Devlin. (1947-) Irish civil rights activist, political activist. GUL; HAC7.

McAuliffe, Christa. (1948-1986) Astronaut, educator. ALTE; BAIR; BUCH; SCHR; WYB.

McBee, Cecil. (1935-) Jazz musician. GOU2.

McBride, Mary Margaret. (Martha Deane) (1899-1976) Broadcast journalist, journalist. PRI.

McCabe, William. (1915-1976) World War II Navajo code talker. Medal of Honor recipient. RAPD2.

McCandless, Bruce, II. (1932-) Astronaut, Navy aviator. PRE.

McCarthy, Henry. (Billy the Kid) (1859-1881) Outlaw. GLA; KRAL; SAV; THOM2; THRA; WAL.

McCarthy, Joe. (1887-1978) Baseball manager. PIE.

McCarthy, Joseph. (1908-1957) Hatemonger, senator. STRE3.

McCartney, Paul. (1942-) English singer, songwriter. CRO4; VEN.

McCauley, Mary Ludwig Hays. (Molly Pitcher) (1754-1832) American Revolutionary War heroine. LEVE; SCHM2; SHEA; SILC; ZEI4.

McClelland, George Brinton. (1826-1885) Civil War general. GREEC3; YAN.

McClintock, Barbara. (1909-1992) Geneticist. Nobel Prize winner. CAM; CEL; CUS2; DAS; HAC6; HAV; HEA; REY; STI; STI2; TIN; VAR; VEG; YOUNT6.

McCloskey, Robert. (1914-2003) Children's author, illustrator. MARC; MARC3.

McClure, Ron. (1941-) Jazz musician. GOU2.

McCormick, Anne O'Hare. (1880-1954) Journalist. Pulitzer Prize winner. PRI.

McCormick, Cyrus Hall. (1809-1884) Inventor, philanthropist. LOM2; NOO.

McCormick, Patricia Keller. (1930-) Olympic diver. HASD; JACT.

McCovey, Willie Lee. (1938-) Baseball player. DEA2; SULG8.

McCoy, Elijah. (1843-1929) Inventor. AAS4; AFR2; ALTMS; AMR; BECKN; HASK8; HAY2; HUD2; MCK; SULO.

McCoy, Millie-Christine. (1851-1912) Siamese twins, singers, slaves. TAT.

McCray, Nikki. (1971-) Olympic basketball player. PON; RUT.

McCrea, Jane. (1752-1777) American Revolutionary War Indian captive. SCHM2.

McCullagh, Joseph B. (1842-1896) Civil War correspondent, journalist, born Ireland. RIT.

McCullough, J. F. (1871-1936) Entrepreneur restaurants. AAS6.

McDaniel, Hattie. (1895-1952) Actor, singer. AFR; GREA; PARJ; PLO; POT.

McDonald, Maurice. (1902-1971) Entrepreneur restaurants. AAS6.

McDonald, Richard. (1909-1998) Entrepreneur restaurants. AAS6.

McDoulet, Annie "Cattle Annie." (1879-1898) Outlaw. KRO.

McEnroe, John. (1959-) Sportscaster, tennis player. CHRIST; CRO4; LEVE.

McGee, Anita Newcomb. (1864-1940) Army nurse corps founder, physician. STI.

McGibbon, Al. (1919-) Jazz musician. GOU2.

McGrady, Tracy. (1979-) Basketball player. PAU.

McGraw, John. (1873-1934) Baseball manager. PIE.

McGriff, Fred. (1963-) Baseball player. DEA2.

McGrory, Mary. (1918-) Journalist. PRI.

McGuire, Edith. (1944-) Olympic sprinter, track and field athlete. MOL.

McGwire, Mark. (1963-) Baseball player. SCHER; SCHWAR; TOR2; USC2.

McHale, Kevin. (1957-) Basketball player. SAV6.

McJunkin, George. (1851-1922) Cowboy, slave. MILR.

McKane, Alice Woodby. (1865-1948) Physician. AFR2.

McKay, Claude. (1890-1948) Author, poet, born Jamaica. BECKN; HARD.

McKean, Thomas. (1734-1817) American Revolutionary War patriot, attorney, congressman, Declaration of Independence signer. FRA2; QUI.

McKenner, George, III. (1940-) Educator. AFR2.

McKinney, Nina Mae. (1909-1967) Jazz singer. MON.

McKinley, Ida Saxton. (1847-1907) First Lady. BARB; GOR; PAST.

McKinley, Ray. (1910-1995) Jazz musician. GOU6.

McKinley, William. (1843-1901) Attorney, Civil War major, congressman, governor, 25th president of U.S. ADA; BARB; BAU; BLASS; CRO6; DAV2; JONR; MORR; STG.

McKinstry, Carolyn. (1949-) Civil rights activist. HOOS.

McLachlan, Sarah. (1968-) Canadian singer, songwriter. KEEL.

McLaughlin, James. (1842-1923) Frontiersman, Indian agent. CALV.

McLaughlin, John. (1942-) English bandleader, jazz musician. SHIP.

McLean, Gordon. (1934-) Author, children's rights activist, human rights activist, born Canada. JACKD3.

McLoughlin, John. (1784-1857) Canadian fur trader, physician. DOH2.

McLuhan, Herbert Marshall. (1911-1980) Canadian educator, visionary. KRULL7.

McMillan, Terry. (1951-) Author. WILKB.

McNair, Ronald. (1950-1986) Astronaut, physicist. AFR2; BUR; HASK7.

McNamara, Robert Strange. (1916-) Army Air Force, cabinet member, World War II lieutenant colonel. Presidential Medal of Freedom recipient. RIC2.

McNelly, Leander H. (1844-1877) Crime fighter, Texas Rangers captain. ITA3.

McNutt, Marcia. (1952-) Geologist, physicist. KAH8.

McQueen, Thelma "Butterfly." (1911-1995) Actor. PARJ.

McRae, Carmen. (1922-1994) Jazz musician, singer. GOU5; HAC3.

McTell, "Blind" Willie. (1901-1959) Jazz musician, singer. GOU3.

McWhorter, "Free" Frank. (1777-1854) Entrepreneur saltpeter, slave. HASK; HASK4.

Meacham, Joseph. (d. 1796) Spiritual leader, co-founder of Shaker community. STRE6.

Mead, Margaret. (1901-1978) Anthropologist. Presidential Medal of Freedom recipient. BRED2; CUS2; DE; HAC8; HARN; HAV; HER; KNI; LEVE; MCD; POLK; ROL; STI2; TIN; VEG; WEI.

Meade, George Gordon. (1815-1872) Civil War general. GREEC3.

Means, Gaston. (1879-1938) Swindler. BLACG5.

Medawar, Sir Peter Brian. (1915-1987) English medical researcher, zoologist. Nobel Prize winner. SPA.

Medici, Lorenzo de. (1449-1492) Italian nobleman, patron of the arts. WILKP2.

Mee, Margaret Ursula Brown. (1909-1988) English botanist, painter. POLK.

Mehmed II "The Conqueror." (1432-1481) Mongol military leader. CRO3; WILKP.

Mehta, Zubin. (1936-) Conductor, born India. GAN; SIN.

Meinhof, Ulrike. (1934-1976) German journalist, revolutionary. DUN.

Meir, Golda. (1898-1978) Israeli prime minister, born Russia. AXEC; CUS2; DUN; HER; JACW2; KRULL; NAR4; PARJ2; PASA; PRI3; ROE; ROL; TAI.

Meitner, Lise. (1878-1968) Swedish inventor, nuclear physicist, born Germany. HAV; STI2; TIN; YOUNT6.

Melba, Nellie. (1861-1931) Australian opera

singer. BLACA2.

Mella. African warrior queen. MAYE2.

Mellon, Andrew. (1855-1937) Entrepreneur oil, philanthropist. AAS7.

Melville, Herman. (1819-1891) Author. CRO4; FAB2; OFT2; PER; SAW.

Memphis Minnie. *See* Douglas, Lizzie.

Menchú, Rigoberta. (1959-) Guatemalan human rights activist. Nobel Peace Prize winner. HAC7; HER; KEEN2; KRULL; LUC; ROL; SCHR2.

Mencia, Carlos. (unknown) Comedian, born Honduras. MARV8.

Mencius. (371-289 B.C.) Chinese philosopher, spiritual leader, co-founder of Confucianism. GOLDM.

Mencken, Henry Louis "H.L." (1880-1956) Author, editor, journalist. RIT.

Mendel, Gregor. (1822-1884) Austrian geneticist. AAS13; TIN.

Mendeleyev, Dimitri Ivanovich. (1843-1907) Russian chemist. TIN.

Mendelssohn, Moses. (1729-1786) German educator, philosopher, scholar. CRO5; PASA.

Mendes, Aristides. (d. 1954) Portuguese Holocaust rescuer. FREM.

Mendes, Chico. (1944-1988) Brazilian environmentalist, human rights activist. BOY; KRE.

Mendez, José. (1887-1928) Cuban baseball player. WIN.

Mendlovic, Leopold. (unknown) Czech Jewish Holocaust survivor. GID.

Mendoza, Juana Belen Gutierrez. (1875-1942) Mexican journalist, political activist, revolutionary. COOL.

Menedéz de Aviles, Pedro. (1519-1574) Spanish explorer, founder of St. Augustine, naval officer. CRO2; DOH5; LAE; SIN2.

Menendez, Francisco. (1700-1772) Colonist, military hero, slave, born Africa. CRO2.

Menes. (3100-3038 B.C.) Egyptian king. YEN.

Mengele, Josef. (1911-1979) German Nazi war criminal, physician. LAND2; SCHM4.

Mercator, Gerardus. (1512-1594) Belgian geographer. POD.

Mercury, Freddie. (1946-1991) English rock musician. GON.

Mergler, Marie Josepha. (1851-1901) Physician, born Germany. STI.

Merian, Anna Marie Sibylla. (1647-1717) Dutch illustrator, naturalist. POLK.

Merman, Ethel. (1908-1984) Singer. ORG.

Merrick, Joseph "Elephant Man." (1862-1890) English showman. DRI; KRAL.

Merton, Thomas. (Father M. Louis) (1915-1968) French poet, spiritual leader. CRO5.

Messner, Reinhold. (1944-) Italian mountaineer. PRE.

Metacomet. *See* Philip, King.

Metchnikoff, Élie. (1845-1916) Russian bacteriologist, physiologist. CURT.

Methodius. (815-885) Greek saint, spiritual leader. CRO5.

Metoyer, Marie-Therese. (1742-1816) Colonist, slave. HASK; HASK4.

Metz, Christian. (1795-1867) Founder of Amana utopian society, born Germany. STRE6.

Mexia, Ynes. (1870-1938) Botanist, explorer. MCLO3; POLK.

Meyer, Anna "Pee Wee." (1929-) Baseball player. HOOS.

Meyer, Annie Nathan. (1867-1951) Women's rights activist. TAI.

Meyers, Ann. (1955-) Olympic basketball player, sportscaster. KELLY; SAV13.

Meyers, Nancy. (1950-) Screenwriter. SMIL.

Michael. Saint. ARM.

Micheaux, Garrett Oscar. (1884-1951) Filmmaker. AFR; BECKN; HASK; HASK5; TUR2.

Michelangelo. (Michelangelo Buonarotti) (1475-1564) Italian painter, sculptor. BART; BLACA; BRIL; CRO4; CUM; CUS; GLU; HOOB3; KRULL2; KRY; REN; YEN.

Michelson, Albert Abraham. (1852-1931) Physicist, born Poland. Nobel Prize winner. HAV; TIN.

Michener, James. (1907-1997) Author. Presidential Medal of Freedom recipient, Pulitzer Prize winner. PER.

Middleton, Arthur. (1742-1787) American Revolutionary War patriot, congressman, Declaration of Independence signer. FRA2; QUI.

Midler, Bette. (1945-) Actor, singer. ORG.

Midori. (1971-) Japanese musician. BRIL; SIN; STRU2.

Mies van der Rohe, Ludwig. (1886-1969)
Architect, born Germany. CUS.

Miguel, Luis. (singer) *See* Gallego, Luis Miguel.

Mikan, George. (1924-) Basketball player.
JACT; KNA5; RAPK2.

Mikita, Stan. (1940-) Hockey player, born
Czechoslovakia. KNA8.

Mikulski, Barbara. (1936-) Congresswoman,
senator. FIR; GUL; MORI2.

Millais, John Everett. (1829-1896) Educator,
painter. BRIL.

Millay, Edna St.Vincent. (1892-1950) Playwright, poet. Pulitzer Prize winner. PER;
SMIL2.

Millbrett, Tiffany. (1972-) Olympic soccer
player. LAY2; MILM.

Miller, Arthur. (1915-) Playwright. Pulitzer
Prize winner. BRO; TWEPO.

Miller, Cheryl. (1964-) Olympic basketball
player, sportscaster. GREA; KELLY;
SAV13; SAV14.

Miller, Dorie. (1919-1943) Navy seaman,
World War II hero. HASK2; POT; REE2.

Miller, Inger. (1972-) Olympic track and field
athlete. RUT6.

Miller, Lee. (1907-1977) Photographer,
World War II photojournalist. COLM.

Miller, Reggie. (1965-) Basketball player.
PAU; TOR3.

Miller, Shannon. (1977-) Olympic gymnast.
ALTE2; BAIL; GREES; HASD; KLE;
RUT3.

Mills, Billy. (1938-) Oglala Lakota Indian
olympic track and field athlete. AVE;
KNA4.

Mills, Enos. (1870-1922) Author, naturalist.
KEEN.

Millwood, Kevin. (1974-) Baseball player.
SCHWAR2.

Milne, Alan Alexander "A. A." (1882-1956)
English children's author, World War I soldier. MAS.

Milo of Crotona. (c. 558 B.C.) Greek olympic
weightlifter, wrestler. JACT.

Milton, John. (1608-1674) English poet.
KEND; SEV.

Minamoto, Yoritomo. (1147-?) Japanese
samurai warrior. HOOB4.

Minamoto, Yoshitsune. (1160-?) Japanese
samurai warrior. HOOB4.

Mineta, Norman. (1931-) Cabinet member,
congressman. RAG.

Mingus, Charles. (1922-) Bandleader, composer, jazz musician. GOU2; MON; SHIP.

Mink, Patsy Takemoto. (1927-2002) Attorney, congresswoman. SIN.

Minke, Willy. (unknown) German Jewish
Holocaust survivor. PET.

Minoka-Hill, Lillie Rosa. (1876-1952) Mohawk Indian physician. STI.

Minoso, Saturnino Orestes "Minnie." (1922-)
Baseball player, born Cuba. WIN.

Minuit, Peter. (1580-1638) Colonist, born
Holland. CRO2; DOH3.

Mirabal, Robert. (unknown) Taos Indian musician, painter. MOO.

Mirabi. (1498-1565) Indian poet. KNI.

Miranda, Carmen. (1909-1955) Brazilian actor, singer. LAE.

Miriam. Biblical character. TAI.

Miriam the Scribe. (15th century) Yemenite
scribe. TAI.

Miro, Joan. (1893-1983) Spanish painter and
sculptor. KRY.

Mistral, Gabriela Lucila Godoy y Alcayága.
(1889-1957) Chilean diplomat, educator,
poet. Nobel Prize winner. HER; HOOB6;
KNI; MARZ; ROL.

Mitchell, Arthur. (1934-) Choreographer,
dancer. POT.

Mitchell, Edgar. (1930-) Astronaut, Navy
pilot. PRE.

Mitchell, Keith Moore "Red." (1927-1992)
Jazz musician. GOU2.

Mitchell, Margaret. (1900-1948) Author.
KNI.

Mitchell, Maria. (1818-1889) Astronomer.
BRIL; CEL; HEA; HER; POLK; STI2.

Mitchell, Thecla. (unknown) Marathon runner. RAPD.

Mitsui, Shuho. (1590-1676) Japanese businesswoman. HOOB4.

Miyamura, Hiroshi. (1925-) Korean War
Army hero. Medal of Honor recipient.
DOH.

Mize, Johnny. (1913-1993) Baseball player.
SULG8.

Mizrahi, Asenath Barazani. (16th century)
Kurdistani educator, scholar. TAI.

Moceanu, Dominique. (1981-) Olympic gymnast. KLE; KRAMS5; LAY; RUT3.

Mock, Geraldine Fredritz. (1925-) Aviation pioneer. YOUNT7.

Modligliani, Amedeo. (1884-1920) Italian painter. CUM.

Mohammed. *See* Muhammad.

Mohr, Nicholasa. (1935-) Children's author. AUT; HILC; LAE.

Moise, Penina. (1797-1880) Educator, poet. TAI.

Molière. *See* Poquelin, Jean Baptiste.

Molina, Mario. (1943-) Chemist, environmentalist, born Mexico. Nobel Prize winner. OLE.

Momaday, N. Scott. (1934-) Kiowa Indian author, painter. Pulitzer Prize winner. AVE.

Monaghan, Tom. (1937-) Entrepreneur restaurants. AAS6.

Mondesi, Raúl. (1971-) Baseball player, born Dominican Republic. STEWM.

Mondrian, Piet. (1872-1944) Dutch painter. TWEPR.

Moneta, Ernesto. (1833-1918) Italian journalist, peace activist. Nobel Peace Prize winner. KEEN2.

Monet, Claude. (1840-1926) French painter. BLACA; CUM; CUS; GLU; IMP; KRY; SAB.

Mongkut, Maha. (1804-1868) Siamese king. CRO4.

Monk, Art. (1957-) Football player. THOR.

Monk, Thelonious. (1917-1982) Bandleader, composer, jazz musician. AFR; GOU4; HAC3; MON; SHIP.

Monroe, Bill. (1911-1996) Bluegrass musician. SAW.

Monroe, Elizabeth Kortright. (1768-1830) First Lady. BARB; GOR; PAST.

Monroe, George. (1844-1886) Stagecoach driver, pioneer. MON2.

Monroe, Harriet. (1860-1936) Poet, publisher. SAW.

Monroe, James. (1758-1831) Ambassador, cabinet member, 5th president of U.S. ADA; BARB; BAU; BLASS; CRO6; DAV2; FAB; MORR; SAW.

Monroe, Marilyn. (1926-1962) Actor. DUN; KRAL.

Montagu, Ewen. (1901-1985) English attorney, author, World War II spy. MART.

Montagu, Lily. (1873-1963) English spiritual leader, founder of Liberal Judaism. PASA; TAI.

Montagu, Lady Mary Wortley. (1689-1762) English author. POLK; ROL.

Montalbán, Ricardo. (1920-) Actor, born Mexico. LAE.

Montana, Joe. (1956-) Football player. BUCK3; HUNT; JACT; JAN; KNA9; LAC2; SULG7.

Montcalm, Louis-Joseph. (1712-1759) Canadian colonist, born France. CRO2.

Montefiore, Lady Judith Cohen. (1784-1862) English human rights activist, philanthropist. TAI.

Montefiore, Sir Moses. (1784-1885) English human rights activist, philanthropist. PASA.

Montelius, Oscar. (1843-1921) Swedish archaeologist. FAG.

Montessori, Maria. (1870-1952) Italian educator, physician. CUS2; DUN; HER; HOOB3; HUNTE2; KIR; ROL; STI.

Monteverdi, Claudio. (1567-1643) Italian composer. BLACA2; SEV; VEN.

Montezuma II. (1466-1520) Mexican aztec king. KRAL; POD.

Montgolfier, Jacques Étienne. (1745-1799) French aviation pioneer, inventor. BERL; ZAU2.

Montgolfier, Joseph Michel. (1740-1810) French aviation pioneer, inventor. BERL; WILLI; ZAU2.

Montgomery, Benjamin. (1819-1877) Inventor, slave. SULO.

Montgomery, Bernard Law. (1887-1976) English military leader, World War II field marshal. CRO3; LAC.

Montgomery, Lucy Maud "L. M." (1874-1942) Canadian children's author. HUNTE4.

Montgomery, Monk. (1921-1982) Jazz musician. GOU2.

Montgomery, Wes. (1925-1968) Jazz musician. GOU3.

Moodie, Geraldine Fitzgibbon. (1854-1945) Canadian photographer. POLK.

Moody, Dwight Lyman. (1837-1899) Spiritual leader. CRO5; JACKD.

Moody, Helen Wills. (1906-1998) Olympic tennis player. HASD; JACT.

Moon, John P. (1938-) Computer pioneer, engineer, inventor. SULO; YOUNT2.

Moon, Lottie. (1840-1912) Missionary.
JACKD3.

Moon, Sun Myung. (1920-) Korean cult
leader, Unification Church. KELLA;
STRE.

Moon, Warren. (1956-) Football player.
LAC2.

Moore, Alice Ruth. (1875-1935) Author,
poet. LYO.

Moore, Alonzo. (d. 1914) Magician, showman. HASK6.

Moore, Ann. (1940-) Inventor. THI.

Moore, Audley. (1898-1997) Civil rights activist, women's rights activist. GREA;
RED2.

Moore, Gordon. (1929-) Computer pioneer,
physicist. Presidential Medal of Freedom
recipient. AAS5.

Moore, Henry Spencer. (1898-1986) English
sculptor. BLACA; CUS.

Moore, Oscar. (1916-1981) Jazz musician.
GOU3.

Moore, Sara Jane. (1930-) Assassin, attempted to kill President Gerald Ford.
JONR; STG; SULG9.

Moorer, Thomas H. (1912-2004) Navy chief
of operations, World War II admiral. BOR.

Morani, Alma Dea. (1907-2001) Physician,
plastic surgeon, born Italy. KENJ.

More, Sir Thomas. (1478-1535) English political activist, statesman. CLA2; GOLDM.

Moreau, Gustave. (1826-1898) French
painter. KRY.

Moreno, Rita. (1931-) Actor, dancer, born
Puerto Rico. GAI2; LAE; SIN2.

Morgan, Ann Haven. (1882-1966) Ecologist,
zoologist. KEEN; LEU.

Morgan, Barbara. (1900-1992) Photographer.
HOR.

Morgan, Garrett A. (1877-1963) Inventor.
AAS4; AFR2; ALTMS; AMR; BECKN;
HAC2; HASK8; HAY2; HUD2; MCK;
POT; SULO; TUR2.

Morgan, Henry. (1635-1688) English pirate.
POD; YOUNT5.

Morgan, Jill. (unknown) Mechanical engineer. KAH5.

Morgan, Joe. (1943-) Baseball player. BJA2;
SULG2.

Morgan, John Pierpont "J. P." (1837-1913)
Entrepreneur steel, financier, philanthropist.

CRO; GREEC.

Morgan, Julia. (1872-1957) Architect.
ALTE2; ROL; STU.

Morgan, Rose. (1913-) Entrepreneur beauty
salons. RED.

Morgan, Thomas Hunt. (1866-1945) Biologist, geneticist, zoologist. Nobel Prize winner. AAS13; SHER.

Mori, Kyoko. (1957-) Young adult author,
born Japan. ISH.

Mori, Toshio. (1910-1980) Author, born Japan. SIN.

Morisot, Berthe. (1841-1895) French painter.
BLACA; CUM; KRY.

Morissette, Alanis. (1974-) Canadian pop
singer. ROBB.

Morita, Akio. (1921-) Japanese entrepreneur
electronics, inventor. HOOB4.

Morley, Sylvanus Griswold. (1883-1948)
Archaeologist, World War I spy. FAG.

Morozova, Feodosia. (1630-1675) Russian
noblewoman. HOOB5.

Morpurgo, Rachel Luzzatto. (1790-1871)
Italian poet. TAI.

Morrigan. Celtic goddess of war. MAYE2.

Morrill, Justin. (1810-1898) Congressman,
senator. FAB.

Morris, Esther. (1814-1902) Suffragist,
women's rights activist. ALTE2; LAK;
THIR.

Morris, Gouverneur. (1752-1816) American
Revolutionary War patriot, attorney, congressman, diplomat, senator. MEI.

Morris, Lewis. (1726-1798) American Revolutionary War patriot, military leader, congressman, Declaration of Independence
signer. FRA2; QUI.

Morris, Robert. (1734-1806) American Revolutionary War patriot, congressman, Declaration of Independence signer, financier,
born England. FRA2; QUI.

Morris, Samuel. (1827-1893) Liberian missionary. JACKD.

Morrison, Toni. (1931-) Author, educator.
Nobel Prize winner, Pulitzer Prize winner.
AFR; ALTMS; ARO; BECKN; BOL;
BRED; FEM2; GREA; HAN; HARN;
HEA; HER; KNI; MEE; PER; POT;
RED4; ROL; TWEPO; WILKB.

Morrow, Bobby Joe. (1935-) Olympic track
and field athlete. KNA3.

Morse, Samuel Finley Breese. (1791-1872) Inventor. CRO; LOM2; NOO; STRE2; YEN.

Morton, Ferdinand Joseph "Jelly Roll." (1885-1941) Bandleader, composer, jazz musician. GOU4; SHIP.

Morton, John. (1724-1777) American Revolutionary War patriot, congressman, Declaration of Independence signer. FRA2; QUI.

Morton, William T. G. (1819-1868) Dentist, medical researcher. CURT; FRA3; MUL2.

Mosconi, Willie. (1913-1993) Pocket billards player. JACT.

Moseley-Braun, Carol. (1947-) Presidential candidate, senator. DUD; FEM; GUL; JONV; POT; THRO.

Moser-Proell, Annemarie. (1953-) Austrian olympic skier. JACT.

Moses. (1392?-1272? B.C.E,) Hebrew spiritual leader, founder Judaism. CRO5; GOLDM; JACW2; YEN.

Moses, Anna Mary Robertson "Grandma Moses." (1860-1961) Painter. KRY.

Moses, Bob. (1935-) Civil rights activist, educator. AFR2.

Moses de Leon. (1240-1305) Spanish mystic, spiritual leader. CRO5.

Moses, Edwin. (1955-) Olympic track and field athlete. HUNTE; KNA3.

Moses, Frank. (1931-) German Jewish Holocaust survivor. LAND.

Moss, Cynthia. (1940-) Wildlife biologist, journalist. HAV; POLK.

Moss, Randy. (1977-) Football player. DEI.

Mossell, Gertrude Bustill. (1855-1948) Educator, journalist, women's rights activist. PRI.

Mossell, Nathan Francis. (1856-1946) Physician. COX.

Motley, Archibald, Jr. (1891-1981) Painter. HARD.

Motley, Constance Baker. (1921-) Attorney, civil rights activist, jurist. DUD; GREA; MORI; PLO; ZEI5.

Moton, Robert Russa. (1867-1940) Educator. COX2.

Mott, John Raleigh. (1865-1955) Social worker, missionary, spiritual leader, YMCA head. Nobel Peace Prize winner. KEEN2.

Mott, Lucretia Coffin. (1793-1880) Abolition-

ist, women's rights activist. ROL.

Motte, Rebecca. (d. 1815) American Revolutionary War heroine, patriot. SILC.

Mouhot, Henri. (1826-1861) French archaeologist. SCHEL.

Mourning, Alonzo. (1970-) Basketball player. BJA; PAU.

Mourning Dove (Christine Quintasket) (1888-1936) Okanogan Indian author, Native American rights activist. SMIL2.

Moutoussamy-Ashe, Jeanne. (1951-) Photographer. HOR.

Mowat, Farley. (1921-) Canadian children's author, naturalist. KEEN.

Moxon, June. (unknown) Mixed-media artist, sculptor. THI2.

Mozart, Wolfgang Amadeus. (1756-1791) Austrian composer. BLACA2; BOY; BRIL; EIG; HAZ; KAL; KRULL4; MARZ; VEN; YEN.

Mozhaiski, Alexander. (1825-1890) Russian aviation pioneer, engineer, navy officer. BERL2.

Mraz, George. (1945-) Czech jazz musician. GOU2.

Mubarak, Mohamed Hosni. (1929-) Egyptian president. WAK.

Mugabe, Robert. (1924-) Zimbabwean political leader. RAS.

Muhammad. (570?-632) Arab prophet, founder of Islam religion. CLA2; CRO4; CRO5; GOLDM; JACW2; WILKP2; YEN.

Muhammad, Elijah. (1897-1975) Civil rights activist, leader Nation of Islam. CRO4; GOLDM.

Muir, John. (1838-1914) Author, conservationist, naturalist, born Scotland. BYR; CALV; CRO; CRO4; DEN; FAB3; HAV; KEEN; KRE; LUC2; SAW; STA.

Mukherjee, Bharti. (1940-) Author, born India. CHI; ISH.

Muldowney, Shirley. (1940-) Auto drag racer. COOL; JEN2.

Mulhall, Lucille. (1855-1940) Cowgirl. ALTE2.

Mullaney, Kate. (1845-1906) Workers' rights activist. THIR.

Mullens, Priscilla. (1604-1680) Colonist, born England. KRAL.

Müller, George. (1805-1898) English children's rights activist, human rights activist, born Germany. JACKD.

Müller, Heinrich. (1901-1945) German Nazi war criminal. SCHM4.

Mulligan, Gerald "Gerry." (1927-1996) Bandleader, composer, jazz musician. SHIP.

Münch, Edvard. (1863-1944) Norwegian painter. KRY; NIN.

Münch-Nielsen, Preben. (1926-) Danish Holocaust rescuer. AXE.

Münchhassen, Baron von. (1720-1797) German storyteller. KRAL.

Muniz, Maria Antonia. (1762-1870) Brazilian matriarch. HOOB6.

Munk, Walter. (1917-) Oceanographer, born Austria. POLKI.

Mura, David. (1952-) Poet. CHI.

Murasaki, Shikibu. (978?-1030?) Japanese author. HAZ2; HER; HOOB4; KRULL6; LEO2; SMIL2.

Murdoch, Iris. (1919-1999) English author, born Ireland. KNI.

Murdoch, Rupert. (1931-) Entrepreneur media mogul, publisher. RIT.

Murie, Margaret Thomas. (1902-2003) Author, conservationist. Presidential Medal of Freedom recipient. BYR; KEEN; LUC2; SIR.

Murie, Olaus. (1889-1963) Biologist, illustrator, ornithologist. BYR; KEEN; LUC2.

Murieta, Joaquin. (1832-1853) Mexican gold miner, outlaw. GLA; LAE.

Murphy, Audie. (1924-1971) Actor, World War II Army hero. KRAL.

Murphy, Dervla. (1931-) Irish author, explorer. MCLO2; ZAU.

Murphy, Eddie. (1961-) Actor, comedian. AFR; KAL2.

Murphy, Isaac. (1861-1896) Jockey. KUH.

Murphy, John H., Sr. (d. 1922) Publisher newspapers, slave. AFR.

Murray, David. (1955-) Bandleader, composer, jazz musician. SHIP.

Murray, Joseph E. (1919-) Physician. Nobel Prize winner. CURT.

Murray, Judith Sargent. (1751-1820) Author, editor. SCHM2.

Murray, Mary Lindley. (unknown) American Revolutionary War heroine, patriot. SILC.

Murray, Pauli. (1910-1985) Civil rights activist. MORI3.

Murrow, Edward R. (1908-1965) Broadcast journalist. Presidential Medal of Freedom recipient. CRO; RIT; SAT.

Musgrove, Mary. (1700-1763) Creek Indian colonist, Indian interpreter. CRO2.

Musial, Stan. (1920-) Baseball player. DEA; SULG8.

Musick, Edwin C. (1893-1938) New Zealander World War I aviator. ROS.

Musolino-Alber, Ella. (unknown) Entrepreneur sports promotion. PIL2.

Mussolini, Benito. (1883-1945) Italian dictator, political activist. CRO4; SCHM4.

Mussorgsky, Modest Petrovich. (1839-1881) Russian composer, musician. VEN.

Mutombo, Dikembe. (1966-) Zaire basketball player. BJA; YOUNG.

Mutsuhito. (1852-1912) Japanese emperor Meiji ruler. WILKP4; YEN.

Myers, Walter Dean. (1937-) Children's and young adult author. YUN.

Myrdal, Alva. (1902-1986) Swedish peace activist, sociologist, UNESCO founder. Nobel Peace Prize winner. KEEN2; SCHR2.

N

Nader, Ralph. (1934-) Attorney, presidential candidate, reformer. LEVE

Nahmanides. (Moses ben Nahman) Spanish scholar, spiritual leader. PASA.

Nair, Malathy. (unknown) Chemist, born India. KAH2.

Namath, Joe Willie. (1943-) Football player, sportscaster. KNA9; LEVE; SULG7.

Nanak. (1469-1538) Indian spiritual leader, founder Sikh religion. CRO5; GOLDM; JACW2.

Nansen, Fridtjof. (1861-1930) Norwegian explorer, statesman, zoologist. Nobel Peace Prize winner. KEEN2; PRE.

Naomi. Biblical character. ARM2.

Narahashi, Keiko. (1959-) Children's author, illustrator, born Japan. TALAR3.

Naranjo, Michael. (1944-) Pueblo Indian sculptor, Vietnam War soldier. ALLP.

Naropa. (1016-1100) Indian Buddhist spiritual leader. CRO5.

Nascimento, Edson Arantes do. (Pelé) (1940-) Brazilian soccer player. BOY; BRIL;

HOOB6; JACT; KRULL3; LIT; SULG3.

Nash, Diane. (1938-) Civil rights activist as young person. ROC.

Nasi, Dona Gracia. (1510-1568) Portuguese entrepreneur banking, shipping, philanthropist. LEO3; PASA; TAI.

Nasser, Gamal Abdel. (1918-1970) Egyptian president, United Arab Republic president. MAYB2; RAS.

Nast, Thomas. (1840-1902) Cartoonist, born Germany. RIT.

Nation, Cary. (1846-1911) Reformer. ALTE2; DUN; HARN; HER; LAK.

Natori, Josefina "Josie" Cruz. (1947-) Entrepreneur financier, fashion designer, born Philippines. RAG.

Navratilova, Martina. (1956-) Czech tennis player. HARR; HASD; JACT; SCHWAR; STRU; SULG3.

Naylor, Phyllis Reynolds. (1933-) Children's and young adult author. HILC2.

Naylor, Rosamund. (unknown) Agricultural economist. KAH.

Neave, Richard. (unknown) English forensic scientist, medical illustrator. DON.

Nebhepetre Mentuhotep I. (fl. 2060-2010 B.C.) Egyptian king. BAKR.

Nechaev, Sergei. (1847-1882) Russian terrorist. STRE4.

Nee, Watchman. (1903-1972) Chinese evangelical spiritual leader. JACKD2.

Neel, Alice. (1900-1984) Painter. SILL2.

Nefertari. (fl. 1270 B.C.) Egyptian queen. BAKR.

Nefertiti. (fl. 1372-1350 B.C.) Egyptian queen. BAKR; DUN.

Nehru, Jawaharlal. (1889-1964) Indian prime minister. WAKI.

Nekhebet. Egyptian goddess of royal protection. FIS.

Nell, William Cooper. (1816-1874) Abolitionist, historian. AFR2.

Nelson, Don. (1940-) Basketball coach. KNA10.

Nelson, Gaylord. (1916-) Attorney, environmentalist, governor, senator, World War II Army hero. Presidential Medal of Freedom recipient. BYR; LUC2.

Nelson, Horatio. (1758-1805) English naval leader. CRO3.

Nelson, Prince Rogers. (Prince) (1958-)

Singer, songwriter. AFR.

Nelson, Thomas, Jr. (1738-1789) American Revolutionary War patriot, congressman, Declaration of Independence signer, governor. FRA2; QUI.

Nepatys. Egyptian goddess of the morning. FIS.

Nero. (Nero Claudius Caesar) (37-68) Roman emperor. BAKR3; COOLI; NAR2.

Ness, Eliot. (1903-1957) Crime fighter. DON; ITA3; KRAL.

Nestorius. (c. 381-451) Turkish spiritual leader, founder of Nestorian Church. CRO5.

Neuharth, Allen. (1924-) Editor, journalist, publisher. RIT.

Nevelson, Louise. (1899-1988) Sculptor, born Russia. BRO; STU; TAI.

Nevksy, Alexander. (1220-1263) Russian military leader, Saint. HOOB5.

Newby-Fraser, Paula. (1962-) Zimbabwean olympic track and field athlete, triathlon. HASD; SAV14.

Newman, Lydia D. (unknown) Inventor. SULO2.

Newman, Paul. (1925-) Actor, entrepreneur foods, philanthropist. KRAMB.

Newman, Sarah Jane "Sally Skull." (1817-1866) Civil War heroine, outlaw, pioneer. ALTE2.

Newton, Sir Isaac. (1642-1727) English mathematician, physicist. POD; TIN; WILKP3; WILLS; YEN.

Newton, John. (1725-1807) English songwriter, spiritual leader. JACKD2.

Ney, Elisabet. (1833-1907) Sculptor. ALTE2.

Ng Poon Chew. (1866-1931) Publisher newspaper, spiritual leader, born China. HOOS.

Ngor, Haing. (1947?-1996) Actor, human rights activist, physican, born Cambodia. MORE.

Nguyen, Dustin. (1962-) Actor, born Vietnam. MORE.

Niccacci, Padre Rufino. (unknown) Italian Holocaust rescuer, spiritual leader. FREM; PET.

Nichiren. (1222-1282) Japanese Buddhist monk, spiritual leader. HOOB4.

Nicholaevna, Anastasia. (1901-1918) Russian princess. BREW; KRAL.

Nicholaevna, Olga. (1895-1918) Russian princess. BREW.

Nicholaevna, Tatiana. (1897-1918) Russian princess. BREW.

Nicholas II. (1868-1918) Russian czar. CRO4.

Nicholas. "Santa Claus." (d. 345) Bishop of Myra (Southern Asia Minor—Turkey) saint. KRAL.

Nicholson, Eliza Jane Poitevent Holbrook. (1849-1896) Poet, publisher newspaper. PRI.

Nicholson, Francis. (1655-1728) Colonist, born England. CRO2.

Nicholson, John. (1757-1800) Entrepreneur financier, real estate, born Wales. AAS8.

Nicholson, Vanessa-Mae. (1978-) English musician. STRU2; WEL.

Nicklaus, Jack. (1940-) Golfer. CRO4; ITA5; JACT; SULG3.

Nidal, Abu. (1937-2002) Arab terrorist. STRE4.

Niekro, Joe. (1944-) Baseball player. SLO.

Niekro, Phil. (1939-) Baseball player. SLO.

Nightingale, Florence. (1820-1910) English nurse. BLASH; CEL; CLA; DUN; HER; JACKD2; ROE; ROL; STI.

Niles, Mary Blair. (1880-1959) Explorer. MCLO3.

Nimitz, Chester W. (1885-1966) World War I Navy, World War II Navy admiral, commander of pacific fleet. CRO3; LAC; OLE2.

Niard. Norse God of the ocean. FIS3.

Nixon, Richard Milhous. (1913-1994) Congressman, 37th president of U.S., senator, vice-president, World War II Navy. ADA; BARB; BAU; BLASS; CRO; CRO6; DAV2; FAB; KRULL5; MORR; ROBE2.

Nixon, Thelma "Pat" Ryan. (1912-1993) First Lady. ANT; BARB; GOR; PAST.

Nkrumah, Kwame. (1909-1972) Ghanian prime minister, president. RAS.

Noah, Mordecai Manuel. (1785-1851) Attorney, journalist, playwright. BRO.

Nobel, Alfred Bernhard. (1833-1896) Swedish inventor, philanthropist. KEEN2; TRAU.

Nobile, Umberto. (1885-1978) Italian air force general, arctic explorer, aviator. TES.

Noble, Jordan. (1801-?) Drummer boy War of 1812 and Seminole War. REE2.

Nobunaga, Oda. (1534-1582) Japanese shogun warrior. CRO3.

Noel-Baker, Philip. (1889-1982) English diplomat, peace activist. Nobel Peace Prize winner. KEEN2.

Noether, Emmy. (1882-1935) German mathematician. CEL; HENH; ROL.

Noguchi, Constance Tom. (1948-) Chemist, medical researcher. YOUNT.

Noguchi, Isamu. (1904-1988) Sculptor. GAN; GREENBJ; KRULL2; SIN.

Nolan, Sidney. (1917-1988) Australian painter. BLACA.

Nordenskjöld, Nils Adolf Erik. (1832-1901) Swedish explorer, geologist. LOM.

Nordenskjöld, Nils Otto. (1869-1928) Swedish explorer, geologist. PRE.

Norgay, Tenzig. (1914-1986) Nepalese Sherpa mountaineer. CRO4.

Norman, Dorothy. (1905-1997) Author, photographer. HOR.

Norman, Jessye. (1945-) Singer. TAT.

Norris, George. (1861-1944) Congressman, senator. FAB.

North, Marianne. (1830-1890) English illustrator. POLK.

Northup, Solomon. (1808-1861?) Slave. HAM.

Norton, Alice Mary. (Andre) (1912-) Author, librarian. DAT.

Norton, Daniel. (1840-1918) Civil rights activist, fugitive slave, state legislator. AFR2.

Norton, Eleanor Holmes. (1937-) Attorney, civil rights activist, congresswoman. GREA; LINL2.

Norwood, Brandy. (Brandy) (1979-) Pop singer. ROBB.

Nostradamus. (1503-1566) French physician, visionary. KRAL; KRULL7.

Novacek, Michael. (1948-) Author, paleontologist. TALAD.

Novello, Antonia C. (1944-) Physician, surgeon general of U.S., born Puerto Rico. DEA; HARN; HER; HUNTE2; KRAMB2; LAE; MARV2; MORE2; PAL; ROBE; SIN2; STI.

Novykh, Girgori Yefimovich. (Rasputin) (1871-1916) Russian monk. KRAL.

Noyce, Robert Norton. (1927-1990) Computer scientist, physicist. AAS5; LOM2; NOR.

Noyes, John Humphrey. (1811-1886) Oneida utopian community founder. STRE6.

Nudel, Ida. (1931-) Russian human rights activist, political activist. SEG.

Nuñez, Tommy. (1939-) Basketball referee. MARV2.

Nur, Nawrose. (1981-) Chess champion, born India. BRIL.

Nureyev, Rudolf. (1938-1993) Russian ballet dancer. GON.

Nurmi, Paavo. (1897-1973) Finnish olympic runner, track and field athlete. JACT; USC4.

Nurse, Rebecca. (1621-1692) Colonist, accused of being witch, born England. CRO2.

Nussbaum, Susan. (1953-) Actor, disability rights activist, playwright. KEND.

Nut. Egyptian goddess of the sky. FIS.

Nuttall, Thomas. (1786-1859) Author, botanist, educator, ornithologist, born England. KEEN.

Nuvolari, Tazio. (1892-1953) Italian auto racer. JACT.

Nuxhall, Joe. (1929-) Baseball player, sportscaster. HOOS.

Nyad, Diana. (1949-) Marathon swimmer, sportscaster. LINL.

Nye, Bill. (1955-) Television personality. HAV.

Nyerere, Julius K. (1922-1999) Tanzanian prime minister. RAS.

Nykanen, Matti. (1963-) Finnish olympic ski jumper. JACT.

Nzinga, Anna. (also known as Jinga Mbandi) (1580-1663) West African queen. AFR2; COOL; DUN; GREA; KRULL; POD; ROL.

O

Oakley, Annie. (1860-1926) Cowgirl, showman. ALTE2; COOL; CRO4; DUN; HARN; JAN; KRAL; KRO; LAK; LEVE.

Oates, Joyce Carol. (1938-) Author, educator. KNI; PER; SMIL.

Obata, Chiura. (1888-1975) Painter, born Japan. SIN.

Oberhauser, Karen. (unknown) Biologist.

KAH6.

O'Brien, Dan. (1966-) Olympic track and field athlete, decathlon. KAM; KNA4; SAV12.

Ocampo, Adriana. (1955-) Planetary geologist, born Colombia. OLE.

O'Casey, Sean. (1880-1964) Irish playwright. WEI2.

Occom, Samuel. (1723-1792) Oneida Indian spiritual leader. JACKD4.

Ochoa, Ellen. (1959-) Astronaut, electrical engineer. ALTE2; LAE; MARV; MORE2; OLE; SIN2; STI2; STJ.

Ochoa, Estevan. (1831-1888) Mayor. SIN2.

Ochoa, Severo. (1905-1993) Biochemist, physician, physiologist, born Spain. Nobel Prize winner. LAE; PAL.

O'Connor, Flannery. (1925-1964) Author. GOM; KNI; MEE; VERD.

O'Connor, Sandra Day. (1930-) Attorney, Supreme Court justice. ALTE2; DEN; GUL; HARN; HEA; JONV; KRAMB2; LEVE; ZEI5.

O'Day, Anita. (1919-) Jazz singer. GOU5; ORG.

Odell, Jonathan. (1737-1818) American Revolutionary War traitor, author, physician, spiritual leader, spy. SCHM2.

Odhimabo, Thomas. (1931-2003) Kenyan entomologist. GRAH.

Odin. Norse god of skies. FIS3.

Odum, Eugene. (1913-2002) Ecologist, educator, ornithologist. LEU.

Odum, Lamar. (1979-) Basketball player. PAU.

Odysseus. Greek adventurer. ALTE.

Offenbach, Genia. (unknown) Polish Jewish Holocaust survivor. LAND.

Offenbach, Jacques. (1819-1880) French opera composer, musician. VEN.

Offenbach, Rubin. (unknown) Polish Jewish Holocaust survivor. LAND.

Oglethorpe, James. (1696-1785) Colonist, settled Georgia, born England. CRO2; DON5.

O'Hara, Mary. (1935-) Irish musician, singer. STRU2.

O'Keefe, Georgia. (1887-1986) Painter. Presidential Medal of Freedom recipient. ALTE2; COOL; CUS; DAN; GLU;

GREENBJ; HARN; HEA; HER; HUNTE3; KRULL2; KRY; SILL3; TWEPO.

Okita, Dwight. (1958-) Musician, playwright, poet. CHI.

Okuni. (1571-1610) Japanese kabuki actor. HOOB4.

Olajuwon, Hakeem. (1963-) Basketball player, born Nigeria. BJA; KNA5; KRAMS3; TOR4.

Oliver, Joseph "King." (1885-1938) Bandleader, composer, jazz musician. SHIP.

Olivier, Sir Laurence. (1907-1989) English actor, director. WEI2.

Olmos, Edward James. (1947-) Actor. LAE.

Olmstead, Frederick Law. (1822-1903) Landscape architect, environmentalist. CRO; FAB3.

O'Malley, Grace. (1530-1603) Irish pirate queen. LEO3; SHAR; WEA.

Omidyar, Pierre. (1967-) Entrepreneur online shopping, Internet pioneer, born France. HENH2.

O'Mullan, John. (1670-1722) Irish outlaw. BLACG2.

Onassis, Jacqueline Lee Bouvier Kennedy. (1929-1994) Editor, First Lady. ANT; BARB; CRO4; DUN; GOR; HARN; HER; PAST; TAYS; USC3.

Oñate, Juan de. (1550-1630) Colonist, explorer, born Spain. CRO2; DOH2; LAE; SIN2.

Ondaatje, Michael. (1943-) Author, filmmaker, playwright, poet, born Sri Lanka. CHI.

O'Neal, Shaquille. (1972-) Basketball player. BJA; KRAMS3; PAU; RED6.

O'Neill, Cecilia Rose. (1874-1944) Cartoonist, illustrator, inventor. BRIL; CURR2.

O'Neill, Eugene Gladstone. (1888-1953) Playwright. Nobel Prize winner, Pulitzer Prize winner. FAB2; LEVE; TWEPR; WEI2.

Onizuka, Ellison. (1946-1986) Astronaut. MORE; RAG; SIN.

Opdyke, Irene. (1921-2003) Polish author, Holocaust rescuer. LYM; PET.

Opechancanough. (1556-1646) Lenape Indian chief. CRO2.

Opie, Iona. (1923-) English children's author, folklorist, illustrator, scholar. MARC3.

Oppenheim, Meret. (1913-1985) Swiss jewelry designer, painter, poet, sculptor, born Germany. KNI.

Oppenheimer, J. Robert. (1904-1967) Inventor, physicist. CRO; FOX; HAV; LEVE; SHER.

Ordóñez, Magglió. (1974-) Baseball player, born Venezuela. STEWM.

Ordóñez, Rey. (1971-) Baseball player, born Cuba. STEWM.

Ordway, Katherine. (1899-1979) Conservationist, ecologist. KEEN.

O'Ree, Willie. (1935-) Canadian hockey player. KAM.

Orellana, Francisco de. (1511-1546) Spanish explorer. ALTE; LANG; LOM; PRE.

Orkin, Ruth. (1921-1985) Photographer. HOR.

Orr, Bobby. (1948-) Canadian hockey player. KNA8; SULG3.

Orr, John Boyd. (1880-1971) Scottish agricultural scientist, author, educator, nutritionist, U.N. Food and Agricultural Organization director. Nobel Peace Prize winner. KEEN2.

Orsted Pedersen, Niels-Henning. (unknown) Norwegian jazz musician. GOU2.

Ortega, Beatriz Gonzalez. (unknown) Mexican nurse during Revolution 1910. COOL.

Ortiz, Simon. (1941-) Acoma Indian author, poet. AVE.

Orwell, George. (1903-1950) English author. PER.

Osborn, Albert Sherman. (1858-1946) Forensic scientist. YEA.

Osborn, Henry. (1857-1935) Paleontologist. AAS.

Osborn, June. (1937-) AIDS activist, physician. STI.

Osborne, Mary. (1921-1992) Jazz musician. GOU3.

Osceola. (1804-1838) Seminole Indian chief. AVE; RAPD2.

Osiris. Egyptian god of the underworld. FIS.

Osler, Sir William. (1849-1919) Canadian educator, physician. CURT.

Ossietzky, Carl von. (1889-1938) German author, peace activist. Nobel Peace Prize winner. KEEN2.

Ossoli, Margaret Fuller. (1810-1850) Journalist, suffragist, women's rights activist. HER; PRI; RIT.

Osterman, Edward. (Monk Eastman) (1873-1920) Gangster. BLACG.

Oswald, Lee Harvey. (1939-1963) Assassin of President John F. Kennedy. JONR; NET; STG; SULG9.

Otis, Elisha Graves. (1811-1861) Inventor. AAS3.

Ott, Mel. (1909-1958) Baseball player, manager. SULG8.

Otto I, the Great. (912-973) German Holy Roman Emperor. CRO3; YEN.

Otto, Kristen. (1966-) German olympic swimmer. JACT.

Ouray. (1820-1880) Ute Indian chief. SHER2.

Overbeck, Carla. (1969-) Olympic soccer player. LAY2; MILM; RUT4.

Ovid. (Publius Ovidius Naso) (43 B.C.-17 A.D.) Roman poet. BAKR3.

Owen, Robert. (1771-1858) Welsh Harmonist utopian society cofounder, philanthropist, social reformer. STRE6.

Owens, Dana Elaine. (Queen Latifah) (1970-) Actor, singer. TAT.

Owens, Jesse. (1913-1980) Olympic track and field athlete. ALTMS; BECKN; BOOK2; BOY; DON2; JACT; JAN; KNA3; KNA4; KRULL3; MARZ; POT; RED6; SAV4; SULG3; USC4.

Owens-Adair, Bethenia. (1840-1926) Physician. KET; LAK.

Oxenbury, Helen. (1938-) English children's author, illustrator. MARC3.

Oya. African goddess. COOL.

Ozawa, Seiji. (1935-) Conductor, born Japan. SIN.

Ozick, Cynthia. (1928-) Author. TAI.

P

Paca, William. (1740-1795) American Revolutionary War patriot, attorney, colonial governor, congressman, Declaration of Independence signer, jurist. FRA2; QUI.

Pacelli, Eugenio Maria Guiseppe. *See* Pius XII.

Pacheco, Romualdo. (1831-1899) Congressman, gold miner, pioneer. LAE

Pack, Amy Thorne "Betty." (1910-1963) World War II spy. COOL; SULG4.

Packard, David. (1912-1996) Computer pioneer, entrepreneur computers, government employee, philanthropist. Presidential Medal of Freedom recipient. AAS12.

Paddleford, Clementine Haskin. (1900-1967) Journalist. PRI.

Paddock, Charlie. (1900-1943) Olympic sprinter, track and field athlete. KNA3.

Paganini, Niccolo. (1782-1840) Italian composer, musician. BLACA2; VEN.

Page, Alan. (1945-) Attorney, football player. SAV7.

Page, Walter. (1900-1957) Jazz musician. GOU2.

Paige, Leroy "Satchel." (1906-1982) Baseball player. LIT; POT; SLO; SULG5; SULM; TUR2; WIN2.

Paik, Nam June. (1932-) Composer, mixed-media artist, born Korea. SIN.

Paine, Robert Treat. (1731-1814) American Revolutionary War patriot, attorney, congressman, Declaration of Independence signer, jurist. FRA2; QUI.

Paine, Thomas. (1737-1809) Author, journalist, philosopher, born England. JACW; RIT; SCHM2; THOM.

Paisiello, Giovanni. (1740-1816) Italian opera composer. VEN.

Palamas, Gregory. (1296-1359) Greek Orthodox spiritual leader. CRO5.

Palau, Luis. (1934-) Author, spiritual leader, born Argentina. JACKD3.

Palestrina, Giovanni. (1525-1594) Italian composer, singer. VEN.

Paley, Grace. (1922-) Author. PER.

Palmer, Anyim. (unknown) Educator. AFR2.

Palmer, Arnold. (1929-) Golfer. CRO4; ITA5; JACT.

Palmer, Jim. (1945-) Baseball player. SULG5.

Palmeiro, Rafael. (1964-) Baseball player, born Dominican Republic. MARV6; STEWM2.

Palmier, Remo. (1923-2002) Jazz musician. GOU3.

Pankhurst, Christabel. (1880-1958) English suffragist. ROL; THOM.

Pankhurst, Emmeline. (1858-1928) English suffragist. DUN; HAC7; ROL; THOM.

Pantoja, Antonio. (1922-2002) Educator, human rights activist, social worker, born Puerto Rico. Presidential Medal of Freedom recipient. LAE.

Pappenheim, Berta. (1859-1936) German organization founder, social reformer, social worker. TAI.

Paradis, Maria Theresia von. (1759-1824) Austrian composer, musician. WEL.

Paré, Ambroise. (1510-1590) French physician. CURT; POD.

Pariseau, Esther. (Mother Joseph) (1832-1902) Human rights activist, spiritual leader. ALTE2.

Parker, Bonnie. (1911-1934) Outlaw. BLACG; CRO4; DUN; KRAL; THOM2.

Parker, Charles Christopher "Bird" Jr. (1920-1955) Bandleader, composer, jazz musician. AFR; GOU; HAC3; JAZ; MON; MOU; SHIP.

Parker, Dorothy. (1893-1967) Author, poet, screenwriter. COOL; KNI.

Parker, Ely Samuel. (1828-1895) Seneca Indian chief, Civil War assistant to General Grant, Commissioner of Indian Affairs. AVE; MON2.

Parker, Henriette. (1932-) Belgian Jewish Holocaust survivor. KUS.

Parker, John. (1827-1900) Inventor, slave. MCK.

Parker, Robert Leroy. (Butch Cassidy) (1866-1937) Outlaw. SAV.

Parkerson, Michelle. (1953-) Filmmaker. AFR.

Parkhurst, Charlotte Darkey. (1812-1879) Pioneer, stagecoach driver. CALV; FUR2.

Parkman, Francis. (1823-1893) Frontiersman, historian. CALV.

Parks, Gordon. (1912-) Photographer. GAI; HAC4; JACKN.

Parks, Henry G. (1916-1989) Entrepreneur food services. HASK.

Parks, Paul. (1923-) Civil engineer, Holocaust rescuer, World War II soldier. TIT.

Parks, Rosa. (1913-) Civil rights activist. Presidential Medal of Freedom recipient. ALLZ; ALTMS; BECKN; CRO; DEN; DUB; FEM; GREA; HARM; HEA; MARZ; PIN; PLO; RED2; ROL; TUR2.

Parlow, Cindy. (1978-) Olympic soccer player. LAY2; MILM.

Parris, Betty. (1682-1760) Colonist, puritan, accused others of witchcraft. HOOS.

Parris, Samuel. (1653-1720) Colonist, puritan, accused others of witchcraft, spiritual leader, born England. STRE3.

Parsons, Benny. (1941-) Nascar auto racer. RIL.

Parsons, Elsie Clews. (1875-1941) Anthropologist, folklorist, sociologist. WEI.

Parsons, Lucy. (1853-1943) Civil rights activist, revolutionary, slave, workers' rights activist. KAT.

Parton, Sara Payne. (Fanny Fern) (1811-1872) Author, journalist. PRI.

Pascal, Blaise. (1623-1662) French mathematician, philosopher, physicist. TIN.

Pass, Joe. (1929-1994) Jazz musician. GOU3.

Passy, Frédéric. (1822-1912) French International League of Peace and Freedom founder, peace activist. Nobel Peace Prize winner. KEEN2.

Pasteur, Louis. (1822-1895) French chemist, microbiologist. CURT; MUL; TIN.

Pastorius, Jaco. (1951-1987) Composer, jazz musician. GOU2.

Pastrana, Julia. (1832-1860) Mexican "bearded lady" showperson. DRI.

Paterson, Katherine. (1932-) Children's and young adult author. HILC2; YUN.

Paterson, William. (1745-1806) American Revolutionary War patriot, attorney, congressman, senator, Supreme Court justice, born Ireland. MEI.

Patino, Simon I. (1865-1947) Bolivian entrepreneur tin mines. HOOB6.

Paton, John G. (1824-1906) Scottish missionary. JACKD4.

Patrick. (389?-461?) Irish folk hero, slave, saint, spiritual leader. CRO5; JACW2; KRAL.

Patrick, Ruth. (1907-) Freshwater biologist, ecologist. STI2.

Patton, George C. (1885-1945) Olympic track and field athlete, pentathlon, World War II Army general. CRO3; CRO4; KNA; OLE2; SCHM4.

Paul. (10?-62?) Saint. ARM; CLA2; CRO5; GOLDM; JACW2; YEN.

Paul, Alice. (1885-1977) Attorney, suffragist, women's rights activist. DUM; HARN; HEL; ZEI5.

Paul, Les. (1916-) Jazz musician. GOU3.

Pauli, Wolfgang. (1900-1958) Austrian physicist. Nobel Prize winner. HAV.

Pauling, Linus Carl. (1901-1994) Chemist, educator, medical researcher. Nobel Peace Prize winner, Nobel Prize winner. HAV; KEEN2; SHER; TIN.

Paulsen, Gary. (1939-) Children's and young adult author. AUT; HILC2; YUN.

Paumann, Konrad. (1415-1473) German composer. VEN.

Pavlov, Ivan Petrovich. (1849-1936) Russian physiologist. Nobel Prize winner. TIN.

Pavlova, Anna. (1881-1931) Russian ballet dancer. DUN; HER; HOOB5; ROE.

Payne, Ethel L. (1911-1991) Journalist. RIT.

Payne, Katy. (1937-) Acoustic biologist. POLK; SAY; SIR.

Payne-Gaspochkin, Cecilia. (1900-1979) Astronomer, born England. CAM.

Payton, Gary. (1968-) Basketball player. PAU.

Payton, Philip A. (1876-1917) Entrepreneur real estate. HASK; HASK5.

Payton, Walter. (1954-) Football player. BUCK; HUNT; LAC3.

Peacock, Gary. (1935-) Jazz musician. GOU2.

Peake, Mary Smith. (1823-1862) Educator. COX2.

Pearson, Lester. (1897-1972) Canadian ambassador, diplomat, prime minister. Nobel Peace Prize winner. KEEN2.

Peary, Robert. (1856-1920) Arctic explorer, naval officer. ALTE; CRO4; CURR; LEVE; LOM; PRE; SCHEL2; SCHR; WAT.

Peck, Annie Smith. (1850-1935) Adventurer, archaeologist, mountaineer. BRY; HAC; HARN; HASD; MCLO3; POLK; RAPD; ZAU.

Peck, Ellen. (1829-1915) Swindler. BLACG5.

Peck, Richard. (1934-) Children's and young adult author. YUN.

Pedro II. (1825-1891) Brazilian emperor, king. PAP.

Peel, Sir Robert. (1788-1850) English crimefighter, statesman. ITA3.

Pei, Ieah Ming "I. M." (1917-) Architect, born China. Presidential Medal of Freedom recipient. DEN; MORE; RAG; SIN.

Peizerat, Gwendal. (1972-) French olympic figure skater. MILT.

Pelé. *See* Nascimento, Edson Arantes do.

Pelletier, David. (1974-) Canadian olympic figure skater. MILT.

Peña, Federico. (1947-) Attorney, cabinet member, mayor. LAE; MARV; MORE2.

Penn, Gillette. (Penn) (1956-) Magician. WOO2.

Penn, John. (1740-1788) American Revolutionary War patriot, attorney, congressman, Declaration of Independence signer. FRA2; QUI.

Penn, William. (1644-1718) Colonist, founder Pennsylvania colony, born England. CRO2; DOH3; GOLDM.

Penney, James Cash. (1875-1971) Entrepreneur retail stores. AAS12.

Penniman, Richard Wayne. (Little Richard) (1932-) Rock singer. LES.

Pennington, James W. C. (1809-1870) Abolitionist, civil rights activist, educator, slave, spiritual leader. AFR2.

Pennington, Mary Engle. (1872-1952) Chemist. STI2.

Penrose, Roger. (1931-) English mathematician. HAV.

Penry, Jacques. (unknown) French forensic scientist. YEA.

Pepi II. (fl. 2278-2184 B.C.) Egyptian king. BAKR.

Pepperell, William. (1696-1759) Army officer, colonist. CRO2.

Perera, Hilda. (1926-) Children's author, born Cuba. MARV6.

Peres, Shimon. (1923-) Israeli prime minister, born Poland. Nobel Peace Price winner. KEEN2; WAK.

Pérez, Neifi. (1973-) Baseball player, born Dominican Republic. STEWM.

Perez, Rosie. (1964-) Actor, choreographer, dancer. MARV5.

Perez, Selena Quintanilla. (Selena) (1971-1995) Pop singer. LAE; MARV4; ROBB.

Pergolesi, Giovanni Battista. (1710-1736) Italian composer. VEN.

Pericles. (495-429 BC) Greek architect, political activist. BAKR2; CRO4; NAR; WILKP2; YEN.

Perkin, Sir William Henry. (1838-1907) English chemist. TIN.

Perkins, Anthony. (1932-1992) Actor. GON.

Perkins, Frances. (1882-1965) Cabinet member, social worker. HARN; KRAMB2;

MORI; ROL; ZEI5.

Perkins, John. (1930-) Civil rights activist, spiritual leader. JACKD2.

Perkins, Maxwell. (1884-1947) Editor. LEVE.

Perkins, Nancy. (1949-) Inventor. BLASH4.

Perl, Gisella. (1910-1985) Hungarian Jewish Holocaust survivor, physician. TAI.

Perlasca, Giorgio. (1910-1992) Italian Holocaust rescuer. FREM.

Perlman, Itzhak. (1945-) Israeli musician. BRO; KEND.

Perón, Eva "Evita." (1919-1952) Argentine actor, political activist. COOL; DUN; GUL; HER; HOOB6; KRAL; KRULL; PARJ2; PRI3; ROE.

Péron, Juan Domingo. (1895-1974) Argentine dictator, president. PAP.

Perot, Ross. (1930-) Entrepreneur electronics, presidential candidate. AAS2.

Perry, Carrie Saxon. (1931-) Mayor. AFR2.

Perry, Christopher J. (d. 1921) Publisher newspapers. AFR.

Perry, Gaylord. (1938-) Baseball player. SULG5.

Pershing, John Joseph. (1860-1948) Historian, World War I Army general. Pulitzer Prize winner. CRO4.

Person, Chuck. (1964-) Basketball player. TOR3.

Pert, Candace Beebe. (1946-) Biochemist, medical researcher. YOUNT3.

Pestalozzi, Johann. (1746-1827) Swiss educator. CLA.

Pétain, Henri Phillipe. (1856-1951) French World War I, World War II military leader. CRO3.

Peter. (d. 67 A.D?) Apostle, saint. ARM; MAYE.

Peter I the Great. (1672-1725) Russian czar. CRO3; HOOB5; MARZ; MEL.

Peters, C.J. (1940-) Medical researcher, physician. YOUNT4.

Peterson, Esther. (1906-1997) Consumer Affairs Director, women's rights activist, workers' rights activist. THIR.

Peterson, Oscar. (1925-) Canadian jazz musician. SHIP.

Petitclerc, Chantal. (1969-) Canadian wheelchair racer. BRY.

Petrie, William Matthew Fliders. (1853-1942) English archaeologist. FAG.

Petrovic, Drazen. (1964-) Yugoslavian olympic basketball player. TOR3.

Petry, Ann. (1911-1997) Children's and adult author. WILKB.

Pettiford, Oscar. (1922-1960) Jazz musician. GOU2.

Pettit, Bob. (1932-) Basketball player. RAPK2.

Petty, Richard. (1937-) Nascar auto racer. JACT; RIL.

Pfeiffer, Ida. (1797-1858) Austrian adventurer, author. MCLO4; POLK; STEFO2.

Phayllos of Cortona. (c. 480 B.C.) Greek olympic track and field athlete, pentathlon. JACT.

Phelps, Jaycie. (1979-) Olympic gymnast. KLE.

Phidias. (c. 490-432 B.C.) Greek sculptor. BAKR2; KRY.

Phidippides. (505-490? B.C.) Greek olympic track and field athlete. BAKR2; JACT.

Philby, Harold Arlen Russell "Kim." (1912-1988) English spy. MART; THOM4.

Philip. Apostle, saint. MAYE.

Philip, King. (Metacom, Metacomet, Pometacom) (1638-1676) Wampanoag Indian chief. CRO2; KAL3; POD.

Philip II. (383-336 B.C.) Greek general, king. BAKR2; CRO3.

Philip II. (1165-1223) French king. PAP.

Philip II. (1527-1598) Spanish king. PAP.

Phillips, Frank. (1873-1950) Entrepreneur oil. AAS7.

Phillips, Pauline Esther "Popo." (Abigail Van Buren) (1918-) Journalist. PRI.

Phips, William. (1651-1695) Colonial governor. CRO2.

Piazza, Mike. (1968-) Baseball player. SCHER; SCHWAR.

Picasso, Pablo. (1881-1973) Spanish ceramicist, painter, sculptor. BLACA; BOY; CUM; CUS; GLU; KRULL2; KRY; TWEPR; YEN.

Piccard, Jacques. (1922-) Swiss oceanographer. PRE.

Piccinni, Noccolo. (1728-1800) Italian opera composer. VEN.

Pickering, William. (1858-1938) Astronomer, space scientist. RIC3.

Pickett, Bill. (1870-1932) Rodeo star. KAT2;

MON2; POT.

Pickett, George Edward. (1825-1875) Civil War general. GREEC2.

Pickford, Mary. (1893-1979) Canadian actor. GAI2; HARN; MCLU; ROE.

Pico, Pio de Jesus. (1801-1894) Mexican governor. LAE.

Picotte, Susan La Flesche. (1865-1915) Ponca and Omaha Indian physician. AVE; KENJ2; KET; KIR; RAPD2; ROBE; STI.

Pierce, Ambrose. (1842-1914) Author, Civil War soldier. MAD.

Pierce, Franklin. (1804-1869) Army general Mexican War, attorney, congressman, 14th President of U.S. ADA; BARB; BAU; BLASS; CRO6; DAV2; MORR.

Pierce, Jane Appleton. (1806-1863) First Lady. BARB; GOR; PAST.

Pierce, Mary. (1975-) Tennis player, born Canada. RUT5.

Pierce, Naomi. (1954-) Biologist. POLK.

Pike, Zebulon Montgomery. (1779-1813) Explorer, military leader War of 1812. BAKS; POD; PRE.

Pilatre de Rozier, Jean-François. (1756-1785) French aviation pioneer. WILLI.

Pilecki, Witold. (1900-1948) Polish Holocaust Resistance leader. GRAN.

Pincay, Laffit, Jr. (1946-) Jockey, born Panama. JACT.

Pinchback, Pinckney Benton Stewart "P. B. S." (1837-1921) Civil War captain, congressman, governor. ALTMS; BECKN; HASK2.

Pinchot, Gifford. (1865-1946) Conservationist, forester, governor. FAB3; KEEN.

Pinckney, Eliza Lucas. (1722-1793) Agronomist, colonist, entrepreneur indigo crops, born West Indies. CRO2; FUR; HEA; HOOS; VAR; WEL.

Pindar. (518-446 B.C.) Greek poet. BAKR2.

Pineda, Álonzo Alvarez de. (1792-1872) Spanish explorer, Navy admiral. SIN2.

Pinel, Philippe. (1745-1826) French disability rights activist, physician, reformer. CURT.

Pinkerton, Allan. (1818-1884) Private detective, born Scotland. CRO; DON; ITA3; MART; SAW.

Pinkney, Brian. (1961-) Children's author, illustrator. TALAR2.

Pinkney, Jerry. (1939-) Children's author, illustrator. MARC2; MARC3; TALAR.

Pinzón, Martin. (1440-1493) Spanish explorer. PRE.

Pinzón, Vicente. (1463-1514) Spanish explorer. PRE.

Pippin, Horace. (1888-1946) Painter, World War I soldier. AFR; HARD; KEND.

Pippin, Scottie. (1965-) Basketball player. AAS17; BJA; BJA3; PAU.

Pire, Dominique-Georges. (1910-1969) Belgian peace activist, spiritual leader, founded University of Peace. Nobel Peace Prize winner. KEEN2.

Pissarro, Camille. (1830-1903) French painter. IMP; KRY.

Pitcher, Harriet Brooks. (1876-1933) Canadian physicist. DID.

Pitcher, Molly. *See* McCauley, Mary Ludwig Hays.

Pitt, William. (1708-1778) English prime minister during American Revolutionary War. SCHM2.

Pitt-Rivers, Augustus Lane Fox. (1827-1900) English archaeologist. FAG.

Pius XII. (Eugenio Maria Guiseppe Pacelli) (1867-1958) Italian pope during World War II. SCHM4.

Pizan, Christine de. (1365-1430) French author, poet. DUN; HER; KNI.

Pizarro, Francisco. (1475-1541) Spanish explorer, military leader. ALTE; CRO3; POD; PRE; WAT.

Pizzarelli, John, Jr. (1960-) Jazz musician. GOU3.

Place, Etta. (1875-1940) Outlaw. ALTE2; SAV2.

Planck, Max Karl Ernst Ludwig. (1858-1947) German physicist. Nobel Prize winner. HAV.

Plantain, James. (fl. 1720) Jamaican pirate. BLACG4.

Plante, Jacques. (1929-1986) Canadian hockey player. JACT; SPI.

Platearius, Trotula. (fl. 1080) Italian physician. LEO2.

Plato. (427-347 B.C.) Greek mathematician, philosopher. BAKR2; NAR3; YEN.

Plautus. (Titus Maccius Plautus) (254-184 B.C.) Roman playwright. BAKR3.

Pleasant, Mary Ellen "Mammy." (1814-1904) Abolitionist, civil rights activist, entrepreneur real estate, pioneer. KAT.

Pliny the Elder. (23-79) Roman historian. AND.

Pliny the Younger. (Gaius Plinius Caecilius) (61-113) Roman attorney, sttorney, author. BAKR3.

Plummer, Edouard E. (unknown) Educator. AFR2.

Plunkett, Jim. (1947-) Football player. Heisman trophy winner. DEV.

Plushenko, Evgeny. (1982-) Russian olympic figure skater. MILT.

Pocahontas. (1595-1617) Powhatan Indian princess. CRO2; CRO4; DOH5; HARN; HEA; HOOS; KRAL; LEVE; MCD; MON2; POD; ROL.

Podkopayeva, Lilia. (1978-) Ukrainian olympic gymnast. GREES.

Poe, Edar Allan. (1809-1849) Author, poet. FAB2; KRULL6; LEVE; MAD; OFT2; PER; ROM.

Pohl, Frederik. (1919-) Author. DAT.

Poitier, Sidney. (1924-) Actor, filmmaker. POT; RED3.

Polak, Ina. (1923-) Dutch Jewish Holocaust survivor. LAND4.

Polak, Jack. (unknown) Dutch Jewish Holocaust survivor. LAND4.

Polk, James. (1795-1849) Congressman, governor, 11th president of U.S. ADA; BARB; BAU; BLASS; CRO; CRO6; DAV2; FAB; MORR.

Polk, Sarah Childress. (1803-1891) First Lady. BARB; GOR; PAST; TAYS.

Pollack, Ben. (1903-1971) Bandleader, jazz musician. GOU6.

Pollock, Jackson. (1912-1956) Painter. CUM; GREENBJ; KRY; TWEPO.

Polo, Marco. (1254-1324) Italian adventurer, explorer. ALTE; CRO4; LANG; LOM; POD; PRE; WAT; WILKP2; YEN.

Polovchak, Walter. (1967-) Political activist, born Russia. BRIL.

Polydamus. (c. 408 B.C.) Greek olympic boxer, wrestler. JACT.

Pompey. (Gnaeus Pompeius Magnus) (106-48 B.C.) Roman military leader, political activist. BAKR3; CRO3.

Ponce, Carlos. (1972-) Puerto Rican pop singer. KRULI.

Ponce de Léon, Juan. (1460-1521) Spanish explorer. ALTE; CRO2; FRIT; LAE; PARN; PRE; SIN2.

Pontiac. (1720-1769) Ottawa Indian chief, colonist, French and Indian War military leader. AVE; CRO2; KAL3.

Poodry, Clifton. (1943-) Seneca Indian biologist, geneticist. STJ3.

Pool, Judith Graham. (1919-1975) Physiologist. STI2.

Poor, Salem. (1747-1780) American Revolutionary War soldier. SCHM2.

Pop-Pank. (1790-?) Native American girl, friend of Sacagawea. ROE.

Popé. (c.1650-1692) San Juan Pueblo Indian medicine man, military leader. AVE; CRO2.

Popieluszk, Father Jerzy. (1947-1984) Polish political activist, spiritual leader. CLA; TRAC2.

Poquelin, Jean Baptiste. (Molière) French actor, playwright. HOOB2; WEI2.

Porsche, Ferdinand. (1875-1952) Czech auto maker. ITA6.

Porter, Katherine Anne. (1890-1980) Author. BRED; GOM.

Porter, William Sydney. (O. Henry) (1862-1910) Author. FAB2; PER.

Portola, Gaspar de. (1723-1784) Colonist, born Spain. CRO2.

Posada, Jorge. (1971-) Baseball player, born Puerto Rico. STEWM.

Post, Wiley. (1899-1935) Aviation pioneer. WILLI.

Potter, Beatrix. (1866-1943) English children's author and illustrator. HER; HUNTE4; MARZ; THI2.

Potter, Richard. (1783-1835) Magician. HASK6.

Potter, Tommy. (1918-1988) Jazz musician. GOU2.

Poussaint, Alvin Francis. (1934-) Civil rights activist, psychiatrist. COX.

Poussin, Nicolas. (1594-1665) Italian painter, born France. CUM; SEV.

Powdermaker, Hortense. (1900-1970) Anthropologist. WEI.

Powell, Adam Clayton, Jr. (1908-1972) Civil rights activist, congressman, spiritual leader. AFR2; BECKN; CIV; DUD.

Powell, Clilan Bethany. (1894-1977) Physician, publisher newspapers. AFR.

Powell, Colin. (1937-) Army Chair Joint Chiefs of Staff, cabinet member, Gulf War general, Vietnam War infantry officer. Presidential Medal of Freedom recipient. BECKN; BOOK; BOR; BRED2; DUD; HASK2; MED; RIC.

Powell, Cristen. (1979-) Drag racer. WEL.

Powell, Dawn. (1897-1965) Author. KNI.

Powell, Earl "Bud." (1924-1966) Composer, jazz musician. GOU4; SHIP.

Powell, John Wesley. (1834-1902) Civil War soldier, explorer, geologist. CALV; FAB3; KEEN; KEND; PRE.

Powell, William J. (1897?-1942) Author, engineer, World War I Army pilot. HART; JONS2.

Powhatan. (1550-1618) Algonquin Lenape Indian chief, colonist. CRO2.

Pozo, Chano. (1915-1948) Jazz musician, born Cuba. GOU6.

Prabhupada, A. C. Bhaktivedanta. (1896-1977) Indian cult leader, spiritual leader, established Hare Krishnas. STRE.

Pran, Dith. (1942-) Journalist, born Cambodia. SIN.

Praxiteles. (390?-330 BC) Greek sculptor. KRY.

Preisand, Sally. (1946-) Spiritual leader. TAI.

Prekerowa, Teresa. (1921-) Polish historian, Holocaust rescuer. AXE.

Prendergast, Franklyn G. (1945-) Biochemist, physician. STJ.

Presley, Elvis. (1935-1977) Rock singer. BOY; CRO; KNA2; KRAL; LEVE; WOO3.

Preston, Ann. (1813-1872) Abolitionist, educator, physician, reformer. STI.

Pretty Shield. (1850-1930) Crow Indian healer. ALTE2.

Price, Florence. (1888-1953) Composer. NIC2.

Price, John. (1840-?) Fugitive slave. FRA.

Price, Leontyne. (1927-) Opera singer. Presidential Medal of Freedom recipient. BOL; GREA; PLO; TUR2.

Price, Mark. (1964-) Basketball player. TOR3.

Pride, Charley. (1938-) Entrepreneur banks, music publishing, singer. RED5.

Priestly, Joseph. (1773-1804) English chemist, spiritual leader. TIN.

Primavera, Elise. (1955-) Children's author, illustrator. TALAR3.

Prince. (singer) *See* Nelson, Prince Rogers.

Prince, Lucy Terry. (1733-1821) Poet. ALTMS; KNI.

Prince, Mary. (1788-?) Author, fugitive slave. FRA.

Printz, Johan. (1592-1663) Colonial governor, born Sweden. CRO2.

Pritchard, Marion van Binsbergen. (1920-) Dutch Holocaust rescuer. LYM.

Procope, Ernesta. (1932-) Entrepreneur insurance company. RED.

Proctor, Barbara Gardner. (1933-) Entrepreneur advertising. RED.

Proctor, William. (1801-1884) Entrepreneur soap company. AAS12.

Prokofiev, Sergei Sergeevich. (1891-1953) Russian composer. KRULL4.

Pronger, Chris. (1974-) Canadian olympic hockey player. BREH.

Prophet, Nancy Elizabeth. (1890-1960) Sculptor. HARD.

Prosser, Gabriel. (1776-1800) Slave insurrectionist. ALTMS; HAM.

Prothrow-Stith, Deborah. (1954-) Human rights activist, physician, state public health commissioner. COX.

Provensen, Alice. (1918-) Children's author, illustrator. MARC2.

Provensen, Martin. (1916-1987) Children's author, illustrator. MARC2.

Pryor, Richard. (1940-) Actor, comedian. PARJ.

Ptahhotep. (fl. 2400 B.C.) Egyptian author. BAKR.

Ptolemy. (100-170) Greek astronomer, geographer. AND; NAR3; WILLS.

Ptolemy I. (Ptolemy Soter) (c. 367-283 B.C.) Greek military leader, ruler. BAKR2.

Puccini, Giacomo. (1858-1924) Italian opera composer. VEN.

Puckett, Kirby. (1961-) Baseball player. SEHN; SULG2.

Pudaite, Rochunga. (1927-) Bible translator, born India. JACKD3.

Puente, Tito. (1923-2000) Bandleader, jazz musician. LAE.

Pukui, Mary Kawena. (1895-1986) Hawaiian folklorist, linquist. SIN; WEI.

Pulaski, Casimir. (1747-1779) Polish American Revolutionary War military leader. SCHM2.

Pulitzer, Joseph. (1847-1911) Philanthropist, publisher, born Hungary. CRO4; RIT.

Pulwer, Miriam. (unknown) Polish Jewish Holocaust survivor. LAND.

Purtell, Edna. (1900-1986) Human rights activist, suffragist, women's rights activist. HOOS

Purvis, Charles Burleigh. (1842-1929) Civil War surgeon, educator. COX.

Purvis, Melvin. (1903-1960) Crime fighter. ITA3.

Pusey, Anne. (1948-) Ecologist, primatologist, born England. KAH6.

Pushkin, Alexander. (Alexsandr Seergeevich Pushkin) (1799-1837) Russian poet. HOOB5.

Pyle, Ernest Taylor "Ernie." (1900-1945) Journalist, World War II correspondent. Pulitzer Prize winner. GRAN; RIT.

Pyrrhus. (319-272 B.C.) Greek military leader. BAKR2; NAR.

Pythagoras. (c. 580-500 B.C.) Greek mathematician, philosopher. AND; BAKR2; TIN.

Pytheas. (fl. 300 B.C.) Greek astronomer, explorer, geographer, mathematician. ALTE; BAKR2; LOM.

Q

Qaddafi, Muammar-al. (1942-) Libyan military leader, terrorist. WAK.

Qiu Jin. (1875-1907) Poet, revolutionary, women's rights activist.

Quant, Mary. (1934-) English fashion designer. KENJ.

Quick, Flora. (Tom King) (unknown) Outlaw, disguised as man. SAV2.

Quidde, Ludwig. (1858-1941) German historian, organization founder, peace activist. Nobel Peace Prize winner. KEEN2.

Quimby, Doug. (1936-) Jazz singer. TAT.

Quimby, Edith Hinkley. (1891-1982) Biophysicist. VEG.

Quimby, Frankie. (1937-) Jazz singer. TAT.

Quimby, Harriet. (1884-1912) Aviation pioneer, journalist. HARN; KRAMB2; MCLE2; MCLO5; WILLI.

Quindlen, Anna. (1953-) Journalist. PRI.

Quinn, Anthony. (1915-2001) Actor, born Mexico. LAE.

Quisling, Vidkun. (1887-1945) Norwegian Nazi war criminal, political activist, World War II traitor. SCHM4.

R

Ra. Egyptian god of all creation. FIS.

Rabassa, Gregory. (1922-) Educator, translator. SIN2.

Rabe, Karin. (unknown) Physicist. KAH8.

Rabelais, François. (1495-1553) French author, physician. PER.

Rabi'ah of Basra. (717-801) Indian Islamic prophet. CRO5; GOLDM.

Rabin, Yitzhak. (1922-1995) Israeli prime minister. Nobel Peace Prize winner. CRO4; KEEN2; PASA; WAK.

Rachel. Biblical character. ARM2; TAI.

Radisson, Pierre Esprit. (1636-1710) French explorer. BAKS; PRE.

Radnitzky, Emmanuel. (Man Ray) (1890-1976) Photographer, sculptor. GAI; KRY.

Ragnarok. Norse god of the last battle. FIS3.

Rahr, Tammy. (unknown) Cayuga Indian beadworker. MOO.

Rai, Jitbahadur. (d. 1949) Nepal ghurka, World War II hero, born India. GRAN.

Raine, Kathleen. (1908-2003) English mystic, poet. KNI.

Raines, Tim. (1959-) Baseball player. BJA2.

Rainey, Gertrude "Ma." (1886-1939) Singer, songwriter. AFR; HASK5; JONH; MON; ORG; TAT.

Rainier, Prince, III. (1923-) Monacan prince. CRO4.

Rajalakshmi, R. (1926-) Indian biochemist. YOUNT6.

Raleigh, Sir Walter. (1554-1618) English adventurer, colonist, explorer, founder of Virginia and North Carolina colonies, poet. ALTE; DOH5; POD; PRE.

Ralph, Julian. (1853-1903) Journalist. RIT.

Ramabai, Pandita. (1858-1922) Indian human rights activist. JACKD4.

Ramakrishna, Sri. (1836-1886) Indian Hindu spiritual leader. CRO5.

Ramanujan. Srinivasa. (1887-1920) Indian mathematician. HENH.

Rameau, Jean-Philippe. (1683-1764) French composer, musician. VEN.

Ramesses II. (fl. 1279-1212 B.C.) Egyptian king. BAKR; ROBE3.

Ramesses III. (fl. 1182-1151 B.C.) Egyptian king. BAKR.

Ramirez, Carlos A. (1953-) Chemical engineer, medical researcher. STJ2.

Ramirez, Francisco. (1830-1890) Editor, publisher newspapers. SIN2.

Ramirez, Manny. (1972-) Baseball player, born Dominican Republic. SCHWAR; STEWM2.

Ramirez, Sara Estela. (1881-1910) Poet, political activist, women's rights activist, born Mexico. LAE.

Ramos-Horta, José. (1949-) East Timor journalist, political activist. Nobel Peace Prize winner. KEEN2.

Ramsay, Sir William. (1852-1916) Scottish chemist. Nobel Prize winner. TIN.

Randall, Dudley. (1914-2000) Poet. RED4.

Randolph, Asa Philip. (1889-1979) Civil rights activist, labor leader. Presidential Medal of Freedom recipient. AFR2; ALTMS; BECKN; CIV; DUB; RED2; STRE5; VERN.

Raney, Jimmy. (1927-1995) Jazz musician. GOU3.

Rangada. Hindu women warrior. MAYE2.

Rankin, Jeanette. (1880-1973) Congresswoman, peace activist, social worker, suffragist. ALTE2; FAB; FIR; GUL; HARN; HEL; KRAMB2; KRULL; MORI2; SAW; THIR; ZEI2; ZEI5.

Raphael. (Raffallo Sanzio) (1483-1520) Italian painter. BART; CUM; KRY; REN.

Rapp, George. (1757-1847) Harmonist utopian society cofounder, born Germany. STRE6.

Rashi. (Solomon ben Issac) (1040-1105) French author, educator, scholar. PASA.

Rasputin. *See* Novykh, Grigori Yefimovich.

Ravel, Maurice. (1875-1937) French composer. VEN.

Rawlings, Marjorie Kinnan. (1896-1953) Children's and adult author. Pulitzer Prize winner. KNI.

Rawlinson, Sir Henry Creswicke. (1810-1895) English archaeologist. FAG.

Ray, Charlotte E. (1850-1911) Attorney, community activist, educator. GREA.

Ray, Elise. (1982-) Olympic gymnast. LAY.

Razia, Sultana. (fl. 1236-1240) Indian Muslim warrior princess. HER.

Read, George. (1733-1798) American Revolutionary patriot, attorney, congressman, Declaration of Independence signer, jurist, senator. FRA2; QUI.

Read, Mary. (1690-1720) English pirate, disguised as man. BLACG4; COOL; DUN; SHAR; THOM3; WEA.

Reagan, Anne Robbins "Nancy." (1921-) First Lady. Presidential Medal of Freedom recipient. ANT; BARB; GOR; PAST.

Reagan, Ronald. (1911-2004) Actor, governor, 40th president of U.S., World War II Army Air Force. Presidential Medal of Freedom recipient. ADA; BARB; BAU; BLASS; CRO4; CRO6; DAV2; JONR; KRULL5; MORR; ROBE2; STG.

Ream, Vinnie. (1847-1914) Sculptor. HOOS.

Reaves, Bass. (1824-1910) Crimefighter. MON2.

Rebekah (Rebecca). Biblical character. ARM2; TAI.

Red Cloud. (1822-1909) Lakota Sioux Indian chief. MON2.

Red Cloud, Mitchell, Jr. (1924-) Ho-Chunk Indian Korean Conflict Army hero. Medal of Honor recipient. DOI1.

Red Jacket. (1756-1830) Seneca Indian chief, orator. AVE.

Redman, Joshua. (1969-) Jazz musician. SHIP.

Redmond, Mary. (unknown) American Revolutionary War patriot, spy. HOOS.

Reed, Dale. (unknown) Space scientist. RIC3.

Reed, Esther DeBeerdt. (1746-1780) American Revolutionary War patriot. FUR; FUR3; SCHM2; SILC; ZEI4.

Reed, Judy W. (unknown) Inventor. SULO2.

Reed, Virginia. (1833-1921) Pioneer. KRO; STEFO3; WEL.

Reed, Walter. (1851-1902) Medical researcher, physician. YOUNT4.

Reed, Willis. (1942-) Basketball player. TOR4.

Reeve, Christopher. (1952-2004) Actor, filmmaker. DEN.

Rego, Paula. (1935-) Portuguese illustrator, painter, printmaker. DUN.

Reich, Steve. (1936-) Composer. NIC.

Reich, Wilhelm. (1897-1957) Psychoanalyst, born Austria. HAV.

Reiche, Maria. (1903-1998) German mathematician. POLK.

Reichmann, Paul. (1930-) Entrepreneur real estate, born Austria. AAS8.

Reid, Clarice D. (1931-) Medical researcher, physician. GREA.

Reid, Helen Rogers. (1882-1970) Publisher magazines. PRI.

Reid, Rufus. (1944-) Jazz musician. GOU2.

Reifel, Ben. (1906-1990) Brule Lakota congressman, World War II lieutenant colonel. AVE.

Reinhardt, Django. (1910-1953) Belgian jazz musician. GOU3.

Reinhart, Johann. (1943-) Anthropologist. TALAD.

Reisberg, Mira. (1953-) Painter, born Australia. HON.

Reitsch, Hanna. (1912-1979) German aviator. DUN.

Rekhmire. (fl. 1460 B.C.) Egyptian tax collector, jurist. BAKR.

Rembrandt. (Harmen Szoon van Rijn) (1606-1669) Dutch engraver, painter. BLACA; CUM; CUS; GLU; KRULL2; KRY; SEV.

Remington, Frederic. (1861-1909) Painter, sculptor. CALV; KRY.

Remond, Sarah P. (1826-1894) Abolitionist, physician, women's rights activist. STI.

Renault, Louis. (1843-1918) French attorney. Nobel Peace Prize winner. KEEN2.

Reno, Janet. (1938-) Attorney, cabinet member, state attorney general. JONV.

Renoir, Pierre Auguste. (1841-1919) French painter. HOOB2; IMP; KRY; SAB.

Rentería, Édgar. (1975-) Baseball player, born Colombia. STEWM.

Resnick, Judith. (1949-1986) Astronaut, electrical engineer. BRO; STI2; TAI.

Reston, James. (1909-1995) Editor, journalist, born Scotland. Pulitzer Prize winner. RIT.

Retton, Mary Lou. (1968-) Olympic gymnast. DIT; GREES; SAV14.

Reuss, Allan. (1915-1988) Jazz musician. GOU3.

Revelle, Roger. (1909-1991) Oceanographer. POLKI.

Revels, Hiram Rhoades. (1822-1901) Senator. POT.

Revere, Paul. (1735-1818) American Revolutionary War military, folk hero, silversmith. CRO; CRO2; JAN; KRAL; SCHM2.

Reynolds, "Lonesome" Charley. (1844-1876) Indian scout, pioneer. SAV3.

Reynolds, Sir Joshua. (1723-1792) English painter. CUM; EIG; KRY.

Reynolds, Mary. (fl. 1854-1866) Lighthouse keeper. FLE.

Rheaume, Manon. (1972-) Canadian hockey player. BRIL4; HASD.

Rhodes, Cecil John. (1853-1902) English entrepreneur diamonds, financier, philanthropist, political activist. TRAU.

Ribaut, Jean. (1520-1565) French colonist, explorer, navy officer. CRO2.

Ricci, Matteo. (1552-1610) Italian missionary. POD.

Rice, Anne. (1941-) Author. KNI; MAD; PER.

Rice, Glen. (1967-) Basketball player. AAS17; KNA11.

Rice, Jerry. (1962-) Football player. HUNT; THOR.

Rich, Anna M. (1956-) Illustrator. TALAR3.

Rich, Buddy. (1917-1987) Jazz musician. GOU6.

Richard I. (The Lionhearted) (1157-1199) English military leader king. CRO3; KRAL.

Richard, Maurice. (1921-2000) Canadian hockey player. KNA8; KRULL3.

Richards, Ann. (1933-) Governor. ALTE2; GUL; THRO.

Richards, Ellen Swallow. (1842-1911) Chemist, ecologist, nutritionist. STA; STI2.

Richardson, Bill. (1947-) Ambassador, cabinet member, congressman. MARV8.

Richardson, Dorothy "Dot." (1961-) Olympic softball player, physician. BRIL2.

Richter, Charles. (1900-1985) Seismologist. HAV.

Richthofen, Baron Manfred von "The Red Baron." (1892-1918) German World War I aviator. KRAL.

Rickenbacker, Edward Vernon "Eddie." (1890-1973) Entrepreneur airline, World War I and II Air Force aviator. Medal of Honor recipient. DOH; ROS.

Rickey, Wesley Branch. (1881-1965) Baseball team president, civil rights activist. DEN.

Rickover, Hyman George. (1900-1986) Navy rear admiral, born Russia. Presidential Medal of Freedom recipient. BRO.

Rider, Isaiah, Jr. (1971-) Basketball player. BJA.

Ridderhof, Joy. (1903-1984) Missionary, bible translator. JACKD4.

Ride, Sally Kristen. (1951-) Astronaut, astrophysicist. ALTE; BAIR; BRIGG2; BUCH; HARN; HAV; PRE; SCHR; STI2; WYB; YOUNT7.

Ridesel, Baroness Frederika von. (1746-1808) German American Revolutionary War camp follower, author. SCHM2.

Ridgway, Matthew Bunker. (1895-1993) Army chief of staff, World War II Army general, Supreme Commander of Allied Forces in Europe. Presidential Medal of Freedom recipient. BOR; KNA.

Riefenstahl, Leni. (1902-2003) German filmmaker. DUN; POLK.

Riggs, Lillian. (1888-1977) Rancher. ALTE2.

Riis, Jacob August. (1849-1914) Human rights activist, journalist, orator, photographer, social reformer, born Denmark. GAI; JACW.

Riiser-Larsen, Hjalmar. (1890-1965) Norwegian aviator, Navy pilot. TES.

Rijnhart, Susie Carson. (1868-1908) Canadian explorer, missionary. MCLO2.

Rikyu, Senno. (1522-1591) Japanese tea ceremony expert. HOOB4.

Riley, Bridget. (1931-) English painter. DUN.

Riley, Pat. (1945-) Basketball coach. KNA10.

Rillieux, Norbert. (1806-1894) Engineer, inventor. AAS4; ALTMS; HASK8; HAY2; MCK; SULO.

Rimes, LeAnn. (1982-) Country music singer. MILM.

Rimsky-Korsakov, Nikolay Andreevich. (1844-1908) Russian composer, educator. VEN.

Rinehart, Mary Roberts. (1876-1958) Author, journalist, World War I correspondent. ZEI2.

Ringgold, Faith. (1930-) Children's author, educator, illustrator, sculptor. AFR; SILL2.

Ripken, Cal, Jr. (1960-) Baseball player. DEA3; DEN; SCHWAR.

Ripley, George. (1802-1880) Brook Farm Society utopian community founder, editor, social reformer. STRE6.

Ripoll, Shakira Mebarak. (Shakira) (1977-) Colombian pop singer. KRULI.

Rivera, Diego. (1886-1957) Mexican painter. CRO4; CUS; GLU; KRULL2; KRY; TWEPR.

Rivera, Geraldo. (1943-) Broadcast journalist, television personality. LAE; MARV.

Rivera, Mariano. (1969-) Baseball player, born Panama. SCHWAR.

Rivers, Ruben. (1918-1944) World War II Army hero. Medal of Honor recipient. REE2.

Rivington, James. (1727-1802) English printer, publisher, American Revolutionary War spy. SCHM2.

Rivlin, Alice. (1931-) Economist. JEF2.

Roach, Max. (1924-) Composer, jazz musician. GOU6.

Robbins, Jerome. (1918-1998) Choreographer, dancer. FOR.

Robert-Houdin, Jean Eugene. (1805-1871) French magician. WOO2.

Roberts, Bartholomew. (Black Bart) (1682-1722) Welsh pirate. BLACG4; YOUNT5.

Roberts, Corinne Boggs "Cokie." (1943-) Author, broadcast journalist. PRI; RIT.

Roberts, Ed. (1939-1995) Disability rights activist. KEND.

Roberts, Edward "Fireball." (1929-1964) Nascar auto racer. RIL.

Roberts, Robin. (1926-) Baseball player. SULG5.

Roberts, Stanley Corvet. (1970-) Basketball player. BJA.

Roberts, Tiffany. (1977-) Olympic soccer player. MILM.

Robertson, Alice Mary. (1854-1931) Congresswoman, educator, social worker. ZEI5.

Robertson, Oscar. (1938-) Basketball player. RAPK2; SAV5.

Robertson, Ruth Agnes McCall. (1905-1998) Photographer. POLK.

Robeson, Paul. (1898-1976) Actor, football player, political activist, singer. ALTMS; BECKN; HARD; HASK5; TAT; WEI2.

Robespierre, Maximilien François Marie Isidore de. (1758-1794) French political activist, revolutionary. HOOB2.

Robinson, Betty. (1911-1999) Olympic sprinter, track and field athlete. MOL.

Robinson, Bill "Bojangles." (1878-1949) Dancer, showman. HARD.

Robinson, Brooks. (1937-) Baseball player. SULG2.

Robinson, Daniel Louis "Satchmo." (1900?-1971) Jazz musician. MOU.

Robinson, David. (1965-) Basketball player. BJA; KNA5; KRAMS3; PAU; YOUNG.

Robinson, Eddie Gay. (1919-) Football coach. HASK7.

Robinson, Frank. (1936-) Baseball player. BOOK2; SEHN.

Robinson, John Roosevelt "Jackie." (1919-1972) Baseball player. Presidential Medal of Freedom recipient. ALTMS; BECKN; BJA2; CRO; DEN; JACT; JACW3; KRULL3; LEVE; RED6; SAV4; SLO; SULG3; TOR2.

Robinson, Jennifer. (1976-) Canadian olympic figure skater. MILT.

Robinson, Julia Bowman. (1919-1985) Mathematician. CEL; HENH.

Robinson, Mary. (1944-) Irish president. GUL.

Robinson, Smokey. (1940-) Singer, songwriter. AFR.

Robinson, Walker Smith, Jr. "Sugar Ray." (1921-1989) Boxer. ITA2.

Robles, Alfonso Garcíá. (1911-1991) Mexican diplomat. Nobel Peace Prize winner. KEEN2.

Robota, Róza. (1921-1945) Polish Jewish Holocaust resistance worker, victim. SCHM4.

Roc, John S. (1825-1866) Abolitionist, attorney, civil rights activist, physician. COX.

Rock, Chris. (1966-) Comedian. KAL2.

Rockefeller, John Davison. (1839-1937) Entrepreneur oil, philanthropist. AAS7; CRO; GREEC; MAYB; TRAU.

Rockwell, George Lincoln. (1918-1967) American Nazi Party head, hatemonger, political activist. STRE3.

Rockwell, Norman. (1894-1978) Painter. Presidential Medal of Honor recipient. KRY.

Rodale, Jerome Irving "J. I." (1898-1971) Agricultural scientist, environmentalist, publisher. FAB3.

Roddick, Anita. (1942-) English entrepreneur beauty supplies. DUN; GRAH; MAYB; MCLU.

Rodgers, Calbraith Perry. (1879-1912) Aviation pioneer. WILLI; ZAU2.

Rodgers, Richard. (1902-1979) Composer, musician, songwriter. Pulitzer Prize winner. CRO4.

Rodin, Auguste. (1840-1917) French sculptor. CUS; KRY.

Rodman, Dennis. (1961-) Basketball player. SAV6.

Rodney, Caesar. (1728-1784) American Revolutionary War patriot, military leader, congressman, Declaration of Independence signer. FRA2; QUI.

Rodriguez, Alex "A-Rod." (1975-) Baseball player. BUCK4; SCHWAR; SCHWAR2; STEWM2.

Rodriguez, Eloy. (1947-) Agricultural scientist, botanist, educator. STJ2.

Rodriguez, Ivan. (1971-) Baseball player, born Puerto Rico. SCHWAR; STEWM.

Rodriguez, Matt. (1936-) Crimefighter, police commissioner. MORE2.

Rodriguez, Paul. (1955-) Actor, born Mexico. MORE2.

Rodriguez, Richard. (1944-) Author, broadcast journalist, editor, educator. HILC; LAE; SIN2.

Rodriguez, Robert. (1968-) Filmmaker, screenwriter. MARV4.

Rodriguez de Tio, Lola. (1843-1924) Puerto Rican poet, political activist, women's rights activist. LAE.

Roebling, John Augustus. (1806-1869) Civil engineer, born Germany. AAS11.

Roebling, Washington Augustus. (1837-1926) Civil engineer. AAS11.

Roentgen, Wilhelm Conrad. (1845-1923) German physician, physicist. Nobel Prize winner. AAS15; CURT; MUL2; TIN.

Rogers, Ginger. (1911-1995) Actor, dancer. CRO4.

Rogers, Patricia. (unknown) Geologist. KAH4.

Rogers, Robert. (1731-1795) Frontiersman, soldier. CRO3.

Rogers, Roy. (1911-1998) Actor, cowboy, folk hero. DEN; KRAL.

Rogers, Will. (1879-1935) Cherokee Indian

actor, author, showman. ALLP; AVE.

Rogers, Woodes. (1679-1732) English pirate. YOUNT5.

Rohde, Ruth Bryan Owen. (1885-1954) Congresswoman, diplomat. MORI.

Röhm, Ernst. (1887-1934) German Nazi military leader. SCHM4.

Roland, Madame Jeanne-Marie "Manon." (1754-1793) French political activist, revolutionary. DUN; KNI.

Rolen, Scott. (1975-) Baseball player. SCHWAR.

Rolfe, John. (1585-1622) Colonist, pilgrim, married Pocahontas, born England. CRO2.

Rollins, Charlemae. (1897-1979) Librarian, storyteller. TUR.

Rollins, Theodore Walter "Sonny." (1930-) Bandleader, jazz musician. SHIP.

Rollins, Tree. (1955-) Basketball player. YOUNG.

Rolls, Charles. (1877-1910) English automaker, aviation pioneer. AAS3.

Romero, Jacy. (1965-) Chumash Indian dancer. MOO.

Romero, Oscar. (1917-1980) El Salvadorian political activist, spiritual leader. CLA2; CRO5.

Rommel, Erwin "Desert Fox." (1891-1944) German World War II commander. CRO3; LAC; SCHM4.

Ronge, Maximilian. (unknown) Austrian World War I spy. MART.

Ronstadt, Frederico. (1862-1954) Entrepreneur. SIN2.

Ronstadt, Linda. (1946-) Singer. LAE; SIN2.

Roosevelt, Anna Curtenius. (1946-) Archaeologist. POLK.

Roosevelt, (Anna) Eleanor. (1884-1962) Author, First Lady, human rights activist, orator. ANT; BARB; CRO; CUS2; DEN; DUN; FAB; GOR; GUL; HAC5; HARN; HEA; HER; JACW; KRULL; LEVE; MARZ; MCD; PAST; ROE; ROL; TAYS; THIR; WILKP4; ZEI3.

Roosevelt, Edith Kermit Carow. (1861-1948) First Lady. BARB; GOR; PAST.

Roosevelt, Franklin Delano. (1882-1945) Attorney, governor, Navy assistant secretary, 32nd president of U.S. ADA; BARB; BAU; BLASS; CRO; CRO4; CRO6; DAV2; DEN; FAB; JONR; KEND; KRULL5;

MARZ; MAYB2; MORR; SCHM4; STG; YEN.

Roosevelt, Theodore. (1858-1919) Conservationist, governor, 26th president of U.S. Nobel Peace Prize winner. AAS2; ADA; BARB; BAU; BLASS; CRO; CRO4; CRO6; DAV2; DEN; FAB; FAB3; JAN; JONR; KEEN; KEEN2; KRULL5; LINE; MORR; STG; YEN.

Root, Elihu. (1845-1937) Attorney, cabinet member, peace activist. Nobel Peace Prize winner. KEEN2; RIC2.

Roper, Margaret More. (1505-1544) English scholar. LEO3.

Ros-Lentinen, Ileana. (1952-) Congresswoman, state legislator, born Cuba. LAE; MORE2; THRO.

Rose of Lima. (1586-1617) Peruvian saint, spiritual leader. HOOB6.

Rose, Edward. (1780?-1820?) Native American frontiersman, fur trapper. KAT2.

Rose, Ernestine Potowski. (1810-1892) Abolitionist, orator, reformer, women's rights activist, born Poland. TAI.

Rose, Mary Swartz. (1874-1941) Educator, nutritionist. REY.

Rose, Pete. (1941-) Baseball player, manager. DEA.

Roseanne. *See* Arnold, Roseanne.

Rosenbach, Larry. (1929-) Polish Jewish Holocaust survivor. GREENF.

Rosenberg, Ethel. (1915-1953) Traitor. AAS18; BRO.

Rosenberg, Julius. (1918-1953) Traitor. AAS18; BRO.

Rosenfeld, Bobbie. (1904-1969) Canadian olympic track and field athlete. BRY.

Rosenthal, Ida. (1886-1973) Inventor, born Russia. ALTML.

Rosenwald, Julius. (1862-1932) Entrepreneur retail stores, philanthropist. TRAU.

Rosenzweig, Franz. (1886-1939) German educator, scholar. PASA.

Ross, Alexander. (1783-1856) Canadian abolitionist, naturalist, physician. HAM.

Ross, Barney. (1907-1967) Boxer, World War II marine hero. BRO.

Ross, Betsy. (1752-1836) American Revolutionary War patriot, folk hero. HARN; KRAL; SCHM2; TIN; ZEI4.

Ross, Diana. (1944-) Actor, entrepreneur music business, singer. RED3.

Ross, George. (1730-1779) American Revolutionary War patriot, attorney, congressman, Declaration of Independence signer. FRA2; QUI.

Ross, Sir James Clark. (1800-1862) Scottish explorer. PRE.

Ross, John. (1790-1866) Cherokee Indian chief. SHER2.

Ross, Sir John. (1777-1856) Scottish arctic explorer. PRE.

Rossetti, Christina Georgina. (1830-1894) English art model, poet. KNI.

Rossetti, Dante Gabriel. (1828-1882) Italian painter, poet. KRY.

Rossi, Europa di. (Madame Europa) (16th century) Italian singer. TAI.

Rossini, Gioaccino. (1792-1868) Italian opera composer. VEN.

Rotblat, Joseph. (1908-) English peace activist, physicist, born Poland. Nobel Peace Prize winner. KEEN2.

Roth, Irving. (1930-) Czech Jewish Holocaust survivor. TIT.

Roth-Hano, Renée. (1931-) Author, Holocaust survivor, social worker, born France. SCHM4.

Rothschild, Miriam. (1908-) Author, conservationist, entomologist, naturalist, born England. KEEN.

Rotmil, Bernard. (1926-) French Jewish Holocaust survivor. KUS.

Roualt, Georges. (1871-1958) French painter. KRY.

Rousseau, Henri. (1844-1910) French painter. KRY; ORE.

Rousso, Harilyn. (1946-) Disability rights activist, psychotherapist. KEND.

Rowland, Frank Sherwood. (1927-) Atmospheric chemist. Nobel Prize winner. LEU.

Rowlandson, Mary. (1635-1682) Colonist, Indian captive. CRO2.

Rowling, Joanne Kathleen "J. K." (1965-) English children's author. KNI.

Rowny, Edward L. (1917-) Army career officer, Korean War general, Vietnam War Deputy Chief of Staff, World War II lieutenant general. BOR.

Roy, Patrick. (1965-) Canadian hockey player. KRAMS2; SPI.

Royall, Anne Newport. (1769-1854) Adventurer, journalist. PRI.

Roybal, Edward Ross. (1916-) Congressman. LAE.

Roybal-Allard, Lucille. (1941-) Congresswoman, women's rights activist. LAE.

Royce, Henry. (1863-1933) English automaker. AAS3.

Rubens, Peter Paul. (1577-1640) Flemish painter. CUM; GLU; KRY; SEV.

Rubin, Vera Cooper. (1928-) Astronomer. CAM; STI2; THI2; YOUNT3.

Rubinowicz, David. (1927-1942) Polish Jewish author, Holocaust victim. WE.

Rucker, Herman. (Black Herman) (1892-1934) Magician. HASK6.

Rudashevski, Yitzak. (1927-1943) Polish Jewish author, Holocaust victim. WE.

Rudin, Mary Ellen Estill. (1924-) Mathematician. CEL.

Rudkin, Margaret Fogharty. (1897-1967) Entrepreneur foods. AAS3; KRAMB.

Rudolph, Wilma. (1940-1994) Olympic track and field athlete. ALTMS; BECKN; BRIL; DIT; GAI3; GREA; HARN; HASD; HER; JEN2; KEND; KRULL3; MOL; OCO; PLO; RED6; SAV10; SAV14; STRU; WEL.

Ruffin, Josephine St. Pierre. (1842-1924) Abolitionist, civil rights activist, organizations founder, suffragist. THIR.

Ruggles, David. (1810-1849) Abolitionist, publisher magazine. HASK.

Rumi, Jalal al-Din. (1207-1273) Afghan mystic, philosopher, poet. CRO5.

Rumsfeld, Donald H. (1932-) Aviator, cabinet member, naval career, state legislator. Presidential Medal of Freedom recipient. RIC2.

Rush, Benjamin. (1745-1813) American Revolutionary War patriot, author, congressman, Declaration of Independence signer, physician. FRA2; QUI; SCHM2.

Rushing, Jimmy. (1903-1972) Jazz singer. MON.

Russell, Bill. (1934-) Basketball player. BOOK2; CRO4; KNA5; KNA10; SULG3; TOR4.

Russell, Curly. (1917-1986) Jazz musician. GOU2.

Russell, Harold. (1914-2002) Actor, disability

rights activist, World War II soldier, born Canada. KEND.

Russell, Herman J. (1930-) Entrepreneur construction. AFR2.

Russworm, John B. (1799-1851) Publisher newspaper. BECKN.

Rustin, Bayard. (1910?-1987) Civil rights activist, labor leader. BECKN; JACW; RED2.

Rutan, Dick. (1938-) Aviator,Vietnam War Air Force pilot. PRE.

Ruth. Biblical character. ARM2; TAI.

Ruth, George Herman "Babe." (1895-1948) Baseball player. CRO4; DEA; DEA2; ITA; JACW3; JAN; KRAL; KRAMS; KRULL3; LEVE; SEHN; SLO; SULG3; SULG8; TOR2; USC2; YEN.

Rutherford, Baron Ernest. (1871-1938) New Zealand physicist. Nobel Prize winner. FOX; TIN.

Rutledge, Edward. (1749-1800) American Revolutionary War patriot, congressman, Declaration of Independence signer. FRA2; QUI.

Ryan, Katherine "Klondike Kate." (1869-1932) Chef, gold miner, pioneer. KET.

Ryan, Nolan. (1947-) Baseball player. BUCK2; SLO; SULG5; SULM; TOR2.

S

Saadia Gaon. (882-942) Hebrew scholar, spiritual leader. PASA.

Saar, Alison. (1956-) Mixed-media artist. AFR.

Saar, Betye. (1926-) Mixed-media artist. AFR; SILL3.

Sabatini, Gabriela. (1970-) Argentine tennis player. HAR.

Sabin, Albert Bruce. (1906-1993) Medical researcher, physician, born Poland. Presidential Medal of Freedom recipient. CURT; HAV; SPA.

Sabin, Florence Rena. (1871-1953) Anatomist, medical researcher, physician, suffragist. HAV; HUNTE2; REY; STI; STI2.

Sacagawea. (1788-1884) Lemhi Shoshone Indian guide, interpreter. ALTE; ALTE2; AVE; CALV; DEN; FUR2; HARN; HAZ2; HER; HOOS; LAK; POD; RAPD2; ROL;

SAV2; SAV3; WEL.

Sadat, Anwar. (1918-1981) Egyptian political activist, president. Nobel Peace Prize winner, Presidential Medal of Freedom recipient. KEEN2; MAYB2.

Saenz, Manuela. (1797-1856) Spanish political activist. CRO4.

Safransky, Eddie. (1914-1974) Jazz musician. GOU2.

Sagan, Carl. (1934-1996) Astronomer, author. Pulitzer Prize winner. CAM; HAV.

Sager, Ruth. (1918-1997) Biologist, geneticist. REY.

Saigo, Takemori. (1827-1877) Japanese samurai warrior. HOOB4.

Saint-Exupéry, Antoine de. (1900-1944) French adventurer, author, aviator. ZAU.

Sainte-Marie, Buffy. (1941-) Cree Indian actor, peace activist, singer, songwriter, born Canada. AVE; GOLDE; HUNTE3.

Sakharov, Andrei. (1921-1989) Russian nuclear physicist, political activist. Nobel Peace Prize winner. FOX; HOOB5; KEEN2; TRAC2.

Saladin, Salah al-Din. (1138-1193) Kurdish military leader, ruler, spiritual leader. CLA; CRO3.

Salavarrieta, Policarpa "La Pola." (1795-1817) Colombian political activist. HER.

Salazar, Rubén. (1928-1970) Broadcast journalist, civil rights activist, journalist, born Mexico. LAE; SIN2.

Salchow, Ulrich. (1877-1949) Swedish olympic figure skater. JACT.

Salé, Jamie. (1977-) Canadian olympic figure skater. MILT.

Salem, Peter. (1750-1816) American Revolutionary War soldier. ALTMS; HASK2; HASK4; MED.

Salinger, J. D. (1919-) Author. TWEPO; VERD.

Salk, Jonas. (1914-1995) Educator, medical researcher, physician. BRO; CRO; CURT; DEN; HAV; LEVE; MUL; SPA.

Salome. Biblical character. ARM2.

Salter, Fanny. (1883-?) Lighthouse keeper. FLE.

Salvador, Sal. (1925-1999) Jazz musician. GOU3.

Sampras, Pete. (1971-) Tennis player. CHRIST.

Sampson, Deborah. (Robert Shurtliff) (1760-1827) American Revolutionary War soldier, disguised as man. FUR; FUR3; HARN; HASK2; HASK4; HEA; HER; HOOS; SCHM2; SILC; ZEI4.

Sampson, Edith. (1901-1980) Attorney, diplomat, social worker. GREA.

Sampson, Henry. (1934-) Aerospace engineer, inventor, space scientist. HENS2.

Sampson, Will. (1934-1987) Creek Indian actor, painter.

Samuel, Sir Marcus. (1853-1927) English entrepreneur oil. AAS7.

Samuelson, Joan Benoit. (1957-) Olympic marathon runner, track and field athlete. HASD; LINL; LIT.

Sanchez, Ilich Ramirez "Carlos." (1949-) Venezuelan terrorist. STRE4.

Sanchez, Loreta. (1960-) Congresswoman. LAE.

Sanchez, Oscar Arias. *See* Arias Sanchez, Oscar.

Sanchez, Pedro. (1940-) Soil scientist. OLE.

Sanchez Vicario, Arantza. (1971-) Spanish tennis player. RUT5.

Sand, George. *See* Dupin, Amandine Aurore Lucia.

Sandburg, Carl. (1878-1967) Children's and adult author, historian, poet. Presidential Medal of Freedom recipient, Pulitzer Prize winner. KRULL6; PER; TWEPR.

Sander, Sally. (1925-) Polish Jewish Holocaust survivor. LAND4.

Sander, Zelik. (unknown) Polish Jewish Holocaust survivor. LAND4.

Sanders, Barry. (1968-) Football player. Heisman Trophy winner. BUCK; DEV; HUNT; LAC3; SAV8.

Sanders, Deion. (1967-) Baseball player, football player. SAV4.

Sanders, Fetague. (1915-1992) Magician. HASK6.

Sanders, Colonel Harland. (1890-1980) Entrepreneur restaurants. AAS6; AAS16; KRAL; KRAMB.

Sanders, Marlene. (1931-) Broadcast journalist. KRAMB2.

Sandoz, Mari. (1896-1966) Author, historian. ALTE2.

Sanger, Frederick. (1918-) English biochemist. Nobel Prize winner. TIN.

Sanger, Margaret. (1879-1966) Nurse, reformer, women's rights activist. ARC; COOL; CRO; DUN; HARN; HER; ROL; STI; THIR.

Santana, Carlos. (1947-) Musician, born Mexico. LAE.

Santayana, George. (1863-1952) Philosopher, poet, born Spain. LAE; SIN2.

Santiago, Esmeralda. (1948-) Puerto Rican author. HILC.

Santorio, Santorio. (1561-1636) Italian medical researcher, physician. MUL2.

Santos, Bienvenido N. (1911-1992) Author, born Philippines. SIN.

Santos, Miriam. (1956-) City official, born Puerto Rico. PAL.

Santos-Dumont, Alberto. (1873-1932) Brazilian aviation pioneer. ZAU2.

Sapp, Warren. (1971-) Football player. DEI.

Sappho of Lesbos. (625-570 B.C.) Greek poet. BAKR2; DUN; HER; KNI; LEO; ROL.

Saragossa, La. *See* Agostin, Maria.

Sarah. Biblical character. TAI.

Sarah. Duchess of York. (1959-) English princess. LEVI.

Sarah bat Tovim. (18th century) Ukrainian Jewish prayer book author. TAI.

Sarah of Yemen. (7th century) Yemenite poet. TAI.

Saralegui, Cristina. (1948-) Television personality, born Cuba. LAE; MEN.

Sarashina, Lady. (1008-?) Japanese adventurer, author, poet. POLK.

Sargent, John Singer. (1856-1925) Painter. CUM.

Sargon the Great. (c. 2300 B.C.) Mesopotamian king. PAP.

Sarkisian, Cherilyn. (Cher) (1946-) Pop singer. KEEL.

Sarmiento, Domingo Faustino. (1811-1888) Argentine political activist, president. HOOB6.

Sarnoff, David. (1891-1971) Entrepreneur broadcasting media, born Russia. MAYB.

Sartre, Jean Paul. (1905-1980) French philosopher. Nobel Prize winner. CRO4.

Saruhashi, Katsuku. (1920-) Japanese chemist. YOUNT7.

Sasso, Sandy Eisenberg. (1947-) Children's author, spiritual leader. TAI.

Satcher, David. (1941-) Medical researcher, physician, surgeon general of U.S. COX.

Satie, Erik. (1866-1925) French composer. KRULL4.

Sato, Eisaku. (1901-1975) Japanese attorney, peace activist, prime minister. Nobel Peace Prize winner. KEEN2.

Saund, Dalip Singh. (1899-1973) Congressman, born India. SIN.

Saunders, Cicely. (1918-) English physician. HUNTE2.

Sauñe, Rómulo. (1953-1992) Peruvian Quechua Indian missionary, spiritual leader. JACKD4.

Savage, Augusta Christine. (1892-1962) Educator, sculptor. AFR; GREA; HARD; HASK5.

Savage, Tom. (1595-1627) Colonist. HOOS.

Savitskaya, Svetlana. (1948-) Russian cosmonaut. BRIGG2.

Sawchuck, Terry. (1925-1970) Canadian hockey player. SPI.

Sawyer, Diane. (1945-) Broadcast journalist. HILA.

Say, Allen. (1937-) Children's author, illustrator, photographer, born Japan. SIN.

Say, Thomas. (1787-1834) Author, educator, entomologist. KEEN.

Sayers, Dorothy L. (1893-1957) English author. KNI.

Sayers, Gale. (1943-) Football player. LAC3.

Scarlatti, Domenico. (1685-1757) Italian sacred music composer, musician. VEN.

Scathach. Celtic warrior goddess. MAYE2.

Schayes, Dolph. (1928-) Basketball player, coach. SAV6.

Schechter, Matilde Roth. (1859-1924) Jewish organizational founder, born Germany. TAI.

Schechter, Solomon. (1849-1915) Author, educator, spiritual leader, founder of Conservative Judaism, born Romania. PASA.

Schele, Linda. (1942-1998) Lexicographer. POLK.

Schiff, Charlene. (1930-) Polish Jewish Holocaust survivor. KUS.

Schindler, Emilie. (1909-2001) Czech Holocaust rescuer. PET.

Schindler, Oskar. (1908-1974) Czech Holocaust rescuer. FREM; LYM; PET; SCHM4.

Schirra, Walter Marty "Wally," Jr. (1923-) Astronaut. RIC4.

Schliemann, Heinrich. (1822-1890) German archaeologist. FAG; POD; SCHEL; WEI.

Schloss, Lewis. (1921-) German Jewish Holocaust survivor. LAND4.

Schmandt-Besserat, Denise. (1933-) Archaeologist, lexicographer, born France. THI2.

Schmidt, Harrison "Jack." (1935-) Astronaut, geologist. PRE.

Schmidt, Mike. (1949-) Baseball player. DEA2; SULG2; SULG8; TOR; YOUNG2.

Schmirler, Sandra. (1964-2000) Canadian olympic curler. BRY.

Schneiderman, Rose. (1882-1972) Labor leader, worker's rights activist, born Poland. HEA; HER; SEG; TAI.

Schnirer, Sarah. (1833-1935) Polish educator, established schools for religious Jewish girls. TAI.

Scholl, Hans. (1918-1943) German Holocaust resistance leader, victim. GRAN; SCHM4.

Scholl, Sophie. (1921-1943) German Holocaust resistance leader, victim. GRAN; SCHM4.

Schomburg, Arthur. (1874-1938) Educator, historian, born Puerto Rico. BECKN; SIN2; TUR2.

Schönberg, Arnold. (1874-1951) Composer, conductor, born Austria. VEN.

Schrank, John. (1876-1943) Assassin, attempted to kill President Theodore Roosevelt. JONR; STG; SULG9.

Schreiner, Olive. (1855-1920) South African author, women's rights activist. HER.

Schuijn, Eric. (1979-) In-line skater. SAV9.

Schroeder, Becky. (1962-) Inventor. BLASH3; THI.

Schroeder, Patricia. (1940-) Attorney, congresswoman, publisher. ALTE2; FIR; GUL; THRO.

Schubert, Franz Peter. (1797-1828) Austrian composer. ROM; VEN.

Schulte, Eduard Reinhold Karl. (1891-1966) German attorney, political activist, spy. SCHM4.

Schultz, Sigrid "Lillian." (1899-1980) Journalist, World War II correspondent. PRI.

Schultz, Ted. (unknown) Entomologist. KALLN.

Schulz, Charles. (1922-2000) Cartoonist. STEFF.

Schumann, Clara. (1819-1896) German composer, musician. BLACA2; CRO4; DUN; HER; KRULL4; ROE.

Schumann, Robert. (1810-1856) German composer, musician. CRO4; VEN.

Schuyler, Peter. (1657-1724) Colonist, Indian agent. CRO2.

Schwab, George. (1931-) Latvian Jewish Holocaust survivor. GREENF.

Schwabe, Stephanie. (1957-) Geomicrobiologist, explorer, geologist, born Germany. POLK.

Schwartz, Amy. (1954-) Children's author, illustrator. TALAR.

Schwarzkopf, Norman. (1934-) Gulf War Army general, Vietnam War Army commander. Presidential Medal of Freedom recipient. CRO3.

Schweitzer, Albert. (1875-1965) French missionary, musician, physician, spiritual leader. Nobel Peace Prize winner. CLA; CRO5; CURT; HAV; KEEN2; SHAW.

Scieszka, Jon. (1954-) Children's author. AUT; MARC2.

Scifi, Claire of Assisi. (1193-1252) Saint. LEO2.

Scipio Africanus. (Publius Cornelius Scipio Africanus) (236-183 B.C.) Roman general, statesman. BAKR3; CRO3.

Scorsese, Martin. (1942-) Filmmaker. HILA2.

Scott, David. (1932-) Aeronautical engineer, Air Force pilot, astronaut. PRE.

Scott, Dennis. (1968-) Basketball player. TUR3.

Scott, Dred. (1795-1858) Slave. ALTMS; BECKN; HAM; KAT; MCK.

Scott, Harriet. (unknown) Slave, wife of Dred Scott. KAT.

Scott, Robert Falcon. (1868-1912) English explorer, naval officer. CURR; PRE.

Scott, Roland. (1909-2002) Medical researcher, physician. AFR2.

Scott, Sheila. (1927-1988) English aviation pioneer, World War II nurse. BRIGG.

Scott, Sir Walter. (1771-1832) Scottish author, poet. PER.

Scott, William Alexander, II. (1903-1934) Publisher newspaper. AFR.

Scott, Winfield. (1786-1866) Army general War of 1812, Mexican War, presidential candidate. CRO3.

Scurlock, Addison. (1883-1964) Photographer. SULG.

Scurry, Brianna. (1971-) Olympic soccer player. BRIL5; LAY2; MILM; RUT4.

Seaborg, Glenn Theodore. (1912-1999) Nuclear chemist. Nobel Prize Winner. HAV.

Seacole, Mary. (1805-1881) Jamaican nurse. DUN.

Seager, Joy Debenham. (1899-1991) Australian human rights activist, physician. KIR.

Sears, Richard. (1863-1914) Entrepreneur mail order catalogs, retail stores. AAS12; MAC; MAYB.

Seathl. (1788-1866) Duwamish Indian chief, orator. AVE; SHER2.

Seaver, Tom. (1944-) Baseball player. SLO; SULG5; SULM.

Secada, Jon. (1963-) Singer, born Cuba. MARV3.

Seddon, Margaret Rhea. (1947-) Astronaut, physician. BRIGG2.

See, Carolyn. (1934-) Author. SMIL.

Seeger, Ruth Crawford. (1901-1953) Composer. NIC.

Seerey, Pat. (1923-1986) Baseball player. TOR.

Segni, Lothario de. *See* Innocent III, Pope.

Seguín, Juan N. (1806-1890) Mexican mayor, military leader, state legislator. LAE.

Seinfeld, Jerry. (1954-) Comedian. BRO.

Sejr, Arne. (1922-) Danish Holocaust resistance worker. BERS.

Sela, Princess. (c. 420 A.D.) Viking pirate. SHAR.

Selassie, Haile. (1892-1975) Ethiopian emperor. RAS.

Selena. (singer) *See* Perez, Selena Quintanilla.

Seles, Monica. (1973-) Tennis player, born Yugoslavia. HARR; LINL; MILE; RUT5; SCHWAB.

Selim III, Sultan. (1761-1808) Turkish archer, ruler. JACT.

Semiramis. (c. 2000 B.C.) Assyrian warrior queen, legendary. LEO; MAYE2.

Semmelweis, Ignaz Phillipp. (1818-1865) Hungarian medical researcher, physician. CURT.

Sendak, Maurice. (1928-) Children's author, illustrator. BRO; MARC; MARC3; MAS; PER.

Seneca. (Lucius Annaeus Seneca) (4 B.C.- 65

A.D.) Roman philosopher, playwright, statesman. BAKR3; COOLI.

Senenmut. (fl. 1495 B.C.) Egyptian architect, educator. BAKR.

Senesh, Hannah. (1921-1944) Hungarian Jewish Holocaust resistance fighter, author, poet, victim. MAN; SCHM4; TAI.

Senghor, Léopold. (1906-2001) African Senegal president. RAS.

Senwosret I. (1971-1928 B.C.) Egyptian king. BAKR.

Senwosret III. (fl. 1874-1841 B.C.) Egyptian king. BAKR.

Septimius, Severus Lucius. (146-211) Roman emperor, general. BAKR3.

Sequoyah. (1770-1843) Cherokee Indian chief, Creek War soldier, linguist. AVE; HAZ; MARZ.

Seraphim. St. of Sarov. (1759-1833) Russian Orthodox saint, spiritual leader. CRO5.

Serio, Suzie McConnell. (1966-) Olympic basketball player. PON.

Serling, Rod. (1924-1975) Author, World War II Army. MAD.

Serra, Father Junipero. (1713-1784) Spanish missionary. CRO2; DOH2; GOLDM; LAE; POD; SIN2.

Serrano, Lupe. (1930-) Dancer, educator, born Chile. LAE.

Serturner, Friedrich. (1783-1841) German chemist, medical researcher. CURT.

Set. Egyptian god of the desert. FIS.

Seti I. (fl. 1291-1278 B.C.) Egyptian king. BAKR.

Seton, Elizabeth Ann. (1774-1821) Educator, saint, spiritual leader. GOLDM.

Seton, Ernest Thompson. (1860-1946) Author, cofounder Boy Scouts of America, illustrator, Native American rights activist, naturalist, born England. KEEN.

Seurat, Georges. (1859-1890) French painter. IMP; KRY; ORE; SAB.

Seuss, Dr. See Geisel, Theodor Seuss.

Sevier, John. (1745-1815) Frontiersman, governor. DOH4.

Sewall, Samuel. (1652-1730) Colonist, Salem Witch Trials jurist. CRO2.

Seward, William. (1801-1872) Attorney, cabinet member, governor. RIC.

Seymour, William Joseph. (1870-1922) Spiritual leader, founder Pentecostal Church. JACKD4.

Shaarawi, Huda. (1879-1947) Egyptian women's rights activist. HER.

Shackleton, Ernest. (1874-1922) Irish arctic explorer. ALTE; LANG; WAT; ZAU.

Shaka. (1787-1828) African zulu warrior and king. POD.

Shakespeare, William. (1564-1616) English playwright. HAZ; KRULL6; MARZ; PER; SEV; WEI2; YEN.

Shakira. (singer) See Ripoll, Shakira Mebarak.

Shange, Ntozake. (1948-) Author. HAC4; WILKB.

Shannon, Larry. (1933-) Biologist. STJ.

Shantz, Bobby. (1925-) Baseball player. SULG2.

Shapira-Luria, Miriam. (15th century) Italian Jewish educator. TAI.

Shapley, Harlow. (1885-1972) Astronomer. CAM.

Sharma, Prem. (1943-) Human rights activist, women's rights activist, born India. GOLDE.

Sharpe, Avery. (1954-) Jazz musician. GOU2.

Sharpe, Sterling. (1965-) Football player. THOR.

Shavelson, Clara Lemlich. (1886-1982) Workers' rights activist, born Russia. TAI.

Shaw, Anna Howard. (1847-1919) Physician, reformer, suffragist, born England. DUM.

Shaw, Artie. (1910-) Bandleader, jazz musician. SHIP.

Shaw, Bernard. (1940-) Broadcast journalist. RIT.

Shaw, Earl D. (1937-) Inventor, physicist. SULO.

Shaw, George Bernard. (1856-1950) Irish author, playwright. Nobel Prize winner. WEI2.

Shays, Daniel. (1747-1825) American Revolutionary War military. SCHM2.

Sheen, Martin. (1940-) Actor. SIN2.

Sheldon, May French. (1847-1936) Explorer. POLK.

Shelley, Mary. (1797-1851) English author. KNI; ROM.

Shepard, Alan B. (1923-1998) Astronaut, Navy test pilot. BAIR; PRE.

Shepard, Sam. (1943-) Actor, author, playwright. Pulitzer Prize winner. PER.

Sheptitsky, Andrew. (1865-1944) Polish Holocaust rescuer, spiritual leader. LYM.

Sheridan, Philip Henry. (1831-1888) Civil War general. GREEC3; TRAC; YAN.

Sherman, Cindy. (1954-) Photographer. HOR; SILL.

Sherman, Patsy O. (1930-) Chemist, inventor. THI.

Sherman, Roger. (1721-1793) American Revolutionary War patriot, attorney, congressman, Declaration of Independence signer. FRA2; MEI; QUI.

Sherman, William Tecumseh. (1820-1891) Civil War general. CRO3; GREEC3; TRAC; YAN.

Shih Huang Di. (259-210 B.C.) Chinese emperor. HOOB; WILKP4; YEN.

Shilts, Randy. (1951-1994) AIDS activist, author, journalist. GON.

Shimomura, Tsutomu. (1965-) Computer scientist, physicist, born Japan. YOUNT.

Shirley, Donna. (1941-) Aerospace engineer, space scientist. THI2.

Shirley, William. (1694-1771) Colonial governor, born England. CRO2.

Shochat, Manya. (1880-1961) Israeli settler, Russian revolutionary, born Russia. TAI.

Shockley, William. (1910-1989) English inventor, physicist. Nobel Prize winner. AAS15; TIN.

Shoemaker, Gene. (1928-1997) Geologist, space scientist. CARR.

Shoemaker, Willie. (1931-2003) Jockey. JACT; KUH; SAV12.

Sholes, Christopher. (1819-1890) Editor, inventor, publisher. DIN.

Shonagon, Sei. (960?-) Japanese author. HOOB4.

Shoong, Joe. (1879-1961) Entrepreneur financier, philanthropist. SIN.

Shore, Ann Goldman. (1929-) Polish Jewish Holocaust survivor. GREENF.

Shotoku, Taishi. (574-622) Japanese prince. HAZ; HOOB4.

Shu. Egyptian god of the air. FIS.

Shula, Don. (1930-) Football coach. SAV11.

Shurney, Robert. (1921-) Aeronautical engineer, inventor, space scientist. AFR2; JEF.

Shurtliff, Robert. *See* Sampson, Deborah.

Sibelius, Jean. (1865-1957) Finnish composer. BLACA2; VEN.

Sichelgaita. (d. 1090) Italian military leader, princess. CRO3.

Siegel, Ben "Bugsy." (1906-1947) Gangster. WOO.

Signac, Paul. (1863-1935) French painter. KRY.

Sigur, Wanda. (1958-) Inventor, space scientist. HENS.

Sikharulidze, Anton. (1976-) Russian olympic figure skater. MILT.

Sikorsky, Igor. (1889-1972) Aeronautical engineer, aviation pioneer, born Russia. BERL.

Sills, Beverly. (1929-) Opera singer. Presidential Medal of Freedom recipient. BRO; STU.

Simmons, Jake, Jr. (1901-1981) Entrepreneur oil. HASK.

Simmons, John. (1918-1979) Jazz musician. GOU2.

Simmons, William. (1880-1946) Hatemonger, KKK Imperial Wizard. STRE3.

Simon. Apostle, saint. MAYE.

Simon, Seymour. (1931-) Children's author. AUT.

Simone, Nina. (1933-2003) Composer, jazz musician, singer. GREA; HAC3; MON.

Simons, Menno. (1524-1561) Dutch spiritual leader. JACKD.

Simpkins, Andy. (1932-1999) Jazz musician. GOU2.

Simpson, Lorna. (1960-) Photographer. GREA; HOR; WOL.

Simpson, Orenthal James "O. J." (1947-) Football player. Heisman Trophy Winner. DEV; LAC3.

Simpson, Bessie Wallis Warfield Spencer. (1896-1986) English Duchess of Windsor, born U.S. CRO4.

Sims, Naomi. (1949-) Entrepreneur cosmetics, fashion model. RED.

Sinatra, Francis "Frank." (1915-1998) Singer. Presidential Medal of Freedom recipient. GOU5.

Singer, Isaac Bashevis. (1904-1991) Children's and adult author, born Poland. Nobel Prize winner. PER; TWEPO.

Singer, Isaac Merritt. (1811-1875) Entrepreneur sewing machines, inventor. LOM2.

Singh, Sirdar Jagdit. (1897-1976) Entrepreneur textiles, born India. SIN.

Singleton, Arthur "Zutty." (1898-1975) Jazz musician. GOU6.

Singleton, John. (1968-) Filmmaker, screenwriter. PARJ.

Sirani, Elizabeth. (1638-1665) Italian painter. KRY; LEO3.

Sis, Peter. (1949-) Children's author, illustrator, born Czechoslovakia. TALAR3.

Sisler, George. (1893-1973) Baseball player. SULG2.

Sissle, Noble. (1889-1970) Songwriter. HASK5; TAT.

Sitting Bull. (Tatanka Yotanka) (1831-1890) Sioux Indian chief. AVE; CRO; JAN; LEVE; MON2; WAL.

Skoblikova, Lydia. (1939-) Russian olympic speed skater. AAS20.

Skoglund, Sandy. (1946-) Painter, photographer. WOL.

Slayton, Donald K. "Deke." (1924-1993) Astronaut. BAIR.

Sleet, Moneta, Jr. (1926-1996) Photographer. Pulitzer Prize winner. POT.

Slessor, Mary. (1848-1915) Scottish missionary. JACKD.

Slew, Jenny. (1719-?) Slave. HAM.

Sloan, Alfred Pritchard, Jr. (1875-1966) Automaker. ITA6.

Slocum, Melissa. (1961-) Jazz musician. GOU2.

Slutskaya, Irina. (1979-) Russian olympic figure skater. MILT.

Smalls, Robert. (1839-1915) Civil War military hero, congressman, slave. ALTMS; BECKN; GAR; HASK2; MED.

Smetana, Bedrich. (1824-1884) Czech composer. VEN.

Smetanina, Raisa. (1953-) Russian olympic skier. JACT.

Smith, Ada "Bricktop." (1894-1984) Entrepreneur nightclub, jazz singer. HASK.

Smith, Adam. (1723-1790) Scottish economist. BUS.

Smith, Amanda. (1837-1915) Slave, spiritual leader. JACKD2.

Smith, Anna Deavere. (1950-) Actor, playwright. GOLDE.

Smith, Bessie. (1894-1937) Jazz singer. AFR; ALTMS; BECKM; BECKN; COOL; HAC3; HARD; HASK5; HER; JONH; LES; MON; ORG; SHIP; TAT; WEL.

Smith, Billy. (1950-) Canadian hockey player. SPI.

Smith, Charles Kingsford. (1897-1935) Australian aviation pioneer. WILLI.

Smith, Clara. (1894-1935) Jazz singer. AFR.

Smith, David. (1906-1965) Sculptor. GREENBJ; KRY.

Smith, Emmitt. (1969-) Football player. BUCK; KNA9; LAC3.

Smith, Floyd. (1917-1982) Jazz musician. GOU3.

Smith, Holland M. (1882-1967) Attorney, World War II Marine Corps general. KNA.

Smith, Jabbo. (1908-1991) Jazz musician. GOU.

Smith, James. (1719-1806) American Revolutionary War patriot, congressman, Declaration of Independence signer, born Ireland. FRA2; QUI.

Smith, James L. (1881-?) Author, slave. LAND3.

Smith, James McCune. (1813-1865) Physician. COX; MCK2.

Smith, Jedediah Strong. (1799-1831) Explorer, fur trader, pioneer. ALTE; BAKS; COLL; GLA2; JAN; PRE; TAYS2.

Smith, Jefferson Randolph "Soapy." (1860-1898) Swindler. BLACG5.

Smith, John. (1580-1631) English adventurer, colonist, settler of Jamestown colony, military leader. CRO2; CRO4; DOH5; POD.

Smith, Johnny. (1922-1997) Jazz musician. GOU3.

Smith, Joseph, Jr. (1805-1844) Spiritual leader, founder of Mormon Church. CRO4; CRO5; GOLDM; JACW2; STRE.

Smith, Katie. (1964-) Basketball player. PON.

Smith, Lane. (1959-) Children's author, illustrator. MARC2; TALAR.

Smith, Liz. (1923-) Journalist. PRI.

Smith, Madelaine. (1835-1928) Scottish criminal. DUN.

Smith, Mamie. (1883-1946) Jazz singer. AFR; MON.

Smith, Margaret Chase. (1897-1995) Congresswoman, senator, World War II Air Force lieutenant colonel. Presidential Medal of Freedom recipient. BRED2; FAB; FIR; GUL; MORI2; THRO.

Smith, Mildred Davidson Austin. (1916-1993) Disability rights activist, inventor.

BLASH5; SULO2.

Smith, Ozzie. (1954-) Baseball player. DEA3; SULG2.

Smith, Samantha Reed. (1972-1985) Youth ambassador to Soviet Union, peace activist. BRIL.

Smith, Tommie. (1944-) Olympic track and field athlete. KNA3.

Smith, Walter Wellesley "Red." (1905-1982) Journalist. Pulitzer Prize winner. RIT.

Smith, Will. (1948-1987) Fashion designer. AFR.

Smith, Will. (1969-) Actor, rap singer. PARJ.

Smits, Jimmy. (1955-) Actor. MEN.

Smyth, Ethel. (1858-1944) English composer, suffragist. STRU2.

Snead, Sam. (1912-2002) Golfer. ITA5.

Snefru. (fl. 2613-1589 B.C.) Egyptian king. BAKR.

Snow, Clyde. (1932-) Anthropologist, forensic scientist. FRID.

Snow, Eliza. (1804-1887) Pioneer, poet, spiritual leader, women's rights activist. FUR2.

Snow, John. (1813-1858) English medical researcher, physician. YOUNT4.

Snowe, Olympia. (1947-) Senator. GUL.

Sobrero, Kate. (1976-) Olympic soccer player. LAY2.

Socrates. (470-399 B.C.) Greek philosopher. BAKR2; CRO5; HAZ; YEN.

Söderblom, Nathan. (1866-1931) Swedish spiritual leader. Nobel Peace Prize winner. KEEN2.

Sofaer, Anna. (unknown) Painter, sculptor. THI2.

Sokolow, Yvonne Kray. (1927-) Dutch Jewish Holocaust survivor. KUS.

Solomon, Haym. (1740-1785) American Revolutionary War patriot, financier, born Poland. BRO.

Solon. (610-580 B.C.) Greek military leader, statesman. BAKR2; NAR.

Soloveitchik, Joseph Dov. (1903-1993) Spiritual leader, born Poland. PASA.

Somersett. (1600s) Slave. HAM.

Somerville, Mary Fairfax. (1780-1872) Scottish astronomer, mathematician, scholar, women's rights activist. CEL; ROL.

Sonduk. (610-647) Korean queen. LEO2.

Soong Ai-Ling. (1889-1973) Chinese financier, philanthropist. HOOB.

Soong Charlie. (1866-1918) Chinese entrepreneur. HOOB.

Soong Ching-ling. (1893-1981) Peace activist, wife of Sun Yat-Sen. HAZ2; HOOB.

Soong May-Ling. (1897-2003) Chinese sociologist, wife of Chiang Kai-Shek. HOOB.

Sophocles. (496-405 B.C.) Greek playwright. BAKR2.

Sorge, Richard. (1895-1944) German journalist, World War II spy. GRAN.

Sosa, Sammy. (1968-) Baseball player, born Dominican Republic. BOY; LAE; SCHWAR; STEWM2; USC2.

Soto, Gary. (1952-) Children's and young adult author. HILC; HILC2; LAE.

Sousa, John Philip. (1854-1932) Bandleader, composer, Marine Corps bandleader. BRED3; BRIL; NIN.

Soyinka, Wole. (1934-) Nigerian author, playwright, poet, political activist. Nobel Prize winner. TWEPO.

Spahn, Warren. (1921-2003) Baseball player. SULG5.

Spalding, Albert Goodwill. (1850-1915) Baseball player, entrepreneur sporting goods. AAS9.

Spartacus. (109-71 B.C.) Roman gladiator. BAKR3.

Spaulding, Charles Clinton. (1874-1952) Entrepreneur banks, life insurance. HASK.

Speaker, Tris. (1888-1958) Baseball player. SULG2.

Spears, Britney. (1981-) Pop singer. ROBB.

Sperry, Roger. (1913-1994) Anatomist, medical researcher, physiologist, zoologist. Nobel Prize winner. HAV.

Spielberg, Steven. (1947-) Filmmaker. BRO; HILA2; LEVE.

Spikes, Frederick McKinley. (c. late 1800s) Inventor. MCK.

Spitz, Mark. (1950-) Olympic swimmer. BRO; JACT; JAN; KNA4; USC4.

Spivey, Victoria. (1906-1976) Composer, jazz singer. AFR.

Spizer, Randy. (1980-) In-line skater. SAV9.

Spock, Benjamin. (1903-1998) Author, physician, presidential candidate. CRO; LEVE.

Spoerry, Anne. (1918-1999) French medical missionary, physician, World War II resistance. HUNTE2.

Spotted Tail. (1823-1881) Brulé Sioux Indian

military leader, peace activist. SHER2.

Springsteen, Bruce. (1949-) Composer, rock musician. KNA2; LEVE; WOO3.

Squanto. (Tisquantum) (1580-1622) Wampanoag Indian colonist, guide, negotiator. CRO2; POD; RAPD2.

Staedler, Michelle. (unknown) Marine biologist. KAH6.

Stael, Madame Anna Louise Germaine de. (1766-1817) French author, noblewoman. KNI.

Stafford, Jo. (1917-) Jazz singer. GOU5.

Staley, Dawn. (1970-) Olympic basketball player. PON; RUT; SAV13.

Stalin, Joseph. (1879-1953) Russian dictator. GREER; MAYB2; YEN.

Stam, Betty. (d. 1934) Missionary. JACKD4.

Stam, John. (d. 1934) Missionary. JACKD4.

Standing Bear. (1829-1908) Ponca Indian chief. MON2.

Standish, Miles. (1584-1656) Colonist, pilgrim, born England. CRO2.

Stangl, Franz. (1908-1971) Austrian Nazi war criminal. SCHM4.

Stanley, Sir Henry Morton. (1841-1904) Civil War soldier, explorer, journalist, born Wales. LANG; POD; PRE.

Stanton, Edwin. (1814-1869) Attorney, cabinet member. RIC2.

Stanton, Elizabeth Cady. (1815-1902) Suffragist, women's rights activist. CRO4; DUM; GUL; HARN; HEA; HEL; HER; JACW; MARZ; MCD; ROL; ZEI5.

Starbird, Kate. (1975-) Basketball player. RUT.

Stark, Freya. (1893-1993) English adventurer, explorer. DUN; HAC; LANG; MCLO2; STEFO2.

Starks, John. (1965-) Basketball player. RAPK.

Starr, Bart. (1934-) Football player. KNA9; LAC2; SULG7.

Starr, Myra "Belle" Shirley. (1848-1889) Outlaw, pioneer. COOL; DUN; GLA; KRAL; KUH; SAV2; THOM2; WAL.

Starr, Henry. (1873-1921) Outlaw. BLACG3.

Starrs, James. (1930-) Attorney, forensic scientist. HAV.

Staubach, Roger. (1942-) Football player. Heisman Trophy winner. DEV; LAC2; SAV8; SULG7.

Stauffenberg, Claus von. (1907-1944) German World War II military and resistance leader. THOM4.

Steel, Danielle. (1947-) Author. KNI.

Steele, Samuel. (1851-1919) Canadian crime fighter. ITA3.

Steffens, Lincoln. (1866-1936) Author, journalist. RIT.

Steig, Jeanne. (1930-) Children's author, illustrator. MARC3.

Steig, William. (1907-2003) Children's author, cartoonist, illustrator. MARC; MARC3.

Stein, Aurel. (1862-1943) Hungarian archaeologist. FAG.

Stein, Gertrude. (1874-1946) Author, playwright. CRO4; GOM; KNI; PER; SMIL2.

Steinbeck, John. (1902-1968) Author. Nobel Prize winner, Presidential Medal of Freedom recipient, Pulitzer Prize winner. BRED; CRO; FAB2; MEE; PER; TWEPR.

Steinem, Gloria. (1934-) Journalist, women's rights activist. BRO; GUL; HARN; LEVE; MORI3; PRI.

Steiner, Rudolf. (1861-1925) Austrian author, educator, spiritual leader, founder theosophical movement. CRO5.

Stengel, Casey. (1890-1975) Baseball manager. PIE.

Stephen I. (975-1038) Hungarian king. PAP.

Stephens, Helen. (1918-1994) Olympic track and field athlete. MOL.

Stephens, John Lloyd. (1805-1852) Adventurer, attorney, explorer. FAG.

Stephenson, George. (1781-1848) English engineer, inventor. DIN; LOM2.

Sternberg, Charles. (1850-1943) Paleontologist. AAS.

Stevens, Gary. (1963-) Jockey. KUH.

Stevens, Jennie "Little Britches." (1879-) Outlaw. KRO.

Stevens, Nettie Maria. (1861-1912) Biologist, medical researcher. REY; STI2; TIN; VEG.

Stevens, Thaddeus. (1792-1868) Attorney, civil rights activist, congressman. JACW; KEND.

Stevenson, Adlai. (1900-1965) Ambassador, governor, presidential candidate, World War II Assistant Secretary of Navy. CRO.

Stevenson, Robert Louis. (1850-1894) Scottish children's and adult author, poet.

KRULL6; NIN; PER.

Steward, Austin. (1794-1860) Abolitionist, author, slave. LAND3.

Steward, Susan McKinney. (1847-1918) Physician. AFR2; JONL.

Stewart, Elinoire Pruitt. (1876-1933) Author, pioneer. STEFO3.

Stewart, Larry Elliot "Slam." (1914-1987) Jazz musician, singer. GOU2.

Stewart, Martha. (1941-) Author, entrepreneur home goods, television personality. HARN; LUT; MCL.

Stieglitz, Alfred. (1864-1946) Photographer. BRO; GAI; JACKN; KRY.

Still, Peter. (1800-1868) Fugitive slave. FRA.

Still, Susan. (1961-) Astronaut, Navy pilot. BRIGG2.

Still, Valerie. (1961-) Basketball player. PON.

Still, Vina. (unknown) Slave. FRA.

Still, William Grant. (1895-1978) Composer, conductor. POT.

Stillwell, Hallie Crawford. (1897-1997) Rancher. ALTE2.

Stillwell, Joseph W. (1883-1946) World War II general. KNA.

Stimson, Henry. (1867-1950) Attorney, cabinet member. RIC2.

Stine, Robert Lawrence "R. L." (1943-) Young adult author. HILC2; MAD.

Stinson, Katherine. (1891-1977) Aviator, World War I Red Cross pilot. YOUNT7.

Stockton, John. (1962-) Basketball player. PAU; SAV5.

Stockton, Richard. (1730-1781) American Revolutionary War patriot, attorney, congressman, Declaration of Independence signer. FRA2; QUI.

Stockwell, Elisha. (1846-?) Civil War teen soldier. HOOS.

Stojka, Karl. (1931-) Austrian gypsy Holocaust survivor. SCHM4.

Stojko, Elvis. (1972-) Canadian olympic figure skater. MILT.

Stommel, Henry. (1920-1992) Oceanographer. POLKI.

Stommer, Helga Edelstein. (1926-) German Jewish Holocaust survivor. GID.

Stone, Isidor Feinstein "I. F." (1907-1989) Editor magazines and newspapers. RIT.

Stone, Lucy. (1818-1893) Abolitionist, suffragist, women's rights activist. DUM; HARN; HEL; ROL.

Stone, Thomas. (1743-1787) American Revolutionary War patriot, attorney, congressman, Declaration of Independence signer. FRA2; QUI.

Stone, Toni. (1921-1966) Baseball player. HASD.

Storm, Hannah. (1962-) Sportscaster. HILA.

Stowe, Emily Jennings. (1831-1903) Canadian abolitionist, physician, suffragist, women's rights activist. KIR; STI.

Stowe, Harriet Beecher. (1811-1896) Abolitionist, author. BLASH; CHA; CRO; FAB2; HEA; HER; JACW; KNI; PER; ROL.

Stowers, Freddie. (1896-1918) World War I Army corporal. Medal of Honor recipient. REE2.

Stradivari, Antonio. (1644-1737) Italian instrument designer, musician. KRAL.

Straker, David Augustus. (1842-1908) Attorney, civil rights activist. AFR2.

Stratton, Charles Sherwood. (Tom Thumb) (1838-1883) Showman. DRI; KRAL.

Strauss, Levi. (1829-1902) Entrepreneur blue jeans, born Germany. AAS16; BRO; KENJ; MAYB.

Strauss, Richard. (1864-1949) German composer, conductor. VEN.

Stravinsky, Igor Fedorovich. (1882-1971) Composer, born Russia. BLACA2; KRULL4; TWEPR; VEN.

Strayhorn, Billy. (1915-1967) Composer, jazz musician. CRO4.

Street, Picabo. (1971-) Olympic skier. DIT.

Streichen, Edward. (1879-1973) Photographer, World War I and II photojournalist, born Luxembourg. Presidential Medal of Freedom recipient. JACKD.

Streisand, Barbra. (1942-) Actor, singer. BRO.

Stresemann, Gustav. (1878-1929) German statesman. Nobel Peace Prize winner. KEEN2.

Stringer, Ann. (1918-1990) Journalist, World War II correspondent. COLM.

Stringfellow, John. (1799-1883) English aviation pioneer. BERL2.

Strozzi, Barbara. (1619-1664) Italian composer. NIC2.

Strug, Kerri. (1977-) Olympic gymnast. DON2; GREES; KLE.

Stuart, James Ewell Brown "Jeb." (1833-1864) Civil War general. GREEC2; REG; TRAC.

Stuart, Miranda. (James Barry) (1795-1865) English Civil War soldier, physician, disguised as man. DUN; STI; WEL.

Stuart, Robert. (1785-1848) Explorer, fur trapper, born Scotland. BAKS.

Stubbs, George. (1724-1806) English painter. EIG.

Stukeley, William. (1687-1765) English archaeologist. FAG.

Stuyvesant, Peter. (1610-1672) Dutch colonist, settler of New Netherlands (New York). CRO2; DOH3.

Subotai. (1176-1248) Mongol general. CRO3.

Suchocka, Hanna. (1946-) Polish political leader. GUL.

Suetonius. (Gaius Suetonius Tranquillus) (69-135) Roman journalist. HOOB3.

Sugihara, Sempo. (1900-1986) Japanese Holocaust rescuer. FREM; LYM.

Sukarno, Achmad. (1901-1970) Indonesian president. PAP; WAKI.

Suleiman I, the Magnificent. (1494-1566) Turkish military leader, ruler. CRO3.

Sulla. (Lucius Cornelius Sulla) (138-78 B.C.) Roman general, statesman. BAKR3.

Sullam, Sara Coppio. (1592-1641) Italian poet, scholar. TAI.

Sullivan, Annie. (1866-1936) Educator. CRO4; CUS2; DEN; DUN; MARZ.

Sullivan, Sir Arthur. (1842-1900) English opera composer. CRO4; KRULL4.

Sullivan, John L. (1858-1918) Boxer. KNA7.

Sullivan, Kathryn. (1951-) Astronaut, oceanographer. POLKI.

Sullivan, Leon. (1922-2001) Civil rights activist, entrepreneur automaker, workers' rights activist. BECKN.

Summitt, Pat Head. (1952-) Basketball coach. GAI3.

Sun Yat-Sen. (1866-1925) President Republic of China. PAP; WAKI.

Surovov, Aleksandr. (1792-1800) Russian military commander. CRO3.

Susanna. (d. 295) Biblical character, saint. ARM2.

Sutter, John Augustus. (1803-1880) Gold-miner, pioneer, born Germany, lived Mexico. DOH2; TAYS2.

Suttles, George "Mule." (1901-1968) Baseball player. WIN2.

Suttner, Bertha von. (1843-1914) Austrian author, cofounder International Peace Bureau, peace activist. Nobel Peace Prize winner. KEEN2.

Suu Kyi, Daw Aung San. (1945-) Burmese peace activist. Nobel Peace Prize winner, Presidential Medal of Freedom recipient. CUS2; DUN; GUL; HAC6; HER; KEEN2; KRULL; LUC; PRI3; SCHR2.

Suzuki, Daisetz Teitan "D. T." (1870-1966) Educator, philosopher, translator, born Japan. SIN.

Swain, Clara A. (1834-1910) Medical missionary, physician. STI.

Swallow, Steve. (1940-) Composer, jazz musician. GOU2.

Swann, Lynn. (1952-) Football player, sportscaster. KNA9; THOR.

Swedenborg, Emanuel. (1688-1772) Swedish mystic, philosopher. CRO5.

Swift, Jonathan. (1667-1745) English author. EIG; PER.

Swinton, Ernest. (1868-1951) English inventor, military leader. RIC5.

Swisshelm, Jane Grey Cannon. (1815-1884) Abolitionist, journalist, women's rights activist. PRI; RIT.

Swoopes, Sheryl. (1971-) Olympic basketball player. BRIL3; GAI3; JACK; KELLY; PON; RUT; SAV13; WEL.

Szcerbiak, Wally. (1977-) Basketball player. PAU.

Szold, Henrietta. (1860-1945) Editor, founder of Hadassah, Zionist organization. PASA; TAI.

T

Tabei, Junko. (1939-) Japanese mountaineer. MCLO6.

Tacitus. (Publius Cornelius Tacitus) (55-115) Roman historian, orator, statesman. BAKR3.

Taft, Helen Herron "Nellie." (1861-1943) First Lady. ANT; BARB; GOR; PAST.

Taft, Robert Alphonse. (1889-1953) Senator.

FAB.

Taft, William H. (1857-1930) Attorney, Supreme Court chief justice, 27th president of U.S. ADA; BARB; BAU; BLASS; CRO6; DAV2; KRULL5; MORR.

Tagore, Rabindranth. (1861-1941) Indian author, composer, painter, poet. Nobel Prize winner. BLACA.

Tallchief, Maria. (1925-) Osage Indian ballet dancer. ALLP; ALTE2; BRIL; HARN; MARZ; RAPD2; STU.

Tamara. (1156-1212) Russian medieval queen. ROL.

Tamerlane. (1336-1405) Mongol conqueror. CRO3.

Tan, Amy. (1952-) Author. ALTE2; CHI; ISH; PER; SIN.

Taney, Roger Brooke. (1777-1864) Attorney, Supreme Court justice. AAS14; CRO.

Tanner, Henry Ossawa. (1859-1937) Painter. AFR; BLACA; HAC4; HARD; POT.

Tape, Mary McGladery. (1857-1928) Children's rights activist, painter, photographer, born China. KET.

Tarantino, Quentin. (1963-) Filmmaker. HILA2.

Tarbell, Ida. (1857-1944) Journalist. HILA; PRI; RIT; SAT; THIR; WHI.

Tarkenton, Francis. (1940-) Football player. SULG7.

Tarter, Jill Cornell. (1944-) Astrophysicist. POLK.

Tasman, Abel. (1603-1659) Dutch explorer. POD; PRE.

Tatis, Fernando. (1975-) Baseball player, born Dominican Republic. STEWM2.

Tatum, Art. (1910-1956) Jazz musician. GOU4; MON; SHIP.

Taussig, Helen Brooke. (1898-1986) Medical researcher, physician. Presidential Medal of Freedom recipient. CURT; HUNTE2; KENJ; LINL3; REY; STI; YOUNT3.

Tay, Jannie. (1945-) Singaporean entrepreneur. MCLU.

Taylor, Annie Edson. (1838-1921) Adventurer. RAPD.

Taylor, Billy, Jr. (1925-1977) Jazz musician. GOU2.

Taylor, Cecil. (1929-) Jazz musician. GOU4.

Taylor, Elizabeth. (1932-) Actor, AIDS activist, born England. CRO4.

Taylor, George. (1716-1781) American Revolutionary War patriot, congressman, Declaration of Independence signer, manufacturer, born Ireland. FRA2; QUI.

Taylor, James Hudson. (1832-1905) English missionary. JACKD.

Taylor, Lawrence. (1959-) Football player. SAV7.

Taylor, Margaret Mackell Smith. (1788-1852) First Lady. BARB; GOR; PAST.

Taylor, Mildred. (1943-) Children's author. RED4.

Taylor, Susan. (1946-) Editor magazine, television personality. GREA; RED.

Taylor, Susie King. (1848-1912) Civil War nurse, educator, slave. COX; COX2; GAR; GREA; HOOS; ROBE; ZEI.

Taylor, Telford. (1908-1998) Army brigadier general, attorney, Nuremberg Trials chief counsel, World War II colonel. SCHM4.

Taylor, Zachary. (1784-1850) Army general Seminole War, War of 1812, 12th president of U.S. ADA; BARB; BAU; BLASS; CRO6; DAV2; MORR.

Tchaikovsky, Peter Ilyich. (1840-1893) Russian composer. BLACA2; HOOB5; KAL; KRULL4; ROM.

Tchernyshev, Peter. (1971-) Olympic figure skater, born Russia. MILT.

Te Ata. (1897-1995) Chickasaw Indian folklorist, storyteller. AVE.

Teach, Edward. (Blackbeard) (1680-1718) English outlaw, pirate. BLACG4; CRO2; THOM2; YOUNT5.

Teasdale, Lucille. (1929-1996) Canadian human rights activist, physician. KIR.

Teasdale, Sara. (1844-1933) Poet. KNI.

Tebe, Marie. (d. 1901) Civil War soldier, disguised as man, born France. BLASH; ZEI.

Tecumseh. (1768-1813) Shawnee Indian chief, American Revolutionary War soldier, War of 1812 soldier, orator. AVE; CRO; DEN; LEVE.

Tefnut. Egyptian goddess of the morning dew. FIS.

Tejada, Miguel. (1976-) Baseball player, born Dominican Republic. STEWM.

Tell, William. (1282-?) Swiss political activist, possibly legendary. KRAL; THOM2.

Teller, Raymond Joseph. (Teller) (1948-) Comedian, magician. WOO2.

Temin, Howard. (1934-) Medical researcher, physician, virologist. Nobel Prize winner. HAV.

Temple, Lewis. (1800-1854) Inventor. AAS4; ALTMS; HASK8; HAY2; MCK.

Temple, Shirley. (1928-) Actor, ambassador. BRIL.

Ten Boom, Corrie. (1892-1979) Dutch author, Holocaust rescuer. JACKD2.

Tenayuca, Emma. (1916-1999) Workers' rights activist. BERS; LAE.

tenBroek, Jacobus. (1911-1968) Attorney, disability rights activist, educator, born Canada. KEND.

Tenebaum, Frieda. (1934-) Holocaust survivor. NIE.

Tennyson, Alfred Lord. (1809-1892) English poet. PER.

Ter Bosch, Gerard. (1617-1681) Dutch painter. CUM.

Terence. (Publius Terentius Afer) (185-159 B.C.) Roman playwright. BAKR3.

Teresa, Mother. *See* Bojaxhiu, Agnes.

Teresa of Avila. (1515-1582) Spanish mystic, saint. CRO5; KNI.

Tereshakova, Valentina V. (1937-) Russian cosmonaut. BRIGG2; DUN; HAC; HER; PRE; RIC4; ROL; STI2.

Terrell, Mary Church. (1863-1954) Civil rights activist, suffragist, women's rights activist. ALTMS; BECKN; COX2; DUB; GREA; HEL; TAYK; THIR.

Terry, Ellen. (1847-1928) English actor. WEI2.

Terry, Ellen. (unknown) Entrepreneur real estate. PIL2.

Tesla, Nikola. (1856-1943) Electrical engineer, inventor, born Yugoslavia. HAV.

Teters, Charlene. (1950-) Spokane Indian mixed-media artist, Native American rights activist, painter. MOO.

Thackeray, William Makepeace. (1811-1863) English author. PER.

Tharp, Marie. (1920-) Oceanographer. POLK.

Tharp, Twyla. (1941-) Choreographer. FOR.

Tharpe, Sister Rosetta. (1921-1973) Jazz singer. MON.

Thatcher, Margaret. (1925-) English prime minister. Presidential Medal of Freedom recipient. AXEC; DUN; GUL; HER; MAYB2; NAR4; PARJ2; PRI3; ROL.

Thayer, Eli. (1819-1899) Abolitionist, educator, settled Kansas, state legislator. DOH4.

Thayer, Helen. (1938-) Arctic explorer, mountaineer, olympic track and field athlete, born New Zealand. MCLO4.

Themistocles. (523?-463 B.C.) Greek naval commander, politician, statesman. BAKR2; CRO3; NAR.

Theni, Gustavo. (1951-) Italian olympic skier. JACT.

Theodora. (497-548) Turkish actor, empress of Eastern Roman Empire, women's rights activist. CRO4; DUN; HER; ROL.

Theodoric the Great. (454-526) Italian conqueror, king. PAP.

Theodosius I. (347-395) Roman emperor. BAKR3.

Theophrastus. (371-287 B.C.) Greek botanist. NAR3.

Theotokópoulous, Doménikos. (El Greco) (1541-1614) Greek painter. BLACA; GLU; KRY.

Theroux, Paul. (1941-) Author. PER.

Thible, Elizabeth. (fl. 1784) French aviation pioneer. WILLI.

Thomas Aquinas. (1225-1274) Italian philosopher, saint, spiritual leader. CRO5; JACW2; YEN.

Thomas, Dave. (1932-2002) Entrepreneur restaurants. KRAMB.

Thomas, Debi. (1967) Olympic figure skater, physician. GAI3; HUNTE; POY.

Thomas, Frank. (1968-) Baseball player. DEA; DEA2.

Thomas, George Henry. (1816-1870) Civil War general. GREEC3; TRAC.

Thomas, Helen. (1920-) Journalist. HILA.

Thomas, Isaiah. (1961-) Basketball player. KNA11; SAV5; TOR4.

Thomas, Piri. (1928-) Author. HILC.

Thomas, Valerie. (1943-) Inventor, mathematician, physicist. HAY2; HENS2; SULO2; THI.

Thomas, Vivien. (1910-1985) Medical researcher. AFR2.

Thompson, Ben. (1843-1884) Civil War soldier, crimefighter, frontiersman, gunfighter. SAV; THRA.

Thompson, Daley. (1958-) English olympic decathlon, track and field athlete. DON2.

Thompson, David. (1770-1857) English explorer, fur trader, geographer. PRE.

Thompson, Dorothy. (1893-1961) Journalist, suffragist. PRI; RIT; WHI.

Thompson, Edward. (1840-1935) Archaeologist, historian. SCHEL.

Thompson, Jennie. (1981-) Olympic gymnast. LAY.

Thompson, Mary Harris. (1829-1895) Educator, physician. STI.

Thompson, William. (1927-1950) Korean War hero. Medal of Honor recipient. REE2.

Thoms, Adah Belle. (1870-1943) Public health pioneer, World War I nurse. COX.

Thomsen, Christian Jurgenson. (1786-1865) Danish archaeologist. FAG.

Thomson, Joseph John. (1856-1940) English inventor, physicist. Nobel Prize winner. LOM2; TIN.

Thomson, Roy Herbert. (1894-1973) Canadian entrepreneur newspapers and broadcasting. MAYB.

Thomson, William. (1824-1907) Scottish mathematician, physicist. TIN.

Thor. Norse god of thunder. FIS3.

Thoreau, Henry David. (1817-1862) Author, naturalist. CRO4; FAB2; FAB3; KEEN; OFT2; PER; STA.

Thornton, Joe. (1979-) Canadian hockey player. BREH.

Thornton, Matthew. (1714-1803) American Revolutionary War patriot, congressman, Declaration of Independence signer, physician, born Ireland. FRA2; QUI.

Thorpe, Jim. (1888-1953) Chippewa/Sac/Fox Indian baseball player, decathlon, football player, olympic track and field athlete, pentathlon. ALLP; AVE; KRULL3; RAPD2; SULG3; USC4.

Thorpe, Otis Henry. (1962-) Basketball player. BJA.

Thorvaldson, Erik "Erik the Red." (950-1010) Viking explorer. POD; PRE.

Thucydides. (454-404? B.C.) Greek historian. BAKR2.

Thurman, Howard. (1900-1981) Educator, peace activist, scholar, spiritual leader. AFR2.

Thurman, Wallace. (1902-1934) Author, editor. HARD.

Thurmond, Strom. (1902-2003) Governor,

presidential candidate, senator. AAS2.

Thutmose III. (fl. 1504-1450 B.C.) Egyptian king. BAKR.

Tiant, Luis. Sr. (1906-1977) Baseball player, born Cuba. WIN.

Tibbles, Suzette LaFlesche. (1854-1903) Ponca and Omaha Indian Native American rights activist. KET.

Tiberius. (Tiberius Claudius Nero) (42 B.C.-37 A.D.) Roman emperor. BAKR3.

Tiburzi, Bonnie Linda. (1948-) Pilot. BRIGG; YOUNT7.

Tien, Chang-Lin. (1935-) Educator, born China. RAG.

Tijerina, Rejes López. (1926-) Mexican civil rights activist. LAE.

Tiktiner, Rivkah bat Meir "Rebecca." (16th century) Czech Jewish author. TAI.

Tilden, William Tatem, Jr. "Bill." (1893-1953) Tennis player. CHRIST; JACT.

Tilles, Helen. (unknown) Austrian Jewish Holocaust survivor. TIT.

Tillich, Paul. (1886-1965) Philosopher, spiritual leader, World War I chaplain, born Germany. CRO5.

Timms, Michele. (1965-) Australian olympic basketball player, sportscaster. JACK.

Ting, Samuel Chao Chung. (1936-) Physicist. Nobel Prize winner. MORE; YOUNT.

Tingley, Katherine. (1847-1929) Human rights activist, spiritual leader, utopian community founder. STRE6.

Tinker, Clarence L. (1887-1942) Osage Indian World War I Army Air Corps pilot, World War II Army Air Corps major general. AVE.

Tinne, Alexandrine. (1839-1869) Dutch explorer. MCLO; POLK.

Tintoretto. (Jacopo Robusti) (1518-1594) Italian painter. KRY.

Titian. (Tiziano Vecellio.) (1457-1576) Italian painter. CUM; GLU; REN.

Tito, Josip Broz. (1892-1980) Yugoslavian president, World War I Austro-Hungarian army, World War II political activist, anti-Nazi. SCHM4; THOM4.

Titov, Vladimir. (1947-) Russian cosmonaut. PRE.

Tiye. (fl. 1370 B.C.) Egyptian queen. BAKR.

Togo, Heihachiro. (1848-1934) Japanese naval leader. CRO3.

Toguri, Iva "Tokyo Rose." (1916-1988) World War II traitor. AAS18.

Tokes, Laszlo. (unknown) Romanian political activist, spiritual leader. TRAC2.

Toklas, Alice B. (1877-1967) Author, partner of Gertrude Stein. CRO4; KNI.

Tolan, Eddie. (1908-1967) Olympic sprinter, track and field athlete. KNA3.

Tolliver, Peter. (1927-) Engineer, physicist. HENS2.

Tolstoy, Leo. (Lev Nikolaevich) (1828-1910) Russian author. HOOB5; NIN; PER.

Tom Thumb. *See* Stratton, Charles Sherwood.

Tomara, Sonia. (d. 1982) Journalist, World War II correspondent, born Russia. COLM.

Tomjanovich, Rudy. (1948-) Basketball coach. KNA10.

Tonegawa, Susumu. (1939-) Molecular biologist, immunologist, medical researcher, born Japan. Nobel Prize winner. SPA; YOUNT.

Tonty, Henri de. (1649-1704) French explorer, settler of Arkansas, born Italy. DOH4.

Toomer, Jean. (1894-1967) Author, poet. HARD.

Topham, Thomas. (1710-1749) English weightlifter, wrestler. JACT.

Torrence, Gwen. (1965-) Olympic sprinter, track and field athlete. HUNTE; MOL.

Torresola, Griselio. (1925-1950) Puerto Rican assassin, attempted to kill President Harry Truman. JONR; STG; SULG9.

Torriente, Cristobal. (1895-1938) Baseball player, born Cuba. WIN.

Torrio, John. (1882-1957) Gangster, born Italy. BLACG.

Torvalds, Linus. (1970-) Finnish computer scientist, Internet pioneer, software engineer. FREN.

Totino, Rose. (1915-1994) Entrepreneur food/restaurants. PIL.

Tough, Davey. (1907-1948) Jazz musician. GOU6.

Touissant L'Ouverture, Pierre Dominique. (1743-1803) Haitian general, slave insurrectionist. CRO3; MON2.

Touissant, Pierre. (1766-1853) Entrepreneur hair salons, philanthropist, slave. HASK; HASK5.

Toulouse-Lautrec, Henride. (1864-1901) French painter. IMP; KRY; ORE.

Tower, Joan. (1938-) Composer. NIC2.

Townes, Charles Hard. (1915-) Inventor, physicist. Nobel Prize winner. AAS15; TIN.

Townsend, Cameron. (1896-1982) Missionary, bible translator. JACKD2.

Townshend, Charles. (1725-1767) English statesman. SCHMR2.

Tracy, Benjamin. (1830-1915) Attorney, cabinet member. RIC2.

Trajan. (Marcus Ulpius Traianus) (53-117) Roman emperor, general. BAKR3; COOLI.

Travis, Dempsey J. (1920-) Author, cabinet member, entrepreneur real estate. HASK.

Traylor, Bill. (1854-1947) Painter, slave. AFR.

Traynor, Harold "Pie." (1899-1972) Baseball player. SULG2.

Trevino, Lee. (1939-) Golfer. ITA5; LAE.

Trinh, Eugene H. (1950-) Astronaut, physicist, born Vietnam. SIN.

Trocme, André. (unknown) French Holocaust rescuer, spiritual leader. FREM; PET.

Trocme, Magda. (unknown) French Holocaust rescuer, spiritual leader. FREM; PET.

Tromp, Maarten von. (1597-1653) Dutch naval admiral. CRO3.

Trotsky, Leon. (1879-1940) Russian revolutionary. CRO4.

Trotter, Mildred. (1899-1991) Anatomist, anthropologist, forensic scientist. YEA.

Trotter, William Monroe. (1872-1934) Civil rights activist, editor. BECKN; DUB; RIT.

Trudeau, Garry. (1948-) Cartoonist. STEFF.

Truman, Elizabeth "Bess" Wallace. (1885-1982) First Lady. BARB; GOR; PAST.

Truman, Harry S. (1884-1972) 33rd president of U.S., senator, vice president, World War I captain. ADA; BARB; BAU; BLASS; CRO4; CRO6; DAV2; DEN; FAB; JONR; KRULL5; LEVE; LINE; MORR; STG.

Trung Nhi. (14-43) Vietnamese warrior queen. HER; LEO; ROE.

Trung Trac. (14-43) Vietnamese warrior queen. HER; LEO; ROE.

Truth, Sojourner. (1797-1883) Abolitionist, author, spiritual leader, suffragist, women's rights activist. ALTMS; BECKN; DUN; GAR; GREA; GUL; HAC2; HAM; HEL; HER; JACW; KAT; PIN; PLO; SHAP;

TAYK; WILKB; ZEI5.

Tryphosa. Roman olympic track and field athlete. LEO.

Tsai, Gerard, Jr. (1928-) Financier, born China. SIN.

Tsinhnahjinnie, Hulleah. (1954-) Navajo/ Creek/Seminole Indian photographer. HOR.

Tsui, Lap-Chee. (1950-) Canadian molecular biologist, medical researcher, born China. SPA.

Tubman, Harriet. (1820-1913) Abolitionist, Civil War spy, nurse, slave. ALTMS; BECKN; CHA; CLA; COOL; DEN; DUN; FRA; GREA; HAC2; HAM; HARN; HASK2; HAZ2; HEA; HER; JACKD; JAN; KEND; KRULL; LEVE; LIL; MARZ; MCD; MED; PIN; PLO; POT; ROE; ROL; SHAP; TAYK; THOM4; ZEI.

Tuchman, Barbara Wertheim. (1912-1989) Historian. Pulitzer Prize winner. KNI.

Tucker, Sophie. (1887-1966) Singer. ORG.

Tupou, Salote, III. (1900-1965) Tonga queen. WEL.

Tupper, Earl. (1907-1983) Entrepreneur storage containers. AAS3.

Turing, Alan. (1912-1954) English computer pioneer, mathematician, World War II code breaker. HENH; WILKP3.

Turner, Charles Henry. (1867-1923) Biologist, educator, entomologist. HAY3; MCK2.

Turner, Henry McNeal. (1834-1915) Orator, spiritual leader. AFR2; BECKN.

Turner, James Milton. (1840-1915) Abolitionist, diplomat, educator, slave. COX2.

Turner, Joseph Mallord William "J. M. W." (1775-1851) English painter. BLACA; CUM; CUS; ROM.

Turner, Nat. (1800-1831) Slave insurrectionist. ALTMS; BECKN; HAM; LIL; TAYK.

Turner, Ted. (1938-) Entrepreneur news media. MAC; MAYB.

Turner, Tina. See Bullock, Anna Mae.

Turpin, Dick. (1705-1739) English highway robber. BLACG2; THOM2.

Turpin, Tom. (unknown) Educator, entomologist. KALLN.

Tussaud, Marie. (1761-1850) French sculptor. DUN.

Tutankhamun. (1347-1329 B.C.) Egyptian king, pharoah. BAKR; BOY; KRAL; ROBE3.

Tutu, Desmond Mpilo. (1931-) South African human rights activist, spiritual leader. Nobel Peace Prize winner. BLU; CRO5; GOLDM; KEEN2; LUC; SHAW.

Twain, Mark. See Clemens, Samuel.

Twain, Shania. See Edwards, Eileen Regina.

Twilight, Alexander Lucius. (1795-1857) Educator, state legislator. COX2; POT.

Two Leggings. (fl.1840s) Crow Indian military leader, warrior. WE2.

Tyler, Anne. (1941-) Author. Pulitzer Prize winner. SMIL.

Tyler, John. (1790-1862) Governor, 10th president of U.S., senator, vice president. ADA; BARB; BAU; BLASS; CRO6; DAV2; LINE; MORR.

Tyler, Julia Gardiner. (1820-1889) First Lady. BARB; PAST; ZEI.

Tyler, Letitia Christian. (1790-1842) First Lady. BARB; GOR; PAST.

Tyndale, William. (1494-1536) English scholar, translator. CRO5; JACKD.

Tyner, McCoy. (1938-) Jazz musician. GOU4.

Typhoid Mary. See Mallon, Mary.

Tyr. Norse god of war. FIS3.

Tyson, Cicely. (1933-) Actor. GREA; PARJ.

Tyson, Michael "Mike." (1966-) Boxer. ITA2; KNA7; SAV12.

Tyus, Wyomia. (1945-) Olympic track and field athlete. HUNTE; MOL.

Tz-u-hsi. (1835-1908) Chinese dowager empress. DUN; GUL; HER; KRULL.

U

Uccello, Paolo. (1397-1475) Italian painter. REN.

Uchida, Yoshiko. (1921-1992) Children's author. ISH; SIN.

Ulam, Stanislaw. (1909-1984) Mathematician, physicist, born Poland. HENH.

Ung, Han. (1968-) Author, playwright, born Philippines. CHI.

Unitas, Johnny. (1933-2002) Football player. HUNT; LAC2; SULG3; SULG7.

Unthan, Hermann. (1848-1929) Musician. DRI.

Updike, John. (1932-) Author. Pulitzer Prize winner. VERD.

Urania of Worms, Lady. (13th century) German Jewish cantor. TAI.

V

Vaccarelli, Paulo Antonio. (Paul Kelly) (1876-1927) Boxer, gangster, born Italy. BLACG.

Valadez, Mariano. (fl. 1950s) Huichol Indian yarn painter. MOO.

Valdez, Luis. (1940-) Actor, playwright, poet. LAE; SIN2; WEI2.

Valdez, Patssi. (1951-) Painter. HON.

Valens, Ritchie. (1942-1959) Singer, songwriter. KNA2; SIN2.

Valenzuela, Fernando. (1960-) Baseball player, born Mexico. SLO.

Vallejo, Mariano Guadalupe. (1808-1890) Rancher, settler of California. LAE; SIN2.

Van Allen, James. (1914-) Physicist, space scientist. HAV.

Van Allsburg, Chris. (1949-) Children's author, illustrator. MARC; TALAR.

Van Buren, Abigail. *See* Phillips, Pauline Esther.

Van Buren, Hannah Hoes. (1783-1819) First Lady. BARB; GOR; PAST.

Van Buren, Martin. (1782-1862) Attorney, 8th president of U.S. ADA; BARB; BAU; BLASS; CRO6; DAV2; MORR.

Van der Goes, Hugo. (1440-1482) Flemish painter. CUM; KRY.

Van der Woude, Elizabeth. (1657-1694) Dutch adventurer. POLK.

Van der Zee, James. (1886-1983) Photographer. AFR; HARD; HASK5.

Van Dyck, Sir Anthony. (1599-1641) Flemish painter. KRY; SEV.

Van Dyken, Amy. (1973-) Olympic swimmer. DIT; KRAMS5.

Van Eyck, Jan. (1390-1441) Flemish painter. CUM; KRY; REN.

Van Gogh, Vincent. (1853-1890) Dutch painter. BLACA; CUM; GLU; IMP; KRULL2; KRY; ORE.

Van Horn, Keith. (1975-) Basketball player. NEL.

Van Hoosen, Bertha. (1863-1952) Medical researcher, physician. STI.

Van Lew, Elizabeth. (1818-1900) Civil War spy. BLASH; CARA; CHA; ZEI.

Van Meegeren, Hans. (1889-1947) Dutch painter, swindler. BLACG5.

Van Peebles, Mario. (1957-) Actor, filmmaker, screenwriter. PARJ.

Van Peebles, Melvin. (1932-) Actor, filmmaker. AFR.

Van Raalte, Jim. (unknown) World War II Army soldier, Holocaust rescuer. TIT.

Van Vechten, Carl. (1880-1964) Author, photographer. HARD.

Vancouver, George. (1757-1798) English explorer. PRE.

Vanderbilt, Cornelius. (1794-1877) Entrepreneur financier, steamships, trains. CRO; GREEC.

Vanderbilt, Harold. (1884-1976) Yachtsman. JACT.

Vann, Robert. (1879-1940) Publisher newspaper. AFR.

Vardon, Harry. (1870-1937) English golfer. JACT.

Vargas, Diego de. (1643-1704) Governor. SIN2.

Vargas, Jay. (1937-) Vietnam War hero. Medal of Honor recipient. DOH.

Vargas, Tetelo. (1906-1971) Baseball player, born Dominican Republic. WIN.

Vashon, John Bathan. (1792-1854) Seaman, War of 1812. HASK2.

Vasquez, Tiburcio. (1835-1875) Outlaw. BLACG3; SIN2.

Vauban, Sebastien le preste de. (1633-1707) French engineer, military leader. CRO3.

Vaughan, Joseph Floyd "Arky." (1912-1952) Baseball player. DEA3.

Vaughan, Sarah. (1924-1991) Jazz musician, singer. AFR; GOU5; GREA; MON; RED5; SHIP.

Vaughn, Mo. (1967-) Baseball player. SCHER; SCHWAR.

Vaux-Walcott, Mary. (1860-1940) Canadian mountaineer, naturalist. MCLO6.

Vaz, Katherine. (unknown) Author, born Portugal. SMIL2.

Veeck, Bill. (1914-1986) Baseball team owner, World War II Marine. KEND.

Vega, Bernardo. (1885-1965) Entrepreneur cigars. SIN2.

Vega, Garcilaso de la. (1539-1616) Peruvian author, historian. HOOB6.

Velarde, Pablita. (1918-) Santa Clara Pueblo Indian painter. AVE.

Velasquez, William C. (1944-1988) Civil rights activist. Presidential Medal of Freedom recipient. LAE.

Velázquez, Diego de Rodriguez Silva y. (1599-1660) Spanish painter. CUM; GLU; KRY; SEV.

Velazquez, Loreta Janeta. (1842-?) Civil War soldier, disguised as man. BLASH; CHA; SIN2; ZEI.

Velazquez, Nydia. (1953-) Congresswoman, born Puerto Rico. LAE; MEN.

Veney, Bethany. (1815-?) Author, slave. LAND3.

Veniaminov, Innokentii. (1797-1879) Russian Orthodox missionary, spiritual leader. CRO5.

Venizélos, Eleutherios. (1864-1936) Greek political activist, statesman. PAP.

Ventris, Michael. (1922-1956) English architect, linguist. WEI.

Venturini, Tisha. (1973-) Olympic soccer player. MILM.

Vera, Joseph Azlor Vitro de. (d. 1723) Mexican military leader, defender of Texas. SIN2.

Vercingetorix. (75-46 B.C.) Roman ruler. CRO4.

Verdi, Giuseppe. (1813-1901) Italian opera composer. BLACA2; HOOB3; KRULL4; NIN; VEN.

Verendrye, Pierre. (1685-1749) French colonist in Canada. CRO2; PRE.

Vergoose, Elizabeth "Mother Goose." (unknown) Colonial storyteller. KRAL.

Vermeer, Johannes. (1632-1675) Dutch painter. GLU; SEV.

Verne, Jules. (1828-1905) French author. KRULL7; PER; YEN.

Vernon, Mickey. (1918-) Baseball player. SULG2.

Verrazzano, Giovanni da. (1458-1528) Italian explorer. ALTE; PARN; POD; PRE.

Vesalius, Andreas. (1514-1564) Belgian anatomist, illustrator, physician. CURT; POD; PRE.

Vesey, Denmark. (1767-1822) Slave insurrectionist. ALTMS; MED.

Vespasian. (Titus Flavius Vespasianus) (9-79) Roman emperor. BAKR3.

Vespucci, Amerigo. (1454-1512) Italian explorer. ALTE; FRIT; LOM; PARN; PRE.

Victoria. (1819-1901) English queen. BREW; CRO4; GUL; HER; KRULL; ROL; WEL.

Vigee-Le Brun, Elisabeth. (1755-1842) French painter. KRY; ROE

Villa-Komaroff, Lydia. (1947-) Molecular biologist, medical researcher, physician. STJ2.

Villa-Lobos, Heitor. (1887-1959) Brazilian composer, educator. HOOB6.

Villagra, Gaspar Perez de. (1558-1620) Colonist, historian, poet. SIN2.

Villaseñsor, Victor. (1940-) Author, screenwriter. LAE.

Viña, Fernando. (1969-) Baseball player. STEWM.

Vine, Allyn. (1914-1994) Inventor, oceanographer. POLKI.

Vinnegar, Leroy. (1928-1999) Jazz musician. GOU2.

Vinson, Phyllis Tucker. (1948-) Television filmmaker. GREA.

Virchow, Rudolph. (1821-1902) German medical researcher, pathologist, physician. CURT.

Virgil. (Publius Vergilius Maro) (70-19 B.C.) Roman poet. BAKR3; PER.

Vivaldi, Antonio. (1678-1741) Italian composer. EIG; KRULL4; VEN.

Vivekananda. (1863-1902) Indian spiritual leader, Ramakrishna movement founder. CRO5.

Vizquel, Omar. (1967-) Baseball player, born Venezuela. STEWM.

Vlad the Impaler. (Vlad Dracul) (1431-1477) Romanian terrorist. KRAL.

Vogelsang, Peter. (1815-1887) Civil War lieutenant. HASK2.

Voigt, Cynthia. (1942-) Young adult author. SMIL2.

Volta, Alessandro. (1746-1827) Italian educator, physicist. TIN.

Voltaire. *See* Arouet, François Marie.

Von Braun, Werner. (1912-1977) Engineer, inventor, born Germany. DIN; HAV; RIC3; RIC5; YEN.

Von Manstein, Erich. (1887-1973) German World War II field marshal, anti-Nazi.

LAC.

Von Mason, Stephen. (1954-) Painter. HON.

Von Moltke, Helmut. (1800-1891) German military leader. CRO3.

Von Neumann, John. (1903-1957) Computer pioneer, mathematician, born Hungary. NOR.

Von Ribbentrop, Joachim. (1893-1946) German diplomat, foreign minister, Nazi war criminal. SCHM4.

Vonnegut, Kurt. (1922-) Author. PER; VERD.

W

Waddell, George Edward "Rube." (1876-1914) Baseball player. SULG5.

Wade, Cheryl Marie. (unknown) Disability rights activist, poet. SMIL2.

Wadhwa, Meenakshi. (1967-) Astronomer, space scientist, born India. POLK.

Wadlow, Robert. (1918-1940) Showman, circus performer. DRI.

Wagner, Billy. (1971-) Baseball player. SCHWAR.

Wagner, John Peter "Honus." (1874-1955) Baseball player. DEA; DEA3; KRAMS; SULG2.

Wagner, Richard. (1813-1883) German composer. BLACA2; NIN; VEN.

Waheene. (1841-?) Hidatsa Indian historian. WE2.

Wait, Bethany. (1973-1991) Young rescuer of people in storm. BRIL.

Waite, Charles. (fl. 1920s) Forensic scientist. YEA.

Wakefield, Ruth. (1905-1977) Entrepreneur cookies, inventor. THI.

Waksman, Selman Abraham. (1888-1973) Bacteriologist, microbiologist, medical researcher, born Russia. Nobel Prize winner. TIN.

Wald, Lillian. (1867-1940) Nurse, public health worker, social worker. BRO; STI; TAI; THIR.

Walden, Barbara. (1936-) Entrepreneur cosmetics. AFR2.

Waldheim, Kurt. (1918-) Austrian president, Nazi war criminal, Secretary-General of U.N. LAND2.

Walesa, Lech. (1943-) Polish political activist, president. Nobel Peace Prize winner, Presidential Medal of Freedom recipient. KEEN2; MAYB2; TRAC2.

Walker, Alice. (1944-) Author. Pulitizer Prize winner. AFR; ARO; FEM2; GREA; HAN; KNI; PER; RED4; WILKB.

Walker, Herschel. (1962-) Football player. Heisman Trophy winner. DEV.

Walker, Joe. (1799-1876) Explorer, frontiersman. ALTE.

Walker, John. (1937-) Traitor. AAS18.

Walker, Judith Cary. (1889-1973) Radio broadcaster. PRI.

Walker, Kate. (1842-1931) Lighthouse keeper. FLE.

Walker, Kenny. (1967-) Football player. SAV10.

Walker, Larry. (1966-) Canadian baseball player. SCHWAR.

Walker, Madame C. J. *See* Walker, Sarah Breedlove McWilliams.

Walker, Maggie Lena. (1867-1934) Entrepreneur banker, journalist. AFR2; GREA; HASK; JEF2; PLO; RED; THIR; TUR2.

Walker, Margaret. (1915-1998) Author. GREA; WILKB.

Walker, Mary Edwards. (1832-1919) Civil War surgeon, physician, women's rights activist. Medal of Honor recipient. BLASH; DOH; KENJ2; ROBE; SHEA; STI; THIR; ZEI.

Walker, Moses Fleetwood. (1857-1924) Baseball player. POT.

Walker, Sarah Breedlove McWilliams "Madame C. J." (1867-1919) Entrepreneur cosmetics, human rights activist, inventor. AAS4; AFR2; ALTML; ALTMS; BECKN; BLASH; COOL; CURR2; FEM; GREA; GREEC; HARN; HASK; HASK7; HASK8; HUD2; JEF2; KRAMB2; LUT; MAYB; POT; RED; ROL; SULO; SULO2; VAR.

Walker, Thomas. (1715-1794) American Revolutionary War patriot, colonist, physician. CRO2.

Walker, Thomas. (1850-1935) Attorney, entrepreneur real estate, philanthropist, state legislator. AFR2.

Wall, Rachel. (1760-1789) Pirate. SHAR; WEA.

Wallace, Alfred Russel. (1823-1913) English naturalist. FAB3; KEEN.

Wallace, George. (1919-1998) Governor, presidential candidate. AAS2.

Wallace, Henry. (1888-1965) Presidential candidate, vice-president. AAS2.

Wallace, Sippie. (1898-1986) Jazz singer. AFR.

Wallenberg, Raoul. (1912-?) Swedish Holocaust rescuer, victim. FREM; LYM; SCHM4; THOM4.

Wallenstein, Albrecht von. (1583-1634) Bohemian military leader. CRO3.

Waller, Thomas Wright "Fats." (1904-1943) Bandleader, composer, jazz musician. AFR; GOU4; SHIP.

Wally, Augustus. (unknown) Spanish American War buffalo soldier. REE2.

Walpole, Horace. (1717-1797) English author, historian, political activist. SCHM2.

Walsh, Bill. (1931-) Football coach. SAV11.

Walsh, Christian. See Cavanagh, Kit.

Walsh, Don. (1931-) Oceanographer, navy officer. PRE.

Walsh, Mary. (1950-) Vietnam War Army physical therapist. SHEA.

Walt, Lewis W. (1913-1989) Marine general, World War II, Korean War, Vietnam War. BOR.

Walters, Barbara. (1931-) Broadcast journalist. HARN; HILA; PRI.

Walton, Bill. (1952-) Basketball player. KNA5; KNA11; TOR4.

Walton, George. (1741-1804) American Revolutionary War patriot, congressman, Declaration of Independence signer. FRA2; QUI.

Walton, Sam. (1918-1992) Entrepreneur discount stores. MAC; MAYB; PIL.

Waltrip, Darrell. (1947-) Nascar auto racer. RIL.

Wang, An. (1920-1990) Computer pioneer, electrical engineer, entrepreneur computers, born China. AAS5; GREEC; HAV; MORE; SIN.

Wang, Vera. (1949-) Fashion designer. KENJ.

Wang, Wayne. (1949-) Filmmaker, born Hong Kong. GAN; SIN.

Ward, Catherine Barnes. (1851-1913) Photographer. HOR.

Ward, Nancy. (1738-1822) American Revolutionary War patriot, Cherokee Indian leader, peace activist. AVE; CALV; SILC.

Ward, Samuel Ringgold. (1817-1878) Abolitionist, slave, spiritual leader. AFR2.

Warhol, Andy. (1928-1987) Filmmaker, painter, publisher. BLACA; GREENBJ; KRULL2; KRY; LEVE; TWEPO.

Waring, Laura Wheeler. (1877-1948) Painter. HARD.

Warner, Kurt. (1971-) Football player. DEI.

Warren, Adelina Otero. (1881-1965) Author, educator. SIN2.

Warren, Charles. (unknown) English archaeologist. FAG.

Warren, Earl. (1891-1974) Attorney, governor, Supreme Court chief justice. Presidential Medal of Freedom recipient. AAS14; CRO; FAB.

Warren, Mercy Otis. (1728-1814) American Revolutionary War patriot, playwright. FUR3; HARN; HEA; SCHM2; SILC; ZEI.

Warren, William Whipple. (1825-1853) Objway Indian historian, interpreter. WE2.

Washakie. (1800-1900) Shoshone Indian chief. SHER2.

Washington, Augustus. (1820-?) Civil rights activist, educator, photographer. SULG.

Washington, Booker T. (1856-1915) Educator, slave, statesman. AFR2; ALTMS; BECKN; CLA; COX2; CRO; GAR; HAC2; JACW; JAN; POT; SHAP; TAYK; UNG.

Washington, Denzel. (1954-) Actor. AFR; PARJ.

Washington, Dinah. (1925-1959) Jazz singer. AFR.

Washington, George. (1732-1799) American Revolutionary War general, 1st president of U.S. ADA; BARB; BAU; BLASS; CRO; CRO3; CRO4; CRO6; DAV2; DEN; FAB; JAN; KRULL5; LEVE; MARZ; MORR; SCHM2; USC; WILKP; YEN.

Washington, George. (1817-1905) Pioneer. ALTMS.

Washington, Madison. (unknown) Slave insurrectionist. ALTMS.

Washington, Martha Dandridge Curtis. (1731-1802) First Lady. BARB; GOR; PAST; ZEI4.

Washington, Ora. (1898-1971) Basketball

player, tennis player. HASD.

Washington, Warren. (1936-) Meteorologist. AFR2.

Washow, Omar. (1970-) Entrepreneur computer services. HASK.

Wasserstein, Wendy. (1950-) Playwright. Pulitzer Prize winner. SMIL2.

Waters, Ethel. (1896-1977) Actor, jazz singer. AFR; GOU5; HARD; MON; WEI2.

Waters, Maxine. (1938-) Congresswoman, state legislator. GREA; THRO.

Waters, McKinley Morganfield "Muddy." (1915-1983) Jazz musician, singer. LES.

Waterton, Charles. (1782-1865) English adventurer, naturalist. ZAU.

Watson, Ella "Cattle Kate." (1861-1889) Outlaw, pioneer. SAV2.

Watson, James Dewey. (1928-) Biologist, geneticist, zoologist. Nobel Prize winner, Presidential Medal of Freedom recipient. AAS13; CRO4; CURT; SHER; TIN.

Watson, Thomas. (1856-1922) Hatemonger, journalist, political activist. CRO; STRE4.

Watson, Thomas, Jr. (1914-1993) Computer pioneer, entrepreneur computers, World War II fighter pilot. Presidential Medal of Freedom recipient. AAS5.

Watson-Schutze, Eva. (1867-1935) Photographer. HOR.

Watson-Watt, Sir Robert Alexander. (1892-1973) Scottish inventor, physicist. TIN.

Watt, James. (1736-1819) Scottish inventor. DIN; LOM2; WILKP3.

Watteau, Jean Antoine. (1684-1721) Flemish painter. EIG; KRY.

Watterson, Henry. (1840-1921) Editor newspapers. RIT.

Wattleton, Faye. (1943-) President of Planned Parenthood, women's rights activist. GREA.

Watts, Alan. (1915-1973) Spiritual leader. CRO5.

Wauneka, Annie Dodge. (1910-1997) Navajo Indian public health educator. Presidential Medal of Freedom recipient. HAV; HUNTE2; SHER2.

Wayans, Keenen Ivory. (1958-) Actor, comedian, filmmaker, screenwriter. PARJ.

Wayne, Chuck. (1923-1997) Jazz musician. GOU3.

Wayne, John. (1907-1979) Actor. Presidential

Medal of Freedom recipient. JAN.

Weatherspoon, Teresa. (1965-) Olympic basketball player. PON.

Weaver, Jeff. (1976-) Baseball player. SCHWAR.

Webb, Del. (1899-1974) Entrepreneur real estate. AAS8.

Webb, Sheyann. (1957-) Civil rights activist as young person. ROC.

Webb, Spud. (1963-) Basketball player. BJA; BJA3; JEN2.

Webb, William Henry "Chick." (1909-1939) Jazz musician. GOU6.

Webber, Andrew Lloyd. (1948-) English composer. KAL.

Webber, Chris. (1973-) Basketball player. BJA; PAU; SAV6; SAV12.

Weber, Karl Maria Friedrich Ernst von. (1786-1826) German opera composer. VEN.

Weber, Lois. (1881-1939) Filmmaker. THIR.

Webern, Anton von. (1883-1945) Austrian composer. VEN.

Webster, Daniel. (1782-1852) Attorney, cabinet member, congressman, orator, senator. CRO; FAB.

Webster, Noah. (1758-1843) Lexicographer. CRO; LEVE.

Wecht, Cyril. (1931-) Attorney, forensic scientist, physician. HAV.

Weddington, Sarah. (1945-) Attorney, women's rights activist. CALA.

Wedener, Alfred. (1880-1930) German explorer, meteorologist. CARR.

Weekly, Frieda von Richthofen. (1870-1956) German wife of D. H. Lawrence. CRO4.

Weeks, Kent R. (unknown) Archaeologist, author, egyptologist. GREENBL.

Weems, Ann Marie. (1840-?) Fugitive slave, disguised as man. FRA; HOOS.

Weems, Carrie Mae. (1951-) Photographer. SILL.

Weetamoo. (1640-1676) Pocasset Indian warrior. ALLP; FUR.

Weidner, John. (unknown) French Holocaust rescuer. PET.

Weihenmayer, Eric. (1968-) Mountaineer. KAM.

Weil, Joseph "Yellow Kid." (1877-1977) Swindler. BLACG5.

Weil, Simone. (1909-1943) French author,

political activist, revolutionary. KNI.

Weinberg, Stefan. (1923-) Polish Jewish Holocaust survivor. LAND4.

Weinberger, Caspar W. (1917-) Attorney, cabinet member. Presidential Medal of Freedom recipient. RIC2.

Weinsberg, Alicia Fajnsztejn. (1929-) Polish Jewish Holocaust survivor. GREENF.

Weiser, Johann Conrad. (1696-1760) Colonist, Indian interpreter, born Germany. CRO2.

Weiss, Michael. (1976-) Olympic figure skater. MILT.

Weissmuller, Johnny. (1904-1984) Olympic swimmer. KRULL3.

Weizmann, Chaim. (1874-1952) Israeli chemist, president, political activist, born Russia. PASA.

Welch, Bob. (1956-) Baseball player. KAM.

Welch, Joseph. (1890-1960) Attorney, jurist, McCarthy trials judge. EME.

Weldon, Fay. (1931-) English author. SMIL2.

Wellesley, Arthur. (1880-1959) English military leader, born Ireland. CRO3.

Wellman, Walter. (1858-1934) Aviation pioneer, journalist. TES.

Wells, David. (1963-) Baseball player. SCHWAR.

Wells, Herbert George "H. G." (1866-1946) English author, historian. KRULL7; PER.

Wells, Horace. (1815-1848) Dentist, medical researcher. FRA3.

Wells, James Lesesne. (1902-1993) Painter, printmaker. HARD.

Wells, Rebecca. (1952-) Author. KNI.

Wells, Rosemary. (1943-) Children's author, illustrator. MARC3.

Wells-Barnett, Ida B. (1862-1931) Civil rights activist, journalist, reformer. ALTMS; BECKN; BOL; DEN; DUB; FEM; GOLDE; GREA; HAC2; HAN; HARN; HER; LYO; MED; MORI3; PIN; PLO; PRI; RIT; THIR; TUR2; WILKB.

Welty, Eudora. (1909-2001) Author. Pulitzer Prize winner. BRED; GOM; VERD.

Wen-Chi, Lady. (c. 178 A.D.) Chinese poet. POLK.

Wengeroff, Pauline. (1833-1916) Russian author. TAI.

Weni. (fl. 2300 B.C.) Egyptian general, jurist. BAKR.

Wentworth, Benning. (1696-1770) Colonial governor. DOH3.

Wertheimer, Henry. (1927-) German Jewish Holocaust survivor. KUS.

Wesley, John. (1703-1791) English spiritual leader, founded Methodist religion. CRO5; JACKD; JACW2.

West, Benjamin. (1738-1820) Painter. BRIL; EIG.

West, Dorothy. (1907-1998) Author. HASK5; WILKB.

West, Jerry. (1938-) Basketball player. RAPK2; TOR4.

West, Mae. (1893-1980) Actor, showwoman. COOL.

West, Rick C. (1951-) Canadian arachnologist. TALAD.

West, W. Richard, Sr. (1912-1996) Cheyenne Indian painter, sculptor. AVE.

West, W. Richard, Jr. (1943-) Cheyenne Indian attorney. AVE.

Westinghouse, George. (1846-1914) Inventor. NOO.

Westmoreland, William C. (1914-) Army chief of staff, Korean War commander, Vietnam War, World War II colonel. BOR.

Westover, Cynthia. (1885-1931) Inventor. BLASH2.

Wettling, George. (1907-1968) Jazz musician. GOU6.

Wharton, Edith. (1862-1937) Author. Pulitzer Prize winner. ARO; FAB2; GOM; KNI; NIN.

Wheatley, Phillis. (1754-1784) American Revolutionary War patriot, poet. ALTMS; ARO; BECKN; BRIL; FEM2; FUR; FUR3; GREA; HAN; HARN; HEA; HOOS; KNI; OFT; PLO; POT; SCHM2; SILC; STRI; WEL; WILKB; ZEI4.

Wheeler, Robert Eric Mortimer. (1890-1976) English archaeologist. FAG; GREENBL; WEI.

Wheelwright, John. (1592-1679) Puritan spiritual leader, settled New Hampshire. DOH3.

Whipple, William. (1730-1785) American Revolutionary War military leader, congressman, Declaration of Independence signer. FRA2; QUI.

Whistler, James Abbott McNeill. (1834-1903) Engraver, painter. CUM; GLU; IMP.

White, Charles. (1918-1979) Painter. TUR2.

White, Elwyn Brooks "E. B." (1899-1985) Children's author. Presidential Medal of Freedom recipient, Pulitzer Prize winner. FAB2; KRULL6; MAS; RYL.

White, George Henry. (1852-1918) Attorney, congressman, entrepreneur banker, slave. KAT2.

White, Gilbert. (1720-1793) English naturalist. FAB3.

White, John. (1557-1593) English explorer. CRO2.

White, Morgan. (1983-) Olympic gymnast. LAY2.

White, Reggie. (1961-) Football player. HUNT.

White, Ryan. (1971-1990) AIDS activist and victim. BRIL; GON; HOOS.

White, Tom. (unknown) Spiritual leader. JACKD4.

White, Walter. (1893-1955) Author, civil rights activist. BECKN; CIV.

White, William Allen. (1868-1944) Editor, journalist. Pulitzer Prize winner. RIT.

Whiten, Mark. (1966-) Baseball player. TOR.

Whitefield, George. (1714-1770) Colonist, spiritual leader. CRO2; CRO5.

Whitehead, Gustave. (1874-1927) Aviation pioneer, born Germany. BERL2.

Whitehead, Robert. (1823-1905) English inventor. RIC5.

Whitestone, Heather. (1973-) Beauty queen. KEND.

Whitewolf, Jim. (1878-?) Kiowa-Apache Indian historian. WE2.

Whitfield, Mark. (1966-) Jazz musician. GOU3.

Whitfield, Princess. (1937-) Educator. AFR2.

Whitman, Christine Todd. (1946-) Environmental Protection Agency head, governor. GUL; THRO.

Whitman, Marcus. (1802-1847) Missionary, physician, pioneer. CALV; DOH2.

Whitman, Narcissa. (1808-1847) Missionary, pioneer. ALTE; CALV; DOH2; FUR2; LAK; SAV2; TAYS2.

Whitman, Walt. (1819-1892) Poet. FAB2; LEVE; NIN; OFT2.

Whitney, Eli. (1765-1825) Inventor. CRO; LEVE; LOM2.

Whitney, Mary Watson. (1847-1920) Astronomer. STI2.

Whitten, Charles. (1922-) Medical researcher, physician. AFR2.

Whittle, Sir Frank. (1907-1996) English aeronautical engineer, inventor, royal air force fighter pilot. DIN.

Whitton, Erin. (1971-) Olympic hockey player. BRIL4.

Whitworth, Kathy. (1939-) Golfer. HASD.

Whyte, Edna Gardner. (1902-1993) Aviator, nurse, World War II Naval Nurse Corps. YOUNT7.

Wichman, Carl Eric. (1887-?) Entrepreneur bus line, born Sweden. AAS16.

Wickenheiser, Hayley. (1969-) Canadian olympic hockey player. BRIL4; BRY.

Wiesel, Elie. (1928-) Holocaust survivor, author, born Romania. Nobel Peace Prize winner, Presidential Medal of Freedom recipient. BRO; DEN; KEEN2; MAN; SCHM4.

Wiesenthal, Simon. (1908-) Austrian Jewish Holocaust survivor, author, Nazi hunter, born Poland. Presidential Medal of Freedom recipient. ITA3; SCHM4.

Wiesner, David. (1956-) Children's author, illustrator. MARC; TALAR.

Wijsmuller, Gertrude. (unknown) Dutch Holocaust rescuer, social worker. MARX.

Wilberforce, William. (1759-1833) English abolitionist for British slave trade. JACKD4.

Wilde, Oscar. (1854-1900) Irish playwright, poet. PER.

Wilder, L. Douglas. (1931-) Attorney, chemist, governor, Korean War military, state legislator. BOOK; DUD; POT.

Wilder, Laura Ingalls. (1867-1957) Children's author, pioneer. HARN; KNI; KRO; PER.

Wilder, Thornton. (1897-1975) Author, playwright. Presidential Medal of Freedom recipient, Pulitzer Prize winner. PER.

Wilhelm II. (1859-1941) German emperor, World War I general. WILKP.

Wilkes, Charles. (1798-1877) Explorer, naval officer. ALTE; PRE.

Wilkes, John. (1725-1797) American Revolutionary War English political leader, reformer. SCHM2.

Wilkins, Dominique. (1960-) Basketball player, born France. BJA.

Wilkins, Sir George Hubert. (1888-1958) Australian adventurer, aviator, explorer, World War I photographer. TES.

Wilkins, Roy. (1901-1981) Civil rights activist. Presidential Medal of Freedom recipient. ALTMS; BECKN.

Wilkinson, Rupert. (1936-) English author. MARX.

Willard, Emma Hart. (1787-1870) Educator, women's rights activist. HEA; HER; UNG.

Willard, Frances Elizabeth. (1839-1898) Reformer, suffragist. MORI3; THIR.

Willey, Gordon Randolph. (1913-2002) Archaeologist, author. FAG.

William I, The Conqueror. (1027-1087) English general, king. CRO3; DAV; WILKP; YEN.

William I, The Silent. (1533-1584) Dutch count of Nassau and prince of Orange. WILKP.

William III. (1650-1702) English king. DAV.

Williams, Abigail. (1680-?) Colonist, puritan, accused others of witchcraft. HOOS.

Williams, Angela. (1980-) Track and field athlete. RUT6.

Williams, Bernie. (1968-) Baseball player, born Puerto Rico. SCHWAR; STEWM.

Williams, Bert. (1874-1922) Actor, comedian, dancer, singer. POT.

Williams, Betty. (1943-) Irish peace activist, reformer. Nobel Peace Prize winner. BLU; HER; KEEN2; SCHR2.

Williams, Charles "Buck." (1960-) Basketball player. RAPK.

Williams, Daniel Hale. (1856-1931) Educator, physician. AFR2; ALTMS; BECKN; COX; HAC2; HAY; MCK2; POT; SULO; YOUNT2.

Williams, Doug. (1955-) Football player. BUCK; KNA9.

Williams, Eunice. (1697-1787) Colonist, Indian captive. HOOS.

Williams, George Washington. (1849-1891) Attorney, Civil War soldier, historian, spiritual leader. AFR2; ALTMS; BECKN; HASK2.

Williams, Jason. (1975-) Basketball player. NEL.

Williams, Jody. (1950-) Human rights activist, reformer. Nobel Peace Prize winner. KEEN2.

Williams, Joe. (1918-1999) Jazz singer. GOU5.

Williams, John. (1664-1729) Colonist, puritan spiritual leader. CRO2.

Williams, John "Hot Rod." (1962-) Basketball player. RAPK.

Williams, Lucinda. (1953-) Country singer. ORG.

Williams, Mary Lou. (1910-1981) Jazz musician. GOU4; GREA; MON; MOU; SHIP; STRU2.

Williams, Moses. (d. 1899) Indian War Army soldier. MON2.

Williams, Ozzie. (1921-) Space scientist. AFR2.

Williams, Paul Revere. (1894-1980) Architect. POT.

Williams, Ricky. (1977-) Football player. Heisman Trophy winner. DEI.

Williams, Roger. (1603-1683) Founder Rhode Island, human rights activist, spiritual leader, born England. CRO2; JACW; JACW2; POD.

Williams, Serena. (1981-) Tennis player. BRY; MILE; RUT5.

Williams, Ted. (1918-2002) Baseball player. Presidential Medal of Freedom recipient. DEA; ITA; JACT; KRAMS; SULG3; SULG8.

Williams, Tennessee. (1911-1983) Playwright. Pulitzer Prize winner. FAB2; TWEPO; WEI2.

Williams, Tony. (1945-1997) Jazz musician. GOU6.

Williams, Venus. (1980-) Tennis player. BRY; MILE; RUT5.

Williams, Vera. (1927-) Children's author, illustrator. TALAR2.

Williams, William. (1731-1811) American Revolutionary War patriot, congressman, Declaration of Independence signer. FRA2; QUI.

Wills, Maurice Morning "Maury." (1932) Baseball player. BJA2.

Wills, William John. (1833-1861) Australian explorer, born England. LANG.

Wilson, Alexander. (1766-1813) Author, ornithologist, born Scotland. KEEN.

Wilson, August. (1935-) Playwright. Pulitzer Prize winner. AFR.

Wilson, Ellen Louisa Axson. (1860-1914)

First Lady. BARB; GOR; PAST.

Wilson, Ernest Judson "Boojum." (1899-1963) Baseball player. WIN2.

Wilson, Franny. (unknown) Civil War soldier, disguised as man. CHA.

Wilson, Harriet E. Adams. (1827?-1863?) Author. KNI.

Wilson, James. (1742-1798) American Revolutionary War patriot, attorney, congressman, Declaration of Independence signer, born Scotland. FRA2; QUI.

Wilson, Lewis "Hack." (1900-1948) Baseball player. SULG8.

Wilson, Luzena Stanley. (1821-?) Author, pioneer. FUR2.

Wilson, Sharifa. (unknown) City official. AFR2.

Wilson, Theodore "Teddy." (1912-1986) Bandleader, jazz musician. GOU4; SHIP.

Wilson, Woodrow. (1856-1924) Educator, governor, 28th president of U.S. Nobel Peace Prize winner. ADA; BARB; BAU; BLASS; BLU; CRO; CRO6; DAV2; FAB; KEEN2; KRULL5; MAYB2; MORR; SAW.

Wilson-Hawkins, Carla. (unknown) Educator. AFR2.

Winblad, Ann. (1950-) Internet pioneer, financier. FREN.

Winchell, Walt. (1897-1972) Journalist. RIT.

Winckelmann, Johann Joachim. (1717-1768) German archaeologist. FAG.

Winema. (Tobey Riddle) (1836-1932) Modoc Indian Native American rights activist, peace activist. SHER2.

Winfrey, Oprah. (1954-) Entrepreneur media conglomerate, filmmaker, television personality. CUS2; GREA; HARN; HASK; JEF2; LUT; MCLU; POT; RED5; ROE.

Winkler-Kühne, Ruth. (1931-) German Holocaust rescuer. AXE.

Winnemucca, Sarah. (1844-1891) Paiute Indian Native American rights activist. ALTE2; AVE; FUR2; HARN; HEA; HER; LAK.

Winslow, Anna Green. (1760-1779) Colonist. HOOS.

Winslow, Edward. (1595-1655) Colonist, pilgrim. CRO2.

Winthrop, John. (1588-1649) English colonial governor, puritan. CRO2; DOH3; WILKP2.

Winyan Ohitika. Sioux Indian legendary heroine. MAYE2.

Winzeler, Henry Simon. (unknown) Entrepreneur toy and picture frame company. AAS10.

Wise, Isaac Mayer. (1819-1900) Spiritual leader, founder Reform Judaism in U.S., born Czechoslovakia. GOLDM; JACW2; PASA.

Wise, Stephen S. (1874-1949) Spiritual leader, born Hungary. BRO.

Wisniewski, David. (1953-2002) Children's author, illustrator. TALAR2.

Witherspoon, John. (1723-1794) American Revolutionary War patriot, congressman, Declaration of Independence signer, educator, spiritual leader, born Scotland. FRA2; QUI; SAW.

Witt, Katarina. (1965-) German olympic figure skater. HASD; RUT2; SMIP.

Woerner, Louise. (unknown) Entrepreneur home health care. PIL2.

Wolcott, Oliver. (1726-1797) American Revolutionary War military, patriot, congressman, Declaration of Independence signer. FRA2; QUI.

Wolde, Mamo. (1931-) Ethiopian olympic track and field athlete. DON2.

Wolfe, James. (1727-1759) English army general, colonist in Canada. CRO2; CRO3; WILKP.

Wolfe, Tom. (1931-) Author, journalist. PER.

Wollstonecraft, Mary. (1759-1797) English author, women's rights activist. HER; ROL; SMIL2.

Wonder, Stevie. (1950-) Jazz musician. AFR; KEND; RED5; TAT.

Wong, Anna May. (1905-1961) Actor. GAN; SIN.

Wong, Jade Snow. (1922-) Author, ceramicist. SIN.

Wong-Staal, Flossie. (1947-) Medical researcher, born China. CAM2; HUNTE2; YOUNT; YOUNT3.

Woodard, Alfre. (1953-) Actor. PARJ.

Woodard, Lynette. (1959-) Basketball player. LINL.

Woodhull, Victoria. (1838-1927) Journalist, presidential candidate, suffragist, women's rights activist. HARN; HEL; PRI.

Woodruff, Hale Aspacio. (1900-1980) Educator, painter. HARD.

Woods, Granville T. (1856-1910) Inventor. AAS4; AFR2; ALTMS; BECKN; HASK; HASK8; HAY2; HUD2; MCK; SULO.

Woods, Tiger. (1975-) Golfer. BOY; BRIL; SAV4.

Woodson, Carter G. (1875-1950) Educator, historian. AFR2; COX2; HASK5; POT; TUR.

Woodward, Robert Upshur "Bob." (1943-) Journalist. RIT; SAT.

Woodward, Henry. (1646-1685) Colonist, settled Carolinas. CRO2; DOH5.

Woolf, Virginia. (1882-1941) English author. HER; KNI; PER; SMIL.

Woolley, Charles Leonard. (1880-1960) English archaeologist. FAG; WEI.

Woolworth, Frank Winfield. (1852-1919) Entrepreneur retail stores. AAS10.

Wordsworth, Dorothy. (1771-1855) English poet. KNI.

Wordsworth, William. (1770-1850) English poet. PER; ROM.

Workman, Fanny Bullock. (1859-1925) Explorer, mountaineer, women's rights activist. MCLO6; STEFO2.

Worsaae, Jens Jacob A. (1821-1885) Danish archaeologist. FAG.

Worth, Charles Frederick. (1825-1895) French fashion designer. KENJ.

Worthy, James. (1961-) Basketball player. KNA11.

Wovoka. (Jack Wilson) (1858-1932) Paiute Indian mystic, spiritual leader. AVE.

Wozniak, Stephen. (1950-) Computer pioneer, entrepreneur computers. AAS12; CRO; HAV; NOR; YEN.

Wren, Christopher. (1632-1723) English architect. CUS.

Wright, Eugene. (1923-) Jazz musician. GOU2.

Wright, Frank Lloyd (1869-1959) Architect. CRO; LEVE.

Wright, Jane Cooke. (1919-) Medical researcher, physician. AFR2; GREA; HAY; SULO; SULO2; STI; YOUNT2.

Wright, Jonathan Jasper. (1840-1885) Attorney, jurist. AFR2.

Wright, Louis Tompkins. (1891-1932) Civil rights activist, medical researcher, physician. AFR2; COX; HAY.

Wright, Orville. (1871-1948) Aviation pioneer. ALTE; BERL; BERL2; CRO; DEN; DIN; JAN; LOM2; ROS; SCHR; WILKP3; WILLI; YEN.

Wright, Patience Lovell. (1725-1786) American Revolutionary War patriot, sculptor, spy. ZEI4.

Wright, Richard. (1908-1960) Author. ALTMS; BECKN; MAL; OFT; TWEPO.

Wright, Wilbur. (1867-1912) Aviation pioneer. ALTE; BERL; BERL2; CRO; DEN; DIN; JAN; LOM2; ROS; SCHR; WILKP3; WILLI; YEN.

Wu Chao. (625-705) Chinese empress. COOL; HER; HOOB.

Wu, Chien-Shiung. (1912-1997) Nuclear physicist, born China. CAM; DID; HAC8; HAV; LINL3; REY; SIN; STI2; YOUNT; YOUNT3.

Wuhsha. (11th century) Egyptian entrepreneur banker. TAI.

Wurmbrand, Richard. (1909-2001) Romanian missionary. CLA2.

Wycliffe, John. (1320-1384) English educator, spiritual leader. CRO5.

Wyeth, Andrew. (1917-) Painter. LEVE.

Wythe, George. (1726-1806) American Revolutionary War patriot, attorney, congressman, Declaration of Independence signer. FRA2; QUI.

X

Xaman Ek. Mayan god of the north star. FIS2.

Xavier, Francis. (1506-1552) Portuguese missionary, saint. CLA2; CRO5.

Xenophon. (fl. 428-355 B.C.) Greek historian. BAKR2; CRO3; PRE.

Xerxes I. (519-465 B.C.) Persian military leader, king. YEN.

Y

Yadin, Yigael. (1917-1984) Israeli archaeologist, deputy prime minister. WEI.

Yagudin, Alexei. (1980-) Russian olympic figure skater. MILT.

Yakami. Japanese legendary heroine. MAYE2.

Yakel, Jerrell. (1959-) La Jolla Indian neuroscientist. STJ3.

Yalow, Rosalyn Sussman. (1921-) Medical researcher, physicist. Nobel Prize winner. CAM; DAS; HAV; LINL3; REY; STI2; TAI; TIN; VEG.

Yamaguchi, Kristi. (1971-) Olympic figure skater. DIT; GAN; HASD; KRAMS4; LINL; POY; RUT2; SAV14; SIN; SMIP.

Yamamoto, Hisaye. (1921-) Author. SMIL.

Yamamoto, Isoroku. (1884-1943) Japanese military leader, led attack on Pearl Harbor. CRO3; LAC.

Yamasaki, Minoru. (1912-1986) Architect. SIN.

Yamauchi, Hiroshi. (1928-) Japanese entrepreneur, inventor computer games. AAS9.

Yang, Chen Ning. (1922-) Physicist, born China. Nobel Prize winner. SIN; YOUNT.

Yang, Jerry. (1968-) Entrepreneur computers, Internet pioneer. FREN; HENH2.

Yani, Wang. (1975-) Chinese painter. BRIL; WEL.

Yarborough, Cale. (1940-) Nascar auto racer. RIL.

Ybor, Vincente Martinez. (1818-1896) Cuban entrepreneur cigars, founder Ybor City, Fl. SIN2.

Yeager, Chuck. (1923-) Test pilot, World War II Air Force pilot. Presidential Medal of Freedom recipient. ALTE; JAN; ROS.

Yeager, Jenna L. (1952-) Aviator. PRE; YOUNT7.

Yeats, William Butler. (1865-1939) Irish folklorist, poet. Nobel Prize winner. PER.

Yeltsin, Boris. (1931-) Russian president. TRAC2.

Yener, Kutlu Aslihan. (1946-) Turkish archaeologist. YOUNT6.

Yep, Laurence. (1948-) Children's author. AUT; CHI; HILC2; ISH; SIN.

Yepremian. Garo. (1944-) Football player, born Cyprus. SAV7.

Yermak. (Vasily Timofeyovich) (1540-1585) Russian explorer, pirate. HOOB5.

Yglesias, José. (1919-1995) Author. LAE.

Yin, Luoth. (1950-) Community activist, social worker, born Cambodia. SIN.

Yorinks, Arthur. (1953-) Children's author. MARC2.

York. (1770-1832) Slave to Lewis and Clark. ALTMS; HASK3.

York, Alvin Cullum. (1887-1964) World War I military hero. Medal of Honor recipient. DOH.

Young, Andrew Jackson. (1932-) Civil rights activist, congressman, diplomat, mayor. Presidential Medal of Freedom recipient. HARM; POT; TAYK2.

Young, Ann Eliza Webb. (1844-1908) Pioneer, reformer. ALTE2.

Young, Brigham. (1801-1877) Spiritual leader of Mormon Church. CRO; CRO4; DOH2.

Young, Charles. (1864-1922) Army career soldier, Spanish American War, World War I colonel. ALTMS; HASK2; REE.

Young, Chavonda J. Jacobs. (1967-) Paper science engineer. SULO2.

Young, Coleman. (1918-1997) Mayor. AFR2.

Young, Denton True "Cy." (1867-1955) Baseball player. JACT; SULG5; TUR2.

Young, John Watts. (1930-) Astronaut. BAIR; PRE; RIC4.

Young, Lester Willis. (1909-1959) Jazz musician. GOU; MON; SHIP.

Young, Plummer Bernard, Sr. (1884-1962) Publisher newspapers. AFR.

Young, Roger Arliner. (1889-1964) Educator, zoologist. SULO2.

Young, Sheila. (1950-) Bicyclist, olympic speed skater. HASD.

Young, Steve. (1961-) Football player. SULG7.

Young, Whitney Moore, Jr. (1921-1971) Civil rights activist. Presidential Medal of Freedom recipient. BECKN.

Youngblood, Jack. (1950-) Football player. SAV7.

Younger, Maud. (1870-1936) Community activist, human rights activist, women's rights activist, workers' rights activist. THIR.

Younghans, Maria. (1867-1918) Lighthouse keeper. FLE.

Younghans, Miranda. (fl. 1918-1929) Lighthouse keeper. FLE.

Yuan Me. (1716-?) Chinese author, chef. HOOB.

Yum Kaax. Mayan god of corn. FIS2.

Z

Zacuto, Abraham. (1452-1515) Spanish astronomer, explorer. POD.

Zaharias, Mildred "Babe" Didrikson. (1913-1956) Golfer, olympic track and field athlete. AAS20; ALTE2; COOL; DIT; HARN; HASD; HER; JACT; KRULL3; MARZ; ROL; SAV14; STRU; SULG3; WEL.

Zais, Karen. (unknown) Mechanical engineer. KAH5.

Zakrzewska, Marie Elizabeth. (1829-1902) Physician, born Germany. STI.

Zallman, Elijah ben Solomon. (1720-1797) Polish scholar, spiritual leader. PASA.

Zamboni, Frank J. (1901-1988) Entrepreneur ice resurfacing machine. AAS3.

Zangara, Giuseppe "Joe." (1900-1933) Assassin, attempted to kill President Franklin Delano Roosevelt, born Italy. JONR; STG; SULG9.

Zapata, Carmen. (1927-) Actor. LAE.

Zapata, Emiliano. (1879-1919) Mexican revolutionary. THOM3.

Zarins, Juris. (1945-) Archaeologist, born Latvia. TALAD.

Zasulich, Vera. (1849-1919) Russian revolutionary. HOOB5.

Zavala, Maria Elena. (unknown) Botanist, educator. STJ2.

Zawinul, Joe. (1932-) Jazz musician, born Austria. GOU4.

Zeisberger, David. (1721-1808) Missionary, born Moravia. JACKD2.

Zelinsky, Paul. (1953-) Children's author, illustrator. TALAR3.

Zelle, Margareta Gertrude. (Mata Hari) (1876-1917) Dutch dancer, World War I spy. KRAL; SULG4; THOM4; ZEI2.

Zenger, John Peter. (1697-1746) Journalist, printer, born Germany. CRO2; JACW; RIT.

Zeno. (335-263 B.C.) Greek philosopher. BAKR2; CRO2.

Zenobia. (fl. 267-272) Syrian queen. LEO; MEL2; ROL.

Zernike, Frits. (1888-1966) Dutch chemist, inventor, physicist. Nobel Prize winner. AAS15.

Zheng, Haixia. (1967-) Chinese olympic basketball player. JACK.

Zheng He. (1371-1433) Chinese navy admiral. HOOB; POD.

Zhukov, Georgi. (1896-1974) Russian World War II general. CRO3; LAC.

Zimmerman, John. (1973-) Olympic figure skater. MILT.

Ziska, Jan. (1358-1424) Bohemian military leader. CRO3.

Zmeskal, Kim. (1976-) Olympic gymnast. LINL.

Zola, Emile. (1840-1902) French author. IMP.

Zollar, Attila. (1927-1998) Jazz musician, born Hungary. GOU3.

Zolotow, Charlotte. (1915-) Children's author, illustrator. MARC3.

Zorich, Chris. (1969-) Football player, philanthropist. KAM.

Zoroaster. (Zarathrustra) (628-551 B.C.) Persian spiritual leader. CRO2; GOLDM; JACW2.

Zughaib, Helen. (1959-) Painter, born Lebanon. HON.

Zunz, Leopold. (1794-1886) German educator. PASA.

Zurbriggen, Pirmin. (1963-) Swiss olympic alpine skater. JACT.

Zwilich, Ellen. (1939-) Composer, jazz musician. Pulitzer Prize winner. BRED3.

Zwingli, Ulrich. (1484-1531) Swiss spiritual leader. CRO4.

Part III

LIST OF
SUBJECT HEADINGS

List of Subject Headings

Abolitionists
Actors
Adventurers
Afghans
African-Americans
Africans
Agricultural Scientists
AIDS Activists
Air Force Personnel
Alexandrians
Ambassadors and Diplomats
American Revolutionary War Figures
Anatomists
Anthropologists
Apostles
Arabs
Arachnologists
Archaeologists
Archers
Architects
Archivists
Argentines
Army Personnel
Artists
Arts, Patrons of
Asian-Americans
Assassins, Presidential
Assyrians
Astronauts
Astronomers
Athletes
Attorneys
Australians
Austrians
Cabinet Members

Authors
    Children's and Young Adult
    Fiction
    Nonfiction
Auto Racers
Automakers
Aviation Pioneers
Aviators
Aztecs
Babylonians
Bacteriologists
Bandleaders
Bankers
Baseball Players
Baseball Team Management
Basketball Players
Basketball Team Management
Belgians
Biathlon, Decathlon . . . Athletes
Biblical Figures
Bicyclists
Billiards Players
Biologists
Blacks, International
Boaters
Bobsledders
Bolivians
Botanists and Horticulturalists
Bowlers
Boxers
Brazilians
Broadcast Journalists
Burmese
Byzantians
Cambodians

Canadians
Carthaginians
Cartoonists and Caricaturists
Celts
Chefs
Chemists
Chiefs, Native American
Children's Rights Activists
Chileans
Chinese
City Government Officials
Civil Rights Activists
Civil War Figures
Colombians
Colonists
Comedians
Community Activists
Composers
Computer Pioneers
Conductors, Musical
Congressmen/Women
Costa Ricans
Cowboys and Ranchers
Crimefighters
Criminals
Cubans
Cult Leaders
Curlers
Czechs
Dancers and Choreographers
Danes
Declaration of Independence Signers
Dentists
Dictators
Directors, Theatrical
Disability Rights Activists
Divers
Dominicans
Dutch
East Timorians
Economists
Editors and Publishers
Educators
Egyptians, Ancient
Egyptians, Modern
Egyptologists
Emotionally Disabled
Engineers
English
Engravers and Etchers
Entomologists

Entrepreneurs and Industrialists
   Bankers and Financiers
   Computers, Electronics, and Media
   Cosmetics and Fashion
   Food Industry
   Household and Decorative Items
   Oil, Chemicals, and Steel
   Real Estate
   Retail Establishments
   Toys and Sporting Goods
   Transportation
   Unclassified
Environmentalists
Ethiopians
Explorers
Filipinos
Filmmakers
Finns
First Ladies of United States
Folk Heroes and Legendary Characters
Football Players
Football Team Management
Forensic Scientists
Founders of Cities and Colonies
French
Fur Traders, Trappers, and Hunters
Gangsters
Gay Rights Activists
Geneticists
Geographers
Geologists
Germans
Gjamoams
Gods and Goddesses
Gold Miners
Golfers
Government Workers
   National
   State
Governors, United States
Greeks, Ancient
Greeks, Modern
Guatemalans
Gulf War Figures
Gymnasts
Haitians
Hatemongers
Hawaiians
Hearing Impaired
Hebrews, Ancient
Heisman Trophy Winners

Hispanic-Americans
Historians
Hockey Players
Holocaust Figures
   Rescuers and Resistance Workers
   Survivors
   Victims
Hondurans
Human Rights Activists
Hungarians
Icelanders and Greenlanders
Icthyologists
Illustrators
Immigrants to United States
Immunologists
Incas
Indian Captives
Indian Guides, Scouts, and Agents
Indians, Asian
Indonesians
Internet Pioneers
Inventors
Iraqis and Iranians
Irish
Israelis
Italians
Jamaicans
Japanese
Jewelry and Metal Designers
Jewish-Americans
Jews, International
Jockeys
Jordanians
Journalists
Judo Athletes
Jurists
Kenyans
Korean Conflict Figures
Koreans
Kurds
Labor Leaders
Latvians
Learning Disabled
Lebanese
Lepidopterists
Lexicographers and Linguists
Liberians
Librarians
Libyans
Lighthouse Keepers
Lithuanians

Magicians
Marine Corps Personnel
Martial Artists
Mathematicians
Medal of Honor Recipients
Medical Researchers
Mesopotamians
Meteorologists
Mexicans
Military Leaders
Mineralogists
Missionaries
Mixed-Media Artists
Models, Art, and Fashion
Mongols
Mountaineers
Mozambicans
Musical Groups
Musicians
    Classical
    Jazz and Blues
    Rock, Other
Muslims
Native American Rights Activists
Native Americans
Navy Personnel
Nazi Hunters
Nazi War Criminals
Nepalese
Neuroscientists
New Zealanders
Nicaraguans
Nigerians
Nobel Prize Winners
    Chemistry
    Economics
    Literature
    Medicine and Physiology
    Peace
    Physics
Norwegians
Nurses
Nutritionists
Oceanographers
Olympic Athletes
Orators
Organizational Founders and Heads
Ornithologists
Outlaws
Painters
Pakistanis

Paleontologists
Palestinians
Panamanians
Pathologists
Peace Activists
Persians
Peruvians
Philanthropists
Philosophers
Photographers and photojournalists
Physical Therapists
Physically Challenged
Physicians
Physicists
Physiologists
Pilots
Pioneers and Frontierspeople
Pirates
Playwrights
Poets
Poles
Political Activists and World Leaders
Portuguese
Potters and Ceramicists
Presidential Candidates, American
Presidential Medal of Freedom
    Recipients
Presidents, United States
Primatologists
Printers and Printmakers
Psychics, Mystics, and Visionaries
Psychiatrists, Psychologists, and
    Psychotherapists
Public Health Workers
Puerto Ricans
Pulitzer Prize Winners
Racquetball Players
Reformers
Revolutionaries
Rock Climbers
Romanians
Romans, Ancient
Rulers and Royalty
Runners and Sprinters
Russians
Saints
Salvadorians
Scholars
Scots
Screenwriters
Scribes and Translators

Sculptors
Seismologists
Senators, United States
Serial Killers
Showmen and Women
Singaporeans
Singers
Skaters
Skiers
Slave Insurrectionists
Slaves
Sled Dog Racers
Soccer Players
Social Workers
Sociologists
Softball Players
Soil Scientists
Songwriters
Space Scientists
Spaniards
Spies and Secret Agents
Spiritual Leaders
Sportscasters
Sri Lankans
Storytellers and Folklorists
Suffragists
Sumerians, Ancient
Surfers
Swedish
Swimmers
Swindlers
Swiss
Syrians
Tanzanians
Tartars
Television and Radio Personalities
Tennis Players
Terrorists
Thais
Tibetans
Track and Field Athletes
Traitors
Turks
Ugandans
Ukrainians
Utopian Community Founders
Venezuelans
Veterinarians
Vice Presidents, United States
Vietnam War Figures
Vietnamese

Vikings, Ancient
Virgin Islanders
Virologists
Visually Disabled
Volcanologists
Volleyball Players
Weight Lifters
Welsh
Wheelchair Athletes
Women
Women Disguised as Men
Women's Rights Activists

Workers' Rights Activists
World War I Figures
World War II Figures
Wrestlers
X-Ray Crystallographers
Yemenites
Young People
Yugoslavians
Zairians
Zimbabweans
Zoologists

Part IV

SUBJECT GUIDE
TO
BIOGRAPHEES

Subject Guide To Biographees

Abolitionists

See also Civil Rights Activists; Slave Insurrectionists.

Allen, Richard. (1760-1831)
Banneker, Benjamin. (1731-1806)
Brown, John. (1800-1859)
Brown, William Wells. (1814-1884)
Burns, Anthony. (1834-1862)
Cartwright, Peter. (1785-1872)
Cary, Mary Ann Shadd. (1822-1893)
Coffin, Katie. (unknown)
Coffin, Levi. (1798-1877)
Coker, Daniel. (1780-1846)
Copeland, John Anthony, Jr. (1836-1859)
Craft, Ellen. (1826-1897)
Delaney, Martin Robison. (1812-1885)
Dickinson, Anna Elizabeth. (1842-1932)
Douglass, Frederick. (1817-1895)
Field, Kate. (1838-1896)
Forten, Charlotte. *See* Grimke, Charlotte
Forten.
Forten, James. (1766-1842)
Foster, Abby Kelley. (1811-1887)
Freeman, Elizabeth "Mumbet." (1742-1829)
Garnet, Henry Highland. (1815-1882)
Garrison, William Lloyd. (1805-1879)
Gibbs, Mifflin. (1823-1915)
Grimke, Angelina. (1805-1879)
Grimke, Charlotte Forten. (1837-1914)
Grimke, Sarah Moore. (1792-1873)
Harper, Frances E. W. (1825-1911)
Hayden, Lewis. (1815-1889)
Henson, Josiah. (1789-1883)
Jacobs, Harriet. (1813-1897)
Jay, Allen. (1831-1910)

Keckley, Elizabeth. (1818-1907)
Loguen, Jermain Wesley. (1813-1872)
Lovejoy, Elijah P. (1802-1837)
Lundy, Benjamin. (1789-1839)
Mann, Horace. (1796-1859)
Mott, Lucretia Coffin. (1793-1880)
Nell, William Cooper. (1816-1874)
Pennington, James W. C. (1809-1870)
Pleasant, Mary Ellen "Mammy." (1814-
1904)
Preston, Ann. (1813-1872)
Remond, Sarah P. (1826-1894)
Roc, John S. (1825-1866)
Rose, Ernestine Potowski. (1810-1892) born
Poland.
Ross, Alexander. (1783-1856) Canadian.
Ruffin, Josephine St. Pierre. (1842-1924)
Ruggles, David. (1810-1849)
Steward, Austin. (1794-1860)
Stone, Lucy. (1818-1893)
Stowe, Emily Jennings. (1831-1903) Cana-
dian.
Stowe, Harriet Beecher. (1811-1896)
Swisshelm, Jane Grey Cannon. (1815-1884)
Terrell, Mary Church. (1863-1954)
Thayer, Eli. (1819-1899)
Truth, Sojourner. (1797-1883)
Tubman, Harriet. (1820-1913)
Turner, James Milton. (1840-1915)
Ward, Samuel Ringgold. (1817-1878)
Wilberforce, William. (1759-1833) English.

Actors

See also Comedians; Dancers; Showmen;
Singers; Television Personalities.

Ahn, Philip. (1911-1978)
Allen, Debbie. (1956-)
Allen, Woody. (1935-)
Andrews, Julie. (1935-) born England
Arnaz y de Acha, Desiderio Alberto, III.
   (Desi Arnaz) (1917-1986) born Cuba.
Astaire, Fred. (1899-1987)
Barrault, Jean-Louis. (1910-1994) French.
Barrymore, Ethel. (1879-1959)
Bassett, Angela. (1959-)
Bernhardt, Sarah. (1844-1923) French.
Blades, Ruben. (1948-)
Booth, William. (1833-1893)
Burke, Chris. (1965-)
Burns, George. (1896-1996)
Burton, Richard. (1925-1984) Welsh.
Carrey, Jim. (1962-)
Carroll, Diahann. (1935-)
Childress, Alice. (1920-1994)
Cho, Margaret. (1969-)
Cooper, Jackie. (1922-)
Cosby, Bill. (1937-)
Crabtree, Lotta. (1847-1924)
Cruise, Tom. (1962-)
Dandridge, Dorothy. (1923-1965)
Davis, Ossie. (1917-)
Davis, Sammy, Jr. (1925-1990)
De Generes, Ellen. (1958-)
Dean, James. (1931-1955)
Dee, Ruby. (1924-)
Deneuve, Catherine. (1943-) French.
Douglas, Helen Gahagan. (1900-1980)
Duke, Patty. (1946-)
Duse, Eleanora. (1859-1924) Italian.
Echohawk, Brummett. (1922-) Pawnee
   Indian.
Espinel, Luisa Ronstadt. (1892-1963)
Evans, Dale. (1912-2001)
Foster, Jodie. (1962-)
Freeman, Morgan. (1937-)
Gable, Clark. (1901-1960)
Garbo, Greta. (1905-1990) born Sweden.
Garcia, Andy. (1957-) born Cuba.
Garrick, David. (1717-1779) English.
Gilpin, Charles. (1878-1930)
Glover, Savion. (1974-)
Goldberg, Whoopi. (1950-)
Gonzalez, Melissa Eve. (1980-)
Greaves, William. (1926-)
Guerra, Jackie. (1967-)
Hayakawa, Sessue. (Kintaro) (1890-1973)

born Japan.
Hepburn, Katherine. (1907-2003)
Hope, Leslie Townes " Bob." (1903-2003)
   born England.
Houston, Whitney. (1963-)
Irving, Henry. (1838-1905) English.
Jackson, Janet. (1966-)
Johnson, Noble. (1881-1978)
Julia, Raul. (1940-1994) born Puerto Rico.
Kaminska, Ida. (1899-1980) born Russia.
Kean, Edmund. (1787-1833) English.
Kelly, Grace. (1929-1982)
Latifah, Queen. *See* Owens, Dana Elaine.
Lee, Bruce. (1940-1973)
Lincoln, Abbey. (1930-)
Lopez, Jennifer. (1970-)
Marin, Richard Anthony "Cheech." (1946-)
Matlin, Marlee. (1965-)
McDaniel, Hattie. (1895-1952)
McQueen, Thelma "Butterfly." (1911-1995)
Midler, Bette. (1945-)
Miranda, Carmen. (1909-1955) Brazilian.
Molière. *See* Poquelin, Jean Baptiste.
Monroe, Marilyn. (1926-1962)
Montalbán, Ricardo. (1920-) born Mexico.
Moreno, Rita. (1931-) born Puerto Rico.
Murphy, Audie. (1924-1971)
Murphy, Eddie. (1961-)
Newman, Paul. (1925-)
Ngor, Haing. (1947-1996) born Cambodia.
Nguyen, Dustin. (1962-) born Vietnam.
Nussbaum, Susan. (1953-)
Okuni. (1571-1610) Japanese kabuki.
Olivier, Sir Laurence. (1907-1989) English.
Olmos, Edward James. (1947-)
Owens, Dana Elaine. (Queen Latifah)
   (1970-)
Perez, Rosie. (1964-)
Perkins, Anthony. (1932-1992)
Perón, Eva "Evita." (1919-1952) Argentine.
Pickford, Mary. (1893-1979) Canadian.
Poitier, Sidney. (1924-)
Poquelin, Jean Baptiste. (Molière) (1622-
   1673) French.
Pryor, Richard. (1940-)
Quinn, Anthony. (1915-2001) born Mexico.
Reagan, Ronald. (1911-2004)
Reeve, Christopher. (1952-2004)
Robeson, Paul. (1898-1976)
Rodriguez, Paul. (1955-) born Mexico.
Rogers, Ginger. (1911-1995)

Rogers, Roy. (1911-1998)
Rogers, Will. (1879-1935) Cherokee Indian.
Ross, Diana. (1944-)
Russell, Harold. (1914-2002)
Sainte-Marie, Buffy. (1941-) Cree Indian,
  born Canada.
Sampson, Will. (1934-1987) Creek Indian.
Sheen, Martin. (1940-)
Shepard, Sam. (1943-)
Smith, Anna Deavere. (1950-)
Smith, Will. (1969-)
Smits, Jimmy. (1955-)
Streisand, Barbra. (1942-)
Taylor, Elizabeth. (1932-) born England.
Temple, Shirley. (1928-)
Terry, Ellen. (1847-1928) English.
Theodora. (497-548) Turkish.
Tyson, Cicely. (1933-)
Valdez, Luis. (1940-)
Van Peebles, Mario. (1957-)
Van Peebles, Melvin. (1932-)
Washington, Denzel. (1954-)
Waters, Ethel. (1896-1977)
Wayans, Keenen Ivory. (1958-)
Wayne, John. (1907-1979)
West, Mae. (1893-1980)
Williams, Bert. (1874-1922)
Wong, Anna May. (1905-1961)
Woodard, Alfre. (1953-)
Zapata. Carmen. (1927-)

Adventurers

Adams, Harriet Chalmers. (1875-1937)
Aebi, Tania. (1966-)
Bell, Gertrude. (1868-1926) English.
Bishop, Isabella Lucy " Bird." (1831-1904)
  English.
Bowie, James. (1796-1836)
Cannary, Martha Jane. (Calamity Jane)
  (1852-1903)
Casanova de Seingalt, Giovanni Giacomo.
  (1725-1798) Italian.
Cochrane, Elizabeth. (Nellie Bly) (1865-
  1922)
Dampier, William. (1652-1715) English.
David-Neel, Alexandra. (1868-1969)
  French.
Davison, Anne. (1913-1992) born England.
Dixie, Florence. (1857-1905) English.
Dodwell, Christina. (1951-) English.
Drake, Sir Francis. (1540-1596) English.

Egeria. (4th century) Spanish.
Gilgamesh. (2700 B.C.) Babylonian.
Grandmaison y Bruno Godin, Isabel. (1729-
  1792) Peruvian.
Hadley, Leila Eliott Burton. (1925-)
Hahn, Emily. (1905-1997)
Harkhuf. (c. 2275 B.C.) Egyptian.
Harrison, Marguerite Baker. (1879-1967)
Hendrickson, Sue. (1950-)
Hercules. Greek.
Heyerdahl, Thor. (1914-2002) Norwegian.
Hillary, Sir Edmund. (1919-) New Zea-
  lander.
Ibn-Battuta, Muhammad. (1304-1369) Mus-
  lim Berber, born Morocco.
James, Naomi. (1949-) New Zealander.
Jason. Greek.
Joliet, Louis. (1645-1700) Canadian.
Kingsley, Mary. (1862-1900) English.
Layard, Austen Henry. (1817-1894) English.
London, Jack. (1876-1916)
Odysseus. Greek.
Peck, Annie Smith. (1850-1935)
Pfeiffer, Ida. (1757-1858) Austrian.
Polo, Marco. (1254-1324) Italian.
Raleigh, Sir Walter. (1554-1618) English.
Royall, Anne Newport. (1769-1854)
Saint-Exupéry, Antoine de. (1900-1944)
  French.
Sarashina, Lady. (1008-?) Japanese.
Smith, John. (1580-1631) English
Stark, Freya. (1893-1993) English.
Stephens, John Lloyd. (1805-1852)
Taylor, Annie Edson. (1838-1921)
Van der Woude, Elizabeth. (1657-1694)
  Dutch.
Waterton, Charles. (1782-1865) English.
Wilkins, Sir George Hubert. (1888-1958)
  Australian.

Afghans

Rumi, Jalal al-Din. (1207-1273) Mystic,
  philosopher, poet.

African-Americans

See also Blacks, International.
Aaron, Henry "Hank." (1934-) Baseball
  player. Presidential Medal of Freedom recipient.
Abbott, Robert Sengstacke. (1870-1940)

Civil rights activist, newspaper editor.

Abdul-Jabbar, Kareem. (1947-) Basketball player.

Abdul-Rauf, Mahmoud. (Chris Jackson) (1969-) Basketball player.

Abdur-Rahim, Ahareef. (1976-) Basketball player.

Abernathy, Ralph David. (1926-1990) Civil rights activist, spiritual leader.

Adams, Eugene W. (1920-) Medical researcher, pathologist, veterinarian.

Adams, Michael. (1963-) Basketball player.

Ailey, Alvin. (1931-1989) Choreographer, dancer.

Alexander, William. (1916-) Filmmaker.

Ali, Muhammad. (1942-) Olympic boxer.

Allen, Debbie. (1956-) Actor, dancer, singer.

Allen, Geri. (1957-) Bandleader, jazz musician.

Allen, Henry "Red." (1908-1967) Jazz musician.

Allen, Marcus. (1960-) Football player. Heisman Trophy winner.

Allen, Richard. (1760-1831) Abolitionist, spiritual leader.

Ammons, Albert. (1907-1949) Bandleader, jazz musician.

Amos, Wally. (1936-) Entrepreneur cookies.

Anderson, Garland. (1886-1939) Playwright.

Anderson, Ivie. (1904-1949) Jazz singer.

Anderson, John. (1831-?) Fugitive slave.

Anderson, Marian. (1897-1993) Opera singer. Presidential Medal of Freedom recipient.

Angelou, Maya. (1928-) Author, poet.

Archibald, Nate "Tiny." (1948-) Basketball player.

Armistead, James. (1760-1832) American Revolutionary War soldier, patriot.

Armstrong, Ellen. (1914-) Cartoonist, magician.

Armstrong, John Hartford. (1886-1939) Magician.

Armstrong, Louis. (1901-1971) Bandleader, composer, jazz musician.

Arrington, Richard, Jr. (1934-) Mayor.

Ashe, Arthur. (1943-1993) Tennis player. Presidential Medal of Freedom winner.

Ashford, Evelyn. (1957-) Olympic track and field athlete.

Attucks, Crispus. (1732-1770) American

Revolutionary War military hero.

Augusta, Alexander T. (1825-1890) Civil War physician.

Avery, Byllye. (1937-) Women's rights activist.

Bailey, Pearl. (1918-1990) Jazz singer. Presidential Medal of Freedom recipient.

Baker, Ella Josephine. (1903-1986) Civil rights activist.

Baker, George, Jr. "Father Divine." (1882-1965) Cult leader.

Baker, Josephine. (1906-1975) Jazz singer, World War II resistance worker.

Baker, Vernon J. (1919-) World War II lieutenant. Medal of Honor recipient.

Baldwin, James. (1924-1987) Author, civil rights activist, playwright.

Ball, James P. (1825-1904) Entrepreneur photo studios, photographer.

Bambera, Toni. (1939-1995) Author.

Banks, Ernie. (1931-) Baseball player.

Banneker, Benjamin. (1731-1806) Abolitionist, astronomer, inventor, mathematician.

Banning, James Herman. (1900-1933) Aviation pioneer, engineer.

Baraka, Amiri. (1934-) Poet.

Barbarin, Louis. (1902-1997) Jazz musician.

Barden, Don. (1943-) Entrepreneur cable television.

Barker, Danny. (1908-1994) Jazz musician.

Barkley, Charles. (1963-) Basketball player.

Barnes, Sharon J. (1955-) Chemist.

Barnett, Claude. (1890-1967) Publisher.

Barthé, Richmond. (1901-1989) Sculptor.

Basie, William "Count." (1904-1984) Bandleader, composer, jazz musician. Presidential Medal of Freedom recipient.

Bassett, Angela. (1959-) Actor.

Bates, Daisy. (1914-1999) Civil rights activist.

Bath, Patricia. (1942-) Medical researcher, physician.

Battey, Cornelius M. (1873-1927) Photographer.

Baylor, Elgin. (1934-) Basketball player.

Beals, Melba Pattilo. (1941-) Civil rights activist.

Beard, Andrew Jackson. (1849-1941) Inventor, slave.

Bearden, Romare. (1912-1988) Painter.

Bechet, Sidney. (1897-1959) Bandleader, composer, educator, jazz musician.

Beckwourth, James. (1798-1866) Fur trapper, pioneer, slave, Seminole War soldier.

Becoat, Bill. (1938-) Inventor.

Belafonte, Harry. (1927-) Singer.

Bell, James Thomas "Cool Papa." (1903-1991) Baseball player.

Belle, Albert. (1966-) Baseball player.

Benjamin, Miriam E. (unknown) Inventor.

Bennett, Lerone, Jr. (1928-) Author, historian, journalist.

Benson, George. (1943-) Jazz musician.

Berry, Chuck. (1926-) Composer, rock musician, singer.

Bethune, Mary McLeod. (1875-1955) Civil rights activist, educator.

Bethune, Thomas "Blind Tom" Greene. (1849-1908) Musician, slave.

Bibb, Henry. (unknown) Slave.

Black Herman. *See* Rucker, Herman.

Blackburn, Robert. (1920-2003) Educator, painter, printmaker.

Blackman, Cindy. (1959-) Composer, jazz musician.

Blackwell, Otis. (1931-2002) Songwriter.

Blake, James Hubert "Eubie." (1883-1983) Composer, jazz musician. Presidential Medal of Freedom recipient.

Blakey, Art. (1919-1990) Bandleader, jazz musician.

Blakey, Michael L. (1953-) Anthropologist.

Blanton, Jimmy. (1918-1942) Jazz musician.

Bluford, Guion Steward. (1942-) Astronaut, Vietnam War pilot.

Bogues, Tyrone "Muggsy." (1965-) Basketball player.

Bolden, Bucky. (1868-1931) Bandleader, jazz musician.

Bolden, Charles. (1946-) Astronaut, Marine Corps pilot.

Bolton-Holifield, Ruthie. (1967-) Basketball player.

Bond, Julian. (1940-) Civil rights activist, governor.

Bonds, Barry. (1964-) Baseball player.

Bonga, George. (1802-1880) Fur trader.

Bontemps, Arnaud "Arna." (1902-1973) Author, educator, librarian, poet.

Boone, Sarah. (unknown) Inventor.

Bosley, Freeman R., Jr. (1954-) Mayor.

Bourne, St. Clair. (unknown) Filmmaker.

Boyd, Henry. (1802-1886) Inventor, slave.

Boyd, Richard Henry. (1843-1922) Entrepreneur banking and dolls, slave.

Bradley, Benjamin. (1830-?) Inventor.

Bradley, Thomas. (1917-1998) Mayor.

Bragg, Janet Harmon. (1907-1993) Aviator, nurse.

Brand, Elton. (1979-) Basketball player.

Brandy. (singer) *See* Norwood, Brandy.

Braud, Wellman. (1891-1966) Jazz musician.

Braxton, Anthony. (1945-) Bandleader, composer, jazz musician.

Brents, Frank. (1926-) Magician.

Brisco-Hooks, Valerie. (1960-) Olympic sprinter, track and field athlete.

Brock, Lou. (1939-) Baseball player.

Brooks, Gwendolyn. (1917-2000) Poet. Pulitzer Prize winner.

Broonzy, "Big" Bill. (1893-1959) Jazz musician, singer.

Brown, Clara. (1803-1885) Pioneer, slave.

Brown, Dorothy Lavinia. (1919-) Physician, state legislator.

Brown, Henry "Box." (1816-?) Magician, slave.

Brown, James. (1933-) Civil rights activist, jazz musician, singer.

Brown, Jim. (1936-) Football player.

Brown, John "Fed." (1810-1876) Author, slave.

Brown, Marie Van Brittan. (fl. 1969) Inventor.

Brown, Ray. (1926-2002) Jazz musician.

Brown, Ronald. (1941-1996) Attorney, cabinet member.

Brown, Sterling Allen. (1901-1989) Author, poet.

Brown, Tim. (1966-) Football player. Heisman Trophy winner.

Brown, Wesley A. (1927-) Navy lieutenant commander.

Brown, William Wells. (1814-1884) Abolitionist, author, playwright, slave.

Browne, Marjorie Lee. (1914-1979) Mathematician.

Bruce, Blanche K. (1841-1898) Senator.

Bryan, Ashley. (1923-) Children's author, illustrator.

Bryant, Kobe. (1978-) Basketball player.

Bullett, Vicki. (unknown) Basketball player.

Bullock, Anna Mae. (Tina Turner) (1939) Pop singer.

Bunche, Ralph. (1904-1971) Diplomat, statesman. Nobel Peace Prize winner. Presidential Medal of Freedom recipient.

Burke, Yvonne Braithwaite. (1932-) Attorney, congresswoman, human rights activist.

Burnett, Charles. (1944-) Filmmaker.

Burns, Anthony. (1834-1862) Abolitionist, slave.

Burns, Ursula. (1958-) Engineer.

Burrell, Stanley Kirk. (Hammer) (1962-) Dancer, rap singer, songwriter.

Bush, George W. (1791-1867) Cattle trader, explorer, pioneer.

Butler, Octavia. (1947-) Author.

Byrdsong, Ricky. (1957-1999) Basketball coach, human rights activist.

Byrdsong, Sherialyn. (1957-) Basketball coach, human rights activist.

Cadoria, Sherian. (1940-) Army brigadier general, Vietnam War military police.

Callendar, George "Red." (1916-) Jazz musician.

Calloway, Cab. (1907-1994) Bandleader, composer, jazz singer.

Campanella, Roy. (1921-1993) Baseball player.

Campbell, Bebe Moore. (1950-) Author.

Campbell, Earl. (1955-) Football player. Heisman Trophy winner.

Campbell, Naomi. (1970-) Fashion model.

Campbell, Tunis G. (1812-1891) State legislator.

Canady, Alexa. (1950-) Physician.

Cardozo, Francis Louis. (1837-1903) Educator.

Carl, William. (unknown) Magician.

Carney, William H. (1840-1908) Civil War military hero. Medal of Honor recipient.

Carr, Henry. (1942-) Olympic sprinter, track and field athlete.

Carroll, Diahann. (1935-) Actor.

Carruthers, George. E. (1939-) Astrophysicist.

Carson, Benjamin Solomon. (1951-) Human rights activist, physician.

Carter, Benny. (1907-) Jazz musician.

Carter, Iola O. (unknown) Inventor.

Carter, Pamela. (1950-) Attorney, state attorney general.

Carter, Ron. (1937-) Jazz musician.

Carter, Vince. (1977-) Basketball player.

Carver, George Washington. (1864-1943) Agricultural scientist.

Cary, Mary Ann Shadd. (1822-1893) Abolitionist, attorney, educator, journalist.

Casey, Al. (1915-) Jazz musician.

Castner, Mattie. (1848-1920) Pioneer hotelkeeper.

Catlett, Elizabeth. (1915-) Painter, printmaker, sculptor.

Catlett, "Big" Sid. (1910-1951) Jazz musician.

Ceballos, Cedric. (1969-) Basketball player.

Chamberlain, Wilt. (1936-) Basketball player.

Chambers, Paul. (1935-1969) Jazz musician.

Charles, Ray. (1930-2004) Jazz musician, singer.

Charleston, Oscar McKinley. (1896-1954) Baseball player.

Charlot, Olivia. (1913-) Jazz singer.

Cheeks, Maurice. (1956-) Basketball player.

Chenzira, Ayoka. (1956-) Filmmaker.

Cherry, Fred V. (1928-) Vietnam War soldier.

Chesnutt, Charles. (1858-1932) Author.

Childress, Alice. (1920-1994) Actor, author, playwright.

Chinn, May Edward. (1896-1980) Physician.

Chisholm, Shirley. (1924-) Congresswoman, presidential candidate.

Christian, Charlie. (1916-1942) Jazz musician.

Cinque, Joseph. (1817-1879) Slave insurrectionist.

Clark, Kenneth B. (1914-) Civil rights activist, psychologist.

Clark, Joan. (unknown) Inventor.

Clark, Marcellus R. (d. 1971) Magician.

Clark, Peter Humphries. (1829-1925) Civil rights activist, educator.

Clark, Septima Poinsette. (1898-1987) Civil rights activist, educator.

Clarke, Kenny. (1914-1985) Jazz musician.

Clarke, Kim. (1954-) Jazz musician.

Clifton, Lucille. (1936-) Children's author.

Coachman, Alice. (1923-) Olympic track

and field athlete.

Cobb, Jewel Plummer. (1924-) Cell biologist, educator, medical researcher.

Cobb, William Montague. (1904-1990) Anatomist, educator, historian, physician.

Coker, Daniel. (1780-1846) Abolitionist, civil rights activist, educator.

Cole, Nat King. (1916-1965) Jazz musician, singer.

Cole, Natalie. (1950-) Singer.

Cole, Rebecca J. (1846-1922) Civil rights activist, human rights activist, physician.

Cole, William "Cozy." (1909-1981) Jazz musician.

Coleman, Bessie. (1893-1926) Aviator.

Coleman, Derrick. (1967-) Basketball player.

Coleman, Ornette. (1930-) Bandleader, composer, jazz musician.

Collins, Cardiss. (1931-) Congresswoman.

Collins, Daniel A. (1916-) Dentist, medical researcher, physician.

Collins, Kathleen. (1942-1988) Filmmaker.

Collins, Marva Delores. (1936-) Children's rights activist, educator.

Coltrane, John. (1926-1967) Bandleader, jazz musician.

Colvin, Claudette. (1940-) Civil rights activist.

Comer, James P. (1934-) Community activist, physician, psychiatrist.

Conly, Elvira. (1845-?) Pioneer, slave.

Cooley, Chloe. (unknown) Slave.

Cooper, Anna Julia. (1858-1964) Educator.

Cooper, Chuck. (1926-1984) Basketball player.

Cooper, Cynthia. (1963-) Olympic basketball player.

Cooper, Floyd. (1959-) Children's author, illustrator.

Copeland, John Anthony, Jr. (1836-1859) Abolitionist.

Coppin, Fannie Jackson. (1836-1913) Educator, slave.

Cornelius, Don. (1936-) Entrepreneur television.

Cornish, Samuel E. (1795-1858) Editor newspaper, journalist.

Cosby, Bill. (1937-) Actor, comedian. Presidential Medal of Freedom recipient.

Cowings, Patricia. (1948-) Physiologist, psychologist, space scientist.

Cox, Ida. (1889-1967) Jazz singer.

Craft, Ellen. (1826-1897) Abolitionist, slave, disguised self as man.

Craft, William. (1824-1900) Slave.

Craig, Lulu Sadler. (1868-1972?) Educator.

Crawford, Jimmy. (1910-1980) Jazz musician.

Crosby, Israel. (1919-1962) Jazz musician.

Croslin, Michael. (1933-) Mechanical engineer, inventor, medical researcher, Korean War, Vietnam War Air Force, born Virgin Islands.

Crosthwait, David Nelson, Jr. (1898-1976) Engineer, inventor.

Crumpler, Rebecca Lee. (1833-1895) Physician.

Cuffe, Paul. (1759-1817) Colonist, entrepreneur sailmaker, founder Sierre Leone, philanthropist.

Cullen, Countee. (1903-1946) Children's and adult author, educator, poet.

Curtis, Austin Maurice. (1868-1939) Physician.

Dabney, Austin. (1799-1821) American Revolutionary War soldier, slave.

Dandridge, Dorothy. (1923-1965) Actor, singer.

Darden, Christine. (1942-) Engineer, mathematician, space scientist.

Dash, Julie. (1952-) Filmmaker.

Davis, Angela. (1944-) Educator, political activist.

Davis, Benjamin O., Jr. (1912-2002) Air Force career officer, Korean War general, World War II Tuskegee airman.

Davis, Benjamin O., Sr. (1877-1970) Army career officer, Spanish American War, World War I, World War II brigadier general.

Davis, Ernie. (1939-1963) Football player. Heisman Trophy winner.

Davis, John. (1921-1984) Olympic weightlifter.

Davis, Lonnie. (1958-) Gulf War military hero.

Davis, Miles Dewey III. (1926-1991) Bandleader, composer, jazz musician.

Davis, Ossie. (1917-) Actor, civil rights activist.

Davis, Richard. (1930-) Educator, jazz musician.

Davis, Sammy, Jr. (1925-1990) Actor, showman, singer.

Davis, Terrell. (1972-) Football player.

Davis, Tice. (unknown) Slave.

Dawes, Dominique. (1976-) Olympic gymnast.

Dawkins, Darryl. (1957-) Basketball player.

De Moss, Edward "Bingo." (1889-1965) Baseball player.

De Passe, Suzanne. (1946-) Filmmaker.

De Priest, Oscar. (1871-1951) Congressman.

Dede, Edmund. (1827-1903) Jazz musician.

Dee, Ruby. (1924-) Actor.

DeFrantz, Anita. (1952-) Olympic rower.

Delaney, Annie Elizabeth. (1891-1995) Author, educator.

Delaney, Martin Robison. (1812-1885) Abolitionist, Civil War major, journalist, physician.

Delaney, Sarah Louise "Sadie." (1889-1998) Author, educator.

Derham, James. (1762-1804) Physician, slave.

Devers, Gail. (1966-) Olympic track and field athlete.

Dickerson, Eric. (1960-) Football player.

Dihigo, Martin "El Maestro." (1905-1971) Baseball player, born Cuba.

Dillon, Leo. (1933-) Children's author, illustrator.

Dinkins, David. (1927-) Attorney, mayor.

Divine, Father. *See* Baker, George F., Jr.

Doby, Larry. (1923-2003) Baseball player.

Dodds, Warren "Baby." (1898-1959) Jazz musician.

Dolphy, Eric. (1928-1964) Jazz musician.

Dorsett, Tony. (1954-) Football player. Heisman Trophy winner.

Dorsey, Thomas Andrew. (1899-1993) Composer, gospel musician.

Douglas, Aaron. (1899-1979) Painter.

Douglas, Lizzie. (Memphis Minnie) (1897-1973) Jazz musician.

Douglass, Frederick. (1817-1895) Abolitionist, journalist, orator, slave.

Douglass, Sarah Mapps. (1806-1882) Educator.

Dove, Rita. (1952-) Poet. Pulitzer Prize winner.

Dowling, Arthur. (d.1922) Magician.

Drew, Charles Richard. (1904-1950) Educator, medical researcher, physician.

Du Bois, W. E. B. (1868-1963) Author, civil rights activist, editor, educator, founder of NAACP.

Du Sable, Jean Baptiste Pointe. (1745-1818) Frontiersman, fur trapper.

Duke, Mark. (1958-) Painter.

Dunbar, Paul Laurence. (1872-1906) Poet.

Duncan, Tim. (1976-) Basketball player, born Virgin Islands.

Duncanson, Robert Scott. (1821-1872) Painter.

Dunham, Katherine. (1909-) Anthropologist, choreographer, dancer.

Dunn, Oscar. (1820-1871) Civil War Army captain, state lieutenant governor.

Dunn, Warrick. (1975-) Football player.

Durham, Eddie. (1906-1987) Jazz musician.

Duvivier, George. (1920-1985) Jazz musician.

Dwight, Edward J., Jr. (1933-) Air Force pilot, astronaut, sculptor.

Earley, Charity Adams. (1918-2002) World War II WAAC lieutenant colonel.

Eckford, Elizabeth. (1942-) Civil rights activist.

Eckstine, Billy. (1904-1993) Jazz singer.

Edelman, Marian Wright. (1939-) Attorney, children's rights activist, civil rights activist, human rights activist. Presidential Medal of Freedom recipient.

Edwards, Teresa. (1964-) Olympic basketball player.

Eglin, Ellen F. (1849-?) Inventor.

Elders, Jocelyn Jones. (1933-) Physician, surgeon general of U.S.

Eldridge, Roy. (1911-1989) Jazz musician.

Ellington, Edward Kennedy "Duke." (1899-1974) Bandleader, composer, jazz musician. Presidential Medal of Honor recipient.

Ellis, Dale. (1960-) Basketball player.

Ellison, Ralph. (1919-1994) Author, educator. Presidential Medal of Freedom recipient.

Emeagwali, Philip. (1954-) Computer scientist, engineer, born Nigeria.

English, Alex. (1954-) Basketball player.

Equiano, Olaudah. (1745-1799) Author, slave, born Nigeria.

Ericsson-Jackson, Aprille Joy. (unknown) Aerospace engineer, space scientist.

Erving, Julius. (1950-) Basketball player.

Eubanks, Kevin. (1957-) Jazz musician.

Europe, James Reese. (1881-1939) Bandleader, composer, jazz musician, World War I military hero.

Evans, Henry. (1760-1810) Spiritual leader.

Evans, Matilda Arabella. (1872-1935) Human rights activist, physician.

Everett, Milton Hutchins "M. H." (mid 1800s-early 1900s) Magician, showman.

Evers, Medgar. (1925-1963) Civil rights activist.

Evers-Williams, Myrlie. (1933-) Civil rights activist.

Ewing, Patrick. (1962-) Basketball player.

Farmer, James. (1920-1999) Civil rights activist. Presidential Medal of Freedom recipient.

Farrakhan, Louis. (1933-) Civil rights activist, hatemonger.

Fauset, Jessie Redmon. (1882-1961) Author.

Feelings, Tom. (1933-2003) Children's author, illustrator.

Ferguson, Angella D. (1925-) Medical researcher, physician.

Ferguson, Catherine "Katy." (1779-1854) Educator, slave.

Ferlette, Diane. (1945-) Storyteller.

Fields, Mary. (1832-1914) Pioneer businesswoman, slave, disguised as man.

Fitzgerald, Ella. (1918-1996) Jazz singer. Presidential Medal of Freedom recipient.

Flaggs, Gail. (unknown) Geneticist, medical researcher.

Fleetwood, Christian A. (1840-1914) Civil War Army major. Medal of Honor recipient.

Fletcher, Alphonse "Buddy," Jr. (1966-) Entrepreneur stock brokerage, mathematician.

Flipper, Henry O. (1856-1940) Army career officer, slave, World War I lieutenant.

Ford, Justina Laurena. (1871-1952) Physician.

Foreman, George. (1949-) Olympic boxer.

Forsythe, Ruby Middleton. (1905-1992) Educator.

Forten, Charlotte. *See* Grimke, Charlotte Forten.

Forten, James. (1766-1842) Abolitionist, entrepreneur sailmaker.

Fortune, T. Thomas. (1856-1928) Civil rights activist, journalist, state legislator.

Foster, Andrew "Rube." (1879-1930) Baseball player, manager.

Foster, George Murphy "Pops." (1892-1969) Jazz musician.

Foster, William Hendrick "Willie." (1904-1978) Baseball player.

Francis, Steve. (1977-) Basketball player.

Franklin, Aretha. (1942-) Jazz singer.

Franklin, Chester A. (1880-1955) Publisher newspaper.

Franklin, John Hope. (1915-) Historian. Presidential Medal of Freedom recipient.

Fraser-Reid, Bertram O. (1934-) Organic chemist.

Frazier, E. Franklin. (1894-1962) Educator, sociologist.

Frazier, Joe. (1944-) Boxer.

Freeman, Elizabeth "Mumbet." (1742-1829) Abolitionist, nurse, slave.

Freeman, Louis. (1952-) Airline pilot.

Freeman, Morgan. (1937-) Actor.

Fuller, Meta Vaux Warrick. (1877-1968) Sculptor.

Fuller, Solomon Carter. (1872-1953) Medical researcher, pathologist, physician, born Africa.

Futrell, Mary Hatwood. (1940-) Educator.

Gaines, Ernest. (1933-) Author.

Galloway, Abraham. (1837-1870) Slave, state legislator.

Gantt, Harvey B. (1943-) Architect, civil rights activist, mayor.

Garcia. (c. 1813) Seminole War soldier, slave.

Garner, Margaret. (1833-?) Slave.

Garnet, Henry Highland. (1815-1882) Abolitionist, orator, spiritual leader.

Garnett, Kevin. (1976-) Basketball player.

Garrison-Jackson, Zina. (1963-) Tennis player.

Garvey, Amy-Jacques. (1896-1973) Civil rights activist.

Garvey, Marcus. (1887-1940) Civil rights activist, born Jamaica.

Gaston, Arthur George. (1892-1996) Entrepreneur multi-businesses, World War I Army.

George, Eddie. (1973-) Football player. Heisman Trophy winner.

George, Eliza Davis. (1879-1979) Missionary.

Gerima, Haile. (1946-) Filmmaker, born Ethiopia.

Gibbs, Mifflin. (1823-1915) Abolitionist, attorney, educator, jurist.

Gibson, Althea. (1927-2003) Tennis player.

Gibson, Bob. (1935-) Baseball player.

Gibson, Josh. (1911-1947) Baseball player.

Gillespie, John Birks "Dizzy." (1917-1993) Bandleader, composer, jazz musician.

Gillom, Jennifer. (1964-) Olympic basketball player.

Gilpin, Charles. (1878-1930) Actor.

Giovanni, Nikki. (1943-) Children's author, poet.

Glover, Savion. (1974-) Actor, dancer.

Goldberg, Whoopi. (1950-) Actor, comedian.

Goode, Mal. (1908-1995) Broadcast journalist.

Goode, Sara E. (1850-?) Inventor, slave.

Goode, W. Wilson. (1938-) Army captain, mayor.

Goodman, Robert O. (1956-) Navy commander, born Puerto Rico.

Goodridge, Glenalvin. (1829-1866) Entrepreneur photo studios, photographer.

Goodridge, Wallace. (1841-1922) Entrepreneur photo studios, photographer.

Goodridge, William. (1846-1891) Entrepreneur photo studios, photographer.

Gordy, Berry, Jr. (1929-) Entrepreneur music business.

Gourdine, Meredith. (1929-1998) Electrical engineer, inventor, olympic track and field athlete.

Goyens, William. (1794-1856) Army military leader Texas Revolution.

Grant, Horace Junior. (1965-) Basketball player.

Grant, Jehu. (1752?-?) American Revolutionary War soldier, slave.

Granville, Evelyn Boyd. (1924-) Educator, government employee, mathematician.

Gravely, Samuel L., Jr. (1922-) Navy admiral, World War II military.

Graves, Earl G. (1935-) Publisher magazines.

Gray, William H. "Bill." (1941-) Congressman, educator.

Greaves, William. (1926-) Actor, filmmaker.

Green, Dannellia Gladden. (1966-) Engineer.

Green, Freddie. (1911-1987) Jazz musician.

Green, Grant. (1931-1978) Jazz musician.

Green, Lear. (c. 1830-1850) Slave.

Greene, Charles Edward "Mean Joe." (1946-) Football player.

Greenfield, Elizabeth Taylor. (1809-1876) Singer.

Greenfield, Eloise. (1929-) Children's author, poet.

Greer, William Alexander "Sunny." (1895?-1982) Jazz musician.

Gregory, Dick. (1932-) Civil rights activist, comedian, presidential candidate.

Gregory, Frederick. (1941-) Air Force colonel, astronaut, aviator.

Griffey, Ken, Jr. (1969-) Baseball player.

Griffin, Archie. (1954-) Football player. Heisman Trophy winner.

Griffin, Bessie Blount. (1913-) Inventor.

Griffith, Darrell. (1958-) Baseball player.

Grimes, Tiny. (1916-1989) Jazz musician.

Grimke, Charlotte Forten. (1837-1914) Abolitionist, author, educator.

Guy, Fred. (1897-1971) Jazz musician.

Gwaltney, John Langston. (1928-1998) Anthropologist.

Gwynn, Tony. (1960-) Baseball player.

Hale, Clara. (1905-1992) Children's rights activist, human rights activist.

Haley, Alex. (1921-1992) Author, journalist, World War II Coast Guard. Pulitzer Prize winner.

Haley, Charles. (1964-) Football player.

Hall, Al. (1915-) Jazz musician.

Hall, George Cleveland. (1864-1930) Physician.

Hamer, Fannie Lou. (1917-1977) Civil rights activist.

Hamilton, Richard. (1978-) Basketball player.

Hamilton, Virginia. (1936-2002) Children's and young adult author.

Hammer. See Burrell, Stanley Kirk.

Hammonds, Julia T. (unknown) Inventor.

Hammons, David. (1943-) Mixed-media artist.

Hancock, Herbie. (1940-) Bandleader, jazz musician.

Handy, William Christopher. (1873-1958) Composer, jazz musician.

Hannah, Marc. (1956-) Computer pioneer.

Hansberry, Lorraine. (1930-1965) Playwright.

Hansberry, William Leo. (1894-1965) Anthropologist, educator.

Hardaway, Anfernee. (1972-) Basketball player.

Hardaway, Tim. (1966-) Basketball player.

Harper, Frances E. W. (1825-1911) Abolitionist, author, poet, suffragist, women's rights activist.

Harris, Bernard. (1956-) Astronaut, physician.

Harris, Betty Wright. (1940-) Chemist.

Harris, Eliza. (unknown) Slave.

Harris, Franco. (1950-) Football player.

Harris, Patricia Roberts. (1924-1985) Attorney, cabinet member, diplomat.

Harris, Wesley. (1941-) Aerospace engineer, civil rights activist, educator, space scientist.

Harvard, Beverly. (1950-) Police Chief.

Harvard, Claude. (1911-1999) Inventor.

Hastie, William H. (1904-1976) Attorney, jurist.

Hawkins, Coleman. (1904-1969) Jazz musician.

Hawkins, Connie. (1942-) Basketball player.

Hayden, Lewis. (1815-1889) Abolitionist, state legislator.

Hayden, Palmer C. (1890-1973) Painter.

Hayes, Bob. (1942-2002) Football player, Olympic sprinter, track and field athlete.

Hayes, Elvin. (1945-) Basketball player.

Hayes, Isaac. (1943-) Jazz musician, singer.

Haynes, Lemuel. (1753-1833) American Revolutionary War soldier, spiritual leader.

Haynes, Ray. (1925-) Jazz musician.

Healy, Michael. (1839-1904) Captain U.S. Revenue Cutter Service.

Healy, Patrick Francis. (1834-1910) Educator, spiritual leader.

Heard, J. C. (1917-1988) Jazz musician.

Heath, Percy. (1923-) Jazz musician.

Height, Dorothy Irene. (1912-) Civil rights activist, National Council of Negro Women director, social worker. Presidential Medal of Freedom recipient.

Henderson, Fletcher. (1897-1952) Bandleader, jazz musician, singer.

Henderson, Rickey. (1958-) Baseball player.

Henry, Caryl. (1955-) Painter.

Henry, John. (1840-1871) Railroad worker, folk hero.

Henry, Warren. (1909-2001) Physical chemist.

Henson, Josiah. (1789-1883) Abolitionist, slave, spiritual leader.

Henson, Matthew. (1866-1955) Arctic explorer.

Hill, Grant. (1972-) Basketball player.

Hill, Lauryn. (1975-) Pop singer, songwriter.

Hill, Mozell Clarence. (1911-1969) Civil rights activist, educator.

Himes, Chester. (1909-1984) Author, criminal.

Hines, Earl "Fatha." (1903-1983) Bandleader, jazz musician.

Hines, Jim. (1946-) Olympic track and field athlete.

Hinton, Milt. (1910-2000) Jazz musician.

Hinton, William Augustus. (1883-1959) Educator, medical researcher, physician.

Hoagland, Jesse. (1939-) Inventor.

Holdsclaw, Chamique. (1977-) Basketball player.

Holiday, Billie. (1915-1959) Jazz singer.

Holley, Major. (1924-1991) Jazz musician, singer.

Holmes, Larry. (1949-) Boxer.

Hope, John. (1868-1936) Civil rights activist, educator.

Horne, Lena. (1917-) Jazz singer.

Hosier, Harry "Black Harry." (1750-1806) Spiritual leader.

Houston, Charles H. (1895-1950) Attorney, civil rights activist, educator.

Houston, Whitney. (1963-) Actor, singer.

Howard, Mildred. (1945-) Mixed-media artist.

Huddleston, Ned. (1849-1900) Outlaw, slave.

Hughes, James Mercer Langston. (1902-1967) Poet.

Hughes, Louis. (1832-?) Author, slave.

Hunt, Fern. (unknown) Computer scientist, mathematician.

Hunter, Alberta. (1895-1984) Jazz singer.

Hunter, Clarence. (1920-1993) Magician.

Hunter, Clementine. (1886-1988) Painter.

Hunter-Gault, Charlayne. (1942-) Broadcast journalist, civil rights activist.

Hurston, Zora Neale. (1901-1960) Anthropologist, author.

Hutson, Jean Blackwell. (1914-1998) Librarian.

Hyman, Flo. (1954-1986) Olympic volleyball player.

Iverson, Allen. (1975-) Basketball player.

Jackson, "Blind Lemon." (1897-1930) Jazz musician.

Jackson, Bo. (1962-) Baseball player, football player. Heisman Trophy winner.

Jackson, Janet. (1966-) Actor, dancer, singer.

Jackson, Janis. (unknown) Biologist, medical researcher, physician.

Jackson, Jesse. (1941-) Civil rights activist, political activist, spiritual leader. Presidential Medal of Freedom recipient.

Jackson, Jim. (1970-) Basketball player.

Jackson, Mahalia. (1911-1972) Jazz singer.

Jackson, May Howard. (1877-1931) Sculptor.

Jackson, Michael. (1958-) Showman, singer.

Jackson, Reggie. (1946-) Baseball player.

Jackson, Shirley Ann. (1946-) Educator, Nuclear Regulatory Head, physicist.

Jacobs, Harriet. (1813-1897) Abolitionist, author, slave.

James, Daniel "Chappie," Jr. (1920-1978) Air Force general, Korean War, Vietnam War, World War II.

James, Edgerrin. (1978-) Football player.

Jamison, Judith. (1944-) Choreographer, dancer.

Jasper, John. (1812-1901) Slave, spiritual leader.

Jemison, Mae C. (1956-) Astronaut, educator, physician.

Jennings, Thomas L. (1791-1859) Entrepreneur tailoring/dry cleaning businesses.

Jeter, Derek. (1974-) Baseball player.

Joel, Lawrence. (1928-1984) Vietnam War Army hero. Medal of Honor recipient.

JoeSam. (1939-) Painter, sculptor.

Johnetta. (1927-1983) Jazz singer.

Johns, Barbara. (1935-1991) Civil rights activist.

Johnson, Anthony. (c. 1678) Civil rights activist, slave.

Johnson, Bill. (c. 1870) Jazz musician.

Johnson, Earvin "Magic." (1959-) Basketball player.

Johnson, Francis "Hall." (1883?-1970) Composer, conductor.

Johnson, George. (1948-) Basketball player.

Johnson, Halle Tanner Dillon. (1864-1901) Physician.

Johnson, Hazel W. (1927-) Army Nurse Corps chief, brigadier general, educator.

Johnson, Henry. (1897-1929) World War I military hero.

Johnson, Jack. (1878-1946) Boxer.

Johnson, James P. (1891-1976) Composer, jazz musician.

Johnson, James Weldon. (1871-1938) Attorney, author, civil rights activist, diplomat, educator, journalist, songwriter.

Johnson, John H. (1918-) Publisher magazines. Presidential Medal of Freedom recipient.

Johnson, Katherine. (1918-) Aerospace engineer, space scientist.

Johnson, Keyshawn. (1972-) Football player.

Johnson, Larry. (1969-) Basketball player.

Johnson, Lonnie. (1889-1970) Jazz musician.

Johnson, Lonnie. (1949-) Inventor.

Johnson, Michael. (1967-) Olympic track and field athlete.

Johnson, Mordecai. (1890-1976) Educator, spiritual leader.

Johnson, Noble. (1881-1978) Actor, entrepreneur film studio, filmmaker.

Johnson, Rafer. (1935-) Olympic track and field athlete.

Johnson, Robert. (1911-1938) Jazz singer.

Johnson, Sargent Claude. (1887-1967) Sculptor.

Johnson, William Henry. (1901-1970) Painter.

Johnson, William Julius "Judy." (1900-1989) Baseball player.

Jones, Albert Jose. (unknown) Marine biologist, explorer, Korean War military.

Jones, Andruw. (1977-) Baseball player.

Jones, David "Deacon." (1938-) Football

player.

Jones, Elvin. (1927-) Jazz musician.

Jones, Frederick McKinley. (1892-1961) Inventor.

Jones, Jonathan "Papa Jo." (1911-1985) Jazz musician.

Jones, Marion. (1975-) Basketball player, olympic track and field athlete.

Jones, Quincy. (1933-) Entrepreneur music companies, jazz musician.

Jones, Robert. (1951-) Food science chemist.

Jones, Sam. (1924-1981) Jazz musician.

Joplin, Scott. (1868-1917) Composer, jazz musician. Pulitzer Prize winner.

Jordan, Barbara. (1936-1996) Attorney, civil rights activist, congresswoman. Presidential Medal of Freedom recipient.

Jordan, George. (1847-1904) Indian War soldier.

Jordan, Lynda. (unknown) Chemist, medical researcher.

Jordan, Michael. (1963-) Basketball player.

Jordan, Vernon E., Jr. (1935-) Attorney, civil rights activist, National Urban League organizer.

Joyner, Florence Griffith. (1959-1998) Olympic track and field athlete.

Joyner-Kersee, Jackie. (1962-) Olympic track and field athlete.

Joyner, Marjorie Stewart. (1896-1994) Entrepreneur beauty supplies.

Julian, Hubert Fauntleroy. (1897-?) Aviation pioneer, born Trinidad.

Julian, Percy Lavon. (1899-1975) Chemist, medical researcher.

Just, Ernest Everett. (1883-1941) Biologist, educator.

Kearse, Jevon. (1976-) Football player.

Keckley, Elizabeth. (1818-1907) Abolitionist, entrepreneur dressmaking, slave.

Kelly, Patrick. (1954-1990) Fashion designer.

Kelly, Sharon Pratt. (1944-) Attorney, mayor.

Kelly, Wynton. (1931-1971) Jazz musician, born Jamaica.

Kemp, Shawn. (1969-) Basketball player.

Kennedy, Cortez. (1968-) Football player.

Kennedy, Florence. (1916-2000) Attorney, women's rights activist.

Kenner, Beatrice. (1912-) Inventor.

Kessel, Barney. (1923-) Jazz musician.

Kidd, Jason. (1973-) Basketball player.

King, B.B. (1925-) Jazz musician, singer.

King, Coretta Scott. (1927?-) Author, civil rights activist, singer.

King, Martin Luther, Jr. (1929-1968) Civil rights activist, orator. Nobel Peace Prize winner.

King, Reatha Clark. (1938-) Chemist, National Bureau of Standards employee.

Kirby, John. (1908-1952) Jazz musician.

Koontz, Elizabeth Duncan. (1919-1989) Civil rights activist, educator, organization president.

Laney, Lucy Craft. (1854-1933) Educator, slave.

Lanier, Bob. (1948-) Basketball player.

Larkin, Barry. (1964-) Baseball player.

Lars, Byron. (1965-) Fashion designer.

Larsen, Nella. (1891-1964) Author.

Latifah, Queen. See Owens, Dana Elaine.

Latimer, Lewis Howard. (1848-1928) Inventor.

Lawless, Theodore K. (1892-1971) Physician, philanthropist.

Lawrence, Jacob. (1917-2000) Painter.

Ledbetter, Huddy "Leadbelly." (1885-1949) Jazz musician, singer, songwriter.

Lee, Jarena. (1783-1850) Spiritual leader.

Lee, Shelton Jackson "Spike," (1957-) Filmmaker, screenwriter.

Leisdorff, William A. (1810-1848) Diplomat, entrepreneur steamboats.

Leonard, Charles "Sugar Ray." (1956-) Olympic boxer.

Leonard, Walter Fenner "Buck." (1907-1997) Baseball player.

Leslie, Lisa. (1972-) Olympic basketball player.

Lester, Julius. (1939-) Children's and adult author.

Lewis, Carl. (1961-) Olympic track and field athlete.

Lewis, Mary Edmonia. (1845-1890) Sculptor.

Lewis, Reginald. (1942-1993) Attorney, entrepreneur foods conglomerate.

Lincoln, Abbey. (1930-) Actor, composer, singer.

Lindsay, John. (1894-1950) Jazz musician.

Lion, Jules. (1810-1866) Photographer.

Little, Larry. (1945-) Football player.

Little Richard. *See* Penniman, Richard Wayne.

Llewellyn, J. Bruce. (1927-) Entrepreneur media conglomerate, soft drink bottler.

Lloyd, John Henry "Pop." (1884-1965) Baseball player.

Locke, Alain Leroy. (1886-1954) Composer, educator.

Lofton, Kenny. (1967-) Baseball player.

Logan, Arthur C. (1909-1973) Physician.

Loguen, Jermain Wesley. (1813-1872) Abolitionist.

Lord, Audre. (1934-1992) Human rights activist, poet.

Louis, Joe. (1914-1981) Boxer.

Love, Nat. (1854-1921) Cowboy.

Lowe, Ann. (1899-?) Fashion designer.

Lynch, John R. (1847-1939) Congressman, slave.

Mackey, Raleigh "Biz." (1897-1965) Baseball player.

Madhubuti, Hadi R. (1942-) Poet.

Mahoney, Mary Eliza. (1845-1926) Civil rights activist, nurse, women's rights activist.

Malcolm X. (1925-1965) Civil rights leader.

Malone, Annie Turnbo. (1869-1957) Inventor.

Malone, Karl. (1963-) Basketball player.

Malone, Russell. (1963-) Jazz musician.

Mangin, Anna M. (unknown) Inventor.

Marbury, Stephon. (1977-) Basketball player.

Marchbanks, Vance. (1905-1988) Air Force colonel, medical researcher, physician, space scientist, World War II Tuskegee airman.

Marsalis, Wynton. (1961-) Bandleader, composer, educator, jazz musician. Pulitzer Prize winner.

Marshall, Andrew Cox. (1775-1856) Spiritual leader.

Marshall, Jim. (1937-) Football player.

Marshall, Paule. (1929-) Author.

Marshall, Thurgood. (1908-1993) Attorney, civil rights activist, Supreme Court justice. Presidential Medal of Freedom recipient.

Martin, Louise. (1911-) Photographer.

Mason, Biddy. (1818-1891) Civil rights activist, entrepreneur businesses, pioneer, slave.

Massey, Walter. (1938-) Physicist.

Mathis, Johnny. (1935-) Singer.

Matzeliger, Jan Ernst. (1852-1889) Inventor.

Mays, Benjamin. (1895-1984) Educator, spiritual leader.

Mays, Willie. (1931-) Baseball player.

McBee, Cecil. (1935-) Jazz musician.

McCovey, Willie Lee. (1938-) Baseball player.

McCoy, Elijah. (1843-1929) Inventor.

McCoy, Millie-Christine. (1851-1912) Siamese twins, singers, slaves.

McDaniel, Hattie. (1895-1952) Actor, singer.

McGibbon, Al. (1919-) Jazz musician.

McGrady, Tracy. (1979-) Basketball player.

McGriff, Fred. (1963-) Baseball player.

McGuire, Edith. (1944-) Olympic sprinter, track and field athlete.

McJunkin, George. (1851-1922) Cowboy, slave.

McKane, Alice Woodby. (1865-1948) Physician.

McKay, Claude. (1890-1948) Author, poet, born Jamaica.

McKenner, George, III. (1940-) Educator.

McKinney, Nina Mae. (1909-1967) Jazz singer.

McKinstry, Carolyn. (1949-) Civil rights activist.

McMillan, Terry. (1951-) Author.

McNair, Ronald. (1950-1986) Astronaut, physicist.

McQueen, Thelma "Butterfly." (1911-1995) Actor.

McRae, Carmen. (1922-1994) Jazz musician, singer.

McTell, "Blind Willie." (1901-1959) Jazz musician, singer.

McWhorter, "Free" Frank. (1777-1854) Entrepreneur mining saltpeter, slave.

Memphis Minnie. *See* Douglas, Lizzie.

Menendez, Francisco. (1700-1772) Colonial military hero, slave, born Africa.

Metoyer, Marie-Therese. (1742-1816) Colonist, landowner, slave.

Micheaux, Garrett Oscar. (1884-1951) Filmmaker.

Miller, Cheryl. (1964-) Olympic basketball player, sportscaster.

Miller, Dorie. (1919-1943) World War II naval hero.

Miller, Inger. (1972-) Olympic track and field athlete.

Miller, Reggie. (1965-) Basketball player.

Mingus, Charles. (1922-1979) Bandleader, composer, jazz musician.

Mitchell, Arthur. (1934-) Choreographer, dancer.

Monk, Art. (1957-) Football player.

Monk, Thelonious. (1917-1982) Bandleader, composer, jazz musician.

Monroe, George. (1844-1886) Stagecoach driver, pioneer.

Montgomery, Benjamin. (1819-1877) Inventor, slave.

Montgomery, Monk. (1921-1982) Jazz musician.

Montgomery, Wes. (1925-1968) Jazz musician.

Moon, John P. (1938-) Computer scientist, engineer, inventor.

Moon, Warren. (1956-) Football player.

Moore, Alice Ruth. (1875-1935) Author, poet.

Moore, Alonzo. (d. 1914) Magician, showman.

Moore, Audley. (1898-1997) Civil rights activist, women's rights activist.

Morgan, Garrett A. (1877-1963) Inventor.

Morgan, Joe. (1943-) Baseball player.

Morgan, Rose. (1913-) Entrepreneur beauty salons.

Morrison, Toni. (1931-) Author, educator. Nobel Prize winner, Pulitzer Prize winner.

Morton, Ferdinand Joseph "Jelly Roll." (1885-1941) Bandleader, composer, jazz musician.

Moseley-Braun, Carol. (1947-) Presidential candidate, senator.

Moses, Bob. (1935-) Civil rights activist, educator.

Moses, Edwin. (1955-) Olympic track and field athlete.

Moss, Randy. (1977-) Football player.

Mossell, Gertrude Bustill. (1855-1948) Educator, journalist, women's rights activist.

Mossell, Nathan Francis. (1856-1946) Physician.

Motley, Archibald, Jr. (1891-1981) Painter.

Motley, Constance Baker. (1921-) Attorney, civil rights activist, jurist.

Moton, Robert Russa. (1867-1940) Educator.

Mourning, Alonzo. (1970-) Basketball player.

Moutoussamy-Ashe, Jeanne. (1951-) Photographer.

Muhammad, Elijah. (1897-1975) Civil rights activist, leader Nation of Islam.

Murphy, Eddie. (1961-) Actor, comedian.

Murphy, Isaac. (1861-1896) Jockey.

Murphy, John H., Sr. (d. 1922) Publisher newspapers.

Murray, David. (1955-) Bandleader, composer, jazz musician.

Murray, Pauli. (1910-1985) Attorney, civil rights activist.

Myers, Walter Dean. (1937-) Children's and young adult author.

Nash, Diane. (1938-) Civil rights activist as young person.

Nell, William Cooper. (1816-1874) Abolitionist, historian.

Nelson, Prince Rogers. (Prince) (1958-) Rock singer, songwriter.

Newman, Lydia D. (unknown) Inventor.

Noble, Jordan. (1801-?) Drummer Boy in War of 1812 and Seminole War.

Norman, Jessye. (1945-) Opera singer.

Northup, Solomon. (1808-1861) Slave.

Norton, Daniel. (1840-1918) Civil rights activist, slave, state legislator.

Norton, Eleanor Holmes. (1937-) Attorney, civil rights activist, congresswoman.

Norwood, Brandy. (Brandy) (1979-) Pop singer.

O'Brien, Dan. (1966-) Olympic track and field athlete, decathlon.

Odum, Lamar. (1979-) Basketball player.

Olajuwon, Hakeem. (1963-) Basketball player, born Nigeria.

Oliver, Joseph "King." (1885-1938) Bandleader, composer, jazz musician.

O'Neal, Shaquille. (1972-) Basketball player.

Owens, Dana Elaine. (Queen Latifah) (1970-) Actor, singer.

Owens, Jesse. (1913-1980) Olympic track and field athlete.

Page, Alan. (1945-) Attorney, football
  player.
Page, Walter. (1900-1957) Jazz musician.
Paige, Leroy "Satchel." (1906-1982) Base-
  ball player.
Palmer, Anyim. (unknown) Educator.
Parker, Charles Christopher "Bird" Jr.
  (1920-1955) Bandleader, composer, jazz
  musician.
Parker, John. (1827-1900) Inventor, slave.
Parkerson, Michelle. (1953-) Filmmaker.
Parks, Gordon. (1912-) Photographer.
Parks, Henry G. (1916-1989) Entrepreneur
  food services.
Parks, Paul. (1923-) Civil engineer, Holo-
  caust rescuer, World War II soldier.
Parks, Rosa. (1913-) Civil rights activist.
  Presidential Medal of Freedom recipient.
Parsons, Lucy. (1853-1943) Civil rights ac-
  tivist, revolutionary, slave, workers' rights
  activist.
Payne, Ethel L. (1911-1991) Journalist.
Payton, Gary. (1968-) Basketball player.
Payton, Philip A. (1876-1917) Entrepreneur
  real estate.
Payton, Walter. (1954-) Football player.
Peake, Mary Smith. (1823-1862) Educator.
Penniman, Richard Wayne. (Little Richard)
  (1932-) Rock singer.
Pennington, James W. C. (1809-1870) Abo-
  litionist, civil rights activist, educator,
  slave, spiritual leader.
Pennington, Mary Engle. (1872-1952)
  Chemist. STI2.
Perkins, John. (1930-) Civil rights activist,
  spiritual leader.
Perry, Carrie Saxon. (1931-) Mayor.
Perry, Christopher J. (d. 1921) Publisher
  newspapers.
Person, Chuck. (1964-) Basketball player.
Petry, Ann. (1911-1997) Children's and
  adult author.
Pettiford, Oscar. (1922-1960) Jazz musician.
Pickett, Bill. (1870-1932) Rodeo star.
Pinchback, Pinckney Benton Stewart
  "P. B. S." (1837-1921) Civil War captain,
  congressman, governor.
Pinkney, Brian. (1961-) Children's author,
  illustrator.
Pinkney, Jerry. (1939-) Children's author,
  illustrator.

Pippin, Horace. (1888-1946) Painter, World
  War I Army soldier.
Pippin, Scottie. (1965-) Basketball player.
Pleasant, Mary Ellen "Mammy." (1814-
  1904) Abolitionist, civil rights activist, en-
  trepreneur real estate, pioneer.
Plummer, Edouard E. (unknown) Educator.
Poitier, Sidney. (1924-) Actor, filmmaker.
Poor, Salem. (1747-1780) American Revo-
  lutionary War soldier.
Potter, Richard. (1783-1835) Magician.
Potter, Tommy. (1918-1988) Jazz musician.
Poussaint, Alvin Francis. (1934-) Civil
  rights activist, psychiatrist.
Powell, Adam Clayton, Jr. (1908-1972)
  Civil rights activist, congressman, spiri-
  tual leader.
Powell, Clilan Bethany. (1894-1977) Physi-
  cian, publisher newspapers.
Powell, Colin. (1937-) Army Chair Joint
  Chiefs of Staff, cabinet member, Gulf
  War general, Vietnam War infantry offi-
  cer. Presidential Medal of Freedom re-
  cipient.
Powell, Earl "Bud." (1924-1966) Composer,
  jazz musician.
Powell, William J. (1897?-1942) Author,
  engineer, World War I Army pilot.
Pozo, Chano. (1915-1948) Jazz musician,
  born Cuba.
Prendergast, Franklyn G. (1945-) Biochem-
  ist, physician.
Price, Florence. (1888-1953) Composer.
Price, John. (1840-?) Slave.
Price, Leontyne. (1927-) Opera singer.
  Presidential Medal of Freedom recipient.
Pride, Charley. (1938-) Entrepreneur banks
  and music publishing, singer.
Prince. (singer) See Nelson, Prince Rogers.
Prince, Lucy Terry. (1733-1821) Poet.
Prince, Mary. (1788-?) Author, slave.
Procope, Ernesta. (1932-) Entrepreneur in-
  surance.
Proctor, Barbara Gardner. (1933-) Entrepre-
  neur advertising.
Prophet, Nancy Elizabeth. (1890-1960)
  Sculptor.
Prosser, Gabriel. (1776-1800) Slave insur-
  rectionist.
Prothrow-Stith, Deborah. (1954-) Human
  rights activist, physician, state Public

Health Commissioner.

Pryor, Richard. (1940-) Actor, comedian.

Puckett, Kirby. (1961-) Baseball player.

Purvis, Charles Burleigh. (1842-1929) Civil War surgeon, physician.

Quimby, Doug. (1936-) Jazz singer.

Quimby, Frankie. (1937-) Jazz singer.

Raines, Tim. (1959-) Baseball player.

Rainey, Gertrude "Ma." (1886-1939) Jazz singer, songwriter.

Randall, Dudley. (1914-2000) Poet.

Randolph, Asa Philip. (1889-1979) Civil rights activist, labor leader. Presidential Medal of Freedom recipient.

Ray, Charlotte E. (1850-1911) Attorney, community activist, educator.

Reaves, Bass. (1824-1910) Crimefighter.

Redman, Joshua. (1969-) Jazz musician.

Reed, Judy W. (unknown) Inventor.

Reed, Willis. (1942-) Basketball player.

Reid, Clarice D. (1931-) Medical researcher, physician.

Reid, Rufus. (1944-) Jazz musician.

Remond, Sarah P. (1826-1894) Abolitionist, physician, women's rights activist.

Revels, Hiram Rhoades. (1822-1901) Senator.

Rice, Glen. (1967-) Basketball player.

Rice, Jerry. (1962-) Football player.

Rich, Anna M. (1956-) Illustrator.

Rider, Isaiah, Jr. (1971-) Basketball player.

Rillieux, Norbert. (1806-1894) Engineer, inventor.

Ringgold, Faith. (1930-) Children's author, educator, illustrator, sculptor.

Rivers, Ruben. (1918-1944) World War II Army hero. Medal of Honor recipient.

Roach, Max. (1924-) Composer, jazz musician.

Roberts, Stanley Corvet. (1970-) Basketball player.

Robertson, Oscar. (1938-) Basketball player.

Robeson, Paul. (1898-1976) Actor, football player, political activist, singer.

Robinson, Bill "Bojangles." (1878-1949) Dancer, showman.

Robinson, Daniel Louis "Satchmo." (1900?-1971) Jazz musician.

Robinson, David. (1965-) Basketball player.

Robinson, Eddie Gay. (1919-) Football coach.

Robinson, Frank. (1936-) Baseball player.

Robinson, John Roosevelt "Jackie." (1919-1972) Baseball player. Presidential Medal of Freedom recipient.

Robinson, Smokey. (1940-) Singer, songwriter.

Robinson, Walker Smith, Jr. "Sugar Ray." (1921-1989) Boxer.

Roc, John S. (1825-1866) Abolitionist, attorney, civil rights activist, physician.

Rock, Chris. (1966-) Comedian.

Rodman, Dennis. (1961-) Basketball player.

Rollins, Charlemae. (1897-1979) Librarian, storyteller.

Rollins, Theodore Walter "Sonny." (1930-) Bandleader, jazz musician.

Rollins, Tree. (1955-) Basketball player.

Ross, Diana. (1944-) Actor, entrepreneur music, singer.

Rucker, Herman. (Black Herman) (1892-1934) Magician.

Rudin, Mary Ellen Estill. (1924-) Mathematician.

Rudolph, Wilma. (1940-1994) Olympic track and field athlete.

Ruffin, Josephine St. Pierre. (1842-1924) Abolitionist, civil rights activist, organizational head, women's rights activist.

Ruggles, David. (1810-1849) Abolitionist, publisher magazines.

Rushing, Jimmy. (1903-1972) Jazz singer.

Russell, Bill. (1934-) Basketball player.

Russell, Curly. (1917-1986) Jazz musician.

Russell, Herman J. (1930-) Entrepreneur construction.

Russworm, John B. (1799-1851) Publisher newspaper.

Rustin, Bayard. (1910-1987) Civil rights activist, labor leader.

Saar, Alison. (1956-) Mixed-media artist.

Saar, Betye. (1926-) Mixed-media artist.

Salem, Peter. (1750-1816) American Revolutionary War patriot, soldier.

Sampson, Deborah. (Robert Shurtliff) (1760-1827) American Revolutionary war patriot, soldier, disguised as man.

Sampson, Edith. (1901-1980) Attorney, diplomat, social worker.

Sampson, Henry. (1934-) Aerospace engineer, inventor, space scientist.

Sanders, Barry. (1968-) Football player.

Heisman Trophy winner.

Sanders, Deion. (1967-) Baseball player, football player.

Sanders, Fetague. (1915-1992) Magician.

Sapp, Warren. (1971-) Football player.

Satcher, David. (1941-) Medical researcher, physician, surgeon general of U.S.

Savage, Augusta Christine. (1892-1962) Educator, sculptor.

Sayers, Gale. (1943-) Football player.

Schomburg, Arthur. (1874-1938) Educator, historian, born Puerto Rico.

Scott, Dennis. (1968-) Basketball player.

Scott, Dred. (1795-1858) Slave.

Scott, Harriet. (unknown) Slave, wife of Dred Scott.

Scott, Roland. (1909-2002) Medical researcher, physician.

Scott, William Alexander II. (1903-1934) Publisher newspaper.

Scurlock, Addison. (1883-1964) Photographer.

Scurry, Brianna. (1971-) Olympic soccer player.

Seymour, William Joseph. (1870-1922) Spiritual leader, founder of Pentecostal Church.

Shange, Ntozake. (1948-) Author.

Shannon, Larry. (1933-) Biologist.

Sharpe, Avery. (1954-) Jazz musician.

Sharpe, Sterling. (1965-) Football player.

Shaw, Bernard. (1940-) Broadcast journalist.

Shaw, Earl D. (1937-) Inventor, physicist.

Shurney, Robert. (1921-) Aeronautical engineer, inventor, space scientist.

Sigur, Wanda. (1958-) Inventor, space scientist.

Simmons, Jake, Jr. (1901-1981) Entrepreneur oil industry.

Simmons, John. (1918-1979) Jazz musician.

Simone, Nina. (1933-2003) Composer, jazz musician, singer.

Simpkins, Andy. (1932-1999) Jazz musician.

Simpson, Lorna. (1960-) Photographer.

Simpson, Orenthal James "O. J." (1947-) Football player. Heisman Trophy winner.

Sims, Naomi. (1949-) Entrepreneur beauty products, fashion model.

Singleton, Arthur "Zutty." (1898-1975) Jazz musician.

Singleton, John. (1968-) Filmmaker, screenwriter.

Sissle, Noble. (1889-1970) Songwriter.

Sleet, Moneta, Jr. (1926-1996) Photojournalist. Pulitzer Prize winner.

Slew, Jenny. (1719-?) Slave.

Smalls, Robert. (1839-1915) Civil War naval hero, congressman, slave.

Smith, Ada "Bricktop." (1894-1984) Entrepreneur nightclub, singer.

Smith, Amanda. (1837-1915) Spiritual leader, slave.

Smith, Anna Deavere. (1950-) Actor, playwright.

Smith, Bessie. (1894-1937) Jazz singer.

Smith, Clara. (1894-1935) Jazz singer.

Smith, Emmitt. (1969-) Football player.

Smith, Floyd. (1917-1982) Jazz musician.

Smith, Jabbo. (1908-1991) Jazz musician.

Smith, James L. (1881-?) Author, slave.

Smith, James McCune. (1813-1865) Physician.

Smith, Johnny. (1922-1997) Jazz musician.

Smith, Mamie. (1883-1946) Jazz singer.

Smith, Mildred Davidson Austin. (1916-1993) Disability rights activist, inventor.

Smith, Ozzie. (1954-) Baseball player.

Smith, Tommie. (1944-) Olympic track and field athlete.

Smith, Will. (1948-1987) Fashion designer.

Smith, Will. (1969-) Actor, rap singer.

Somersett. (1600s) Slave.

Spaulding, Charles Clinton. (1874-1952) Entrepreneur banks, insurance.

Spikes, Frederick McKinley. (c. late 1800s) Inventor.

Spivey, Victoria. (1906-1976) Composer, singer.

Staley, Dawn. (1970-) Olympic basketball player.

Starks, John. (1965-) Basketball player.

Steward, Austin. (1794-1860) Abolitionist, author, slave.

Steward, Susan McKinney. (1847-1918) Physician.

Stewart, Leroy Elliot "Slam." (1914-1987) Jazz musician, singer.

Still, Peter. (1800-1868) Slave.

Still, Valerie. (1961-) Basketball player.

Still, Vina. (unknown) Slave, wife of Peter Still.

Still, William Grant. (1895-1978) Composer, conductor.

Stone, Toni. (1921-1966) Baseball player.

Stowers, Freddie. (1896-1918) World War I Army hero. Medal of Honor recipient.

Straker, David Augustus. (1842-1908) Attorney, civil rights activist.

Strayhorn, Billy. (1915-1967) Composer, jazz musician.

Sullivan, Leon. (1922-2001) Civil rights activist, entrepreneur auto company, workers' rights activist.

Suttles, George "Mule." (1901-1968) Baseball player.

Swann, Lynn. (1952-) Football player, sportscaster.

Swoopes, Sheryl. (1971-) Olympic basketball player.

Tanner, Henry Ossawa. (1859-1937) Painter.

Tatum, Art. (1910-1956) Jazz musician.

Taylor, Billy, Jr. (1925-1977) Jazz musician.

Taylor, Cecil. (1929-) Jazz musician.

Taylor, Lawrence. (1959-) Football player.

Taylor, Mildred. (1943-) Children's author.

Taylor, Susan. (1946-) Editor magazine, television personality.

Taylor, Susie King. (1848-1912) Civil War nurse, educator, slave.

Temple, Lewis. (1800-1854) Inventor.

Terrell, Mary Church. (1863-1954) Civil rights activist, women's rights activist.

Tharpe, Sister Rosetta. (1921-1973) Jazz singer.

Thomas, Debi. (1967-) Olympic figure skater, physician.

Thomas, Frank. (1968-) Baseball player.

Thomas, Isaiah. (1961-) Basketball player.

Thomas, Valerie. (1943-) Inventor, mathematician, physicist.

Thomas, Vivien. (1910-1985) Medical researcher.

Thompson, William. (1927-1950) Korean War Army hero. Medal of Honor recipient.

Thoms, Adah Belle. (1870-1943) World War I nurse, public health pioneer.

Thorpe, Otis Henry. (1962-) Basketball player.

Thurman, Howard. (1900-1981) Educator, peace activist, scholar, spiritual leader.

Thurman, Wallace. (1902-1934) Author, editor.

Tolan, Eddie. (1908-1967) Olympic track and field athlete.

Tolliver, Peter. (1927-) Engineer, physicist.

Toomer, Jean. (1894-1967) Author, poet.

Torrence, Gwen. (1965-) Olympic track and field athlete.

Touissant, Pierre. (1766-1853) Entrepreneur hairdresser, philanthropist, slave.

Travis, Dempsey J. (1920-) Author, cabinet member, entrepreneur real estate.

Traylor, Bill. (1854-1947) Painter, slave.

Trotter, William Monroe. (1872-1934) Civil rights activist, editor.

Truth, Sojourner. (1797-1883) Abolitionist, author, slave, spiritual leader, suffragist, women's rights activist.

Tubman, Harriet. (1820-1913) Abolitionist, Civil War spy, nurse, slave.

Turner, Charles Henry. (1867-1923) Biologist, educator, entomologist.

Turner, Henry McNeal. (1834-1915) Orator, spiritual leader.

Turner, James Milton. (1840-1915) Abolitionist, diplomat, educator, slave.

Turner, Nat. (1800-1831) Slave insurrectionist.

Turner, Tina. *See* Bullock, Anna Mae.

Twilight, Alexander Lucius. (1795-1857) Educator, state legislator.

Tyner, McCoy. (1938-) Jazz musician.

Tyson, Cicely. (1933?-) Actor.

Tyson, Michael. (1966-) Boxer.

Tyus, Wyomia. (1945-) Olympic track and field athlete.

Van der Zee, James. (1886-1983) Photographer, photojournalist.

Van Peebles, Mario. (1957-) Actor, filmmaker, screenwriter.

Van Peebles, Melvin. (1932-) Actor, filmmaker.

Van Vechten, Carl. (1880-1964) Author, photographer.

Vann, Robert. (1879-1940) Publisher newspaper.

Vaughan, Sarah. (1924-1991) Jazz musician, singer.

Vaughn, Mo. (1967-) Baseball player.

Veney, Bethany. (1815-?) Author, slave.

Vesey, Denmark. (1767-1822) Slave insurrectionist.

Vinnegar, Leroy. (1928-1999) Jazz musician.

Vinson, Phyllis Tucker. (1948-) Television filmmaker.

Von Mason, Stephen. (1954-) Painter.

Walden, Barbara. (1936-) Entrepreneur beauty supplies.

Walker, Alice. (1944-) Author. Pulitzer Prize winner.

Walker, Herschel. (1962-) Football player. Heisman Trophy winner.

Walker, Madame C. J. *See* Walker, Sarah Breedlove McWilliams.

Walker, Maggie Lena. (1867-1934) Entrepreneur banker, journalist.

Walker, Margaret. (1915-1998) Author.

Walker, Moses Fleetwood. (1857-1924) Baseball player.

Walker, Sarah Breedlove McWilliams. (Madame C. J.) (1867-1919) Entrepreneur beauty supplies, human rights activist, inventor.

Walker, Thomas. (1850-1935) Attorney, entrepreneur real estate, philanthropist, state legislator.

Wallace, Sippie. (1898-1986) Jazz singer.

Waller, Thomas Wright "Fats." (1904-1943) Bandleader, composer, jazz musician.

Wally, Augustus. (unknown) Spanish American War buffalo soldier.

Ward, Samuel Ringgold. (1817-1878) Abolitionist, slave, spiritual leader.

Waring, Laura Wheeler. (1877-1948) Painter.

Washington, Augustus. (1820-?) Civil rights activist, educator, photographer.

Washington, Booker T. (1856-1915) Educator, slave, statesman.

Washington, Denzel. (1954-) Actor.

Washington, Dinah. (1925-1959) Jazz singer.

Washington, George. (1817-1905) Pioneer.

Washington, Madison. (unknown) Slave insurrectionist.

Washington, Ora. (1898-1971) Basketball player, tennis player.

Washington, Warren. (1936-) Meteorologist.

Washow, Omar. (1970-) Entrepreneur computer services.

Waters, Ethel. (1896-1977) Actor, singer.

Waters, Maxine. (1938-) Congresswoman, state legislator.

Waters, McKinley Morganfield "Muddy." (1915-1983) Jazz musician, singer.

Wattleton, Faye. (1943-) President of Planned Parenthood, women's rights activist.

Wayans, Keenen Ivory. (1958-) Actor, comedian, filmmaker, screenwriter.

Weatherspoon, Teresa. (1965-) Olympic basketball player.

Webb, William Henry "Chick." (1909-1939) Jazz musician.

Webber, Chris. (1973-) Basketball player.

Weems, Ann Marie. (1840-?) Slave, disguised as male.

Weems, Carrie Mae. (1951-) Photographer.

Wells, James Lesesne. (1902-1993) Painter, printmaker.

Wells-Barnett, Ida B. (1862-1931) Civil rights activist, journalist, reformer.

West, Dorothy. (1907-1998) Author.

Wheatley, Phillis. (1754-1784) American Revolutionary War patriot, poet.

White, Charles. (1918-1979) Painter.

White, George Henry. (1852-1918) Attorney, banker, congressman, slave.

White, Reggie. (1961-) Football player.

White, Walter. (1893-1955) Author, civil rights activist.

Whiten, Mark. (1966-) Baseball player.

Whitfield, Princess. (1937-) Educator.

Whitten, Charles. (1922-) Medical researcher, physician.

Wilder, L. Douglas. (1931-) Attorney, chemist, governor, Korean War military, state legislator.

Wilkins, Dominique. (1960-) Basketball player, born France.

Wilkins, Roy. (1901-1981) Civil rights activist. Presidential Medal of Freedom recipient.

Williams, Angela. (1980-) Olympic track and field athlete.

Williams, Bert. (1874-1922) Actor, comedian, dancer, singer.

Williams, Charles "Buck." (1960-) Basketball player.

Williams, Daniel Hale. (1856-1931) Educator, physician.

Williams, Doug. (1955-) Football player.

Williams, George Washington. (1849-1891) Attorney, Civil War soldier, historian, spiritual leader.

Williams, Joe. (1918-1999) Jazz singer.

Williams, John "Hot Rod." (1962-) Basketball player.

Williams, Mary Lou. (1910-1981) Jazz musician.

Williams, Moses. (d. 1899) Indian Wars soldier.

Williams, Ozzie. (1921-) Space scientist.

Williams, Paul Revere. (1894-1980) Architect.

Williams, Ricky. (1977-) Football player.

Williams, Serena. (1981-) Tennis player.

Williams, Tony. (1945-1997) Jazz musician.

Williams, Venus. (1980-) Tennis player.

Wills, Maurice Morning "Maury." (1932-) Baseball player.

Wilson, August. (1935-) Playwright. Pulitzer Prize winner.

Wilson, Ernest Judson "Boojum." (1899-1963) Baseball player.

Wilson, Harriet E. Adams. (1827?-1863?) Author.

Wilson, Sharifa. (unknown) City official.

Wilson, Theodore "Teddy." (1912-1986) Bandleader, jazz musician.

Wilson-Hawkins, Carla. (unknown) Educator.

Winfrey, Oprah. (1954-) Entrepreneur media conglomerate, filmmaker, television personality.

Wonder, Stevie. (1950-) Jazz musician.

Woodard, Alfre. (1953-) Actor.

Woodard, Lynette. (1959-) Basketball player.

Woodruff, Hale Aspacio. (1900-1980) Educator, painter.

Woods, Granville T. (1856-1910) Inventor.

Woods, Tiger. (1975-) Golfer.

Woodson, Carter G. (1875-1950) Educator, historian.

Worthy, James. (1961-) Basketball player.

Wright, Eugene. (1923-) Jazz musician.

Wright, Jane Cooke. (1919-) Medical researcher, physician.

Wright, Jonathan Jasper. (1840-1885) Attorney, jurist.

Wright, Louis Tompkins. (1891-1952) Civil rights activist, medical researcher, physician.

Wright, Richard. (1908-1960) Author.

York. (1770-1832) Explorer.

Young, Andrew Jackson. (1932-) Ambassador, civil rights activist, congressman, mayor. Presidential Medal of Freedom recipient.

Young, Charles. (1864-1922) Army career officer, Spanish American War, World War I.

Young, Chavonda J. Jacobs. (1967-) Paper science engineer.

Young, Coleman. (1918-1997) Mayor.

Young, Lester Willis. (1909-1959) Jazz musician.

Young, Plummer Bernard, Sr. (1884-1962) Publisher newspaper.

Young, Roger Arliner. (1889-1964) Educator, zoologist.

Young, Whitney Moore, Jr. (1921-1971) Civil rights activist. Presidential Medal of Freedom recipient.

Zorich, Chris. (1969-) Football player.

Africans

See also African Americans; Blacks, International.

Anokye, Okomfo. (17th century) West African priest.

Askia the Great. (1444?-1538) King.

Augustine. (354-430) North African saint, spiritual leader.

Barsosio, Sally. (1978-) Kenyan olympic track and field athlete.

Bol, Manute. (1962-) Sudanese basketball player.

Cinque, Joseph. (1817-1879) Patriot, slave insurrectionist.

Dahia al-Kahina. (fl. 680) North African freedom fighter, queen.

de Klerk, Fredrik Willem " F. W." (1936) South African attorney, civil rights activist, political activist. Nobel Peace Prize winner.

Elizabeth. (1941-) Princess of Toro (Uganda).

Esu-Williams. Eku. (1956-) Nigerian AIDS educator, community leader, immunologist, physician.

Gordimer, Nadine. (1923-) South African author, playwright. Nobel Prize winner.

Gronniosaw, Ukawsaw. (1725-1786) Prince, kingdom of Borneo, captured slave.

Judith of Ethiopia. (Tenth century) Warrior queen.

Kenyatta, Jomo. (1894-1978) Kenyan president, prime minister.

Kenyatta, Julius K. (1922-) Tanzanian prime minister.

Kivengere, Festo. (1919-1988) Ugandan human rights activist, spiritual leader.

Kruger, Paul. (1825-1904) South African general in Boer War, statesman.

Leakey, Richard. (1944-) Kenyan archaeologist, paleontologist.

Lucas, Adetokonbo. (1931-) Nigerian medical researcher, physician.

Luthuli, Albert. (c. 1898-1967) South African political activist. Nobel Peace Prize winner.

Luwum, Janani. (1922-1977) Ugandan archbishop, political activist.

Maathai, Wangari. (1940-) Kenyan environmental activist, human rights activist, political activist.

Machel, Gracia Simbine. (1945-) Mozambican children's rights activist.

Makeba, Miriam. (1932-) South African political activist, singer.

Makeda. (960-930 B.C.) Ethiopian Queen of Sheba.

Makhubu, Lydia Phindile. (1937-) Swasiland chemist, educator.

Mandela, Nelson. (1918-) South African attorney, human rights activist, political activist. Nobel Peace Prize winner, Presidential Medal of Freedom recipient.

Mandela, Winnie Madikizela. (1934-) South African political activist.

Mansa Musa I. (1312-1337) King of Mali.

Mbandi, Jinga. *See* Nzinga, Anna.

Mella. African warrior queen.

Morris, Samuel. (1827-1893) Liberian missionary.

Mugabe, Robert. (1924-) Zimbabwean prime minister.

Mutombo, Dikembe. (1966-) Zairian basketball player.

Newby-Fraser, Paula. (1962-) Zimbabwean olympic track and field athlete, triathlon.

Nkrumah, Kwame. (1909-1972) Ghanian president, prime minister.

Nyerere, Julius K. (1922-1999) Tanzanian prime minister.

Nzinga, Anna. (1580-1663) West African queen.

Odhiambo, Thomas. (1931-2003) Kenyan entomologist.

Oya. African Goddess.

Qaddafi, Muammar-al. (1942-) Libyan head of state, terrorist.

Schreiner, Olive. (1855-1920) South African author, women's rights activist.

Selassie, Haile. (1892-1975) Ethiopian emperor.

Senghor, Léopold. (1906-2001) Senegal president.

Shaka. (1787-1828) Zulu warrior king.

Soyinka, Wole. (1934-) Nigerian author, playwright, poet, political activist. Nobel Prize winner.

Tupou, Queen Salote III. (1900-1965) Ruler of Tonga.

Tutu, Desmond Mpilo. (1931-) South African archbishop, human rights activist. Nobel Peace Prize winner.

Wolde, Mamo. (1931-) Ethiopian olympic track and field athlete, marathon runner.

Agricultural Scientists

Borlaug, Norman Ernest. (1914-) Wheat strains to increase food supply.

Carver, George Washington. (1864-1943) Peanuts.

Chapman, Jonathan. (Johnny Appleseed) (1774-1845) Orchardist.

Durgan, Beverly. (unknown) Weeds.

Hoben, Patricia. (unknown) Bovine diseases.

Holland, Elizabeth. (unknown) Biogeochemist.

Kapuscinski, Anne. (unknown) Fisheries, born France.

Naylor, Rosamond. (unknown) Agricultural economist.

Orr, John Boyd. (1880-1971) Scottish agricultural nutritionist.

Pinckney, Eliza Lucas. (1722-1793) Agronomist, born West Indies.

Rodale, Jerome Irving "J. I." (1898-1971) Organic farm movement.

Rodriguez, Eloy. (1947-)

AIDS Activists

See also Medical Researchers.

Barré-Sinoussi, Francoise. (1947-) French medical researcher.

Esu-Williams, Eku. (1956-) Nigerian AIDS educator, immunologist.

Gertz, Alison. (1966-1992)

Glaser, Elizabeth. (1947-1994)

Haring, Keith. (1958-1990)

Ho, David. (1952-) Medical researcher, physician, born Taiwan.

James, Ryan. (1975-)

Lifshitz, Aliza. (1951-) Mexican physician.

Osborn, June. (1937-) Physician, National Commission on AIDS chairwoman.

Shilts, Randy. (1951-1994)

Taylor, Elizabeth. (1932-) born England.

White, Ryan. (1971-1990)

Wong-Staal, Flossie. (1947-) Medical researcher, born China. Discovered HIV virus.

Air Force Personnel

See also Gulf War; Korean War; Medal of Honor recipients; Military Leaders; Vietnam War; World War One; World War Two.

Abrahamson, James A. (1933-) Lieutenant general.

Arnold, Henry H. (1886-1950) World War II general.

Bader, Sir Douglas. (1910-1982) English World War II pilot, hero.

Balchen, Bernt. (1899-1973) World War II pilot, born Norway.

Brown, George S. (1918-1978) Korean War, Vietnam War, World War II general, Joint Chiefs of Staff.

Chennault, Claire Lee. (1890-1958) World War I, II fighter pilot, major general.

Cochran, Jacqueline. (1910-1980) World War II Women's Air Force Service Pilots director.

Collins, Eileen. (1956-) Pilot.

Croslin, Michael. (1933-) Korean War, Vietnam War pilot, born Virgin Islands.

Davis, Benjamin O., Jr. (1912-2002) Career officer, Korean War commander, brigadier general, World War II Tuskegee airman.

Doolittle, Jimmy. (1886-1993) World War II Army Air Corps pilot. Medal of Honor recipient.

Duke, Charles. (1935-) Pilot.

Dwight, Edward J., Jr. (1933-) Jet pilot.

Fort, Cornelia. (1919-1943) World War II pilot.

Göring, Hermann. (1893-1946) German general.

Gregory, Frederick. (1941-) Colonel.

Grissom, Virgil I. "Gus." (1926-1967) Korean War combat pilot.

Irwin, James. (1930-1991) Test pilot.

James, Daniel "Chappie," Jr. (1920-1978) Korean War, Vietnam War, World War II, four star general.

Lee, Mark C. (1952-) Lieutenant.

LeMay, Curtis E. (1906-1990) World War II general.

Marchbanks, Vance. (1905-1988) Colonel, World War II Tuskegee airman.

Nobile, Umberto. (1885-1978) Italian air force general.

Richthofen, Baron Manfred von "The Red Baron." (1892-1918) German World War I fighter pilot

Rickenbacker, Edward Vernon "Eddie." (1890-1973) World War I, II pilot. Medal of Honor recipient.

Rutan, Dick. (1938-) Vietnam War fighter pilot.

Scott, David. (1932-) Pilot.

Smith, Margaret Chase. (1897-1995) World War II lieutenant colonel.

Whittle, Sir Frank. (1907-1996) English royal air force pilot.

Yeager, Chuck. (1923-) World War II pilot.

Alexandrians

See also Egyptians, Ancient.

Arius (c. 256-336) Alexandrian spiritual leader, founder of Arianism.

Catherine of Alexandria. (4th century) Saint.

Mary Prophetetissa of Alexandria. (1st century) Chemist, inventor.

Ambassadors and Diplomats

Adams, John Quincy. (1767-1848)

Bernadotte, Folke. (1895-1948) Swedish.

Bunche, Ralph. (1904-1971)

Chaucer, Geoffrey. (1343-1400) English.

Constant, Paul D'Estournelles. (1852-1924)

French.
Dawes, Charles Gates. (1865-1951)
Dayan, Moshe. (1915-1981) Israeli foreign
    minister.
Dulles, John Foster. (1888-1959)
Fenwick, Millicent. (1910-1992)
Franklin, Benjamin. (1706-1790)
Galbraith, John Kenneth. (1908-) born Can-
    ada.
Gallatin, Albert. (1761-1849) born Switzer-
    land.
Hammarskjöld, Dag. (1905-1961) Swedish.
Harris, Patricia Roberts. (1924-1985)
Harte, Bret. (1836-1902)
Hay, John. (1838-1905)
Jay, John. (1745-1829)
Johnson, James Weldon. (1871-1938)
Kellogg, Frank Billings. (1856-1937)
Kennedy, Joseph Patrick. (1888-1969)
Kirkpatrick, Jeane. (1926-)
Kollontai, Alexandra. (1872-1952) Russian.
Leisdorff, William A. (1810-1848)
Luce, Clare Boothe. (1903-1987)
Marsh, George Perkins. (1801-1882)
Mistral, Gabriela Lucila Godoy y Alcayága.
    (1889-1957) Chilean.
Monroe, James. (1758-1831)
Morris, Gouverneur. (1752-1816)
Noel-Baker, Philip. (1889-1982) English.
Pearson, Lester. (1897-1972) Canadian.
Richardson, Bill. (1947-)
Robles, Alfonso García. (1911-1991) Mexi-
    can.
Rohde, Ruth Bryan Owen. (1885-1954)
Sampson, Edith. (1901-1980)
Smith, Samantha Reed. (1972-1985) Youth
    ambassador to Soviet Union.
Stevenson, Adlai. (1900-1965)
Temple, Shirley. (1928-)
Turner, James Milton. (1840-1915)
Von Ribbentrop, Joachim. (1893-1946) Ger-
    man.
Waldheim, Kurt. (1918-) Austrian.
Wing Yung. (1828-1912) born China.
Young, Andrew Jackson. (1932-)

American Revolutionary War
  Figures

British, Military
Amherst, Jeffrey. (1717-1797)

Burgoyne, John. (1732-1792)
Gage, Thomas. (1721-1787)
Howe, William. (1729-1814)
Tecumseh. (1768-1813) Shawnee chief.

British, Spies and Traitors
André, Captain John. (1750-1780)
Girty, Simon. (1741-1818)
Rivington, James. (1727-1802)

British, Statesmen
Burke, Edmund. (1729-1797)
George III. (1738-1820) King.
Pitt, William. (1708-1778) Prime minister.
Townshend, Charles. (1725-1767)
Wilkes, John. (1725-1797)

French
Louis XVI. (1754-1792) King.

Loyalists
Brant, Joseph. (1742-1807) Mohawk chief.
Draper, Margaret Green. (1727-1804) News-
    paper publisher.
Odell, Jonathan. (1737-1818)

Patriots, Military
Allen, Ethan. (1738-1789)
Armistead, James. (1760-1832)
Arnold, Benedict. (1741-1801)
Attucks, Crispus. (1732-1770)
Crevecouer, Hector St. John de. (1735-1813)
Dabney, Austin. (1799-1821)
Dickinson, John. (1732-1808)
Grant, Jehu. (1752-?)
Greene, Nathanael. (1742-1786)
Haynes, Lemuel. (1753-1833)
Jones, John Paul. (1747-1792)
Kosciuszko, Thaddeus. (1746-1817) Polish.
Lafayette, Marie Joseph Paul Yves Roch
    Gilbert du Motier, Marquis de. (1757-
    1834) French.
L'Enfant, Pierre Charles. (1754-1825) born
    France.
Martin, Joseph Plumb. (1762-1852)
McCauley, Mary Ludwig Hays. (Molly
    Pitcher) (1754-1832)
Poor, Salem. (1747-1780)
Pulaski, Casimir. (1747-1779) Polish no-
    bleman.
Revere, Paul. (1735-1818)

Rodney, Caesar. (1728-1784)
Salem, Peter. (1750-1816)
Sampson, Deborah. (Robert Shurtliff)
  (1760-1827) disguised as man.
Shays, Daniel. (1747-1825)
Washington, George. (1732-1799)
Whipple, William. (1730-1785) General.
Wolcott, Oliver. (1726-1797)

Patriots, Spies and Traitors
Armistead, James. (1760-1832)
Arnold, Benedict. (1741-1801)
Arnold, Peggy Shippen. (1760-1804)
Bailey, Anne Trotter. (1743-1825)
Darragh, John. (unknown)
Darragh, Lydia. (1725-1789)
Hale, Nathan. (1755-1776)
Hart, Nancy. (1744-1841)
Langston, Dicey. (1766-1837)
Odell, Jonathan. (1737-1818)
Redmond, Mary. (unknown)
Wright, Patience Lovell. (1725-1786)

Patriots, Statesmen
Adams, John. (1735-1826)
Adams, Samuel. (1722-1803)
Bartlett, Josiah. (1729-1795)
Braxton, Carter. (1736-1797)
Carroll, Charles. (1737-1832)
Chase, Samuel. (1741-1811)
Clymer, George. (1739-1813)
Ellery, William. (1727-1820)
Floyd, William. (1734-1821)
Franklin, Benjamin. (1706-1790)
Freneau, Philip. (1752-1832)
Gálvez, Bernardo de. (1746-1782)
Gerry, Elbridge. (1744-1814)
Gwinnett, Button. (1735-1777)
Hall, Lyman. (1724-1790)
Hamilton, Alexander. (1753-1804)
Hancock, John. (1737-1793)
Hart, John. (1711-1779)
Henry, Patrick. (1736-1799)
Hewes, Joseph. (1730-1779)
Heyward, Thomas, Jr. (1746-1809)
Hooper, William. (1742-1790)
Hopkins, Stephen. (1707-1785)
Hopkinson, Francis. (1737-1791)
Huntingdon, Samuel. (1731-1796)
Jay, John. (1745-1829)
Jefferson, Thomas. (1743-1826)

Lee, Francis Lightfoot. (1734-1797)
Lee, Richard Henry. (1732-1794)
Lewis, Francis. (1713-1802)
Livingston, Philip. (1716-1778)
Lynch, Thomas, Jr. (1749-1779)
Mason, George. (1725-1792)
McKean, Thomas. (1734-1817)
Middleton, Arthur. (1742-1787)
Morris, Gouverneur. (1752-1816)
Morris, Lewis. (1726-1798)
Morris, Robert. (1734-1806)
Morton, John. (1724-1777)
Nelson, Thomas, Jr. (1738-1789)
Paca, William. (1740-1795)
Paine, Robert Treat. (1731-1814)
Paterson, William. (1745-1806)
Penn, John. (1740-1788)
Read, George. (1733-1798)
Revere, Paul. (1735-1818)
Rodney, Caesar. (1728-1784)
Ross, George. (1730-1779)
Rush, Benjamin. (1745-1813)
Rutledge, Edward. (1749-1800)
Sherman, Roger. (1721-1793)
Smith, James. (1719-1806)
Solomon, Haym. (1740-1785) Financier.
Stockton, Richard. (1730-1781)
Stone, Thomas. (1743-1787)
Taylor, George. (1716-1781)
Thornton, Matthew. (1714-1803)
Walker, Thomas. (1715-1794)
Walton, George. (1741-1804)
Whipple, William. (1730-1785)
Williams, William. (1731-1811)
Wilson, James. (1742-1798)
Witherspoon, John. (1723-1794)
Wolcott, Oliver. (1726-1797)
Wythe, George. (1726-1806)

Patriots, Women
Adams, Abigail. (1744-1818)
Arnett, Hannah. (unknown)
Barker, Penelope. (unknown)
Barry, Catherine Moore. (unknown)
Brant, Mary "Molly." (Degonwadanti)
  (1736-1796) Mohawk Indian.
Bratton, Martha. (unknown)
Burgin, Elizabeth. (unknown)
Corbin, Margaret. (1751-1800)
Franklin, Deborah Read. (1707-1774) Busi-
  nesswoman.

Geiger, Emily. (1760-1813)
Goddard, Mary Katherine. (1738-1816) Printer, publisher.
Hart, Nancy. (1744-1841)
Jemison, Mary. (1742-1833) Indian captive.
Langston, Dicey. (1766-1837)
Ludington, Sybil. (1761-1839)
Macdonald, Flora. (1723-1790) Scottish musician.
Martin, Grace. (unknown)
Martin, Rachel. (unknown)
McCrea, Jane. (1752-1777) Indian captive.
Motte, Rebecca. (d. 1815)
Murray, Judith Sargent. (1751-1820) Author, editor.
Murray, Mary Lindley. (unknown)
Redmond, Mary. (unknown)
Reed, Esther DeBeerdt. (1746-1780)
Ridesel, Baroness Frederika von. (1746-1808) German camp follower.
Ross, Betsy. (1752-1836)
Ward, Nancy. (1728-1822)
Warren, Mercy Otis. (1728-1814)
Wheatley, Phillis. (1754-1784)
Wright, Patience Lovell. (1725-1786)

Anatomists
Cavazos, Lauro F. (1927-)
Cobb, William Montague. (1904-1990)
Cuvier, Georges. (1769-1832) French.
Harvey, William. (1578-1657) English.
Sabin, Florence Rena. (1871-1953)
Sperry, Roger. (1913-1994)
Trotter, Mildred. (1899-1991)
Vesalius, Andreas. (1514-1564) Belgian.

Anthropologists
Abrams, George. (1939-)
Benedict, Ruth. (1887-1948)
Blakey, Michael L. (1953-)
Boaz, Franz. (1858-1942) German.
Deloria, Ella Cara. (1889-1971) Yankton Dakota Indian.
Dockstader, Frederick L. (1919-1998) Oneida and Navajo Indian.
Dunham, Katherine. (1909-)
Eiseley, Loren. (1907-1977)
Fletcher, Alice Cunningham. (1838-1923)
Gwaltney, John Langston. (1928-1998)
Hansberry, William Leo. (1894-1965)
Hurston, Zora Neale. (1901-1960)

Kroeber, Alfred. (1875-1960)
La Flesche, Francis. (1857-1932) Ponca and Omaha Indian.
Leakey, Louis S.B. (1903-1972) English.
Leakey, Mary. (1913-1996) English.
Livingstone, David. (1813-1873) Scottish.
Lowie, Robert Henry. (1883-1957) born Austria.
Mead, Margaret. (1901-1978)
Parsons, Elsie Clews. (1875-1941)
Powdermaker, Hortense. (1900-1970)
Reinhart, Johann. (1943-)
Snow, Clyde. (1932-)
Trotter, Mildred. (1899-1991)

Apostles
See also Saints.
Andrew. (1st century)
Bartholomew.
James the Elder.
James the Younger.
John the Evangelist.
Judas.
Jude Thaddeus.
Matthew.
Matthias.
Peter.
Philip.
Simon.

Arabs
Arafat, Yasir. (1929-) Palestinian political activist, terrorist. Nobel Peace Prize winner.
Assad, Hafez-al. (1930-2000) Syrian president.
Dahia al-Kahina. (fl. 680) North African freedom fighter, queen.
Ghazali-al. (1058-1111) Spiritual leader.
Hussein, Ibn Talal. (1935-1999) Jordanian king.
Ibn al-Walid, Khalid. (d. 642) General.
Ibn-Battuta, Muhammad. (1304-1369) Adventurer, explorer.
Ibn-e-Sina, Hakim. (980-1037) Physician.
Ibn Ziyvad, Tariq. (d. 700) Military leader.
Khadijah. (Khadika bint Khuwaylid) (555-620) wife of Muhammad.
Khwarizmi, Abu Jafar Muhammad Ibn Musa-al. (780-850) Astronomer, mathematician.

Mansur, Abu Jafar ibn Muhammad al-. (714-775) Military leader.

Muhammad. (570?-632) Prophet, founder Islam religion.

Nasser, Gamal Abdel. (1918-1970) Egyptian president, president of United Arab Republic.

Nidal, Abu. (1937-2002) Terrorist.

Qaddafi, Muammar-al. (1942-) Libyan military leader, terrorist.

Sharki, Amatalrauf-al. (1958-) Yemenite women's rights activist.

Arachnologists
West, Rick C. (1951-) Canadian.

Archaeologists
See also Egyptologists.

Bell, Gertrude. (1868-1926) English.

Belzoni, Giovanni. (1778-1823) Italian.

Biaggi, Cristina Shelley. (1937-)

Bingham, Hiram. (1878-1956)

Breasted, James Henry. (1865-1935)

Breuil, Henri. (1877-1961) French.

Carter, Howard. (1873-1939) English.

Caton-Thompson, Gertrude. (1888-1985) English.

Childe, Vere Gordon. (1892-1957) Australian.

Clark, Grahame. (1907-1995) English.

Clark, John Desmond. (1916-2002)

Connelly, Joan Breton. (1954-)

Evans, Arthur. (1851-1941) English.

Evans, John. (1823-1908) English.

Fletcher, Alice Cunningham. (1838-1923)

Garrod, Dorothy. (1892-1968) English.

Gimbutas, Marija Birute Alseikaite. (1921-1994) born Lithuania.

Hadjidaki-Marder, Elpida. (1948-) Greek.

Hawes, Harriet Ann Boyd. (1871-1945)

Herbert, George. (1866-1923) English.

Kenyon, Kathleen. (1906-1978) English.

Kidder, Alfred Vincent. (1885-1963)

Lawrence, Thomas Edward. (Lawrence of Arabia) (1888-1935) English.

Layard, Austen Henry. (1817-1894) English.

Leakey, Louis S. B. (1903-1972) English.

Leakey, Mary. (1913-1996) English.

Leakey, Richard. (1944-) Kenyan.

Mallowan, Max. (1904-1978) English.

Mariette, Auguste. (1821-1881) French.

Montelius, Oscar. (1843-1921) Swedish.

Morley, Sylvanus Griswold. (1883-1948)

Mouhot, Henri. (1826-1861) French.

Peck, Annie Smith. (1850-1935)

Petrie, William Matthew Fliders. (1853-1942) English.

Pitt-Rivers, Augustus Lane Fox. (1827-1900) English.

Rawlinson, Sir Henry Creswicke. (1810-1895) English.

Roosevelt, Anna Curtenius. (1946-)

Schliemann, Heinrich. (1822-1890) German.

Schmandt-Besserat, Denise. (1933-) born France.

Stein, Aurel. (1862-1943) Hungarian.

Stukeley, William. (1687-1765) English.

Thompson, Edward. (1840-1935)

Thomsen, Christian Jurgenson. (1786-1865) Danish.

Warren, Charles. (unknown) English.

Weeks, Kent R. (unknown)

Wheeler, Robert Eric Mortimer. (1890-1976) English.

Willey, Gordon Randolph. (1913-2002)

Wincklemann, Johann Joachim. (1717-1768) German.

Wooley, Charles Leonard. (1880-1960) English.

Worsaae, Jens Jacob A. (1821-1885) Danish.

Yadin, Yigael. (1917-1984) Israeli.

Yener, Rutlu Aslihan. (1946-) Turkish.

Zarins, Juris. (1945-) born Latvia.

Archers
Selim III, Sultan. (1761-1808) Turkish.

Architects
Brunelleschi. (1377-1466) Italian.

Fuller, R. Buckminster. (1895-1983)

Gantt, Harvey B. (1943-)

Guastavino, Rafael. (1842-1908) born Spain.

Hayden, Sophia. (1868-1953) born Chile.

Imhotep. (3000-2950 B.C.) Egyptian.

Jefferson, Thomas. (1743-1826)

Lamb, William Frederick. (1883-1952)

L'Enfant, Pierre Charles. (1754-1825) born France.

Leonardo da Vinci. (1452-1519) Italian.

Lin, Maya Ying. (1960-)

Lisboa, Antonio Francisco. (1738-1814) Brazilian.

Mies van der Rohe, Ludwig. (1886-1969) born Germany.

Morgan, Julia. (1872-1957)

Olmstead, Frederick Law. (1822-1903) Landscape architect.

Pei, Ieah Ming "I. M." (1917-) born China.

Pericles. (495-429 B.C.) Greek.

Senenmut. (fl. 1495 B.C.) Egyptian.

Ventris, Michael. (1922-1956) English.

Williams, Paul Revere. (1894-1980)

Wren, Christopher. (1632-1723) English.

Wright, Frank Lloyd. (1869-1959)

Yamasaki, Minoru. (1912-1986)

Archivists
See Historians.

Argentines
See also Hispanic-Americans.

Alvarez, Eduardo. (unknown) Crime fighter, forensic scientist.

Antokoletz, Maria Adele de. (unknown) Human rights activist.

Bonafini, Hebe de. (unknown) Human rights activist.

Borges, Jorge Luis. (1899-1986) Author, poet.

Cortazar, Julio. (1914-1984) Author.

de Vincenzo, Roberto. (1923-) Golfer.

Esquivel, Adolfo Pérez. (1931-) Human rights activist, sculptor. Nobel Peace Prize winner.

Guevara, Che. (1928-1967) Revolutionary.

Lamas, Carlos Saavedra. (1878-1959) Attorney, educator, peace activist, statesman. Nobel Peace Prize winner.

Maradona, Diego. (1960-) Soccer player.

Perón, Eva "Evita." (1919-1952) Actor, political activist.

Perón, Juan. (1895-1974) Dictator, president.

Sabatini, Gabriela. (1970-) Tennis player.

Sarmiento, Domingo Faustina. (1811-1888) Political activist, president.

Army Personnel
See also Civil War; Gulf War; Korean War, Medal of Honor Recipients; Military

Leaders; Vietnam War; World War I; World War II.

Abrams, Creighton W. (1914-1974) Vietnam War Chief of Staff, World War II general.

Baker, Vernon J. (1919-) World War II second lieutenant, military hero. Medal of Honor recipient.

Benavidez, Roy. (1935-) Vietnam War military hero. Medal of Honor recipient.

Bingham, Hiram. (1878-1956) World War I pilot.

Blanchfield, Florence Aby. (1882-1971) World War I nurse, World War II superintendent nurses.

Bradley, Omar N. (1893-1981) World War II general.

Bridger, Jim. (1804-1881) Civil War soldier.

Burnside, Ambrose Everett. (1824-1881) Civil War general.

Butler, Benjamin David. (1818-1893) Civil War general.

Cadoria, Sherian. (1940-) Brigadier general, Vietnam War military police.

Cammermeyer, Margarethe. (1942) Army colonel, Vietnam War nurse.

Carlson, Evans. (1896-1947) World War I soldier.

Carney, William H. (1840-1908) Civil War sergeant, military hero. Medal of Honor recipient.

Carson, Christopher "Kit." (1809-1868) Civil War soldier.

Chacon, Rafael. (1833-1925) Civil War soldier.

Cherry, Fred V. (1928-) Vietnam War soldier.

Clalin, Frances. (unknown) Civil War soldier,disguised as man.

Clark, William. (1770-1838)

Clem, Johnny. (1852-1937) Civil War soldier as child.

Cody, William "Buffalo Bill." (1846-1917) Civil War soldier.

Custer, George Armstrong. (1839-1876) Civil War soldier.

Davis, Benjamin O., Sr. (1877-1970) Career officer, World War I, II, Spanish American War, brigadier general.

Davis, Lonnie. (1958-) Gulf War hero.

Delaney, Martin Robison. (1812-1885) Civil

War major.

Delano, Jane Arminda. (1862-1919) World War I Superintendent Army Air Corps nurses.

Dix, Dorothea. (1802-1887) Civil War superintendent nurses.

Dole, Robert. (1923-) World War II second lieutenant.

Dunn, Oscar. (1820-1871) Civil War captain.

Earley, Charity Adams. (1918-2002) World War II WAAC lieutenant colonel.

Edmonds, Sarah Emma. (1841-1898) Civil War soldier, disguised as man.

Eisenhower, Dwight David. (1890-1969) World War II Allied Military Commander.

Ferenz, Ludmilla "Lou." (1921-) World War II Army Nurse Corps pilot.

Fleetwood, Christian A. (1840-1914) Civil War major. Medal of Honor recipient.

Flipper, Henry O. (1856-1914) Career soldier.

Foch, Ferdinand. (1851-1929) French World War I general.

Forrest, Nathan Bedford. (1821-1877) Civil War general.

Fremont, John Charles. (1813-1890) Civil War general.

Garcia, Hector Perez. (1914-1996) World War II hero.

Garfield, James A. (1831-1881) Civil War soldier.

Gaston, Arthur George. (1892-1996) World War I.

Goethals, George W. (1858-1928) Career soldier.

Goode, W. Wilson. (1938-) Captain.

Goyens, William. (1794-1856) Texas Revolution military leader.

Grant, Ulysses S. (1822-1885) Civil War general.

Greene, Nathanael. (1742-1786) American Revolutionary War general.

Halloren, Mary. (1907-) Career soldier, World War II WAAC.

Halleck, Henry Wager. (1815-1872) Civil War general.

Hancock, Winfield Scott. (1824-1886) Civil War general.

Hardee, William Joseph. (1815-1873) Civil War general.

Harrison, Benjamin. (1833-1901) Civil War colonel.

Harrison, William Henry. (1773-1862) War of 1812 general.

Hayes, Rutherford B. (1822-1893) Civil War soldier.

Hill, Ambrose Powell. (1825-1865) Civil War general.

Hobby, Oveta Culp. (1905-1995) World War II commander WAACS.

Hodgers, Jenny. (1844-1915) Civil War soldier, disguised as man, born Ireland.

Hood, John Bell. (1821-1879) Civil War general.

Hooker, Joseph. (1814-1878) Civil War general.

Inouye, Daniel. (1924-) World War II captain.

Jackson, Thomas "Stonewall." (1824-1863) Civil War general.

Jans, Megan C. (1952-) Gulf War lieutenant colonel.

Joel, Lawrence. (unknown) Vietnam War hero.

John III Sobieski. (1624-1696) Polish general.

Johnson, Hazel W. (1927-) Brigadier general, Chief of nurse corps.

Johnson, Henry. (1897-1929) World War I soldier.

Johnston, Joe. (1807-1891) Civil War general.

Jordan, George. (1847-1904) Indian Wars soldier.

King, Dick. (1845-?) Civil War soldier as child.

Lee, Robert E. (1807-1870) Civil War general.

Lippmann, Walter. (1889-1974) World War II captain military intelligence.

Locklear, Ormer. (1891-1929) World War I Army Air Services pilot.

Longstreet, James. (1821-1904) Civil War general.

Louis II de Bourbon. (1621-1686) French commander.

MacArthur, Douglas. (1880-1964) World War I officer, World War II commander general.

Marshall, George Catlett. (1880-1959)

World War II general, Chief of Staff.

Matsunaga, Masayuki "Spark." (1916-1990) World War II captain.

McCabe, William. (1915-1976) World War II Navajo code talker. Medal of Honor recipient.

McClelland, George Brinton. (1826-1885) Civil War general.

McGee, Anita Newcombe. (1846-1940) Army nurse corps founder, Spanish American War.

McKinley, William. (1843-1901) Civil War major.

McNamara, Robert Strange. (1916) World War II Army Air Force.

Meade, George Gordon. (1815-1872) Civil War general.

Miyamura, Hiroshi. (1925-) Korean War hero. Medal of Honor recipient.

Murphy, Audie. (1924-1971) World War II hero.

Nelson, Gaylord. (1916-) World War II hero.

Noble, Jordan. (1801-?) Drummer Boy Seminole War, War of 1812.

Parker, Ely Samuel. (1828-1895) Assistant to Ulysses S. Grant.

Patton, George C. (1885-1945) World War I, World War II general.

Pepperell, William. (1696-1759) Colonial officer.

Pershing, John Joseph. (1860-1948) World War I general.

Pickett, George Edward. (1825-1875) Civil War general.

Pierce, Ambrose. (1842-1914) Civil War soldier.

Pierce, Franklin. (1804-1869) Mexican War general.

Pinchback, Pinckeny Benton Stewart "P. B. S." (1837-1921) Civil War captain.

Pippin, Horace. (1888-1946) World War I soldier.

Powell, Colin. (1937-) Chair Joint Chiefs of Staff, Vietnam War infantry officer, Gulf War general.

Powell, John Wesley. (1834-1902) Civil War soldier.

Powell, William J. (1897-1942) World War I pilot.

Reagan, Ronald. (1911-2004) World War II

Army Air Force second lieutenant.

Red Cloud, Mitchell, Jr. (1924-) Korean War hero. Medal of Honor recipient.

Reifel, Ben. (1906-1990) World War II lieutenant colonel.

Ridgway, Matthew Bunker. (1895-1993) World War II general, Supreme Commander of Allied Forces in Europe, Chief of Staff.

Rivers, Ruben. (1918-1944) World War II hero. Medal of Honor recipient.

Rogers, Robert. (1731-1795) French-Indian War soldier.

Rommel, Erwin. (1891-1944) German World War II commander.

Rowny, Edward L. (1917-) Career soldier. Korean War, Vietnam War, World War II.

Russell, Harold. (1914-2002) World War II.

Schwarzkopf, Norman. (1934-) Gulf War general, Vietnam War commander.

Scott, Winfield. (1786-1866) War of 1812 general, Mexican War.

Sequoyah. (1770-1843) Creek War soldier.

Serling, Rod. (1924-1975) World War II.

Sheridan, Philip Henry. (1831-1888) Civil War general.

Sherman, Willliam Tecumseh. (1820-1891) Civil War general.

Stillwell, Joseph W. (1883-1946) World War II general.

Stowers, Freddie. (1896-1918) World War I corporal. Medal of Honor recipient.

Stuart James Ewell Brown. "Jeb." (1833-1864) Civil War general.

Swinton, Ernest. (1868-1951) English major general.

Taylor, Telford. (1908-1998) World War II brigadier general, colonel, Nuremberg Trials jurist.

Taylor, Zachary. (1784-1850) Seminole War general, War of 1812.

Thomas, George Henry. (1816-1870) Civil War general.

Thompson, William. (1927-1950) Korean War hero. Medal of Honor recipient.

Tinker, Clarence L. (1887-1942) Osage Indian World War I Army Air Corps pilot, World War II major general.

Truman, Harry S. (1884-1972) World War I captain.

Van Raalte, Jim. (unknown) World War II

soldier, liberator of concentration camps.

Veeck, Bill. (1914-1986) World War II soldier.

Velazquez, Loreta Janeta. (1842-?) Civil War soldier, disguised as man.

Vogelsang, Peter. (1815-1887) Civil War lieutenant.

Walker, Mary Edwards. (1832-1919) Civil War surgeon.

Wally, Augustus. (unknown) Spanish American War buffalo soldier.

Walsh, Mary. (1950-) Vietnam War physical therapist.

Westmoreland, William C. (1914-) Vietnam War Chief of Staff, World War II.

Williams, Moses. (d. 1899) Indian War soldier.

Wolfe, James. (1727-1759) English army general.

York, Alvin Cullum. (1887-1964) World War I hero.

Young, Charles. (1864-1922) Career soldier, World War I officer.

Artists

See Cartoonists and Caricaturists; Engravers; Illustrators; Jewelry Designers; Mixed-Media Artists; Painters; Potters and Ceramicists; Printmakers; Sculptors.

Arts, Patrons of

D'Este, Beatrice. (1475-1497) Italian.

D'Este, Isabella. (1474-1539) Italian.

Geoffrin, Thérèse Roget. (1699-1777) French.

Macdowell, Marian. (1857-1956)

Medici, Lorenzo de. (1449-1492) Italian.

Asian-Americans

Ahn, Chang-Ho. (1878-1938) Human rights activist, born Korea.

Ahn, Philip. (1911-1978) Actor.

Akiyoshi, Toshiko. (1929-) Bandleader, composer, jazz musician, born China.

Aruego, Jose. (1932-) Children's author, illustrator, born Philippines.

Bemis, Polly. (Lalu Nathay) (1853-1933) Pioneer, born China.

Boissonnault, Masako. (1944-) Entrepreneur interior design.

Bulosan, Carlos. (1911-1956) Author, born Philippines.

Chandrasekhar, Subrahmanyan. (1910-1995) Astrophysicist, born Pakistan. Nobel Prize winner.

Chang, Michael. (1972-) Tennis player.

Cheng, Nien. (1915-) Author, political activist and prisoner, born China.

Chennault, Anna. (1925-) Political activist, born China.

Chern, Shiing-Shen. (1911-) Educator, mathematician, born China.

Chin, Karen. (1952-) Paleontologist, born Canada.

Chin, Leann. (1933-) Entrepreneur restaurants.

Cho, Margaret. (1969-) Actor.

Choi, Sook Nyul. (1937-) Children's and young adult author, born Korea.

Chow, Amy. (1978-) Olympic gymnast.

Chu, Paul Ching-Wu. (1941-) Physicist, born China.

Chung, Contance Vu-Hwa "Connie." (1946-) Broadcast journalist.

Chung, Myung-Whun. (1953-) Conductor, musician, born Korea.

Cordova, Dorothy. (1932-) Archivist, community activist.

Cordova, Fred. (1931-) Archivist, community activist.

Cruz, Philip Vera. (1904-) Labor leader, born Philippines.

Fong, Hiram. (1907-) Senator.

Gramm, Wendy. (1945-) Economist.

Grimmesey, Tevry. (1931-) World War II girl in detainee camp for Japanese-Americans.

Hagedorn, Jessica. (1949-) Author, born Philippines.

Hamanaka, Sheila. (1949-) Children's author, illustrator.

Hayakawa, Samuel Ichiye. (1906-1992) Educator, senator, scholar, born Canada.

Hayakawa, Sessue. (Kintaro) (1890-1973) Actor, born Japan.

Ho, David. (1952-) AIDS researcher, medical researcher, physician, born Taiwan.

Hom, Nancy. (1949-) Painter.

Howe, James Wong. (1899-1976) Filmmaker.

Hwang, David Henry. (1957-) Playwright.

Inouye, Daniel. (1924-) Attorney, senator, World War II Army captain.

Kahanamoku, Duke. (1890-1968) Hawaiian surfer, olympic swimmer.

Ka'lulani. (1875-1899) Hawaiian princess.

Kang, Younghill. (1903-1973) Author, educator, born Korea.

Khorana, Har Gobind. (1922-) Chemist, geneticist, born India. Nobel Prize winner.

Kim, Willyce. (1946-) Author, poet.

King, Charles Edward. (1879-1950) Bandleader, composer, publisher, born Hawaii.

Kingman, Dong. (1911-2000) Painter.

Kingston, Maxine Hong. (1940-) Author, educator.

Kuramato, June. (1948-) Jazz musician, born Japan.

Kwan, Michelle. (1980-) Olympic figure skater.

Kyoko, Ina. (1972-) Olympic figure skater, born Japan.

Lee, Bruce. (1940-1973) Actor, martial artist.

Lee, K.W. (1928-) Journalist, born Korea.

Lee, Li-Young. (1957-) Poet, born Indonesia.

Lee, Marie G. (1964-) Young adult author.

Lee, Sammy. (1920-) Olympic diver, physician.

Lee, Tsung Dao. (1926-) Physicist, born China. Nobel Prize winner.

Leonard, Andy. (1968-) Weightlifter, born Vietnam.

Lew Chew. (1866-?) Gold miner, born China.

Lewis, Loida Nicolas. (1942-) Attorney, author, entrepreneur food conglomerate, born Philippines.

Liliuokalani, Lydia. (1838-1917) Hawaiian composer, musician, queen.

Lin, Maya Ying. (1960-) Architect, sculptor.

Liu, Hung. (1948-) Painter, born China.

Lord, Bette Bao. (1938-) Author, born China.

Louganis, Greg. (1960-) Olympic diver.

Ma, Yo-Yo. (1955-) Musician, born France.

Malo, Davida. (1795-1853) Hawaiian translator.

Manalapit, Pablo. (1891-1969) Hawaiian labor leader, born Philippines.

Mathai-Davis, Prema. (1950-) Human rights activist, women's rights activist, Director YWCA, born India.

Matsui, Robert. (1941-) Congressman.

Matsunaga, Masayuki "Spark." (1916-1990) Hawaiian attorney, senator, World War II Army captain.

Mehta, Zubin. (1936-) Conductor, born India.

Midori. (1971-) Musician, born Japan.

Mineta, Norman. (1931-) Cabinet member, congressman.

Mink, Patsy Takemoto. (1927-2002) Attorney, congresswoman.

Miyamura, Hiroshi. (1925-) Korean War Army hero. Medal of Honor recipient.

Mori, Kyoko. (1957-) Young adult author, born Japan.

Mori, Toshio. (1910-1980) Author, born Japan.

Mukherjee, Bharti. (1940-) Author, born India.

Mura, David. (1952-) Poet.

Nair, Malathy. (unknown) Chemist, food scientist, born India.

Narahashi, Keiko. (1959-) Children's author, illustrator, born Japan.

Natori, Josefina "Josie" Cruz. (1947-) Entrepreneur fashion designer, financier, born Philippines.

Ng Poon Chew. (1866-1931) Editor newspaper, spiritual leader, born China.

Ngor Haing. (1951-1996) Actor, human rights activist, physician, born Cambodia.

Nguyen, Dustin. (1962-) Actor, born Vietnam.

Noguchi, Constance Tom. (1948-) Chemist, medical researcher.

Noguchi, Isamu. (1904-1988) Sculptor.

Nur, Nawrose. (1981-) Chess player, born India.

Obata, Chiura. (1888-1975) Painter, born Japan.

Okita, Dwight. (1958-) Musician, playwright, poet.

Ondaatje, Michael. (1943-) Author, filmmaker, playwright, poet, born Sri Lanka.

Onizuka, Ellison. (1946-1986) Astronaut.

Ozawa, Seiji. (1935-) Conductor, born Japan.

Paik, June. (1932-) Composer, mixed media artist, born Korea.

Pei, Ieah Ming "I. M." (1917-) Architect, born China. Presidential Medal of Freedom recipient.

Pran, Dith. (1942-) Journalist, born Cambodia.

Pudaite, Rochunga. (1927-) Bible translator, born India.

Pukui, Mary Kawena. (1895-1986) Hawaiian folklorist, linguist.

Santos, Bienvenido N. (1911-1992) Author, born Philippines.

Saund, Dalip Singh. (1899-1973) Congressman, born India.

Say, Allen. (1937-) Children's author, illustrator, photographer, born Japan.

Sharma, Prem. (1943-) Human rights activist, women's rights activist, born India.

Shimomura, Tsutomu. (1965-) Computer scientist, physicist, born Japan.

Shoong, Joe. (1879-1961) Entrepreneur financier, philanthropist.

Singh, Sirdar Jagjit. (1897-1976) Entrepreneur fabrics, born India.

Suzuki, Daisetz Teitan "D. T." (1870-1966) Educator, philosopher, translator, born Japan.

Tan, Amy. (1952-) Author.

Tape, Mary McGladery. (1857-1928) Children's rights activist, painter, photographer, born China.

Tien, Chang-Lin. (1935-) Educator, born China.

Ting, Samuel Chao Chung. (1936) Physicist. Nobel Prize winner.

Tonegawa, Susumu. (1939-) Molecular biologist, immunologist, medical researcher, born Japan. Nobel Prize winner.

Trinh, Eugene H. (1950-) Astronaut, physicist, born Vietnam.

Tsai, Gerard, Jr. (1928-) Financier, born China.

Uchida, Yoshiko. (1921-1992) Children's author.

Ung, Han. (1968-) Author, playwright, born Philippines.

Wadhwa, Meenakshi. (1967-) Astronomer, space scientist, born India.

Wang, An. (1920-1990) Electrical engineer, entrepreneur computers, born China.

Wang, Vera. (1949-) Fashion designer.

Wang, Wayne. (1949-) Filmmaker.

Wong, Anna May. (1905-1961) Actor.

Wong, Jade Snow. (1922-) Author, ceramicist.

Wong-Staal, Flossie. (1947-) Medical researcher, born China.

Wu, Chien Shiung. (1912-1997) Nuclear physicist, born China.

Yamaguchi, Kristi. (1971-) Olympic figure skater.

Yamamoto, Hisaye. (1921-) Author.

Yamasaki, Minoru. (1912-1986) Architect.

Yang, Chen Ning. (1922-) Physicist, born China. Nobel Prize winner.

Yang, Jerry. (1968-) Entrepreneur Internet.

Yep, Laurence. (1948-) Children's author.

Yin, Luoth. (1950-) Community worker, social worker, born Cambodia.

Assassins, Presidential

Includes those who attempted to kill the President of the United States but did not succeed.

Booth, John Wilkes. (1838-1865) Killed Abraham Lincoln.

Collazo, Oscar. (1914-1994) Puerto Rican, attempted to kill Harry S. Truman.

Czolgosz, Leon. (1873-1901) Killed William McKinley, born Poland.

Frome, Lynette "Squeaky." (1948-) Attempted to kill Gerald Ford.

Guiteau, Charles Julius. (1841-1882) Killed James Garfield.

Hinckley, John Warnock, Jr. (1966-) Attempted to kill Ronald Reagan.

Lawrence, Richard. (1800-1861) Attempted to kill Andrew Jackson.

Moore, Sara Jane. (1930-) Attempted to kill Gerald Ford.

Oswald, Lee Harvey. (1939-1963) Killed John Fitzgerald Kennedy.

Schrank, John. (1876-1943) Attempted to kill Theodore Roosevelt.

Torresola, Griselio. (1925-1950) Puerto Rican, attempted to kill Harry S. Truman.

Zangara, Giuseppe "Joe." (1900-1933) Attempted to kill Franklin Delano Roosevelt, born Italy.

Assyrians
Semiramis. (c. 2000 B.C.) Warrior queen,
  legendary.

Astronauts
Aldrin, Edwin, Jr. "Buzz." (1930-)
Armstrong, Neil. (1930-)
Bean, Alan. (1932-)
Bluford, Guion Steward. (1942-)
Bolden, Charles. (1946-)
Cernan, Eugene. (1934-)
Chang-Diaz, Franklin R. (1950-) born Vene-
  zuela.
Collins, Eileen M. (1956-)
Conrad, Charles "Pete," Jr. (1930-1999)
Davis, N. Jan. (1953-)
Duke, Charles. (1935-)
Dunbar, Bonnie. (1949-)
Dwight, Edward J., Jr. (1933-)
Gagarin, Yuri. (1934-1968) Russian cosmo-
  naut.
Glenn, John. (1921-)
Gregory, Frederick. (1941-)
Grissom, Virgil I. "Gus." (1926-1967)
Harris, Bernard. (1956-)
Irwin, James. (1930-1991)
Ivins, Marsha. (1951-)
Jemison, Mae. (1956-)
Lee, Mark C. (1952-)
Leonov, Alexei. (1934-) Russian.
Lucid, Shannon. (1943-)
McAuliffe, Christa. (1948-1986)
McCandless, Bruce, II. (1932-)
McNair, Ronald. (1950-1986)
Mitchell, Edgar. (1930-)
Ochoa, Ellen. (1959-)
Onizuka, Ellison. (1946-1986)
Resnick, Judith. (1949-1986)
Ride, Sally. (1951-)
Savitskaya, Svetlana. (1948-) Russian cos-
  monaut.
Schirra, Walter Marty "Wally," Jr. (1923-)
Schmidt, Harrison "Jack." (1935-)
Scott, David. (1932-)
Seddon, Margaret Rhea. (1947-)
Shepard, Alan B. (1923-1998)
Slayton, Donald K. "Deke." (1924-1993)
Still, Susan. (1961-)
Sullivan, Kathryn. (1951-)
Tereshkova, Valentina V. (1937-) Russian
  cosmonaut.

Titov, Vladimir. (1947-) Russian cosmo-
  naut.
Trinh, Eugene H. (1950-) born Vietnam.
Young, John Watts. (1930-)

Astronomers
Banneker, Benjamin. (1731-1806)
Brahe, Sophie. (1556-1643) Danish.
Brahe, Tycho. (1546-1601) Danish.
Branting, Karl. (1860-1925) Swedish.
Burbridge, E. Margaret. (1919-) English.
Burnell, Jocelyn Bell. (1943-) Irish.
Cannon, Annie Jump. (1863-1941)
Copernicus, Nicolaus. (1473-1543) Polish.
Eratostheses. (276-194 B.C.) Greek.
Faber, Sandra. (unknown)
Fleming, Williamina Patron Stevens. (1857-
  1911) born Scotland.
Galilei, Galileo. (1564-1642) Italian.
Hale, George Ellery. (1868-1938)
Halley, Edmund. (1656-1742) English.
Herschel, Caroline. (1750-1848) English.
Herschel, Sir John. (1792-1871) English.
Herschel, William. (1738-1822) English.
Hogg, Helen Battles Sawyer. (1905-1993)
  Canadian.
Hubble, Edwin. (1889-1953)
Huygens, Christiaan. (1629-1695) Dutch.
Hypathia. (355-415) Egyptian.
Jernigan, Tamara. (1955-)
Kepler, Johannes. (1571-1630) German.
Khayyam, Omar. (1048-1131) Persian.
Khwarizmi, Abu Ja-Far Muhammad Ibn
  Musa-al. (780-850) Arab Muslim.
Langley, Samuel Pierpont. (1834-1906)
Leavitt, Henrietta Swan. (1868-1921)
Livingstone, David. (1813-1873) Scottish.
Lowell, Percival. (1855-1916)
Maury, Antonia C. (1866-1952)
Mitchell, Maria. (1818-1889)
Payne-Gasposchkin, Cecilia. (1900-1979)
  born England.
Pickering, William. (1858-1938)
Ptolemy. (100-170) Greek.
Pytheas. (fl. 300 B.C.) Greek.
Rubin, Vera Cooper. (1928-)
Sagan, Carl. (1934-1996)
Shapley, Harlow. (1885-1972)
Somerville, Mary Fairfax. (1780-1872) Scot.
Wadhwa, Meenakshi. (1967-) born India.
Whitney, Mary Watson. (1847-1920)

Zacuto, Abraham. (1452-1515) Spanish.

Athletes

See Baseball Players; Basketball Players;
   Biathlon, Decathlon; Pentathlon Athletes;
   Bicyclists; Boaters; Bobsledders; Bowlers;
   Boxers; Curlers; Divers; Football Players;
   Golfers; Gymnasts; Hockey Players;
   Jockeys; Judo; Kayakers; Martial Artists;
   Olympic Athletes; Racquetball Players;
   Runners and Sprinters; Skaters; Skiers;
   Soccer Players; Softball Players; Swim-
   mers; Tennis Players; Track and Field
   Athletes; Volleyball Players; Weight-
   lifters; Wheel Chair Athletes; Wrestlers.

Attorneys

Abzug, Bella. (1920-1988)
Acheson, Dean. (1893-1971)
Adams, John. (1735-1826)
Allen, Florence Ellinwood. (1884-1966)
Arthur, Chester A. (1829-1886)
Asser, Tobias. (1838-1913) Dutch.
Bailey, F. Lee. (1933-)
Baker, James. (1930-)
Beernaert, Auguste. (1829-1912) Belgian.
Benenson, Peter. (1921-)
Benjamin, Judah Philip. (1811-1884)
Black, Hugo. (1886-1971)
Bourgeois, Léon. (1851-1925) French.
Brandeis, Louis. (1856-1941)
Briand, Aristide. (1862-1932) French.
Brown, Ronald. (1941-1996)
Burke, Yvonne Braithwaite. (1932-)
Burr, Aaron. (1756-1836)
Butler, Benjamin Franklin. (1818-1893)
Campbell, Bonnie. (1948-)
Carter, Pamela. (1950-)
Cary, Mary Ann Shadd. (1822-1893)
Cassin, René. (1887-1976) French.
Catlin, George. (1796-1872)
Cecil, Robert. (1864-1958) English.
Cicero. (106-43 B.C.) Roman.
Clinton, Hillary Rodham. (1947-)
Clinton, William Jefferson "Bill." (1946)
Conley, Lyda. (1869-1946)
Coolidge, Calvin. (1872-1923)
D'Arcy, William Knox. (1849-1917)
   English.
Darrow, Clarence. (1857-1938)
Davis, John W. (1873-1955)

Dawes, Charles G. (1865-1951)
de Klerk, Fredrik Willem "F. W." (1936)
   South African.
Deer, Ada. (1935-) Menominee Indian.
Dees, Morris. (1936-)
Deloria, Philip Sam (unknown) Yankton
   Dakota Indian.
Dickinson, John. (1732-1808)
Dinkins, David. (1927-)
Dulles, John Foster. (1888-1959)
Eastman, Crystal. (1881-1928)
Echohawk, John. (1945-) Pawnee Indian.
Echohawk, Larry. (1948-) Pawnee Indian.
Edelman, Marian Wright. (1939-)
Esquiroz, Margarita. (1945-)
Fairstein, Linda. (1947-)
Ferraro, Geraldine. (1935-)
Fielding, Henry. (1707-1754) English.
Fillmore, Millard. (1800-1874)
Ford, Gerald R. (1913-)
Frank, Hans. (1900-1946) German.
Gibbs, Mifflin. (1823-1915)
Ginsburg, Ruth Bader. (1933-)
Gobat, Albert. (1843-1914) Swiss.
Hamilton, Andrew. (1676-1741)
Harlan, John. (1833-1911)
Harrison, Benjamin. (1833-1901)
Haskells, Ella Knowles. (1860-1911)
Hastie, William H. (1904-1976)
Hayes, Rutherford B. (1822-1893)
Heyward, Thomas, Jr. (1746-1809)
Hiss, Alger. (1904-1996)
Holmes, Oliver Wendell. (1841-1935)
Hooper, William. (1742-1790)
Hopkinson, Francis. (1737-1791)
Houston, Charles. H. (1895-1950)
Hughes, Charles Evan. (1862-1948)
Hull, Cordell. (1871-1955)
Huntingdon, Samuel. (1731-1796)
Inouye, Daniel. (1924-)
Ireland, Patricia. (1945-)
Jackson, Robert H. (1892-1954)
Jay, John. (1745-1829)
Johnson, James Weldon. (1871-1938)
Jordan, Barbara. (1936-1996)
Jordan, Vernon E., Jr. (1935-)
Kelley, Florence. (1859-1932)
Kellogg, Frank Billings. (1856-1937)
Kelly, Sharon Pratt. (1944-)
Kennedy, Florence. (1916-2000)
Kennedy, John F., Jr. (1960-1998)

Kennedy, Robert Francis. (1925-1968)
Kuntzler, William. (1919-1995)
La Fontaine, Henri. (1854-1943) Belgian.
Lamas, Carlos Saavedra. (1878-1959) Argentine.
Lewis, Loida Nicolas. (1942-) born Philippines.
Lewis, Reginald F. (1942-1993)
Lincoln, Abraham. (1809-1865)
Lockwood, Belva Ann. (1830-1917)
Lyell, Sir Charles. (1797-1875) English.
Lynch, Thomas, Jr. (1749-1779)
MacBride, Seán. (1904-1988) Irish.
Mandela, Nelson. (1918-) South African.
Marsh, George Perkins. (1801-1882)
Marshall, John. (1755-1835)
Marshall, Thurgood. (1908-1993)
Martinez, Vilma. (1943-)
Matsunaga, Masayuki "Spark." (1916-1990)
McKean, Thomas. (1734-1817)
McKinley, William. (1843-1901)
Mink, Patsy Takemoto. (1927-2002)
Montagu, Ewen. (1901-1985) English.
Morris, Gouverneur. (1752-1816)
Motley, Constance Baker. (1921-)
Murray, Pauli. (1910-1995)
Nader, Ralph. (1934-)
Nelson, Gaylord. (1916-)
Noah, Mordecai Manuel. (1785-1851)
Norton, Eleanor Holmes. (1937-)
O'Connor, Sandra Day. (1930-)
Paca, William. (1740-1795)
Page, Alan. (1945-)
Paine, Robert Treat. (1731-1814)
Paterson, William. (1745-1806) born Ireland.
Paul, Alice. (1885-1977)
Peña, Federico. (1947-)
Penn, John. (1740-1788)
Pierce, Franklin. (1804-1869)
Pliny the Younger. (61-113) Roman.
Ray, Charlotte E. (1850-1911)
Read, George. (1733-1798)
Renault, Louis. (1843-1918) French.
Reno, Janet. (1938-)
Roc, John S. (1825-1866)
Roosevelt, Franklin Delano. (1882-1945)
Root, Elihu. (1845-1937)
Ross, George. (1730-1779)
Sampson, Edith. (1901-1980)
Sato, Eisaku. (1901-1975) Japanese.

Schroeder, Patricia. (1940-)
Schulte, Eduard Reinhold Karl. (1891-1966) German.
Seward, William. (1801-1872)
Sherman, Roger. (1721-1793)
Smith, Holland M. (1882-1967)
Smith, James. (1719-1806) born Ireland.
Starrs, James. (1930-)
Stephens, John Lloyd. (1805-1852)
Stimson, Henry. (1867-1950)
Stockton, Richard. (1730-1781)
Stone, Thomas. (1743-1787)
Straker, David Augustus. (1842-1908)
Taft, William H. (1857-1930)
Taney, Roger Brooke. (1777-1864)
Taylor, Telford. (1908-1998)
tenBroek, Jacobus. (1911-1968) born Canada.
Tracy, Benjamin. (1830-1915)
Van Buren, Martin. (1782-1862)
Walker, Thomas. (1850-1935)
Warren, Earl. (1891-1974)
Webster, Daniel. (1782-1852)
Wecht, Cyril. (1931-)
Weddington, Sarah. (1945-)
Weinberger, Caspar W. (1917-)
Welch, Joseph. (1890-1960)
West, W. Richard, Jr. (1943-)
White, George Henry. (1852-1918)
Wilder, L. Douglas. (1931-)
Williams, George Washington. (1849-1891)
Wilson, James. (1742-1798) born Scotland.
Wright, Jonathan Jasper. (1840-1885)
Wythe, George. (1726-1806)

Australians

See also Immigrants to United States, Australian.
Billiris, Manuel. (1975-) In-line skater.
Burnet, Sir Frank MacFarlane. (1899-1985) Medical researcher, physician. Nobel Prize winner.
Childe, Vere Gordon. (1892-1957) Archaeologist.
Court, Margaret Smith. (1942-) Tennis player.
Florey, Lord Howard Walter. (1898-1968) Medical researcher, pathologist. Nobel Prize winner.
Fraser, Dawn. (1937-) Olympic swimmer.
Freeman, Cathy. (1973-) Olympic track and

field athlete.

Gatty, Harold Charles. (1903-1957) Aviation pioneer.

George, Emma. (1974-) Olympic track and field athlete.

Hume, Hamilton. (1797-1873) Explorer.

Kelly, Ned. (1855-1880) Outlaw.

Kenny, Elizabeth. (1880-1952) Medical researcher, World War I nurse.

Laver, Rod. (1938-) Tennis player.

Melba, Nellie. (1861-1931) Opera singer.

Nolan, Sidney. (1917-1988) Painter.

Seager, Joy Debenham. (1899-1991) Human rights activist, physician.

Smith, Charles Kingsford. (1897-1935) Aviation pioneer.

Timms, Michele. (1965-) Olympic basketball player.

Wilkins, Sir George Hubert. (1888-1958) Adventurer, aviator, explorer, World War I photographer.

Wills, John. (1833-1861) Explorer.

Austrians

See also Immigrants to United States, Austrian.

Berg, Alan Alban. (1885-1935) Composer.

Buber, Martin. (1878-1965) Philosopher.

Chotek, Sophie. (1868-1914) Political activist, wife of Archduke Ferdinand, World War I victim.

Frankl, Viktor. (1905-1997) Holocaust survivor, psychotherapist.

Freud, Sigmund. (1856-1939) Physician, psychoanalyst.

Fried, Alfred. (1864-1921) Journalist, peace activist, publisher. Nobel Peace Prize winner.

Haydn, Franz Joseph. (1732-1809) Composer.

Herzl, Theodor. (1860-1904) Author, journalist, spiritual leader, born Hungary.

Kino, Eusebio. (1645-1711) Explorer, missionary, spiritual leader.

Klimt, Gustav. (1862-1918) Painter.

Loeb, Ilse. (unknown) Holocaust survivor.

Mahler, Gustav. (1860-1911) Composer, conductor.

Maria Theresa. (1717-1780) Archduchess, empress.

Mendel, Gregor. (1822-1884) Geneticist.

Moser-Proell, Annemarie. (1953-) Olympic skier.

Mozart, Wolfgang Amadeus. (1756-1791) Composer.

Paradis, Maria Theresia von. (1759-1824) Composer, musician.

Pauli, Wolfgang. (1900-1958) Physicist. Nobel Prize winner.

Pfeiffer, Ida. (1797-1858) Adventurer, author.

Ronge, Maximilian. (unknown) World War I spy.

Schubert, Franz Peter. (1797-1828) Composer.

Stangl, Franz. (1908-1971) Nazi war criminal.

Steiner, Rudolf. (1861-1925) Author, educator, spiritual leader.

Stojka, Karl. (1931-) Holocaust survivor.

Suttner, Bertha von. (1843-1914) Author, peace activist. Nobel Peace Prize winner.

Tilles, Helen. (unknown) Holocaust survivor.

Waldheim, Kurt. (1918-) Nazi war criminal, president, secretary general of United Nations.

Webern, Anton von. (1883-1945) Composer.

Wiesenthal, Simon. (1908-) Author, Holocaust survivor, Nazi hunter, born Poland. Presidential Medal of Freedom recipient.

Authors

See also Historians; Journalists; Playwrights; Poets; Screenwriters; Songwriters.

Authors, Children and Young Adult

Alcott, Louisa May. (1832-1888)

Alger, Horatio. (1832-1899)

Allen, Thomas B. (1928-)

Andersen, Hans Christian. (1805-1875) Danish.

Anno, Mitsumasa. (1926-) Japanese.

Aruego, Jose. (1932-) born Philippines.

Baum, L. Frank. (1856-1919)

Blume, Judy. (1938-)

Brooks, Bruce. (1950-)

Brown, Marcia. (1918-)

Brown, Margaret Wise. (1910-1952)

Bryan, Ashley. (1923-)

Burnett, Frances Hodgson. (1849-1924) born England.
Butler, Beverly. (1932-)
Byars, Betsy. (1928-)
Carle, Eric. (1929-)
Carroll, Lewis. *See* Dodgson, Charles.
Catalanotto, Peter. (1959-)
Chess, Victoria. (1939-)
Choi, Sook Nyul. (1937-) born Korea.
Cleary, Beverly. (1912-)
Clifton, Lucille. (1936-)
Cole, Joanna. (1944-)
Cooper, Floyd. (1959-)
Cullen, Countee. (1903-1946)
Cummings, Pat. (1950-)
Cushman, Karen. (1941-)
Dahl, Roald. (1916-1990) English.
Desimini, Lisa. (1964-)
Dillon, Diane. (1933-)
Dillon, Leo. (1933-)
Dodgson, Charles. (Lewis Carroll) (1832-1898) English.
Downing, Julie. (1956-)
Egielski, Richard. (1952-)
Ehlert, Lois. (1934-)
Ernst, Lisa Campbell. (1957-)
Feelings, Tom. (1933-2003)
Fink, Ida. (1921-) Israeli, born Poland.
Fleming, Denise. (1950-)
Freedman, Russell. (1929-)
Geisel, Theodor Seuss. (Dr. Seuss) (1904-1991)
Giovanni, Nikki. (1943-)
Greenfield, Eloise. (1929-)
Hale, Sarah Josepha Buell. (1788-1879)
Hamanaka, Sheila. (1949-)
Hamilton, Virginia. (1936-2002)
Hawkes, Kevin. (1959-)
Henkes, Kevin. (1960-)
Hinton, Susan "S. E." (1949-)
Hoban, Tana. (unknown)
Hopkins, Lee Bennett. (1938-)
Howe, James. (1946-)
Hurwitz, Johanna. (1937-)
Joyce, William. (1957-)
Kalman, Maira. (1949-)
Karas, G. Brian. (1957)
Kellogg, Steven. (1941-)
Kipling, Rudyard. (1865-1936) English.
Klein, Norma. (1938-1989)
Koningsburg, Elaine "E. L." (1930-)

Korczak, Janusz. (1878-1942) Polish.
Kuskin, Karla. (1933-)
Lattimore, Deborah Nourse. (1949-)
Le Guin, Ursula K. (1929-)
Le Sueur, Meridel. (1900-1996)
Lee, Marie G. (1964-)
L'Engle, Madeline. (1918-)
Lester, Julius. (1939-)
Lewin, Betsy. (1937-)
Lewin, Ted. (1935-)
Lewis, Clive Staples "C. S." (1898-1963) Irish.
Lindgren, Astrid. (1902-2002) Swedish.
Little, Jean. (1932-) Canadian.
Lord, Bette Bao. (1938-) born China.
Lowry, Lois. (1937-)
Marshall, James. (1942-1992)
Martin, Ann M. (1955-)
McCloskey, Robert. (1914-2003)
Milne, Alan Alexander "A. A." (1882-1956) English.
Mohr, Nicholasa. (1938-)
Montgomery, Lucy Maud "L. M." (1874-1942) Canadian.
Mori, Kyoko. (1957-) born Japan.
Mowat, Farley. (1921-) Canadian.
Myers, Walter Dean. (1937-)
Narahashi, Keiko. (1959-) born Japan.
Naylor, Phyllis Reynolds. (1933-)
Opie, Iona. (1923-) English.
Oxenbury, Helen. (1938-) English.
Paterson, Katherine. (1932-)
Paulsen, Gary. (1939-)
Peck, Richard. (1934-)
Perera, Hilda. (1926-) born Cuba.
Petry, Ann. (1911-1997)
Pinkney, Brian. (1961-)
Pinkney, Jerry. (1939-)
Potter, Beatrix. (1866-1943) English.
Primavera, Elise. (1955-)
Provensen, Alice. (1918-)
Provensen, Martin. (1916-1987)
Rawlings, Marjorie Kinnan. (1896-1953)
Ringgold, Faith. (1930-)
Rowling, Joanne Kathleen "J. K." (1965-)
Sandburg, Carl. (1878-1967)
Sasso, Sandy Eisenberg. (1947-)
Say, Allen. (1937-) born Japan.
Schwartz, Amy. (1954-)
Scieszka, Jon. (1954-)
Sendak, Maurice. (1928-)

Seuss, Dr. *See* Geisel, Theodor Seuss.
Simon, Seymour. (1931-)
Singer, Isaac Bashevis. (1904-1991) born Poland.
Sis, Peter. (1949-) born Czechoslovakia.
Smith, Lane. (1959-)
Soto, Gary. (1952-)
Steig, Jeanne. (1930-)
Steig, William. (1907-2003)
Stevenson, Robert Louis. (1850-1894) Scot.
Stine, Robert Lawrence "R. L." (1943-)
Taylor, Mildred. (1943-)
Uchida, Yoshiko. (1921-1992)
Van Allsburg, Chris. (1949-)
Voigt, Cynthia. (1942-)
Wells, Rosemary. (1943-)
White, Elwyn Brooks "E. B." (1899-1985)
Wiesner, David. (1956-)
Wilder, Laura Ingalls. (1867-1957)
Williams, Vera B. (1927-)
Wisniewski, David. (1953-2002)
Yep, Laurence. (1948-)
Yorinks, Arthur. (1953-)
Zelinsky, Paul. (1953-)
Zolotow, Charlotte. (1915-)

Authors, Fiction, African
Gordimer, Nadine. (1923-) South African.
Schreiner, Olive. (1855-1920) South African.
Soyinka, Wole. (1934-) Nigerian.

Authors, Fiction, American
Alcott, Louisa May. (1832-1888)
Alexie, Sherman. (1966-) Spokane-Coeur D'Alene Indian.
Allen, Paula Gunn. (1939-) Laguna Pueblo/Sioux Indian.
Alvarez, Julia. (1950-)
Anaya, Rudolfo. (1937-)
Anderson, Poul. (1926-2001)
Arthur, Elizabeth Ann. (1953-)
Asimov, Isaac. (1920-1992)
Baldwin, James. (1924-1987)
Bambera, Toni. (1939-1995)
Barnes, Djuna. (1892-1982)
Bellow, Saul. (1915-)
Bloch, Robert. (1917-1994)
Blume, Judy. (1938-)
Bontemps, Arnaud "Arna." (1902-1973)
Bradbury, Ray. (1920-)

Bromfield, Louis. (1896-1956)
Brown, Christy. (1932-1981)
Brown, Sterling Allen. (1901-1989)
Brown, William Wells. (1814-1884)
Buck, Pearl. (1892-1973)
Bulosan, Carlos. (1911-1956) born Philippines.
Burroughs, Edgar Rice. (1875-1950)
Butler, Octavia. (1947-)
Cahan, Abraham. (1860-1951) born Lithuania.
Campbell, Bebe Moore. (1950-)
Cather, Willa. (1873-1947)
Cheever, Susan. (1943-)
Chesnutt, Charles. (1858-1932)
Childress, Alice. (1920-1994)
Chopin, Kate. (1850-1904)
Cisneros, Sandra. (1954-)
Clancy, Tom. (1947-)
Clemens, Samuel. (Mark Twain) (1835-1910)
Cofer, Judith Ortiz. (1952-)
Cooper, James Fenimore. (1789-1851)
Crane, Stephen. (1871-1900)
Crichton, Michael. (1942-)
Cullen, Countee. (1903-1946)
Davis, Richard Harding. (1864-1916)
Dillard, Annie. (1945-)
Doolittle, Hilda "H. D." (1886-1961)
Douglas, Marjorie Stoneman. (1890-1998)
Dreiser, Theodore. (1871-1945)
Ellison, Ralph. (1919-1994)
Emerson, Ralph Waldo. (1803-1882)
Erdrich, Louise. (1954-)
Fairstein, Linda. (1947-)
Faulkner, William. (1897-1962)
Fitzgerald, F. Scott. (1896-1940)
Flagg, Fannie. (1944-)
Foote, Mary Hallock. (1847-1938)
Gaines, Ernest. (1933-)
Grafton, Sue. (1940-)
Gygax, Gary. (1938-)
Hagedorn, Jessica. (1949-) born Philippines.
Haley, Alex. (1921-1992)
Hammett, Dashiell. (1894-1961)
Harper, Frances E. W. (1825-1911)
Harte, Bret. (1836-1902)
Hawthorne, Nathaniel. (1804-1864)
Hay, John. (1838-1905)
Heinlein, Robert. (1907-1988)
Hemingway, Ernest Miller. (1899-1961)

Henry, O. *See* Porter, William Sydney.
Herbert, Frank. (1920-1986)
Hijuelos, Oscar. (1948-)
Himes, Chester. (1909-1984)
Irving, John. (1942-)
Irving, Washington. (1783-1859)
Isaacs, Susan. (1943-)
Jackson, Shirley. (1919-1965)
James, Henry. (1843-1916)
Janowitz, Tama. (1957-)
Johnson, James Weldon. (1871-1938)
Jong, Erica. (1942-)
Kang, Younghill. (1903-1973) born Korea.
Kerouac, Jack. (1922-1969)
Kim, Willyce. (1946-)
King, Stephen. (1947-)
Kingston, Maxine Hong. (1940-)
Koontz, Dean. (1945-)
Kosinski, Jerzy. (1933-1991) born Poland.
Larsen, Nella. (1891-1964)
Lawrence, D. H. (1885-1930) English.
Le Guin, Ursula K, (1929-)
Le Sueur, Meridel. (1900-1996)
Lewis, Sinclair. (1885-1951)
London, Jack. (1876-1916)
Lord, Bette Bao. (1938-) born China.
Lovecraft, H. P. (1890-1937)
MacLeish, Archibald. (1892-1982)
Mailer, Norman. (1923-)
Marshall, Paule. (1929-)
McKay, Claude. (1890-1948)
McMillan, Terry. (1951-)
Melville, Herman. (1819-1891)
Michener, James. (1907-1997)
Mitchell, Margaret. (1900-1948)
Mohr, Nicholasa. (1938-)
Momaday, N. Scott. (1934-) Kiowa Indian.
Moore, Alice Ruth. (1875-1935)
Mori, Toshio. (1910-1980) born Japan.
Morrison, Toni. (1931-)
Mourning Dove. (Christine Quintasket)
    (1888-1936) Okanogan Indian.
Mukherjee, Bharti. (1940-) born India.
Norton, Alice Mary. (Andre) (1912-)
Oates, Joyce Carol. (1938-)
O'Connor, Flannery. (1925-1964)
Ondaatje, Michael. (1943-) born Sri Lanka.
Ortiz, Simon. (1941-) Acoma Indian.
Ozick, Cynthia. (1928-)
Paley, Grace. (1922-)
Parker, Dorothy. (1893-1967)

Parton, Sara Payson. (Fanny Fern) (1811-
    1872)
Petry, Ann. (1911-1997)
Pierce, Ambrose. (1842-1914)
Poe, Edgar Allan. (1809-1849)
Pohl, Frederik. (1919-)
Porter, Katherine Anne. (1890-1980)
Porter, William Sydney. (O. Henry) (1862-
    1910)
Powell, Dawn. (1897-1965)
Rawlings, Marjorie Kinnan. (1896-1953)
Rice, Anne. (1941-)
Rinehart, Mary Roberts. (1876-1958)
Salinger, J. D. (1919-)
Sandburg, Carl. (1878-1967)
Sandoz, Mari. (1896-1966)
Santiago, Esmeralda. (1948-) Puerto Rican.
Santos, Bienvenido N. (1911-1992) born
    Philippines.
See, Carolyn. (1934-)
Serling, Rod. (1924-1975)
Shange, Ntozake. (1948-)
Shepard, Sam. (1943-)
Singer, Isaac Bashevis. (1904-1991) born
    Poland.
Steel, Danielle. (1947-)
Stein, Gertrude. (1874-1946)
Steinbeck, John. (1902-1968)
Stowe, Harriet Beecher. (1811-1896)
Tan, Amy. (1952-)
Toomer, Jean. (1894-1967)
Twain, Mark. *See* Clemens, Samuel.
Tyler, Anne. (1941-)
Ung, Han. (1968-) born Philippines.
Updike, John. (1932-)
Van Vechten, Carl. (1880-1964)
Vaz, Katherine. (unknown) born Portugal.
Villasensor, Victor. (1940-)
Vonnegut, Kurt. (1922-)
Walker, Alice. (1944-)
Walker, Margaret. (1915-1998)
Wells, Rebecca. (1952-)
Welty, Eudora. (1909-2001)
West, Dorothy. (1907-1998)
Wharton, Edith. (1862-1937)
White, Walter. (1893-1955)
Wiesel, Elie. (1928-) born Transylvania
    (Romania)
Wilder, Thornton. (1897-1975)
Wilson, Harriet E. Adams. (1827?-1863?)
Wolfe, Tom. (1931-)

Wright, Richard. (1908-1960)
Yamamoto, Hisaye. (1921-)
Yglesias, José. (1919-1995)

Authors, Fiction, Asian
Murasaki, Shikibu. (970?-1030?) Japanese.
Tagore, Rabindranth. (1861-1941) Indian.

Authors, Fiction, Canadian
Atwood, Margaret. (1939-)
Montgomery, Lucy Maud "L. M." (1874-1942)

Authors, Fiction, English
Austen, Jane. (1775-1817)
Bronte, Anne. (1820-1849)
Bronte, Charlotte. (1816-1855)
Bronte, Emily. (1818-1848)
Bulwer-Lytton, Edward. (1803-1873)
Bunyan, John. (1628-1688)
Cartland, Barbara. (1901-2000)
Christie, Agatha. (1891-1976)
Conrad, Joseph. (1857-1924) born Poland.
Defoe, Daniel. (1660-1731)
Dickens, Charles. (1812-1870)
Eliot, George. *See* Evans, Mary Ann.
Evans, Mary Ann. (George Eliot) (1819-1880)
Fielding, Henry. (1707-1754)
Hall, Radclyffe. (1886-1943)
Hardy, Thomas. (1840-1928)
Huxley, Aldous. (1894-1963)
Kempe, Margery. (1373-1440)
Kipling, Rudyard. (1865-1936)
Lawrence, D.H. (1885-1930)
Manley, Mary. (1663-1724)
Mansfield, Katherine. (1888-1923) born New Zealand.
Maugham, W. Somerset. (1874-1965)
Murdoch, Iris. (1919-1999)
Orwell, George. (1903-1950)
Sayers, Dorothy L. (1893-1957)
Shelley, Mary. (1797-1851)
Swift, Jonathan. (1667-1745)
Thackeray, William Makepeace. (1811-1863)
Weldon, Fay. (1931-)
Wells, Hubert George "H. G." (1866-1946)
Wollstonecraft, Mary. (1759-1797)

Woolf, Virginia. (1882-1941)

Authors, Fiction, European
Appelfeld, Aharon. (1932-) Ukrainian.
Arouet, François Marie. (Voltaire) (1694-1778) French.
Beauvoir, Simone de. (1908-1986) French.
Boccaccio, Giovanni. (1313-1375) Italian.
Cervantes, Miguel de. (1547-1616) Spanish.
Deledda, Grazia. (1871-1936) Italian.
Dupin, Amandine Aurore Lucie. (George Sand) (1804-1876) French.
Hesse, Herman. (1877-1962) Swiss, born Germany.
Hugo, Victor. (1802-1885) French.
Lustig, Arnost. (1926-) Czech.
Pizan, Christine de. (1365-1430) French.
Rabelais, François. (1495-1553) French.
Saint-Exupéry, Antoine de. (1900-1944) French.
Sand, George. *See* Dupin, Amandine Aurore Lucie.
Stael, Madame Anna Louise Germaine de. (1766-1817) French.
Verne, Jules. (1828-1905) French.
Voltaire. *See* Arouet, François Marie.
Zola, Emile. (1840-1902) French.

Authors, Fiction, Irish/Scottish
Doyle, Sir Arthur Conan. (1859-1930) Scottish.
Joyce, James. (1882-1941) Irish.
Scott, Sir Walter. (1771-1832) Scottish.
Shaw, George Bernard. (1856-1950) Irish.
Stevenson, Robert Louis. (1850-1894) Scottish.

Authors, Fiction, Latin
Allende, Isabel. (1942-) Chilean.
Amado, Jorge. (1912-2001) Brazilian.
Borges, Jorge Luis. (1899-1986) Argentine.
Castellanos, Rosario. (1925-1974) Mexican.
Cortazar, Julio. (1914-1984) Argentine.
Fuentes, Carlos. (1928-) Mexican.
Llosa, Mario Vargas. (1936-) Peruvian.
Marquez, Gabriel Garcia. (1928-) Colombian.
Vega, Garcilaso de la. (1539-1616) Peruvian.

Authors, Fiction, Russian
Chekhov, Anton. (1860-1904)
Dostoevski, Fyodor. (1821-1881)
Tolstoy, Leo. (1828-1910)

Authors, Nonfiction, American
Acheson, Dean. (1893-1971)
Allen, Paula Gunn. (1939-) Laguna
   Pueblo/Sioux Indian.
Angelou, Maya. (1928-)
Barton, Bruce. (1886-1967)
Beecher, Catherine. (1800-1878)
Bennett, Lerone, Jr. (1928-)
Bombeck, Erma. (1927-1996)
Bonnin, Gertrude Simmons. (1876-1938)
   Yankton Dakota Indian.
Brody, Jane. (1941-1987)
Bromfield, Louis. (1896-1956)
Brown, John "Fed." (1810-1876)
Brown, William Wells. (1814-1884)
Burroughs, John. (1837-1921)
Carson, Rachel. (1907-1964)
Cheever, Susan. (1943-)
Cheng, Nien. (1915-) born China.
Chesnut, Mary Boykin. (1823-1886)
Cofer, Judith Ortiz. (1952-)
Condon, Eddie. (1905-1973)
Crevecoeur, Hector St. John de. (1735-1813)
   born France.
Custer, Libbie. (1842-1933)
Davis, Varina Howell. (1826-1906)
Delaney, Annie Elizabeth. (1891-1995)
Delaney, Sarah Louise "Sadie." (1889-1998)
Deloria, Vine, Jr. (1939-) Yankton Dakota
   Indian.
Dillard, Annie. (1945-)
Dockstader, Frederick L. (1919-1998)
   Oneida and Navajo Indian.
Douglas, Marjorie Stoneman. (1890-1998)
Du Bois, W. E. B. (1868-1963)
Durant, Ida Kaufman "Ariel." (1898-1981)
   born Russia.
Durant, Will. (1885-1981)
Eastman, Charles Alexander. (1858-1939)
   Santee Dakota Indian.
Echohawk, Brummett. (1922-) Pawnee In-
   dian.
Egeria. (4th century) Spanish.
Ehrlich, Paul. (1932-)
Eiseley, Loren. (1907-1977)
Equiano, Olaudeh. (1745-1799) born Nige-

ria.
Estés, Clarissa Pinkol. (1943-)
Farmer, Fannie Merritt. (1857-1915)
Fauset, Jessie Redmon. (1882-1961)
Forten, Charlotte. *See* Grimke, Charlotte
   Forten.
Franklin, Benjamin. (1706-1790)
Fremont, Jessie Benton. (1824-1902)
Gaes, Jason. (1978-)
Galbraith, John. (1908-) born Canada.
Gilman, Charlotte Perkin. (1860-1935)
Graham, Billy. (1918-)
Graham, Katharine. (1917-2001)
Greeley, Horace. (1811-1872)
Griffin, Susan. (1943-)
Grimke, Charlotte Forten. (1837-1914)
Grinnell, George Bird. (1849-1938)
Hadley, Leila Eliott Burton. (1925-)
Hahn, Emily. (1905-1997)
Hay, John. (1838-1905)
Hernandez, Maria Latigo. (1893-1986) born
   Mexico.
Heschel, Abraham Joshua. (1907-1972) born
   Poland.
Hockenberry, John. (1956-)
Hubbard, L. Ron. (1911-1986)
Hughes, Louis. (1832-?)
Hurston, Zora Neale. (1901-1960)
Jacobs, Harriet. (1813-1897)
James, Alice. (1848-1892)
Jong, Erica. (1942-)
Keillor, Garrison. (1942-)
Keller, Helen. (1880-1968)
Kerr, Barbara. (unknown)
King, Coretta Scott. (1927?-)
Kübler-Ross, Elisabeth. (1926-2004) born
   Switzerland.
La Flesche, Francis. (1857-1932) Ponca and
   Omaha Indian.
Leitner, Isabella Katz. (1924-) born Hun-
   gary.
Leopold, Aldo. (1886-1948)
Lester, Julius. (1939-)
Lewis, Loida Nicolas. (1942-) born Philip-
   pines.
Lindbergh, Anne Morrow. (1906-2001)
Lippmann, Walter. (1889-1974)
Marsh, George Perkins. (1801-1882)
Martin, Joseph Plumb. (1762-1852)
Masters, William. (1915-2001)
Mather, Cotton. (1663-1728)

McKay, Claude. (1890-1948)
McLean, Gordon. (1934-) born Canada.
Mencken, Henry Louis "H. L." (1880-1956)
Mills, Enos. (1870-1922)
Muir, John. (1838-1914) born Scotland.
Murie, Margaret Thomas. (1902-2003)
Murray, Judith Sargent. (1751-1820)
Norman, Dorothy. (1905-1997)
Novacek, Michael. (1948-)
Nuttall, Thomas. (1786-1859) born England.
Odell, Jonathan. (1737-1818)
Paine, Thomas. (1737-1809) born England.
Palau, Luis. (1934-) born Argentina.
Parker, Dorothy. (1893-1967)
Powell, William J. (1897-1942)
Prince, Mary. (1788-?)
Roberts, Corinne Boggs "Cokie." (1943-)
Rodriguez, Richard. (1944-)
Rogers, Will. (1879-1935) Cherokee Indian.
Roosevelt, (Anna) Eleanor. (1884-1962)
Roth-Hano, Renée. (1931-) born France.
Rothschild, Miriam. (1908-) born England.
Rowlandson, Mary. (1635-1682)
Rush, Benjamin. (1745-1813)
Sagan, Carl. (1934-1996)
Santiago, Esmeralda. (1948-) Puerto Rican.
Say, Thomas. (1787-1834)
Schechter, Solomon. (1849-1915) born Romania.
Seton, Ernest Thompson. (1860-1946) born England.
Shilts, Randy. (1951-1994)
Smith, James L. (1881-?)
Spock, Benjamin. (1903-1998)
Steffens, Lincoln. (1866-1936)
Steward, Austin. (1794-1860)
Stewart, Elinoire Pruitt. (1876-1933)
Stewart, Martha. (1941-)
Theroux, Paul. (1941-)
Thomas, Piri. (1928-)
Thoreau, Henry David. (1817-1862)
Thurman, Wallace. (1902-1934)
Toklas, Alice B. (1877-1967)
Toomer, Jean. (1894-1967)
Truth, Sojourner. (1797-1883)
Veney, Bethany. (1815-?)
Warren, Adelina Otero. (1881-1965)
Weeks, Kent R. (unknown)
Wiesel, Elie. (1928-) born Transylvania (Romania).
Willey, Gordon Randolph. (1913-2002)

Wilson, Alexander. (1766-1813) born Scotland.
Wilson, Luzena Stanley. (1821-?)
Wing, Yuan. (1828-1912) born China.
Wolfe, Tom. (1931-)

Authors, Nonfiction, Ancient
Apollonius Rhodius. (c. 290-247 B.C.) Greek.
Juvenal. (Decimus Junius Juvenalis) (55?-127) Roman.
Pliny the Younger. (Gaius Plinius Caecilius Secundus) (61-113) Roman.
Ptahhotep. (fl. 2400 B.C.) Egyptian.

Authors, Nonfiction, Asian
Hanh, Thich Nhat. (1926-) Vietnamese.
Sarashina, Lady. (1008-?) Japanese.
Shonagon, Sei. (960s) Japanese.
Tagore, Rabindranth. (1861-1941) Indian.
Yuan Me. (1716-?) Chinese.

Authors, Nonfiction, English
Aguilar, Grace. (1816-1847)
Angell, Sir Norman. (1873-1967)
Burke, Edmund. (1729-1797)
Churchill, Sir Winston Leonard Spencer. (1874-1965)
Clark, Grahame. (1907-1995)
Dixie, Florence. (1857-1905)
Dodwell, Christina. (1951-)
Durrell, Gerald. (1925-1995)
Fountaine, Margaret. (1862-1940)
Kempe, Margery. (1373-1440)
Kingsley, Mary. (1862-1900)
Markham, Beryl. (1902-1986)
Montagu, Ewen. (1901-1985)
Montagu, Lady Mary Wortley. (1689-1712)
Walpole, Horace. (1717-1797)
Wilkinson, Rupert. (1936-)

Authors, Nonfiction, European
Baeck, Leo. (1873-1956) German.
Buffon, Georges. (1707-1788) French.
Egeria. (fourth century) Spanish.
Filipovic, Zlata. (1980-) Yugoslavian.
Flinker, Moshe. (1926-1944) Dutch.
Frank, Anne. (1929-1945) Dutch.
Gluckel of Hameln. (1646-1724) German.
Herzl, Theodor. (1860-1904) Austrian.
Heyman, Eva. (1931-1944) Hungarian.

Hirsch, Samson Raphael. (1808-1888) German.
John XXIII. (Angelo Roncalli) (1881-1963) Italian.
Katznelson, Yitzhak. (1886-1944) Polish.
Lamarck, Jean Baptiste. (1744-1829) French.
Lange, Christian. (1869-1938) Norwegian.
Levi, Primo. (1919-1987) Italian.
Opdyke, Irene. (1921-2003) Polish.
Ossietzky, Carl von. (1889-1938) German.
Pfeiffer, Ida. (1797-1858) Austrian.
Rashi (Solomon Ben Isaac) (1040-1105) French.
Ridesel, Baroness Fredrika von. (1746-1808) German.
Rubinowicz, David. (1927-1942) Polish.
Rudashevski, Yitzhak. (1927-1943) Polish.
Senesh, Hannah. (1921-1944) Hungarian.
Steiner, Rudolf. (1861-1925) Austrian.
Suttner, Bertha von. (1843-1914) Austrian.
Ten Boom, Corrie. (1892-1979) Dutch.
Tiktiner, Rivkah bat Meir "Rebecca." (16th century) Czech.
Weil, Simone. (1909-1943) French.
Wiesenthal, Simon. (1908-) born Poland.

Authors, Nonfiction, Irish/Scottish/Welsh
Boswell, James. (1740-1795) Scottish.
Leonowens, Anna. (1834-1915) Welsh.
Murphy, Dervla. (1931-) Irish.
Orr, John Boyd. (1880-1971) Scottish.
Shaw, George Bernard. (1856-1950) Irish.

Authors, Nonfiction, Latin
Lifshitz, Aliza. (1951-) Mexican.

Authors, Nonfiction, Middle Eastern
Fink, Ida. (1921-) Israeli, born Poland.
Gibran, Kahlil. (1883-1931) Lebanese.
Saadia Gaon. (882-942) Hebrew.

Authors, Nonfiction, New Zealandic
Hillary, Sir Edmund. (1919-)

Authors, Nonfiction, Russian
Sarah bat Tovim. (18th century) Ukrainian.
Wengeroff, Pauline. (1833-1916)

Auto Racers
Allison, Bobby. (1937-)

Andretti, Mario. (1940-) born Italy.
Bonnett, Neil. (1946-1994)
Christian, Sara. (1920-)
Elliott, Bill. (1956-)
Foyt, A. J. (1935-)
Guthrie, Janet. (1938-)
Marlin, Sterling. (1957-)
Muldowney, Shirley. (1940-) Drag racer.
Nuvolari, Tazio. (1892-1953) Italian.
Parsons, Benny. (1941-)
Petty, Richard. (1937-)
Powell, Cristen. (1979-)
Roberts, Edward "Fireball." (1929-1964)
Waltrip, Darrell. (1947-)
Yarborough, Cale. (1940-)

Automakers
See also Entrepreneurs and Industrialists-Transportation.
Benz, Karl. (1844-1929) German.
Buick, David Dunbar. (1854-1929) born Scotland.
Chrysler, Walter P. (1875-1940)
Daimler, Gottlieb. (1834-1900) German.
Dodge, Horace. (1868-1920)
Dodge, John. (1864-1920)
Ferrari, Enzo. (1898-1988) Italian.
Ford, Henry. (1863-1947)
Honda, Soichiro. (1906-1991) Japanese.
Lamborghi, Feruccio. (1916-1993) Italian.
Lyons, Sir William. (1901-1985) English.
Porsche, Ferdinand. (1875-1952) Czech.
Rolls, Charles. (1877-1910) English.
Royce, Henry. (1863-1933) English.
Sloan, Alfred Pritchard, Jr. (1875-1966)

Aviation Pioneers
See also Pilots.
Ader, Clement. (1841-1926) French.
Alcock, Sir John. (1892-1919) English.
Andrée, August. (1854-1897) Swedish.
Banning, James Herman. (1900-1933)
Blanchard, Jean-Pierre. (1754-1809) French.
Blériot, Louis. (1872-1936) French.
Bragg, Janet Harmon. (1907-1993)
Brown, Arthur Whitten. (1886-1948)
Byrd, Richard Evelyn. (1888-1957)
Cayley, George. (1773-1857) English.
Chanute, Octave. (1832-1910) born France.
Coleman, Bessie. (1873-1926)
Curtiss, Glenn H. (1878-1930)

Du Temple, Felix. (1823-1890) French.
Earhart, Amelia. (1897-1937)
Gatty, Harold Charles. (1903-1957) Australian.
Girrard, Henri. (1825-1882) French.
Henson, William. (1812-1888) born England.
Herring, Augustus. (1867-1926)
Jathro, Karl. (1873-1933) German.
Langley, Samuel Pierpont. (1834-1906)
Laroche, Raymonde de. (1886-1919) French.
Latham, Hubert. (1883-1912) French.
Lilienthal, Otto. (1848-1896) German.
Markham, Beryl. (1902-1986) English.
Maxim, Sir Hiram Stevens. (1840-1916) English.
Mock, Geraldine Fredritz. (1925-)
Montgolfier, Jacques Étienne. (1745-1799) French.
Montgolfier, Joseph Michel. (1740-1810) French.
Mozhaiski, Alexander. (1825-1890) Russian.
Pilatre de Rozier, Jean- François. (1756-1785) French.
Quimby, Harriet. (1884-1912)
Post, Wiley. (1899-1935)
Rodgers, Calbraith Perry. (1879-1912)
Rolls, Charles. (1877-1910) English.
Santos-Dumont, Alberto. (1873-1932) Brazilian.
Scott, Sheila. (1927-1988) English.
Sikorsky, Igor. (1889-1972) born Russia.
Smith, Charles Kingsford. (1897-1935) Australian.
Stringfellow, John. (1799-1883) English.
Thible, Elizabeth. (fl. 1784) French.
Wellman, Walter. (1858-1934)
Whitehead, Gustave. (1874-1927) born Germany.
Wright, Orville. (1871-1948)
Wright, Wilbur. (1867-1912)

Aviators
See Pilots.

Aztecs
See also Mexicans.
Montezuma II. (1466-1520) King.

Babylonians
Gilgamesh. (2700 B.C.) Adventurer, king.
Hammurabi. (fl. 1792-1750 B.C.) Mesopotamian king.
Hillel. (60 B.C.-10 A.D.) Scholar, spiritual leader.
Sargon the Great. (c. 2300 B.C.) Mesopotamian king.

Bacteriologists
Alexander, Hattie Elizabeth. (1901-1968)
Avery, Oswald. (1877-1955) Canadian.
Ehrlich, Paul. (1854-1915) German.
Fleming, Sir Alexander. (1881-1955) Scottish.
Hazen, Elizabeth. (1885-1975)
Koch, Robert. (1843-1910) German.
Laveran, Charles Louis Alphonse. (1845-1932) French.
Metchnikoff, Élie. (1845-1916) Russian.
Pasteur, Louis. (1822-1895) French.
Waksman, Selman Abraham. (1888-1973) born Russia.

Bandleaders
See also Conductors.
Akiyoshi, Toshiko. (1929-) born China.
Allen, Geri. (1957-)
Ammons, Albert. (1907-1949)
Armstrong, Louis. (1901-1971)
Arnaz y de Acha, Desiderio Alberto, III. (Desi Arnaz) (1917-1986) born Cuba.
Basie, William "Count." (1904-1984)
Bechet, Sidney. (1897-1959)
Blakcy, Art. (1919 1990)
Bolden, Buddy. (1868-1931)
Braxton, Anthony. (1945-)
Brecker, Michael. (1949-)
Calloway, Cab. (1907-1994)
Coleman, Ornctte. (1930)
Coltrane, John. (1926-1967)
Condon, Eddie. (1905-1973)
Corea, Anthony "Chick." (1941-)
Cugat, Xavier. (1900-1990) born Spain.
Davis, Miles Dewey III. (1926-1991)
Dorsey, James "Jimmy." (1904-1957)
Dorsey, Thomas "Tommy." (1905-1956)
Ellington, Edward Kennedy "Duke." (1899-1974)
Europe, James Reese. (1881-1939)

Garbarek, Jan. (1947-) Norwegian.
Getz, Stan. (1927-1991)
Gillespie, John Birks "Dizzy." (1917-1993)
Hancock, Herbie. (1940-)
Henderson, Fletcher. (1877-1952)
Hines, Earl "Fatha." (1903-1983)
King, Charles Edward. (1879-1950) born
 Hawaii.
Marsalis, Wynton. (1961-)
McLaughlin, John. (1942-) English.
Mingus, Charles. (1922-1979)
Monk, Thelonius. (1917-1982)
Morton, Ferdinand Joseph "Jelly Roll."
 (1885-1941)
Mulligan, Gerald "Gerry." (1927-1996)
Murray, David. (1955-)
Oliver, Joseph "King." (1885-1938)
Parker, Charles Christopher "Bird" Jr.
 (1920-1955)
Pollack, Ben. (1903-1971)
Puente, Tito. (1923-2000)
Rollins, Theodore Walter "Sonny." (1930-)
Shaw, Artie. (1910-)
Sousa, John Philip. (1854-1932)
Waller, Thomas Wright "Fats." (1904-1943)
Wilson, Theodore "Teddy." (1912-1986)

Bankers

See Entrepreneurs and Industrialists-
 Banking and Finance.

Baseball Players

Aaron, Henry "Hank." (1934-)
Abbott, Jim. (1967-)
Abreu, Bobby. (1974-) born Venezuela.
Adcock, Joe. (1927-)
Aleu, Moises. (1966-) born Dominican Re-
 public.
Alexander, Grover Cleveland. (1887-1950)
Alfonzo, Edgardo. (1974-) born Venezuela.
Alomar, Roberto. (1968-) born Puerto Rico.
Aparicio, Luis. (1934-) born Venezuela.
Appling, Luke. (1907-1991)
Ashburn, Richie. (1927-1997)
Avila, Bobby. (1924-) born Mexico.
Bagwell, Jeff. (1968-)
Baker, John Franklin "Home Run." (1886-
 1964)
Banks, Ernie. (1931-)
Bell, James Thomas "Cool Papa." (1903-
 1991)

Belle, Albert. (1966-)
Beltran, Carlos. (1977-) born Puerto Rico.
Beltré, Adrián. (1979-) born Dominican
 Republic.
Bench, Johnny. (1947-)
Bender, Charles Albert "Chief." (1884-
 1954) Chippewa Indian.
Biggio, Craig. (1965-)
Blyleven, Bert. (1951-) born Netherlands.
Bonds, Barry. (1964-)
Borders, Ila. (1975-)
Boudreau, Lou. (1917-2001)
Brock, Lou. (1939-)
Brosius, Scott. (1966-)
Brown, Kevin. (1968-)
Brown, Mordecai Peter Centennial "Three
 Finger." (1876-1948)
Buckner, Bill. (1949-)
Campanella, Roy. (1921-1993)
Canseco, Jose. (1964-) born Cuba.
Carlton, Steve. (1944-)
Casey, Sean. (1974-)
Castillo, Luis. (1975-) born Dominican Re-
 public.
Cepeda, Perucho. (1906-1955) born Puerto
 Rico.
Charleston, Oscar McKinley. (1896-1954)
Chase, Hal. (1883-1947)
Clemens, Roger. (1962-)
Clemente, Roberto. (1934-1972) born Puerto
 Rico.
Cobb, Ty. (1886-1961)
Coimbre, Pancho. (1909-1989) born Puerto
 Rico.
Colavito, Rocky. (1933-)
Collins, Eddie. (1887-1951)
Connor, Roger. (1857-1931)
Crawford, Samuel Earl "Wahoo Sam."
 (1880-1968)
Cronin, Joe. (1906-1984)
Croteau, Julie. (1970-)
Cruz, Jose, Jr. (1974-) born Puerto Rico.
De Moss, Edward "Bingo." (1889-1965)
Dean, Jay Hanna "Dizzy." (1911-1974)
Dean, Paul "Daffy." (1914-1981)
Delgado, Carlos. (1972-) born Puerto Rico.
Dihigo, Martin "El Maestro." (1905-1971)
 born Cuba.
Dimaggio, Joe. (1914-1999)
Doby, Larry. (1923-2003)
Dravecky, Dave. (1956-)

Drysdale, Don. (1936-)
Eisenreich, Jim. (1959-)
Feller, Bob. (1918-)
Fingers, Rollie. (1946-)
Ford, Edward Charles "Whitey." (1928-)
Foster, Andrew "Rube." (1879-1930)
Foster, William Hendrick "Willie." (1904-1978)
Foxx, Jimmie. (1907-1967)
Fryman, Travis. (1969-)
Furcal, Rafael, (1980-)
Galarraga, Andrés. (1962-) born Venezuela.
Garciaparra, Nomar. (1973-)
Gehrig, Lou. (1903-1941)
Gibson, Bob. (1935-)
Gibson, Josh. (1911-1947)
Glavine, Tom. (1966-)
Gonzalez, Juan. (1969-) born Puerto Rico.
Gonzalez, Luis. (1967-)
Gray, Pete. (1915-2002)
Green, Shawn. (1972-)
Greenberg, Hank. (1911-1986)
Griffey, Ken, Jr. (1969-)
Grove, Robert Moses "Lefty." (1900-1975)
Guerrero, Vladimir. (1976-) born Dominican Republic.
Guzman, Cristian. (1978-) born Dominican Republic.
Gwynn, Tony. (1960-)
Henderson, Rickcy. (1958-)
Hernandez, Keith. (1953-)
Hershiser, Orel. (1958-)
Hidalgo, Richard. (1975-) born Venezuela.
Hodges, Gil. (1924-1972)
Hoffman, Trevor. (1967-)
Horner, Bob. (1957-)
Hornsby, Rogers. (1896-1963)
Hubbell, Carl. (1903-1988)
Hunter, Jim "Catfish." (1946-)
Jackson, Bo. (1962-)
Jackson, Reggie. (1946-)
Jeter, Derek. (1974-)
Johnson, Randy. (1963-)
Johnson, Walter. (1887-1946)
Johnson, William Julius "Judy." (1900-1989)
Jones, Andruw. (1977-)
Jones, Chipper. (1972-)
Justice, David. (1966-)
Kaat, Jim. (1938-)
Kendall, Jason. (1974-)

Killebrew, Harmon. (1936-)
Kiner, Ralph. (1922-)
Klein, Chuck. (1904-1958)
Koufax, Sandy. (1935-)
Lajoie, Nap. (1874-1959)
Larkin, Barry. (1964-)
Larsen, Don. (1929-)
Lee, Carlos. (1976-) born Panama.
Leonard, Walter Fenner "Buck." (1907-1997)
Lloyd, John Henry "Pop." (1884-1965)
Lofton, Kenny. (1967-)
López, Javy. (1970-) born Puerto Rico.
Luque, Dolf. (1890-1957) born Cuba.
Mackey, Raleigh "Biz." (1897-1965)
Maddux, Greg. (1966-)
Mantle, Mickey. (1931-1995)
Marichal, Juan. (1937-) born Dominican Republic.
Marion, Marty. (1917-)
Maris, Roger. (1934-1985)
Marquard, Richard Williams "Rube." (1889-1980)
Martin, Billy. (1928-1989)
Martinez, Edgar. (1963-) born Puerto Rico.
Martinez, Pedro. (1971-) born Dominican Republic.
Martinez, Tino. (1967-)
Mathewson, Christopher "Christy." (1880-1925)
Matthews, Eddie. (1931-2001)
Mattingly, Don. (1961-)
Mays, Willie. (1931-)
Mazeroski, Bill. (1936-)
McCovey, Willie Lee. (1938-)
McGriff, Fred. (1963-)
McGwire, Mark. (1963-)
Mendez, José. (1887-1928) Cuban.
Meyer, Anna "Pee Wee." (1929-)
Millwood, Kevin. (1974-)
Minoso, Saturnino Orestes "Minnie." (1923-) born Cuba.
Mize, Johnny. (1913-1993)
Mondesi, Raúl. (1971-) born Dominican Republic.
Morgan, Joe. (1943-)
Musial, Stan. (1920-)
Niekro, Joe. (1944-)
Niekro, Phil. (1939-)
Nuxhall, Joe. (1929-)
Ordóñez, Magglió. (1974-) born Venezuela.

Ordóñez, Rey. (1971-) born Cuba.
Ott, Mel. (1909-1958)
Paige, Leroy "Satchel." (1906-1982)
Palmer, Jim. (1945-)
Palmeiro, Rafael. (1964-) born Dominican Republic.
Pérez, Neifi. (1973-) born Dominican Republic.
Perry, Gaylord. (1938-)
Piazza, Mike. (1968-)
Posada, Jorge. (1971-) born Puerto Rico.
Puckett, Kirby. (1961-)
Raines, Tim. (1959-)
Ramirez, Manny. (1972-) born Dominican Republic.
Rentería, Édgar. (1975-) born Colombia.
Ripken, Cal, Jr. (1960-)
Rivera, Mariano. (1969-) born Panama.
Roberts, Robin. (1926-)
Robinson, Brooks. (1937-)
Robinson, Frank. (1936-)
Robinson, John Roosevelt "Jackie." (1919-1972)
Rodriguez, Alex "A-Rod." (1975-)
Rodriguez, Ivan. (1971-)
Rolen, Scott. (1975-)
Rose, Pete. (1941-)
Ruth, George Herman "Babe." (1895-1948)
Ryan, Nolan. (1947-)
Sanders, Deion. (1967-)
Schmidt, Mike. (1949-)
Seaver, Tom. (1944-)
Seerey, Pat. (1923-1986)
Shantz, Bobby. (1925-)
Sisler, George. (1893-1973)
Smith, Ozzie. (1954-)
Sosa, Sammy. (1968-) born Dominican Republic.
Spahn, Warren. (1921-2003)
Spalding, Albert Goodwill. (1850-1915)
Speaker, Tris. (1888-1958)
Stone, Toni. (1921-1966)
Suttles, George "Mule." (1901-1968)
Tatis, Fernando. (1975-) born Dominican Republic.
Tejada, Miguel. (1976-) born Dominican Republic.
Thomas, Frank. (1968-)
Thorpe, Jim. (1888-1953)

Tiant, Luis, Sr. (1906-1977) born Cuba.
Torriente, Cristobal. (1895-1938) born Cuba.
Traynor, Harold "Pie." (1899-1972)
Triant, Luis, Sr. (1906-1977) born Cuba.
Valenzuela, Fernando. (1960-) born Mexico.
Vargas, Tetelo. (1906-1971) born Dominican Republic.
Vaughan, Joseph Floyd "Arky." (1912-1952)
Vaughn, Mo. (1967-)
Vernon, Mickey. (1918-)
Viña, Fernando. (1969-)
Vizquel, Omar. (1967-) born Venezuela.
Waddell, George Edward "Rube." (1876-1914)
Wagner, Billy. (1971-)
Wagner, John Peter "Honus." (1874-1955)
Walker, Larry. (1966-) Canadian.
Walker, Moses Fleetwood. (1857-1924)
Weaver, Jeff. (1976-)
Welch, Bob. (1956-)
Wells, David. (1963-)
Whiten, Mark. (1966-)
Williams, Bernie. (1968-) born Puerto Rico.
Williams, Ted. (1918-2002)
Wills, Maurice Morning "Maury." (1932-)
Wilson, Ernest Judson "Boojum." (1899-1963)
Wilson, Lewis "Hack." (1900-1948)
Young, Denton True "Cy." (1867-1955)

Baseball Team Management
Alou, Felipe. (1935-) born Dominican Republic.
Boudreau, Lou. (1917-2001)
Cox, Bobby. (1941-)
Cuza, Fernando. (unknown)
Durocher, Leo. (1908-1991)
Foster, Andrew "Rube." (1879-1930)
Lasorda, Tommy. (1927-)
Mack, Connie. (1862-1956)
Martin, Billy. (1928-1989)
McCarthy, Joe. (1887-1978)
McGraw, John. (1873-1934)
Ott, Mel. (1909-1958)
Rickey, Wesley Branch. (1881-1965)
Rose, Pete. (1941-)
Stengel, Casey. (1890-1975)
Veeck, Bill. (1914-1986)

Basketball Players

Abdul-Jabbar, Kareem. (1947-)
Abdul-Rauf, Mahmoud. (Chris Jackson) (1969-)
Abdur-Rahim, Ahareef. (1976-)
Adams, Michael. (1963-)
Ainge, Danny. (1959-)
Archibald, Nate "Tiny." (1948-)
Arizin, Paul. (1928-)
Azzi, Jennifer. (1968-)
Baranova, Elena. (1976-) Russian.
Barkley, Charles. (1963-)
Barry, Rick. (1944-)
Baylor, Elgin. (1934-)
Bird, Larry. (1956-)
Bogues, Tyrone "Muggsy." (1965-)
Bol, Manute. (1962-) African.
Bolton-Holifield, Ruthie. (1967-)
Bradley, Bill. (1943-)
Bradley, Shawn. (1972-)
Brand, Elton. (1979-)
Bryant, Kobe. (1978-)
Bullett, Vicki. (unknown)
Carter, Vince. (1977-)
Ceballos, Cedric. (1969-)
Chamberlain, Wilt. (1936-)
Cheeks, Maurice. (1956-)
Coleman, Derrick. (1967-)
Cooper, Chuck. (1926-1984)
Cooper, Cynthia. (1963-)
Cousy, Bob. (1928-)
Cowens, Dave. (1948-)
Dawkins, Darryl. (1957-)
DeBusschere, Dave. (1940-2002)
Donovan, Anne. (1961-)
Drexler, Clyde. (1962-)
Duncan, Tim. (1976-) born Virgin Islands.
Eaton, Mark. (1957-)
Edwards, Teresa. (1964-)
Ellis, Dale. (1960-)
English, Alex. (1954-)
Erving, Julius. (1950-)
Ewing, Patrick. (1962-)
Francis, Steve. (1977-)
Garnett, Kevin. (1976-)
Gillom, Jennifer. (1964-)
Grant, Horace Junior. (1965-)
Griffith, Darrell. (1958-)
Hamilton, Richard. (1978-)
Hardaway, Anfernee. (1972-)

Hardaway, Tim. (1966-)
Havlicek, John. (1940-)
Hawkins, Connie. (1942-)
Hayes, Elvin. (1945-)
Hill, Grant. (1972-)
Holdsclaw, Chamique. (1977-)
Hurley, Bobby. (1971-)
Iverson, Allen. (1975-)
Jackson, Jim. (1970-)
Johnson, Earvin "Magic." (1957-)
Johnson, George. (1948-)
Johnson, Larry. (1969-)
Jones, Marion. (1975-)
Jordan, Michael. (1963-)
Kemp, Shawn. (1969-)
Kidd, Jason. (1973-)
Laettner, Christian. (1969-)
Lanier, Bob. (1948-)
Leslie, Lisa. (1972-)
Lieberman-Cline, Nancy. (1958-)
Lobo, Rebecca. (1973-)
Lucas, John. (1953-)
Majerle, Dan. (1968-)
Malone, Karl. (1963-)
Maravich, Pete. (1947-1988)
Marbury, Stephon. (1977-)
McCray, Nikki. (1971-)
McGrady, Tracy. (1979-)
McHale, Kevin. (1957-)
Meyers, Ann. (1955-)
Mikan, George. (1924-)
Miller, Cheryl. (1964-)
Miller, Reggie. (1965-)
Mourning, Alonzo. (1970-)
Mutombo, Dikembe. (1966-) Zairian.
Odum, Lamar. (1979-)
Olajuwon, Hakeem. (1963-) born Nigeria.
O'Neal, Shaquille. (1972-)
Payton, Gary. (1968-)
Person, Chuck. (1964-)
Petrovic, Drazen. (1964-) Yugoslavian.
Pettit, Bob. (1932-)
Pippin, Scottie. (1965-)
Price, Mark. (1964-)
Reed, Willis. (1942-)
Rice, Glen. (1967-)
Rider, Isaiah, Jr. (1971-)
Roberts, Stanely Corvet. (1970-)
Robertson, Oscar. (1938-)
Robinson, David. (1965-)
Rodman, Dennis. (1961-)

Rollins, Tree. (1955-)
Russell, Bill. (1934-)
Schayes, Dolph. (1928-)
Scott, Dennis. (1968-)
Serio, Suzie McConnell. (1966-)
Smith, Katie. (1964-)
Staley, Dawn. (1970-)
Starbird, Kate. (1975-)
Starks, John. (1965-)
Still, Valerie. (1961-)
Stockton, John. (1962-)
Swoopes, Sheryl. (1971-)
Szcerbiak, Wally. (1977-)
Thomas, Isaiah. (1961-)
Thorpe, Otis Henry. (1962-)
Timms, Michele. (1965-)
Van Horn, Keith. (1975-)
Walton, Bill. (1952-)
Washington, Ora. (1898-1971)
Weatherspoon, Teresa. (1965-)
Webb, Spud. (1963-)
Webber, Chris. (1973-)
West, Jerry. (1938-)
Wilkins, Dominique. (1960-) born France.
Williams, Charles "Buck." (1960-)
Williams, Jason. (1975-)
Williams, John "Hot Rod." (1962-)
Woodard, Lynette. (1959-)
Worthy, James. (1961-)
Zheng, Haixia. (1967-) Chinese.

Basketball Team Management
Auerbach, Arnold Jacob "Red." (1917-)
Byrdsong, Ricky. (1957-1999)
Byrdsong, Sherialyn. (1957-)
Conradt, Jody. (1941-)
Daly, Chuck. (1930-)
DeBusschere, Dave. (1940-2002)
Hannum, Alex. (1923-2002)
Holzman, William "Red." (1920-1998)
Jackson, Phil. (1945-)
Kundla, John. (1916-)
Lieberman-Cline, Nancy. (1958-)
Lucas, John. (1953-)
Nelson, Don. (1940-)
Nuñez, Tommy. (1939-)
Riley, Pat. (1945-)
Schayes, Dolph. (1928-)
Summitt, Pat Head. (1952-)
Tomjanovich, Rudy. (1948-)

Belgians
See also Immigrants to United States, Belgian.
Beernaert, Auguste. (1829-1912) Attorney, peace activist, political activist. Nobel Peace Prize winner.
Belline, Germaine. (unknown) Holocaust rescuer.
Brueghel, Jan. (1568-1625) Painter.
Brueghel, Pieter. (1525-1569) Painter.
Damien, Father. *See* De Veuster, Joseph.
De Veuster, Joseph. (Father Damien) (1840-1889) Human rights activist, missionary, spiritual leader.
di Lasso, Orlando. (1532-1594) Composer, singer.
La Fontaine, Henri. (1854-1943) Attorney, educator, political activist. Nobel Peace Prize winner.
Leopold II. (1835-1909) King.
Magritte, René. (1896-1967) Painter.
Mercator, Gerardus. (1512-1594) Geographer.
Parker, Henriette. (1932-) Holocaust survivor.
Pire, Dominique-Georges. (1910-1969) Peace activist, spiritual leader, founded University of Peace. Nobel Peace Prize winner.
Reinhardt, Django. (1910-1953) Jazz musician.
Rubens, Peter Paul. (1577-1640) Painter.
Van der goes, Hugo. (1440-1482) Painter.
Van Dyck, Sir Anthony. (1599-1641) Painter.
Van Eyck, Jan. (1390-1441) Painter.
Vesalius, Andreas. (1514-1564) Anatomist, illustrator, physician.
Watteau, Jean Antoine. (1684-1721) Painter.

Biathlon, Decathlon, Pentathlon, and Triathlon Athletes
See also Olympic Athletes; Track and Field Athletes.
Bedard, Myriam. (1969-) Canadian biathlon.
Mathias, Bob. (1930-) Decathlon.
Newby-Fraser, Paula. (1962-) Zimbabwean triathlon athlete.
O'Brien, Dan. (1966-) Decathlon.
Patton, George C. (1885-1945) Pentathlon.

Phayllos of Cortona. (c. 480) Greek pentathlon.
Thompson, Daley. (1958-) English decathlon.
Thorpe, Jim. (1888-1953) Chip-
pewa/Sac/Fox Indian decathlon, pentathlon.

Biblical Figures

New Testament
Elisabeth.
Herodias.
Jesus Christ.
Joseph, Saint.
Martha.
Mary.
Mary Magdalen.
Mary, Virgin.
Susanna.

Old Testament
Abigail.
Abraham. Patriarch.
Bathsheba.
David. King of Israel.
Deborah. (c. 1150 B.C.) Mother of Israel.
Delilah.
Esther. (5th century B.C.)
Eve.
Hagar.
Hannah.
Jeremiah.
Judith.
Leah.
Miriam.
Moses.
Naomi.
Rachel.
Rebekah.
Ruth.
Salome.
Sarah.

Bicyclists
LeMond, Greg. (1961-)
Young, Sheila. (1950-)

Billiards Players
Mosconi, Willie. (1913-1993)

Biologists
Aristotle. (384-322 B.C.) Greek.
Barkow, Bill. (unknown) Acoustic biolo-
gist.
Bowles, Ann. (1956-) Acoustic biologist.
Chisholm, Sallie. (unknown)
Clark, Christopher. (unknown) Acoustic
biologist.
Claude, Albert. (1899-1983) English cell
biologist.
Cobb, Jewel Plummer. (1924-) Cell biolo-
gist.
Commoner, Barry. (1917-) Environmental
biologist.
Crick, Francis H.C. (1916-2004) English
molecular biologist.
Dallmeier, Francisco. (1953-) Wildlife bi-
ologist, born Venezuela.
Earle, Sylvia. (1935-) Marine biologist.
Evans, Bill. (unknown) Acoustic biologist.
Franklin, Rosalind Elsie. (1920-1958)
English molecular biologist.
Heyerdahl, Thor. (1914-2002) Norwegian.
Hoben, Patricia. (unknown)
Jackson, Janis. (unknown)
Jones, Albert Jose. (unknown) Marine bi-
ologist.
Just, Ernest Everett. (1883-1941) Cell biolo-
gist.
Leeuwenhoek, Anton van. (1632-1723)
Dutch.
Levi-Montalcini, Rita. (1909-) Cell biolo-
gist, born Italy.
Mahowald, Misha. (1963-)
Maxwell, Nicole Hughes. (1905-1998) Eth-
nobiologist.
Morgan, Thomas Hunt. (1866-1945)
Moss, Cynthia. (1940-) Wildlife biologist.
Murie, Olaus. (1889-1963)
Oberhauser, Karen. (unknown)
Patrick, Ruth. (1907-) Freshwater biologist.
Payne, Katy. (1937-) Acoustic biologist.
Pierce, Naomi. (1954-)
Poodry, Clifton. (1943-) Seneca Indian.
Sager, Ruth. (1918-1997)
Schwabe, Stephanie. (1957-) Geomicrobi-
ologist, born Germany.
Shannon, Larry. (1933-)
Staedler, Michelle. (unknown) Marine bi-
ologist.

Stevens, Nettie Marie. (1861-1912)
Tonegawa, Susumu. (1939-) Molecular biologist, born Japan.
Tsui, Lap-Chee. (1950-) Canadian molecular biologist, born China.
Turner, Charles Henry. (1867-1923)
Villa-Komaroff, Lydia. (1947-) Molecular biologist.
Waksman, Selman Abraham. (1888-1973) Microbiologist, born Russia.
Watson, James Dewey. (1928-)
Wong-Staal, Flossie. (1947-) Molecular biologist, born China.

Blacks, International

See also African-Americans.
Anoyke, Okomfo. (17th century) West African spiritual leader.
Askia the Great. (1444?-1538) African king.
Barsosio, Sally. (1978-) Kenyan olympic track and field athlete.
Bol, Manute. (1962-) Sudanese basketball player.
Cinque, Joseph. (1817-1879) African patriot, slave insurrectionist.
Dorantz, Stephen. (Esteban, Estevanico) (1500-1539) Black Spanish explorer, colonist in America.
Elizabeth. (1941-) Princess of Toro. (Uganda)
Esu-Williams, Eku. (1956-) Nigerian AIDS activist, educator, immunologist, physician.
Freeman, Cathy. (1973-) Australian olympic track and field athlete.
Fuhr, Grant. (1962-) Canadian hockey player.
Gronniosaw, Ukawsaw. (1725-1786) Prince of Borneo, captured slave.
Jean-Murat, Carolle. (1950-) Haitian educator, human rights activist, physician, public health worker.
Kenyatta, Jomo. (1894-1978) Kenyan prime minister, president.
Kenyatta, Julius K. (1922-) Tanzanian prime minister.
Kivengere, Festo. (1919-1988) Ugandan political activist, spiritual leader.
Lucas, Adetokonbo. (1931-) Nigerian medical researcher, physican.
Luthuli, Albert. (1898-1967) South African educator, political activist, tribal chief.
Luwum, Janani, (1922-1977) Ugandan political activist, spiritual leader.
Maathai, Wangari. (1940-) Kenyan environmental activist, human rights activist, political activist.
Machel, Gracia Simbone. (1945-) Mozambican children's rights activist.
Makeba, Miriam. (1932-) South African political activist, singer.
Makeda, Miriam. (960-930 B.C.) Ethiopian queen.
Makhubu, Lydia Phindile. (1937-) Swaziland chemist, educator.
Mandela, Nelson. (1918-) South African attorney, human rights activist, political activist. Nobel Peace Prize winner, Presidential Medal of Honor recipient.
Mandela, Winnie Madikizela. (1934) South African political activist.
Mansa Musa I. (1312-1337) King of Mali.
Mbandi, Jinga. *See* Nzinga, Anna.
Mella. African warrior queen.
Morris, Samuel. (1827-1893) Liberian missionary.
Mugabe, Robert. (1924-) Zimbabwean prime minister.
Mutombo, Dikembe. (1966-) Zairian basketball player.
Nkrumah, Kwame. (1909-1972) Ghanian prime minister, president.
Nyerere, Julius. (1922-1999) Tanzanian prime minister.
Nzinga, Anna. (Jinga Mbandi) (1580-1663) African queen.
Odhiambo, Thomas. (1931-2003) Kenyan entomologist.
Olajuwon, Hakeem. (1963-) Nigerian basketball player.
O'Ree, Willie. (1935-) Canadian hockey player.
Peterson, Oscar. (1925-) Canadian jazz musician.
Seacole, Mary. (1805-1881) Jamaican nurse.
Selassie, Haile. (1892-1975) Ethiopian emperor.
Senghor, Léopold. (1906-2001) Senegal president.
Shaka. (1787-1828) Zulu warrior king.
Soyinka, Wole. (1934-) Nigerian author, political activist. Nobel Prize winner.

Tupou, Queen Salote III. (1900-1965) Tonga ruler.

Tutu, Desmond Mpilo. (1931-) South African human rights activist, spiritual leader.

Wolde, Mamo. (1931-) Ethiopian olympic marathon runner, track and field athlete.

Boaters

Aebi, Tania. (1966-) Sailed solo around world.

Barton, Greg. (1959-) Olympic kayaker.

Davison, Anne. (1913-1992) Sailed solo across Atlantic, born England.

DeFrantz, Anita. (1952-) Olympic rower.

Hanauer, Chip. (1954-) Power boat racer.

James, Naomi. (1949-) Sailed solo around world.

Laumann, Silken. (1965-) Canadian olympic rower.

Bobsledders

Eagan, Eddie. (1898-1967)

Bolivians

See also Hispanic-Americans.

Escalante, Jaime. (1930-) Educator.

Patino, Simon J. (1865-1947) Entrepreneur tin mining.

Botanists and Horticulturalists

See also Agricultural Scientists; Environmentalists.

Arvigo, Rosita. (1941-)

Bailey, Liberty Hyde. (1858-1954)

Bartram, John. (1699-1777)

Bartram, William. (1739-1822)

Burbank, Luther. (1849-1926)

Carver, George Washington. (1864-1943)

Chapman, Jonathan. (Johnny Appleseed) (1774-1845)

Dietrich, Amalie Nelle. (1821-1891) German.

Duggar, Benjamin. (1872-1956)

Eastwood, Alice. (1859-1953) Canadian.

Gray, Asa. (1810-1888)

Humboldt, Alexander von. (1769-1859) German.

Lamarck, Jean Baptiste. (1744-1829) French.

Linnaeus, Carl. (1707-1778) Swedish.

Livingstone, David. (1813-1873) Scottish.

Mee, Margaret Ursula Brown. (1909-1988) English.

Mexia, Ynes. (1870-1938)

Nuttall, Thomas. (1786-1859) born England.

Rodriguez, Eloy. (1947-)

Sanchez, Pedro. (1940-) born Cuba.

Theophrastus. (371-287 B.C.) Greek.

Bowlers

Carter, Don. (1926-)

Ludewig, Marion. (1914-)

Boxers

Ali, Muhammad. (1942-)

Carbajal, Michael. (1968-)

de la Hoya, Oscar. (1973-)

Dempsey, Jack. (1895-1983)

Eagan, Eddie. (1898-1967)

Foreman, George. (1949-)

Frazier, Joe. (1944-)

Gonzales, Rodolfo "Corkey." (1928-)

Holmes, Larry. (1949-)

Johnson, Jack. (1878-1946)

Kelly, Paul. *See* Vaccarelli, Paulo Antonio.

Leonard, Charles "Sugar Ray." (1956-)

Louis, Joe. (1914-1981)

Marciano, Rocky. (Rocco Francis Marchegiano) (1923-1969)

Polydamus. (c. 408 B.C.) Greek.

Robinson, Walker Smith, Jr. "Sugar Ray." (1921-1989)

Ross, Barney. (1907-1967)

Sullivan, John L. (1858-1918)

Tyson, Michael "Mike." (1966-)

Vaccarelli, Paulo Antonio. (Paul Kelly) (1876-1927) born Italy.

Brazilians

See also Hispanic-Americans.

Amado, Jorge. (1912-2001) Author.

da Silva, Fabriola. (1979-) In-line skater.

Lisboa, Antonio Francisco. (1738-1814) Architect, sculptor.

Marcovaldi, Maria "Neca." (1948-) Conservationist.

Mendes, Chico. (1944-1988) Environmentalist, human rights activist.

Miranda, Carmen. (1909-1955) Actor, singer.

Muniz, Maria Antonia. (1762-1870) Matriarch.

Nascimento, Edson Arantes do. (Pelé)
(1940-) Soccer player.

Pedro II. (1825-1891) King.

Pelé. *See* Nascimento, Edson Arantes do.

Santos-Dumont, Alberto. (1873-1932) Aviation pioneer.

Villa-Lobos, Heitor. (1887-1959) Composer,
educator.

British

See English; Irish; Scottish; Welsh.

Broadcast Journalists

See also Journalists; Sportscasters; Television and Radio Personalities.

Amanpour, Christiane. (1958-) English.

Breckinridge, Mary Marvin. (1905-2002)

Chung, Constance Vu-Hwa "Connie."
(1946-)

Coughlin, Father Charles Edward. (1891-
1979) born Canada.

Cronkite, Walter. (1916-)

Fernandez, Giselle. (1961-) born Mexico.

Goode, Mal. (1908-1995)

Hockenberry, John. (1956-)

Hunter-Gault, Charlayne. (1942-)

Jones, Charles Wesley. (1900-1986)

Leibowitz, Nehama. (1905-1997) Israeli.

McBride, Mary Margaret. (Martha Deane)
(1899-1976)

Murrow, Edward R. (1908-1965)

Rivera, Geraldo. (1943-)

Roberts, Corinne Boggs " Cokie." (1943-)

Rodriguez, Richard. (1944-)

Salazar, Rubén. (1928-1970) born Mexico.

Sanders, Marlene. (1931-)

Sawyer, Diane. (1945-)

Shaw, Bernard. (1940-)

Walker, Judith Cary. (1889-1973)

Walters, Barbara. (1931-)

Burmese

Aung San. (1915-1947) Political leader.

Suu Kyi, Daw Aung San. (1945-) Human
rights activist, peace activist. Nobel Peace
Prize winner, Presidential Medal of Freedom recipient.

Byzantians

Belisarius. (505-565) Military leader.

Comnena, Anna. (1083-1148) Historian,
princess, religious reformer.

Justinian I, the Great. (482-565) Emperor.

Cabinet Members

See also Government Workers.

Acheson, Dean. (1893-1971) Secretary of
State.

Adams, John Quincy. (1767-1848) Secretary
of State.

Albright, Madeleine. (1937-) Secretary of
State, born Czechoslovakia.

Baker, James. (1930-) Secretary of State.

Brown, Ronald. (1941-1996) Secretary of
Commerce.

Bryan, William Jennings. (1860-1925) Secretary of State.

Buchanan, James. (1791-1868) Secretary of
State.

Calhoun, John Caldwell. (1782-1850) Secretary of War.

Cavazos, Lauro F. (1927-) Secretary of
Education.

Cisneros, Henry. (1947-) Secretary Housing
and Urban Development.

Clay, Henry. (1777-1852) Secretary of State.

Davis, Jefferson. (1808-1889) Secretary of
War.

Dulles, John Foster. (1888-1959) Secretary
of State.

Forrestal, James. (1892-1949) Secretary of
Defense, Secretary of War.

Gallatin, Albert. (1761-1849) Secretary of
the Treasury, born Switzerland.

Hamilton, Alexander. (1753-1804) Secretary
of the Treasury.

Harris, Patricia Roberts. (1924-1985) Secretary of Health, Education and Welfare,
Secretary of Housing and Urban Development.

Hay, John. (1838-1905) Secretary of State.

Hobby, Oveta. (1905-1995) Secretary of
Health, Education and Welfare.

Hoover, Herbert. (1874-1964) Secretary of
Commerce.

Hughes, Charles Evan. (1862-1948) Secretary of State.

Hull, Cordell. (1871-1955) Secretary of State.

Jefferson, Thomas. (1743-1826) Secretary of State.

Kellogg, Frank B. (1856-1937) Secretary of State.

Kissinger, Henry. (1923-) Secretary of State, born Germany.

Madison, James. (1751-1836) Secretary of State.

Marshall, George Catlett. (1880-1959) Secretary of Defense, Secretary of State.

Marshall, John. (1755-1835) Secretary of State.

McNamara, Robert Strange. (1916-) Secretary of Defense.

Mineta, Norman. (1931-) Secretary of Transportation.

Monroe, James. (1758-1831) Secretary of State.

Peña, Federico. (1947-) Secretary of Transportation.

Perkins, Frances. (1882-1965) Secretary of Labor.

Powell, Colin. (1937-) Secretary of State.

Reno, Janet. (1938-) Attorney General.

Richardson, Bill. (1947-) Secretary of Energy.

Root, Elihu. (1845-1937) Secretary of War.

Rumsfeld, Donald H. (1932-) Secretary of Defense.

Seward, William. (1801-1872) Secretary of State.

Stanton, Edwin. (1814-1869) Attorney General, Secretary of War.

Stimson, Henry. (1867-1950) Secretary of State, Secretary of War.

Tracy, Benjamin, (1830-1915) Secretary of the Navy.

Travis, Dempsey J. (1920-) Secreatary of Housing and Urban Development.

Webster, Daniel. (1782-1852) Secretary of State.

Weinberger, Caspar. (1917-) Secretary of Defense.

Cambodians

See also Immigrants to United States, Cambodian.

Chorn, Arn. (1967-) Political activist and prisoner.

Canadians

See also Immigrants to United States, Canadian.

Abbott, Maude Elizabeth Seymour. (1869-1940) Medical researcher, physician.

Atwood, Margaret. (1939-) Author, poet.

Avery, Oswald. (1877-1955) Bacteriologist.

Banting, Sir Frederick Grant. (1891-1941) Medical researcher, physician. Nobel Prize winner.

Bateman, Ray, Jr. (1974-) Teenage medical researcher.

Bedard, Myriam. (1969-) Olympic biathlon, track and field athlete.

Belaney, Archibald. (Grey Owl) (1888-1938) Fur trapper, naturalist, born England.

Belfour, Ed. (1965-) Hockey player.

Bloomfield, Michael. (unknown) Environmentalist, founder Harmony Foundation of Canada.

Bourne, Shae-Lynn. (1976-) Olympic figure skater.

Boyd, Liona. (1949-) Musician.

Brodeur, Martin. (1972-) Hockey player.

Brown, George. (1818-1880) Editor, publisher.

Campbell, Kim. (1947-) Prime Minister.

Caron, Nadine. (1970-) Physician.

Champlain, Samuel de. (1567-1635) Explorer.

Dryden, Ken. (1947-) Hockey player.

Eastwood, Alice. (1859-1953) Botanist.

Edwards, Eileen Regina. (Shania Twain) (1965-) Singer, songwriter.

Esposito, Phil. (1942-) Hockey player.

Esposito, Tony. (1944-) Hockey player.

Friezen, Jeff. (1976-) Hockey player.

Fuhr, Grant. (1962-) Hockey player.

Galdikas, Birute. (1946-) Primatologist, born West Germany.

Ghermezian, Bahman. (1946-) Entrepreneur real estate, born Iran.

Ghermezian, Eskander. (1940-) Entrepreneur real estate, born Iran.

Ghermezian, Nader. (1941-) Entrepreneur real estate, born Iran.

Ghermezian, Raphael. (1944-) Entrepreneur real estate, born Iran.

Goforth, Jonathan. (1859-1936) Missionary.

Goforth, Rosalind Smith. (1864-1942) Missionary.

Gretzky, Wayne. (1961-) Hockey player.

Grey Owl. *See* Belaney, Archibald.

Hall, Glenn. (1931-) Hockey player.

Hart, Pearl. (1871-1925) Outlaw.

Hickson, Catherine. (1955-) Geologist, volcanologist.

Hogg, Helen Battles Sawyer. (1905-1993) Astronomer.

Howe, Gordie. (1928-) Hockey player.

Hubbard, Mina Benson. (1870-1956) Explorer.

Hull, Bobby. (1939-) Hockey player.

Hull, Brett. (1964-) Hockey player.

Iberville, Pierre le Moyne. (1661-1706) Colonist, naval captain, founder of Louisiana, born France.

Joliet, Louis. (1645-1700) Adventurer, explorer.

Kariya, Paul. (1974-) Hockey player.

Karpis, Alvin. (1908-1979) Gangster.

Kraatz, Victor. (1971-) Olympic figure skater.

Lafleur, Guy. (1951-) Hockey player.

Laumann, Silken. (1965-) Olympic rower.

Lecavalier, Vincent. (1980-) Hockey player.

Leitch, Peter. (1944-) Jazz musician.

Lemieux, Mario. (1965-) Hockey player.

Lindros, Eric. (1973-) Hockey player.

Little, Jean. (1932-) Children's author.

McLachlan, Sarah. (1968-) Singer, songwriter.

McLoughlin, John. (1784-1857) Fur trader, physician.

McLuhan, Marshall. (1911-1980) Educator, visionary.

Montcalm, Louis-Joseph. (1712-1759) Colonist, born France.

Montgomery, Lucy Maud "L. M." (1874-1942) Children's author, novelist.

Moodie, Geraldine Fitzgibbon. (1854-1945) Photographer.

Morissette, Alanis. (1974-) Pop singer.

Mowat, Farley. (1921-) Children's author, naturalist.

O'Ree, Willie. (1935-) Hockey player.

Orr, Bobby. (1948-) Hockey player.

Osler, Sir William. (1849-1919) Educator, physician.

Pearson, Lester. (1897-1972) Ambassador, diplomat, prime minister, president. Nobel Peace Prize winner.

Pelletier, David. (1974-) Olympic figure skater.

Peterson, Oscar. (1925-) Jazz musician.

Petitclerc, Chantal. (1969-) Wheelchair athlete.

Pickford, Mary. (1893-1979) Actor.

Pitcher, Harriet Brooks. (1876-1933) Physicist.

Plante, Jacques. (1929-1986) Hockey player.

Pronger, Chris. (1974-) Olympic hockey player.

Rheaume, Manon. (1972-) Hockey player.

Richard, Maurice. (1921-2000) Hockey player.

Rijnhart, Susie Carson. (1868-1908) Explorer, missionary.

Robinson, Jennifer. (1976-) Olympic figure skater.

Rosenfeld, Bobbie. (1904-1969) Olympic track and field athlete.

Ross, Alexander. (1783-1856) Abolitionist, naturalist, physician.

Roy, Patrick. (1965-) Hockey player.

Salé, Jamie. (1977-) Olympic figure skater.

Sawchuck, Terry. (1925-1970) Hockey player.

Schmirler, Sandra. (1964-2000) Olympic curler.

Smith, Billy. (1950-) Hockey player.

Steele, Samuel. (1851-1919) Crime fighter.

Stojko, Elvis. (1972-) Olympic figure skater.

Stowe, Emily Jennings. (1831-1903) Abolitionist, physician, suffragist, women's rights activist.

Teasdale, Lucille. (1929-1996) Human rights activist, physician.

Thomson, Roy Herbert. (1894-1973) Entrepreneur media conglomerate, publisher newspaper.

Thornton, Joe. (1979-) Hockey player.

Tsui, Lap-Chee. (1950-) Molecular biologist, medical researcher, born China.

Twain, Shania. *See* Edwards, Eileen Regina.

Vaux-Walcott, Mary. (1860-1940) Mountaineer, naturalist.

Walker, Larry. (1966-) Baseball player.

West, Ricky. (1951-) Arachnologist.

Wickenheiser, Hayley. (1969-) Olympic hockey player.

Carthaginians

Hannibal. (247-183 B.C.) General.
Hanno. (c. 450 B.C.) Explorer.

Cartoonists and Caricaturists

Adams, Scott. (1957-)
Armstrong, Ellen. (1914-)
Callahan, John. (1951-)
Darling, Jay Norwood "Ding." (1876-1962)
Daumier, Honoré. (1808-1879) French.
Groening, Matt. (1954-)
Guisewite, Cathy. (1950-)
Haring, Keith. (1958-1990)
Jones, Charles Martin "Chuck." (1912-2002)
Nast, Thomas. (1840-1902) born Germany.
O'Neill, Cecilia Rose. (1874-1944)
Schulz, Charles. (1922-2000)
Steig, William. (1907-2003)
Trudeau, Garry. (1948-)

Celts

Boudicca. (28-62) Queen.
Morrigan. Goddess of war.
Scathach. Warrior goddess.

Chefs

Careme, Antonin. (1784-1833) French.
Farmer, Fannie Merritt. (1857-1915)
Mallon, Mary "Typhoid Mary." (1870-1938)
  Irish cook said to spread typhoid disease.
Ryan, Katherine "Klondike Kate." (1869-
  1932)
Yuan Me. (1916-) Chinese.

Chemists

Baekeland, Leo. (1863-1944) Industrial
  chemist, born Belgium.
Barnes, Sharon J. (1955-)
Barré-Sinoussi, Françoise. (1947-) French.
Benerito, Ruth. (1916-) Physical chemist.
Bennett, Hugh Hammond. (1881-1960) Ag-
  ricultural chemist.
Berzelius, Jöns Jakob. (1779-1848) Swed-
  ish.
Blodgett, Katherine. (1898-1979)
Bordin, Alexander Porfiervich. (1833-1889)
  Russian.
Borlaug, Norman Ernest. (1914-) Agricul-
  tural chemist, biochemist.
Boyle, Robert. (1627-1691) English.

Brill, Yvonne. (1924-) Aerospace chemist,
  born Canada.
Brown, Rachel. (1898-1980) Biochemist.
Carothers, Wallace. (1896-1937) Organic
  chemist.
Carr, Emma Perry. (1880-1972) Physical
  chemist.
Cavendish, Henry. (1731-1810) English.
Chain, Sir Ernst Boris. (1906-1979) English
  biochemist.
Cohen, Stanley. (1922-) Biochemist.
Cori, Gerty Radnitz. (1896-1957) Biochem-
  ist.
Crespi, Ann. (unknown)
Curie, Marie Sklodowska. (1867-1934)
  French, born Poland.
Curie, Pierre. (1859-1906) French.
Dalton, John. (1766-1844) English.
Davy, Humphrey. (1778-1829) English.
Elion, Gertrude Belle. (1918-1999) Bio-
  chemist.
Faraday, Michael. (1791-1867) English.
Fieldler, Molly. (unknown)
Fraser-Reid, Bertram O. (1934-) Organic
  chemist.
Gay-Lussac, Joseph Louis. (1778-1850)
  French.
Good, Mary. (1931-)
Harris, Betty Wright. (1940-)
Henry, Warren. (1909-2001) Physical chem-
  ist.
Hodgkin, Dorothy Crowfoot. (1910-1994)
  English physical chemist.
Holland, Elizabeth. (unknown)
  Biogeochemist.
Jackson, Charles T. (1805-1880)
Joliot-Curie, Irène. (1897-1956) French.
Jones, Robert. (1951-) Food science chem-
  ist.
Jordan, Lynda. (unknown)
Julian, Percy Lavon. (1899-1975)
Kekulé, Friedrich August. (1829-1896) Ger-
  man.
Khorana, Har Gobind. (1922-) born India.
King, Reatha Clark. (1938-)
Kwolek, Stephanie. (1923-)
Lavoisier, Antoine Laurent. (1743-1794)
  French.
Lavoisier, Marie. (1758-1836) French.
Levi, Primo. (1919-1987) Italian.
Libby, Willard F. (1908-1980)

Livingstone, David. (1813-1873) Scottish.
Lucid, Shannon. (1943-) Biochemist.
Makhubu, Lydia Phindile. (1937-) Swazi-
   land, African.
Marsh, James. (fl. 1832) Scottish.
Mary Prophetetissa of Alexandria. (1st cen-
   tury A.D.) Alexandrine, Egyptian.
Mendeleyev, Dimitri Ivanovich. (1843-
   1907) Russian.
Molina, Mario. (1943-) born Mexico.
Nair, Malathy. (unknown) born India.
Noguchi, Constance Tom. (1948-)
Ochoa, Severo. (1905-1993) Biochemist,
   born Spain.
Pasteur, Louis. (1822-1895) French.
Pauling, Linus Carl. (1901-1994) Physical
   chemist.
Pennington, Mary Engle. (1872-1952)
Perkin, Sir William Henry. (1838-1907)
   English.
Pert, Candace Beebe. (1946-) Biochemist.
Prendergast, Franklyn G. (1945-) Biochem-
   ist.
Priestly, Joseph. (1773-1804) English.
Rajalakshmi, R. (1926-) Indian biochemist.
Ramsay, Sir William. (1852-1916) Scottish.
Richards, Ellen Swallow. (1842-1911)
Rowland, Frank Sherwood. (1927-)
   Atmospheric chemist.
Sanger, Frederick. (1918-) English biochem-
   ist.
Saruhashi, Katsuku. (1920-) Japanese.
Seaborg, Glenn Theodore. (1912-1999) Nu-
   clear chemist.
Serturner, Friedrich. (1783-1841) German.
Sherman, Patsy. (1930-)
Weizmann, Chaim. (1874-1952) Israeli.
Wilder, L. Douglas. (1931-)
Zernike, Frits. (1888-1966) Dutch.

Chiefs, Native American

See also Native American Rights Activists;
   Native Americans.
Black Kettle. (1807-1868) Cheyenne.
Brant, Joseph. (1742-1807) Mohawk.
Cochise. (1812-1874) Apache.
Crazy Horse. (1841-1877) Lakota Oglala
   Sioux.
Crowfoot. (1821-1890) Blackfoot.
Deganwidah. (c. 1400) Huron.
Geronimo. (1829-1909) Apache.

Hayenwatha. (c. 1400) Mohawk.
Hiawatha. (fl. 1440) Iroquois.
Joseph. (1840-1904) Nez Percé.
Kintpuash. (Captain Jack) (1837-1873)
   Modoc.
Little Raven. (d. 1889) Arapaho.
Luther Standing Bear. (1868-1937) Oglala
   Lakota Sioux.
Mankiller, Wilma. (1945-) Cherokee.
Massasoit. (1606-1661) Wampanoag.
Metacomet. *See* Philip, King.
Opechancanough. (1556-1646) Lenape.
Osceola. (1804-1838) Seminole.
Ouray. (1820-1880) Ute.
Parker, Ely Samuel. (1828-1895) Seneca.
Philip, King. (Metacom, Metacomet,
   Pometacom) (1638-1676) Wampanoag.
Pontiac. (1720-1769) Ottawa.
Powhatan. (1550-1618) Lenape.
Red Cloud. (1822-1909) Lakota Sioux.
Red Jacket. (1756-1830) Seneca.
Ross, John. (1790-1866) Cherokee.
Seathl. (1788-1866) Duwamish.
Sequoyah. (1770-1843) Cherokee.
Sitting Bull. (Tatanka Yotanka) (1831-1890)
   Sioux.
Standing Bear. (1829-1908) Ponca.
Tecumseh. (1768-1813) Shawnee.
Washakie. (1800-1900) Shoshone.
Weetamoo. (1640-1676) Pocasset.

Children's Rights Activists

Bonafini, Hebe de. (unknown) Argentine.
Byrdsong, Ricky. (1957-1999)
Byrdsong, Sherialyn. (1957-)
Collins, Marva Delores. (1936-)
Coram, Thomas. (1668-1751) English.
Edelman, Marian Wright. (1939-)
Glaser, Elizabeth. (1947-1994)
Hale, Clara. (1905-1992)
Hamilton, Alice. (1869-1970)
Lathrop, Julia. (1858-1932)
Machel, Gracia Simbone. (1945-) Mozambi-
   can.
Masih, Isbal. (1982-1995) Pakistani.
McLean, Gordon. (1934-) born Canada.
Müller, George. (1805-1898) English, born
   Germany.
Tape, Mary McGladery. (1857-1928) born
   China.

Chileans

See also Hispanic-Americans.

Allende, Isabel. (1942-) Author.

Mistral, Gabriela Lucila Godoy y Alcayága. (1889-1957) Educator, poet. Nobel Prize winner.

Serrano, Lupe. (1930-) Dancer, educator, born Chile.

Chinese·

See also Immigrants to United States, Chinese.

Ban Chao. (d. 102) Historian, military leader.

Ban Gu. (32-92) Historian.

Ban Piao. (unknown) Historian, scholar.

Ban Zhao. (45-116) Historian.

Cheng I Sao. (Lady Ching) (1775-1844) Pirate.

Chiang Kai-Shek. (1887-1975) Military leader.

Chin Ch'iu. (1879-1907) Women's rights activist.

Chou En-Lai. (1898-1976) Communist leader.

Chuang Tzu. (369-286 B.C.) Philosopher, spiritual leader, cofounder of Taoism.

Confucius. (551-479 B.C.) Philosopher, spiritual leader, cofounder of Confucianism.

Da Fu. (712-?) Poet.

Dorgon. (1612-1650) Emperor, prince.

Fang, Lizhi. (1936-) Astrophysicist, human rights activist.

Hoei-Shin. (5th century) Explorer, spiritual leader.

Hsüan-tsang. (c. 602-664) Spiritual leader.

Hua Mu-lan. (c. 400) Warrior, disguised as man.

Jie, Ling. (1982-) Olympic gymnast.

Kublai Khan. (1215-1294) Mongol emperor.

Lai Cho San. (1922-1939) Pirate.

Lao-Tzu. (604-531 B.C.) Philosopher, spiritual leader, cofounder of Taoism.

Li Po (or Li Bo) (701-762) Poet.

Li Ch'ing Chao. (1084-1151) Poet.

Lin Xezu. (1785-1850) Educator, reformer.

Ling, Chai. (1966-) Political activist.

Liu Pang. (256-195 B.C.) Emperor.

Lu, Chen. (1976-) Olympic figure skater.

Ma Yuan. (1165-1225) Painter.

Mao Tse-tung. (1893-1976) Communist dictator, military leader.

Mencius. (371-289 B.C.) Philosopher, spiritual leader, cofounder of Confucianism.

Nee, Watchman. (1903-1972) Spiritual leader.

Qui Jin. (1875-1907) Poet, revolutionary, women's rights activist.

Shih Huang Di. (259-210 B.C.) Emperor.

Soong Ai-ling. (1889-1973) Financier, philanthropist.

Soong Charlie. (1866?-1918) Entrepreneur.

Soong Ching-ling. (1893-1981) Peace activist, wife of Sun Yat-Sen.

Soong May-ling. (1897-2003) Sociologist, wife of Chaing Kai Shek.

Sun Yat-Sen. (1866-1925) President China.

Tz-u-hsi. (1835-1908) Empress.

Wen-Chi, Lady. (c. 178) Poet.

Wu Chao. (625-705) Empress.

Yani, Wang. (1975-) Painter.

Yuan Me. (1716-?) Chef.

Zheng, Haixia. (1967-) Olympic basketball player.

Zheng He. (1371-1433) Navy admiral.

Choreographers

See Dancers and Choreographers.

City Government Officials

Arrington, Richard, Jr. (1934-) Mayor Birmingham, AL.

Bosley, Freeman R., Jr. (1954-) Mayor St. Louis.

Bradley, Thomas. (1917-1998) Mayor Los Angeles.

Brodie, William. (1741-1798) Scottish city official.

Byrne, Jane. (1934-) Mayor Chicago.

Cisneros, Henry. (1947-) Mayor San Antonio.

Cleveland, Grover. (1837-1908) Mayor Buffalo, NY.

Dinkins, David. (1927-) Mayor New York City.

Feinstein, Dianne. (1933-) Mayor San Francisco.

Gantt, Harvey B. (1943-) Mayor Charlotte, N.C.

Goode, W. Wilson. (1938-) Mayor Philadelphia.

Harvard, Beverly. (1950-) Police chief At
    lanta.
Kelly, Sharon Pratt. (1944-) Mayor Wash-
    ington D.C.
Ochoa, Estevan. (1831-1888) Mayor Tuc-
    son.
Peña, Federico. (1947-) Mayor Denver.
Perry, Carrie Saxon. (1931-) Mayor Hart-
    ford, CT.
Rodriguez, Matt. (1936-) Police superinten-
    dent Chicago.
Santos, Miriam. (1956-) City treasurer Chi-
    cago, born Puerto Rico.
Seguín, Juan N. (1806-1890) Mayor San
    Antonio.
Wilson, Sharifa. (unknown) City Council
    Palo Alto, CA.
Young, Andrew Jackson. (1932-) Mayor
    Atlanta.
Young, Coleman. (1918-1997) Mayor De-
    troit.

Civil Rights Activists

*Unless otherwise indicated, all these indi-
    viduals were activists for the civil rights of
    African-American people.*
See also Abolitionists; Human Rights Activ-
    ists.
Abbott, Robert Sengstacke. (1870-1940)
Abernathy, Ralph David. (1926-1990)
Ames, Jessie Daniel. (1883-1972)
Baker, Ella Josephine. (1903-1986)
Balch, Emily Greene. (1867-1961)
Baldwin, James. (1924-1987)
Bates, Daisy. (1914-1999)
Beals, Melba Pattilo. (1941-)
Bethune, Mary McLeod. (1875-1955)
Bolling, Thomas Spottswood, Jr. (1939-
    1990)
Bond, Julian. (1940-)
Brown, James. (1933-)
Clark, Kenneth B. (1914-)
Clark, Peter Humphries. (1829-1925)
Clark, Septima Poinsette. (1898-1987)
Coker, Daniel. (1780-1846)
Cole, Rebecca J. (1846-1922)
Colvin, Claudette. (1940-)
Cotera, Martha P. (1938-) Mexican-
    American civil rights.
Davis, Ossie. (1917-)

de Klerk, Fredrik Willem "F. W." (1936)
    South African Black rights.
Dees, Morris. (1936-)
Du Bois, W. E. B. (1868-1963)
Eckert, Elizabeth. (1942-)
Edelman, Marian Wright. (1939-)
Evers, Medger. (1925-1963)
Evers-Williams, Myrlie. (1933-)
Farmer, James. (1920-1999)
Farrakhan, Louis. (1933-)
Fortune, T. Thomas. (1856-1928)
Foster, Sarah Jane. (1839-1868)
Gantt, Harvey B. (1943-)
Garcia, Hector Perez. (1914-1996) Mexican-
    American civil rights, born Mexico.
Garvey, Amy-Jacques. (1896-1973)
Garvey, Marcus. (1887-1940) born Jamaica.
Gonzales, Rodolfo "Corkey." (1928-)
    Mexican-American civil rights.
Gregory, Dick. (1932-)
Guiterrez, Jose Angel. (1944-) Mexican-
    American civil rights.
Hamer, Fannie Lou. (1917-1977)
Hanson, Harriet. (1825-1911)
Harris, Wesley. (1941-)
Height, Dorothy. (1912-)
Hernandez, Maria Latigo. (1893-1986)
    Mexican-American civil rights, born Mex-
    ico.
Heschel, Abraham Joshua. (1907-1972) born
    Poland.
Hill, Mozell Clarence. (1911-1969)
Hope, John. (1868-1936)
Houston, Charles H. (1895-1950)
Hunter-Gault, Charlayne. (1942-)
Jackson, Jesse. (1941-)
Jay, Allen. (1831-1910)
Johns, Barbara. (1935-1991)
Johnson, Anthony. (1678?-)
Johnson, James Weldon. (1871-1938)
Jordan, Barbara. (1936-1996)
Jordan, Vernon E., Jr. (1935-)
King, Coretta Scott. (1927?-)
King, Martin Luther, Jr. (1929-1968)
Koontz, Elizabeth Duncan. (1919-1989)
Kuntzler, William. (1919-1995)
Mahoney, Mary Eliza. (1845-1926)
Malcolm X. (1925-1965)
Marshall, Thurgood. (1908-1993)
Martinez, Vilma. (1943-) Hispanic-
    American civil rights.

Mason, Biddy. (1818-1891)

McAliskey, Bernadette Devlin. (1947-) Irish civil rights.

McKinstry, Carolyn. (1949-)

Moore, Audley. (1898-1997)

Moses, Bob. (1935-)

Motley, Constance Baker. (1921-)

Muhammad, Elijah. (1897-1975)

Murray, Pauli. (1910-1985)

Nash, Diane. (1938-)

Norton, Daniel. (1840-1918)

Norton, Eleanor Holmes. (1937-)

Parks, Rosa. (1913-)

Parsons, Lucy. (1853-1943)

Pennington, James W. C. (1809-1870)

Perkins, John. (1930-)

Pleasant, Mary Ellen "Mammy." (1814-1904)

Poussaint, Alvin Francis. (1934-)

Powell, Adam Clayton, Jr. (1908-1972)

Randolph, Asa Philip. (1889-1979)

Rickey, Wesley Branch. (1881-1965)

Roc, John S. (1825-1866)

Ruffin, Josephine St. Pierre. (1842-1924)

Rustin, Bayard. (1910?-1987)

Salazar, Rubén. (1928-1970) Mexican-American civil rights, born Mexico.

Straker, David Augustus. (1842-1908)

Sullivan, Leon. (1922-2001)

Tape, Mary McGladery. (1857-1928) Chinese-American civil rights, born China.

Terrell, Mary Church. (1863-1954)

Tijerina, Rejes López. (1926-) Mexican-American civil rights

Trotter, William Monroe. (1872-1934)

Velasquez, William C. (1944-1988) Hispanic-American civil rights.

Washington, Augustus. (1820-?)

Webb, Sheyann. (1957-)

Wells-Barnett, Ida B. (1862-1931)

White, Walter. (1893-1955)

Wilkins, Roy. (1901-1981)

Wright, Louis Tompkins. (1891-1952)

Young, Andrew Jackson. (1932-)

Young, Whitney Moore, Jr. (1921-1971)

Civil War Figures

See also Army Personnel; Medal of Honor recipients; Military Leaders.

Females

Barton, Clara. (1821-1912) Union nurse, founder American Red Cross.

Berry, Carrie. (1854-?) Southern girl during siege of Atlanta.

Bickerdyke, Mary Ann "Mother." (1817-1901) Union nurse.

Boyd, Belle. (1843-1900) Confederate spy.

Brownell, Kady. (1842-?) Union heroine.

Chesnut, Mary Boykin. (1823-1886) Confederate author.

Clalin, Frances. (unknown) Union soldier, disguised as man.

Cushman, Pauline (Harriet Wood) (1833-1893) Union spy.

Davis, Varina Howell. (1826-1906) Author, First Lady of Confederacy.

Dix, Dorothea. (1802-1887) Superintendent union army nurses.

Edmonds, Sarah Emma. (1841-1898) Union nurse, soldier, spy, disguised as man.

Edmondson, Belle. (1840-1873) Confederate spy.

Frietchie, Barbara Hauer. (1766-1862) Union flag bearer.

Greenhow, Rose O'Neal. (1817-1864) Confederate spy.

Hodgers, Jenny. (1844-1915) Union soldier, disguised as man, born Ireland.

Lincoln, Mary Todd. (1818-1882) First Lady of Union.

Newman, Sarah Jane "Sally Skull." (1817-1866) Confederate heroine.

Stowe, Harriet Beecher. (1811-1896) Author.

Stuart, Miranda. (James Barry) (1795-1865) English union soldier, disguised as man.

Taylor, Susie King. (1848-1912) Educator, union nurse.

Tebe, Marie. (d. 1901) Union flag bearer, born France.

Tubman, Harriet. (1820-1913) Union spy.

Tyler, Julia Gardiner. (1820-1889) Confederate author, First Lady.

Van Lew, Elizabeth. (1818-1900) Union spy.

Velazquez, Loreta Janeta. (1842-?) Confederate soldier, disguised as man.

Walker, Mary Edwards. (1832-1919) Union physician. Medal of Honor recipient.

Wilson, Franny. (unknown) Soldier, disguised as man.

Military

Bates, Billy. (1843-1909) Soldier, POW.

Bridger, Jim. (1804-1881) Soldier.

Burnside, Ambrose Everett. (1824-1881) Union general.

Butler, Benjamin Franklin. (1818-1893) Union general.

Carney, William H. (1840-1908) Union soldier. Medal of Honor recipient.

Carson, Christopher "Kit." (1809-1868) Soldier.

Chacon, Rafael. (1833-1925) Soldier.

Clalin, Frances. (unknown) Union soldier, disguised as man.

Clem, Johnny. (1852-1937) Soldier as child.

Cody, William. (Buffalo Bill) (1846-1917) Confederate soldier.

Custer, George Armstrong. (1839-1876) Union general.

Delaney, Martin Robison. (1812-1885) Union major, physician.

Dunn, Oscar. (1820-1871) Union captain.

Edmonds, Sarah Emma. (1841-1898) Union soldier.

Ericsson, John. (1803-1889) Union navy.

Farragut, David Glasgow. (1801-1870) Union Navy admiral.

Fleetwood, Christian A. (1840-1914) Union sergeant major. Medal of Honor recipient.

Forrest, Nathan Bedford. (1821-1877) Confederate general.

Fremont, John Charles. (1813-1890) Union general.

Garfield, James A. (1831-1881) Union general.

Grant, Ulysses G. (1822-1885) Union general.

Halleck, Henry Wager. (1815-1872) Union general.

Hancock, Winfield Scott. (1824-1886) Union general.

Hardee, William Joseph. (1815-1873) Confederate general.

Harrison, Benjamin. (1833-1901) Union colonel.

Hayes, Rutherford B. (1822-1893) Union lieutenant colonel.

Hill, Ambrose Powell. (1825-1865) Confederate general.

Hodgers, Jenny. (1844-1915) Union soldier, disguised as man, born Ireland.

Hood, John Bell. (1821-1879) Confederate general.

Hooker, Joseph. (1814-1878) Union general.

Jackson, Thomas "Stonewall."(1824-1863) Confederate general.

Johnston, Joe. (1807-1891) Confederate general.

King, Dick. (1845-) Soldier as teenager.

Lee, Robert E. (1807-1870) Confederate general.

Longstreet, James. (1821-1904) Confederate general.

McClelland, George Brinton. (1826-1885) Union general.

McKinley, William. (1843-1901) Union major.

Meade, George Gordon. (1815-1872) Union general.

Parker, Ely Samuel. (1828-1895) Union assistant to General Grant.

Pickett, George Edward. (1825-1875) Confederate general.

Pierce, Ambrose. (1842-1914) Union soldier.

Pinchback, Pinckney Benton Stewart "P. B. S." (1837-1921) Union captain.

Powell, John Wesley. (1834-1902) Union soldier.

Sheridan, Philip Henry. (1831-1888) Union general.

Sherman, William Tecumseh. (1820-1891) Union general.

Smalls, Robert. (1839-1915) Union naval hero.

Stanley, Sir Henry Morton. (1841-1904) English confederate soldier.

Stockwell, Elisha. (1846-?) Teenage soldier.

Stuart, James Ewell Brown "Jeb." (1833-1864) Confederate general.

Stuart, Miranda. (1795-1865) English union soldier, disguised as man.

Tebe, Marie. (d. 1901) Union soldier, disguised as man.

Thomas, George Henry. (1816-1870) Union general.

Thompson, Ben. (1843-1884) Confederate soldier.

Velazquez, Loreta Janeta. (1842-?) Confederate soldier, disguised as man.

Vogelsang, Peter. (1815-1887) Lieutenant.

Williams, George Washington. (1849-1891) Union soldier.

Wilson, Franny. (unknown) Soldier, disguised as man.

Others

Augusta, Alexander T. (1825-1890) Union physician.

Barnard, George N. (1819-1902) Photographer.

Benjamin, Judah Philip. (1811-1884) Confederate attorney, statesman.

Brady, Matthew B. (1823-1896) Photographer.

Cook, George S. (1819-1902) Photographer.

Davis, Jefferson. (1808-1889) President of Confederacy.

Delaney, Martin Robison. (1812-1885) Union physician.

Ericsson, John. (1803-1889) Inventor of battleship.

Gardner, Alexander. (1821-1882) Photographer, born Scotland.

Gibson, James F. (unknown) Photographer, born Scotland.

Hickok, James Butler "Wild Bill." (1837-1876) Union scout.

Lincoln, Abraham. (1809-1865) President of U.S.

McCullagh, Joseph B. (1842-1896) Journalist, born Ireland.

Purvis, Charles Burleigh. (1842-1929) Surgeon.

Stanton, Edwin. (1814-1869) Secretary of War.

Colombians

See also Hispanic-Americans.

Marquez, Gabriel Garcia. (1928-) Author. Nobel Prize winner.

Rentería, Édgar. (1975-) Baseball player, born Colombia.

Ripoll, Shakira Mebarek. (Shakira) Pop singer.

Salavarrieta, Policarpa. "La Pola." (1795-1817) Political activist.

Colonists

Alden, John. (1599-1687) English.

Amherst, Jeffrey. (1717-1797) English.

Andros, Edmund. (1637-1714) born England.

Bacon, Nathaniel. (1647-1676)

Bailey, Anne Trotter. (1743-1875)

Berkeley, John. (1602-1678)

Berkeley, William. (1606-1677) born England.

Bienville, Jean Baptiste le Moyne. (1680-1767) French.

Boyd, William. (1674-1744)

Boylston, Zabadiel. (1679-1766) Physician.

Bradford, William. (1590-1657) Pilgrim, governor.

Bradstreet, Anne. (1612-1672)

Bradstreet, Simon. (1603-1697)

Brebeuf, Jean de, Father. (1593-1649) Jesuit missionary, priest.

Brent, Margaret. (1601-1671)

Brewster, William. (1567-1643) Pilgrim.

Buade, Louis de. (Frontenac et Palluau, Comte) (1622-1698) French colonist to Canada.

Byrd, William. (1674-1744)

Calvert, Cecil. (1606-1675) settled Maryland.

Calvert, Leonard. (1607-1647) settled Maryland.

Carter, Robert. (1663-1732) settled Virginia.

Carteret, Sir George. (1610-1680) settled New Jersey.

Church, Benjamin. (1639-1718) Massachusetts.

Claiborne, William. (1587-1677) Maryland.

Cornstalk. (1720-1777) Shawnee warrior.

Cromwell, Oliver. (1599-1658) Puritan colonist.

Cuffe, Paul. (1759-1817) Mariner, merchant.

Dorantz, Stephen. (Esteban, Estevanico) (1500-1539) Spanish.

Dudley, Joseph. (1647-1720)

Duston, Hannah. (1657-1736) Indian captive.

Dyer, Mary. (1610-1660) Hung for religious beliefs.

Edwards, Jonathan. (1703-1758)

Eliot, John. (1604-1690) Puritan missionary.

Endicott, John. (1589-1665) Puritan leader, colonial governor.

Galvez, Bernardo de. (1746-1786) Colonial governor, born Spain.

Gardiner, Lion. (1599-1663)

Gist, Christopher. (1706-1759)

Hamilton, Andrew. (1676-1741)

Hooker, Thomas. (1586-1647) Puritan preacher.

Hutchinson, Thomas. (1711-1780)

Iberville, Pierre le Moyne de. (1661-1706) Canadian, settled Los Angeles.

Ingles, Mary Draper. (1731-1815) Indian captive.

Johnson, William. (1714-1774) Superintendent of Indian Affairs.

Joques, Isaac. (1607-1646) French colonist in Canada.

La Tour, Charles Turquis de Sainte-Étienne de. (1593-1666) French colonist in Canada.

Leisler, Jacob. (1640-1691) New York.

Logan, James. (1674-1751) Pennsylvania.

Maisonneuve, Paul. (1612-1676) French colonial founder of Montreal.

Massasoit. (1600-1661) Wampanoag Indian chief.

Mather, Cotton. (1663-1728) Puritan minister.

Mather, Increase. (1639-1723) Puritan minister.

Menedéz de Aviles, Pedro. (1519-1574) Spanish explorer, founder of St. Augustine, FL.

Menendez, Francisco. (1700-1772) Colonial military hero, former African slave.

Metoyer, Marie-Therese. (1742-1816) Slave, landowner.

Minuit, Peter. (1580-1638) Dutch.

Montcalm, Louis-Joseph. (1712-1759) French colonist in Canada.

Mullens, Priscilla. (1604-1680) Wife of John Alden.

Musgrove, Mary. (1700-1763) Indian interpreter.

Nicholson, Francis. (1655-1728) Colonial governor.

Nurse, Rebecca. (1621-1692) Accused of witchcraft.

Oglethorpe, James. (1696-1785) settled Georgia.

Oñate, Juan de. (1550-1630) Spanish.

Opechancanough. (1556-1646) Lenape chief.

Parris, Betty. (1682-1760) Puritan, accused others of witchcraft.

Parris, Samuel. (1653-1720) Puritan minister, accused others of witchcraft, born England.

Penn, William. (1644-1718) settled Pennsylvania

Pepperell, William. (1696-1759) Massachusetts military leader.

Philip, King. (Metacom, Metacomet, Pometacom) (1638-1676) Wampanoag Indian chief.

Phips, William. (1651-1695) Colonial governor.

Pinckney, Eliza Lucas. (1722-1793) Agronomist, born West Indies.

Pontiac. (1720-1769) Ottawa chief.

Popé. (d. 1692) San Juan Pueblo military leader.

Portola, Gaspar de. (1723-1784) born Spain.

Powhatan. (1550-1608) Lenape chief.

Printz, Johan. (1592-1663) born Sweden.

Raleigh, Sir Walter. (1554-1618)

Ribaut, Jean. (1520-1565) French explorer, naval officer.

Rolfe, John. (1585-1622) Pilgrim, married Pocahontas.

Rowlandson, Mary. (1635-1682) Indian captive.

Savage, Tom. (1595-1627)

Schuyler, Peter. (1657-1724)

Sewall, Samuel. (1652-1730) Salem witch trials jurist.

Shirley, William. (1694-1771) Colonial governor, military leader.

Smith, John. (1580-1631) Colonial governor.

Squanto. (Tisquantum) (1580-1622) Wampanoag chief.

Standish, Miles. (1584-1656) Pilgrim.

Stuyvesant, Peter. (1610-1672) Settled New York.

Verendrye, Pierre. (1685-1749) French colonist in Canada.

Vergoose, Elizabeth "Mother Goose." (unknown) Storyteller.

Villagra, Gaspar Perez de. (1558-1620)

Walker, Thomas. (1715-1794)

Weetamoo. (1640-1676) Pocasset chief.

Weiser, Johann Conrad. (1696-1760) Indian interpreter, born Germany.

Wentworth, Benning. (1696-1770) Colonial

governor.

Wheelwright, John. (1592-1679) Puritan spiritual leader, settled New Hampshire.

Whitefield, George. (1714-1770) Spiritual leader.

Williams, Abigail. (1680-?) Puritan, accused others of witchcraft.

Williams, Eunice. (1697-1787) Puritan, Indian captive.

Williams, John. (1664-1729) Puritan minister.

Williams, Roger. (1603-1686) Spiritual leader, founder of Rhode Island.

Winslow, Anna Green. (1760-1779) Colonial girl.

Winslow, Edward. (1595-1655) Pilgrim.

Winthrop, John. (1588-1649) Colonial governor, puritan.

Wolfe, James. (1727-1759) English colonist in Canada.

Woodward, Henry. (1646-1685) Settled Carolinas.

Comedians

Allen, Gracie. (1900-1964)

Arnold, Roseann. (1952-)

Ball, Lucille. (1911-1989)

Benny, Jack. (1894-1974)

Burns, George. (1896-1996)

Carrey, Jim. (1962-)

Chaplin, Charlie. (1889-1997)

Cosby, Bill. (1937-)

De Generes, Ellen. (1958-)

Goldberg, Whoopi. (1950-)

Gregory, Dick. (1932-)

Guerra, Jackie. (1967-)

Hardy, Oliver. (1892-1957)

Hope, Leslie Townes " Bob." (1903-2003) born England.

Jefferson, Arthur Stanley. (Stan Laurel) (1890-1965) born England.

Keaton, Buster. (1895-1966)

Marin, Richard Anthony "Cheech." (1946-)

Marx, Groucho. (1890-1977)

Mencia, Carlos. (unknown) born Honduras.

Murphy, Eddie. (1961-)

Pryor, Richard. (1940-)

Rock, Chris. (1966-)

Roseann. *See* Arnold, Roseann.

Seinfeld, Jerry. (1954-)

Teller, Raymond Joseph "Teller." (1948-)

Wayans, Keenen Ivory. (1958-)

Williams, Bert. (1874-1922)

Community Activists

See also Human Rights Activists; Public Health Workers; Social Workers.

Addams, Jane. (1860-1935)

Comer, James P. (1934-)

Cordova, Dorothy. (1932-)

Cordova, Fred. (1931-)

Esu-Williams, Eka. (1956-) Nigerian.

Garcia, Emma. (1972-)

Ray, Charlotte E. (1850-1911)

Yin, Luoth. (1950-) born Cambodia.

Composers

American

Akiyoshi, Toshiko. (1929-) born China.

Anderson, Laurie. (1947-)

Armstrong, Louis. (1901-1971)

Babbitt, Milton. (1916-)

Ballard, Louis. (1931-) Quapaw and Cherokee Indian.

Barber, Samuel. (1910-1981)

Basie, William "Count." (1904-1984)

Beach, Amy. (1867-1944)

Bechet, Sidney. (1897-1959)

Berlin, Irving. (1888-1989) born Russia.

Bernstein, Leonard. (1918-1990)

Berry, Chuck. (1926-)

Blackman, Cindy. (1959-)

Blades, Ruben. (1948-)

Blake, James Hubert "Eubie." (1883-1983)

Braxton, Anthony. (1945-)

Byrne, David. (1952-) born Scotland.

Calloway, Cab. (1907-1994)

Casals, Pablo. (1876-1973) born Spain.

Coleman, Ornette. (1930-)

Copland, Aaron. (1900-1990)

Corea, Anthony "Chick." (1941-)

Cowell, Henry. (1897-1965)

Crumb, George. (1929-)

Davis, Miles Dewey III. (1926-1991)

Dorsey, Thomas Andrew. (1899-1993) Gospel music.

Dylan, Bob. (1941-)

Ellington, Edward Kennedy "Duke." (1899-1974)

Europe, James Reese. (1881-1939)

Fine, Vivian. (1913-)

Foster, Stephen. (1826-1864)
Gershwin, George. (1898-1937)
Gershwin, Ira. (1896-1983)
Gillepsie, John Birks "Dizzy." (1917-1993)
Glass, Philip. (1937-)
Goodman, Benjamin David "Benny." (1909-
    1986)
Gottschalk, Louis Moreau. (1829-1869)
Handy, William Christopher. (1873-1958)
Hopkinson, Francis. (1737-1791)
Ives, Charles. (1874-1954)
Johnson, Francis "Hall." (1883?-1970)
Johnson, James P. (1891-1976)
Joplin, Scott. (1868-1917)
King, Charles Edward. (1879-1950) born
    Hawaii.
Liliuokalani, Lydia. (1838-1917) Hawaiian.
Lincoln, Abbey. (1930-)
Locke, Alain Leroy. (1886-1954)
MacDowell, Edward. (1861-1908)
Marsalis, Wynton. (1961-)
Mingus, Charles. (1922-1979)
Monk, Thelonius. (1917-1982)
Morton, Ferdinand Joseph "Jelly Roll."
    (1885-1941)
Mulligan, Gerald "Gerry." (1927-1996)
Murray, David. (1955-)
Oliver, Joseph "King." (1885-1938)
Paik, Nam June. (1932-) born Korea.
Parker, Charles Christopher "Bird" Jr.
    (1920-1955)
Pastorius, Jaco. (1951-1987)
Powell, Earl "Bud." (1924-1966)
Price, Florence. (1888-1953)
Reich, Steve. (1936-)
Roach, Max. (1924-)
Rodgers, Richard. (1902-1979)
Schönberg, Arnold. (1874-1951) born Aus-
    tria.
Seeger, Ruth Crawford. (1901-1953)
Shaw, Artie. (1910-)
Simone, Nina. (1933-2003)
Sousa, John Philip. (1854-1932)
Spivey, Victoria. (1906-1976)
Springsteen, Bruce. (1949-)
Still, William Grant. (1895-1978)
Stravinsky, Igor Fedorovich. (1882-1971)
    born Russia.
Strayhorn, Billy. (1915-1967)
Swallow, Steve. (1940-)
Tower, Joan. (1938-)

Waller, Thomas Wright "Fats." (1904-1943)
Zwilich, Ellen. (1939-)

Austrian
Berg, Alan Alban. (1885-1935)
Haydn, Franz Joseph. (1732-1809)
Mahler, Gustav. (1860-1911)
Mozart, Wolfgang Amadeus. (1756-1791)
Paradis, Maria Theresia von. (1759-1824)
Schubert, Franz. (1797-1828)
Webern, Anton von. (1883-1945)

Belgian
di Lasso, Orlando. (1532-1594)

Brazilian
Villa-Lobos, Heitor. (1887-1959)

Czechoslovakian
Dvorak, Antonin. (1841-1904)
Smetana, Bedrich. (1824-1884)

English
Britten, Benjamin. (1913-1976) Opera.
Dowland, John. (1562-1626)
Elgar, Edward. (1857-1934)
Gilbert, Sir William. (1836-1911) Comic
    opera.
Handel, George Frideric. (1685-1759)
Smyth, Ethel. (1858-1944)
Sullivan, Sir Arthur. (1842-1900) Comic
    opera.
Webber, Andrew Lloyd. (1948-)

Finnish
Sibelius, Jean. (1865-1957)

French
Berlioz, Hector. (1803-1869)
Bizet, Georges. (1838-1875) Opera.
Boulanger, Nadia. (1887-1979)
Clugney, Odode. (879-942)
Debussy, Claude. (1862-1918)
Despres, Josquin. (1440-1521)
Gounod, Charles. (1818-1893) Sacred music
    and opera.
Mauchaut, Guillaume de. (1300-1377)
Offenbach, Jacques. (1819-1880) Operettas.
Rameau, Jean-Philippe. (1683-1764)
Ravel, Maurice. (1875-1937)
Satie, Erik. (1866-1925)

German
Bach, Johann Sebastian. (1685-1750)
Beethoven, Ludwig von. (1770-1827)
Brahms, Johannes. (1833-1897)
Gluck, Christoph Willibald. (1714-1787)
 Opera.
Hensel, Fanny Mendelssohn. (1805-1847)
Paumann, Konrad. (1415-1473)
Schumann, Clara. (1819-1896)
Schumann, Robert. (1810-1856)
Strauss, Richard. (1864-1949)
Wagner, Richard. (1813-1883)
Weber, Karl Maria Friedrich Ernst von.
 (1786-1826) Opera.

Hungarian
Bartok, Bela. (1861-1945)
Liszt, Franz. (1811-1886)

Indian
Tagore, Rabindranth. (1861-1941)

Italian
Bellini, Vincenzo. (1801-1835)
Boccherini, Luigi. (1741-1805)
Cimarosa, Domenico. (1749-1801) Comic
 opera.
D'Aresso, Guido. (992-1050) Liturgical
 music.
Donizetti, Gaetano. (1797-1848) Opera.
Gabrieli, Andrea. (1510-1586)
Galluppi, Baldassarre. (1706-1785) Opera.
Gregory I. (Gregory the Great) (540-604)
Marcello, Benedetto. (1686-1739) Opera.
Monteverdi, Claudio. (1567-1643)
Paganini, Niccolo. (1782-1840)
Paisiello, Giovanni. (1740-1816) Opera.
Palestrina, Giovanni Pierluigi da. (1525-
 1594)
Pergolesi, Giovanni Battista. (1710-1736)
Piccinni, Noccolo. (1728-1800) Opera.
Puccini, Giacomo. (1858-1924) Opera.
Rossini, Gioaccino. (1792-1868) Opera.
Scarlatti, Domenico. (1685-1757) Sacred
 music.
Strozzi, Barbara. (1619-1664)
Verdi, Giuseppe. (1813-1901)
Vivaldi, Antonio. (1678-1741)

Norwegian
Grieg, Edvard. (1843-1907)

Polish
Chopin, Frederic. (1810-1849)

Russian
Bordin, Alexander Porfiervich. (1833-1889)
 Opera.
Mussorgsky, Modest Petrovich. (1839-1881)
Prokofiev, Sergei Sergeevich. (1891-1953)
Rimsky-Korsakov, Nikolay Andreevich.
 (1844-1908)
Tchaikovsky, Peter Ilyich. (1840-1893)

Spanish
Albéniz, Isaac. (1860-1909)
Falla, Manuel de. (1876-1946) Ballet.
Granados, Enrique. (1867-1916)

Computer Pioneers
See also Entrepreneurs, Computers, Elec-
 tronics, and Media; Internet Pioneers.
Aiken, Howard. (1900-1973)
Allen, Paul. (1953-)
Babbage, Charles. (1791-1871) English.
Bezos, Jeffrey. (1964-)
Cray, Seymour. (1925-1996)
Eckert, J. Presper. (1919-1995)
Emeagwali, Philip. (1954-) born Nigeria.
Gates, Bill. (1955-)
Gini, Mari. (unknown) born Italy.
Hannah, Marc. (1956-)
Hewlett, Bill. (1913-2001)
Hodgins, Jessica. (unknown)
Hoff, Ted. (1937-)
Hollerith, Herman. (1860-1929)
Hopper, Grace. (1906-1972)
Hunt, Fern. (unknown)
Jobs, Steven. (1955-)
Kilby, Jack St. Clair. (1923-)
Labosky, Bonnie. (unknown)
Lovelace, Lady Ada Byron. (1815-1852)
 English.
Mahowald, Misha. (1963-)
Mauchly, John W. (1907-1980)
Moon, John P. (1938-)
Moore, Gordon. (1929-)
Noyce, Robert Norton. (1927-1990)
Packard, David. (1912-1996)
Shimomura, Tsutomu. (1965-) born Japan.
Torvalds, Linus. (1969-) Finnish.
Turing, Alan. (1912-1954) English.
Von Neumann, John. (1903-1957) born

Hungary.

Wang, An. (1920-1990) born China.

Watson, Thomas, Jr. (1914-1993)

Wozniak, Stephen. (1950-)

Conductors, Musical

See also Bandleaders.

Bernstein, Leonard. (1918-1990)

Boulanger, Nadia. (1887-1979) French.

Casals, Pablo. (1876-1973) born Spain.

Chung, Myung-Whun. (1953-) born Korea.

Despres, Josquin. (1440-1521) French.

Grieg, Edvard. (1843-1907) Norwegian.

Johnson, Francis " Hall." (1883?-1970)

Mahler, Gustav. (1860-1911) Austrian.

Mehta, Zubin. (1936-) born India.

Ozawa, Seiji. (1935-) born Japan.

Schönberg, Arthur. (1874-1951) born Austria.

Still, William Grant. (1895-1978)

Strauss, Richard. (1864-1949) German.

Congressional Medal of Honor Recipients

See Medal of Honor Recipients.

Congressmen/Women

Abzug, Bella. (1920-1988) New York.

Adams, John Quincy. (1767-1848) Massachusetts.

Bartlett, Josiah. (1729-1795) New Hampshire.

Barton, Bruce. (1886-1967) New York.

Boxer, Barbara. (1940-) California.

Braxton, Carter. (1736-1797) Virginia.

Bryan, William Jennings. (1860-1925) Nebraska.

Buchanan, James. (1791-1868) Pennsylvania.

Burke, Yvonne Braithwaite. (1932-) California.

Butler, Benjamin Franklin. (1818-1893) Massachusetts.

Calhoun, John Caldwell. (1782-1850) South Carolina.

Carroll, Charles. (1737-1832) Maryland.

Chase, Samuel. (1741-1811) Maryland.

Chisholm, Shirley. (1924-) New York.

Clay, Henry. (1777-1852) Kentucky.

Clymer, George. (1739-1813) Pennsylvania.

Collins, Cardiss. (1931-) Illinois.

Crockett, Davy. (1786-1836) Tennessee.

Davis, Jefferson. (1808-1889) Mississippi.

Davis, John W. (1873-1955) West Virginia.

De Priest, Oscar. (1871-1951) Illinois.

Dole, Robert. (1923-) Kansas.

Douglas, Helen Gahagan. (1900-1980) California.

Ellery, William. (1727-1820) Rhode Island.

Fenwick, Millicent. (1910-1992) New Jersey.

Ferraro, Geraldine. (1935-) New York.

Fillmore, Millard. (1800-1874) New York.

Floyd, William. (1734-1821) New York.

Ford, Gerald R. (1913-) Michigan.

Gallatin, Albert. (1761-1849) Pennsylvania.

Garfield, James A. (1831-1881) Ohio.

Gerry, Elbridge. (1744-1814) Massachusetts.

Gonzáles, Henry Barbosa. (1916-2000) Texas.

Gray, William H. "Bill." (1941-) Pennsylvania.

Gwinnett, Button. (1735-1777) Georgia.

Hall, Lyman. (1724-1790) Georgia.

Harrison, William Henry. (1773-1862) Ohio.

Hart, John. (1711-1779) New Jersey.

Hayes, Rutherford B. (1822-1893) Ohio.

Hewes, Joseph. (1730-1779) North Carolina.

Heyward, Thomas, Jr. (1746-1809) South Carolina.

Hooper, William. (1742-1790) North Carolina.

Hopkins, Stephen. (1707-1785) Rhode Island.

Hopkinson, Francis. (1737-1791) New Jersey.

Houston, Samuel. (1793-1863) Texas.

Hull, Cordell. (1871-1955) Tennessee.

Huntingdon, Samuel. (1731-1796) Connecticut.

Hutchinson, Thomas. (1711-1780) Massachusetts.

Jackson, Andrew. (1767-1863) Tennessee.

Jefferson, Thomas. (1743-1826) Virginia.

Johnson, Lyndon Baines. (1908-1973) Texas.

Jordan, Barbara. (1936-1996) Texas.

La Follette, Robert. (1855-1925) Wisconsin.

Lee, Francis Lightfoot. (1734-1797) Virginia.

Lee, Richard Henry. (1732-1794) Virginia.

Lewis, Francis. (1713-1802) New York.

Lincoln, Abraham. (1809-1865) Illinois.

Livingston, Philip. (1716-1778) New York.

Luce, Clare Boothe. (1903-1987) Connecticut.

Lynch, John R. (1847-1939) Mississippi.

Lynch, Thomas, Jr. (1749-1779) South Carolina.

Mann, Horace. (1796-1859) Massachusetts.

Matsui, Robert. (1941-) California.

McKean, Thomas. (1734-1817) Delaware.

McKinley, William. (1843-1901) Ohio.

Middleton, Arthur. (1742-1787) South Carolina.

Mikulski, Barbara. (1936-) Maryland.

Mineta, Norman. (1931-) California.

Mink, Patsy Takemoto. (1927-2002) Hawaii.

Morrill, Justin. (1810-1898) Vermont.

Morris, Gouverneur. (1752-1816) New York.

Morris, Lewis. (1726-1798) New York.

Morris, Robert. (1734-1806) Pennsylvania.

Morton, John. (1724-1777) Pennsylvania.

Nelson, Thomas, Jr. (1738-1789) Virginia.

Nixon, Richard Milhous. (1913-1994) California.

Norris, George. (1861-1944) Ohio.

Norton, Eleanor Holmes. (1937-)

Paca, William. (1740-1795) Maryland.

Pacheco, Romualdo. (1831-1899) California.

Paine, Robert Treat. (1731-1814) Massachusetts.

Penn, John. (1740-1788) North Carolina.

Pierce, Franklin. (1804-1869) New Hampshire.

Pinchback, Pinckney Benton Stewart "P. B. S." (1837-1921) Louisiana.

Polk, James K. (1795-1849) Tennessee.

Powell, Adam Clayton, Jr. (1908-1972) New York.

Rankin, Jeanette. (1880-1973) Montana.

Read, George. (1733-1798) Delaware.

Reifel, Ben. (1906-1990) South Dakota.

Richardson, Bill. (1947-) New Mexico.

Robertson, Alice Mary. (1854-1931) Oklahoma.

Rodney, Caesar. (1728-1784) Delaware.

Rohde, Ruth Bryan Owen. (1885-1954) Florida.

Ros-Lentinen, Ileana. (1952-) Florida.

Ross, George. (1730-1779) Pennsylvania.

Roybal, Edward Ross. (1916-) California.

Roybal-Allard, Lucille. (1941-) California.

Rush, Benjamin. (1745-1813) Pennsylvania.

Rutledge, Edward. (1749-1800) South Carolina.

Sanchez, Loreta. (1960-) California.

Saund, Dalip Singh. (1899-1973) California.

Schroeder, Patricia. (1940-) Colorado.

Sherman, Roger. (1721-1793) Connecticut.

Smalls, Robert. (1839-1915) South Carolina.

Smith, James. (1719-1806) Pennsylvania.

Smith, Margaret Chase. (1897-1995) Maine.

Stevens, Thaddeus. (1792-1868) Pennsylvania.

Stockton, Richard. (1730-1781) New Jersey.

Stone, Thomas. (1743-1787) Maryland.

Taylor, George. (1716-1781) Pennsylvania.

Thornton, Matthew. (1714-1803) New Hampshire.

Velazquez, Nydia. (1953-) New York.

Walton, George. (1741-1804) Georgia.

Waters, Maxine. (1938-) California.

Webster, Daniel. (1782-1852) New Hampshire and Massachusetts.

Whipple, William. (1730-1785) New Hampshire.

White, George Henry. (1852-1918) North Carolina.

Williams, William. (1731-1811) Connecticut.

Wilson, James. (1742-1798) Pennsylvania.

Witherspoon, John. (1723-1794) New Jersey.

Wolcott, Oliver. (1726-1797) Connecticut.

Wythe, George. (1726-1806) Virginia.

Young, Andrew Jackson. (1932-) Georgia.

Conservationists

See Environmentalists.

Costa Ricans

See also Hispanic-Americans.

Arias Sánchez, Oscar. (1941-) President. Nobel Peace Prize winner.

Cowboys and Ranchers

See also Pioneers and Frontiersmen.
Abbott, Teddy Blue. (1860-?)
Briones, Juana. (1802-1889)
Evans, Dale. (1912-2001)
Goodnight, Molly. (1839-1926)
Horn, Tom. (1806-1903)
James-Rodman, Charmayne. (1970-) Rodeo rider.
Love, Nat. (1854-1921)
Lucas, Tad. (1902-1990) Rodeo rider.
Mahan, Larry. (1943-) Rodeo cowboy.
McJunkin, George. (1851-1922) Cowboy.
Mulhall, Lucille. (1855-1940) Cowgirl.
Oakley, Annie. (1860-1926)
Pickett, Bill. (1870-1932) Rodeo rider.
Riggs, Lillian. (1888-1977)
Rogers, Roy. (1911-1998)
Stillwell, Hallie Crawford. (1897-1997)
Vallejo, Mariano Guadalupe. (1808-1890)

Crimefighters

See also Forensic Scientists.
Alvarez, Eduardo. (unknown) Argentine police inspector.
Bean, Judge Roy. (1825-1903) Western.
Bowie, James. (1796-1836) Texas Ranger.
Brown, Henry. (1857-1884) Marshal.
Earp, Wyatt. (1848-1929) Western lawman.
Fairstein, Linda. (1947-) District Attorney.
Fielding, Henry. (1707-1754) English.
Fisher, John King. (1854-1884)
Hickok, James Butler "Wild Bill." (1837-1876) Western sheriff.
Hoover, J. Edgar. (1895-1972) FBI director.
Kefauver, Estes. (1903-1969)
Klarsfeld, Beate. (1939-) German.
Klarsfeld, Serge. (1935-) Hungarian.
Masterson, William Barclay "Bat." (1853-1921) Marshal.
McNelly, Leander H. (1844-1877) Texas Rangers captain.
Ness, Eliot. (1903-1957)
Peel, Sir Robert. (1788-1850) English Scotland Yard.
Pinkerton, Allan. (1819-1884) born Scotland.
Purvis, Melvin. (1903-1960) Federal agent.
Reaves, Bass. (1824-1910) Marshal.
Rodriguez, Matt. (1936-)
Steele, Samuel. (1851-1919) Canadian mounty.
Thompson, Ben. (1843-1884)
Wiesenthal, Simon. (1908-) Austrian.

Criminals

See also Assassins; Gangsters; Outlaws; Serial Killers.
Borden, Lizzie. (1860-1927) Murdered parents, folk hero.
Borgia, Lucrezia. (1480-1519) Italian villainess.
Buck, Rufus. (d. 1896) Gang leader.
Cooper, Dan "D. B." (unknown) Hijacker.
Devi, Phoolan. (1963-) Indian robber.
Frith, Mary "Moll Cutpurse." (1590-1659) English pickpocket.
Goldsby, Crawford. (1876-1896)
Himes, Chester. (1909-1984)
Locusta of Gaul. (fl. 50 A.D.) Roman poisoner.
Smith, Madelaine. (1835-1928) Scottish poisoner.

Cubans

See also Hispanic-Americans.
Alonso, Alicia. (1921-) Ballet dancer.
Arnaz y de Acha, Desiderio Alberto, III. (Desi Arnaz) (1917-1986) Actor, bandleader, born Cuba.
Canseco, Jose. (1964-) Baseball player, born Cuba.
Castro, Fidel. (1926-) Dictator.
Cruz, Celia. (1924-2003) Salsa singer, born Cuba.
de Dios Unanue, Manuel. (1943-1992) Editor, publisher, born Cuba.
Dihigo, Martin "El Maestro." (1905-1971) Baseball player, born Cuba.
Estefan, Gloria. (1957-) Singer, born Cuba.
Finlay, Carlos Juan. (1833-1915) Medical researcher, physician.
Fornés, Maria Irene. (1930-) Playwright, born Cuba.
Garcia, Andy. (1957-) Actor, born Cuba.
Goizueta, Roberto C. (1931-1997) Entrepreneur cola, born Cuba.
Guiteras, Juan. (1852-1925) Medical researcher, physician, born Cuba.
Lopez, Lourdes. (1958-) Dancer, born Cuba.
Luque, Dolf. (1890-1957) Baseball player, born Cuba.

Martí, José. (1853-1895) Political activist, revolutionary.

Mendez, José. (1887-1928) Baseball player.

Minoso, Saturnine Orestes "Minnie." (1922-) Baseball player, born Cuba.

Ordóñez, Rey. (1971-) Baseball player, born Cuba.

Perera, Hilda. (1926-) Children's author, born Cuba.

Pozo, Chano. (1915-1948) Jazz musician.

Ros-Lentinen, Ileana. (1952-) Congress-woman, state legislator, born Cuba.

Pozo, Chano. (1915-1948) Jazz musician, born Cuba.

Sanchez, Pedro. (1940-) Soil scientist, born Cuba.

Saralegui, Cristina. (1948-) Television personality, born Cuba.

Secada, Jon. (1963-) Singer, born Cuba.

Tiant, Luis, Sr. (1906-1977) Baseball player, born Cuba.

Torriente, Cristobal. (1895-1938) Baseball player.

Ybor, Vincente Martinex. (1818-1896) Entrepreneur cigars, founder of Ybor City, FL.

Cult Leaders

See also Utopian Community Founders.

Baker, George F., Jr. (Father Divine) (1882-1965)

Beukels, Jan. (John of Leiden) (1509-1536) German.

Hubbard, L. Ron. (1911-1986) Church of Scientology.

Jones, Jim. (1931-1978) Peoples Temple.

Koresh, David. (1959-1993) Branch Davidians.

Moon, Sun Myung. (1920-) Korean Unification Church founder, "Moonies."

Prabhupada, A. C. Bhaktivedanta. (1896-1977) Hare Kirshnas.

Curlers

Schmirler, Sandra. (1964-2000) Canadian.

Czechs

See also Immigrants to United States, Czechoslovakian.

Berk, Allan. (1918-) Holocaust survivor.

Caslavska, Vera. (1942-) Olympic gymnast.

Dubcek, Alexander. (1921-1992) Political activist.

Dvorak, Antonin. (1841-1904) Composer.

Elias, Patrick. (1976-) Hockey player.

Gutman, Sarel. (17th century) Merchant.

Havel, Vaclav. (1936-) Human rights activist, playwright, president.

Hejduk, Milan. (1976-) Olympic hockey player.

Hus, Jan. (1369-1415) Scholar, spiritual leader.

Laitman, Helen Kornitzer. (unknown) Holocaust survivor.

Lustig, Arnost. (1926-) Author, Holocaust survivor, screenwriter.

Mendlovic, Leopold. (unknown) Holocaust survivor.

Mikita, Stan. (1940-) Hockey player.

Mraz, George. (1945-) Jazz musician.

Navratilova, Martina. (1956-) Tennis player.

Porsche, Ferdinand. (1875-1952) Automaker.

Roth, Irving. (1930-) Holocaust survivor.

Schindler, Emilie. (1909-2001) Holocaust rescuer.

Schindler, Oskar. (1908-1974) Holocaust rescuer.

Smetana, Bedrich. (1824-1884) Composer.

Tiktiner, Rivkah bat Meir "Rebecca." (16th century) Author.

Wallenstein, Albrecht von. (1583-1634) Bohemian military leader.

Ziska, Jan. (1358-1424) Bohemian military leader.

Dancers and Choreographers

Ailey, Alvin. (1931-1989)

Allen, Debbie. (1956-)

Alonso, Alicia. (1921-) Cuban.

Astaire, Fred. (1899-1987)

Balanchine, George. (1904-1983) born Russia.

Baryshnikov, Mikhail. (1948-) born Russia.

Bujones, Fernando. (1955-)

Burrell, Stanley Kirk. (Hammer) (1962-)

Cisneros, Evelyn. (1958-)

De Mille, Agnes. (1905-1993)

Dunham, Katherine. (1909-)

Fosse, Bob. (1927-1987)

Glover, Savion. (1974-)
Graham, Martha. (1894-1991)
Hammer. *See* Burrell, Stanley Kirk.
Jackson, Janet. (1966-)
Jamison, Judith. (1944-)
Limón, José Arcadia. (1908-1972) born
   Mexico.
Lopez, Lourdes. (1958-) born Cuba.
Makarova, Natalia. (1940-) born Russia.
Mata Hari. *See* Zelle, Margareta Gertrude.
Mitchell, Arthur. (1934-)
Moreno, Rita. (1931-) born Puerto Rico.
Nureyev, Rudolf. (1938-1993) Russian.
Pavlova, Anna. (1881-1931) Russian.
Perez, Rosie. (1964-)
Robbins, Jerome. (1918-1998)
Robinson, Bill "Bojangles." (1878-1949)
Rogers, Ginger. (1911-1995)
Romero, Jacy. (1965-) Chumash Indian.
Serrano, Lupe. (1930-) born Chile.
Tallchief, Maria. (1925-) Osage Indian.
Tharp, Twyla. (1941-)
Williams, Bert. (1874-1922)
Zelle, Margareta Gertrude. (Mata Hari)
   (1876-1917)

Danes

See also Immigrants to United States, Dan-
   ish.
Andersen, Hans Christian. (1805-1875)
   Children's author, storyteller.
Bajer, Fredrik. (1837-1922) Peace activist,
   political leader. Nobel Peace Prize winner.
Bamberger, Niels. (1928-) Holocaust survi-
   vor.
Bering, Vitus Jonassen. (1681-1741) Ex-
   plorer.
Bohr, Niels. (1885-1962) Physicist. Nobel
   Prize winner.
Brahe, Sophie. (1556-1643) Astronomer.
Brahe, Tycho. (1546-1601) Astronomer.
Canute II. (994-1035) Military leader.
Christiansen, Ole Kirk. (1891-1958) Entre-
   preneur toy manufacturer.
Kieler, Jorgen. (1920-) Holocaust rescuer.
Münch -Nielsen, Preben. (1926-) Holocaust
   rescuer.
Sejr, Arne. (1922-) Holocaust resistance
   worker.
Thomsen, Christian Jurgenson. (1786-1865)
   Archaeologist.

Worsaae, Jens Jacobs A. (1821-1885) Archaeologist.

Deaf
See Hearing Impaired.

Declaration of Independence Sign-
ers
Adams, Samuel. (1722-1803) Massachu-
   setts.
Bartlett, Josiah. (1729-1795) New Hamp-
   shire.
Braxton, Carter. (1736-1797) Virginia.
Carroll, Charles. (1737-1832) Maryland.
Chase, Samuel. (1741-1811) Maryland.
Clymer, George. (1739-1813) Pennsylvania.
Ellery, William. (1727-1820) Rhode Island.
Floyd, William. (1734-1821) New York.
Franklin, Benjamin. (1706-1790) Pennsyl-
   vania.
Gerry, Elbridge. (1744-1814) Massachu-
   setts.
Gwinnett, Button. (1735-1777) Georgia.
Hall, Lyman. (1724-1790) Georgia.
Hart, John. (1711-1779) New Jersey.
Hewes, Joseph. (1730-1779) North Carolina.
Heyward, Thomas, Jr. (1746-1809) South
   Carolina.
Hooper, William. (1742-1790) North Caro-
   lina.
Hopkins, Stephen. (1707-1785) Rhode Is-
   land.
Hopkinson, Francis. (1737-1791) New Jer-
   sey.
Huntingdon, Samuel. (1731-1796) Con-
   necticut.
Jefferson, Thomas. (1743-1826) Virginia.
Lee, Francis Lightfoot. (1734-1797) Vir-
   ginia.
Lee, Richard Henry. (1732-1794) Virginia.
Lewis, Francis. (1713-1802) New York.
Livingston, Philip. (1716-1778) New York.
Lynch, Thomas, Jr. (1749-1779) South
   Carolina.
McKean, Thomas. (1734-1817) Delaware.
Middleton, Arthur. (1742-1787) South Caro-
   lina.
Morris, Gouverneur. (1752-1816) New
   York.
Morris, Lewis. (1726-1798) New York.

Morris, Robert. (1734-1806) Pennsylvania.
Morton, John. (1724-1777) Pennsylvania.
Nelson, Thomas, Jr. (1738-1789) Virginia.
Paca, William. (1740-1795) Maryland.
Paine, Robert Treat. (1731-1814) Massachusetts.
Penn, John. (1740-1788) North Carolina.
Read, George. (1733-1798) Delaware.
Rodney, Caesar. (1728-1784) Delaware.
Ross, George. (1730-1779) Pennsylvania.
Rush, Benjamin. (1745-1813) Pennsylvania.
Rutledge, Edward. (1749-1800) South Carolina.
Sherman, Roger. (1721-1793) Connecticut.
Smith, James. (1719-1806) Pennsylvania.
Stockton, Richard. (1730-1781) New Jersey.
Stone, Thomas. (1743-1787) Maryland.
Taylor, George. (1716-1781) Pennsylvania.
Thornton, Matthew. (1714-1803) New Hampshire.
Walton, George. (1741-1804) Georgia.
Whipple, William. (1730-1785) New Hampshire.
Williams, William. (1731-1811) Connecticut.
Wilson, James. (1742-1798) Pennsylvania.
Witherspoon, John. (1723-1794) New Jersey.
Wolcott, Oliver. (1726-1797) Connecticut.
Wythe, George. (1726-1806) Virginia.

Dentists
Collins, Daniel A. (1916-)
Holliday, John "Doc." (1852-1887)
Morton, William T. G. (1819-1868)
Wells, Horace. (1815-1848)

Dictators
See also Hatemongers; Military Leaders; Revolutionaries; Terrorists.
Caesar, Julius. (100-44 B.C.) Roman.
Castro, Fidel. (1926-) Cuban.
Franco, Francisco. (1892-1975) Spanish.
Hitler, Adolf. (1889-1945) German.
Ho Chi Minh. (1890-1969) Vietnamese.
Hussein, Saddam. (1937-) Iraqian.
Mao Tse-Tung. (1893-1976) Chinese.
Marcos, Ferdinand. (1917-1989) Filipino.
Mussolini, Benito. (1883-1945) Italian.
Perón, Juan Domingo. (1895-1974) Argentine.

Stalin, Joseph. (1879-1953) Russian.

Directors, Theatrical
Barrault, Jean-Louis. (1910-1994) French.
Olivier, Sir Laurence. (1907-1989) English.

Disability Rights Activists
See also AIDS activists.
Callahan, John. (1951-)
Chamberlin, Judi. (1944-)
Cochrane, Elizabeth. (Nellie Bly) (1865-1922)
Driscoll, Jean. (1966-)
Hamilton, Marilyn. (1947-)
Keller, Helen. (1880-1968)
Nussbaum, Susan. (1953-)
Pinel, Philippe. (1745-1826) French.
Roberts, Ed. (1939-1995)
Rousso, Harilyn. (1946-)
Russell, Harold. (1914-2002)
Smith, Mildred Davidson Austin. (1916-1993)
ten Broek, Jacobus. (1911-1968) born Canada.
Wade, Cheryl Marie. (unknown)

Disabled
See Emotionally Disabled; Hearing Impaired; Learning Disabled; Physically Challenged; Visually Impaired.

Divers
Lee, Sammy. (1920-)
Louganis, Greg. (1960-)
McCormick, Patricia Keller. (1930-)

Doctors
See Physicians.

Dominicans
See also Hispanic-Americans.
Aleu, Moises. (1966-) Baseball player, born Dominican Republic.
Alou, Felipe. (1935-) Baseball manager, born Dominican Republic.
Beltré, Adrián. (1979-) Baseball player, born Dominican Republic.
Castillo, Luis. (1975-) Baseball player, born Dominican Republic.
Charles, Eugenia. (1919-) Prime minister of

Dominica.

de la Renta, Oscar (1932-) Fashion designer, born Dominican Republic.

Fernandez, Mary Joe. (1971-) Tennis player, born Dominican Republic.

Furcal, Rafael. (1980-) Baseball player, born Dominican Republic.

Guerrero, Vladimir. (1976-) Baseball player, born Dominican Republic.

Guzman, Cristian. (1978-) Baseball player, born Dominican Republic.

Marichal, Juan. (1937-) Baseball player, born Dominican Republic.

Martinez, Pedro. (1971-) Baseball player, born Dominican Republic.

Mondesi, Rául. (1971-) Baseball player, born Dominican Republic.

Palmeiro, Rafael. (1964-) Baseball player, born Dominican Republic.

Pérez, Neifi. (1973-) Baseball player, born Dominican Republic.

Ramirez, Manny. (1972-) Baseball player, born Dominican Republic.

Sosa, Sammy. (1968-) Baseball player, born Dominican Republic.

Tatis, Fernando. (1975-) Baseball player, born Dominican Republic.

Tejada, Miguel. (1976-) Baseball player, born Dominican Republic.

Vargas, Tetelo. (1906-1971) Baseball player, born Dominican Republic.

Dutch

See also Immigrants to United States, Dutch.

Andrew, Brother. (1928-) Holocaust resistance worker, missionary.

Asser, Tobias. (1838-1913) Attorney. Nobel Peace Prize winner.

Barents, Willem. (1550-1597) Arctic explorer.

Blankers-Koen, Fanny. (1918-2004) Olympic track and field athlete.

Bosch, Hieronymous. (1450-1516) Painter.

Einthoven, Willem. (1860-1927) Medical researcher, physician. Nobel Prize winner.

Erasmus, Desiderius. (1469-1536) Philosopher, scholar, spiritual leader.

Flinker, Moshe. (1926-1944) Author, Holocaust victim.

Frank, Anne. (1929-1945) Author, Holocaust victim, born Germany.

Gies, Miep. (1909-) Holocaust rescuer, born Austria.

Hals, Frans. (1581-1666) Painter.

Hasselaar, Kenau. (1526-1588) Political activist.

Huygens, Christiaan. (1629-1695) Astronomer.

Leeuwenhoek, Anton van. (1632-1723) Biologist, medical researcher, physician.

Leyster, Judith. (1609-1660) Painter.

Limbourg, Herman. (fl. 1400s) Painter.

Limbourg, Jean. (fl. 1400s) Painter.

Limbourg, Paul. (fl. 1400s) Painter.

Maurice of Nassau. (1567-1625) Military leader, Prince of Orange.

Merian, Anna Marie Sibylla. (1647-1717) Illustrator, naturalist.

Minuit, Peter. (1580-1638) Colonist.

Mondrian, Piet. (1872-1944) Painter.

Polak, Ina. (1923-) Holocaust survivor.

Polak, Jack. (unknown) Holocaust survivor.

Pritchard, Marion van Binsbergen. (1920-) Holocaust rescuer.

Rembrandt. (Harmen Szoon van Rijn) (1606-1669) Painter.

Simons, Menno. (1524-1561) Spiritual leader, founder Mennonites.

Sokolow, Yvonne Kray. (1927-) Holocaust survivor.

Stuyvesant, Peter. (1610-1672) Colonist, settled New York.

Tasman, Abel. (1603-1659) Explorer.

Ten Boom, Corrie. (1892-1979) Author, Holocaust rescuer.

Ter Bosch, Gerard. (1617-1681) Painter.

Tinne, Alexandrine. (1839-1869) Explorer.

Tromp, Maarten von. (1597-1653) Navy admiral.

Van der Woude, Elizabeth. (1657-1694) Adventurer.

Van Gogh, Vincent. (1853-1890) Painter.

Van Meegeren, Hans. (1889-1947) Painter, swindler.

Vermeer, Johannes. (1632-1675) Painter.

Wijsmuller, Gertrude. (unknown) Holocaust rescuer.

William I, the Silent. (1533-1584) Prince of Orange.

Zernike, Frits. (1888-1966) Chemist, inventor, physicist. Nobel Prize winner.

East Timorians

See also Indonesians.

Belo, Carlos Felipe Ximenes. (1948-) Peace
activist, spiritual leader. Nobel Peace
Prize winner.

Ramos-Horta, José. (1949-) Journalist, political activist. Nobel Peace Prize winner.

Ecologists

See Environmentalists.

Economists

Friedman, Milton. (1912-)

Galbraith, John Kenneth. (1908-) born Canada.

Gramm, Wendy Lee. (1945-)

Greenspan, Alan. (1926-)

Keynes, John Maynard. (1883-1946)
English.

Malthaus, Thomas Robert. (1766-1834)
English.

Marx, Karl. (1818-1883) German.

Naylor, Rosamond. (unknown) Agricultural
economist.

Rivlin, Alice. (1931-)

Smith, Adam. (1723-1790) Scottish.

Editors and Publishers

See also Journalists.

Abbott, Robert Sengstacke. (1870-1940)

Adams, Samuel. (1722-1803)

Annenberg, Walter. (1908-2002)

Bache, Benjamin Franklin. (1769-1798)

Barnett, Claude. (1890-1967)

Bennett, James Gordon. (1795-1872) born
Scotland.

Bloomer, Amelia Jenks. (1818-1894)

Boudinot, Elias. (1803-1839) Cherokee Indian.

Brown, George. (1818-1880) Canadian.

Brown, Helen Gurley. (1922-)

Cahan, Abraham. (1860-1951) born Lithuania.

Carothers, Wallace. (1896-1937)

Cornish, Samuel E. (1795-1858)

Cousins, Margaret. (1905-1996)

de dios Unanue, Manuel. (1943-1992) born
Cuba.

Draper, Margaret Green. (1727-1804)

Du Bois, W. E. B. (1868-1963)

Estrada, Alfredo. (unknown)

Fenno, John. (1751-1798)

Fielding, Henry. (1707-1754) English.

Franklin, Chester A. (1880-1955)

Freneau, Philip. (1752-1832)

Fried, Alfred. (1864-1921) Austrian.

Garrison, William Lloyd. (1805-1879)

Goddard, Mary Katherine. (1738-1816)

Graham, Katharine. (1917-2001)

Graves, Earl G. (1935-)

Greeley, Horace. (1811-1872)

Hale, Sarah Josepha Buell. (1788-1879)

Harmsworth, Alfred. (1865-1922) English.

Hearst, William Randolph. (1863-1951)

Hobby, Oveta Culp. (1905-1995)

Hopkins, Stephen. (1707-1785)

Johnson, John H. (1918-)

Kennedy, John Fitzgerald, Jr. (1960-1998)

King, Charles Edward. (1879-1950) born
Hawaii.

Leslie, Miriam Florence Folline "Frank."
(1836-1914)

Lifshitz, Aliza. (1951-) Mexican.

Lovejoy, Elijah. (1802-1837)

Lozano, Ignacio E. (1886-1953) Mexican.

Luce, Henry R. (1898-1967)

Mencken, Henry Louis "H. L." (1880-1956)

Monroe, Harriet. (1860-1936)

Murdoch, Rupert. (1931-) born Australia.

Murphy, John H., Sr. (d. 1922)

Murray, Judith Sargent. (1751-1820)

Neuharth, Allen. (1924-)

Ng Poon Chew. (1866-1931) born China.

Nicholson, Eliza Jane Poitevent Holbrook.
(1849-1896)

Onassis, Jacqueline Lee Bouvier Kennedy.
(1929-1994)

Perkins, Maxwell. (1884-1947)

Perry, Christopher J. (d. 1921)

Powell, Clilan Bethany. (1894-1977)

Pride, Charley. (1938-) Music publishing.

Pulitzer, Joseph. (1847-1911) born Hungary.

Ramirez, Francisco. (1830-1890)

Reid, Helen Rogers. (1882-1970)

Reston, James. (1909-1995) born Scotland.

Ripley, George. (1802-1880)

Rivington, James. (1727-1802) English.

Rodale, Jerome Irving "J. I." (1898-1971)

Rodriguez, Richard. (1944-)

Ruggles, David. (1810-1849)

Russworm, John B. (1799-1851)

Schroeder, Patricia. (1940-)

Scott, William Alexander. (1903-1934)

Sholes, Christopher. (1819-1890)

Stone, Isidor Feinstein "I. F." (1907-1989)

Szold, Henrietta. (1860-1945)

Taylor, Susan. (1946-)

Thomson, Roy Herbert. (1894-1973) Canadian.

Thurman, Wallace. (1902-1934)

Trotter, William Monroe. (1872-1934)

Vann, Robert. (1879-1940)

Warhol, Andy. (1928-1987)

Watterson, Henry. (1840-1921)

White, William Allen. (1868-1944)

Young, Plummer Bernard, Sr. (1884-1962)

Educators

Agassiz, Louis. (1807-1873) Natural history, born Switzerland.

Alving, Amy. (unknown) Engineering.

Bailey, Liberty Hyde. (1858-1954) Botany.

Balanchine, George. (1904-1983) Dance.

Barnard, Henry. (1811-1900) Established public schools in Connecticut, U.S. Commissioner of Education.

Barnhart, Cynthia. (unknown) Engineering.

Bascom, Florence. (1862-1945) Geology.

Beach, Sheryl Luzzader. (unknown) Geography, geology.

Beadle, George. (1903-1989) College president, genetics.

Bechet, Sidney. (1897-1959) Music.

Beecher, Catherine. (1800-1878) Teacher training.

Bethune, Mary McLeod. (1875-1955)

Blackburn, Robert. (1920-2003) Art.

Bontemps, Arnaud, "Arna." (1902-1973)

Butler, Nicholas Murray. (1862-1947) College president.

Cannon, Walter Bradford. (1871-1945) Physiology.

Cardozo, Francis Louis. (1837-1903) Established public schools in South Carolina, college for African American students.

Cary, Mary Ann Shadd. (1822-1893)

Cavazos, Lauro F. (1927-) Physiology.

Cavell, Edith. (1865-1915) Nursing.

Chern, Shiing-Shen. (1911-) Mathematics.

Clapp, Cornelia. (1849-1934) Zoology.

Clark, Christopher. (unknown) Biology.

Clark, Peter Humphries. (1829-1925) High school teacher.

Clark, Septima Poinsette. (1898-1987)

Cobb, Jewel Plummer. (1924-) Biology.

Cobb, William Montague. (1904-1990) Medicine.

Cofer, Judith Ortiz. (1952-) Writing.

Coker, Daniel. (1780-1846) Schools for African American students.

Collins, Marva Delores. (1936-) Inner city schools.

Comer, James P. (1934-) Public health.

Cooper, Anna Julia. (1858-1964)

Coppin, Fannie Jackson. (1836-1913)

Cotera, Martha P. (1938-) born Mexico.

Craig, Lulu Sadler. (1868-1972?)

Cullen, Countee. (1903-1946) Writing.

Davis, Angela.(1944-) University.

Davis, Richard. (1930-) Music.

Delaney, Annie Elizabeth. (1891-1995)

Delaney, Sarah Louise "Sadie." (1889-1998)

Dewey, John. (1859-1952) Education.

Dix, Dorothea. (1802-1887) Nursing.

Douglass, Sarah Mapps. (1806-1882) Schools for African American children.

Drew, Charles Richard. (1904-1950) Medicine.

Du Bois, W. E. B. (1868-1963)

Dukepoo, Frank C. (1943-) Biology.

Edwards, Jonathan. (1703-1758) College president.

Ehrlich, Paul. (1932-) Zoology.

Eisenstein, Judith Kaplan. (1909-1996) Music.

Ellison, Ralph. (1919-1994) Writing.

Escalante, Jaime. (1930-) High School mathematics, born Bolivia.

Esu-Williams, Eku. (1956-) Nigerian AIDS educator.

Ferguson, Catherine "Katy." (1779-1854) Teacher of poor children.

Forsythe, Ruby Middleton. (1905-1992)

Forten, Charlotte. *See* Grimke, Charlotte Forten.

Foster, Sarah Jane. (1839-1868)

Frazier, E. Franklin. (1894-1962) Sociology.

Futrell, Mary Hatwood. (1940-)

Gabrieli, Andrea. (1510-1586) Italian music educator.

Gibbs, Mifflin. (1823-1915) College president.

Gini, Mari. (unknown) Computer science.

Goodrich, Annie W. (1866-1954) Nursing.

Granville, Evelyn Boyd. (1924-) Mathematics.

Gratz, Rebecca. (1781-1869) Sunday schools for Jewish children.

Gray, Asa. (1810-1888) Botany.

Gray, William "Bill." (1941-)

Gray, Martha. (unknown) Engineering.

Grimke, Charlotte Forten. (1837-1914)

Hamilton, Alice. (1869-1970) Public health, industrial medicine.

Hansberry, William Leo. (1894-1965) History.

Harris, Wesley. (1941-) Aeronautics.

Hata, Prateep Ungsongtham. (1952-) Thai educator.

Hauptman, Judith. (unknown) Talmud.

Hayakawa, Samuel Ichiye. (1906-1992) College president.

Healy, Patrick Francis. (1834-1910) College president.

Heschel, Abraham Joshua. (1907-1972) Theology.

Hilda of Whitby. (614-680) English.

Hill, Mozell Clarence. (1911-1969) Sociology.

Hinton, William Augustus. (1883-1959) Medicine.

Hirsch, Samson Raphael. (1808-1888) German educator.

Hope, John. (1868-1936)

Houston, Charles H. (1895-1950)

Jackson, Shirley Ann. (1946-) Physics.

Jacobi, Mary Putnam. (1842-1906) Medicine.

Jean-Murat, Carolle. (1950-) Haitian public health educator.

Jemison, Mae C. (1956-)

Jex-Blake, Sophia. (1840-1912) English medical educator.

Johnson, Hazel W. (1927-) Nursing.

Johnson, James Weldon. (1871-1938)

Johnson, Mordecai. (1890-1976) College president.

Jordan, Irving King. (1943-) College president.

Just, Ernest Everett. (1883-1941) Biology.

Kang, Younghill. (1903-1973) born Korea.

Kaplan, Mordecai. (1881-1983) born Lithuania.

Kapuscinski, Anne. (unknown) Agricultural science, born France.

Kerr, Barbara. (unknown) Environmental concerns.

Kingston, Maxine Hong. (1940-) Writing.

Koontz, Elizabeth Duncan. (1919-1989) President of National Education Association.

La Fontaine, Henri. (1854-1943) Belgian.

Lamas, Carlos Saavedra. (1878-1959) Argentine.

Laney, Lucy Craft. (1854-1933)

Lange, Christian. (1869-1938) Norwegian.

Leonowens, Anna. (1834-19150 Welsh teacher of King of Siam's children.

Lifshitz, Aliza. (1951-) Mexican medical educator.

Lin Xezu. (1785-1850) Drug education.

Locke, Alain Leroy. (1886-1954) Music.

Longshore, Hannah E. Myers. (1810-1901) Medicine.

Luria, Isaac. (1534-1572) Israeli theology.

Luthuli, Albert. (1898-1967) South African.

Lyon, Mary. (1797-1849) Founded first college for women.

Makhubu, Lydia Phindile. (1937-) Swaziland chemistry educator.

Mann, Horace. (1796-1859) College president.

Marsalis, Wynton. (1961-) Music.

Martinez, Father Antonio José. (1793-1867) Mexican.

Mather, Increase. (1639-1723) College president.

Mays, Benjamin E. (1895-1984)

McAuliffe, Christa. (1948-1986)

McKenner, George, III. (1940-)

McLuhan, Marshall. (1911-1980) Canadian.

Mendelssohn, Moses. (1729-1786) German.

Millais, John Everett. (1829-1896) Art.

Mistral, Gabriela Lucila y Alcayága. (1889-1957) Chilean poetry educator.

Mizrahi, Asenath Barazani. (16th century) Kurdistani.

Moise, Penina. (1797-1880) Hebrew.

Montessori, Maria. (1870-1952) Italian education theorist.

Morrison, Toni. (1931-) Writing.

Moses, Bob. (1935-)

Mossell, Gertrude Bustill. (1855-1948)

Moton, Robert Russa. (1867-1940) College president.

Nuttall, Thomas. (1786-1859) Environmental science educator, born England.

Oates, Joyce Carol. (1938-) Literature.

Odum, Eugene. (1913-2002) Ecology.

Orr, John Boyd. (1880-1971) Scottish nutrition educator.

Osler, Sir William. (1849-1919) Canadian medical educator.

Palmer, Anyim. (unknown)

Pantoja, Antonio. (1922-2002) born Puerto Rico.

Pauling, Linus Carl. (1901-1994) Chemistry.

Peake, Mary Smith. (1823-1862) Teacher of poor children.

Pennington, James W. C. (1809-1870)

Pestalozzi, Johann. (1746-1827) Swiss theorist on education.

Plummer, Edouard E. (unknown)

Poodry, Clifton. (1943-) Seneca Indian biology teacher.

Preston, Ann. (1813-1872) Medical education for women.

Purvis, Charles Burleigh. (1842-1929) Medicine.

Rabassa, Gregory. (1922-) Languages.

Rashi. (Solomon ben Isaac) (1040-1105) French Jewish theology.

Ray, Charlotte E. (1850-1911)

Rimsky-Korsakoff, Nikolai Andreevich. (1844-1908) Russian music educator.

Ringgold, Faith. (1930-) Art.

Robertson, Alice Mary. (1854-1931)

Rodriguez, Eloy. (1947-) Plant science.

Rodriguez, Richard. (1944-)

Rose, Mary Swartz. (1874-1941) Nutrition.

Rosenzweig, Franz. (1886-1939) German.

Salk, Jonas. (1914-1995) Medicine.

Savage, Augusta Christine. (1892-1962) Sculpture.

Say, Thomas. (1787-1834) Entomology.

Schechter, Solomon. (1849-1915) Theology, born Romania.

Schnirer, Sarah. (1833-1935) Polish educator, established schools for Jewish girls.

Schomburg, Arthur. (1874-1938) born Puerto Rico.

Senenmut. (fl. 1495 B.C.) Egyptian.

Serrano. Lupe. (1930-) Dance, born Chile.

Seton, Elizabeth Ann. (1774-1821) Catholic education for children.

Shapira-Luria, Miriam. (15th century) Italian educator Talmud.

Steiner, Rudolf. (1861-1925) Austrian education theorist.

Suzuki, Daisetz Teitan "D. T." (1870-1966) born Japan.

Taylor, Susie King. (1848-1912) Teacher of soldiers during Civil War.

Temin, Howard. (1934-) Medicine.

tenBroek, Jacobus. (1911-1968) born Canada.

Thayer, Eli. (1819-1899)

Thompson, Mary Harris. (1829-1895)

Thurman, Howard. (1900-1981)

Tien, Chang-Lin. (1935-) University chancellor, born China.

Turner, Charles Henry. (1867-1923) High school biology.

Turner, James Milton. (1840-1915) Schools for African American children.

Turpin, Tom. (unknown) Entomology.

Twilight, Alexander Lucius. (1795-1857)

Villa-Lobos, Heitor. (1887-1959) Brazilian educator music.

Volta, Alessandro. (1746-1827) Italian educator physics.

Warren, Adelina Otero. (1881-1965) School administrator.

Washington, Augustus. (1820-?)

Washington, Booker T. (1856-1915) College president, teachers college.

Wauneka, Annie Dodge. (1910-1997) Public health.

Whitfield, Princess. (1937-)

Willard, Emma Hart. (1787-1870) First college for women.

Williams, Daniel Hale. (1856-1931) Medicine.

Wilson, Woodrow. (1856-1924)

Wilson-Hawkins, Carla. (unknown)

Wing, Yung. (1828-1912) born China.

Witherspoon, John. (1723-1794) College president.

Woodruff, Hale Aspacio. (1900-1980) Art.

Woodson, Carter G. (1875-1950) History.

Wycliffe, John. (1320-1384) English educator at Oxford.

Young, Roger Arliner. (1889-1964) Zoology.

Zunz, Leopold. (1794-1886) German educator Jewish theology.

Egyptians, Ancient

See also Gods and Goddesses, Egyptian.
Ahmose. (fl. 1535 B.C.) Naval captain.
Amenemhet I. (f. 1991-1962 B.C.) King.
Amenemhet III. (1842-1797 B.C.) King.
Amenhotep III. (1886-1849 B.C.) King.
Amenhotep IV. (Akhaneten) (1370?-1340?
    B.C.) King, spiritual leader.
Arius. (c. 256-336) Spiritual leader, founder
    of Arianism.
Cleopatra VII. (69-30 B.C.) Ruler.
Cleopatra Selene of Mauretania. (40 B.C.-6
    A.D.) Daughter of Cleopatra VII.
Djoser. (fl. 2668-2649 B.C.) King.
Harkhuf. (c. 2275 B.C.) Adventurer.
Hatshepsut. (1500-1460 B.C.) Pharoah.
Horemheb. (fl. 1321-1293 B.C.) King.
Hypathia. (355-415) Astronomer, mathema-
    tician, philosopher.
Imhotep. (3000-2950 B.C.) Architect.
Khufu. (fl. 2589-2566 B.C.) King.
Mary Prophetetissa of Alexandria. (1st cen-
    tury A.D.) Chemist, inventor.
Menes. (3100-3038 B.C.) Pharoah.
Nebhepetre Mentuhotep I. (fl. 2060-2010
    B.C.) King.
Nefertari. (fl. 1270 B.C.) Queen.
Nefertiti. (fl. 1372-1350 B.C.) Queen.
Pepi II. (fl. 2278-2184 B.C.) King.
Ptahhotep. (fl. 2400 B.C.) Author.
Ramesses II. (fl. 1279-1212 B.C.) King.
Ramesses III. (fl. 1182-1151 B.C.) King.
Rekhmire. (fl. 1460 B.C.) Jurist, tax collec-
    tor.
Senenmut. (fl. 1495 B.C.) Architect, educa-
    tor.
Senwosret I. (1971-1928 B.C.) King.
Senwosret III. (fl. 1874-1841 B.C.) King.
Seti I. (fl. 1291-1278 B.C.) King.
Snefru. (fl. 2613-2589 B.C.) King.
Thutmose III. (fl. 1504-1450 B.C.) King.
Tiye. (fl. 1370 B.C.) Queen.
Tutankhamun. (1347-1329 B.C.) King.
Weni. (fl. 2300 B.C.) General, judge.

Egyptians, Modern

Mubarak, Mohamad Hosni. (1929-) Presi-
    dent.
Nasser, Gamal Abdel. (1918-1970) Presi-
    dent.
Sadat, Anwar. (1918-1981) President. Nobel
Peace Prize winner, Presidential Medal of
    Freedom recipient.
Shaarawi, Huda. (1879-1947) Women's
    rights activist.
Wuhsha. (11th Century) Businesswoman.

Egyptologists

See also Archaeologists.
Breasted, James Henry. (1865-1935)
Carter, Howard. (1873-1939) English.
Champollion, Jean-François. (1790-1832)
    French.
Herbert, George. (1866-1923) English.
Weeks, Kent R. (unknown)

Emotionally Disabled

Barnes, Djuna. (1892-1982) Author, journal-
    ist, playwright.
Bizet, Georges. (1838-1875) French opera
    composer.
Campbell, Earl. (1955-) Football player.
Carrington, Leonora. (1917-) Painter.
Chamberlin, Judi. (1944-) Disability rights
    activist.
Duke, Patty. (1946-) Actor.
Duncanson, Robert Scott. (1821-1872)
    Painter.
Fitzgerald, Zelda Sayre. (1900-1948) Wife
    of F. Scott.
Jackson, Shirley. (1919-1965) Author.
James, Alice. (1848-1892) Author.
Kempe, Margery. (1373-1440) Author.
Kerouac, Jack. (1922-1969) Author.
Mistral, Gabriela Lucila Godoy y Alcayága.
    (1889-1957) Chilean educator, poet.
Mourning Dove. (Christine Quintasket)
    (1888-1936) Okanogan Indian author, Na-
    tive American rights activist.
Münch, Edvard. (1863-1944) Norwegian
    painter.
Oppenheim, Meret. (1913-1985) Swiss jew-
    elry designer, painter, poet, sculptor, born
    Germany.
Pastorius, Jaco. (1951-1987) Composer, jazz
    musician.
Pollock, Jackson. (1912-1956) Painter.
Rossini, Gioaccino. (1792-1868) Italian
    composer.
Schumann, Robert. (1810-1856) German
    composer, musician.
Smetana, Bedrich. (1824-1884) Czech com-

poser.

Van der Goes, Hugo. (1440-1482) Belgian painter.

Whittle, Sir Frank. (1907-1996) English inventor, Royal Air Force pilot.

Woolf, Virginia. (1882-1941) English author.

Young, Roger Arliner. (1889-1964) Educator, zoologist.

Engineers

Aeronautical

Alving, Amy. (unknown)

Andrée, August. (1854-1897) Swedish.

Banning, James Herman. (1900-1933)

Bean, Alan. (1932-)

Brill, Yvonne. (1924-) born Canada.

Crews, Jeanne Lee. (unknown)

Darden, Christine. (1942-)

Duke, Charles. (1935-)

Ericsson-Jackson, Aprille Joy. (unknown)

Faget, Maxim. (1921-2004)

Glenn, John. (1921-)

Harris, Wesley. (1941-)

Henson, William. (1812-1888) born England.

Houbolt, John. (fl. 1960)

Irwin, James. (1930-1991)

Ivins, Marsha. (1951-)

Johnson, Katherine. (1918-)

Korolev, Sergei. (1906-1966) Russian.

Lear, William. (1902-1978)

Lilienthal, Otto. (1848-1896) German.

Mozhaiski, Alexander. (1825-1890) Russian.

Sampson, Henry. (1934-)

Scott, David. (1932-)

Shirley, Donna. (1941-)

Shurney, Robert. (1921-)

Sikorsky, Igor. (1889-1972) born Russia.

Von Braun, Werner. (1912-1977) born Germany.

Whittle, Sir Frank. (1907-1996) English.

Automotive

Benz, Karl. (1844-1929) German.

Daimler, Gottlieb. (1834-1900) German.

Biomedical

Dunbar, Bonnie. (1949-)

Gray, Martha. (unknown)

Greatbatch, Wilson. (1919-)

Hounsfield, Sir Godfrey N. (1919-) English.

Ceramic

Dunbar, Bonnie. (1949-)

Chemical

Griffith, Linda. (unknown)

Ramirez, Carlos A. (1953-)

Rillieux, Norbert. (1806-1894)

Civil

Barnhart, Cynthia. (unknown)

Brunel, Marc. (1769-1849) French.

Chanute, Octave. (1832-1910) born France.

Crowe, Frank. (1882-1946)

Emeagwali, Philip. (1941-) born Nigeria.

Fulton, Robert. (1765-1815)

Goethals, George W. (1858-1928)

L'Enfant, Pierre Charles. (1754-1825) born France.

Parks, Paul. (1923-)

Roebling, John Augustus. (1806-1869) born Germany.

Roebling, Washington Augustus. (1837-1926)

Electrical

Ader, Clement. (1841-1926) French.

Armstrong, Edwin Howard. (1890-1954)

Bushnell, Nolan. (1943-)

Cray, Seymour. (1925-1996)

Crosthwait, David Nelson, Jr. (1898-1976)

Farnsworth, Philo Taylor. (1906-1971)

Gabor, Dennis. (1900-1979) Hungarian.

Hoff, Ted. (1937-)

Kilby, Jack St. Clair. (1923-)

Moon, John P. (1938-)

Ochoa, Ellen. (1959-)

Resnick, Judith. (1949-1986)

Tesla, Nikola. (1856-1943) born Yugoslavia.

Wang, An. (1920-1990) born China.

Engineering Physics

Gourdine, Meredith. (1929-1998)

Environmental

Colmenaaves, Margarita. (1957-)

Mechanical
Croslin, Michael. (1933-)
Daimler, Gottlieb. (1834-1900) German.
Davis, N. Jan. (1953-)
Dunbar, Bonnie. (1949-)
Eiffel, Alexandre Gustave. (1832-1923)
  French.
Eriksson-Jackson, Aprille Joy. (unknown)
Estrada, Alfredo. (unknown)
Green, Dannellia Gladden. (1966-)
Lee, Mark C. (1952-)
Lucas, Anthony Francis. (1855-1896) born
  Austria.
Morgan, Jill. (unknown)
Stephenson, George. (1781-1848) English.
Zais, Karen. (unknown)

Military
Vauban, Sebastien LePreste de. (1633-1707)
  French.

Mining
Girard, Jami. (unknown)
Hoover, Herbert. (1874-1964)

Paper Science
Young, Charonda J. Jacobs. (1967-)

Unspecified
Burns, Ursula. (1958-)
Leonardo da Vinci. (1452-1519)
Powell, William J. (1897?-1942)
Tolliver, Peter. (1927-)

English

See also Immigrants to United States, Eng-
  lish.
Adams, William. (1564-1620) Explorer.
Aguilar, Grace. (1816-1847) Author,
  scholar.
Albert. (1819-1861) Prince, husband of
  Queen Victoria.
Alcock, Sir John. (1892-1919) Aviation pio-
  neer, World War I captain.
Alcuin of York. (732-804) Scholar.
Alfred the Great. (849-901) Navy founder.
Amanpour, Christiane. (1958-) Broadcast
  journalist, Gulf War correspondent.
Amherst, Jeffrey. (1717-1797) American
  Revolutionary War military leader.

Anderson, Elizabeth Garrett. (1836-1917)
  Physician.
Angell, Sir Norman. (1873-1967) Author,
  peace activist. Nobel Peace Prize winner.
Anne. (1665-1714) Queen.
Anning, Mary. (1799-1847) Paleontologist.
Arkwright, Sir Richard. (1732-1792) Inven-
  tor.
Arthur. (6th century) King, folk hero.
Austen, Jane. (1775-1817) Author.
Aylward, Gladys. (1902-1970) Missionary,
  World War I spy.
Babbage, Charles. (1791-1871) Computer
  pioneer, mathematician.
Bader, Sir Douglas. (1910-1982) Pilot,
  World War II hero.
Baird, John Logie. (1888-1946) Inventor.
Baker, Florence von Sass. (1841-1916) Ex-
  plorer, born Romania.
Baker, Sir Samuel White. (1821-1893) Ex-
  plorer.
Bannister, Roger. (1929-) Olympic track and
  field athlete.
Behn, Aphra Johnson. (1640?-1689) Play-
  wright, poet, spy.
Bell, Gertrude. (1868-1926) Adventurer,
  archaeologist, explorer.
Benham, Gertrude. (1867-1938) Mountain-
  eer.
Berners-Lee, Tim. (1955-) Internet pioneer.
Besant, Annie. (1847-1933) Human rights
  activist, journalist, orator, reformer.
Bishop, Isabella Lucy "Bird." (1831-1904)
  Adventurer.
Blackbeard. *See* Teach, Edward.
Blake, William. (1757-1827) Engraver,
  painter, poet.
Blunt, Lady Anne. (1837-1917) Explorer.
Boleyn, Anne. (1507-1536) Wife of Henry
  VIII.
Boole, George. (1815-1864) Mathematician.
Booth, Catherine. (1829-1890) Co-founder
  of Salvation Army, human rights activist.
Booth, William. (1829-1912) Co-founder of
  Salvation Army, human rights activist,
  spiritual leader.
Born, Max. (1882-1970) Physicist, born
  Poland. Nobel Prize winner.
Boyle, Robert. (1627-1691) Chemist, inven-
  tor, physicist.

Bradford, William. (1590-1657) Colonial governor.

Brewster, William. (1567-1643) Pilgrim.

Britten, Benjamin. (1913-1976) Composer.

Bronte, Anne. (1820-1849) Author.

Bronte, Branwell. (1817-1848) Painter.

Bronte, Charlotte. (1816-1855) Author, poet.

Bronte, Emily. (1818-1848) Author, poet.

Browning, Elizabeth Barrett. (1806-1861) Poet.

Browning, Robert. (1812-1889) Poet.

Bulwer-Lytton, Edward. (1803-1873) Author.

Bunyan, John. (1628-1688) Author, spiritual leader.

Burbridge, E. Margaret. (1919-) Astronomer.

Burgoyne, John. (1723-1792) Military leader, playwright.

Burke, Edmund. (1729-1797) Author, orator, philosopher, political activist.

Burton, Sir Richard Francis. (1821-1890) Explorer, linguist, soldier, translator.

Byron, Lord. *See* Gordon, George.

Cabot, John. (1450-1499) Explorer, born Italy.

Carpenter, Iris. (unknown) Journalist, World War II correspondent.

Carroll, Lewis. *See* Dodgson, Charles.

Carter, Howard. (1873-1939) Archaeologist, egyptologist.

Cartland, Barbara. (1901-2000) Author.

Catherine of Aragon. (1485-1536) Queen.

Caton-Thompson, Gertrude. (1888-1985) Archaeologist.

Cavanagh, Kit. (Christian Walsh) (1667-1739) Soldier, disguised as man.

Cavell, Edith. (1865-1915) Educator, World War I nurse and heroine.

Cavendish, Henry. (1731-1810) Chemist, physicist.

Cayley, George. (1773-1857) Aviation pioneer.

Cecil, Robert. (1864-1958) Attorney, peace activist, statesman. Nobel Peace Prize winner.

Chain, Sir Ernst Boris. (1906-1979) Biochemist, medical researcher. Nobel Prize winner.

Chamberlain, J. Austen. (1863-1937) Political activist, statesman. Nobel Peace Prize winner.

Chamberlain, Neville. (1869-1940) Prime Minister.

Charles. (1947-) Prince of Wales.

Charles I. (1600-1649) King.

Charles II. (1630-1685) King.

Chaucer, Geoffrey. (1343-1400) Diplomat, poet, scholar.

Cheesman, Lucy Evelyn. (1881-1969) Entomologist.

Christie, Agatha. (1891-1976) Author.

Churchill, John. (1650-1722) Military leader.

Churchill, Sir Winston Leonard Spencer. (1874-1965) Author, prime minister. Nobel Prize winner.

Clark, Grahame. (1907-1995) Archaeologist, author.

Claude, Albert. (1899-1983) Biologist, World War I Intelligence, born Belgium. Nobel Prize winner.

Conrad, Joseph. (1857-1924) Author, born Poland.

Constable, John. (1776-1837) Painter.

Conway, John H. (1937-) Mathematician.

Cook, James. (1728-1779) Explorer.

Coram, Thomas. (1668-1751) Children's rights activist, human rights activist.

Cranmer, Thomas. (1489-1556) Spiritual leader.

Cremer, Sir William. (1828-1908) Labor leader, organization cofounder, workers' rights activist. Nobel Peace Prize winner.

Crick, Francis H. C. (1916-2004) Molecular biologist. Nobel Prize winner.

Cromwell, Oliver. (1599-1658) Military leader.

Dahl, Roald. (1916-1990) Children's author.

Dalton, John. (1766-1844) Chemist.

Dampier, William. (1652-1715) Adventurer, explorer, pirate.

D'Arcy, William Knox. (1849-1917) Attorney, entrepreneur oil.

Darling, Grace. (1815-1842) Lighthouse keeper's daughter who rescued people when very young.

Darwin, Charles. (1809-1882) Naturalist.

Davy, Humphrey. (1778-1829) Chemist, inventor.

Defoe, Daniel. (1660-1731) Author, secret agent.

Diana. (1961-1997) Princess of Wales. Human rights activist.

Dickens, Charles. (1812-1870) Author.

Dirac, Paul Adrien Maurice. (1902-1984) Physicist. Nobel Prize winner.

Disraeli, Benjamin. (1804-1881) Prime Minister.

Dixie, Florence. (1857-1905) Adventurer, author, women's rights activist.

Dodgson, Charles. (Lewis Carroll) (1832-1898) Children's author.

Dodwell, Christina. (1951-) Adventurer, author.

Donne, John. (1572-1631) Poet, spiritual leader.

Dowland, John. (1562-1626) Composer, musician.

Durrell, Gerald. (1925-1995) Environmentalist, zoologist.

Edward I. (1239-1307) Military leader, king.

Edward II. (1287-1327) King.

Edward VIII. (1894-1972) Duke of Windsor.

Edward the Black Prince. (1330-1376) Prince of Wales.

Elgar, Edward. (1857-1934) Composer.

Eliot, George. See Evans, Mary Ann.

Eliot, John. (1604-1690) Puritan missionary.

Eliot, Thomas Stearns "T. S." (1888-1965) Playwright, poet. Nobel Prize winner, Presidential Medal of Honor recipient.

Elizabeth I. (1533-1603) Queen.

Elizabeth II. (1926-) Queen.

Epstein, Sir Michael Anthony. (1921-) Medical researcher, physician.

Evans, Arthur. (1851-1941) Archaeologist.

Evans, John. (1823-1908) Archaeologist.

Evans, Mary Ann. (George Eliot) (1819-1880) Author.

Every, Henry. (1653-?) Pirate.

Faraday, Michael. (1791-1867) Chemist, inventor.

Faulds, Henry. (fl. 1880) Forensic scientist, physician.

Fawkes, Guy. (1570-1606) Undercover agent, folk hero.

Fegen, Edward Fogarty. (1895-1940) World War II Navy commander.

Fielding, Henry. (1707-1754) Attorney, author, crime fighter, editor, jurist, playwright.

Fleming, John Ambrose. (1849-1945) Physicist.

Fountaine, Margaret. (1862-1940) Author, environmentalist, lepidopterist.

Fox, George. (1624-1691) Spiritual leader, founder Quaker religion.

Franklin, Sir John. (1786-1847) Arctic explorer.

Franklin, Rosalind Elsie. (1920-1958) Molecular biologist, x-ray crystallographer.

Freud, Anna. (1895-1982) Physician, psychoanalyst, born Austria.

Frith, Mary "Moll Cutpurse." (1590-1659) Pickpocket.

Frobisher, Martin. (1535-1594) Explorer.

Fry, Elizabeth. (1780-1845) Human rights activist, prison reformer.

Gainsborough, Thomas. (1727-1788) Painter.

Galahad, Sir. (6th century) Knight, folk hero.

Garrick, David. (1717-1779) Actor, playwright.

Garrod, Dorothy. (1892-1968) Archaeologist.

George III. (1738-1820) King.

George V. (1865-1936) King.

George VI. (1895-1952) King.

George, David Lloyd. (1863-1945) Prime Minister, World War I military leader.

Gilbert, Sir Humphrey. (1539-1583) Explorer.

Gilbert, Sir William. (1836-1911) Composer, songwriter.

Gladstone, William. (1809-1898) Prime Minister.

Godiva, Lady. (1010-1067) Countess, reformer, folk heroine.

Goodall, Jane. (1934-) Primatologist.

Goodwin, Jan. (1944-) Journalist.

Gordon, George. (Lord Byron) (1788-1824) Poet.

Gresham, Thomas. (1518-1579) Financier.

Guinevere. (6th century) Princess, married to King Arthur, folk heroine.

Gwendolen. (fl. 1075-1060 B.C.) Warrior queen.

Hall, Radclyffe. (1886-1943) Author, poet, dressed as man.

Halley, Edmund. (1656-1742) Astronomer.

Handel, George Frideric. (1685-1759) Composer.

Hardy, Thomas. (1840-1928) Author, poet.

Harmsworth, Alfred. (1865-1922) Publisher.

Harvey, William. (1578-1657) Anatomist.

Hawking, Stephen. (1942-) Astrophysicist.

Henry II. (1133-1189) King.

Henry III. (1207-1272) King.

Henry V. (1387-1422) King.

Henry VI. (1421-1471) King.

Henry VII. (1457-1509) King.

Henry VIII. (1491-1547) King.

Henry, Sir Edward. (1859-1931) Forensic scientist.

Hepworth, Barbara. (1903-1975) Sculptor.

Herbert, George. (1866-1923) Archaeologist, egyptologist.

Herschel, Caroline. (1750-1848) Astronomer.

Herschel, Sir John. (1792-1871) Astronomer.

Herschel, William. (1738-1822) Astronomer.

Hilda of Whitby. (614-680) Educator, saint, spiritual leader.

Hodgkin, Dorothy Crowfoot. (1910-1994) Chemist, x-ray crystallographer. Nobel Prize winner.

Hogarth, William. (1697-1764) Painter.

Holland, Dave. (1946-) Jazz musician.

Holmes, Arthur. (1890-1965) Geologist.

Hood, Robin. (1290-1346) Outlaw, political activist, folk hero.

Hooke, Robert. (1635-1703) Inventor.

Hounsfield, Sir Godfrey N. (1919-) Biomedical engineer, inventor. Nobel Prize winner.

Howard, John. (1726-1790) Prison reformer.

Howe, William. (1729-1814) American Revolutionary War Commander in Chief of British forces.

Hudson, Henry. (1565-1631) Explorer.

Huxley, Aldous. (1894-1963) Author.

Ireland, William Henry. (1777-1835) Swindler.

Irvine, Andrew. (1896-1924) Explorer, mountaineer.

Irving, Henry. (1838-1905) Actor.

James I. (1566-1625) King.

Jeffreys, Sir Alec. (1950-) Forensic scientist, geneticist.

Jenner, Edward. (1749-1823) Medical researcher, physician.

Jex-Blake, Sophia. (1840-1912) Educator, physician.

John. (1167-1216) King.

Johnson, Amy. (1903-1941) Aviator, World War II pilot.

Johnson, Samuel. (1709-1784) Journalist, lexicographer.

Johnson, William. (1714-1774) Colonist, superintendent of Indian Affairs.

Joule, James Prescott. (1818-1889) Physicist.

Julian of Norwich. (1342-1416) Nun, religious mystic.

Kean, Edmund. (1787-1833) Actor.

Keats, John. (1795-1821) Poet.

Kempe, Margery. (1373-1440) Author.

Kenyon, Kathleen. (1906-1978) Archaeologist.

Keynes, John Maynard. (1883-1946) Economist.

Killigrew, Lady Elizabeth. (1530-1570) Pirate.

Kingsley, Mary. (1862-1900) Adventurer, author, explorer.

Kipling, Rudyard. (1865-1936) Author, born India. Nobel Prize winner.

Lancelot, Sir. (6th century) Knight of Round Table, legendary.

Lawrence, D. H. (1885-1930) Author.

Lawrence, Thomas Edward. (Lawrence of Arabia) (1888-1935) Archaeologist, World War I military leader.

Layard, Austen Henry. (1817-1894) Adventurer, archaeologist.

Lead, Jane. (1624-1704) Mystic.

Leakey, Louis S.B. (1903-1972) Anthropologist, archaeologist, paleontologist.

Leakey, Mary. (1913-1996) Anthropologist, archaeologist.

Leigh, Samuel. (1785-1852) Missionary.

Lennon, John. (1940-1980) Musician, singer.

Lister, Joseph. (1827-1912) Medical researcher, physician.

Lloyd George, David. (1863-1945) Prime Minister, World War I military leader.

Lovelace, Lady Ada Byron. (1815-1852) Computer scientist, mathematician.

Lyell, Sir Charles. (1797-1875) Attorney, geologist.

Lyons, Sir William. (1901-1985) Auto-maker.

Mallory, George. (1886-1924) Explorer, mountaineer.

Mallowan, Max. (1904-1978) Archaeologist.

Malthaus, Thomas Robert. (1766-1834) Economist.

Manley, Mary. (1663-1724) Author, journalist, women's rights activist.

Mansfield, Katherine. (1888-1923) Author, born New Zealand.

Mantell, Gideon. (1790-1852) Geologist, physician.

Margaret. (1930-2002) Princess.

Markham, Beryl. (1902-1986) Author, aviation pioneer, pilot.

Marlowe, Christopher. (1564-1593) Playwright.

Mary I. (Mary Tudor) (1516-1558) Queen of England and Ireland.

Mary II. (1662-1694) Queen of England, Scotland, and Ireland.

Mary Tudor. *See* Mary I.

Maskelyne, Jasper. (1902-1973) Magician, World War II hero.

Matilda of England. (1102-1167) Princess, empress Holy Roman Empire.

Maugham, W. Somerset. (1874-1965) Author, playwright.

Maxim, Sir Hiram Stevens. (1840-1916) Aviation pioneer, inventor.

Mazuchelli, Nina. (1832-1914) Explorer, mountaineer.

McCartney, Paul. (1942-) Singer, songwriter.

McLaughlin, John. (1942-) Bandleader, jazz musician.

Medawar, Sir Peter Brian. (1915-1987) Medical researcher, zoologist. Nobel Prize winner.

Mee, Margaret Ursula Brown. (1909-1988) Botanist, painter.

Mercury, Freddie. (1946-1991) Rock musician.

Merrick, Joseph "Elephant Man." (1862-1890) Showman, folk hero.

Milne, Alan Alexander "A. A." (1882-1956) Children's author.

Milton, John. (1608-1674) Poet.

Montagu, Ewen. (1901-1985) Attorney, author, World War II spy.

Montagu, Lily. (1873-1963) Spiritual leader, established Liberal Judaism.

Montagu, Lady Mary Wortley. (1689-1762) Author.

Montefiore, Lady Judith Cohen. (1784-1862) Human rights activist, philanthropist.

Montefiore, Sir Moses. (1784-1885) Human rights activist, philanthropist.

Montgomery, Bernard. (1887-1976) World War I and II military leader.

Moore, Henry. (1898-1986) Sculptor.

More, Sir Thomas. (1478-1535) Political activist, statesman.

Morgan, Henry. (1635-1688) Pirate.

Müller, George. (1805-1898) Children's rights activist, human rights activist, born Germany.

Murdoch, Iris. (1919-1999) Author, born Ireland.

Neave, Richard. (unknown) Forensic scientist, medical illustrator.

Nelson, Horatio. (1758-1805) Naval leader.

Newton, Sir Isaac. (1642-1727) Mathematician, physicist.

Newton, John. (1725-1807) Songwriter, spiritual leader.

Nicholson, Vanessa-Mae. (1978-) Musician.

Nightingale, Florence. (1820-1910) Nurse, Crimean War head of nurses.

Noel-Baker, Philip. (1889-1982) Diplomat, peace activist. Nobel Peace Prize winner.

North, Marianne. (1830-1890) Illustrator.

Oglethorpe, James. (1696-1785) Colonist, settled Georgia.

Olivier, Sir Laurence. (1907-1989) Actor, director.

Opie, Iona. (1923-) Children's author, folklorist, illustrator, scholar.

Orwell, George. (1903-1950) Author.

Oxenbury, Helen. (1938-) Children's author, illustrator.

Pankhurst, Christabel. (1880-1958) Suffragist.

Pankhurst, Emmeline. (1858-1928) Suffragist.

Peel, Sir Robert. (1788-1850) Crimefighter, political activist.

Penn, William. (1644-1718) Colonist, founder Pennsylvania.

Penrose, Roger. (1931-) Mathematican.

Perkin, Sir William Henry. (1838-1907) Chemist.

Petrie, William Matthew Fliders. (1853-1942) Archaeologist.

Philby, Harold Arlen Russell "Kim." (1912-1988) Spy.

Pitt, William. (1708-1778) Prime Minister.

Pitt-Rivers, Augustus Lane Fox. (1827-1900) Archaeologist.

Potter, Beatrix. (1866-1943) Children's author, illustrator.

Priestly, Joseph. (1773-1804) Chemist, spiritual leader.

Quant, Mary. (1934-) Fashion designer.

Raine, Kathleen. (1908-2003) Mystic, poet.

Raleigh, Sir Walter. (1554-1618) Adventurer, explorer, founder of Virginia and North Carolina.

Rawlinson, Sir Henry Creswicke. (1810-1895) Archaeologist.

Read, Mary. (1690-1720) Pirate, disguised as man.

Reynolds, Sir Joshua. (1723-1792) Painter.

Rhodes, Cecil John. (1853-1902) Entrepreneur diamonds, financier, philanthropist, political leader.

Richard I. (The Lion Hearted) (1157-1199) Military leader, king.

Riley, Bridget. (1931-) Painter.

Rivington, James. (1727-1802) American Revolutionary War spy, printer, publisher.

Roddick, Anita. (1942-) Entrepreneur beauty supplies.

Rogers, Woodes. (1679-1732) Pirate.

Rolfe, John. (1585-1622) Colonist, pilgrim.

Rolls, Charles. (1877-1910) Automaker, aviation pioneer.

Roper, Margaret More. (1505-1544) Scholar.

Rossetti, Christina Georgina. (1830-1894) Art model, poet.

Rotblat, Joseph. (1908-) Peace activist, physicist, born Poland. Nobel Peace Prize winner.

Rowling, Joanne Kathleen "J. K." (1965-) Children's author.

Royce, Henry. (1863-1933) Automaker.

Rutherford, Baron Ernest. (1871-1930) Physicist.

Samuel, Sir Marcus. (1853-1927) Entrepreneur oil.

Sanger, Frederick. (1918-) Biochemist. Nobel Prize winner.

Sarah. Duchess of York. (1959-) Princess.

Sass-Baker, Florence von. (1841-1916) Explorer.

Saunders, Cicely. (1918-) Physician.

Sayers, Dorothy L. (1893-1957) Author.

Scott, Robert Falcon. (1868-1912) Explorer, naval officer.

Scott, Sheila. (1927-1988) Aviation pioneer, World War II nurse.

Shakespeare, William. (1564-1616) Playwright.

Shelley, Mary. (1797-1851) Author.

Shirley, William. (1694-1771) Colonial governor.

Shockley, William. (1910-1989) Inventor, physicist. Nobel Prize winner.

Smith, John. (1580-1631) Adventurer, colonist, settler of Jamestown, military leader.

Smyth, Ethel. (1858-1944) Composer, suffragist.

Snow, John. (1813-1858) Medical researcher, physician.

Standish, Miles. (1584-1656) Colonist, pilgrim.

Stanley, Sir Henry Morton. (1841-1904) Civil War soldier, explorer, journalist.

Stark, Freya. (1893-1993) Adventurer, explorer.

Stephenson, George. (1781-1848) Engineer, inventor.

Stringfellow, John. (1799-1883) Aviation pioneer.

Stuart, Miranda. (James Barry) (1795-1865) Civil War soldier disguised as man, physician.

Stubbs, George. (1724-1806) Painter.

Stukeley, William. (1687-1765) Archaeologist.

Sullivan, Sir Arthur. (1842-1900) Composer.

Swift, Jonathan. (1667-1745) Author.

Swinton, Ernest. (1868-1951) Army major general, inventor.

Taylor, James Hudson. (1832-1905) Missionary.

Tennyson, Alfred Lord. (1809-1892) Poet.

Terry, Ellen. (1847-1928) Actor.

Thackeray, William Makepeace. (1811-1863) Author.

Thatcher, Margaret. (1925-) Prime Minister. Presidential Medal of Freedom recipient.

Thompson, Daley. (1958-) Olympic decathlon athlete.

Thompson, David. (1770-1857) Explorer, fur trader, geographer.

Thomson, Joseph John. (1856-1940) Inventor, physicist. Nobel Prize winner.

Topham, Thomas. (1710-1749) Weightlifter, wrestler.

Townshend, Charles. (1725-1767) Parliament member.

Turing, Alan. (1912-1954) Computer pioneer, mathematician, World War II code breaker.

Turner, Joseph Mallord William "J. M. W." (1775-1851) Painter.

Turpin, Dick. (1705-1739) Highway robber.

Tyndale, William. (1494-1536) Scholar, bible translator.

Vancouver, George. (1757-1798) Explorer.

Vardon, Harry. (1870-1937) Golfer.

Ventris, Michael. (1922-1956) Architect, linguist.

Victoria. (1819-1901) Queen.

Wallace, Alfred Russel. (1823-1913) Naturalist.

Walpole, Horace. (1717-1797) Author, historian, political activist.

Warren, Charles. (unknown) Archaeologist.

Waterton, Charles. (1782-1865) Adventurer, naturalist.

Webber, Andrew Lloyd. (1948-) Composer.

Weldon, Fay. (1931-) Author.

Wellesley, Arthur. (1880-1959) Military leader, born Ireland.

Wells, Herbert George "H. G." (1866-1946) Author, historian.

Wesley, John. (1703-1791) Spiritual leader, founded Methodist religion.

Wheeler, Robert Eric Mortimer. (1890-1976) Archaeologist.

White, Gilbert. (1720-1793) Naturalist.

White, John. (1557-1593) Explorer.

Whitefield, George. (1714-1770) Colonist, spiritual leader.

Whitehead, Robert. (1823-1905) Inventor.

Whittle, Sir Frank. (1907-1996) Engineer, inventor, fighter pilot.

Wilberforce, William. (1759-1833) Abolitionist for British slave trade.

Wilkes, John. (1725-1797) Political activist, reformer.

Wilkinson, Rupert. (1936-) Author.

William I, the Conqueror. (1027-1087) General, king.

William III. (1650-1702) King.

Winthrop, John. (1588-1649) Colonial governor, pilgrim.

Wollstonecraft, Mary. (1759-1797) Author, women's rights activist.

Woodward, Henry. (1646-1685) Colonist, settled Carolinas.

Woolf, Virginia. (1882-1941) Author.

Woolley, Charles Leonard. (1880-1960) Archaeologist.

Wordsworth, Dorothy. (1771-1855) Poet.

Wordsworth, William. (1770-1850) Poet.

Wren, Christopher. (1632-1723) Architect.

Wycliffe, John. (1320-1384) Educator, spiritual leader.

Engravers and Etchers

See also Illustrators; Painters; Printers and Printmakers.

Blake, William. (1757-1827) English.

Dürer, Albrecht. (1471-1528) German.

Rembrandt. (Harmen Szoon van Rijn) (1606-1669) Dutch.

Whistler, James Abbott McNeill. (1834-1903)

Entomologists

Cervenka, Valerie. (unknown)

Cheesman, Lucy Evelyn. (1881-1969) English.

Comstock, Anna Botsford. (1854-1930)

Ehrlich, Paul. (1932-)

Fabre, Jean Henri. (1823-1915) French.

Odhiambo, Thomas. (1931-2003) Kenyan.

Rothschild, Miriam. (1908-) born England.

Say, Thomas. (1787-1834)

Schultz, Ted. (unknown)

Turner, Charles Henry. (1867-1923)

Turpin, Tom. (unknown)

West, Rick C. (1951-) Canadian.

Entrepreneurs and Industrialists

Bankers and Financiers

Banuelos, Romana Acosta. (1925-)

Boyd, Richard Henry. (1843-1922)

Brady, James "Diamond Jim." (1856-1917)

Buffet, Warren. (1930-)

Crassus. (Marcus Licinius Crassus) (c. 115-53 B.C.) Roman.

Dawes, Charles Gates. (1865-1951)

DeMédici. Cosimo. (1389-1464) Italian.

Dow, Charles Henry. (1851-1902)

Dulcie of Worms. (12th century) German.

Ellsworth, Lincoln. (1880-1951)

Fletcher, Alphonse "Buddy," Jr. (1966-) Stock brokerage firm.

Forrestal, James. (1892-1949)

Garzarelli, Elaine. (1952-) Financial analyst.

Gianninni, A.P. (1870-1949)

Green, Hetty. (1834-1916)

Gresham, Thomas. (1518-1579) English.

Jones, Edward. (1856-?) Financial reports.

Kennedy, Joseph Patrick. (1888-1969)

MacArthur, John D. (1897-1978)

Mellon, Andrew. (1855-1937)

Morgan, John Pierpont "J. P." (1837-1913)

Morris, Robert. (1734-1806) born England.

Nasi, Dona Gracia. (1510-1568) Portuguese.

Nicholson, John. (1757-1800) born Wales.

Pride, Charley. (1938-)

Procope, Ernesta. (1932-) Insurance company.

Rhodes, Cecil John. (1853-1902) English.

Solomon, Haym. (1740-1785) born Poland.

Soong Ai-ling. (1889-1973) Chinese.

Spaulding, Charles Clinton. (1874-1952) Banks, life insurance.

Tsai, Gerard, Jr. (1928-) born China.

Vanderbilt, Cornelius. (1794-1877)

Walker, Maggie Lena. (1867-1934)

White, George Henry. (1852-1918)

Winblad, Ann. (1950-)

Wuhsha. (11th century) Egyptian.

Computers, Electronics, and Media

Allen, Paul. (1953-) Computer operating systems.

Annenberg, Walter. (1908-2002) Newspapers, media.

Barden, Don. (1943-) Cable television.

Barton, Bruce. (1886-1967) Advertising.

Bezos, Jeffrey. (1964) Internet merchandiser.

Bushnell, Nolan. (1943-) Video arcade games.

Case, Steve. (1958-) Computer systems.

Cornelius, Don. (1936-) Black music television.

Craig, Daniel H. (1811-1895) News service.

Ellison, Lawrence. (1944-) Computer systems.

Gates, Bill. (1955-) Computer operating systems.

Gordy, Berry, Jr. (1929-) Music producer.

Grove, Andrew. (1936-) Computer, internet.

Hewlett, Bill. (1913-2001) Computers.

Job, Steven. (1955-) Computers.

Johnson, Noble. (1881-1978) Black motion picture company.

Jones, Quincy. (1933-) Music companies.

Llewellyn, J. Bruce. (1927-) Media conglomerate.

Morita, Akio. (1921-) Japanese electronics.

Murdoch, Rupert. (1931-) Media conglomerate, born Australia.

Omidyar, Pierre. (1967-) Internet merchandiser, born France.

Packard, David. (1912-1996) Computers.

Perot, Ross. (1930-) Electronic data systems.

Proctor, Barbara Gardner. (1933-) Advertising.

Ross, Diana. (1944-) Music businesses.

Sarnoff, David. (1891-1971) Radio and television broadcasting, born Russia.

Tay, Jannie. (1945-) Singaporean wrist watches.

Thomson, Roy Herbert. (1894-1973) Canadian media conglomerate.

Turner, Ted. (1938-) Television news.

Wang, An. (1920-1990) Computers, born China.

Washow, Omar. (1970-) Computer online services.

Watson, Thomas, Jr. (1914-1993) Computers.

Wozniak, Stephen. (1950-) Computers.

Yang, Jerry. (1968-) Computers, internet.

Cosmetics and Fashion

Arden, Elizabeth. (1878-1966) Cosmetics, born Canada.

Ash, Mary Kay. (1915-2001) Cosmetics.

Chanel, Gabrielle "Coco." (1883-1971) French fashion designer.

de la Renta, Oscar. (1932-) Fashion designer, born Dominican Republic.

Dior, Christian. (1905-1957) French fashion designer.

Ford, Eileen. (1922-) Modeling agency owner.

Herrera, Caroline. (1939-) Fashion designer, born Venezuela.

Joyner, Marjorie Stewart. (1896-1994) Cosmetics.

Karan, Donna. (1948-) Fashion designer.

Keckley, Elizabeth. (1818-1907) Dressmaker.

Kelly, Patrick. (1954-1990) Fashion designer.

Knight, Phil. (1938-) Shoe designer.

Lars, Byron. (1965-) Fashion designer.

Lowe, Ann. (1899-?) Fashion designer.

Morgan, Rose. (1913-) Beauty salons.

Natori, Josefina "Josie" Cruz. (1947) Fashion designer, born Philippines.

Quant, Mary. (1934-) English fashion designer.

Roddick, Anita. (1942-) English, beauty supplies.

Sims, Naomi. (1949-) Fashion model.

Singh, Sirdar Jagdit. (1897-1976)

Smith, Will. (1948-1987)

Strauss, Levi. (1829-1902) born Germany.

Touissant, Pierre. (1766-1853)

Walden, Barbara. (1936-) Cosmetics.

Walker, Sarah Breedlove McWilliams "Madame C. J." (1867-1919)

Wang, Vera. (1949-) Fashion designer.

Worth, Charles Frederick. (1825-1895) French fashion designer.

Food Industry
See also Entrepreneurs-Retail Establishments.

Adams, Samuel. (1722-1803) Brewer.

Allyón, Lucas Vásquez de. (1475-1526) Spanish sugar mill owner.

Amos, Wally. (1936-) Cookies.

Clicquot-Ponsardin, Nicole Barbe. (1777-1866) French winemaker.

Cummings, Nathan. (1896-1985) Food conglomerate chair, born Canada.

Fields, Debbi. (1956-) Cookies.

Folger, James A. (1835-1889) Coffee and spices.

Goizueta, Roberto C. (1931-1997) Soft drink bottler, born Cuba.

Heinz, Henry John. (1844-1919) Foods and sauces.

Hershey, Milton. (1857-1945) Chocolate.

Kellogg, Will Keith. (1860-1951) Cereals.

Lewis, Loida Nicolas. (1942-) Food conglomerate chair, born Philippines.

Lewis, Reginald. (1942-1993) Food conglomerate chair.

Llewellyn, J. Bruce. (1927-) Soft drink bottler.

Newman, Paul. (1925-) Salad dressings and sauces.

Parks, Henry G. (1916-1989) Catering, food services.

Rudkin, Margaret Fogharty. (1897-1967) Cakes and cookies.

Totino, Rose. (1915-1994) Pizza.

Wakefield, Ruth. (1905-1977) Cookies.

Household and Decorative Items
Boehm, Helen. (1909-) Porcelain art.

Boissonnault, Masako. (1944-) Interior design.

Burpee, W. Atlee. (1858-1915) Gardening seeds and supplies.

Eastman, George. (1854-1932) Cameras.

Fuller, Alfred. (1855-1973) Household brushes, born Canada.

Gamble, James. (1803-1891) Soaps.

Gillette, King C. (1855-1932) Razors.

Hall, Joyce C. (1891-1982) Greeting cards.

Proctor, William. (1801-1884) Soaps.

Singer, Isaac Merritt. (1811-1875) Sewing machines.

Stewart, Martha. (1941-) Household items.

Tupper, Earl. (1907-1983) Storage containers.

Woerner, Louise. (unknown) Home health care.

Oil, Chemicals, and Steel
Anderson, Robert O. (1917-) Oil.

Bush, George Herbert Walker. (1924-) Oil.

Carnegie, Andrew. (1835-1919) Steel, born Scotland.

D'Arcy, William Knox. (1849-1917) English, oil.

Dow, Herbert Henry. (1866-1930) Chemicals.

Du Pont, Eleuthere Ireneee. (1771-1834) Chemicals, born France.

Getty, J(ean) Paul. (1892-1976) Oil.
Guffey, James M. (1839-1930) Oil.
Guggenheim, Meyer. (1828-1905) Copper.
Higgins, Patillo. (1863-1955) Oil.
Lucas, Anthony Francis. (1855-1921) Oil,
born Austria.
McWhorter, "Free Frank." (1777-1854)
Saltpeter.
Mellon, Andrew. (1855-1937) Oil.
Morgan, John Pierpont "J. P." (1837-1913)
Steel.
Patino, Simon J. (1865-1947) Bolivian tin
miner.
Phillips, Frank. (1873-1950) Oil.
Rhodes, Cecil John. (1853-1902) English,
diamonds.
Rockefeller, John Davison. (1839-1937) Oil.
Samuel, Sir Marcus. (1853-1927) English,
oil.
Simmons, Jake, Jr. (1901-1981) Oil.
Taylor, George. (1716-1781) Ironworks
owner, born Ireland.

Real Estate
Aster, John Jacob. (1763-1848) born Ger-
many.
Disney, Walt. (1901-1966) Theme parks.
Ghermezian, Bahman. (1946-) Canadian,
born Iran. Mega-malls.
Ghermezian, Eskander. (1940-) Canadian,
born Iran. Mega-malls.
Ghermezian, Nader. (1941-) Canadian, born
Iran. Mega-malls.
Ghermezian, Raphael. (1944-) Canadian,
born Iran. Mega-malls.
Hilton, Conrad. (1887-1979) Hotels.
Levitt, William. (1907-1994) Planned com-
munities.
Marriott, John Willard. (1900-1985) Hotels,
restaurants.
Nicholson, John. (1787-1800) Philadelphia
developer, born Wales.
Payton, Philip A. (1876-1917) Harlem de-
veloper.
Pleasant, Mary Ellen "Mammy." (1814-
1904) Boarding houses.
Reichmann, Paul. (1930-) New York City
developer, born Austria.
Russell, Herman J. (1930-) Construction.
Smith, Ada "Bricktop." (1894-1984) Night-
club.

Terry, Ellen. (unknown) Dallas real estate.
Travis, Dempsey J. (1920-)
Walker, Thomas. (1850-1935)
Webb, Del. (1899-1974) Planned communi-
ties for senior citizens.

Retail Establishments
Anderson, Walter. (1880-?) White Castle
hamburgers.
Axene, Harry. (1905-) Dairy Queen and
Tastee Freeze ice cream.
Ball, James P. (1825-1904) Photo studios.
Bean, Leon Leonwood "L. L." (1872-1967)
Clothing and sports supplies.
Bushnell, Nolan. (1943-) Chuck E. Cheese
restaurants.
Chin, Leann. (1933-) Chinese restaurants.
Cohen, Ben. (1951-) Ben & Jerry's ice
cream.
Fields, Debbi. (1956-) Mrs. Field's cookies.
Gimbel, Adam. (1817-1896) Department
stores, born Germany.
Goodridge, Glenalvin. (1829-1866) Photo
studios.
Goodridge, Wallace. (1841-1922) Photo
studios.
Goodridge, William. (1846-1891) Photo
studios.
Greenfield, Jerry. (1951-) Ben & Jerry's ice
cream.
Gutman, Sarel. (17th century) Czech mer-
chant.
Harvey, Fred. (1835-1901) Fred Harvey
restaurants, born England.
Ingram, Billy. (1880-?) White Castle ham-
burgers.
Jennings, Thomas L. (1791-1859) Tailoring
and dry cleaning.
Kroc, Ray. (1902-1984) McDonald's ham-
burgers.
Lewis, Francis. (1713-1802) Clothing mer-
chant..
Livingston, Philip. (1716-1778) Revolution-
ary War merchant.
McCullough, J. F. (1871-1936) Dairy
Queen.
McDonald, Maurice. (1902-1971) McDon-
ald's hamburgers founder.
McDonald, Richard. (1909-1998) McDon-
ald's hamburgers co-founder.
Monaghan, Tom. (1937-) Domino's Pizza.

Penney, James Cook. (1875-1971) Discount department stores.

Roddick, Anita. (1942-) English, Body Shops.

Rosenwald, Julius. (1862-1932) Sears Department Stores.

Sanders, Colonel Harland. (1890-1980) Kentucky Fried Chicken.

Sears, Richard. (1863-1914) Mail order and Sears Department Stores.

Shoong, Joe. (1879-1961) National Dollar Stores.

Thomas, Dave. (1932-2002) Wendy's hamburgers.

Walton, Sam. (1918-1992) Wal-Mart discount stores.

Woolworth, Frank Winfield. (1852-1919) General "dime" stores.

Toys and Sporting Goods

Boyd, Richard Henry. (1843-1922) Black dolls.

Bradley, Milton. (1836-1911) Board games.

Christiansen, Ole Kirk. (1891-1958) Danish building toys.

Coleman, William. (1870-1957) Camping supplies.

Cowen, Joshua Lionel. (1880-1965) Toy trains.

Edwards, Chris. (1973-) In-line skates.

Eisenberg, Arlo. (1973-) In-line skates.

Gygax, Gary. (1938-) Dungeons and Dragons games.

Handler, Ruth. (1912-2002) Barbie dolls.

Hillerich, Bud. (1866-1946) Baseball bats.

Spalding, Albert Goodwill. (1850-1915) Sporting goods.

Bushnell, Nolan. (1943-) Atari video games company.

Winzeler, Henry Simon. (unknown) Ohio Art company toys.

Yamauchi, Hiroshi. (1928-) Japanese Nintendo games.

Zamboni, Frank J. (1901-1988) Ice resurfacing machines.

Transportation

See also Automakers.

Almonaster y Rojas, Andrés. (1725-1798) Shipping.

Beech, Olive Ann. (1903-1993) Aircraft.

Best, Daniel. (1838-1923) Tractors.

Brittin, Louis. (fl. 1926) Airline founder.

Cuffe, Paul. (1759-1817) Sailmaker.

Curtiss, Glenn H. (1878-1930) Aircraft.

Deere, John. (1804-1886) Tractors.

Forten, James. (1766-1842) Sailmaker.

Hill, James J. (1838-1916) Railroads, born Canada.

Holt, Benjamin. (1849-1920) Tractors.

Hughes, Howard. (1905-1976) Aircraft.

Iacocca, Lee. (1924-) Chrysler Automotive CEO.

Lear, William. (1902-1978) Aircraft.

Leisdorff, William A. (1810-1848) Steamboats.

Nasi, Dona Gracia. (1510-1568) Portuguese shipping.

Rickenbacker, Edward Vernon "Eddie." (1890-1973) Airline owner.

Sullivan, Leon. (1922-2001) General Motors CEO.

Vanderbilt, Cornelius. (1794-1877) Steamships, trains.

Wichman, Carl Eric. (1887-?) Greyhound busses, born Sweden.

Unclassified

Fields, Mary. (1832-1914) Pioneer businesswoman.

Franklin, Deborah Read. (1707-1774) American Revolutionary War businesswoman.

Gaston, Arthur George. (1892-1996) Multibusinesses.

Hancock, John. (1737-1793) American Revolutionary War businessman.

Krupp, Alfried. (1907-1967) German arms manufacturer.

Mason, Biddy. (1818-1891)

Mitsui, Shuho. (1590-1676) Japanese businesswoman.

Musolino-Alber, Ella. (unknown) Sports promotion.

Pinckney, Eliza Lucas. (1722-1793) Indigo crop producer.

Ronstadt, Frederico. (1862-1954) Businessman.

Soong Charlie. (1866-1918) Chinese.

Stradivari, Antonio. (1644-1737) Italian violin maker.

Vega, Bernardo. (1885-1965) Cigar manufacturer.

Wuhsha. (11th Century) Egyptian businesswoman.

Ybor, Vincente Martinez. (1818-1896) Cuban cigar manufacturer.

Environmentalists

*Includes Conservationists, Ecologists, Natu-
ralists.*

Agassiz, Louis. (1807-1873) born Switzerland.

Alexander, Annie Montague. (1867-1950)
Naturalist.

Allen, Christina M. (1970-) Rain forest
ecologist.

Andrews, Roy Chapman. (1884-1960) Naturalist.

Baret, Jeanne. (1740?-1803?) French naturalist.

Beebe, Charles William. (1877-1962) Naturalist.

Belaney, Archibald. (Grey Owl) (1888-
1938) Canadian naturalist.

Berry, Wendell. (1934-) Ecologist.

Blom, Gertrude Elizabeth Loertscher Doby.
(1901-1993) Swiss conservationist.

Bloomfield, Michael. (unknown) Canadian.

Braun, E. Lucy. (1889-1971) Ecologist.

Bromfield, Louis. (1896-1956) Ecologist.

Brower, David. (1912-2000)

Brundtland, Gro Harlem. (1939-) Norwegian.

Buffon, Georges. (1707-1788) French naturalist.

Burroughs, John. (1837-1921)

Carson, Rachel. (1907-1964)

Commoner, Barry. (1917-) Environmentalist.

Comstock, Anna Botsford. (1854-1930)
Naturalist.

Cousteau, Jacques-Yves. (1910-1997)
French.

Darling, Jay Norwood "Ding." (1876-1962)
Conservationist.

Darwin, Charles. (1809-1882) English naturalist.

Douglas, Marjorie Stoneman. (1890-1998)
Conservationist.

Durrell, Gerald. (1925-1995) English wildlife preservationist.

Edge, Rosalie. (1877-1962) Conservationist.

Fountaine, Margaret. (1862-1940) English.

Fowler-Billings, Katharine Stevens. (1902-
1997) Conservationist.

Fuertes, Louis Agassiz. (1874-1927) Naturalist.

Gibbs, Lois Marie. (1951-) Environmental
activist.

Grey Owl. *See* Belaney, Archibald.

Grinnell, George Bird. (1849-1938) Naturalist.

Hayes, Randy. (unknown)

Hornaday, William Temple. (1854-1937)
Wildlife conservationist.

Johnson, Kory. (1979-)

Krecek, Joseph. (unknown)

Lamarck, Jean Baptiste. (1744-1829)
French.

Leopold, Aldo. (1886-1948)

Maathai, Wangari. (1940-) Kenyan.

MacKaye, Benton. (1879-1975) Conservationist, forester.

Marcovaldi, Maria "Neca." (1948-) Brazilian conservationist.

Marsh, George Perkins. (1801-1882) Conservationist.

Mendes, Chico. (1944-1988) Brazilian.

Merian, Anna Marie Sibylla. (1647-1717)
Dutch naturalist.

Mills, Enos. (1870-1922) Naturalist.

Molina, Mario. (1943-) born Mexico.

Morgan, Ann Haven. (1882-1966) Ecologist.

Mowat, Farley. (1921-) Canadian naturalist.

Muir, John. (1838-1914) Conservationist,
naturalist, born Scotland.

Murie, Margaret Thomas. (1902-2003) Conservationist.

Murie, Olaus. (1889-1963) Wildlife researcher.

Nelson, Gaylord. (1916-)

Nuttall, Thomas. (1786-1859) English.

Odum, Eugene. (1913-2002) Ecologist.

Olmstead, Frederick Law. (1822-1903)

Ordway, Katherine. (1899-1979) Conservationist, ecologist.

Patrick, Ruth. (1907-) Ecologist.

Pinchot, Gifford. (1865-1946) Conservationist, forester.

Pusey, Anne. (1948-)

Richards, Ellen Swallow. (1842-1911)

Rodale, Jerome Irving "J.I." (1898-1971)

Roosevelt, Theodore. (1858-1919) Conservationist.

Ross, Alexander. (1783-1856) Canadian naturalist.

Rothschild, Miriam. (1908-) Conservationist, naturalist, born England.

Seton, Ernest Thompson. (1860-1946) Naturalist, born England.

Thoreau, Henry David. (1817-1862)

Vaux-Walcott, Mary. (1860-1940) Canadian.

Wallace, Alfred Russel. (1823-1913) English.

Waterton, Charles. (1782-1865) English.

White, Gilbert. (1720-1793) English.

Ethiopians

See also Africans; Blacks, International.

Makeda. (960-930 B.C.) Queen of Sheba.

Selassie, Haile. (1892-1975) Emperor.

Wolde, Mamo. (1931-) Olympic track and field athlete, marathon runner.

Explorers

See also Adventurers; Archaeologists; Pioneers and Frontierspeople.

American

Akeley, Delia. (1875-1970) Africa.

Akeley, Mary Leonore Jobe. (1878-1966) Africa.

Atkinson, Lucy. (1820-1863?) Asia.

Bancroft, Ann. (1955-) Arctic.

Beckwourth, James. (1798-1866) Western United States.

Bennett, Floyd. (1890-1928) Arctic.

Boyd, Louise Arner. (1887-1972) Arctic.

Bush, George W. (1791-1867) Oregon.

Byrd, Richard Evelyn. (1888-1957) Arctic.

Cameron, Agnes Deans. (1863-1912) Arctic.

Cashman, Nellie. (1845-1925) Western United States.

Clark, William. (1770-1838) Western United States.

Colter, John. (1775-1813) Western United States.

Cressy-Marcks, Violet. (1890-1976) World traveler.

Du Chaillu, Paul. (1836-1903) Africa, born France.

Ellsworth, Lincoln. (1880-1951) Arctic.

Fremont, John Charles. (1813-1890) Westward expansion to Pacific.

Gist, Christopher. (1706-1759) Western United States.

Henson, Matthew. (1866-1955) Arctic.

Johnson, Osa Leighty. (1894-1953) Africa, South Seas.

Jones, Albert Jose. (unknown) Underwater exploration.

Lewis, Meriwether. (1774-1809) Western United States.

Lisa, Manuel. (1772-1820) Western United States.

Marsden, Kate. (1859-1931) Arctic.

Mexia, Ynes. (1870-1938) Central and South America.

Niles, Mary Blair. (1880-1959) South America.

Peary, Robert. (1856-1920) Arctic.

Pike, Zebulon Montgomery. (1779-1813) Western United States.

Powell, John Wesley. (1834-1902) American frontier.

Sacagawea. (1788-1884) Indian guide for Lewis and Clark.

Schwabe, Stephanie. (1957-) Bahamas, Black Holes of Andros.

Sheldon, May French. (1847-1936) East Africa.

Smith, Jedediah Strong. (1799-1831) Western United States.

Stephens, John Lloyd. (1805-1852) Mayan ruins.

Stuart, Robert. (1785-1848) Oregon Trail, born Scotland.

Walker, Joe. (1799-1876) Mississippi region.

Wilkes, Charles. (1798-1877) Antarctic.

Workman, Fanny Bullock. (1859-1925) Mountains.

York. (1770-1832) William Clark's slave.

Ancient Civilizations

Hanno. (c. 450 B.C.) Carthaginian explorer of west coast of Africa

Harkhuf. (c. 2275 B.C.) Egyptian.

Hoei-shin. (5th century) Chinese explorer of North and Central America.

Pytheas. (c. 300 B.C.) Greek explorer of Straits of Gibralter, Arctic Circle.

Arab
Ibn-Battuta, Muhammad. (1304-1369) Muslim Berber Morrocan explorer.

Australian and New Zealandic
Hume, Hamilton. (1797-1873) Australia.
Thayer, Helen. (1938-) Arctic.
Wilkins, Sir George Hubert. (1888-1958) Arctic.
Wills, William John. (1833-1861) Northward route across Australia.

Canadian
Hubbard, Mina Benson. (1870-1956) Labrador.
Joliet, Louis. (1645-1700) Rights for France to land in America.
Rijnhart, Susie Carson. (1868-1908) Tibet.

Dutch
Barents, Willem. (1550-1597) Arctic.
Tasman, Abel. (1603-1659) East Indies.
Tinne, Alexandrine. (1839-1869) Africa.

English
Adams, William. (1564-1620) Japan.
Baker, Florence von Sass. (1841-1916) Nile River.
Baker, Sir Samuel White. (1821-1893) Africa, Upper Nile.
Bell, Gertrude. (1868-1926) Middle East.
Blunt, Lady Anne. (1837-1917) Arabia.
Burton, Sir Richard Francis. (1821-1890) Africa and Arab lands.
Cabot, John. (1450-1499) Newfoundland.
Cook, James. (1728-1779) Antarctic Circle, Australia, Hawaii.
Dampier, William. (1652-1715) Australia and New Guinea.
Drake, Sir Francis. (1540-1596) Africa.
Franklin, Sir John. (1786-1847) Arctic.
Frobisher, Martin. (1535-1594) Northwest Passage.
Gilbert, Sir Humphrey. (1539-1583) Newfoundland, Northwest Passage.
Hudson, Henry. (1565-1631) Northwest Passage.
Irvine, Andrew. (1896-1924) Mount Everest.
Kingsley, Mary. (1862-1900) Africa.
Mallory, George. (1886-1924) Mount Everest.
Mazuchelli, Nina. (1832-1914) Mountains.
Raleigh, Sir Walter. (1554-1618) Eastern United States.
Scott, Robert Falcon. (1868-1912) Arctic.
Stanley, Sir Henry Morton. (1841-1904) Africa.
Stark, Freya. (1893-1993) Asia.
Thompson, David. (1770-1857) Canada.
Vancouver, George. (1757-1798) Canada.
White, John. (1557-1593) New World.

European, Assorted
De Smet, Pierre Jean. (1801-1873) Belgian, Western United States.
Kino, Eusebio. (1645-1711) Austrian, Southwest United States.
Wedener, Alfred. (1880-1930) German, Greenland.

French
Brule, Etienne. (1592-1632) Canada.
Cailliaud, Frederic. (1787-1869) North Africa.
Caillié, René. (1799-1838) North Africa.
Cartier, Jacques. (1491-1557) St. Lawrence River.
Champlain, Samuel de. (1567-1635) Canada.
Cousteau, Jacques-Yves. (1910-1997) Amazon River underwater explorations.
David-Neel, Alexandra. (1868-1969) Asia.
Groseilliers, Médard Chouat des. (1618?-1695?) Hudson's Bay.
La Salle, René Robert Cavalier. (1643-1687) Mississippi River.
Laclède Liguest, Pierre de. (1729-1778) Western United States.
Marquette, Jacques. (1637-1675) North America.
Radisson, Pierre Esprit. (1636-1710) St. Lawrence River.
Ribaut, Jean. (1520-1565) South Carolina.
Tonty, Henri de. (1649-1704) born Italy, explored Mississippi River.

Irish
Brendan the Navigator. (484-577) North America.
Burke, Robert O'Hara. (1820-1861) Australia.

Murphy, Dervla. (1931-) Asia.
Shackleton, Ernest. (1874-1936) Arctic.

Italian
Cabot, Sebastian. (1476-1557) Newfound-
land.
Columbus, Christopher. (1451-1506) Amer-
ica.
Nobile, Umberto. (1885-1978) Arctic.
Polo, Marco. (1254-1324) Asia.
Verrazzano, Giovanni da. (1458-1528) East-
ern United States.
Vespucci, Amerigo. (1454-1512) North
America, South America.

Portuguese
Alburquerque, Afonso de. (1453-1515) In-
dia.
Cabral, Pedro Álvares. (1460-1526) Mo-
zambique.
Cabrillo, Juan Rodriguez. (1520?-1543)
West Coast of North America.
Corte Real, Gaspar. (1455-1501) Northeast
coast of North America.
Corte Real, Miguel. (1450-1502) Northeast
coast of North America.
Covilla, Peroda. (1460-1526) India.
Cunha, Tristao da. (1460-1540) India, South
Atlantic.
Gama, Gaspar da. (1458-1526) born Poland,
explored India.
Gama, Vasco. (1460-1524) Orient.
Dias, Bartholomeu. (1450-1500) Africa,
Indian Ocean.
Henry. Prince of Portugal. (Henry the Navi-
gator) (1394-1460) South Atlantic.
Magellan, Ferdinand. (1480-1521) First ex-
ploration around globe.

Russian
Dezhnev, Semyon. (1610-1672) American
West.
Kuznetsova, Irina Mihailovna. (1961-) Arc-
tic.
Kuznetsova, Valentina Mihailovna. (1937-)
Arctic.
Yermak (Vasily Timofeyovich) (1540-1585)
Siberia.

Scandinavian
Amundsen, Roald Engebreth Gravning.

(1872-1928) Norwegian South Pole ex-
plorer.
Andrée, August. (1854-1897) Swedish arctic
explorer.
Bering, Vitus Jonassen. (1681-1741) Danish
Asia and American explorer.
Dietrichson, Leif. (d.1928) Norwegian ex-
plorer of South Pole.
Hedin, Sven. (1865-1952) Swedish explorer
of Tibet and Western China.
Nansen, Fridtjof. (1861-1930) Norwegian
explorer of Arctic Circle and Greenland.
Nordenskjöld, Nils Adolf Erik. (1832-1901)
Swedish Arctic explorer.
Nordenskjöld, Nils Otto. (1869-1928) Swed-
ish Arctic explorer.

Scottish
Livingstone, David. (1813-1873) Canada.
MacKenzie, Sir Alexander. (1764-1820)
Canada.
Ross, Sir James Clark. (1800-1862) Arctic.
Ross, Sir John. (1777-1856) Arctic.

Spanish
Africanus, Leo. (Giovanni Leone) (1495-
1553) Spanish Moor.
Alaminos, Antón de. (1482-1520) Ship pilot
for Columbus and Ponce de Leon.
Allyón, Lucas Vásquez de. (1475-1526)
South Carolina.
Balboa, Vasco Nunez de. (1475-1519) Pa-
cific Ocean.
Bermúdez, Diego. (1480-?) Page for Co-
lumbus.
Cabeza de Vaca, Álvar Núñez. (1490-1557)
American Southwest.
Coronado, Francisco Vásquez de. (1510-
1554) American West.
Cortes, Hernan. (1485-1547) Mexico.
de Soto, Hernando. (1496?-1542) Southeast
America.
Dorantz, Stephen. (Estevanico, Esteban)
(1500-1539) American West.
Menedéz de Aviles, Pedro. (1519-1574)
Florida.
Oñate, Juan de. (1550-1630) New Mexico.
Orellana, Francisco de. (1511-1546) Ama-
zon River.
Pineda, Álonzo Alvarez de. (1792-1872)
Colorado, Mississippi River.

Pinzón, Martin. (1440-1493) Sailed with
  Columbus.
Pinzón, Vincente. (1463-1514) Sailed with
  Columbus.
Pizarro, Francisco. (1475-1541) Inca Empire
  of Peru.
Ponce de Léon, Juan. (1460-1521) Florida.
Zacuto, Abraham. (1452-1515) Navigator
  for Columbus.

Viking
Ericsson, Leif. (970-1020) Viking explorer
  of North America.
Eriksdottir, Freydis. (971-1010) Viking explorer of Greenland.
Thorvaldson, Erik "Erik the Red." (950-
  1010) Viking explorer.

Fashion Designers
See Entrepreneurs, Cosmetics and Fashion.

Fashion Models
See Models, Art, and Fashion.

Filipinos
See also Immigrants to United States, Filipino.
Aguinaldo, Emilio. (1869-1964) Military
  leader, revolutionary.
Aquino, Corazon. (1933-) President.
del Mundo, Fe. (1911-) Human rights activist, physician.
Marcos, Ferdinand. (1917-1989) Dictator,
  political activist.

Filmmakers
See also Actors; Screenwriters.
Alexander, William. (1916-)
Allen, Woody. (1935-)
Bourne, St. Clair. (unknown)
Burnett, Charles. (1944-)
Capra, Frank. (1897-1991) born Italy.
Chenzira, Ayoka. (1956-)
Collins, Kathleen. (1942-1988)
Coppola, Francis Ford. (1939-)
Crowe, Cameron. (1957-)
Dash, Julie. (1952-)
De Mille, Cecil B. (1881-1959)
De Palma, Brian. (1940-)
De Passe, Suzanne. (1946-)

Disney, Walt. (1901-1966)
Eisenstein, Sergei. (1898-1948) Russian.
Ford, John. (1895-1973)
Gerima, Haile. (1946-) born Ethiopia.
Goldwyn, Samuel. (1882-1974) born Po-
  land.
Greaves, William. (1926-)
Hitchcock, Alfred. (1899-1980) born
  England.
Howe, James Wong. (1899-1976) born
  China.
Hughes, Howard. (1905-1976)
Johnson, Noble. (1881-1978)
Johnson, Osa Leighty. (1894-1953)
Lansing, Sherry. (1944-)
Lear, Norman. (1922-)
Lee, Shelton Jackson "Spike." (1957-)
Lucas, George. (1944-)
Marin, Richard Anthony "Cheech." (1946-)
Mayer, Louis B. (1885-1957)
Micheaux, Garrett Oscar. (1884-1951)
Ondaatje, Michael. (1943-) born Sri Lanka.
Parkerson, Michelle. (1953-)
Poitier, Sidney. (1924-)
Reeve, Christopher. (1952-2004)
Riefenstahl, Leni. (1902-2003) German.
Rodriguez, Robert. (1968-)
Scorsese, Martin. (1942-)
Singleton, John. (1968-)
Spielberg, Steven. (1947-)
Tarantino, Quentin. (1963-)
Van Peebles, Mario. (1957-)
Van Peebles, Melvin. (1932-)
Vinson, Phyllis Tucker. (1948-)
Wang, Wayne. (1949-) born China.
Warhol, Andy. (1928-1987)
Wayans, Keenen Ivory. (1958-)
Weber, Lois. (1881-1939)
Winfrey, Oprah. (1954-)

Financiers
See Entrepreneurs and Industrialists, Bankers and Financiers.

Finns
Nurmi, Paavo. (1897-1973) Olympic runner,
  track and field athlete.
Nykanen, Matti. (1963-) Olympic ski
  jumper.
Sibelius, Jean. (1865-1957) Composer.
Torvalds, Linus. (1970-) Computer scien-

tist, internet pioneer, software engineer.

First Ladies of United States
Adams, Abigail. (1744-1818)
Adams, Louisa Catherine Johnson. (1775-1852)
Arthur, Ellen Lewis Herndon. (1837-1880)
Bush, Barbara Pierce. (1925-)
Bush, Laura Welch. (1946-)
Carter, Rosalynn Smith. (1927-)
Cleveland, Frances Folsom. (1864-1947)
Clinton, Hillary Rodham. (1947-)
Coolidge, Grace Anna Goodhue. (1879-1957)
Eisenhower, Mamie Geneva Doud. (1896-1979)
Fillmore, Abigail Powers. (1798-1853)
Ford, Elizabeth Bloomer "Betty." (1918-)
Garfield, Lucretia Rudolph. (1832-1918)
Grant, Julia Dent. (1826-1902)
Harding, Florence Kling DeWolfe. (1860-1924)
Harrison, Anna Tuthill Symmes. (1775-1864)
Harrison, Caroline Scott. (1832-1892)
Hayes, Lucy Ware Webb. (1831-1889)
Hoover, Lou Henry. (1874-1944)
Jackson, Rachel Donelson Robards. (1767-1828)
Jefferson, Martha Waylee Skelton. (1748-1782)
Johnson, Claudia Alta "Lady Bird." (1912-)
Johnson, Eliza McCardle. (1810-1876)
Kennedy, Jacqueline Bouvier. *See* Onassis, Jacqueline Bouvier Kennedy.
Lane, Harriet. (1830-1903) Niece of James Buchanan.
Lincoln, Mary Todd. (1818-1882)
Madison, Dolley Payne Todd. (1768-1849)
McKinley, Ida Saxton. (1847-1907)
Monroe, Elizabeth Kortright. (1768-1830)
Nixon, Thelma "Pat" Ryan. (1912-1993)
Onassis, Jacqueline Bouvier Kennedy. (1929-1994)
Pierce, Jane Appleton. (1806-1863)
Polk, Sarah Childress. (1803-1891)
Reagan, Anne Robbins "Nancy." (1921-)
Roosevelt, (Anna) Eleanor. (1884-1962)
Roosevelt, Edith Kermit Carow. (1861-1948)
Taft, Helen Herron "Nellie." (1861-1943)

Taylor, Margaret Mackell Smith. (1788-1852)
Truman, Elizabeth "Bess" Wallace. (1885-1982)
Tyler, Julia Gardiner. (1820-1889)
Tyler, Letitia Christian. (1790-1842)
Van Buren, Hannah Hoes. (1783-1819)
Washington, Martha Dandridge Curtis. (1731-1802)
Wilson, Ellen Louisa Axson. (1860-1914)

Flemish
See Belgians.

Folk Heroes and Legendary Characters
Abelard. (1097-1142) French orator.
Aliquipso. Oneida Indian legendary heroine.
Arthur, King. (6th century) English king, possibly legendary.
Barrow, Claude. (1909-1934) Gangster.
Borden, Lizzie. (1860-1927) Criminal, allegedly killed parents with ax.
Borgia, Lucrezia. (1480-1519) Italian villainess.
Chapman, Jonathan. (Johnny Appleseed) (1774-1845) Agricultural scientist, botanist, frontiersman.
Cooper, Dan "D.B." (unknown) Hijacker.
Crockett, Davy. (1786-1836) Frontiersman.
Dean, James. (1931-1955) Actor, comedian.
Devi. East Indian legendary warrior princess.
Earp, Wyatt. (1848-1929) Wild West lawman.
Fawkes, Guy. (1570-1606) English undercover agent.
Frietchie, Barbara Hauer. (1766-1862) Civil war heroine, flag bearer for Union.
Galahad, Sir. (6th century) Knight of Round Table, legendary.
Godiva, Lady. (1010-1067) English countess, reformer.
Grimm, Jacob. (1785-1863) German folktale collector.
Grimm, Wilhelm. (1786-1859) German folktale collector.
Guinevere. (6th century) Wife of King Arthur, legendary.
Helen of Troy. (1200-1150 B.C.) Greek

heroine, legendary.

Héloise. (1098-1164) French abbess, lover of Abelard.

Henry, John. (1840-1871) Railroad worker.

Hiawatha. (fl. 1440) Iroquois chief.

Hickok, James Butler "Wild Bill." (1837-1876) Crime fighter, gunfighter.

Hiera. Amazon warrior queen, legendary.

Hood, Robin. (1290-1346) English outlaw, legendary.

Hughes, Howard. (1905-1976) Entrepreneur aircraft, filmmaker.

Jason. Greek adventurer.

Jones, Casey. (1863-1900) Railroad man.

Kidd, William "Captain." (1645-1701) Scottish pirate.

Lafitte, Jean. (1781-1826) Pirate.

Lancelot, Sir. (6th century) Knight of Round Table, warrior.

Mallon, Mary "Typhoid Mary." (1870-1938) Irish maid and cook thought to spread typhoid.

Merrick, Joseph "Elephant Man." (1862-1890) English physically deformed showman.

Monroe, Marilyn. (1926-1962) Actor.

Mullens, Priscilla. (1604-1680) Colonist, wife of John Alden.

Münchhassen, Baron von. (1720-1797) German storyteller.

Murphy, Audie. (1924-1971) World War II military hero.

Nicholaevna, Anastasia. (1901-1918) Russian princess.

Nicholas, St. "Santa Claus." (d. 345) Bishop of Myra (Turkey), saint.

Nostradamus. (1503-1566) French physician, psychic.

Novykh, Girgori Yefimovich. (Rasputin) (1871-1916) Russian monk.

Parker, Bonnie. (1911-1934) Gangster.

Patrick. (389?-461?) Irish saint, slave.

Rasputin. *See* Novykh, Girgori Yefimovich.

Revere, Paul. (1735-1818) American Revolutionary War patriot and soldier, silversmith.

Richthofen, Baron Manfred von "Red Baron." (1892-1918) German World War I aviator.

Rogers, Roy. (1911-1998) Actor, cowboy.

Ross, Betsy. (1752-1836) American Revolu-

tionary War patriot.

Semiramis. (c. 2000 B.C.) Queen of Assyria, legendary heroine.

Stratton, Charles Sherwood "Tom Thumb." (1838-1883) Showman.

Tell, William. (1282-?) Swiss political activist.

Tutankhamun. (1347-1329 B.C.) Egyptian pharoah.

Typhoid Mary. *See* Mallon, Mary.

Vergoose, Elizabeth "Mother Goose." (unknown) Storyteller.

Vlad the Impaler "Vlad Dracul." (1431-1477) Romanian terrorist.

Winyan Ohitika. Sioux legendary heroine.

Yakami. Japanese legendary heroine.

Folklorists
See Storytellers and Folklorists.

Football Players
See also Heisman Trophy Winners.

Aikman, Troy. (1966-)

Allen, Marcus. (1960-)

Alworth, Lance. (1940-)

Baugh, Sammy. (1914-)

Berry, Raymond, (1933-)

Blanchard, Felix Anthony "Doc." (1924-)

Bleier, Robert Patrick "Rocky." (1946-)

Bradshaw, Terry. (1948-)

Brown, Jim. (1936-)

Brown, Tim. (1966-)

Butkus, Dick. (1942-)

Campbell, Earl. (1955-)

Davis, Ernie. (1939-1963)

Davis, Glenn. (1925-)

Davis, Terrell. (1972-)

Dawson, Len. (1935-)

Dempsey, Tom. (1947-)

Dickerson, Eric. (1960-)

Dorsett, Tony. (1954-)

Dunn, Warrick. (1975-)

Elway, John. (1960-)

Favre, Brett. (1969-)

Flutie, Doug. (1962-)

George, Eddie. (1973-)

Graham, Otto. (1921-2003)

Grange, Red. (1903-1991)

Greene, Charles Edward "Mean Joe." (1946-)

Griffin, Archie. (1954-)

Haley, Charles. (1964-)
Harris, Franco. (1950-)
Hayes, Bob. (1942-2002)
Hirsch, Elroy "Crazy Legs." (1923-2004)
Hornung, Paul. (1935-)
Hutson, Don. (1913-1997)
Jackson, Bo. (1962-)
James, Edgerrin. (1978-)
Johnson, Keyshawn. (1972-)
Jones, David "Deacon." (1938-)
Kearse, Jevon. (1976-)
Kelly, Jim. (1960-)
Kennedy, Cortez. (1968-)
Larguent, Steve. (1954-)
Layne, Bobby. (1920-1986)
Lilly, Bob. (1939-)
Little, Larry. (1945-)
Luckman, Sid. (1916-1990)
Manning, Peyton. (1976-)
Marchetti, Gino. (1927-)
Marino, Dan. (1961-)
Marshall, Jim. (1937-)
Maynard, Don. (1937-)
Monk, Art. (1957-)
Montana, Joe. (1956-)
Moon, Warren. (1956-)
Moss, Randy. (1977-)
Namath, Joe. (1943-)
Page, Alan. (1945-)
Payton, Walter. (1954-)
Plunkett, Jim. (1947)
Rice, Jerry. (1962-)
Robeson, Paul. (1898-1976)
Sanders, Barry. (1968-)
Sanders, Deion. (1967-)
Sapp, Warren. (1971-)
Sayers, Gale. (1943-)
Sharpe, Sterling. (1965-)
Simpson, Orenthal James "O. J." (1947-)
Smith, Emmitt. (1969-)
Starr, Bart. (1934-)
Staubach, Roger. (1942-)
Swann, Lynn. (1952-)
Tarkenton, Francis "Fran." (1940-)
Taylor, Lawrence "L. T." (1959-)
Thorpe, Jim. (1888-1953)
Unitas, Johnny. (1933-2002)
Walker, Herschel. (1962-)
Walker, Kenny. (1967-)
Warner, Kurt. (1971-)
White, Reggie. (1961-)

Williams, Doug. (1955-)
Williams, Ricky. (1977-)
Yepremian, Garo. (1944-) born Cyprus.
Young, Steve. (1961-)
Youngblood, Jack. (1950-)
Zorich, Chris. (1969-)

Football Team Management

Brown, Paul. (1908-1996)
Gibbs, Joe. (1940-)
Graham, Otto. (1921-2003)
Grant, Bud. (1927-)
Halas, George. (1895-1983)
Johnson, Jimmy. (1943-)
Lambeau, Earl Louis "Curly." (1898-1965)
Landry, Tom. (1924-2000)
Lombardi, Vincent. (1913-1970)
Robinson, Eddie Gay. (1919-)
Shula, Don. (1930-)
Walsh, Bill. (1931-)

Forensic Scientists

See also Crimefighters.
Alvarez, Eduardo. (unknown) Argentine.
Bertillon, Alphonse. (1853-1914) French.
Cervenka, Valerie. (unknown) Forensic entomologist.
Faulds, Henry. (fl. 1880) English.
Goddard, Calvin Hooker. (1891-1955)
Henry, Sir Edward. (1859-1931) English.
Jeffreys, Sir Alec. (1950-) English.
Khreiss, Betty Jane. (unknown)
Landsteiner, Karl. (1868-1943) born Austria.
Locard, Edmond. (1877-1966) French.
Marsh, James. (fl. 1832) Scottish.
Neave, Richard. (unknown) English.
Osborn, Albert Sherman. (1858-1946)
Penry, Jacques. (unknown) French.
Snow, Clyde. (1932-)
Starrs, James. (1930-)
Trotter, Mildred. (1899-1991)
Waite, Charles. (fl. 1920)
Wecht, Cyril. (1931-)

Founders of Cities and Colonies

See also Colonists; Pioneers and Frontiersmen.
Anza, Juan Bautista de. (1735-1788) Mexican settler of California

Austin, Stephen Fuller. (1793-1836) Texas.

Calvert, Cecil. (1606-1675) Maryland.

Calvert, Leonard. (1607-1647) Maryland.

Carter, Robert. (1663-1732) Virginia.

Carteret, Sir George. (1610-1680) New Jersey.

Cuffe, Paul. (1759-1817) Sierra Leone.

Du Sable, Jean Baptiste Pointe. (1745-1818) Chicago.

Hooker, Thomas. (1586-1647) Connecticut.

Iberville, Pierre le Moyne de. (1661-1706) Louisiana.

Maisonneuve, Paul. (1612-1676) Montreal.

Menedéz de Aviles, Pedro. (1519-1574) St. Augustine.

Oglethorpe, James Edward. (1696-1785) Georgia.

Penn, William. (1644-1718) Pennsylvania.

Raleigh, Sir Walter. (1554-1618) Virginia and North Carolina.

Smith, John. (1580-1631) Jamestown.

Stuyvesant, Peter. (1610-1672) New York.

Thayer, Eli. (1819-1899) Kansas.

Tonty, Henri de. (1649-1704) Arkansas.

Vallejo, Mariano Guadalupe. (1808-1890) California.

Wheelwright, John. (1592-1679) New Hampshire.

Williams, Roger. (1603-1683) Rhode Island.

Woodward, Henry. (1646-1685) Carolinas.

Ybor, Vincente Martinez. (1818-1896) Ybor City, FL.

French

See also Immigrants to United States, French.

Abelard, Pierre. (1097-1142) Orator.

Ader, Clement. (1841-1926) Aviation pioneer, engineer, inventor.

Arouet, François Marie. (Voltaire) (1694-1778) Author, philosopher, playwright.

Baret, Jeanne. (1740?-1803?) Naturalist.

Barrault, Jean-Louis. (1910-1994) Actor, theatrical director and producer.

Barré-Sinoussi, Françoise. (1947-) Chemist, medical researcher.

Beauharnais, Josephine. (1763-1814) Empress, wife of Napoleon Bonaparte.

Beauvoir, Simone de. (1908-1986) Author, philosopher, women's rights activist.

Becquerel, Antoine Henri. (1852-1908) Physicist. Nobel Prize winner.

Berlioz, Hector. (1803-1869) Composer.

Bernard of Clairvaux. Monk, saint.

Bernhardt, Sarah. (1844-1923) Actor.

Bertillon, Alphonse. (1853-1914) Forensic scientist.

Bizet, Georges. (1838-1875) Composer.

Blanchard, Jean-Pierre. (1754-1809) Aviation pioneer.

Blériot, Louis. (1872-1936) Aviation pioneer.

Bonaly, Surya. (1973-) Olympic figure skater.

Bonaparte, Napoleon. (1768-1821) Conqueror, political activist.

Bonheur, Rosa. (1822-1899) Painter.

Boulanger, Nadia. (1887-1979) Composer, conductor.

Bourgeois, Léon. (1851-1925) Attorney, prime minister, statesman. Nobel Peace Prize winner.

Braille, Louis. (1809-1852) Inventor.

Braque, Georges. (1882-1963) Painter.

Brebeuf, Jean de, Father. (1593-1649) Missionary, spiritual leader.

Breuil, Henri. (1877-1961) Archaeologist.

Briand, Aristide. (1862-1932) Attorney, prime minister, statesman. Nobel Peace Prize winner.

Brule, Etienne. (1592-1632) Explorer.

Brunel, Marc. (1769-1849) Civil engineer.

Buade, Louis de. (Frontenac et Palluau, Comte) (1622-1698) Colonist, military leader.

Buffon, Georges. (1707-1788) Author, naturalist.

Cailliaud, Frederic. (1787-1869) Explorer.

Caillié, René. (1799-1838) Explorer.

Calvin, John. (1509-1564) Protestant theologian.

Careme, Antonin. (1784-1833) Chef.

Carnot, Lazare Nicolas Marguerite. (1753-1823) Military leader.

Carré, Lily. (1908-) World War II spy.

Cartier, Jacques. (1491-1557) Explorer.

Cassin, René. (1887-1976) Attorney, legal scholar, UNESCO cofounder. Nobel Peace Prize winner.

Catherine de Medici. (1519-1589) Queen.

Cézanne, Paul. (1839-1906) Painter.

Chagall, Marc. (1887-1985) Painter, born

Russia.

Champlain, Samuel de. (1567-1635) Explorer.

Champollion, Jean-François. (1790-1832) Egyptologist.

Chanel, Gabrielle "Coco." (1883-1971) Fashion designer.

Churchill, Odette Brailly Sansom. (1912-1995) World War II resistance worker.

Claudel, Camille. (1864-1943) Sculptor.

Clémenceau, Georges. (1841-1929) Prime minister, World War I military leader.

Clicquot-Ponsardin, Nicole-Barbe. (1777-1866) Winemaker.

Clotilda. (470-545) Saint, spiritual leader, wife of Clovis.

Clovis. (466-511) Military leader, spiritual leader.

Clugney, Odode. (879-942) Composer, singer, spiritual leader.

Constant, Paul D'Estournelles. (1852-1924) Diplomat, peace activist, statesman. Nobel Peace Prize winner.

Courbet, Gustave. (1819-1877) Painter.

Cousteau, Jacques-Yves. (1910-1997) Environmentalist, underwater explorer, inventor, World War II resistance fighter. Presidential Medal of Freedom recipient.

Cresson, Edith. (1934-) Prime minister.

Curie, Marie Sklodowska. (1867-1934) Chemist, inventor, physicist, born Poland. Nobel Prize winner.

Curie, Pierre. (1859-1906) Chemist, physicist. Nobel Prize winner.

Cuvier, Georges. (1769-1832) Anatomist, paleontologist.

Danton, Georges. (1759-1794) Military leader, revolutionary.

Daumier, Honoré. (1808-1879) Caricaturist, painter, sculptor.

Dausset, Jean. (1916-) Immunologist, physician, physiologist. Nobel Prize winner.

David, Jacques-Louis. (1784-1825) Painter.

David-Neel, Alexandra. (1868-1969) Adventurer, explorer.

De Gaulle, Charles. (1890-1970) World War I and II military leader.

Debussy, Claude. (1862-1918) Composer.

Degas, Edgar. (1834-1917) Painter.

Delacroix, Eugène. (1798-1863) Painter.

Deneuve, Catherine. (1943-) Actor.

Descartes, René. (1596-1650) Mathematician, philosopher.

Despres, Josquin, (1440-1521) Composer, conductor.

Diderot, Denis. (1713-1784) Scholar.

Dior, Christian. (1905-1957) Fashion designer.

du Chatelet, Marquise Gabrielle-Emilie. (1706-1749) Mathematician, physicist.

Du Temple, Felix. (1823-1890) Aviation pioneer, naval officer.

Duchamp, Marcel. (1887-1968) Painter.

Dupin, Amandine Aurore Lucie. (George Sand) (1804-1876) Author.

Eiffel, Alexandre Gustave. (1832-1923) Mechanical engineer.

Eleanor of Aquitaine. (1122-1204) Queen.

Fabre, Jean Henri. (1823-1915) Entomologist.

Foch, Ferdinand. (1851-1929) World War I army general.

Foucault, Jean Bernard Léon. (1819-1868) Physicist.

Fragonard, Jean-Honoré. (1732-1806) Painter.

Gauguin, Paul. (1848-1903) Painter.

Gay-Lussac, Joseph Louis. (1778-1850) Chemist.

Geoffrin, Thérese Roget. (1699-1777) Patron of the arts.

Germain, Sophie. (1776-1831) Mathematician.

Girrard, Henri. (1825-1882) Inventor.

Gounod, Charles. (1818-1893) Composer.

Groseilliers, Médard Chouat des. (1618?-1695?) Explorer.

Guiscard, Robert. (1015-1085) Military leader.

Héloise. (1098-1164) Spiritual leader, lover of Abelard.

Hugo, Victor. (1802-1885) Author, playwright, poet.

Ingres, Jean-Auguste. (1780-1867) Painter.

Joan of Arc. (1412-1431) Military leader, saint.

Joliot-Curie, Irène. (1897-1956) Chemist, physicist. Nobel Prize winner.

Joques, Isaac. (1607-1646) Colonist.

Jouhaux, Léon. (1879-1954) Labor leader, International Labor Organization cofounder, political activist. Nobel Peace

Prize winner.

Killy, Jean-Claude. (1943-) Olympic skier.

Kouchner, Bernard. (1939-) Human rights activist, physician, political activist.

La Salle, René Robert Cavalier. (1643-1687) Explorer.

La Tour, Charles Turquis de Sainte-Étienne de. (1593-1666) Colonist.

Laclède Liguest, Pierre de. (1729-1778) Explorer.

Lafayette, Marie Joseph Paul Yves Roch Gilbert du Motier, Marquis de. (1757-1834) Military leader.

Lamarck, Jean Baptiste. (1744-1829) Author, botanist, environmentalist.

Lanennec, René T.H. (1781-1826) Medical researcher, physician.

Laroche, Raymonde de. (1886-1919) Aviation pioneer

Latham, Hubert. (1883-1912) Aviation pioneer.

Laveran, Charles Louis Alphonse. (1845-1932) Bacteriologist, medical researcher. Nobel Prize winner.

Lavoisier, Antoine Laurent. (1743-1794) Chemist.

Lavoisier, Marie. (1758-1836) Chemist.

Locard, Edmond. (1877-1966) Forensic scientist.

L'Olonnois, François. (1630-1671) Pirate.

Lorrain, Claude. (1605-1682) Painter.

Louis II de Bourbon. (1621-1686) Army commander.

Louis XIV. (1638-1715) King.

Louis XVI. (1754-1792) King.

Mahaut, Countess de Artois. (1275-1329) Noblewoman.

Maisonneuve, Paul. (1612-1676) Colonist in Montreal.

Manet, Édouard. (1832-1883) Painter.

Maria, "Madame." (unknown) Holocaust rescuer.

Marie Antoinette. (1755-1793) Princess, queen.

Marie-Benoit, Father. (unknown) Holocaust rescuer, capucin monk.

Mariette, Auguste. (1821-1881) Archaeologist.

Marquette, Jacques. (1637-1675) Missionary, explorer, spiritual leader.

Martel, Charles. (689-741) Military leader.

Martin of Tours. (316?-397) Saint.

Mason, Andrée-Paule. (1923-1991) World War II resistance fighter.

Matisse, Henri. (1869-1954) Painter, sculptor.

Mauchaut, Guillaume de. (1300-1377) Composer.

Merton, Thomas. (Father M. Louis) (1915-1968) Poet, spiritual leader.

Molière. See Poquelin, Jean Baptiste.

Monet, Claude. (1840-1926) Painter.

Montgolfier, Jacques Étienne. (1745-1799) Aviation pioneer, inventor.

Montgolfier, Joseph Michel. (1740-1810) Aviation pioneer, inventor.

Moreau, Gustave. (1826-1898) Painter.

Morisot, Berthe. (1841-1895) Painter.

Mouhot, Henri. (1826-1861) Archaeologist.

Nostradamus. (1503-1566) Physician, folk hero, visionary.

Offenbach, Jacques. (1819-1880) Composer, musician.

Paré, Ambroise. (1510-1590) Physician.

Pascal, Blaise. (1623-1662) Mathematician, philosopher, physicist.

Passy, Frédéric. (1822-1912) International League of Peace and Freedom founder, peace activist. Nobel Peace Prize winner.

Pasteur, Louis. (1822-1895) Chemist.

Peizerat, Gwendal. (1972-) Olympic figure skater.

Penry, Jacques. (unknown) Forensic scientist.

Pétain, Henri Phillipe. (1856-1951) World War I and II military leader.

Philip II. (1165-1223) King.

Pilatre de Rozier, Jean- François. (1756-1785) Aviation pioneer.

Pinel, Philippe. (1745-1826) Human rights activist, physician, reformer.

Pissarro, Camille. (1830-1903) Painter.

Pizan, Christine de. (1365-1430) Author, poet.

Poquelin, Jean Baptiste. (Molière) (1622-1673) Actor, playwright.

Poussin, Nicolas. (1594-1665) Painter.

Rabelais, François. (1495-1553) Author, physician.

Radisson, Pierre Esprit. (1636-1710) Explorer.

Rameau, Jean-Phillippe. (1683-1764) Composer, musician.

Rashi. (Solomon ben Isaac) (1040-1105) Author, educator, Hebrew scholar.

Ravel, Maurice. (1875-1937) Composer.

Renault, Louis. (1843-1918) Attorney. Nobel Peace Prize winner.

Renoir, Pierre Auguste. (1841-1919) Painter.

Ribaut, Jean. (1520-1565) Colonist, explorer, naval officer.

Robert-Houdin, Jean Eugene. (1805-1871) Magician.

Robespierre, Maximilien François Marie Isisdore de. (1758-1794) Political activist, revolutionary.

Rodin, Auguste. (1840-1917) Sculptor.

Roland, Madame Jeanne-Marie "Manon." (1754-1793) Political activist, revolutionary.

Rotmil, Bernard. (1926-) Holocaust survivor.

Rouault, Georges. (1871-1958) Painter.

Rousseau, Henri. (1844-1910) Painter.

Saint-Exupéry, Antoine de. (1900-1944) Adventurer, author, aviator.

Sand, George. *See* Dupin, Amandine Aurore Lucie.

Sartre, Jean Paul. (1905-1980) Philosopher. Nobel Prize winner.

Satie, Erik. (1866-1925) Composer.

Schweitzer, Albert. (1875-1965) Missionary, musician, spiritual leader. Nobel Peace Prize winner.

Seurat, Georges. (1859-1890) Painter.

Signac, Paul. (1863-1935) Painter.

Spoerry, Anne. (1918-1999) Missionary, physician, World War II resistance worker.

Stael, Madame Anna Louise Germaine de. (1766-1817) Author, noblewoman.

Thible, Elizabeth. (fl. 1784) Aviation pioneer.

Tonty, Henri de. (1649-1704) Explorer, born Italy.

Toulouse-Lautrec, Henride. (1864-1901) Painter.

Trocme, André. (unknown) Holocaust rescuer, spiritual leader.

Trocme, Magda. (unknown) Holocaust rescuer, spiritual leader.

Tussaud, Marie. (1761-1850) Sculptor.

Vauban, Sebastien le preste de. (1633-1707) Military leader.

Verendrye, Pierre. (1685-1749) Colonist.

Verne, Jules. (1828-1905) Author.

Vigee-Le Brun, Elisabeth. (1755-1842) Painter.

Voltaire. *See* Arouet, François Marie.

Weidner, John. (unknown) Holocaust rescuer.

Weil, Simone. (1909-1943) Author, political activist, revolutionary.

Worth, Charles Frederick. (1825-1895) Fashion designer.

Zola, Emile. (1840-1902) Author.

Frontiersmen
See Pioneers and Frontierspeople.

Fur Traders, Trappers, and Hunters.
See also Indian Agents and Scouts; Pioneers and Frontierspeople.

Beckwourth, James. (1798-1866)

Belaney, Archibald. (Grey Owl) (1888-1938) Canadian trapper, born England.

Bonga, George. (1802-1880) African American and Ojibwa Indian.

Boone, Daniel. (1734-1820)

Bridger, Jim. (1804-1881)

Carson, Christopher "Kit." (1809-1868)

Chouteau, Auguste. (1749-1829)

Cody, William. (Buffalo Bill) (1846-1917)

Colter, John. (1775-1813)

Crockett, Davy. (1786-1836)

Dezhnev, Semyon. (1610-1672) Russian.

Du Sable, Jean Baptiste Pointe. (1745-1818)

Fink, Mike. (1770?-1823?)

Fitzpatrick, Tom "Broken Hand." (1799-1854)

Gist, Christopher. (1706-1759)

Glass, Hugh. (1780-1833)

Leroux, Antoine. (1635-1708) born France.

Lisa, Manuel. (1772-1820)

Mackenzie, Sir Alexander. (1764-1820) born Scotland.

McLoughlin, John. (1784-1857) Canadian.

Rose, Edward. (1780?-1820?)

Smith, Jedediah Strong. (1799-1831)

Stuart, Robert. (1785-1848) Scottish.

Thompson, David. (1770-1857) English.

Gangsters

See also Criminals; Outlaws.
Capone, Al. (1899-1947)
Colosimo, James "Big Jim." (1878-1920)
  born Italy.
Dillinger, John. (1903-1934)
Eastman, Monk. *See* Osterman, Edward.
Giancana, Salvatore "Sam." (1908-1975)
  born Italy.
Gotti, John. (1940-2002)
Karpis, Alvin. (1908-1979) Canadian.
Kelly, Paul. *See* Vaccarelli, Paulo Antonio.
Lansky, Meyer. (1902-1983) born Russia.
Luciano, Salvatore "Lucky." (1897-1962)
  born Italy.
Osterman, Edward. (Monk Eastman) (1873-
  1920)
Siegel, Ben "Bugsy." (1906-1947)
Torrio, John. (1882-1957) born Italy.
Vaccarelli, Paulo Antonio. (Paul Kelly)
  (1876-1927) born Italy.

Gay Rights Activists

Hardy-Garcia, Dianne. (1965-)
Hirschfeld, Magnus. (1868-1935) Polish.

Geneticists

Beadle, George. (1903-1989)
Flaggs, Gail. (unknown)
Jeffreys, Sir Alec. (1950-) English.
Khorana, Har Gobind. (1922-) born India.
King, Mary-Claire. (1946-)
McClintock, Barbara. (1909-1992)
Mendel, Gregor. (1822-1884) Austrian.
Morgan, Thomas Hunt. (1866-1945)
Poodry, Clifton. (1943-) Seneca Indian.
Sager, Ruth. (1918-1997)
Watson, James Dewey. (1928-)

Geographers

Adams, Harriet Chalmers. (1875-1937)
Beach, Sheryl Luzzader. (unknown)
Eratostheses. (276-194 B.C.) Greek.
Hedin, Sven. (1865-1952) Swedish.
Humboldt, Alexander von. (1769-1859) German.
Livingstone, David. (1813-1873) Scottish.
Mercator, Gerardus. (1512-1594) Belgian.
Ptolemy. (100-170) Greek.
Pytheas. (fl. 300 B.C.) Greek.
Thompson, David. (1770-1857) English.

Geologists

Bascom, Florence. (1862-1945)
Beach, Sheryl Luzzader. (unknown)
Braun, E. Lucy. (1889-1971)
Denetclaw, Wilfred F., Jr. (1959-) Navajo
  Indian.
Ewing, Maurice. (1906-1974)
Fowler-Billings, Katharine Stevens.
  (1902-1997)
Gilbert, G. K. (1843-1918)
Hayden, Ferdinand Vandeveer. (1829-
  1887)
Hess, Harry. (1906-1969)
Hickson, Catherine. (1955-) Canadian.
Hitchcock, Edward. (1793-1864)
Holmes, Arthur. (1890-1965) English.
Hose, Louise. (1952-)
Hutton, James. (1726-1797) Scottish.
Lucas, Anthony Francis. (1855-1921)
  born Austria.
Lyell, Sir Charles. (1797-1875) English.
Maclure, William. (1763-1840) born Scot-
  land.
Mantell, Gideon. (1790-1852) English.
McNutt, Marcia. (1952-)
Nordenskjöld, Nils Adolf Erik. (1822-
  1901) Swedish.
Nordenskjöld, Nils Otto. (1869-1928)
  Swedish.
Ocampo, Adriana. (1955-) Planetary ge-
  ologist, born Colombia.
Powell, John Wesley. (1834-1902)
Rogers, Patricia. (unknown)
Schmidt, Harrison "Jack." (1935-)
Schwabe, Stephanie. (1957-) born Ger-
  many.
Shoemaker, Gene. (1928-1997)

Germans

See also Immigrants to United States,
  German.
Adler, Henny. (1925-) Holocaust survivor.
Adler, Sam. (unknown) Holocaust survi-
  vor.
Attila the Hun. (400-453) Conqueror,
  king.
Bach, Johann Sebastian. (1685-1750)
  Composer, musician.
Baeck, Leo. (1873-1956) Author, Holo-
  caust resistance fighter, survivor.
Barbie, Klaus. (1913-1991) Nazi war

criminal.

Beckenbauer, Franz. (1946-) Soccer player.

Beckmann, Max. (1884-1950) Painter, printmaker.

Beethoven, Ludwig von. (1770-1827) Composer.

Benz, Karl. (1844-1929) Automaker, engineer, inventor.

Beukels, Jan. (John of Leiden) (1509-1536) Cult leader, spiritual leader.

Bismarck, Otto Eduard Leopold von. (1815-1898) Chancellor, political activist.

Boaz, Franz. (1858-1942) Anthropologist, linguist.

Bonhoeffer, Dietrich. (1906-1945) Holocaust resistance fighter, victim, spiritual leader.

Boniface. (672-754) Missionary, saint.

Bormann, Martin. (1900-1945) Nazi war criminal.

Brahms, Johannes. (1833-1897) Composer.

Brandt, Karl. (1904-1948) Nazi war criminal, physician.

Brandt, Willy. (1913-1992) Journalist, statesman. Nobel Peace Prize winner.

Braun, Eva. (1912-1945) Hitler's mistress.

Brecht, Bertolt. (1898-1956) Playwright, poet.

Cantor, Georg. (1845-1918) Mathematician.

Clausewitz, Karl von. (1780-1831) Military leader.

Clifford, Esther. (1921-) Holocaust survivor.

Cohn, Marianne. (1924-1944) Holocaust resistance worker, victim.

Daimler, Gottlieb. (1834-1900) Automaker, mechanical engineer, inventor.

Dietrich, Amalie Nelle. (1821-1891) Botanist.

Dornberger, Walter. (1895-1980) Inventor, World War I military.

Dulcie of Worms. (12th century) Moneylender, scholar.

Dürer, Albrecht. (1471-1528) Engraver, painter.

Eckhart, Meister. (1280-1327) Mystic, spiritual leader.

Ehrlich, Paul (1854-1915) Bacteriologist, medical researcher. Nobel Prize winner.

Eichmann, Adolf. (1906-1962) Nazi war criminal.

Ella bat Moses. (17th century) Printer.

Engels, Friedrich. (1820-1895) Political activist.

Frank, Hans. (1900-1946) Attorney, Nazi political activist.

Frank, Henry. (unknown) Holocaust survivor.

Frank, Irene. (1927-) Holocaust survivor.

Frederick I. (Barbarossa) (1123-1190) King Holy Roman Empire.

Frederick II "The Great." (1712-1786) King.

Friedrich, Caspar David. (1774-1840) Painter.

Frommet of Arwyller. (15th century) Scribe.

Gauss, Carl Friedrich. (1777-1855) Mathematician.

Geiger, Abraham. (1810-1874) Reform Judaism spiritual leader.

Geiger, Hans. (1882-1945) Inventor, physicist.

Gela bat Moses. (18th century) Printer.

Gloria von Thum und Taxis. (1960-) Princess.

Gluck, Christoph Willibald. (1714-1787) Opera composer.

Gluckel of Hameln. (1646-1724) Author.

Goebbels, Joseph. (1897-1945) Nazi war criminal.

Göring, Hermann. (1893-1946) Air Force general, Nazi war criminal.

Graf, Steffi. (1969-) Tennis player.

Grimm, Jakob. (1785-1863) Folklorist, storyteller.

Grimm, Wilhelm. (1786-1859) Folklorist, storyteller.

Grotefend, Georg Friedrich. (1775-1853) Scholar, translator.

Gruenewald, Matthias. (1475-1528) Painter.

Grynszpan, Herschel. (1921-1942) Holocaust resistance fighter, victim.

Guderian, Heinz. (1888-1954) World War II military leader.

Gutenberg, Johann. (1399-1468) Inventor, printer.

Heisenberg, Werner. (1901-1976) Physicist. Nobel Prize winner.

Henry IV. (1050-1106) Emperor.

Hensel, Fanny Mendelssohn. (1805-1847) Composer.

Hess, Rudolf. (1894-1987) Aviator, Nazi war criminal.

Heydrich, Reinhard. (1904-1942) Nazi war criminal.

Hildegarde von Bingen. (1098-1179) Spiritual leader, visionary.

Himmler, Heinrich. (1900-1945) Nazi war criminal.

Hindenburg, Paul von. (1847-1934) President, World War I military leader.

Hirsch, Samson Raphael. (1808-1888) Author, educator.

Hitler, Adolf. (1889-1945) Chancellor, dictator, Nazi war criminal.

Höss, Rudolf. (1900-1947) Nazi war criminal.

Hübener, Helmut. (1925-1942) Youth who protested against Nazis in World War II.

Humboldt, Alexander von. (1769-1859) Botanist, geographer.

Janensch, Werner. (1878-1969) Paleontologist.

Jathro, Karl. (1873-1933) Aviation pioneer.

Katz, Ralph. (1932-) Holocaust survivor.

Kekulé, Friedrich August. (1829-1896) Chemist.

Kepler, Johannes. (1571-1630) Astronomer.

Klarsfeld, Beate. (1939-) Nazi hunter.

Koch, Ilse. (1906-1967) Nazi war criminal.

Koch, Karl. (1897-1945) Nazi war criminal.

Koch, Robert. (1843-1910) Bacteriologist. Nobel Prize winner.

Kolbe, Fritz. (1903-1961) World War II spy for allies.

Kollwitz, Kaethe. (1867-1945) Painter, sculptor.

Krupp, Alfried. (1907-1967) Entrepreneur arms manufacturer, Nazi war criminal.

Kuehn, Ruth. (unknown) World War II spy.

Levy, Hans. (1928-) Holocaust survivor.

Liebmann, Hanne Eve Hirsch. (1924-) Holocaust survivor.

Lilienthal, Otto. (1848-1896) Aeronautical engineer, aviation pioneer.

Luther, Martin. (1483-1546) Spiritual leader, reformer.

Luxemburg, Rosa. (1870-1919) Peace activist, political activist, born Poland.

Marx, Karl Heinrich. (1818-1883) Economist, philosopher.

Mata Hari. *See* Zeller, Margareta Gertrude.

Meinhof, Ulrike. (1934-1976) Journalist, revolutionary.

Mendelssohn, Moses. (1729-1786) Educator, philosopher, scholar.

Mengele, Josef. (1911-1979) Nazi war criminal, physician.

Minke, Willy. (unknown) Holocaust survivor.

Moses, Frank. (1931-) Holocaust survivor.

Müller, Heinrich. (1901-1945) Nazi war criminal.

Münchhassen, Baron von. (1720-1797) Storyteller.

Noether, Emmy. (1882-1935) Mathematician.

Ossietzky, Carl von. (1889-1938) Author, peace activist. Nobel Peace Prize winner.

Otto I, the Great. (912-973) Holy Roman Emperor.

Otto, Kristen. (1966-) Olympic swimmer.

Pappenheim, Berta. (1859-1936) Organization founder, social reformer, social worker.

Paumann, Konrad. (1415-1473) Composer.

Planck, Max Karl Ernst Ludwig. (1858-1947) Physicist. Nobel Prize winner.

Quidde, Ludwig. (1858-1941) Historian, organization founder, peace activist. Nobel Peace Prize winner.

Reiche, Maria. (1903-1998) Mathematician.

Reitsch, Hanna. (1912-1979) Aviator, test pilot.

Richthofen, Baron Manfred von "Red Baron." (1892-1918) World War I aviator.

Ridesel, Baroness Frederika von. (1746-1808) American Revolutionary War camp follower, author.

Riefenstahl, Leni. (1902-2003) Filmmaker.

Roentgen, Wilhelm Conrad. (1845-1923) Physican, physicist. Nobel Prize winner.

Röhm, Ernst. (1887-1934) Nazi military leader.

Rommel, Erwin "Desert Fox." (1891-1944) World War II Army commander.

Rosenzweig, Franz. (1886-1939) Educator, scholar.

Schliemann, Heinrich. (1822-1890) Archaeologist.

Schloss, Louis. (1921-) Holocaust survivor.

Scholl, Hans. (1918-1943) Holocaust resistance fighter, victim.

Scholl, Sophie. (1921-1943) Holocaust resistance fighter, victim.

Schulte, Eduard Reinhold Karl. (1891-1966)
Attorney, political activist, World War II
anti-Nazi spy.

Schumann, Clara. (1819-1896) Composer,
musician.

Schumann, Robert. (1810-1856) Composer,
musician.

Serturner, Friedrich. (1783-1841) Chemist,
medical researcher.

Sorge, Richard. (1895-1944) Journalist,
World War II spy.

Stauffenberg, Claus von. (1907-1944) World
War II anti-Nazi political leader.

Stommer, Helga Edelstein. (1926-) Holocaust survivor.

Strauss, Richard. (1864-1949) Composer,
conductor.

Stresemann, Gustav. (1878-1929) Statesman. Nobel Peace Prize winner.

Urania of Worms, Lady. (13th Century)
Cantor.

Virchow, Rudolph. (1821-1902) Medical
researcher, pathologist, physician.

Von Manstein, Erich. (1887-1973) World
War II field marshal.

Von Moltke, Helmut. (1800-1891) Military
leader.

Von Ribbentrop, Joachim. (1893-1946) Diplomat, foreign minister, Nazi war criminal.

Wagner, Richard. (1813-1883) Composer.

Weber, Karl Maria Friedrich Ernst von.
(1786-1826) Composer.

Wedener, Alfred. (1880-1930) Explorer,
mcterologist.

Weekly, Frieda von Richthofen. (1870-
1956) Wife of D. H. Lawrence.

Wertheimer, Henry. (1927-) Holocaust survivor.

Wilhelm II. (1859-1941) Emperor, World
War I general.

Winckelmann, Johann Joachim. (1717-
1768) Archaeologist.

Winkler-Kühne, Ruth. (1931-) Holocaust
rescuer.

Witt, Katarina. (1965-) Olympic figure
skater.

Zunz, Leopold. (1794-1886) Educator.

Ghanians

See also Africans; Blacks, International;
Immigrants to United States, African.

Nkrumah, Kwame. (1909-1972) President,
prime minister.

Gods and Goddesses

African
Oya. Goddess.

Egyptian
Anubis. God of the dead.
Geb. God of the earth.
Hathhor. Goddess of love.
Horus. God of life.
Isis. (3000 B.C.)
Nekhebet. Goddess of royal protection.
Nepatys. Goddess of the morning.
Nut. Goddess of the sky.
Osiris. God of the underworld.
Ra. (The Sun) God of all creation.
Set. God of the desert.
Shu. God of air.
Tefnut. Goddess of the morning dew.

Greek
Athena
Diana

Mayan
Ah Puch. God of death.
Bolontiku. God of the lower world.
Chac. God of rain.
Ek Chuah. God of war.
Itzámna. God of all.
Ix Chel. Goddess of childbirth.
Ix Tab. Goddess of suicide.
Kinich Ahau. God of the sun.
Kukulcán. God of the wind.
Manik. God of human sacrifice.
Xaman Ek. God of the north star.
Yum Kaax. God of corn.

Norse
Baldur. God of peace and light.
Bragi. God of poetry.
Frey. God of rain and sunshine.
Freya. Goddess of love and beauty.

Frigga. Goddess of marriage.
Heimdall. The watchman.
Hela. Goddess of death.
Hermod. God of courage.
Idunn. Goddess of youth.
Loki. God of mischief.
Niord. God of the ocean.
Odin. God of the skies.
Ragnarok. The last battle.
Thor. God of thunder.
Tyr. God of war.

Gold Miners

See also Cowboys and Ranchers; Pioneers
and Frontierspeople.
Cashman, Nellie. (1845-1925)
Clappe, Louise Amelia. (1819-1906)
Murieta, Joaquin. (1832-1853) born Mexico.
Pacheco, Romualdo. (1831-1899)
Ryan, Katherine "Klondike Kate." (1869-
    1932)
Sutter, John Augustus. (1803-1880) born
    Germany.

Golfers

Berg, Patty. (1918-)
Collett-Vare, Glenna. (1903-1989)
de Vicenzo, Roberto. (1923-) Argentine.
Didrikson, Mildred "Babe." *See* Zaharias,
    Mildred "Babe" Didrikson.
Hogan, Ben. (1912-1997)
Jones, Bobby. (1902-1971)
Lopez, Nancy. (1957-)
Martin, Casey. (1972-)
Nicklaus, Jack. (1940-)
Palmer, Arnold. (1929-)
Snead, Sam. (1912-2002)
Trevino, Lee. (1939-)
Vardon, Harry. (1870-1937) English.
Whitworth, Kathy. (1939-)
Woods, Tiger. (1975-)
Zaharias, Mildred "Babe" Didrikson. (1913-
    1956)

Government Workers

See also Ambassadors and Diplomats; Cabi-
    net Members; City Government Officials;
    Congressmen/women; Governors; Sena-
    tors.

National
Anderson, Mary. (1872-1964) Director U.S.
    Women's Bureau, born Sweden.
Banuelos, Romana Acosta. (1925-)
    Treasurer.
Barnard, Henry. (1811-1900) U.S. Commis-
    sioner of Education.
Campbell, Bonnie. (1948-) Director of Vio-
    lence Against Women campaign.
Dee, Ada. (1935-) Assistant Secretary of
    Indian Affairs.
Edelman, Marian Wright. (1939-) Director,
    Children's Defense Fund.
Elders, Jocelyn Jones. (1933-) Surgeon Gen-
    eral.
Granville, Evelyn Boyd. (1924-) National
    Bureau of Standards.
Healy, Bernardine. (1944-) Director, Na-
    tional Institute of Health.
Heuman, Judy. (1947-) Assistant Secretary
    of Education.
Hiss, Alger. (1904-1996) Department of
    Justice.
Hoover, J. Edgar. (1895-1972) Federal Bu-
    reau of Investigation director.
Hopkins, Harry. (1890-1946) Director of
    President Franklin D. Roosevelt's relief
    efforts.
Jackson, Shirley Ann. (1946-) Director, Nu-
    clear Regulatory Commission.
Johnson, William. (1714-1774) Superinten-
    dent of Indian Affairs, born England.
King, Reatha Clark. (1938-) National Bu-
    reau of Standards.
Lathrop, Julia. (1858-1932) Director, U.S.
    Children's Bureau.
Novello, Antonio C. (1944-) Surgeon Gen-
    eral of U.S., born Puerto Rico.
Packard, David. (1912-1996) Deputy Secre-
    tary of Defense.
Parker, Ely Samuel. (1828-1895) Commis-
    sioner of Indian Affairs.
Peterson, Esther. (1906-1997) Director,
    Consumer Affairs.
Satcher, David. (1941-) Surgeon General.
Travis, Dempsey J. (1920-) Head, Housing
    and Urban Development.
Whitman, Christine Todd. (1946-) Head,
    Environmental Protection Agency.

State

Bond, Julian. (1940-) Legislator, Georgia.

Brown, Dorothy Lavinia. (1919-) Legislator, Tennessee.

Campbell, Tunis G. (1812-1891) Legislator, Georgia.

Carter, Pamela. (1950-) Attorney General, Indiana.

Chavez, Dennis. (1888-1962) Legislator, New Mexico.

Dunn, Oscar. (1820-1871) Lieutenant Governor, Louisiana.

Echohawk, Larry. (1948-) Legislator, Idaho.

Fenwick, Millicent. (1910-1992) Legislator, New Jersey.

Fortune, T. Thomas. (1856-1928) Legislator, Florida.

Galloway, Abraham. (1837-1870) Legislator, North Carolina.

Grasso, Ella. (1919-1981) Legislator, Connecticut.

Hayden, Lewis. (1815-1889) Legislator, Massachusetts.

Hilton, Conrad. (1887-1979) Legislator, New Mexico.

Lincoln, Abraham. (1809-1865) Legislator, Illinois.

Mann, Horace. (1795-1859) Legislator, Massachusetts.

Marsh, George Perkins. (1801-1882) Legislator, Vermont.

Norton, Daniel. (1840-1918) Legislator, Virginia.

Prothrow-Stith, Deborah. (1954-) Commissioner of Public Health, Massachusetts.

Reno, Janet. (1938-) Attorney General, Florida.

Ros-Lentinen, Ileana. (1952-) Legislator, Florida, born Cuba.

Rumsfeld, Donald H. (1932-) Legislator, Illinois.

Seguín, Juan N. (1806-1890) Legislator, Texas.

Thayer, Eli. (1819-1899) Legislator, Massachusetts.

Twilight, Alexander Lucius. (1795-1857) Legislator, Vermont.

Walker, Thomas. (1850-1935) Legislator.

Waters, Maxine. (1938-) Legislator, California.

Wilder, L. Douglas. (1931-) Legislator, Vir-

ginia.

Governors, United States

Adams, Samuel. (1722-1803) Massachusetts.

Andros, Edmund. (1637-1714) New York,Virginia.

Berkeley, William. (1606-1677) Virginia.

Bienville, Jean Baptiste le Moyne. (1680-1767) Louisiana, born France.

Bradford, William. (1590-1657) Plymouth colony.

Brown, Dorothy Lavinia. (1919-) Tennessee.

Bush, George Walker. (1946-) Texas.

Butler, Benjamin Franklin. (1818-1893) Massachusetts.

Carter, James Earl "Jimmy." (1924-) Georgia.

Cleveland, Grover. (1837-1908) New York.

Clinton, William Jefferson "Bill." (1946) Arkansas.

Coolidge, Calvin. (1872-1923) Massachusetts.

Dudley, Joseph. (1647-1720) Massachusetts.

Endicott, John. (1589-1665) Massachusetts.

Ferguson, Miriam "Mo." (1875-1961) Texas.

Gage, Thomas. (1721-1787) Massachusetts.

Gálvez, Bernardo de. (1746-1786) Louisiana.

Gerry, Elbridge. (1744-1814) Massachusetts.

Grasso, Ella. (1919-1981) Connecticut.

Gwinnett, Button. (1735-1777) Georgia.

Hall, Lyman. (1724-1790) Georgia.

Harrison, William Henry. (1773-1862) Indiana.

Hayes, Rutherford B. (1822-1893) Ohio.

Henry, Patrick. (1736-1799) Virginia.

Houston, Samuel. (1793-1863) Texas.

Hughes, Charles Evan. (1862-1948) New York.

Hutchinson, Thomas. (1711-1780) Massachusetts.

Jay, John. (1745-1829) New York.

Kunin, Madeleine. (1933-) Vermont.

La Follette, Robert. (1855-1925) Wisconsin.

McKinley, William. (1843-1901) Ohio.

Nelson, Gaylord. (1916-) Wisconsin.

Nelson, Thomas, Jr. (1738-1789) Virginia.

Nicholson, Francis. (1655-1728) South Carolina, Virginia.

Paca, William. (1740-1795) Maryland.

Phips, William. (1651-1695) Massachusetts Bay.

Pico, Pio de Jesus. (1801-1894) California.

Pinchback, Pinckney Benton Stewart "P. B. S." (1837-1921) Louisiana.

Pinchot, Gifford. (1865-1946) Pennsylvania.

Polk, James K. (1795-1849) Tennessee.

Printz, Johan. (1592-1663) Delaware.

Reagan, Ronald. (1911-2004) California.

Richards, Ann. (1933-) Texas.

Roosevelt, Franklin Delano. (1882-1945) New York.

Roosevelt, Theodore. (1858-1919) New York.

Sevier, John. (1745-1815) Tennessee.

Seward, William. (1801-1872) New York.

Shirley, William. (1694-1771) Massachusetts.

Stevenson, Adlai. (1900-1965) Illinois.

Thurmond, Strom. (1902-2003) South Carolina.

Tyler, John. (1790-1862) Virginia.

Vargas, Diego de. (1643-1704) New Mexico.

Wallace, George. (1919-1998) Alabama.

Warren, Earl. (1891-1974) California.

Wentworth, Benning. (1696-1770) New Hampshire.

Whitman, Christine Todd. (1946-) New Jersey.

Wilder, L. Douglas. (1931-) Virginia.

Wilson, Woodrow. (1856-1924) New Jersey.

Winthrop, John. (1588-1649) Massachusetts Bay.

Greeks, Ancient

Aeschylus. (c. 525-456 B.C.) Playwright.

Aesop. (c. 600 B.C.) Storyteller.

Agnodice. (c. 300 B.C.) Physician.

Alicbiades. (450-405 B.C.) General, traitor.

Alexander the Great. (356-323 B.C.) King.

Anacreon. (c. 570-485 B.C.) Poet.

Antigonus I. (c. 382-301 B.C.) General.

Apollonius Rhodius. (c. 290-247 B.C.) Author, scholar.

Archimedes. (287-212 B.C.) Inventor, mathematician.

Aristophanes. (c. 455-388 B.C.) Playwright.

Aristotle. (384-322 B.C.) Biologist, philosopher, scholar.

Aspasia. (c. 470-410 B.C.) Women's rights activist.

Darius III. (380-330 B.C.) Ruler.

Demetrius. (336-283 B.C.) Military leader, ruler.

Democritus. (460-370 B.C.) Scientist.

Demosthenes. (384-322 B.C.) Orator.

Epaminondas. (410-323 B.C.) Military leader.

Epicurus. (341-270 B.C.) Philosopher.

Eratostheses. (276-194 B.C.) Astronomer, geographer.

Euclid. (325-270 B.C.) Mathematician.

Euripides. (484-406 B.C.) Playwright.

Galen. (130-200) Physician.

Helen of Troy. (1200-1150 B.C.) Heroine Troy War, legendary.

Hercules. (unknown) Adventurer.

Herodotus. (c. 484-420 B.C.) Historian.

Hipparchia of Athens. (c. 330 B.C.) Philosopher.

Hippocrates. (460?-370? B.C.) Physician.

Homer. (c. 750 B. C.) Poet.

Jason. (unknown) Adventurer.

Leonidas I. (c. 505-490 B.C.) General, king.

Lycurgus. (7th century B.C.) Statesman.

Milo of Crotona. (c. 558 B.C.) Olympic weightlifter, wrestler.

Odysseus. (unknown) Adventurer.

Pericles. (495-429 B.C.) Architect, political activist.

Phayllos of Cortona. (c. 480 B.C.) Olympic pentathlon, track and field athlete.

Phidias. (c. 490-432 B.C.) Sculptor.

Phidippides. (c. 505-490 B.C.) Olympic track and field athlete, runner.

Philip II. (383-336 B.C.) General, king.

Pindar. (c. 518-446 B.C.) Poet.

Plato. (427-347 B.C.) Mathematician, philosopher.

Polydamus. (c. 408 B.C.) Olympic boxer, wrestler.

Praxiteles. (390?-330 B.C.) Sculptor.

Ptolemy. (100-170) Astronomer, geographer.

Ptolemy I. (Ptolemy Soter) (367-283 B.C.) General, king.

Pyrrhus. (319-272 B.C.) Military leader.

Pythagoras. (c. 580-500 B.C.) Mathematician, philosopher.
Pytheas. (fl. 300 B.C.) Astronomer, explorer, geographer, mathematician.
Sappho of Lesbos. (625-570 B.C.) Poet.
Socrates. (470-399 B.C.) Philosopher.
Solon. (610-580 B.C.) Military leader, political activist.
Sophocles. (496-405 B.C.) Playwright.
Themistocles. (523-463 B.C.) Naval commander, political activist, statesman.
Theophrastus. (371-287 B.C.) Botanist.
Thucydides. (c. 454-404 B.C.) Historian.
Xenophon. (c. 428-355 B.C.) Historian.
Zeno. (335-263 B.C.) Philosopher.

Greeks, Modern
Callas, Maria. (1923-1977) Opera singer.
Cyril. (827-869) Missionary, saint, spiritual leader.
Greco, El. *See* Theotokópoulous, Doménikos.
Hadjidaki-Marder, Elpida. (1948-) Marine archaeologist.
Methodius. (815-885) Saint, spiritual leader.
Palamas, Gregory. (1296-1359) Spiritual leader.
Theotokópoulous, Doménikos.(El Greco) (1541-1614) Painter.
Venizélos, Eleutherios. (1864-1936) Statesman.

Guatemalans
Menchú, Rigoberta. (1959-) Human rights activist. Nobel Peace Prize winner.

Gulf War Figures
Amanpour, Christine. (1958-) English broadcast journalist, war correspondent.
Davis, Lonnie. (1958-) Army military hero.
Dorman, Pamela Davis. (1952-) Navy chaplain.
Jans, Megan. (1952-) Helicoptor pilot, lieutenant colonel.
Powell, Colin. (1937-) General.
Schwarzkopf, Norman. (1934-) General.

Gymnasts
See also Olympic Athletes.
Amanar, Simona. (1979-) Romanian.

Andrianov, Nikolai. (1952-) Russian.
Antolin, Jeanette. (1981-)
Atler, Vanessa. (1982-)
Beckerman, Alyssa. (1981-)
Boguinskaia, Svetlana. (1973-) Russian.
Borden, Amanda. (1977-)
Caslavska, Vera. (1942-) Czech.
Chow, Amy. (1978-)
Comaneci, Nadia. (1961-) Romanian.
Conner, Bart. (1958-)
Dantzscher, Jamie. (1982-)
Dawes, Dominique. (1976-)
Dimas, Trent. (1970-)
Jie, Ling. (1982-) Chinese.
Kato, Sawao. (1946-) Japanese.
Khorkina, Svetlana. (1979-) Russian.
Korbut, Olga. (1955-) Russian.
Latynina, Larissa. (1934-) Russian.
Maloney, Kris. (1981-)
Miller, Shannon. (1977-)
Moceanu, Dominique. (1981-)
Phelps, Jaycie. (1979-)
Podkopayeva, Lilia. (1978-) Ukrainian.
Ray, Elise. (1982-)
Retton, Mary Lou. (1968-)
Strug, Kerri. (1977-)
Thompson, Jennie. (1981-)
White, Morgan. (1983-)
Zmeskal, Kim. (1976-)

Haitians
Jean-Murat, Carolle. (1950-) Educator, human rights activist, physician, public health worker.
Touissant L'Ouverture, Pierre Dominique. (1743-1803) General, slave insurrectionist.

Handicapped
See Emotionally Disabled; Hearing Impaired; Learning Disabled; Physically Challenged; Visually Impaired.

Hatemongers
See also Cult Leaders; Dictators; Nazi War Criminals; Terrorists.
Beecher, Lyman. (1775-1863) Puritan religious zealot.
Coughlin, Father Charles Edward. (1891-1979) Radio broadcaster, spiritual leader,

born Canada.

Farrakhan, Louis. (1933-) Black Power
leader.

Hitler, Adolf. (1889-1945) German dictator,
Nazi war criminal.

McCarthy, Joseph. (1908-1957) Senator,
Communist purge.

Parris, Betty. (1682-1760) Puritan, accused
others of witchcraft in Salem witch trials.

Parris, Samuel. (1653-1720) Clergyman,
Salem Witch Trials.

Rockwell, George Lincoln. (1918-1967)
American Nazi Party leader.

Simmons, William. (1880-1946) Ku Klux
Klan Imperial Wizard.

Trotter, William Monroe. (1872-1934) Mili-
tant black rights leader.

Watson, Thomas. (1856-1922) Journalist,
racial and religious hatred.

Williams, Abigail. (1680-?) Puritan, accused
others of witchcraft.

Hawaiians
See also Asian-Americans.

Kahanamoku, Duke. (1890-1968) Surfer,
olympic swimmer.

Ka'lulani. (1875-1899) Princess.

King, Charles Edward. (1879-1950) Bandleader, composer.

Liliuokalani, Lydia. (1838-1917) Composer, musician, queen.

Malo, Davida. (1795-1853) Translator.

Manalapit, Pablo. (1891-1969) Labor
leader, born Philippines.

Matsunaga, Masayuki "Spark." (1916-1990)
Attorney, senator, World War II Army
captain.

Mink, Patsy Takemoto. (1927-2002) Attorney, congresswoman.

Pukui, Mary Kawena. (1895-1986) Hawaiian folklorist, linguist.

Hearing Impaired
Alexander, Grover Cleveland. (1887-1950)
Baseball player.

Beethoven, Ludwig von. (1770-1827) German composer.

Cerf, Vinton. (1943-) Internet pioneer.

Ederle, Gertrude. (1905-2003) Olympic
swimmer.

Edison, Thomas Alva. (1847-1931) Inven-

tor.

Jordan, Irving King. (1943-) Educator.

Keller, Helen. (1880-1968) Author, disability rights activist.

Kisor, Henry. (1940-)

Low, Juliette Gordon "Daisy." (1860-1927)
Founder of Girl Scouts of America.

Matlin, Marlee. (1965-) Actor.

O'Brien, Dan. (1966-) Olympic decathlon
athlete.

Stone, Isidor Feinstein "I. F." (1907-1989)
Editor.

Walker, Kenny. (1967-) Football player.

Whitestone, Heather. (1973-) Beauty queen.

Hebrews, Ancient
See also Israelis; Jews.

Akiba ben Joseph. (c. 50-135) Scholar, spiritual leader.

Beruriah. (2nd century) Scholar.

David. (fl. 1010-970 B.C.E.) King.

Deborah. (c. 1150 B.C. E.) Mother of Israel.

Esther. (5th century) Queen.

Hanasi, Judah. (135-217) Scholar, spiritual
leader.

Herodias. (1st century C.E.) Israeli queen.

Hillel. (60 B.C.E.-10 C.E.) Scholar, spiritual
leader.

Ima Shalom. (50-?) Talmudic woman.

Jael of Israel. (120-100 B.C.E.) Political
activist.

Jeremiah. (650-585 B.C.E.) Scholar, spiritual leader.

Johanah ben Zakkai. (15-70) Spiritual
leader.

Moses. (1392?-1272? B.C.E.) Prophet, spiritual leader, founder Judaism.

Saadia Gaon. (882-942) Scholar, spiritual
leader.

Sarah of Yemen. (unknown) Yemenite poet.

Heisman Trophy Winners
See also Football Players.

Allen, Marcus. (1960-) Winner 1981.

Blanchard, Felix Anthony "Doc." (1924-)
Winner 1945.

Brown, Tim. (1966-) Winner 1987.

Campbell, Earl. (1955-) Winner 1977.

Davis, Ernie. (1939-1963) Winner 1961.

Davis, Glenn. (1925-) Winner 1946.

Dorsett, Tony. (1954-) Winner 1976.

Flutie, Doug. (1962-) Winner 1984.

George, Eddie. (1973-) Winner 1995.

Griffin, Archie. (1954-) Winner 1974, 1975.

Hornung, Paul. (1935-) Winner 1956.

Jackson, Bo. (1962-) Winner 1985.

Plunkett, Jim. (1947-) Winner 1970.

Sanders, Barry. (1968-) Winner 1988.

Simpson, Orenthal James "O. J." (1947-) Winner 1968.

Staubach, Roger. (1942-) Winner 1963.

Walker, Herschel. (1962-) Winner 1982.

Williams, Ricky. (1977-) Winner 1998.

Hispanic-Americans

These individuals were either born in the United States or moved to the United States from Spanish speaking countries. It is not known if many of the Latin sports figures playing on American teams became citizens of the United States or retained citizenship in their home countries.

Abreu, Bobby. (1974-) Baseball player, born Venezuela.

Aguilera, Christina. (1966-) Pop singer.

Aleu, Moises. (1966-) Baseball player, born Dominican Republic.

Alfonzo, Edgardo. (1974-) Baseball player, born Venezuela.

Allyón, Lucas Vásquez de. (1475-1526) Spanish entrepreneur foods, explorer.

Almonaster y Rojas, Andrés. (1725-1798) Entrepreneur shipping, philanthropist, born Spain.

Almonaster y Rojas, Michaela. (1795-1874) Baroness of Pontalba, philanthropist.

Alomar, Roberto. (1968-) Baseball player, born Puerto Rico.

Alonso, Alicia. (1921-) Cuban ballet dancer.

Alou, Felipe. (1935-) Baseball manager, born Dominican Republic.

Alvarez, Everett, Jr. (1937-) Vietnam War Navy pilot.

Alvarez, Julia. (1950-) Author.

Alvarez, Luis Walter. (1911-1988) Physicist. Nobel Prize winner.

Anaya, Rudolfo. (1937-) Author.

Angel, Carl. (1968-) Painter.

Anthony, Marc. (1968-) Pop singer.

Anza, Juan Bautista de. (1735-1788) Explorer, born Mexico.

Aparicio. Luis. (1934-) Baseball player, born Venezuela.

Arce, Elmer Figuero. (Chayanne) (1968-) Puerto Rican pop singer.

Arnaz y de Acha, Desiderio Alberto, III. (Desi Arnaz) (1917-1986) Actor, bandleader, born Cuba.

Arvigo, Rosita. (1941-) Botanist.

Avila, Bobby. (1924-) Baseball player, born Mexico.

Baca, Judy. (1946-) Human rights activist.

Baez, Joan. (1941-) Political activist, singer.

Banuelos, Romana Acosta. (1925-) Banker, treasurer of U.S.

Barceló, Maria Gertrudes "Tules." (1800-1852) Pioneer, women's rights activist.

Beltran, Carlos. (1977-) Baseball player, born Puerto Rico.

Beltré, Adrián. (1979-) Baseball player, born Dominican Republic.

Benavidez, Roy. (1935-) Vietnam War hero. Medal of Honor recipient.

Blades, Ruben. (1948-) Actor, composer, singer.

Bori, Lucrezia. (1887-1960) Opera singer, born Spain.

Bravo, Lola Alvarez. (1907-1993) Photographer, photojournalist, born Mexico.

Briones, Juana. (1802-1889) Human rights activist, pioneer, rancher.

Bujones, Fernando. (1955-) Ballet dancer.

Cabeza de Vaca, Álvar Núñez. (1490-1557) Spanish explorer.

Canseco, Jose. (1964-) Baseball player, born Cuba.

Carbajal, Michael. (1968-) Boxer.

Cardona, Manuel. (1934-) Physicist, born Spain.

Cardus, David. (1922-) Physician, born Spain.

Carey, Mariah. (1969-) Singer.

Carr, Vicki. (1940-) Singer.

Casals, Pablo. (1876-1973) Composer, conductor, musician, born Spain. Presidential Medal of Freedom recipient.

Casals, Rosemary. (1948-) Tennis player.

Castaneda, Carlos. (1896-1958) Historian, born Mexico.

Castillo, Luis. (1975-) Baseball player, born Dominican Republic.

Cavazos, Lauro F. (1927-) Anatomist, cabinet member, educator, physiologist.

Cepada, Perucho. (1906-1955) Baseball player, born Puerto Rico.

Chacon, Rafael. (1833-1925) Civil War soldier.

Chagoya, Enrique. (1953-) Painter.

Chang-Diaz, Franklin R. (1950-) Astronaut, physicist, born Venezuela.

Chávez, César. (1927-1993) Workers' rights activist. Presidential Medal of Freedom recipient.

Chavez, Denise. (1948-) Playwright.

Chavez, Dennis. (1888-1962) Senator, state legislator.

Chavez-Thompson, Linda. (1944-) Workers' rights activist.

Cisneros, Evelyn. (1958-) Ballet dancer.

Cisneros, Henry. (1947-) Cabinet member, mayor.

Cisneros, Sandra. (1954-) Author.

Clemente, Roberto. (1934-1972) Baseball player, born Puerto Rico.

Cofer, Judith Ortiz. (1952-) Author, educator, poet.

Coimbre, Pancho. (1909-1989) Baseball player, born Puerto Rico.

Collazo, Oscar. (1914-1994) Attempted assassin of President Harry S. Truman, born Puerto Rico.

Colmenaaves, Margarita. (1957-) Environmental engineer.

Colon, Raul. (1952-) Illustrator, born Puerto Rico.

Cordero, Angel, Jr. (1942-) Jockey.

Corona, Bert. (1918-2001) Labor leader, workers' rights activist.

Cotera, Martha P. (1938-) Civil rights activist, educator, historian, born Mexico.

Crespo, Elvis. (1970-) Puerto Rican pop singer.

Crespo, George. (1962-) Painter.

Cruz, Celia. (1924-2003) Singer, born Cuba.

Cruz, Jose, Jr. (1974-) Baseball player, born Puerto Rico.

Cruz, Juana Inés de, Sister. (1651-1695) Mexican poet, scholar, spiritual leader.

Cugat, Xavier. (1900-1990) Bandleader, musician, born Spain.

Cuza, Fernando. (unknown) Baseball agent.

Dallmeier, Francisco. (1953-) Wildlife biologist, born Venezuela.

de Dios Unanue, Manuel. (1943-1992) Editor, publisher, born Cuba.

de la Cruz, Jessie Lopez. (1919-) Workers' rights activist.

de la Hoya, Oscar. (1973-) Boxer.

de la Renta, Oscar. (1932-) Fashion designer, born Dominican Republic.

De Vicenzo, Roberto. (1923-) Argentine golfer.

Delgado, Carlos. (1972-) Baseball player, born Puerto Rico.

Diaz, Henry. (1948-) Meteorologist.

Dihigo, Martin "El Maestro." (1905-1971) Baseball player, born Cuba.

Dimas, Trent. (1970-) Olympic gymnast.

Dorantz, Stephen. (Esteban, Estevanico) (1500-1539) Explorer, born Spain.

Durazo, Maria Elena. (1954-) Labor leader, workers rights activist, born Mexico.

Escalante, Jaime. (1930-) Educator, born Bolivia.

Escobar, Marisol. (Marisol) (1930-) Sculptor, born Venezuela.

Espinel, Luisa Ronstadt. (1892-1963) Actor, singer.

Esquiroz, Margarita. (1945-) Attorney, jurist.

Estefan, Gloria. (1957-) Singer, born Cuba.

Estés, Clarissa Pinkol. (1943-) Author, psychologist, storyteller.

Estrada, Alfredo. (unknown) Mechanical engineer, publisher magazines.

Farragut, David Glasgow. (1801-1870) Civil War Navy admiral.

Fernandez, Beatriz Christina "Gigi." (1967-) Tennis player, born Puerto Rico.

Fernandez, Giselle. (1961-) Broadcast journalist, journalist, born Mexico.

Fernandez, Lisa. (1971-) Olympic softball player.

Fernandez, Mary Joe. (1971-) Tennis player, born Dominican Republic.

Finlay, Carlos Juan. (1833-1915) Medical researcher, physician, born Cuba.

Fornés, Maria Irene. (1930-) Playwright, born Cuba.

Fuertes, Louis Agassi. (1874-1927) Naturalist, painter.

Furcal, Rafael. (1980-) Baseball player, born Dominican Republic.

Galarraga, Andrés. (1962-) Baseball player, born Venezuela.

Gallego, Luis Miguel. (Luis Miguel) (1970-) Puerto Rican pop singer.

Gálvez, Bernardo de. (1746-1786) American Revolutionary War patriot, colonial governor, born Spain.

Garcia, Andy. (1957-) Actor, born Cuba.

Garcia, Dawn. (unknown) Journalist.

Garcia, Emma. (1972-) Community activist.

Garcia, Hector Perez. (1914-1996) Civil rights activist, physician, World War II Army hero, born Mexico. Presidential Medal of Freedom recipient.

Garciaparra, Nomar. (1973-) Baseball player.

Goizueta, Roberto C. (1931-1997) Entrepreneur soft drinks, born Cuba.

Gomez, Eddie. (1944-) Jazz musician.

Gomez, Scott. (1979-) Hockey player.

Gonzáles, Henry Barbosa (1916-2000) Congressman.

Gonzáles, Jovita Mireles. (1904-1983) Historian, storyteller.

Gonzales, Richard "Pancho." (1928-1995) Tennis player.

Gonzales, Rodolfo "Corkey." (1928-) Boxer, civil rights activist, poet.

Gonzalez, Juan. (1969-) Baseball player, born Puerto Rico.

Gonzalez, Luis. (1967-) Baseball player.

Gonzalez, Maya Christina. (1964-) Painter.

Gonzalez, Melissa Eve. (1980-) Actor.

Gonzalez, Ruben. (1951-) Racquetball player.

Govea, Jessica. (c. 1950) Workers' rights activist.

Greer, Pedro Jose, Jr. (1956-) Human rights activist, physician.

Guastavino, Rafael. (1842-1908) Architect, born Spain.

Guerra, Jackie. (1967-) Actor, comedian, human rights activist, workers' rights activist.

Guerrero, Vladimir. (1976-) Baseball player, born Dominican Republic.

Guiteras, Juan. (1852-1925) Medical researcher, physician, born Cuba.

Guiterrez, Jose Angel. (1944-) Civil rights activist for Mexican-Americans.

Guzman, Cristian. (1978-) Baseball player, born Dominican Republic.

Hayden, Sophia. (1868-1953) Architect, born Chile.

Hernandez, Keith. (1953-) Baseball player.

Hernandez, Maria Latigo. (1893-1986) Author, political activist, television personality, born Mexico.

Herrera, Caroline. (1939-) Fashion designer, born Venezuela.

Hidalgo, Richard. (1975-) Baseball player, born Venezuela.

Hijuelos, Oscar. (1948-) Author. Pulitzer Prize winner.

Huerta, Dolores. (1930-) Labor leader.

Iglesias, Enrique. (1975-) Pop singer, born Spain.

Johnson, Kory. (1979-) Environmental activist, half Hispanic.

Jones, Andruw. (1977-) Baseball player.

Julia, Raul. (1940-1994) Actor, born Puerto Rico.

Lee, Carlos. (1976-) Baseball player, born Panama.

Lifshitz, Aliza. (1951-) Mexican AIDS activist, author, editor, educator, physician.

Limón, José Arcadia. (1908-1972) Choreographer, dancer, born Mexico.

Lisa, Manuel. (1772-1820) Explorer, fur trader.

Lobo, Rebecca. (1973-) Olympic basketball player.

López, Javy. (1970-) Baseball player, born Puerto Rico.

Lopez, Jennifer. (1969-) Actor, pop singer.

Lopez, Josefina. (1969-) Playwright, born Mexico.

Lopez, Lourdes. (1958-) Ballet dancer, born Cuba.

Lopez, Nancy. (1957-) Golfer.

Lozano, Ignacio E. (1886-1953) Publisher newspaper, born Mexico.

Luque, Dolf. (1890-1957) Baseball player, born Cuba.

Mantilla, Ray. (1934-) Jazz musician.

Marichal, Juan. (1937-) Baseball player, born Dominican Republic.

Marcos de Niza, Fray. (1495-1558) Spanish missionary.

Marin, Richard Anthony "Cheech." (1946-) Actor, comedian, filmmaker.

Martin, Ricky. (1971-) Puerto Rican pop singer.

Martinez, Father Antonio José. (1793-1867)

Educator, human rights activist, spiritual
leader, born Mexico.

Martinez, Edgar. (1963-) Baseball player,
born Puerto Rico.

Martinez, José P. (1920-1943) World War II
military hero.

Martinez, Pedro. (1971-) Baseball player,
born Dominican Republic.

Martinez, Tino. (1967-) Baseball player.

Martinez, Vilma. (1943-) Attorney, civil
rights activist.

Martinez-Canas, Maria. (1960-) Puerto Rican photographer, born Cuba.

Mencia, Carlos. (unknown) Comedian, born
Honduras.

Mendez, José. (1887-1928) Cuban baseball
player.

Menedéz de Aviles, Pedro. (1519-1574)
Explorer, founder of St. Augustine, naval
officer, born Spain.

Mexia, Ynes. (1870-1938) Botanist, explorer.

Minoso, Saturnino Orestes "Minnie."
(1922-) Baseball player, born Cuba.

Miranda, Carmen. (1909-1955) Brazilian
actor, singer.

Mohr, Nicholasa. (1938-) Author.

Molina, Mario. (1943-) Chemist, environmental scientist, born Mexico. Nobel
Prize winner.

Mondesi, Raúl. (1971-) Baseball player,
born Dominican Republic.

Montalbán, Ricardo. (1920-) Actor, born
Mexico.

Moore, Oscar. (1916-1981) Jazz musician.

Moreno, Rita. (1931-) Actor, dancer, born
Puerto Rico.

Murieta, Joaquin. (1832-1853) Gold miner,
outlaw, born Mexico.

Novello, Antonia C. (1944-) Physician, surgeon general of U.S., born Puerto Rico.

Nuñez, Tommy. (1939-) Basketball referee.

Ocampo, Adriana. (1955-) Planetary geologist, born Colombia.

Ochoa, Ellen. (1959-) Astronaut, electrical
engineer.

Ochoa, Estevan. (1831-1888) Mayor.

Ochoa, Severo. (1905-1993) Biochemist,
physician, physiologist, born Spain. Nobel
Prize winner.

Olmos, Edward James. (1947-) Actor.

Oñate, Juan de. (1550-1630) Colonist, explorer.

Ordóñez, Magglió. (1974-) Baseball player,
born Venezuela.

Ordóñez, Rey. (1971-) Baseball player, born
Cuba.

Pacheco, Romualdo. (1831-1899) Congressman, gold miner, pioneer.

Palau, Luis. (1934-) Author, spiritual leader,
born Argentina.

Palmeiro, Rafael. (1964-) Baseball player,
born Dominican Republic.

Pantoja, Antonio. (1922-2002) Educator,
human rights activist, social worker, born
Puerto Rico. Presidential Medal of Freedom recipient.

Pastrana, Julia. "Bearded Lady." (1832-
1860) Mexican showman.

Peña, Federico. (1947-) Attorney, cabinet
member, mayor.

Perera, Hilda. (1926-) Children's author,
born Cuba.

Pérez, Neifi. (1973-) Baseball player, born
Dominican Republic.

Perez, Rosie. (1964-) Actor, choreographer,
dancer.

Perez, Selena Quintanilla. (Selena) (1971-
1995) Pop singer.

Pico, Pio de Jesus. (1801-1894) Governor,
born Mexico.

Pincay, Laffit, Jr. (1946-) Jockey, born
Panama.

Pineda, Álonzo Alvarez de. (1792-1872).
Spanish explorer, Navy admiral.

Ponce, Carlos. (1972-) Pop singer.

Ponce de Léon, Juan. (1460-1521) Spanish
explorer.

Portola, Gaspar de. (1723-1784) Colonist,
born Spain.

Posada, Jorge. (1971-) Baseball player, born
Puerto Rico.

Pozo, Chano. (1915-1948) Jazz musician,
born Cuba.

Puente, Tito. (1923-2000) Bandleader, jazz
musician.

Quinn, Anthony. (1915-2001) Actor, born
Mexico.

Rabassa, Gregory. (1922-) Educator, translator.

Ramirez, Carlos A. (1953-) Chemical engineer, medical researcher.

Ramirez, Francisco. (1830-1890) Editor, publisher.

Ramirez, Manny. (1972-) Baseball player, born Dominican Republic.

Ramirez, Sara Estela. (1881-1910) Poet, political activist, women's rights activist, born Mexico.

Rentería, Édgar. (1975-) Baseball player, born Colombia.

Richardson, Bill. (1947-) Ambassador, cabinet member, congressman.

Ripoll, Shakira Mebarek. (Shakira) (1977-) Colombian pop singer.

Rivera, Geraldo. (1943-) Broadcast journalist, television personality.

Rivera, Mariano. (1969-) Baseball player, born Panama.

Rodriguez, Alex "A-Rod." (1975-) Baseball player.

Rodriguez, Eloy. (1947-) Agricultural scientist, botanist, educator.

Rodriguez, Ivan. (1971-) Baseball player, born Puerto Rico.

Rodriguez, Matt. (1936-) Police superintendent.

Rodriguez, Paul. (1955-) Actor, born Mexico.

Rodriguez, Richard. (1944-) Author, broadcast journalist, editor, educator.

Rodriguez, Robert. (1968-) Filmmaker, screenwriter.

Rodriguez de Tio, Lola. (1843-1924) Poet, political activist, women's rights activist, born Puerto Rico.

Ronstadt, Frederico. (1862-1954) Businessman.

Ronstadt, Linda. (1946-) Singer.

Ros-Lentinen, Ileana. (1952-) Congresswoman, state senator, born Cuba.

Roybal, Edward Ross. (1916-) Congressman.

Roybal-Allard, Lucille. (1941-) Congresswoman, women's rights activist.

Salazar, Rubén. (1928-1970) Broadcast journalist, civil rights activist, journalist, born Mexico.

Sanchez, Loreta. (1960-) Congresswoman.

Sanchez, Pedro. (1940-) Soil scientist, born Cuba.

Santana, Carlos. (1947-) Musician, born Mexico.

Santayana, George. (1863-1952) Philosopher, poet, born Spain.

Santiago, Esmeralda. (1948-) Author, born Puerto Rico.

Santos, Miriam. (1956-) Chicago treasurer, born Puerto Rico.

Saralegui, Cristina. (1948-) Television personality, born Cuba.

Schomburg, Arthur. (1874-1938) Educator, historian, born Puerto Rico.

Secada, Jon. (1963-) Singer, born Cuba.

Seguín, Juan N. (1806-1890) Mayor, military leader, political activist, state senator.

Selena. *See* Perez, Selena Quintanilla.

Serra, Father Junipero. (1713-1784) Missionary, born Spain.

Serrano, Lupe. (1930-) Dancer, educator, born Chile.

Sheen, Martin. (1940-) Actor.

Smits, Jimmy. (1955-) Actor.

Soto, Gary. (1952-) Children's and young adult author.

Tatis, Fernando. (1975-) Baseball player, born Dominican Republic.

Tejada, Miguel. (1976-) Baseball player, born Dominican Republic.

Tenayuca, Emma. (1916-1999) Workers' rights activist.

Thomas, Piri. (1928-) Author.

Tiant, Luis, Sr. (1906-1977) Baseball player, born Cuba.

Tijerina, Rejes López. (1926-) Civil rights activist.

Torresola, Griselio. (1925-1950) Puerto Rican attempted assasin of President Harry Truman.

Torriente, Cristobal. (1895-1938) Baseball player, born Cuba.

Trevino, Lee. (1939-) Golfer.

Valdez, Luis. (1940-) Actor, playwright, poet.

Valdez, Patssi. (1951-) Painter.

Valens, Ritchie. (1942-1959) Singer, songwriter.

Valenzuela, Fernando. (1960-) Baseball player, born Mexico.

Vallejo, Mariano Guadalupe. (1808-1890) Founder California, rancher.

Vargas, Diego de. (1643-1704) Governor.

Vargas, Jay. (1937-) Vietnam War hero. Medal of Honor recipient.

Vargas, Tetelo. (1906-1971) Baseball
player, born Dominican Republic.
Vasquez, Tiburcio. (1835-1875) Outlaw.
Vaz, Katherine. (unknown) Author, born
Portugal.
Vega, Bernardo. (1885-1965) Entrepreneur
cigars.
Velasquez, William C. (1944-1988) Civil
rights activist. Presidential Medal of Free-
dom recipient.
Velazquez, Loreta Janeta. (1842-?) Civil
War soldier, disguised as man.
Velazquez, Nydia. (1953-) Congresswoman,
born Puerto Rico.
Vera, Joseph Azlor Vitro de. (d. 1723?)
Mexican military leader, defender of
Texas.
Villa-Komaroff, Lydia. (1947-) Medical
researcher, molecular biologist.
Villagra, Gaspar Perez de. (1558-1620)
Colonist, historian, poet.
Villaseñsor, Victor. (1940-) Author, screen-
writer.
Viña, Fernando. (1969-) Baseball player.
Vizquel, Omar. (1967-) Baseball player,
born Venezuela.
Warren, Adelina Otero. (1881-1965) Au-
thor, educator.
Williams, Bernie. (1968-) Baseball player,
born Puerto Rico.
Ybor, Vincente Martinez. (1818-1896) En-
trepreneur cigars, founder Ybor City, FL.
Yglesias, José. (1919-1995) Author.
Zapata, Carmen. (1927-) Actor.
Zavala, Maria Elena. (unknown) Botanist,
educator.

Historians
See also Authors, Nonfiction
Ban Chao. (d. 102) Chinese.
Ban Gu. (32-92) Chinese.
Ban Piao. (unknown) Chinese.
Ban Zhao. (45-116) Chinese.
Bennett, Lerone, Jr. (1928-)
Biaggi, Cristina Shelley. (1937-)
Castaneda, Carlos. (1896-1958) born
Mexico.
Cobb, William Montague. (1904-1990)
Comnena, Anna. (1083-1148) Byzantian.
Cordova, Dorothy. (1932-)
Cordova, Fred. (1931-)

Cotera, Martha P. (1938-) born Mexico.
Debo, Angie. (1890-1988)
Durant, Ida Kaufman "Ariel." (1898-1981)
Durant, Will. (1885-1981)
Franklin, John Hope. (1915-)
Goddard, Calvin Hooker. (1891-1955)
Gonzáles, Jovita Mireles. (1904-1983)
Herodotus. (c. 484-420 B.C.) Greek.
John Stands in Timber. (1884-1967) Chey-
enne Indian.
Livy. (Titus Livius) (59? B.C.-17 A.D.)
Roman.
Lone Dog. (Shunka-Ishnala) (1780-1871)
Yankton Dakota Indian.
Machiavelli, Niccolo. (1469-1527) Italian.
Nell, William Cooper. (1816-1874)
Parkman, Francis. (1823-1893)
Pershing, John Joseph. (1860-1948)
Pliny the Elder. (23-79) Roman.
Prekerowa, Teresa. (1921-) Polish.
Quidde, Ludwig. (1858-1941) German.
Sandburg, Carl. (1878-1967)
Sandoz, Mari. (1896-1966)
Schomburg, Arthur. (1874-1938) born
Puerto Rico.
Tacitus. (Publius or Gaius Cornelius Taci-
tus) (55-115) Roman.
Thompson, Edward. (1840-1935)
Thucydides. (c. 454-404 B.C.) Greek.
Tuchman, Barbara Wertheim. (1912-1989)
Vega, Garcilaso de la (1539-1616) Peruvian.
Villagra, Gaspar Perez de. (1558-1620)
Waheenee. (1841-?) Hidatsa Indian.
Walpole, Horace. (1717-1797) English.
Warren, William Whipple. (1825-1853)
Obijway Indian.
Wells, Herbert George "H. G." (1866-1946)
English.
Whitewolf, Jim. (1878-?) Kiowa-Apache
Indian.
Williams, George Washington. (1849-1891)
Woodson, Carter G. (1875-1950)
Xenophon. (c. 428-355 B.C.) Greek.

Hockey Players
*Some of the Canadian players may now be
American citizens.*
Belfour, Ed. (1965-) Canadian.
Brodeur, Martin. (1972-) Canadian.
Drury, Chris. (1976-)
Dryden, Ken. (1947-) Canadian.

Elias, Patrick. (1976-) Czech.
Esposito, Phil. (1942-) Canadian.
Esposito, Tony. (1944-) Canadian.
Friezen, Jeff. (1976-) Canadian.
Fuhr, Grant. (1962-) Canadian.
Gomez, Scott. (1979-)
Granato, Cammi. (1971-)
Gretzky, Wayne. (1961-) Canadian.
Hall, Glenn. (1931-) Canadian.
Hejduk, Milan. (1976-) Czech.
Howe, Gordie. (1928-) born Canada.
Hull, Bobby. (1939-) Canadian.
Hull, Brett. (1964-) Canadian.
Kariya, Paul. (1974-) Canadian.
Kolzig, Olaf. (1970-) born Germany.
Lafleur, Guy. (1951-) Canadian.
Lecavalier, Vincent. (1980-) Canadian.
Lemieux, Mario. (1965-) Canadian.
Lindros, Eric. (1973-) Canadian.
Mikita, Stan. (1940-) born Czechoslovakia.
O'Ree, Willie. (1935-) Canadian.
Orr, Bobby. (1948-) Canadian.
Plante, Jacques. (1929-1986) Canadian.
Pronger, Chris. (1974-) Canadian.
Rheaume, Manon. (1972-) Canadian.
Richard, Maurice. (1921-2000) Canadian.
Roy, Patrick. (1965-) Canadian.
Sawchuck, Terry. (1925-1970) Canadian.
Smith, Billy. (1950-) Canadian.
Thornton, Joe. (1979-) Canadian.
Whitton, Erin. (1971-)
Wickenheiser, Hayley. (1969-) Canadian.

Holocaust Figures

See also Nazi Hunters; Nazi War Criminals; World War II Participants.

Rescuers and Resistance Workers
Andrew, Brother. (1928-) Dutch.
Anielewicz, Mordecai. (1919-1943) Polish.
Baeck, Leo. (1873-1956) German.
Baker, Josephine. (1906-1975) French resistance.
Belline, Germaine. (unknown) Belgian.
Bernadotte, Folke. (1895-1948) Swedish.
Bonhoeffer, Dietrich. (1906-1945) German.
Borkowska, Anna. (c. 1900-) Polish.
Brizi, Luigi. (unknown) Italian.
Cohn, Marianne. (1924-1944) German.
Czerniaków, Adam. (1880-1942) Polish.
Draenger, Shimson. (1917-1943) Polish.

Draenger, Tova. (1917-1943) Polish.
Fry, Varian. (1907-1967)
Gies, Miep. (1909-) Dutch, born Austria.
Grossman, Mendel. (1917-1945) Polish.
Grynszpan, Herschel. (1921-1942) German.
Hardaga, Mustafa. (unknown) Muslim.
Hübener, Helmut. (1925-1942) German.
Khan, Noor Inayar. (1914-1944) Indian.
Kieler, Jorgen. (1920-) Danish.
Korczak, Janusz. (1878-1942) Polish.
Kosmodemianskaya, Zoya. (1925-1943) Polish.
Kovner, Abba. (1918-1987) Russian.
Kovner, Vitka. (1920-) Polish.
Kowalyk, Jonka. (unknown) Ukrainian.
Lazebnik, Faye. (unknown) Polish.
Lubetkin, Zivia. (1914-1978) Polish.
Maria, "Madame." (unknown) French.
Marie-Benoit, Father. (unknown) French.
Mason, Andréé-Paule. (1923-1991) French.
Mendes, Aristides. (d. 1954) Portuguese.
Minke, Willy. (unknown) German.
Münch-Nielsen, Preben. (1926-) Danish.
Niccacci, Padre Rufino. (unknown) Italian.
Opdyke, Irene. (1921-2003) Polish.
Parks, Paul. (1923-)
Perlasca, Giorgio. (1910-1992) Italian.
Pilecki, Witold. (1900-1948) Polish.
Prekerowa, Teresa. (1921-) Polish.
Pritchard, Marion van Binsbergen. (1920-) Dutch.
Robota, Róza. (1921-1945) Polish.
Schindler, Emilie. (1909-2001) Czech.
Schindler, Oskar. (1908-1974) Czech.
Scholl, Hans. (1918-1943) German.
Scholl, Sophie. (1921-1943) German.
Sejr, Arne. (1922-) Danish.
Senesh, Hannah. (1921-1944) Hungarian.
Sheptitsky, Andrew. (1865-1944) Polish.
Spoerry, Anne. (1918-1999) French.
Stauffenberg, Claus von. (1904-1944) German.
Sugihara, Sempo. (1900-1986) Japanese.
Ten Boom, Corrie. (1892-1979) Dutch.
Trocme, André. (unknown) French.
Trocme, Magda. (unknown) French.
Van Raalte, Jim. (unknown)
Wallenberg, Raoul. (1912-?) Swedish.
Weidner, John. (unknown) French.
Wijsmuller, Gertrude. (unknown) Dutch.
Winkler-Kühne, Ruth. (1931-) German.

Survivors

It is not known where most of the survivors lived after the war. Many moved to the United States; some made their new home in Israel; a few remained in Europe or moved to England. The nationality listed is from the country of origin.

Adler, Henny. (1925-) German.
Adler, Sam. (unknown) German.
Appelfeld, Aharon. (1932-) Ukrainian.
Baeck, Leo. (1873-1956) German.
Bamberger, Niels. (1928-) Danish.
Basch, Civia Gelber. (1928-) Romanian.
Berk, Allan. (1918-) Czech.
Bettelheim, Bruno. (1903-1990) Austrian.
Bihaly, Judith. (1934-) Hungarian.
Blair, Tonia Rotkopf. (1925-) Polish.
Clifford, Esther. (1921-) German.
Cukier, Sam. (1920-) Polish.
Eisen, Renata. (1929-) Yugoslavian.
Fink, Ida. (1921-) Polish.
Fleischman, Solomon. (1928-) Hungarian.
Frank, Henry. (unknown) German.
Frank, Irene. (1927-) German.
Frankl, Viktor. (1905-1997) Austrian.
Friedman, Tova Grossman. (1938-) Polish.
Hyams, Rachel. (1937-)
Katz, Ralph. (1932-) German.
Knopfler, Clara. (unknown) Transylvanian.
Kohane, Akiva. (1929-) Polish.
Kosinski, Jerzy. (1933-1991) Polish.
Kovner, Abba. (1918-1989) Russian.
Laitman, Helen Kornitzer. (unknown) Czech.
Leitner, Isabella Katz. (1924-) Hungarian.
Lerner, Bianca. (1929-) Polish.
Levi, Primo. (1919-1987) Italian.
Levy, Hans. (1928-) German.
Liebmann, Hanne Eve Hirsch. (1924-) German.
Loeb, Ilse. (unknown) Austrian.
Lubetkin, Zivia. (1914-1978) Polish.
Lustig, Arnost. (1926-) Czech.
Mandel, Basia. (1925-) Polish.
Mendlovic, Leopold. (unknown) Czech.
Moses, Frank. (1931-) German.
Offenbach, Genia. (unknown) Polish.
Offenbach, Rubin. (unknown) Polish.
Parker, Henriette. (1932-) Belgian.
Perl, Gisella. (1910-1985) Hungarian.

Polak, Ina. (1923-) Dutch.
Polak, Jack. (unknown) Dutch.
Pulwer, Miriam. (unknown) Polish.
Rosenbach, Larry. (1929-) Polish.
Roth, Irving. (1930-) Czech.
Roth-Hano, Renée. (1931-) French.
Rotmil, Bernard. (1926-) French.
Sander, Sally. (1925-) Polish.
Sander, Zelik. (unknown) Polish.
Schiff, Charlene. (1930-) Polish.
Schloss, Lewis. (1921-) German.
Schwab, George. (1931-) Latvian.
Shore, Ann Goldman. (1929-) Polish.
Sokolow, Yvonne Kray. (1927-) Dutch.
Stojka, Karl. (1931-) Austrian.
Stommer, Helga Edelstein. (1926-) German.
Tenebaum, Frieda. (1934-)
Tilles, Helen. (unknown) Austrian.
Weinberg, Stefan. (1923-) Polish.
Weinsberg, Alicia Fajnstejn. (1929-) Polish.
Wertheimer, Henry. (1927-) German.
Wiesel, Elie. (1928-) Romanian.
Wiesenthal, Simon. (1908-) Austrian.

Victims

Anielewicz, Mordecai. (1919-1943) Polish.
Bonhoeffer, Dietrich. (1906-1945) German.
Cohn, Marianne. (1924-1944) German.
Czerniaków, Adam. (1880-1942) Polish.
Draenger, Shimson. (1917-1943) Polish.
Draenger, Tova. (1917-1943) Polish.
Flinker, Moshe. (1926-1944) Dutch.
Frank, Anne. (1929-1945) Dutch, born Germany.
Grossman, Mendel. (1917-1945) Polish.
Grynszpan, Herschel. (1921-1942) German.
Heyman, Eva. (1931-1944) Hungarian.
Hübener, Helmut. (1925-1942) German.
Katznelson, Yitzhak. (1886-1944) Polish.
Khan, Noor Inayar. (1914-1944) Indian.
Korczak, Janusz. (1878-1942) Polish.
Kosmodemianskaya, Zoya. (1925-1943) Polish.
Robota, Rósa. (1921-1945) Polish.
Rubinowicz, David. (1927-1942) Polish.
Rudashevski, Yitzak. (1927-1943) Polish.
Scholl, Hans. (1918-1943) German.
Scholl, Sophie. (1921-1943) German.
Senesh, Hannah. (1921-1944) Hungarian.
Wallenberg, Raoul. (1912-?) Swedish.

Hondurans

See also Hispanic-Americans
Mencia, Carlos. (unknown) Comedian.

Horticulturalists

See Botanists and Horticulturalists.

Human Rights Activists

See also Abolitionists; Children's Rights
   Activists; Civil Rights Activists; Holo-
   caust Rescuers and Resistance Workers;
   Nobel Peace Prize winners; Peace Activ-
   ists; Reformers; Social Workers;
   Women's Rights Activists; Workers'
   Rights Activists.
Addams, Jane. (1860-1935)
Ahn, Chang-Ho. (1878-1938) born Korea.
Antokoletz, Maria Adele de. (unknown)
   Argentine.
Baca, Judy. (1946-)
Benenson, Peter. (1921-)
Besant, Annie. (1847-1933) English.
Bojaxhiu, Agnes. (Mother Teresa) (1910-
   1997) Indian, born Yugoslavia.
Bonafini, Hebe de. (unknown) Argentine.
Booth, Catherine. (1829-1890) English.
Booth, Eva. (1865-1950) born England.
Booth, William. (1829-1912) English.
Briones, Juana. (1802-1889)
Bryan, William Jennings. (1860-1925)
Bukovsky, Vladimir. (1942-) Russian.
Burke, Yvonne Braithwaite. (1932-)
Byrdsong, Ricky. (1957-1999)
Byrdsong, Sherialyn. (1957-)
Burke, Yvonne Braithwaite. (1932-)
Campbell, Bonnie. (1948-)
Carson, Benjamin Solomon. (1951-)
Cassin, René. (1887-1976) French.
Catherine of Siena. (1353-1386) Italian.
Cochrane, Elizabeth. (Nellie Bly) (1865-
   1922)
Cole, Rebecca J. (1846-1922)
Coram, Thomas. (1668-1751) English.
Darrow, Clarence. (1857-1938)
De Veuster, Joseph. (Father Damien) (1840-
   1889) Belgian.
del Mundo, Fe. (1911-) Filipino.
Diana. (1961-1997) English.
Dix, Dorothea. (1802-1887)
Dunant, Henri. (1828-1910) Swiss.

Edelman, Marian Wright. (1939-)
Esquivel, Adolfo Pérez. (1931-) Argentine.
Evans, Matilda Arabella. (1872-1935)
Fang, Lizhi. (1936-) Chinese.
Fry, Elizabeth. (1780-1845) English.
Gladney, Edna Kahly. (1886-1961)
Goldman, Emma. (1869-1940) born Lithua-
   nia.
Greer, Pedro Jose, Jr. (1956-)
Grimke, Angelina. (1805-1879)
Grimke, Sarah Moore. (1792-1873)
Guerra, Jackie. (1967-)
Hale, Clara. (1905-1992)
Hamilton, Alice. (1869-1970)
Handali, Esther Kiera. (16th century) Turk-
   ish.
Hardy-Garcia, Dianne. (1965-)
Hata, Prateep Ungsongtham. (1952-) Thai.
Havel, Vaclav. (1936-) Czech.
Hirschfeld, Magnus. (1868-1935) Polish.
Hope, Leslie Townes " Bob." (1903-2003)
   born England.
Hutchinson, Anne Marbury. (1591-1643)
   born England.
Ireland, Patricia. (1945-)
Jean-Murat, Carolle. (1950-) Haitian.
Kelley, Florence. (1859-1932)
Kivengere, Festo. (1919-1988) Ugandan.
Kohut, Rebekah Bettelheim. (1864-1951)
Kollontai, Alexandra. (1872-1952) Russian.
Korczak, Janusz. (1878-1942) Polish.
Kouchner, Bernard. (1939-) French.
Kuhn, Maggie. (1905-1995)
Lathrop, Julia. (1858-1932)
Lord, Audre. (1934-1992)
Maathai, Wangari. (1940-) Kenyan.
Mandela, Nelson. (1918-) South African.
Martinez, Father Antonio José. (1793-1867)
   Mexican.
Mathai-Davis, Prema. (1950-) born India.
McLean, Gordon. (1934-) born Canada.
Mendes, Chico. (1944-1988) Brazilian.
Menchú, Rigoberta. (1959-) Guatemalan.
Montefiore, Lady Judith Cohen. (1784-
   1862) English.
Montefiore, Sir Moses. (1784-1885)
   English.
Müller, George. (1805-1898) English, born
   Germany.
Ngor, Haing. (1947-1996) born Cambodia.
Noyes, John Humphrey. (1811-1886)

Nudel, Ida. (1931-) Russian.

Pantoja, Antonio. (1922-2002) born Puerto Rico.

Pariseau, Esther. (Mother Joseph) (1832-1902)

Prothrow-Stith, Deborah. (1954-)

Purtell, Edna. (1900-1986)

Ramabai, Pandita. (1858-1922) Indian.

Riis, Jacob August. (1849-1914) born Denmark.

Roosevelt, (Anna) Eleanor. (1884-1962)

Seager, Joy Debenham. (1899-1991) Australian.

Sharma, Prem. (1943-) born India.

Stevens, Thaddeus. (1792-1868)

Suu Kyi, Daw Aung San. (1945-) Burmese.

Teasdale, Lucille. (1929-1996) Canadian.

Theodora, Empress. (497-548) Turkish.

Tingley, Katherine. (1847-1929)

Tutu, Desmond Mpilo. (1931-) South African.

Walker, Sarah Breedlove McWilliams "Madame C. J." (1867-1919)

Williams, Jody. (1950-)

Williams, Roger. (1603-1683)

Younger, Maud. (1870-1936)

Hungarians

See also Immigrants to United States, Hungarian.

Bartok, Bela. (1861-1945) Composer.

Bihaly, Judith. (1934-) Holocaust survivor.

Biro, Ladislao. (1900-1944) Inventor.

Fleischman, Solomon. (1928-) Holocaust survivor.

Gabor, Dennis. (1900-1979) Electrical engineer, inventor, physicist. Nobel Prize winner.

Heyman, Eva. (1931-1944) Author, Holocaust victim.

Klarsfeld, Serge. (1935-) Nazi hunter, scholar.

Lincoln, Trebitsch. (1872-1943) Spy.

Liszt, Franz. (1811-1886) Composer.

Perl, Gisella. (1910-1985) Holocaust survivor, physician.

Semmelweis, Ignaz Phillipp. (1818-1865) Medical researcher, physician.

Senesh, Hannah. (1921-1944) Author, Holocaust resistance fighter, victim, poet.

Stein, Aurel. (1862-1943) Archaeologist.

Stephen I. (975-1038) King.

Icelanders and Greenlanders

Ericsson, Leif. (960-?) Icelandic explorer.

Eriksdottir, Freydis. (971-1010) Greenlander explorer.

Finnbogadottir, Vigadis. (1930-) Icelandic president.

Gudmundsdottir, Bjork. (Bjork) (1966-) Icelandic pop singer.

Icthyologists

Clark, Eugenie. (1922-)

Illustrators

See also Cartoonists and Caricaturists; Engravers; Painters.

Allen, Thomas B. (1928-)

Anno, Mitsumasa. (1926-) Japanese.

Aruego, Jose. (1932-) born Philippines.

Baskin, Leonard. (1922-)

Begin, Mary Jane. (1963-)

Brown, Marcia. (1918-)

Bryan, Ashley. (1923-)

Carle, Eric. (1929-)

Catalanotto, Peter. (1959-)

Chess, Victoria. (1939-)

Colon, Raul. (1952-) born Puerto Rico.

Cooper, Floyd. (1959-)

Cummings, Pat. (1950-)

Degen, Bruce. (1945-)

Desimini, Lisa. (1964-)

Dillon, Diane. (1933-)

Dillon, Leo. (1933-)

Downing, Julie. (1956-)

Dyer, Jane. (1945-)

Egielski, Richard. (1952-)

Ehlert, Lois. (1934-)

Ernst, Lisa Campbell. (1957-)

Feelings, Tom. (1933-2003)

Fleming, Denise. (1950-)

Geisel, Theodor Seuss. (Dr. Seuss) (1904-1991)

Hamanaka, Sheila. (1949-)

Hawkes, Kevin. (1959-)

Henkes, Kevin. (1960-)

Hoban, Tana. (unknown)

Joyce, William. (1957-)

Kalman, Maira. (1949-)

Karas, G. Brian. (1957-)

Kellogg, Steven. (1941-)
Kuskin, Karla. (1933-)
Lattimore, Deborah Nourse. (1949-)
Leach, Molly. (1960-)
Lewin, Betsy. (1937-)
Lewin, Ted. (1935-)
Marshall, James. (1942-1992)
McCloskey, Robert. (1914-2003)
Merian, Anna Marie Sibylla. (1647-1717) Dutch wildlife illustrator.
Murie, Olaus. (1889-1963) Wildlife.
Narahashi, Keiko. (1959-) born Japan.
Neave, Richard. (unknown) English medical illustrator.
North, Marianne. (1830-1890) English.
O'Neill, Cecilia Rose. (1874-1944)
Opie, Iona. (1923-) English.
Oxenbury, Helen. (1938-) English.
Pinkney, Brian. (1961-)
Pinkney, Jerry. (1939-)
Potter, Beatrix. (1866-1943) English.
Primavera, Elise. (1955-)
Provensen, Alice. (1918-)
Provensen, Martin. (1916-1987)
Rego, Paula. (1935-) Portuguese.
Rich, Anna M. (1956-)
Ringgold, Faith. (1930-)
Say, Allen. (1937-) born Japan.
Schwartz, Amy. (1954-)
Sendak, Maurice. (1928-)
Seton, Ernest Thompson. (1860-1946) Wildlife illustrator, born England.
Seuss, Dr. *see* Geisel, Theodor Seuss.
Sis, Peter. (1949-) born Czechoslovakia.
Smith, Lane. (1959-)
Steig, Jeanne. (1930-)
Steig, William. (1907-2003)
Van Allsburg, Chris. (1949-)
Vesalius, Andreas. (1514-1564) Belgian medical illustrator.
Wells, Rosemary. (1943-)
Wiesner, David. (1956-)
Williams, Vera B. (1927-)
Wisniewski, David. (1953-2002)
Zelinsky, David. (1953-)
Zolotow, Charlotte. (1915-)

Immigrants to United States

African
Emeagwali, Philip. (1954-) Computer scientist, engineer, born Nigeria.
Equiano, Olaudah. (1745-1799) Author, slave, born Nigeria.
Fuller, Solomon Carter. (1872-1953) Medical researcher, pathologist, physician, born Liberia.
Gerima, Haile. (1946-) Filmmaker, born Ethiopia.
Olajuwon, Hakeem. (1963-) Basketball player, born Nigeria.
Menedez, Francisco. (1700-1772) Colonist, slave.

Australian and New Zealandic
Murdoch, Rupert. (1931-) Media mogul, born Australia.
Reisberg, Mira. (1953-) Painter, born Australia.
Thayer, Helen. (1938-) Arctic explorer, mountaineer, olympic track and field and luge, born New Zealand.

Austrian
Bettelheim, Bruno. (1903-1990) Holocaust survivor, psychotherapist.
Landsteiner, Karl. (1868-1943) Forensic scientist, pathologist, physician, physiologist. Nobel Prize winner.
Lowie, Robert Henry. (1883-1957) Anthropologist.
Lucas, Anthony Francis. (1855-1921) Engineer, entrepreneur oil, geologist.
Munk, Walter. (1917-) Oceanographer.
Reich, Wilhelm. (1897-1957) Psychoanalyst.
Reichmann, Paul. (1930-) Real estate entrepreneur.
Schönberg, Arthur. (1874-1951) Composer, conductor.
Zawinul, Joe. (1932-) Jazz musician.

Belgian
Baekeland, Leo. (1863-1944) Industrial chemist, inventor.
De Smet, Pierre-Jean. (1801-1873) Missionary, Jesuit priest.

Cambodian
Ngor, Haing. (1947-1996) Actor, human rights activist, physician.
Pran, Dith. (1942-) Journalist.

Yin, Luoth. (1950-) Community activist, social worker.

Canadian

Arden, Elizabeth. (1878-1966) Entrepreneur cosmetics.

Brill, Yvonne. (1924-) Aerospace chemist, inventor, space scientist.

Chin, Karen. (1952-) Paleontologist.

Coughlin, Father Charles. (1891-1979) Broadcast journalist, hatemonger, radio broadcaster, spiritual leader.

Cummings, Nathan. (1896-1985) Entrepreneur food industry.

Fuller, Alfred. (1885-1973) Entrepreneur brushes.

Galbraith, John Kenneth. (1908-) Author, diplomat, economist.

Hayakawa, Samuel Ichiye. (1906-1992) Educator, senator, scholar.

Hill, James J. (1838-1916) Entrepreneur railroads.

Howe, Gordie. (1928-) Hockey player.

Jones, Mary "Mother." (1830-1930) Labor leader, workers' rights activist, born Ireland.

McLean, Gordon. (1934-) Author, children's rights activist, human rights activist.

Pierce, Mary. (1975-) Tennis player.

Russell, Harold. (1914-2002) Actor, disability rights activist, World War II soldier.

Sainte-Marie, Buffy. (1941-) Cree Indian actor, Native American rights activist, peace activist, singer, songwriter.

tenBroek, Jacobus. (1911-1968) Attorney, disability rights activist, educator.

Chilean

Hayden, Sophia. (1868-1953) Architect.

Serrano, Lupe. (1930-) Dancer, educator.

Chinese

Akiyoshi, Toshiko. (1929-) Jazz pianist.

Bemis, Polly. (Lalu Nathay) (1853-1933) Pioneer.

Cheng, Nien. (1915-) Author, political activist.

Chennault, Anna. (1925-) Journalist, political activist.

Chern, Shiing-Shen. (1911-) Educator, mathematician.

Chu, Paul Ching-Wu. (1941-) Physicist.

Ho, David. (1952-) Medical researcher, physician, born Taiwan.

Howe, James Wong. (1899-1976) Filmmaker.

Lee, Tsung Dao. (1926-) Physicist. Nobel Prize winner.

Lew Chew. (1866-?) Gold miner.

Liu, Hung. (1948-) Painter.

Lord, Bette Bao. (1938-) Author.

Ng Poon Chew. (1866-1931) Editor, publisher, spiritual leader.

Pei, Ieah Ming "I. M." (1917-) Architect. Presidential Medal of Freedom recipient.

Tape, Mary McGladery. (1857-1928) Children's rights activist, civil rights activist, painter, photographer.

Tien, Chang-Lin. (1935-) Educator.

Tsai, Gerard, Jr. (1928-) Financier.

Wang, An. (1920-1990) Computer pioneer, electrical engineer, entrepreneur computers.

Wang, Wayne. (1949-) Filmmaker, born Hong Kong.

Wing, Yung. (1828-1912) Author, diplomat, educator.

Wong-Staal, Flossie. (1947-) Medical researcher.

Wu, Chien-Shiung. (1912-1997) Nuclear physicist.

Yang, Chen Ning. (1922-) Physicist. Nobel Prize winner.

Colombian

Ocampo, Adriana. (1955-) Geologist.

Cuban

Arnaz y de Acha, Desiderio Alberto, III. (Desi Arnaz) (1917-1986) Actor, bandleader.

Cruz, Celia. (1924-2003) Salsa singer.

de Dios Unanue, Manuel. (1943-1992) Editor, publisher.

Estefan, Gloria. (1957-) Singer.

Fornés, Maria Irene. (1930-) Playwright.

Garcia, Andy. (1957-) Actor.

Goizueta, Roberto C. (1931-1997) Entrepreneur soft drinks.

Guiteras, Juan. (1852-1925) Medical researcher, physician.

Lopez, Lourdes. (1958-) Ballet dancer.

Perera, Hilda. (1926-) Children's author.

Pozo, Chano. (1915-1948) Jazz musician.

Ros-Lentinen, Ileana. (1952-) Congress woman, state senator.

Sanchez, Pedro. (1940-) Soil scientist.

Saralegui, Cristina. (1948-) Television personality.

Secada, Jon. (1963-) Singer.

Cypriot

Yepremian, Garo. (1944-) Football player.

Czechoslovakian (Czech Republic)

Albright, Madeleine. (1937-) Cabinet member.

Cori, Gerty Radnitz. (1896-1957) Biochemist. Nobel Prize winner.

Mikita, Stan. (1940-) Hockey player.

Navratilova, Martina. (1956-) Tennis player.

Sis, Peter. (1949-) Children's author, illustrator.

Wise, Isaac Mayer. (1819-1900) Spiritual leader.

Zeisberger, David. (1721-1808) Indian guide, missionary, born Moravia.

Danish

Riis, Jacob August. (1849-1914) Human rights activist, journalist, orator, photographer.

Dutch

Blyleven, Bert. (1951-) Baseball player.

de Kooning, Willem. (1904-1997) Painter, sculptor.

English

See also American Revolutionary War Patriots and Colonists for arrivals from that time period.

Andrews, Julie. (1935-) Actor, singer.

Blackwell, Elizabeth. (1821-1910) Physician.

Blackwell, Emily. (1826-1910) Physician.

Booth, Eva. (1865-1950) Human rights activist, brought Salvation Army movement to U.S.

Burland, Rebecca. (1793-1872) Pioneer.

Burnett, Frances Hodgson. (1849-1924) Children's author.

Cole, Thomas. (1801-1848) Painter.

Davison, Anne. (1913-1992) Adventurer, aviator, sailor.

Gompers, Samuel. (1850-1924) Labor leader, workers' rights activist.

Harvey, Fred. (1835-1901) Entrepreneur restaurants.

Henson, William. (1812-1888) Aviation pioneer, engineer.

Hitchcock, Alfred. (1899-1980) Filmmaker.

Hope, Leslie Townes " Bob." (1903-2003) Actor, comedian, human rights activist. Presidential Medal of Freedom recipient.

Hutchinson, Anne Marbury. (1591-1643) Human rights activist, spiritual leader, women's rights activist.

Jacobi, Mary Putnam. (1842-1906) Educator, physician.

Jefferson, Arthur Stanley. (Stan Laurel) (1890-1965) Comedian.

Lee, Ann. (1736-1784) Shaker spiritual leader.

Levertov, Denise. (1923-1997) Poet.

Nuttall, Thomas. (1786-1859) Author, botanist, educator, ornithologist.

Paine, Thomas. (1737-1809) Author, journalist, philosopher, political activist.

Parris, Samuel. (1653-1720) Hatemonger, spiritual leader.

Payne-Gasposchkin, Cecilia. (1900-1979) Astronomer.

Pusey, Anne. (1948-) Ecologist, primatologist.

Rothschild, Miriam. (1908-) Author, conservationist, entomologist.

Seton, Ernest Thompson. (1860-1946) Author, cofounder Boy Scouts, Native American rights activist, naturalist.

Shaw, Anna Howard. (1847-1919) Physician, reformer, suffragist.

Taylor, Elizabeth. (1932-) Actor, AIDS activist.

Williams, Roger. (1603-1683) Spiritual leader.

Filipino

Aruego, Jose. (1932-) Children's author, illustrator.

Bulosan, Carlos. (1911-1956) Author.

Cruz, Philip Vera. (1904-) Labor leader.

Hagedorn, Jessica. (1949-) Author.

Lewis, Loida Nicolas. (1942-) Attorney,

author, entrepreneur food products.

Manalapit, Pablo. (1891-1969) Labor leader.

Natori, Josefina "Josie" Cruz. (1947-) Fashion designer, financier.

Santos, Bienvenido N. (1911-1992) Author.

Ung, Han. (1968-) Author, playwright.

French

See also American Revolutionary War Patriots and Colonists for arrivals from that time period.

Chanute, Octave. (1832-1910) Aviation pioneer, civil engineer.

Du Chaillu, Paul. (1836-1903) Explorer.

Du Pont, Eleuthere Irenee. (1771-1834) Entrepreneur chemicals.

Kapuscinski, Anne. (unknown) Agricultural scientist, educator.

Leroux, Antoine. (1635-1708) Fur trader, Indian scout.

Ma, Yo-Yo. (1955-) Musician.

Omidyar, Pierre. (1967-) Entrepreneur Internet, Internet pioneer.

Roth-Hano, Renée. (1931-) Author, Holocaust survivor, social worker.

Schmandt-Besserat, Denise. (1933-) Archaeologist, lexicographer.

Tebe, Marie. (d. 1901) Civil War soldier.

Wilkins, Dominique. (1960-) Basketball player.

German

Aster, John Jacob. (1763-1848) Entrepreneur real estate.

Einstein, Albert. (1879-1955) Physicist. Nobel Prize winner.

Gimbel, Adam. (1817-1896) Entrepreneur department stores.

Goeppert-Mayer, Maria. (1906-1972) Physicist. Nobel Prize winner.

Hesse, Eva. (1936-1970) Painter, sculptor.

Horney, Karen Danielsen. (1885-1952) Psychiatrist.

Kissinger, Henry. (1923-) Cabinet member. Nobel Peace Prize winner.

Kolzig, Olaf. (1970-) Olympic hockey player.

Mergler, Marie Josepha. (1851-1901) Physician.

Metz, Christian. (1795-1867) Utopian community founder.

Mies van der Rohe, Ludwig. (1886-1969) Architect.

Nast, Thomas. (1840-1902) Cartoonist.

Rapp, George. (1757-1847) Harmonist community cofounder.

Roebling, John Augustus. (1806-1869) Civil engineer.

Schechter, Matilde Roth. (1859-1924) Women's organization founder.

Schwabe, Stephanie. (1957-) Geomicrobiologist, geologist.

Strauss, Levi. (1829-1902) Entrepreneur blue jeans.

Sutter, John Augustus. (1803-1880) Gold miner, pioneer.

Tillich, Paul. (1886-1965) Philosopher, spiritual leader.

Von Braun, Werner. (1912-1977) Engineer, inventor.

Whitehead, Gustave. (1874-1927) Aviation pioneer.

Zakrzewska, Marie Elizabeth. (1829-1902) Physician.

Zenger, John Peter. (1697-1746) Journalist, printer.

Haitian

Audubon, John James. (1785-1851) Ornithologist, painter.

Du Sable, Jean Baptiste Pointe. (1745-1818) Founder of Chicago, frontiersman, fur trapper.

Hungarian

Capa, Robert. (1913-1954) Photojournalist.

Leitner, Isabella Katz. (1924-) Author, Holocaust survivor.

Pulitzer, Joseph. (1847-1911) Philanthropist, publisher newspapers.

Von Neumann, John. (1903-1957) Computer pioneer, mathematician.

Wise, Stephen S. (1874-1949) Spiritual leader.

Zollar, Attila. (1927-1998) Jazz musician.

Indian

Khorana, Har Gobind. (1922-) Chemist, geneticist. Nobel Prize winner.

Mathai-Davis, Prema. (1950-) Human rights activist, organizational head, women's rights activist.

Mehta, Zubin. (1936-) Conductor.
Mukherjee, Bharti. (1940-) Author.
Nair, Malathy. (unknown) Chemist.
Nur, Nawrose. (1981-) Chess champ.
Pudaite, Rochunga. (1927-) Bible translator.
Saund, Dalip Singh. (1899-1973) Congressman.
Sharma, Prem. (1943-) Human rights activist, women's rights activist.
Singh, Sirdar Jagdit. (1897-1976) Entrepreneur textiles.
Wadhwa, Meenakshi. (1967-) Astronomer, space scientist.

Indonesian
Lee, Li-Young. (1957-) Poet.

Irish
See also American Revolutionary War Patriots and Colonists for arrivals from that time period.
Godkin, Edwin L. (1831-1902) Journalist.
Hodgers, Jenny. (Albert Cashier) (1844-1915) Civil War soldier, disguised as man.
McCullagh, Joseph B. (1842-1896) Civil War correspondent, journalist.

Italian
Andretti, Mario. (1940-) Auto racer.
Capra, Frank. (1897-1991) Filmmaker.
Colosimo, James "Big Jim." (1878-1920) Gangster.
Fermi, Enrico. (1901-1954) Inventor, physicist. Nobel Prize winner.
Giancana, Salvatore "Sam." (1908-1975) Gangster.
Gini, Mari. (unknown) Computer scientist, educator, physicist.
Kelly, Paul. *See* Vaccarelli, Paulo Antonio.
Levi-Montalcini, Rita. (1909-) Cell biologist. Nobel Prize winner.
Luciano, Salvatore "Lucky." (1897-1962) Gangster.
Morani, Alma Dea. (1907-2001) Physician.
Tonty, Henry de. (1649-1704) Explorer, founder Arkansas.
Torrio, John. (1882-1957) Gangster.
Vaccarelli, Paulo Antonio. (Paul Kelly) (1876-1927) Boxer, gangster.
Zangara, Giuseppe "Joe." (1900-1933) Assassin.

Jamaican
Garvey, Marcus. (1887-1940) Civil rights activist, orator.
Kelly, Wynton. (1931-1971) Jazz musician.
McKay, Claude. (1890-1948) Author, poet.

Japanese
Hayakawa, Sessue. (Kintaro) (1890-1973) Actor.
Kuramato, June. (1948-) Jazz musician.
Kyoko, Ina. (1972-) Olympic figure skater.
Mori, Kyoko. (1957-) Young adult author.
Mori, Toshio. (1910-1980) Author.
Narahashi, Keiko. (1959-) Children's author, illustrator.
Obata, Chiura. (1888-1975) Painter.
Ozawa, Seiji. (1935-) Conductor.
Say, Allen. (1937-) Children's author, illustrator, photographer.
Shimomura, Tsutomu. (1965-) Computer scientist, physicist.
Suzuki, Daisetz Teitan "D. T." (1870-1966) Educator, philosopher, translator.
Tonegawa, Susumu. (1939-) Molecular biologist, immunologist, medical researcher. Nobel Prize winner.

Korean
Ahn, Chang-Ho. (1878-1938) Human rights activist.
Choi, Sook Nyul. (1937-) Children's author.
Chung, Myung-Whun. (1953-) Conductor, musician.
Kang, Younghill. (1903-1973) Author, educator.
Lee, K. W. (1928-) Journalist.
Paik, Nam June. (1932-) Composer, mixed media artist.

Latvian
Zarins, Juris. (1945-) Archaeologist.

Lebanese
Zughaib, Helen. (1959-) Painter.

Lithuanian
Cahan, Abraham. (1860-1951) Author, editor newspapers.
Gimbutas, Marija Birute Alseikaite. (1921-

1994) Archaeologist.

Goldman, Emma. (1869-1940) Human rights activist, political activist, women's rights activist.

Kaplan, Mordecai. (1881-1983) Educator, spiritual leader.

Luxembourgian

Streichen, Edward. (1879-1973) World War I and II photojournalist. Presidential Medal of Freedom recipient.

Mexican

Castaneda, Carlos. (1896-1958) Historian.

Cotera, Martha P. (1938-) Civil rights activist, educator, historian.

Durazo, Maria Elena. (1954-) Labor leader, workers' rights activist.

Fernandez, Giselle. (1961-) Broadcast journalist, journalist.

Garcia, Hector Perez. (1914-1996) Civil rights activist, physician, World War II Army hero.

Hernandez, Maria Latigo. (1893-1986) Author, political activist, television personality.

Limón, José Arcadia. (1908-1972) Choreographer, dancer.

Lopez, Josefina. (1969-) Playwright.

Lozano, Ignacio E. (1886-1953) Publisher newspaper.

Molina, Mario. (1943-) Chemist, environmental scientist. Nobel Prize winner.

Montalbán, Ricardo. (1920-) Actor.

Quinn, Anthony. (1915-2001) Actor.

Ramirez, Sara Estela. (1881-1910) Poet, political activist, women's rights activist.

Rodriguez, Paul. (1955-) Actor.

Salazar, Rubén. (1928-1970) Broadcast journalist, civil rights activist, journalist.

Santana, Carlos. (1947-) Musician.

Norwegian

Balchen, Bernt. (1899-1973) World War II Army Air Force aviator.

Pakistani

Chandrasekhar, Subrahmayan. (1910-1995) Astrophysicist. Nobel Prize winner.

Panamanian

Pincay, Laffit, Jr. (1946-) Jockey.

Polish

Czolgosz, Leon. (1873-1901) Assassin of President William McKinley.

Friedman, Tova Grossman. (1938-) Holocaust survivor, social worker.

Goldwyn, Samuel. (1882-1974) Filmmaker. Presidential Medal of Freedom recipient.

Heschel, Abraham Joshua. (1907-1972) Author, civil rights activist, educator, political activist.

Kosinski, Jerzy. (1933-1991) Author, Holocaust survivor.

Michelson, Albert Abraham. (1852-1931) Physicist. Nobel Prize winner.

Rose, Ernestine Potowski. (1810-1892) Abolitionist, orator, reformer, women's rights activist.

Sabin, Albert Bruce. (1906-1993) Medical researcher, physician. Presidential Medal of Freedom recipient.

Schneiderman, Rose. (1882-1972) Labor leader, workers' rights activist.

Singer, Isaac Bashevis. (1904-1991) Children's and adult author. Nobel Prize winner.

Soloveitchik, Joseph Dov. (1903-1993) Spiritual leader.

Ulam, Stanislaw. (1909-1984) Mathematician, physicist.

Portuguese

Vaz, Katherine. (unknown) Author.

Puerto Rican

Colon, Raul. (1952-) Illustrator.

Goodman, Robert O. (1956-) Navy commander, born Puerto Rico.

Julia, Raul. (1940-1994) Actor.

Moreno, Rita. (1931-) Actor, dancer.

Novello, Antonia C. (1944-) Physician, Surgeon General of U.S.

Pantoja, Antonio. (1922-2002) Educator, human rights activist, social worker.

Santos, Miriam. (1956-) City official.

Schomburg, Arthur. (1874-1938) Educator, historian.

Velazquez, Nydia. (1953-) Congresswoman, born Puerto Rico.

Romanian

Schechter, Solomon. (1849-1915) Author, educator, spiritual leader, founder of Conservative Judaism.

Wiesel, Elie. (1928-) Author, Holocaust survivor. Nobel Peace Prize winner, Presidential Medal of Freedom recipient.

Russian

Balanchine, George. (1904-1983) Choreographer, dancer, educator. Presidential Medal of Freedom recipient.

Baryshnikov, Mikhail. (1948-) Dancer.

Berlin, Irving. (1888-1989) Composer. Presidential Medal of Freedom recipient.

Durant, Ida Kaufman "Ariel." (1898-1981) Author, historian. Presidential Medal of Freedom recipient, Pulitzer Prize winner.

Heifetz, Jascha. (1901-1987) Musician.

Kaminska, Ida. (1899-1980) Actor.

Lansky, Meyer. (1902-1983) Gangster.

Makarova, Natalia. (1940-) Ballet dancer.

Nevelson, Louise. (1899-1988) Sculptor.

Polovchak, Walter. (1967-) Dissident.

Rickover, Hyman George. (1900-1986) Navy rear admiral. Presidential Medal of Freedom recipient.

Rosenthal, Ida. (1886-1973) Inventor.

Sarnoff, David. (1891-1971) Entrepreneur broadcasting media.

Shavelson, Clara Lemlich. (1886-1982) Workers' rights activist.

Sikorsky, Igor. (1889-1972) Aeronautical engineer, aviation pioneer,

Stravinsky, Igor Fedorovich. (1882-1971) Composer.

Tchernyshev, Peter. (1971-) Olympic figure skater.

Tomara, Sonia. (d. 1982) Journalist, World War II correspondent.

Waksman, Selman Abraham. (1888-1973) Bacteriologist, medical researcher, micro biologist. Nobel Prize winner.

Scottish

See also American Revolutionary War Patriots and Colonists for arrivals from that time period.

Bell, Alexander Graham. (1847-1922) Inventor.

Bennett, James Gordon. (1795-1872) Editor, publisher.

Buick, David Dunbar. (1854-1929) Automaker.

Byrne, David. (1952-) Composer, singer, songwriter.

Carnegie, Andrew. (1835-1919) Entrepreneur steel, philanthropist.

Fleming, Williamina Patron Stevens. (1857-1911) Astronomer.

Garden, Mary. (1874-1967) Opera singer.

Gardner, Alexander. (1821-1882) Civil War photographer.

Gibson, James F. (unknown) Civil War photographer.

Maclure, William. (1763-1840) Geologist, utopian community founder.

Muir, John. (1838-1914) Author, conservationist, naturalist.

Pinkerton, Allan. (1819-1884) Private detective.

Reston, James. (1909-1995) Editor, journalist. Pulitzer Prize winner.

Stuart, Robert. (1785-1848) Explorer, fur trapper.

Wilson, Alexander. (1766-1813) Author, ornithologist.

Spanish

Bori, Lucrezia. (1887-1960) Opera singer.

Cardona, Manuel. (1934-) Physicist.

Cardus, David. (1922-) Physician.

Casals, Pablo. (1876-1973) Composer, conductor, musician. Presidential Medal of Freedom recipient.

Cugat, Xavier. (1900-1990) Bandleader, musician.

Guastavino, Rafael. (1842-1908) Architect.

Iglesias, Enrique. (1975-) Pop singer.

Ochoa, Severo. (1905-1993) Biochemist, physician, physiologist. Nobel Prize winner.

Santayana, George. (1863-1952) Philosopher, poet.

Sri Lankan

Ondaatje, Michael. (1943-) Author, filmmaker, playwright, poet.

Swedish

Anderson, Mary. (1872-1964) Director of U.S. Women's Bureau, labor leader.

Bjerknes, Jacob. (1897-1975) Meteorologist.

Ericsson, John. (1803-1889) Civil War Navy, inventor.

Garbo, Greta. (1905-1990) Actor.

Wichman, Carl Eric. (1887-?) Entrepreneur bus line.

Swiss

Agassiz, Louis. (1807-1873) Educator, naturalist.

Chouet, Bernard. (1945-) Geophysicist, volcanologist.

Gallatin, Albert. (1761-1849) Cabinet member, congressman, diplomat.

Guggenheim, Meyer. (1828-1905) Entrepreneur copper.

Khan, Yasmin Aga. (1949-) Princess.

Kübler-Ross, Elisabeth. (1926-2004) Author, psychiatrist.

Kunin, Madeleine. (1933-) Governor.

Trinidadian

Julian, Hubert Fauntleroy. (1897-?) Aviation pioneer.

Ukrainian

Demjanjuk, John "Ivan the Terrible." (1920-) Nazi war criminal.

Venezuelan

Chang-Diaz, Franklin R. (1950-) Astronaut, physicist.

Dallmeier, Francisco. (1953-) Wildlife biologist.

Escobar, Marisol. (Marisol) (1930-) Sculptor.

Herrera, Caroline. (1939-) Fashion designer.

Vietnamese

Leonard, Andy. (1968-) Weightlifter.

Nguyen, Dustin. (1962-) Actor.

Trinh, Eugene H. (1950-) Astronaut, physicist.

Virgin Islander

Croslin, Michael. (1933-) Mechanical engineer, inventor, Korean War Air Force, medical researcher, Vietnam War Air Force.

Duncan, Tim. (1976-) Basketball player.

Welsh

Nicholson, John. (1757-1800) Entrepreneur real estate, financier.

Stanley, Sir Henry Morton. (1841-1904) Civil War soldier, explorer, journalist.

West Indian

Pinckney, Eliza Lucas. (1722-1793) Agronomist, colonist, entrepreneur indigo crops.

Yugoslavian

Seles, Monica. (1973-) Tennis player.

Tesla, Nikola. (1856-1943) Electrical engineer, inventor.

Immunologists

Dausset, Jean. (1916-) French.

Esu-Williams, Eku. (1956-) Nigerian.

Tonegawa, Susumu. (1939-) born Japan.

Incas

Atahualpa. (1502-1533) Emperor.

Indian Captives

Duston, Hannah. (1657-1736)

Ingles, Mary Draper. (1731-1815)

Jemison, Mary. (1742-1833)

McCrea, Jane. (1752-1777)

Rowlandson, Mary. (1635-1682)

Williams, Eunice. (1697-1787)

Indian Guides, Scouts, and Agents

See also Pioneers and Frontiersmen.

Bailey, Anne Trotter. (1743-1825)

Bridger, Jim. (1804-1881)

Cannary, Martha Jane. (Calamity Jane) (1852-1903)

Carson, Christopher "Kit." (1809-1868)

Clark, William. (1770-1838)

Cody, William. (Buffalo Bill) (1846-1917)

Comstock, Will. (1842-1868)

Fitzpatrick, Tom "Broken Hand." (1799-1854)

Girty, Simon. (1741-1818)

Gist, Christopher. (1706-1759)

Horn, Tom. (1806-1903)

Leroux, Antoine. (1635-1708) born France.

McLaughlin, James. (1842-1923)

Musgrove, Mary. (1700-1763) Creek Indian.

Reynolds, "Lonesome" Charley. (1844-1876)

Sacagawea. (1788-1884) Lemhi Shoshone.

Schuyler, Peter. (1657-1724)

Squanto. (Tisquantum) (1580-1622)

Warren, William Whipple. (1825-1853) Obijway Indian.

Weiser, Johann Conrad. (1696-1760) born Germany.

Zeisberger, David. (1721-1808) born Moravia.

Indians, American

See Native Americans.

Indians, Asian

See also Immigrants to United States, Indian.

Asóka the Great. (292?-232 B.C.) King.

Babur, Zahir un-Din Muhammed. (Babur the Conqueror) (1483-1530) Emperor, general.

Bai, Lakshmi. (1830-1858) Military leader, ruler, disguised as man.

Bojaxhiu, Agnes. (Mother Teresa) (1910-1997) Human rights activist, missionary, born Yugolavia. Nobel Peace Prize winner, Presidential Medal of Freedom recipient.

Devi. Legendary East Indian goddess/warrior queen.

Devi, Gayatri "Ayesha." (1919-) Political activist, princess.

Devi, Phoolan. (1963-) Criminal, political activist.

Gandhi, Indira. (1917-1984) Prime Minister.

Gandhi, Mohandas. (1869-1948) Ruler, peace activist, spiritual leader.

Gautama, Siddhartha (Buddha) (560-480 B.C.) Philosopher, founder Buddhism.

Jahan, Shah. (1592-1666) Ruler.

Jhirad, Jerusha. (1891-1948) Physician.

Jinnah, Mohammed Ali. (1876-1948) Governor general of Pakistan.

Kabir. (1440-1518) Philosopher, poet.

Khan, Noor Inayat. (1914-1944) Holocaust resistance worker, victim.

Mahavira, Vardhamana. (599-527 B.C.)

Founder Jainism religion.

Mangeshkar, Lata. (1929-2001) Singer.

Mirabi. (1498-1565) Poet.

Nanak. (1469-1538) Founder Sikh religion.

Naropa. (1016-1100) Buddhist saint.

Nehru, Jawaharlal. (1889-1964) Prime minister.

Prabhupada, A. C. Bhaktivedanta. (1896-1977) Cult leader, spiritual leader.

Rabi'ah of Basra. (717-801) Spiritual leader, founder of Sufi movement of Islam.

Rai, Jitbahadur. (d. 1949) World War II military leader, Nepal ghurka.

Rajalakshmi, R. (1926-) Biochemist.

Ramabai, Pandita. (1858-1922) Human rights activist.

Ramakrishna, Sri. (1836-1886) Spiritual leader, brought Hinduism to North America.

Ramanujan, Srinivasa. (1887-1920) Mathematician.

Rangada. Hindu woman warrior.

Razia, Sultana. (fl. 1236-1240) Muslim warrior princess.

Tagore, Rabindranth. (1861-1941) Author, composer, painter, poet. Nobel Prize winner.

Vivekananda. (1863-1902) Spiritual leader, Ramakrishna movement.

Indonesians

See also Immigrants to United States, Indonesian.

Sukarno, Achmad. (1901-1970) President.

Internet Pioneers

See also Computer Pioneers; Entrepreneurs, Computers, Electronics, and Media.

Andreessen, Marc. (1971-)

Berners-Lee, Tim. (1955-) English.

Bezos, Jeffrey. (1964-)

Case, Steve. (1958-)

Cerf, Vinton. (1943-)

Ellison, Lawrence. (1944-)

Gates, Bill. (1955-)

Grove, Andrew. (1936-)

Jobs, Steven. (1955-)

Omidyar, Pierre. (1967-) born France.

Torvalds, Linus. (1970-) Finnish.

Winblad, Ann. (1950-) Financier.

Yang, Jerry. (1968-)

Inventors

See also Aviation Pioneers; Medical Researchers; Space Scientists.

American

Anderson, Mary. (1866-1953) Windshield wipers.

Armstrong, Edwin Howard. (1890-1954) Radio co-inventor.

Baekeland, Leo. (1863-1944) Plastics, born Belgium.

Banneker, Benjamin. (1731-1806) Astronomical tables, clock.

Bardeen, John. (1908-1991) Transistor co-inventor.

Beard, Andrew Jackson. (1849-1941) Railroad car coupling system.

Becoat, Bill. (1938-) Two wheel drive bicycle.

Bell, Alexander Graham. (1847-1922) Telephone, born Scotland.

Benerito, Ruth. (1916-) Wrinkle free fabrics.

Benjamin, Miriam E. (unknown) Chair with emergency call button.

Blodgett, Katherine. (1898-1979) Monomolecular layers.

Boone, Sarah. (unknown) Ironing board.

Boyd, Henry. (1802-1886) Wooden bed frame.

Boyle, Robert. (1627-1691) Improved air pump.

Bradley, Benjamin. (1830-?) Steam engine.

Brattain, Walter Houser. (1902-1987) Transistor co-inventor.

Brill, Yvonne. (1924-) Electronic propulsion, born Canada.

Brown, Marie Van Brittan. (fl. 1969) Home security system.

Bushnell, David. (1742-1824) Submarine.

Bushnell, Nolan. (1943-) Video arcade games.

Carlson, Chester. (1906-1968) Xerography.

Carothers, Wallace. (1896-1937) Nylon.

Carter, Iola O. (unknown) Folding nursery chair.

Clark, Joan. (unknown) Medicine tray.

Colt, Samuel. (1814-1862) Revolver.

Coston, Martha. (1826-1886) Signal flares for Navy.

Crews, Jeanne Lee. (unknown) Space bumper.

Croslin, Michael. (1933-) Blood pressure and pulse monitors.

Crosthwait, David Nelson, Jr. (1898-1976) Heating systems.

De Forest, Lee. (1873-1961) Radio co-inventor.

Deere, John. (1804-1886) Plows, tractors.

Eastman, George. (1854-1932) Camera.

Edison, Thomas Alva. (1847-1931) Light bulb, phonograph, motion picture camera.

Eglin, Ellen. (1849-?) Clothes wringer.

Ericsson, John. (1803-1889) Battleship, born Sweden.

Everson, Carrie. (1842-1914) Mining industry inventions.

Farnsworth, Philo Taylor. (1906-1971) Television.

Fermi, Enrico. (1901-1954) Atomic reactor, born Italy.

Fuller, R. Buckminster. (1895-1983) Geodesic dome.

Fulton, Robert. (1765-1815) Steamboat, submarine.

Gabe, Frances. (1915-) Self-cleaning house.

Gillette, King C. (1855-1932) Disposable razors.

Ginsburg, Charles. (1920-1992) Videotape recorder.

Goddard, Robert. (1882-1945) Rocket.

Goode, Sara E. (1850-?) Folding bed-cabinet.

Goodyear, Charles. (1800-1860) Vulcanized rubber.

Gould, Gordon. (1920-) Lasers.

Gourdine, Meredith. (1929-1998) Electricity inventions.

Graham, Bette Nesmith. (1924-1980) Liquid paper.

Grandin, Temple. (1974-) Livestock handling equipment.

Greatbatch, Wilson. (1919-) Heart pacemaker.

Greene, Catherine Littlefield. (1755-1814) Cotton gin co-inventor.

Griffin, Bessie Blount. (1913-) Automatic invalid feeder.

Hamilton, Marilyn. (1947-) Wheelchair design improvements.

Hammonds, Julia T. (unknown) Knitting yarn holder.

Handler, Ruth. (1916-2002) Barbie Dolls.

Harvard, Claude. (1911-1999) Auto and radio inventions.

Henry, Joseph. (1797-1878) Electricity inventions.

Hoagland, Jesse. (1939-) Safety squat bar for weightlifting.

Hoff, Ted. (1937-) Microprocessor.

Hosmer, Harriet. (1830-1908) Artificial marble.

Jacob, Mary Phelps. (Caresse Crosby) (1892-1970) Brassiere.

Jefferson, Thomas. (1743-1826)

Johnson, Lonnie. (1949-) Super Soaker.

Jones, Amanda Theodosia. (1835-1914) Vacuum canning process.

Jones, Frederick McKinley. (1892-1961) Refrigerator.

Kenner, Beatrice. (1912-) Kitchen and household gadgets.

Kerr, Barbara. (unknown) Solar box cooker.

Knight, Margaret. (1838-1914) Paper bag folding machine.

Kwolek, Stephanie. (1923-) Kevlar fabrics.

Land, Edwin. (1909-1991) Polaroid cameras.

Latimer, Lewis Howard. (1848-1928) Carbon filaments in light bulbs.

Lawrence, Ernest Orlando. (1901-1958) Cyclotron.

Lear, William. (1902-1978) Aircraft inventions.

Libby, Willard F. (1908-1980) Radioactive dating.

Malone, Annie Turnbo. (1869-1957) Hair and skin products.

Mangin, Anna M. (unknown) Party forks.

Masters, Sybilla. (d. 1720) Cornmeal processing.

Matzeliger, Jan Ernst. (1852-1889) Shoe lasting machines.

McCormick, Cyrus Hall. (1809-1884) Reaper.

McCoy, Elijah. (1843-1929) Lubricator for steam machines.

Montgomery, Benjamin. (1819-1877) Propellor.

Moon, John P. (1938-) Computer technology.

Moore, Ann. (1940-) Baby holder.

Morgan, Garrett A. (1877-1963) Gas mask, traffic lights.

Morse, Samuel Finley Breese. (1791-1872) Telegraph.

Newman, Lydia D. (unknown) Hairbrush design.

O'Neill, Cecilia Rose. (1874-1944) Kewpie doll.

Oppenheimer, J. Robert. (1904-1967) Atomic bomb.

Otis, Elisha Graves. (1811-1861) Elevator.

Parker, John. (1827-1900) Tobacco screw press.

Perkins, Nancy. (1949-) Industrial design.

Reed, Judy W. (unknown) Dough kneader and roller.

Rillieux, Norbert. (1806-1894) Sugar refining vacuum.

Rosenthal, Ida. (1886-1973) Brasserie, born Russia.

Sampson, Henry. (1934-) Process for making rocket fuel.

Schroeder, Becky. (1962-) Phosphorescent chemical glo-sheets.

Shaw, Earl D. (1937-) Lasers.

Sherman, Patsy O. (1930-) Scotchgard process.

Sholes, Christopher. (1819-1890) First practical typewriter.

Shurney, Robert. (1921-) Space industry inventions.

Sigur, Wanda. (1958-) Space industry inventions.

Singer, Isaac Merritt. (1811-1875) Sewing machines.

Smith, Mildred Davidson. (1916-1993) Game.

Spikes, Frederick McKinley. (fl. late 1880s) Automatic safety brake.

Temple, Lewis. (1800-1854) Whaling harpoon.

Tesla, Nikola. (1856-1943) A.C. current system, born Yugoslavia.

Thomas, Valerie. (1943-) Illusion transmitter.

Townes, Charles Hard. (1915-) Laser.

Vine, Allyn. (1914-1994) Deep sea submersible.

Von Braun, Werner. (1912-1977) Rockets, born Germany.

Wakefield, Ruth. (1905-1977) Chocolate chip cookies.

Walker, Sarah Breedlove McWilliams "Madame C. J." (1867-1919) Cosmetics.

Westinghouse, George. (1846-1914) A.C. electrical system, railroad air brake.

Westover, Cynthia. (1885-1931) Dumping cart.

Whitney, Eli. (1765-1825) Cotton gin.

Woods, Granville T. (1856-1910) Railway telegraph.

Ancient Civilizations

Archimedes. (287-212 B.C.) Pumps and levers, Greek.

Mary Prophetetissa of Alexandria. (1st century A.D.) Alloys, Egyptian.

Dutch

Zernike, Frits. (1888-1966) Phase contrast microscope.

English

Arkwright, Sir Richard. (1732-1792) Waterproof spinning machine.

Baird, John Logie. (1888-1946) Television transmitter.

Boyle, Robert. (1627-1691) Improved air pumps.

Davy, Humphrey. (1778-1829) Safety lamp for miners.

Faraday, Michael. (1791-1867) Dynamo.

Hooke, Robert. (1635-1703) Weather instruments.

Maxim, Sir Hiram Stevens. (1840-1916) Automatic machine gun.

Shockley, William. (1910-1989) Transistor.

Stephenson, George. (1781-1848) Railroad locomotive.

Swinton, Ernest. (1868-1951) Military tank.

Thomson, Joseph John. (1856-1940) Electron.

Whitehead, Robert. (1823-1905) Torpedo.

Whittle, Sir Frank. (1907-1996) Jet engine.

French

Ader, Clement. (1841-1926) Flying machines.

Braille, Louis. (1809-1852) Reading system for blind.

Cousteau, Jacques-Yves. (1910-1997) Aqualung.

Curie, Marie. (1867-1934) Radium co-inventor, born Poland.

Curie, Pierre. (1859-1906) Radium co-inventor.

Girrard, Henri. (1825-1882) Dirigible.

Montgolfier, Jacques Étienne. (1745-1799) Hot air balloon.

Montgolfier, Joseph Michel. (1740-1810) Hot air balloon.

German

Benz, Karl. (1844-1929) Automobile with internal combustion engine.

Daimler, Gottlieb. (1834-1900) Gasoline driven automobile.

Dornberger, Walter. (1895-1980) Ballistic missiles.

Geiger, Hans. (1882-1945) Geiger counter.

Gutenberg, Johann. (1399-1468) Printing press.

Hungarian

Biro, Ladislao. (1900-1944) Ball point pen.

Gabor, Dennis. (1900-1979) Holography.

Italian

Marconi, Guglielmo. (1874-1937) Wireless telegraph.

Japanese

Morita, Akio. (1921-) Cassette player, transistor radio.

Yamauchi, Hiroshi. (1928-) Computer games.

Scottish

Dunlop, John. (1840-1921) Pneumatic tires.

Watson-Watt, Sir Robert Alexander. (1892-1973) Radar.

Watt, James. (1736-1819) Steam engine improvements.

Swedish

Meitner, Lise. (1878-1968) Nuclear fission for atom bomb.

Nobel, Alfred Bernhard. (1833-1893) Dynamite.

Iraqis and Iranians

Al-Ghazali. (1058-1111) Islamic Iranian spiritual leader.

Bahrami, Mansoor. (1956-) Iranian tennis player.

Bat Ha-Levi. (12th century) Iraqi scholar.

Hussein, Saddam. (1937-) Dictator, Iraqi president.

Khomeini, Ayatollah Ruhollah. (1900-1989) Iranian political leader, spiritual leader.

Irish

See also Immigrants to United States, Irish.

Barnardo, Thomas. (1845-1905) Missionary.

Bonney, Anne. (1697-1721) Pirate.

Boru, Brian. (941-1014) Military leader.

Brendan the Navigator. (Saint Brendan) (484-577) Explorer, saint.

Burke, Robert O'Hara. (1820-1861) Explorer.

Burkitt, Denis Parsons. (1911-1993) Medical researcher, physician.

Burnell, Jocelyn Bell. (1943-) Astronomer.

Carmichael, Amy. (1867-1951) Missionary.

Collins, Michael. (1890-1922) Revolutionary, terrorist.

Columba. (521-597) Missionary, saint.

Corrigan, Mairead. (1944-) Peace activist. Nobel Peace Prize winner.

Joyce, James. (1882-1941) Author, playwright.

Lewis, Clive Staples "C. S." (1898-1963) Children's author.

MacBride, Séan. (1904-1988) Attorney, peace activist, statesman. Nobel Peace Prize winner.

Mallon, Mary "Typhoid Mary." (1870-1938) Cook, maid, folk hero.

Markiewiecz, Constance. (1867-1927) Political activist.

McAliskey, Bernadette Devlin. (1947-) Civil rights activist, political activist.

Murphy, Dervla. (1931-) Author, explorer.

O'Casey, Sean. (1880-1964) Playwright.

O'Hara, Mary. (1935-) Musician, singer.

O'Malley, Grace. (1530-1603) Pirate queen.

O'Mullan, John. (1670-1722) Outlaw.

Patrick. (389?-461?) Folk hero, saint, slave, spiritual leader.

Robinson, Mary. (1944-) President.

Shackleton, Ernest. (1874-1922) Explorer.

Shaw, George Bernard. (1856-1950) Author, playwright. Nobel Prize winner.

Wilde, Oscar. (1854-1900) Playwright, poet.

Williams, Betty. (1943-) Peace activist, reformer. Nobel Peace Prize winner.

Yeats, William Butler. (1865-1939) Folklorist, poet. Nobel Prize winner.

Israelis

See also Hebrews, Ancient.

Arad, Yael. (1967-) Olympic judo athlete.

Begin, Menachem. (1913-1992) Prime minister, born Poland. Nobel Peace Prize winner.

Ben-Gurion, David. (1886-1973) Prime Minister.

Ben-Yehuda, Eliezer. (1858-1922) Linguist.

Caro, Joseph Ben Ephraim. (1488-1575) Scholar, born Spain.

Chizick, Sarah. (1897-) Political activist, settler.

Dayan, Moshe. (1915-1981) Foreign Minister, military leader.

Fink, Ida. (1921-) Author, Holocaust survivor, playwright, born Poland.

Leibowitz, Nehama. (1905-1997) Broadcast journalist, scholar.

Luria, Isaac. (1534-1572) Educator, mystic, scholar.

Meir, Golda. (1898-1978) Prime Minister, born Russia.

Peres, Shimon. (1923-) Prime Minister, born Poland. Nobel Peace Prize winner.

Perlman, Itzhak. (1945-) Musician.

Rabin, Yitzhak. (1922-1995) Prime Minister. Nobel Peace Prize winner.

Shochat, Manya. (1880-1961) Settler, former Russian revolutionary, born Russia.

Weizman, Chaim. (1874-1952) President.

Yadin, Yigael. (1917-1984) Archaeologist, political activist, deputy prime minister.

Italians

See also Immigrants to United States, Italian.

Abrabanel, Benvenida. (d. 1560) Political activist, scholar, born Spain.

Agnesi, Maria Gaetana. (1718-1799) Mathematician.

Anguissola, Sofonisba. (1532-1625) Painter.

Arcimboldo, Giuseppe. (1527-1593) Painter.

Ascarelli, Devorah. (16th century) Poet, scholar.

Bassi, Laura. (1711-1778) Physicist.

Bellini, Giovanni. (1430-1516) Painter.

Bellini, Vincenzo. (1801-1835) Composer.

Belzoni, Giovanni. (1778-1823) Archaeologist.

Benedict of Nursia. (480-550) Monk, saint.

Bernini, Gian Lorenzo. (1598-1680) Sculptor.

Boccaccio, Giovanni. (1313-1375) Author.

Boccherini, Luigi. (1741-1805) Composer.

Boccioni, Umberto. (1882-1916) Painter, sculptor.

Borgia, Lucrezia. (1480-1519) Villainess, folk hero.

Botticelli, Sandro. (1444-1510) Painter.

Brizi, Luigi. (unknown) Holocaust rescuer.

Brunelleschi. (1377-1466) Architect.

Bruno, Giordano. (1548-1600) Scholar.

Cabot, Sebastian. (1476-1557) Explorer.

Caglistro, Alessandro di. (1743-1795) Magician.

Canaletto. (Giovanni Antonio Canale) (1697-1768) Painter.

Caravaggio. (Michelangelo Merisi) (1573-1610) Painter.

Caruso, Enrico. (1873-1921) Opera singer.

Casanova de Seingalt, Giovanni Giacomo. (1725-1798) Adventurer.

Catherine of Siena. (1353-1386) Human rights activist, mystic, poet, spiritual leader.

Cellini, Benvenuto. (1500-1571) Goldsmith, jewelry designer, sculptor.

Cimabue. (1240?-1302) Painter.

Cimarosa, Domenico. (1749-1801) Composer.

Colonna, Vittoria. (1490-1547) Reformer.

Columbus, Christopher. (1451-1506) Explorer.

Correggio. (Antonio Allegri) (1489-1534) Painter.

Dante Alighieri. (1265-1321) Poet.

D'Aresso, Guido. (992-1050) Composer, monk.

Deledda, Grazia. (1871-1936) Author. Nobel Prize winner.

deMédici, Cosimo. (1389-1464) Financier.

D'Este, Beatrice. (1475-1497) Patron of arts.

D'Este, Isabella. (1474-1539) Patron of arts.

Donatello. (Donato de Betto di Bordi) (1387-1466) Sculptor.

Donizetti, Gaetano. (1797-1848) Opera composer.

Duse, Eleanora. (1859-1924) Actor.

Ferrari, Enzo. (1898-1988) Automaker.

Fontana, Lavinia. (1552-1614) Painter.

Francesca, Piero Della. (c. 1415-1492) Mathematician, painter.

Francis of Assisi. (1181-1226) Saint, spiritual leader.

Gabrieli, Andrea. (1510-1586) Composer, educator, musician.

Galilei, Galileo. (1564-1642) Astronomer, mathematician, physicist.

Galluppi, Baldassarre. (1706-1785) Opera composer.

Garibaldi, Giuseppe. (1807-1882) Military leader.

Gentileschi, Artemisia. (1593-1652) Painter.

Giaconda, Lisa. (1479-1509) Model for Mona Lisa.

Giorgione. (Giorgio Barbarelli) (1447-1510) Painter.

Giotto di Bondone. (1276-1337) Painter.

Gregory I. (Pope Gregory the Great) (540-604) Composer, pope, saint.

Gregory VII. (1015-1085) Pope.

Innocent III. (Segni da Lothario) (1160-1216) Pope.

John XXIII. (Angelo Roncalli) (1881-1963) Pope. Presidential Medal of Freedom recipient.

Julius II. (1443-1513) Pope.

Kauffmann, Angelica. (1741-1807) Painter.

Lamborghi, Feruccio. (1916-1993) Automaker.

Leo X. (1475-1521) Pope.

Leonardo da Vinci. (1452-1519) Architect, engineer, painter, sculptor.

Levi, Primo. (1919-1987) Author, chemist, Holocaust survivor.

Luria, Isaac. (1534-1572) Israeli educator, mystic, scholar.

Machiavelli, Niccolo. (1469-1527) Historian, political activist.

Mansi, Paula dei. (13th century) Italian scribe, scholar.

Marcello, Benedetto. (1686-1739) Composer.

Marconi, Guglielmo. (1874-1937) Inventor, physicist. Nobel Prize winner.

Massaccio, Tommaso. (1401-1428) Painter.

Medici, Lorenzo de. (1449-1492) Nobleman, patron of arts.

Messner, Reinhold. (1944-) Mountaineer.

Michelangelo, Buonarotti. (1475-1564) Painter, sculptor.

Modligliani, Amedeo. (1884-1920) Painter.

Moneta, Ernesto. (1833-1918) Journalist, peace activist. Nobel Peace Prize winner.

Montessori, Maria. (1870-1952) Educator, physician.

Monteverdi, Claudio. (1567-1643) Composer.

Morpurgo, Rachel Luzzatto. (1790-1871) Poet.

Mussolini, Benito. (1883-1945) Dictator, political activist.

Niccacci, Padre Rufino. (unknown) Holocaust rescuer, spiritual leader.

Nobile, Umberto. (1885-1978) Air Force general, arctic pilot.

Nuvolari, Tazio. (1892-1953) Auto racer.

Pacelli, Eugenio Maria Guiseppe. *See* Pius XII.

Paganini, Niccolo. (1782-1840) Composer, musician.

Paisiello, Giovanni. (1740-1816) Composer.

Palestrina, Giovanni Pierluigi da. (1525-1594) Composer, singer.

Pergolesi, Giovanni Battista. (1710-1736) Composer.

Perlasca, Giorgio. (1910-1992) Holocaust rescuer.

Piccinni, Noccolo. (1728-1800) Opera composer.

Pius XII. (Eugenio Maria Giuseppe) (1867-1958) Pope.

Platearius, Trotula. (c. 1080) Physician.

Polo, Marco. (1254-1324) Adventurer, explorer.

Puccini, Giacomo. (1858-1924) Opera composer.

Raphael. (Raffaello Sanzio) (1483-1520) Painter.

Ricci, Matteo. (1552-1610) Missionary.

Rossetti, Dante Gabriel. (1828-1882) Painter, poet, born England.

Rossi, Europa di. (Madame Europa) (16th century) Singer.

Rossini, Gioaccino. (1792-1868) Composer.

Santorio, Santorio. (1561-1636) Medical researcher, physician.

Scarlatti, Domenico. (1685-1757) Composer, musician.

Scifi, Claire of Assisi. (1193-1252) Saint, spiritual leader.

Shapira-Luria, Miriam. (15th century) Educator.

Sichelgaita. (d. 1090) Princess of Lombard.

Sirani, Elizabeth. (1638-1665) Painter.

Stradivari, Antonio. (1644-1737) Musician, instrument maker.

Strozzi, Barbara. (1619-1664) Composer.

Sullam, Sara Coppio. (1592-1641) Poet, scholar.

Theni, Gustavo. (1951-) Olympic skier.

Theodoric the Great. (454-526) Roman conqueror.

Thomas Aquinas. (1224-1274) Philosopher, saint, theologian.

Tintoretto. (Jacobo Robusti) (1518-1594) Painter.

Titian. (Tiziano Vecellio) (1477-1576) Painter.

Uccello, Paolo. (1397-1475) Painter.

Verdi, Giuseppe. (1813-1901) Composer.

Verrazzano, Giovanni da. (1458-1528) Explorer.

Vespucci, Amerigo. (1454-1512) Explorer.

Vivaldi, Antonio. (1678-1741) Composer.

Volta, Alessandro. (1746-1827) Educator, physicist.

Jamaicans

See also Immigrants to United States, Jamaican.

Plantain, James. (fl. 1720) Pirate.

Seacole, Mary. (1805-1881) Nurse.

Japanese

See also Immigrants to United States, Japanese.

Anno, Mitsumasa. (1926-) Children's author, illustrator.

Basho. (1644-1694) Poet.

Dogen. (1200-1253) Spiritual leader, founder of Soto Zen school of Buddhism.

Hani Motoko. (1873-1957) Journalist.

Hirohito. (1901-1989) Emperor.

Hokusai, Katsushika. (1760-1849) Painter, printmaker.

Honda, Soichiro. (1906-1991) Automaker.

Ichikawa Fusae. (1893-1981) Political activist, suffragist, women's rights activist.

Kato, Sawao. (1946-) Olympic gymnast.

Koken. (718-770) Empress, Buddhist nun.

Komyo. (701-760) Empress.

Kukai. (774-835) Spiritual leader, founder of Shingon sect of Buddhism.

Manjiro. (1827-1898) Fisherman.

Midori. (1971-) Musician.

Minamoto, Yoritomo. (1147-?) Samurai warrior.

Minamoto, Yoshitsune. (1160-?) Samurai warrior.

Mitsui, Shuho. (1590-1676) Businesswoman.

Morita, Akio. (1921-) Entrepreneur electronics, inventor.

Murasaki, Shikibu. (978?-1030?) Author.

Mutsuhito. (1852-1912) Emperor.

Nichiren. (1222-1282) Buddhist monk.

Nobunaga, Oda. (1534-1582) Shogun warrior.

Okuni. (1571-1610) Actor.

Rikyu, Senno. (1522-1591) Tea ceremony expert.

Saigo, Takemori. (1827-1877) Samurai warrior.

Sarashina, Lady. (1008-?) Adventurer, author, poet.

Saruhashi, Katsuku. (1920-) Chemist.

Sato, Eisaku. (1901-1975) Attorney, peace activist, prime minister. Nobel Peace Prize winner.

Shonagon, Sei. (960s-?) Author.

Shotoku, Tashi. (574-622) Prince.

Sugihara, Sempo. (1900-1986) Holocaust rescuer.

Tabei Junko. (1939-) Mountaineer.

Togo, Heihachiro. (1848-1934) Naval leader.

Yakami. Legendary heroine.

Yamamoto, Isoroku. (1884-1943) World War II military leader.

Yamauchi, Hiroshi. (1928-) Entrepreneur, inventor computer games.

Jewelry and Metal Designers

Campbell, Ben Nighthorse. (1933-) Cheyenne Indian.

Celleni, Benvenuto. (1500-1571) Italian goldsmith.

Dockstader, Frederick L. (1919-1998) Oneida and Navajo Indian.

Oppenheim, Meret. (1913-1985) Swiss, born Germany.

Rahr, Tammy. (unknown) Cayuga Indian beadworker.

Revere, Paul. (1735-1818) Silversmith.

Jewish-Americans

See also Biblical Figures; Hebrews, Ancient; Holocaust Figures; Israelis; Jews, International.

Abzug, Bella. (1920-1998) Attorney, congresswoman, peace activist.

Allen, Woody. (1935-) Actor, filmmaker, screenwriter.

Annenberg, Walter. (1908-2002) Entrepreneur broadcasting media, philanthropist, publisher. Presidential Medal of Freedom recipient.

Arbus, Diane. (1923-1971) Photographer.

Arnold, Roseanne. (1952-) Comedian.

Asimov, Isaac. (1920-1992) Author.

Auerbach, Arnold Jacob "Red." (1917-) Basketball coach.

Baskin, Leonard. (1922-) Illustrator, printmaker, sculptor.

Bellow, Saul. (1915-) Author. Nobel Prize winner, Pulitzer Prize winner.

Benjamin, Judah Philip. (1811-1884) Attorney, confederate statesman.

Benny, Jack. (1894-1974) Comedian.

Berlin, Irving. (1888-1989) Composer, born Russia. Presidential Medal of Freedom recipient.

Bernstein, Carl. (1944-) Journalist.

Bernstein, Leonard. (1918-1990) Composer, conductor.

Bernstein, Peter. (1967-) Jazz musician.

Bettelheim, Bruno. (1903-1990) Holocaust survivor, psychotherapist, born Austria.

Blume, Judy. (1938-) Children's and young adult author.

Boxer, Barbara. (1940-) Congresswoman, women's rights activist.

Brandeis, Louis. (1856-1941) Attorney, Supreme Court chief justice.

Brody, Jane. (1941-1987) Author, journalist, nutritionist.

Burns, George. (1896-1996) Actor, comedian.

Cahan, Abraham. (1860-1951) Author, editor, born Lithuania.

Capa, Robert. (1913-1954) Photojournalist, born Hungary.

Cardin, Shoshana. (1926-) Organizational head.

Cohen, Ben. (1951-) Entrepreneur ice cream.

Cohen, Rose. (1880-1925) Labor leader, workers' rights activist.

Cohen, Sasha. (1984-) Olympic figure skater.

Cohen, Stanley. (1922-) Biochemist. Nobel Prize winner.

Commoner, Barry. (1917-) Biologist, environmentalist.

Copland, Aaron. (1900-1990) Composer. Presidential Medal of Freedom recipient, Pulitzer Prize winner.

Cori, Gerty Radnitz. (1896-1957) Biochemist, born Czechoslovakia. Nobel Prize winner.

Cowan, Ruth. (1902-) Journalist, World War II correspondent.

Cowen, Joshua Lionel. (1880-1965) Entrepreneur toy trains.

Cummings, Nathan. (1896-1985) Entrepreneur food industry.

Davis, Sammy, Jr. (1925-1990) Actor, showman, singer.

Dorfman, Elsa. (1937-) Photographer.

Dresselhaus, Mildred. (1930-) Physicist.

Durant, Ida Kaufman "Ariel." (1898-1981) Author, historian, born Russia. Presidential Medal of Freedom recipient, Pulitzer Prize winner.

Dylan, Bob. (1941-) Composer, folksinger.

Eilberg, Amy. (1954-) First Conservative Jewish female rabbi.

Einstein, Albert. (1879-1955) Physicist, born Germany. Nobel Prize winner.

Eisenberg, Arlo. (1973-) In-line skater.

Eisenstein, Judith Kaplan. (1909-1996) Educator, songwriter.

Elion, Gertrude Belle. (1918-1999) Biochemist. Nobel Prize winner.

Ellison, Lawrence. (1944-) Entrepreneur Internet, Internet pioneer.

Fairstein, Linda. (1947-) Attorney, author, crimefighter.

Feinstein, Dianne. (1933-) Mayor, senator.

Fine, Vivian. (1913-) Composer.

Friedan, Betty Goldstein. (1921-) Women's rights activist.

Friedman, Milton. (1912-) Economist. Nobel Prize winner, Presidential Medal of Honor recipient.

Friedman, Tova Grossman. (1938-) Holocaust survivor, social worker, born Poland.

Gershwin, George. (1898-1937) Composer.

Gershwin, Ira. (1896-1983) Composer.

Gertz, Alison. (1966-1992) AIDS activist.

Getz, Stan. (1927-1991) Bandleader, jazz musician.

Gimbel, Adam. (1817-1896) Entrepreneur department stores, born Germany.

Ginsberg, Allen. (1926-1997) Poet.

Ginsburg, Ruth Bader. (1933-) Attorney, Supreme Court justice.

Glaser, Elizabeth. (1947-1994) AIDS activist, children's rights activist.

Glass, Philip. (1937-) Composer.

Goldman, Emma. (1869-1940) Human rights activist, political activist, women's rights activist, born Lithuania.

Goldwyn, Samuel. (1882-1974) Filmmaker, born Poland. Presidential Medal of Freedom recipient.

Gompers, Samuel. (1850-1924) Labor leader, workers' rights activist, born England.

Goodman, Benjamin David "Benny." (1909-1986) Composer, jazz musician.

Gould, Gordon. (1920-) Inventor, physicist.

Gould, Stephen Jay. (1941-) Paleontologist.

Gratz, Rebecca. (1781-1869) Educator, philanthropist.

Greenberg, Hank. (1911-1986) Baseball player.

Greenfield, Jerry. (1951-) Entrepreneur ice cream.

Greenspan, Alan. (1926-) Economist.

Grove, Andrew. (1936-) Entrepreneur Internet, Internet pioneer.

Guggenheim, Meyer. (1828-1905) Entrepreneur copper, born Switzerland.

Hammerstein, Oscar, II. (1895-1960) Playwright, songwriter.

Handler, Ruth. (1916-2002) Entrepreneur dolls, inventor.

Hauptman, Judith. (unknown) Educator.

Heifetz, Jascha. (1901-1987) Musician, born Russia.

Heschel, Abraham Joshua. (1907-1972) Author, civil rights activist, educator, political activist, born Poland.

Heuman, Judy. (1947-) Assistant Secretary of Education.

Hoban, Tana. (unknown) Children's author, illustrator.

Holzman, William "Red." (1920-1998) Basketball coach.

Houdini, Harry. (1874-1926) Magician.

Hughes, Sarah. (1985-) Olympic figure skater.

Hurwitz, Johanna. (1937-) Children's author.

Hyman, Libbie. (1888-1969) Zoologist.

Isaacs, Susan. (1943-) Author.

Janowitz, Tama. (1957-) Author.

Jolson, Al. (1886-1950) Showman, singer.

Jong, Erica. (1942-) Author, poet.

Kalman, Maira. (1949-) Children's author, illustrator.

Kaminska, Ida. (1899-1980) Actor, born Russia.

Kaplan, Mordecai Menahem. (1881-1983) Educator, founder of Reconstructionist movement of Judaism, born Lithuania.

Karan, Donna. (1948-) Fashion designer.

King, Larry. (1933-) Television personality.

Kissinger, Henry. (1923-) Cabinet member, born Germany. Nobel Peace Prize winner.

Klein, Norma. (1938-1989) Young adult author.

Kohut, Rebekah Bettelheim. (1864-1951) Human rights activist.

Koningsburg, Elaine "E. L." (1930-) Children's author.

Kosinski, Jerzy. (1933-1991) Author, Holocaust survivor, born Poland.

Koufax, Sandy. (1935-) Baseball player.

Kunin, Madeleine. (1933-) Governor, born Switzerland.

Kuntzler, William. (1919-1995) Attorney, civil rights activist.

Kuskin, Karla. (1933-) Children's author, illustrator.

Land, Edwin. (1909-1991) Inventor, physicist.

Landers, Ann. See Lederer, Esther Pauline.

Lansing, Sherry. (1944-) Filmmaker.

Lansky, Meyer. (1902-1983) Gangster, born Russia.

Lazarus, Emma. (1849-1887) Poet.

Lear, Norman. (1922-) Filmmaker.

Lederer, Esther Pauline "Eppie." (Ann Landers) (1918-2002) Journalist.

Leibovitz, Annie. (1949-) Photographer.

Leitner, Isabella Katz. (1924-) Author, Holocaust survivor, born Hungary.

Lester, Julius. (1939-) Children's and adult author.

Levi-Montalcini, Rita. (1909-) Cell biologist, born Italy. Nobel Prize winner.

Levitt, William. (1907-1994) Entrepreneur real estate.

Levy, Uriah P. (1792-1862) Naval commander.

Lewin, Ted. (1935-) Children's author, illustrator.

Lieberman-Cline, Nancy. (1958-) Olympic basketball player, coach.

Lippmann, Walter. (1889-1974) Author, journalist, World War I Army captain. Presidential Medal of Freedom recipient, Pulitzer Prize winner.

Luckman, Sid. (1916-1990) Football player.

Mailer, Norman. (1923-) Author, playwright. Pulitzer Prize winner.

Man, Ray. See Radnitsky, Emmanuel.

Marx, Groucho. (1890-1977) Comedian.

Matlin, Marlee. (1965-) Actor.

Mayer, Louis B. (1885-1957) Filmmaker.

Meyer, Annie Nathan. (1867-1951) Women's rights activist.

Michelson, Albert Abraham. (1852-1931) Physicist, born Poland. Nobel Prize winner.

Midler, Bette. (1945-) Actor, singer.

Miller, Arthur. (1915-) Playwright.

Moise, Penina. (1797-1880) Educator, poet.

Nevelson, Louise. (1899-1988) Sculptor, born Russia.

Noah, Mordecai Manuel. (1785-1851) Attorney, journalist, playwright.

Nussbaum, Susan. (1953-) Actor, disability rights activist, playwright.

Oppenheimer, J. Robert. (1904-1967) Inventor, physicist.

Ozick, Cynthia. (1928-) Author.

Paley, Grace. (1922-) Author.

Parker, Dorothy. (1893-1967) Author, poet, screenwriter.

Phillips, Pauline Esther "Popo." (Abigail Van Buren) (1918-) Journalist.

Preisand, Sally. (1946-) First female rabbi in U.S.

Radnitsky, Emmanuel. (Man Ray) (1890-1976) Photographer, sculptor.

Redman, Joshua. (1969-) Jazz musician.

Reich, Steve. (1936-) Composer.

Reichmann, Paul. (1930-) Entrepreneur real estate, born Austria.

Reisberg, Mira. (1953-) Painter, born Australia.

Resnick, Judith. (1949-1986) Astronaut, electrical engineer.

Rich, Buddy. (1917-1987) Jazz musician.

Rickover, Hyman. (1900-1986) Navy rear admiral, born Russia. Presidential Medal of Freedom recipient.

Robbins, Jerome. (1918-1998) Choreographer, dancer.

Rose, Ernestine Potowski. (1810-1892) Abolitionist, orator, reformer, women's rights activist, born Poland.

Rosenberg, Ethel. (1915-1953) Traitor.

Rosenberg, Julius. (1918-1953) Traitor.

Rosenthal, Ida. (1886-1973) Fashion designer, inventor, born Russia.

Rosenwald, Julius. (1862-1932) Entrepreneur department stores, philanthropist.

Ross, Barney. (1907-1967) Boxer, World War II Marine hero.

Roth-Hano, Renée. (1931-) Author, Holocaust survivor, social worker, born France.

Rothschild, Miriam (1908-) Author, conservationist, entomologist, naturalist, born England.

Rubin, Vera Cooper. (1928-) Astronomer.

Sabin, Albert Bruce. (1906-1993) Medical researcher, physician, born Poland. Presidential Medal of Freedom recipient.

Sagan, Carl. (1934-1996) Astronomer, author. Pulitzer Prize winner.

Sager, Ruth. (1918-1997) Biologist, geneticist.

Salk, Jonas. (1914-1995) Educator, medical researcher, physician.

Sarnoff, David. (1891-1971) Entrepreneur broadcasting media, born Russia.

Sasso, Sandy Eisenberg. (1947-) First female Reconstructionist rabbi.

Schayes, Dolph. (1928-) Basketball player, coach.

Schechter, Matilde Roth. (1859-1924) Organizational head, born Germany.

Schechter, Solomon. (1849-1915) Author, educator, spiritual leader, born Romania.

Schneiderman, Rose. (1882-1972) Labor leader, workers' rights activist, born Poland.

Schönberg, Arnold. (1874-1951) Composer, conductor, born Austria.

Schwartz, Amy. (1954-) Children's author, illustrator.

Seinfeld, Jerry. (1954-) Comedian.

Sendak, Maurice. (1928-) Children's author, illustrator.

Shavelson, Clara Lemlich. (1886-1982) Workers' rights activist, born Russia.

Shaw, Artie. (1910-) Bandleader, jazz musician.

Siegel, Ben "Bugsy." (1906-1947) Gangster.

Sills, Beverly. (1929-) Opera singer. Presidential Medal of Freedom recipient.

Singer, Isaac Bashevis. (1904-1991) Author, born Poland. Nobel Prize winner.

Solomon, Haym. (1740-1785) American Revolutionary War financier, born Poland.

Soloveitchik, Joseph Dov. (1903-1993) Spiritual leader, born Poland.

Spielberg, Steven. (1947-) Filmmaker.

Spitz, Mark. (1950-) Olympic swimmer.

Stein, Gertrude. (1874-1946) Author, playwright.

Steinem, Gloria. (1934-) Journalist, women's rights activist.

Stieglitz, Alfred. (1864-1946) Photographer.

Stine, Robert Lawrence "R. L." (1943) Young adult author.

Stone, Isidor Feinstein "I. F." (1907-1989) Editor newspapers and magazines.

Strauss, Levi. (1829-1902) Entrepreneur, inventor blue jeans, born Germany.

Streisand, Barbra. (1942-) Actor, singer.

Szold, Henrietta. (1860-1945) Editor, organizational founder.

Taylor, Elizabeth. (1932-) Actor, AIDS activist.

Temin, Howard. (1934-) Medical researcher, physician, virologist. Nobel Prize winner.

Toklas, Alice B. (1877-1967) Author, partner of Gertrude Stein.

Tuchman, Barbara Wertheim. (1912-1989) Historian. Pulitzer Prize winner.

Tucker, Sophie. (1887-1966) Singer.

Ulam, Stanislaw. (1909-1984) Mathematician, physicist, born Poland.

Van Buren, Abigail. *See* Phillips, Pauline Esther.

Waksman, Selman Abraham. (1888-1973) Bacteriologist, microbiologist, medical researcher, born Russia. Nobel Prize winner.

Wald, Lillian. (1867-1940) Nurse, social worker.

Walters, Barbara. (1931-) Broadcast journalist.

Wasserstein, Wendy. (1950-) Playwright. Pulitzer Prize winner.

Wecht, Cyril. (1931-) Attorney, forensic scientist, physician.

Wiesel, Elie. (1928-) Author, Holocaust survivor, born Romania. Nobel Peace Prize winner, Presidential Medal of Freedom recipient.

Williams, Vera B. (1927-) Children's author, illustrator.

Winchell, Walt. (1897-1972) Journalist.

Wise, Isaac Mayer. (1819-1900) Reform Judaism pioneer, born Czechoslovakia.

Wise, Stephen S. (1874-1949) Spiritual leader, born Hungary.

Yalow, Rosalyn Sussman. (1921-) Medical researcher, physicist. Nobel Prize winner.

Yorinks, Arthur. (1953-) Children's author.

Zolotow, Charlotte. (1915-) Children's author, illustrator.

Jews, International

See also Hebrews, Ancient; Holocaust Figures; Israelis.

Abrabanel, Benvenida. (d. 1560) Italian political activist, scholar, born Spain.

Aguilar, Grace. (1816-1847) English author, scholar.

Ahad Ha'am. *See* Ginzberg, Asher.

Akiba ben Joseph. (c. 50-135) Hebrew scholar, spiritual leader, founder of Rabbinic Judaism.

Appelfeld, Aharon. (1932-) Ukrainian author, Holocaust survivor.

Arad, Yael. (1967-) Israeli olympic judo athlete.

Ascarelli, Devorah. (16th century) Italian poet, scholar.

Asser, Tobias. (1838-1913) Dutch attorney, peace activist.

Ba'al Shem Tov, Israel. (Israel ben Eliezer) Polish founder of Hasidic movement of Judaism.

Baeck, Leo. (1873-1956) German author, Holocaust resistance worker, survivor.

Bat Ha-Levi. (12th century) Iraqi scholar.

Begin, Menachem. (1913-1992) Israeli prime minister, born Poland. Nobel Peace Prize winner.

Ben-Gurion, David. (1886-1973) Israeli prime minister.

Ben-Yehuda, Eliezer. (1858-1922) Israeli linguist.

Bernhardt, Sarah. (1844-1923) French actor.

Born, Max. (1882-1970) English physicist, born Poland.

Brecht, Bertolt. (1898-1956) German playwright, poet.

Buber, Martin. (1878-1965) Austrian philosopher.

Caro, Joseph. (1488-1579) Scholar.

Cassin, René. (1887-1976) French attorney, human rights activist, legal scholar, UNESCO cofounder.

Chagall, Marc. (1887-1985) French painter, born Russia.

Chain, Sir Ernst Boris. (1906-1979) English biochemist, medical researcher, born Germany. Nobel Prize winner.

Da Gama, Gaspar. (1458-1526) Portuguese explorer, born Poland.

Dahia al-Kahina. (fl. 680) North African political activist, queen

Dayan, Moshe. (1915-1981) Israeli foreign minister, military leader.

Disraeli, Benjamin. (1804-1881) English prime minister.

Dulcie of Worms. (12th century) German banker, scholar.

Ehrlich, Paul. (1854-1915) German bacteriologist, medical researcher. Nobel Prize winner.

Eisenstein, Sergei. (1898-1948) Russian filmmaker.

Elijah ben Solomon. (1720-1797) Polish scholar, spiritual leader.

Ella bat Moses. (17th century) German printer.

Fink, Ida. (1921-) Israeli author, Holocaust survivor, playwright, born Poland.

Flinker, Moshe. (1926-1944) Dutch author, Holocaust victim.

Frank, Anne. (1929-1945) Dutch author, Holocaust victim, born Germany.

Frankl, Viktor E. (1905-1997) Austrian Holocaust survivor, physician, psychotherapist.

Franklin, Rosalind Elsie. (1920-1958) English molecular biologist, x-ray crystallographer.

Freud, Anna. (1895-1982) English physician, psychoanalyst, born Austria.

Freud, Sigmund. (1856-1939) Austrian physician, psychoanalyst.

Fried, Alfred. (1864-1921) Austrian journalist, peace activist, publisher. Nobel Peace Prize winner.

Frommet of Arwyller. (15th century) German scribe.

Geiger, Abraham. (1810-1874) German Reform Judaism leader.

Gela bat Moses. (18th century) German printer.

Ginzberg, Asher. (Ahad Ha'am) (1856-1922) Russian spiritual leader, Spiritual Judaism founder.

Gluckel of Hameln. (1646-1724) German author.

Gutman, Sarel. (17th century) Czech merchant.

Ghermezian, Bahman. (1946-) Canadian entrepreneur real estate, born Iran.

Ghermezian, Eskander. (1940-) Canadian entrepreneur real estate, born Iran.

Ghermezian, Nader. (1941-) Canadian entrepreneur real estate, born Iran.

Ghermezian, Raphael. (1944-) Canadian entrepreneur real estate, born Iran.

Grossman, Mendel. (1917-1945) Polish Holocaust photographer, victim.

Halevi, Judah. (1075-1141) Spanish physician, poet, scholar, spiritual leader.

Hanagid, Samuel. (993-1056) Spanish military leader, scholar.

Hanasi, Judah. (135-217) Hebrew scholar, spiritual leader.

Handali, Esther Kiera. (16th century) Turkish human rights activist.

Hensel, Fanny Mendelssohn. (1805-1847) German composer.

Herodias. (1st century C.E.) Israeli queen.

Herschel, Caroline. (1750-1848) English astronomer.

Herschel, Sir William. (1738-1822) English astronomer.

Herzl, Theodor. (1860-1904) Austrian author, journalist, born Hungary.

Heyman, Eva. (1931-1944) Hungarian author, Holocaust victim.

Hillel. (60 B.C.E.-10 C.E.) Hebrew scholar, spiritual leader.

Hirsch, Samson Raphael. (1808-1888) German author, educator.

Hirschfield, Magnus. (1868-1935) Polish gay rights activist, human rights activist, physician.

Horowitz, Sarah Rebecca Rachel Leah. (18th century) Polish scholar.

Ima Shalom. (50-?) Hebrew woman of Talmud.

Jhirad, Jerusha. (1891-1948) Indian physician.

Judith of Ethiopia. (10th century) Warrior queen.

Karpis, Alvin. (1908-1979) Canadian gangster.

Katznelson, Yitzhak. (1886-1944) Polish author, Holocaust victim, poet, political activist.

Klarsfeld, Beate. (1938-) German Nazi hunter.

Klarsfeld, Serge. (1935-) Hungarian Nazi hunter.

Korczak, Janusz. (1878-1942) Polish author, Holocaust rescuer and victim, human rights activist, physician.

Kovner, Abba. (1918-1987) Russian Holocaust resistance worker, survivor, poet.

Leibowitz, Nehama. (1905-1997) Israeli broadcast journalist, scholar.

Levi, Primo. (1919-1987) Italian author, chemist, Holocaust survivor.

Lifshitz, Aliza. (1951-) Mexican AIDS activist, author, educator, editor, physician.

Luria, Isaac. (1534-1572) Israeli educator, scholar.

Lustig, Arnost. (1926-) Czech author, Holocaust survivor, screenwriter.

Luxemburg, Rosa. (1870-1919) German political activist, revolutionary, workers' rights activist, born Poland.

Mahler, Gustav. (1860-1911) Austrian composer, conductor.

Maimonides. (Moses ben Maimon) (1135-1204) Spanish philosopher.

Mandelbrot, Benoit. (1924-) Polish mathematician.

Mansi, Paula dei. (13th century) Italian scribe, scholar.

Meir, Golda. (1898-1978) Israeli prime minister, born Russia.

Meitner, Lise. (1878-1968) Swedish nuclear physicist, born Germany.

Mendelssohn, Moses. (1729-1786) German educator, philosopher, scholar.

Metchnikoff, Élie. (1845-1916) Russian bacteriologist, physiologist.

Miriam the Scribe. (15th century) Yemenite scribe.

Mizrahi, Asenath Barazani. (16th century) Kurdistani educator, scholar.

Modligliani, Amedeo. (1884-1920) Italian painter.

Montagu, Lily. (1873-1963) English founder of Liberal Judaism.

Montefiore, Lady Judith Cohen. (1784-1862) English human rights activist, philanthropist.

Montefiore, Sir Moses. (1784-1885) English human rights activist, philanthropist.

Morpurgo, Rachel Luzzatto. (1790-1871) Italian poet.

Moses de Leon. (1240-1305) Spanish mystic, spiritual leader.

Nahmanides. (Moses ben Nahman) (1194-1270) Spanish scholar, spiritual leader.

Nasi, Dona Gracia. (1510-1568) Portuguese entrepreneur banking, shipping, philanthropist.

Noether, Emmy. (1882-1935) German mathematician.

Nostradamus. (1503-1566) French physician, visionary.

Nudel, Ida. (1931-) Russian human rights activist, political activist.

Offenbach, Jacques. (1819-1880) French composer, musician.

Pappenheim, Berta. (1859-1936) German organizational founder, social reformer, social worker.

Peres, Shimon. (1923-) Israeli prime minister, born Poland. Nobel Peace Prize winner.

Perl, Gisella. (1910-1985) Hungarian Holocaust survivor, physician.

Perlman, Itzhak. (1945-) Israeli musician.

Rabin, Yitzhak. (1922-1995) Israeli prime minister. Nobel Peace Prize winner.

Rashi. (Solomon ben Isaac) (1040-1105) French author, educator, scholar.

Rosenfeld, Bobbie. (1904-1969) Canadian olympic track and field athlete.

Rosenzweig, Franz. (1886-1939) German educator, scholar.

Rossi, Europa di. (Madame Europa) (16th century) Italian singer.

Rotblat, Joseph. (1908-) English peace activist, physicist, born Poland. Nobel Peace Prize winner.

Rubinowicz, David. (1927-1942) Polish author, Holocaust victim.

Rudashevski, Yitzak. (1927-1943) Polish author, Holocaust victim.

Saadia Gaon. (882-942) Hebrew scholar, spiritual leader.

Samuel, Sir Marcus. (1853-1927) English entrepreneur oil.

Sarah bat Tovim. (18th century) Ukrainian prayer book author.

Sarah of Yemen. (7th century) Yemenite poet.

Schnirer, Sarah. (1833-1935) Polish educator.

Senesh, Hannah. (1921-1944) Hungarian author, Holocaust resistance fighter, victim, poet.

Shapira-Luria, Miriam. (15th century) Italian educator.

Shochat, Manya. (1880-1961) Israeli settler, revolutionary, born Russia.

Slutskaya, Irina. (1979-) Russian olympic figure skater.

Stein, Aurel. (1862-1943) Hungarian archaeologist.

Sullam, Sara Coppio. (1592-1641) Italian poet, scholar.

Tiktiner, Rivkah Bat Meir "Rebecca." (16th century) Czech author.

Trotsky, Leon. (1879-1940) Russian revolutionary.

Urania of Worms, Lady. (13th century) German cantor.

Weil, Simone. (1909-1943) French author, political activist, revolutionary.

Weizmann, Chaim. (1874-1952) Israeli chemist, president, born Russia.

Wengeroff, Pauline. (1833-1916) Russian author.

Wiesenthal, Simon. (1908-) Austrian Nazi hunter, born Poland. Presidential Medal of Freedom recipient.

Wuhsha. (11th century) Egyptian businesswoman.

Yadin, Yigael. (1917-1984) Israeli archaeologist, deputy prime minister, political activist.

Zacuto, Abraham. (1452-1515) Spanish astronomer, explorer.

Zallman, Elijah ben Solomon. (1720-1797) Polish scholar, spiritual leader.

Zunz, Leopold. (1794-1886) German educator.

Jockeys
Arcaro, Eddie. (1916-1997)
Bailey, Jerry. (1957-)
Cauthen, Steve. (1960-)
Cordero, Angel, Jr. (1942-)
Day, Pat. (1953-)
Desormeaux, Kent. (1970-)
Krone, Julie. (1963-)
Murphy, Isaac. (1861-1896)
Pincay, Laffit, Jr. (1946-) born Panama.
Shoemaker, Willie. (1931-2003)
Stevens, Gary. (1963-)

Jordanians
Hussein, Ibn Talal. (1935-1999) King.

Journalists
See also Editors and Publishers.
Alsop, Joseph. (1910-1989)
Arnoldson, Klas. (1844-1916) Swedish.
Barnes, Djuna. (1892-1982)
Bennett, Lerone, Jr. (1928-)
Bernstein, Carl. (1944-)
Besant, Annie. (1847-1933) English.
Bly, Nellie. *See* Elizabeth Cochrane.
Bombeck, Erma. (1927-1996)
Brandt, Willy. (1913-1992) German.

Branting, Karl. (1860-1925) Swedish.
Brody, Jane. (1941-1987)
Bugbee, Emma. (1888-1981)
Carpenter, Iris. (unknown) English.
Cary, Mary Ann Shadd. (1822-1893)
Chennault, Anna. (1925-) born China.
Clappe, Louise Amelia. (1819-1906)
Clemens, Samuel. (Mark Twain) (1835-1910)
Cochrane, Elizabeth. (Nellie Bly) (1865-1922)
Condon, Eddie. (1905-1973)
Cornish, Samuel E. (1795-1858)
Cousins, Margaret. (1905-1996)
Cowan, Ruth. (1902-) World War II.
Craig, Daniel H. (1811-1895)
Croly, Jane Cunningham. (Jennie June) (1829-1901)
Crowe, Cameron. (1957-)
Davis, Richard Harding. (1864-1916)
Davison, Martin Robison. (1812-1885)
Day, Dorothy. (1897-1980)
Delaney, Martin Robison. (1812-1885)
Dix, Dorothy. *See* Gilmer, Elizabeth Meriwether.
Dorr, Rheta Childe. (1866-1948)
Douglass, Frederick. (1817-1895)
Dow, Charles Henry. (1851-1902)
Ducommon, Élie. (1833-1906) Swiss.
Duniway, Abigail Scott. (1834-1915)
Fern, Fanny. *See* Parton, Sara Payne.
Fernandez, Giselle. (1961-) born Mexico.
Field, Kate. (1838-1896)
Flanner, Janet. (Genét) (1892-1978)
Fortune, T. Thomas. (1856-1928)
Fried, Alfred. (1864-1921) Austrian.
Garcia, Dawn. (unknown)
Gellhorn, Martha. (1908-1998)
Genét. *See* Flanner, Janet.
Geyer, Georgie Anne. (1933-)
Gilmer, Elizabeth Meriwether. (Dorothy Dix) (1861-1951)
Gobright, Lawrence A. (1816-1879)
Godkin, Edwin L. (1831-1902) born Ireland.
Goodman, Ellen. (1941-)
Goodwin, Jan. (1944-) English.
Greeley, Horace. (1811-1872)
Haley, Alex. (1921-1992)
Hani Motoko. (1873-1957) Japanese.
Herzl, Theodor. (1860-1904) Austrian.
Hockenberry, John. (1956-)

Hull, Peggy. (1890-1967)
Johnson, James Weldon. (1871-1938)
Johnson, Samuel. (1709-1784) English.
Jones, Jennie. *See* Croly, Jane Cunningham.
Kilgallen, Dorothy. (1913-1965)
Kirkpatrick, Helen. (1909-1997)
Kisor, Henry. (1940-)
Landers, Ann. *See* Lederer, Esther Pauline.
Le Sueur, Meridel. (1900-1996)
Lederer, Esther Pauline "Eppie." (Ann
    Landers) (1918-2002)
Lee, K. W. (1928-) born Korea.
Lippmann, Walter. (1889-1974)
Lundy, Benjamin. (1789-1839)
Manley, Mary. (1663-1724) English.
McBride, Mary Margaret. (Martha Deane)
    (1899-1976)
McCormick, Anne O'Hare. (1880-1954)
McCullagh, Joseph B. (1842-1896) born
    Ireland.
McGrory, Mary. (1918-)
Meinhof, Ulrike. (1934-1976) German.
Mencken, Henry Louis "H. L." (1880-1956)
Mendoza, Juana Belen Gutierrez. (1875-
    1942) Mexican.
Moneta, Ernesto. (1833-1918) Italian.
Moss, Cynthia. (1940-)
Mossell, Gertrude Bustill. (1855-1948)
Neuharth, Allen. (1924-)
Noah, Mordecai Manuel. (1785-1851)
Ossoli, Margaret Fuller. (1810-1850)
Paddleford, Clementine Haskin. (1900-
    1967)
Paine, Thomas. (1737-1809) born England.
Parton, Sara Payson. (Fanny Fern) (1811-
    1872)
Payne, Ethel L. (1911-1991)
Phillips, Pauline Esther "Popo." (Abigail
    Van Buren) (1918-)
Pran, Dith. (1942-) born Cambodia.
Pyle, Ernest Taylor "Ernie." (1900-1945)
Quimby, Harriet. (1884-1912)
Quindlen, Anna. (1953-)
Ralph, Julian. (1853-1903)
Ramos-Horta, José. (1949-) East Timorian.
Reston, James. (1909-1995) born Scotland.
Riis, Jacob August. (1849-1914) born Den-
    mark.
Rinehart, Mary Roberts. (1876-1958)
Royall, Anne Newport. (1769-1854)
Salazar, Rubén. (1928-1970) born Mexico.

Schultz, Sigrid "Lillian." (1899-1980)
Shilts, Randy. (1951-1994)
Smith, Liz. (1923-)
Smith, Walter Wellesley "Red." (1905-
    1982)
Sorge, Richard. (1895-1944) German.
Stanley, Sir Henry Morton. (1841-1904)
    English.
Steffens, Lincoln. (1866-1936)
Steinem, Gloria. (1934-)
Stringer, Ann. (1918-1990) World War II
    correspondent.
Suetonius. (Gaius Suetonius Tranquillus)
    (69-135) Roman.
Swisshelm, Jane Grey Cannon. (1815-1884)
Tarbell, Ida. (1857-1944)
Thomas, Helen. (1920-)
Thompson, Dorothy. (1893-1961)
Tomara, Sonia. (d. 1982) born Russia.
Twain, Mark. *See* Clemens, Samuel.
Van Buren, Abigail. *See* Phillips, Pauline
    Esther.
Walker, Maggie Lena. (1867-1934)
Watson, Thomas. (1856-1922)
Wellman, Walter. (1858-1934)
Wells-Barnett, Ida B. (1862-1931)
White, William Allen. (1868-1944)
Winchell, Walter. (1897-1972)
Wolfe, Tom. (1931-)
Woodhull, Victoria. (1838-1927)
Woodward, Robert Upshur "Bob." (1943-)
Zenger, John Peter. (1697-1746) born Ger-
    many.

Judo Athletes

Arad, Yael. (1967-) Israeli.
Campbell, Ben Nighthorse. (1953-) Chey-
    enne Indian.

Jurists

Allen, Florence Ellinwood. (1884-1966)
    U.S. Appeals Court judge.
Bean, Roy. (1825-1903)
Black, Hugo. (1886-1971) Supreme Court
    justice.
Brandeis, Louis. (1856-1941) Supreme
    Court chief justice.
Esquiroz, Margarita. (1945-)
Fielding, Henry. (1707-1754) English.
Gibbs, Mifflin. (1823-1915)
Ginsburg, Ruth Bader. (1933-) Supreme

Court justice.

Harlan, John. (1833-1911) Supreme Court justice.

Hastie, William H. (1904-1976) Federal Appeals court.

Heyward, Thomas, Jr. (1746-1809) Circuit judge.

Holmes, Oliver Wendell. (1841-1935) Supreme Court justice.

Hughes, Charles Evan. (1862-1948) Supreme Court justice.

Huntingdon, Samuel. (1731-1796)

Jackson, Robert H. (1892-1954) Supreme Court justice, Nuremberg trial judge.

Jay, John. (1745-1829) Supreme Court justice.

Marshall, John. (1755-1835) Supreme Court justice.

Marshall, Thurgood. (1908-1993) Supreme Court justice.

Motley, Constance Baker. (1921-) Federal judge.

O'Connor, Sandra Day. (1930-) Supreme Court justice.

Paca, William. (1740-1795)

Paine, Robert Treat. (1731-1814)

Paterson, William. (1745-1806) Supreme Court justice, born Ireland.

Read, George. (1733-1798) Supreme Court chief justice.

Rekhmire. (fl. 1460 B.C.) Egyptian.

Sewall, Samuel. (1652-1730) Salem Witch trials judge.

Taft, William H. (1857-1930) Supreme Court justice.

Taney, Roger Brooke. (1777-1864) Supreme Court justice.

Taylor, Telford. (1908-1998) Nuremberg trial judge.

Warren, Earl. (1891-1974) Supreme Court chief justice.

Welch, Joseph. (1890-1960) McCarthy trial judge.

Weni. (fl. 2300 B.C.) Egyptian.

Wright, Jonathan Jasper. (1840-1885)

Kayakers

See Boaters; Olympic Athletes, Kayakers.

Kenyans

See also Africans; Blacks, International.

Barsosio, Sally. (1978-) Olympic track and field athlete.

Kenyatta, Jomo. (1894-1978) President, prime minister.

Leakey, Richard. (1944-) Archaeologist, paleontologist.

Maathai, Wangari. (1940-) Environmental activist, human rights activist, political activist.

Odhiambo, Thomas. (1931-2003) Entomologist.

Korean Conflict Figures

Brown, George S. (1918-1978) Air Force general.

Burke, Arleigh A. (1901-1996) Navy Chief of Naval Operations.

Campbell, Ben Nighthorse. (1933-) Cheyenne Indian soldier.

Croslin, Michael. (1933-) Air Force pilot.

Davis, Benjamin O., Jr. (1912-2002) Air Force commander.

Grissom, Virgil I. "Gus." (1926-1967) Air Force combat pilot.

Higgins, Marguerite. (1920-1966) Photojournalist.

James, Daniel "Chappie," Jr. (1920-1978) Air Force combat pilot.

Jones, Albert Jose. (unknown)

Miyamura, Hiroshi. (1925-) Army hero. Medal of Honor recipient.

Red Cloud, Mitchell, Jr. (1924-) Army hero. Medal of Honor recipient.

Rowny, Edward L. (1917-) Army general.

Thompson, William. (1927-1950) Army hero. Medal of Honor recipient.

Walt, Lewis W. (1913-1989) Marine general.

Westmoreland, William C. (1914-) Army commander.

Wilder, L. Douglas. (1931-)

Koreans

See also Immigrants to United States, Korean.

Moon, Sun Myung. (1920-) Cult leader founder of Unification Church "moonies," spiritual leader.

Sonduk. (610-647) Queen.

Kurds

Mizrahi, Asenath Barazani. (16th century)
Educator, scholar.

Saladin, Salah al-Din. (1138-1193) Military
leader, ruler, spiritual leader.

Labor Leaders

See also Workers' Rights Activists.

Anderson, Mary. (1872-1964) born Sweden.

Chávez, César. (1927-1993)

Cohen, Rose. (1880-1925)

Corona, Bert. (1918-2001)

Cremer, Sir William. (1828-1908) English.

Cruz, Philip Vera. (1904-) born Philippines.

Debs, Eugene. (1855-1926)

Durazo, Maria Elena. (1954-) born Mexico.

Gompers, Samuel. (1850-1924) born
England.

Haywood, William "Big Bill." (1869-1928)

Henderson, Arthur. (1863-1935) Scottish.

Hoffa, James R. (1913-1975)

Huerta, Dolores. (1930-)

Jones, Mary "Mother." (1830-1930) born
Ireland.

Jouhaux, Léon. (1879-1954) French.

Lewis, John L. (1880-1969)

Little, Frank. (1879-1917) Cherokee Indian.

Manalapit, Pablo. (1891-1969) Hawaiian,
born Philippines.

Randolph, Asa Philip. (1889-1979)

Rustin, Bayard. (1910?-1987)

Schneiderman, Rose. (1882-1972) born Poland.

Latin Americans

See individual countries.

Latvians

Schwab, George. (1931-) Holocaust survivor.

Lawmen

See Crime Fighters.

Lawyers

See Attorneys.

Learning Disabled

Adams, Ansel. (1902-1984) Photographer.

Ali, Muhammad. (1942-) Olympic boxer.

Bancroft, Ann. (1955-) Arctic explorer.

Beethoven, Ludwig von. (1770-1827) German composer.

Bell, Alexander Graham. (1847-1922) Inventor, born Scotland.

Burke, Chris. (1965-) Actor.

Cruise, Tom. (1962-) Actor.

Disney, Walt. (1901-1966) Filmmaker,
showman.

Einstein, Albert. (1879-1955) Physicist,
born Germany.

Eisenhower, Dwight David. (1890-1969)
Army military leader, president, World
War II Allied Military Commander.

Faraday, Michael. (1791-1867) English
chemist, inventor.

Fitzgerald, F. Scott. (1896-1940) Author.

Ford, Henry. (1863-1947) Automaker.

Galilei, Galileo. (1564-1642) Italian astronomer, mathematician, physicist.

Jackson, Andrew. (1767-1863) Congressman, president, senator.

Kennedy, John Fitzgerald. (1917-1963)
President, senator, World War II Navy
commander.

Leonard, Andy. (1968-) Weightlifter, born
Vietnam.

Leonardo da Vinci. (1452-1519) Italian architect, painter, sculptor.

Louganis, Greg. (1960-) Olympic diver.

Mozart, Wolfgang Amadeus. (1756-1791)
Austrian composer.

Pasteur, Louis. (1822-1895) French chemist,
microbiologist.

Patton, George Smith, Jr. (1885-1945)
Olympic track and field athlete, pentathlon, World War II Army general.

Picasso, Pablo. (1881-1973) Spanish ceramicist, painter, sculptor.

Sarkisian, Cherilyn. (Cher) (1946-) Singer.

Taussig, Helen Brooke. (1898-1986) Physician.

Washington, George. (1732-1799) American
Revolutionary War general, president.

Wilson, Woodrow. (1856-1924) Governor,
president.

Wright, Orville. (1871-1948) Aviation pioneer.

Wright, Wilbur. (1867-1912) Aviation pioneer.

Lebanese

See also Immigrants to United States, Lebanese.

Gibran, Kahlil. (1883-1931) Author, mystic.

Lepidopterists

Fountaine, Margaret. (1862-1940) English.

Lexicographers and Linguists

Ahyokah. (1811-?) Cherokee Indian, daughter of Sequoyah.

Ben-Yehuda, Eliezer. (1858-1922) Israeli.

Boaz, Franz. (1858-1942) German.

Burton, Sir Richard Francis. (1821-1890) English.

Deloria, Ella Cara. (1889-1971) Yankton Dakota

Johnson, Samuel. (1709-1784) English.

Pukui, Mary Kawena. (1895-1986) Hawaiian.

Schele, Linda. (1942-1998)

Schmandt-Besserat, Denise. (1933-) born France.

Sequoyah. (1770-1843) Cherokee.

Ventris, Michael. (1922-1956)

Webster, Noah. (1758-1843)

Liberians

See also Africans; Blacks, International.

Morris, Samuel. (1827-1893) Missionary.

Librarians

Bontemps, Arnaud "Arna." (1902-1973)

Bush, Laura Welch. (1946-)

Hutson, Jean Blackwell. (1914-1998)

Norton, Alice Mary. (Andre) (1912-)

Rollins, Charlemae. (1897-1979)

Libyans

Qaddafi, Muammar al-. (1942-) Military leader, terrorist

Lighthouse Keepers

Bates, Abigail. (1799-?)

Bates, Rebecca. (1795-?)

Burgess, Abbie. (1839-1892)

Colfax, Harriet. (1824-1904)

Darling, Grace. (1815-1842) English.

Fish, Emily. (1843-1931)

Fish, Juliet. (1859-1947)

Hecox, Laura. (1854-1919)

Lewis, Ida. (1842-1911)

Reynolds, Mary. (fl. 1854-1866)

Salter, Fanny. (1883-?)

Walker, Kate. (1842-1931)

Younghans, Maria. (fl. 1867-1918)

Younghans, Miranda. (fl. 1918-1929)

Linguists

See Lexicographers and Linguists.

Lithuanians

Borkowska, Anna. (c. 1900-?) Holocaust rescuer, spiritual leader.

Magicians

Armstrong, Ellen. (1914-)

Armstrong, John. (1886-1939)

Black Herman. *See* Rucker, Herman.

Brents, Frank. (1926-)

Brown, Henry "Box." (1816-?)

Caglistro, Alessandro di. (1743-1795) Italian.

Carl, William. (unknown)

Clark, Marcellus R. (d. 1971)

Copperfield, David. (1956-)

Dowling, Arthur. (d.1922)

Everett, Milton Hutchins "M. H." (mid 1800's-early 1900's)

Houdini, Harry. (1874-1926)

Hunter, Clarence. (1920-1993)

Kellar, Harry. (1849-1922)

Maskelyne, Jasper. (1902-1973) English.

Moore, Alonzo. (d. 1914)

Penn, Gillette. (Penn) (1956-)

Potter, Richard. (1783-1835)

Robert-Houdin, Jean Eugene. (1805-1871) French.

Rucker, Herman. (Black Herman) (1892-1934)

Sanders, Fetague. (1915-1992)

Teller, Raymond Joseph. (Teller) (1948-)

Marine Corps Personnel

Berg, Patty. (1918-) World War II lieutenant.

Bolden, Charles. (1946-) Pilot.

Carlson, Evans. (1896-1947) World War II
  commander.
Hayes, Ira. (1922-1955) Pim Indian World
  War II hero.
Hodges, Gil. (1924-1972) World War II.
Red Cloud, Mitchell, Jr. (1924-) Ho-Chunk
  Indian World War II.
Ross, Barney. (1907-1967) World War II
  hero.
Smith, Holland M. (1882-1967) World War
  II general.
Sousa, John Philip. (1854-1932) Bandleader.
Veeck, Bill. (1914-1986) World War II.
Walt, Lewis W. (1913-1989) World War II,
  Korean Conflict, Vietnam War.

Martial Artists
Lee, Bruce. (1940-1973)

Mathematicians
Agnesi, Maria Gaetana. (1718-1799) Italian.
Archimedes. (287-212 B.C.) Greek.
Babbage, Charles. (1791-1871) English.
Banneker, Benjamin. (1731-1806)
Bernoulli, Daniel. (1700-1782) Swiss.
Boole, George. (1815-1864) English.
Browne, Marjorie Lee. (1914-1979)
Cantor, Georg. (1845-1918) German.
Chern, Shiing-Shen. (1911-) born China.
Conway, John H. (1937-) English.
Darden, Christine. (1942-)
Descartes, René. (1596-1650) French.
du Chatelet, Marquise Gabrielle-Emilie.
  (1706-1749) French.
Euclid. (325-270 B.C.) Greek.
Euler, Leonard. (1707-1783) Swiss.
Fletcher, Alphonse "Buddy," Jr. (1966-)
Francesca, Piero Della. (c. 1415-1492) Ital-
  ian.
Galilei, Galileo. (1564-1642) Italian.
Gauss, Carl Friedrich. (1777-1855) German.
Germain, Sophie. (1776-1831) French.
Granville, Evelyn Boyd. (1924-)
Gray, Mary. (1938-)
Houbolt, John. (fl. 1960s)
Hunt, Fern. (unknown)
Hypathia. (355-415) Egyptian.
Khayyam, Omar. (1048-1131) Persian.
Khwarizmi, Abu Ja-far Muhammad Ibn
  Musa-al. (780-850) Arab.
Kovalevskaia, Sofia. (1850-1891) Russian.

Labosky, Bonnie. (unknown)
Lovelace, Lady Ada Byron. (1815-1852)
  English.
Mandelbrot, Benoit. (1924-) Polish.
Newton, Sir Isaac. (1642-1727) English.
Noether, Emmy. (1882-1935) German.
Pascal, Blaise. (1623-1662) French.
Penrose, Roger. (1931-) English.
Plato. (427-347 B.C.) Greek.
Pythagoras. (c. 530-500 B.C.) Greek.
Pytheas. (fl. 300 B.C.) Greek.
Ramanujan, Srinivasa. (1887-1920) Indian.
Reiche, Maria. (1903-1998) German.
Robinson, Julia Bowman. (1919-1985)
Rudin, Mary Ellen Estill. (1924-)
Somerville, Mary Fairfax. (1780-1872)
  Scottish.
Thomas, Valerie. (1943-)
Thomson, William. (1824-1907) Scottish.
Turing, Alan. (1912-1954) English.
Ulam, Stanislaw. (1909-1984) born Poland.
Von Neumann, John. (1903-1957) born
  Hungary.

Mayors, United States
See City Government Officials.

Medal of Honor Recipients
Baker, Vernon J. (1919-) World War II.
Benavidez, Roy. (1935-) Vietnam War.
Bulkeley, John. (1911-1996) World War II.
Carney, William H. (1840-1908) Civil War.
Doolittle, Jimmy. (1896-1993) World War
  II.
Fleetwood, Christian A. (1840-1914) Civil
  War.
Joel, Lawrence. (1928-1984) Vietnam War.
McCabe, William. (1915-1976) World War
  II.
Miyamura, Hiroshi. (1925-) Korean War.
Red Cloud, Mitchell, Jr. (1924-) Korean
  War.
Rickenbacker, Edward Vernon "Eddie."
  (1890-1973) World War I.
Rivers, Ruben. (1918-1944) World War II.
Stowers, Freddie. (1896-1918) World War I.
Thompson, William. (1927-1950) Korean
  War.
Vargas, Jay. (1937-) Vietnam War.
Walker, Mary Edwards. (1832-1919) Civil
  War.

York, Alvin. (1887-1968) World War I.

Medical Researchers

See also Inventors; Physicians.

American

Adams, Eugene W. (1920-) Cancer in dogs.

Alexander, Hattie Elizabeth. (1901-1968) Meningitis.

Andersen, Dorothy. (1901-1963) Cystic fibrosis.

Apgar, Virginia. (1909-1974) Neonatal testing.

Bath, Patricia. (1942-) Cataract removal.

Brown, Rachel. (1898-1980) Antibiotics and fungal drugs.

Cobb, Jewel Plummer. (1924-) Cells.

Collins, Daniel A. (1916-) Chromosomes, pain.

Crespi, Ann. (unknown) Machine for people with heart problems.

Croslin, Michael. (1933-) Blood pressure and pulse monitors.

Dick, Gladys Rowena. (1881-1963) Scarlet fever.

Drew, Charles Richard. (1904-1950) Blood.

Duggar, Benjamin. (1872-1956) Aureomycin antibiotic.

Ferguson, Angella D. (1925-) Sickle cell anemia in children.

Flaggs, Gail. (unknown) Cancer cells and genetic disease.

Fuller, Solomon Carter. (1872-1953) Mental illness and changes in brain cells, Alzheimers Disease, born Liberia.

Gray, Martha. (unknown) Cartilage damage.

Greatbatch, Wilson. (1919-) Pacemakers.

Griffith, Linda. (unknown) Artificial organs.

Hazen, Elizabeth. (1885-1975) Fungal drugs.

Hinton, William Augustus. (1883-1959) Syphillis testing.

Ho, David. (1952-) AIDS research.

Hoben, Patricia. (unknown) Dairy cow diseases.

Hostetter, Margaret. (unknown) Pneumonia.

Jackson, Charles T. (1805-1880) Anesthesia.

Jackson, Janis. (unknown) RAS gene in cancer.

Jordan, Lynda. (unknown) PLA2 protein.

Julian, Percy Lavon. (1899-1975) Arthritis, glaucoma.

Long, Crawford. (1815-1878) Anesthesia.

Love, Susan. (1948-) Breast cancer.

Maass, Clara. (1875-1901) Yellow fever.

Marchbanks, Vance. (1905-1988) Space science effects.

Masters, William. (1915-2001) Sexual behavior.

Morton, William T. G. (1819-1868) Ether.

Noguchi, Constance Tom. (1948-) Blood cells.

Pauling, Linus Carl. (1901-1994) Sickle cell anemia, cancer, viruses.

Pert, Candace Beebe. (1946-) AIDS, brain chemistry, opiates.

Peters, C. J. (1940-) Ebola virus.

Ramirez, Carlos A. (1953-) Pancreas.

Reed, Walter. (1851-1902) Yellow fever.

Reid, Clarice D. (1931-) Sickle cell anemia.

Sabin, Albert Bruce. (1906-1993) Polio vaccine, born Poland.

Sabin, Florence Rena. (1871-1953) Embryonic blood cells.

Salk, Jonas. (1914-1995) Polio vaccine.

Satcher, David. (1941-) Sickle cell anemia.

Scott, Roland. (1909-2002) Sickle cell anemia.

Sperry, Roger. (1913-1994) Brain.

Stevens, Nettie Marie. (1861-1912) Male-female chromosomes.

Taussig, Helen Brooke. (1898-1986) Congenital heart disease repair.

Temin, Howard. (1934-) Viruses.

Thomas, Vivien. (1910-1985)

Tonegawa, Susumu. (1939-) Immune system, born Japan.

Van Hoosen, Bertha. (1863-1952) Painless childbirth.

Villa-Komaroff, Lydia. (1944-)

Waksman, Selman Abraham. (1888-1973) Streptomycins, born Russia.

Wells, Horace. (1815-1848) Anesthesia.

Whitten, Charles. (1922-) Sickle cell anemia.

Wong-Staal, Flossie. (1947-) HIV virus, born China.

Wright, Jane Cooke. (1919-) Chemotherapy.

Wright, Louis Tompkins. (1891-1952) Schick test for diphtheria, surgical devices.

Yalow, Rosalyn Sussman. (1921-) Radioimmuno assays.

Australian and New Zealandic
Burnet, Sir Frank MacFarlane. (1899-1985) Immunity.
Florey, Lord Howard Walter. (1898-1968) Co-discoverer penicillin.
Kenny, Elizabeth. (1880-1952) Polio research.

Canadian
Abbott, Maude Elizabeth Seymour. (1869-1940) Congenital heart defects.
Banting, Sir Frederick Grant. (1891-1941) Insulin discoverer.
Bateman, Ray, Jr. (1974-) Teenage researcher.
Tsui, Lap-Chee. (1950-) Cystic fibrosis, born China.

Cuban
Finlay, Carlos Juan. (1833-1915) Yellow fever.
Guiteras, Juan. (1852-1925) Yellow fever.

Dutch
Einthoven, Willem. (1860-1927) Electrocardiogram inventor.
Leeuwenhoek, Anton van. (1632-1723) Smallpox vaccine.

English
Chain, Ernst Boris. (1906-1979) Co-discoverer penicillin.
Epstein, Sir Michael Anthony. (1921-) Epstein-Barr Disease.
Hounsfield, Sir Godfrey N. (1919-) CT scanner.
Jenner, Edward. (1749-1823) Smallpox vaccine.
Lister, Joseph. (1827-1912) Use of antisepsis in surgery.
Medawar, Sir Peter Brian. (1915-1987) Skin grafts, organ donations.
Snow, John. (1813-1858) Cholera.

French
Barré-Sinoussi, Françoise. (1947-) AIDS research.
Lanennec, Réne T. H. (1781-1826) Stethescope inventor.

Laveran, Charles Louis Alphonse. (1845-1932) Malaria.

German
Ehrlich, Paul. (1854-1915) Chemotherapy founder.
Serturner, Friedrich. (1783-1841) Morphine inventor.
Virchow, Rudolph. (1821-1902) Cells.

Hungarian
Semmelweis, Ignaz Phillipp. (1818-1865) Antiseptics in hospital care.

Irish
Burkitt, Denis Parsons. (1911-1993) Geographic patterns of disease.

Italian
Santorio, Santorio. (1561-1636) Thermometer inventor.

Nigerian
Lucas, Adetokonbo. (1931-) Leprosy.

Scottish
Fleming, Sir Alexander. (1881-1955) Penicillin co-discoverer.
Lind, James. (1716-1794) Scurvy.

Mentally Ill
See Emotionally Disabled.

Mesopotamians, Ancient
Hammurabi. (fl. 1792-1750 B.C.) King.
Sargon the Great. (c. 2300 B.C.) King.

Meteorologists
Bjerknes, Jacob. (1897-1975) born Sweden.
Diaz, Henry. (1948-)
Lorenz, Edward. (1917-)
Washington, Warren. (1936-)
Wedener, Alfred. (1880-1930) German.

Mexicans
See also Hispanic-Americans; Immigrants to United States, Mexican.
Anza, Juan Bautista de. (1735-1788). Explorer, settled California.
Avila, Bobby. (1924-) Baseball player.

Bravo, Lola Alvarez. (1907-1993) Photographer, photojournalist.

Castellanos, Rosario. (1925-1974) Author.

Cotera, Martha P. (1938-) Civil rights activist, educator, historian.

Cruz, Juana Inés de, Sister. (1651-1695) Poet, scholar, spiritual leader.

Fuentes, Carlos. (1928-) Author.

Garduño, Flor. (1957-) Photographer.

Hernandez, Maria Latigo. (1893-1986) Author, civil rights activist, political activist, television personality, born Mexico.

Jimenez y Muro, Dolores. (1848-1925) Revolutionary.

Juarez, Benito. (1806-1872) President.

Kahlo, Frida. (1907-1954) Painter.

Lifshitz, Aliza. (1951-) AIDS activist, author, editor, educator, physician.

Lozano, Ignacio E. (1886-1953) Publisher newspapers, born Mexico.

Malinche. (Malintzin) (1500-1527) Princess, slave, translator.

Martinez, Father Antonio José. (1793-1867) Educator, human rights activist, spiritual leader.

Mendoza, Juana Belen Guiterrez. (1875-1942) Journalist, revolutionary.

Montalbán, Ricardo. (1920-) Actor, born Mexico.

Montezuma II. (1466-1520) Aztec king.

Murieta, Joaquin. (1832-1853) Gold miner, outlaw, born Mexico.

Ortega, Beatriz Gonzalez. (unknown) Nurse during Revolution of 1910.

Pastrana, Julia. (1832-1860) Bearded lady.

Pico, Pio de Jesus. (1801-1894) Governor.

Rivera, Diego. (1886-1957) Painter.

Robles, Alfonso Garcíá. (1911-1991) Diplomat. Nobel Peace Prize winner.

Santana, Carlos. (1947-) Musician, born Mexico.

Seguín, Juan N. (1806-1890) Mayor San Antonio, military leader, state legislator.

Valenzuela, Fernando. (1940-) Baseball player, born Mexico.

Vera, Joseph Azlar Vitro de. (d. 1723) Military leader.

Zapata, Emiliano. (1879-1919) Revolutionary.

Microbiologists
See Biologists; Chemists.

Military Leaders
See also Air Force; American Revolutionary War Figures; Army; Civil War Figures; Gulf War Figures; Korean Conflict Figures; Marine Corps; Medal of Honor recipients; Navy; Revolutionaries; World War I Figures; World War II Figures.

African

Judith of Ethiopia. (10th century) Warrior queen.

Kruger, Paul. (1825-1904) South African Boer War general.

Shaka. (1787-1828) Zulu warrior.

American

Abrahamson, James A. (1933-)

Abrams, Creighton W. (1914-1974)

Allen, Ethan. (1738-1789)

Bradley, Omar N. (1893-1981)

Brown, George S. (1918-1978) General, Joint Chiefs of Staff.

Burke, Arleigh A. (1901-1996)

Davis, Benjamin O., Jr. (1912-2002)

Davis, Benjamin O., Sr. (1877-1970)

Eisenhower, Dwight David. (1890-1969)

Farragut, David Glasgow. (1801-1870) Navy admiral.

Geronimo. (1829-1909) Apache Indian Chief, military leader.

Goyens, William. (1794-1856) Texas Revolution.

Greene, Nathanael. (1742-1786) American Revolutionary War Army commander.

Halsey, William F. "Bull." (1882-1959) Navy commander.

Harrison, William Henry. (1773-1862) War of 1812 general.

Hayward, John T. (1908-1999) Navy admiral.

Healy, Michael A. (1839-1904) U.S. Revenue Cutter Service captain.

Horse, John. (1812-1852) Seminole Indian leader of Seminole War.

Lozen. (1840s-1890s) Apache woman warrior.

MacArthur, Douglas. (1880-1964) World
    War II army commander general.
Marshall, George Catlett. (1880-1959) Army
    Chief of Staff.
Nimitz, Chester W. (1885-1966) World War
    II navy admiral, commander of Pacific
    Fleet.
Patton, George Smith, Jr. (1885-1945)
    World War II general.
Pershing, John Joseph. (1860-1948) World
    War I general.
Pierce, Franklin. (1804-1869) Mexican War
    general.
Pike, Zebulon Montgomery. (1779-1813)
    Brigadier general War of 1812.
Pontiac. (1720-1769) Ottawa Indian.
Popé. (d. 1692) San Juan Pueblo resistance
    leader.
Powell, Colin. (1937-) Army Chair Joint
    Chiefs of Staff, Gulf War general.
Ridgway, Matthew Bunker. (1895-1993)
    Army Chief of Staff. World War II su-
    preme commander allied forces in Europe.
Rogers, Robert. (1731-1795) French-Indian
    War.
Schwarzkopf, Norman. (1934-) Gulf War
    general, Vietnam War commander.
Scott, Winfield. (1786-1866) General War
    of 1812, Mexican War.
Seguín, Juan N. (1806-1890) Mexican
    leader for Texas independence.
Sequoyah. (1770-1843) Cherokee Creek
    War soldier.
Spotted Tail. (1823-1881) Brulé Sioux war-
    rior.
Taylor, Zachary. (1784-1850) Seminole
    War, War of 1812 general.
Tecumseh. (1768-1813) Shawnee military
    leader.
Two Leggings. (fl. 1840s) Crow Indian war-
    rior.
Wally, Augustus. (unknown) Spanish
    American War buffalo soldier.
Walt, Lewis W. (1913-1989)
Weetamoo. (1640-1676) Pocasset Indian
    warrior.
Westmoreland, William C. (1914-) Korean
    War commander, Vietnam War Chief of
    Staff, World War II colonel.

Ancient Civilizations

Agrippa. (Marcus Vippsarius Agrippa) 63-
    12 B.C.) Roman general.
Ahmose. (fl. 1535 B.C.) Egyptian.
Alaric the Goth. (370-410) Romanian war-
    lord.
Alcibiades. (450-405 B.C.) Greek general.
Alexander the Great. (356-323 B.C.) Greek
    conqueror.
Antigonus I. (c. 382-301 B.C.) Greek gen-
    eral.
Antony, Marc. (Marcus Antonius) (83?-30
    B.C.) Roman general.
Camillus. (Marcus Furius Camillus) (450-
    363 B.C.) Roman general.
Constantine. (c. 280-337) Roman.
Crassus. (Marcus Licinius Crassus)
    (c. 115-53 B.C.) Roman general.
Cyrus the Great. (600-530 B.C.) Persian
    warrior.
Demetrius. (336-283 B.C.) Greek general.
Epaminondas. (410-323 B.C.) Greek.
Hadrian. (Publius Aelius Handriansu) (76-
    138) Roman general.
Hannibal. (247-183 B.C.) Carthaginian gen-
    eral.
Leonidas I. (575-450 B.C.) Greek general.
Morrigan. Celtic goddess of war.
Philip II. (383-336 B.C.) Greek general.
Pompey. (Gnaeus Pompeius Magnus) (106-
    48 B.C.) Roman general.
Ptolemy I. (Ptolemy Soter) (c. 367-283
    B.C.) Greek general.
Pyrrhus. (319-272 B.C.) Greek.
Rangada. Hindu woman warrior.
Scathach. Celtic warrior goddess.
Scipio Africanus (Publius Cornelius Scipio
    Africanus) (236-183 B/C.) Roman gen-
    eral.
Semiramis. (c. 2000 B.C.) Assyrian woman
    warrior.
Septimius Severus, Lucius. (146-211) Ro-
    man.
Solon. (610-580 B.C.) Greek warrior.
Spartacus. (109-71 B.C.) Roman gladiator.
Sulla. (Lucius Cornelius Sulla) (138-78
    B.C.) Roman general.
Themistocles. (523-463 B.C.) Greek naval
    commander.

Trajan. (Marcus Ulpius Traianus) (53-117)
  Roman general.
Weni. (fl. 2300 B.C.) Egyptian general.
Xerxes I. (519-465 B.C.) Persian general.

Arab, Iranian, Islamic, Mongolian, Russian,
  and Turk
Abu Bakr. (1050-1087) Islamic general.
Babur, Zahir un-Din Muhammed. (Babur
  the Conqueror) (1483-1530) Indian
  Mughal general.
Bayerzid I. (1354-1403) Turk.
Belisaurius. (505-565) Byzantian.
Genghis Khan. (1165-1227) Mongol gen-
  eral, conqueror.
Ibn al-Walid, Khalid. (d. 642) Arab general.
Ibn Ziyad, Tariq. (d. 700) Arab Berber gen-
  eral.
Mansur, Abu Jafar ibn Muhammad al-.
  (714-775) Islamic leader Muslim Empire.
Mehmed II. (1482-1481) Mongol conqueror.
Nevsky, Alexander. (1220-1263) Russian
  warrior hero.
Qaddafi, Muammar-al. (1942-) Libyan
  leader, terrorist.
Saladin, Salah al-Din. (1138-1193) Kurdish
  Muslim.
Subotai. (1176-1248) Mongol general.
Suleiman I, the Magnificient. (1494-1566)
  Turkish warrior.
Surovov, Aleksandr. (1792-1800) Russian
  commander.
Tamerlane. (1336-1405) Mongol conqueror.
Zhukov, Georgi. (1896-1974) Russian gen-
  eral.

Asian
Aguinaldo, Emilio. (1869-1964) Philippine
  leader, revolutionary.
Bai, Lakshmi. (1830- 1858) Indian, dis-
  guised as man.
Ban Chao. (d. 102) Chinese.
Chiang Kai-Shek. (1887-1975) Chinese.
Giap, Vo Nguygen. (1911-) Vietnamese.
Hua Mu-lan. (c. 400) Chinese.
Mao Tse Tung. (1893-1976) Chinese.
Minamoto, Yoritomo. (1147-?) Japanese
  samurai warrior.
Minamoto, Yoshitsune. (1160-?) Japanese

samurai warrior.
Nobunaga, Oda. (1534-1582) Japanese sho-
  gun warrior.
Saigo, Takemori. (1827-1877) Japanese
  samurai warrior.
Togo, Heihachiro. (1848-1934) Japanese
  naval leader.
Trung Nhi. (14-43) Vietnamese warrior
  queen.
Trung Trac. (14-43) Vietnamese warrior
  queen.
Yamamoto, Isoroku. (1884-1943) Japanese;
  led attack on Pearl Harbor.
Zheng He. (1371-1433) Chinese admiral.

Canadian
Iberville, Pierre le Moyne de. (1661-1706)
  born France.

English and British
Alfred the Great. (849-901) English.
Boru, Brian. (941-1014) Irish warrior.
Bruce, Robert. (1274-1329) Scottish war-
  rior.
Burgoyne, John. (1723-1792) English.
Burton, Sir Richard Francis. (1821-1890)
  English.
Churchill, John. (1650-1722) English.
Cromwell, Oliver. (1599-1658) English gen-
  eral.
Drake, Sir Francis (1540-1596) English.
Edward I. (1239-1307) English.
Fegen, Edward Fogarty. (1895-1940)
  English navy commander.
Gwendolen. (fl. 1075-1060 B.C.) Warrior
  queen.
Howe, William. (1729-1814) English.
Lloyd George, David. (1863-1945) World
  War I.
Montgomery, Bernard. (1887-1976) English
  World War I, World War II field marshal.
Nelson, Horatio. (1758-1805) English navy
  leader.
Richard I. (The Lion Hearted) (1157-1199)
  English warrior.
Wellesley, Arthur. (1880-1959) English.
William I, The Conqueror. (1027-1087)
  English general.
Wolfe, James. (1727-1759) English.

European

Agustin, Maria. (La Saragossa) (1786-1857) Spanish.

Alvarez de Toledo, Fernando. (Duke of Alva) (1507-1583) Spanish.

Attila the Hun. (400-453) German.

Bonaparte, Napoleon. (1768-1821) French conqueror.

Buade, Louis de. (1622-1698) French.

Carnot, Lazare Nicolas Marguerite. (1753-1823) French.

Charlemagne. (742-814) French conqueror.

Cid Campedor, El. (Rodrigo Diaz de Viver) (1043-1099) Spanish.

Clausewitz, Karl von. (1780-1831) German.

Clémenceau, Georges. (1841-1929) French.

Clovis. (466-511) French.

Danton, Georges. (1759-1794) French.

De Gaulle, Charles. (1890-1970) French general.

Garibaldi, Giuseppe. (1807-1882) Italian.

Guderian, Heinz. (1888-1954) German.

Guiscard, Robert. (1015-1085) French Norman warrior.

Hanagid, Samuel. (993-1056) Spanish army leader.

Hindenburg, Paul von. (1847-1934) German World War I leader.

Ignatius of Loyola. (1491-1556) Spanish.

Joan of Arc. (1412-1431) French.

La Tour, Charles Turquis de Sainte-Étienne de. (1593-1666) French military leader.

John III Sobieski. (1624-1696) Polish army commander.

Lafayette, Marie Joseph Paul Yves Roch Gilbert du Motier, Marquis de. (1757-1834) French.

Louis II de Bourbon. (1621-1686) French army commander.

Martel, Charles. (689-741) French.

Maurice of Nassau. (Prince of Orange) (1567-1625) Dutch.

Pétain, Henri Phillipe. (1856-1951) French World War I, World War II leader.

Pizarro, Francisco. (1475-1541) Spanish conqueror.

Richthofen, Baron Manfred von "Red Baron." (1892-1918) German aviator.

Sichelgaita. (d. 1090) Italian.

Theodoric the Great. (454-526) Roman conqueror.

Tromp, Maarten von. (1597-1653) Dutch naval admiral.

Vauban, Sebastien de preste de. (1633-1707) French.

Von Manstein, Erich. (1887-1973) German field marshal, anti-Nazi.

Von Moltke, Helmut. (1800-1891) German.

Wallenstein, Albrecht von. (1583-1634) Bohemian soldier.

Wilhelm II. (1859-1941) German general.

William I, The Silent. (Prince of Orange) (1533-1584) Dutch.

Ziska, Jan. (1358-1424) Bohemian.

Latin

Vera, Joseph Azlor Vitro de. (d. 1723) Mexican leader, defender of Texas.

Middle Eastern

Arafat, Yasir. (1929-) Palestinian.

Dayan, Moshe. (1915-1981) Israeli.

Lawrence, Thomas Edward. (Lawrence of Arabia) (1888-1935)

Leo III, the Isaurian. (680-741) Syrian.

Scandinavian

Gustavus Adolphus II. (1594-1632) Swedish.

Canute II. (994-1035) Danish.

Mineralogists

Hess, Harry. (1906-1969)

Missionaries

See also Spiritual Leaders.

Andrew, Brother. (1928-) Dutch.

Aylward, Gladys. (1902-1970) English.

Barnardo, Thomas. (1845-1905) Irish.

Bojaxhiu, Agnes. (Mother Teresa) (1910-1997) Indian, born Yugoslavia.

Boniface. (672-754) German.

Brebeuf, Jean de, Father. (1593-1649) French.

Carmichael, Amy. (1867-1951) Irish.

Cobb, Geraldyn. (1931-)

Columba, Saint. (521-597)

Cyril, Saint. (827-869) Greek.

De Smet, Pierre Jean. (1801-1873) born Belgium.

De Veuster, Joseph. (Father Damien) (1840-1889) Belgian.

Eliot, John. (1604-1690) English.
Elliot, Jim. (1927-1956)
George, Eliza Davis. (1879-1979)
Goforth, Jonathan. (1859-1936) Canadian.
Goforth, Rosalind Smith. (1864-1942) Canadian.
Greene, Betty. (1920-1997)
Jones, Charles Wesley. (1900-1986)
Judson, Adoniram. (1788-1850)
Judson, Ann Hasseltine. (unknown)
Kino, Eusebio. (1645-1711) Austrian.
Leigh, Samuel. (1785-1852) English.
Liddell, Eric. (1902-1945) Scottish.
Livingstone, David. (1813-1873) Scottish.
Marcos de Niza, Fray. (1495-1558) Spanish.
Marquette, Jacques. (1637-1675) French.
Moon, Lottie. (1840-1912)
Morris, Samuel. (1827-1906) Liberian.
Mott, John Raleigh. (1865-1955)
Paton, John G. (1824-1906) Scottish.
Ricci, Matteo. (1552-1610) Italian.
Ridderhof, Joy. (1903-1984)
Rijnhart, Susie Carson. (1868-1908) Canadian.
Sauñe, Rómulo. (1953-1992) Peruvian Quechua Indian.
Schweitzer, Albert. (1875-1965) French.
Serra, Father Junipero. (1713-1784) Spanish.
Slessor, Mary. (1848-1915) Scottish.
Spoerry, Anne. (1918-1999) French.
Stam, Betty. (d. 1934)
Stam, John. (d. 1934)
Swain, Clara A. (1834-1910)
Taylor, James Hudson. (1832-1905) English.
Teresa, Mother. *See* Bojaxhiu, Agnes.
Townsend, Cameron. (1896-1982)
Veniaminov, Innokentii. (1797-1879) Russian.
Whitman, Marcus. (1802-1847)
Whitman, Narcissa. (1808-1847)
Wurmbrand, Richard. (1909-2001) Romanian.
Xavier, Francis. (1506-1552) Portuguese.
Zeisberger, David. (1721-1808) born Moravia.

Mixed-Media Artists
Hammons, David. (1943-)
Howard, Mildred. (1945-)

Moxon, June. (unknown)
Paik, Nam June. (1932-) born Korea.
Saar, Alison. (1956-)
Saar, Betye. (1926-)
Teters, Charlene. (1952-) Spokane Indian.

Models, Art, and Fashion
Campbell, Naomi. (1970-)
Ford, Eileen. (1922-)
Giaconda, Lisa. (1479-1509) Italian model for Mona Lisa.
Rossetti, Christina Georgina. (1830-1894) English.
Sims, Naomi. (1949-)
Whitestone, Heather. (1973-) Beauty queen.

Mongols
Babur, Zahir un-Din Muhammed. (Babur the Conqueror) (1483-1530) Indian Mughal military leader.
Genghis Khan. (1165-1227) Military conqueror.
Kublai Khan. (1215-1294) Emperor.
Mehmed II. (1432-1481) Conqueror.
Subotai. (1176-1248) General.
Tamerlane. (1336-1405) Conqueror.

Mountaineers
Benham, Gertrude. (1867-1938) English.
Brower, David. (1912-2000)
Hill, Lynn. (1961-) Rock climber.
Hillary, Sir Edmund. (1919-) New Zealand.
Irvine, Andrew. (1896-1924) English.
Mallory, George. (1886-1924) English.
Mazuchelli, Nina. (1832-1914) English.
Messner, Reinhold. (1944-) Italian.
Norgay, Tenzig. (1914-1986) Nepalese.
Peck, Annie Smith. (1850-1935)
Tabei Junko. (1939-) Japanese.
Thayer, Helen. (1938-) born New Zealand.
Vaux-Walcott, Mary. (1860-1940) Canadian.
Weihenmayer, Eric. (1968-)
Workman, Fanny Bullock. (1859-1925)

Mozambicans
See also Africans; Blacks, International.
Machel, Gracia Simbone. (1945-) Children's rights activist.

Musical Groups
Beach Boys.
Beatles.
C Note.
Doors.

Musicians
See also Bandleaders; Composers; Conductors; Singers; Songwriters.

Classical
Albéniz, Isaac. (1860-1909) Spanish.
Babbitt, Milton. (1916-)
Bach, Johann Sebastian. (1685-1750) German.
Casals, Pablo. (1876-1973) born Spain.
Chung, Myung-Whun. (1953-) born Korea.
Crumb, George. (1929-)
Dowland, John. (1562-1626) English.
Gabrieli, Andrea. (1510-1586) Italian.
Grieg, Edvard. (1843-1907) Norwegian.
Heifetz, Jascha. (1901-1987) born Russia.
Ma, Yo-Yo. (1955-) born France.
Macdonald, Flora. (1722-1790) Scottish.
MacDowell, Edward. (1861-1908)
Midori. (1971-) Japanese.
Mussorgsky, Modest Petrovich. (1839-1881) Russian.
Nicholson, Vanessa-Mae. (1978-) English.
Offenbach, Jacques. (1819-1880) French.
O'Hara, Mary. (1935-) Irish.
Okita, Dwight. (1958-)
Paganini, Niccolo. (1782-1840) Italian.
Paradis, Maria Theresia von. (1759-1824) Austrian.
Perlman, Itzhak. (1945-) Israeli.
Rameau, Jean-Philippe. (1683-1764) French.
Scarlatti, Domenico. (1685-1757) Italian.
Schumann, Clara. (1819-1896) German.
Schumann, Robert. (1810-1856) German.
Schweitzer, Albert. (1875-1965) French.
Stradivari, Antonio. (1644-1737) Italian.
Zwilich, Ellen. (1939-)

Jazz and Blues
Akiyoshi, Toshiko. (1929-) born China.
Alden, Howard. (1948-)
Allen, Geri. (1957-)
Allen, Henry "Red." (1908-1967)
Ammons, Albert. (1907-1949)

Armstrong, Louis. (1901-1971)
Ashby, Irving. (1920-1987)
Barbarin, Louis. (1902-1997)
Barker, Danny. (1908-1994)
Basie, William "Count." (1904-1984)
Bauduc, Ray. (1909-1988)
Bauer, Billy. (1915-)
Bechet, Sidney. (1897-1959)
Beiderbecke, Leon "Bix." (1903-1931)
Benson, George. (1943-)
Bernstein, Peter. (1907-)
Bertoncini, Gene. (1937-)
Bethune, Thomas "Blind Tom" Greene. (1849-1908)
Blackman, Cindy. (1959-)
Blake, James Hubert "Eubie." (1883-1983)
Blakey, Art. (1919-1990)
Blanton, Jimmy. (1918-1942)
Bolden, Buddy. (1868-1931)
Braud, Wellman. (1891-1966)
Braxton, Anthony. (1945-)
Brecht, Sidney. (1897-1959)
Becker, Michael. (1949-)
Broonzy, "Big" Bill. (1893-1959)
Brown, James. (1933-)
Brown, Ray. (1926-2002)
Brown, Steve. (1890-1965)
Bunn, Teddy. (1909-1978)
Burrell, Kenny. (1931-)
Byrd, Charlie. (1925-1999)
Callendar, George "Red." (1916-)
Carter, Benny. (1907-)
Carter, Ron. (1937-)
Casey, Al. (1915-)
Catlett, "Big" Sid. (1910-1951)
Chambers, Paul. (1935-1969)
Charles, Ray. (1930-2004)
Christian, Charlie. (1916-1942)
Clarke, Kenny. (1914-1985)
Clarke, Kim. (1954-)
Cole, Nat King. (1916-1965)
Cole, William "Cozy." (1909-1981)
Coleman, Ornette. (1930-)
Coltrane, John. (1926-1967)
Condon, Eddie. (1905-1973)
Corea, Anthony "Chick." (1941-)
Crawford, Jimmy. (1910-1980)
Crosby, Israel. (1919-1962)
Davis, Miles Dewey III. (1926-1991)
Davis, Richard. (1930-)
Dede, Edmund. (1827-1903)

Dodds, Warren "Baby." (1898-1959)
Dolphy, Eric. (1928-1964)
Dorsey, James "Jimmy." (1904-1957)
Dorsey, Thomas "Tommy." (1905-1956)
Dorsey, Thomas Andrew. (1899-1993)
Douglas, Lizzie. (Memphis Minnie) (1897-1973)
Durham, Eddie. (1906-1987)
Duvivier, George. (1920-1985)
Eldridge, Roy. (1911-1989)
Ellington, Edward Kennedy "Duke." (1899-1974)
Ellis, Herb. (1921-)
Eubanks, Kevin. (1957-)
Europe, James Reese. (1881-1939)
Evans, William "Bill." (1929-1980)
Farlow, Tal. (1921-1998)
Foster, George Murphy "Pops." (1892-1969)
Garbarek, Jan. (1947-) Norwegian.
Getz, Stan. (1927-1991)
Gillepsie, John Birks "Dizzy." (1917-1993)
Gomez, Eddie. (1944-)
Goodman, Benjamin David "Benny." (1909-1986)
Green, Freddie. (1911-1987)
Green, Grant. (1931-1978)
Greer, William Alexander "Sunny." (1895?-1982)
Grimes, Lloyd " Tiny." (1916-1989)
Guy, Fred. (1897-1971)
Haden, Charlie. (1937-)
Hall, Al. (1915-)
Hall, Jim. (1930-)
Hancock, Herbie. (1940-)
Handy, William Christopher. (1873-1958)
Hawkins, Coleman. (1904-1969)
Hayes, Isaac. (1943-)
Haynes, Ray. (1925-)
Heard, J. C. (1917-1988)
Heath, Percy. (1923-)
Henderson, Fletcher. (1897-1952)
Hines, Earl "Fatha." (1903-1983)
Hinton, Milt. (1910-2000)
Holland, Dave. (1946-) English.
Holley, Major. (1924-1991)
Jackson, "Blind Lemon." (1897-1930)
Jarrett, Keith. (1945-)
Johnson, Bill. (c. 1870)
Johnson, James P. (1891-1976)
Johnson, Lonnie. (1889-1970)
Jones, Elvin. (1927-)

Jones, Jonathan "Papa Jo." (1911-1985)
Jones, Quincy. (1933-)
Jones, Sam. (1924-1981)
Joplin, Scott. (1868-1917)
Kelly, Wynton. (1931-1971) born Jamaica.
Kessel, Barney. (1923-)
King, B. B. (1925-)
Kirby, John. (1908-1952)
Krupa, Gene. (1900-1973)
Kuramato, June. (1948-) born Japan.
La Faro, Scott. (1940-1969)
Lang, Eddie. (1903-1933)
Ledbetter, Huddy "Leadbelly." (1885-1949)
Leitch, Peter. (1944-) Canadian.
Lindsay, John. (1894-1950)
Lowe, Mundell. (1922-)
Malone, Russell. (1963-)
Mantilla, Ray. (1934-)
Marsalis, Wynton. (1961-)
Martino, Pat. (1944-)
McBee, Cecil. (1935-)
McClure, Ron. (1941-)
McGibbon, Al. (1919-)
McKinley, Ray. (1910-1995)
McLaughlin, John. (1942-) English.
McRae, Carmen. (1922-1994)
McTell, "Blind" Willie. (1901-1959)
Mingus, Charles. (1922-1979)
Mitchell, Keith Moore "Red." (1927-1992)
Monk, Thelonius. (1917-1982)
Montgomery, Monk. (1921-1982)
Montgomery, Wes. (1925-1968)
Moore, Oscar. (1916-1981)
Morton, Ferdinand Joseph "Jelly Roll." (1885-1941)
Mraz, George. (1945-) Czech.
Mulligan, Gerald "Gerry." (1927-1996)
Murray, David. (1955-)
Oliver, Joseph "King" (1885-1938)
Orsted Pedersen, Niels-Henning. (unknown) Norwegian.
Osborne, Mary. (1921-1992)
Page, Walter. (1900-1957)
Palmier, Remo. (1923-2002)
Parker, Charles Christopher "Bird" Jr. (1920-1955)
Pass, Joe. (1929-1994)
Pastorius, Jaco. (1951-1987)
Paul, Les. (1916-)
Peacock, Gary. (1935-)
Peterson, Oscar. (1925-) Canadian.

Pettiford, Oscar. (1927-1960)
Pizzarelli, John, Jr. (1960-)
Pollack, Ben. (1903-1971)
Potter, Tommy. (1918-1988)
Powell, Earl "Bud." (1924-1966)
Pozo, Chano. (1915-1948) born Cuba.
Puente, Tito. (1923-2000)
Raney, Jimmy. (1927-1995)
Redman, Joshua. (1969-)
Reid, Rufus. (1944-)
Reinhardt, Django. (1910-1953) Belgian.
Reuss, Allan. (1915-1988)
Rich, Buddy. (1917-1987)
Roach, Max. (1924-)
Robinson, Daniel Louis "Satchmo." (1900?-
    1971)
Rollins, Theodore Walter "Sonny." (1930-)
Russell, Curly. (1917-1986)
Safransky, Eddie. (1914-1974)
Salvador, Sal. (1925-1999)
Sharpe, Avery. (1954-)
Shaw, Artie. (1910-)
Simmons, John. (1918-1979)
Simone, Nina. (1933-2003)
Simpkins, Andy. (1932-1999)
Singleton, Arthur "Zutty." (1898-1975)
Slocum, Melissa. (1961-)
Smith, Floyd. (1917-1982)
Smith, Jabbo. (1908-1991)
Smith, Johnny. (1922-1997)
Stewart, Leroy Elliot "Slam." (1914-1987)
Strayhorn, Billy. (1915-1967)
Swallow, Steve. (1940-)
Tatum, Art. (1910-1956)
Taylor, Billy, Jr. (1925-1977)
Taylor, Cecil. (1929-)
Tough, Davey. (1907-1948)
Tyner, McCoy. (1938-)
Unthan, Hermann. (1848-1929)
Vaughan, Sarah. (1924-1991)
Vinnegar, Leroy. (1928-1999)
Waller, Thomas Wright "Fats." (1904-1943)
Waters, McKinley Morganfield "Muddy."
    (1915-1983)
Wayne, Chuck. (1923-1997)
Webb, William Henry "Chick." (1909-1939)
Wettling, George. (1907-1968)
Whitfield, Mark. (1966-)
Williams, Mary Lou. (1910-1981)
Williams, Tony. (1945-1997)
Wilson, Theodore "Teddy." (1912-1986)

Wonder, Stevie. (1950-)
Wright, Eugene. (1923-)
Young, Lester Willis. (1909-1959)
Zawinul, Joe. (1932-) born Austria.
Zollar, Attila. (1927-1998) born Hungary.

Rock
Beach Boys.
Beatles. English.
Berry, Chuck. (1926-)
Byrne, David. (1952-) born Scotland.
Cobain, Kurt. (1967-1994)
Doors.
Hendrix, Jimi. (1942-1970)
Joplin, Janis. (1943-1970)
Lennon, John. (1940-1980) English.
Lydon, John Joseph. (Johnny Rotten)
    (1956-)
Mercury, Freddie. (1946-1991) English.
Springsteen, Bruce. (1949-)

Other
Boyd, Liona. (1949-) Canadian guitarist.
Cugat, Xavier. (1900-1990) Spanish music.
Liliuokalani, Lydia. (1838-1917) Hawaiian
    folk music.
Mirabal, Robert. (unknown) Taos Indian
    musician.
Monroe, Bill. (1911-1996) Bluegrass musi-
    cian.
Rodgers, Richard. (1902-1979) Show music.
Santana, Carlos. (1947-) Latin music, born
    Mexico.

Muslims
Abu Bakr. (1050-1087) Islamic general.
Africanus, Leo. (Giovannie Leone) (1495-
    1553) Spanish explorer.
al-Ghazali. (1058-1111) Islamic Iranian
    spiritual leader.
Cyrus the Great. (600-530 B.C.) Iranian
    (Persian) warrior.
Hardaga, Mustafa. (unknown) Holocaust
    rescuer.
Ibn al-Walid, Khalid. (d. 642) Arab general.
Ibn- Battuta, Muhammad. (1304-1369)
    Berber adventurer, explorer, born Mo-
    rocco.
Ibn-e-Sina, Hakim. (980-1037) Islamic phy-
    sician.
Ibn Ziyad, Tariq. (d. 700) Arab Berber gen-

eral.

Kabir. (1440-1518) Indian poet, philosopher.

Khomeini, Ayatollah Ruhollah. (1900-1989) Iranian religious and political leader.

Mansur, Abu Jafar ibn Muhammad al-. (714-775) Military leader.

Muhammad. (570?-632) Arab prophet, founder of Islam religion.

Razia, Sultana. (f. 1236-1240) Indian princess.

Saladin, Salah al-Din. (1138-1193) Kurdish ruler, sultan Egypt and Syria.

Mystics

See Psychics, Mystics, and Visionaries.

Native American Rights Activists

Bonnin, Gertrude Simmons. (1876-1938) Yankton Dakota.

Conley, Helena. (1867-1958) Wyandotte.

Conley, Ida. (1862-1948) Wyandotte.

Conley, Lyda. (1869-1946) Wyandotte.

Deer, Ada. (1935-) Menominee.

Deloria, Vine, Jr. (1939-) Yankton Dakota.

Harris, LaDonna. (1931-) Comanche.

Johnson, William. (1714-1774) English, Superintendent of Indian Affairs.

Joseph, Chief. (1840-1904) Nez Percé.

Little, Frank. (1879-1917) Cherokee Indian.

Lockwood, Belva Ann. (1830-1917)

Mourning Dove. (Christine Quintasket) (1888-1936) Okanogan Indian.

Parker, Ely Samuel. (1828-1895) Commissioner of Indian Affairs.

Sainte-Marie, Buffy. (1941-) Cree Indian, born Canada.

Seton, Ernest Thompson. (1860-1946) born England.

Teters, Charlene. (1952-) Spokane Indian.

Tibbles, Suzette LaFlesche. (1854-1903) Ponca and Omaha Indian.

Winema. (Tobey Riddle) (1836-1932) Modoc Indian.

Winnemucca, Sarah. (1844-1891) Paiute Indian.

Native Americans

See also Chiefs, Native American; Native American Rights Activists.

Abrams, George. (1939-) Seneca anthropologist.

Ahyokah. (1811-?) Cherokee linguist, daughter of Sequoyah.

Alexie, Sherman. (1966-) Spokane-Coeur author, poet, screenwriter.

Aliquipso. (unknown) Oneida legendary heroine.

Allen, Paula Gunn. (1939-) Laguna Pueblo/Sioux author, poet.

Ballard, Louis. (1931-) Quapaw and Cherokee composer.

Begay, Fred. (1932-) Navajo and Ute physicist.

Bender, Charles Albert "Chief." (1884-1954) Chippewa baseball player.

Black Elk. (1863-1950) Oglala Lakota Sioux mystic and medicine man, showman.

Black Kettle. (1807-1868) Cheyenne chief, peace activist.

Bonga, George. (1802-1880) Ojibwa fur trader.

Bonnin, Gertrude Simmons. (1876-1938) Yankton Dakota author, Native American rights activist, reformer.

Boudinot, Elias. (1800-1839) Cherokee editor newspaper.

Brant, Joseph. (1742-1807) Mohawk war chief, American Revolutionary War patriot.

Brant, Mary "Molly." (Degonwadonti) (1736-1796) Mohawk American Revolutionary War patriot.

Buck, Rufus. (d. 1896) Gang leader.

Campbell, Ben Nighthorse. (1933-) Cheyenne jewelry designer, Korean Conflict hero, Olympic judo athlete, senator.

Chuka. (c. 1890) Hopi boy sent to boarding school.

Cochise. (1812-1874) Apache chief.

Conley, Helena. (1867-1958) Wyandotte Native American rights activist.

Conley, Ida. (1862-1948) Wyandotte Native American rights activist.

Conley, Lyda. (1869-1946) Wyandotte attorney, Native American rights activist.

Cornstalk. (1720-1777) Shawnee warrior.

Crazy Horse. (1841-1877) Lakota Oglala Sioux chief.

Crowfoot. (1821-1890) Blackfoot chief, peace activist.

Crown, Frank Fools. (1890-1989) Oglala spiritual leader.

Deer, Ada. (1935-) Menominee attorney, Native American rights activist, Assistant Secretary of Indian Affairs, social worker.

Deganwidah. (c. 1400) Huron chief, peace activist.

Deloria, Ella Cara. (1889-1971) Yankton Dakota anthropologist, linguist.

Deloria, Philip Sam. (unknown) Yankton Dakota attorney.

Deloria, Vine, Jr. (1939-) Yankton Dakota author, Native American rights activist.

Deloria, Vine, Sr. (1901-1990) Yankton Dakota spiritual leader.

Denetclaw, Wilfred F., Jr. (1959-) Navajo geologist.

Dockstader, Frederick L. (1919-1998) Oneida and Navajo anthropologist, author, silversmith artist.

Dukepoo, Frank C. (1943-) Hopi educator.

Eastman, Charles Alexander. (1858-1939) Santee Dakota author, physician.

Echohawk, Brummett. (1922-) Pawnee actor, author, painter, World War II hero.

Echohawk, John. (1945-) Pawnee attorney.

Echohawk, Larry. (1948-) Pawnee attorney, state legislator.

Erdrich, Louise. (1954-) Chippewa author.

Garcia. (fl. 1813) Seminole War soldier.

Geronimo. (1829-1909) Apache chief.

Goldsby, Crawford. (1876-1896) Cherokee criminal.

Handsome Lake. (1735-1818) Iroquois prophet, spiritual leader.

Harris, LaDonna. (1931-) Comanche Native American rights activist.

Hayenwatha. (c. 1400) Mohawk chief, peace activist.

Hayes, Ira. (1922-1955) Pim World War II Marine hero.

Hiawatha. (fl. 1440) Iroquois chief, spiritual leader, legendary.

Horse, John. (1812-1852) Black Seminole military leader.

Howe, Oscar. (1915-1983) Yankton Dakota painter.

Ishi. (1862-1916) Yani Indian.

John Stands in Timber. (1884-1967) Cheyenne historian.

Johnson, Kory. (1979-) Environmental activist, half Native American.

Joseph, Chief. (1840-1904) Nez Percé chief, Native American rights activist.

Juarez, Benito. (1806-1872) Zapotec president of Mexico.

Kintpuash. (Captain Jack) (1837-1873) Modac chief.

La Flesche, Francis. (1857-1932) Ponca and Omaha anthropologist, author.

Lang, Naomi. (1978-) Karuk olympic figure skater.

Little, Frank. (1879-1917) Cherokee labor leader, Native American rights activist, workers' rights activist.

Little Raven. (d. 1889) Arapaho chief.

Lone Dog. (Shunka-Ishnala) (1780-1871) Yankton Dakota historian.

Lowry, Judith. (1948-) Pit River painter.

Lozen. (1840s-1890s) Apache woman warrior.

Luther Standing Bear. (1868-1937) Oglala Lakota Sioux chief.

Mankiller, Wilma. (1945-) Cherokee chief. Presidential Medal of Freedom recipient.

Martinez, Julian. (1897-1943) San Idlefonso Pueblo potter.

Martinez, Maria Montoya. (1887-1980) San Idlefonso Pueblo potter.

Massasoit. (1600-1661) Wampanoag chief.

McCabe, William. (1915-1976) World War II Navajo code talker.

Metacomet. See Philip, King.

Mills, Billy. (1938-) Oglala Lakota Sioux olympic track and field athlete.

Minoka-Hill, Lillie Rosa. (1876-1952) Mohawk physician.

Mirabal, Robert. (unknown) Taos musician, painter.

Momaday, N. Scott. (1934-) Kiowa author, painter. Pulitzer Prize winner.

Mourning Dove. (Christine Quintasket) (1888-1936) Okanogan author, Native American rights activist.

Musgrove, Mary. (1700-1763) Creek interpreter.

Naranjo, Michael. (1944-) Pueblo sculptor, Vietnam War soldier.

Occom, Samuel. (1723-1792) Oneida Indian spiritual leader.

Opechancanough. (1556-1646) Pamunkey Lenape chief.

Ortiz, Simon. (1941-) Acoma Indian author, poet.

Osceola. (1804-1838) Seminole chief.

Ouray. (1820-1880) Ute chief.

Parker, Ely Samuel. (1828-1895) Seneca chief, Civil War assistant to General Grant, Commisioner of Indian Affairs.

Parks, Paul. (1923-) Civil engineer, Holocaust rescuer, World War II soldier.

Philip, King. (Metacom, Metacomet, Pometacom) (1638-1676) Wampanoag chief.

Pickett, Bill. (1870-1932) Cheyenne and African-American rodeo rider.

Picotte, Susan LaFlesche. (1865-1915) Ponca and Omaha physician.

Pocahontas. (1595?-1617) Powhatan princess.

Pometacom. *See* Philip, King.

Pontiac. (1720-1769) Ottawa chief and military leader.

Poodry, Clifton. (1943-) Seneca biologist, educator, geneticist.

Pop-Pank. (1790-?) Friend of Sacagawea.

Popé. (c. 1650- 1692) San Juan Pueblo medicine man, military leader.

Powhatan. (1550-1618) Algonguin Lenape chief, colonist.

Pretty Shield. (1850-1930) Crow healing woman.

Rahr, Tammy. (unknown) Cayuga beadworker.

Red Cloud. (1822-1909) Lakota Sioux chief.

Red Cloud, Mitchell, Jr. (1924-) Ho-Chunk World War II Marine, Korean Conflict Army hero. Medal of Honor recipient.

Red Jacket. (1756-1830) Seneca chief, orator.

Reifel, Ben. (1906-1990) Brule Lakota congressman, World War II lieutenant colonel.

Rogers, Will. (1879-1935) Cherokee actor, author, showman.

Romero, Jacy. (1965-) Chumash dancer.

Rose, Edward. (1780?-1820?) Frontiersman, fur trapper.

Ross, John. (1790-1866) Cherokee chief.

Sacagawea. (1788-1884) Lemhi Shoshone guide and interpreter.

Sainte-Marie, Buffy. (1941-) Cree actor, Native American rights activist, peace activist, singer, songwriter, born Canada.

Sampson, Will. (1934-1987) Creek actor, painter.

Seathl. (1788-1866) Duwamish chief, orator.

Sequoyah. (1770-1843) Cherokee chief, Creek War Army soldier, linguist.

Sitting Bull. (Tatanka Yotanka) (1831-1890) Sioux chief.

Spotted Tail. (1823-1881) Brulé Sioux peace activist, warrior.

Squanto. (Tisquantum) (1580-1622) Wampanoag guide, negotiator.

Standing Bear. (1829-1908) Ponca chief.

Tallchief, Maria. (1925-) Osage ballet dancer.

Te Ata. (1897-1995) Chickasaw folklorist, storyteller.

Tecumseh. (1768-1813) Shawnee chief, military leader, orator.

Teters, Charlene. (1952-) Spokane mixed media artist, Native American rights activist, painter.

Thorpe, Jim. (1888-1953) Chippewa/ Sac/Fox baseball player, decathlon, football player, Olympic track and field athlete, penthalon.

Tibbles, Suzette LaFlesche. (1854-1903) Ponca and Omaha Native American rights activist.

Tinker, Clarence L. (1887-1942) Osage World War I Army pilot, World War II major general.

Tsinhnahjinnie, Hulleah. (1954-) Navajo/ Creek/Seminole photographer.

Two Leggings. (fl. 1840s) Crow military leader, warrior.

Valadez, Mariano. (1950s) Huichol yarn painter.

Velarde, Pablita. (1918-) Santa Clara Pueblo painter.

Waheenee. (1841-) Hidatsa historian.

Ward, Nancy. (1738-1822) Cherokee leader, peace activist.

Warren, William Whipple. (1825-1853) Obijway historian, interpreter.

Washakie. (1800-1900) Shoshone chief.

Wauneka, Annie Dodge. (1910-1997) Navajo public health educator. Presidential Medal of Freedom recipient.

Weetamoo. (1640-1676) Pocasset warrior.

West, W. Richard, Sr. (1912-1996) Cheyenne painter, sculptor.

West, W. Richard, Jr. (1943-) Cheyenne
attorney.

Whitewolf, Jim. (1878-?) Kiowa-Apache
historian..

Winema. (Tobey Riddle) (1836-1932) Modoc Native American rights activist, peace
activist.

Winnemucca, Sarah. (1844-1891) Paiute
Native American rights activist.

Winyan Ohtika. Sioux legendary heroine.

Wovoka. (Jack Wilson) (1858-1932) Paiute
mystic, spiritual leader.

Yakel, Jerrell. (1959-) La Jolla neuroscientist.

Youngblood, Jack. (1950-) Football player.

Naturalists

See Environmentalists.

Navy Personnel

See also Civil War; Gulf War; Korean Conflict; Military Leaders; Vietnam War;
World War I, World War II.

American

Alvarez, Everett, Jr. (1937-) Vietnam War
pilot.

Bean, Alan. (1932-) Pilot.

Bennett, Floyd. (1890-1928) Pilot.

Brown, Wesley A. (1927-) Lieutenant commander.

Bulkeley, John. (1911-1996) Career Navy,
vice admiral. World War II lieutenant.
Medal of Honor recipient.

Burke, Arleigh A. (1901-1996) Admiral,
Korean War Chief of Naval Operations.

Bush, George Herbert Walker. (1924-)
World War II pilot.

Byrd, Richard Evelyn. (1888-1957) World
War I pilot, World War II admiral.

Carter, James Earl "Jimmy." (1924-) World
War II Nuclear Submarine Service.

Cernan, Eugene. (1934-) Pilot.

Dorman, Pamela Davis. (1952-) Gulf War
chaplain.

Douglas, Marjorie Stoneman. (1890-1958)
World War I.

Ericsson, John. (1803-1889) Battleship in
ventor for Civil War, born Sweden.

Farragut, David Glasgow. (1801-1870) Civil

War admiral.

Ford, Gerald R. (1913-) World War II.

Goodman, Robert O. (1956-) Commander,
born Puerto Rico.

Graham, Calvin. (1929-1992) World War II
at age 12.

Gravely, Samuel L., Jr. (1922-) Admiral,
World War II ensign.

Halsey, William F. "Bull." (1882-1959)
World War II admiral, commander.

Hancock, Joy Bright. (1898-1986) World
War I reserves, World War II director of
WAVES.

Hayward, John T. (1908-1999) World War
II admiral, Cuban Missile Crisis.

Hess, Harry. (1906-1969) World War II
commander.

Johnson, Lyndon Baines. (1908-1973)
World War II.

Jones, John Paul. (1747-1792) American
Revolutionary War military, father of
American Navy, born Scotland.

Kennedy, John Fitzgerald. (1917-1963)
World War II commander.

Levy, Uriah P. (1792-1862) War of 1812
commander.

McCandless, Bruce, II. (1932-) Pilot.

Miller, Dorie. (1919-1943) Seaman at Pearl
Harbor.

Mitchell, Edgar. (1930-) Pilot.

Moorer, Thomas H. (1912-2004) Admiral,
World War II Chief of Naval Operations.

Nimitz, Chester W. (1885-1966) World
War I, World War II admiral, commander
of Pacific Fleet.

Nixon, Richard Milhous. (1913-1994)
World War II.

Peary, Robert. (1856-1920)

Rickover, Hyman. (1900-1986) Rear admiral, born Russia.

Roosevelt, Franklin Delano. (1882-1945)
Assistant secretary.

Rumsfeld, Donald H. (1932-) Career officer.

Shepard, Alan B. (1923-1998) Test pilot.

Smalls, Robert. (1839-1915) Civil War hero.

Stevenson, Adlai. (1900-1965) World War
II Assistant Secretary of Navy.

Still, Susan. (1961-) Pilot.

Tracy, Benjamin. (1830-1915) Secretary of
Navy.

Vashon, John Batham. (1792-1854) War of

1812 seaman.

Walsh, Don. (1931-) Officer.

Whyte, Edna Gardner. (1902-1993) World War II Naval Nurse Corps.

Wilkes, Charles. (1798-1877) Officer.

Other

Ahmose. (fl. 1535 B.C.) Egyptian captain.

Alfred the Great. (849-901) English founder of Navy.

Dietrichson, Leif. (d.1928) Norwegian.

Drake, Sir Francis. (1540-1596) English admiral.

Du Temple, Felix. (1823-1890) French officer.

Fegen, Edward Fogarty. (1895-1940) English World War II commander.

Hanno. (c. 450 B.C.) Carthagian.

Iberville, Pierre le Moyne de. (1661-1706) Canadian captain, born France.

Menendéz de Aviles, Pedro. (1519-1574) Spanish officer.

Mozhaiski, Alexander. (1825-1890) Russian officer.

Nelson, Horatio. (1758-1805) English.

Pineda, Álonzo Alvarez de. (1792-1872) Spanish admiral.

Ribaut, Jean. (1520-1565) French officer.

Riiser-Larsen, Hjalmar. (1890-1965) Norwegian pilot.

Scott, Robert Falcon. (1868-1912) English officer.

Themistocles. (523-463 B.C.) Greek commander and admiral.

Togo, Heihachiro. (1848-1934) Japanese officer.

Tromp, Maarten von. (1597-1653) Dutch admiral.

Zheng He. (1371-1433) Chinese admiral.

Nazi Hunters

See also Crime Fighters; Holocaust Figures; World War II Figures.

Klarsfeld, Beate. (1939-) German.

Klarsfeld, Serge. (1935-) Hungarian.

Wiesenthal, Simon. (1908-) Austrian, born Poland.

Nazi War Criminals

See also Hatemongers, Holocaust Figures;

World War II Figures.

Barbie, Klaus. (1913-1991) German.

Bormann, Martin. (1900-1945) German.

Brandt, Karl. (1904-1948) German.

Braun, Eva. (1912-1945) German.

Denjamjuk, John "Ivan the Terrible." (1920-) born Ukraine.

Eichmann, Adolf. (1906-1962) German.

Goebbels, Joseph. (1897-1945) German.

Göring, Hermann. (1893-1946) German.

Hess, Rudolf. (1894-1987) German.

Heydrich, Reinhard. (1904-1942) German.

Himmler, Heinrich. (1900-1945) German.

Hitler, Adolf. (1889-1945) German.

Höss, Rudolf. (1900-1947) German.

Koch, Ilse. (1906-1967) German.

Koch, Karl. (1897-1945) German.

Krupp, Alfried. (1907-1967) German.

Mengele, Josef. (1911-1979) German.

Müller, Heinrich. (1901-1945) German.

Quisling, Vidkun. (1887-1945) Norwegian.

Röhm, Ernst. (1887-1934) German.

Stangl, Franz. (1908-1971) Austrian.

Von Ribbentrop, Joachim. (1893-1946) German.

Waldheim, Kurt. (1918-) Austrian.

Nepalese

Norgay, Tenzig. (1914-1986) Mountaineer.

Rai, Jitbahadur. (d. 1949) World War II ghurka.

Neuroscientists

Yakel, Jerrell. (1959-) La Jolla Indian.

New Zealanders

See also Immigrants to United States, New Zealandic.

Hillary, Sir Edmund. (1919-) Adventurer, author, mountaineer.

Hodgson, Tasha. (1972-) In-line skater.

James, Naomi. (1949-) Adventurer, sailor.

Musick, Edwin C. (1893-1938) World War I pilot.

Rutherford, Baron Ernest. (1871-1938) Physicist. Nobel Prize winner.

Newscasters

See Broadcast Journalists.

Nicaraguans

Chamorro, Violeta Barrios de. (1929-) President.

Nigerians

See also Africans; Blacks, International.

Esu-Williams, Eku. (1956-) AIDS educator, immunologist, physician.

Lucas, Adetokonbo. (1931-) Medical researcher, physician.

Olajuwon, Hakeem. (1963-) Basketball player, born Nigeria.

Soyinka, Wole. (1934-) Author, playwright, poet, political activist.

Nobel Prize Winners

Chemistry

Curie, Marie Sklodowska. (1867-1934) French, born Poland. Prize 1911.

Hodgkin, Dorothy Crowfoot. (1910-1994) English. Prize 1964.

Joliot-Curie, Irène. (1897-1956) French. Prize 1935.

Libby, Willard Frank. (1908-1980) Prize 1960.

Molina, Mario. (1943-) born Mexico. Prize 1995.

Pauling, Linus Carl. (1901-1994) Prize 1954.

Ramsay, Sir William. (1852-1916) Scottish. Prize 1904.

Rowland, Frank Sherwood. (1927-) Prize 1995.

Rutherford, Baron Ernest. (1871-1938) New Zealander. Prize 1908.

Sanger, Frederick. (1918-) English. Prize 1958, 1980.

Seaborg, Glenn Theodore. (1912-1999) Prize 1951.

Economics

Friedman, Milton. (1912-) Prize 1976.

Literature

Bellow, Saul. (1915-) Prize 1976.

Buck, Pearl. (1892-1973) Prize 1938.

Churchill, Sir Winston Leonard Spencer. (1874-1965) English. Prize 1953.

Deledda, Grazia. (1871-1936) Italian.

Eliot, Thomas Stearns "T. S." (1888-1965) English. Prize 1948.

Faulkner, William. (1897-1962) Prize 1949.

Gordimer, Nadine. (1923-) South African. Prize 1991.

Hemingway, Ernest Miller. (1899-1961) Prize 1954.

Hesse, Herman. (1877-1962) Swiss, born Germany. Prize 1946.

Kipling, Rudyard. (1865-1936) English. Prize 1907.

Lewis, Sinclair. (1885-1951) Prize 1930.

Marquez, Gabriel Garcia. (1928-) Colombian. Prize 1982.

Mistral, Gabriela Lucila y Alcayága. (1889-1957) Chilean. Prize 1945.

Morrison, Toni. (1931-) Prize 1993.

O'Neill, Eugene Gladstone. (1888-1953) Prize 1936.

Sartre, Jean-Paul. (1905-1980) French. Prize 1964.

Shaw, George Bernard. (1856-1950) Irish. Prize 1925.

Singer, Isaac Bashevis. (1904-1991) born Poland. Prize 1978.

Soyinka, Wole. (1934-) Nigerian. Prize 1986.

Steinbeck, John. (1902-1968) Prize 1962.

Tagore, Rabindranth. (1861-1941) Indian. Prize 1913.

Yeats, William Butler. (1865-1939) Irish. Prize 1923.

Medicine and Physiology

Banting, Sir Frederick Grant. (1891-1941) Canadian. Prize 1923.

Beadle, George. (1903-1989) Prize 1958.

Burnet, Sir Frank MacFarlane. (1899-1985) Australian. Prize 1960.

Chain, Sir Ernst Boris. (1906-1979) English. Prize 1945.

Claude, Albert. (1899-1983) English. Prize 1974.

Cohen, Stanley. (1922-) Prize 1986.

Cori, Gerty Radnitz. (1896-1957) Prize 1947.

Crick, Francis Harry Compton. (1916-2004) English. Prize 1962.

Dausset, Jean. (1916-) French. Prize 1980.

Ehrlich, Paul. (1854-1915) German. Prize 1908.

Einthoven, Willem. (1860-1927) Dutch. Prize 1924.

Elion, Gertrude Belle. (1918-1999) Prize 1988.

Fleming, Sir Alexander. (1881-1955) Scottish. Prize 1945.

Florey, Lord Howard Walter. (1898-1968) Australian. Prize 1945.

Hounsfield, Sir Godfrey N. (1919-) English. Prize 1979.

Khorana, Har Gobind. (1922-) born India. Prize 1968.

Koch, Robert. (1843-1910) German. Prize 1905.

Landsteiner, Karl. (1868-1943) born Austria. Prize 1930.

Laveran, Charles Louis Alphonse. (1845-1932) French. Prize 1907.

Levi-Montalcini, Rita. (1909-) born Italy. Prize 1986.

McClintock, Barbara. (1908-1992) Prize 1983.

Medawar, Sir Peter Brian. (1915-1987) English. Prize 1960.

Morgan, Thomas Hunt. (1866-1945) Prize 1933.

Murray, Joseph E. (1919-) Prize 1990.

Ochoa, Severo. (1905-1993) born Spain. Prize 1959.

Pavlov, Ivan Petrovich. (1849-1936) Russian. Prize 1904.

Sperry, Roger W. (1913-1994) Prize 1981.

Temin, Howard Martin. (1934-) Prize 1975.

Tonegawa, Susumu. (1939-) born Japan. Prize 1987.

Waksman, Selman Abraham. (1888-1973) born Russia. Prize 1952.

Watson, James Dewey. (1928-) Prize 1962.

Yalow, Rosalyn Sussman. (1921-) Prize 1977.

Peace Prize
See also Peace Activists.

Peace, African
de Klerk, Fredrik Willem "F. W." (1936-) South African. Prize 1993.

Luthuli, Albert. (1898-1967) South African. Prize 1960.

Mandela, Nelson. (1918-) South African. Prize 1993.

Tutu, Desmond Mpilo. (1931-) South African. Prize 1984.

Peace, American
Addams, Jane. (1860-1935) Prize 1931.

Balch, Emily Greene. (1867-1961) Prize 1946.

Borlaug, Norman Ernest. (1914-) Prize 1970.

Bunche, Ralph. (1904-1971) Prize 1950.

Butler, Nicholas Murray. (1862-1947) Prize 1931.

Carter, James Earl "Jimmy." (1924-) Prize 2002.

Dawes, Charles Gates. (1865-1951) Prize 1925.

Hull, Cordell. (1871-1955) Prize 1945.

Kellogg, Frank Billings. (1856-1937) Prize 1929.

King, Martin Luther, Jr. (1929-1968) Prize 1964.

Kissinger, Henry. (1923-) born Germany. Prize 1973.

Marshall, George Catlett. (1880-1959) Prize 1953.

Mott, John Raleigh. (1865-1955) Prize 1946.

Pauling, Linus Carl. (1901-1994) Prize 1962.

Roosevelt, Theodore. (1858-1919) Prize 1906.

Root, Elihu. (1845-1937) Prize 1912.

Wiesel, Elie. (1928-) born Romania. Prize 1986.

Williams, Jody. (1950-) Prize 1997.

Wilson, Woodrow. (1856-1924) Prize 1919.

Peace, Canadian
Pearson, Lester. (1897-1972) Prize 1957.

Peace, English and British
Angell, Sir Norman. (1873-1967) Prize 1933.

Cecil, Robert. (1864-1958) Prize 1937.

Chamberlain, J. Austen. (1863-1937) Prize 1925.

Corrigan, Mairead. (1944-) Irish. Prize 1976.

Cremer, Sir William Randel. (1828-1908) Prize 1903.

Henderson, Arthur. (1863-1935) Scottish. Prize 1934.

MacBride, Seán. (1904-1988) Irish. Prize 1974.

Noel-Baker, Philip. (1889-1982) Prize 1959.

Orr, John Boyd. (1880-1971) Scottish. Prize 1949.

Williams, Betty. (1943-) Irish. Prize 1976.

Peace, European

Asser, Tobias. (1838-1913) Dutch. Prize 1911.

Beernaert, Auguste. (1829-1912) Belgian. Prize 1909.

Bourgeois, Léon. (1851-1925) French. Prize 1920.

Brandt, Willy. (1913-1992) German. Prize 1971.

Briand, Aristide. (1862-1932) French Prize 1926.

Cassin, René. (1887-1976) French. Prize 1968.

Constant, Paul D'Estournelles. (1852-1924) French. Prize 1909.

Ducommon, Élie. (1833-1906) Swiss. Prize 1902.

Dunant, Henri. (1828-1910) Swiss. Prize 1901.

Fried, Alfred. (1864-1921) Austrian. Prize 1911.

Gobat, Albert. (1843-1914) Swiss. Prize 1902.

Jouhaux, Léon. (1879-1954) French. Prize 1951.

La Fontaine, Henri. (1854-1943) Belgian. Prize 1913.

Moneta, Ernesto. (1833-1918) Italian. Prize 1907.

Ossietzky, Carl von. (1889-1938) German. Prize 1935.

Passy, Frédéric. (1822-1912) French. Prize 1901.

Pire, Dominiques-Georges. (1910-1969) Belgian. Prize 1958.

Quidde, Ludwig. (1858-1941) German. Prize 1927.

Renault, Louis. (1843-1918) French. Prize 1907.

Rotblat, Joseph. (1908-) English, born Poland. Prize 1995.

Schweitzer, Albert. (1875-1965) French. Prize 1952.

Stresemann, Gustav. (1878-1929) German. Prize 1926.

Suttner, Bertha von. (1843-1914) Austrian. Prize 1905.

Walesa, Lech. (1943-) Polish. Prize 1983.

Peace, Far Eastern and Middle Eastern

Arafat, Yasir. (1929-) Palestinian. Prize 1994.

Begin, Menachem. (1913-1992) Israeli. Prize 1978.

Bojaxhiu, Agnes. (Mother Teresa) (1910-1997) Indian, born Yugoslavia. Prize 1979.

Gyatso, Tenzin. (1935-) Tibetan. Prize 1989.

Le-Duc-Tho. (1911-1990) Vietnamese. Prize 1973.

Peres, Shimon. (1923-) Israeli. Prize 1994.

Rabin, Yitzhak. (1922-1995) Israeli. Prize 1994.

Sadat, Anwar. (1918-1981) Egyptian. Prize 1978.

Sato, Eisaku. (1901-1975) Japanese. Prize 1974.

Suu Kyi, Daw Aung San. (1945-) Burmese. Prize 1991.

Teresa, Mother. *See* Bojaxhiu, Agnes.

Peace, Latin

Arias Sánchez, Oscar. (1941-) Costa Rican. Prize 1987.

Belo, Carlos Felipe Ximenes. (1948-) East Timor. Prize 1996.

Esquivel, Adolfo Pérez. (1931-) Argentine. Prize 1980.

Lamas, Carlos Saavedra. (1878-1959) Argentine. Prize 1936.

Menchú, Rigoberta. (1959-) Guatemalan. Prize 1992.

Ramos-Horta, José. (1949-) East Timor. Prize 1996.

Robles, Alfonso García. (1911-1991) Mexican. Prize 1982.

Peace, Russian

Gorbachev, Mikhail. (1931-) Prize 1990.

Sakharov, Andrei. (1921-1989) Prize 1975.

Peace, Scandinavian

Arnoldson, Klas. (1844-1916) Swedish. Prize 1908.

Bajer, Fredrik. (1837-1922) Danish. Prize

1908.

Branting, Karl. (1860-1925) Swedish. Prize 1921.

Hammarskjöld, Dag. (1905-1961) Swedish. Prize 1961.

Lange, Christian. (1869-1938) Norwegian. Prize 1921.

Myrdal, Alva. (1902-1986) Swedish. Prize 1982.

Nansen, Fridtjof. (1861-1930) Norwegian. Prize 1922.

Söderblom, Nathan. (1866-1931) Swedish. Prize 1930.

Physics

Alvarez, Luis Walter. (1911-1988) Prize 1968.

Bardeen, John. (1908-1991) Prize 1956, 1972.

Becquerel, Antoine Henri. (1852-1908) French. Prize 1903.

Bohr, Niels. (1885-1962) Danish. Prize 1922.

Born, Max. (1882-1970) English. Prize 1954.

Brattain, Walter Houser. (1902-1987) Prize 1956.

Chandrasekhar, Subramanyan. (1910-1995) born Pakistan. Prize 1983.

Compton, Arthur Holly. (1892-1962) Prize 1927.

Crick, Francis H. C. (1916-) English.

Curie, Marie. (1867-1934) French, born Poland. Prize 1903.

Curie, Pierre. (1859-1906) French. Prize 1903.

Dirac, Paul Adrien Maurice. (1902-1984) English. Prize 1933.

Einstein, Albert. (1879-1955) born Germany. Prize 1921.

Fermi, Enrico. (1901-1954) born Italy. Prize 1938.

Feynman, Richard Philips. (1918-1988) Prize 1965.

Gabor, Dennis. (1900-1979) Hungarian. Prize 1971.

Goeppert-Mayer, Maria. (1906-1972) born Germany. Prize 1963.

Heisenberg, Werner. (1901-1976) German. Prize 1932.

Hofstadter, Robert. (1915-1990) Prize 1961.

Kilby, Jack S. (1923-) Prize 2000.

Lawrence, Ernest Orlando. (1901-1958) Prize 1939.

Lee, Tsung-Dao. (1926-) born China. Prize 1957.

Marconi, Guglielmo. (1874-1937) Italian. Prize 1909.

Michelson, Albert Abraham. (1852-1931) born Poland. Prize 1907.

Pauli, Wolfgang. (1900-1958) Austrian. Prize 1945.

Planck, Max Karl Ernst Ludwig. (1858-1947) German. Prize 1918.

Roentgen, Wilhelm Conrad. (1845-1923) German. Prize 1901.

Shockley, William. (1910-1989) English. Prize 1956.

Thomson, Joseph John. (1856-1940) English. Prize 1906.

Ting, Samuel Chao Chung. (1936-) Prize 1976.

Townes, Charles Hard. (1915-) Prize 1964.

Yang, Chen Ning. (1922-) born China. Prize 1957.

Zernike, Frits. (1888-1966) Dutch. Prize 1953.

Norwegians

See also Immigrants to United States, Norwegian; Viking.

Amundsen, Roald Engebreth Gravning. (1872-1928) Arctic explorer.

Brundtland, Gro Harlem. (1939-) Environmental activist, physician, prime minister.

Dietrichson, Leif. (d.1928) Arctic explorer

Ericsson, Leif. (970-1020) Viking explorer, navy officer.

Garbarek, Jan. (1947-) Bandleader, jazz musician.

Grieg, Edvard. (1843-1907) Composer, conductor, musician.

Henie, Sonia. (1912-1969) Figure skater.

Heyerdahl, Thor. (1914-2002) Adventurer, biologist.

Ibsen, Henrik. (1828-1906) Playwright, poet.

Lange, Christian. (1869-1938) Author, educator, peace activist. Nobel Peace Prize winner.

Martha Louise. (1971-) Princess.

Münch, Edvard. (1863-1944) Painter.

Nansen, Fridtjof. (1861-1930) Explorer, statesman, zoologist. Nobel Peace Prize winner.

Orsted Pedersen, Niels-Henning. (unknown) Jazz musician.

Quisling, Vidkun. (1887-1945) Nazi war criminal, political activist, traitor.

Riiser-Larsen, Hjalmar. (1890-1965) Navy pilot.

Thorvaldson, Erik "Erik the Red." (950-1010) Viking explorer.

Nurses

See also Civil War; Vietnam War; World War I; World War II.

Barton, Clara. (1821-1912) Civil War.

Bickerdyke, Mary Ann "Mother." (1817-1901) Civil War.

Blanchfield, Florence Aby. (1882-1971) World War I and II army.

Bragg, Janet Harmon. (1907-1993)

Cammermeyer, Margarethe. (1942-) Vietnam War.

Cavell, Edith. (1865-1915) English World War I.

Chisholm, Mairí. (1896-?) Scottish World War I.

Delano, Jane Arminda. (1862-1919) World War I superintendent Army Air Corps Nurses.

Dempsey, Sister Mary Joseph. (1856-1939)

Dix, Dorothea. (1802-1887) Civil War superintendent of Army Nurses.

Edmonds, Sarah Emma. (1841-1898) Civil War.

Ferenz, Ludmilla "Lou." (1921-) World War II Army Nurse Corp flight nurse.

Freeman, Elizabeth "Mumbet." (1742-1829)

Goodrich, Annie W. (1866-1954)

Johnson, Hazel W. (1927-) Army Nurse Corps Chief.

Kenny, Elizabeth. (1880-1952) Australian World War I.

Maass, Clara. (1875-1901)

Mahoney, Mary Eliza. (1845-1926)

Nightingale, Florence. (1820-1910) English Crimean War head of nurses.

Ortega, Beatriz Gonzalez. (unknown) Mexican nurse during Revolution of 1910.

Sanger, Margaret. (1879-1966)

Scott, Sheila. (1927-1988) English World War II.

Seacole, Mary. (1805-1881) Jamaican.

Taylor, Susie King. (1848-1912) Civil War.

Thoms, Adah Belle. (1870-1943) World War I.

Tubman, Harriet. (1820-1913) Civil War.

Wald, Lillian. (1867-1940)

Whyte, Edna Gardner. (1902-1993) World War II Navy Nurse Corps.

Nutritionists

Brody, Jane. (1941-1987)

Lappe, Frances Moore. (1944-)

Orr, John Boyd. (1880-1971) Scottish.

Richards, Ellen Swallow. (1842-1911)

Rose, Mary Swartz. (1874-1941)

Oceanographers

Ballard, Robert. (1942-)

Clarke, Eugenie. (1922-)

Corso, Sandra. (unknown)

Earle, Sylvia. (1935-)

Ewing, Maurice. (1906-1974)

Maury, Matthew Fontaine. (1806-1873)

Munk, Walter. (1917-) born Austria.

Piccard, Jacques. (1922-) Swiss.

Revelle, Roger. (1909-1991)

Stommel, Henry. (1920-1992)

Sullivan, Kathryn. (1951-)

Tharp, Marie. (1920-)

Vine, Allyn. (1914-1994)

Walsh, Don. (1931-)

Olympic Athletes

Basketball

Azzi, Jennifer. (1968-)

Bradley, Bill. (1943-)

Cooper, Cynthia. (1963-)

Donovan, Anne. (1961-)

Edwards, Teresa. (1964-)

Gillom, Jennifer. (1964-)

Laettner, Christian. (1969-)

Leslie, Lisa. (1972-)

Lieberman-Cline, Nancy. (1958-)

Lobo, Rebecca. (1973-)

McCray, Nikki. (1971-)

Meyers, Ann. (1955-)

Miller, Cheryl. (1964-)

Petrovic, Drazen. (1964-1993) Yugoslavian.
Serio, Suzie McConnell. (1966-)
Staley, Dawn. (1970-)
Swoopes, Sheryl. (1971-)
Timms, Michele. (1965-) Australian.
Weatherspoon, Teresa. (1965-)
Zheng, Haixia. (1967-) Chinese.

Biathlon, Decathlon, and Triathlon
Bedard, Myriam. (1969-) Canadian.
Mathias, Bob. (1930-)
Newby-Fraser, Paula. (1962-) Zimbabwean.
O'Brien, Dan. (1966-)
Patton, George Smith, Jr. (1885-1945)
Phayllos of Cortona. (c. 480) Greek.
Thompson, Daley. (1958-) English.
Thorpe, Jim. (1888-1953) Chip-
    pewa/Fox/Sac Indian.

Bobsledding
Eagan, Eddie. (1898-1967)

Boxing
Ali, Muhammad. (1942-)
Eagan, Eddie. (1898-1967)
Foreman, George. (1949-)
Leonard, Charles "Sugar Ray." (1956-)
Polydamus. (c. 408 B.C.) Greek.

Curling
Schmirler, Sandra. (1964-2000) Canadian.

Diving
Lee, Sammy. (1920-)
Louganis, Greg. (1960-)
McCormick, Patricia Keller. (1930-)

Gymnastics
Amanar, Simona. (1979-) Romanian.
Andrianov, Nikolai. (1952-) Russian.
Antolin, Jeanette. (1981-)
Atler, Vanessa. (1982-)
Beckerman, Alyssa. (1981-)
Boguinskaia, Svetlana. (1973-) Russian.
Borden, Amanda. (1977-)
Caslavska, Vera. (1942-) Czech.
Chow, Amy. (1978-)
Comaneci, Nadia. (1961-) Romanian.
Conner, Bart. (1958-)
Dantzscher, Jamie. (1982-)
Dawes, Dominique. (1976-)

Dimas, Trent. (1970-)
Jie, Ling. (1982-) Chinese.
Kato, Sawao. (1946-) Japanese.
Khorkina, Svetlana. (1979-) Russian.
Korbut, Olga. (1955-) Russian.
Latynina, Larissa. (1934-) Russian.
Maloney, Kris. (1981-)
Miller, Shannon. (1977-)
Moceanu, Dominique. (1981-)
Phelps, Jaycie. (1979-)
Podkopayeva, Lilia. (1978-) Ukrainian.
Ray, Elise. (1982-)
Retton, Mary Lou. (1968-)
Strug, Kerri. (1977-)
Thompson, Jennie. (1981-)
White, Morgan. (1983-)
Zmeskal, Kim. (1976-)

Hockey
Granato, Cammi. (1971-)
Hejduk, Milan. (1976-) Czech.
Kolzig, Olaf. (1970-) born Germany.
Pronger, Chris. (1974-) Canadian.
Whitton, Erin. (1971-)
Wickenheiser, Hayley. (1969-) Canadian.

Judo
Arad, Yael. (1967-) Israeli.
Campbell, Bell Nighthorse. (1933-) Chey-
    enne Indian.

Kayaking and Rowing
Barton, Greg. (1959-)
DeFrantz, Anita. (1952-)
Laumann, Silken. (1965-) Canadian.

Skating
Albright, Tenley. (1935-)
Anissina, Mariana. (1975-) Russian.
Baiul, Oksana. (1977-) Ukrainian.
Berezhnaya, Elena. (1977-) Russian.
Blair, Bonnie. (1964-)
Bonaly, Surya. (1973-) French.
Bourne, Shae-Lynn. (1976-) Canadian.
Button, Dick. (1929-)
Cohen, Sasha. (1984-)
Eldredge, Todd. (1971-)
Fleming, Peggy. (1948-)
Fratianne, Linda. (1960-)
Goebel, Timothy. (1980-)
Hamill, Dorothy. (1956-)

Harding, Tonya. (1970-)
Heiden, Eric. (1958-)
Heiss, Carol. (1940-)
Henie, Sonia. (1912-1969) Norwegian.
Hughes, Sarah. (1985-)
Kerrigan, Nancy. (1969-)
Kraatz, Victor. (1971-) Canadian.
Kwan, Michelle. (1980-)
Kyoko, Ina. (1972-) born Japan.
Lang, Naomi. (1978-) Karuk Indian.
Lipinski, Tara. (1982-)
Lu, Chen. (1976-) Chinese.
Peizerat, Gwendal. (1972-) French.
Pelletier, David. (1974-) Canadian.
Plushenko, Evgeny. (1982-) Russian.
Robinson, Jennifer. (1976-) Canadian.
Salchow, Ulrich. (1877-1949) Swedish.
Salé, Jamie. (1977-) Canadian.
Sikharulidze, Anton. (1976-) Russian.
Skoblikova, Lydia. (1939-) Russian.
Slutskaya, Irina. (1979-) Russian.
Stojko, Elvis. (1972-) Canadian.
Tchernyshev, Peter. (1971-) born Russia.
Thomas, Debi. (1967-)
Weiss, Michael. (1976-)
Witt, Katarina. (1965-) German.
Yagudin, Alexei. (1980-) Russian.
Yamaguchi, Kristi. (1971-)
Young, Sheila. (1950-)
Zimmerman, John. (1973-)

Skiing
Golden, Diana. (1963-2001)
Killy, Jean-Claude. (1943-) French.
Moser-Proell, Annemarie. (1953-) Austrian.
Nykanen, Matti. (1963-) Finnish.
Smetanina, Raisa. (1953-) Russian.
Street, Picabo. (1971-)
Theni, Gustavo. (1951-) Italian.
Zurbriggen, Pirmin. (1963-) Swiss.

Soccer
Akers, Michelle. (1966-)
Chastain, Brandi. (1968-)
Fair, Lorrie. (1978-)
Fawcett, Joy. (1968-)
Foudy, Julie. (1971-)
Hamm, Mia. (1972-)
Heinrichs, April. (1964-)
Lilly, Kristine. (1971-)
Millbrett, Tiffany. (1972-)

Overbeck, Carla. (1969-)
Parlow, Cindy. (1978-)
Roberts, Tiffany. (1977-)
Scurry, Brianna. (1971-)
Sobrero, Kate. (1976-)
Venturini, Tisha. (1973-)

Softball
Fernandez, Lisa. (1971-)
Richardson, Dorothy "Dot." (1961-)

Swimming
Caulkins, Tracy. (1963-)
Ederle, Gertrude. (1905-2003)
Evans, Janet. (1971-)
Fraser, Dawn. (1937-) Australian.
Kahanamoku, Duke. (1890-1968) Hawaiian.
Mann, Shelley. (1939-)
Otto, Kristen. (1966-) German.
Spitz, Mark. (1950-)
Van Dyken, Amy. (1973-)
Weissmuller, Johnny. (1904-1984)

Tennis
Agassi, Andre. (1970-)
Capriati, Jennifer. (1976-)
Moody, Helen Wills. (1906-1998)

Track and Field
Includes long jumpers, pole vaulters, runners, sprinters. See also Biathlon, Decathlon, and Triathlon.
Ashford, Evelyn. (1957-)
Bannister, Roger. (1929-) English.
Barsosio, Sally. (1978-) Kenyan.
Blankers-Koen, Fanny. (1918-2004) Dutch.
Brisco-Hooks, Valerie. (1960-)
Carr, Henry. (1942-)
Coachman, Alice. (1923-)
Devers, Gail. (1966-)
Didrikson, Mildred "Babe" *see* Zaharias, Mildred "Babe."
Dionysia. (unknown) Ancient Roman.
Dragila, Stacy. (1971-)
Freeman, Cathy. (1973-) Australian.
George, Emma. (1974-) Australian.
Gourdine, Meredith. (1929-1998) Long jump.
Hayes, Bob. (1942-2002)
Hedea. (unknown) Roman.
Hines, Jim. (1946-)

Johnson, Michael. (1967-)
Johnson, Rafer. (1935-)
Jones, Marion. (1975-)
Joyner, Florence Griffith. (1959-1998)
Joyner-Kersee, Jackie. (1962-)
Lewis, Carl. (1961-)
Liddell, Eric. (1902-1945) Scottish.
Maximinus, Gaius Valerius. (186-238) Roman.
McGuire, Edith. (1944-)
Miller, Inger. (1972-)
Mills, Billy. (1938-) Oglala Lakota Sioux Indian.
Morrow, Bobby Joe. (1935-)
Moses, Edwin. (1955-)
Newby-Fraser, Paula. (1962-) Zimbabwean.
Nurmi, Paavo. (1897-1973) Finnish.
O'Brien, Dan. (1966-)
Owens, Jesse. (1913-1980)
Paddock, Charlie. (1900-1943)
Patton, George Smith, Jr. (1885-1945)
Phayllos of Cortona. (c. 480) Greek.
Phidippides. (c. 505-490 B.C.) Greek.
Robinson, Betty. (1911-1999)
Rosenfeld, Bobbie. (1904-1969) Canadian.
Rudolph, Wilma. (1940-1994)
Samuelson, Joan Benoit. (1957-)
Smith, Tommie. (1944-)
Stephens, Helen. (1918-1994)
Thayer, Helen. (1938-) born New Zealand.
Thompson, Daley. (1958-)
Thorpe, Jim. (1888-1953) Chippewa/Sac/Fox Indian.
Tolan, Eddie. (1908-1967)
Torrence, Gwen. (1965-)
Tryphosa. (unknown) Roman.
Tyus, Wyomia. (1945-)
Wolde, Mamo. (1931-) Ethiopian.
Zaharias, Mildred "Babe" Didrikson. (1913-1956)

Volleyball
Hyman, Flo. (1954-1986)

Weight Lifting
Alexeyev, Vasily. (1942-) Russian.
Davis, John. (1921-1984)
Milo of Crotona. (c. 558 B.C.) Greek.

Wrestling
Gable, Dan. (1948-)

Milo of Crotona. (c. 558 B.C.) Greek.

Orators
Abelard, Pierre. (1097-1142) French.
Besant, Annie. (1847-1933) English.
Burke, Edmund. (1729-1797) English.
Cicero. (Marcus Tollius Cicero) (106-43 B.C.) Roman.
Demosthenes. (384-322 B.C.) Greek.
Dickinson, Anna Elizabeth. (1842-1932)
Douglass, Frederick. (1817-1895)
Garnet, Henry Highland. (1815-1882)
Garvey, Marcus. (1887-1940)
Harper, John. (1872-1912) Scottish.
Henry, Patrick. (1736-1799)
Hortensia. (1st century) Roman.
King, Martin Luther, Jr. (1929-1968)
Pliny the Younger. (Gaius Plinius Caecilius Secundus) (61-113) Roman.
Red Jacket. (1756-1830) Seneca Indian.
Riis, Jacob August. (1849-1914) born Denmark.
Roosevelt, (Anna) Eleanor. (1884-1962)
Rose, Ernestine Potowski. (1810-1892) born Poland.
Seathl. (1788-1866) Duwamish chief.
Tacitus. (Publius or Gaius Cornelius Tacitus) (55-115) Roman.
Tecumseh. (1768-1813) Shawnee chief.
Turner, Henry McNeal. (1834-1915)
Webster, Daniel. (1782-1852)

Organizational Founders and Heads
Asser, Tobias. (1838-1913) Institute of International Law co-founder.
Barton, Clara. (1821-1912) American Red Cross.
Benenson, Peter. (1921-) Amnesty International founder.
Bloomfield, Michael. (unknown) Canadian founder of Harmony Foundation of Canada.
Bond, Julian. (1940-) NAACP head.
Booth, Catherine. (1829-1890) English co-founder of Salvation Army.
Booth, Eva. (1865-1950) Brought Salvation Army movement to U.S.
Booth, William. (1829-1912) English co-founder of Salvation Army.

Brower, David. (1912-2000) Sierra Club president.

Brundtland, Gro Harlem. (1939-) World Health Organization head.

Campbell, Bonnie. (1948-) Women Against Violence.

Cardin, Shoshana. (1926-) Jewish organizations.

Cassin, René. (1887-1976) French UNESCO cofounder.

Cremer, Sir William. (1828-1908) English National Arbitration League cofounder.

Du Bois, W. E. B. (1868-1963) NAACP founder.

Ducommon, Élie. (1833-1906) Swiss International Peace Bureau founder.

Dunant, Henri. (1828-1910) Swiss International Red Cross founder.

Edelman, Marian Wright. (1939-) Children's Defense Fund.

Flynn, Elizabeth Gurley. (1890-1964) American Civil Liberties Union co-founder.

Gobat, Albert. (1843-1914) Swiss Director of International Peace Bureau.

Height, Dorothy Irene. (1912-) National Council Negro Women director.

Ireland, Patricia. (1945-) National Organization for Women president.

Jordan, Vernon E., Jr. (1935-) National Urban League head, United Negro College Fund head.

Jouhaux, Léon. (1879-1954) French International Labor Organization cofounder.

Koontz, Elizabeth Duncan. (1919-1989) National Education Association president.

Kouchner, Bernard. (1939-) French Doctors Without Walls founder.

Low, Juliette Gordon "Daisy." (1860-1927) Girl Scouts of America founder.

Lucas, Adetokunbo. (1931-) Nigerian World Health Organization founder.

MacBride, Séan. (1904-1988) Irish International Peace Bureau president.

Mathai-Davis, Prema. (1950-) YWCA executive director, born India.

Mott, John Raleigh. (1865-1955) YMCA executive director.

Myrdal, Alva. (1902-1986) Swiss UNESCO founder.

Orr, John Boyd. (1880-1971) Scottish U.N. Food and Agricultural Organization director.

Osborn, June. (1937-) National Commission on AIDS chair.

Pappenheim, Berta. (1859-1936) German Jewish women's organization founder.

Passy, Frédéric. (1822-1912) French International League of Peace and Freedom founder.

Pire, Dominique-Georges. (1910-1969) Belgian University of Peace founder.

Quidde, Ludwig. (1858-1941) German World Peace Congress founder.

Ruffin, Josephine St. Pierre. (1842-1924) African American women's organizations founder.

Schechter, Matilde Roth. (1859-1924) Women's League of Conservative Judaism founder.

Seton, Ernest Thompson. (1860-1946) Boy Scouts of America co-founder, born England.

Suttner, Bertha von. (1843-1914) Austrian International Peace Bureau co-founder.

Szold, Henrietta. (1860-1945) Hadassah Women's Zionist Organization founder.

Wattleton, Faye. (1943-) Planned Parenthood president.

Ornithologists

Audubon, John James. (1785-1851) born Haiti.

Beebe, Charles William. (1877-1962)

Murie, Olaus. (1889-1963)

Nuttall, Thomas. (1786-1859) born England.

Odum, Eugene. (1913-2002)

Wilson, Alexander. (1766-1813) born Scotland.

Outlaws

Allison, Clay. (1840-1877)

Barrow, Clyde. (1909-1934)

Billy the Kid. *See* McCarthy, Henry.

Black Bart. *See* Boles, Charles.

Blackbeard. *See* Teach, Edward.

Boles, Charles. (Black Bart) (1829-1917)

Brown, Henry. (1857-1884)

Cassidy, Butch. *See* Parker, Robert Leroy.

Dalton, Bob. (1870-1892)

Dalton, Emmett. (1871-1937)

Dalton, Grattan. (1861-1892)

Erauso, Catalina de. (1585-1650) Spanish.
Fisher, John King. (1854-1884)
Hardin, John Wesley. (1853-1895)
Hare, Joseph Thompson. (1780-1818)
Hart, Pearl. (1871-1925) Canadian.
Hickok, James Butler "Wild Bill." (1837-1876)
Holliday, John "Doc" (1852-1887)
Hood, Robin. (1290-1346) English.
Huddleston, Ned. (1849-1900)
James, Frank. (1843-1915)
James, Jesse. (1847-1882)
Kelly, Ned. (1855-1880) Australian.
Longabaugh, Harry "Sundance Kid." (1863-1909)
McCarthy, Henry. (Billy the Kid) (1859-1881)
McDoulet, Annie "Cattle Annie." (1879-1898)
Murieta, Joaquin. (1832-1853) born Mexico.
Newman, Sarah Jane "Sally Skull." (1817-1866)
O'Mullan, John. (1670-1722) Irish.
Parker, Bonnie. (1911-1934)
Parker, Robert Leroy. (Butch Cassidy) (1866-1937)
Place, Etta. (1875-1940)
Quick, Flora. (Tom King) (unknown) disguised as man.
Starrr, Myra "Belle" Shirley. (1848-1889)
Starr, Henry. (1873-1921)
Stevens, Jennie "Little Britches." (1879-)
Teach, Edward. (Blackbeard) (1680-1718) English.
Turpin, Dick. (1705-1739) English highway robber.
Vasquez, Tiburcio. (1835-1875)
Watson, Ella "Cattle Kate." (1861-1889)

Painters

American
Allston, Washington. (1779-1843)
Angel, Carl. (1968-)
Audubon, John James. (1785-1851) born Haiti.
Bearden, Romare. (1912-1988)
Bellows, George Wesley. (1882-1925)
Benton, Thomas Hart. (1889-1975)
Bingham, George Caleb. (1811-1879)
Blackburn, Robert. (1920-2003)

Calder, Alexander. (1898-1966)
Carrington, Lenora. (1917-)
Cassatt, Mary. (1844-1926)
Catlett, Elizabeth. (1915-)
Catlin, George. (1796-1872)
Chagoya, Enrique. (1953-)
Church, Frederick E. (1826-1900)
Cole, Thomas. (1801-1848) born England.
Colton, Mary-Russell. (1889-1971)
Copley, John Singleton. (1738-1815)
Crespo, George. (1962-)
Davis, Stuart. (1894-1964)
de Kooning, Willem. (1904-1997) born Holland.
Douglas, Aaron. (1899-1979)
Dove, Arthur. (1880-1946)
Duke, Mark. (1958-)
Duncanson, Robert Scott. (1821-1872)
Echohawk, Brummett. (1922-) Pawnee Indian.
Frank, Mary. (1933-)
Fuertes, Louis Agassiz. (1874-1927)
Gonzalez, Maya Christina. (1964-)
Haring, Keith. (1958-1990)
Hayden, Palmer C. (1890-1973)
Henri, Robert. (1865-1929)
Henry, Caryl. (1955-)
Hesse, Eva. (1936-1970) born Germany.
Hom, Nancy. (1949-)
Homer, Winslow. (1836-1910)
Hopper, Edward. (1882-1967)
Howe, Oscar. (1915-1983) Yankton Dakota Indian.
Hunter, Clementine. (1886-1988)
Hurd, Henriette Wyatt. (1907-1997)
JoeSam. (1939-)
Johnson, William Henry. (1901-1970)
Kingman, Dong. (1911-2000)
Lawrence, Jacob. (1917-2000)
Liu, Hung. (1948-) born China.
Lowry, Judith. (1948-)
Millais, John Everett. (1829-1896)
Mirabal, Robert. (unknown) Taos Indian.
Momaday, N. Scott. (1934-) Kiowa Indian.
Moses, Anna Mary Robertson "Grandma." (1860-1961)
Motley, Archibald, Jr. (1891-1981)
Neel, Alice. (1900-1984)
Obata, Chiura. (1888-1975) born Japan.
O'Keefe, Georgia. (1887-1986)
Pippin, Horace. (1888-1946)

Pollock, Jackson. (1912-1956)
Reisberg, Mira. (1953-) born Australia.
Remington, Frederic. (1861-1909)
Rockwell, Norman. (1894-1978)
Sampson, Will. (1934-1987) Creek Indian.
Sargent, John Singer. (1856-1925)
Skoglund, Sandy. (1946-)
Sofaer, Anna. (unknown)
Tanner, Henry Ossawa. (1859-1937)
Tape, Mary McGladery. (1857-1928) born China.
Teters, Charlene. (1952-) Spokane Indian.
Traylor, Bill. (1854-1947)
Valadez, Mariano. (fl. 1950s) Huichol Indian.
Valdez, Patssi. (1951-)
Velarde, Pablita. (1918-) Santa Clara Pueblo Indian.
Von Mason, Stephen. (1954-)
Warhol, Andy. (1928-1987)
Waring, Laura Wheeler. (1877-1948)
Wells, James Lesesne. (1902-1993)
West, Benjamin. (1738-1820)
West, W. Richard, Sr. (1912-1996)
Whistler, James Abbott McNeill. (1834-1903)
White, Charles. (1918-1979)
Woodruff, Hale Aspacio. (1900-1980)
Wyeth, Andrew. (1917-)
Zughaib, Helen. (1959-) born Lebanon.

Asian
Hokusai, Katsushika. (1760-1849) Japanese.
Ma Yuan. (1165-1225) Chinese.
Tagore, Rabindranth. (1861-1941) Indian.
Yani, Wang. (1975-) Chinese.

Belgian (Flemish)
Brueghel, Jan. (1568-1625)
Brueghel, Pieter. (1525-1569)
Magritte, René. (1896-1967)
Rubens, Peter Paul. (1577-1640)
Van Der Goes, Hugo. (1440-1482)
Van Dyck, Sir Anthony. (1599-1641)
Van Eyck, Jan. (1390-1441)
Watteau, Jean Antoine. (1684-1721)

Dutch
Bosch, Hieronymous. (1450-1516)
Hals, Frans. (1581-1666)
Leyster, Judith. (1609-1660)

Limbourg, Herman. (fl. 1400s)
Limbourg, Jean. (fl 1400s)
Limbourg, Paul. (fl. 1400s)
Mondrian, Piet. (1872-1944)
Rembrandt. (Harmen Szoon van Rijn) (1606-1669)
Ter Bosch, Gerard. (1617-1681)
Van Gogh, Vincent. (1853-1890)
Van Meegeren, Hans. (1889-1947)
Vermeer, Johannes. (1632-1675)

English
Blake, William. (1757-1827)
Bronte, Branwell. (1817-1848)
Constable, John. (1776-1837)
Gainsborough, Thomas. (1727-1788)
Hogarth, William. (1697-1764)
Mee, Margaret Ursula Brown. (1909-1988)
Reynolds, Sir Joshua. (1723-1792)
Riley, Bridget. (1931-)
Stubbs, George. (1724-1806)
Turner, Joseph Mallord William "J. M. W." (1775-1851)

French
Bonheur, Rosa. (1822-1899)
Braque, Georges. (1882-1963)
Cézanne, Paul. (1839-1906)
Chagall, Marc. (1887-1985) born Russia.
Courbet, Gustave. (1819-1877)
Daumier, Honoré. (1808-1879)
David, Jacques-Louis. (1784-1825)
Degas, Edgar. (1834-1917)
Delacroix, Eugène. (1798-1863)
Duchamp, Marcel. (1887-1968)
Fragonard, Jean-Honoré. (1732-1806)
Gauguin, Paul. (1848-1903)
Ingres, Jean-Auguste. (1780-1867)
Lorrain, Claude. (1605-1682)
Manet, Édouard. (1832-1883)
Matisse, Henri. (1869-1954)
Monet, Claude. (1840-1926)
Moreau, Gustave. (1826-1898)
Morisot, Berthe. (1841-1895)
Pissarro, Camille. (1830-1903)
Poussin, Nicolas. (1594-1665) born France.
Renoir, Pierre Auguste. (1841-1919)
Roualt, Georges. (1871-1958)
Rousseau, Henri. (1844-1910)
Seurat, Georges. (1859-1890)
Signac, Paul. (1863-1935)

Toulouse-Lahtrec, Henride. (1864-1901)
Vigee-Le Brun, Elisabeth. (1755-1842)

German
Beckmann, Max. (1884-1950)
Dürer, Albrecht. (1471-1528)
Friedrich, Caspar David. (1774-1840)
Gruenewald, Matthias. (1475-1528)
Kollwitz, Kaethe. (1867-1945)

Greek and Turk
Iaia of Cyzicus. (fl. 90 B.C.) Turk.
Theotokópoulous, Doménikos. (El Greco)
  (1541-1614) Greek.

Italian
Anguissola, Sofonisba. (1532-1625)
Arcimboldo, Giuseppe. (1527-1593)
Bellini, Giovanni. (1430-1516)
Boccioni, Umberto. (1882-1916)
Botticelli, Sandro. (1444-1510)
Canaletto. (Giovanni Antonio Canale)
  (1697-1768)
Caravaggio. (Michelangeo Merisi) (1573-
  1610)
Cimabue. (1240?-1302)
Correggio. (Antonio Allegri) (1489-1534)
Fontana, Lavinia. (1552-1614)
Francesca, Piero Della. (c. 1415-1492)
Gentileschi, Artemisia. (1593-1652)
Giorgione. (Giorgio Barbarclli) (1447-1510)
Giotto di Bondone. (1276-1337)
Kauffmann, Angelica. (1741-1807)
Leonardo da Vinci. (1452-1519)
Massaccio, Tommaso. (1401-1428)
Michelangelo Buonarotti. (1475-1564)
Modligliani, Amedeo. (1884-1920)
Raphael. (Raffaello Sanzio) (1483-1520)
Rossetti, Dante Gabriel. (1828-1882)
Sirani, Elizabeth. (1638-1665)
Tintoretto. (Jacopo Robusti) (1518-1594)
Titian. (Tiziano Vecellio) (1477-1576)
Uccello, Paolo. (1397-1475)

Mexican
Kahlo, Frida. (1907-1954)
Rivera, Diego. (1886-1957)

Portuguese and Spanish
Dali, Salvador. (1904-1989) Spanish.
Goya, Francisco de. (1746-1828) Spanish.

Miro, Joan. (1893-1983) Spanish.
Picasso, Pablo. (1881-1973) Spanish.
Rego, Paula. (1935-) Portuguese.
Velázquez, Diego Rodriguez Silva y. (1599-
  1660) Spanish.

Russian
Gabo, Naum. (1890-1977)
Kandinsky, Wassily. (1866-1944)

Ungrouped
Klee, Paul. (1879-1940) Swiss.
Klimt, Gustav. (1862-1918) Austrian.
Münch, Edvard. (1863-1944) Norwegian.
Oppenheim, Meret. (1913-1985) Swiss, born
  Germany.
Nolan, Sidney. (1917-1988) Australian.

Pakistanis
See also Immigrants to United States, Paki-
  stani.
Bhutto, Benazir. (1953-) Prime minister.
Masih, Igbal. (1982-1995) Slave, workers'
  rights activist.

Paleontologists
See also Archaeologists.
Alexander, Annie Montague. (1867-1950)
Andrews, Roy Chapman. (1884-1960)
Anning, Mary. (1799-1847) English.
Bakker, Robert. (1945-)
Brown, Barnum. (1873-1963)
Chin, Karen. (1952-) born Canada.
Cope, Edward. (1840-1897)
Cuvier, Georges. (1769-1832) French.
Douglass, Earl. (1862-1931)
Edinger, Tilly. (1897-1967)
Gittis, Kelley Anne. (unknown)
Gould, Stephen Jay. (1941-)
Hendrickson, Sue. (1950-)
Horner, Jack. (1946-)
Janensch, Werner. (1878-1969) German.
Leakey, Louis S. B. (1903-1972) English.
Leakey, Richard. (1944-) Kenyan.
Leidy, Joseph. (1823-1891)
Marsh, Othniel Charles. (1831-1899)
Novacek, Michael. (1948-)
Osborn, Henry. (1857-1935)
Sternberg, Charles. (1850-1943)

Palestinians
Arafat, Yasir. (1929-) Political leader, terrorist. Nobel Peace Prize winner.

Panamanians
See also Hispanic-Americans.
Lee, Carlos. (1976-) Baseball player.
Pincay, Laffit, Jr. (1946-) Jockey, born Panama.
Rivera, Mariano. (1969-) Baseball player.

Pathologists
See also Physicians.
Adams, Eugene W. (1920-)
Andersen, Dorothy. (1901-1963)
Florey, Lord Howard Walter. (1898-1968) Australian.
Fuller, Solomon Carter. (1872-1953) born Liberia.
Hamilton, Alice. (1869-1970)
Landsteiner, Karl. (1868-1943) born Austria.
L'Esperance, Elsie Strong. (1878-1959)
Virchow, Rudolph. (1821-1902) German.

Peace Activists
See also Nobel Prize Winners, Peace.
Abzug, Bella. (1920-1988)
Angell, Sir Norman. (1873-1967) English.
Arnoldson, Klas. (1844-1916) Swedish.
Bajer, Fredrik. (1837-1922) Danish.
Balch, Emily Greene. (1867-1961)
Beernaert, Auguste. (1829-1912) Belgian.
Belo, Carlos Felipe Ximenes. (1948-) East Timorian.
Black Kettle. (1807-1868) Cheyenne Indian.
Bojaxhiu, Agnes. (Mother Theresa) (1910-1997) Indian, born Yugoslavia.
Butler, Nicholas Murray. (1862-1947)
Carter, James Earl "Jimmy." (1924-)
Cecil, Robert. (1864-1958) English.
Constant, Paul D'Estournelles. (1852-1924) French.
Corrigan, Mairead. (1944-) Irish.
Crowfoot. (1821-1890) Blackfoot Indian.
Deganwidah. (c. 1400) Huron Indian.
Ducommon, Élie. (1833-1906) Swiss.
Fried, Alfred. (1864-1921) Austrian.
Gandhi, Mohandas. (1869-1948) Indian.

Gobat, Albert. (1843-1914) Swiss.
Hammarskjöld, Dag. (1905-1961) Swedish.
Hanh, Thich Nhat. (1926-) Vietnamese.
Hayenwatha. (c. 1400) Mohawk Indian.
Lamas, Carlos Saavedra. (1878-1959) Argentine.
Lange, Christian. (1869-1938) Norwegian.
Little Raven. (d. 1889) Arapaho Indian.
MacBride, Seán. (1904-1988) Irish.
Moneta, Ernesto. (1833-1918) Italian.
Myrdal, Alva. (1902-1986) Swedish.
Noel-Baker, Philip. (1889-1982) English.
Ossietzky, Carl von. (1889-1938) German.
Passy, Frédéric. (1822-1912) French.
Pire, Dominique-Georges. (1910-1969) Belgian.
Quidde, Ludwig. (1858-1941) German.
Rankin, Jeannette. (1880-1973)
Root, Elihu. (1845-1937)
Rotblat, Joseph. (1908-) English, born Poland.
Sainte-Maire, Buffy. (1941-) Cree Indian, born Canada.
Sato, Eisaku. (1901-1975) Japanese.
Smith, Samantha Reid. (1972-1985)
Soong Ching-ling. (1893-1981) Chinese.
Spotted Tail. (1823-1881) Sioux Indian.
Suttner, Bertha von. (1843-1914) Austrian.
Suu Kyi, Daw Aung San. (1945-) Burmese.
Thurman, Howard. (1900-1981)
Ward, Nancy. (1738-1822) Cherokee Indian.
Williams, Betty. (1943-) Irish.
Winema. (Tobey Riddle) (1836-1932) Modoc Indian.

Persians, Ancient
Cyrus the Great. (600-530 B.C.) Warrior.
Esther. (5th century B.C.) Queen.
Khayyam, Omar. (1048-1131) Astronomer, mathematician, poet.
Mani. (216-277) Prophet, founder of Manichaeism religion.
Xerxes I. (519-465 B.C.) Military leader, king.
Zoroaster. (628-551 B.C.) Spiritual leader.

Persians, Modern
Bahaullah. (1817-1892) Spiritual leader, founder Baha'i religion.

Peruvians

See also Hispanic-Americans.

Atahualpa. (1502-1533) Inca emperor.

Grandmaison y Bruno Godin, Isabel. (1729-1792) Adventurer.

Llosa, Mario Vargas. (1936-) Author.

Martin de Porres. (1579-1639) Saint.

Rose of Lima. (1586-1617) Saint, spiritual leader.

Sauñe, Rómulo. (1953-1992) Quechua Indian missionary, spiritual leader.

Vega, Garcilaso de la. (1539-1616) Author, historian.

Philanthropists

See also Human Rights Activists.

Almonaster y Rojas, Andrés. (1725-1798)

Almonaster y Rojas, Michaela. (1795-1874)

Annenberg, Walter. (1908-2002)

Carnegie, Andrew. (1835-1919) born Scotland.

Cuffe, Paul. (1759-1817)

Dawes, Charles Gates. (1865-1951)

Eastman, Charles. (1854-1932)

Gratz, Rebecca. (1781-1869)

Hearst, William Randolph. (1863-1951)

Kellogg, Will Keith. (1860-1951)

Lawless, Theodore. (1892-1971)

Livingston, Philip. (1716-1778)

MacArthur, Catherine. (1906-1981)

MacArthur, John D. (1897-1978)

Marriott, John Willard. (1900-1985)

McCormick, Cyrus Hall. (1809-1884)

Mellon, Andrew. (1855-1937)

Montefiore, Lady Judith Cohen. (1784-1862) English.

Montefiore, Sir Moses. (1784-1885) English.

Morgan, John Pierpont "J. P." (1837-1913)

Nasi, Dona Gracia. (1510-1568) Portuguese.

Newman, Paul. (1925-)

Nobel, Alfred Bernhard. (1833-1896) Swedish.

Owen, Robert. (1771-1858) Welsh.

Packard, David. (1912-1996)

Pulitzer, Joseph. (1847-1911) born Hungary.

Rhodes, Cecil John. (1853-1902) English.

Rockefeller, John Davison. (1839-1937)

Rosenwald, Julius. (1862-1932)

Shoong, Joe. (1879-1961)

Soong Ai-Ling. (1889-1973) Chinese.

Touissant, Pierre. (1766-1853)

Walker, Thomas. (1850-1935)

Zorich, Chris. (1969-)

Philosophers

See also Scholars; Spiritual Leaders.

Aristotle. (384-322 B.C.) Greek.

Arouet, François Maire. (Voltaire) (1694-1778) French.

Aud the Deep Minded. (c. 900) Viking.

Beauvoir, Simone de. (1908-1986) French.

Buber, Martin. (1878-1965) Austrian.

Burke, Edmund. (1729-1797) English.

Chuang Tzu. (369-286 B.C.) Chinese.

Cicero. (Marcus Tollius Cicero) (106-43 B.C.) Roman.

Confucius. (551-479 B.C.) Chinese.

Descartes, René. (1596-1650) French.

Dewey, John. (1859-1952)

Emerson, Ralph Waldo. (1803-1882)

Epicurus. (341-270 B.C.) Greek.

Erasmus, Desiderius. (1469-1536) Dutch.

Gautama, Siddhartha. (Buddha) (560-480 B.C.) Indian.

Hipparchia of Athens. (330 B.C.) Greek.

Hypathia. (355-415) Egyptian.

Kabir. (1440-1518) Indian.

Lao-Tzu. (604-531 B.C.) Chinese.

Maimonides. (Moses ben Maimon) (1135-1204) Spanish.

Marx, Karl Heinrich. (1818-1883) German.

Mencius. (371-289 B.C.) Chinese.

Mendelssohn, Moses. (1729-1786) German.

Paine, Thomas. (1737-1809) born England.

Pascal, Blaise. (1623-1662) French.

Plato. (427-347 B.C.) Greek.

Pythagoras. (c. 580-500 B.C.) Greek.

Rumi, Jalal al-Din. (1207-1273) Afghan.

Santayana, George. (1863-1952) born Spain.

Sartre, Jean Paul. (1905-1980) French.

Seneca. (Lucius Annaeus Seneca) (4 B.C.-65 A.D.) Roman.

Socrates. (470-399 B.C.) Greek.

Suzuki, Daisetz Teitan "D. T." (1870-1966) born Japan.

Swedenborg, Emanuel. (1688-1772) Swedish.

Thomas Aquinas. (1224-1274) Italian.

Tillich, Paul. (1886-1965) born Germany.

Zeno. (335-263 B.C.) Greek.

Photographers and Photojournalists

Abbott, Berenice. (1898-1991)
Adams, Ansel. (1902-1984)
Adams, Harriet Chalmers. (1875-1937)
Arbus, Diane. (1923-1971)
Arnold, Eve. (1913-)
Ball, James P. (1825-1904)
Barnard, George N. (1819-1902) Civil War.
Battey, Cornelius M. (1873-1927)
Blom, Gertrude Elizabeth Loertscher Doby. (1901-1993) Swiss.
Bourke-White, Margaret. (1906-1971) World War II.
Brady, Matthew B. (1823-1896) Civil War.
Bravo, Lola Alvarez. (1907-1993) Mexican.
Breckinridge, Mary Marvin. (1905-2002) World War II.
Bridges, Marilyn. (1948-)
Brigman, Anne. (1869-1950)
Burson, Nancy. (1948-)
Cameron, Evelyn. (1868-1928)
Cameron, Julia Margaret. (1815-1878)
Capa, Robert. (1913-1954) born Hungary.
Chappelle, Georgette "Dickey" Meyer. (1918-1965) World War II.
Cook, George S. (1819-1902) Civil War.
Cunningham, Imogen. (1883-1976)
Curtis, Edward S. (1868-1952)
Dahl-Wolfe, Louise. (1895-1989) Fashion.
Dater, Judy. (1941-)
Dorfman, Elsa. (1937-)
Doubilet, David. (1946-) Underwater.
Gardner, Alexander. (1821-1882) Civil War, born Scotland.
Garduño, Flor. (1957-) Mexican.
Gibson, James F. (unknown) Civil War, born Scotland.
Gilpin, Laura. (1891-1979)
Goodridge, Glenalvin. (1829-1866)
Goodridge, Wallace. (1841-1922)
Goodridge, William. (1846-1891)
Grossman, Mendel. (1917-1945) Polish Holocaust.
Higgins, Marguerite. (1920-1966) Korean, Vietnam War, World War II.
Hine, Lewis W. (1874-1940)
Johnston, Frances Benjamin. (1864-1952)
Joubert, Beverly. (1957-) Wildlife.

Joubert, Dereck. (1956-) Wildlife.
Kasebier, Gertrude. (1852-1934)
Lange, Dorothea. (1895-1965)
Leibovitz, Annie. (1949-)
Lion, Jules. (1810-1866)
Man Ray. *See* Radnitsky, Emmanuel.
Mark, Mary Ellen. (1940-)
Martin, Louise. (1911-)
Martinez-Canas, Maria. (1960-) Puerto Rican, born Cuba.
Miller, Lee. (1907-1977) World War II.
Moodie, Geraldine Fitzgibbon. (1854-1945) Canadian.
Morgan, Barbara. (1900-1992)
Moutoussamy-Ashe, Jeanne. (1951-)
Norman, Dorothy. (1905-1997)
Orkin, Ruth. (1921-1985)
Parks, Gordon. (1912-)
Radnitsky, Emmanuel. (Man Ray) (1890-1976)
Riis, Jacob August. (1849-1914) born Denmark.
Robertson, Ruth Agnes McCall. (1905-1998)
Say, Allen. (1937-) born Japan.
Scurlock, Addison. (1883-1964)
Sherman, Cindy. (1954-)
Simpson, Lorna. (1960-)
Skoglund, Sandy. (1946-)
Sleet, Moneta, Jr. (1926-1996)
Stieglitz, Alfred. (1864-1946)
Streichen, Edward. (1879-1973) World War I and II, born Luxembourg.
Tape, Mary McGladery. (1857-1928) born China.
Tsinhnahjinnie, Hulleah. (1954-) Navajo/Creek/Seminole Indian.
Van der Zee, James. (1886-1983)
Van Vechten, Carl. (1880-1964)
Ward, Catherine Barnes. (1851-1913)
Washington, Augustus. (1820-?)
Watson-Schutze, Eva. (1867-1935)
Weems, Carrie Mae. (1951-)
Wilkins, Sir George Hubert. (1888-1958) Australian World War I.

Physical Therapists

Griffin, Bessie Blount. (1913-)
Walsh, Mary. (1950-) Vietnam War army therapist.

Physically Challenged

These individuals persevered and succeeded in their respective fields despite physical limitations caused by birth defects, accidents, war injuries, or acute or chronic illness.

Abbott, Jim. (1967-) Baseball player. (missing a hand)

Abdul-Rauf, Mahmoud. (Chris Jackson) (1969-) Basketball player. (tourette's syndrome)

Akers, Michelle. (1966-) Olympic soccer player. (Chronic fatigue syndrome)

Alexander, Grover Cleveland. (1887-1950) Baseball player. (epilepsy)

Ashe, Arthur. (1943-1993) Tennis player. Presidential Medal of Freedom recipient. (AIDS)

Bader, Sir Douglas. (1910-1982) English pilot, World War II hero. (war injury)

Barton, Greg. (1959-) Olympic kayaker. (club feet, leg deformities)

Bernhardt, Sarah. (1844-1923) French actor. (leg amputated due to knee injury)

Bleier, Rocky. (1946-) Football player. (injuries from Vietnam War)

Brown, Christy. (1932-1981) Author, poet. (cerebral palsy)

Brown, Mordecai Peter Centennial "Three Finger." (1876-1948) Baseball player.

Browning, Elizabeth Barrett. (1806-1861) English poet. (nervous disorders)

Callahan, John. (1951-) Cartoonist, disability rights activist. (quadriplegic after accident)

Campanella, Roy. (1921-1993) Baseball player. (quadriplegic after accident)

Carmichael, Amy. (1867-1951) Irish missionary. (invalid from serious fall)

Conner, Bart. (1958-) Olympic gymnast.

Dempsey, Tom. (1947-) Football player. (birth defects; missing limbs)

Devers, Gail. (1966-) Olympic track and field athlete. (Graves disease)

Dole, Robert. (1923-) Congressman, presidential candidate, senator, World War II lieutenant. Presidential Medal of Freedom recipient. (war injury)

Dravecky, Dave. (1956-) Baseball player. (cancer)

Driscoll, Jean. (1966-) Wheelchair athlete. (spina bifida)

Eisenreich, Jim. (1959-) Baseball player. (Tourette's syndrome)

Eng and Chang. (1811-1874) Showmen, Siamese twins.

Fraser, Dawn. (1937-) Australian olympic swimmer. (asthma)

Gaes, Jason. (1978-) Author. (cancer)

Galarraga, Andrés. (1962-) Baseball player, born Venezuela. (cancer)

Garrison-Jackson, Zina. (1963-) Tennis player. (eating disorders)

Gertz, Alison. (1966-1992) AIDS activist. (AIDS)

Glaser, Elizabeth. (1947-1994) AIDS activist, children's rights activist. (AIDS)

Golden, Diana. (1963-2001) Olympic skier. (cancer)

Grandin, Temple. (1974-) Inventor. (autism)

Gray, Pete. (1915-2002) Baseball player. (arm removed from childhood accident)

Hamilton, Marilyn. (1947-) Disability rights activist, inventor. (paralyzed)

Haring, Keith. (1958-1990) AIDS activist, cartoonist, painter. (AIDS)

Hawking, Stephen. (1942-) English astrophysicist. (ALS disease)

Heuman, Judy. (1947-) Asst. Secretary of Education. (polio)

Higgins, Patillo. (1863-1955) Entrepreneur oil. (missing arm)

Hockenberry, John. (1956-) Author, broadcast journalist. (paralyzed following accident)

Hogan, Ben. (1912-1997) Golfer. (injured in automobile accident)

Holliday, John "Doc." (1852-1887) Dentist, outlaw. (physical ailments)

Hunter, Jim "Catfish." (1946-) Baseball player. (physically injured)

Hurley, Bobby. (1971-) Basketball player. (serious accident)

Inouye, Daniel. (1924-) Attorney, senator, World War II Army captain. (war injury)

Johnson, Earvin "Magic" (1959-) Basketball player. (AIDS)

Joyner, Florence Griffith. (1959-1998) Olympic track and field athlete. (heart disease)

Joyner-Kersee, Jackie. (1962-) Olympic track and field athlete. (asthma)

Kahlo, Frida. (1907-1954) Mexican painter. (injured in accident)

Kariya, Paul. (1974-) Canadian hockey player. (injured)

Keats, John. (1795-1821) English poet. (chronic illness)

Kelly, Patrick. (1954-1990) Fashion designer. (AIDS)

Kelly, Wynton. (1931-1971) Jazz musician, born Jamaica. (epilepsy)

Kenner, Beatrice. (1912-) Inventor. (facial deformities from burns)

Lange, Dorothea. (1895-1965) Photographer. (polio)

Laroche, Raymonde de. (1886-1919) Aviation pioneer. (injured severely in crash)

Lemieux, Mario. (1965-) Canadian hockey player. (Hodgkins Disease)

LeMond, Greg. (1961-) Bicyclist. (cancer)

Lewis, Clive Staples "C. S." (1898-1963) Irish children's author. (World War I injury)

Lisboa, Antonio Francisco. (1738-1814) Brazilian architect, sculptor. (leprosy)

Logan, James. (1674-1751) Colonist, born Ireland. (injured in fall)

Lord, Audre. (1934-1992) Human rights activist, poet. (cancer)

Lucas, John. (1953-) Basketball player, coach. (drug and alcohol abuse)

Luxemburg, Rosa. (1870-1919) German political activist, workers' rights activist, born Poland. (crippled since childhood)

Mankiller, Wilma. (1945-) Cherokee Nation chief. Presidential Medal of Freedom recipient. (serious car accident)

Mann, Shelley. (1939-) Olympic swimmer. (polio)

Mansfield, Katherine. (1888-1923) English author, born New Zealand. (chronic illness)

Martin, Casey. (1972-) Golfer. (birth defects)

McCoy, Millie-Christine. (1851-1912) Siamese twins, singers, slaves.

Medawar, Sir Peter Brian. (1915-1987) English medical researcher, zoologist. Nobel Prize winner. (massive stroke)

Mendelssohn, Moses. (1729-1786) German

educator, philosopher, scholar. (curvature of the spine from childhood illness)

Mercury, Freddie. (1946-1991) English rock musician. (AIDS)

Merrick, Joseph. (1862-1890) English "Elephant Man," showman. (birth abnormalities)

Mistral, Gabriela Lucila Godoy y Alcayága. (1889-1957) Chilean educator, poet. Nobel Prize winner. (diabetes)

Mitchell, Thecla. (unknown) Marathon runner. (triple amputee)

Murdoch, Iris. (1919-1999) English author, born Ireland. (Alzheimer's Disease)

Nureyev, Rudolf. (1938-1993) Russian ballet dancer. (AIDS)

Nussbaum, Susan. (1953-) Actor, disability rights activist, playwright. (quadriplegic)

O'Connor, Flannery. (1925-1964) Author. (lupus)

Pastrana, Julia. (1832-1860) Mexican showperson. ("bearded lady")

Peacock, Gary. (1935-) Jazz musician. (chronic fatigue syndrome)

Perkins, Anthony. (1932-1992) Actor. (AIDS)

Perlman, Itzhak. (1945-) Israeli musician. (polio)

Peron, Eva "Evita." (1919-1952) Argentine actor, political activist. (cancer)

Petitclerc, Chantal. (1969-) Canadian wheelchair racer. (paraplegic)

Pippin, Horace. (1888-1946) Painter, World War I soldier. (paralyzed from war injuries)

Poussin, Nicolas. (1594-1665) Italian painter, born France. (chronic illness)

Powell, John Wesley. (1834-1902) Civil War soldier, explorer, geologist. (one arm)

Powell, William J. (1897?-1942) Author, engineer, World War I Army pilot. (gassed during war)

Reeve, Christopher. (1952-2004) Actor, filmmaker. (paralyzed by fall from horse)

Reinhardt, Django. (1910-1953) Belgian jazz musician. (only two fingers on hand from fire injury)

Roberts, Ed. (1939-1995) Disability rights activist. (quadriplegic)

Roosevelt, Franklin Delano. (1882-1945)

Attorney, governor, Navy assistant secretary, 32nd president of U.S. (polio)

Rossetti, Christina Georgina. (1830-1894) English art model, poet. (Graves Disease)

Rousso, Harilyn. (1946-) Disability rights activist, psychotherapist. (cerebral palsy)

Rudolph, Wilma. (1940-1994) Olympic track and field athlete. (one leg paralzyed)

Russell, Harold. (1914-2002) Actor, disability rights activist, World War II soldier, born Canada. (lost arm from war injury)

Sawchuck, Terry. (1925-1970) Canadian hockey player. (one leg shorter than other)

Sequoyah. (1770-1843) Cherokee chief, Creek War Army soldier, linguist. (war injury)

Serling, Rod. (1924-1975) Author, World War II Army. (war injury)

Shilts, Randy. (1951-1994) AIDS activist, author, journalist. (AIDS)

Smith, Mildred Davidson Austin. (1916-1993) Disability rights activist, inventor. (multiple sclerosis)

Smith, Will. (1948-1987) Fashion designer. (AIDS)

Stevens, Thaddeus. (1792-1868) Attorney, civil rights activist, congressman. (clubfoot)

Stratton, Charles Sherwood. (Tom Thumb) (1838-1883) Showman. (dwarf)

Toulouse-Lautrec, Henride. (1864-1901) French painter. (permanently deformed legs resulting from falls)

Tubman, Harriet. (1820-1913) Abolitionist, Civil War spy, nurse, slave. (comas)

Unthan, Hermann. (1848-1929) Musician. (armless)

Veeck, Bill. (1914-1986) Baseball team owner, World War II Marine. (war injury)

Wade, Cheryl Marie. (unknown) Disability rights activist, poet.

Wadlow, Robert. (1918-1940) Showman, circus performer. (tallest man)

White, Ryan. (1971-1990) AIDS activist and victim.

Physicians

See also Anatomists; Geneticists; Medical Researchers; Nobel Prize Winners-Medicine and Physiology; Pathologists; Psychiatrists and Psychotherapists.

American

Albright, Tenley. (1935-)

Alexander, Hattie Elizabeth. (1901-1968)

Andersen, Dorothy. (1901-1963)

Apgar, Virginia. (1909-1974)

Augusta, Alexander T. (1825-1890)

Baker, Sara Josephine. (1873-1945)

Barringer, Emily Dunning. (1876-1961)

Bartlett, Josiah. (1729-1795)

Bath, Patricia. (1942-)

Blackwell, Elizabeth. (1821-1910) born England.

Blackwell, Emily. (1826-1910) born England.

Boylston, Zabadiel. (1679-1766)

Brown, Dorothy Lavinia. (1919-)

Canady, Alexa. (1950-)

Cardus, David. (1922-) born Spain.

Carson, Benjamin Solomon. (1951-)

Chinn, May Edward. (1896-1980)

Cleveland, Emeline Horton. (1829-1878)

Cobb, William Montague. (1904-1990)

Cole, Rebecca J. (1846-1922)

Collins, Daniel A. (1916-)

Comer, James P. (1934-)

Crichton, Michael. (1942-)

Crumpler, Rebecca Lee. (1833-1895)

Curtis, Austin Maurice. (1868-1939)

Delaney, Martin Robison. (1812-1885)

Derham, James. (1762-1804)

Dick, Gladys Rowena. (1881-1963)

Drew, Charles Richard. (1904-1950)

Duggar, Benjamin. (1872-1956)

Eastman, Charles Alexander. (1858-1939)

Elders, Jocelyn Jones. (1933-)

Evans, Matilda Arabella. (1872-1935)

Ferguson, Angella D. (1925-)

Fix, Georgia Arbuckle. (1852-1918)

Ford, Justina Laurena. (1871-1952)

Fowler, Lydia Folger. (1822-1879)

Fuller, Solomon Carter. (1872-1953) born Liberia.

Garcia, Hector Perez. (1914-1996) born Mexico.

Greer, Pedro Jose, Jr. (1956-)

Guiteras, Juan. (1852-1925) born Cuba.

Hall, George Cleveland. (1864-1930)

Hall, Lyman. (1724-1790)

Hamilton, Alice. (1869-1970)

Harris, Bernard. (1956-)

Healy, Bernadine. (1944-)

Hinton, William Augustus. (1883-1959)

Ho, David. (1952-) born Taiwan.

Holmes, Herman Mudget "H. H." (1860-1896)

Hostetter, Margaret. (unknown)

Jackson, Janis. (unknown)

Jacobi, Mary Putnam. (1842-1906) born England.

Jemison, Mae C. (1956-)

Johnson, Halle Tanner Dillon. (1864-1901)

Kübler-Ross, Elisabeth. (1926-) born Switzerland.

Landsteiner, Karl. (1868-1943) born Austria.

Lawless, Theodore. (1892-1971)

Lee, Sammy. (1920-)

Leidy, Joseph. (1823-1891)

L'Esperance, Elsie Strong. (1878-1959)

Logan, Arthur C. (1909-1973)

Long, Crawford. (1815-1878)

Longshore, Hannah E. Myers. (1810-1901)

Love, Susan. (1948-)

Lovejoy, Esther Pohl. (1869-1967)

Marchbanks, Vance. (1905-1988)

Masters, William. (1915-2001)

McGee, Anita Newcomb. (1864-1940)

McKane, Alice Woodby. (1865-1948)

Mergler, Marie Josepha. (1851-1901) born Germany.

Minoka-Hill, Lillie Rosa. (1876-1952)

Morani, Alma Dea. (1907-2001) Plastic surgeon, born Italy.

Mossell, Nathan Francis. (1856-1946)

Murray, Joseph E. (1919-)

Ngor, Haing. (1947-1996) born Cambodia.

Novello, Antonia C. (1944-) Surgeon General, born Puerto Rico.

Ochoa, Severo. (1950-1993) born Spain.

Odell, Jonathan. (1737-1818)

Osborn, June. (1937-)

Owens-Adair, Bethenia. (1840-1926)

Peters, C. J. (1940-)

Picotte, Susan La Flesche. (1865-1915) Ponca and Omaha Indian.

Popé. (d. 1692) San Juan Pueblo Indian.

Powell, Clilan Bethany. (1894-1977)

Prendergast, Franklyn G. (1945-)

Preston, Ann. (1813-1872)

Pretty Shield. (1850-1930) Crow Indian healer.

Prothrow-Stith, Deborah. (1954-)

Purvis, Charles Burleigh. (1842-1929)

Reed, Walter. (1851-1902)

Reid, Clarice D. (1931-)

Remond, Sarah P. (1826-1894)

Richardson, Dorothy "Dot." (1961-)

Roc, John S. (1825-1866)

Rush, Benjamin. (1745-1813)

Sabin, Albert Bruce. (1906-1993) born Poland.

Sabin, Florence Rena. (1871-1953)

Salk, Jonas. (1914-1995)

Satcher, David. (1941-)

Scott, Roland. (1909-2002)

Seddon, Margaret Rhea. (1947-)

Shaw, Anna Howard. (1847-1919) born England.

Smith, James McCune. (1813-1865)

Spock, Benjamin. (1903-1998)

Steward, Susan McKinney. (1847-1918)

Swain, Clara A. (1834-1910)

Taussig, Helen Brooke. (1898-1986)

Temin, Howard. (1934-)

Thomas, Debi. (1967-)

Thompson, Mary Harris. (1829-1895)

Thornton, Matthew. (1714-1803) born Ireland.

Van Hoosen, Bertha. (1863-1952)

Villa-Komoroff, Lydia. (1947-)

Walker, Mary Edwards. (1832-1919)

Walker, Thomas. (1715-1794)

Wecht, Cyril. (1931-)

Whitman, Marcus. (1802-1847)

Whitten, Charles. (1922-)

Williams, Daniel Hale. (1856-1931)

Wright, Jane Cooke. (1919-)

Wright, Louis Tompkins. (1891-1952)

Zakrzewska, Marie Elizabeth. (1829-1902) born Germany.

Ancient Civilizations

Agnodice. (c. 300 B.C.) Greek.

Galen. (130-200) Greek.

Hippocrates. (460?-370? B.C.) Greek.

Arab and Muslim

Ibn-e-Sina, Hakim. (980-1037) Islamic.

Australian

Burnet, Sir Frank MacFarlane. (1899-1985)

Seager, Joy Debenham. (1899-1991)

Canadian

Abbott, Maude Elizabeth Seymour. (1869-1940)

Banting, Sir Frederick Grant. (1891-1941)

Caron, Nadine. (1970-)

McLoughlin, John. (1784-1857)

Osler, Sir William. (1849-1919)

Ross, Alexander. (1783-1856)

Stowe, Emily Jennings. (1831-1903)

Teasdale, Lucille. (1929-1996)

Cuban

Finlay, Carlos Juan. (1833-1915)

English, Irish, and Scottish

Anderson, Elizabeth Garrett. (1836-1917) English.

Burkitt, Denis Parsons. (1911-1993) Irish.

Doyle, Sir Arthur Conan. (1859-1930) Scottish.

Epstein, Sir Michael Anthony. (1921-) English.

Faulds, Henry. (fl. 1880s) English.

Freud, Anna. (1895-1982) Psychoanalyst, born Austria.

Hutton, James. (1726-1797) Scottish.

Inglis, Elsie. (1864-1917) Scottish.

Jenner, Edward. (1749-1823) English.

Jex-Blake, Sophia. (1840-1912) English.

Lind, James. (1716-1794) Scottish.

Lister, Joseph. (1827-1912) English.

Mantell, Gideon. (1790-1852) English.

Saunders, Cicely. (1918-) English.

Snow, John. (1813-1858)

Stuart, Miranda. (James Barry) (1795-1865)

European and Scandinavian

Brandt, Karl. (1904-1948) German.

Brundtland, Gro Harlem. (1939-) Norwegian.

Dausset, Jean. (1916-) French.

Einthoven, Willem. (1860-1927) Dutch.

Frankl, Viktor E. (1905-1997) Austrian.

Freud, Sigmund. (1856-1939) Austrian.

Halevi, Judah. (1075-1141) Spanish.

Hirschfeld, Magnus. (1868-1935) Polish.

Korczak, Janusz. (1878-1942) Polish.

Kouchner, Bernard. (1939-) French.

Lanennec, Réne T. H. (1781-1826) French.

Leeuwenhoek, Anton van. (1632-1723) Dutch.

Mengele, Josef. (1911-1979) German.

Montessori, Maria. (1870-1952) Italian.

Nostradamus. (1503-1566) French.

Paré, Ambroise. (1510-1590) French.

Perl, Gisella. (1910-1985) Hungarian.

Pinel, Philippe. (1745-1826) French.

Platearius, Trotula. (c. 1080) Italian.

Rabelais, François. (1495-1553) French.

Roentgen, Wilhelm Conrad. (1845-1923) German.

Santorio, Santorio. (1561-1636) Italian.

Schweitzer, Albert. (1875-1965) French.

Semmelweis, Ignaz Phillipp. (1818-1865) Hungarian.

Spoerry, Anne. (1918-1999) French.

Vesalius, Andreas. (1514-1564) Belgian.

Virchow, Rudolph. (1821-1902) German.

Other

Bordin, Alexander Porfiervich. (1833-1889) Russian.

del Mundo, Fe. (1911-) Filipino.

Esu-Williams, Eku. (1956-) Nigerian.

Jean-Murat, Carolle. (1950-) Haitian.

Jhirad, Jerusha. (1891-1948) Indian.

Lifshitz, Aliza. (1951-) Mexican.

Lucas, Adetokonbo. (1931-) Nigerian.

Physicists

See also Nobel Prize Winners, Physics.

American

Alvarez, Luis Walter. (1911-1988)

Bardeen, John. (1908-1991)

Begay, Fred. (1932-) Navajo and Ute Indian.

Brattain, Walter Houser. (1902-1987)

Cardona, Manuel. (1934-) born Spain.

Carruthers, George E. (1939-) Astrophysicist.

Chandrasekhar, Subrahmanyan. (1910-1995) born Pakistan.

Chang-Diaz, Franklin R. (1950-) born Venezuela.

Chouet, Bernard. (1945-) born Switzerland.

Chu, Paul Ching-wu. (1941-) born China.

Compton, Arthur Holly. (1892-1962)

Cordova, France. (unknown)

Corso, Sandra. (unknown)

Dresselhaus, Mildred. (1930-)

Einstein, Albert. (1879-1955) born Germany.

Ewing, Maurice. (1906-1974)
Fermi, Enrico. (1901-1954) born Italy.
Feynman, Richard Philips. (1918-1988)
Gini, Mari. (unknown) born Italy.
Goddard, Robert. (1882-1945)
Goeppert-Mayer, Maria. (1906-1972) born
    Germany.
Gould, Gordon. (1920-)
Henry, Joseph. (1797-1878)
Hofstadter, Robert. (1915-1990)
Jackson, Shirley Ann. (1946-)
Jernigan, Tamara. (1955-)
Land, Edwin. (1909-1991)
Langley, Samuel Pierpont. (1834-1906)
Lawrence, Ernest Orlando. (1901-1958)
Lee, Tsung Dao. (1926-) born China.
Massey, Walter. (1938-)
McNair, Ronald. (1950-1986)
McNutt, Marcia. (1952-)
Michelson, Albert Abraham. (1852-1931)
    born Germany.
Moore, Gordon. (1929-)
Noyce, Robert Norton. (1927-1990)
Oppenheimer, J. Robert. (1904-1967)
Quimby, Edith Hinkley. (1891-1982) Bio-
    physicist.
Rabe, Karin. (unknown)
Ride, Sally Kristen. (1951-) Astrophysicist.
Shaw, Earl D. (1937-)
Shimomura, Tsutomu. (1965-) born Japan.
Tarter, Jill Cornell. (1944-) Astrophysicist.
Thomas, Valerie. (1943-)
Ting, Samuel Chao Chung. (1936-)
Tolliver, Peter. (1927-)
Townes, Charles Hard. (1915-)
Trinh, Eugene H. (1950-) born Vietnam.
Ulam, Stanislaw. (1909-1984) born Poland.
Van Allen, James. (1914-)
Wu, Chien Shiung. (1912-1997) Nuclear
    physicist, born China.
Yalow, Rosalyn Sussman. (1921-) Medical
    physicist.
Yang, Chen Ning. (1922-) born China.

English and Scottish
Born, Max. (1882-1970) born Poland.
Boyle, Robert. (1627-1691)
Cavendish, Henry. (1731-1810)
Dirac, Paul Adrien Maurice. (1902-1984)
Fleming, John Ambrose. (1849-1945)

Hawking, Stephen. (1942-)
Joule, James Prescott. (1818-1889)
Maxwell, James Clerk. (1831-1879) Scot-
    tish.
Newton, Sir Isaac. (1642-1727)
Rotblat, Joseph. (1908-) born Poland.
Shockley, William. (1910-1989)
Thomson, Joseph John. (1856-1940)
Thomson, William. (1824-1907) Scottish.
Watson-Watt, Sir Robert Alexander. (1892-
    1973) Scottish.

European
Bassi, Laura. (1711-1778) Italian.
Becquerel, Antoine Henri. (1852-1908)
    French.
Bohr, Niels. (1885-1962) Danish.
Curie, Marie. (1867-1934) French, born
    Poland.
Curie, Pierre. (1859-1906) French.
du Chatelet, Marquise Gabriele-Emilie.
    (1706-1749) French.
Foucault, Jean Bernard Léon. (1819-1868)
    French.
Gabor, Dennis. (1900-1979) Hungarian.
Galilei, Galileo. (1564-1642) Italian.
Geiger, Hans. (1882-1945) German.
Heisenberg, Werner. (1901-1976) German.
Joliot-Curie, Irène. (1897-1956) French.
Marconi, Guglielmo. (1874-1937) Italian.
Meitner, Lise. (1878-1968) Swedish, born
    Germany.
Pascal, Blaise. (1623-1662) French.
Pauli, Wolfgang. (1900-1958) Austrian.
Planck, Max Karl Ernst Ludwig. (1858-
    1947) German.
Roentgen, Wilhelm Conrad. (1845-1923)
    German.
Volta, Alessandro. (1746-1827) Italian.
Zernike, Frits. (1888-1966) Dutch.

Other
Fang, Lizhi. (1936-) Chinese.
Pitcher, Harriet Brooks. (1876-1933) Cana-
    dian.
Rutherford, Baron Ernest. (1871-1938) New
    Zealand.
Sakharov, Andrei. (1921-1989) Russian
    nuclear physicist.

Physiologists

See also Nobel Prize Winners, Medicine and Physiology.

Cannon, Walter Bradford. (1871-1945)

Cavazos, Lauro F. (1927-)

Cowings, Patricia. (1948-)

Dausset, Jean. (1916-) French.

Hyde, Ida Henrietta. (1857-1945)

Landsteiner, Karl. (1868-1943) born Austria.

Metchnikoff, Élie. (1845-1916) Russian.

Ochoa, Severo. (1905-1993) born Spain.

Pavlov, Ivan Petrovich. (1849-1936) Russian.

Pool, Judith Graham. (1917-1975)

Sperry, Roger. (1913-1994)

Pilgrims

See Colonists.

Pilots

See also Aviation Pioneers.

Aliengena, Tony. (1978-) Child pilot.

Arnold, Henry. (1886-1950) World War I.

Bader, Sir Douglas. (1910-1982) English World War II.

Balchen, Bernt. (1899-1973) World War II Army Air Force, born Norway.

Bean, Alan. (1932-) Navy.

Bennett, Floyd. (1890-1928) Navy, co-pilot with Byrd.

Bolden, Charles. (1946-) Marine Corps.

Bragg, Janet Harmon. (1907-1993)

Bush, George Herbert Walker. (1924-) World War II Navy.

Byrd, Richard Evelyn. (1888-1957) World War I and II Navy.

Cernan, Eugene. (1934-) Navy.

Chennault, Claire Lee. (1890-1958) World War I and II.

Cobb, Geraldyn. (1931-)

Cochran, Jacqueline. (1910-1980) World War II Women's Air Force.

Coleman, Bessie. (1893-1926)

Collins, Eileen M. (1956-)

Corrigan, Douglas "Wrong Way." (1907-1995)

Davis, Benjamin O., Jr. (1912-2002) World War II Tuskegee airman.

Davison, Anne. (1913-1992) born England.

Doolittle, Jimmy. (1886-1993) Daredevil pilot, World War II pilot.

Duke, Charles. (1935-) Air Force.

Dwight, Edward J., Jr. (1933-) Air Force.

Earhart, Amelia. (1897-1937)

Eielson, Carl Ben. (1897-1929) Arctic pilot, World War I pilot.

Ferenz, Ludmilla "Lou." (1921-) World War II Army Nurse Corps flight nurse.

Fort, Cornelia. (1919-1943) World War II.

Freeman, Louis. (1952-) Commercial pilot.

Gagarin, Yuri. (1934-1968) Russian.

Greene, Betty. (1920-1997) Medical missionary.

Gregory, Frederick. (1941-) Air Force.

Grissom, Virgil I. "Gus." (1926-1967) Korean War Air Force combat.

Hess, Rudolf. (1894-1987) German.

Hughes, Howard. (1905-1976)

Irwin, James. (1930-1991) Air Force test pilot.

James, Daniel "Chappie," Jr. (1920-1978) Air Force combat pilot, World War II Tuskegee airman.

Jans, Megan. (1952-) Gulf War helicoptor pilot.

Johnson, Amy. (1903-1941) English World War II.

Julian, Hubert Fauntelroy. (1897-?) born Trinidad.

LeMay, Curtis E. (1906-1990) Air Force.

Lindbergh, Anne Morrow. (1906-2001)

Lindbergh, Charles A., Jr. (1902-1974)

Litvak, Lily. (1921-1943) Russian World War II.

Locklear, Ormer. (1891-1929) Daredevil stunt.

Love, Nancy Harkness. (1914-1976) World War II.

Marchbanks, Vance. (1905-1988) World War II Tuskegee airman.

Markham, Beryl. (1902-1986) English.

McCandless, Bruce II. (1932-) Navy.

Mitchell, Edgar. (1930-) Navy.

Mock, Geraldine Fredritz. (1925-)

Musick, Edwin C. (1893-1930) New Zealand World War I.

Nobile, Umberto. (1885-1978) Italian air force pilot, arctic explorer.

Powell, William J. (1897-1942) World War I army.

Reitsch, Hanna. (1912-1979) German test
    pilot.
Richthofen, Baron Manfred von "Red
    Baron." (1892-1918) German World War
    I.
Rickenbacker, Edward Vernon "Eddie."
    (1890-1973) World War I and II.
Riiser-Larsen, Hjalmar. (1890-1965) Nor-
    wegian navy.
Rumsfeld, Donald H. (1932-) Navy.
Rutan, Dick. (1938-) Distance pilot, Viet-
    nam War pilot.
Saint-Exupéry, Antoine de. (1900-1944)
    French World War II.
Scott, David. (1932-) Air Force.
Scott, Sheila. (1927-1988) English.
Shepard, Alan B. (1923-1998) Navy test
    pilot.
Still, Susan. (1961-) Navy.
Stinson, Katherine. (1891-1977) World
    War I.
Tiburzi, Bonnie Linda. (1948-)
Tinker, Clarence L. (1887-1942) Osage In-
    dian World War I army pilot.
Whittle, Sir Frank. (1907-1996) English
    Royal Air Force.
Whyte, Edna Gardner. (1902-1993) Air
    racer.
Wilkins, Sir George Hubert. (1888-1958)
    Australian aviator.
Yeager, Chuck. (1933-) Test pilot.
Yeager, Jenna L. (1952-)

Pioneers and Frontierspeople

See also Colonists; Fur Traders, Trappers
    and Hunters.
Austin, Stephen Fuller. (1793-1836)
Barceló, Maria Gertrudes "Tules." (1800-
    1852)
Beckwourth, James. (1798-1866)
Bemis, Polly. (Lalu Nathay) (1853-1933)
    born China.
Boone, Daniel. (1734-1820)
Bowie, James. (1796-1836)
Bridger, Jim. (1804-1881)
Briones, Juana. (1802-1889)
Brown, Clara. (1803-1885)
Brown, Tabitha. (1780-1858)
Burland, Rebecca. (1793-1872) born
    England.
Bush, George W. (1791-1867)

Cannary, Martha Jane. (Calamity Jane)
    (1852-1903)
Carson, Christopher "Kit." (1809-1868)
Cashman, Nellie. (1845-1925)
Castner, Mattie. (1848-1920)
Chapman, John. (Johnny Appleseed) (1774-
    1845)
Chouteau, Auguste. (1749-1829)
Clappe, Louise Amelia. (1819-1906)
Cody, William. (Buffalo Bill) (1846-1917)
Colter, John. (1775-1813)
Comstock, Will. (1842-1868)
Conly, Elvira. (1845-?)
Crockett, Davy. (1786-1836)
Custer, George Armstrong. (1839-1876)
Custer, Libbie. (1842-1933)
Deere, John. (1804-1886)
Dezhnev, Semyon. (1610-1672) Russian.
Du Sable, Jean Baptiste Pointe. (1745-1818)
    born Haiti.
Fergus, Pamelia. (1824-1902)
Fields, Mary. (1832-1914)
Fink, Mike. (1770?-1823?)
Fremont, Jessie Benton. (1824-1902)
Fremont, John Charles. (1813-1890)
Girty, Simon. (1741-1818)
Glass, Hugh. (1780-1833?)
Horn, Tom. (1806-1903)
Hutton, May Arkwright. (1860-1915)
Lew Chew. (1866-) born China.
Magoffin, Susan Shelby. (1827-1855)
Mason, Biddy. (1818-1891)
Masterson, Martha Gay. (1837-1916)
McLaughlin, James. (1842-1923)
Monroe, George. (1844-1886) Stagecoach
    driver.
Murietta, Joaquin. (1832-1853) Mexican.
Newman, Sarah Jane "Sally Skull." (1817-
    1866)
Pacheco, Romualdo. (1831-1899)
Parkhurst, Charlotte Darkey. (1812-1879)
    Stagecoach driver.
Parkman, Francis. (1823-1893)
Place, Etta. (1875-1940)
Pleasant, Mary Ellen "Mammy." (1814-
    1904)
Reed, Virginia. (1833-1921)
Reynolds, "Lonesome" Charley. (1844-
    1876)
Rogers, Robert. (1731-1795)
Rose, Edward. (1780?-1820?)

Ryan, Katherine "Klondike Kate." (1869-1932)
Sevier, John. (1745-1815)
Smith, Jedediah Strong. (1797-1831)
Snow, Eliza. (1804-1887)
Starr, Myra "Belle" Shirley. (1848-1889)
Stewart, Elinoire Pruitt. (1876-1933)
Sutter, John Augustus. (1803-1880) born Germany.
Thompson, Ben. (1843-1884) Gunfighter.
Walker, Joe. (1799-1876)
Washington, George. (1817-1905)
Watson, Ella "Cattle Kate." (1861-1889)
Whitman, Marcus. (1802-1847)
Whitman, Narcissa. (1808-1847)
Wilder, Laura Ingalls. (1867-1957)
Wilson, Luzena Stanley. (1821-?)
Young, Ann Eliza Webb. (1844-1908)

Pirates

Alfhild. (Alvida) (c. 1000) Viking.
Black Bart. *See* Roberts, Bartholomew.
Blackbeard. *See* Teach, Edward.
Bonney, Anne. (1697-1721) Irish.
Campbell, Fanny. (1755-?)
Cheng I Sao. (Lady Ching) (1775-1844) Chinese.
Dampier, William. (1652-1715) English.
Every, Henry. (1653-?) English.
Kidd, William "Captain." (1645-1701) Scottish.
Killigrew, Lady Elizabeth. (1530-1570) English.
Lafitte, Jean. (1781-1826)
Lai Cho San. (1922-1939) Chinese.
L'Olonnois, François. (1630-1671) French.
Morgan, Henry. (1635-1688) English.
O'Malley, Grace. (1530-1603) Irish.
Plantain, James. (fl. 1720) Jamaican.
Read, Mary. (1690-1720) English.
Roberts, Bartholomew. (Black Bart) (1682-1722) Welsh.
Rogers, Woodes. (1679-1732) English.
Sela, Princess. (c. 420 A.D.) Viking.
Teach, Edward. (Blackbeard) (1680-1718) English.
Wall, Rachel. (1760-1789)
Yermak. (Vasily Timofeyovich) (1540-1585) Russian.

Playwrights

African
Gordimer, Nadine. (1923-) South African.
Soyinka, Wole. (1934-) Nigerian.

American
Anderson, Garland. (1886-1939)
Baldwin, James. (1924-1987)
Barnes, Djuna. (1892-1982)
Brown, William Wells. (1818-1884)
Chávez, Denise. (1948-)
Childress, Alice. (1920-1994)
Fornés, Maria Irene. (1930-) born Cuba.
Hammerstein, Oscar II. (1895-1960)
Hansberry, Lorraine. (1930-1965)
Henley, Beth. (1952-)
Hwang, David Henry. (1957-)
Lopez, Josefina. (1969-) born Mexico.
Luce, Clare Boothe. (1903-1987)
Mailer, Norman. (1923-)
Millay, Edna St.Vincent. (1892-1950)
Miller, Arthur. (1915-)
Noah, Mordecai Manuel. (1785-1851)
Nussbaum, Susan. (1953-)
Okita, Dwight. (1958-)
Ondaatje, Michael. (1943-) born Sri Lanka.
O'Neill, Eugene Gladstone. (1888-1953)
Shepard, Sam. (1943-)
Smith, Anna Deavere. (1950-)
Stein, Gertrude. (1874-1946)
Ung, Han. (1968-) born Philippines.
Valdez, Luis. (1940-)
Warren, Mercy Otis. (1728-1814)
Wasserstein, Wendy. (1950-)
Wilder, Thornton. (1897-1975)
Williams, Tennessee. (1911-1983)
Wilson, August. (1935-)

Ancient Civilizations
Aeschylus. (c. 525-456 B.C.) Greek.
Aristophanes. (c. 455-388 B.C.) Greek.
Euripides. (484-406 B.C.) Greek.
Plautus. (Titus Maccius Plautus) (254-184 B.C.) Roman.
Seneca. (Lucius Annaeus Seneca) (4 B.C.-65 A.S.) Roman.
Sophocles. (496-405 B.C.) Greek.
Terence. (Publius Terentius Afer) (185-159 B.C.) Roman.

English and Irish
Behn, Aphra Johnson. (1640?-1689)
Burgoyne, John. (1723-1792)
Eliot, Thomas Stearns. "T. S." (1888-1965)
Fielding, Henry. (1707-1754)
Garrick, David. (1717-1779)
Joyce, James. (1882-1941) Irish.
Marlowe, Christopher. (1564-1593)
Maugham, W. Somerset. (1874-1965)
O'Casey, Sean. (1880-1964) Irish.
Shakespeare, William. (1564-1616)
Shaw, George Bernard. (1856-1950) Irish.
Wilde, Oscar. (1854-1900) Irish.

European
Arouet, François Marie. (Voltaire) (1694-
    1778) French.
Brecht, Bertolt. (1898-1956) German.
Havel, Vaclav. (1936-) Czech.
Hugo, Victor. (1802-1885) French.
Ibsen, Henrik. (1828-1906) Norwegian.
Moliere. *See* Poquelin, Jean Baptiste.
Poquelin, Jean Baptiste. (Moliere) (1622-
    1673) French.
Voltaire. *See* Arouet, François Marie.

Israeli
Fink, Ida. (1921-) born Poland.

Russian
Chekhov, Anton. (1860-1904)

Poets

American
Alexie, Sherman. (1966-) Spokane-Coeur
    D'Alene Indian.
Allen, Paula Gunn. (1939-) Laguna
    Pueblo/Sioux Indian.
Angelou, Maya. (1928-)
Baraka, Amiri. (1934-)
Berry, Wendell. (1934-)
Bontemps, Arnaud "Arna." (1902-1973)
Bradstreet, Anne. (1612-1672)
Brooks, Gwendolyn. (1917-2000)
Brown, Christy. (1932-1981)
Brown, Sterling Allen. (1901-1989)
Cofer, Judith Ortiz. (1952-)
Cullen, Countee. (1903-1946)
Dickinson, Emily. (1830-1886)
Dillard, Annie. (1945-)

Doolittle, Hilda "H. D." (1886-1961)
Dove, Rita. (1952-)
Dunbar, Paul Laurence. (1872-1906)
Freneau, Philip. (1752-1832)
Frost, Robert. (1874-1963)
Ginsberg, Allen. (1926-1997)
Giovanni, Nikki. (1943-)
Gonzales, Rodolfo "Corky." (1928-)
Greenfield, Eloise. (1929-)
Griffin, Susan. (1943-)
Harper, Frances E. W. (1825-1911)
Harte, Bret. (1836-1902)
Hopkins, Lee Bennett. (1938-)
Hughes, James Mercer Langston. (1902-
    1967)
Jong, Erica. (1942-)
Kandel, Lenore. (1932-)
Kim, Willyce. (1946-)
Lawson, Louisa. (1848-1920)
Lazarus, Emma. (1849-1887)
Lee, Li-Young. (1957-) born Indonesia.
Levertov, Denise. (1923-1997) born
    England.
Longfellow, Henry Wadsworth. (1807-
    1882)
Lord, Audre. (1934-1992)
Lowell, Amy. (1874-1925)
MacLeish, Archibald. (1892-1982)
Madhubuti, Hadi R. (1942-)
McKay, Claude. (1890-1948)
Millay, Edna St.Vincent. (1892-1950)
Moise, Penina. (1797-1880)
Monroe, Harriet. (1860-1936)
Moore, Alice Ruth. (1875-1935)
Mura, David. (1952-)
Nicholson, Eliza Jane Poitevent Holbrook.
    (1849-1896)
Okita, Dwight. (1958-)
Ondaatje, Michael. (1943-) born Sri Lanka.
Ortiz, Simon. (1941-) Acoma Indian.
Parker, Dorothy. (1893-1967)
Poe, Edgar Allan. (1809-1849)
Prince, Lucy Terry. (1733-1821)
Ramirez, Sara Estela. (1881-1910) born
    Mexico.
Randall, Dudley. (1914-2000)
Sandburg, Carl. (1878-1967)
Santayana, George. (1863-1952) born Spain.
Snow, Eliza. (1804-1887)
Teasdale, Sara. (1884-1933)
Toomer, Jean. (1894-1967)

Valdez, Luis. (1940-)
Villagra, Gaspar Perez de. (1558-1620)
Wade, Cheryl Marie. (unknown)
Wheatley, Phillis. (1754-1784)
Whitman, Walt. (1819-1892)

Ancient Civilizations
Anacreon. (570-485 B.C.) Greek.
Catullus. (Gaius Valerius Catullus) (84-54
    B.C.) Roman.
Enheduana of Sumer. (fl. 2300 B.C.)
    Sumerian.
Homer. (c. 750 B.C.) Greek.
Horace. (Quintus Horatius Flaccus) (65-8
    B.C.) Roman.
Martial. (Marcus Valerius Martialis) (40-
    103) Roman.
Ovid. (Publisu Ovidius Naso) (43 B.C.-17
    A.D.) Roman.
Pindar. (c. 518-446 B.C.) Greek.
Sappho of Lesbos. (625-570 B.C.) Greek.
Virgil. (Publius Vergilius Maro) (70-19
    B.C.) Roman.

Asian and Far Eastern
Basho. (1644-1694) Japanese.
Da Fu. (712-?) Chinese.
Kabir. (1440-1518) Indian.
Li Po. (701-762) Chinese.
Li Ch'ing Chao. (1084-1151) Chinese.
Mirabi. (1498-1565) Indian.
Qiu Jin. (1875-1907) Chinese.
Sarashina, Lady. (1008-?) Japanese.
Tagore, Rabindranth. (1861-1941) Indian.
Wen-Chi, Lady. (c. 178) Chinese.

English, Irish, and Scottish
Behn, Aphra Johnson. (1640?-1689)
Blake, William. (1757-1827)
Bronte, Charlotte. (1816-1855)
Bronte, Emily. (1818-1848)
Browning, Elizabeth Barrett. (1806-1861)
Browning, Robert. (1812-1889)
Burns, Robert. (1759-1796) Scottish.
Byron, Lord. *See* Gordon, George.
Chaucer, Geoffrey. (1343-1400)
Donne, John. (1572-1631)
Eliot, Thomas Stearns "T. S." (1888-1965)
Gordon, George. (Lord Byron) (1788-1824)
Hall, Radclyffe. (1886-1943)
Hardy, Thomas. (1840-1928)

Keats, John. (1795-1821)
Milton, John. (1608-1674)
Raine, Kathleen. (1908-2003)
Raleigh, Sir Walter. (1554-1618)
Rossetti, Christina Georgina. (1830-1894)
Scott, Sir Walter. (1771-1832) Scottish.
Stevenson, Robert Louis. (1850-1894) Scot-
    tish.
Tennyson, Alfred Lord. (1809-1892)
Wilde, Oscar. (1854-1900) Irish.
Wordsworth, Dorothy. (1771-1855)
Wordsworth, William. (1770-1850)
Yeats, William Butler. (1865-1939) Irish.

European
Ascarelli, Devorah. (16th century) Italian.
Brecht, Bertolt. (1898-1956) German.
Catherine of Siena. (1353-1386) Italian.
Dante Alighieri. (1265-1321) Italian.
Halevi, Judah. (1075-1141) Spanish.
Hugo, Victor. (1802-1885) French.
Ibsen, Henrik. (1828-1906) Norwegian.
Katznelson, Yitzhak. (1886-1944) Polish.
Merton, Thomas. (1915-1968) French.
Morpurgo, Rachel Luzzatto. (1790-1871)
    Italian.
Oppenheim, Meret. (1913-1985) Swiss, born
    Germany.
Pizan, Christine de. (1365-1430) French.
Rossetti, Dante Gabriel. (1828-1882) Italian.
Senesh, Hannah. (1921-1944) Hungarian.
Sullam, Sara Coppio. (1592-1641) Italian.

Latin
Borges, Jorge Luis. (1899-1986) Argentine.
Cruz, Juana Inés de la, Sister. (1651-1695)
    Mexican.
Mistral, Gabriela Lucila y Alcayága. (1889-
    1957) Chilean.
Rodriguez de Tio, Lola. (1843-1924) Puerto
    Rican.

Russian
Akhmatova, Anna. (1889-1966)
Kovner, Abba. (1918-1987)
Pushkin, Alexander. (Aleksandr Seergee-
    vich) (1799-1837)

Other
Atwood, Margaret. (1939-) Canadian.
Khayyam, Omar. (1048-1131) Persian.

Rumi, Jalal al-Din. (1207-1273) Afghan.

Sarah of Yemen. (7th century) Yemenite.

Soyinka, Wole. (1934-) Nigerian.

Poles

See also Immigrants to United States, Polish.

Anielewicz, Mordecai. (1919-1943) Holocaust resistance worker, victim.

Ba'al Shem Tov, Israel. (Israel ben Eliezer) (1700-1760) Spiritual leader, founder Hasidic Judaism.

Blair, Tonia Rothkopf. (1925-) Holocaust survivor.

Borkowska, Anna. (c. 1900-) Holocaust rescuer, spiritual leader.

Chopin, Frederic. (1810-1849) Composer.

Copernicus, Nicolaus. (1473-1543) Astronomer.

Cukier, Sam. (1920-) Holocaust survivor.

Czerniakóv, Adam. (1880-1942) Holocaust resistance worker, victim.

Draenger, Shimson. (1917-1943) Holocaust resistance worker, victim.

Draenger, Tova. (1917-1943) Holocaust resistance worker, victim.

Elijah ben Solomon. (1720-1797) Scholar, spiritual leader.

Grossman, Mendel. (1917-1945) Holocaust resistance worker, victim, photographer.

Hirschfeld, Magnus. (1868-1935) Gay rights activist, human rights activist, physician.

Horowitz, Sarah Rebecca Rachel Leah. (18th century) Jewish scholar.

John III Sobieski. (1624-1696) Army military commander, king.

John Paul II, Pope. (Karol Wojtyla) (1920-) Pope.

Katznelson, Yitzhak. (1886-1944) Author, Holocaust victim, poet.

Kohane, Akiva. (1929-) Holocaust survivor.

Korczak, Janusz. (1878-1942) Children's author, Holocaust rescuer and victim, human rights activist, physician.

Kosciuszko, Thaddeus. (1746-1817) American Revolutionary War general.

Kosmodemianskaya, Zoya. (1925-1943) Holocaust resistance worker, victim.

Kovner, Vitka Kempner. (1920-) Holocaust resistance worker, survivor.

Lazebnik, Faye. (unknown) Holocaust resistance worker, survivor.

Lerner, Bianca. (1929-) Holocaust survivor.

Lubetkin, Zivia. (1914-1978) Holocaust resistance worker, survivor.

Mandel, Basia. (1925-) Holocaust survivor.

Mandelbrot, Benoit. (1924-) Mathematician.

Offenbach, Genia. (unknown) Holocaust survivor.

Offenbach, Rubin. (unknown) Holocaust survivor.

Opdyke, Irene. (1921-2003) Author, Holocaust resistance worker.

Pilecki, Witold. (1900-1948) Holocaust resistance worker.

Popieluszk, Jerzy, Father. (1947-1987) Political activist, spiritual leader.

Prekerowa, Teresa. (1921-) Historian, Holocaust resistance worker.

Pulaski, Casimir. (1747-1779) American Revolutionary War military leader.

Pulwer, Miriam. (unknown) Holocaust survivor.

Robota, Róza. (1921-1945) Holocaust resistance worker, victim.

Rosenbach, Larry. (1929-) Holocaust survivor.

Rubinowicz, David. (1927-1942) Author, Holocaust victim.

Rudashevski, Yitzak. (1927-1943) Author, Holocaust victim.

Sander, Sally. (1925-) Holocaust survivor.

Sander, Zelik. (unknown) Holocaust survivor.

Schiff, Charlene. (1930-) Holocaust survivor.

Schnirer, Sarah. (1833-1935) Educator.

Sheptitsky, Andrew. (1865-1944) Holocaust rescuer, spiritual leader.

Shore, Ann Goldman. (1929-) Holocaust survivor.

Suchocka, Hanna. (1946-) Political leader.

Walesa, Lech. (1943-) Political activist, president. Nobel Peace Prize winner, Presidential Medal of Freedom recipient.

Weinberg, Stefan. (1923-) Holocaust survivor.

Weinsberg, Alicia Fajnsztein. (1929-) Holocaust survivor.

Zallman, Elijah ben Solomon. (1720-1797) Scholar, spiritual leader.

Political Activists and World Leaders

See also Congressmen/Women; City Government Officials; Declaration of Independence Signers; Dictators; Government Workers; Governors, United States; Hatemongers; Presidents United States; Revolutionaries; Terrorists.

African
de Klerk, Fredrik Willem "F. W." (1936) South African president.
Kenyatta, Jomo. (1894-1978) Kenyan president, prime minister.
Kenyatta, Julius K. (1922-) Tanzanian prime minister.
Kruger, Paul. (1825-1904) South African statesman.
Luthuli, Albert. (1898-1967) South African activist.
Luwum, Janani. (1922-1977) Ugandan political victim.
Maathai, Wangari. (1940-) Kenyan.
Makeba, Miriam. (1932-) South African activist.
Mandela, Nelson. (1918-) South African political activist, prisoner.
Mandela, Winnie Madikizela. (1934-) South African activist.
Mugabe, Robert. (1924-) Zimbabwe prime minister.
Nkrumah, Kwame. (1909-1972) Ghanian president, prime minister.
Nyerere, Julius. (1922-1999) Tanzanian prime minister.
Senghor, Léopold. (1906-2001) Senegal president.
Soyinka, Wole. (1934-) Nigerian activist.

American
Baez, Joan. (1941-)
Chennault, Anna. (1925-) born China.
Chizick, Sarah. (1897-)
Davis, Angela. (1944-)
Franklin, Benjamin. (1706-1790) Statesman.
Goldman, Emma. (1869-1940) born Lithuania.
Hamilton, Alexander. (1753-1804)
Hancock, John. (1737-1793)
Henry, Patrick. (1736-1799) Statesman.

Hernandez, Maria Latigo. (1893-1986) born Mexico.
Heschel, Abraham Joshua. (1907-1972) born Poland.
Houston, Samuel. (1793-1863)
Hutchinson, Thomas. (1711-1780)
Jackson, Jesse. (1941-)
Kennedy, Robert Francis. (1925-1968)
Paine, Thomas. (1737-1809) born England.
Pontiac. (1720-1769) Ottawa Indian activist.
Ramirez, Sara Estela. (1881-1910) born Mexico.
Robeson, Paul. (1898-1976)
Rockwell, George Lincoln. (1918-1967) American Nazi party leader.
Watson, Thomas. (1856-1922)
Washington, Booker T. (1856-1915)

Ancient Civilizations
Antony, Marc. (Marcus Antonius) (83?-30 B.C.) Roman statesman.
Camillus. (Marcus Furius Camillus) (450-365 B.C.) Roman statesman.
Cato the Elder. (Marcus Porcius Cato) (234-149 B.C.) Roman statesman.
Crassus. (Marcus Licinius Crassus) (c. 115-53 B.C.) Roman statesman.
Dahia al-Kahina. (fl. 680) North African.
Gracchus, Gaius. (153-121 B.C.) Roman statesman.
Gracchus, Tiberius. (167-133 B.C.) Roman statesman.
Jael of Israel. (120-100 B.C.) Hebrew.
Lycurgus. (7th century B.C.) Greek statesman.
Pericles. (495-429 B.C.) Greek politician.
Pompey. (Gnaeus Pompey Magnus) (106-48 B.C.) Roman statesman.
Scipio Africanus. (Publius Cornelius Scipio Africanus) (236-183 B.C.) Roman statesman.
Seneca. (Lucius Annaeus Seneca) (4 B.C.-65 A.D.) Roman statesman.
Solon. (610-580 B.C.) Greek statesman.
Sulla. (Lucius Cornelius Sulla) (138-78 B.C.) Roman statesman.
Tacitus. (Publius or Gaius Cornelius Tacitus) (55-115) Roman statesman.
Themistocles. (523-463 B.C.) Greek politician, statesman.

Asian

Aquino, Corazon. (1933-) Filipino president.

Aung San. (1915-1947) Burmese.

Bandaranaike, Sirimavo. (1916-2000) Sri Lankan prime minister.

Bhutto, Benazir. (1953-) Pakistani prime minister.

Cheng, Nien. (1915-) Chinese political prisoner.

Chorn, Arn. (1967) Cambodian political prisoner.

Chou En-Lai. (1898-1976) Chinese Communist leader.

Devi, Gayatri "Ayesha." (1919-) Indian activist.

Devi, Phoolan. (1963-) Indian activist.

Gandhi, Indira. (1917-1984) Indian prime minister.

Genghis Khan. (1165-1227) Mongol political leader.

Ho Chi Minh. (1890-1969) Vietnamese dictator, revolutionary, statesman.

Ichikawa Fusae. (1893-1981) Japanese parliament member.

Jinnah, Mohammed Ali. (1876-1948) Indian Governor General of Pakistan.

Le-Duc-Tho. (1911-1990) Vietnamese political leader.

Ling, Chai. (1966-) Chinese political dissident.

Mao Tse-Tung. (1893-1976) Chinese dictator, revolutionary.

Marcos, Ferdinand. (1917-1989) Filipino dictator.

Nehru, Jawaharlal. (1889-1964) Indian prime minister.

Ramos-Horta, José. (1949-) East Timor activist.

Sato, Eisaku. (1901-1975) Japanese prime minister.

Sukarno, Achmed. (1901-1970) Indonesian president.

Sun Yat-Sen. (1866-1925) Chinese president.

Canadian

Campbell, Kim. (1947-) Prime minister.

Pearson, Lester. (1897-1972) Prime minister, president.

English and Irish

Burke, Edmund. (1729-1797) English.

Cecil, Robert. (1864-1958) English parliament, statesman.

Chamberlain, J. Austen. (1863-1937) English parliament.

Chamberlain, Neville. (1869-1940) English prime minister.

Churchill, Sir Winston Leonard Spencer. (1874-1965) English prime minister.

Collins, Michael. (1890-1922) Irish Republican Army revolutionary.

Cromwell, Oliver. (1599-1658) Statesman.

Disraeli, Benjamin. (1804-1881) English prime minister.

Gladstone, William. (1809-1898) English prime minister.

Hood, Robin. (1270-1346) English.

Lloyd George, David. (1863-1945) English prime minister.

McAliskey, Bernadette Devlin. (1947-) Irish.

MacBride, Seán. (1904-1988) Irish statesman.

Markiewiecz, Constance. (1867-1927) Irish.

More, Sir Thomas. (1478-1535) English activist, statesman.

Peel, Sir Robert. (1788-1850) English statesman.

Pitt, William. (1708-1778) English prime minister.

Rhodes, Cecil John. (1853-1902) English statesman.

Robinson, Mary. (1944-) Irish president.

Thatcher, Margaret. (1925-) English prime minister.

Townshend, Charles. (1725-1767) English parliament.

Walpole, Horace. (1717-1797) English statesman.

Wilkes, John. (1725-1797) English political reformer.

European and Scandinavian

Abrabanel, Benvenida. (d. 1560) Italian, born Spain.

Bajer, Fredrik. (1837-1932) Danish politician.

Beernaert, Auguste. (1829-1912) Belgian.

Bismarck, Otto Eduard Leopold von. (1815-1898) German chancellor.

Bourgeois, Léon. (1851-1925) French prime minister.

Brandt, Willy. (1913-1992) German chancellor.

Branting, Karl. (1860-1925) Swedish prime minister.

Briand, Aristide. (1862-1932) French prime minister.

Brundtland, Gro Harlem. (1939-) Norwegian prime minister.

Chotek, Sophie. (1868-1914) Austrian activist, World War I victim.

Clémenceau, Georges. (1841-1929) French prime minister.

Constant, Paul D'Estournelles. (1852-1924) French statesman.

Cresson, Edith. (1934-) French prime minister.

Dubcek, Alexander. (1921-1992) Czech activist.

Engels, Friedrich. (1820-1895) German communist leader.

Franco, Francisco. (1892-1975) Spanish dictator.

Frank, Hans. (1900-1946) German Nazi politician.

Hasselaar, Kenau. (1526-1588) Dutch.

Havel, Vaclav. (1936-) Czech president.

Hindenburg, Paul von. (1847-1934) German president Weimar Republic.

Hitler, Adolf. (1889-1945) German dictator.

Hübener, Helmut. (1925-1942) World War II anti-Nazi activist.

Ibarurri, Dolores. (1895-1989) Spanish revolutionary and political leader.

Jouhaux, Léon. (1879-1954) French politician.

Katznelson, Yitzhak. (1886-1944) Polish.

La Fontaine, Henri. (1854-1943) Belgian statesman.

Luxemburg, Rosa. (1870-1919) German political victim, revolutionary, born Poland.

Machiavelli, Niccolo. (1469-1527) Italian.

Meinhof, Ulrike. (1934-1976) German revolutionary.

Mussolini, Benito. (1883-1945) Italian dictator.

Nansen, Fridtjof. (1861-1930) Norwegian statesman.

Popieluszk, Jerzy, Father. (1947-1984) Polish activist, antigovernment.

Quisling, Vidkun. (1887-1945) Norwegian Nazi supporter.

Robespierre, Maximilien François Marie Isisdore de. (1758-1794) French revolutionary.

Roland, Madame Jeanne-Marie "Manon." (1754-1793) French revolutionary.

Saenz, Manuela. (1797-1856) Spanish.

Schulte, Eduard Reinhold Karl. (1891-1966) German antinazi activist.

Stresemann, Gustav, (1878-1929) German statesman.

Suchocka, Hanna. (1946-) Polish.

Tell, William. (1282-?) Swiss.

Tito, Josip Broz. (1892-1980) Yugoslavian president.

Tokes, Laszlo. (unknown) Romanian.

Von Ribbentrop, Joachim. (1893-1946) German foreign minister.

Waldheim Kurt. (1918-) Austrian president.

Walesa, Lech. (1943-) Polish president.

Weil, Simone. (1909-1943) French revolutionary.

Greek and Turkish

Atatürk, Mustapha Kemal. (1881-1938) Turkish president.

Ciller, Tansu. (1946-) Turkish prime minister.

Venizélos, Eleutherios. (1864-1936) Greek statesman.

Latin

Arias Sánchez, Oscar. (1941-) Costa Rican president.

Bolivar, Simón. (1783-1830) Venezuelan revolutionary.

Castro, Fidel. (1926-) Cuban dictator.

Chamorro, Violeta Barrios de. (1929-) Nicaraguan president.

Charles, Eugenia. (1919-) Dominican prime minister.

Guevara, Che. (1928-1967) Argentine revolutionary.

Jimenez y Muro, Dolores. (1848-1925) Mexican revolutionary.

Juarez, Benito. (1806-1872) Mexican president.

Lamas, Carlos Saavedra. (1878-1959) Argentine statesman.

Martí, José. (1853-1895) Cuban revolutionary.

Mendoza, Juana Belen Gutierrez. (1875-1942) Mexican revolutionary.

Perón, Eva "Evita." (1919-1952) Argentine.

Perón, Juan Domingo. (1895-1974) Argentine dictator, president.

Rodriguez de Tio, Lola. (1843-1924) Puerto Rican.

Romero, Oscar. (1917-1980) El Salvadorian activist.

Salavarrieta, Policarpa "La Pola." (1795-1817) Colombian patriot and fighter.

Sanchez, Ilrich Ramirez "Carlos." (1949) Venezuelan terrorist.

Sarmiento, Domingo Faustino. (1811-1888) Argentine president.

Zapata, Emiliano. (1879-1919) Mexican revolutionary.

Middle Eastern

Arafat, Yasir. (1929-) Palestinian terrorist, born Egypt.

Assad, Hafiz-al. (1930-2000) Syrian president.

Begin, Menachem. (1913-1992) Israeli prime minister, born Poland.

Ben-Gurion, David. (1886-1973) Israeli prime minister.

Chizick, Sarah. (1897-) Israeli.

Dayan, Moshe. (1915-1981) Israeli foreign minister.

Hussein, Ibn Talal. (1935-1999) Jordanian king.

Hussein, Saddam. (1937-) Iraqi dictator, president.

Khomeini, Ayatollah Ruholla. (1900-1989) Iranian Muslim.

Meir, Golda. (1878-1978) Israeli prime minister, born Russia.

Mubarak, Mohamad Hosni. (1929-) Egyptian president.

Nasser, Gamal Abdel. (1918-1970) Egyptian president, president United Arab Emirates.

Peres, Shimon. (1923-) Israeli prime minister, born Poland.

Rabin, Yitzhak. (1922-1995) Israeli prime minister.

Sadat, Anwar. (1918-1981) Egyptian president.

Weizmann, Chaim. (1874-1952) Israeli president.

Yadin, Yigael. (1917-1984) Israeli deputy prime minister.

Russian

Bonner, Elena. (1923-)

Gorbachev, Mikhail. (1931-) President.

Khrushchev, Nikita. (1894-1971) Communist leader.

Kollontai, Alexandra. (1872-1952)

Lenin, Nikolai. (Vladimir Ilich) (1870-1924) Communist leader.

Nudel, Ida. (1931-) Dissident.

Sakharov, Andrei. (1921-1989) Dissident and political prisoner.

Stalin, Joseph. (1879-1953) Dictator.

Trotsky, Joseph. (1879-1940) Revolutionary.

Yeltsin, Boris. (1931-) President.

Zasulich, Vera. (1849-1919) Russian revolutionary.

Other

Finnbogadottir, Vigadis. (1930-) Icelandic president.

Popes
See Spiritual Leaders.

Portuguese
See also Immigrants to United States, Portuguese.

Alburquerque, Afonso de. (1453-1515) Explorer.

Cabral, Pedro Álvares. (1460-1526) Explorer.

Cabrillo, Juan Rodriguez. (1520?-1543) Explorer.

Corte Real, Gaspar. (1455-1501) Explorer.

Corte Real, Miguel. (1450-1502) Explorer.

Covilla, Peroda. (1460-1526) Explorer.

Cunha, Tristao da. (1460-1540) Explorer.

Da Gama, Gaspar. (1458-1526) Explorer, born Poland.

Da Gama, Vasco. (1460-1524) Explorer.

Dias, Bartholomeu. (1450-1500) Explorer.

Henry. Prince of Portugal. (Henry the Navigator) (1394-1460) Explorer, prince.

Magellan, Ferdinand. (1480-1521) Explorer.

Mendes, Aristides. (d. 1954) Holocaust rescuer.

Nasi, Dona Gracia. (1510-1568) Entrepreneur banking, shipping, philanthropist.

Rego, Paula. (1935-) Illustrator, painter, printmaker.

Xavier, Francis. (1506-1552) Missionary, saint.

Potters and Ceramicists

See also Sculptors.

Martinez, Julian. (1897-1943) San Idlefonso Pueblo Indian.

Martinez, Maria Montoya. (1887-1980) San Idlefonso Pueblo Indian.

Picasso, Pablo. (1881-1973) Spanish.

Wong, Jade Snow. (1922-)

Presidential Candidates, American

Anderson, John. (1922-)

Bradley, Bill. (1943-)

Burr, Aaron. (1756-1836)

Chisholm, Shirley. (1924-)

Davis, John W. (1873-1955)

Debs, Eugene. (1855-1926)

Dole, Robert. (1923-)

Douglas, Stephen A. (1813-1861)

Fremont, John Charles. (1813-1890)

Gregory, Dick. (1932-)

Jackson, Jesse. (1941-)

Kennedy, Robert Francis. (1925-1968)

La Follette, Robert. (1855-1925)

Lockwood, Belva Ann. (1830-1917)

Moseley-Braun, Carol. (1947-)

Nader, Ralph. (1934-)

Perot, Ross. (1930-)

Scott, Winfield. (1786-1866)

Spock, Benjamin. (1903-1998)

Stevenson, Adlai. (1900-1965)

Thurmond, Strom. (1902-2003)

Wallace, George. (1919-1998)

Wallace, Henry A. (1888-1965)

Woodhull, Victoria. (1838-1927)

Presidential Medal of Freedom Recipients

Aaron, Henry "Hank." (1934-) Baseball player.

Acheson, Dean. (1893-1971) Cabinet member.

Adams, Ansel. (1902-1984) Photographer.

Aldrin, Edwin, Jr. "Buzz." (1930-) Astronaut.

Anderson, Marian. (1897-1993) Opera singer.

Annenberg, Walter. (1908-2002) Editor, media entrepreneur, philanthropist, publisher.

Armstrong, Neil. (1930-) Astronaut.

Ashe, Arthur. (1943-1993) Tennis player.

Bailey, Pearl. (1918-1990) Jazz singer.

Baker, James. (1930-) Cabinet member.

Balanchine, George. (1904-1983) Choreographer, dancer, born Russia.

Ball, Lucille. (1911-1989) Comedian.

Bardeen, John. (1908-1991) Physicist.

Basie, William "Count." (1904-1984) Jazz musician.

Berlin, Irving. (1888-1989) Composer, born Russia.

Blake, James Hubert "Eubie." (1883-1983) Composer, jazz musician.

Bojaxhiu, Agnes. (Mother Teresa) (1910-1997) Indian human rights activist, missionary, born Yugoslavia.

Borlaug, Norman Ernest. (1914-) Agricultural scientist, biochemist.

Bradley, Omar N. (1893-1981) World War II general.

Bunche, Ralph. (1904-1971) Diplomat, statesman.

Burke, Arleigh A. (1901-1996) Navy admiral.

Calder, Alexander. (1898-1966) Painter, sculptor.

Carson, Rachel. (1907-1964) Author, environmentalist.

Carter, James Earl "Jimmy." (1924-) President of U.S.

Carter, Rosalyn. (1927-) First Lady of U.S.

Casals, Pablo. (1876-1973) Composer, musician, born Spain.

Chávez, César. (1927-1993) Workers' rights activist.

Copland, Aaron. (1900-1990) Composer.

Cosby, Bill. (1937-) Actor, comedian.

Cousteau, Jacques-Yves. (1910-1997) French environmentalist, underwater explorer, inventor, World War II resistance fighter.

Cronkite, Walter. (1916-) Broadcast journalist.

Dimaggio, Joe. (1914-1999) Baseball player.

Disney, Walt. (1901-1966) Entrepreneur real estate, filmmaker.

Dole, Robert. (1923-) Congressman, presidential candidate, senator.

Doolittle, Jimmy. (1896-1993) World War II aviator.

Douglas, Marjorie Stoneman. (1890-1998) Author, conservationist.

Durant, Ida Kaufman "Ariel." (1898-1981) Author, historian, born Russia.

Durant, Will. (1885-1981) Author, historian.

Edelman, Marian Wright. (1939-) Attorney, children's rights activist, civil rights activist, human rights activist.

Eliot, Thomas Stearns "T. S." (1888-1965) English playwright, poet.

Ellington, Edward Kennedy "Duke." (1899-1974) Composer, jazz musician.

Ellison, Ralph. (1919-1994) Author, educator.

Farmer, James. (1920-1999) Civil rights activist.

Fitzgerald, Ella. (1918-1996) Jazz singer.

Ford, Gerald R. (1913-) President of U.S.

Ford, John. (1895-1973) Filmmaker.

Franklin, John Hope. (1915-) Historian.

Friedman, Milton. (1912-) Economist.

Fuller, R. Buckminster. (1895-1983) Architect.

Galbraith, John Kenneth. (1908-) Economist.

Garcia, Hector Perez. (1914-1996) Civil rights activist, physician, World War II Army hero, born Mexico.

Goldwyn, Samuel. (1882-1974) Filmmaker, born Poland.

Graham, Billy. (1918-) Author, spiritual leader.

Graham, Katharine. (1917-2001) Author, publisher.

Grasso, Ella. (1919-1981) Governor.

Height, Dorothy Irene. (1912-) Civil rights activist, social worker.

Hope, Leslie Townes "Bob." (1903-2003) Actor, comedian, born England.

Jackson, Jesse. (1941-) Civil rights activist, political activist, spiritual leader.

John XXIII. (1881-1963) Italian pope.

Johnson, Claudia "Lady Bird" Alta. (1912-) First Lady of U.S.

Johnson, John H. (1918-) Publisher.

Johnson, Lyndon Baines. (1908-1973) President of U.S.

Jordan, Barbara. (1936-1996) Attorney, civil rights activist, congresswoman.

Keller, Helen. (1880-1968) Author, disability rights activist.

Kennedy, John Fitzgerald. (1917-1963) President of U.S.

Kirkpatrick, Jeane. (1926-) Ambassador.

Land, Edwin. (1909-1991) Inventor, physicist.

Lewis, John L. (1880-1969) Labor leader.

Lippmann, Walter. (1889-1974) Journalist.

Luce, Clare Boothe. (1903-1987) Ambassador, congresswoman, playwright.

MacLeish, Archibald. (1892-1982) Author, poet.

Mandela, Nelson. (1918-) South African attorney, human rights activist, political prisoner.

Mankiller, Wilma. (1945-) Cherokee chief.

Marriott, John Willard. (1900-1985) Entrepreneur hotels and restaurants, philanthropist.

Marshall, Thurgood. (1908-1993) Civil rights activist, Supreme Court justice.

McNamara, Robert Strange. (1916-) Cabinet member.

Mead, Margaret. (1901-1978) Anthropologist.

Michener, James. (1907-1997) Author.

Moore, Gordon. (1929-) Computer pioneer, physicist.

Murie, Margaret. (1902-2003) Author, conservationist.

Murrow, Edward R. (1908-1965) Broadcast journalist.

Nelson, Gaylord. (1916-) Environmentalist, governor, senator, World War II hero.

O'Keefe, Georgia. (1887-1986) Painter.

Packard, David. (1912-1996) Computer entrepreneur and pioneer.

Pantoja, Antonio. (1922-2002) Educator, human rights activist, social worker, born Puerto Rico.

Parks, Rosa. (1913-) Civil rights activist.

Pei, Ieah Ming. (1917-) Architect, born China.

Powell, Colin. (1937-) Army Chair Joint Chiefs of Staff, cabinet member, Gulf War general.

Price, Leontyne. (1927-) Opera singer.

Randolph, Asa Philip. (1889-1979) Civil rights activist, labor leader.

Reagan, Anne Robbins "Nancy." (1921-) First Lady.

Reagan, Ronald. (1911-2004) President of U.S.

Rickover, Hyman. (1900-1986) Navy rear admiral.

Ridgway, Matthew Bunker. (1895-1993) Army Chief of Staff.

Robinson, John Roosevelt "Jackie." (1919-1972) Baseball player.

Rockwell, Norman. (1894-1978) Painter.

Rumsfeld, Donald H. (1932-) Cabinet member.

Sabin, Albert Bruce. (1906-1993) Medical researcher, physician, born Poland.

Sadat, Anwar. (1918-1981) Egyptian president.

Sandburg, Carl. (1878-1967) Author, poet.

Schwarzkopf, Norman. (1934-) Gulf War Army general, Vietnam Army commander.

Sills, Beverly. (1929-) Opera singer.

Sinatra, Frank. (1915-1998) Singer.

Smith, Margaret Chase. (1897-1995) Congresswoman, senator.

Steinbeck, John. (1902-1968) Author.

Streichen, Edward. (1879-1973) Photojournalist, born Luxembourg.

Suu Kyi, Daw Aung San. (1945-) Burmese peace activist.

Taussig, Helen Brooke. (1898-1986) Physician.

Teresa, Mother. *See* Bojaxhiu, Agnes.

Thatcher, Margaret. (1925-) English prime minister.

Velasquez, William. (1944-1988) Civil rights activist.

Walesa, Lech. (1943-) Polish political activist, president.

Warren, Earl. (1891-1974) Supreme Court chief justice.

Watson, James Dewey. (1928-) Biologist, geneticist, zoologist.

Watson, Thomas, Jr. (1914-1992) Computer entrepreneur and pioneer.

Wauneka, Annie Dodge. (1910-1997) Navajo public health educator.

Wayne, John. (1907-1979) Actor.

Weinberger, Caspar. (1917-) Cabinet member.

White, Elwyn Brooks "E. B." (1899-1985) Children's author.

Wiesel, Elie. (1928-) Author, Holocaust survivor, born Romania.

Wiesenthal, Simon. (1908-) Austrian author, Holocaust survivor, Nazi hunter.

Wilder, Thornton. (1897-1975)

Wilkins, Roy. (1901-1981) Civil rights activist.

Williams, Ted. (1918-2002) Baseball player.

Wyeth, Andrew. (1917-) Painter.

Yeager, Chuck. (1923-) World War II air force pilot.

Young, Andrew Jackson. (1932-) Civil rights activist, diplomat, mayor.

Young, Whitney M. (1921-1971) Civil rights activist.

Presidents, United States

Adams, John. (1735-1826) 2nd president.

Adams, John Quincy. (1767-1848) 6th president.

Arthur, Chester A. (1829-1886) 21st president.

Buchanan, James. (1791-1868) 15th president.

Bush, George Herbert Walker. (1924-) 41st president.

Bush, George Walker. (1946-) 43rd president.

Carter, James Earl "Jimmy." (1924-) 39th president.

Cleveland, Grover. (1837-1908) 22nd and 24th president.

Clinton, William Jefferson "Bill." (1946) 42nd president.

Coolidge, Calvin. (1872-1923) 30th president.

Eisenhower, Dwight David. (1890-1969) 34th president.

Fillmore, Millard. (1800-1874) 13th president.

Ford, Gerald R. (1913-) 38th president.

Garfield, James A. (1831-1881) 20th president.

Grant, Ulysses S. (1822-1885) 18th president.

Harding, Warren G. (1865-1923) 29th president.

Harrison, Benjamin. (1833-1901) 23rd president.

Harrison, William Henry. (1773-1862) 9th president.

Hayes, Rutherford B. (1822-1893) 19th president.

Hoover, Herbert. (1874-1964) 31st president.

Jackson, Andrew. (1767-1863) 7th president.

Jefferson, Thomas. (1743-1826) 3rd president.

Johnson, Andrew. (1808-1875) 17th president.

Johnson, Lyndon Baines. (1908-1973) 36th president.

Kennedy, John Fitzgerald. (1917-1963) 35th president.

Lincoln, Abraham. (1809-1865) 16th president.

Madison, James. (1751-1836) 4th president.

McKinley, William. (1843-1901) 25th president.

Monroe, James. (1758-1831) 5th president.

Nixon, Richard Milhous. (1913-1994) 37th president.

Pierce, Franklin. (1804-1869) 14th president.

Polk, James K. (1795-1849) 11th president.

Reagan, Ronald. (1911-2004) 40th president.

Roosevelt, Franklin Delano. (1882-1945) 32nd president.

Roosevelt, Theodore. (1858-1919) 26th president.

Taft, William H. (1857-1930) 27th president.

Taylor, Zachary. (1784-1850) 12th president.

Truman, Harry S. (1884-1972) 33rd president.

Tyler, John. (1790-1862) 10th president.

Van Buren, Martin. (1782-1862) 8th president.

Washington, George. (1732-1799) 1st president.

dent.

Wilson, Woodrow. (1856-1924) 28th president.

Priests
See Spiritual Leaders.

Primatologists
Fossey, Dian. (1932-1985)

Galdikas, Birute. (1946-) Canadian, born Germany.

Goodall, Jane. (1934-) English.

Pusey, Anne. (1948-) born England.

Printers and Printmakers
Baskin, Leonard. (1922-)

Beckmann, Max. (1884-1950) German.

Blackburn, Robert. (1920-2003)

Catlett, Elizabeth. (1915-)

Ella bat Moses. (17th century) German.

Franklin, Benjamin. (1706-1790)

Gela bat Moses. (18th century) German.

Goddard, Mary Katherine. (1738-1816)

Gutenberg, Johann. (1399-1468) German.

Hokusai, Katsushika. (1760-1849) Japanese.

Rego, Paula. (1935-) born Portugal.

Rivington, James. (1727-1802) English.

Wells, James Lesesne. (1902-1993)

Zenger, John Peter. (1697-1746) born Germany.

Psychics, Mystics, and Visionaries
Black Elk. (1863-1950) Oglala Lakota Sioux Indian mystic.

Catherine of Siena. (1353-1386) Italian.

Cayce, Edgar. (1877-1945)

Dixon, Jeane. (1918-1997)

Eckhart, Meister. (1280-1327) German mystic.

Gibran, Kahlil. (1883-1931) Lebanese mystic.

Hildegarde von Bingen. (1098-1179) German religious visionary.

Julian of Norwich. (1342-1416) English religious mystic.

Lead, Jane. (1624-1704) English mystic.

Luria, Isaac. (1534-1572) Israeli mystic.

McLuhan, Marshall. (1911-1980) Canadian visionary.

Moses de Leon. (1240-1305) Spanish mystic.

Nostradamus. (1503-1566) French visionary.

Raine, Kathleen. (1908-2003) English.

Rumi, Jalal al-Din. (1207-1273) Afghan mystic.

Swedenborg, Emanuel. (1688-1772) Swedish religious mystic.

Teresa, St. of Avila. (1515-1582) Spanish religious mystic.

Wovoka. (Jack Wilson) (1858-1932) Paiute Indian mystic.

Psychiatrists, Psychologists, and Psychotherapists.

Bettleheim, Bruno. (1903-1990) born Austria.

Clark, Kenneth B. (1914-)

Comer, James P. (1934-)

Cowings, Patricia. (1948-)

Estés, Clarissa Pinkol. (1943-)

Frankl, Viktor E. (1905-1997) Austrian.

Freud, Anna. (1895-1982) English, born Austria.

Freud, Sigmund. (1856-1939) Austrian.

Horney, Karen Danielsen. (1885-1952) born Germany.

Jung, Carl. (1875-1961) Swiss.

Kübler-Ross, Elisabeth. (1926-2004) born Switzerland.

Poussaint, Alvin Francis. (1934-)

Reich, Wilhelm. (1897-1957) born Austria.

Rousso, Harilyn. (1946-)

Public Health Workers

See also Social Workers.

Baker, Sara Josephine. (1873-1945) Physician, public health pioneer in well baby care.

Hamilton, Alice. (1869-1970) Physician, specialized work with very poor people and those who had work-related illnesses.

Jean-Murat, Carolle. (1950-) Haitian public health educator.

Prothrow-Stith, Deborah. (1954-) Public Health Commissioner Massachusetts.

Thoms, Adah Belle. (1870-1943) Nurse, public health pioneer.

Wald, Lillian. (1867-1940) Nurse, social worker, social activist.

Wauneka, Annie Dodge. (1910-1997) Navajo Indian public health educator.

Publishers

See Editors and Publishers.

Puerto Ricans

See also Hispanic-Americans.

Alomar, Roberto. (1968-) Baseball player.

Arce, Elmer Figuero. (Chayanne) (1968-) Pop singer.

Beltran, Carlos. (1977-) Baseball player.

Cepeda, Perucho. (1906-1955) Baseball player.

Clemente, Roberto. (1934-1972) Baseball player.

Coimbre, Pancho. (1909-1989) Baseball player.

Collazo, Oscar. (1914-1994) Assassin (attempted) of President Harry S. Truman

Colon, Raul. (1952-) Illustrator, born Puerto Rico.

Crespo, Elvis. (1970-) Pop singer.

Cruz, Jose, Jr. (1974-) Baseball player.

Delgado, Carlos. (1972-) Baseball player.

Fernandez, Beatriz Christina "Gigi." (1967-) Tennis player.

Gallego, Luis Miguel. (Luis Miguel) (1970-) Pop singer.

Gonzalez, Juan. (1969-) Baseball player.

Julia, Raul. (1940-1994) Actor, born Puerto Rico.

López, Javy. (1970-) Baseball player.

Martin, Ricky. (1971-) Pop singer.

Martinez, Edgar. (1963-) Baseball player.

Martinez-Canas, Maria. (1960-) Photographer, born Cuba.

Moreno, Rita. (1931-) Actor, dancer, born Puerto Rico.

Novello, Antonia C. (1944-) Physician, surgeon general of U.S., born Puerto Rico.

Pantoja, Antonio. (1922-2002) Educator, human rights activist, social worker, born Puerto Rico. Presidential Medal of Freedom recipient.

Ponce, Carlos. (1972-) Pop singer.

Posada, Jorge. (1971-) Baseball player.

Rodriguez, Ivan. (1971-) Baseball player.

Rodriguez de Tio, Lola. (1843-1924) Poet, political activist, women's rights activist.

Santiago, Esmeralda. (1948-) Author.

Schomburg, Arthur. (1874-1938) Educator, historian, born Puerto Rico.

Torresola, Griselio. (1925-1950) Attempted assassin.

Velazquez, Nydia. (1953-) Congresswoman, born Puerto Rico.

Williams, Bernie. (1968-) Baseball player.

Pulitzer Prize Winners

Biography or Autobiography
Graham, Katharine. (1917-2001)
Lindbergh, Charles A. (1902-1974)

Drama
Hammerstein, Oscar, II. (1895-1960)
MacLeish, Archibald. (1892-1982)
Miller, Arthur. (1915-)
O'Neill, Eugene Gladstone. (1888-1953)
Rodgers, Richard. (1902-1979)
Shepard, Sam. (1943-)
Wasserstein, Wendy. (1950-)
Wilder, Thornton. (1897-1975)
Williams, Tennessee. (1911-1983)
Wilson, August. (1935-)

Fiction
Bellow, Saul. (1915-)
Bromfield, Louis. (1896-1956)
Buck, Pearl S. (1892-1973)
Cather, Willa. (1873-1947)
Faulkner, William. (1897-1962)
Hemingway, Ernest Miller. (1899-1961)
Hijuelos, Oscar. (1948-)
Lewis, Sinclair. (1885-1951)
Mailer, Norman. (1923-)
Michener, James. (1907-1997)
Momaday, N. Scott. (1934-) Kiowa Indian.
Morrison, Toni. (1931-)
Rawlings, Marjorie Kinnan. (1896-1953)
Steinbeck, John. (1902-1968)
Tyler, Anne. (1941-)
Updike, John. (1932-)
Walker, Alice. (1944-)
Welty, Eudora. (1909-2001)
Wharton, Edith. (1862-1937)
Wilder, Thornton. (1897-1975)

History
Acheson, Dean. (1893-1971)
Durant, Ida Kaufman "Ariel." (1898-1981)

Durant, Will. (1885-1981)
Pershing, John Joseph. (1860-1948)
Sandburg, Carl. (1878-1967)
Tuchman, Barbara Wertheim. (1912-1989)

Journalism
Darling, Jay Norwood "Ding." (1876-1962)
Higgins, Marguerite. (1920-1966)
Lippmann, Walter. (1889-1974)
McCormick, Anne O'Hare. (1880-1954)
Pyle, Ernest Taylor "Ernie." (1900-1945)
Reston, James. (1909-1995) born Scotland.
Sleet, Moneta, Jr. (1926-1996)
Smith, Walter Wellesley "Red." (1905-1982)
White, William Allen. (1868-1944)

Music
Barber, Samuel. (1901-1981)
Copland, Aaron. (1900-1990)
Ives, Charles. (1874-1954)
Joplin, Scott. (1868-1917)
Marsalis, Wynton. (1961-)
Zwilich, Ellen. (1939-)

Nonfiction
Dillard, Annie. (1945-)
Durant, Ariel. (Ida Kaufman Durant) (1898-1981)
Durant, Will. (1885-1981)
Mailer, Norman. (1923-)
Sagan, Carl. (1934-1996)

Poetry
Brooks, Gwendolyn. (1917-2000)
Dove, Rita. (1952-)
Frost, Robert. (1874-1963)
Lowell, Amy. (1874-1925)
Millay, Edna St.Vincent. (1892-1950)
Sandburg, Carl. (1878-1967)

Special Citation
Geisel, Theodor Seuss. (Dr. Seuss) (1904-1991)
Haley, Alex. (1921-1992)
Hammerstein, Oscar, II. (1895-1960)
Rodgers, Richard. (1902-1979)
White, Elwyn Brooks "E. B." (1899-1985)

Puritans
See Colonists.

Rabbis
See Spiritual Leaders.

Racquetball Players
Gonzalez, Ruben. (1951-)

Ranchers
See Cowboys and Ranchers.

Reformers
See also Children's Rights Activists; Disability Rights Activists; Human Rights Activists; Peace Activists; Social Workers; Suffragists; Utopian Community Founders; Women's Rights Activists; Workers' Rights Activists.
Besant, Annie. (1847-1933) English.
Bonnin, Gertrude Simmons. (1876-1938) Yankton Dakota Indian.
Colonna, Vittoria. (1490-1547) Italian religious reformer.
Comnena, Anna. (1083-1148) Byzantine.
Dix, Dorothea. (1802-1887) Treatment for insane.
Fry, Elizabeth. (1780-1845) English prison reformer.
Gladney, Edna Kahly. (1886-1961) Adoption reform.
Godiva, Lady. (1010-1067) English tax relief reformer.
Howard, John. (1726-1790) English prison reformer.
Kuhn, Maggie. (1905-1995) Rights for older people.
Lathrop, Julia. (1858-1932)
Lin Xezu. (1785-1850) Chinese antidrug and opium.
Lovejoy, Esther Pohl. (1869-1967) Temperance movement.
Nader, Ralph. (1934-) Consumer activist.
Nation, Cary. (1846-1911) Temperance movement.
Owen, Robert. (1771-1858) Welsh.
Pappenheim, Berta. (1859-1936) German.
Pinel, Philippe. (1745-1826) French, humane care for mentally ill.
Preston, Ann. (1813-1872) Temperance movement.
Riis, Jacob August. (1849-1914) Conditions of poor, born Denmark.

Ripley, George. (1802-1880) Social reformer.
Rose, Ernestine Potowski. (1810-1892) Property rights for married women, born Poland.
Sanger, Margaret. (1879-1966) Birth control proponent.
Shaw, Anna Howard. (1847-1919) Temperance movement, born England.
Wells-Barnett, Ida B. (1862-1931) Antilynching crusade.
Wilkes, John. (1725-1797) English.
Willard, Frances Elizabeth. (1839-1898) Temperance movement.
Williams, Betty. (1943-) Irish social reformer.
Williams, Jody. (1950-) Campaign to end landmines.
Young, Ann Eliza Webb. (1844-1908) Antipolygamy campaign.

Revolutionaries
See also Dictators; Military Leaders; Political Activists and Leaders.
Aguinaldo, Emilio. (1869-1964) Filipino.
Bolivar, Simón. (1783-1830) Venezuelan.
Collins, Michael. (1890-1922) Irish.
Danton, Georges. (1759-1794) French.
Guevara, Che. (1928-1967) Argentine.
Ho Chi Minh. (1890-1969) Vietnamese.
Ibarurri, Dolores. (1895-1989) Spanish.
Jimenez y Muro, Dolores. (1848-1925) Mexican.
Kollontai, Alexandra. (1872-1952) Russian.
Le Sueur, Meridel. (1900-1996)
Luxemburg, Rosa. (1870-1919) German, born Poland.
Mao Tse-Tung. (1893-1976) Chinese.
Martí, José. (1853-1895) Cuban.
Meinhof, Ulrike. (1934-1976) German.
Mendoza, Juana Belen Guiterrez. (1875-1942) Mexican.
Parsons, Lucy. (1853-1943)
Qiu Jin. (1875-1907) Chinese.
Robespierre, Maximilien François Marie Isisdore de. (1758-1794) French.
Roland, Madame Jeanne-Marie "Manon." (1754-1793) French.
Shochat, Manya. (1880-1961) Israeli, former Russian revolutionary, born Russia.
Sukarno, Achmed. (1901-1970) Indonesian.

Trotsky, Leon. (1879-1940) Russian.
Weil, Simone. (1909-1943) French.
Zapata, Emiliano. (1879-1919) Mexican.
Zasulich, Vera. (1849-1919) Russian.

Rock Climbers
See also Mountaineers.
Hill, Lynn. (1961-)

Romanians
Alaric the Goth. (370-410) Military leader.
Amanar, Simona. (1979-) Olympic gymnast.
Basch, Civia Gelber. (1928-) Holocaust survivor.
Comaneci, Nadia. (1961-) Olympic gymnast.
Tokes, Laszlo. (unknown) Political activist, spiritual leader.
Vlad the Impaler "Vlad Dracul." (1431-1477) Terrorist.
Wiesel, Elie. (1928-) Author, Holocaust survivor.
Wurmbrand, Richard. (1909-2001) Missionary.

Romans, Ancient
Agrippa. (Marcus Vippsanius Agrippa) (63-12 B.C.) General.
Agrippina the Young. (Agrippina Minor) (15-59) Mother of Nero, wife of Claudius.
Antony, Marc. (Marcus Antonius) (83?-30 B.C.) General, statesman.
Augustus. (31 B.C.-14 A.D.) Emperor.
Caesar, Julius. (100-44 B.C.) Dictator, ruler.
Camillus. (Marcus Furius Camillus) (450-365 B.C.) General, statesman.
Cato the Elder. (Marus Porcius Cato) (234-149 B.C.) Statesman.
Catullus. (Gaius Valerius Catullus) (84-54 B.C.) Poet.
Cicero. (Marcus Tollius Cicero) (106-43 B.C.) Attorney, orator, philosopher.
Claudius. (Tiberius Claudius Nero Germanicus) (10 B.C.-13 A.D.) Emperor.
Constantine. (c. 280-337) Emperor, military leader, spiritual leader.
Crassus. (Marcus Licinius Crassus) (c. 115-53 B.C.) Financier, military leader, statesman.
Diocletian. (Diocles) (245-313) Emperor.

Dionysia. (unknown) Olympic track and field athlete.
Domitian. (Titus Flavius Domitianus) (51-96) Emperor.
Fabius. (d. 203 B.C.) Ruler.
Gracchus, Gaius. (153-121 B.C.) Statesman.
Gracchus, Tiberius. (167-133 B.C.) Statesman.
Hadrian. (Publius Aelius Handrianus) (76-138) Emperor, general.
Hedea. (unknown) Olympic track and field athlete.
Helena, St. (250-330) Mother of Christianity.
Horace. (Quintus Horatius Flaccus) (65-8 B.C.) Poet.
Hortensia. (1st century B.C.) Orator, women's rights activist.
Juvenal. (Decimus Junius Juvenalis) (55?-127) Author.
Livia. (Livia Drusilla) (58 B.C.-29 A.D.) Wife of Augustus.
Livy. (Titus Livius) (59? B.C.-17 A.D.) Historian.
Locusta of Gaul. (fl. 50 A.D.) Poisoner.
Marcus Aurelius. (Marcus Annius Verus) (121-180) Emperor.
Marius. (Gaius Marius) (157-86 B.C.) Emperor.
Martial. (Marcus Valerius Martialis) (40-103) Poet.
Maximinus, Gaius Valerius. (186-238) Olympic track and field athlete, wrestler.
Nero. (Nero Claudius Caesar) (37-68) Emperor.
Ovid. (Publius Ovidius Naso) (43 B.C.-17 A.D.) Poet.
Plautus. (Titus Maccius Plautus) (254-184 B.C.) Playwright.
Pliny the Elder. (23-79 A.D.) Historian.
Pliny the Younger. (Gaius Plinius Caecilius Secundus) (61-113) Attorney, author, orator.
Pompey. (Gnaeus Pompeius Magnus) (106-48 B.C.) General, statesman.
Scipio Africanus. (Publius Cornelius Scipio Africanus) (236-183 B.C.) General, statesman.
Seneca. (Lucius Annaeus Seneca) (4 B.C.-65 A.D.) Philosopher, playwright, statesman.

Septimius Severus, Lucius. (146-211) Emperor, general.

Spartacus. (109-71 B.C.) Gladiator.

Suetonius. (Gaius Suetonius Tranquillus) (69-135) Journalist.

Sulla. (Lucius Cornelius Sulla) (138-78 B.C.) General, statesman.

Tacitus. (Publius or Gaius Cornelius Tacitus) (55-115) Historian, orator, statesman.

Terence. (Publius Terentius Afer) (185-159 B.C.) Playwright.

Theodosius I. (347-395) Emperor.

Tiberius. (Tiberius Claudius Nero) (42 B.C.-37 A.D.) Emperor.

Trajan. (Marcus Ulpius Trajanus) (53-117) Emperor, general.

Tryphosa. (unknown) Olympic track and field athlete.

Vercingetorix. (75-46 B.C.) Ruler.

Vespasian. (Titus Flavius Vespasianus) (9-79) Emperor.

Virgil. (Publius Vergilius Maro) (70-19 B.C.) Poet.

Rowers
See Boaters.

Rulers and Royalty

African
Askia the Great. (1444?-1538). King.
Dahia al-Kahina. (fl. 680) North African queen.
Elizabeth, Princess of Toro (Uganda). (1941-) Princess.
Gronniosaw, Ukawsaw. (1725-1786) Prince, Kingdom of Borneo.
Makeda. (960-930 B.C.) Ethiopian Queen of Sheba.
Mansa Musa I. (1312-1337) King of Mali.
Mbandi, Jinga. *See* Nzinga, Anna.
Mella. Warrior queen.
Nzinga, Anna. (1580-1663) West African queen.
Selassie, Haile. (1892-1975) Ethiopian emperor.
Shaka. (1787-1828) Zulu King.
Tupou, Salote III. (1900-1965) Queen of Tonga.

Assyrian, Babylonian, and Mesopotamian
Gilgamesh. (2700 B.C.) Babylonian king.
Hammurabi. (fl. 1792-1750 B.C.) Mesopotamian king.
Sargon the Great. (c. 2300 B.C.) Mesopotamian king.
Semiramis. (c. 2000 B.C.) Assyrian queen.

Austrian
Maria Theresa. (1717-1780) Archduchess, empress.

Aztec and Incan
Atahualpa. (1502-1533) Inca emperor.
Montezuma II. (1466-1520) Aztec king.

Belgian
Leopold II. (1835-1909) King.

Byzantian
Comnena, Anna. (1083-1148) Princess.
Justinian I, the Great. (482-565) Emperor.

Chinese
Dorgon. (1612-1650) Emperor, prince.
Liu Pang. (256-195 B.C.) Emperor.
Shih Huang Di. (259-210 B.C.) Emperor.
Tz-u-hsi. (1835-1908) Empress Dowager.
Wu Chao. (625-705) Empress.

Dutch
Maurice of Nassau. (1567-1625) Prince of Orange.
William I, The Silent. (1533-1584) Prince of Orange.

Egyptian, Ancient
Akhaneten. (Amenhotep IV) (1370?-1340?) King.
Amenemhet I. (fl. 1991-1962 B.C.) King.
Amenemhet II. (fl. 1842-1797 B.C.) King.
Amenemhet III. (fl. 1886-1849 B.C.) King.
Cleopatra VII. (69-30 B.C.)
Djoser. (fl. 2668-2649 B.C.) King.
Hatshepsut. (1500-1460 B.C.) Pharoah.
Horemheb. (fl. 1321-1293 B.C.) King.
Khufu. (fl. 2589-2566 B.C.) King.
Menes. (3100-3038 B.C.) Pharoah.
Nebheptre Mentuhotep I. (fl. 2060-2010 B.C.) King.
Nefertari. (fl. 1270 B.C.) Queen.

Nefertiti. (fl. 1372-1350 B.C.) Queen.
Pepi II. (fl. 2278-2184 B.C.) King.
Ptolemy I. (Ptolemy Soter) (367-283 B.C.)
    King.
Ramesses II. (fl. 1279-1212 B.C.) King.
Ramesses III. (fl. 1182-1151 B.C.) King.
Senwosret I. (1971-1928 B.C.) King
Senwosret III. (fl. 1874-1841 B.C,) King.
Seti I. (fl. 1291-1278 B.C.) King.
Snefru. (fl. 2613-2589 B.C.) King.
Thutmose III. (fl. 1504-1450 B.C.) King.
Tiye. (fl. 1370 B.C.) Queen.
Tutankhamun. (1347-1329 B.C.) Pharoah.

English and British
Albert. (1819-1861) Prince.
Alfred the Great. (849-901)
Anne. (1665-1714) Queen.
Arthur. (6th century) King, legendary.
Boleyn, Anne. (1507-1536) Second wife of
    Henry VIII.
Boudicca. (28-62) Celtic queen.
Catherine of Aragon. (1485-1536) Queen.
Charles. (1947-) Prince of Wales.
Charles I. (1600-1649) King.
Charles II. (1630-1685) King.
Diana. (1961-1997) Princess of Wales.
Edward I. (1239-1307) King.
Edward II. (1287-1327) King.
Edward VIII. (1894-1972) Duke of
    Windsor.
Edward the Black Prince. (1330-1376)
    Prince of Wales.
Elizabeth I. (1533-1603) Queen.
Elizabeth II. (1926-) Queen.
George III. (1738-1820) King.
George V. (1865-1936) King.
George VI. (1895-1952) King.
Godiva, Lady. (1010-1067) Countess.
Guinevere. (6th century) Princess, wife of
    King Arthur, legendary.
Gwendolen. (fl. 1075-1060 B.C.) Warrior
    queen.
Henry II. (1133-1189) King.
Henry III. (1207-1272) King.
Henry V. (1387-1422) King.
Henry VI. (1421-1471) King.
Henry VII. (1457-1509) King.
Henry VIII. (1491-1547) King.
Herbert, George. (1866-1903) Fifth Earl of
    Carnavon.

James I. (1566-1625) King.
John. (1167-1216) King.
Margaret. (1930-2002) Princess.
Mary I. (Mary Tudor) (1516-1558) Princess,
    queen.
Mary II. (1662-1694) Queen.
Mary, Queen of Scots. (1547-1587)
Mary Tudor. *See* Mary I.
Matilda of England. (1102-1167) Princess.
Richard I. (The Lionhearted) (1157-1199)
    King.
Sarah. Duchess of York. (1959-) Princess
    Victoria. (1819-1901) Queen.
William I, the Conqueror. (1027-1087)
    King.
William III. (1650-1702) King.

French
Beauharnais, Josephine. (1763-1814) Em-
    press.
Bonaparte, Napoleon. *See* Napoleon I.
Catherine de Medici. (1519-1589) Queen.
Charlemagne. (742-814) Emperor.
Eleanor of Aquitaine. (1122-1204) Queen.
Louis XIV. (1638-1715) King.
Louis XVI. (1754-1792) King.
Mahaut, Countess de Artois. (1275-1329)
    Noblewoman.
Marie Antoinette. (1755-1793) Princess,
    queen.
Philip II. (1165-1223) King.

German
Attila the Hun. (400-453) King.
Frederick I. (Barbarossa) (1123-1190) King,
    Holy Roman Empire.
Frederick II "The Great." (1712-1786) King.
Gloria von Thum und Taxis. (1960-) Prin-
    cess.
Henry IV. (1050-1106) Emperor.
Otto I, the Great. (912-973) Holy Roman
    Emperor.
Ridesel, Fredrika von. (1746-1808) Baron-
    ess.
Wilhelm II. (1859-1941) Emperor, kaiser.

Greek, Ancient
Alexander the Great. (356-323 B.C.) King.
Darius III. (380-330 B.C.)
Demetrius. (336-283 B.C.)
Leonidas I. (c. 505-490 B.C.) King Sparta.

Philip II. (383-336 B.C.) King.
Ptolemy I. (Ptolemy Suter) (367-283 B.C.)

Hawaiian
Ka'lulani. (1875-1899) Princess.
Liliuokalani, Lydia. (1838-1917) Queen.

Hebrew, Ancient
David. (fl. 1010-970 B.C.)
Herodias. (1st century C.E.) Queen.

Holy Roman Empire
Charles V. (1500-1558) Emperor.
Frederick I. (Barbarossa) (1123-1190) King.
Matilda of England. (1102-1167) Empress.
Otto I, the Great. (912-973) Emperor.

Hun
Attila the Hun. (400-453) King.

Hungarian
Stephen I. (975-1038) King.

Indian
Asóka the Great. (290-232 B.C.) King.
Babur, Zahir un-Din Muhammed. (Babur
   the Conqueror) (1483-1530) Indian
   Mughal emperor.
Bai, Lakshmi. (1830-1858)
Devi, Gayatri "Ayesha." (1919-) Princess.
Gandhi, Mohandas. (1869-1948)
Jahan, Shah. (1592-1666)
Razia, Sultana. (fl. 1236-1240) Muslim war-
   rior princess.

Italian
Borgia, Lucrezia. (1480-1519) Duchess of
   Ferrara, villainess.
Sichelgaita. (d. 1090) Princess.
Theodoric the Great. (454-526) Conqueror,
   king.

Japanese
Hirohito. (1901-1989) Emperor.
Koken. (718-770) Empress.
Komyo. (701-760) Empress.
Mutsuhito. (1852-1912) Emperor.
Shotoku, Toshi. (574-622) Prince.

Korean
Sonduk of Korea.(610-647) Queen.

Latin
Castro, Fidel. (1926-) Cuban dictator.
Malinche, La. (Malintzin) Mexican princess.
Pedro II. (1825-1891) Brazilian emperor,
   king.

Mongolian
Ghenghis Khan. (1162-1227)
Kublai Khan. (1215-1294) Emperor.
Mehmed II. (1432-1481) Conqueror.

Monacan
Kelly, Grace. (1929-1982) Princess.
Rainier, Prince, III. (1923-) Prince.

Persian
Esther. (5th century B.C.) Queen.
Xerxes I. (519-465 B.C.) King.

Polish
John III Sobieski. (1624-1696) King.

Roman, Ancient
Augustus. (31 B.C.-14 A.D.) Emperor.
Caesar, Julius. (100-44 B.C.) Dictator.
Claudius. (Tiberius Claudius Nero Germani-
   cus) (10 B.C.-13 A.D.) Emperor.
Constatine. (c. 280-337) Emperor.
Diocletian. (Diocles) (245-313) Emperor.
Domitian. (Titus Flavius Domitianus) (51-
   96) Emperor.
Fabius. (d. 203 B.C.)
Hadrian. (Publius Aelius Handrianus) (76-
   138) Emperor.
Marcus Aurelius. (Marcus Annius Verus)
   (121-180) Emperor.
Marius. (Gaius Marius) (157-86 B.C.) Em-
   peror.
Nero. (37-68) Emperor.
Septimius, Severus Lucius. (146-211) Em-
   peror.
Theodoric the Great. (454-526) King.
Theodosius I. (347-395) Emperor.
Tiberius. (Tiberius Claudius Nero) (42 B.C.-
   37 A.D.) Emperor.
Trajan. (Marcus Ulpius Traianus) (53-117)
   Emperor.
Vercingetorix. (75-46 B.C.)
Vespasian (Titus Flavius Vespasianus) (9-
   79) Emperor.

Romanian
Alaric the Goth. (370-410)

Russian
Alexandra. (1872-1918) Czarina.
Catherine the Great. (1729-1796) Empress.
Ivan IV. (Ivan the Terrible) (1530-1584)
    Czar.
Morozova, Feodosia. (1630-1675) Noble-
    woman.
Nicholaevna, Anastasia. (1901-1918) Prin-
    cess.
Nicolaevna, Olga. (1895-1918) Princess.
Nicolaevna, Tatiana. (1897-1918) Princess.
Nicholas II. (1868-1918) Czar.
Peter I the Great. (1672-1725) Czar.
Tamara. (1156-1212) Queen.

Scandinavian
Charles XII. (1682-1718) Swedish king.
Christina. (1626-1689) Swedish queen.
Gustavus Adolphus II. (1594-1632) Swed-
    ish ruler.
Margaret I. (1353-1412) Queen.
Martha Louise. (1971-) Norwegian princess.

Siamese
Mongkut, Maha. (1804-1868) King.

Spanish and Portuguese
Alvarez de Toledo, Fernando. (Duke of
    Alba) (1507-1583)
Cristina. (1965-) Princess.
Elena. (1964-) Princess.
Ferdinand. (1452-1516) King.
Franco, Francisco. (1892-1975) Dictator.
Henry. Prince of Portugal. (Henry the Navi-
    gator) (1394-1460) Prince.
Isabella I. (1451-1504) Queen.
Philip II. (1527-1598) King.

Syrian
Saladin, Salal al-Din. (1138-1193) Kurdish
    Muslim sultan.
Zenobia. (fl. 267-272) Queen.

Turkish
Selim III. (1761-1808) Sultan.
Suleiman I, the Magnificent. (1494-1566)
Theodora. (497-548) Empress.

Runners and Sprinters

See also Olympic Athletes, Track and Field;
    Track and Field Athletes.
Bannister, Roger. (1929-) English.
Brisco-Hooks, Valerie. (1960-)
Carr, Henry. (1942-)
Hayes, Bob. (1942-2002)
Hines, Jim. (1946-)
Lewis, Carl. (1961-)
Liddell, Eric. (1902-1945) Scottish.
Maximinus, Gaius Valerius. (186-233) Ro-
    man.
McGuire, Edith. (1944-)
Mitchell, Thecla. (unknown) Marathon run-
    ner.
Morrow, Bobby Joe. (1935-)
Nurmi, Paavo. (1897-1973) Finnish.
Paddock, Charlie. (1900-1943) Sprinter.
Phidippides. (c. 505-490 B.C.) Greek long
    distance runner.
Robinson, Betty. (1911-1999) Sprinter.
Samuelson, Joan Benoit. (1957-) Long dis-
    tance and marathon runner.
Smith, Tommie. (1944-) Sprinter.
Stephens, Helen. (1918-1994) Sprinter.
Tolan, Eddie. (1908-1967) Sprinter.
Torrence, Gwen. (1965-) Sprinter.
Wolde, Mamo. (1931-) Ethiopian marathon
    runner.

Russians

See also Immigrants to United States, Rus-
    sian.
Abel, Rudolf Ivanovich. (1920-1971) Spy.
Ahad Ha'am. *See* Ginzberg, Asher.
Akhmatova, Anna. (1889-1966) Poet.
Alexandra. (1872-1918) Czarina.
Alexeyev, Vasily. (1942-) Olympic weight
    lifter.
Andrianov, Nikolai. (1952-) Olympic gym-
    nast.
Anissina, Mariana. (1975-) Olympic figure
    skater.
Appelfeld, Aharon. (1932-) Author, Holo-
    caust survivor.
Avvakum. (1620-1682) Spiritual leader.
Baranova, Elena. (1976-) Basketball player.
Berezhnaya, Elena. (1977-) Olympic figure
    skater.
Blavatsky, Helena Petrovna. (1831-1891)
    Spiritual leader, founder Theosophical

Movement.

Boguinskaia, Svetlana. (1973-) Olympic gymnast.

Bonner, Elena. (1923-) Political activist and dissident.

Bordin, Alexander Porfiervich. (1833-1889) Chemist, opera composer, physician.

Bukovsky, Vladimir. (1942-) Human rights activist.

Catherine the Great. (1729-1796) Empress.

Chekhov, Anton. (1860-1904) Author, playwright.

Chikatilo, Andrei. (1936-1994) Serial killer.

Dezhnev, Semyon. (1610-1672) Explorer, fur trapper, pioneer.

Dostoevski, Fyodor. (1821-1881) Author.

Eisenstein, Sergei. (1898-1948) Filmmaker.

Gabo, Naum. (1890-1977) Painter, sculptor.

Gagarin, Yuri. (1934-1968) Aviator, cosmonaut.

Ginzberg, Asher. (Ahad Ha'am) (1856-1927) Spiritual leader, founder Spiritual Judaism.

Gorbachev, Mikhail. (1931-) President. Nobel Peace Prize winner.

Ivan IV. (Ivan the Terrible) (1530-1584) Czar.

Kandinsky, Wassily. (1866-1944) Painter.

Khorkina, Svetlana. (1979-) Olympic gymnast.

Khrushchev, Nikita. (1894-1971) Communist leader.

Kollontai, Alexandra. (1872-1952) Ambassador, human rights activist, political activist, revolutionary, women's rights activist.

Korbut, Olga. (1955-) Olympic gymnast.

Korolev, Sergei. (1906-1966) Engineer, space scientist.

Kournikova, Anna. (1981-) Tennis player.

Kovalevskaia, Sofia. (1850-1891) Mathematician.

Kovner, Abba. (1918-1987) Holocaust resistance worker, survivor, poet.

Kowalyk, Jonka. (unknown) Ukrainian Holocaust resistance worker.

Kuznetsova, Irina Mihailovna. (1961-) Arctic explorer.

Kuznetsova, Valentina Mihailovna. (1937-) Arctic explorer.

Latynina, Larissa. (1934-) Olympic gymnast.

Lenin, Nikolai. (Vladimir Ilich) (1870-1924) Communist leader.

Leonov, Alexei. (1934-) Cosmonaut.

Litvak, Lily. (1921-1943) World War II fighter pilot.

Mendeleyev, Dimitri Ivanovich. (1843-1907) Chemist.

Metchnikoff, Élie. (1845-1916) Bacteriologist, physiologist.

Morozova, Feodosia. (1630-1675) Noblewoman.

Mozhaiski, Alexander. (1825-1890) Aviation pioneer, engineer, navy officer.

Mussorgsky, Modest Petrovich. (1839-1881) Composer, musician.

Nechavev, Sergei. (1847-1882) Terrorist.

Nevsky, Alexander. (1720-1763) Saint, warrior hero.

Nicholaevna, Anastasia. (1901-1918) Princess.

Nicholaevna, Olga. (1895-1918) Princess.

Nicholaevna, Tatiana. (1897-1918) Princess.

Nicholas II. (1868-1918) Czar.

Novykh, Girgori Yefimovich. (Rasputin) (1871-1916) Monk.

Nudel, Ida. (1931-) Human rights activist, dissident.

Nureyev, Rudolf. (1938-1993) Dancer.

Pavlov, Ivan Petrovich. (1849-1936) Physiologist. Nobel Prize winner.

Pavlova, Anna. (1881-1931) Ballet dancer.

Peter I the Great. (1672-1725) Czar.

Plushenko, Evgeny. (1982-) Olympic figure skater.

Podkopayeva, Lilia. (1978-) Ukrainian olympic gymnast.

Prokofiev, Sergei Sergeevich. (1891-1953) Composer.

Pushkin, Alexander. (Aleksandr Seergeevich) (1799-1837) Poet.

Rasputin. *See* Novykh, Girgori Yefimovich.

Rimsky-Korsakov, Nikolay Andreevich. (1844-1908) Composer, educator.

Sakharov, Andrei. (1921-1989) Nuclear physicist, political prisoner. Nobel Peace Prize winner.

Sarah bat Tovim. (18th century) Ukrainian prayer book author.

Savitskaya, Svetlana. (1948-) Cosmonaut.

Seraphim, St. of Sarov. (1759-1833) Russian

Orthodox saint and spiritual leader.

Sikharulidze, Anton. (1976-) Olympic figure skater.

Skoblikova, Lydia. (1939-) Olympic speed skater.

Slutskaya, Irina. (1979-) Olympic figure skater.

Smetanina, Raisa. (1953-) Olympic skier.

Stalin, Joseph. (1879-1953) Dictator, head of state.

Surovov, Aleksandr. (1792-1800) Military commander.

Tamara, Queen. (1156-1212) Medieval queen.

Tchaikovsky, Peter Ilyich. (1840-1893) Composer.

Tereshkova, Valentina. (1937-) Cosmonaut.

Titov, Vladimir. (1947-) Cosmonaut.

Tolstoy, Leo. (Lev Nikolaevich) (1828-1910) Author.

Trotsky, Leon. (1879-1940) Communist leader, revolutionary.

Veniaminov, Innokentii. (1797-1879) Russian Orthodox missionary, priest.

Wengeroff, Pauline. (1833-1916) Author.

Yagudin, Alexei. (1980-) Olympic figure skater.

Yeltsin, Boris. (1931-) President.

Yermak. (Vasily Timofeyovich) (1540-1585) Explorer, pirate.

Zasulich, Vera. (1849-1919) Revolutionary.

Zhukov, Georgi. (1896-1974) World War II general.

Sailors

See Boaters.

Saints

See also Apostles; Spiritual Leaders.

Andrew. (1st century)

Apollonia.

Augustine. (354-430)

Bartholomew.

Benedict of Nursia. (480-550) Italian monk.

Bernard of Clairvaux. (1090-1153) French.

Boniface. (672-754) German.

Brendan the Navigator. (484-577) Irish.

Catherine of Alexandria. (4th century)

Cecilia.

Christopher. (3rd century)

Clotilda. (470-545)

Columba. (521-597) Irish.

Cyril. (827-869) Greek Christian Orthodox.

Dorothy.

Eustace.

Francis of Assisi. (1181-1226) Italian founder of Franciscan Christianity.

George.

Gregory I. (Pope Gregory the Great) (540-604) Italian.

Helena. (250-330) Roman mother of Christianity.

Hilda of Whitby. (614-680) English.

Ignatius of Loyola. (1491-1556) Spanish.

James the Elder.

James the Younger.

Jerome. (342-420)

Joan of Arc. (1412-1431) French.

John the Baptist.

John the Evangelist.

Joseph.

Jude Thaddeus.

Lucy. (d. 304)

Luke.

Martin de Porres. (1579-1639) Peruvian.

Martin of Tours. (316?-397) French.

Mary Magdalen.

Matthew.

Matthias.

Methodius. (815-885) Greek.

Michael.

More, Saint Thomas. (1478-1535) English.

Naropa. (1016-1100) Indian Buddhist.

Nevsky, Alexander. (1220-1263) Russian.

Nicholas "Santa Claus." (d. 345) Bishop of Myra, Southern Asia Minor.

Patrick. (389?-461?) Irish.

Paul. (10?-62?)

Peter. (d. 67?)

Philip.

Rose of Lima. (1586-1617) Peruvian nun.

Scifi, Claire of Assisi. (1193-1252) Italian.

Seraphim of Sarov. (1759-1833) Russian.

Seton, Elizabeth Ann. (1774-1821)

Simon.

Susanna. (d. 295)

Teresa of Avila. (151-1582) Spanish.

Thomas Aquinas. (1224-1274) Italian.

Xavier, Francis. (1506-1552) Portuguese.

Salvadorians

See also Hispanic-Americans

Romero, Oscar. (1917-1980) Political activist, spiritual leader.

Scandinavians
See also Danish; Norwegian; Swedish; Viking.
Margaret I. (1353-1412) Queen.

Scholars
See also Historians; Philosophers; Spiritual Leaders.
Abrabanel, Benvenida. (d. 1560) Italian, born Spain.
Aguilar, Grace. (1816-1847) English.
Akiba ben Joseph. (c. 50-135) Hebrew.
Alcuin of York. (732-804) English.
Apollonius Rhodius. (c. 290-247 B.C.) Greek.
Aristotle. (384-322 B.C.) Greek.
Ascarelli, Devorah. (16th century) Italian.
Aud the Deep Minded. (c. 900) Viking.
Ban Piao. (unknown) Chinese.
Bat Ha-Levi. (12th century) Iraqi.
Beruriah. (2nd century) Hebrew.
Bruno, Giordano. (1548-1600) Italian.
Cassin, René. (1887-1976) French legal scholar.
Caro, Joseph Ben Ephraim. (1488-1575) Israeli, born Spain.
Chaucer, Geoffrey. (1343-1400) English.
Cruz, Juana Inés de la, Sister. (1651-1695) Mexican.
Diderot, Denis. (1713-1784) French.
Dulcie of Worms. (12th century) German.
Elijah ben Solomon. (1720-1797) Polish.
Erasmus, Desiderius. (1469-1536) Dutch.
Grotefend, Georg Friedrich. (1775-1853) German.
Halevi, Judah. (1075-1141) Spanish.
Hanagid, Samuel. (993-1056) Spanish.
Hanasi, Judah. (135-217) Hebrew.
Hayakawa, Samuel Ichiye. (1906-1992)
Hillel. (60 B.C.-10 A.D.) Hebrew.
Horowitz, Sarah Rebecca Rachel Leah. (18th century) Polish Jewish.
Hus, Jan. (1369-1415) Czech.
Jeremiah. (650-585 B.C.E.) Hebrew.
Judah Ha-Nasi. (135-217) Hebrew.
Leibowitz, Nehama. (1905-1997) Israeli.
Luria, Isaac. (1534-1572) Israeli.
Mansi, Paula dei. (13th century) Italian.

Mendelssohn, Moses. (1729-1786) German.
Mizrahi, Asenath Barazani. (16th century) Kurdistani.
Nahmanides. (Moses ben Nahman) (1194-1270) Spanish.
Opie, Iona. (1923-) English.
Rashi. (Solomon ben Isaac) (1040-1105) French.
Roper, Margaret More. (1505-1544) English.
Rosenzweig, Franz. (1886-1939) German.
Saadia Gaon. (882-942) Hebrew.
Somerville, Mary Fairfax. (1780-1872) Scottish.
Sullam, Sara Coppio. (1592-1641) Italian.
Thurman, Howard. (1900-1981)
Tyndale, William. (1494-1536) English.
Zallman, Elijah ben Solomon. (1720-1797) Polish.

Scots
See also Immigrants to United States, Scottish.
Boswell, James. (1740-1795) Author.
Brodie, William. (1741-1798) City official.
Brown, Arthur Whitten. (1886-1948) Aviation pioneer.
Bruce, Robert. (1274-1329) Warrior.
Burns, Robert. (1759-1796) Poet.
Chisholm, Mairí. (1896-?) Suffragist, World War I nurse.
Doyle, Sir Arthur Conan. (1859-1930) Author, physician.
Dunlop, John. (1840-1921) Inventor.
Fleming, Sir Alexander. (1881-1955) Bacteriologist, medical researcher. Nobel Prize winner.
Harper, John. (1872-1912) Orator, spiritual leader.
Henderson, Arthur. (1863-1935) Labor leader. Nobel Peace Prize winner.
Hutton, James. (1726-1797) Geologist, physician.
Inglis, Elsie. (1864-1917) Physician, women's rights activist, World War I surgeon.
Kidd, William "Captain." (1645-1701) Pirate.
Liddell, Eric. (1902-1945) Missionary, olympic track and field athlete, runner.
Lind, James. (1716-1794) Medical re-

searcher, physician.

Livingstone, David. (1813-1873) Anthropologist, astronomer, botanist, chemist, explorer, geographer, missionary.

MacDonald, Flora. (1722-1790) American Revolutionary War musician.

MacKenzie, Sir Alexander. (1764-1820) Explorer, fur trader.

Marsh, James. (fl. 1832) Chemist, forensic scientist.

Mary, Queen of Scots. (1547-1587) Queen.

Maxwell, James Clerk. (1831-1879) Physicist.

Orr, John Boyd. (1880-1971) Agricultural scientist, author, educator, nutritionist, U.N. Food and Agricultural Organization director. Nobel Peace Prize winner.

Paton, John G. (1824-1906) Missionary.

Ramsay, Sir William. (1852-1916) Chemist. Nobel Prize winner.

Ross, Sir James Clark. (1800-1862) Explorer.

Ross, Sir John. (1777-1856) Arctic explorer.

Scott, Sir Walter. (1771-1832) Author, poet.

Slessor, Mary. (1848-1915) Missionary.

Smith, Adam. (1723-1790) Economist.

Smith, Madelaine. (1835-1928) Criminal.

Somerville, Mary Fairfax. (1780-1872) Astronomer, mathematician, scholar, women's rights activist.

Stevenson, Robert Louis. (1850-1894) Author, poet.

Stuart, Robert. (1785-1848) Explorer, fur trapper.

Thomson, William. (1824-1907) Mathematician, physicist.

Watson-Watt, Sir Robert Alexander. (1892-1973) Inventor, physicist.

Watt, James. (1736-1819) Inventor.

Screenwriters

See also Filmmakers; Playwrights.

Alexie, Sherman. (1966-) Spokane Coeur D'Alene Indian.

Allen, Woody. (1935-)

Bloch, Robert. (1917-1994)

Crichton, Michael. (1942-)

Flagg, Fannie. (1944-)

Hammett, Dashiell. (1894-1961)

Lee, Shelton Jackson "Spike." (1957-)

Lustig, Arnost. (1926-) Czech.

Mathison, Melissa. (1949-)

Meyers, Nancy. (1950-)

Parker, Dorothy. (1893-1967)

Rodriguez, Robert. (1968-)

Singleton, John. (1968-)

Van Peebles, Mario. (1957-)

Villaseñsor, Victor. (1940-)

Wayans, Keenen Ivory. (1958-)

Scribes and Translators

See also Lexicographers and Linguists.

Burton, Sir Richard Francis. (1821-1890) English.

Doolittle, Hilda "H. D." (1886-1961)

Frommet of Arwyller. (15th century) German scribe.

Girty, Simon. (1741-1818)

Grotefend, Georg Friedrich. (1775-1853) German translator Sumerian writing.

Malinche, La. (Malintzin) (1500-1527) Mexican.

Malo, Davida. (1795-1853) Hawaiian.

Mansi, Paula dei. (13th century) Italian.

Miriam the Scribe. (15th century) Yemenite.

Pudaite, Rochunga. (1927-) Bible translator, born India.

Rabassa, Gregory. (1922-)

Ridderhof, Joy. (1903-1984) Bible translator.

Schele, Linda. (1942-1998)

Suzuki, Daisetz Teitan "D. T." (1870-1966) born Japan.

Townsend, Cameron. (1896-1982) Bible translator.

Tyndale, William. (1494-1536) English bible translator.

Sculptors

Barthé, Richmond. (1901-1989)

Baskin, Leonard. (1922-)

Bernini, Gian Lorenzo. (1598-1680) Italian.

Boccioni, Umberto. (1882-1916) Italian.

Borglum, Gutzon. (1867-1941)

Calder, Alexander. (1898-1966)

Catlett, Elizabeth. (1915-)

Celleni, Benvenuto. (1500-1571) Italian.

Claudel, Camille. (1864-1943) French.

Colton, Mary-Russell. (1889-1971)

Daumier, Honoré. (1808-1879) French.

de Kooning, Willem. (1904-1997) born Holland.

Donatello. (Donato de Betto di Bardi) (1387-1466) Italian.
Dwight, Edward J., Jr. (1933-)
Escobar, Marisol. (Marisol) (1930-) Venezuelan.
Esquivel, Adolfo Pérez. (1931-) Argentine.
Fuller, Meta Vaux Warrick. (1877-1968)
Gabo, Naum. (1890-1977) Russian.
Hepworth, Barbara. (1903-1975) English.
Hesse, Eva. (1936-1970) born Germany.
Hosmer, Harriet. (1830-1908)
Jackson, May Howard. (1877-1931)
JoeSam. (1939-)
Johnson, Sargent Claude. (1887-1967)
Kollwitz, Kaethe. (1867-1945) German.
Leonardo da Vinci. (1452-1519) Italian.
Lewis, Mary Edmonia. (1845-1890)
Lin, Maya Ying. (1960-)
Lisboa, Antonio Francisco. (1738-1814) Brazilian.
Man Ray. *See* Radnitsky, Emmanuel.
Marisol. S*ee* Escobar, Marisol.
Matisse, Henri. (1869-1954) French.
Michelangelo Buonarotti. (1475-1564) Italian.
Miro, Joan. (1893-1983) Spanish.
Moore, Henry. (1898-1986) English.
Moxon, June. (unknown)
Naranjo, Michael. (1944-)
Nevelson, Louise. (1899-1988) born Russia.
Ney, Elisabet. (1833-1907)
Noguchi, Isamu. (1904-1988)
Oppenheim, Meret. (1913-1985) Swiss, born Germany.
Phidias. (c. 490-432) Greek.
Picasso, Pablo. (1881-1973) Spanish.
Praxiteles. (390?-330 B.C.) Greek.
Prophet, Nancy Elizabeth. (1890-1960)
Radnitsky, Emmanuel. (Man Ray) (1890-1976)
Ream, Vinnie. (1847-1914)
Remington, Frederic. (1861-1909)
Ringgold, Faith. (1930-)
Rodin, Auguste. (1840-1917) French.
Savage, Augusta Christine. (1892-1962)
Smith, David. (1906-1965)
Sofaer, Anna. (unknown)
Tussaud, Marie. (1761-1850) French.
West, W. Richard, Sr. (1912-1996)
Wright, Patience Lovell. (1725-1786)

Secretaries of Commerce, Defense, State, and War

See Cabinet Members.

Seismologists

See also Meterologists.
Richter, Charles. (1900-1985)

Senators, United States

Adams, John Quincy. (1767-1848) Massachusetts.
Bingham, Hiram. (1878-1956) Connecticut.
Bradley, Bill. (1943-) New Jersey.
Bruce, Blanche K. (1841-1898) Mississippi.
Burr, Aaron. (1756-1836) New York.
Calhoun, John Caldwell. (1782-1850) South Carolina.
Campbell, Ben Nighthorse. (1933-) Colorado.
Chavez, Dennis. (1888-1962) New Mexico.
Clay, Henry. (1777-1852) Missouri.
Clinton, Hillary Rodham. (1947-) New York.
Davis, Jefferson. (1808-1889) Mississippi.
Dole, Robert. (1923-) Kansas.
Douglas, Stephen A. (1813-1861) Illinois.
Feinstein, Dianne. (1933-) California.
Fong, Hiram. (1907-) Hawaii.
Galloway, Abraham. (1837-1870) North Carolina.
Garfield, James. (1831-1881) Tennessee.
Harding, Warren G. (1865-1923) Ohio.
Harrison, Benjamin. (1833-1901) Indiana.
Hayakawa, Samuel Ichiye. (1906-1992) California.
Houston, Samuel. (1793-1863) Texas.
Hull, Cordell. (1871-1955) Tennessee.
Inouye, Daniel. (1924-) Hawaii.
Jackson, Andrew. (1767-1863) Tennessee.
Johnson, Lyndon Baines. (1908-1973) Texas.
Kassebaum, Nancy Landon. (1932-) Kansas.
Kefauver, Estes. (1903-1963) Tennessee.
Kellogg, Frank Billings. (1856-1937) New York.
Kennedy, Edward Moore "Ted." (1932-) Massachusetts.
Kennedy, John Fitzgerald. (1917-1963) Massachusettts.
Kennedy, Robert Francis. (1925-1968) Mas-

sachusetts.

La Follette, Robert. (1855-1925) Wisconsin.

Lee, Richard Henry. (1732-1794) Virginia.

Matsunaga, Masayuki "Spark." (1916-1990) Hawaii.

McCarthy, Joseph. (1908-1957) Wisconsin.

Mikulski, Barbara. (1936-) Maryland.

Morrill, Justin. (1810-1898) Vermont.

Morris, Gouverneur. (1752-1816) New York.

Moseley-Braun, Carol. (1947-) Illinois.

Nelson, Gaylord. (1916-) Wisconsin.

Nixon, Richard Milhous. (1913-1994) California.

Norris, George. (1861-1944) Nebraska.

Paterson, William. (1745-1806) New Jersey.

Read, George. (1733-1798) Delaware.

Revels, Hiram Rhoades. (1822-1901) Mississippi.

Smith, Margaret Chase. (1897-1995) Maine.

Snowe, Olympia. (1947-) Maine.

Taft, Robert Alphonse. (1889-1953) Ohio.

Thurmond, Strom. (1902-2003) South Carolina.

Truman, Harry S. (1884-1972) Missouri.

Tyler, John. (1790-1862) Virginia.

Webster, Daniel. (1782-1852) Massachusetts.

Serial Killers

Bundy, Ted. (1946-1989)

Chikatilo, Andrei. (1936-1994) Russian.

Dahmer, Jeffrey. (1960-1994)

Fish, Albert. (1870-1936)

Gacy, John Wayne. (1942-1994)

Gein, Ed. (1906-1984)

Holmes, Herman Mudget "H. H." (1860-1896)

Showmen and Women

See also Actors; Comedians; Dancers; Magicians; Singers.

Barnum, Phineas " P. T." (1810-1891) Circus.

Black Elk. (1863-1950) Oglala Lakota Sioux medicine man performer.

Chaplin, Charlie. (1889-1997)

Cody, William "Buffalo Bill." (1846-1917) Wild West show.

Davis, Sammy, Jr. (1925-1990)

Disney, Walt. (1901-1966)

Eng and Chang. (1811-1874) Conjoined twins, born Siam.

Everett, Milton Hutchins "M. H." (mid 1800s-early 1900s) Minstrel performer.

Jackson, Michael. (1958-)

Jolson, Al. (1886-1950)

Kelly, Emmett. (1898-1979) Circus clown.

Merrick, Joseph. (1862-1890) English "Elephant Man."

Moore, Alonzo. (d. 1914) Minstrel performer.

Oakley, Annie. (1860-1926) Wild West.

Pastrana, Julia. (1832-1860) Mexican "bearded lady" in circus.

Robinson, Bill "Bojangles." (1878-1949)

Rogers, Will. (1879-1935) Cherokee Indian humorist.

Stratton, Charles Sherwood. (Tom Thumb) (1838-1883)

Wadlow, Robert. (1918-1940) Tallest man.

West, Mae. (1893-1980)

Siamese
See Thais.

Singaporeans

Tay, Jannie. (1945-) Entrepreneur wristwatch boutiques.

Singers

Aguilera, Christina. (1966-) Pop.

Allen, Debbie. (1956-)

Anderson, Ivie. (1904-1949) Jazz.

Anderson, Marian. (1897-1993) Opera.

Andrews, Julie. (1935-) born England.

Anthony, Marc. (1968-) Pop.

Arce, Elmer Figuero. (Chayanne) (1968-) Puerto Rican pop.

Baez, Joan. (1941-) Folk.

Bailey, Pearl. (1918-1990) Jazz.

Baker, Josephine. (1906-1975) Jazz.

Belafonte, Harry. (1927-)

Berry, Chuck. (1926-) Rock.

Bjork. *See* Gudmondsdottir, Bjork.

Blades, Ruben. (1948-)

Bori, Lucrezia. (1887-1960) Opera singer, born Spain.

Brandy. *See* Norwood, Brandy.

Broonzy, "Big" Bill. (1893-1959) Blues.

Brown, James. (1933-) Blues.

Bullock, Anna Mae. (Tina Turner) (1939) Pop.

Burrell, Stanley Kirk. (Hammer) (1962-) Rap.

Byrne, David. (1952-) Rock singer, born Scotland.

Callas, Maria. (1923-1977) Greek opera singer.

Calloway, Cab. (1907-1994) Jazz.

Carey, Mariah. (1969-) Pop.

Carr, Vicki. (1940-)

Caruso, Enrico. (1873-1921) Italian opera singer.

Charles, Ray. (1930-2004) Jazz.

Charlot, Olivia. (1913-) Jazz.

Chayanne. *See* Arce, Elmer Figuero.

Cher. *See* Sarkisian, Cherilyn.

Ciccione, Madonna Louise Veronica. (Madonna) (1958-)

Clugney, Odode. (879-942) French liturgical music.

Cole, Nat King. (1916-1965) Jazz.

Cole, Natalie. (1950-) Pop.

Cox, Ida. (1889-1967) Jazz.

Crespo, Elvis. (1970-) Puerto Rican pop singer.

Crosby, Bing. (1904-1977)

Cruz, Celia. (1924-2003) Salsa singer, born Cuba.

Dandridge, Dorothy. (1923-1965)

Davis, Sammy, Jr. (1925-1990)

di Lasso, Orlando. (1532-1594) Belgian.

Douglas, Helen Gahagan. (1900-1980)

Dylan, Bob. (1941-) Folksinger.

Eckstine, Billy. (1904-1993) Jazz.

Edwards, Eileen Regina. (Shania Twain) (1965-) Canadian pop singer.

Espinel, Luisa Ronstadt. (1892-1963)

Estefan, Gloria. (1957-) born Cuba.

Fitzgerald, Ella. (1918-1996) Jazz.

Franklin, Aretha. (1942-) Jazz.

Gallego, Luis Miguel. (Luis Miguel) (1970-) Puerto Rican pop singer.

Garden, Mary. (1874-1967) Opera singer, born Scotland.

Garland, Judy. (1922-1969)

Greenfield, Elizabeth Taylor. (1809-1876)

Gudmundsdottir, Bjork. (Bjork) (1966-) Icelandic pop.

Guthrie, Woody. (1912-1967) Folksinger.

Hammer. *See* Burrell, Stanley Kirk.

Hayes, Isaac. (1943-) Jazz.

Haymes, Dick. (1917-1980) Crooner.

Henderson, Fletcher. (1897-1952) Jazz.

Hill, Lauryn. (1975-) Pop.

Holiday, Billie. (1915-1959) Blues.

Holley, Major. (1924-1991) Jazz.

Holly, Buddy. (1936-1959) Rock.

Horne, Lena. (1917-) Jazz.

Houston, Whitney. (1963-) Pop.

Hunter, Alberta. (1895-1984) Jazz.

Iglesias, Enrique. (1975-) Pop singer, born Spain.

Jackson, Janet. (1966-) Pop.

Jackson, Mahalia. (1911-1972) Blues.

Jackson, Michael. (1958-) Rock.

Johnetta. (1927-1983) Jazz.

Johnson, Robert. (1911-1938) Jazz.

Jolson, Al. (1886-1950)

Joplin, Janis. (1943-1970) Rock.

King, B. B. (1925-) Jazz.

King, Coretta Scott. (1927-)

Latifah, Queen. *See* Owens, Dana Elaine.

Ledbetter, Huddy "Leadbelly." (1885-1949) Jazz.

Lennon, John. (1940-1980) English rock singer.

Lincoln, Abbey. (1930-) Jazz.

Little Richard. *See* Penniman, Richard Wayne.

Lopez, Jennifer. (1970-) Pop.

Luis Miguel. *See* Gallego, Luis Miguel.

Madonna. *see* Ciccione, Madonna Louise Veronica.

Makeba, Miriam. (1932-) South African.

Mangeshkar, Lata. (1929-2001) Indian.

Martin, Ricky. (1971-) Puerto Rican pop.

Mathis, Johnny. (1935-)

McCartney, Paul. (1942-) English rock.

McCoy, Millie and Christine. (1851-1912)

McDaniel, Hattie. (1895-1952) Blues.

McKinney, Nina Mae. (1909-1967) Jazz.

McLachlan, Sarah. (1968-) Canadian pop.

McRae, Carmen. (1922-1994) Jazz.

McTell, "Blind Willie." (1901-1959) Blues.

Melba, Nellie. (1861-1931) Australian.

Merman, Ethel. (1908-1984)

Midler, Bette. (1945-)

Miranda, Carmen. (1909-1955) Brazilian.

Morissette, Alanis. (1974-) Canadian pop.

Nelson, Prince Rogers. (Prince) (1958-) Rock singer.

Norman, Jessye. (1945-) Opera.
Norwood, Brandy. (Brandy) (1979-) Pop
    singer.
O'Day, Anita. (1919-) Jazz.
O'Hara, Mary. (1935-) Irish.
Owens, Dana Elaine. (Queen Latifah)
    (1970-)
Palestrina, Giovanni Pierluigi da. (1525-
    1594) Italian.
Penniman, Richard Wayne. (Little Richard)
    (1932-)
Perez, Selena Quintanilla. (Selena) (1971-
    1995) Pop singer.
Ponce, Carlos. (1972-) Puerto Rican pop.
Presley, Elvis. (1935-1977) Rock.
Price, Leontyne. (1927-) Opera.
Pride, Charley. (1938-) Jazz.
Prince. *See* Nelson, Prince Rogers.
Quimby, Doug. (1936-) Jazz.
Quimby, Frankie. (1937-) Jazz.
Rainey, Gertrude "Ma." (1886-1939) Blues.
Rimes, LeAnn. (1982-) Country music.
Ripoll, Shakira Mebarak. (Shakira) (1977-)
    Colombian.
Robeson, Paul. (1898-1976)
Robinson, Smokey. (1940-)
Ronstadt, Linda. (1946-)
Ross, Diana. (1944-)
Rossi, Europa di. (Madame Europa) (16th
    century) Italian.
Rushing, Jimmy. (1903-1972) Jazz.
Sainte-Marie, Buffy. (1941-) Cree Indian,
    born Canada.
Sarkisian, Cherilyn. (Cher) (1946-) Pop.
Secada, Jon. (1963-) born Cuba.
Selena. *See* Perez, Selena Quintanilla.
Shakira. *See* Ripoll, Shakira Mebarak.
Sills, Beverly. (1929-) Opera.
Simone, Nina. (1933-2003) Jazz.
Sinatra, Frank. (1915-1998) Crooner.
Smith, Ada "Bricktop." (1894-1984) Jazz.
Smith, Bessie. (1894-1937) Jazz.
Smith, Clara. (1894-1935) Jazz.
Smith, Mamie. (1883-1946) Jazz.
Smith, Will. (1969-) Rap.
Spears, Britney. (1981-) Pop.
Spivey, Victoria. (1906-1976) Jazz.
Stafford, Jo. (1917-) Jazz.
Stewart, Leroy Elliot "Slam." (1914-1987)
    Jazz.
Streisand, Barbra. (1942-)

Tharpe, Sister Rosetta. (1921-1973) Jazz.
Tucker, Sophie. (1887-1966)
Turner, Tina. *See* Bullock, Anna Marie.
Twain, Shania. *See* Edwards, Eileen Regina.
Urania of Worms, Lady. (13th century) Ger-
    man liturgical singer.
Valens, Ritchie. (1942-1959) Rock.
Vaughan, Sarah. (1924-1991) Jazz.
Wallace, Sippie. (1898-1986) Jazz.
Washington, Dinah. (1925-1959) Jazz.
Waters, Ethel. (1896-1977) Jazz.
Waters, McKinley Morganfield "Muddy."
    (1915-1983) Blues.
Williams, Bert. (1874-1922)
Williams, Joe. (1918-1999) Jazz.
Williams, Lucinda. (1953-) Country.

Skaters
See also Olympic Athletes, Skaters.

Figure
Albright, Tenley. (1935-)
Anissina, Mariana. (1975-) Russian.
Baiul, Oksana. (1977-) Ukrainian.
Berezhnaya, Elena. (1977-) Russian.
Bonaly, Surya. (1973-) French.
Bourne, Shae-Lynn. (1976-) Canadian.
Button, Dick. (1929-)
Cohen, Sasha. (1984-)
Eldredge, Todd. (1971-)
Fleming, Peggy. (1948-)
Fratianne, Linda. (1960-)
Goebel, Timothy. (1980-)
Hamill, Dorothy. (1956-)
Harding, Tonya. (1970-)
Heiss, Carol. (1940-)
Henie, Sonia. (1912-1969) Norwegian.
Hughes, Sarah. (1985-)
Kerrigan, Nancy. (1969-)
Kraatz, Victor. (1971-) Canadian.
Kwan, Michelle. (1980-)
Kyoko, Ina. (1972-) born Japan.
Lang, Naomi. (1978-) Karuk Indian.
Lipinski, Tara. (1982-)
Lu, Chen. (1976-) Chinese.
Peizerat, Gwendal. (1972-) French.
Pelletier, David. (1974-) Canadian.
Plushenko, Evgeny. (1982-) Russian.
Robinson, Jennifer. (1976-) Canadian.
Salchow, Ulrich. (1877-1949) Swedish.
Salé, Jamie. (1977-) Canadian.

Sikharulidze, Anton. (1976-) Russian.
Slutskaya, Irina. (1979-) Russian.
Stojko, Elvis. (1972-) Canadian.
Tchernyshev, Peter. (1971-) born Russia.
Thomas, Debi. (1967-)
Weiss, Michael. (1976-)
Witt, Katarina. (1965-) German.
Yagudin, Alexei. (1980-) Russian.
Yamaguchi, Kristi. (1971-)
Zimmerman, John. (1973-)

In-Line
Billiris, Manuel. (1975-) Australian.
da Silva, Fabriola. (1979-) Brazilian.
Edwards, Chris. (1973-)
Eisenberg, Arlo. (1973-)
Everett, Dawn. (1979-)
Gengo, Kate. (1964-)
Hodgson, Tasha. (1972-) New Zealander.
Mantz, Matt. (1981-)
Schrijn, Eric. (1979-)
Spizer, Randy. (1980-)

Skateboarding
Hawk, Tony. (1968-)

Speed
Blair, Bonnie. (1964-)
Heiden, Eric. (1958-)
Skoblikova, Lydia. (1939-) Russian.
Young, Sheila. (1950-)

Skiers
See also Olympic Athletes, Skiers.
Golden, Diana. (1963-2001)
Killy, Jean-Claude. (1943-) French.
Moser-Proell, Annemarie. (1953-) Austrian.
Nykanen, Matti. (1963-) Finnish.
Smetanina, Raisa. (1953-) Russian.
Street, Picabo. (1971-)
Theni, Gustavo. (1951-) Italian.
Zurbriggen, Pirmin. (1963-) Swiss.

Slave Insurrectionists
See also Abolitionists.
Cinque, Joseph. (1817-1879) African.
Drayton, Daniel. (unknown) Seaman.
Prosser, Gabriel. (1776-1800)
Touissant L'Ouverture, Pierre Dominique. (1743-1803) Haitian.
Turner, Nat. (1800-1831)

Vesey, Denmark. (1767-1822)
Washington, Madison. (unknown)

Slaves
Anderson, John. (1831-?)
Beard, Andrew Jackson. (1849-1941)
Beckwourth, James. (1798-1866)
Bethune, Thomas "Blind Tom" Greene. (1849-1908)
Bibb, Henry. (unknown)
Boyd, Henry. (1802-1886)
Boyd, Richard Henry. (1843-1922)
Brown, Clara. (1803-1885)
Brown, Henry "Box." (1816-?)
Brown, John "Fed." (1810-1876)
Brown, William Wells. (1814-1884)
Burns, Anthony. (1834-1862)
Conly, Elvira. (1845-?)
Cooley, Chloe. (unknown)
Coppin, Fannie Jackson. (1836-1913)
Craft, Ellen. (1826-1897)
Craft, William. (1824-1900)
Dabney, Austin. (1799-1821)
Davis, Tice. (unknown)
Derham, James. (1762-1804)
Douglass, Frederick. (1817-1895)
Equiano, Olaudah. (1745-1799) born Nigeria.
Ferguson, Catherine "Katy." (1779-1854)
Fields, Mary. (1832-1914)
Flipper, Henry O. (1856-1940)
Freeman, Elizabeth "Mumbet." (1742-1829)
Galloway, Abraham. (1837-1870)
Garcia. (fl. 1813)
Garner, Margaret. (1833-?)
Goode, Sara E. (1850-?)
Grant, Jehu. (1752-?)
Green, Lear. (c. 1830-1850)
Gronniosaw, Ukawsaw. (1725-1786) African.
Harris, Eliza. (unknown)
Henson, Josiah. (1789-1883)
Huddleston, Ned. (1849-1900)
Hughes, Louis. (1832-?)
Jacobs, Harriet. (1813-1897)
Jasper, John. (1812-1901)
Johnson, Anthony. (c. 1678)
Keckley, Elizabeth. (1818-1907)
Laney, Lucy Craft. (1854-1933)
Lynch, John R. (1847-1939)
Malinche, La. (Malintzin) (1500-1527)

Mexican.
Masih, Igbal. (1982-1995) Pakistani.
Mason, Biddy. (1818-1891)
McCoy, Millie and Christine. (1851-1912)
McJunkin, George. (1851-1922)
McWhorter, "Free Frank." (1777-1854)
Menendez, Francisco. (1700-1772) born
   Africa.
Metoyer, Marie-Therese. (1742-1816)
Montgomery, Benjamin. (1819-1877)
Murphy, John H., Sr. (d. 1922)
Northup, Solomon. (1808-1861?)
Norton, Daniel. (1840-1918)
Parker, John. (1827-1900)
Parsons, Lucy. (1853-1943)
Patrick. (389?-461?) Irish.
Pennington, James W. C. (1809-1870)
Price, John. (1840-?)
Prince, Mary. (1788-?)
Scott, Dred. (1795-1858)
Scott, Harriet. (unknown)
Slew, Jenny. (1719-?)
Smalls, Robert. (1839-1915)
Smith, Amanda. (1837-1915)
Smith, James L. (1881-?)
Somersett. (1600s)
Steward, Austin. (1794-1860)
Still, Peter. (1800-1868)
Still, Vina. (unknown)
Taylor, Susie King. (1848-1912)
Touissant, Pierre. (1766-1853)
Traylor, Bill. (1854-1947)
Tubman, Harriet. (1820-1913)
Turner, James Milton. (1840-1915)
Veney, Bethany. (1815-?)
Ward, Samuel Ringgold. (1817-1878)
Washington, Booker T. (1856-1915)
Weems, Ann Marie. (1840-?)
White, George Henry. (1852-1918)
York. (1770-1832)

Sled Dog Racers
Butcher, Susan. (1956-)

Soccer Players
See also Olympic Athletes, Soccer.
Akers, Michelle. (1966-)
Beckenbauer, Franz. (1946-) German.
Chastain, Brandi. (1968-)
Fair, Lorri. (1978-)
Fawcett, Joy. (1968-)

Foudy, Julie. (1971-)
Hamm, Mia. (1972-)
Heinrichs, April. (1964-)
Lilly, Kristine. (1971-)
Macmillan, Shannon. (1974-)
Maradona, Diego. (1960-) Argentine.
Millbrett, Tiffany. (1972-)
Nascimento, Edson Arantes do. (Pelé)
   (1940-) Brazilian.
Overbeck, Carla. (1969-)
Parlow, Cindy. (1978-)
Pelé. *See* Nascimento, Edson Arnates do.
Roberts, Tiffany. (1977-)
Scurry, Brianna. (1971-)
Sobrero, Kate. (1976-)
Venturini, Tisha. (1973-)

Social Workers
See also Children's Rights Activists; Human
   Rights Activists.
Addams, Jane. (1860-1935)
Deer, Ada. (1935-) Menominee Indian.
Friedman, Tova Grossman. (1938-) born
   Poland.
Hardy-Garcia, Dianne. (1965-)
Height, Dorothy Irene. (1912-)
Hopkins, Harry L. (1890-1946)
Lathrop, Julia. (1858-1932)
Mott, John Raleigh. (1865-1955)
Pantoja, Antonio. (1922-2002) born Puerto
   Rico.
Pappenheim, Berta. (1859-1936) German.
Perkins, Frances. (1882-1965)
Rankin, Jeanette. (1880-1973)
Robertson, Alice Mary. (1854-1931)
Roth-Hano, Renée. (1931-) born France.
Sampson, Edith. (1901-1980)
Wald, Lillian. (1867-1940)
Wijsmuller, Gertrude. (unknown) Dutch.
Yin, Luoth. (1950-) born Cambodia.

Sociologists
Frazier, E. Franklin. (1894-1962)
Myrdal, Alva. (1902-1986) Swedish.
Parsons, Elsie Clews. (1875-1941)
Soong May-Ling. (1897-2003) Chinese.

Softball Players
Fernandez, Lisa. (1971-)
Richardson, Dorothy "Dot." (1961-)

Soil Scientists
Sanchez, Pedro. (1940-) born Cuba.

Songwriters
Blackwell, Otis. (1931-2002)
Burrell, Stanley Kirk. (Hammer) (1962-)
Byrne, David. (1952-) born Scotland.
Edwards, Eileen Regina. (Shania Twain)
(1965-) Canadian.
Eisenstein, Judith Kaplan. (1909-1996) Li-
turgical songs.
Gershwin, George. (1898-1937)
Gershwin, Ira. (1896-1983)
Gilbert, Sir William. (1836-1911) English.
Guthrie, Woody. (1912-1967)
Hammer. *See* Burrell, Stanley Kirk.
Hammerstein, Oscar, II. (1895-1960)
Hill, Lauryn. (1975-)
Johnson, James Weldon. (1871-1938)
Ledbetter, Huddy "Leadbelly." (1885-1949)
McCartney, Paul. (1942-) English.
McLachlan, Sarah. (1968-) Canadian.
Nelson, Prince Rogers. (Prince) (1958-)
Newton, John. (1725-1807) English liturgi-
cal music.
Prince. *See* Nelson, Prince Rogers.
Rainey, Gertrude "Ma." (1886-1939)
Robinson, Smokey. (1940-)
Rodgers, Richard. (1902-1979)
Sainte-Marie, Buffy. (1941-) Cree Indian,
born Canada.
Sissle, Noble. (1889-1970)
Twain, Shania. *See* Edwards, Eileen Regina.
Valens, Ritchie. (1942-1959)

Space Scientists
See also Astronauts; Engineers, Aeronauti-
cal.
Abrahamson, James A. (1933-)
Brill, Yvonne. (1924-) born Canada.
Cowings, Patricia. (1948-)
Crews, Jeanne Lee. (unknown)
Darden, Christine. (1942-)
Ericsson-Jackson, Aprille Joy. (unknown)
Faget, Maxim. (1921-2004)
Goddard, Robert. (1882-1945)
Harris, Wesley. (1941-)
Houbolt, John. (fl. 1960s)
Irwin, James. (1930-1991)
Ivins, Marsha. (1951-)

Johnson, Katherine. (1918-)
Korolev, Sergei. (1906-1966) Russian.
Marchbanks, Vance. (1905-1988)
Pickering, William. (1858-1938)
Reed, Dale. (unknown)
Sampson, Henry. (1934-)
Shirley, Donna. (1941-)
Shoemaker, Gene. (1928-1997)
Shurney, Robert. (1921-)
Sigur, Wanda. (1958-)
Van Allen, James. (1914-)
Wadhwa, Meenakshi. (1967-) born India.
Williams, Ozzie. (1921-)

Spaniards
See also Hispanic-Americans, Immigrants to
United States, Spanish.
Africanus, Leo. (Giovanni Leone) (1495-
1553) Explorer.
Agustin, Maria. (La Saragossa) (1786-1857)
Military leader.
Alaminos, Antón de. (1482-1520) Explorer,
ship captain for Columbus and Ponce de
Leon.
Albéniz, Isaac. (1860-1909) Composer, mu-
sician.
Allyón, Lucas Vásquez de. (1475-1526)
Entrepreneur sugar mill owner, explorer.
Alvarez de Toledo, Fernando. (Duke of
Alva) (1507-1583) Military leader.
Balboa, Vasco Nuncz dc. (1475-1519) Ex-
plorer.
Bermúdez, Diego. (1480-?) Page for Co-
lumbus.
Cabeza de Vaca, Álvar Núñez. (1490-1557)
Explorer.
Casals, Pablo. (1876-1973) Composer, con-
ductor, musician.
Cervantes, Miguel de. (1547-1616) Author.
Cid Campeador, El. (Rodrigo Diaz de Viver)
(1043-1099) Military leader.
Coronado, Francisco Vásquez de. (1510-
1554) Explorer.
Cortes, Hernan. (1485-1547) Explorer.
Cristina. (1965-) Princess.
Dali, Salvador. (1904-1989) Painter.
de Soto, Hernando. (1496?-1542) Explorer.
Egeria. (4th century) Adventurer, author,
religious pilgrim.
Elena. (1964-) Princess.
Erauso, Catalina de. (1585-1650) Outlaw,

disguised self as man.

Falla, Manuel de. (1876-1946) Composer.

Ferdinand. (1452-1516) King.

Franco, Francisco. (1892-1975) Dictator, political leader.

Goya, Francisco de. (1746-1828) Painter.

Granados, Enrique. (1867-1916) Composer.

Halevi, Judah. (1075-1141) Physician, poet, scholar, spiritual leader.

Hanagid, Samuel. (993-1056) Military leader, scholar.

Ibarurri, Dolores. (1895-1989) Political leader, revolutionary.

Ignatius of Loyola. (1491-1556) Military leader, saint, spiritual leader.

Isabella I. (1451-1504) Queen.

Las Casas, Bartolomé de. (1474-1566) Soldier, spiritual leader.

Maimonides. (Moses ben Maimon) (1135-1204) Philosopher.

Marcos de Niza, Frey. (1495-1558) Missionary.

Menedéz de Aviles, Pedro. (1519-1574) Explorer, founder St. Augustine, naval officer.

Miro, Joan. (1893-1983) Painter, sculptor.

Moses de Leon. (1240-1305) Mystic, spiritual leader.

Nahmanides. (Moses ben Nahman) (1194-1270) Scholar, spiritual leader.

Oñate, Juan de. (1550-1630) Colonist, explorer, born Spain.

Orellana, Francisco de. (1511-1546) Explorer.

Philip II. (1527-1598) King.

Picasso, Pablo. (1881-1973) Ceramicist, painter, sculptor.

Pineda, Álonzo Alvarez de. (1792-1872) Explorer, navy admiral.

Pinzón, Martin. (1440-1493) Explorer.

Pinzón, Vincente. (1463-1514) Explorer.

Pizarro, Francisco. (1475-1541) Explorer, military leader.

Ponce de León, Juan. (1460-1521) Explorer.

Saenz, Manuela. (1797-1856) Political activist.

Sanchez Vicario, Arantza. (1971-) Tennis player.

Saragossa, La. *See* Agostin, Maria.

Serra, Father Junipero. (1713-1784) Missionary.

Teresa of Avila. (1515-1582) Mystic, saint.

Vega, Garcilaso de la. (1539-1616) Author.

Velázquez, Diego Rodriguez Silva y. (1599-1660) Painter.

Zacuto, Abraham. (1452-1515) Astronomer, navigator for Columbus.

Spies and Secret Agents

See also Traitors.

Abel, Rudolf Ivanovich. (1920-1971) Russian.

Ames, Aldrich. (1941-)

André, Captain John. (1750-1780) American Revolutionary War.

Aylward, Gladys. (1902-1970) World War I.

Behn, Aphra Johnson. (1640?-1689) English.

Beurton, Ruth Kuczynski. (1907-) World War II.

Boyd, Belle. (1843-1900) Civil War.

Carré, Lily. (1908-) French World War II.

Cushman, Pauline. (Harriet Wood) (1833-1893) Civil War.

Darragh, John. (unknown) American Revolutionary War.

Darragh, Lydia. (1725-1789) American Revolutionary War.

Davies, Henry. (unknown) worked with Allen Pinkerton.

Defoe, Daniel. (1660-1731) English.

Edmonds, Sarah Emma. (1841-1898) Civil War.

Edmondson, Belle. (1840-1873) Civil War.

Fawkes, Guy. (1570-1606) English.

Greenhow, Rose O'Neal. (1817-1864) Civil War.

Hale, Nathan. (1755-1776) American Revolutionary War.

Harrison, Marguerite Baker. (1879-1967)

Hart, Nancy. (1744-1841) American Revolutionary War.

Hiss, Alger. (1904-1996)

Howard, Edward Lee. (1951-2002)

Kolbe, Fritz. (1903-1961) German World War II spy for allies.

Kuehn, Ruth. (unknown) German World War II.

Langston, Dicey. (1766-1837) American Revolutionary War.

Lincoln, Trebitsch. (1872-1943) Hungarian.

Mata Hari. *See* Zelle, Margareta Gertrude.

Montagu, Ewen. (1901-1985) English World War II.

Morley, Sylvanus Griswold. (1883-1948) World War I.

Odell, Jonathan. (1737-1818) American Revolutionary War.

Pack, Amy Thorne "Betty." (1910-1963) World War II.

Philby, Harold Arlen Russell "Kim." (1912-1988) English.

Redmond, Mary. (unknown) American Revolutionary War.

Rivington, James. (1727-1802) English Revolutionary War.

Ronge, Maximilian. (unknown) Austrian World War I.

Schulte, Eduard Reinhold Karl. (1891-1966) German World War II.

Sorge, Richard. (1895-1944) German World War II.

Tubman, Harriet. (1820-1913) Civil War.

Van Lew, Elizabeth. (1818-1900) Civil War.

Wright, Patience Lovell. (1725-1786) American Revolutionary War.

Zelle, Margareta Gertrude. (Mata Hari) (1876-1917) Dutch World War I.

Spiritual Leaders

African

Anoyke, Okomfo. (17th century) West African priest.

Kivengere, Festo. (1919-1988) Ugandan bishop.

Luwum, Janani. (1922-1977) Ugandan archbishop.

Tutu, Desmond Mpilo. (1931-) South African archbishop.

American

Abernathy, Ralph David. (1926-1990)

Allen, Richard. (1760-1831)

Baker, George F. (Father Divine) (1882-1965) Cult leader.

Beecher, Lyman. (1775-1863) Puritan zealot.

Blackwell, Antoinette Brown. (1825-1921) First American woman minister.

Brebeuf, Jean de, Father. (1593-1649) Jesuit priest, born France.

Cartwright, Peter. (1785-1872)

Cayce, Edgar. (1877-1945) Psychic.

Coughlin, Father Charles Edward. (1891-1979) Catholic leader, hatemonger, born Canada.

Crown, Frank Fools. (1890-1989) Oglala Indian.

Day, Dorothy. (1897-1980) Catholic journalist on religious matters.

De Smet, Pierre-Jean. (1801-1873) Jesuit priest, born Belgium.

Deloria, Vine, Sr. (1901-1990) Yankton Dakota Indian.

Dempsey, Sister Mary Joseph. (1856-1939)

Dorman, Pamela Davis. (1952-) Gulf War chaplain.

Eddy, Mary Baker. (1821-1910) founder Christian Science religion.

Edwards, Jonathan. (1703-1758)

Eilberg, Amy. (1954-) First Conservative Jewish female rabbi.

Evans, Henry. (1760-1810) Preacher.

Garnet, Henry Highland. (1815-1882) Minister.

Graham, Billy. (1918-) Protestant leader.

Handsome Lake. (1735-1818) Iroquois Indian prophet.

Haynes, Lemuel. (1753-1833) Preacher.

Healy, Patrick Francis. (1834-1910) Jesuit priest.

Henson, Josiah. (1789-1883) Minister.

Hiawatha. (fl. 1440) Iroquois Indian chief.

Hitchcock, Edward. (1793-1864) Minister.

Hooker, Thomas. (1586-1647) Puritan preacher.

Hosier, Harry "Black Harry." (1750-1806) Preacher.

Hubbard, L. Ron. (1911-1986) Scientology Church founder.

Hutchinson, Anne Marbury. (1591-1643) Advocate for religious freedom, born England.

Jackson, Jesse. (1941-) Minister.

Jasper, John. (1812-1901) Minister.

Jay, Allen. (1831-1910) Quaker leader.

Johnson, Mordecai. (1890-1976) Minister.

Kaplan, Mordecai. (1881-1983) Reconstructionist Judaism founder.

Lee, Ann. (1736-1784) Shaker leader, born England.

Lee, Jarena. (1783-1850) Preacher.

Marshall, Andrew Cox. (1775-1856)

Preacher.

Mather, Cotton. (1663-1728) Puritan minister, Protestant leader.

Mather, Increase. (1639-1723) Puritan minister.

Mays, Benjamin E. (1895-1984) Minister.

Meacham, Joseph. (d. 1796) Shaker community founder.

Metz, Christian. (1795-1867) Amana utopian society founder, born Germany.

Moody, Dwight Lyman. (1837-1899) Evangelical minister.

Mott, John R. (1865-1955) Foreign missions founder.

Muhammad, Elijah. (1897-1975) Nation of Islam leader.

Ng Poon Chew. (1866-1931) Minister, born China.

Occom, Samuel. (1723-1792) Oneida Indian Christian preacher.

Odell, Jonathan. (1737-1818) American Revolutionary War minister.

Palau, Luis. (1934-) Evangelist, minister, born Argentina.

Pariseau, Esther "Mother Joseph." (1832-1902) Catholic nun, Good Samaritan.

Parris, Samuel. (1653-1720) Puritan minister, born England.

Pennington, James W. C. (1809-1870) Minister.

Perkins, John. (1930-) Minister.

Powell, Adam Clayton, Jr. (1908-1972) Minister.

Preisand, Sally. (1946-) First female rabbi in U.S.

Rapp, George. (1757-1847) Harmonist community leader, born Germany.

Sasso, Sandy Eisenberg. (1947-) Rabbi.

Schechter, Solomon. (1849-1915) Conservative Judaism leader, born Romania.

Seton, Elizabeth Ann. (1774-1821) Catholic nun.

Seymour, William Joseph. (1870-1922) Pentecostal Church founder.

Smith, Amanda. (1837-1915) Minister.

Smith, Joseph, Jr. (1805-1844) Mormon Church founder.

Snow, Eliza. (1804-1887) Mormon leader.

Soloveitchik, Joseph Dov. (1903-1993) Orthodox Judaism leader, born Poland.

Thurman, Howard. (1900-1981) Protestant

theologian.

Tillich, Paul. (1886-1965) Protestant theologian, born Germany.

Tingley, Katherine. (1847-1929) Theosophical movement founder.

Truth, Sojourner. (1797-1883) Preacher.

Turner, Henry McNeal. (1834-1915) Bishop.

Ward, Samuel Ringgold. (1817-1878) Preacher.

Watts, Alan. (1915-1973) Episcopalian priest.

Wheelwright, John. (1592-1679) Puritan minister.

White, Tom. (unknown) Minister, leader of persecuted Christians.

Williams, George Washington. (1849-1891) Minister.

Williams, John. (1664-1729) Puritan minister.

Williams, Roger. (1603-1683) Advocate for religious freedom, born England.

Wise, Isaac Mayer. (1819-1900) Reform Judaism leader, born Czechoslovakia.

Wise, Stephen S. (1874-1949) Reform Judaism leader, born Hungary.

Witherspoon, John. (1723-1794) Minister, born Scotland.

Wovoka. (1858-1932) Paiute Indian mystic and spiritual leader.

Young, Brigham. (1801-1877) Mormon Church founder.

Ancient Civilizations

Akiba ben Joseph. (50-135) Hebrew Rabbinic Judaism founder.

Amenhotep IV. (Akhantenen) (1370-1340 B.C.) Egyptian.

Arius. (c. 256-336) Egyptian priest, Arianism founder.

Asóka the Great. (292?-232 B.C.) Indian king, made Buddhism state religion.

Augustine. (354-430) North African convert to Christianity.

Chuang Tzu. (369-286 B.C.) Chinese, Taoism cofounder.

Confucius. (551-479 B.C.) Chinese, Confucianism cofounder.

Constantine. (280-337) Roman.

Enheduana of Sumer. (fl. 2300 B.C.) Sumerian priestess.

Gautama, Siddhartha. (Buddah) (560-480 B.C.) Indian Buddhism founder.

Helena. (250-330) Roman Mother of Christianity.

Hillel. (60 B.C.E.-10 C.E.) Hebrew spiritual leader.

Jeremiah. (650-585 B.C.E.) Hebrew prophet.

Jesus Christ. Christianity founder.

Johanan ben Zakkai. (15-70) Hebrew rabbi.

Judah Ha-Nasi. (135-217) Hebrew rabbi.

Lao-Tzu. (604-531 B.C.) Chinese Taoism cofounder.

Mahavira, Vardhamana. (599-527 B.C.) Indian Jainism founder.

Mani. (216-277) Persian prophet, Manichaeism founder.

Mencius. (371-289 B.C.) Chinese Confucianism cofounder.

Moses. (1392?-1272? B.C.E.) Egyptian Hebrew prophet, Judaism founder.

Zoroaster. (628-551 B.C.) Persian spiritual leader.

Asian

Dogen. (1200-1253) Japanese Soto Zen Buddhism founder.

Gandhi, Mohandas. (1869-1948) Indian Hindu moral and spiritual leader.

Gyatso, Sonam. (1543-1588) Tibetan Buddhist Dalai Lama.

Gyatso, Tenzin. (1935-) Tibetan Buddhist Dalai Lama.

Hanh, Thich Nhat. (1926-) Vietnamese Buddhist monk.

Hoei-shin. (5th century) Chinese Buddhist monk.

Hsüan-tsang. (c. 602-664) Chinese Buddhist pilgrim.

Koken. (718-770) Japanese Buddhist nun.

Komyo. (701-760) Japanese Buddhist nun.

Kukai. (774-835) Japanese Shingon Buddhism founder.

Moon, Sun Myung. (1920-) Korean Unification Church founder.

Nanak. (1469-1538) Indian Sikh religion founder.

Naropa. (1016-1100) Indian Buddhist saint.

Nee, Watchman. (1903-1972) Chinese Evangelical Christian minister.

Nichiren. (1222-1282) Japanese Buddhist

monk.

Prabhupada, A. C. Bhaktivedanta. (1896-1977) Indian Hare Krishna cult founder.

Rabi'ah of Basra. (717-801) Indian Sufi Islam movement founder.

Ramakrishna, Sri. (1836-1886) Indian Hindu leader.

Vivekananda. (1863-1902) Indian Ramakrishna movement founder.

East Timorian

Belo, Carlos Felipe Ximenes. (1948-) Priest.

English and British

Booth, William. (1829-1912) Minister, Salvation Army founder.

Bunyan, John. (1628-1688) Minister.

Cranmer, Thomas. (1489-1556) Archbishop.

Donne, John. (1572-1631)

Fox, George. (1624-1691) Quaker religion founder.

Harper, John. (1872-1912) Scottish evangelist.

Hilda of Whitby. (614-680) English abbess.

Julian of Norwich. (1342-1416) Mystic, nun.

Montagu, Lily. (1873-1963) Liberal Judaism founder.

Newton, John. (1725-1807) Minister.

Patrick. (389?-461?) Irish evangelist for Christianity, saint.

Priestly, Joseph. (1773-1804) Minister.

Wesley, John. (1703-1791) Methodist religion founder.

Whitefield, George. (1714-1770) Evangelist and minister.

Wycliffe, John. (1320-1384) Priest.

European

Ba'al Shem Tov. (Israel ben Eliezer) (1700-1760) Polish Hasidic Judaism founder.

Benedict of Nursia. (480-550) Italian monk.

Bernard of Clairaux. (1090-1153) French monk.

Beukels, Jan. (John of Leiden) (1509-1536) German cult founder.

Bonhoeffer, Dietrich. (1906-1945) German theologian.

Borkowska, Anna. (c. 1900-) Polish nun.

Breubeuf, Jean de, Father. (1593-1649) French missionary, Jesuit priest.

Calvin, John. (1509-1564) French spiritual

leader, Protestant theologian.

Catherine of Siena. (1353-1386) Italian mystic, nun.

Clotilda. (470-545) French religious leader, saint.

Clovis. (466-511) French.

Clugney, Odode. (879-942) French Benedictine monk.

D'Aresso, Guido. (992-1050) Italian monk.

De Veuster, Joseph. (Father Damien) (1840-1889) Belgian priest.

Eckhart, Meister. (1280-1327) German mystic.

Egeria. (4th century) Spanish religious pilgrim.

Elijah ben Solomon. (1720-1797) Polish rabbi.

Erasmus, Desiderius. (1469-1536) Dutch humanistic movement founder.

Francis of Assisi. (1181-1226) Italian Franciscan order founder.

Geiger, Abraham. (1810-1874) German Reform Judaism leader.

Grebel, Conrad. (1798-1526) Swiss Protestant reform leader.

Gregory I. (Pope Gregory the Great) (540-604) Italian pope.

Gregory VII. (1015-1085) Italian pope.

Halevi, Judah. (1075-1141) Spanish Jewish leader.

Héloise. (1098-1164) French abbess.

Hildegarde von Bingen. (1098-1179) German nun, visionary.

Hus, Jan. (1369-1415) Czech theologian.

Ignatius of Loyola. (1491-1556) Spanish Jesuit order founder.

Innocent III. (Lothario de Segni) (1160-1216) Italian pope.

John XXIII. (Angelo Roncalli) (1881-1963) Italian pope.

John Paul II. (Karol Wojtyla) (1920-) Polish pope.

Julius II. (1443-1513) Italian pope.

Kino, Eusebio. (1645-1711) Austrian Jesuit priest.

Las Casas, Bartolomé de. (1474-1566) Spanish priest.

Leo X. (1475-1521) Italian pope.

Luther, Martin. (1483-1546) German Lutheran religion founder.

Marie-Benoit, Father. (unknown) French

Capucin monk.

Marquette, Jacques. (1637-1675) French Jesuit priest.

Merton, Thomas. (Father M. Louis) (1915-1968) French trappist monk.

Moses de Leon. (1240-1305) Spanish mystic.

Nahmanides. (Moses ben Nahman) (1194-1270) Spanish rabbi.

Niccacci, Padre Rufino. (unknown) Italian priest.

Pire, Dominique-Georges. (1910-1969) Belgian priest.

Pius XII. (Eugenio Maria Guiseppe Pacelli) (1867-1958) Italian pope.

Popieluszko, Jerzy, Father. (1947-1984) Polish priest.

Schweitzer, Albert. (1875-1965) French theologian.

Sheptitsky, Andrew. (1865-1944) Polish Greek Catholic Church leader.

Simons, Menno. (1524-1561) Dutch Mennonite Church founder.

Söderblom, Nathan. (1866-1931) Swedish spiritual leader.

Steiner, Rudolf. (1861-1925) Austrian Theosophical movement founder.

Thomas Aquinas. (1224-1274) Italian theologian.

Tokes, Laszlo. (unknown) Romanian bishop.

Trocme, André. (unknown) French minister.

Trocme, Magda. (unknown) French.

Urania, Lady. (13th century) Geman cantor.

Zallman, Elijah ben Solomon. (1720-1797) Polish rabbi.

Zwingli, Ulrich. (1484-1531) Swiss Protestant leader.

Greek and Turk

Cyril. (827-869) Greek Christian Orthodox.

Methodius. (815-885) Greek Christian Orthodox leader.

Nestorius. (c. 381-451) Turkish Nestorian Church founder.

Nicholas. "Santa Claus." (d. 345) Bishop of Myra (Southern Asia Minor, Turkey), saint.

Palamas, Gregory. (1296-1359) Greek Orothodox spiritual leader.

Latin

Cruz, Juana Inés de la . (1651-1695) Mexican nun.

Martinez, Father Antonio José. (1793-1867) Priest.

Romero, Oscar. (1917-1980) El Salvadorian priest and bishop.

Rose of Lima. (1586-1617) Peruvian nun, saint.

Sauñe, Rómulo. (1953-1992) Peruvian minister.

Middle Eastern

Gibran, Kahlil. (1883-1931) Lebanese mystic.

Hanasi, Judah. (135-217) Hebrew.

Saadia Gaon. (882-942) Hebrew rabbi.

Muslim and Persian

al-Ghazali. (1058-1111) Iranian Islamic spiritual leader.

Bahaullah. (1817-1892) Persian founder of Baha'i religion.

Khomeini, Ayatollah Ruholla. (1900-1989) Iranian Muslim leader.

Muhammad. (570?-632) Arab prophet and founder of Islam.

Saladin, Salah al-din. (1138-1193) Kurdish Muslim religious leader.

Russian

Avvakum. (1620-1682) Priest.

Blavatsky, Helena Petrovna. (1831-1891) Theosophical movement founder.

Ginzberg, Asher. (Ahad Ha'am) (1856-1922) Jewish spiritual leader.

Novykh, Girgori Yefimovich. (Rasputin) (1871-1916) Monk.

Rasputin. *See* Novykh, Grigori Yefimovich.

Seraphim, St. of Sarov. (1759-1833) Russian Orthodox priest.

Veniaminov, Innokentii. (1797-1879) Russian Orthodox priest.

Sportscasters

See also Broadcast Journalists; Television and Radio Personalities.

Boudreau, Lou. (1917-2001)

Bradshaw, Terry. (1948-)

Button, Dick. (1929-)

Granato, Cammi. (1971-)

Hernandez, Keith. (1953-)

Kiner, Ralph. (1922-)

McEnroe, John. (1959-)

Meyers, Ann. (1955-)

Miller, Cheryl. (1964-)

Namath, Joe. (1943-)

Nuxhall, Joe. (1929-)

Nyad, Diana. (1949-)

Storm, Hannah. (1962-)

Swann, Lynn. (1952-)

Timms, Michele. (1965-) Australian.

Sprinters

See Runners and Sprinters.

Sri Lankans

Bandaranaike, Sirimavo. (1916-2000) Prime Minister.

Storytellers and Folklorists

Aesop. (c. 600 B.C.) Greek storyteller.

Andersen, Hans Christian. (1805-1875) Danish storyteller.

Estés, Clarissa Pinkol. (1943-) Storyteller.

Ferlette, Diane. (1945-) Storyteller.

Gonzáles, Jovita Mireles. (1904-1983) Storyteller.

Grimm, Jakob. (1785-1863) German folklorist.

Grimm, Wilhelm. (1786-1859) German folklorist.

Keillor, Garrison. (1942-) Storyteller.

Münchhassen, Baron von. (1720-1797) German.

Opie, Iona. (1923-) English folklorist.

Parsons, Elsie Clews. (1875-1941) Folklorist.

Pukui, Mary Kawena. (1895-1986) Hawaiian folklorist.

Rollins, Charlemae. (1897-1979) Storyteller.

Te Ata. (1897-1995) Chicksaw Indian storyteller.

Vergoose, Elizabeth "Mother Goose." (unknown) Colonial storyteller.

Yeats, William Butler. (1865-1939) Irish folklorist.

Suffragists

See also Women's Rights Activists.

Ames, Jessie Daniel. (1883-1972)

Anthony, Susan B. (1820-1906)
Blackwell, Antoinette Brown. (1825-1921)
Bloomer, Amelia Jenks. (1818-1894)
Boissevain, Inez Milholland. (1886-1916)
Catt, Carrie Chapman. (1859-1947)
Chisholm, Mairí. (1896-?) Scottish.
Dewson, Molly. (1874-1962)
Dickinson, Anna Elizabeth. (1842-1932)
Dorr, Rheta Childe. (1866-1948)
Duniway, Abigail Scott. (1834-1915)
Edge, Rosalie. (1877-1962)
Flynn, Elizabeth Gurley. (1890-1964)
Hanson, Harriet. (1825-1911)
Harper, Frances E.W. (1825-1911)
Hutton, May Arkwright. (1860-1915)
Ichikawa Fusae. (1893-1981) Japanese.
Lawson, Louisa. (1848-1920)
Morris, Esther. (1814-1902)
Ossoli, Margaret Fuller. (1810-1850)
Pankhurst, Christabel. (1880-1958) English.
Pankhurst, Emmeline. (1858-1928) English.
Paul, Alice. (1885-1977)
Purtell, Edna. (1900-1986)
Rankin, Jeanette. (1880-1973)
Ruffin, Josephine St. Pierre. (1842-1924)
Sabin, Florence Rena. (1871-1953)
Shaw, Anna Howard. (1847-1919) born
    England.
Smyth, Ethel. (1858-1944) English.
Stanton, Elizabeth Cady. (1815-1902)
Stone, Lucy. (1818-1893)
Stowe, Emily Jennings. (1831-1903) Canadian.
Terrell, Mary Church. (1863-1954)
Thompson, Dorothy. (1893-1961)
Truth, Sojourner. (1797-1883)
Willard, Frances Elizabeth. (1839-1898)
Woodhull, Victoria. (1838-1927)

Sumerians, Ancient

Enheduana of Sumer. (fl. 2300 B.C.) Poet,
    priestess.

Surfers

Kahanamoku, Duke. (1890-1968) Hawaiian.

Surgeons

See Physicians.

Swedes

See also Immigrants to United States, Swedish.

Andrée, August. (1854-1897) Aviation pioneer, engineer, arctic explorer.
Arnoldson, Klas. (1844-1916) Journalist, peace activist. Nobel Peace Prize winner.
Bernadotte, Folke. (1895-1948) Diplomat, Holocaust rescuer.
Berzelius, Jöns Jakob. (1779-1848) Chemist.
Born, Björn. (1956-) Tennis player.
Branting, Karl. (1860-1925) Astronomer, journalist, prime minister. Nobel Peace Prize winner.
Charles XII. (1682-1718) King.
Christina. (1626-1689) Queen.
Gustavus Adolphus II. (1594-1632) Military leader, ruler.
Hammarskjöld, Dag. (1905-1961) Diplomat, peace activist. Nobel Peace Prize winner.
Hedin, Sven. (1865-1952) Explorer, geographer.
Lindgren, Astrid. (1902-2002) Children's author.
Linnaeus, Carl. (1707-1778) Botanist.
Meitner, Lise. (1878-1968) Inventor, nuclear physicist, born Germany.
Montelius, Oscar. (1843-1921) Archaeologist.
Myrdal, Alva. (1902-1986) Peace activist, sociologist, UNESCO founder. Nobel Peace Prize winner.
Nobel, Alfred Bernhard. (1833-1896) Inventor, philanthropist.
Nordenskjöld, Nils Adolf Erik. (1832-1901) Arctic explorer, geologist.
Nordenskjöld, Nils Otto. (1869-1928) Explorer, geologist.
Printz, Johan. (1592-1663) Colonial governor, born Sweden.
Salchow, Ulrich. (1877-1949) Olympic figure skater.
Söderblom, Nathan. (1866-1931) Minister. Nobel Peace Prize winner.
Swedenborg, Emanuel. (1688-1772) Mystic, philosopher.
Wallenberg, Raoul. (1912-?) Holocaust rescuer, victim.

Swimmers
See also Divers; Olympic Athletes, Swimming.
Caulkins, Tracy. (1963-)
Ederle, Gertrude. (1905-2003)
Evans, Janet. (1971-)
Fraser, Dawn. (1937-) Australian.
Kahanamoku, Duke. (1890-1968) Hawaiian.
Mann, Shelley. (1939-)
Nyad, Diana. (1949-)
Otto, Kristen. (1966-) German.
Spitz, Mark. (1950-)
Van Dyken, Amy. (1973-)
Weissmuller, Johnny. (1904-1984)

Swindlers
DeMara, Fred. (1921-1982)
Ireland, William Henry. (1777-1835) English.
Means, Gaston. (1879-1938)
Peck, Ellen. (1829-1915)
Smith, Jefferson Randolph "Soapy." (1860-1898)
Van Meegeren, Hans. (1889-1947) Dutch.
Weil, Joseph "Yellow Kid." (1877-1977)

Swiss
See also Immigrants to United States, Swedish.
Bernoulli, Daniel. (1700-1782) Mathematician.
Blom, Gertrude Elizabeth Loertscher Doby. (1901-1993) Conservationist, photographer.
Ducommon, Élie. (1833-1906) Journalist, peace activist. Nobel Peace Prize winner.
Dunant, Henri. (1828-1910) Human rights activist, organization founder. Nobel Peace Prize winner.
Euler, Leonard. (1707-1783) Mathematician.
Gobat, Albert. (1843-1914) Attorney, International Peace Bureau director, peace activist. Nobel Peace Prize winner.
Grebel, Conrad. (1498-1526) Protestant reform leader.
Hesse, Herman. (1877-1962) Author, born Germany. Nobel Prize winner.
Hingis, Martina. (1980-) Tennis player, born Czechoslovakia.
Jung, Carl. (1875-1961) Psychiatrist.

Klee, Paul. (1879-1940) Painter.
Oppenheim, Meret. (1913-1985) Jewelry designer, painter, poet, sculptor.
Pestalozzi, Johann. (1746-1827) Educator.
Piccard, Jacques. (1922-) Oceanographer.
Tell, William. (1282-?) Political activist, legendary.
Zurbriggen, Pirmin. (1963-) Olympic alpine skater.
Zwingli, Ulrich. (1484-1931) Protestant priest.

Syrians
Assad, Hafiz al-. (1930-2000) President.
Leo III, the Isaurian. (680-741) Military leader.
Zenobia. (fl. 267-272) Queen.

Tanzanians
See also Africans; Blacks, International; Immigrants to United States, African.
Nyerere, Julius K. (1922-1999) Prime Minister.

Tartars
Aiyaruk, Princess. (c. 1280) Wrestler.

Television and Radio Personalities
See also Broadcast Journalists; Sportscasters.
Coughlin, Father Charles Edward. (1891-1979) Spiritual leader who used radio broadcasts to spread message of hate, born Canada.
Henson, Jim. (1937-1990) Puppeteer.
Hernandez, Maria Latigo. (1893-1986) born Mexico.
Keillor, Garrison. (1942-)
Kilgallen, Dorothy. (1913-1965)
King, Larry. (1933-)
Nye, Bill. (1955-)
Rivera, Geraldo. (1943-)
Saralegui, Cristina. (1948-) born Cuba.
Stewart, Martha. (1941-)
Taylor, Susan. (1946-)
Walters, Barbara. (1932-)
Winfrey, Oprah. (1954-)

Tennis Players
Agassi, Andre. (1970-)

Ashe, Arthur. (1943-1993)
Bahrami, Mansour. (1956-) Iranian.
Borg, Björn. (1956-) Swedish.
Budge, Don. (1915-2000)
Capriati, Jennifer. (1976-)
Casals, Rosemary. (1948-)
Chang, Michael. (1972-)
Connolly, Maureen. (1934-1969)
Connors, Jimmy. (1952-)
Court, Margaret Smith. (1942-) Australian.
Davenport, Lindsay. (1976-)
Evert, Chris. (1954-)
Fernandez, Beatriz Christina "Gigi." (1967-)
    Puerto Rican.
Fernandez, Mary Joe. (1971-) born Domini-
    can Republic.
Garrison-Jackson, Zina. (1963-)
Gibson, Althea. (1927-2003)
Gonzales, Richard "Pancho." (1928-1995)
Graf, Steffi. (1969-) German.
Hingis, Martina. (1980-) Swiss, born
    Czechoslovakia.
King, Billie Jean. (1943-)
Kournikova, Anna. (1981-) Russian.
Laver, Rod. (1938-) Australian.
McEnroe, John. (1959-)
Moody, Helen Wills. (1906-1998)
Navratilova, Martina. (1956-) Czech.
Pierce, Mary. (1975-) born Canada.
Sabatini, Gabriela. (1970-) Argentine.
Sampras, Pete. (1971-)
Sanchez Vicario, Arantza. (1971-) Spanish.
Seles, Monica. (1973-) born Yugoslavia.
Tilden, William Tatem, Jr. "Bill." (1893-
    1953)
Washington, Ora. (1898-1971)
Williams, Serena. (1981-)
Williams, Venus. (1980-)

Terrorists
See also Dictators; Hatemongers; Military
    Leaders; Revolutionaries.
Arafat, Yasir. (1929-) Palestinian political
    leader.
Collins, Michael. (1890-1922) Irish Repub-
    lican Army.
Nechavev, Sergei. (1847-1882) Russian.
Nidal, Abu. (1937-2002) Arab.
Qaddafi, Muammar-al. (1942-) Libyan.
Sanchez, Ilrich Ramirez "Carlos." (1949-)
    Venezuelan.

Vlad the Impaler "Vlad Dracul." (1431-
    1477) Romanian.

Thais
Eng and Chang. (1811-1874) Conjoined
    twins, born Siam.
Hata, Prateep Ungsongtham. (1952-) Educa-
    tor, human rights activist.
Mongkut, Maha. (1804-1868) King of Siam.

Theologians
See Spiritual Leaders.

Tibetans
Gyatso, Sonam. (1543-1588) Dalai Lama.
Gyatso, Tenzin. (1935-) Dalai Lama. Nobel
    Peace Prize winner.

Track and Field Athletes
See also Olympic Athletes, Track and Field;
    Runners and Sprinters.
Ashford, Evelyn. (1957-)
Bannister, Roger. (1929-) English.
Barsosio, Sally. (1978-) Kenyan.
Blankers-Koen, Fanny. (1918-2004) Dutch.
Brisco-Hooks, Valerie. (1960-)
Carr, Henry. (1942-)
Coachman, Alice. (1923-)
Devers, Gail. (1966-)
Didrikson, Mildred "Babe." *See* Zaharias,
    Mildred "Babe" Didrikson.
Dionysia. (unknown) Roman.
Dragila, Stacy. (1971-) Pole vaulting.
Freeman, Cathy. (1973-) Australian.
George, Emma. (1974-) Australian.
Gourdine, Meredith. (1929-1998) Long
    jump.
Hayes, Bob. (1942-2002)
Hedea. (unknown) Roman.
Hines, Jim. (1946-)
Johnson, Michael. (1967-)
Johnson, Rafer. (1935-)
Jones, Marion. (1975-)
Joyner, Florence Griffith. (1959-1998)
Joyner-Kersee, Jackie. (1962-)
Lewis, Carl. (1961-)
Liddell, Eric. (1902-1945) Scottish.
Maximinus, Gaius Valerius. (186-238) Ro-
    man.
Miller, Inger. (1972-)

Mills, Billy. (1938-) Oglala Lakota Sioux Indian.
Morrow, Bobby Joe. (1935-)
Moses, Edwin. (1955-)
Newby-Fraser, Paula. (1962-) Zimbabwean.
Nurmi, Paavo. (1897-1973) Finnish runner.
O'Brien, Dan. (1966-) Decathlon.
Owens, Jesse. (1913-1980)
Paddock, Charlie. (1900-1943)
Patton, George Smith, Jr. (1885-1945) Pentathlon.
Phayllos of Cortona. (c. 480) Greek pentathlon.
Phidippides. (c. 505-490? B.C.) Greek long distance runner.
Robinson, Betty. (1911-1999)
Rosenfeld, Bobbie. (1904-1969) Canadian.
Rudolph, Wilma. (1940-1994)
Samuelson, Joan Benoit. (1957-)
Smith, Tommie. (1944-)
Stephens, Helen. (1918-1994)
Thayer, Helen. (1938-) born New Zealand.
Thompson, Daley. (1958-) English.
Thorpe, Jim. (1888-1953) Chippewa/Sac/Fox Indian.
Tolan, Eddie. (1908-1967)
Torrence, Gwen. (1965-)
Tryphosa. (unknown) Roman.
Tyus, Wyomia. (1945-)
Williams, Angela. (1980-)
Woldc, Mamo. (1931) Ethiopian.
Zaharias, Mildred "Babe" Didrikson. (1913-1956)

Traitors

See also Spies.
Alcibiades. (450-405 B.C.) Greek.
Ames, Aldrich. (1941-)
Arnold, Benedict. (1741-1801) American Revolutionary War.
Arnold, Peggy Shippen. (1760-1804) American Revolutionary War.
Gillars, Mildred "Axis Sally." (1900-1988) World War II.
Girty, Simon. (1741-1818) American Revolutionary War.
Hiss, Alger. (1904-1996)
Howard, Edward Lee. (1951-2002)
Quisling, Vidkun. (1887-1945) Norwegian World War II.
Rosenberg, Ethel. (1915 1953)

Rosenberg, Julius. (1918-1953)
Toguri, Iva "Tokyo Rose." (1916-1988) World War II.
Walker, John. (1937-)

Translators

See Scribes and Translators.

Turks

Atatürk, Mustapha Kemal. (1881-1938) President.
Bayerzid I. (1354-1403) Military leader.
Ciller, Tansu. (1946-) Prime Minister.
Handali, Esther Kiera. (16th century) Human rights activist.
Iaia of Cyzicus. (fl. 90 B.C.) Painter.
Justinian I, the Great. (482-565) Emperor.
Nestorius. (c. 381-451) Spiritual leader, founder Nestorian Church.
Nicholas, St. (d. 345) Bishop of Myra, Southern Asia Minor, saint.
Selim, III, Sultan. (1761-1808) Archer, ruler.
Suleiman I, the Magnificent. (1494-1566) Military leader, ruler.
Theodora. (497-548) Empress, human rights activist.
Yener, Kutlu Aslihan. (1946-) Archaeologist.

Ugandans

See also Africans.
Elizabeth. (1941-) Princess of Toro
Kivengere, Festo. (1919-1988) Human rights activist, spiritual leader.
Luwum, Janani. (1922-1977) Archbishop, political activist.

Ukrainians

Appelfeld, Aharon. (1932-) Author, Holocaust survivor.
Baiul, Oksana. (1977-) Olympic figure skater.
Kowalyk, Jonka. (unknown) Holocaust rescuer.
Podkopayeva, Lilia. (1978-) Olympic gymnast.
Sarah bat Tovim. (18th century) Prayer book author.

Utopian Community Founders

See also Cult Leaders; Spiritual Leaders.

Lee, Ann. (1736-1784) Shaker movement, born England.

Maclure, William. (1763-1840) Harmonist Society, born Scotland.

Meacham, Joseph. (d. 1796) Shaker community.

Metz, Christian. (1795-1867) Amana Society, born Germany.

Noyes, John Humphrey. (1811-1886) Oneida community.

Owen, Robert. (1771-1858) Welsh Harmonist Society cofounder.

Rapp, George. (1757-1847) Harmonist Society cofounder, born Germany.

Ripley, George. (1802-1880) Brook Farm Society.

Tingley, Katherine. (1847-1929) Point Loma.

Venezuelans

See also Hispanic-Americans.

Abreu, Bobby. (1974-) Baseball player.

Alfonzo, Edgardo. (1974-) Baseball player.

Aparicio, Luis. (1934-) Baseball player.

Bolivar, Simón. (1783-1830) Political leader, revolutionary.

Escobar, Marisol. (Marisol) (1930-) Sculptor, born Venezuela.

Galarraga, Andrés. (1962-) Baseball player.

Herrera, Caroline. (1939-) Fashion designer, born Venezuela.

Hidalgo, Richard. (1975-) Baseball player.

Marisol. *See* Escobar, Marisol.

Ordóñez, Magglió. (1974-) Baseball player.

Sanchez, Ilrich Ramirez "Carlos." (1949) Terrorist.

Vizquel, Omar. (1967-) Baseball player.

Veterinarians

Adams, Eugene W. (1920-)

Hamer, Victoria. (unknown)

Vice Presidents, U.S.

Arthur, Chester A. (1829-1886)

Burr, Aaron. (1756-1836)

Bush, George Herbert Walker. (1924-)

Calhoun, John Caldwell. (1782-1850)

Coolidge, Calvin. (1872-1923)

Davies, Charles Gates. (1865-1951)

Fillmore, Millard. (1800-1874)

Ford, Gerald R. (1913-)

Gerry, Elbridge. (1744-1814)

Johnson, Andrew. (1808-1875)

Johnson, Lyndon Baines. (1908-1973)

Nixon, Richard Milhous. (1913-1994)

Stevenson, Adlai Ewing. (1900-1965)

Truman, Harry S. (1884-1972)

Tyler, John. (1790-1862)

Wallace, Henry A. (1888-1965)

Vietnam War Figures

Abrahamson, James A. (1933-) Air Force lieutenant general.

Abrams, Creighton. (1914-1974) Army Chief of State.

Alvarez, Everett, Jr. (1937-) Navy pilot.

Benavidez, Roy. (1935-) Army hero. Medal of Honor recipient.

Bleier, Robert Patrick "Rocky." (1946-) Army soldier, injured in battle.

Bluford, Guion Steward. (1942-) Pilot.

Brown, George S. (1918-1978) Joint Chiefs of Staff.

Cadoria, Sherian. (1940-) Military police.

Cammermeyer, Margarethe. (1942-) Army nurse.

Cherry, Fred V. (1928-) POW.

Croslin, Michael. (1933-) Air Force pilot.

Giap, Vo Nguygen. (1911-) North Vietnamese military leader.

Hanh, Thich Nhat. (1926-) Vietnamese peace activist.

Higgins, Marguerite. (1920-1966) Photojournalist.

Ho Chi Minh. (1890-1969) Vietnamese dictator, political leader.

James, Daniel "Chappie," Jr. (1920-1978) Four Star General.

Joel, Lawrence. (1928-1984) Army hero. Medal of Honor recipient.

Le-Duc-Tho. (1911-1990) Vietnamese political leader.

Naranjo, Michael. (1944-) Pueblo Indian soldier.

Powell, Colin. (1937-) Army infantry officer.

Rowny, Edward L. (1917-) Army Deputy Chief of Staff.

Rutan, Dick. (1938-) Air Force pilot.

Schwarzkopf, Norman. (1934-) Army commander.

Vargas, Jay. (1937-) Military hero. Medal of Honor recipient.

Walsh, Mary. (1950-) Army physical therapist.

Walt, Lewis W. (1913-1989) Marine general.

Westmoreland, William C. (1914-) Army Chief of Staff.

Vietnamese

Giap, Vo Nguygen. (1911-) Military leader.

Hanh, Thich Nhat. (1926-) Author, Buddhist monk, peace activist.

Ho Chi Minh. (1890-1969) Dictator, politcal leader.

Le-Duc-Tho. (1911-1990) Political leader. Nobel Peace Prize winner.

Trung Nhi. (14-43) Warrior queen.

Trung Trac. (14-43) Warrior queen.

Vikings, Ancient

Alfhild. (Alvida) (c. 1000) Pirate.

Aud the Deep Minded. (c. 900) Philosopher, scholar.

Ericsson, Leif. (970-1020) Explorer.

Erik the Red. *See* Thorvaldson, Erik.

Eriksdottir, Freydis. (971-1010) Explorer.

Sela. (c. 420) Pirate, Princess.

Thorvaldson, Erik "Erik the Red." (950-1010) Explorer.

Virgin Islanders

Duncan, Tim. (1976-) Basketball player.

Virologists

See also Bacteriologists; Physicians.

Burnet, Sir Frank MacFarlane. (1899-1985) Australian.

Sabin, Albert Bruce. (1906-1993) born Poland.

Salk, Jonas Edward. (1914-1995)

Temin, Howard. (1934-)

Visually Disabled

Alexander, Grover Cleveland. (1887-1950) Baseball player.

Alonso, Alicia. (1921-) Cuban ballet dancer.

Bethune, "Blind Tom" Thomas Greene. (1849-1908) Musician, slave.

Blackwell, Elizabeth. (1821-1910) Physician, born England.

Braille, Louis. (1809-1852) French inventor.

Brown, John "Fed." (1810-1876) Author, slave.

Burkitt, Denis Parsons. (1911-1993) Irish medical researcher, physician.

Butler, Beverly. (1932-) Children's author.

Charles, Ray. (1930-) Jazz musician, singer.

Davis, Sammy, Jr. (1925-1990) Actor, showman, singer.

Dayan, Moshe. (1915-1981) Israeli foreign minister, military leader.

Dulles, John Foster. (1888-1959) Attorney, cabinet member, diplomat.

Fuller, Solomon Carter. (1872-1953) Medical researcher, pathologist, physician, born Liberia.

Goldsby, Crawford. (1876-1896) Cherokee Indian criminal.

Gourdine, Meredith. (1929-1998) Electrical engineer, inventor, olympic track and field athlete.

Gwaltney, John Langston. (1928-1998) Anthropologist.

Jackson, "Blind Lemon." (1897-1930) Jazz musician.

Keller, Helen. (1880-1968) Author, disability rights activist. Presidential Medal of Freedom recipient.

Little, Jean. (1932-) Canadian children's author.

Lowe, Ann. (1899-?) Fashion designer.

Lyell, Sir Charles. (1797-1875) English attorney, geologist.

Marsh, George Perkins. (1801-1882) Ambassador, attorney, author, conservationist, state legislator.

McTell, "Blind" Willie. (1901-1959) Jazz musician, singer.

Milton, John. (1608-1674) English poet.

Naranjo, Michael. (1944-) Pueblo Indian sculptor, Vietnam War soldier. (blinded from war injury)

Paradis, Maria Theresia von. (1759-1824) Austrian composer, musician.

Paumann, Konrad. (1415-1473) German composer.

Seymour, William Joseph. (1870-1922) Spiritual leader, founder Pentecostal Church.

Spikes, Frederick McKinley. (c. late 1800s) Inventor.

Sullivan, Annie. (1866-1936) Educator.

Tatum, Art. (1910-1956) Jazz musician.

tenBroek, Jacobus. (1911-1968) Attorney, disability rights activist, educator, born Canada.

Weihenmayer, Eric. (1968-) Mountaineer.

Wonder, Stevie. (1950-) Jazz musician.

Ziska, Jan. (1358-1424) Bohemian military leader.

Volcanologists
See also Geologists; Meteorologists.
Chouet, Bernard. (1945-) born Switzerland.
Hickson, Catherine. (1955-) Canadian.

Volleyball Players
Hyman, Flo. (1954-1986)

Weight Lifters
See also Olympic Athletes, Weight Lifting.
Alexeyev, Vasily. (1942-) Russian.
Davis, John. (1921-1984)
Leonard, Andy. (1968-) born Vietnam.
Milo of Crotona. (c. 558 B.C.) Greek.
Topham, Thomas. (1710-1749) English.

Welsh
See also Immigrants to United States, Welsh.
Black Bart. *See* Roberts, Bartholomew.
Burton, Richard. (1925-1984) Actor.
Lawrence, Thomas Edward. (Lawrence of Arabia) (1888-1935) Archaeologist, World War I intelligence officer.
Leonowens, Anna. (1834-1915) Author, educator.
Owen, Robert. (1771-1858) Harmonist Society cofounder, philanthropist, social reformer.
Roberts, Bartholomew "Black Bart." (1682-1722) Pirate.
Stanley, Sir Henry Morton. (1841-1904) Civil War soldier, explorer, journalist.

Wheelchair Athletes
Driscoll, Jean. (1966-)
Petitclerc, Chantal. (1969-) Canadian.

Women

African
Barsosio, Sally. (1978-) Kenyan olympic track and field athlete.
Dahia al-Kahina. (fl. 680) North African freedom fighter, queen.
Elizabeth. (1941-) Princess of Toro (Uganda).
Esu-Williams. Eku. (1956-) Nigerian AIDS educator, immunologist, physician.
Gordimer, Nadine. (1923-) South African author. Nobel Prize winner.
Judith of Ethiopia. (10th century) Warrior queen.
Maathai, Wangari. (1940-) Kenyan environmentalist, human rights activist, political activist.
Machel, Gracia Simbine. (1945-) Mozambican children's rights activist.
Makeba, Miriam. (1932-) South African political activist, singer.
Makeda. (960-930 B.C.) Ethiopian Queen of Sheba.
Makhubu, Lydia Phindile. (1937-) Swaziland chemist, educator.
Mandela, Winnie Madikizela. (1934-) South African political activist.
Mbandi, Jinga. *See* Nzinga, Anna.
Mella. Warrior Queen.
Newby-Fraser, Paula. (1962-) Zimbabwe olympic track and field athlete, triathlon.
Nzinga, Anna. (1580-1663) West African queen.
Oya. African Goddess.
Schreiner, Olive. (1855-1920) South African author, women's rights activist.
Tupou, Queen Salote III. (1900-1965) Ruler of Tonga.

American
Abbott, Berenice. (1898-1991) Photographer.
Abbott, Maude Elizabeth Seymour. (1869-1940) Medical researcher.
Abzug, Bella. (1920-1998) Attorney, con-

gresswoman, peace activist.

Adams, Abigail. (1744-1818) American Revolutionary War patriot, First Lady, women's rights activist.

Adams, Harriet Chalmers. (1875-1937) Adventurer, geographer, photographer.

Adams, Louisa Catherine Johnson. (1775-1852) First Lady.

Addams, Jane. (1860-1935) Community activist, human rights activist, social worker. Nobel Peace Prize winner.

Aebi, Tania. (1966-) Adventurer, sailor.

Aguilera, Christina. (1966-) Pop singer.

Ahyokah. (1811-?) Cherokee Indian lexicographer, daughter of Sequoyah.

Akeley, Delia. (1875-1970) Explorer.

Akeley, Mary Leonore Jobe. (1878-1966) Explorer.

Akers, Michelle. (1966-) Olympic soccer player.

Akiyoshi, Toshiko. (1929-) Bandleader, composer, jazz musician, born China.

Albright, Madeleine. (1937-) Cabinet member, born Czechoslovakia.

Albright, Tenley. (1935-) Olympic figure skater, physician.

Alcott, Louisa May. (1832-1888) Children's and adult author.

Alexander, Annie Montague. (1867-1950) Naturalist, paleontologist.

Alexander, Hattie Elizabeth. (1901-1968) Bacteriologist, medical researcher, physician.

Aliquipso. (unknown) Oneida Indian legendary heroine.

Allen, Christina M. (1970-) Ecologist.

Allen, Debbie. (1956-) Actor, dancer, singer.

Allen, Florence Ellinwood. (1884-1966) Attorney, U.S. Appeals Court jurist.

Allen, Geri. (1957-) Bandleader, jazz musician.

Allen, Gracie. (1900-1964) Comedian.

Allen, Paula Gunn. (1939-) Laguna Pueblo/Sioux Indian author, poet.

Almonaster y Rojas, Michaela. (1795-1874) Baroness of Pontalba, philanthropist.

Alvarez, Julia. (1950-) Author.

Alving, Amy. (unknown) Aerospace engineer, educator.

Ames, Jessie Daniel. (1883-1972) Civil rights activist, suffragist, women's rights activist.

Andersen, Dorothy. (1901-1963) Medical researcher, pathlogist, physician.

Anderson, Ivie. (1904-1949) Jazz singer.

Anderson, Laurie. (1947-) Composer.

Anderson, Marian. (1897-1993) Opera singer. Presidential Medal of Freedom recipient.

Anderson, Mary. (1866-1953) Inventor.

Anderson, Mary. (1872-1964) Director U.S. Women's Bureau, labor leader, born Sweden.

Andrews, Julie. (1935-) Actor, singer, born England.

Angelou, Maya. (1928-) Author, poet.

Anthony, Susan B. (1820-1906) Suffragist, women's rights activist.

Antolin, Jeanette. (1981-) Olympic gymnast.

Apgar, Virginia. (1909-1974) Medical researcher, physician.

Arbus, Diane. (1923-1971) Photographer.

Arden, Elizabeth. (1878-1966) Entrepreneur cosmetics industry, born Canada.

Armstrong, Ellen. (1914-) Cartoonist, magician.

Arnett, Hannah. (unknown) American Revolutionary War patriot.

Arnold, Eve. (1913-) Photographer.

Arnold, Peggy Shippen. (1760-1804) American Revolutionary War traitor, wife of Benedict Arnold.

Arnold, Roseanne. (Roseanne) (1952-) Comedian.

Arthur, Elizabeth Ann. (1953-) Author.

Arthur, Ellen Lewis Herndon. (1837-1880) First Lady.

Arviga, Rosita. (1941-) Botanist.

Ash, Mary Kay. (1915-2001) Entrepreneur cosmetics industry.

Ashford, Evelyn. (1957-) Olympic track and field athlete.

Atkinson, Lucy. (1820-1863?) Explorer.

Atler, Vanessa. (1982-) Olympic gymnast.

Avery, Byllye. (1937-) Women's rights activist.

Azzi, Jennifer. (1968-) Olympic basketball player.

Baca, Judy. (1946-) Human rights activist.

Baez, Joan. (1941-) Political activist, singer.

Bailey, Anne Trotter. (1743-1825) American Revolutionary War patriot, colonist, Indian scout.

Bailey, Liberty Hyde. (1858-1954) Botanist, educator.

Bailey, Pearl. (1918-1990) Jazz singer. Presidential Medal of Freedom recipient.

Baker, Ella Josephine. (1903-1986) Civil rights activist.

Baker, Josephine. (1906-1975) Jazz singer, World War II resistance worker.

Baker, Sara Josephine. (1873-1945) Physician, public health pioneer.

Balch, Emily Greene. (1867-1961) Civil rights activist, peace activist, women's rights activist. Nobel Peace Prize winner.

Ball, Lucille. (1911-1989) Comedian. Presidential Medal of Freedom recipient.

Bambera, Toni Cade. (1939-1995) Author.

Bancroft, Ann. (1955-) Arctic explorer.

Banuelos, Romana Acosta. (1925-) Banker, treasurer of U.S.

Barceló, Maria Gertrudes "Tules." (1800-1852) Pioneer, women's rights activist.

Barker, Penelope. (unknown) American Revolutionary War patriot.

Barnes, Djuna. (1892-1982) Author, journalist, playwright.

Barnes, Sharon J. (1955-) Chemist.

Barnhart, Cynthia. (unknown) Civil and transportation engineer, educator.

Barringer, Emily Dunning. (1876-1961) World War II physician.

Barry, Catherine Moore. (unknown) American Revolutionary War patriot.

Barrymore, Ethel. (1879-1959) Actor.

Barton, Clara. (1821-1912) Civil War nurse, founder American Red Cross.

Bascom, Florence. (1862-1945) Educator, geologist.

Bassett, Angela. (1959-) Actor.

Bates, Abigail. (1799-?) Lighthouse keeper.

Bates, Daisy. (1914-1999) Civil rights activist.

Bates, Rebecca. (1795-?) Lighthouse keeper.

Bath, Patricia. (1942-) Medical researcher, physician.

Beach, Amy. (1867-1944) Composer.

Beach, Sheryl Luzzader. (unknown) Educator, geographer, geologist.

Beals, Melba Pattilo. (1941-) Civil rights activist.

Beckerman, Alyssa. (1981-) Olympic gym-

nast.

Beech, Olive Ann. (1903-1993) Entrepreneur aircraft.

Beecher, Catherine. (1800-1878) Author, educator, women's rights activist.

Begin, Mary Jane. (1963-) Illustrator.

Bemis, Polly. (Lulu Nathay) (1853-1933) Pioneer, born China.

Benedict, Ruth. (1887-1948) Anthropologist.

Benerito, Ruth. (1916-) Physical chemist, inventor.

Benjamin, Miriam E. (unknown) Inventor.

Berg, Patty. (1918-) Golfer, World War II Marine Corps lieutenant.

Berry, Carrie. (1854-?) Southern girl during Civil War.

Bethune, Mary McLeod. (1875-1955) Civil rights activist, educator.

Beurton, Ruth Kuczynski. (1907-) World War II spy.

Biaggi, Cristina Shelley. (1937-) Archaeologist, historian.

Bickerdyke, Mary Ann "Mother." (1817-1901) Civil War nurse.

Blackman, Cindy. (1959-) Composer, jazz musician.

Blackwell, Antoinette Brown. (1825-1921) Spiritual leader, suffragist.

Blackwell, Elizabeth. (1821-1910) Physician, born England.

Blackwell, Emily. (1826-1910) Physician, born England.

Blair, Bonnie. (1964-) Olympic speed skater.

Blanchfield, Florence Aby. (1882-1971) World War I and II Army nurse.

Blodgett, Katherine. (1898-1979) Chemist.

Bloomer, Amelia Jenks. (1818-1894) Editor, publisher, suffragist, women's rights activist.

Blume, Judy. (1938-) Children's and young adult author.

Bly, Nellie. *See* Cochrane, Elizabeth.

Boehm, Helen. (1909-) Entrepreneur porcelain art.

Boissevain, Inez Milholland. (1886-1916) Suffragist, women's rights activist.

Boissonnault, Masako. (1944-) Interior designer.

Bolton-Holifield, Ruthie. (1967-) Basketball

player.

Bombeck, Erma. (1927-1996) Journalist.

Bonnin, Gertrude Simmons. (1876-1938) Yankton Dakota Indian author, Native American rights activist, social reformer.

Boone, Sarah. (unknown) Inventor.

Booth, Eva. (1865-1950) Brought Salvation Army movement to U.S., human rights activist, born England.

Borden, Amanda. (1977-) Olympic gymnast.

Borden, Lizzie. (1860-1927) Allegedly killed parents, folk hero.

Borders, Ila. (1975-) Baseball player.

Bori, Lucrezia. (1887-1960) Opera singer, born Spain.

Bourke-White, Margaret. (1906-1971) Photographer, World War II photojournalist.

Bowles, Ann. (1956-) Acoustic biologist.

Boxer, Barbara. (1940-) Congresswoman, women's rights activist.

Boyd, Belle. (1843-1900) Civil War spy.

Boyd, Louise Arner. (1887-1972) Arctic explorer.

Bradstreet, Anne. (1612-1672) Colonist, poet.

Bragg, Janet Harmon. (1907-1993) Aviator, nurse.

Brandy. *See* Norwood, Brandy.

Brant, Mary "Molly." (Degonwadonti) (1736-1796) Mohawk Indian American Revolutionary War patriot.

Bratton, Martha. (unknown) American Revolutionary War patriot.

Braun, E. Lucy. (1889-1971) Ecologist, geologist.

Breckinridge, Mary Marvin. (1905-2002) World War II broadcast journalist, photojournalist.

Brent, Margaret. (1601-1671) Colonist, women's rights activist.

Bridges, Marilyn. (1948-) Photographer.

Brigman, Anne. (1869-1950) Photographer.

Brill, Yvonne. (1924-) Aerospace chemist, inventor, space scientist, born Canada.

Briones, Juana. (1802-1889) Human rights activist, pioneer, rancher.

Brisco-Hooks, Valerie. (1960-) Olympic sprinter, track and field athlete.

Brody, Jane. (1941-1987) Author, journalist, nutritionist.

Brooks, Gwendolyn. (1917-2000) Poet.

Pulitzer Prize winner.

Brown, Clara. (1803-1885) Pioneer, slave.

Brown, Dorothy Lavinia. (1919-) Physician, state legislator.

Brown, Helen Gurley. (1922-) Editor magazine.

Brown, Marcia. (1918-) Children's author, illustrator.

Brown, Margaret Tobin "Molly." (1867-1932) Women's rights activist.

Brown, Margaret Wise. (1910-1952) Children's author.

Brown, Marie Van Brittan. (fl. 1969) Inventor.

Brown, Rachel. (1898-1980) Biochemist, medical researcher.

Brown, Tabitha. (1780-1858) Pioneer.

Browne, Marjorie Lee. (1914-1979) Mathematician.

Brownell, Kady. (1842-?) Civil War heroine.

Buck, Pearl S. (1892-1973) Author. Nobel Prize and Pulitzer Prize winner.

Bugbee, Emma. (1888-1981) Journalist.

Bullett, Vicki. (unknown) Basketball player.

Bullock, Anna Mae. (Tina Turner) (1939-) Singer.

Burgess, Abbie. (1839-1892) Lighthouse keeper.

Burgin, Elizabeth. (unknown) American Revolutionary War heroine.

Burke, Yvonne Braithwaite. (1932-) Attorney, congresswoman, human rights activist.

Burland, Rebecca. (1793-1872) Pioneer, born England.

Burnett, Frances Hodgson. (1849-1924) Children's author, born England.

Burns, Ursula. (1958-) Engineer.

Burson, Nancy. (1948-) Photographer.

Bush, Barbara Pierce. (1925-) First Lady.

Bush, Laura Welch. (1946-) First Lady.

Butcher, Susan. (1956-) Sled dog racer.

Butler, Beverly. (1932-) Children's author.

Butler, Octavia. (1947-) Author.

Byars, Betsy. (1928-) Children's author.

Byrdsong, Sherialyn. (1957-) Basketball coach, human rights activist.

Byrne, Jane. (1934-) Mayor.

Cadoria, Sherian. (1940-) Army brigadier general, Vietnam War military police.

Calamity Jane. *See* Cannary, Martha Jane.

Cameron, Agnes Deans. (1863-1912) Arctic explorer.

Cameron, Evelyn. (1868-1928) Photographer.

Cameron, Julia Margaret. (1815-1878) Photographer.

Cammermeyer, Margarethe. (1942-) Army colonel, Vietnam War nurse.

Campbell, Bebe Moore. (1950-) Author.

Campbell, Bonnie. (1948-) Attorney, government agency director, women's rights activist.

Campbell, Fanny. (1755-?) Pirate.

Campbell, Naomi. (1970-) Fashion model.

Canady, Alexa. (1950-) Physician.

Cannary, Martha Jane. (Calamity Jane) (1852-1903) Adventurer, Indian scout, pioneer.

Cannon, Annie Jump. (1863-1941) Astronomer.

Capriati, Jennifer. (1976-) Olympic tennis player.

Cardin, Shoshana. (1926-) Organizational head.

Carey, Mariah. (1969-) Singer.

Carr, Emma Perry. (1880-1972) Physical chemist.

Carr, Vicki. (1940-) Singer.

Carrington, Leonora. (1917-) Painter.

Carroll, Diahann. (1935-) Actor.

Carson, Rachel. (1907-1964) Author, environmental activist. Presidential Medal of Freedom recipient.

Carter, Iola O. (unknown) Inventor.

Carter, Pamela. (1950-) Attorney, state Attorney General.

Carter, Rosalynn Smith. (1927-) First Lady. Presidential Medal of Freedom recipient.

Cary, Mary Ann Shadd. (1822-1893) Abolitionist, author, educator, journalist.

Casals, Rosemary. (1948-) Tennis player.

Cashman, Nellie. (1845-1925) Gold miner, explorer, pioneer.

Cassatt, Mary. (1844-1926) Painter.

Castner, Mattie. (1848-1920) Pioneer hotelkeeper.

Cather, Willa. (1873-1947) Author. Pulitzer Prize winner.

Catlett, Elizabeth. (1915-) Painter, printmaker, sculptor.

Catt, Carrie Chapman. (1859-1947) Suffragist, women's rights activist.

Caulkins, Tracy. (1963-) Olympic swimmer.

Cervenka, Valerie. (unknown) Forensic entomologist.

Chamberlin, Jodi. (1944-) Disability rights activist.

Chappelle, Georgette "Dickey" Meyer. (1918-1965) World War II photojournalist.

Charlot, Olivia. (1913-) Jazz singer.

Chastain, Brandi. (1968-) Olympic soccer player.

Chávez, Denise. (1948-) Playwright.

Chávez-Thompson, Linda. (1944-) Workers' rights activist.

Cheever, Susan. (1943-) Author.

Cheng, Nien. (1915-) Author, political activist and prisoner, born China.

Chennault, Anna. (1925-) Journalist, political activist, born China.

Chenzira, Ayoka. (1956-) Filmmaker.

Cher. *See* Sarkisan, Cherilyn.

Chesnut, Mary Boykin. (1823-1886) Author, Civil War diarist.

Chess, Victoria. (1939-) Children's author, illustrator.

Childress, Alice. (1920-1994) Actor, author, playwright.

Chin, Karen. (1952-) Paleontologist, born Canada.

Chin, Leann. (1933-) Entrepreneur restaurants.

Chinn, May Edward. (1896-1980) Physician.

Chisholm, Sallie. (unknown) Biologist.

Chisholm, Shirley. (1924-) Congresswoman, presidential candidate.

Cho, Margaret. (1969-) Actor.

Choi, Sook Nyul. (1937-) Children's and young adult author, born Korea.

Chopin, Kate. (1850-1904) Author, women's rights activist.

Chow, Amy. (1978-) Olympic gymnast.

Christian, Sara. (1920-) Auto racer.

Chung, Constance Vu-Hwa "Connie." (1946-) Television broadcast journalist.

Ciccione, Madonna Louise Veronica. (Madonna) (1958-) Singer.

Cisneros, Evelyn. (1958-) Ballet dancer.

Cisneros, Sandra. (1954-) Author.

Clalin, Frances. (unknown) Civil War soldier, disguised as man.

Clapp, Cornelia. (1849-1934) Educator, zoologist.

Clappe, Louise Amelia. (1819-1906) Gold mine camp owner, journalist, pioneer.

Clark, Eugenie. (1922-) Ichthyologist, oceanographer.

Clark, Joan. (unknown) Inventor.

Clark, Septima Poinsette. (1898-1987) Civil rights activist, educator.

Clarke, Kim. (1954-) Jazz musician.

Cleary, Beverly. (1912-) Children's author.

Cleveland, Emeline Horton. (1829-1878) Physician.

Cleveland, Frances Folsom. (1864-1947) First Lady.

Clifton, Lucille. (1936-) Children's author.

Clinton, Hillary Rodham. (1947-) Attorney, First Lady, senator.

Coachman, Alice. (1923-) Olympic track and field athlete.

Cobb, Geraldyn. (1931-) Aviator, missionary.

Cobb, Jewel Plummer. (1924-) Cell biologist, educator, medical researcher.

Cochran, Jacqueline. (1910-1980) Aviator, World War II Air Force Female Service Pilots director.

Cochrane, Elizabeth. (Nellie Bly) (1865-1922) Adventurer, disability rights activist, human rights activist, journalist.

Cofer, Judith Ortiz. (1952-) Author, educator, poet.

Coffin, Katie. (unknown) Abolitionist.

Cohen, Rose. (1880-1925) Labor leader, workers' rights activist.

Cohen, Sasha. (1984-) Olympic figure skater.

Cole, Joanna. (1944-) Children's author.

Cole, Natalie. (1950-) Singer.

Cole, Rebecca J. (1846-1922) Civil rights activist, human rights activist, physician.

Coleman, Bessie. (1893-1926) Aviator.

Colfax, Harriet. (1824-1904) Lighthouse keeper.

Collett-Vare, Glenna. (1903-1989) Golfer.

Collins, Cardiss. (1931-) Congresswoman.

Collins, Eileen M. (1956-) Air Force pilot, astronaut.

Collins, Kathleen. (1942-1988) Filmmaker.

Collins, Marva Delores. (1936-) Educator.

Colmenaaves, Margarita. (1957-) Environmental engineer.

Colton, Mary-Russell. (1889-1971) Painter, sculptor.

Colvin, Claudette. (1940-) Civil rights activist.

Comstock, Anna Botsford. (1854-1930) Entomologist, naturalist.

Conley, Helena. (1867-1958) Wyandotte Indian Native American rights activist.

Conley, Ida. (1862-1948) Wyandotte Indian Native American rights activist.

Conley, Lyda. (1869-1946) Wyandotte Indian attorney, Native American rights activist.

Conly, Elvira. (1845-?) Pioneer, slave.

Connelly, Joan Breton. (1954-) Archaeologist.

Connolly, Maureen. (1934-1969) Tennis player.

Conradt, Jody. (1941-) Basketball coach.

Cooley, Chloe. (unknown) Slave.

Coolidge, Grace Anna Goodhue. (1879-1957) First Lady.

Cooper, Anna Julia. (1858-1964) Educator.

Cooper, Cynthia. (1963-) Olympic basketball player.

Coppin, Fannie Jackson. (1836-1913) Educator, slave.

Corbin, Margaret. (1751-1800) American Revolutionary War heroine.

Cordova, Dorothy. (1932-) Archivist, community leader.

Cordova, France. (unknown) Physicist.

Cori, Gerty Radnitz. (1896-1957) Biochemist, born Czechoslovakia. Nobel Prize winner.

Corso, Sandra. (unknown) Geophysicist, oceanographer.

Coston, Martha. (1826-1886) Inventor.

Cotera, Martha P. (1938-) Civil rights activist, educator, historian, born Mexico.

Cousins, Margaret. (1905-1996) Editor, journalist.

Cowan, Ruth. (1902-) Journalist, World War II correspondent.

Cowings, Patricia. (1948-) Physiologist, psychologist, space scientist.

Cox, Ida. (1889-1967) Singer.

Crabtree, Lotta. (1847-1924) Actor.

Craft, Ellen. (1826-1897) Abolitionist, slave, disguised as man.

Craig, Lulu Sadler. (1868-1972?) Educator.

Crespi, Ann. (unknown) Chemist, medical researcher.

Cressy-Marcks, Violet. (1890-1976) Explorer.

Crews, Jeanne Lee. (unknown) Aerospace engineer, space scientist.

Croly, Jane Cunningham. (Jennie June) (1829-1901) Journalist.

Croteau, Julie. (1970-) Baseball player.

Crumpler, Rebecca Lee. (1833-1895) Physician.

Cruz, Celia. (1924-2003) Singer, born Cuba.

Cummings, Pat. (1950-) Children's author, illustrator.

Cunningham, Imogen. (1883-1976) Photographer.

Curtis, Jennie. (c. 1878) Child laborer.

Cushman, Karen. (1941-) Children's and young adult author.

Cushman, Pauline. (Harriet Wood) (1833-1893) Civil War spy.

Custer, Libbie. (1842-1933) Author, pioneer, women's rights activist.

Dahl-Wolfe, Louise. (1895-1989) Photographer.

Dandridge, Dorothy. (1923-1965) Actor, singer.

Dantzscher, Jamie. (1982-) Olympic gymnast.

Darden, Christine. (1942-) Aeronautical engineer, mathematician, space scientist.

Darragh, Lydia. (1725-1789) American Revolutionary War spy.

Dash, Julie. (1952-) Filmmaker.

Dater, Judy. (1941-) Photographer.

Davenport, Lindsay. (1976-) Tennis player.

Davis, Angela. (1944-) Educator, political activist.

Davis, N. Jan. (1953-) Astronaut, mechanical engineer.

Davis, Varina Howell. (1826-1906) Civil War author, wife of Jefferson Davis.

Davison, Anne. (1913-1992) Adventurer, aviator, sailor, born England.

Dawes, Dominique. (1976-) Olympic gymnast.

Day, Dorothy. (1897-1980) Journalist, spiritual leader, women's rights activist.

De Generes, Ellen. (1958-) Actor, comedian.

de la Cruz, Jessie Lopez. (1919-) Workers' rights activist.

De Mille, Agnes. (1905-1993) Choreographer.

De Passe, Suzanne. (1946-) Filmmaker.

Debo, Angie. (1890-1988) Historian.

Dee, Ruby. (1924-) Actor.

Deer, Ada. (1935-) Menominee Indian attorney, Asst. Secretary Indian Affairs, Native American rights activist, social worker.

DeFrantz, Anita. (1952-) Olympic rower.

Deganwidah. (c. 1400) Huron Indian chief, peace activist.

Delaney, Annie Elizabeth. (1891-1995) Author, educator.

Delaney, Sarah Louise "Sadie." (1889-1998) Author, educator.

Delano, Jane Arminda. (1862-1919) World War I superintendent Army Air Corps nurses.

Deloria, Ella Cara. (1889-1971) Yankton Dakota Indian anthropologist, linguist.

Dempsey, Sister Mary Joseph. (1856-1939) Nurse, spiritual leader.

Desimini, Lisa. (1964-) Children's author, illustrator.

Devers, Gail. (1966-) Olympic track and field athlete.

Dewson, Molly. (1874-1962) Suffragist, women's rights activist.

Dick, Gladys Rowena. (1881-1963) Medical researcher, physician.

Dickinson, Anna Elizabeth. (1842-1932) Abolitionist, orator, suffragist.

Dickinson, Emily. (1830-1886) Poet.

Didrikson, Mildred "Babe." See Zaharias, Mildred "Babe" Didrikson.

Dillard, Annie. (1945-) Author, poet. Pulitzer Prize winner.

Dillon, Diane. (1933-) Children's author, illustrator.

Dix, Dorothea. (1802-1887) Civil War Army nurse superintendent, educator, human rights activist, social reformer.

Dix, Dorothy. See Gilmer, Elizabeth Meriwether.

Dixon, Jeane. (1918-1997) Psychic.

Donovan, Anne. (1961-) Olympic basketball player.

Doolittle, Hilda "H. D." (1886-1961) Author, poet, translator.

Dorfman, Elsa. (1937-) Photographer.

Dorman, Pamela Davis. (1952-) Gulf War Navy chaplain.

Dorr, Rheta Childe. (1866-1948) Journalist, suffragist, World War I correspondent.

Douglas, Helen Gahagan. (1900-1980) Actor, congresswoman, singer.

Douglas, Lizzie. (Memphis Minnie) (1897-1973) Jazz musician.

Douglas, Marjorie Stoneman. (1890-1998) Author, conservationist, World War I Navy. Presidential Medal of Freedom recipient.

Douglass, Sarah Mapps. (1806-1882) Educator.

Dove, Rita. (1952-) Poet. Pulitzer Prize winner.

Downing, Julie. (1956-) Children's author, illustrator.

Dragila, Stacy. (1971-) Olympic track and field athlete.

Draper, Margaret Green. (1727-1804) American Revolutionary War loyalist, newspaper publisher.

Dresselhaus, Mildred. (1930-) Physicist.

Driscoll, Jean. (1966-) Wheelchair athlete.

Duke, Patty. (1946-) Actor.

Dunbar, Bonnie. (1949-) Astronaut, mechanical engineer.

Dunham, Katherine. (1909-) Anthropologist, choreographer, dancer.

Duniway, Abigail Scott. (1834-1915) Journalist, suffragist, women's rights activist.

Durant, Ida Kaufman "Ariel." (1898-1981) Author, historian, born Russia. Presidential Medal of Freedom recipient, Pulitzer Prize winner.

Durazo, Maria Elena. (1954-) Labor leader, born Mexico.

Durgan, Beverly. (unknown) Agricultural scientist.

Duston, Hannah. (1657-1736) Colonist, Indian captive.

Dyer, Jane. (1945-) Illustrator.

Dyer, Mary. (1610-1660) Colonist.

Earhart, Amelia. (1897-1937) Aviation pioneer, aviator.

Earle, Sylvia. (1935-) Marine biologist, oceanographer.

Earley, Charity Adams. (1918-2002) World War II WAAC lieutenant colonel.

Eastman, Crystal. (1881-1928) Attorney, women's rights activist, workers' rights activist.

Eckford, Elizabeth. (1942-) Civil rights activist.

Eddy, Mary Baker. (1821-1910) Spiritual leader, founder Christian Science religion.

Edelman, Marian Wright. (1939-) Attorney, children's rights activist, civil rights activist, human rights activist. Presidential Medal of Freedom recipient.

Ederle, Gertrude. (1905-2003) Olympic swimmer.

Edge, Rosalie. (1877-1962) Conservationist, suffragist.

Edinger, Tilly. (1897-1967) Paleontologist.

Edmonds, Sarah Emma. (1841-1898) Civil War soldier disguised as man, nurse, spy.

Edmondson, Belle. (1840-1873) Civil War spy.

Edwards, Teresa. (1964-) Olympic basketball player.

Eglin, Ellen F. (1849-?) Inventor.

Ehlert, Lois. (1934-) Children's author, illustrator.

Eilberg, Amy. (1954-) Spiritual leader.

Eisenhower, Mamie Geneva Doud. (1896-1979) First Lady.

Eisenstein, Judith Kaplan. (1909-1996) Educator, songwriter.

Elders, Jocelyn Jones. (1933-) Physician, surgeon general of U.S.

Elion, Gertrude Belle. (1918-1999) Biochemist. Nobel Prize winner.

Erdrich, Louise. (1954-) Chippewa Indian author.

Ericsson-Jackson, Aprille Joy. (unknown) Aerospace engineer, space scientist.

Ernst, Lisa Campbell. (1957-) Children's author, illustrator.

Escobar, Marisol. (Marisol) (1930-) Sculptor, born Venezuela.

Espinel, Luisa Ronstadt. (1892-1963) Actor, singer.

Esquiroz, Margarita. (1945-) Attorney, jurist.

Estefan, Gloria. (1957-) Singer, born Cuba.

Estés, Clarissa Pinkol. (1943-) Author, psychologist, storyteller.

Evans, Dale. (1912-2001) Actor, cowgirl.

Evans, Janet. (1971-) Olympic swimmer.

Evans, Matilda Arabella. (1872-1935) Human rights activist, physician.

Everett, Dawn. (1979-) In-line skater.

Evers-Williams, Myrlie. (1933-) Civil rights activist.

Everson, Carrie. (1842-1914) Inventor.

Evert, Chris. (1954-) Tennis player.

Faber, Sandra. (unknown) Astronomer.

Fair, Lorrie. (1978-) Olympic soccer player.

Fairstein, Linda. (1947-) Attorney, author, crimefighter.

Farmer, Fannie Merritt. (1857-1915) Author, chef.

Fauset, Jessie Redmon. (1882-1961) Author.

Fawcett, Joy. (1968-) Olympic soccer player.

Feinstein, Dianne. (1933-) Mayor, senator.

Fenwick, Millicent. (1910-1992) Ambassador, congresswoman, state legislator.

Ferenz, Ludmilla "Lou." (1921-) World War II Army Nurse Corps flight nurse.

Fergus, Pamelia. (1824-1902) Pioneer.

Ferguson, Angella D. (1925-) Medical researcher, physician.

Ferguson, Catherine "Katy." (1779-1854) Educator, slave.

Ferguson, Miriam "Mo." (1875-1961) Governor.

Ferlette, Diane. (1945-) Storyteller.

Fernandez, Giselle. (1961-) Broadcast journalist, journalist, born Mexico.

Fernandez, Lisa. (1971-) Olympic softball player.

Fernandez, Mary Joe. (1971-) Tennis player, born Dominican Republic.

Ferraro, Geraldine. (1935-) Attorney, congresswoman.

Field, Kate. (1838-1896) Abolitionist, journalist.

Fieldler, Molly. (unknown) Chemist.

Fields, Debbi. (1956-) Entrepreneur cookies.

Fields, Mary. (1832-1914) Pioneer businesswoman, slave, disguised as man.

Fillmore, Abigail Powers. (1798-1853) First Lady.

Fine, Vivian. (1913-) Composer.

Fish, Emily. (1843-1931) Lighthouse keeper.

Fish, Juliet. (1859-1947) Lighthouse keeper.

Fitzgerald, Ella. (1918-1996) Jazz singer. Presidential Medal of Freedom recipient.

Fitzgerald, Zelda Sayre. (1900-1948) Wife of F. Scott Fitzgerald.

Fix, Georgia Arbuckle. (1852-1918) Physician.

Flagg, Fannie. (1944-) Author, screenwriter.

Flaggs, Gail. (unknown) Geneticist, medical researcher.

Flanner, Janet. (Genét) (1892-1978) Journalist.

Fleming, Denise. (1950-) Children's author, illustrator.

Fleming, Peggy. (1948-) Olympic figure skater.

Fleming, Williamina Patron Stevens. (1857-1911) Astronomer, born Scotland.

Fletcher, Alice Cunningham. (1838-1923) Anthropologist, archaeologist.

Flynn, Elizabeth Gurley. (1890-1964) Suffragist, workers' rights activist.

Foote, Mary Hallock. (1847-1938) Author.

Ford, Eileen. (1922-) Entrepreneur modeling agency.

Ford, Elizabeth Bloomer "Betty." (1918-) First Lady.

Ford, Justina Laurena. (1871-1952) Physician.

Fornés, Maria Irene. (1930-) Playwright, born Cuba.

Forsythe, Ruby Middleton. (1905-1992) Educator.

Fort, Cornelia. (1919-1943) World War II pilot.

Forten, Charlotte. *See* Grimke, Charlotte Forten.

Fossey, Dian. (1932-1985) Primatologist.

Foster, Abby Kelley. (1811-1887) Abolitionist.

Foster, Jodie. (1962-) Actor.

Foster, Sarah Jane. (1839-1868) Civil rights activist, educator.

Foudy, Julie. (1971-) Olympic soccer player.

Fowler, Lydia Folger. (1822-1879) Physician.

Fowler-Billings, Katharine Stevens. (1902-1997) Conservationist, geologist.

Frank, Mary. (1933-) Painter.

Franklin, Aretha. (1942-) Jazz singer.

Franklin, Deborah Read. (1707-1774) American Revolutionary War patriot, entrepreneur.

Fratianne, Linda. (1960-) Olympic figure skater.

Freeman, Elizabeth "Mumbet." (1742-1829) Abolitionist, nurse, slave.

Fremont, Jessie Benton. (1824-1902) Author, pioneer.

Friedan, Betty Goldstein. (1921-) Women's rights activist.

Friedman, Tova Grossman. (1938-) Holocaust survivor, social worker, born Poland.

Frietchie, Barbara Hauer. (1766-1862) Civil War heroine, perhaps legendary.

Frome, Lynette "Squeaky." (1948-) Assassin (attempted) of President Gerald Ford.

Fuller, Meta Vaux Warrick. (1877-1968) Sculptor.

Futrell, Mary Hatwood. (1940-) Educator.

Gabe, Frances. (1915-) Inventor.

Garbo, Greta. (1905-1990) Actor, born Sweden.

Garcia, Dawn. (unknown) Journalist.

Garcia, Emma. (1972-) Community activist.

Garden, Mary. (1874-1967) Opera singer, born Scotland.

Garfield, Lucretia Rudolph. (1832-1918) First Lady.

Garland, Judy. (1922-1969) Singer.

Garner, Margaret. (1833-?) Fugitive slave.

Garrison-Jackson, Zina. (1963-) Tennis player.

Garvey, Amy-Jacques. (1896-1973) Civil rights activist.

Garzarelli, Elaine. (1952-) Financial analyst.

Geiger, Emily. (1760-1813) American Revolutionary War patriot.

Gellhorn, Martha. (1908-1998) Journalist, World War II correspondent.

Genét. *See* Flanner, Janet.

Gengo, Kate. (1964-) In-line skater.

George, Eliza Davis. (1879-1979) Missionary.

Gertz, Alison. (1966-1992) AIDS activist.

Geyer, Georgie Anne. (1933-) Journalist.

Gibbs, Lois Marie. (1951-) Environmental activist.

Gibson, Althea. (1927-2003) Tennis player.

Gillars, Mildred "Axis Sally." (1900-1988) World War II traitor.

Gillom, Jennifer. (1964-) Olympic basketball player.

Gilman, Charlotte Perkins. (1860-1935) Author, women's rights activist.

Gilmer, Elizabeth Meriwether. (Dorothy Dix) (1861-1951) Journalist.

Gilpin, Laura. (1891-1979) Photographer.

Gimbutas, Marija Birute Alseikaite. (1921-1994) Archaeologist, born Lithuania.

Gini, Mari. (unknown) Computer scientist, educator, physicist, born Italy.

Ginsburg, Ruth Bader. (1933-) Attorney, Supreme Court justice.

Giovanni, Nikki. (1943-) Children's author, poet.

Girard, Jami. (unknown) Mining engineer.

Gittis, Kelley Anne. (unknown) Paleontologist.

Gladney, Edna Kahly. (1886-1961) Human rights activist, reformer.

Glaser, Elizabeth. (1947-1994) AIDS activist, children's rights activist.

Goddard, Mary Katherine. (1738-1816) American Revolutionary War patriot, printer, publisher.

Goeppert-Mayer, Maria. (1906-1972) Physicist, born Germany. Nobel Prize winner.

Goldberg, Whoopi. (1950-) Actor, comedian.

Golden, Diana. (1963-2001) Olympic skier.

Goldman, Emma. (1869-1940) Human rights activist, political activist, women's rights activist.

Gonzáles, Jovita Mireles. (1904-1983) Historian, storyteller.

Gonzalez, Maya Christina. (1964-) Painter.

Gonzalez, Melissa Eve. (1980-) Actor.

Good, Mary. (1931-) Chemist.

Goode, Sara E. (1850-?) Inventor, slave.

Goodman, Ellen. (1941-) Journalist.

Goodnight, Molly. (1839-1926) Rancher.

Goodrich, Annie W. (1866-1954) Educator, nurse.

Govea, Jessica. (c. 1950) Workers' rights activist.

Grafton, Sue. (1940-) Author.

Graham, Bette Nesmith. (1924-1980) Inventor.

Graham, Katharine. (1917-2001) Author, publisher. Presidential Medal of Freedom recipient. Pulitzer Prize winner.

Graham, Martha. (1894-1991) Choreographer, dancer.

Gramm, Wendy Lee. (1945-) Economist.

Granato, Cammi. (1971-) Olympic hockey player, sportscaster.

Grandin, Temple. (1974-) Inventor.

Grant, Julia Dent. (1826-1902) First Lady.

Granville, Evelyn Boyd. (1924-) Educator, government employee, mathematician.

Grasso, Ella. (1919-1981) Governor, state legislator. Presidential Medal of Freedom recipient.

Gratz, Rebecca. (1781-1869) Educator, philanthropist.

Gray, Martha. (unknown) Medical engineer, educator, medical researcher.

Gray, Mary. (1938-) Mathematician.

Green, Dannellia Gladden. (1966-) Engineer.

Green, Hetty. (1834-1916) Financier.

Green, Lear. (c. 1830-1850) Fugitive slave.

Greene, Betty. (1920-1997) Aviator, missionary.

Greene, Catherine Littlefield. (1755-1814) Inventor.

Greenfield, Elizabeth Taylor. (1809-1876) Singer.

Greenfield, Eloise. (1929-) Children's author, poet.

Greenhow, Rose O'Neal. (1817-1864) Civil War spy.

Griffin, Bessie Blount. (1913-) Inventor.

Griffin, Susan. (1943-) Author, poet.

Griffith, Linda. (unknown) Chemical engineer, medical researcher.

Grimke, Angelina. (1805-1879) Abolitionist, human rights activist.

Grimke, Charlotte Forten. (1837-1914) Abolitionist, author, educator.

Grimke, Sarah Moore. (1792-1873) Abolitionist, human rights activist.

Grimmesey, Tevry. (1931-) World War II girl put in detention camp for Japanese-Americans.

Guerra, Jackie. (1967-) Actor, comedian, human rights activist, workers' rights activist.

Guisewite, Cathy. (1950-) Cartoonist.

Guthrie, Janet. (1938-) Auto racer.

Hadley, Leila Eliott Burton. (1925-) Adventurer, author.

Hagedorn, Jessica. (1949-) Author, born

Philippines.

Hahn, Emily. (1905-1997) Adventurer, author, women's rights activist.

Hale, Clara. (1905-1992) Children's rights activist, human rights activist.

Hale, Sarah Josepha Buell. (1788-1879) Children's author, editor magazine, women's rights activist.

Halloren, Mary. (1907-) Army career officer.

Hamanaka, Sheila. (1949-) Children's author, illustrator.

Hamer, Fannie Lou. (1917-1977) Civil rights activist.

Hamer, Victoria. (unknown) Veterinarian.

Hamill, Dorothy. (1956-) Olympic figure skater.

Hamilton, Alice. (1869-1970) Children's rights activist, educator, human rights activist, pathologist, physician, public health activist.

Hamilton, Marilyn. (1947-) Disability rights activist, inventor.

Hamilton, Virginia. (1936-2002) Children's and young adult author.

Hamm, Mia. (1972-) Olympic soccer player.

Hammonds, Julia T. (unknown) Inventor.

Hancock, Joy Bright. (1898-1986) Naval career, Director WAVES, World War I, World War II.

Handler, Ruth. (1916-2002) Entrepreneur dolls, inventor.

Hansberry, Lorraine. (1930-1965) Playwright.

Hanson, Harriet. (1825-1911) Civil rights activist, suffragist, workers' rights activist.

Harding, Florence Kling De Wolfe. (1860-1924) First Lady.

Harding, Tonya. (1970-) Olympic figure skater.

Hardy-Garcia, Dianne. (1965-) Gay rights activist, human rights activist, social worker.

Harper, Frances E. W. (1825-1911) Abolitionist, author, poet, suffragist, women's rights activist.

Harris, Betty Wright. (1940-) Chemist.

Harris, Eliza. (unknown) Fugitive slave.

Harris, LaDonna. (1931-) Comanche Indian Native American rights activist.

Harris, Patricia Roberts. (1924-1985) Attorney, cabinet member, diplomat.

Harrison, Anna Tuthill Symmes. (1775-1864) First Lady.

Harrison, Caroline Scott. (1832-1892) First Lady.

Harrison, Marguerite Baker. (1879-1967) Adventurer, spy.

Hart, Nancy. (1744-1841) American Revolutionary War patriot, spy.

Harvard, Beverly. (1950-) Police chief.

Haskells, Ella Knowles. (1860-1911) Attorney.

Hauptman, Judith. (unknown) Educator.

Hawes, Harriet Ann Boyd. (1871-1945) Archaeologist.

Hayden, Sophia. (1868-1953) Architect, born Chile.

Hayes, Lucy Ware Webb. (1831-1889) First Lady.

Hazen, Elizabeth. (1885-1975) Bacteriologist, medical researcher.

Healy, Bernadine. (1944-) National Institute of Health director, physician.

Hecox, Laura. (1854-1919) Lighthouse keeper.

Height, Dorothy Irene. (1912-) Civil rights activist, National Council of Negro Women director, social worker. Presidential Medal of Freedom recipient.

Heinrichs, April. (1964-) Olympic soccer player, coach.

Heiss, Carol. (1940-) Olympic figure skater.

Hendrickson, Sue. (1950-) Adventurer, paleontologist.

Henley, Beth. (1952-) Playwright.

Henry, Caryl. (1955-) Painter.

Hepburn, Katharine. (1907-2003) Actor.

Hernandez, Maria Latigo. (1893-1986) Author, civil rights activist, political activist, television personality, born Mexico.

Herrera, Caroline. (1939-) Fashion designer, born Venezuela

Hesse, Eva. (1936-1970) Painter, sculptor, born Germany.

Heuman, Judy. (1947-) Assistant Secretary of Education.

Higgins, Marguerite. (1920-1966) Photojournalist Korean War, Vietnam War, World War II. Pulitzer Prize winner.

Hill, Lauryn. (1975-) Singer, songwriter.

Hill, Lynn. (1961-) Rock climber.

Hinton, Susan E. "S. E." (1949-) Young adult author.

Hoban, Tana. (unknown) Children's author, illustrator.

Hobby, Oveta Culp. (1905-1995) Cabinet member, publisher, World War II Army commander of WAACS.

Hoben, Patricia. (unknown) Agricultural scientist, biologist, medical researcher.

Hodgers, Jenny. (1844-1915) Civil War soldier disguised as man, born Ireland.

Hodgins, Jessica. (unknown) Computer scientist.

Holdsclaw, Chamique. (1977-) Basketball player.

Holiday, Billie. (1915-1959) Jazz singer.

Holland, Elizabeth. (unknown) Biogeochemist.

Hom, Nancy. (1949-) Painter.

Hoover, Lou Henry. (1874-1944) First Lady.

Hopper, Grace. (1906-1972) Computer pioneer.

Horne, Lena. (1917-) Jazz singer.

Horney, Karen Danielsen. (1885-1952) Psychiatrist, born Germany.

Hose, Louise. (1952-) Geologist.

Hosmer, Harriet. (1830-1908) Inventor, sculptor.

Hostetter, Margaret. (unknown) Medical researcher, physician.

Houston, Whitney. (1963-) Actor, singer.

Howard, Mildred. (1945-) Mixed media artist.

Huerta, Dolores. (1930-) Labor leader.

Hughes, Sarah. (1985-) Olympic figure skater.

Hull, Peggy. (1890-1967) World War I correspondent.

Hunt, Fern. (unknown) Computer scientist, mathematician.

Hunter, Alberta. (1895-1984) Jazz singer.

Hunter, Clementine. (1886-1988) Painter.

Hunter-Gault, Charlayne. (1942-) Broadcast journalist, civil rights activist.

Hurd, Henriette Wyeth. (1907-1997) Painter.

Hurston, Zora Neale. (1901-1960) Anthropologist, author.

Hurwitz, Johanna. (1937-) Children's author.

Hutchinson, Anne Marbury. (1591-1643) Human rights activist, women's rights activist, born England.

Hutson, Jean Blackwell. (1914-1998) Librarian.

Hutton, May Arkwright. (1860-1915) Pioneer, suffragist.

Hyde, Ida Henrietta. (1857-1945) Physiologist.

Hyman, Flo. (1954-1986) Olympic volleyball player.

Hyman, Libbie. (1888-1969) Zoologist.

Ingles, Mary Ingles. (1731-1815) Colonist, Indian captive.

Ireland, Patricia. (1945-) Attorney, National Organization for Women president, women's rights activist.

Isaacs, Susan. (1943-) Author.

Ivins, Marsha. (1951-) Aerospace engineer, astronaut, space scientist.

Jackson, Janet. (1966-) Actor, dancer, singer.

Jackson, Janis. (unknown) Biologist, medical researcher, physician.

Jackson, Mahalia. (1911-1972) Blues singer.

Jackson, May Howard. (1877-1931) Sculptor.

Jackson, Rachel Donelson Robards. (1767-1828) First Lady.

Jackson, Shirley. (1919-1965) Author.

Jackson, Shirley Ann. (1946-) Educator, Nuclear Regulatory Commission head, physicist.

Jacob, Mary Phelps. (Caresse Crosby) (1892-1970) Inventor.

Jacobi, Mary Putnam. (1842-1906) Educator, physician, born England.

Jacobs, Harriet. (1813-1897) Abolitionist, author, slave.

James, Alice. (1848-1892) Author.

James-Rodman, Charmayne. (1970-) Rodeo rider.

Jamison, Judith. (1944-) Choreographer, dancer.

Janowitz, Tama. (1957-) Author.

Jans, Megan C. (1952-) Gulf War Army lieutenant colonel, helicopter pilot.

Jefferson, Martha Waylee Skelton. (1748-1782) First Lady.

Jemison, Mae C. (1956-) Astronaut, educator, physician.

Jemison, Mary. (1742-1833) American Revolutionary War patriot, Indian captive.

Jernigan, Tamara. (1955-) Astronomer, physicist.

Johnetta. (1927-1983) Jazz singer.

Johns, Barbara. (1935-1991) Civil rights activist.

Johnson, Claudia "Lady Bird" Alta. (1912-) First Lady. Presidential Medal of Freedom recipient.

Johnson, Eliza McCardle. (1810-1876) First Lady.

Johnson, Halle Tanner Dillon. (1864-1901) Physician.

Johnson, Hazel W. (1927-) Army Nurse Corps chief, brigadier general, educator.

Johnson, Katherine. (1918-) Space scientist.

Johnson, Kory. (1979-) Environmental activist.

Johnson, Osa Leighty. (1894-1953) Explorer, filmmaker.

Johnston, Frances Benjamin. (1864-1952) Photographer.

Johnston, Harriet Lane. *See* Lane, Harriet.

Jones, Amanda Theodosia. (1835-1914) Inventor.

Jones, Marion. (1975-) Basketball player, olympic track and field athlete.

Jones, Mary "Mother." (1830-1930) Labor leader, workers' rights activist, born Ireland.

Jong, Erica. (1942-) Author, poet.

Joplin, Janis. (1943-1970) Rock musician, singer.

Jordan, Barbara. (1936-1996) Attorney, civil rights activist, congresswoman. Presidential Medal of Freedom recipient.

Jordan, Lynda. (unknown) Chemist, medical researcher.

Joubert, Beverly. (1957-) Wildlife photographer.

Joyner, Florence Griffith. (1959-1998) Olympic track and field athlete.

Joyner-Kersee, Jackie. (1962-) Olympic track and field athlete.

Joyner, Marjorie Stewart. (1896-1994) Entrepreneur cosmetics.

Judson, Ann Hassletine. (unknown) Missionary.

Kalman, Maira. (1949-) Children's author, illustrator.

Kaminska, Ida. (1899-1980) Actor, born Russia.

Kandel, Lenore. (1932-) Poet.

Kapuscinski, Anne. (unknown) Agricultural scientist, educator, born France.

Karan, Donna. (1948-) Fashion designer.

Kasebier, Gertrude. (1852-1934) Photographer.

Kassebaum, Nancy Landon. (1932-) Senator.

Keckley, Elizabeth. (1818-1907) Abolitionist, entrepreneur dressmaking, slave.

Keller, Helen. (1880-1968) Author, disability rights activist. Presidential Medal of Freedom recipient.

Kelley, Florence. (1859-1932) Attorney, human rights activist, social worker.

Kelly, Grace. (1929-1982) Actor, wife of Prince Rainier.

Kelly, Sharon Pratt. (1944-) Attorney, mayor.

Kennedy, Florence. (1916-2000) Attorney, women's rights activist.

Kennedy, Jacqueline Lee Bouvier. *See* Onassis, Jacqueline Lee Bouvier Kennedy.

Kennedy, Rose Fitzgerald. (1890-1995) Matriarch Kennedy family.

Kenner, Beatrice. (1912-) Inventor.

Kerr, Barbara. (unknown) Author, educator, inventor.

Kerrigan, Nancy. (1969-) Olympic figure skater.

Khan, Yasmin Aga. (1949-) Princess, born Switzerland.

Khreiss, Betty Jane. (unknown) Forensic scientist.

Kilgallen, Dorothy M. (1913-1965) Journalist, television personality.

Kim, Willyce. (1946-) Author, poet.

King, Billie Jean. (1943-) Tennis player.

King, Coretta Scott. (1927?-) Author, civil rights activist, singer.

King, Mary-Claire. (1946-) Geneticist.

King, Reatha Clark. (1938-) Chemist, National Bureau of Standards government agency employee.

Kingston, Maxine Hong. (1940-) Author, educator.

Kirkpatrick, Helen. (1909-1997) Journalist, World War II correspondent.

Kirkpatrick, Jeane. (1926-) Ambassador. Presidential Medal of Freedom recipient.

Klein, Norma. (1938-1989) Young adult author.

Knight, Margaret. (1838-1914) Inventor.

Knight, Nancy Lopez. *See* Lopez, Nancy.

Kohut, Rebekah Bettleheim (1864-1951) Human rights activist.

Koningsburg, Elaine "E. L." (1930-) Children's author.

Koontz, Elizabeth Duncan. (1919-1989) Civil rights activist, educator, National Education Association president.

Krone, Julie. (1963-) Jockey.

Kübler-Ross, Elisabeth. (1926-2004) Author, psychiatrist, born Switzerland.

Kuhn, Maggie. (1905-1995) Human rights activist, reformer.

Kunin, Madeleine. (1933-) Governor, born Switzerland.

Kuramoto, June. (1948-) Jazz musician, born Japan.

Kuskin, Karla. (1933-) Children's author, illustrator.

Kwan, Michelle. (1980-) Olympic figure skater.

Kwolek, Stephanie. (1923-) Chemist, inventor.

Kyoko, Ina. (1972-) Olympic figure skater, born Japan.

Labosky, Bonnie. (unknown) Computer scientist, mathematician.

Landers, Ann. *See* Lederer, Esther Pauline.

Lane, Harriet. (1830-1903) First Lady. (Niece of James Buchanan).

Laney, Lucy Craft. (1854-1933) Educator, slave.

Lang, Naomi. (1978-) Karuk Indian olympic figure skater.

Lange, Dorothea. (1895-1965) Photographer.

Langston, Dicey. (1766-1837) American Revolutionary War patriot, spy.

Lansing, Sherry. (1944-) Filmmaker.

Lappe, Frances Moore. (1944-) Nutritionist.

Larsen, Nella. (1891-1964) Author.

Lathrop, Julia. (1858-1932) Children's rights activist, U.S. Children's Bureau director, social reformer, social worker.

Latifah, Queen. *See* Owens, Dana Elaine.

Lattimore, Deborah Nourse. (1949-) Chil

dren's author, illustrator.

Lawson, Louisa. (1848-1920) Poet, suffragist.

Lazarus, Emma. (1849-1887) Poet.

Le Guin, Ursula K. (1929-) Young adult author.

Le Sueur, Meridel. (1900-1996) Children's author, novelist, journalist, revolutionary.

Leach, Molly. (1960-) Illustrator.

Leavitt, Henrietta Swan. (1868-1921) Astronomer.

Lederer, Esther Pauline "Eppie." (Ann Landers) (1918-2002) Journalist.

Lee, Ann. (1736-1784) Spiritual leader, founder of Shaker community, born England.

Lee, Jarena. (1783-1850) Spiritual leader.

Lee, Marie G. (1964-) Young adult author.

Leibovitz, Annie. (1949-) Photographer.

Leitner, Isabella Katz. (1924-) Author, Holocaust survivor, born Hungary.

L'Engle, Madeline. (1918-) Children's and young adult author.

Leslie, Lisa. (1972-) Olympic basketball player.

Leslie, Miriam "Frank" Florence Folline. (1836-1914) Editor magazine.

L'Esperance, Elsie Strong. (1878-1959) Pathologist, physician.

Levertov, Denise. (1923-1997) Poet, born England.

Levi-Montalcini, Rita. (1909-) Cell biologist, born Italy. Nobel Prize winner.

Lewin, Betsy. (1937-) Children's author, illustrator.

Lewis, Ida. (1842-1911) Lighthouse keeper.

Lewis, Loida Nicolas. (1942-) Attorney, author, entrepreneur foods conglomerate, born Philippines.

Lewis, Mary Edmonia. (1845-1890) Sculptor.

Lieberman-Cline, Nancy. (1958-) Olympic basketball player, coach.

Lilly, Kristine. (1971-) Olympic soccer player.

Lin, Maya Ying. (1960-) Architect, sculptor.

Lincoln, Abbey. (1930-) Actor, composer, jazz singer.

Lincoln, Mary Todd. (1818-1882) First Lady.

Lindbergh, Anne Morrow. (1906-2001) Author, aviator.

Lipinski, Tara. (1982-) Olympic figure skater.

Liu, Hung. (1948-) Painter, born China.

Lobo, Rebecca. (1973) Olympic basketball player.

Lockwood, Belva Ann. (1830-1917) Attorney, Native American rights activist, presidential candidate, women's rights activist.

Longshore, Hannah E. Myers. (1810-1901) Educator, physician.

Lopez, Jennifer. (1970-) Actor, pop singer.

Lopez, Josefina. (1969-) Playwright, born Mexico.

Lopez, Nancy. (1957-) Golfer.

Lord, Audre. (1934-1992) Human rights activist, poet.

Lord, Bette Bao. (1938-) Author, born China.

Love, Nancy Harkness. (1914-1976) World War II pilot.

Love, Susan. (1948-) Medical researcher, physician.

Lovejoy, Esther Pohl. (1869-1967) Physician, reformer, women's rights activist, World War I Red Cross doctor.

Low, Juliette Gordon "Daisy." (1860-1927) Girl Scouts of America founder.

Lowe, Ann. (1899-?) Fashion designer.

Lowell, Amy. (1874-1925) Poet. Pulitzer Prize winner.

Lowry, Judith. (1948-) Pit River Indian painter.

Lowry, Lois. (1937-) Children's and young adult author.

Lozen. (1840-1890) Apache Indian warrior.

Lucas, Tad. (1902-1990) Rodeo rider.

Luce, Clare Boothe. (1903-1987) Ambassador, congresswoman, playwright. Presidential Medal of Freedom recipient.

Lucid, Shannon W. (1943-) Astronaut.

Ludewig, Marion. (1914-) Bowler.

Ludington, Sybil. (1761-1839) American Revolutionary War patriot.

Lyon, Mary. (1797-1849) Educator.

Maass, Clara. (1875-1901) Medical researcher, nurse.

MacArthur, Catherine. (1906-1981) Philanthropist.

MacDowell, Marian. (1857-1956) Patron of

the arts.

Macmillan, Shannon. (1974-) Soccer player.

Madison, Dolley Payne Todd. (1768-1849) First Lady.

Madonna. *See* Ciccione, Madonna Louise Veronica.

Magoffin, Susan Shelby. (1827-1855) Pioneer.

Mahoney, Mary Eliza. (1845-1926) Civil rights activist, nurse, women's rights activist.

Mahowald, Misha (1963-) Biologist, computer scientist.

Makarova, Natalia. (1940-) Ballet dancer, born Russia.

Malone, Annie Turnbo. (1869-1957) Inventor.

Maloney, Kris. (1981-) Olympic gymnast.

Mangin, Anna M. (unknown) Inventor.

Mankiller, Wilma. (1945-) Cherokee chief. Presidential Medal of Freedom recipient.

Mann, Shelley. (1939-) Olympic swimmer.

Mark, Mary Ellen. (1940-) Photographer.

Marsden, Kate. (1859-1931) Arctic explorer.

Marshall, Paule. (1929-) Author.

Martin, Ann M. (1955-) Children's and young adult author.

Martin, Grace. (unknown) American Revolutionary War patriot.

Martin, Louise. (1911-) Photographer.

Martin, Rachcl. (unknown) American Revolutionary War patriot.

Martinez, Maria Montoya. (1887-1980) San Idlefonso Pueblo Indian potter.

Martinez, Vilma. (1943-) Attorney, civil rights activist.

Mason, Biddy. (1818-1891) Civil rights activist, entrepreneur, pioneer, slave.

Masters, Sybilla. (d. 1720) Inventor.

Masterson, Martha Gay. (1837-1916) Pioneer.

Mata Hari. *See* Zelle, Margareta Gertrude.

Mathai-Davis, Prema. (1950-) Human rights activist, women's rights activist, YWCA Director, born India.

Mathison, Melissa. (1949-) Screenwriter.

Matlin, Marlee. (1965-) Actor.

Maury, Antonia C. (1866-1952) Astronomer.

Maxwell, Nicole Hughes. (1905-1998) Ethnobiologist.

McAuliffe, Christa. (1948-1986) Astronaut, educator.

McBride, Mary Margaret. (Martha Deane) (1899-1976) Broadcast journalist, journalist.

McCauley, Mary Ludwig Hays. (Molly Pitcher) (1754-1832) American Revolutionary War heroine.

McClintock, Barbara. (1909-1992) Geneticist. Nobel Prize winner.

McCormick, Anne O'Hare. (1880-1954) Journalist. Pulitzer Prize winner.

McCormick, Patricia Keller. (1930-) Olympic diver.

McCoy, Millie-Christine. (1851-1912) Siamese twins, singers, slaves.

McCray, Nikki. (1971-) Olympic basketball player.

McCrea, Jane. (1752-1777) American Revolutionary War Indian captive.

McDaniel, Hattie. (1895-1952) Actor, singer.

McDoulet, Annie "Cattle Annie." (1879-1898) Outlaw.

McGee, Anita Newcomb. (1864-1940) Army Nurse Corps founder, physician.

McGrory, Mary. (1918-) Journalist.

McGuire, Edith. (1944-) Olympic track and field athlete.

McKane, Alice Woodby. (1865-1948) Physician.

McKinney, Nina Mae. (1909-1967) Jazz singer.

McKinley, Ida Saxton. (1847-1907) First Lady.

McKinstry, Carolyn. (1949-) Civil rights activist.

McMillan, Terry. (1951-) Author.

McNutt, Marcia. (1952-) Geologist, physician.

McQueen, Thelma "Butterfly." (1911-1995) Actor.

McRae, Carmen. (1922-1994) Jazz musician, singer.

Mead, Margaret. (1901-1978) Anthropologist. Presidential Medal of Freedom recipient.

Memphis Minnie. *See* Douglas, Lizzie.

Mergler, Marie Josepha. (1851-1901) Physician, born Germany.

Merman, Ethel. (1908-1984) Singer.

Metoyer, Marie-Therese. (1742-1816) Colonist, slave.

Mexia, Ynes. (1870-1938) Botanist, explorer.

Meyer, Anna "Pee Wee." (1929-) Baseball player.

Meyer, Annie Nathan. (1867-1951) Women's rights activist.

Meyers, Ann. (1955-) Olympic basketball player, sportscaster.

Meyers, Nancy. (1950-) Screenwriter.

Midler, Bette. (1945-) Actor, singer.

Mikulski, Barbara. (1936-) Congresswoman, senator.

Millay, Edna St.Vincent. (1892-1950) Playwright, poet. Pulitzer Prize winner.

Millbrett, Tiffany. (1972-) Olympic soccer player.

Miller, Cheryl. (1964-) Olympic basketball player, sportscaster.

Miller, Inger. (1972-) Olympic track and field athlete.

Miller, Lee. (1907-1977) Photographer, World War II photojournalist.

Miller, Shannon. (1977-) Olympic gymnast.

Mink, Patsy Takemoto. (1927-2002) Attorney, congresswoman.

Minoka-Hill, Lillie Rosa. (1876-1952) Mohawk Indian physician.

Mitchell, Margaret. (1900-1948) Author.

Mitchell, Maria. (1818-1889) Astronomer.

Mitchell, Thecla. (unknown) Marathon runner.

Moceanu, Dominique. (1981-) Olympic gymnast.

Mock, Geraldine Fredritz. (1925-) Aviation pioneer.

Mohr, Nicholasa. (1935-) Children's author, novelist.

Moise, Penina. (1797-1880) Educator, poet.

Monroe, Elizabeth Kortright. (1768-1830) First Lady.

Monroe, Harriet. (1860-1936) Poet, publisher.

Monroe, Marilyn. (1926-1962) Actor.

Moody, Helen Wills. (1906-1998) Olympic tennis player.

Moon, Lottie. (1840-1912) Missionary.

Moore, Alice Ruth. (1875-1935) Author, poet.

Moore, Ann. (1940-) Inventor.

Moore, Audley. (1898-1997) Civil rights activist, women's rights activist.

Moore, Sara Jane. 91930-) Assassin, attempted to kill President Gerald Ford.

Morani, Alma Dea. (1907-2001) Physician, plastic surgeon, born Italy.

Moreno, Rita. (1931-) Actor, dancer, born Puerto Rico.

Morgan, Ann Haven. (1882-1966) Ecologist, zoologist.

Morgan, Barbara. (1900-1992) Photographer.

Morgan, Jill. (unknown) Mechanical engineer.

Morgan, Julia. (1872-1957) Architect.

Morgan, Rose. (1913-) Entrepreneur beauty salons.

Mori, Kyoko. (1957-) Young adult author, born Japan.

Morris, Esther. (1814-1902) Suffragist, women's rights activist.

Morrison, Toni. (1931-) Author, educator. Nobel Prize winner, Pulitzer Prize winner.

Moseley-Braun, Carol. (1944-) Presidential candidate, senator.

Moses, Anna Mary Robertson "Grandma." (1860-1961) Painter.

Moss, Cynthia. (1940-) Wildlife biologist, journalist.

Mossell, Gertrude Bustill. (1855-1948) Educator, journalist, women's rights activist.

Motley, Constance Baker. (1921-) Attorney, civil rights activist, jurist.

Mott, Lucretia Coffin. (1793-1880) Abolitionist, women's rights activist.

Motte, Rebecca. (d. 1815) American Revolutionary War patriot, heroine.

Mourning Dove. (Christine Quintasket) (1888-1936) Okanogan Indian author, Native American rights activist.

Moutoussamy-Ashe, Jeanne. (1951-) Photographer.

Moxon, June. (unknown) Mixed-media artist, sculptor.

Mukherjee, Bharti. (1940-) Author, born India.

Muldowney, Shirley. (1940-) Auto drag racer.

Mulhall, Lucille. (1855-1940) Cowgirl.

Mullaney, Kate. (1845-1906) Workers' rights activist.

Mullens, Priscilla. (1604-1680) Colonist, born England.

Murie, Margaret Thomas. (1902-2003) Author, conservationist. Presidential Medal of Freedom recipient.

Murray, Judith Sargent. (1751-1820) American Revolutionary War author, editor.

Murray, Mary Lindley. (unknown) American Revolutionary War patriot, heroine.

Murray, Pauli. (1910-1985) Attorney, civil rights activist.

Musgrove, Mary. (1700-1763) Creek Indian colonist, Indian interpreter.

Musolino-Alber, Ella. (unknown) Entrepreneur sports promotion.

Nair, Malathy. (unknown) Chemist, born India.

Narahashi, Keiko. (1959-) Children's author, illustrator, born Japan.

Nash, Diane. (1938-) Civil rights activist.

Nation, Cary. (1846-1911) Reformer.

Natori, Josefina "Josie" Cruz. (1947-) Entrepreneur financier, fashion designer, born Philippines.

Naylor, Phyllis Reynolds. (1933-) Children's and young adult author.

Naylor, Rosamund. (unknown) Agricultural economist.

Neel, Alice. (1900-1984) Painter.

Nevelson, Louise. (1899-1988) Sculptor, born Russia.

Newman, Lydia D. (unknown) Inventor.

Newman, Sarah Jane "Sally Skull." (1817-1866) Civil War heroine, outlaw.

Ney, Elisabet. (1833-1907) Sculptor.

Nicholson, Eliza Jane Poitevent Holbrook. (1849-1896) Poet, publisher newspaper.

Niles, Mary Blair. (1880-1959) Explorer.

Nixon, Thelma "Pat" Ryan. (1912-1993) First Lady.

Noguchi, Constance Tom. (1948-) Chemist, medical researcher.

Norman, Dorothy. (1905-1997) Author, photographer.

Norman, Jessye. (1945-) Opera singer.

Norton, Alice Mary. (Andre) (1912-) Author, librarian.

Norton, Eleanor Holmes. (1937-) Attorney, civil rights activist, congresswoman.

Novello, Antonia C. (1944-) Physician, surgeon general of U.S., born Puerto Rico.

Nurse, Rebecca. (1621-1692) Colonist, accused of being witch, born England.

Nussbaum, Susan. (1953-) Actor, disability rights activist, playwright.

Nyad, Diana. (1949-) Marathon swimmer, sportscaster.

Oakley, Annie. (1860-1926) Cowgirl, showman.

Oates, Joyce Carol. (1938-) Author, educator.

Oberhauser, Karen. (unknown) Biologist.

Ocampo, Adriana. (1955-) Planetary geologist, born Colombia.

Ochoa, Ellen. (1959-) Astronaut, electrical engineer.

O'Connor, Flannery. (1925-1964) Author.

O'Connor, Sandra Day. (1930-) Attorney, Supreme Court justice.

O'Day, Anita. (1919-) Jazz singer.

O'Keefe, Georgia. (1887-1986) Painter. Presidential Medal of Freedom recipient.

Onassis, Jacqueline Lee Bouvier Kennedy. (1929-1994) Editor, First Lady.

O'Neill, Cecilia Rose. (1874-1944) Cartoonist, illustrator, inventor.

Ordway, Katherine. (1899-1979) Conservationist, ecologist.

Orkin, Ruth. (1921-1985) Photographer.

Osborn, June. (1937-) AIDS activist, physician.

Osborne, Mary. (1921-1992) Jazz musician.

Ossoli, Margaret Fuller. (1810-1850) Journalist, suffragist, women's rights activist.

Overbeck, Carla. (1969-) Olympic soccer player.

Owens, Dana Elaine. (Queen Latifah) (1970-) Actor, singer.

Owens-Adair, Bethenia. (1840-1926) Physician.

Ozick, Cynthia. (1928-) Author.

Pack, Amy Thorne "Betty." (1910-1963) World War II spy.

Paddleford, Clementine Haskin. (1900-1967) Journalist.

Paik, Nam June. (1932-) Composer, mixed-media artist, born Korea.

Paley, Grace. (1922-) Author.

Pariseau, Esther. (Mother Joseph) (1832-1902) Human rights activist, spiritual leader.

Parker, Bonnie. (1911-1934) Outlaw.

Parker, Dorothy. (1893-1967) Author, poet, screenwriter.

Parkerson, Michelle. (1953-) Filmmaker.

Parkhurst, Charlotte Darkey. (1812-1879) Pioneer, stagecoach driver.

Parks, Rosa. (1913-) Civil rights activist. Presidential Medal of Freedom recipient.

Parlow, Cindy. (1978-) Olympic soccer player.

Parris, Betty. (1682-1760) Colonist, puritan, accused others of witchcraft.

Parsons, Elsie Clews. (1875-1941) Anthropologist, folklorist, sociologist.

Parsons, Lucy. (1853-1943) Civil rights activist, revolutionary, slave, workers' rights activist.

Parton, Sara Payson. (Fanny Fern) (1811-1872) Author, journalist.

Paterson, Katherine. (1932-) Children's and young adult author.

Patrick, Ruth. (1907-) Freshwater biologist, ecologist.

Paul, Alice. (1885-1977) Attorney, suffragist, women's rights activist.

Payne, Ethel L. (1911-1991) Journalist.

Payne, Katy. (1937-) Acoustic biologist.

Payne-Gaspochkin, Cecilia. (1900-1979) Astronomer, born England.

Peake, Mary Smith. (1823-1862) Educator.

Peck, Annie Smith. (1850-1935) Adventurer, archaeologist, mountaineer.

Peck, Ellen. (1829-1915) Swindler.

Pennington, Mary Engle. (1872-1952) Chemist.

Perera, Hilda. (1926-) Children's author, born Cuba.

Perez, Rosie. (1964-) Actor, choreographer, dancer.

Perez, Selena Quintanilla. (Selena) (1971-1995) Singer.

Perkins, Frances. (1882-1965) Cabinet member, social worker.

Perkins, Nancy. (1949-) Inventor.

Perry, Carrie Saxon. (1931-) Mayor.

Pert, Candace Beebe. (1946-) Biochemist, medical researcher.

Peterson, Esther. (1906-1997) Consumer Affairs director, women's rights activist, workers' rights activist.

Petry, Ann. (1911-1997) Children's and adult author.

Phelps, Jaycie. (1979-) Olympic gymnast.

Phillips, Pauline Esther "Popo." (Abigail Van Buren) (1918-) Journalist.

Picotte, Susan LaFlesche. (1865-1915) Ponca and Omaha Indian physician.

Pierce, Jane Appleton. (1806-1863) First Lady.

Pierce, Mary. (1975-) Tennis player, born Canada.

Pierce, Naomi. (1954-) Biologist.

Pinckney, Eliza Lucas. (1722-1793) Agronomist, colonist, entrepreneur indigo crops, born West Indies.

Pitcher, Mary. *See* McCauley, Mary Ludwig Hays.

Place, Etta. (1875-1940) Outlaw.

Pleasant, Mary Ellen "Mammy." (1814-1904) Abolitionist, civil rights activist, entrepreneur real estate, pioneer.

Pocahontas. (1595?-1617) Powhatan Indian princess.

Polk, Sarah Childress. (1803-1891) First Lady.

Pool, Judith Graham. (1919-1975) Physiologist.

Pop-Pank. (1790-?) Native American friend of Sacagawea.

Porter, Katherine Anne. (1890-1980) Author.

Powdermaker, Hortense. (1900-1970) Anthropologist.

Powell, Cristen. (1979-) Drag racer.

Powell, Dawn. (1897-1965) Author.

Preisand, Sally. (1946-) Spiritual leader.

Preston, Ann. (1813-1872) Abolitionist, educator, physician, reformer.

Pretty Shield. (1850-1930) Crow Indian healer.

Price, Florence. (1888-1953) Composer.

Price, Leontyne. (1927-) Opera singer. Presidential Medal of Freedom recipient.

Primavera, Elise. (1955-) Children's author, illustrator.

Prince, Lucy Terry. (1733-1821) Poet.

Prince, Mary. (1788-?) Author, fugitive slave.

Procope, Ernesta. (1932-) Entrepreneur insurance.

Proctor, Barbara Gardner. (1933-) Entrepreneur advertising.

Prophet, Nancy Elizabeth. (1890-1960)

Sculptor.

Prothrow-Stith, Deborah. (1954-) Human rights activist, physician, Public Health Commissioner Massachusetts.

Provensen, Alice. (1918-) Children's author, illustrator.

Pudaite, Rochunga. (1927-) Bible translator, born India.

Pukui, Mary Kawena. (1895-1986) Hawaiian folklorist, linguist.

Purtell, Edna. (1900-1986) Human rights activist, suffragist, women's rights activist.

Pusey, Anne. (1948-) Ecologist, primatologist, born England.

Quick, Flora. (Tom King) (unknown) Outlaw, disguised as man.

Quimby, Edith Hinkley. (1891-1982) Biophysicist.

Quimby, Frankie. (1937-) Jazz singer.

Quimby, Harriet. (1884-1912) Aviation pioneer, journalist.

Quindlen, Anna. (1953-) Journalist.

Rabe, Karin. (unknown) Physicist.

Rahr, Tammy. (unknown) Cayuga Indian beadworker.

Rainey, Gertrude "Ma." (1886-1939) Singer, songwriter.

Ramirez, Sara Estela. (1881-1910) Poet, political activist, women's rights activist, born Mexico.

Rankin, Jeanette. (1880-1973) Congresswoman, peace activist, social worker, suffragist.

Rawlings, Marjorie Kinnan. (1896-1953) Children's and adult author. Pulitzer Prize winner.

Ray, Charlotte E. (1850-1911) Attorney, community activist, educator.

Ray, Elise. (1982-) Olympic gymnast.

Reagan, Anne Robbins "Nancy." (1921-) First Lady. Presidential Medal of Freedom recipient.

Ream, Vinnie. (1847-1914) Sculptor.

Redmond, Mary. (unknown) American Revolutionary War patriot, spy.

Reed, Esther DeBeerdt. (1746-1780) American Revolutionary War patriot.

Reed, Judy W. (unknown) Inventor.

Reed, Virginia. (1833-1921) Pioneer.

Reid, Clarice D. (1931-) Medical researcher, physician.

Reid, Helen Rogers. (1882-1970) Publisher magazines.

Reisberg, Mira. (1953-) Painter, born Australia.

Remond, Sarah P. (1826-1894) Abolitionist, physician, women's rights activist.

Reno, Janet. (1938-) Attorney, cabinet member.

Resnick, Judith. (1949-1986) Astronaut, electrical engineer.

Retton, Mary Lou. (1968-) Olympic gymnast.

Reynolds, Mary. (fl. 1854-1866) Lighthouse keeper.

Rice, Anne. (1941-) Author.

Rich, Anna M. (1956-) Illustrator.

Richards, Ann. (1933-) Governor.

Richards, Ellen Swallow. (1842-1911) Chemist, ecologist, nutritionist.

Richardson, Dorothy "Dot." (1961-) Olympic softball player, physician.

Ridderhof, Joy. (1903-1984) Missionary, bible translator.

Ride, Sally Kristen. (1951-) Astronaut, astrophysicist.

Riggs, Lillian. (1888-1977) Rancher.

Rimes, LeAnn. (1982-) Country music singer.

Rinehart, Mary Roberts. (1876-1958) Author, journalist, World War I correspondent.

Ringgold, Faith. (1930-) Children's author, educator, illustrator, sculptor.

Rivlin, Alice. (1931-) Economist.

Roberts, Corinne Boggs "Cokie." (1943-) Author, broadcast journalist.

Roberts, Tiffany. (1977-) Olympic soccer player.

Robertson, Alice Mary. (1854-1931) Congresswoman, educator, social worker.

Robertson, Ruth Agnes McCall. (1905-1998) Photographer.

Robinson, Betty. (1911-1999) Olympic sprinter, track and field athlete.

Robinson, Julia Bowman. (1919-1985) Mathematician.

Rogers, Ginger. (1911-1995) Actor, dancer.

Rogers, Patricia. (unknown) Geologist.

Rohde, Ruth Bryan Owen. (1885-1954) Congresswoman, diplomat.

Rollins, Charlemae. (1897-1979) Librarian, storyteller.

Romero, Jacy. (1965-) Chumash Indian dancer.

Ronstadt, Linda. (1946-) Singer.

Roosevelt, Anna Curtenius. (1946-) Archaeologist.

Roosevelt, (Anna) Eleanor. (1884-1962) Author, First Lady, human rights activist, orator.

Roosevelt, Edith Kermit Carow. (1861-1948) First Lady.

Ros-Lentinen, Ileana. (1952-) Congresswoman, state legislator, born Cuba.

Rose, Ernestive Potowski. (1810-1892) Abolitionist, orator, reformer, women's rights activist, born Poland.

Rose, Mary Swartz. (1874-1941) Educator, nutritionist.

Roseanne. *See* Arnold, Roseanne.

Rosenberg, Ethel. (1915-1953) Traitor.

Rosenthal, Ida. (1886-1973) Inventor.

Ross, Betsy. (1752-1836) American Revolutionary War patriot, folk hero.

Ross, Diana. (1944-) Actor, entrepreneur music business, singer.

Roth-Hano, Renée. (1931-) Author, Holocaust survivor, social worker, born France.

Rothschild, Miriam. (1908-) Author, conservationist, entomologist, naturalist, born England.

Rousso, Harilyn. (1946-) Disability rights activist, psychotherapist.

Rowlandson, Mary. (1635-1682) Colonist, Indian captive.

Royall, Anne Newport. (1769-1854) Adventurer, journalist.

Roybal-Allard, Lucille. (1941-) Congresswoman, women's rights activist.

Rubin, Vera Cooper. (1928-) Astronomer.

Rudin, Mary Ellen Estill. (1924-) Mathematician.

Rudkin, Margaret Fogharty. (1897-1967) Entrepreneur foods.

Rudolph, Wilma. (1940-1994) Olympic track and field athlete.

Ruffin, Josephine St. Pierre. (1842-1924) Abolitionist, civil rights activist, organizations founder, suffragist.

Ryan, Katherine "Klondike Kate." (1869-

1932) Chef, gold miner, pioneer.

Saar, Alison. (1956-) Mixed-media artist

Saar, Betye. (1926-) Mixed-media artist.

Sabin, Florence Rena. (1871-1953) Anatomist, medical researcher, physician, suffragist.

Sacagawea. (1788-1884) Lemhi Shoshone Indian guide, interpreter.

Sager, Ruth. (1918-1997) Biologist, geneticist.

Sainte-Marie, Buffy. (1941-) Cree Indian actor, peace activist, singer, songwriter, born Canada.

Salter, Fanny. (1883-?) Lighthouse keeper.

Sampson, Deborah. (1760-1827) American Revolutionary War soldier disguised as man.

Sampson, Edith. (1901-1980) Attorney, diplomat, social worker.

Samuelson, Joan Benoit. (1957-) Olympic marathon runner, track and field athlete.

Sanchez, Loreta. (1960-) Congresswoman.

Sanders, Marlene. (1931-) Broadcast journalist.

Sandoz, Mari. (1896-1966) Author, historian.

Sanger, Margaret. (1879-1966) Nurse, reformer, women's rights activist.

Santos, Miriam. (1956-) City official, born Puerto Rico.

Saralegui, Cristina. (1948-) Television personality, born Cuba.

Sarkisian, Cherilyn. (Cher) (1946-) Pop singer.

Sasso, Sandy Eisenberg. (1947-) Children's author, spiritual leader.

Savage, Augusta Christine. (1892-1962) Educator, sculptor.

Sawyer, Diane. (1945-) Broadcast journalist.

Schechter, Matilde Roth. (1859-1924) Organization founder, born Germany.

Schele, Linda. (1942-1998) Lexicographer.

Schmandt-Besserat, Denise. (1933-) Archaeologist, lexicographer, born France.

Schneiderman, Rose. (1882-1972) Labor leader, workers' rights activist, born Poland.

Schroeder, Becky. (1962-) Inventor.

Schroeder, Patricia. (1940-) Attorney, congresswoman, publisher.

Schultz, Sigrid "Lillian." (1899-1980)

World War II correspondent.

Schwabe, Stephanie. (1957-) Geomicrobiologist, explorer, born Germany.

Schwartz, Amy. (1954-) Children's author, illustrator.

Scott, Harriet. (unknown) Slave, wife of Dred Scot.

Scurry, Brianna. (1971-) Olympic soccer player.

Seddon, Margaret Rhea. (1947-) Astronaut, physician.

See, Carolyn. (1934-) Author.

Seeger, Ruth Crawford. (1901-1953) Composer.

Selena. *See* Perez, Selena Quintanilla.

Seles, Monica. (1973-) Tennis player, born Yugoslavia.

Serio, Suzie McConnell. (1966-) Olympic basketball player.

Serrano, Lupe. (1930-) Dancer, educator, born Chile.

Seton, Elizabeth Ann. (1774-1821) Educator, saint, spiritual leader.

Shange, Ntozake. (1948-) Author.

Sharma, Prem. (1943-) Human rights activist, women's rights activist, born India.

Shavelson, Clara Lemlich. (1886-1982) Workers' rights activist, born Russia.

Shaw, Anna Howard. (1847-1919) Physician, reformer, suffragist, born England.

Sheldon, May French. (1847-1936) Explorer.

Sherman, Cindy. (1954-) Photographer.

Sherman, Patsy O. (1930-) Chemist, inventor.

Shirley, Donna. (1941-) Aerospace engineer, space scientist.

Sigur, Wanda. (1958-) Inventor, space scientist.

Sills, Beverly. (1929-) Opera singer. Presidential Medal of Freedom recipient.

Simone, Nina. (1933-2003) Composer, jazz musician, singer.

Simpson, Lorna. (1960-) Photographer.

Sims, Naomi. (1949-) Entrepreneur cosmetics, fashion model.

Skoglund, Sandy. (1946-) Painter, photographer.

Slew, Jenny. (1719-?) Slave.

Slocum, Melissa. (1961-) Jazz musician.

Smith, Ada "Bricktop." (1894-1984) Entrepreneur nightclub, jazz singer.

Smith, Amanda. (1837-1915) Slave, spiritual leader.

Smith, Anna Deavere. (1950-) Actor, playwright.

Smith, Bessie. (1894-1937) Jazz singer.

Smith, Clara. (1894-1935) Jazz singer.

Smith, Katie. (1964-) Basketball player.

Smith, Liz. (1923-) Journalist.

Smith, Mamie. (1883-1946) Jazz singer.

Smith, Margaret Chase. (1897-1995) Congresswoman, senator, World War II Air Force lieutenant colonel. Presidential Medal of Freedom recipient.

Smith, Mildred Davidson Austin. (1916-1993) Disability rights activist, inventor.

Smith, Samantha Reed. (1972-1985) Youth ambassador to Soviet Union, peace activist.

Snow, Eliza. (1804-1887) Pioneer, poet, spiritual leader, women's rights activist.

Snowe, Olympia. (1947-) Senator.

Sobrero, Kate. (1976-) Olympic soccer player.

Sofaer, Anna. (unknown) Painter, sculptor.

Spears, Britney. (1981-) Pop singer.

Spivey, Victoria. (1906-1976) Composer, jazz singer.

Staedler, Michelle. (unknown) Marine biologist.

Stafford, Jo. (1917-) Jazz singer.

Staley, Dawn. (1970-) Olympic basketball player.

Stam, Betty. (d. 1934) Missionary.

Stanton, Elizabeth Cady. (1815-1902) Suffragist, women's rights activist.

Starbird, Kate. (1975-) Basketball player.

Starr, Myra "Belle" Shirley. (1848-1889) Outlaw, pioneer.

Steel, Danielle. (1947-) Author.

Steig, Jeanne. (1930-) Children's author, illustrator.

Stein, Gertrude. (1874-1946) Author, playwright.

Steinem, Gloria. (1934-) Journalist, women's rights activist.

Stephens, Helen. (1918-1994) Olympic sprinter, track and field athlete.

Stevens, Jennie "Little Britches." (1879-) Outlaw.

Stevens, Nettie Marie. (1861-1912) Biologist, medical researcher.

Steward, Susan McKinney. (1847-1918) Physician.

Stewart, Elinoire Pruitt. (1876-1933) Author, pioneer.

Stewart, Martha. (1941-) Author, entrepreneur home goods, television personality.

Still, Susan. (1961-) Astronaut, Navy pilot.

Still, Valerie. (1961-) Basketball player.

Still, Vina. (unknown) Slave.

Stillwell, Hallie Crawford. (1897-1997) Rancher.

Stinson, Katherine. (1891-1977) Aviator, World War I Red Cross pilot.

Stone, Lucy. (1818-1893) Abolitionist, suffragist, women's rights activist.

Stone, Toni. (1921-1966) Baseball player.

Storm, Hannah. (1962-) Sportscaster.

Stowe, Harriet Beecher. (1811-1896) Abolitionist, author.

Street, Picabo. (1971-) Olympic skier.

Streisand, Barbra. (1942-) Actor, singer.

Stringer, Ann. (1918-1990) Journalist, World War II correspondent.

Strug, Kerri. (1977-) Olympic gymnast.

Sullivan, Annie. (1866-1936) Educator.

Sullivan, Kathryn. (1951-) Astronaut, oceanographer.

Summitt, Pat Head. (1952-) Basketball coach.

Swain, Clara A. (1834-1910) Medical missionary, physician.

Swisshelm, Jane Grey Cannon. (1815-1884) Abolitionist, journalist, women's rights activist.

Swoopes, Sheryl. (1971-) Olympic basketball player.

Szold, Henrietta. (1860-1945) Editor, organizational founder.

Taft, Helen Herron "Nellie." (1861-1943) First Lady.

Tallchief, Maria. (1925-) Osage Indian ballet dancer.

Tan, Amy. (1952-) Author.

Tape, Mary McGladery. (1857-1928) Children's rights activist, painter, photographer, born China.

Tarbell, Ida. (1857-1944) Journalist.

Tarter, Jill Cornell. (1944-) Astrophysicist.

Taussig, Helen Brooke. (1898-1986) Medical researcher, physician. Presidential

Medal of Freedom recipient.

Taylor, Annie Edson. (1838-1921) Adventurer.

Taylor, Elizabeth. (1932-) Actor, AIDS activist, born England.

Taylor, Margaret Mackell Smith. (1788-1852) First Lady.

Taylor, Mildred. (1943-) Children's author.

Taylor, Susan. (1946-) Editor magazine, television personality.

Taylor, Susie King. (1848-1912) Civil War nurse, educator, slave.

Te Ata. (1897-1995) Chicksaw Indian folklorist, storyteller.

Teasdale, Sara. (1884-1933) Poet.

Tebe, Marie. (d. 1901) Civil War soldier, disguised as man, born France.

Temple, Shirley. (1928-) Actor, ambassador.

Tenayuca, Emma. (1916-1999) Workers' rights activist.

Terrell, Mary Church. (1863-1954) Civil rights activist, suffragist, women's rights activist.

Terry, Ellen. (unknown) Entrepreneur real estate.

Teters, Charlene. (1950-) Spokane Indian mixed-media artist, Native American rights activist, painter.

Tharp, Marie. (1920-) Oceanographer.

Tharp, Twyla. (1941-) Choreographer.

Tharpe, Sister Rosetta. (1921-1973) Jazz singer.

Thayer, Helen. (1938-) Arctic explorer, mountaineer, olympic track and field athlete, born New Zealand.

Thomas, Debi. (1967-) Olympic figure skater, physician.

Thomas, Helen. (1920-) Journalist.

Thomas, Piri. (1928-) Author.

Thomas, Valerie. (1943-) Inventor, mathematician, physicist.

Thompson, Dorothy. (1893-1961) Journalist, suffragist.

Thompson, Jennie. (1981-) Olympic gymnast.

Thompson, Mary Harris. (1829-1895) Educator, physician.

Thoms, Adah Belle. (1870-1943) Public health pioneer, World War I nurse.

Tibbles, Suzette LaFlesche. (1854-1903) Ponca and Omaha Indian Native American rights activist.

Tiburzi, Bonnie Linda. (1948-) Pilot.

Tingley, Katherine. (1847-1929) Human rights activist, spiritual leader, utopian community founder.

Toguri, Iva "Tokyo Rose." (1916-1988) World War II traitor.

Toklas, Alice B. (1877-1967) Author, partner of Gertrude Stein.

Tomara, Sonia. (d. 1982) Journalist, World War II correspondent, born Russia.

Torrence, Gwen. (1965-) Olympic sprinter, track and field athlete.

Totino, Rose. (1915-1994) Entrepreneur food/restaurants.

Tower, Joan. (1938-) Composer.

Trotter, Mildred. (1899-1991) Anatomist, anthropologist, forensic scientist.

Truman, Elizabeth "Bess" Wallace. (1885-1982) First Lady.

Truth, Sojourner. (1797-1883) Abolitionist, author, spiritual leader, suffragist, women's rights activist.

Tsinhnahjinnie, Hulleah. (1954-) Navajo/Creek/Seminole Indian photographer.

Tubman, Harriet. (1820-1913) Abolitionist, Civil War spy, nurse, slave.

Tuchman, Barbara Wertheim. (1912-1989) Historian. Pulitzer Prize winner.

Tucker, Sophie. (1887-1966) Singer.

Tyler, Anne. (1941-) Author. Pulitzer Prize winner.

Tyler, Julia Gardiner. (1820-1889) Civil War author, First Lady.

Tyler, Letitia Christian. (1790-1842) First Lady.

Tyson, Cicely. (1933-) Actor.

Tyus, Wyomia. (1945-) Olympic track and field athlete.

Uchida, Yoshiko. (1921-1992) Children's author.

Valdez, Patssi. (1951-) Painter.

Van Buren, Abigail. *See* Phillips, Pauline Esther.

Van Buren, Hannah Hoes. (1783-1819) First Lady.

Van Dyken, Amy. (1973-) Olympic swimmer.

Van Hoosen, Bertha. (1863-1952) Medical researcher, physician.

Van Lew, Elizabeth. (1818-1900) Civil War

spy.

Vaughan, Sarah. (1924-1991) Jazz musician, singer.

Vaz, Katherine. (unknown) Author.

Velarde, Pablita. (1918-) Santa Clara Pueblo Indian painter.

Velazquez, Loreta Janeta. (1842-?) Civil War soldier, disguised as man.

Velazquez, Nydia. (1953-) Congresswoman, born Puerto Rico.

Veney, Bethany. (1815-?) Author, slave.

Venturini, Tisha. (1973-) Olympic soccer player.

Vergoose, Elizabeth "Mother Goose." (unknown) Colonial storyteller.

Villa-Komaroff, Lydia. (1947-) Molecular biologist, medical researcher, physician.

Vinson, Phyllis Tucker. (1948-) Television filmmaker.

Voigt, Cynthia. (1942-) Young adult author.

Wade, Cheryl Marie. (unknown) Disability rights activist, poet.

Wadhwa, Meenakshi. (1967-) Astronomer, space scientist, born India.

Waheenee. (1841-?) Hidatsa Indian historian.

Wait, Bethany. (1973-1991) Young rescuer of people in storm.

Wakefield, Ruth. (1905-1977) Entrepreneur cookies, inventor.

Wald, Lillian. (1867-1940) Nurse, public health worker, social worker.

Walden, Barbara. (1936-) Entrepreneur cosmetics.

Walker, Alice. (1944-) Author. Pulitzer Prize winner.

Walker, Judith Cary. (1889-1973) Radio broadcaster.

Walker, Kate. (1842-1931) Lighthouse keeper.

Walker, Madame C. J. *See* Walker, Sarah Breedlove McWilliams.

Walker, Maggie Lena. (1867-1934) Entrepreneur banker, journalist.

Walker, Margaret. (1915-1998) Author.

Walker, Mary Edwards. (1832-1919) Civil War surgeon, physician, women's rights activist. Congressional Medal of Honor recipient.

Walker, Sarah Breedlove McWilliams "Madame C. J." (1867-1919) Entrepreneur cosmetics, human rights activist, inventor.

Wall, Rachel. (1760-1789) Pirate.

Wallace, Sippie. (1898-1986) Jazz singer.

Walsh, Mary. (1950-) Vietnam War Army physicial therapist.

Walters, Barbara. (1931-) Broadcast journalist.

Wang, Vera. (1949-) Fashion designer.

Ward, Catherine Barnes. (1851-1913) Photographer.

Ward, Nancy. (1738-1822) American Revolutionary War patriot, Cherokee Indian leader, peace activist.

Waring, Laura Wheeler. (1877-1948) Painter.

Warren, Adelina Otero. (1881-1965) Author, educator.

Warren, Mercy Otis. (1728-1814) American Revolutionary War patriot, playwright.

Washington, Dinah. (1925-1959) Jazz singer.

Washington, Martha Dandridge Curtis. (1731-1802) First Lady.

Washington, Ora. (1898-1971) Basketball player, tennis player.

Wasserstein, Wendy. (1950-) Playwright. Pulitzer Prize winner.

Waters, Ethel. (1896-1977) Actor, jazz singer.

Waters, Maxine. (1938-) Congresswoman, state legislator.

Watson, Ella "Cattle Kate." (1861-1889) Outlaw, pioneer.

Watson-Schutze, Eva. (1867-1935) Photographer.

Wattleton, Faye. (1943-) Planned Parenthood president, women's rights activist.

Wauneka, Annie Dodge. (1910-1997) Navajo public health educator. Presidential Medal of Freedom recipient.

Weatherspoon, Teresa. (1965-) Olympic basketball player.

Webb, Sheyann. (1957-) Civil rights activist.

Weber, Lois. (1881-1939) Filmmaker.

Weddington, Sarah. (1945-) Attorney, women's rights activist.

Weems, Ann Marie. (1840-?) Fugitive slave, disguised as man.

Weems, Carrie Mae. (1951-) Photographer.

Weetamoo. (1640-1676) Pocasset Indian warrior.

Wells, Rebecca. (1952-) Author.

Wells, Rosemary. (1943-) Children's author, illustrator.

Wells-Barnett, Ida B. (1862-1931) Civil rights activist, journalist, reformer.

Welty, Eudora. (1909-2001) Author. Pulitzer Prize winner.

West, Dorothy. (1907-1998) Author.

West, Mae. (1893-1980) Actor, showwoman.

Westover, Cynthia. (1885-1931) Inventor.

Wharton, Edith. (1862-1937) Author. Pulitzer Prize winner.

Wheatley, Phillis. (1754-1784) American Revolutionary War patriot, poet.

White, Morgan. (1983-) Olympic gymnast.

Whitestone, Heather. (1973-) Beauty queen.

Whitfield, Princess. (1937-) Educator.

Whitman, Christine Todd. (1946-) Environmental Protection Agency head, governor.

Whitman, Narcissa. (1808-1847) Missionary, pioneer.

Whitney, Mary Watson. (1847-1920) Astronomer.

Whitton, Erin. (1971-) Olympic hockey player.

Whitworth, Kathy. (1939-) Golfer.

Whyte, Edna Gardner. (1902-1993) Aviator, nurse, World War II Naval Nurse Corps.

Wilder, Laura Ingalls. (1867-1957) Children's author, pioneer.

Willard, Emma Hart. (1787-1870) Educator, women's rights activist.

Willard, Frances Elizabeth. (1839-1898) Reformer, suffragist.

Williams, Abigail. (1680-?) Colonist, puritan, accused others of witchcraft.

Williams, Angela. (1980-) Olympic track and field athlete.

Williams, Eunice. (1697-1787) Colonist, Indian captive.

Williams, Jody. (1950-) Human rights activist, reformer. Nobel Peace Prize winner.

Williams, Lucinda. (1953-) Country singer.

Williams, Mary Lou. (1910-1981) Jazz musician.

Williams, Serena. (1981-) Tennis player.

Williams, Venus. (1980-) Tennis player.

Williams, Vera. (1927-) Children's author, illustrator.

Wilson, Ellen Louisa Axson. (1860-1914)

First Lady.

Wilson, Franny. (unknown) Civil War soldier, disguised as man.

Wilson, Harriet E. Adams. (1827?-1863?) Author.

Wilson, Luzena Stanley. (1821-?) Author, pioneer.

Wilson, Sharifa. (unknown) City official.

Wilson-Hawkins, Carla. (unknown) Educator.

Winblad, Ann. (1950-) Internet pioneer, financier.

Winema. (Tobey Riddle) (1836-1932) Modoc Indian Native American rights activist, peace activist.

Winfrey, Oprah. (1954-) Entrepreneur media conglomerate, filmmaker, television personality.

Winnemucca, Sarah. (1844-1891) Paiute Indian Native American rights activist.

Winslow, Anna Green. (1760-1779) Colonist.

Winyan Ohitika. Sioux legendary heroine.

Woerner, Louise. (unknown) Entrepreneur home health care.

Wong, Anna May. (1905-1961) Actor.

Wong, Jade Snow. (1922-) Author, ceramicist.

Wong-Staal, Flossie. (1947-) Medical researcher, born China.

Woodard, Alfre. (1953-) Actor.

Woodard, Lynette. (1959-) Olympic basketball player.

Woodhull, Victoria. (1838-1927) Journalist, presidential candidate, suffragist, women's rights activist.

Workman, Fanny Bullock. (1859-1925) Explorer, mountaineer, women's rights activist.

Wright, Jane Cooke. (1919-) Medical researcher, physician.

Wright, Patience Lovell. (1725-1786) American Revolutionary War patriot, sculptor, spy.

Wu, Chien Shiung. (1912-1997) Nuclear physicist, born China.

Yalow, Rosalyn Sussman. (1921-) Medical reseacher, physicist. Nobel Prize winner.

Yamaguchi, Kristi. (1971-) Olympic figure skater.

Yamamoto, Hisaye. (1921-) Author.

Yeager, Jenna L. (1952-) Aviator.

Young, Ann Eliza Webb. (1844-1908) Pioneer, reformer.

Young, Chavonda J. Jacobs. (1967-) Paper science engineer.

Young, Roger Arliner. (1889-1964) Educator, zoologist.

Young, Sheila. (1950-) Bicyclist, olympic speed skater.

Younger, Maud. (1870-1936) Community activist, human rights activist, women's rights activist, workers' rights activist.

Younghans, Maria. (1867-1918) Lighthouse keeper.

Younghans, Miranda. (fl. 1918-1929) Lighthouse keeper.

Zaharias, Mildred "Babe" Didrikson. (1913-1956) Golfer, olympic track and field athlete.

Zais, Karen. (unknown) Mechanical engineer.

Zakrzewska, Marie Elizabeth. (1829-1902) Physician, born Germany.

Zapata, Carmen. (1927-) Actor.

Zavala, Maria Elena. (unknown) Botanist, educator.

Zmeskal, Kim. (1976-) Olympic gymnast.

Zolotow, Charlotte. (1915-) Children's author, illustrator.

Zughaib, Helen. (1959-) Painter, born Lebanon.

Zwilich, Ellen. (1939-) Composer, jazz musician. Pulitzer Prize winner.

Arab

Khadijah. (Khadika bint Khuwaylid) (555-620) Muhammad's wife.

Argentine

Antokoletz, Maria Adele de. (unknown) Human rights activist.

Bonafini, Hebe de. (unknown) Human rights activist.

Perón, Eva "Evita." (1919-1952) Actor, political activist.

Sabatini, Gabriela. (1970-) Tennis player.

Assyrian

Semiramis. (c. 2000 B.C.) Warrior queen, legendary.

Australian

Court, Margaret Smith. (1942-) Tennis
  player.
Fraser, Dawn. (1937-) Olympic swimmer.
Freeman, Cathy. (1973-) Olympic track and
  field athlete.
George, Emma. (1974-) Olympic track and
  field athlete
Kenny, Elizabeth. (1880-1952) Medical
  researcher, World War I nurse.
Melba, Nellie. (1861-1931) Opera singer.
Seager, Joy Debenham. (1899-1991) Human
  rights activist, physician.
Timms, Michele. (1965-) Olympic basket-
  ball player, sportscaster.

Austrian

Chotek, Sophie. (1868-1914) Political activ-
  ist, wife of Archduke Ferdinand.
Loeb, Ilse. (unknown) Holocaust survivor.
Maria Theresa. (1717-1780) Archduchess,
  empress.
Moser-Proell, Annemarie. (1953-) Olympic
  skier.
Paradis, Maria Theresia von. (1759-1824)
  Composer, musician.
Pfeiffer, Ida. (1797-1858) Adventurer, au-
  thor.
Suttner, Bertha von. (1843-1914) Author,
  peace activist. Nobel Peace Prize winner.
Tilles, Helen. (unknown) Holocaust survi-
  vor.

Belgian

Belline, Germaine. (unknown) Holocaust
  rescuer.
Parker, Henriette. (1932-) Holocaust survivor.

Biblical Figures

New Testament
Elisabeth.
Martha.
Mary.
Mary, Magdalen.
Mary, Virgin.
Susanna.

Old Testament
Abigail.

Bathsheba.
Deborah. (c. 1150 B.C.) Mother of Israel.
Delilah.
Esther. (5th century B.C.) Persian queen.
Eve.
Hagar.
Hannah.
Judith.
Leah.
Miriam.
Naomi.
Rachel.
Rebekah.
Ruth.
Salome.
Sarah.

Brazilian
da Silva, Fabriola. (1979-) In-line skater.
Marcovaldi, Maria "Neca." (1948-) Conservationist.
Miranda, Carmen. (1909-1955) Actor,
  singer.
Muniz, Maria Antonia. (1762-1870) Matriarch.

Burmese
Suu Kyi, Daw Aung San. (1945-) Human
  rights activist, peace activist. Nobel Peace
  Prize winner. Presidential Medal of Freedom recipient.

Byzantian
Comnena, Anna. (1083-1148) Historian,
  princess, religious reformer.

Canadian
Abbott, Maude Elizabeth Seymour. (1869-
  1940) Medical researcher, physician.
Atwood, Margaret. (1939-) Author, poet.
Bedard, Myriam. (1969-) Olympic biathlon
  athlete.
Bourne, Shae-Lynn. (1976-) Olympic figure
  skater.
Boyd, Liona. (1949-) Musician.
Campbell, Kim. (1947-) Prime Minister.
Caron, Nadine. (1970-) Physician.
Eastwood, Alice. (1859-1953) Botanist.
Edwards, Eileen Regina. (Shania Twain)
  (1965-) Singer, songwriter.
Galdikas, Birute. (1946-) Primatologist,

born West Germany.

Goforth, Rosalind Smith. (1864-1942) Missionary.

Hart, Pearl. (1871-1925) Outlaw.

Hickson, Catherine. (1955-) Geologist, volcanologist.

Hogg, Helen Battles Sawyer. (1905-1993) Astronomer.

Hubbard, Mina Benson. (1870-1956) Explorer.

Laumann, Silken. (1965-) Olympic rower.

Little, Jean. (1932-) Children's author.

McLachlan, Sarah. (1968-) Singer, songwriter.

Montgomery, Lucy Maud "L. M." (1874-1942) Children's author, novelist.

Moodie, Geraldine Fitzgibbon. (1854-1945) Photographer.

Morissette, Alanis. (1974-) Pop singer.

Petitclerc, Chantal. (1969-) Wheelchair athlete.

Pickford, Mary. (1893-1979) Actor.

Pitcher, Harriet Brooks. (1876-1933) Physicist.

Rheaume, Manon. (1972-) Hockey player.

Rijnhart, Susie Carson. (1868-1908) Explorer, missionary.

Robinson, Jennifer. (1976-) Olympic figure skater.

Rosenfeld, Bobbie. (1904-1969) Olympic track and field athlete.

Salé, Jamie. (1977-) Olympic figure skater.

Schmirler, Sandra. (1964-2000) Olympic curler.

Stowe, Emily Jennings. (1831-1903) Abolitionist, physician, suffragist, women's rights activist.

Teasdale, Lucille. (1929-1996) Human rights activist, physician.

Twain, Shania. *See* Edwards, Eileen Regina.

Vaux-Walcott, Mary. (1860-1940) Mountaineer, naturalist.

Wickenheiser, Hayley. (1969-) Olympic hockey player.

Celt

Boudicca. (28-62) Queen.

Morrigan. Goddess of war.

Scathach. Warrior goddess.

Chilean

Allende, Isabel. (1942-) Author.

Mistral, Gabriela Lucila Godoy y Alcayága. (1889-1957) Educator, poet. Nobel Prize winner.

Chinese

Ban Zhao. (45-116) Historian.

Cheng I Sao. (Lady Ching) (1775-1844) Pirate.

Chin Ch'iu. (1879-1907) Women's rights activist.

Hua Mu-lan. (c. 400) Warrior, disguised as man.

Jie, Ling. (1982-) Olympic gymnast.

Lai Cho San. (1922-1939) Pirate.

Li Ch'ing Chao. (1084-1151) Poet.

Ling, Chai. (1966-) Political activist.

Lu, Chen. (1976-) Olympic figure skater.

Qiu Jin. (1875-1907) Poet, revolutionary, women's rights activist.

Soong Ai-ling. (1889-1973) Financier, philanthropist.

Soong Ching-ling. (1893-1981) Peace activist, wife of Sun Yat-Sen.

Soong May-Ling. (1897-2003) Sociologist, wife of Chiang Kai-Shek.

Tz-u-hsi. (1835-1908) Empress.

Wen-Chi, Lady. (c. 178) Poet.

Wu Chao. (625-705) Empress.

Yani, Wang. (1975-) Painter.

Zheng, Haixia. (1967-) Olympic basketball player.

Colombian

Ripoll, Shakira Mebarak. (Shakira) (1977-) Pop singer.

Salavarrieta, Policarpa. "La Pola." (1795-1817) Political activist.

Cuban

Alonso, Alicia. (1921-) Ballet dancer.

Lopez, Lourdes. (1958-) Dancer.

Czechoslovakian

Caslavska, Vera. (1942-) Olympic gymnast.

Gutman, Sarel. (17th century) Merchant.

Laitman, Helen Kornitzer. (unknown) Holocaust survivor.

Navratilova, Martina. (1956-) Tennis player.
Schindler, Emilie. (1909-2001) Holocaust
  rescuer.
Tiktiner, Rivkah bat Meir "Rebecca." (16th
  century) Author.

Danish
Brahe, Sophie. (1556-1643) Astronomer.

Dominican
Charles, Eugenia. (1919-) Prime Minister of
  Dominica.

Dutch
Blankers-Koen, Fanny. (1918-2004) Olym-
  pic track and field athlete.
Frank, Anne. (1929-1945) Author, Holo-
  caust victim, born Germany.
Gies, Miep. (1909-) Holocaust rescuer, born
  Austria.
Hasselaar, Kenau. (1526-1588) Political
  activist.
Leyster, Judith. (1609-1660) Painter.
Merian, Anna Marie Sibylla. (1647-1717)
  Illustrator, naturalist.
Polak, Ina. (1923-) Holocaust survivor.
Pritchard, Marion van Binsbergen. (1920-)
  Holocaust rescuer.
Sokolow, Yvonne Kray. (1927-) Holocaust
  survivor.
Ten Boom, Corrie. (1892-1979) Author,
  Holocaust rescuer.
Tinne, Alexandrine. (1839-1869) Explorer.
Van der Woude, Elizabeth. (1657-1694)
  Adventurer.
Wijsmuller, Gertrude. (unknown) Holocaust
  rescuer, social worker.
Zelle, Margareta Gertrude. (Mata Hari)
  (1876-1917) Dancer, World War I spy.

Egyptian
Cleopatra VII. (69-30 B.C.) Ruler.
Cleopatra Selene of Mauretania. (40 B.C.-6
  A.D.) Daughter of Cleopatra VII.
Hatshepsut. (1500-1460 B.C.) Pharoah.
Hypathia. (Hypatia) (355-415) Astronomer,
  mathematician, philosopher.
Mary Prophetetissa of Alexandria. (1st cen-
  tury A.D.) Chemist, inventor.
Nefertari. (fl. 1270 B.C.) Queen.
Nefertiti. (fl. 1372-1350 B.C.) Queen.

Shaarawi, Huda. (1879-1947) Women's
  rights activist.
Tiye. (fl. 1370 B.C.) Queen.
Wuhsha. (11th century) Entrepreneur
  banker.

English
Aguilar, Grace. (1816-1847) Author,
  scholar.
Amanpour, Christiane. (1958-) Broadcast
  journalist, Gulf War correspondent.
Anderson, Elizabeth Garrett. (1836-1917)
  Physician.
Anne. (1665-1714) Queen.
Anning, Mary. (1799-1847) Paleontologist.
Austen, Jane. (1775-1817) Author.
Aylward, Gladys. (1902-1970) Missionary,
  World War I spy.
Baker, Florence von Sass. (1841-1916) Ex-
  plorer, born Romania.
Behn, Aphra Johnson. (1640?-1689) Play-
  wright, poet, spy.
Bell, Gertrude. (1868-1926) Adventurer,
  archaeologist, explorer.
Benham, Gertrude. (1867-1938) Mountain-
  eer.
Besant, Annie. (1847-1933) Human rights
  activist, journalist, orator, reformer.
Bishop, Isabella Bird. (1831-1904) Explorer.
Blunt, Lady Anne. (1837-1917) Explorer.
Boleyn, Anne. (1507-1536) Wife of Henry
  VIII.
Booth, Catherine. (1829-1890) Co-founder
  of Salvation Army, human rights activist.
Bronte, Anne. (1820-1849) Author.
Bronte, Charlotte. (1816-1855) Author, poet.
Bronte, Emily. (1818-1848) Author, poet.
Browning, Elizabeth Barrett. (1806-1861)
  Poet.
Burbridge, E. Margaret. (1919-) Astrono-
  mer.
Carpenter, Iris. (unknown) Journalist, World
  War II correspondent.
Cartland, Barbara. (1901-2000) Author.
Catherine of Aragon. (1485-1536) Queen.
Caton-Thompson, Gertrude. (1888-1985)
  Archaeologist.
Cavanagh, Kit. (Christian Walsh) (1667-
  1739) Soldier, disguised as man.
Cavell, Edith. (1865-1915) Educator, World
  War I nurse and heroine.

Cheesman, Lucy Evelyn. (1881-1969) Entomologist.

Christie, Agatha. (1891-1976) Author.

Darling, Grace. (1815-1842) Lighthouse keeper's daughter who rescued people when she was very young.

Diana. (1961-1997) Princess of Wales. Human rights activist.

Dixie, Florence. (1857-1905) Adventurer, author, women's rights activist.

Dodwell, Christina. (1951-) Adventurer, author.

Eliot, George. *See* Evans, Mary Ann.

Elizabeth I. (1533-1603) Queen.

Elizabeth II. (1926-) Queen.

Evans, Mary Ann. (George Eliot) (1819-1880) Author, disguised as man.

Fountaine, Margaret. (1862-1940) Author, environmentalist, lepidopterist.

Franklin, Rosalind Elsie. (1920-1958) Molecular biologist, x-ray crystallographer.

Freud, Anna. (1895-1982) Physician, psychoanalyst, born Austria.

Frith, Mary "Moll Cutpurse." (1590-1659) Pickpocket.

Fry, Elizabeth. (1780-1845) Human rights activist, prison reformer.

Garrod, Dorothy. (1892-1968) Archaeologist.

Godiva, Lady. (1010-1067) Countess, reformer, folk heroine.

Goodall, Jane. (1934-) Primatologist.

Goodwin, Jan. (1944-) Journalist.

Guinevere. (6th century) Princess, married to King Arthur, folk heroine.

Gwendolen. (fl. 1075-1060 B.C.) Warrior queen.

Hall, Radclyffe. (1886-1943) Author, poet, dressed as man.

Hepworth, Barbara. (1903-1975) Sculptor.

Herschel, Caroline. (1750-1848) Astronomer, born Germany.

Hilda of Whitby. (614-680) Educator, saint, spiritual leader.

Hodgkin, Dorothy Crowfoot. (1910-1994) Chemist, x-ray crystallographer. Nobel Prize winner.

Jex-Blake, Sophia. (1840-1912) Educator, physician.

Johnson, Amy. (1903-1941) Aviator, World War II pilot.

Julian of Norwich. (1342-1416) Nun, religious mystic.

Kempe, Margery. (1373-1440) Author.

Kenyon, Kathleen. (1906-1978) Archaeologist.

Killigrew, Lady Elizabeth. (1530-1570) Pirate.

Kingsley, Mary. (1862-1900) Adventurer, author, explorer.

Leakey, Mary. (1913-1996) Anthropologist, archaeologist.

Lovelace, Lady Ada Byron. (1815-1852) Computer scientist, mathematician.

Manley, Mary. (1663-1724) Author, journalist, women's rights activist.

Mansfield, Katherine. (1888-1923) Author, born New Zealand.

Margaret. (1930-2002) Princess.

Markham, Beryl. (1902-1986) Author, aviation pioneer, pilot.

Mary I. (Mary Tudor) (1516-1558) Queen England and Ireland.

Mary II. (1662-1694) Queen of England, Scotland, and Ireland.

Matilda of England. (1102-1167) Princess, empress.

Mazuchelli, Nina. (1832-1914) Explorer, mountaineer.

Mee, Margaret Ursula Brown. (1909-1988) Botanist, painter.

Montagu, Lily. (1873-1963) Spiritual leader, established Liberal Judaism.

Montagu, Lady Mary Wortley. (1689-1762) Author.

Montefiore, Lady Judith Cohen. (1784-1862) Human rights activist, philanthropist.

Murdoch, Iris. (1919-1999) Author, born Ireland.

Nicholson, Vanessa-Mae. (1978-) Musician.

Nightingale, Florence. (1820-1910) Nurse, Crimean War head of nurses.

North, Marianne. (1830-1890) Illustrator.

Opie, Iona. (1923-) Children's author, folklorist, illustrator, scholar.

Oxenbury, Helen. (1938-) Children's author, illustrator.

Pankhurst, Christabel. (1880-1958) Suffragist.

Pankhurst, Emmeline. (1858-1928) Suffragist.

Potter, Beatrix. (1866-1943) Children's author, illustrator.

Quant, Mary. (1934-) Fashion designer.

Raine, Kathleen. (1908-2003) Mystic, poet.

Read, Mary. (1690-1720) Pirate, disguised as man.

Riley, Bridget. (1931-) Painter.

Roddick, Anita. (1942-) Entrepreneur beauty supplies.

Roper, Margaret More. (1505-1544) Scholar.

Rossetti, Christina Georgina. (1830-1894) Art model, poet.

Rowling, Joanne Kathleen "J. K." (1965-) Children's author.

Sarah. Duchess of York. (1959-) Princess.

Saunders, Cicely. (1918-) Physician.

Sayers, Dorothy L. (1893-1957) Author.

Scott, Sheila. (1927-1988) Aviation pioneer, World War II nurse.

Shelley, Mary. (1797-1851) Author.

Simpson, Bessie Wallis Warfield Spencer. (1896-1986) Duchess of Windsor, born U.S.

Smyth, Ethel. (1858-1944) Composer, suffragist.

Stark, Freya. (1893-1993) Adventurer, explorer.

Stuart, Miranda. (James Barry) (1795-1865) Civil War soldier disguised as man, physician.

Terry, Ellen. (1847-1928) Actor.

Thatcher, Margaret. (1925-) Prime Minister. Presidential Medal of Freedom recipient.

Victoria. (1819-1901) Queen.

Weldon, Fay. (1931-) Author.

Wollstonecraft, Mary. (1759-1797) Author, women's rights activist.

Woolf, Virginia. (1882-1941) Author.

Wordsworth, Dorothy. (1771-1855) Poet.

Filipino

Aquino, Corazon. (1933-) President.

del Mundo, Fe. (1911-) Human rights activist, physician.

French

Baret, Jeanne. (1740?-1803?) Naturalist.

Barré-Sinoussi, Françoise. (1947-) Chemist, medical researcher.

Beauharnais, Josephine. (1763-1814) Empress.

Beauvoir, Simone de. (1908-1986) Author, philosopher, women's rights activist.

Bernhardt, Sarah. (1844-1923) Actor.

Bonaly, Surya. (1973-) Olympic figure skater.

Bonheur, Rosa. (1822-1899) Painter.

Boulanger, Nadia. (1887-1979) Composer, conductor.

Carré, Lily. (1908-) World War II spy.

Catherine de Medici. (1519-1589) Queen.

Chanel, Gabrielle "Coco." (1883-1971) Fashion designer.

Churchill, Odette Brailly Sansom. (1912-1995) World War II Resistance worker.

Claudel, Camille. (1864-1943) Sculptor.

Clicquot-Ponsardin, Nicole-Barbe. (1777-1866) Winemaker.

Clotilda. (470-545) Saint, spiritual leader, wife of Clovis.

Cohn, Marianne. (1924-1944) Holocaust resistance, victim.

Cresson, Edith. (1934-) Prime Minister.

Curie, Marie Sklodowska. (1867-1934) Chemist, inventor, physicist, born Poland. Nobel Prize winner.

David-Neel, Alexandra. (1868-1969) Adventurer, explorer.

Deneuve, Catherine. (1943-) Actor.

du Chatelet, Marquise Gabrielle-Emilie. (1706-1749) Mathematician, physicist.

Dupin, Amandine Aurore Lucie. (George Sand) (1804-1876) Author, disguised as man.

Eleanor of Aquitaine. (1122-1204) Queen.

Geoffrin, Thérese Roget. (1699-1777) Patron of the arts.

Germain, Sophie. (1776-1831) Mathematician.

Héloise. (1098-1164) Abbess, lover of Abelard.

Joan of Arc. (1412-1431) Military leader, Saint.

Joliot-Curie, Irène. (1897-1956) Chemist, physicist.

Laroche, Raymonde de. (1886-1919) Aviation pioneer

Lavoisier, Marie. (1758-1836) Chemist.

Mahaut, Countess de Artois. (1275-1329) Noblewoman.

Maria, "Madame." (unknown) Holocaust rescuer.

Marie Antoinette. (1755-1793) Princess, queen.

Morisot, Berthe. (1841-1895) Painter.

Peizerat, Gwendal. (1972-) Olympic figure skater.

Pizan, Christine de. (1365-1430) Author, poet.

Roland, Madame Jeanne-Marie "Manon." (1754-1793) Political activist, revolutionary.

Sand, George. *See* Dupin, Amandine Aurore Lucie.

Spoerry, Anne. (1918-1999) Missionary, physician, World War II resistance worker.

Stael, Madame Anna Louise Germaine de. (1766-1817) Author, noblewoman.

Thible, Elizabeth. (fl. 1784) Aviation pioneer.

Trocme, Magda. (unknown) Holocaust rescuer.

Tussaud, Marie. (1761-1850) Sculptor.

Vigee-Le Brun, Elisabeth. (1755-1842) Painter.

Weil, Simone. (1909-1943) Author, political activist, revolutionary.

German

Adler, Henny. (1925-) Holocaust survivor.

Braun, Eva. (1912-1945) Hitler's mistress.

Clifford, Esther. (1921-) Holocaust survivor.

Cohn, Marianne. (1924-1944) Holocaust resistance worker, victim.

Dietrich, Amalie Nelle. (1821-1891) Botanist.

Dulcie of Worms. (12th century) Moneylender, scholar.

Ella bat Moses. (17th century) Printer.

Frank, Irene. (1927-) Holocaust survivor.

Frommet of Arwyller. (15th century) Scribe.

Gela bat Moses. (18th century) German printer.

Gloria von Thurn und Taxis. (1960-) Princess.

Gluckel of Hameln. (1646-1724) Author.

Graf, Steffi. (1969-) Tennis player.

Hensel, Fanny Mendelssohn. (1805-1847) Composer.

Hildegarde von Bingen. (1098-1179) Spiritual leader, visionary.

Klarsfeld, Beate. (1939-) Nazi hunter.

Koch, Ilse. (1906-1967) Nazi war criminal.

Kollwitz, Kaethe. (1867-1945) Painter, sculptor.

Kuehn, Ruth. (unknown) World War II spy.

Liebmann, Hanne Eve Hirsch. (1924-) Holocaust survivor.

Luxemburg, Rosa. (1870-1919) Political activist, revolutionary, workers rights activist, born Poland.

Mata Hari. *See* Zelle, Margareta Gertrude.

Meinhof, Ulrike. (1934-1976) Journalist, revolutionary.

Noether, Emmy. (1882-1935) Mathematician.

Otto, Kristen. (1966-) Olympic swimmer.

Pappenheim, Berta. (1859-1936) Organization founder, social reformer, social worker.

Reiche, Maria. (1903-1998) Mathematician.

Reitsch, Hanna. (1912-1979) Aviator, test pilot.

Ridesel, Baroness Frederika von. (1746-1808) American Revolutionary War camp follower, author.

Riefenstahl, Leni. (1902-2003) Filmmaker.

Scholl, Sophie. (1921-1943) Holocaust resistance fighter, victim.

Schumann, Clara. (1819-1896) Composer, musician.

Stommer, Helga Edelstein. (1926-) Holocaust survivor.

Urania of Worms, Lady. (13th Century) Cantor.

Weekly, Frieda von Richthofen. (1870-1956) Wife of D. H. Lawrence.

Winkler-Kühne, Ruth. (1931-) Holocaust rescuer.

Witt, Katarina. (1965-) Olympic figure skater.

Zelle, Margareta Gertrude. (Mata Hari) (1876-1917) Dancer, World War I spy.

Goddesses

Egyptian

Hathhor. Goddess of love.

Isis. (c. 3000 B.C.)

Nekhebet. Goddess of royal protection.

Nepatys. Goddess of the morning.

Nut. Goddess of the sky.

Tefnut. Goddess of the morning dew.

Greek

Athena

Diana

Mayan

Ix Chel. Goddess of childbirth.

Ix Tab. Goddess of suicide.

Norse

Freya. Goddess of love and beauty.

Frigga. Goddess of marriage.

Hela. Goddess of death.

Idunn. Goddess of youth.

Greek, Ancient
Agnodice. (c. 300 B.C.) Physician.
Aspasia. (c. 470-410 B.C.) Women's rights activist.
Helen of Troy. (1200-1150 B.C.) Heroine Troy War, legendary.
Hipparchia of Athens. (c. 330 B.C.) Philosopher.
Sappho of Lesbos. (625-570 B.C.) Poet.

Greek, Modern
Callas, Maria. (1923-1977) Opera singer.
Hadjidaki-Marder, Elpida. (1948-) Marine archaeologist.

Guatemalan
Menchú, Rigoberta. (1959-) Human rights activist.

Haitian
Jean-Murat, Carolle. (1950-) Educator, human rights activist, physician, public health activist.

Hawaiian
Ka'lulani. (1875-1899) Princess.
Liliuokalani, Lydia. (1838-1917) Composer, musician, queen.
Pukui, Mary Kawena. (1895-1986) Hawaiian folklorist, linguist.

Hebrew, Ancient
Beruriah. (2nd century) Talmudic scholar.
Dahia al-Kahina. (fl. 680) North African freedom fighter, queen
Deborah. (c. 1150 B.C.E.) Mother of Israel.
Esther. (5th century) Queen.
Ima Shalom. (50-?) Talmudic woman.
Jael of Israel. (120-100 B.C.E.) Political activist.

Hungarian
Bihaly, Judith. (1934-) Holocaust survivor.
Heyman, Eva. (1931-1944) Author, Holocaust victim.
Leitner, Isabella Katz. (1924-) Holocaust survivor.
Perl, Gisella. (1910-1985) Holocaust survivor, physician.
Senesh, Hannah. (1921-1944) Author, resistance fighter, victim.

Icelandic
Finnbogadottir, Vigadis. (1930-) President.
Gudmundsdottir, Bjork. (Bjork) (1966-) Pop singer.

Indian and Asian
Bai, Lakshmi. (1830-1858) Military leader, ruler.
Bojaxhiu, Agnes. (Mother Teresa) (1910-1997) Human rights activist, missionary, born Yugoslavia. Nobel Peace Prize winner, Presidential Medal of Freedom recipient.
Devi. Legendary East Indian goddess/warrior queen.
Devi, Gayatri "Ayesha." (1919-) Political activist, Princess.
Devi, Phoolan. (1963-) Criminal, political activist.
Gandhi, Indira. (1917-1984) Prime Minister.
Jhirad, Jerusha. (1891-1948) Physician.
Kabir. (1440-1518) Philosopher, poet.
Khan, Noor Inayat. (1914-1944) Holocaust resistance worker, victim.
Mangeshkar, Lata. (1929-2001) Singer.
Mirabi. (1498-1565) Poet.
Rajalakshmi, R. (1926-) Biochemist.
Ramabai, Pandita. (1858-1922) Human rights activist.
Rangada. Hindu woman warrior.
Razia, Sultana. (fl. 1236-1240) Muslim warrior princess.

Iraqi
Bat Ha-Levi. (12th century) Scholar.

Irish
Bonney, Anne. (1697-1721) Pirate.
Burnell, Jocelyn Bell. (1943-) Astronomer.
Carmichael, Amy. (1867-1951) Missionary.
Corrigan, Mairead. (1944-) Peace activist. Nobel Peace Prize winner.
Mallon, Mary "Typhoid Mary." (1870-1938) Cook, maid, folk hero.
Markiewiecz, Constance. (1867-1927) Political activist.
McAliskey, Bernadette Devlin. (1947-) Civil rights activist, political activist.
Murphy, Dervla. (1931-) Author, explorer.
O'Hara, Mary. (1935-) Musician, singer.
O'Malley, Grace. (1530-1603) Pirate.

Robinson, Mary. (1944-) President.

Williams, Betty. (1943-) Peace activist, reformer. Nobel Peace Prize winner.

Israeli

Arad, Yael. (1967-) Olympic judo athlete.

Chizick, Sarah. (1897-) Settler.

Fink, Ida. (1921-) Author, Holocaust survivor, playwright, born Poland.

Herodias. (1st century C.E.) Israeli queen.

Leibowitz, Nehama. (1905-1997) Broadcast journalist, scholar.

Meir, Golda. (1898-1978) Prime Minister, born Russia.

Shochat, Manya. (1880-1961) Settler, former revolutionary in Russia, born Russia.

Italian

Abrabanel, Benvenida. (d. 1560) Political activist, scholar, born Spain.

Agnesi, Maria Gaetana. (1718-1799) Mathematician.

Anguissola, Sofonisba. (1532-1625) Painter.

Ascarelli, Devorah. (16th century) Poet, scholar.

Bassi, Laura. (1711-1778) Physicist.

Borgia, Lucrezia. (1480-1519) Ruler, villainess, folk hero.

Catherine of Siena. (1353-1386) Human rights activist, mystic, poet, spiritual leader.

Colonna, Vittoria. (1490-1547) Reformer.

Deledda, Grazia. (1871-1936) Author. Nobel Prize winner.

D'Este, Beatrice. (1475-1497) Patron of arts.

D'Este, Isabella. (1474-1539) Patron of arts.

Duse, Eleanora. (1859-1924) Actor.

Fontana, Lavinia. (1552-1614) Painter.

Gentileschi, Artemisia. (1593-1652) Painter.

Giaconda, Lisa. (1479-1509) Model for Mona Lisa.

Kauffmann, Angelica. (1741-1807) Painter.

Mansi, Paula dei. (13th century) Italian scribe, scholar.

Montessori, Maria. (1870-1952) Educator, physician.

Morpurgo, Rachel Luzzatto. (1790-1871) Poet.

Platearius, Trotula. (c. 1080) Physician.

Rossi, Europa di. (Madame Europa) (16th century) Singer.

Scifi, Claire of Assisi. (1193-1252) Saint.

Shapira-Luria, Miriam. (15th century) Educator.

Sichelgaita. (d. 1090) Princess of Lombard.

Sirani, Elizabeth. (1638-1665) Painter.

Strozzi, Barbara. (1619-1664?) Composer.

Sullam, Sara Coppio. (1592-1641) Poet, scholar.

Jamaican

Seacole, Mary. (1805-1881) Nurse.

Japanese

Hani Motoko. (1873-1957) Journalist.

Ichikawa Fusae. (1893-1981) Political activist, suffragist, women's rights activist.

Koken. (718-770) Empress, Buddhist nun.

Komyo. (701-760) Empress, Buddhist nun.

Midori. (1971-) Musician.

Mitsui, Shuho. (1590-1676) Businesswoman.

Murasaki, Shikibu. (978?-1030?) Author.

Mutsuhito. (1852-1912) Empress.

Okuni. (1571-1610) Kabuki actor.

Rikyu, Senno. (1522-1591) Tea ceremony expert.

Sarashina, Lady. (1008-?) Adventurer, author, poet.

Saruhashi, Katsuku. (1920-) Chemist.

Shonagon, Sei. (960s-?) Author.

Tabei Junko. (1939-) Mountaineer.

Yakami. Legendary heroine.

Korean

Sonduk. (610-647) Queen.

Kurd

Mizrahi, Asenath Barazani. (16th century) Educator, scholar.

Lithuanian

Borkowska, Anna. (c. 1900-?) Holocaust rescuer, spiritual leader.

Mexican

Bravo, Lola Alvarez. (1907-1993) Photographer, photojournalist.

Cruz, Juana Inés de la, Sister. (1651-1695) Poet, scholar.

Garduño, Flor. (1957-) Photographer.

Jimenez y Muro, Dolores. (1848-1925) Revolutionary.

Kahlo, Frida. (1907-1954) Painter.

Lifshitz, Aliza. (1951-) AIDS activist, author, editor, educator, physician.

Malinche. (Malintzin) (1500-1527) Princess, slave, translator.

Mendoza, Juana Belen Guiterrez. (1875-1942) Journalist, revolutionary.

Ortega, Beatriz Gonzalez. (unknown) Nurse during Revolution of 1910.

Pastrana, Julia. (1832-1860) Mexican "bearded lady" showperson.

New Zealander

Hodgson, Tasha. (1972-) In-line skater.

James, Naomi. (1949-) Adventurer, sailor.

Nicaraguan

Chamorro, Violeta Barrios de. (1929-) President.

Norwegian

Brundtland, Gro Harlem. (1939-) Physician, prime minister, World Health Organization head.

Henie, Sonia. (1912-1969) Figure skater.

Martha Louise. (1971-) Princess.

Pakistani

Bhutto, Benazir. (1953-) Prime Minister.

Peruvian

Grandmaison y Bruno Godin, Isabel. (1729-1792) Adventurer.

Rose of Lima. (1586-1617) Saint, spiritual leader.

Polish

Blair, Tonia Rothkopf. (1925-) Holocaust survivor.

Borkowska, Anna. (c. 1900-) Holocaust rescuer, spiritual leader.

Draenger, Tova. (1917-1943) Holocaust resistance worker, victim.

Horowitz, Sarah Rebecca Rachel Leah. (18th century) Scholar.

Kosmodemianskaya, Zoya. (1925-1943) Holocaust resistance worker, victim.

Kovner, Vitka Kempner. (1920-) Holocaust resistance worker.

Lazebnik, Faye. (unknown) Holocaust resistance worker, survivor.

Lerner, Bianca. (1929-) Holocaust survivor.

Lubetkin, Zivia. (1914-1978) Holocaust resistance worker, survivor.

Mandel, Basia. (1925-) Holocaust survivor.

Offenbach, Genia. (unknown) Holocaust survivor.

Opdyke, Irene. (1921-2003) Author, Holocaust resistance worker.

Prekerowa, Teresa. (1921-) Historian, Holocaust resistance worker.

Pulwer, Miriam. (unknown) Holocaust survivor.

Robota, Róza. (1921-1945) Holocaust resistance worker, victim.

Sander, Sally. (1925-) Holocaust survivor.

Schiff, Charlene. (1930-) Holocaust survivor.

Schnirer, Sarah. (1833-1935) Educator.

Shore, Ann Goldman. (1929-) Holocaust survivor.

Suchocka, Hanna. (1946-) Political leader.

Weinsberg, Alicia Fajnsztein. (1929-) Holocaust survivor.

Portuguese

Nasi, Dona Gracia. (1510-1568) Entrepreneur banking, shipping, philanthropist.

Rego, Paula. (1935-) Illustrator, painter, printmaker.

Puerto Rican

Fernandez, Beatriz Christina "Gigi." (1967-) Tennis player.

Martinez-Canas, Maria. (1960-) Photographer, born Cuba.

Rodriguez de Tio, Lola. (1843-1924) Poet, political activist, women's rights activist.

Santiago, Esmeralda. (1948-) Author.

Romanian

Amanar, Simona. (1979-) Olympic gymnast.

Basch, Civia Gelber. (1928-) Holocaust survivor.

Comaneci, Nadia. (1961-) Olympic gymnast.

Roman, Ancient

Agrippina the Young. (Agrippina Minor) (15-59) Mother of Nero, wife of Claudius.

Dionysia. (unknown) Olympic track and field athlete.

Hedea. (unknown) Olympic track and field athlete.

Helena, St. (250-330) Mother of Christianity.

Hortensia. (1st century B.C.) Orator, women's rights activist.

Livia. (Livia Drusilla) (58 B.C.-29 A.D.) Wife of Augustus.

Locusta of Gaul. (fl. 50 A.D.) Poisoner.

Tryphosa. (unknown) Olympic track and field athlete.

Russian

Akhmatova, Anna. (1889-1966) Poet.

Alexandra. (1872-1918) Czarina.

Anissina, Mariana. (1975-) Olympic figure skater.

Baiul, Oksana. (1977-) Ukrainian olympic figure skater.

Baranova, Elena. (1976-) Basketball player.

Berezhnaya, Elena. (1977-) Olympic figure skater.

Blavatsky, Helena Petrovna. (1831-1891) Spiritual leader, founder Theosophical movement.

Boguinskaia, Svetlana. (1973-) Olympic gymnast.

Bonner, Elena. (1923-) Political activist and dissident.

Catherine the Great. (1729-1796) Empress.

Khorkina, Svetlana. (1979-) Olympic gymnast.

Kollontai, Alexandra. (1872-1952) Ambassador, human rights activist, political activist, revolutionary, women's rights activist.

Korbut, Olga. (1955-) Olympic gymnast.

Kournikova, Anna. (1981-) Tennis player.

Kovalevskaia, Sofia. (1850-1891) Mathematician.

Kuznetsova, Irina Mihailovna. (1961-) Arctic explorer.

Kuznetsova, Valentina Mihailovna. (1937-) Arctic explorer.

Latynina, Larissa. (1934-) Olympic gymnast.

Litvak, Lily. (1921-1943) World War II fighter pilot.

Morozova, Feodosia. (1630-1675) Noblewoman.

Nicholaevna, Anastasia. (1901-1918) Princess.

Nicholaevna, Olga. (1895-1918) Princess.

Nicholaevna,Tatiana. (1897-1918) Princess.

Nudel, Ida. (1931-) Human rights activist, political dissident.

Pavlova, Anna. (1881-1931) Ballet dancer.

Savitskaya, Svetlana. (1948-) Cosmonaut.

Skoblikova, Lydia. (1939-) Olympic speed skater.

Slutskaya, Irina. (1979-) Olympic figure skater.

Smetanina, Raisa. (1953-) Olympic skier.

Tamara, Queen. (1156-1212) Medieval queen.

Tereshkova, Valentina. (1937-) Cosmonaut.

Wengeroff, Pauline. (1833-1916) Author.

Zasulich, Vera. (1849-1919) Revolutionary.

Saints

Apollonia.

Catherine of Alexandria. (4th century)

Cecilia.

Clotilda. (470-545)

Dorothy.

Helena. (250-330) Roman mother of Christianity.

Hilda of Whitby. (614-680) English.

Joan of Arc. (1412-1431) French.

Lucy. (d. 304)

Mary Magdalen.

Rose of Lima. (1586-1617) Peruvian nun.

Scifi, Claire of Assisi. (1193-1252) Italian.

Seton, Elizabeth Ann. (1774-1821)

Susanna. (d. 295)

Teresa of Avila. (151-1582) Spanish.

Scandinavian

Margaret I. (1353-1412) Queen.

Scottish

Chisholm, Mairí. (1896-?) Suffragist, World War I nurse.

Inglis, Elsie. (1864-1917) Physician, women's rights activist, World War I surgeon.

MacDonald, Flora. (1722-1790) American Revolutionary War musician.

Mary, Queen of Scots. (1547-1587) Queen.

Slessor, Mary. (1848-1915) Missionary.

Smith, Madelaine. (1835-1928) Criminal.

Somerville, Mary Fairfax. (1780-1872) Astronomer, mathematician, scholar, women's rights activist.

Singaporean

Tay, Jannie. (1945-) Entrepreneur wristwatch boutiques.

Spanish

Agustin, Maria. (La Saragossa) (1786-1857) Military leader.

Cristina. (1965-) Princess.

Egeria. (4th century) Adventurer, author, religious pilgrim.

Elena. (1964-) Princess.

Erauso, Catalina de. (1585-1650) Outlaw, disguised self as man.

Ibarurri, Dolores. (1895-1989) Political leader, revolutionary.

Isabella I. (1451-1504) Queen.

Saenz, Manuela. (1797-1856) Political activist.

Sanchez Vicario, Arantza. (1971-) Tennis player.

Saragossa, La. *See* Agostin, Maria.

Teresa, St. of Avila. (1515-1582) Mystic, saint.

Sri Lankan

Bandaranaike, Sirimavo. (1916-2000) Prime Minister.

Sumerian

Enheduana of Sumer. (fl. 2300 B.C.) Poet, priestess.

Swedish

Christina. (1626-1689) Queen.

Lindgren, Astrid. (1902-2002) Children's author.

Meitner, Lise. (1878-1968) Nuclear physicist, born Germany.

Myrdal, Alva. (1902-1986) Peace activist, sociologist, UNESCO founder. Nobel Peace Prize winner.

Swiss

Blom, Gertrude Elizabeth Loertscher Doby.

(1901-1993) Conservationist, photographer.

Hingis, Martina. (1980-) Tennis player, born Czechoslovakia.

Oppenheim, Meret. (1913-1985) Jewelry designer, painter, poet, sculptor, born Germany.

Syrian

Zenobia. (fl. 267-272) Queen.

Tarter

Aiyaruk, Princess. (c. 1280) Wrestler.

Thai

Hata, Prateep Ungsongtham. (1952-) Educator, human rights activist.

Transylvanian

Knopfler, Clara. (unknown) Holocaust survivor.

Turk

Ciller, Tansu. (1946-) Prime Minister.

Handali, Esther Kiera. (16th century) Human rights activist.

Iaia of Cyzicus. (fl. 90 B.C.) Painter.

Theodora. (497-548) Actor, empress, women's rights activist.

Yener, Kutlu Aslihan. (1946-) Archaeologist.

Ukrainian

Baiul, Oksana. (1977-) Olympic figure skater.

Kowalyk, Jonka. (unknown) Holocaust rescuer.

Podkopayeva, Lilia. (1978-) Olympic gymnast.

Sarah bat Tovim. (18th century) Prayer book author.

Vietnamese

Trung Nhi. (14-43) Warrior queen.

Trung Trac. (14-43) Warrior queen.

Viking, Ancient

Alfhild. (Alvida) (c. 1000) Pirate.

Aud the Deep Minded. (c. 900) Philosopher, scholar.

Eriksdottir, Freydis. (971-1010) Explorer of

Greenland.

Sela. (c. 420) Pirate, Viking princess.

Welsh

Leonowens, Anna. (1834-1915) Author, educator.

Yemenite

al-Sharki, Amatalrauf. (1958-) Women's rights activist.

Miriam the Scribe. (15th century) Scribe.

Sarah of Yemen. (7th century) Poet.

Yugoslavian

Eisen, Renata. (1929-) Holocaust survivor.

Filipovic, Zlata. (1980-) Author.

Women Disguised as Men

Bai, Lakshmi. (1830-1858) Indian military leader, ruler.

Bailey, Anne Trotter. (1743-1825) American Revolutionary War soldier, Indian scout.

Baret, Jeanne. (Jean Baré) (1740?-1803?) French naturalist.

Bonney, Anne. (1697-1721) Irish pirate.

Cavanagh, Kit. (Christian Walsh) (1667-1739) English soldier.

Clalin, Frances. (unknown) Civil War soldier.

Craft, Ellen. (1826-1897) Abolitionist, fugitive slave.

Dupin, Amandine Aurore Lucie. (George Sand) (1804-1876) French author.

Edmonds, Sarah Emma. (Franklin Thompson) (1841-1898) Civil War soldier, nurse, spy.

Erauso, Catalina de. (1585-1650) Spanish outlaw.

Evans, Mary Ann. (George Eliot) (1819-1880) English author.

Fields, Mary. (1832-1914) Pioneer businesswoman, slave.

Hall, Radclyffe. (1886-1943) English author, poet.

Hodgers, Jenny. (Albert Cashier) (1844-1915) Civil War soldier.

Hua Mu-Lan. (c. 400) Chinese warrior.

Quick, Flora. (Tom King) (unknown) Outlaw.

Read, Mary. (1690-1720) English pirate.

Sampson, Deborah. (Robert Shurtliff) (1760-1827) American Revolutionary War patriot and soldier.

Stuart, Miranda. (James Barry) (1795-1865) English Civil War soldier, physician.

Tebe, Marie. (d. 1901) Civil War soldier.

Velazquez, Loreta Janeta. (1842-?) Civil War soldier.

Weems, Ann Marie. (1840-) Fugitive slave.

Wilson, Franny. (unknown) Civil War soldier.

Women's Rights Activists

See also Suffragists.

Adams, Abigail. (1744-1818)

al-Sharki, Amatalrauf. (1958-) Yemenite.

Ames, Jessie Daniel. (1883-1972)

Anthony, Susan B. (1820-1906)

Aspasia. (c. 470-410 B.C.) Greek.

Avery, Byllye. (1937-)

Balch, Emily Greene. (1867-1961)

Barceló, Maria Gertrudes "Tules." (1800-1852)

Beauvoir, Simone de. (1908-1986) French.

Beecher, Catherine. (1800-1878)

Bloomer, Amelia Jenks. (1818-1894)

Boissevain, Inez Milholland. (1886-1916)

Boxer, Barbara. (1940-)

Brent, Margaret. (1606-1671)

Brown, Margaret Tobin "Molly." (1867-1932)

Campbell, Bonnie. (1948-)

Catt, Carrie Chapman. (1859-1947)

Chin, Ch'iu. (1879-1907) Chinese.

Chopin, Kate. (1850-1904)

Custer, Libbie. (1842-1933)

Day, Dorothy. (1897-1980)

Dewson, Molly. (1874-1962)

Dixie, Florence. (1857-1905) English.

Duniway, Abigail Scott. (1834-1915)

Eastman, Crystal. (1881-1928)

Friedan, Betty Goldstein. (1921-)

Gilman, Charlotte Perkins. (1860-1935)

Goldman, Emma. (1869-1940) born Lithuania.

Hahn, Emily. (1905-1997)

Hale, Sarah Josepha Buell. (1788-1879)

Harper, Frances E. W. (1825-1911)

Hortensia. (1st century B.C.) Roman.

Hutchinson, Anne Marbury. (1591-1643) born England.

Ichikawa, Fusae. (1893-1981) Japanese.
Inglis, Elsie. (1864-1917) Scottish.
Ireland, Patricia. (1945-)
Kennedy, Florence. (1916-2000)
Kollontai, Alexandra. (1872-1952) Russian.
Lockwood, Belva Ann. (1830-1917)
Lovejoy, Esther Pohl. (1869-1967)
Mahoney, Mary Eliza. (1845-1926)
Manley, Mary. (1663-1724) English.
Mann, Horace. (1796-1859)
Mathai-Davis, Prema. (1950-) born India.
Meyer, Annie Nathan. (1867-1951)
Moore, Audley. (1898-1997)
Morris, Esther. (1814-1902)
Mossell, Gertrude Bustill. (1855-1948)
Mott, Lucretia Coffin. (1793-1880)
Ossoli, Margaret Fuller. (1810-1850)
Pankhurst, Christabel. (1880-1928) English.
Pankhurst, Emmeline. (1858-1928) English.
Paul, Alice. (1885-1977)
Peterson, Esther. (1906-1997)
Purtell, Edna. (1900-1986)
Qiu Jin. (1875-1907) Chinese.
Ramirez, Sara Estela. (1881-1910) born
    Mexico.
Remond, Sarah P. (1826-1894)
Rodriguez de Tio, Lola. (1843-1924) Puerto
    Rican.
Rose, Ernestine Potowski. (1810-1892) born
    Poland.
Roybal-Allard, Lucille. (1941-)
Sanger, Margaret. (1879-1966)
Schreiner, Olive. (1855-1920) South Afri-
    can.
Shaarawi, Huda. (1879-1947) Egyptian.
Sharma, Prem. (1943-) born India.
Snow, Eliza. (1804-1887)
Somerville, Mary Fairfax. (1780-1872)
    Scottish.
Stanton, Elizabeth Cady. (1815-1902)
Steinem, Gloria. (1934-)
Stone, Lucy. (1818-1893)
Stowe, Emily Jennings. (1831-1903) Cana-
    dian.
Swisshelm, Jane Cannon. (1815-1884)
Terrell, Mary Church. (1863-1954)
Truth, Sojourner. (1797-1883)
Walker, Mary Edwards. (1832-1919)
Wattleton, Faye. (1943-)
Weddington, Sarah. (1945-)
Willard, Emma Hart. (1787-1870)

Wollstonecraft, Mary. (1759-1797) English.
Woodhull, Victoria. (1838-1927)
Workman, Fanny Bullock. (1859-1925)
Younger, Maud. (1870-1936)

Workers' Rights Activists

See also Labor Leaders.
Chávez, César. (1927-1993)
Chávez-Thompson, Linda. (1944-)
Cohen, Rose. (1880-1925)
Corona, Bert. (1918-2001)
Cremer, Sir William. (1828-1908) English.
Curtis, Jennie. (fl. 1878)
De la Cruz, Jessie Lopez. (1919-)
Durazo, Maria Elena. (1954-) born Mexico.
Eastman, Crystal. (1881-1928)
Flynn, Elizabeth Gurley. (1890-1964)
Gompers, Samuel. (1850-1924) born
    England.
Govea, Jessica. (c. 1950)
Guerra, Jackie. (1967-)
Hanson, Harriet. (1825-1911)
Hine, Lewis W. (1874-1940)
Jones, Mary "Mother." (1830-1930) born
    Ireland.
Little, Frank. (1879-1917) Cherokee Indian.
Luxemburg, Rosa. (1870-1919) German,
    born Poland.
Masih, Igbal. (1982-1995) Pakistani.
Mullaney, Kate. (1845-1906)
Parsons, Lucy. (1853-1943)
Peterson, Esther. (1906-1997)
Schneiderman, Rose. (1882-1972) born Po-
    land.
Shavelson, Clara Lemlich. (1886-1982) born
    Russia.
Sullivan, Leon. (1922-2001)
Tenayuca, Emma. (1916-1999)
Younger, Maud. (1870-1936)

World Leaders

See Military Leaders; Political Activists and
    Leaders; Rulers and Royalty.

World War I Figures

See also Military Leaders.
Alcock, Sir John. (1892-1919) English cap-
    tain.
Alexander, Grover Cleveland. (1887-1950)
Arnold, Henry H. (1856-1950) Pilot.

Aylward, Gladys. (1902-1970) English spy.

Bingham, Hiram. (1878-1956) Army pilot.

Blanchfield, Florence Aby. (1882-1971) Army nurse.

Bromfield, Louis. (1896-1956)

Byrd, Richard Evelyn. (1888-1957) Navy pilot.

Carlson, Evans. (1896-1947) Army.

Cavell, Edith. (1865-1915) English nurse and heroine, executed.

Chennault, Claire Lee. (1890-1958) Air Force fighter pilot.

Chisholm, Mairí. (1896-?) Scottish nurse.

Chotek, Sophie. (1868-1914) Austrian wife of Archduke Ferdinand, assasinated.

Claude, Albert. (1899-1983) English intelligence officer.

Clémenceau, Georges. (1841-1929) French military leader.

Davis, Benjamin O., Sr. (1877-1970) Army officer.

De Gaulle, Charles. (1890-1970) French lieutenant.

Delano, Jane Arminda. (1862-1919) Superintendent Army Air Nurse Corps.

Dornberger, Walter. (1895-1980) German army.

Dorr, Rheta Childe. (1866-1948) Journalist, war correspondent.

Douglas, Marjorie Stoneman. (1890-1998) Navy.

Eielson, Carl Ben. (1897-1929) Pilot.

Eisenhower, Dwight David. (1890-1969)

Europe, James Reese. (1881-1939) Military hero.

Flipper, Henry O. (1856-1940) Lieutenant.

Foch, Ferdinand. (1851-1929) French army general.

Gaston, Arthur George. (1892-1996) Army.

Hancock, Joy Bright. (1898-1986) Naval reserves WAVES.

Hindenburg, Paul von. (1847-1934) German military leader.

Hull, Peggy. (1890-1967) Journalist, war correspondent.

Inglis, Elsie. (1864-1917) Scottish surgeon.

Johnson, Henry. (1897-1929) Military hero.

Kenny, Elizabeth. (1880-1952) Australian nurse.

Lawrence, Thomas Edward. (Lawrence of Arabia) (1888-1935) English intelligence officer.

Lewis, Clive Staples "C. S." (1898-1963) Irish soldier.

Lippmann, Walter. (1889-1974) Captain military intelligence.

Lloyd George, David. (1863-1945) English military leader.

Locklear, Ormer. (1891-1929) Army Air Service pilot.

Lovejoy, Esther Pohl. (1869-1967) Red Cross physician.

MacArthur, Douglas. (1880-1964) Officer.

Marshall, George Catlett. (1882-1959) Army officer.

Mata Hari. *See* Zelle, Margareta Gertrude.

Milne, Alan Alexander "A. A." (1882-1956) English soldier.

Montgomery, Bernard. (1887-1976) English military.

Morley, Sylvanus Griswold. (1883-1948) Spy.

Musick, Edwin C. (1893-1938) New Zealander pilot.

Nimitz, Chester W. (1885-1966) Navy.

Patton, George C. (1885-1945) Army.

Pershing, John Joseph. (1860-1948) Army general.

Pétain, Henri Phillipe. (1856-1951) French military leader.

Pippin, Horace. (1888-1946) Soldier.

Powell, William J. (1897-1942) World War I pilot.

Richthofen, Baron Manfred von "Red Baron." (1892-1918) German aviator.

Rickenbacker, Edward Vernon "Eddie." (1890-1973) Aviator. Medal of Honor recipient.

Rinehart, Mary Roberts. (1876-1958) Journalist, war correspondent.

Ronge, Maximilian. (unknown) Austrian double spy.

Stinson, Katherine. (1891-1977) Red Cross pilot.

Stowers, Freddie. (1896-1918) Corporal. Medal of Honor recipient.

Streichen, Edward. (1879-1973) Photojournalist, born Luxembourg.

Thoms, Adah Belle. (1870-1943) Nurse.

Tillich, Paul. (1886-1965) Chaplain, born Germany.

Tinker, Clarence L. (1887-1942) Army Air

Corps pilot.

Tito, Josip Broz. (1892-1980) Austro-Hungarian Army soldier, born Yugoslavia.

Truman, Harry S. (1884-1972) Captain.

Wilhelm II. (1859-1941) German general, kaiser.

Wilkins, Sir George Hubert. (1888-1958) Australian photojournalist.

York, Alvin. (1887-1964) Military hero. Medal of Honor recipient.

Young, Charles. (1864-1922) Colonel.

Zelle, Margareta Gertrude. (Mata Hari) (1876-1917) German spy.

World War II Figures

See also Holocaust Resistance Workers; Holocaust Survivors; Holocaust Victims; Military Leaders; Nazi War Criminals.

Abrams, Creighton W. (1914-1974) General.

Arnold, Henry H. (1886-1950) Air Force general.

Bader, Sir Douglas. (1910-1982) English pilot.

Baker, Josephine. (1906-1975) Resistance worker in France.

Baker, Vernon J. (1919-) Army lieutenant, military hero. Medal of Honor recipient.

Balchen, Bernt. (1899-1973) Air Force pilot, born Norway.

Barringer, Emily Dunning. (1876-1961) Head of female physicians.

Beech, Olive Ann. (1903-1993) Entrepreneur military planes.

Berg, Patty. (1918-) Marine Corps lieutenant.

Beurton, Ruth Kuczynski. (1907-) Spy.

Blanchfield, Florence Aby. (1882-1971) Superintendent U.S. Army Nurse Corps.

Bourke-White, Margaret. (1906-1971) Photojournalist.

Bradley, Omar N. (1893-1981) General.

Breckinridge, Mary Marvin. (1905-2002) Broadcast journalist, photojournalist.

Brown, George S. (1918-1978) General.

Bulkeley, John. (1911-1996) Naval lieutenant, military hero. Congressional Medal of Honor.

Bush, George Herbert Walker. (1924-) Navy pilot.

Byrd, Richard Evelyn. (1888-1957) Navy admiral.

Carlson, Evans. (1896-1947) Marine commander.

Carpenter, Iris. (unknown) English war correspondent.

Carré, Lily. (1908-) French double spy.

Carter, James Earl "Jimmy." (1924-) Navy Nuclear Submarine service.

Chappelle, Georgette "Dickey" Meyer. (1918-1965) Photojournalist.

Chennault, Claire Lee. (1890-1958) Air Force major general.

Churchill, Odette Brailly Sansom. (1912-1995) French resistance.

Churchill, Sir Winston Leonard Spencer. (1874-1965) English prime minister.

Cochran, Jacqueline. (1910-1980) Women's Air Force Service Pilots director.

Cousteau, Jacques-Yves. (1910-1997) French resistance fighter.

Cowan, Ruth. (1902-) War correspondent.

Cray, Seymour. (1925-1996) Radio operator, decoder.

Davis, Benjamin O., Jr. (1912-2002) Air Force Tuskegee airman.

Davis, Benjamin O., Sr. (1877-1970) Army brigadier general.

De Gaulle, Charles. (1890-1970) French general.

Dole, Robert. (1923-) Lieutenant.

Doolittle, Jimmy. (1896-1993) Air Force lieutenant colonel, military hero. Medal of Honor.

Earley, Charity Adams. (1918-2002) WAAC lieutenant colonel.

Echohawk, Brummett. (1922-) Pawnee Indian military hero.

Eisenhower, Dwight David. (1890-1969) Allied Military Commander, general.

Fegen, Edward Fogarty. (1895-1940) English Royal Navy Commander.

Ferenz, Ludmilla "Lou." (1921-) Army Nurse Corps flight nurse.

Ford, Gerald. (1913-) Navy.

Fort, Cornelia. (1919-1943) Fighter pilot, killed in battle.

Frank, Hans. (1900-1946) German Nazi politician.

Freud, Anna. (1895-1982) English psychoanalyst, born Austria.

Garcia, Hector Perez. (1914-1996) Army military hero, born Mexico.

Gellhorn, Martha. (1908-1998) Journalist, correspondent.

Gillars, Mildred "Axis Sally." (1900-1988) Traitor.

Goddard, Calvin Hooker. (1891-1955) Colonel.

Graham, Calvin. (1929-1992) Navy at age of twelve.

Gravely, Samuel L., Jr. (1922-) Navy ensign.

Grimmesey, Tevry. (1931-) Japanese-American girl detainee.

Guderian, Heinz. (1888-1954) German military leader.

Haley, Alex. (1921-1992) Coast Guard.

Halloren, Mary. (1907-) Women's Army Corps.

Halsey, William F. "Bull." (1882-1959) Navy admiral.

Hancock, Joy Bright. (1898-1986) Navy WAVES Director.

Hayes, Ira. (1922-1955) Pim Indian Marine hero.

Hayward, John T. (1908-1999) Navy admiral.

Hess, Harry. (1906-1969) Navy commander.

Higgins, Marguerite. (1920-1966) Photojournalist.

Hitler, Adolf. (1889-1945) German chancellor, Nazi war criminal.

Hobby, Oveta Culp. (1905-1995) WAACS commander.

Hodges, Gil. (1924-1972) Marine.

Hübener, Helmut. (1925-1942) Anti-Nazi, killed for political beliefs.

Inouye, Daniel. (1924-) Captain.

James, Daniel "Chappie," Jr. (1920-1978) Tuskegee airman.

Johnson, Amy. (1903-1941) English pilot.

Johnson, Lyndon Baines. (1908-1973) Navy.

Kennedy, John Fitzgerald. (1917-1963) Navy commander.

Kirkpatrick, Helen. (1909-1997) War correspondent.

Kolbe, Fritz. (1903-1961) German spy for allies.

Krupp, Alfried. (1907-1967) German arms manufacturer, Nazi war criminal.

Kuehn, Ruth. (unknown) German spy.

LeMay, Curtis E. (1906-1990) Air Force general.

Litvak, Lily. (1921-1943) Russian fighter pilot.

Love, Nancy Harkness. (1914-1976) Pilot.

MacArthur, Douglas. (1880-1964) Army commander general.

Marchbanks, Vance. (1905-1989) Tuskegee airman.

Marshall, George Catlett. (1880-1959) Army Chief of Staff, general.

Martinez, José P. (1920-1943) Military hero.

Maskelyne, Jasper. (1902-1973) English hero.

Mason, Andrée-Paule. (1923-1991) French resistance fighter.

Matsunaga, Masayuki "Spark." (1916-1990) Army captain.

McCabe, William. (1915-1976) Army Navajo code talker. Medal of Honor recipient.

McNamara, Robert Strange. (1916-) Army Air Force lieutenant colonel.

Miller, Dorie. (1919-1943) Navy seaman, military hero.

Miller, Lee. (1907-1977) Photojournalist.

Montagu, Ewen. (1901-1985) English spy.

Montgomery, Bernard Law. (1887-1976) English field marshal.

Moorer, Thomas H. (1912-2004) Admiral, Chief Naval Operations.

Murphy, Audie. (1924-1971) Most decorated Army soldier.

Mussolini, Benito. (1883-1945) Italian political leader.

Nelson, Gaylord. (1916-) Army hero.

Nimitz, Chester W. (1885-1966) Admiral, Commander U.S. Pacific fleet.

Nixon, Richard Milhous. (1913-1994) Navy.

Obata, Chiura. (1888-1975) In internment camp.

Pack, Amy Thorne "Betty." (1910-1963) Spy.

Parks, Paul. (1923-) Concentration camp liberator.

Patton, George Smith, Jr. (1885-1945) General.

Pétain, Henri Phillipe. (1856-1951) French military leader.

Pire, Dominique-Georges. (1910-1969) Belgian who initiated aid to diplaced persons after the war.

Pyle, Ernest Taylor "Ernie." (1900-1945) War correspondent.

Quisling, Vidkun. (1887-1945) Norwegian war criminal, traitor.

Rai, Jitbahadur. (d. 1949) Nepal ghurka, military hero, born India.

Reagan, Ronald. (1911-) Army Air Force second lieutenant.

Red Cloud, Mitchell. (1924-) Ho-Chunk Indian Marine.

Reifel, Ben. (1906-1990) Brule Lakota Indian lieutenant colonel.

Rickenbacker, Edward Vernon "Eddie." (1890-1973) Pilot.

Ridgway, Matthew Bunker. (1895-1993) Army general, Supreme Commander of Allied Forces in Europe.

Rivers, Ruben. (1918-1994) Army hero. Medal of Honor recipient.

Rommel, Erwin "Desert Fox." (1891-1944) German commander.

Ross, Barney. (1907-1967) Marine hero.

Rowny, Edward L. (1917-) Army lieutenant general.

Russell, Harold. (1914-2002) Soldier, born Canada.

Saint-Exupéry, Antoine de. (1900-1944) French pilot.

Schulte, Eduard Reinhold Karl. (1891-1966) German spy.

Schultz, Sigrid "Lillian." (1899-1980) Foreign and war correspondent.

Scott, Sheila. (1927-1988) English nurse.

Serling, Rod. (1924-1975) Soldier.

Smith, Holland M. (1882-1967) Marine Corps general.

Smith, Margaret Chase. (1897-1995) Air Force lieutenant colonel.

Sorge, Richard. (1895-1944) German spy.

Spoerry, Anne. (1918-1999) French resistance.

Stauffenberg, Claus von. (1907-1944) German army colonel, resistance.

Stevenson, Adlai. (1900-1965) Assistant Secretary of Navy.

Stillwell, Joseph W. (1883-1946) Army general.

Streichen, Edward. (1879-1973) Photojour-

nalist, born Luxembourg.

Stringer, Ann. (1918-1900) War correspondent.

Taylor, Telford. (1908-1998) Army brigadier general, colonel, Nuremberg trial judge.

Tinker, Clarence L. (1887-1942) Army Air Corps major general.

Tito, Josip Broz. (1892-1980) Yugoslavian political leader, anti-Nazi.

Toguri, Iva "Tokyo Rose." (1916-1988) Traitor.

Tomara, Sonia. (d. 1982) War correspondent, born Russia.

Turing, Alan. (1912-1954) English code breaker.

Van Raalte, Jim. (unknown) Holocaust camp liberator.

Veeck, Bill. (1914-1986) Marine.

Von Manstein, Erich. (1887-1973) German field marshal.

Walt, Lewis W. (1913-1989) Marine leader.

Watson, Thomas, Jr. (1914-1993) Fighter pilot.

Westmoreland, William C. (1914-) Army colonel.

Whyte, Edna Gardner. (1902-1993) Naval nurse corps.

Yamamoto, Isoroku. (1884-1943) Japanese military leader, led attack on Pearl Harbor.

Yeager, Chuck. (1923-) Air Force pilot.

Zhukov, Georgi. (1896-1974) Russian general.

Wrestlers
See also Olympic Athletes, Wrestling.

Aiyaruk, Princess. (c. 1280) Tartar.

Gable, Dan. (1948-)

Maximinus, Gaius Valerius. (186-233) Roman.

Milo of Crotona. (c. 558 B.C.) Greek.

Polydamus. (c. 408 B.C.) Greek.

Topham, Thomas. (1710-1749) English.

X-Ray Crystallographers
Franklin, Rosalind Elsie. (1920-1958) English.

Hodgkin, Dorothy Crowfoot. (1910-1994) English.

Yemenites

al-Sharki, Amatalrauf. (1958-) Women's rights activist.

Miriam the Scribe. (15th century) Scribe.

Sarah of Yemen. (7th century) Poet.

Young People

Distinguised by their contributions during their youth.

Aliengena, Tony. (1978-) Pilot.

Bateman, Ray J. (1974-) Canadian medical researcher.

Bates, Abigail. (1799-?) Lighthouse keeper.

Bates, Billy. (1848-1909) Teenage Civil War soldier, POW.

Bates, Rebecca. (1795-?) Lighthouse keeper.

Bermúdez, Diego. (1480-?) Spanish page for Christopher Columbus.

Berry, Carrie. (1854-?) Civil War girl.

Bolling, Thomas Spottswood, Jr. (1939-1990) Civil rights activist.

Chorn, Arn. (1967-) Cambodian political activist.

Chuka. (c. 1890) Hopi Indian child sent to boarding school.

Clem, Johnny. (1852-1937) Civil War child soldier.

Cohen, Rose. (1880-1925) Sweatshop worker, workers' rights activist.

Cohn, Marianne. (1924-1944) French Holocaust resistance worker, victim.

Colvin, Claudette. (1940-) Civil rights activist, kept seat on bus.

Cooper, Jackie. (1922-) Child actor.

Curtis, Jennie. (fl. 1878) Child worker, workers' rights activist.

Darling, Grace. (1815-1842) English lighthouse keeper's daughter who rescued people when she was very young.

Eckford, Elizabeth. (1942-) Civil rights activist, integrated high school.

Filipovic, Zlata. (1980-) Yugoslavian author.

Flinker, Moshe. (1926-1944) Dutch author, Holocaust victim.

Frank, Anne. (1929-1945) Dutch author, Holocaust victim, born Germany.

Gaes, Jason. (1978-) Author, cancer patient.

Gantt, Harvey B. (1943-) Civil rights activist.

Garcia, Emma. (1972-) Community activist.

Glover, Savion. (1974-) Actor, dancer.

Govea, Jessica. (c. 1950) Workers' rights activist.

Graham, Calvin. (1929-1992) World War II Navy at age of 12.

Grimmesey, Tevvy. (1931-) Japanese-American detainee World War II.

Heyman, Eva. (1931-1944) Hungarian author, Holocaust victim.

Hübener, Helmut. (1925-1942) German Holocaust political activist, victim.

James, Ryan. (1975-) AIDS activist.

Joan of Arc. (1412-1431) French military leader, saint.

Johns, Barbara. (1935-1991) Civil rights activist.

Johnson, Kory. (1979-) Environmentalist.

King, Dick. (1845-?) Civil War teenage soldier.

Langston, Dicey. (1766-1837) Revolutionary War spy.

Lewis, Ida. (1842-1911) Lighthouse keeper.

Martin, Joseph Plumb. (1762-1852) American Revolutionary War child soldier.

Masih, Iqbal. (1982-1995) Pakistani slave, workers' rights activist.

Midori. (1971-) Japanese musician.

Millais, John Everett. (1829-1896) Painter.

Nash, Diane. (1938-) Civil rights activist.

Nicholson, Vanessa-Mae. (1978-) English musician.

Noble, Jordan. (1801-?) Drummer Boy Seminole War and War of 1812.

Nur, Nawrose. (1981-) Chess champion, born Bangladesh.

Nuxhall, Joe. (1929-) Baseball player for Major Leagues at age fifteen.

O'Neill, Cecilia Rose. (1874-1944) Cartoonist, illustrator.

Parris, Betty. (1682-1760) Puritan colonist, made witchcraft accusations.

Polovchak, Walter. (1967-) Russian boy who refused to return to Russia.

Powell, Cristen. (1979-) Drag racer.

Ream, Vinnie. (1847-1914) Sculptor.

Redmond, Mary. (unknown) American Revolutionary War spy.

Schroeder, Becky. (1962-) Inventor.

Smith, Samantha Reed. (1972-1985) Youth ambassador to Soviet Union, peace activist.

Stockwell, Elisha. (1846-) Civil War teen-age soldier.

Temple, Shirley. (1928-) Child actor.

Tutankhamun. (1347-1329 B.C.) Egyptian pharoah.

Wait, Bethany. (1973-1991) Saved people from storms with emergency radio station.

Webb, Sheyann. (1957-) Civil rights activist.

White, Ryan. (1971-1990) AIDS activist, victim.

Williams, Abigail. (1680-?) Puritan colonist, accused others of witchcraft.

Williams, Eunice. (1697-1787) Puritan, Indian captive.

Winslow, Anna Green. (1760-1779) Colonist.

Yani, Wang. (1975-) Chinese painter.

Yugoslavians

See also Immigrants to United States, Yugoslavian.

Bojaxhiu, Agnes. (Mother Teresa) (1910-1997) Human rights activist, missionary, Saint.

Eisen, Renata. (1929-) Holocaust survivor.

Filipovic, Zlata. (1980-) Author.

Petrovic, Drazen. (1964-1993) Basketball player.

Tito, Josip Broz. (1892-1980) President, World War I soldier, World War II political activist, anti-Nazi.

Zairians

See also Africans; Blacks, International; Immigrants to United States, African.

Mutombo, Dikembe. (1966-) Basketball player.

Zimbabweans

See also Africans; Blacks, International; Immigrants to United States, African.

Mugabe, Robert. (1924-) Prime Minister.

Newby-Fraser, Paula. (1962-) Olympic tri-athlon athlete, track and field athlete.

Zoologists

Clapp, Cornelia. (1849-1934)

Durrell, Gerald. (1925-1995) English.

Ehrlich, Paul. (1932-)

Hyman, Libbie. (1888-1969)

Medawar, Sir Peter Brian. (1915-1987) English.

Morgan, Ann Haven. (1882-1966)

Morgan, Thomas Hunt. (1866-1945)

Nansen, Fridtjof. (1861-1930) Norwegian.

Sperry, Roger. (1913-1994)

Watson, James Dewey. (1928-)

Young, Roger Arliner. (1889-1964)

About the Author

Sue Barancik has had twenty years of public library experience frantically and feverishly searching the shelves for biographical information for countless youngsters doing school reports. She has served for the past eight years as the coordinator of Youth Services for the Somerset County Library System in New Jersey. Previous public library positions include the Evansville Vanderburgh Public Library in Indiana and the New Providence Memorial Library in New Jersey. She was also an enthusiastic instructor of children's literature and storytelling at universities in Michigan and Indiana and a professional storyteller. For her next book, she promises fewer characters and a lot more plot!